The Wordsworth
Dictionary of Quotations

—

Edited by Connie Robertson

Wordsworth Reference

This edition published 1998 by Wordsworth Editions Ltd.
Cumberland House, Crib Street, Ware, Hertfordshire, SG12 9ET

ISBN 1-85326-489-X

Printed and bound in Great Britain by Mackays of Chatham PLC.

Dictionary of Quotations

Editor's Introduction

As in earlier editions of this dictionary, the aim is to provide the reader with, firstly, the means of finding a half-remembered phrase or reference; secondly, examples of what has been said by the famous, the not so famous, and the infamous on a particular subject; and thirdly, when using the dictionary alphabetically by author, a representation of statements made by the author or speaker which have become memorable or remarkable. Whilst fulfilling these criteria it is hoped that the book will also provide a source of entertainment for the browser.

The intention of this newly revised and updated edition with its larger format and new typeface is to make it even easier for the reader to use. The index has been greatly enhanced by the addition of a determining phrase for each entry so that identifying the quotation should be much simpler than in the earlier editions.

The obvious sources of established quotations, such as the Bible, the Classical authors, Shakespeare and the great poets, are all represented here, but these sections have been deliberately pruned to provide only the more useful and relevant quotations since more extensive selections can be found in specialized dictionaries. Instead I have included many contemporary quotations which are perhaps more relevant to our particular time and its readers, including a new section on mottoes and slogans. Many of these come from visual and audio media such as advertising and television which is now an abundant source of well known quotations.

I hope you find it both a useful and informative addition to your reference shelf and fun to read.

Arrangement of Entries

Entries have been arranged alphabetically by author/speaker and also indexed by keywords (usually at least two) so that if the originator is not known it should not prove difficult to find a quotation by using the index.

Authors are listed under their most commonly used name, for example where a pseudonym or titled form is the best known version. Where joint authors are responsible for a quote, they are listed under the first name by which the pairing is commonly known, but this is not intended to diminish the importance of the contribution of the other author.

Foreign language quotations are given together with the English where they are well-known, otherwise only the translation appears.

The source of the quotation is shown where it is known to come from a published work by that author. Where the source is a part-work such as a story or poem within a larger work, it is given within single quotation marks. Notes which clarify the context of the quotation are shown in brackets. Film quotations are given under the name of the actor who spoke the lines, but since they are not the words of that particular person but of the character which they were playing, the lines are given in quotation marks.

The index is also arranged alphabetically by keyword. In most cases singular and plural forms of a noun are grouped separately, but in seeking to locate a quotation it is advisable to check under both forms. Where an unusual spelling of a keyword occurs in the quotation, it is indexed under the more usual form unless there is no equivalent.

Connie Robertson

May 1998

Acknowledgments

I would like to thank Mervyn Edwards, Sheila Mudge and Ena Richards for their invaluable contribution to the making of this dictionary, and Clive Reynard and Marcus Clapham for their encouragement throughout. For this third edition I am particularly grateful to Mervyn Edwards for the work he has done on improving the index.

I am also very grateful to all those who have written in with comments and suggestions after reading the first two editions. This revised edition has taken account of many of these and whether you write to suggest an amendment or to request the inclusion of a favourite quotation, your letters will be most welcome.

Please write to me
c/o Wordsworth Editions Ltd, 6 London Street, LONDON W2 1HL.

Contents

Dictionary of Quotations

ABBEY Edward

1

Growth for the sake of growth is the ideology of the cancer cell.

ABBOTT Diane 1953-

2

Being an MP is the sort of job all working class parents want for their children - clean, indoors and no heavy lifting.

ABSE Dannie 1923-

3 *'Pathology of Colours'*

I know the colour rose, and it is lovely,
But not when it ripens in a tumour;
And healing greens,leaves and grass, so springlike,
In limbs that fester are not springlike.

4 *'Pathology of Colours'*

So in the simple blessing of a rainbow,
In the bevelled edge of a sunlit mirror,
I have seen visible, Death's artifact
Like soldier's ribbon on a tunic tacked.

ACE Goodman

5

The best cure for hypochondria is to forget about your own body and get interested in someone else's.

ACE Jane

6

Doctor, feel my purse.

7

Time wounds all heels.

ACHESON Dean 1893-1971

8

The first requirement of a statesman is that he be dull.

9

The future comes one day at a time.

10

Great Britain has lost an Empire and has not yet found a role.

11

A memorandum is written not to inform the reader but to protect the writer.

12

Negotiation in the classic diplomatic sense assumes parties more anxious to agree than to disagree.

ACTON Lord 1834-1902

13

The most certain test by which we judge whether a country is really free is the amount of security enjoyed by minorities.

14 *Historical Essays and Studies*

Power tends to corrupt, and absolute power corrupts absolutely. Great men are almost always bad men.

15

Truth is the only merit that gives dignity and worth to history.

16

There is no worse heresy than that the office sanctifies the holder of it.

ADAMOV Arthur 1908-1970

17

The only thing to know is how to use your neuroses.

ADAMS Abigail 1744-1818

18

These are times in which a genius would like to live. It is not in the still calm of life, or the repose of a pacific station, that great characters are formed...Great necessities call out great virtues.

ADAMS Cindy

19

Success has made failures of many men.

ADAMS Douglas 1952-

20 *The Hitch Hiker's Guide to the Galaxy*

The Answer to the great Question of...Life, the Universe and Everything...is Forty-two.

ADAMS Frank and HOUGH Will H.

21

I wonder who's kissing her now.

ADAMS Franklin P. 1881-1960

22

Christmas is over, and Business is Business.

23

Health is the thing that makes you feel that now is the best time of the year.

24 *Nods and Becks*

Years ago we discovered the exact point, the dead centre of middle age. It occurs when you are too young to take up golf and too old to rush up to the net.

25 *Nods and Becks*

Elections are won by men and women chiefly because most people vote against somebody rather than for somebody.

26

There are plenty of good five-cent cigars in the country. The trouble is they cost a quarter. What the country really needs is a good five-cent nickle.

ADAMS Henry Brooks 1838-1918

27 *The Education of Henry Adams*
Nothing in education is so astonishing as the amount of ignorance it accumulates in the form of inert facts.

28 *The Education of Henry Adams*
They know enough who know how to learn.

29 *The Education of Henry Adams*
Politics, as a practice, whatever its professions, has always been the systematic organization of hatreds.

30 *The Education of Henry Adams*
Accident counts for much in companionship as in marriage.

31 *The Education of Henry Adams*
A friend in power is a friend lost.

32 *The Education of Henry Adams*
The effect of power and publicity on all men is the aggravation of self, a sort of tumour that ends by killing the victim's sympathies.

33 *The Education of Henry Adams*
Chaos often breeds life, when order breeds habit.

34 *The Education of Henry Adams*
A teacher affects eternity; he can never tell where his influence stops.

35 *The Education of Henry Adams*
One friend in a lifetime is much; two are many; three are hardly possible. Friendship needs a certain parellelism of life, a community of thought, a rivalry of aim.

36 *The Education of Henry Adams*
Morality is a private and costly luxury.

37 *The Education of Henry Adams*
Practical politics consists in ignoring facts.

38 *The Education of Henry Adams*
No one means all he says, and yet very few say all they mean, for words are slippery and thought is viscous.

ADAMS Joey

39
Bankruptcy is a legal proceeding in which you put your money in your pants pocket and give your coat to your creditors.

ADAMS John 1735-1826

40
There is a danger from all men. The only maxim of a free Government ought to be to trust no man living with power to endanger the public liberty.

41 *(letter to Horacio Gates)*
In politics the middle way is none at all.

42 *(letter to Thomas Jefferson)*
You and I ought not to die before we have explained ourselves to each other.

43 *'Novanglus' papers*
A government of laws, and not of men.

44 *(on his presidency)*
The four most miserable years of my life ...

45 *Thoughts on Government*
The happiness of society is the end of government.

46 *Thoughts on Government*
Fear is the foundation of most governments.

ADAMS John Quincy 1767-1848

47
Had I been chosen president again, I am certain I could not have lived another year.

48
In esse I am nothing; in posse I am everything.

49
If I were to go over my life again, I would be a shoemaker rather than an American Statesman.

ADAMSON Harold 1906-1980

50
Comin' in on a wing and a pray'r.

ADCOCK Sir Frank 1886-1968

51
That typically English characteristic for which there is no English name - *esprit de corps.*

ADDISON Joseph 1672-1719

52 *Ancient Medals*
Pray consider what a figure a man would make in the republic of letters.

53 *'A Song for St Cecilia's Day'*
Music, the greatest good that mortals know
And all of heaven we have below.

54 *The Campaign*
And those who paint 'em truest praise 'em most.

55 *Cato*
What pity is it
That we can die but once to serve our country!

56 *Cato*
From hence, let fierce contending nations know
What dire effects from civil discord flow.

57 *Cato*
The woman that deliberates is lost.

58 *(of Cowley)*
He more had pleased us, had he pleased us less.

59 *The Drummer*
There is nothing more requisite in business than dispatch.

60 *(dying words)*
See in what peace a Christian can die.

61
We have in England a particular bashfulness in everything that regards religion.

62
A man should always consider how much he has more than he wants, and how much more unhappy he might be than he really is.

63
Nothing that is not a real crime makes a man appear so contemptible and little in the eyes of the world as inconsistency.

64
A perfect tragedy is the noblest production of human nature.

65 *The Spectator*
The hand that makes us divine

66 *The Spectator*
Sir Roger told them, with the air of a man who would not give his judgement rashly, that much might be said on both sides.

67 *The Spectator*
If we may believe our logicians, man is distinguished from all other creatures by the faculty of laughter.

68 *The Spectator*
A woman seldom asks advice until she has bought her wedding clothes.

69
Sunday clears away the rust of the whole week.

70
I have often thought, says Sir Roger, it happens very well that Christmas should fall out in the Middle of Winter.

71
As vivacity is the gift of women, gravity is that of men.

72
Young men soon give, and soon forget affronts, Old age is slow in both.

ADE George 1866-1944
73 *Fables in Slang*
After being turned down by numerous publishers, he had decided to write for posterity.

74
He had been kicked in the head by a mule when young, and believed everything he read in the Sunday papers.

75
One man's poison ivy is another man's spinach.

76
A people so primitive that they did not know how to get money except by working for it.

77
If it were not for the presents, an elopement would be preferable.

78 *'The Steel Box'*
`Whom are you?' he asked, for he had attended business college.

79 *The Sultan of Sulu.*
R-E-M-O-R-S-E.
Those dry Martinis did the work for me;
Last night at twelve I felt immense,
Today I feel like thirty cents.

80
In uplifting, get underneath.

ADENAUER Konrad 1876-1967
81
The good Lord set definite limits on man's wisdom, but set no limits on his stupidity - and that's just not fair.

82
I havn't asked you to make me young again. All I want is to go on getting older.

83
History is the sum total of the things that could have been avoided.

84
A thick skin is a gift from God.

ADLER Alfred 1870-1937
85
The feeling of inferlority rules the mental life and can be clearly recognized as the sense of incompleteness and unfulfillment, and in the uninterrupted struggle both of individuals and of humanity.

86 *The problems of Neurosis*
The truth is often a terrible weapon of aggression. It is possible to lie, and even to murder, for the truth.

87
Trust only movement. Life happens at the level of events not of words.

ADLER Mortimer J.
88
In the case of good books, the point is not to see how many of them you can get through, but rather how many can get through to you.

89
The telephone book is full of facts but it doesn't contain a single idea.

ADLER Renata 1938-
90
It is always self-defeating to pretend to the style of a generation younger than your own; it simply erases your own experience in history.

ADLER Polly 1900-1962
91 *(referring to a brothel)*
A House is not a Home.

ADY Thomas fl. 1655
92 *A Candle in the Dark*
Matthew, Mark, Luke and John,
The bed be blest that I lie on,
Four angels round my head,
One to watch, and one to pray,
And two to bear my soul away.

AESCHYLUS c.525-456 BC
93 *(of Helen)*
Hell to ships, hell to men, hell to cities.

94
Words are the physicians of a mind diseased.

95
It is always in season for old men to learn.

AESOP c.550 BC
96 *Fables 'The Dog and the Shadow'*
Beware that you do not lose the substance by grasping at the shadow.

97 *Fables 'Hercules and the Waggoner'*
The gods help them that help themselves.

98 *Fables 'The Milkmaid and her Pail'*
Don't count your chickens before they are hatched.

99 *Fables 'The Wolf in Sheep's Clothing'*
The lamb that belonged to the sheep whose skin the wolf was wearing began to follow the wolf in the sheep's clothing.

AGA KHAN III 1877-1957
100 *(defending his taste for alcohol)*
I'm so holy that when I touch wine, it turns into water.

AGAR Herbert 1897-1980
101
Snobs talk as if they had begotten their ancestors.

102 *A Time for Greatness*
The truth which makes men free is for the most part the truth which men prefer not to hear.

AGATE James 1877-1947
103 *Ego 6*
My mind is not a bed to be made and re-made.

104
The English instinctively admire any man who has no talent and is modest about it.

105
Long experience has taught me that in England nobody goes to the theatre unless he or she has bronchitis.

AGATHON c.445-400 BC
106
Even God cannot change the past.

AGNEW Spiro T. 1918-1996
107
To some extent if you've seen one city slum you've seen them all.

108
A spirit of national masochism prevails, encouraged by an effete corps of impudent snobs who characterize themselves as intellectuals.

AHMAD Iqbal
109
When you give the reins to reason then the imagination is repressed.

AHMANSON Howard
110
I'm so happy to be rich, I'm willing to take all the consequences.

AKINS Zoë 1886-1958
111
The Greeks had a word for it.

ALAIN (Émile-Auguste Chartier) 1868-1951
112 *Propos sur la religion*
Nothing is more dangerous than an idea, when you have only one idea.

113
Time must needs call the tune and man must follow it.

ALAIN-FOURNIER (Henri Alban) 1886-1914
114 *Le Grand Meaulnes*
Perhaps when we come to die, death will provide the meaning and the sequel and the ending of this unsuccessful adventure.

115 *Le Grand Meaulnes*
How can a man who has once strayed into Heaven ever hope to make terms with the earth!

116
Life on the farm is a school of patience; you can't hurry the crops or make an ox in two days.

ALBEE Edward 1928-
117 *Who's afraid of Virginia Woolf?*
I have a fine sense of the ridiculous, but no sense of humour.

ALBERT Prince (Consort to Queen Victoria) 1819-1861
118 *(of the French)*
I clearly forsee the day when this vainglorious

and immoral people will have to be put down.

ALBERTI Leon Battista 1404-1472
119
Beauty - the adjustment of all parts
proportionately so that one cannot add or
subtract or change without impairing the
harmony of the whole.

ALCOTT Louisa May 1832-1888
120 *Little Women*
Girls are so queer, you never know what they
mean. They say No when they mean Yes, and
drive a man out of his wits for the fun of it.

ALDEN Robert
121
There is not enough darkness in all the world to
put out the light of even one small candle.

ALDINGTON Richard 1892-1962
122 *The Colonel's Daughter*
Patriotism is a lively sense of collective
responsibility. Nationalism is a silly cock
crowing on its own dunghill.

ALDISS Brian 1925-
123 *Barefoot in the Head*
Keep violence in the mind
Where it belongs.

ALDRICH Henry 1647-1710
124 *A Catch*
If all be true that I do think,
There are five reasons we should drink;
Good wine, a friend, or being dry,
Or lest we should be by and by;
Or any other reason why.

ALDRICH Thomas Bailey 1836-1907
125
The man who suspects his own tediousness has
yet to be born.

126
The possession of gold has ruined fewer men
than the lack of it.

ALDRIN `Buzz' 1930-
127 *(on successful moon landing of Apollo XI)*
Houston, Tranquillity Base here. The Eagle has
landed.

ALEXANDER Cecil Frances 1818-1895
128 *'All things bright and beautiful'*
All things bright and beautiful,
All creatures great and small,
All things wise and wonderful
The Lord God made them all.

129 *'Once in Royal David's city'*
Once in Royal David's City
Stood a lowly cattle shed,
Where a mother laid her baby,
In a manger for its bed:

Mary was that mother mild,
Jesus Christ her little child.

130 *'There is a green hill far away'*
There is a green hill far away,
Without a city wall,
Where the Dear Lord was crucified,
Who died to save us all.

ALEXANDER The Great 356-323 BC
131
I am dying with the help of too many
physicians.

ALFVÉN Hannes 1872-1960
132
As both the Mercury and Apollo programs have
shown, our science and technology are so
powerful that, if an intense effort is made, we
can do almost anything we want in say, ten
years - provided we are not in conflict with the
laws of nature.

ALGREN Nelson 1909-1981
133
A walk on the wild side.

134 *A Walk on the Wild Side*
Never eat at a place called Mom's. Never play
cards with a man called Doc. Never go to bed
with a woman whose troubles are greater than
your own.

ALI Muhammad (Cassius Clay) 1942-
135 *(announcing his retirement)*
I want to get out with my greatness intact.

136
You don't want no pie in the sky when you die.
You want something here on the ground while
you're still around.

137 *(motto)*
Float like a butterfly, sting like a bee.

138 *(his slogan from c.1963)*
I am the greatest.

139
When you're as great as I am, it's hard to be
humble.

ALLAINVAL, Abbé d' 1700-1753
140
L'embarras des richesses
The embarrassment of riches

ALLEN Fred 1894-1956
141 *(attributed)*
Committee - a group of men who individually
can do nothing but as a group decide that
nothing can be done.

142
I don't want to own anything that won't fit into
my coffin.

143
(A gentleman) is any man who wouldn't hit a woman with his hat on.

ALLEN George 1902-1989
144
Every time you win, you're reborn; when you lose you die a little.

145
Winning can be defined as the science of being totally prepared.

ALLEN Marty
146
A study of economics usually reveals that the best time to buy anything is last year.

ALLEN William 1889-1949
147
America - the best poor man's country in the world.

ALLEN Woody 1935-
148 *All You Ever Wanted to Know About Sex*
Is sex dirty? Only if it's done right.

149 *Annie Hall*
[Sex] was the most fun I ever had without laughing.

150 *Annie Hall (of masturbation)*
Don't knock it. It's sex with someone you love.

151
I believe that sex is a beautiful thing between two people. Between five, it's fantastic.

152 *Clown Prince of American Humour*
I want to tell you this terrific story about contraception. I asked this girl to sleep with me, and she said no.

153
I don't want to achieve immortality through my work. I want to achieve immortality through not dying.

154 *Without Feathers*
I'm not afraid to die. I just don't want to be there when it happens.

155 *Without Feathers*
Money is better than poverty, if only for financial reasons.

156
Love is the answer, but while you're waiting for the answer, sex raises some pretty good questions.

157 *'My Philosophy', Getting Even*
Not only is there no God, but try getting a plumber on weekends.

158 *'Notebooks'*
If only God would give me some clear sign! Like making a large deposit in my name at a Swiss bank.

159
Showing up is eighty percent of life.

160 *Sleeper*
My Brain? It's my second favourite organ.

ALLINGHAM Margery 1904-1966
161 *Flowers for the Judge*
Once sex rears its ugly 'ead it's time to steer clear.

ALLINGHAM William 1828-1899
162 *The Fairies*
Up the airy mountain,
Down the rushy glen,
We daren't go a-hunting,
For fear of little men.

ALTMAN Robert 1925-
163
What's a cult? It just means not enough people to make a minority.

AMERY Leo 1873-1955
164 *(of Herbert Asquith)*
For twenty years he has held a season-ticket on the line of least resistance and has gone wherever the train of events has carried him, lucidly justifying his position at whatever point he has happened to find himself.

165 *(in House of Commons)*
Speak for England.

AMES Adelbert
166
The things we see are the mind's best bet as to what is out front.

AMES Fisher 1758-1808
167
A monarchy is a merchantman, which sails well, but will sometimes strike on a rock and go to the bottom, whilst a republic is a raft which will never sink, but then your feet are always in the water.

AMHERST Earl 1773-1857
168
In the bad old days, there were three easy ways of losing money - racing being the quickest, women the pleasantest and farming the most certain.

AMIEL Henri Frédéric 1821-1881
169
Analysis kills spontaneity. The grain once ground into flour springs and germinates no more.

170
Doing easily what others find is difficult is talent; doing what is impossible for talent is genius.

171
To know how to grow old is the master-work of wisdom, and one of the most difficult chapters in the great art of living.

172
Every life is a possession of faith, and exercises an inevitable and silent propaganda.

173
Man *becomes* man only by the intelligence, but he is man only by the heart.

174
A man only understands what is akin to something already existing in himself.

175
The man who has no inner life is the slave of his surroundings.

176
For purposes of action nothing is more useful than narrowness of thought combined with energy of will.

177
A thousand things advance; nine hundred and ninety-nine retreat; that is progress.

AMIS Sir Kingsley 1922-1995
178 *'A Bookshop idyll'*
We men have got love well weighed up; our stuff
Can get by without it.
Women don't seem to think that's good enough;
They write about it.

179 *'A Bookshop idyll'*
Women are really much nicer than men:
No wonder we like them.

180 *'Delivery Guaranteed'*
Death has got something to be said for it:
There's no need to get out of bed for it;
Wherever you may be,
They bring it to you, free.

181
The delusion that there are thousands of young people about who are capable of benefiting from university training, but have somehow failed to find their way there, is...a necessary component of the expansionist case...More will mean worse.

182 *One Fat Englishman*
Outside every fat man there was an even fatter man trying to close in.

183 *One Fat Englishman*
He was of the faith chiefly in the sense that the church he currently did not attend was Catholic.

184 *Lucky Jim*
The light did him harm, but not as much as looking at things did; he resolved, having done it once, never to move his eyeballs again.

AMSTERDAM Maury
185
Our Congressman are the finest body of men money can buy.

ANDERSON Judith
186
There is nothing enduring in life for a woman except what she builds in a man's heart.

ANDERSON Patrick
187
Power is like a woman you want to stay in bed with forever.

ANDERSON Robert 1917-
188 *Tea and Sympathy*
All you're supposed to do is every once in a while give the boys a little tea and sympathy.

ANDREW Prince, The Duke of York 1960-
189 *(on his engagement)*
(I am) over the moon ... We are both over the moon, and will be even more so when this is over.

ANDREWES Bishop Lancelot 1555-1626
190 *Of the Nativity*
The nearer the Church the further from God.

191 *Of the Nativity*
It was no summer progress. A cold coming they had of it, at this time of the year; just, the worst time of the year, to take a journey, and specially a long journey, in. The ways deep, the weather sharp, the days short, the sun farthest off, *in solstitio brumali*, the very dead of Winter.

ANNE Princess, The Princess Royal 1950-
192 *(attributed)*
When I appear in public, people expect me to neigh, grind my teeth and swish my tail.

193 *(on her first encounter with a horse)*
One was presented with a small hairy individual and out of general curiosity, one climbed on.

194 *(on pregnancy)*
It's a very boring time. I am not particularly maternal - it's an occupational hazard of being a wife.

ANONYMOUS
195
Been there, done that, got the T-shirt.

196 *(placard at Countryside March, 1998)*
Eat British Lamb: 50,000 foxes can't be wrong.

197 *(1940s saying)*
If it moves, salute it; if it doesn't move, pick it up; and if you can't pick it up, paint it white.

198 *(at 1972 Only One Earth Conference)*
We have forgotten how to be good guests, how to walk lightly on the earth as other creatures do.

199
Absence makes the heart grow fonder.

200
In the act of loving someone you arm them against you.

201
Alimony: the cash surrender value of a husband.

202
All glory comes from daring to begin.

203
All marriages are happy. It's living together afterwards that is difficult.

204
If all the world were paper,
And all the sea were ink,
And all the trees were bread and cheese
What should we do for drink?

205 *(by an American Lawyer)*
Obscenity is whatever gives a judge an erection.

206 *(annotation to a ministerial brief)*
This is a rotten argument, but it should be good enough for their lordships on a hot summer afternoon.

207
Anything which parents have not learned from experience they can now learn from their children.

208
Every April, God rewrites the Book of Genesis.

209
A-roving! A-roving!
Since roving's been my ru-i-n
I'll go no more a-roving
With you fair maid.

210
Art is all that cannot be suppressed.

211 *Articles of War*
Any Officer who shall behave in a scandalous manner, unbecoming the character of an officer and a gentleman shall....be cashiered.

212
The average girl would rather have beauty than brains because she knows the average man can see much better than he can think.

213
Baby faced people suffer job discrimination like other minorities.

214
The beginning is easy; what happens next is much harder.

215
The bible tells us to forgive our enemies; not our friends.

216
Bigamy is having one husband too many. Monogamy is the same.

217
The bigger they are, the further they fall.

218
Book lovers never go to bed alone.

219
One boy's a boy, two boys are half a boy; three boys are no boy at all.

220
A bred-in-the-bone Boston lady, when asked why she never travelled, said 'Why should I? I'm already there.'

221 *(on the British monarchy)*
At certain times of grave national stress, when that rag-bag called the British Constitution is in grave danger of coming unstuck, thank heaven for the big safety-pin at the top that keeps it together.

222
A camel is a horse designed by a committee.

223 *(car bumper sticker)*
Life is uncertain - eat dessert first

224
In his chamber, weak and dying,
While the Norman Baron lay,
Loud, without, his men were crying,
'Shorter hours and better pay'.

225
Character is like a tree, and reputation like its shadow. The shadow is what we think of it; the tree is the real thing.

226 *(Charles E. Wilson's defence policy)*
A bigger bang for a buck.

227
Child: Mamma, are Tories born wicked, or do they go wicked afterwards?
Mother: They are born wicked, and grow worse.

228
The Church of England is the Tory party at prayer.

229
The cleverest woman finds a need for foolish admirers.

230
If a cluttered desk is an indication of a cluttered mind, what is indicated by an empty desk?

231
Coffee in England is just toasted milk.

232
Confirmation at Eton: like a huge garden party, faintly over-shadowed by a sense of religion.

233
Conscience is a cur that will let you get past it but that you cannot keep from barking.

234 *(said during the coronation of a new Pope)*
Sic transit gloria mundi.
Thus passes the glory of the world.

235 *(of David Lloyd George)*
He uses figures as if they were adjectives.

236
A dead man
Who never caused others to die
Seldom rates a statue.

237
Death is terrible to Cicero, desirable to Cato, and indifferent to Socrates.

238 *(Decca Recording Company rejecting The Beatles)*
We don't like their sound, and guitar music is on the way out.

239
Deep down he is shallow.

240 *(definition of a lie)*
An abomination unto the Lord, but a very present help in time of trouble.

241
There is a difference between a pyschopath and a neurotic. A pyschopath thinks two and two are five. A neurotic knows that two and two are four, but he worries about it.

242
A distinguished diplomat could hold his tongue in ten languages.

243
To dream of the person you would like to be is to waste the person you are.

244
Early one morning, just as the sun was rising, I heard a maid sing in the valley below:

'Oh, don't deceive me; Oh, never leave me! How could you use a poor maiden so?'

245
The early North American Indians made a great mistake by not having an immigration bureau.

246
To eat is human, to digest, divine.

247 *(on Edward VII's accession to the throne)*
We shall not pretend that there is nothing in his long career which those who respect and admire him would wish otherwise.

248
The Eiffel Tower is the Empire State Building after taxes.

249 *(epitaph for Alexander the Great)*
A tomb now suffices him for whom the whole world was not sufficient.

250 *Epperson's Law*
When a man says it's a silly, childish game, it's probably something his wife can beat him at.

251
The eternal triangle.

252 *Everyman*
Everyman, I will go with thee, and be thy guide,
In thy most need to go by thy side.

253
Her face looks as if it had worn out two bodies.

254
A fair price for oil is whatever you can get plus ten to twenty per cent.

255
There was a faith-healer from Deal
Who said, 'Although pain isn't real,
If I sit on a pin
And it punctures my skin,
I dislike what I fancy I feel'.

256
I feel no pain dear mother now
But oh, I am so dry!
O take me to a brewery
And leave me there to die.

257
He that fights and runs away,
May live to fight another day.

258
The final test of fame is to have a crazy person imagine he is you.

259
If it flies, floats or fucks....don't buy it, rent it.

260
Any fool can make a rule, and every fool will mind it.

261 *(forecasting advance of science in 1949)*
Computers in the future will weigh no more
than 1.5 tons.

262
The four-letter word for psychotherapy is 'talk'.

263
The French have a passion for revolution but an
abhorrence of change.

264 *(of the French Foreign Legion)*
They were never defeated, they were only killed.

265 *(of G.B. Shaw)*
John the Baptist pretending to be Karl Marx.

266
A genealogist is one who traces your family
back as far as your money will go.

267
The parting genius is with sighing sent.

268
Gentleman: one who never hurts anyone's
feelings unintentionally.

269
From ghoulies to ghosties and long-leggety
beasties
And things that go bump in the night,
Good Lord, deliver us!

270
He wouldn't give a duck a drink if he owned
Lake Michigan.

271
The glances over cocktails
That seemed to be so sweet
Don't seem quite so amorous
Over Shredded Wheat.

272
If God lived on earth, people would break his
windows.

273
Good children's literature appeals not only to
the child in the adult, but to the adult in the
child.

274
Good judgement comes from experience, and
experience - well, that comes from poor
judgement.

275
There is so much good in the worst of us and so
much bad in the best of us, that it's rather hard
to tell which of us ought to reform the rest of us.

276 *(graffito found on a London Underground)*
Life is a sexually transmitted disease.

277 *(graffito seen on toilet wall at Athens
airport)*
Aestheticism is the last resort of the bourgeois.

278
It's not as great a day for the bride as she thinks.
She's not marrying the best man.

279
Greensleeves was all my joy,
Greensleeves was my delight,
Greensleeves was my heart of gold
And who but my lady Greensleeves.

280 *(on the Gunpowder Plot)*
Please to remember the fifth of November,
Gunpowder Treason and Plot.
We know no reason
Why gunpowder treason
Should ever be forgot.

281
Hail Caesar, those who are about to die salute
you.

282
The hard rubs of the world are what makes a
man bright.

283
Harpists spend half their life tuning and the
other half playing out of tune.

284
He'd give the devil ulcers.

285
Hell is truth seen too late.

286
A hobby is hard work you wouldn't do for a
living.

287
Honour follows those who flee it.

288
A husband always prefers his wife's mother-in-
law to his own.

289 *(IBM engineer on the microchip in 1968)*
But what...is it good for?

290 *(Illinois Institute of Technology)*
After an eight-hour day, workers require three
overtime hours to produce two regular hours of
results.

291 *(on impartiality)*
Like Caesar's wife, all things to all men.

292
Inflation is defined as the quality that makes
balloons larger and candy bars smaller.

293 *(inscription on one of Columbus' caravels)*
Following the sun we left the old world.

294 *(inscription over Dachau concentration camp gates)*
Arbeit macht frei.
Work liberates.

295 *(inscription at Delphi)*
Know thyself.

296 *(inscription at Delphi)*
Nothing in excess.

297 *(inscription on a sundial)*
Time wastes our bodies and our wits;
But we waste time, so we are quits.

298
An Intelligent Russian once remarked to us,
`Every country has its own constitution; ours is
absolutism moderated by assassination'.

299 *(on investing in the radio in 1920s)*
The wireless music box has no imaginable
commercial value. Who would pay for a
message sent to nobody in particular?

300 *(Jacobite toast)*
The King over the water.

301 *(Jaws 2: film advertising copy)*
Just when you thought it was safe to go back in
the water.

302 *(Jesuit maxim- attributed)*
Give me a child for the first seven years, and I'll
give you the man.

303 *(of Julius Ceasar)*
Every woman's man, and every man's woman.

304
If there were any justice in the world, people
would be able to fly over pigeons for a change.

305 *(keyboard checking exercise)*
The quick brown fox jumped over the lazy dog.

306 *King's Regulations*
All present and correct.

307 *(labour and civil rights song)*
We shall not be moved.

308 *(Labour party pamphlet on parenting)*
Children are luxuries rather than investments.

309
No more Latin, no more French,
No more sitting on a hard board bench.
No more beetles in my tea,
Making googly eyes at me;
No more spiders in my bath
Trying hard to make me laugh.

310
The law locks up both man and woman
Who steals the goose from off the common,
But lets the great felon loose
Who steals the common from the goose.

311
Let's all give God a great big hand. I've seen the
last page of the Bible and it's all going to turn
out all right.

312
Liberty is always unfinished business.

313
Here lies Fred,
Who was alive and is dead:
Had it been his father,
I had much rather;
Had it been his brother,
Still better than another;
Had it been his sister,
No one would have missed her;
Had it been the whole generation,
Still better for the nation:

314
Literature is a power to be possessed, not a
body of objects to be studied.

315
There is no such thing as a little garlic.

316
A little nonsense now and then is relished by
the wisest men.

317
There is little serenity comparable to the
serenity of the inexperienced giving advice to
the experienced.

318
Little wit in the head makes much work for the
feet.

319
Lizzie Borden took an axe
And gave her mother forty whacks;
When she saw what she had done
She gave her father forty-one!

320
To lose
Is to learn.

321
Love is the child of illusion and the parent of
disillusion.

322
Let those love now, who never loved before;
Let those who always loved, now love the more.

323
Each man is his own absolute lawgiver and
dispenser of glory or gloom to himself, the
maker of his life, his reward, his punishment.

324
If every man would mend a man, then all the
world would be mended.

325
If a man can remember what he worried about last week, he has a very good memory.

326
If it weren't for marriage, men would spend their lives thinking they had no faults at all.

327
I married my husband for life, not for lunch.

328 *The Masque of Balliol*
My name is George Nathianel Curzon, I am a most superior person.

329
'Mean to' don't pick no cotton.

330 *(on microbes)*
Adam
Had'em.

331
Middle age is when you have a choice of two temptations and choose the one that will get you home earlier.

332
Even moderation ought not to be practised to excess.

333
Modern kitchen - where the pot calls the kettle chartreuse.

334
A mother is a person who if she is not there when you get home from school you wouldn't know how to get your dinner, and you wouldn't feel like eating it anyway.

335
Muscular Christianity.

336 *(Muslim Creed)*
I believe there is no god but Allah alone and Muhammed is his prophet.

337
The nature of God is a circle of which the centre is everywhere and the circumference is nowhere.

338
The nearest thing to death in life
Is David Patrick Maxwell Fyfe,
Though underneath that gloomy shell
He does himself extremely well.

339
Ne'er of the living can the living judge -
Too blind the affection, or too fresh the grudge.

340 *(negro spiritual)*
God gave Noah the rainbow sign,
No more water, the fire next time.

341 *(negro spritual)*
Swing low, sweet chariot
Comin' for to carry me home;
I looked over Jordan and what did I see?
A band of angels comin' after me
Comin' for to carry me home.

342
Never pick a quarrel with a man who buys his ink by the gallon.

343 *(news headline)*
Whose finger do you want on the trigger?

344 *(news headline on evolution findings)*
Man is more mushroom than tulip.

345
Nil carborundum illegitimi
(Cod Latin for) 'Don't let the bastards grind you down'.

346
Nostalgia ain't what it used to be.

347
There is nothing wrong with making mistakes. Just don't respond with encores.

348 *(notice in an English doctor's waiting-room)*
To avoid delay, please have all your symptoms ready.

349
Oboe - an ill woodwind that nobody blows good.

350 *(oil drillers in 1859)*
Drill for oil? You mean drill into the ground to try and find oil? You're crazy.

351
There was an old lady from Riga
Who rode with a smile on a tiger
They returned from the ride
With the lady inside
And a smile on the face of the tiger.

352
Old men and far travellers may lie with authority.

353 *(overheard at a performance of Cleopatra)*
How different, how very different from the home life of our own very dear Queen!

354 *(pamphlet from Chinese Family Planning Centre)*
Marriage is not a finished affair. No matter to what age you live, love must be continuously consolidated. Being considerate, thoughtful and respectful without ulterior motives is the key to a satisfactory marriage.

355 *Passing By*
There is a lady sweet and kind,
Was never a face so pleased my mind;

I did but see her passing by
And yet I love her till I die.

356
Some people handle the truth carelessly;
others never touch it at all.

357 *(Post Office inscription, Washington D.C.)*
Messenger of sympathy and love, servant of
parted friends, consoler of the lonely, bond of
the scattered family, enlarger of the common
life.

358
Pretty much all the honest truthtelling there is
in the world is done by children.

359
Psychiatry is the care of the id by the odd.

360
The rabbit has a charming face:
Its private life is a disgrace.
I really dare not name to you
The awful things that rabbits do.

361
Reality is an illusion caused by lack of alcohol.

362
If you really do put a small value upon yourself,
rest assured that the world will not raise your
price.

363 *(report to Admiralty)*
We shelled the Turks from 9 to 11: and then, it
being Sunday, had Divine Service.

364 *(results of a 1997 tourist survey)*
The overall impression from the British and
Germans is that they love France itself but
would rather that the French didn't live there.

365 *(Rugby Football rules in Toronto)*
If a player continues transgressing the rules, his
side shall lose him.

366 *(Scottish toast)*
Here's tae us; wha's like us? Gey few, and they're
a'deid.

367
The sea hath no king but God alone.

368
The secret of teaching is to appear to have
known all your life what you learned this
afternoon.

369
See the happy moron,
He doesn't give a damn,
I wish I were a moron,
My God! perhaps I am.

370
Keep a thing seven years and you will find a use
for it.

371
His shortcoming is his long staying.

372 *(sign on the desk of President Harry S. Truman)*
The buck stops here.

373 *(sign on lawn, University of Iowa)*
If allowed to survive, this grass will produce
enough oxygen for two students to breathe for
one semester.

374
A smile is a curve that can set things straight.

375 *(song)*
O Death, where is thy sting-a-ling-a-ling
O grave, thy victory?
The bells of hell go ting-a-ling-a-ling
For you but not for me.

376 *(song)*
It's love that makes the world go round.

377 *(song)*
We're here because we're here because we're
here because we're here.

378 *(song)*
John Brown's body lies a mould'ring in the grave
His soul is marching on.

379 *(song)*
It is good to be merry and wise,
It is good to be honest and true,
It is best to be off with the old love,
Before you are on with the new.

380 *Stevins MS*
Thirty days hath September,
April, June and November;
All the rest have thirty-one,
Excepting February alone,
And that has twenty-eight days clear,
And twenty-nine in a leap year.

381
There is one thing stronger than all the armies
in the world; and that is an idea whose time has
come.

382
If the student fails to learn the teacher fails to
teach.

383 *(submission of recorded Presidental Conversations)*
Expletive deleted.

384
Success is not so much what you are, but rather
what you appear to be.

385
Tact is the intelligence of the heart.

386
There is a tavern in the town,
And there my dear love sits him down,
And drinks his wine 'mid laughter free,
And never, never thinks of me.
Fare thee well, for I must leave thee,
Do not let this parting grieve thee,
And remember that the best of friends must
part.

387
Tempora mutantur, et nos mutamur in illis.
Times change, and we change with them.

388
There's no such thing as a free lunch.

389
There's a wonderful family called Stein,
There's Gert, and there's Epp and there's Ein:
Gert's poems are bunk,
Epp's statues are junk,
And no one can understand Ein.

390
Every time a man puts a new idea across he
finds ten men who thought of it before he did -
but they only thought of it.

391
It takes time to be a success, but time is all it
takes.

392
'Tis better than riches
To scratch when it itches.

393 *(title of BBC Television series)*
Not So Much a Programme, More a Way of Life.

394 *(title of a song)*
We Shall Overcome.

395 *(tomb inscription)*
Et in Arcadia ego.
And I too am in Arcadia.

396
Truth is the daughter of time.

397
There are two reasons for doing things - a very
good reason and the real reason.

398 *(two-line comic song)*
Lloyd George knew my father,
My father knew Lloyd George.

399
The United States was born in the country and
moved to the city in the nineteenth century.

400 *Universal Declaration of Human Rights*
All human beings are born free and equal in
dignity and rights.

401
Violence is, essentially, a confession of ultimate
inarticulateness.

402
War does not determine who is right - only who
is left.

403 *(weaver's Song)*
Now I am a bachelor, I live by myself and I work
at the weaving trade,
And the only thing that I ever did wrong
Was to woo a fair young maid.
She sighed, she cried, she damned near died:
She said 'What shall I do?'
So I took her into bed and covered up her head
Just to save her from the foggy, foggy dew.

404 *(Weller's Law)*
Nothing is impossible for the person who
doesn't have to do it.

405 *(Western Union memo, 1876)*
This 'telephone' has too many shortcomings to
be seriously considered as a means of
communication. The device is inherently of no
value to us.

406 *(West Indian calypso)*
The singer not the song.

407
What costs nothing is worth nothing.

408
What men usually ask of God when they pray is
that two and two not make four.

409
When you want really big money, you usually
find yourself talking to people who didn't go to
Eton.

410
When war enters a country
It produces lies like sand.

411
Where is the man who has the power and skill
To stem the torrent of a woman's will?
For if she will, she will, you may depend on't;
And if she won't, she won't; so there's an end
on't.

412
Whilst Adam slept, Eve from his side arose;
Strange his first sleep should be his last repose.

413
Who buys has need of two eyes
But one's enough to sell the stuff.

414
He who would do good to another, must do it in minute particulars.

415
He who drinketh by the inch and speaketh by the yard shall be kicketh by the foot.

416
He who laughs, lasts.

417 *(of the Winchester Cathedral organ)*
Audible at five miles, painful at three, and lethal at one.

418
Wit is far more often a shield than a lance.

419
Some women blush when they are kissed; some call for the police; some swear; some bite. But the worst are those who laugh.

420
Women have their faults
Men have only two
Everything they say,
Everything they do.

421
A word to the wise is infuriating.

422
The world is full of fools, and he who would not see it should live alone and smash his mirror.

423
No one in this world needs a mink coat but a mink.

424
Things could be worse. Suppose your errors were counted and published every day, like those of a baseball player.

425
Write something, even if it's just a suicide note.

426
Yankee Doodle came to town
Riding on a pony;
Stuck a feather in his cap
And called it macaroni.

427
Every year it takes less time to fly across the Atlantic, and more time to drive to the office.

428
There was a young lady from Kent,
Who said she knew what men meant
When they asked her to dine;
Private room, champagne, wine -
She knew what they meant and she went.

429
Young men think old men fools and old men know young men to be so.

430
This is a youth-oriented society, and the joke is on them because youth is a disease from which we all recover.

431
After you've heard two eyewitness accounts of an auto accident it makes you wonder about history.

ANOUILH Jean 1910-1987
432
Things are beautiful if you love them.

433
A good actor must never be in love with anyone but himself.

434
Love is, above all, the gift of oneself.

435
Man dies when he wants, as he wants, of what he chooses.

436
Every man thinks God is on his side. The rich and powerful know he is.

437
Oh, love is real enough, you will find it some day, but it has one arch-enemy - and that is life.

438
We poison our lives with fear of burglary and shipwreck, and, ask anyone, the house is never burgled, and the ship never goes down.

439
What you get free costs too much.

440
When you are forty, half of you belongs to the past ... And when you are seventy, nearly all of you.

ANTHONY Metropolitan of Sourozh 1914-
441 *Beginning to Pray*
So often when we say, 'I love you,' we say it with a huge 'I' and a little 'you'.

ANTHONY Susan B. 1820-1906
442 *Motto, The Revolution*
Men their rights and nothing more; Women their rights and nothing less.

443
The only question left to be settled now is, are women persons?

444
In the schoolroom, more than any other place, does the difference of sex, if there is any, need

to be forgotten.

ANTISTHENES c.445-c.370 BC
445
The investigation of the meaning of words is the beginning of education.

ANTOINETTE Marie 1755-1793
446 *(on the way to the guillotine)*
Courage! I have shown it for years; think you I shall lose it at the moment when my sufferings are to end?

ANTRIM Minna 1861-
447 *Naked Truth and Veiled Allusions*
Experience is a good teacher, but she sends in terrific bills.

448 *Naked Truth and Veiled Allusions*
A fool bolts pleasure, then complains of moral indigestion.

APPLETON Sir Edward 1892-1965
449
I do not mind what language an opera is sung in so long as it is a language I don't understand.

APPLETON Thomas Gold 1812-1884
450
A Boston man is the east wind made flesh.

451
Good Americans, when they die, go to Paris.

APPLEY Lawrence
452
Management is now where the medical profession was when it decided that working in a drug store was not sufficient training to become a doctor.

AQUINAS St. Thomas 1225-1274
453
The End of every maker is himself.

454 *Summa Theologicae*
Therefore it is necessary to arrive at a prime mover, put in motion by no other; and this everyone understands to be God.

455 *Summa Theologicae*
If all evil were prevented, much good would be absent from the universe.

The ARABIAN NIGHTS
456 *The History of Ali Baba*
Open Sesame!

ARBUS Diane 1923-1971
457
My favourite thing is to go where I've never been.

458
I really believe there are things nobody would see if I didn't photograph them.

459
You see someone on the street, and essentially what you notice about them is the flaw.

ARBUTHNOT John 1667-1735
460
Biography is one of the new terrors of death.

461 *The History of John Bull*
Law is a bottomless pit.

ARCHIMEDES 287-212 BC
462 *(on making a discovery)*
Eureka!
I have got it!

463 *(on the lever)*
Give me a firm spot on which to stand, and I will move the earth.

ARDREY Robert
464
Human war has been the most successful of all our cultural traditions.

ARENDT Hannah 1906-1975
465
Under conditions of tyranny it is far easier to act than to think.

466
Equality is the result of human organization. We are not born equal.

467
Ideas, as distinguished from events, are never unprecedented.

468
The most radical revolutionary will become a conservative on the day after a revolution.

ARETINO Pietro 1492-1556
469
Age has a good mind and sorry shanks.

ARISTOTLE 384-322 BC
470
Art not only imitates nature, but also completes its deficiencies.

471
Dignity does not consist in possessing honours, but in deserving them.

472
To enjoy the things we ought, and to hate the things we ought, has the greatest bearing on excellence of character.

473
Without friends no one would choose to live, though he had all other goods.

474
It is Homer who has chiefly taught other poets the art of telling lies skilfully.

475
Humour is the only test of gravity, and gravity of humour, for a subject which will not bear raillery is suspicious, and a jest which will not bear serious examination is false wit.

476
Inferiors revolt in order that they may be equal, and equals that they may be superior.

477
Melancholy men are of all others the most witty.

478 *Nicomachean Ethics*
We make war that we may live in peace.

479 *Poetics*
So poetry is something more philosophical and more worthy of serious attention than history.

480 *Poetics*
Probable impossibilities are to be preferred to improbable possibilities.

481 *Politics*
Man is by nature a political animal.

482 *Politics*
He who is unable to live in society, or who has no need because he is sufficient for himself, must be either a beast or a god.

483 *Politics*
Nature does nothing without purpose or uselessly.

484 *Politics*
Where some people are very wealthy and others have nothing, the result will be either extreme democracy or absolute oligarchy, or despotism will come from either of those excesses.

485
The worst form of inequality is to try to make unequal things equal.

ARMISTEAD Lewis Addison 1817-1863
486 *(during the American Civil War)*
Give them the cold steel, boys!

ARMOUR J. Ogden
487
The young man who wants to marry happily should pick out a good mother and marry one of her daughters - any one will do.

ARMSTRONG Louis 1901-1971
488
All music is folk music, I ain't never heard no horse sing a song.

489
There are some people that if they don't know, you can't tell 'em.

490
What we play is life.

ARMSTRONG Neil 1930-
491 *(on becoming the first man to walk on the Moon)*
That's one small step for man, one giant leap for mankind.

492
Fear is not an unknown emotion to us.

ARMSTRONG Sir Robert 1927-
493 *(during 'Spycatcher' trial)*
It contains a misleading impression, not a lie. It was being economical with the truth.

ARNE T. Augustine 1710-1778
494
Britain's best bulwarks are her wooden walls.

ARNOLD George 1834-1865
495 *'The Jolly Old Pedagone'*
The living need charity more than the dead.

ARNOLD Matthew 1822-1888
496 *Absence*
And we forget because we must
And not because we will.

497
Conduct is three-fourths of our life and its largest concern.

498
Culture is the passion for sweetness and light, and (what is more) the passion for making them prevail.

499 *Culture and Anarchy*
The men of culture are the true apostles of equality.

500 *Culture and Anarchy*
When I want to distinguish clearly the aristocratic class from the Philistines proper or middle class, I name the former, in my own mind the Barbarians.

501 *Dover Beach*
Ah, love, let us be true
To one another.

502 *Empedocles on Etna*
Is it so small a thing
To have enjoyed the sun,
To have lived light in the spring,
To have loved to have thought, to have done.

503 *Essays in Criticism*
[Oxford] whispering from her towers the last enchantments of the Middle Ages... Home of lost causes, and forsaken beliefs, and unpopular names, and impossible loyalties!

504 *Essays in Criticsm*
Poetry is at bottom a criticism of life.

505
The same heart beats in every human breast.

506 *'Isolation. To Marguerite'*
This truth - to prove, and make thine own:
`Thou hast been, shalt be, art, alone'.

507
Journalism is literature in a hurry.

508 *Letters of Matthew Arnold*
I am past thirty, and three parts iced over.

509 *Morality*
We cannot kindle when we will
The fire which in the heart resides,
The spirit bloweth and is still
In mystery our soul abides.

510
Nature, with equal mind,
Sees all her sons at play,
Sees man control the wind,
The wind sweep man away.

511
The nice sense of measure is certainly not one
of nature's gifts to her English children ... we
have all of us yielded to infatuation at some
moment of our lives.

512 *'Parting'*
Say, has some wet bird-haunted English lawn
Lent it the music of its trees at dawn?

513 *'Philomela'*
Hark! ah, the Nightingale!
The tawny-throated!
Hark! from that moonlit cedar what a burst!
What triumph! hark - what pain!

514 *'Philomela'*
Eternal Passion!
Eternal Pain!

515 *'Self-Dependence'*
Resolve to be thyself: and know, that he
Who finds himself, loses his misery.

516
This strange disease of modern life.

517 *'The Scholar-Gipsy'*
Go, for they call you, Shepherd, from the hill.

518 *'The Scholar-Gipsy'*
Still nursing the unconquerable hope, still
Clutching the inviolable shade.

519 *'Thyrsis'*
And that sweet City with her dreaming spires,
She needs not June for beauty's heightening.

520
Tired of knocking at Preferment's door.

521 *'Youth's Agitations'*
And sigh that one thing only has been lent
To youth and age in common - discontent.

ARNOLD Samuel J. 1774-1852
522 *The Death of Nelson*
For England, home and beauty.

ARNOLD Thomas 1795-1842
523 *(address to his scholars at Rugby)*
What we must look for here is, first, religious
and moral principles; secondly, gentlemanly
conduct; thirdly, intellectual ability.

524
My object will be, if possible, to form Christian
men for Christian boys I can scarcely hope to
make.

ASAF George 1880-1951
525 *'Pack up your Troubles in Your Old Kit Bag'*
What's the use of worrying?
It never was worth while,
So pack up your troubles in your old kit bag,
And smile, smile, smile.

ASCH Sholem 1880-1957
526
Not the power to remember, but its very
opposite, the power to forget, is a necessary
condition for our existence.

527
It has been said that writing comes more easily
if you have something to say.

ASHFORD Daisy 1881-1972
528
I am very fond of fresh air and royalties.

ASHRAWI Hanan
529
Women in politics are more honest and
forthright. We are not in it for the ego
gratification.

ASHTON-WARNER Sylvia
530
I tore myself away from the safe comfort of
certainties through my love for truth; and truth
rewarded me.

ASIMOV Isaac 1920-1992
531
Our lifetime may be the last that will be lived
out in a technological society.

ASNAS Max
532
Money is something you got to make in case
you don't die.

ASQUITH Herbert H. 1852-1928
533
You should read it, though there is much that is
skip-worthy.

534
It is fitting that we should have buried the
Unknown Prime Minister [Bonar Law] by the

side of the unknown Soldier.

535
Greatness is a zigzag streak of lightning in the brain.

536 *(phrase used repeatedly in speeches)*
We had better wait and see.

537
[The War office kept three sets of figures:] one to mislead the public, another to mislead the Cabinet, and the third to mislead itself.

ASQUITH Margot 1865-1945
538 *(of David Lloyd George)*
He can't see a belt without hitting below it.

539 *(of F.E. Smith)*
He's very clever, but sometimes his brains go to his head.

540 *(of her husband)*
His modesty amounts to deformity.

541 *(to Jean Harlow, correcting the mispronunciation of her name)*
The 'T' is silent - as in `Harlow'.

542 *(of Lady Desborough)*
She tells enough white lies to ice a wedding cake.

543 *(of Lord Kitchener)*
If Kitchener is not a great man, he is, at least, a great poster.

544 *(of a politician)*
He always has his arm round your waist and his eye on the clock.

545 *(of Sir Stafford Cripps)*
He has a brilliant mind until he makes it up.

ASSISI St Francis of 1181-1226
546 *'Prayer of St Francis'*
Lord, make me an instrument of Your peace!
Where there is hatred let me sow love;
Where there is injury, pardon;
Where there is doubt, faith;
Where there is despair, hope;
Where there is darkness, light;
Where there is sadness, joy.

O divine Master, grant that I may not so much seek
To be consoled as to console;
To be understood as to understand;
To be loved as to love.
For it is in giving that we receive;
It is in pardoning that we are pardoned;
And it is in dying that we are born to eternal life.

ASTAIRE Fred 1899-1987
547
The hardest job kids face today is learning good manners without seeing any.

ASTLEY Sir Jacob 1579-1652
548 *Prayer before the battle of Edgehill*
O Lord! thou knowest how busy I must be this day: if I forget thee, do not thou forget me.

ASTOR Lady 1879-1964
549
The main dangers in this life are the people who want to change everything - or nothing.

550
I married beneath me. All women do.

551
My vigour, vitality and cheek repel me. I am the kind of woman I would run from.

ATKINS Eileen 1934-
552
Fame means absolutely nothing except a good table at a restaurant.

ATKINSON Brooks 1894-1984
553
Life is seldom as unendurable as, to judge by the facts, it logically ought to be.

554
Every man with an idea has at least two or three followers.

555 *Once around the Sun*
After each war there is a little less democracy to save.

556 *Once Around The Sun*
We cheerfully assume that, in some mystic way, love conquers all; that good outweighs evil in the just balances of the universe, and that at the 11th hour, something gloriously triumphant will prevent the worst before it happens.

557
The virtue of the camera is not the power it has to transform the photographer into an artist, but the impulse it gives him to keep on looking.

ATKINSON E.L. and GARRARD Apsley Cherry 1882-1929 and 1882-
558 *(inscription on the burial-place of Captain Oates)*
A very gallant gentleman.....he walked willingly to his death in a blizzard to try to save his comrades beset by hardships.

ATTLEE Clement 1883-1967
559 *(on himself)*
Few thought he was even a starter.
There were many who thought themselves smarter.
But he ended PM, CH and OM.
An Earl and a Knight of the Garter.

560
Democracy means government by discussion, but it is only effective if you can stop people talking.

561
[Russian Communism is] the illegitimate child of Karl Marx and Catherine the Great.

562
I think the British have the distinction above all other nations of being able to put new wine into old bottles without bursting them.

563
The voice we heard was that of Mr. Churchill but the mind was that of Lord Beaverbrook.

564
Winston Churchill - fifty per cent genius, fifty per cent bloody fool.

ATWOOD Margaret 1939-
565
The answers you get from literature depend upon the questions you pose.

566
A divorce is like an amputation; you survive, but there's less of you.

567
Fear has a smell, as
Love does.

568
If the national mental illness of the United States is megalomania, that of Canada is paranoid schizophrenia.

AUBREY John 1626-1697
569 *Brief Lives 'John Milton'*
Oval face. His eye a dark grey. He had auburn hair. His complexion exceeding fair - he was so fair that they called him the lady of Christ's College.

AUDEN W. H. 1907-1973
570 *(of himself)*
My face looks like a wedding-cake left out in the rain.

571
We are all here on earth to help others; what on earth the others are here for I don't know.

572
Almost all of our relationships begin, and most of them continue, as forms of mutual exploitation, a mental or physical barter, to be terminated when one or both parties run out of goods.

573
Art is born of humiliation.

574 *A Certain World*
All sin tends to be addictive, and the terminal point of addiction is what is called damnation.

575 *Dog Beneath the Skin*
Happy the hare at morning, for she cannot read
The Hunter's waking thoughts.

576 *The Dyer's Hand*
Among those whom I like, I can find no common denominator, but among those whom I love, I can: all of them make me laugh.

577 *The Dyer's Hand*
Man is a history-making creature who can neither repeat his past nor leave it behind.

578 *The Dyer's Hand 'Reading'*
Some books are undeservedly forgotten; none are undeservedly remembered.

579
The ear tends to be lazy, craves the familiar and is shocked by the unexpected; the eye, on the other hand, tends to be impatient, craves the novel and is bored by repetition.

580 *'Epitaph for the Unknown Soldier'*
To save your world you asked this man to die:
Would this man, could he see you now, ask why?

581
Geniuses are the luckiest of mortals because what they must do is the same as what they most want to do.

582
To ask the hard question is simple.

583
Let us humour if we can
The vertical man
Though we value none
But the horizontal one.

584 *'In memory of W.B. Yeats'*
Earth, receive an honoured guest:
Willam Yeats is laid to rest.
Let the Irish vessel lie
Emptied of its poetry.

585 *'In memory of W.B. Yeats'*
In the deserts of the heart
Let the healing fountain start
In the prison of his days
Teach the free man how to praise.

586 *'The Love Feast'*
In an upper room at midnight
See us gathered on behalf
Of love according to the gospel
Of the radio-phonograph.

587 *'Lullaby'*
Lay your sleeping head, my love,
Human on my faithless arm.

588 *'This Lunar Beauty'*
Love shall not near
The sweetness here,
Nor sorrow take
His endless look.

589
Any marriage, happy or unhappy, is infinitely
more interesting and significant than any
romance, however passionate.

590 *'In memory of Sigmund Freud'*
To us he is no more a person
now but a whole climate of opinion.

591 *'New Year letter'*
To the man-in-the-street, who, I'm sorry to say,
Is a keen observer of life,
The word `Intellectual' suggests straight away
A man who's untrue to his wife.

592 *'Night train'*
This is the night mail crossing the Border,
Bringing the cheque and the postal order,
Letters for the rich, letters for the poor.
The shop on the corner, the girl next door.

593
It is nonsense to speak of 'higher' and 'lower'
pleasures. To a hungry man it is, rightly, more
important that he eat than that he philosophize.

594 *'Orators'*
Private faces in public places
Are wiser and nicer
Than public faces in private places.

595
My poetry doesn't change from place to place -
it changes with the years. It's very important to
be one's age. You get ideas you have to turn
down - 'I'm sorry, no longer', 'I'm sorry, not yet.'

596
A professor is one who talks in someone else's
sleep.

597 *'September 1, 1939'*
I, and the public know
What all schoolchildren learn
Those to whom evil is done
Do evil in return.

598 *'September 1, 1939'*
There is no such thing as the State
And no one exists alone;
Hunger allows no choice
To the citizen or the police;
We must love one another or die.

599 *'Stop All the Clocks'*
He was my North, my South, my East and West,
My working week and my Sunday rest,
My noon, my midnight, my talk, my song;
I thought that love would last forever: I was
wrong.

600 *'The Unknown Citizen'*
Our researchers into Public Opinion are content
That he held the proper opinions for the time of
year;
When there was peace, he was for peace; when
there was war, he went.

601 *'As I Walked Out One Evening'*
The years shall run like rabbits,
For in my arms I hold
The Flower of the Ages,
And the first love of the world.

602
When we do evil,
We and our victims
Are equally bewildered.

603 *'The Witnesses'*
The sky is darkening like a stain;
Something is going to fall like rain,
And it won't be flowers.

AUGUSTINE St. 354-430
604
Charity is no substitute for justice withheld.

605 *Confessions*
Give me chastity and continence, but not yet.

606 *Contra Epistolam Parmeniani*
The verdict of the world is final.

607 *De Duabus Animabus*
Hear the other side.

608 *(on the Good of Marriage)*
To many, total abstinence is easier than perfect
moderation.

609 *Joannis*
Love and do what you like.

610
Lord, who art always the same, give that I know
myself, give that I know Thee.

611
We make ourselves a ladder out of vices if we
trample the vices themselves underfoot.

612
There is no salvation outside the church.

613 *Sermons*
Rome has spoken; the case is concluded.

AURELIUS Marcus 121-180
614
Accept the things to which fate binds you, and

love the people with whom fate brings you together, but do so with all your heart.

615
All things from eternity are like forms and come round in circles.

616
The art of living is more like that of wrestling than of dancing. The main thing is to stand firm and be ready for an unforeseen attack.

617
To change your mind and to follow him who sets you right is to be nonetheless the free agent that you were before.

618
Every instant of time is a pinprick of eternity. All things are petty, easily changed, vanishing away.

619
Life is a stranger's sojourn, a night at an inn.

620
There is no man so blessed that some who stand by his deathbed won't hail the occasion with delight.

621
Never let the future disturb you. You will meet it, if you have to, with the same weapons of reason which today arm you against the present.

622
Nothing happens to any man that he is not formed by nature to bear.

623
Remember that no man loses any other life than this which he now lives, nor lives any other than this which he now loses.

624
Time is a sort of river of passing events, and strong is its current; no sooner is a thing brought to sight than it is swept by and another takes its place, and this too will be swept away.

625
The Universe is transformation; our life is what our thoughts make it.

626
Whatever may happen to you was prepared for you from all eternity; and the implication of causes was from eternity spinning the thread of your being.

627
Whatever the universal nature assigns to any man at any time is for the good of that man at that time.

AUSTEN Jane 1775-1817
628 *Emma*
An egg boiled very soft is not unwholesome.

629 *Emma*
One half of the world cannot understand the pleasures of the other.

630 *Emma*
With men he can be rational and unaffected, but when he has ladies to please, every feature works.

631 *Emma*
The sooner every party breaks up the better.

632 *Emma*
Surprises are foolish things. The pleasure is not enhanced, and the inconvenience is often considerable.

633 *Emma*
One has great hopes from Birmingham. I always say there is something direful in the sound.

634 *Emma*
Business, you know, may bring money, but friendship hardly ever does.

635 *Emma*
Why not seize the pleasure at once? How often is happiness destroyed by preparation, foolish preparation?

636
It is always incomprehensible to a man that a woman should ever refuse an offer of marriage.

637 *Letter to Fanny Knight*
Single women have a dreadful propensity for being poor - which is one very strong argument in favour of matrimony.

638 *Letters*
What dreadful hot weather we have! It keeps me in a continual state of inelegance.

639 *Letters*
I do not want people to be very agreeable, as it saves me the trouble of liking them a great deal.

640 *Letters*
In nine cases out of ten, a woman had better show more affection than she feels.

641 *Letters*
Men are all so good for nothing, and hardly any women at all.

642 *Mansfield Park*
A large income is the best recipe for happiness I ever heard of. It certainly may secure all the myrtle and turkey part of it.

643 *Northanger Abbey*
Oh! who can ever be tired of Bath!

644 *Northanger Abbey*
From politics, it was an easy step to silence.

645
There is nothing like staying at home for real comfort.

646 *Persuasion*
She had been forced into prudence in her youth, she learned romance as she grew older - the natural sequel of an unnatural beginning.

647 *Persuasion*
Next to being married, a girl likes to be crossed in love a little now and then.

648 *Persuasion*
My sore throats are always worse than anyone's.

649 *Persuasion*
All the privilege I claim for my own sex ... is that of loving longest, when existence or when hope is gone.

650 *Pride and Prejudice*
It is a truth universally acknowledged, that a single man in possession of a good fortune, must be in want of a wife.

651 *Pride and Prejudice*
She was a woman of mean understanding, little information, and uncertain temper.

652 *Pride and Prejudice*
Loss of virtue in a female is irretrievable...one false step involves her in endless ruin.

653 *Pride and Prejudice*
A lady's imagination is very rapid; it jumps from admiration to love, from love to matrimony in a moment.

654
I have been a selfish being all my life, in practice, though not in principle.

655 *Sense and Sensibility*
An annuity is a very serious business.

AUSTIN Alfred 1835-1913
656 *(attributed: on illness of the Prince of Wales)*
Across the wires the electric message came: `He is not better, he is much the same'.

AUSTIN Warren R. 1877-1962
657 *(in a debate on the Middle East)*
[Jews and Arabs should settle their differences] like good Christians.

AVERY Milton 1893-1965
658
The idea is in my head; to put it down is nothing.

AVOT Pirke
659
If I am not myself, who will be?

AWDRY Revd W. V. 1911-1997
660 *Thomas the Tank Engine*
You've a lot to learn about trucks, little Thomas. They are silly things and must be kept in their place. After pushing them about here for a few weeks you'll know almost as much about them as Edward. Then you'll be a Really Useful Engine.

AXELROD George 1922-
661
The Seven Year Itch.

AYCKBOURN Alan 1939-
662 *Bedroom Farce*
My mother used to say, Delia, if S-E-X ever rears its ugly head, close your eyes before you see the rest of it.

663 *How the Other Half Loves*
Do you realize, Mrs Foster, the hours I've put into that woman? When I met her, you know, she was nothing. Nothing at all. With my own hands I have built her up. Encouraging her to join the public library and make use of her non-fiction tickets.

664 *Table Manners*
I always feel with Norman that I have him on loan from somewhere. Like one of his library books.

AYER A. J. 1910-1989
665 *(attributed)*
Why should you mind being wrong if someone can show you that you are?

666 *Language, Truth and Logic*
We offer the theist the same comfort as we gave to the moralist. His assertions cannot possibly be valid, but they cannot be invalid either....It is only when the theist claims that in asserting the existence of a transcendent god he is expressing a genuine proposition that we are entitled to disagree with him.

667
No morality can be founded on authority, even if the authority were divine.

AYRES Pam 1947-
668 *'Oh no, I got a cold'*
Medicinal discovery,
It moves in mighty leaps,
It leaps straight past the common cold,
And gives it us for keeps.

AYTOUN Sir Robert 1570-1638
669 `*To an Inconstant Mistress*'
I loved thee once, I'll love no more,
Thine be the grief, as is the blame;
Thou art not what thou wast before,
What reason I should be the same?

BACALL Lauren 1924-
670
Stardom isn't a profession; it's an accident.

BACH George R.
671
Anger cannot be dishonest.

BACKUS Jim
672
Many a man owes his success to his first wife and his second wife to his success.

BACON Francis 1561-1626
673 *The Advancement of Learning*
For all knowledge and wonder (which is the seed of knowledge) is an impression of pleasure in itself.

674 *The Advancement of Learning*
So let great authors have their due, as time, which is the author of authors, be not deprived of his due, which is further and further to discover truth.

675 *The Advancement of Learning*
If a man will begin with certainties, he shall end in doubts; but if he will be content to begin with doubts, he shall end in certainties.

676 *The Advancement of Learning*
[Knowledge is] a rich storehouse for the glory of the Creator and the relief of man's estate.

677 *The Advancement of Learning*
Antiquities are history defaced, or some remnants of history which have casually escaped the shipwreck of time.

678 *The Advancement of Learning*
Poesy was ever thought to have some participation of divineness, because it doth raise and erect the mind, by submitting the shows of things to the desires of the mind; whereas reason doth buckle and bow the mind unto the nature of things.

679 *The Advancement of Learning*
The knowledge of man is as the waters, some descending from above, and some springing from beneath; the one informed by the light of nature, the other inspired by divine revelation.

680 *The Advancement of Learning*
They are ill discoverers that think there is no land, when they can see nothing but sea.

681 *The Advancement of Learning*
But men must know, that in this theatre of man's life it is reserved only for God and angels to be lookers on.

682
That all things are changed, and that nothing really perishes, and that the sum of matter remains exactly the same, is sufficiently certain.

683
All rising to great places is by a winding stair.

684
Anger makes dull men witty, but it keeps them poor.

685 *'The Antitheta of Things'*
Riches are a good handmaid, but the worst mistress.

686 *'The Antitheta of Things'*
Silence is the virtue of fools.

687
Atheism is rather in the lip than in the heart of Man.

688
As the births of living creatures at first are ill-shapen, so are all innovations, which are the births of time.

689 *The Elements of the Common Law*
I hold every man a debtor to his profession.

690 *Essays*
Some books are to be tasted, others to be swallowed, and some few to be chewed and digested.

691 *Essays*
They do best who, if they cannot but admit Love, yet make it keep quarter; and sever it wholly from their serious affairs and actions of life.

692 *Essays 'Of Adversity'*
Prosperity is the blessing of the Old Testament, adversity is the blessing of the New.

693 *Essays 'Of Adversity'*
Prosperity is not without many fears and distastes; and adversity is not without comforts and hopes.

694 *Essays 'Of Adversity'*
Prosperity doth best discover vice, but adversity doth best discover virtue.

695 *Essays 'Of Atheism'*
A little philosophy inclineth man's mind to atheism, but depth in philosophy bringeth men's minds about to religion.

696 *Essays 'Of Atheism'*
They that deny a God destroy man's nobility; for certainly man is of kin to the beasts by his body; and, if he be not of kin to God by his spirit, he is a base and ignoble creature.

697 *Essays 'Of Beauty'*
That is the best part of beauty, which a picture cannot express.

698 *Essays 'Of Ceremonies and Respects'*
Light gains make heavy purses.

699 *Essays 'Of Ceremonies and Respects'*
He that is too much in anything, so that he giveth another occasion of satiety, maketh himself cheap.

700 *Essays 'Of Counsel'*
Books will speak plain when counsellors blanch.

701 *Essays 'Of Cunning'*
I knew one that when he wrote a letter he would put that which was most material in the postscript, as if it had been a bymatter.

702 *Essays 'Of Cunning'*
Nothing doth more hurt in a state than that cunning men pass for wise.

703 *Essays 'Of Death'*
Men fear death as children fear to go in the dark; and as that natural fear in children is increased with tales, so is the other.

704 *Essays 'Of Death'*
There is no passion in the mind of man so weak, but it mates and masters the fear of death. And therefore death is no such terrible enemy, when a man hath so many attendants about him that can win the combat of him. Revenge triumphs over death; love slights it; honour aspireth to it; grief flieth to it.

705 *Essays 'Of Death'*
It is as natural to die as to be born; and to a little infant, perhaps, the one is as painful as the other.

706 *Essays 'Of Death'*
Above all, believe it, the sweetest canticle is Nunc dimittis, when a man hath obtained worthy ends and expectations. Death hath this also, that it openeth the gate to good fame, and extinguisheth envy.

707 *Essays 'Of Dispatch'*
To choose time is to save time.

708 *Essays 'Of Expense'*
Riches are for spending.

709 *Essays 'Of Expense'*
A man ought warily to begin charges which once begun will continue.

710 *Essays 'Of Followers and Friends'*
There is little friendship in the world, and least of all between equals.

711 *Essays 'Of Fortune'*
Chiefly the mould of a man's fortune is in his own hands.

712 *Essays 'Of Fortune'*
If a man look sharply, and attentively, he shall see Fortune: for though she be blind, yet she is not invisible.

713 *Essays 'Of Friendship'*
A crowd is not company, and faces are but a gallery of pictures, and talk but a tinkling cymbal, where there is no love.

714 *Essays 'Of Friendship'*
It redoubleth joys, and cutteth griefs in halves.

715 *Essays 'Of Gardens'*
God Almighty first planted a garden; and indeed, it is the purest of human pleasures.

716 *Essays 'Of Great Place'*
Men in great place are thrice servants; servants of the sovereign or state, servants of fame, and servants of business.

717 *Essays 'Of Great Place'*
It is a strange desire to seek power and to lose liberty.

718 *Essays 'Of Great Place'*
Severity breedeth fear, but roughness breedeth hate.

719 *Essays 'Of Innovations'*
He that will not apply new remedies must expect new evils; for time is the greatest innovator.

720 *Essays 'Of Love'*
It has been well said that 'the arch-flatterer with whom all the petty flatterers have intelligence is a man's self'.

721 *Essays 'Of Marriage and the Single Life'*
He that hath wife and children hath given hostages to fortune; for they are impediments to great enterprises, either of virtue or mischief.

722 *Essays 'Of Marriage and the Single Life'*
Wives are young men's mistresses, companions for middle age, and old men's nurses.

723 *Essays 'Of Marriage and the Single Life'*
He was reputed one of the wise men that made answer to the question when a man should marry? 'A young man not yet, an elder man not at all.'

724 *Essays 'Of Negotiating'*
It is generally better to deal by speech than by letter.

725 *Essays 'Of Nobility'*
New nobility is but the act of power, but ancient nobility is the act of time.

726 *Essays 'Of Nobility'*
Nobility of birth commonly abateth industry.

727 *Essays 'Of Parents and Children'*
The joys of parents are secret, and so are their griefs and fears.

728 *Essays 'Of Parents and Children'*
Children sweeten labours, but they make
misfortunes more bitter.

729 *Essays 'Of Praise'*
Fame is like a river, that beareth up things light
and swollen, and drowns things weighty and
solid.

730 *Essays 'Of Regimen of Health'*
Age will not be defied.

731 *Essays 'Of Revenge'*
Revenge is a kind of wild justice, which the
more man's nature runs to, the more ought law
to weed it out.

732 *Essays 'Of Revenge'*
A man that studieth revenge keeps his own
wounds green.

733 *Essays 'Of Seditions and Troubles'*
Money is like muck, not good except it be
spread.

734 *Essays 'Of Seditions and Troubles'*
The remedy is worse than the disease.

735 *Essays 'Of Seeming Wise'*
The French are wiser than they seem, and the
Spaniards seem wiser than they are.

736 *Essays 'Of Studies'*
To spend too much time in studies is sloth.

737 *Essays 'Of Studies'*
They perfect nature and are perfected by
experience.

738 *Essays 'Of Studies'*
Read not to contradict and confute, nor to
believe and take for granted, nor to find talk
and discourse, but to weigh and consider.

739 *Essays 'Of Studies'*
Reading maketh a full man; conference a ready
man; and writing an exact man.

740 *Essays 'Of Studies'*
Histories make men wise; poets, witty; the
mathematics, subtile; natural philosophy, deep;
moral, grave; logic and rhetoric, able to
contend.

741 *Essays 'Of Superstition'*
There is a superstition in avoiding superstition.

742 *Essays 'Of Suspicion'*
There is nothing makes a man suspect much,
more than to know little.

743 *Essays 'Of Suspicion'*
Suspicions amongst thoughts are like bats
amongst birds, they ever fly by twilight.

744 *Essays 'Of Travel'*
Travel, in the younger sort, is a part of
education; in the elder, a part of experience. He

that travelleth into a country before he hath
some entrance into the language, goeth to
school, and not to travel.

745 *Essays 'Of the True Greatness of Kingdoms'*
Neither will it be, that a people overlaid with
taxes should ever become valiant and martial.

746 *Essays 'Of Truth'*
A mixture of a lie doth ever add pleasure.

747 *Essays 'Of Vicissitude of Things'*
In the youth of a state arms do flourish; in the
middle age of a state, learning; and then both of
them together for a time; in the declining age of
a state, mechanical arts and merchandise.

748 *Essays 'Of Wisdom for a Man's Self'*
Be so true to thyself as thou be not false to
others.

749 *Essays 'Of Wisdom for a Man's Self'*
It is the wisdom of the crocodiles, that shed
tears when they would devour.

750 *Essays 'Of Youth and Age'*
Young men are fitter to invent than to judge,
fitter for execution than for counsel, and fitter
for new projects than for settled business.

751
There is no excellent beauty that hath not some
strangeness in the proportion.

752
Hope is a good breakfast, but it is a bad supper.

753
Knowledge is power.

754 *'A Letter of Advice to the Duke of
Buckingham'*
I have rather studied books than men.

755 *'A Letter of Advice to the Earl of Essex'*
Opportunity makes a thief.

756
I would live to study, and not study to live.

757 *'To My Lord Treasurer Burghley'*
I have taken all knowledge to be my province.

758
A man that is young in years may be old in
hours, if he has lost no time.

759 *Meditationes Sacrae 'Of Heresies'*
For also knowledge itself is power.

760 *New Atlantis*
God's first Creature, which was Light.

761 *Novum Organum*
For what a man would like to be true, that he
more readily believes.

762 *Novum Organum*
Nature cannot be ordered about, except by obeying her.

763 *Resuscitatio*
Books must follow sciences, and not sciences books.

764
Truth emerges more readily from error than from confusion.

765
Universities incline wits to sophistry and affectation.

766
The virtue of prosperity is temperance; the virtue of adversity is fortitude, which in morals is the heroical virtue.

767 *The World*
What is it then to have or have no wife,
But single thraldom, or a double strife?

BADEN-POWELL Robert 1857-1941
768 *Scouting for Boys*
The scouts' motto is founded on my initials, it is: BE PREPARED, which means, you are always to be in a state of readiness in mind and body to do your DUTY.

BAECK Leo 1873-1956
769
The mark of a mature man is the ability to give love and receive it joyously and without guilt.

BAEDEKER Karl 1801-1859
770 *Great Britain - Route 30*
Oxford is on the whole more attractive than Cambridge to the ordinary visitor· and the traveller is therefore recommended to visit Cambridge first, or to omit it altogether if he cannnot visit both.

BAEZ Joan 1941-
771 *(of 60s contemporaries)*
Everyone is either bald or dead or looks like a plum pudding.

772
The only thing that's been a worse flop than the organization of non-violence has been the organization of violence.

BAGEHOT Walter 1826-1877
773
The best reason why monarchy is a strong government is that it is an intelligible government: the mass of mankind understand it, and they hardly anywhere in the world understand any other.

774
Business is really more agreeable than pleasure; it interests the whole mind ... more deeply. But it does not look as if it did.

775 *The English Constitution 'Its History'*
As soon as we see that England is a disguised republic we must see too that the classes for whom the disguise is necessary must be tenderly dealt with.

776 *The English Constitution*
Women - one half of the human race at least - care fifty times more for a marriage than a ministry.

777 *The English Constitution 'The Cabinet'*
The mystic reverence, the religious allegiance, which are essential to a true monarchy, are imaginative sentiments that no legislature can manufacture in any people.

778 *The English Constitution 'The Cabinet'*
In such constitutions [as England's] there are two parts ... first, those which excite and preserve the reverence of the population - the dignified parts ... and next, the efficient parts - those by which it, in fact, works and rules.

779 *The English Constitution 'The Cabinet'*
A cabinet is a combining committee - a hyphen which joins, a buckle which fastens, the legislative part of the state to the executive part of the state.

780 *The English Constitution 'The Cabinet'*
It has been said that England invented the phrase, 'Her Majesty's Opposition'; that it was the first government which made a criticism of administration as much a part of the polity as adminstration itself. This critical opposition is the consequence of cabinet govenment.

781 *The English Constitution 'The Cabinet'*
'The Times' has made many ministries.

782 *The English Constitution 'Checks & Balances'*
It has been said, not truly, but with a possible approximation to truth, that in 1802 every hereditary monarch was insane.

783 *The English Constitution 'The Monarchy'*
Above all things our royalty is to be reverenced, and if you begin to poke about it you cannot reverence it ... Its mystery is its life. We must not let in daylight upon magic.

784 *The English Constitution 'The Monarchy'*
The Sovereign has, under a constitutional monarchy such as ours, three rights - the right to be consulted, the right to encourage, the right to warn.

785 *Estimates of some Englishmen and Scotchmen*
No real English gentleman, in his secret soul, was ever sorry for the death of a political economist.

786 *Estimates of some Englishmen and Scotchmen*
Writers, like teeth, are divided into incisors and grinders.

787
To a great experience one thing is essential - an experiencing nature.

788
The great pleasure in life is doing what people say you cannot do.

789
Poverty is an anomaly to rich people: it is very difficult to make out why people who want dinner do not ring the bell.

BAILEY David 1938-
790
Women love scallywags, but some marry them and then try to make them wear a blazer.

BAILEY John
791
Politics is not a good location or a vocation for anyone lazy, thin-skinned or lacking a sense of humour.

BAILEY Philip James 1816-1902
792
Art is man's nature; nature is God's art.

793 *Festus*
America, thou half-brother of the world;
With something good and bad of every land.

794
Hell is more bearable than nothingness.

BAILLIE Joanna 1762-1851
795 *Basil*
But woman's grief is like a summer storm,
Short as it violent is.

BAINBRIDGE Beryl 1934-
796 *A Weekend with Cloud*
He is, after all, the reflection of the tenderness I bear for myself. It is always ourselves we love.

BAIRNSFATHER Bruce 1888-1959
797 *Fragments from France*
Well, if you knows of a better 'ole, go to it.

BAKER Bobby
798
Shopping is the perfect model for the Quest.

BAKER Russell
799
Happiness is a small and unworthy goal for something as big and fancy as a whole lifetime, and should be taken in small doses.

800
I've had an unhappy life, thank God.

BALANCHINE George 1904-1983
801
I am a choreographer. A choreographer is a poet. I do not create. God creates. I assemble, and I will steal from everywhere to do it.

BALDWIN James 1924-1987
802
All art is a kind of confession, more or less oblique. All artists, if they are to survive, are forced, at last, to tell the whole story; to vomit the anguish up.

803
Children have never been very good at listening to their elders, but they have never failed to imitate them.

804
It comes as a great shock around the age of 5, 6 or 7 to discover that the flag to which you have pledged allegiance, along with everybody else, has not pledged allegiance to you. It comes as a great shock to see Gary Cooper killing off the Indians and, although you are rooting for Gary Cooper, that the Indians are you.

805 *Another Country*
The face of a lover is unknown, precisely because it is invested with so much of oneself. It is a mystery, containing, like all mysteries, the possibility of torment.

806
Education is indoctrination, if you're white - subjugation if you're black.

807
Experience, which destroys innocence, also leads one back to it.

808
I met a lot of people in Europe. I even encountered myself.

809
Money, it turned out, was exactly like sex, you thought of nothing else if you didn't have it and thought of other things if you did.

810 *Nobody Knows My Name*
Anyone who has ever struggled with poverty knows how extremely expensive it is to be poor.

811 *Nobody Knows My Name*
Freedom is not something that anybody can be given; freedom is something people take and people are as free as they want to be.

812
Most people in action are not worth very much; and yet every human being is an unprecedented miracle.

813
We take our shape, it is true, within and against
that cage of reality bequeathed us at our birth,
and yet it is precisely through our dependence
on this reality that we are most endlessly
betrayed.

814
This world is white no longer, and it will never
be white again.

BALDWIN Roger
815
I always felt from the beginning that you had to
defend people you disliked and feared as well as
those you admired.

BALDWIN Stanley 1867-1947
816
Since the day of the air, the old frontiers are
gone. When you think of the defence of
England you no longer think of the chalk cliffs
of Dover; you think of the Rhine. That is where
our frontier lies.

817 *Economic Consequences of the Peace*
They [parliament] are a lot of hard-faced men
who look as if they had done very well out of
the war.

818
The intelligent are to the intelligentsia what a
gentleman is to a gent.

819
A platitude is simply a truth repeated until
people get tired of hearing it.

820 *(speaking on the Abyssinian crisis)*
I have seldom spoken with greater regret, for
my lips are not yet unsealed. Were these
troubles over I would make a case, and I
guarantee that not a man would go into the
lobby against us. (popularly quoted as: My lips
are sealed.)

821
I think it is well also for the man in the street to
realize that there is no power on earth that can
protect him from being bombed. Whatever
people may tell him, the bomber will always get
through. The only defence is in offence, which
means that you have to kill more women and
children more quickly than the enemy if you
want to save yourselves.

822
There are three classes which need sanctuary
more than others - birds, wild flowers, and
Prime Ministers.

823
War would end if the dead could return.

BALFOUR Arthur James 1848-1930
824 *Letter to Mrs. Drew*
It is unfortunate, considering that enthusiasm
moves the world, that so few enthusiasts can be
trusted to speak the truth.

825
Society, dead or alive, can have no charm
without intimacy and no intimacy without an
interest in trifles.

826
Winston has written four volumes about
himself and called it 'World Crisis'.

BALL George W.
827
Nostalgia is a seductive liar.

BALL John d. 1381
828 *Sermon*
When Adam delved, and Eve span,
Who was then a gentleman?

BALL Lucille 1911-1989
829
I think knowing what you cannot do is more
important than knowing what you can do.

BALLOU Hosea 1771-1852
830
Hatred is self-punishment.

BALMAIN Pierre 1914-1982
831
The trick of wearing mink is to look as though
you were wearing a cloth coat. The trick of
wearing a cloth coat is to look as though you are
wearing mink.

BALZAC Honoré De 1799-1850
832
All happiness depends on courage and work. I
have had many periods of wretchedness, but
with energy and above all with illusions, I
pulled through them all.

833
Bureaucracy is a giant mechanism operated by
pygmies.

834 *Le Peau de Chagrin*
To kill the emotions and so live to old age, or to
accept the martyrdom of our passions and die
young is our doom.

835
The majority of husbands remind me of an
orang-utan trying to play the violin.

836
No man should marry until he has studied
anatomy and dissected at least one woman.

837
Manners are the hypocrisy of a nation.

838
A mother who is really a mother is never free.

BANKHEAD Tallulah 1903-1968
839
I'd rather be strongly wrong than weakly right.

BANKS Tony
840 *(whilst Minister for Sport)*
My mind is very, very open, and so is my mouth.

BANZINI Luigi
841
A gentleman does things no gentleman should do in a way only a gentleman can.

BARAKA Imamu Amiri 1934-
842 *Midstream*
God has been replaced, as he has all over the West, with respectability and air-conditioning.

843 *'Tokenism'*
A man is either free or he is not. There cannot be any apprenticeship for freedom.

BARBER James David
844
Trying to make the presidency work these days is like trying to sew buttons on a custard pie.

BARHAM R.H. ('Thomas Ingoldsby') 1788-1845
845 *The Ingoldsby Legends*
So put that in your pipe, my Lord Otto, and smoke it.

BARING Maurice 1874-1945
846 *Outline of Russian Literature*
In Mozart and Salieri we see the contrast between the genius which does what it must and the talent which does what it can.

847
If you would know what the Lord God thinks of money, you have only to look at those to whom he gives it.

BARING-GOULD Sabine 1834-1924
848 *'Onward, Christian Soldiers'*
Onward, Christian soldiers,
Marching as to war,
With the cross of Jesus
Going on before.

BARKER J.M.
849
Only an incompetent mind is content to express itself incompetently.

850
It is a sobering thought that each of us gives his hearers and his readers a chance to look into the inner working of his mind when he speaks or writes.

BARNARD Christian 1922-
851
The prime goal is to alleviate suffering, and not to prolong life. And if your treatment does not alleviate suffering, but only prolongs life, that treatment should be stopped.

BARNARD Frederick R.
852 *Printers' Ink*
One picture is worth ten thousand words.

BARNES Clive 1927-
853
Television is the first truly democratic culture - the first culture available to everybody and entirely governed by what the people want. The most terrifying thing is what people do want.

BARNES Djuna 1892-1982
854
We are adhering to life now with our last muscle - the heart.

BARNES Julian 1946-
855 *Flaubert's Parrot*
What does this journey seem like to those who aren't British - as they head towards the land of embarrassment and breakfast?

856 *Flaubert's Parrot*
Do not imagine that Art is something which is designed to give gentle uplift and self-confidence. Art is not a brassiere. At least, not in the English sense. But do not forget that brassiere is the French for life-jacket.

857 *Flaubert's Parrot*
Books say: she did this because. Life says: she did this. Books are where things are explained to you; life is where things aren't ... Books make sense of life. The only problem is that the lives they make sense of are other people's lives, never your own.

858 *A History of the World in 10½ Chapters*
Does history repeat itself, the first time as tragedy, the second time as farce? No, that's too grand, too considered a process. History just burps, and we taste again that raw onion sandwich it swallowed centuries ago.

859 *Talking It Over*
Love is just a system for getting someone to call you darling after sex.

BARNES Peter 1931-
860 *The Ruling Class*
CLAIRE: How do you know you're ... God?
EARL OF GURNEY: Simple. When I pray to Him I find I'm talking to myself.

BARNUM Phineas T. 1810-1891
861 *(attributed)*
There's a sucker born every minute.

862
Every crowd has a silver lining.

BARRAULT Jean-Louis 1910-1994
863
Acting consists of the ability to keep an
audience from coughing.

BARRIE J.M. 1860-1937
864 *The Admirable Crichton*
His lordship may compel us to be equal
upstairs, but there will never be equality in the
servants' hall.

865
God gave us memories that we might have roses
in December.

866
Heaven for climate, hell for company.

867 *Peter Pan*
When the first baby laughed for the first time,
the laugh broke into a thousand pieces and they
all went skipping about, and that was the
beginning of fairies.

868 *Peter Pan*
Every time a child says 'I don't believe in fairies'
there is a little fairy somewhere that falls down
dead.

869 *Peter Pan*
To die will be an awfully big adventure.

870
The secret of happiness is not in doing what
one likes, but in liking what one has to do.

871 *What Every Woman Knows*
There are few more impressive sights in the
world than a Scotsman on the make.

872 *What Every Woman Knows*
It's a sort of bloom on a woman. If you have it,
you don't need to have anything else; and if you
don't have it, it doesn't much matter what else
you have.

BARRYMORE John 1882-1942
873
The trouble with life is that there are so many
beautiful women and so little time.

874
I want him ('Hamlet') to be so male that when I
come out on the stage, they can hear my balls
clank.

BARTH John 1930-
875
More history's made by secret handshakes than
by battles, bills and proclamations.

876
'Tis e'er the wont of simple folk to prize the
deed and overlook the motive, and of learned
folk to discount the deed and lay open the soul
of the doer.

BARTH Joseph
877
Marriage is our last, best chance to grow up.

BARTH Karl 1886-1968
878
Laughter is the closest thing to the grace of God.

BARTHES Roland 1915-1980
879
Flaubert had infinite correction to perform.

880 *Mythologies 'La nouvelle Citroën'*
I think that cars today are almost the exact
equivalent of the great Gothic cathedrals: I
mean the supreme creation of an era, conceived
with passion by unknown artists, and
consumed in image if not in usage by a whole
population which appropriates them as a
purely magical object.

BARUCH Bernard 1870-1965
881
Age is only a number, a cipher for the records.
A man can't retire his experience. He must use
it. Experience achieves more with less energy
and time.

882
Let us not be deceived - we are today in the
midst of a cold war.

883
The greatest blessing of our democracy is
freedom. But in the last analysis, our only
freedom is the freedom to discipline ourselves.

884
To me, old age is always fifteen years older than
I am.

885
Vote for the man who promises least; he'll be
the least disappointing.

BARZUN Jacques 1907-
886
In any assembly the simplest way to stop
transacting business and split the ranks is to
appeal to a principle.

887
Teaching is not a lost art, but the regard for it is
a lost tradition.

888
The test and the use of man's education is that
he finds pleasure in the exercise of his mind.

889
Whoever wants to know the hearts and minds
of America had better learn baseball.

BASHO Matsuo 1644-1694
890
Do not seek to follow in the footsteps of the
men of old; seek what they sought.

BASINGER Kim
891
The more flesh you show, the further up the
ladder you go.

BATES Marston
892
Research is the process of going up alleys to see
if they are blind.

BAUDELAIRE Charles 1821-1867
893
I have cultivated my hysteria with joy and
terror.

894
Genius is childhood recaptured.

895
How many years of fatigue and punishment it
takes to learn the simple truth that work, that
disagreeable thing, is the only way of not
suffering in life, or at all events, of suffering less.

896
We love women in proportion to their degree of
strangeness to us.

897
As a remedy against all ills - poverty, sickness,
and melancholy - only one thing is absolutely
necessary: a liking for work.

898
A sweetheart is a bottle of wine, a wife is a wine
bottle.

BAUER Gerard
899
The voice is a second face.

BAUGHMAN M. Dale
900
You can never hope to become a skilled
conversationalist until you learn how to put
your foot tactfully through the television set.

BAX Sir Arnold 1883-1953
901
You should make a point of trying every
experience once, excepting incest and folk-
dancing.

BAYLY Thomas Haynes 1797-1839
902 *Isle of Beauty*
Absence makes the heart grow fonder,
Isle of Beauty, Fare thee well!

BEADLE E.R.
903
Half the work that is done in the world is to
make things appear what they are not.

BEARD Charles A. 1874-1948
904
When it is dark enough, you can see the stars.

BEATON Sir Cecil 1904-1980
905
After twenty annual visits, I am still surprised
each time I return to see this giant asparagus
bed of alabaster and rose and green
skyscrapers.

BEATTY David 1871-1936
906 *(at the Battle of Jutland)*
There's something wrong with our bloody ships
today, Chatfield.

BEAUMARCHAIS Pierre-Augustin Caron de
1732-1799
907 *The Barber of Seville*
Drinking when we are not thirsty and making
love all year round, madam; that is all there is to
distinguish us from the other animals.

908
Nature says to a woman: 'Be beautiful if you
can, wise if you want to, but be respected, that
is essential.'

909
It is not necessary to understand things in order
to argue about them.

910
Vilify! Vilify! Some of it will always stick.

BEAUMONT Francis 1584-1616
911 *The Maid's Tragedy*
Those have most power to hurt us, that we love.

912 *The Scornful Lady*
Kiss till the cow comes home.

BEAVERBROOK Lord 1879-1964
913 *(attributed)*
Buy old masters. They fetch a better price than
old mistresses.

914
Business is more exciting than any game.

915 *The Decline and Fall of Lloyd George*
[He] did not seem to care which way he
travelled providing he was in the driver's seat.

916 *(about Edward VIII)*
Our cock won't fight.

BECKER Carl 1873-1945
917 *Progress and Power*
The significance of man is that he is that part of
the universe that asks the question,' What is the
significance of man?' 'He alone can stand apart
imaginatively and, regarding himself and the
universe in their eternal aspects, pronounce a
judgement: 'The significance of man is that he

is insignificant and is aware of it.'

BECKER Ernest
918
Men use one another to assure their personal victory over death.

BECKER May Lamberton
919
We grow neither better nor worse as we get old, but more like ourselves.

BECKETT Samuel 1906-1989
920 *Malone Dies*
If I had the use of my body I would throw it out of the window.

921
There's never an end for the sea.

922 *Waiting for Godot*
One of the thieves was saved. (Pause) It's a reasonable percentage.

923 *Waiting for Godot*
ESTRAGON: Charming spot. Inspiring prospects. Let's go.
VLADIMIR: We can't.
ESTRAGON: Why not?
VLADIMIR: We're waiting for Godot.

924 *Waiting for Godot*
We all are born mad. Some remain so.

BECON Thomas 1523-1567
925 *Catechism*
For commonly, wheresoever God buildeth a church, the devil will build a chapel just by.

BEDFORD Harry and SULLIVAN Terry
926 *(song written for Marie Lloyd)*
I'm a bit of a ruin that Cromwell knocked about a bit.

BEECHAM Sir Thomas 1879-1961
927 *Beecham Stories*
There are two golden rules for an orchestra: start together and finish together. The public doesn't give a damn what goes on in between.

928 *Beecham Stories (describing the harpsichord)*
Like two skeletons copulating on a corrugated tin roof.

929 *Beecham Stories (of Herbert von Karajan)*
A kind of musical Malcolm Sargent.

930 *(to a cellist - attributed)*
Madam, you have between your legs an instrument capable of giving pleasure to thousands - and all you can do is scratch it.

931
The English may not like music, but they absolutely love the noise it makes.

932
Music first and last should sound well, should allure and enchant the ear. Never mind the inner significance.

933 *Wit of Music*
Why do we have to have all these third-rate foreign conductors around - when we have so many second-rate ones of our own?

BEECHER Henry Ward 1813-1887
934
A Christian is nothing but a sinful man who has put himself to school for Christ for the honest purpose of becoming better.

935
Clothes and manners do not make the man; but, when he is made, they greatly improve his appearance.

936
The difference between perseverance and obstinacy is that one often comes from a strong will, and the other from a strong won't.

937
Do not be afraid of defeat. You are never so near to victory as when defeated in a good cause.

938
The dog is the god of frolic.

939
Flowers have an expression of countenance as much as men or animals. Some seem to smile, some have a sad expression, some are pensive and diffident, others again are plain, honest and upright.

940
It is not well for a man to pray cream and live skim milk.

941
The meanest, most contemptible kind of praise is that which first speaks well of a man, and then qualifies it with a 'but'.

942
Mirthfulness is in the mind and you cannot get it out. It is just as good in its place as conscience or veneration.

943
Never forget what a man says to you when he is angry.

944
You never know till you try to reach them how accessible men are; but you must approach each man by the right door.

945
The philosophy of one century is the common sense of the next.

946
What the mother sings to the cradle goes all the way down to the coffin.

947
Where is human nature so weak as in the bookstore?

948
The worst thing in this world, next to anarchy, is government.

BEECHER John
949
Strength is a matter of the made-up mind.

BEERBOHM Sir Max 1872-1956
950 *(attributed)*
I belong to the generation that says goodbye at the front door.

951 *A Defence of Cosmetics*
Most women are not so young as they are painted.

952 *And Even Now 'Hosts and Guests'*
Mankind is divisible into two great classes: hosts and guests.

953
You cannot make a man by standing a sheep on its hind legs. But by standing a flock of sheep in that position you can make a crowd of men.

954
To mankind in general Macbeth and Lady Macbeth stand out as the supreme type of all that a host and hostess should not be.

955
The past is a work of art, free of irrelevancies and loose ends.

956 *More 'Going Back to School'*
I was not unpopular [at school] ... It is Oxford that has made me insufferable.

957 *More 'Going Back to School'*
Undergraduates owe their happiness chiefly to the consciousness that they are no longer at school. The nonsense which was knocked out of them at school is all put gently back at Oxford or Cambridge.

958 *Zuleika Dobson*
The fading signals and grey eternal walls of that antique station, which, familiar to them and insignificant, does yet whisper to the tourist the last enchantments of the Middle Age.

959 *Zuleika Dobson*
The dullard's envy of brilliant men is always assuaged by the suspicion that they will come to a bad end.

960 *Zuleika Dobson*
Women who love the same man have a kind of bitter freemasonry.

BEETON Mrs 1836-1865
961 *The Book of Household Management*
A place for everything and everything in its place.

BEGLEY Louis
962
The test of the ultimate validity of what you think about is whether you can write it down.

BEHAN Brendan 1923-1964
963 *My Brother Brendan (by Dominic Behan)*
There's no such thing as bad publicity except your own obituary.

964
Critics are like eunuchs in a harem: they know how it's done, they've seen it done every day, but they're unable to do it themselves.

965
We had gone out there to pass the beautiful day of high summer like true Irishmen - locked in the dark Snug of a public house.

966 *The Hostage*
PAT: He was an Anglo-Irishman.
MEG: In the blessed name of God what's that?
PAT: A Protestant with a horse.

967 *The Hostage*
When I came back to Dublin, I was court-martialled in my absence and sentenced to death in my absence, so I said they could shoot me in my absence.

968 *The Hostage*
We're here because we're queer
Because we're queer because we're here.

969
It's not that the Irish are cynical. It's rather that they have a wonderful lack of respect for everything and everybody.

970
A Torontonian is a man who leaves culture to his wife.

971
What the hell difference does it make, left or right? There were good men lost on both sides.

BEHN Aphra 1640-1689
972 *The Emperor of the Moon*
Oh, what a dear ravishing thing is the beginning of an Amour!

973 *The Lover's Watch: Four o'clock*
Love ceases to be a pleasure, when it ceases to be a secret.

974 *Lycidus*
Since man with that inconstancy was born,
To love the absent, and the present scorn,
Why do we deck, why do we dress
For such a short-lived happiness?
Why do we put attraction on,
Since either way 'tis we must be undone?

975 *The Rover*
Variety is the soul of pleasure.

976 *The Rover*
Come away; poverty's catching.

977 *The Rover*
Money speaks sense in a language all nations understand.

BELL, Clive 1881-1964
978 *Art*
Art and Religion are means to similar states of mind.

979 *Civilization*
Only reason can convince us of those three fundamental truths without a recognition of which there can be no effective liberty: that what we believe is not necessarily true; that what we like is not necessarily good; and that all questions are open.

BELLOC, Hilaire 1870-1953
980 *A Bad Child's Book of Beasts 'The Tiger'*
The Tiger, on the other hand, is kittenish and mild,
He makes a pretty play fellow for any little child;
And mothers of large families (who claim to common sense)
Will find a Tiger well repay the trouble and expense.

981 *A Bad Child's Book of Beasts   dedication*
Child! do not throw this book about;
Refrain from the unholy pleasure
Of cutting all the pictures out!
Preserve it as your chiefest treasure.

982 *'To the Balliol Men Still in Africa'*
Balliol made me, Balliol fed me,
Whatever I had she gave me again:
And the best of Balliol loved and led me.
God be with you, Balliol men.

983 *More Beasts for Worse Children 'The Microbe'*
The Microbe is so very small
You cannot make him out at all.
But many sanguine people hope
To see him through a microscope.

984 *More Beasts for Worse Children 'The Microbe'*
Oh! let us never, never doubt
What nobody is sure about!

985 *'On His Books'*
When I am dead, I hope it may be said:
'His sins were scarlet, but his books were read.'

986 *Cautionary Tales 'Henry King'*
Physicians of the Utmost Fame
Were called at once; but when they came
They answered, as they took their Fees,
'There is no Cure for this Disease'.

987 *Cautionary Tales 'Jim'*
And always keep a-hold of Nurse
For fear of finding something worse.

988 *Cautionary Tales 'Lord Lundy'*
In my opinion, Butlers ought
To know their place, and not to play
The Old Retainer night and day.

989 *Cautionary Tales 'Lord Lundy'*
Sir! you have disappointed us!
We had intended you to be
The next Prime Minister but three:
The stocks were sold; the Press was squared;
The Middle Class was quite prepared.
But as it is! ... My language fails!
Go out and govern New South Wales!

990 *Cautionary Tales 'Matilda'*
For every time She shouted 'Fire!'
They only answered 'Little Liar!'
And therefore when her Aunt returned,
Matilda, and the House, were Burned.

991 *Cautionary Tales 'Rebecca'*
A Trick that everyone abhors
In Little Girls is slamming Doors.

992 *Fatigue*
I'm tired of Love: I'm still more tired of Rhyme.
But money gives me pleasure all the Time.

993 *'On a Great Election'*
The accursed power which stands on Privilege
(And goes with Women, and Champagne, and Bridge)
Broke - and Democracy resumed her reign:
(Which goes with Bridge, and Women and Champagne).

994 *'Heroic Poem upon Wine'*
Strong brother in God and last companion,
Wine.

995
Just as there is nothing between the admirable omelette and the intolerable, so with autobiography.

996 *Life of Hilaire Belloc*
Gentlemen, I am a Catholic ... If you reject me on account of my religion, I shall thank God that He has spared me the indignity of being your representative.

997
The Llama is a woolly sort of fleecy hairy goat
With an indolent expression and an undulating
throat
Like an unsuccessful literary man.

998 *The Modern Traveller*
Whatever happens we have got
The Maxim Gun, and they have not.

999 *New Cautionary Tales 'About John'*
Like many of the Upper Class
He liked the Sound of Broken Glass

1000 *New Cautionary Tales 'Peter Goole'*
And even now, at twenty-five,
He has to WORK to keep alive!
Yes! All day long from 10 till 4!
For half the year or even more;
With but an hour or two to spend
At luncheon with a city friend.

1001 *'Newdigate Poem'*
A smell of burning fills the startled Air -
The Electrician is no longer there!

1002 *On Nothing 'On Tea'*
Is there no Latin word for Tea? Upon my soul, if
I had known that I would have let the vulgar
stuff alone.

1003 *More Peers 'Lord Finchley'*
Lord Finchley tried to mend the Electric Light
Himself. It struck him dead: And serve him
right!
It is the business of the wealthy man
To give employment to the artisan.

1004 *'On a Sundial'*
I am a sundial, and I make a botch
Of what is done much better by a watch.

1005 *Verses 'Dedicatory Ode'*
From quiet homes and first beginning,
Out to the undiscovered ends,
There's nothing worth the wear of winning,
But laughter and the love of friends.

BELLOW Saul 1915-
1006
All a writer has to do to get a woman is to say
he's a writer. It's an aphrodisiac.

1007
A man is only as good as what he loves.

1008
I have never turned over a fig leaf yet that didn't
have a price tag on the other side.

1009
Our society, like decadent Rome, has turned
into an amusement society, with writers chief
among the court jesters - not so much above
the clatter as part of it.

1010
The truth is, we've not really developed a fiction
that can accommodate the full tumult, the
zaniness and crazed quality of modern
experience.

1011 *Writers at Work*
Art has something to do with the achievement
of stillness in the midst of chaos. A stillness
which characterizes prayer, too, and the eye of
the storm ... an arrest of attention in the midst
of distraction.

BELLUSCH Pietro
1012
To be truly free, it takes more determination,
courage, introspection and restraint than to be
in shackles.

BELTAIRE Mark
1013
The nicest thing about the promise of spring is
that sooner or later she'll have to keep it.

BENCHLEY Robert 1889-1945
1014
Anyone can do any amount of work provided it
isn't the work he is supposed to be doing at that
moment.

1015 *Chips off the old Benchley 'Safety Second'*
My only solution for the problem of habitual
accidents ... is to stay in bed all day. Even then,
there is always the chance that you will fall out.

1016
It took me fifteen years to discover that I had no
talent for writing, but I couldn't give it up
because by that time I was too famous.

1017 *Pluck and Luck*
In America there are two classes of travel - first
class, and with children.

1018 *Wits End (on Venice)*
Streets Flooded. Please advise.

BENEDICT Francis G.
1019
The extra calories needed for one hour of
intense mental effort would be completely met
by eating one oyster cracker or one half of a
salted peanut.

BENÉT Stephen Vincent 1898-1943
1020
(Abraham Lincoln's) weathered face was homely
as a plowed field.

1021 *'American Names'*
I shall not rest quiet in Montparnasse.
I shall not lie easy at Winchelsea.
You may bury my body in Sussex grass,
You may bury my tongue at Champmédy.
I shall not be there, I shall rise and pass.

Bury my heart at Wounded Knee.

1022
He could fiddle all the bugs off a sweet-potato vine.

1023
Honesty is as rare as a man without self-pity.

1024
As for what you're calling hard luck - well, we made New England out of it. That and codfish.

BENN Tony 1925-
1025 *The Benn Heresy 'Interview with Tony Benn'*
It is as wholly wrong to blame Marx for what was done in his name, as it is to blame Jesus for what was done in his.

1026
Bookshops are the one University everyone can enter.

1027
In developing our industrial strategy for the period ahead, we have the benefit of much experience. Almost everything has been tried at least once.

1028
If you file your waste-paper basket for 50 years you build a public library.

BENNARD George 1873-1958
1029 *'The Old Rugged Cross'*
I will cling to the old rugged cross,
And exchange it some day for a crown.

BENNETT Alan 1934-
1030 *'Place Names of China'*
Here I sit, alone and sixty,
Bald, and fat, and full of sin,
Cold the seat and loud the cistern,
As I read the Harpic tin.

1031 *Dinner at Noon*
What keeps us in our place is embarrassment.

1032 *Enjoy*
I don't want to give you the idea I'm trying to hide anything, or that anything unorthodox goes on between my wife and me. It doesn't. Nothing goes on at all ... No foreplay. No afterplay. And fuck all in between.

1033 *Forty Years On*
HEADMASTER: Of course they're out of date. Standards are always out of date. That is what makes them standards.

1034 *Getting On*
We started off trying to set up a small anarchist community, but people wouldn't obey the rules.

1035 *The Old Country*
We were put to Dickens as children but it never quite took. That unremitting humanity soon had me cheesed off.

1036 *'Take a Pew' from Beyond the Fringe*
Life is rather like a tin of sardines - we are all of us looking for the key. I wonder how many of you have wasted years of your life looking behind the kitchen dressers of this life for the key. Others think they have found the key. They roll back the sardine tin of life, they reveal the sardines, the riches of life therein, they get them out and enjoy them. You know there is always a little bit in the corner you can't quite get out.

BENNETT Arnold 1867-1931
1037 *The Card*
His opinion of himself, having once risen, remained at 'set fair'.

1038 *Things that have Interested Me*
The price of justice is eternal publicity.

1039
A man of sixty has spent twenty years in bed and over three years in eating.

1040 *(attributed to his tailor)*
Trousers should shiver on the shoe, but not break.

1041 *The Title*
Being a husband is a whole-time job. That is why so many husbands fail. They cannot give their entire attention to it.

BENNETT James Gordon 1795-1872
1042
Remember, son, many a good story has been ruined by over-verification.

BENNETT Jill 1931-1990
1043
Never marry a man who hates his mother, because he'll end up hating you.

BENNETT W.A.C.
1044
Yes, I'm 68, but when I was a boy I was too poor to smoke, so knock off ten years. That makes me 58. And since I never developed the drinking habit, you can knock off ten more years. So I'm 48 - in the prime of my life. Retire? Retire to what?

BENOIT Madame
1045
I feel a recipe is only a theme, which an intelligent cook can play each time with a variation.

BENSON A.C. 1862-1925
1046 *Finale to Elgar's Coronation Ode*
Land of Hope and Glory, Mother of the Free,
How shall we extol thee who are born of thee?
Wider still and wider shall thy bounds be set;
God who made thee mighty, make thee mightier

yet.

1047
I have known some quite good people who were unhappy, but never an interested person who was unhappy.

BENSON Stella 1892-1933
1048 *This is the End*
Call no man foe, but never love a stranger.

BENTHAM Jeremy 1748-1832
1049 *Anarchical Fallacies*
Natural rights is simple nonsense: natural and imprescriptible rights, rhetorical nonsense - nonsense upon stilts.

1050 *The Commonplace Book*
The greatest happiness of the greatest number is the foundation of morals and legislation.

1051 *Principles of Morals and Legislation*
All punishment is mischief: all punishment in itself is evil.

BENTLEY E. C. 1875-1956
1052 *Biography for Beginners 'Sir Christopher Wren'*
Sir Christopher Wren
Said, 'I am going to dine with some men.
If anybody calls
Say I am designing St. Paul's.'

1053 *Biography for Beginners 'Clive'*
What I like about Clive
Is that he is no longer alive.
There is a great deal to be said
For being dead.

1054 *Biography for Beginners - Introduction*
The Art of Biography
Is different from Geography.
Geography is about Maps,
But Biography is about Chaps.

1055 *More Biography 'George the Third'*
George the Third
Ought never to have occurred.
One can only wonder
At so grotesque a blunder.

BENTLEY Eric 1916-
1056
Fashion, which elevates the bad to the level of the good, subsequently turns its back on bad and good alike.

1057
Ours is the age of substitutes: instead of language, we have jargon; instead of principles, slogans; and, instead of genuine ideas, Bright Ideas.

BENTLEY John
1058
Making money is fun, but it's pointless if you

don't use the power it brings.

BENTLEY Richard 1662-1742
1059 *Bentley, his judgement on claret*
It would be port if it could.

1060 *The Works of Samuel Johnson*
It is a pretty poem, Mr. Pope, but you must not call it Homer.

BENTLEY Thomas 1730-1780
1061
No man is demolished but by himself.

BERENSON Bernhard 1865-1919
1062
A complete life may be one ending in so full an identification with the not-self that there is no self left to die.

1063
Consistency requires you to be as ignorant today as you were a year ago.

1064
We define genius as the capacity for productive reaction against one's training.

1065
Enemies could become the best companions. Companionship is based on a common interest, and the greater the interest the closer the companionship. What makes enemies of people, if not the eagerness, the passion for the same thing?

1066
Governments last as long as the undertaxed can defend themselves against the overtaxed.

BERESFORD Lord Charles 1846-1919
1067 *The World of Fashion 1837-1922*
Very sorry can't come. Lie follows by post.

BERGLER Edmund
1068
Every writer, without exception, is a masochist, a sadist, a peeping Tom, an exhibitionist, a narcissist, an injustice collector and a depressed person constantly haunted by fears of unproductivity.

BERGSON Henri 1859-1941
1069
Art has no other object than to set aside the symbols of practical utility, the generalities that are conventionally and socially accepted, everything in fact which masks reality from us, in order to set us face to face with reality itself.

BERKELEY George 1685-1753
1070 *Concerning the Principles of Human Knowledge*
We have first raised a dust and then complain we cannot see.

1071 *Concerning the Principles of Human Knowledge*
All the choir of heaven and furniture of earth - in a word, all those bodies which compose the mighty frame of the world - have not any subsistence without a mind.

1072 *Oration at Plymouth*
Westward the course of empire takes its way;
The first four acts already past,
A fifth shall close the drama with the day:
Time's noblest offspring is the last.

1073 *Siris*
Truth is the cry of all, but the game of the few.

1074 *Three Dialogues between Hylas and Philonous*
The same principles which at first lead to scepticism, pursued to a certain point bring men back to common sense.

BERLIN Irving 1888-1989
1075 *Annie Get Your Gun*
There's no business like show business.

1076 *Carefree 'Change Partners'*
Must you dance ev'ry dance
With the same fortunate man?
You have danced with him since the music began.
Won't you change partners and dance with me?

1077 *Follow the Fleet 'Let's Face the Music and Dance'*
There may be trouble ahead,
But while there's moonlight and music and love and romance,
Let's face the music and dance.

1078 *'God Bless America'*
God bless America,
Land that I love,
Stand beside her and guide her
Thru the night with a light from above.
From the mountains to the prairies,
To the oceans white with foam,
God bless America,
My home sweet home.

1079 *Holiday Inn 'White Christmas'*
I'm dreaming of a white Christmas,
Just like the ones I used to know,
Where the tree-tops glisten
And children listen
To hear sleigh bells in the snow.

1080 *Top Hat 'Cheek-to-Cheek'*
Heaven - I'm in Heaven - And my heart beats so that I can hardly speak;
And I seem to find the happiness I seek
When we're out together dancing cheek-to-cheek.

1081
The toughest thing about success is that you've got to keep on being a success.

BERLIN Sir Isaiah 1909-1997
1082
Rousseau was the first militant lowbrow.

1083 *Two Concepts of Liberty*
Liberty is liberty, not equality or fairness or justice or human happiness or a quiet conscience.

BERLIOZ Hector 1803-1869
1084
The luck of having talent is not enough; one must also have a talent for luck.

1085
Time is a great teacher, but unfortunately it kills all its pupils.

BERNANOS Georges 1888-1948
1086
Hell, madame, is to love no longer.

1087 *Journal d'un curé de campagne*
The wish for prayer is a prayer in itself.

BERNARD Claude 1812-1878
1088
Art is I, science is we.

BERNARD Dorothy
1089
Courage - fear that has said its prayers.

BERNE Eric 1910-1970
1090
Games people play: the psychology of human relationships.

BERRA Yogi
1091
You can't think and hit at the same time.

1092
The game isn't over until it's over.

1093
You can observe a lot just by watching.

1094
Ninety per cent of this game is half-mental.

BERRIGAN Daniel 1921-
1095
There are no makers of peace because the making of peace is at least as costly as the making of war - at least as exigent.

BERRYMAN John 1914-1972
1096 *'A Point of Age'*
We must travel in the direction of our fear.

BETJEMAN Sir John 1906-1984
1097 *'Death of King George V'*
Old men who never cheated, never doubted,

Communicated monthly, sit and stare
At the new suburb stretched beyond the run-way
Where a young man lands hatless from the air.

1098 *'Death in Leamington'*
Oh! Chintzy, Chintzy cheeriness,
Half dead and half alive!

1099 *'Henley-on-Thames'*
Oh shall I see the Thames again?
The prow-promoted gems again,
As beefy ATS
Without their hats
Come shooting through the bridge?
And 'cheerioh' or 'cheeri-bye'
Across the waste of waters die
And low the mists of evening lie
And lightly skims the midge.

1100 *'How to get on in Society'*
Phone for the fish-knives, Norman
As Cook is a little unnerved;
You kiddies have crumpled the serviettes
And I must have things daintily served.

1101 *'Middlesex'*
Gaily into Ruislip Gardens
Runs the red electric train,
With a thousand Ta's and Pardon's
Daintily alights Elaine;
Hurries down the concrete station
With a frown of concentration,
Out into the outskirt's edges
Where a few surviving hedges
Keep alive our lost Elysium - rural Middlesex
again.

1102 *'Slough'*
Come friendly bombs, and fall on Slough!
It isn't fit for humans now,
There isn't grass to graze a cow.
Swarm over, Death!

1103 *'A Subaltern's Love-Song'*
Miss J. Hunter Dunn, Miss J. Hunter Dunn,
Furnish'd and burnish'd by Aldershot sun,
What strenuous singles we played after tea,
We in the tournament - you against me.

1104 *'A Subaltern's Love-song'*
Around us are Rovers and Austins afar,
Above us, the intimate roof of the car,
And here on my right is the girl of my choice,
With the tilt of her nose and the chime of her
voice.

1105 *Summoned by Bells*
The dread of beatings! Dread of being late!
And, greatest dread of all, the dread of games!

BETTI Ugo 1882-1954
1106
This free-will business is a bit terrifying anyway.
It's almost pleasanter to obey, and make the

most of it.

1107
A vague uneasiness; the police. It's like when
you suddenly understand you have to undress
in front of the doctor.

BEUDOIN Patricia C.
1108
The toughest thing about being a housewife is
you have no place to stay home from.

BEVAN Aneurin 1897-1960
1109 *Aneurin Bevan*
Damn it all, you can't have the crown of thorns
and the thirty pieces of silver.

1110
No amount of cajolery, and no attempts at
ethical or social seduction, can eradicate from
my heart a deep burning hatred for the Tory
Party ... So far as I am concerned they are lower
than vermin.

1111 *The Consultants*
I stuffed their mouths with gold.

1112 *(debate on Suez crisis)*
I am not going to spend any time whatsoever in
attacking the Foreign Secretary ... If we
complain about the tune, there is no reason to
attack the monkey when the organ grinder is
present.

1113
The language of priorities is the religion of
Socialism.

1114
I have never regarded politics as the arena of
morals. It is the arena of interests.

1115 *(of Robert Boothby)*
Why read the crystal when he can read the
book?

1116 *(speech at Blackpool)*
This island is made mainly of coal and
surrounded by fish. Only an organizing genius
could produce a shortage of coal and fish at the
same time.

1117 *(on unilateral disarmament)*
If you carry this resolution you will send
Britain's Foreign Secretary naked into the
conference chamber.

1118
We know what happens to people who stay in
the middle of the road. They get run down.

BEVERIDGE Karl
1119
My favourite example (of ex-patriotism) is
James Joyce, who left Ireland at nineteen and
never came back. But he spent the rest of his

life writing about Ireland from the perspective of living in Paris.

BEVERIDGE William Henry 1879-1963
1120 *Social Insurance and Allied Services*
The object of government in peace and in war is not the glory of rulers or of races, but the happiness of the common man.

1121 *Voluntary Action*
The state is or can be master of money, but in a free society it is master of very little else.

BEVIN Ernest 1881-1951
1122
The most conservative man in this world is the British Trade Unionist when you want to change him.

1123 *Ernest Bevin and the Foreign Office*
If you open that Pandora's Box, you never know what Trojan 'orses will jump out.

1124
My [foreign] policy is to be able to take a ticket at Victoria Station and go anywhere I damn well please.

1125
There never has been a war yet which, if the facts had been put calmly before the ordinary folk, could not have been prevented ... The common man, I think, is the great protection against war.

The BIBLE (Authorised Version)
1126 *New Testament: Acts of the Apostles ch.9 v.5*
It is hard for thee to kick against the pricks.

1127 *New Testament: Acts of the Apostles ch.10 v.34*
God is no respecter of persons.

1128 *New Testament: I Corinthians ch.8 v.1*
Knowledge puffeth up, but charity edifieth.

1129 *New Testament: I Corinthians ch.13 v.1*
When I was a child, I spake as a child, I understood as a child, I thought as a child: but when I became a man, I put away childish things.
For now we see through a glass, darkly; but then face to face: now I know in part; but then shall I know even as also I am known.
And now abideth faith, hope, charity, these three; but the greatest of these is charity.

1130 *New Testament: I Corinthians ch.15 v.26*
The last enemy that shall be destroyed is death.

1131 *New Testament: I Corinthians ch.15 v.55*
O death, where is thy sting? O grave, where is thy victory?

1132 *New Testament: Ephesians ch.4 v.25*
We are members one of another.

1133 *New Testament: Ephesians ch.4 v.26*
Be ye angry and sin not: let not the sun go down upon your wrath.

1134 *New Testament: Galatians ch.6 v.5*
Every man shall bear his own burden.

1135 *New Testament: Hebrews ch.11 v.1*
Faith is the substance of things hoped for, the evidence of things not seen.

1136 *New Testament: James ch.5 v.3*
Behold, we count them happy which endure. Ye have heard of the patience of Job.

1137 *New Testament: James ch.5 v.12*
Let your yea be yea; and your nay, nay.

1138 *New Testament: I John ch.4 v.18*
There is no fear in love; but perfect love casteth out fear.

1139 *New Testament: Revelation ch.1 v.7*
I am Alpha and Omega, the beginning and the ending, saith the Lord.

1140 *New Testament: Revelation ch.7 v.3*
Hurt not the earth, neither the sea, nor the trees.

1141 *New Testament: Revelation ch.21 v.4*
And God shall wipe away all tears from their eyes, and there shall be no more death, neither sorrow, nor crying, neither shall there be any more pain: for the former things are passed away.

1142 *New Testament: Romans ch.4 v.15*
For where no law is, there is no transgression.

1143 *New Testament: Romans ch.6 v.23*
The wages of sin is death.

1144 *New Testament: Romans ch.12 v.19*
Vengeance is mine; I will repay, saith the Lord.

1145 *New Testament: St John ch.1 v.1*
In the beginning was the Word, and the Word was with God, and the Word was God.

1146 *New Testament: St John ch.1 v.3*
All things were made by him; and without him was not any thing made that was made.

1147 *New Testament: St John ch.4 v.48*
Except ye see signs and wonders, ye will not believe.

1148 *New Testament: St John ch.8 v.7*
He that is without sin among you, let him first cast a stone.

1149 *New Testament: St John ch.8 v.32*
And ye shall know the truth, and the truth shall make you free.

1150 *New Testament: St John ch.10 v.11*
I am the good shepherd: the good shepherd
giveth his life for the sheep.

1151 *New Testament: St John ch.14 v.2*
In my Father's house are many mansions ... I go
to prepare a place for you.

1152 *New Testament: St John ch.14 v.6*
I am the way, the truth, and the life: no man
cometh unto the Father, but by me.

1153 *New Testament: St John ch.15 v.13*
Greater love hath no man than this, that a man
lay down his life for his friends.

1154 *New Testament: St Luke ch.4 v.23*
Physician, heal thyself.

1155 *New Testament: St Luke ch.6 v.27*
Love your enemies, do good to them which hate
you.

1156 *New Testament: St Luke ch.15 v.7*
Joy shall be in heaven over one sinner that
repenteth, more than over ninety and nine just
persons, which need no repentance.

1157 *New Testament: St Luke ch.17 v.21*
The kingdom of God is within you.

1158 *New Testament: St Luke ch.23 v.34*
Father, forgive them: for they know not what
they do.

1159 *New Testament: St Mark ch.2 v.27*
The sabbath was made for man, and not man
for the sabbath.

1160 *New Testament: St Mark ch.3 v.25*
If a house be divided against itself, that house
cannot stand.

1161 *New Testament: St Mark ch.4 v.9*
He that hath ears to hear, let him hear.

1162 *New Testament: St Mark ch.4 v.24*
With what measure ye mete, it shall be
measured to you.

1163 *New Testament: St Mark ch.8 v.36 St
Matthew ch.16 v.26*
For what shall it profit a man, if he shall gain
the whole world, and lose his own soul?

1164 *New Testament: St Matthew ch.5 v.3*
Blessed are the poor in spirit: for theirs is the
kingdom of heaven.
Blessed are they that mourn: for they shall be
comforted.
Blessed are the meek: for they shall inherit the
earth.
Blessed are they which do hunger and thirst
after righteousness: for they shall be filled.
Blessed are the merciful: for they shall obtain
mercy.
Blessed are the pure in heart: for they shall see
God.
Blessed are the peacemakers: for they shall be
called the children of God.

1165 *New Testament: St Matthew ch.5 v.13*
Ye are the salt of the earth: but if the salt have
lost his savour, wherewith shall it be salted?

1166 *New Testament: St Matthew ch.5 v.16*
Let your light so shine before men, that they
may see your good works.

1167 *New Testament: St Matthew ch.5 v.39*
Resist not evil: but whosoever shall smite thee
on thy right cheek, turn to him the other also.

1168 *New Testament: St Matthew ch.6 v.3*
When thou doest alms, let not thy left hand
know what thy right hand doeth.

1169 *New Testament: St Matthew ch.6 v.24*
No man can serve two masters ... Ye cannot
serve God and mammon.

1170 *New Testament: St Matthew ch.6 v.33*
Seek ye first the kingdom of God, and his
righteousness; and all these things shall be
added unto you.

1171 *New Testament: St Matthew ch.7 v.1*
Judge not, that ye be not judged.

1172 *New Testament: St Matthew ch.7 v.7*
Ask, and it shall be given you; seek, and ye shall
find; knock, and it shall be opened unto you.

1173 *New Testament: St Matthew ch.7 v.15*
Beware of false prophets, which come to you in
sheep's clothing, but inwardly they are ravening
wolves.

1174 *New Testament: St Matthew ch.8 v.12*
But the children of the kingdom shall be cast
out into outer darkness: there shall be weeping
and gnashing of teeth.

1175 *New Testament: St Matthew ch.8 v.22*
Let the dead bury their dead.

1176 *New Testament: St Matthew ch.9 v.13*
I am not come to call the righteous, but sinners
to repentance.

1177 *New Testament: St Matthew ch.10 v.8*
Freely ye have received, freely give.

1178 *New Testament: St Matthew ch.11 v.28*
Come unto me, all ye that labour and are heavy
laden, and I will give you rest.

1179 *New Testament: St Matthew ch.12 v.30 St
Luke ch.11 v.23*
He that is not with me is against me.

1180 *New Testament: St Matthew ch.16 v.23*
Get thee behind me, Satan.

1181 *New Testament: St Matthew ch.18 v.3*
Except ye be converted, and become as little children, ye shall not enter into the kingdom of heaven.

1182 *New Testament: St Matthew ch.18 v.20*
For where two or three are gathered together in my name, there am I in the midst of them.

1183 *New Testament: St Matthew ch.19 v.6*
What therefore God hath joined together, let not man put asunder.

1184 *New Testament: St Matthew ch.19 v.30*
But many that are first shall be last; and the last shall be first.

1185 *New Testament: St Matthew ch.22 v.14*
For many are called, but few are chosen.

1186 *New Testament: St Matthew ch.22 v.21*
Render therefore unto Caesar the things which are Caesar's; and unto God the things that are God's.

1187 *New Testament: St Matthew ch.24 v.35*
Heaven and earth shall pass away, but my words shall not pass away.

1188 *New Testament: St Matthew ch.26 v.39*
If it be possible, let this cup pass from me.

1189 *New Testament: St Matthew ch.13 v.57*
A prophet is not without honour save in his own country.

1190 *New Testament: II Thessalonians ch.3 v.10*
If any would not work, neither should he eat.

1191 *New Testament: I Timothy ch.6 v.7*
For we brought nothing into this world, and it is certain we can carry nothing out.

1192 *New Testament: I Timothy ch.6 v.10*
The love of money is the root of all evil.

1193 *Old Testament: Amos ch.3 v.3*
Can two walk together, except they be agreed?

1194 *Old Testament: Apocrypha Ecclesiasticus ch.5 v.15*
Be not ignorant of any thing in a great matter or a small.

1195 *Old Testament: Apocrypha Ecclesiasticus ch.6 v.1*
A faithful friend is the medicine of life.

1196 *Old Testament: Apocrypha Ecclesiasticus ch.18 v.25*
When thou hast enough, remember the time of hunger.

1197 *Old Testament: Apocrypha Ecclesiasticus ch.28 v.18*
Many have fallen by the edge of the sword: but not so many as have fallen by the tongue.

1198 *Old Testament: Apocrypha Ecclesiasticus ch.30 v.24*
Envy and wrath shorten the life.

1199 *Old Testament: Apocrypha Ecclesiasticus ch.31 v.17*
Leave off first for manners' sake.

1200 *Old Testament: Apocrypha Ecclesiasticus ch.44 v.1*
Let us now praise famous men, and our fathers that begat us.

1201 *Old Testament: Numbers ch.32 v.23*
Be sure your sin will find you out.

1202 *Old Testament: Deuteronomy ch.6 v.4*
Hear, O Israel: The Lord our God is one Lord.

1203 *Old Testament: Deuteronomy ch.32 v.10*
He kept him as the apple of his eye.

1204 *Old Testament: Ecclesiastes ch.1 v.2*
Vanity of vanities, saith the Preacher, vanity of vanities; all is vanity.

1205 *Old Testament: Ecclesiastes ch.1 v.7*
All the rivers run into the sea; yet the sea is not full.

1206 *Old Testament: Ecclesiastes ch.3 v.1*
To every thing there is a season, and a time to every purpose under the heaven.

1207 *Old Testament: Ecclesiastes ch.8 v.15*
A man hath no better thing under the sun, than to eat, and to drink, and to be merry.

1208 *Old Testament: Ecclesiastes ch.9 v.11*
The race is not to the swift, nor the battle to the strong.

1209 *Old Testament: Ecclesiastes ch.10 v.8*
He that diggeth a pit shall fall into it.

1210 *Old Testament: Ecclesiasticus ch.3 v.22*
Seek not out the things that are too hard for thee, neither search the things that are above thy strength.

1211 *Old Testament: Ecclesiasticus ch.44 v.7*
All these were honoured in their generations and were the glory of their times.

1212 *Old Testament: Ecclesiastes ch.1 v.9*
There is nothing new under the sun.

1213 *Old Testament: Ecclesiastes ch.1 v.18*
In much wisdom is much grief: and he that increaseth knowledge increaseth sorrow.

1214 *Old Testament: Ecclesiastes: ch.10 v.19*
Wine maketh merry: but money answereth all things.

1215 *Old Testament: Exodus ch.3 v.5*
Put off thy shoes from off thy feet, for the place whereon thou standest is holy ground.

1216 *Old Testament: Exodus ch.3 v.8*
A land flowing with milk and honey.

1217 *Old Testament: Exodus ch.21 v.23*
Life for life,
Eye for eye, tooth for tooth, hand for hand, foot
for foot,
Burning for burning, wound for wound, stripe
for stripe.

1218 *Old Testament: Genesis ch.2 v.23*
This is now bone of my bones, and flesh of my
flesh: she shall be called Woman, because she
was taken out of man.

1219 *Old Testament: Genesis ch.2 v.24*
Therefore shall a man leave his father and his
mother, and shall cleave unto his wife: and they
shall be one flesh.

1220 *Old Testament: Genesis ch.3 v.13*
The serpent beguiled me, and I did eat.

1221 *Old Testament: Genesis ch.3 v.16*
In sorrow thou shalt bring forth children.

1222 *Old Testament: Genesis ch.3 v.19*
For dust thou art, and unto dust shalt thou
return.

1223 *Old Testament: Genesis ch.9 v.6*
Whoso sheddeth man's blood, by man shall his
blood be shed.

1224 *Old Testament: Hosea ch.8 v.7*
They have sown the wind, and they shall reap
the whirlwind.

1225 *Old Testament: Isaiah ch.22 v.13*
Let us eat and drink; for tomorrow we shall die.

1226 *Old Testament: Isaiah ch.40 v.15*
The nations are as a drop of a bucket, and are
counted as the small dust of the balance:

1227 *Old Testament: Jeremiah ch.13 v.23*
Can the Ethiopian change his skin, or the
leopard his spots?

1228 *Old Testament: Job ch.12 v.8*
Speak to the earth, and it shall teach thee.

1229 *Old Testament: Job ch.19 v.20*
I am escaped with the skin of my teeth.

1230 *Old Testament: Job ch.1 v.21*
The Lord gave, and the Lord hath taken away;
blessed be the name of the Lord.

1231 *Old Testament: Job ch.28 v.18*
The price of wisdom is above rubies.

1232 *Old Testament: Job ch.32 v.9*
Great men are not always wise.

1233 *Old Testament: Job ch.5 v.7*
Man is born unto trouble, as the sparks fly
upward.

1234 *Old Testament: Joel ch.2 v.28*
Your old men shall dream dreams, your young
men shall see visions.

1235 *Old Testament: Proverbs ch.10 v.1*
A wise son maketh a glad father: but a foolish
son is the heaviness of his mother.

1236 *Old Testament: Proverbs ch.12 v.4*
A virtuous woman is a crown to her husband.

1237 *Old Testament: Proverbs ch.13 v.19*
The desire accomplished is sweet to the soul.

1238 *Old Testament: Proverbs ch.13 v.24*
He that spareth his rod hateth his son.

1239 *Old Testament: Proverbs ch.14 v.23*
In all labour there is profit.

1240 *Old Testament: Proverbs ch.15 v.1*
A soft answer turneth away wrath.

1241 *Old Testament: Proverbs ch.16 v.18*
Pride goeth before destruction, and an haughty
spirit before a fall.

1242 *Old Testament: Proverbs ch.16 v.32*
He that is slow to anger is better than the
mighty; and he that ruleth his spirit than he
that taketh a city.

1243 *Old Testament: Proverbs ch.17 v.22*
A merry heart doeth good like a medicine.

1244 *Old Testament: Proverbs ch.20 v.11*
Even a child is known by his doings.

1245 *Old Testament: Proverbs ch.21 v.9*
It is better to dwell in a corner of the housetop,
than with a brawling woman in a wide house.

1246 *Old Testament: Proverbs ch.22 v.6*
Train up a child in the way he should go: and
when he is old, he will not depart from it.

1247 *Old Testament: Proverbs ch.24 v.3*
Through wisdom a house is built and through
understanding it is established.

1248 *Old Testament: Proverbs ch.28 v.20*
He that maketh haste to be rich shall not be
innocent.

1249 *Old Testament: Proverbs ch.31 v.6*
Give strong drink unto him that is ready to
perish, and wine unto those that be of heavy
hearts.

1250 *Old Testament: I Samuel ch.13 v.14*
A man after his own heart.

BIDAULT Georges 1899-1983
1251
The weak have one weapon: the errors of those
who think they are strong.

BIERCE Ambrose 1842-c.1914

1252 *The Devil's Dictionary*
Acquaintance, n: a person whom we know well enough to borrow from, but not well enough to lend to.

1253 *The Devil's Dictionary*
Apologize, v: to lay the foundation for a future offence.

1254 *The Devil's Dictionary*
Christian, n: one who believes that the New Testament is a divinely inspired book admirably suited to the spiritual needs of his neighbour.

1255 *The Devil's Dictionary*
Commendation, n: the tribute that we pay to achievements that resemble, but do not equal, our own.

1256 *The Devil's Dictionary*
Cynic, n: a blackguard whose faulty vision sees things as they are, not as they ought to be.

1257 *The Devil's Dictionary*
Destiny, n: a tyrant's authority for crime and a fool's excuse for failure.

1258 *The Devil's Dictionary*
Debauche, n: one who has so earnestly pursued pleasure that he has had the misfortune to overtake it.

1259 *The Devil's Dictionary*
Education, n: that which discloses to the wise and disguises from the foolish their lack of understanding.

1260 *The Devil's Dictionary*
Epitaph, n: an inscription on a tomb showing that virtues acquired by death have a retroactive effect.

1261 *The Devil's Dictionary*
History, n: an account mostly false, of events, mostly unimportant, which are brought about by rulers, mostly knaves, and soldiers, mostly fools.

1262 *The Devil's Dictionary*
Idiot, n: a member of a large and powerful tribe whose influence in human affairs has always been dominant and controlling.

1263 *The Devil's Dictionary*
Ignoramus, n: a person unacquainted with certain kinds of knowledge familiar to yourself, and having certain other kinds that you know nothing about.

1264 *The Devil's Dictionary*
Infidel, n: in New York, one who does not believe in the Christian religion; in Constantinople, one who does.

1265 *The Devil's Dictionary*
Litigant, n: a person about to give up his skin for the hope of retaining his bone.

1266 *The Devil's Dictionary*
Love, n: a temporary insanity often curable by marriage.

1267 *The Devil's Dictionary*
Mausoleum, n: the final and funniest folly of the rich.

1268 *The Devil's Dictionary*
Marriage, n: the state or condition of a community consisting of a master, a mistress, and two slaves, making, in all, two.

1269 *The Devil's Dictionary*
Painting, n: the art of protecting flat surfaces from the weather and exposing them to the critic.

1270 *The Devil's Dictionary*
Peace, n: in international affairs, a period of cheating between two periods of fighting.

1271 *The Devil's Dictionary*
Philanthropist, n: a rich (and usually bald) old gentleman who has trained himself to grin while his conscience is picking his pocket.

1272 *The Devil's Dictionary*
Piracy, n: commerce without its folly-swaddles - just as God made it.

1273 *The Devil's Dictionary*
To be positive: to be mistaken at the top of one's voice.

1274 *The Devil's Dictionary*
Pray, v: to ask that the laws of the universe be annulled in behalf of a single petitioner confessedly unworthy.

BIFFEN John 1930-
1275 *(of Margaret Thatcher)*
She was a tigress surrounded by hamsters.

1276 *(resignation letter)*
In politics I think it wiser to leave five minutes too soon than to continue for five years too long.

BIGOD Roger, Earl of Norfolk 1245-1306
1277 *The Chronicle of Walter of Guisbrough*
By God, O King, I will neither go nor hang!

BILLINGS Josh 1818-1885
1278
Adversity has the same effect on a man that severe training has on the pugilist - it reduces him to his fighting weight.

1279
My advice to those who are about to begin, in earnest, the journey of life, is to take their heart in one hand and a club in the other.

1280
To bring up a child in the way he should go, travel that way yourself once in a while.

1281
It is a very delicate job to forgive a man, without lowering him in his estimation, and yours too.

1282
As a general thing, when a woman wears the pants in a family, she has a good right to them.

1283
The happiest time in any man's life is when he is in red-hot pursuit of a dollar with a reasonable prospect of overtaking it.

1284 *Josh Billings' Wit and Humour*
'Vote early and vote often' is the Politishun's golden rule.

1285
Laughter is the sensation of feeling good all over, and showing it principally in one spot.

1286
Every man has his follies - and often they are the most interesting things he has got.

1287
Most men would rather be charged with malice than with making a blunder.

1288
Nature never makes any blunders; when she makes a fool she means it.

1289
It is not only the most difficult thing to know oneself, but the most inconvenient one, too.

1290
There are some people so addicted to exaggeration that they can't tell the truth without lying.

1291
There are many people who mistake their imagination for their memory.

1292
Pity costs nothin' and ain't worth nothin'.

1293
As scarce as truth is, the supply has always been in excess of the demand.

1294
The trouble ain't that people are ignorant: it's that they know so much that ain't so.

1295
The truly innocent are those who not only are guiltless themselves, but who think others are.

1296
When a man comes to me for advice, I find out the kind of advice he wants, and I give it to him.

1297
When a man gets talking about himself, he seldom fails to be eloquent and often reaches the sublime.

BINGER William
1298
A man is a person who will pay two dollars for a one-dollar item he wants. A woman will pay one dollar for a two-dollar item she doesn't want.

BINYON Laurence 1869-1943
1299 *'For the Fallen'*
They shall grow not old, as we that are left grow old.
Age shall not weary them, nor the years condemn.
At the going down of the sun and in the morning
We will remember them.

BIRNEY Earle 1904-
1300
The essentials of poetry are rhythm, dance and the human voice.

BIRRELL Augustine 1850-1933
1301 *Obiter Dicta 'Carlyle'*
The great dust-heap called 'history'.

BIRT John 1944-
1302
Politicians have a higher claim to speak for the people than journalists.

BISMARCK Prince Otto von 1815-1898
1303
Place in the hands of the King of Prussia the strongest possible military power, then he will be able to carry out the policy you wish; this policy cannot succeed through speeches, and shooting-matches, and songs; it can only be carried out through blood and iron.

1304
Politics is the art of the possible.

1305
Prussia needs only one ally: the German people.

1306
You can trust all Englishmen except those who speak French.

1307
If there is ever another war in Europe, it will come out of some damned silly thing in the Balkans.

1308
When you say that you agree to a thing in principle, you mean that you have not the slightest intention of carrying it out.

BISSONETTE David

1309
I recently read that love is entirely a matter of chemistry. That must be why my wife treats me like toxic waste.

BLACK Conrad 1944-

1310
Humility is a good quality, but it can be overdone.

BLACKBURN Tony

1311
Why should the Pope be any closer to God than I am?

BLACKER Valentine 1728-1823

1312 *'Oliver's Advice'*
Put your trust in God, my boys, and keep your powder dry.

BLACKSTONE Sir William 1723-1780

1313 *Commentaries on the Laws of England*
The king never dies.

1314 *Commentaries on the Laws of England*
The Royal Navy of England hath ever been its greatest defence and ornament; its ancient and natural strength; the floating bulwark of the island.

1315 *Commentaries on the Laws of England*
That the king can do no wrong, is a necessary and fundamental principle of the English constitution.

1316 *Commentaries on the Laws of England*
It is better that ten guilty persons escape than one innocent suffer.

BLADE Toledo

1317
A great many open minds should be closed for repairs.

BLAIR Tony 1953-

1318
The art of leadership is saying no, not yes. It is very easy to say yes.

1319
Attendance at school is non-negotiable.

1320 *(defending the Greenwich Dome project)*
Greenwich is the place the millennium begins...if it was Berlin Mean Time, don't you think the Germans would do likewise?

1321
Labour is the party of law and order in Britain today. Tough on crime and tough on the causes of crime.

1322
We are not the masters; the people are the masters. We are the people's servants. Forget that and the electorate will soon show that what the electorate can give, the electorate can take away.

1323
I think the basic principle here is to say, yes, it is right to be intolerant of people homeless on the streets.

BLAKE Eubie 1883-1983

1324 *(on reaching 100)*
If I'd known I was gonna live this long, I'd have taken better care of myself.

BLAKE William 1757-1827

1325 *'Auguries of Innocence'*
To see a world in a grain of sand
And a heaven in a wild flower
Hold infinity in the palm of your hand
And eternity in an hour.

1326 *'Auguries of Innocence'*
A robin red breast in a cage
Puts all Heaven in a rage.

1327 *'Auguries of Innocence'*
He who shall hurt the little wren
Shall never be beloved by men
He who the ox to wrath has moved
Shall never be by woman loved.

1328 *'Auguries of Innocence'*
A truth that's told with bad intent
Beats all the lies you can invent.

1329 *Book of Thel*
Can Wisdom be put in a silver rod,
Or Love in a golden bowl?

1330
Some are born to sweet delight,
Some are born to endless night.

1331 *'A Divine Image'*
Cruelty has a human heart,
And Jealousy a human face;
Terror the human form divine,
And Secrecy the human dress.

1332 *The Everlasting Gospel*
Was Jesus gentle or did he
Give any marks of gentility
When twelve years old he ran away
And left his parents in dismay.

1333
Improvement makes straight roads; but the crooked roads without improvement are roads of genius.

1334 *Jerusalem*
Ever weeping Paddington.

1335 *Jerusalem*
He who would do good to another, must do it in minute particulars

General good is the plea of the scoundrel, hypocrite and flatterer.

1336 *Jerusalem 'To the Jews'*
The fields from Islington to Marybone,
To Primrose Hill and Saint John's Wood
Were builded over with pillars of gold;
And there Jerusalem's pillars stood.

1337 *The Marriage of Heaven and Hell*
Without contraries is no progression. Attraction and repulsion, reason and energy, love and hate, are necessary to human existence.

1338 *The Marriage of Heaven and Hell*
Energy is Eternal Delight.

1339 *The Marriage of Heaven and Hell*
The road of excess leads to the palace of wisdom.

1340 *The Marriage of Heaven and Hell*
Prudence is a rich, ugly, old maid courted by incapacity.

1341 *The Marriage of Heaven and Hell*
A fool sees not the same tree that a wise man sees.

1342 *The Marriage of Heaven and Hell*
If the fool would persist in his folly he would become wise.

1343 *The Marriage of Heaven and Hell*
Prisons are built with stones of Law, brothels with bricks of Religion.

1344 *The Marriage of Heaven and Hell*
The pride of the peacock is the glory of God.
The lust of the goat is the bounty of God.
The wrath of the lion is the wisdom of God.
The nakedness of woman is the work of God.

1345 *The Marriage of Heaven and Hell*
Damn braces: Bless relaxes.

1346 *The Marriage of Heaven and Hell*
Exuberance is beauty.

1347 *The Marriage of Heaven and Hell*
If the doors of perception were cleansed everything would appear to man as it is, infinite.

1348 *Milton [preface]*
And did those feet in ancient time
Walk upon England's mountains green?
And was the holy Lamb of God
On England's pleasant pastures seen?

And did the Countenance Divine
Shine forth upon our clouded hills?
And was Jerusalem builded here
Among these dark Satanic mills?

1349 *Milton [preface]*
Bring me my bow of burning gold:
Bring me my arrows of desire:
Bring me my spear: O clouds, unfold!
Bring me my chariot of fire.

1350 *Milton [preface]*
I will not cease from mental fight,
Nor shall my sword sleep in my hand,
Till we have built Jerusalem,
In England's green and pleasant land.

1351 *MS Note-Book*
The errors of a wise man make your rule
Rather than the perfections of a fool.

1352 *MS Note-Book*
Great things are done when men and mountains meet
This is not done by jostling in the street.

1353 *Note-book*
Never seek to tell thy love, Love that never told can be.

1354 *Note-book*
What is it men in women do require?
The lineaments of gratified desire.
What is it women do in men require?
The lineaments of gratified desire.

1355
The Old and New Testaments are the Great Code of Art.

1356 *For the Sexes: The Gates of Paradise [prologue]*
Mutual Forgiveness of each vice,
Such are the Gates of Paradise.

1357 *'The Smile'*
There is a Smile of Love,
And there is a Smile of Deceit,
And there is a Smile of Smiles
In which these two Smiles meet.

1358 *Songs of Experience 'The Clod and the Pebble'*
Love seeketh not itself to please,
Nor for itself hath any care;
But for another gives its ease,
And builds a Heaven in Hell's despair.

1359 *Songs of Experience 'The Clod and the Pebble'*
Love seeketh only Self to please,
To bind another to its delight,
Joys in another's loss of ease,
And builds a Hell in Heaven's despite.

1360 *Songs of Experience 'Infant Sorrow'*
My mother groaned! my father wept.
Into the dangerous world I leapt:
Helpless, naked, piping loud;
Like a fiend hid in a cloud.

1361 *Songs of Experience 'A Poison Tree'*
I was angry with my friend;
I told my wrath, my wrath did end.
I was angry with my foe:
I told it not, my wrath did grow.

1362 *Songs of Experience 'The Tiger'*
Tyger Tyger, burning bright,
In the forests of the night;
What immortal hand or eye,
Could frame thy fearful symmetry?

1363 *Songs of Innocence 'On Another's Sorrow'*
Can I see another's woe,
And not be in sorrow too.
Can I see another's grief,
And not seek for kind relief.

1364 *Songs of Innocence 'The Divine Image'*
To Mercy Pity Peace and Love,
All pray in their distress.

1365 *Songs of Innocence 'The Divine Image'*
For Mercy has a human heart
Pity a human face:
And Love, the human form divine,
And peace, the human dress.

1366
He who desires, but acts not, breeds pestilence.

BLANCH Lesley 1907
1367 *The Wilder Shores of Love*
She was an Amazon. Her whole life was spent
riding at breakneck speed towards the wilder
shores of love.

BLESSINGTON Lady 1789-1849
1368
Religion converts despair, which destroys, into
resignation, which submits.

BLIXEN Karen 1885-1962
1369 *Out of Africa*
A herd of elephant ... pacing along as if they had
an appointment at the end of the world.

1370
In the mind and nature of a man a secret is an
ugly thing, like a hidden physical defect.

1371 *Seven Gothic Tales 'The Dreamers'*
What is man, when you come to think upon
him, but a minutely set, ingenious machine for
turning, with infinite artfulness, the red wine of
Shiraz into urine?

BLOCH Arthur
1372
A conclusion is the place where you got tired of
thinking.

BLOOMFIELD Harold H.
1373
The irony of love is that it guarantees some
degree of anger, fear and criticism.

BLUM Norbert
1374
Politics is like football - it doesn't matter
whether you win 3-1 or 1-0, you still get 2
points.

BLUNDEN Edmund 1896-1974
1375 *'The Kiss'*
I am for the woods against the world,
But are the woods for me?

1376 *'Report on Experience'*
I have been young, and now am not too old;
And I have seen the righteous forsaken,
His health, his honour and his quality taken.
This is not what we were formerly told.

1377 *'The Resignation'*
This was my country and it may be yet,
But something flew between me and the sun.

BLY Robert 1926-
1378 *'Driving Through Minnesota During Hanoi
Bombings'*
Terror just before death,
Shoulders torn, shot
From helicopters, the boy
Tortured with the telephone generator,
'I felt sorry for him
And blew his head off with a shotgun.'

BLYTHE Ronald 1922-
1379 *The Age of Illusion*
As for the British churchman, he goes to church
as he goes to the bathroom, with the minimum
of fuss and with no explanation if he can help it.

BODENHEIM Maxwell 1893-1954
1380
Poetry is the impish attempt to paint the colour
of the wind.

BOESE Paul
1381
Nature thrives on patience; man on impatience.

BOETHIUS 476-524
1382 *De Consolatione Philosophiae*
Who can give a law to lovers? Love is a greater
law unto itself.

1383 *De Consolatione Philosophiae*
For in every ill-turn of fortune the most
unhappy sort of unfortunate man is the one
who has been happy.

BOGART Humphrey 1899-1957
1384 *in Casablanca*
"Of all the gin joints in all the towns in all the
world, she walks into mine."

1385 *in Casablanca*
"Here's looking at you, kid."

1386 *in In A Lonely Place*
"I was born when you kissed me. I died when you left me. I lived a few weeks while you loved me."

1387 *in The Maltese Falcon*
"You're an angel. I'll wait for you. If they hang you, I'll always remember you."

1388
The whole world is about three drinks behind.

BOHR Niels 1885-1962
1389
One of the favourite maxims of my father was the distinction between the two sorts of truths, profound truths recognized by the fact that the opposite is also a profound truth, in contrast to trivialities where opposites are obviously absurd.

1390
The opposite of a correct statement is a false statement. But the opposite of a profound truth may well be another profound truth.

BOILEAU Nicolas 1636-1711
1391
Hasten slowly, and without losing heart, put your work twenty times upon the anvil.

1392 *L'Art poétique*
A fool can always find a greater fool to admire him.

1393 *Satire (2) A M.Molière*
Of every four words I write, I strike out three.

BOK Derek 1930-
1394
If you think education is expensive - try ignorance.

BOLINGBROKE 1st Viscount 1678-1751
1395 *Observations, Anecdotes, and Characters*
The great mistake is that of looking upon men as virtuous, or thinking that they can be made so by laws.

1396 *Observations, Anecdotes, and Characters*
The greatest art of a politician is to render vice serviceable to the cause of virtue.

BOLITHO William
1397
A very beautiful woman hardly ever leaves a clear-cut impression of features and shape in the memory: usually there remains only an aura of living colour.

BOLT Robert 1924-1995
1398 *A Man for All Seasons*
Morality's not practical. Morality's a gesture. A complicated gesture learned from books.

1399 *A Man for All Seasons*
It profits a man nothing to give his soul for the whole world ... But for Wales - !

BOLTON Robert
1400
A belief is not merely an idea the mind possesses; it is an idea that possesses the mind.

BOMBECK Erma 1927-
1401
Guilt: the gift that goes on giving.

BONAPARTE Napoleon 1822-1891
1402
All celebrated people lose dignity on a close view.

1403
The art of governing consists in not letting men grow old in their jobs.

1404
My downfall raises me to infinite heights.

1405
Fashion condemns us to many follies; the greatest is to make oneself its slave.

1406
The first virtue in a soldier is endurance of fatigue; courage is only the second virtue.

1407
How many really capable men are children more than once during the day?

1408
A leader is a dealer in hope.

1409
As to moral courage, I have very rarely met with the two o'clock in the morning kind. I mean unprepared courage, that which is necessary on an unexpected occasion, and which, in spite of the most unforeseen events, leaves full freedom of judgement and decision.

1410
There are only two forces that unite men - fear and interest.

1411
Riches do not consist in the possession of treasures, but in the use made of them.

1412
If you start to take Vienna - take Vienna.

1413
If they want peace, nations should avoid the pinpricks that precede cannon shots.

BOND Edward 1934-
1414
Law and order is one of the steps taken to maintain injustice.

BONHOEFFER Dietrich 1906-1945
1415
One's task is not to turn the world upside down, but to do what is necessary at the given place and with a due consideration of reality.

The BOOK of COMMON PRAYER
1416 *Articles of Religion no.37*
The Bishop of Rome hath no jurisdiction in this Realm of England.

1417 *The Burial of the Dead, First Anthem*
Man that is born of a woman hath but a short time to live, and is full of misery.

1418 *The Burial of the Dead, First Anthem*
In the midst of life we are in death.

1419 *The Burial of the Dead, Interment*
Forasmuch as it hath pleased Almighty God of his great mercy to take unto himself the soul of our dear brother here departed, we therefore commit his body to the ground; earth to earth, ashes to ashes, dust to dust; in sure and certain hope of the Resurrection to eternal life, through our Lord Jesus Christ.

1420 *The Litany*
From all evil and mischief; from sin, from the crafts and assaults of the devil; from thy wrath, and from everlasting damnation,
Good Lord, deliver us.

1421 *Morning Prayer, General Confession*
We have erred, and strayed from thy ways like lost sheep. We have followed too much the devices and desires of our own hearts.

1422 *Morning Prayer, General Confession*
We have left undone those things which we ought to have done; And we have done those things which we ought not to have done; And there is no health in us.

1423 *Morning Prayer, The Third Collect, for Grace*
Grant that this day we fall into no sin, neither run into any kind of danger.

1424 *Morning Prayer, Versicle*
Give peace in our time, O Lord.

1425 *Psalm 23 v.1*
The Lord is my shepherd: therefore can I lack nothing.

1426 *Psalm 23 v.4*
Yea, though I walk through the valley of the shadow of death, I will fear no evil: for thou art with me; thy rod and thy staff comfort me.

1427 *Psalm 25 v.6*
O remember not the sins and offences of my youth.

1428 *Psalm 37 v.11*
The meek-spirited shall possess the earth.

1429 *Psalm 46 v.1*
God is our hope and strength: a very present help in trouble.

1430 *Psalm 71 v.8*
Cast me not away in the time of age: forsake me not when my strength faileth me.

1431 *Psalm 90 v.4*
For a thousand years in thy sight are but as yesterday: seeing that is past as a watch in the night.

1432 *Psalm 90 v.12*
So teach us to number our days: that we may apply our hearts unto wisdom.

1433 *Psalm 93 v.1*
He hath made the round world so sure: that it cannot be moved.

1434 *Psalm 98 v.1*
O sing unto the Lord a new song: for he hath done marvellous things.

1435 *Psalm 100 v.1*
Be ye sure that the Lord he is God: it is he that hath made us, and not we ourselves; we are his people, the sheep of his pasture.

1436 *Psalm 122 v.1*
I was glad when they said unto me: We will go into the house of the Lord.

1437 *Psalm 136 v.1*
O give thanks unto the Lord, for he is gracious: and his mercy endureth for ever.

1438 *Psalm 137 v.1*
By the waters of Babylon we sat down and wept: when we remembered thee, O Sion.

1439 *Psalm 139 v.13*
I will give thanks unto thee, for I am fearfully and wonderfully made.

1440 *Solemnization of Matrimony, Wedding*
With this Ring I thee wed, with my body I thee worship, and with all my worldly goods I thee endow.

1441 *Solemnization of Matrimony, Wedding*
Those whom God hath joined together let no man put asunder.

BOORSTIN Daniel J. 1914-
1442
Best-sellerism is the star system of the book world. A (best-seller) is a celebrity among books. It is a book known primarily (sometimes exclusively) for its well-knowness.

1443
Some are born great, some achieve greatness, and some hire public relations officers.

1444
The deeper problems connected with advertising come less from the unscrupulousness of our 'deceivers' than from our pleasure in being deceived; less from the desire to seduce than from the desire to be seduced.

1445 *The Image*
A best-seller was a book which somehow sold well simply because it was selling well.

1446
A sign of a celebrity is often that his name is worth more than his services.

BOOTH Edwin 1833-1893
1447
An actor is a sculptor who carves in snow.

BOOTH John Wilkes 1838-1865
1448 *(having shot President Lincoln)*
The South is avenged.

BOOTHROYD Betty 1929-
1449
My desire to get here (Parliament) was like miners' coal dust; it was under my fingers and I couldn't scrub it out.

BOREN James H. 1925-
1450
Guidelines for bureaucrats:
(1) When in charge, ponder.
(2) When in trouble, delegate.
(3) When in doubt, mumble.

BORGE Victor 1909-
1451
Laughter is the shortest distance between two people.

1452
Ah Mozart! He was happily married - but his wife wasn't.

1453 *(playing to a half-filled house)*
Flint must be an extremely wealthy town; I see that each of you bought two or three seats.

BORGES Jorge Luis 1899-1986
1454
The Falklands thing was a fight between two bald men over a comb.

1455
What you really value is what you miss, not what you have.

BORGIA Cesare 1476-1507
1456 *(Motto inscribed on his sword)*
Caesar or nothing.

BORLAND Hal
1457
Summer ends, and Autumn comes, and he who would have it otherwise would have high tide always and a full moon every night.

BÖRNE Ludwig 1786-1837
1458
Women are most adorable when they are afraid; that's why they frighten so easily.

BORROW George 1803-1881
1459 *Lavengro*
A losing trade, I assure you, sir: literature is a drug.

1460 *Lavengro*
Youth will be served, every dog has his day, and mine has been a fine one.

1461 *Lavengro [preface]*
There are no countries in the world less known by the British than these selfsame British Islands.

BORSODI Ralph
1462
There is less leisure now than in the Middle Ages, when one third of the year consisted of holidays and festivals.

BOSQUET Pierre 1810-1861
1463 *(of the Charge of the Light Brigade at Balaclava)*
It is magnificent, but it is not war.

BOSSIDY John Collins 1860-1928
1464 *(at Holy Cross College)*
And this is good old Boston,
The home of the bean and the cod,
Where the Lowells talk to the Cabots
And the Cabots talk only to God.

BOSSUET Jacques-Bénigne 1627-1704
1465
The inexorable boredom that is at the core of life.

BOSWELL James 1740-1795
1466 *Boswell's London Journal*
We may be in some degree whatever character we choose.

1467 *Journal of a Tour to the Hebrides*
We [Boswell and Johnson] are both Tories; both convinced of the utility of monarchical power, and both lovers of that reverence and affection for a sovereign which constitute loyalty, a principle which I take to be absolutely extinguished in Britain.

1468 *Journal of a Tour to the Hebrides*
A page of my Journal is like a cake of portable soup. A little may be diffused into a considerable portion.

1469 *The Life of Samuel Johnson*
JOHNSON: Well, we had a good talk.
BOSWELL: Yes Sir; you tossed and gored several persons.

1470 *The Life of Samuel Johnson*
A man, indeed, is not genteel when he gets drunk; but most vices may be committed very genteelly: a man may debauch his friend's wife genteelly: he may cheat at cards genteelly.

BOTTOMLEY Gordon 1874-1948
1471 *'To Ironfounders and Others'*
Your worship is your furnaces,
Which, like old idols, lost obscenes,
Have molten bowels; your vision is
Machines for making more machines.

BOTTOMLEY Horatio 1860-1933
1472 *(Speech at the Oxford Union)*
Gentlemen: I have not had your advantages.
What poor education I have received has been gained in the University of Life.

BOTTOMLEY Virginia 1948-
1473
Smoking is a dying habit.

BOUCICAULT Dion c.1820-1890
1474
I wish Adam had died with all his ribs in his body.

BOULDING Kenneth
1475
Canada has no cultural unity, no linguistic unity, no religious unity, no economic unity, no geographic unity. All it has is unity.

1476
In any evolutionary process, even in the arts, the search for novelty becomes corrupting.

1477
Nothing fails like success because we don't learn from it. We learn only from failure.

BOULEZ Pierre 1925-
1478
The function of pop music is to be consumed.

1479
Populism - as we all know - frequently transforms itself into fascism.

BOULTON Sir Harold Edwin 1859-1935
1480 *'Glorious Devon'*
When Adam and Eve were dispossessed
Of the garden hard by Heaven,
They planted another one down in the west,
'Twas Devon, glorious Devon!

1481 *'Skye Boat Song'*
Speed, bonnie boat, like a bird on the wing,
'Onward,' the sailors cry;
Carry the lad that's born to be king,

Over the sea to Skye.

BOURDILLON F.W. 1852-1921
1482 *Among the Flowers 'Light'*
The night has a thousand eyes,
And the day but one;
Yet the light of the bright world dies,
With the dying sun.

The mind has a thousand eyes,
And the heart but one;
Yet the light of a whole life dies,
When love is done.

BOURJAILY Vance
1483
Every man, even the most blessed, needs a little more than average luck to survive this world.

BOWEN Catherine Drinker
1484
Chamber music - a conversation between friends.

BOWEN E.E. 1836-1901
1485 *'Forty Years On'* (Harrow School Song)
Forty years on, when afar and asunder
Parted are those who are singing to-day.

1486 *'Forty Years On'* (Harrow School Song)
Follow up! Follow up! Follow up! Follow up!
Follow up!
Till the field ring again and again,
With the tramp of the twenty-two men,
Follow up!

BOWEN Elizabeth 1899-1973
1487
Each of us keeps, battened down inside himself, a sort of lunatic giant - impossible socially, but full-scale. It's the knockings and batterings we sometimes hear in each other that keep our intercourse from utter banality.

1488 *The Death of the Heart*
The innocent are so few that two of them seldom meet - when they do, their victims lie strewn around.

1489 *The Death of the Heart*
It is about five o'clock in an evening that the first hour of spring strikes - autumn arrives in the early morning, but spring at the close of a winter day.

1490 *The Death of the Heart*
Some people are moulded by their admirations, others by their hostilities.

1491 *(of Edith Sitwell)*
A high altar on the move.

1492 *The House in Paris*
Fate is not an eagle, it creeps like a rat.

1493
In big houses in which things are done properly, there is always the religious element. The diurnal cycle is observed with more feeling when there are servants to do the work.

1494
With three or more people there is something bold in the air: direct things get said which would frighten two people alone and conscious of each inch of their nearness to one another. To be three is to be in public - you feel safe.

BOWEN Ezra
1495
If thee marries for money, thee surely will earn it.

BOWEN Lord 1835-1894
1496
The rain, it raineth on the just
And also on the unjust fella:
But chiefly on the just, because
The unjust steals the just's umbrella.

1497
When I hear of an 'equity' in a case like this, I am reminded of a blind man in a dark room - looking for a black hat - which isn't there.

BOWER Walter
1498
The wolf was sick, he vowed a monk to be;
But when he got well, a wolf once more was he.

BOWERING George
1499
nobody
belongs anywhere,
even the
Rocky Mountains
are still
moving.

BOWIE David 1947-
1500 *'Space Oddity'*
Ground control to Major Tom.

BOWMAN Louis Nelson
1501
Another thing about capitalism - everybody knows who's in Grant's tomb.

BOWMAN Peter
1502
Only man, among living things, says prayers. Or needs to.

BOWRA Sir Maurice 1898-1971
1503 *John Betjeman Summoned by Bells*
I'm a man more dined against than dining.

BOYD-ORR Lord 1880-1971
1504
If people have to choose between freedom and

sandwiches they will take sandwiches.

BOYER Charles 1899-1978
1505
A French woman, when double-crossed, will kill her rival. The Italian woman would rather kill her deceitful lover. The Englishwoman simply breaks off relations - but they will all console themselves with another man.

BOYSE J.F.
1506
It would be a great advantage to some schoolmasters if they would steal two hours a day from their pupils, and give their own minds the benefit of the robbery.

BRACKELL Fogg
1507
Facts in books, statistics in encyclopedias, the ability to use them in men's heads.

BRADBURY Malcolm 1932-
1508 *Eating People is Wrong*
The English have the most rigid code of immorality in the world.

BRADFORD John c.1510-1555
1509 *(on seeing a group of criminals led to execution)*
But for the grace of God there goes John Bradford.

BRADLEE Benjamin 1921-
1510
News is the first rough draft of history.

BRADLEY Bill
1511
Becoming number one is easier than remaining number one.

BRADLEY F.H. 1846-1924
1512
In all of us, the excited amateur has to die before the artist can be born.

1513 *Appearance and Reality [preface]*
Where everthing is bad it must be good to know the worst.

1514
Few people would not be the worse for complete sincerity.

BRADLEY Omar 1893-1981
1515
We have grasped the mystery of the atom, and rejected the Sermon on the Mount.

1516
The world has achieved brilliance without wisdom, power without conscience. Ours is a world of nuclear giants and ethical infants.

BRADSHAW John 1602-1659
1517 *(at the trial of Charles I)*
Rebellion to tyrants is obedience to God.

BRADSTREET Anne c.1612-1672
1518 *'The Prologue'*
Let Greeks be Greeks, and Women what they are,
Men have precedency, and still excel.

1519 *'The Prologue'*
This mean and unrefinèd stuff of mine,
Will make your glistering gold but more to shine.

BRAMAH Ernest 1868-1942
1520 *The Wallet of Kai Lung*
The whole narrative is permeated with the odour of joss-sticks and honourable high-mindedness.

BRAMSTON James c.1694-1744
1521 *The Art of Politics*
What's not destroyed by Time's devouring hand?
Where's Troy, and where's the Maypole in the Strand?

BRANCUSI Constantin 1876-1957
1522
Architecture is inhabited sculpture.

BRANDEIS Louis Dembitz 1856-1941
1523
We can have democracy in this country or we can have great wealth concentrated in the hands of a few, but we can't have both.

1524
The most important office is that of private citizen.

BRANDEN Nathaniel
1525
For the rational, psychologically healthy man, the desire for pleasure is the desire to celebrate his control over reality. For the neurotic, the desire for pleasure is the desire to escape from reality.

BRANDO Marlon 1924-
1526
An actor's a guy who, if you ain't talking about him, ain't listening.

1527 *in On The Waterfront*
"I coulda been a contender. I coulda had class and been somebody."

BRAQUE Georges 1882-1963
1528 *Le Jour et la nuit: Cahiers*
Art is meant to disturb, science reassures.

1529 *Le Jour et la nuit: Cahiers*
Truth exists; only lies are invented.

BRATTON John W. and KENNEDY James B.
1530 *'The Teddy Bear's Picnic'*
If you go down in the woods today
You're sure of a big surprise
If you go down in the woods today
You'd better go in disguise
For every Bear that ever there was
Will gather there for certain because,
Today's the day the Teddy Bears have their Picnic.

BRAUN Wernher von 1912-1977
1531
Basic research is when I'm doing what I don't know what I'm doing.

1532
Everything in space obeys the laws of physics. If you know these laws, and obey them, space will treat you kindly. And don't tell me man doesn't belong out there. Man belongs wherever he wants to go - and he'll do plenty well when he gets there.

BRECHT Bertholt 1898-1956
1533
Fearful is the seductive power of goodness.

1534 *Mother Courage*
Peace is nothing but slovenliness, only war creates order.

1535 *Mother Courage*
Don't tell me peace has broken out, when I've just bought some new supplies.

1536 *Mother Courage*
War is like love. It always finds a way.

1537
People are too durable, that's their main trouble. They can do too much to themselves, they last too long.

1538
Poverty makes you sad as well as wise.

1539
The resistible rise of Arturo Ui.

1540 *The Threepenny Opera*
Food comes first, then morals.

1541 *The Threepenny Opera*
What is robbing a bank compared with founding a bank?

1542
Today every invention is received with a cry of triumph which soon turns into a cry of fear.

1543
What happens to the hole when the cheese is gone?

BRENAN Gerald 1894-1987
1544 *Thoughts in a Dry Season*
Those who have some means think that the
most important thing in the world is love. The
poor know that it is money.

1545 *Thoughts in a Dry Season*
Religions are kept alive by heresies, which are
really sudden explosions of faith.

1546 *Thoughts in a Dry Season*
In a happy marriage, it is the wife who provides
the climate, the husband the landscape.

BRENNAN Lynne
1547
Aggression is showing people you are out of
control.

BRIDGE Ann N.
1548
In any relationship we feel an unconscious need
to create, as it were, a new picture, a new
edition of ourselves to present to the fresh
person who claims our interest; for them, we in
a strange sense wish to, and do, start life anew.

BRIDGES Robert 1844-1930
1549 *The Growth of Love*
Beauty sat with me all the summer day,
Awaiting the sure triumph of her eye;
Nor mark'd I till we parted, how, hard by,
Love in her train stood ready for his prey.

1550 *'London Snow'*
All night it fell, and when full inches seven
It lay in the depth of its uncompacted lightness,
The clouds blew off from a high and frosty
heaven;
And all woke earlier for the unaccustomed
brightness
Of the winter dawning, the strange unheavenly
glare.

BRIDGMAN Percy Williams 1882-1961
1551
There is no adequate defence, except stupidity,
against the impact of a new idea.

BRIGHT John 1811-1889
1552 *(during the American Civil War)*
My opinion is that the Northern States will
manage somehow to muddle through.

1553
England is the mother of Parliaments.

1554
The knowledge of the ancient languages is
mainly a luxury.

1555
I am for 'Peace, retrenchment, and reform'.

BRINKLEY David
1556
This is the first convention of the space age -
where a candidate can promise the moon and
mean it.

BRITTEN Benjamin 1913-1976
1557
I am an arrogant and impatient listener, but in
the case of a few composers, a very few, when I
hear a work I do not like, I am convinced that it
is my own fault. Verdi is one of those
composers.

BROCKWAY George
1558
Labour is not a commodity, or a standard, or a
means to an ulterior end, but an end in itself.

BRONOWSKI Jacob 1908-1974
1559
We are all afraid - for our confidence, for the
future, for the world. That is the nature of the
human imagination. Yet every man, every
civilization, has gone forward because of its
engagement with what it has set itself to do.
The personal commitment and the emotional
commitment working together as one, has
made the Ascent of Man.

1560
We are all shot through with enough motives to
make a massacre, any day of the week that we
want to give them their head.

1561 *The Ascent of Man*
The world can only be grasped by action, not by
contemplation.

1562 *The Ascent of Man*
The essence of science: ask an impertinent
question, and you are on the way to a pertinent
answer.

BRONTÉ Charlotte 1816-1855
1563 *Jane Eyre*
Reader, I married him.

1564 *Shirley*
Of late years an abundant shower of curates has
fallen upon the North of England.

1565 *Shirley*
Be a governess! Better be a slave at once!

BRONTÉ Emily 1818-1848
1566 *'Remembrance'*
Cold in the earth - and fifteen wild Decembers,
From those brown hills, have melted into
spring.

1567 *'Remembrance'*
But when the days of golden dreams had
perished,
And even Despair was powerless to destroy,

Then did I learn how existence could be cherished,
Strengthened, and fed without the aid of joy.

1568 *Wuthering Heights*
My love for Heathcliff resembles the eternal rocks beneath - a source of little visible delight, but necessary.

BROOKE Rupert 1887-1915
1569 *'The Chilterns'*
And I shall find some girl perhaps,
And a better one than you,
With eyes as wise, but kindlier,
And lips as soft, but true.
And I dare say she will do.

1570 *'The Dead'*
Blow out, you bugles, over the rich Dead!
There's none of these so lonely and poor of old,
But, dying, has made us rarer gifts than gold.
These laid the world away; poured out the red
Sweet wine of youth; gave up the years to be
Of work and joy, and that unhoped serene,
That men call age; and those that would have been,
Their sons, they gave, their immortality.

1571 *'The Dead'*
Honour has come back, as a king, to earth,
And paid his subjects with a royal wage;
And Nobleness walks in our ways again;
And we have come into our heritage.

1572 *'Heaven'*
Fish say, they have their stream and pond;
But is there anything beyond?

1573 *'The Hill'*
And when we die
All's over that is ours; and life burns on
Through other lovers, other lips.

1574 *'The Life Beyond'*
I thought when love for you died, I should die.
It's dead. Alone, mostly strangely, I live on.

1575 *'The Old Vicarage, Grantchester'*
Unkempt about those hedges blows
An English unofficial rose.

1576 *'The Old Vicarage, Grantchester'*
Curates, long dust, will come and go
On lissom, clerical, printless toe;
And oft between the boughs is seen
The sly shade of a Rural Dean.

1577 *'The Old Vicarage, Grantchester'*
God! I will pack, and take a train,
And get me to England once again!
For England's the one land, I know,
Where men with Splendid Hearts may go.

1578 *'The Old Vicarage, Grantchester'*
For Cambridge people rarely smile,
Being urban, squat, and packed with guile.

1579 *'The Old Vicarage, Grantchester'*
Stands the Church clock at ten to three
And is there honey still for tea?

1580 *'Peace'*
Now, God be thanked Who has matched us with His hour,
And caught our youth, and wakened us from sleeping,
With hand made sure, clear eye, and sharpened power,
To turn, as swimmers into cleanness leaping.

1581 *'Peace'*
Naught broken save this body, lost but breath;
Nothing to shake the laughing heart's long peace there
But only agony, and that has ending;
And the worst friend and enemy is but Death.

1582 *'The Soldier'*
If I should die, think only this of me:
That there's some corner of a foreign field
That is for ever England. There shall be
In that rich earth a richer dust concealed;
A dust whom England bore, shaped, made aware,
Gave, once, her flowers to love, her ways to roam,
A body of England's, breathing English air,
Washed by the rivers, blest by suns of home.

BROOKNER Anita 1938-
1583 *Hotel du Lac*
Good women always think it is their fault when someone else is being offensive. Bad women never take the blame for anything.

BROOKS Mel 1926-
1584
Every human being has hundreds of separate people living under his skin. The talent of a writer is his ability to give them their separate names, identities, personalities and have them relate to other characters living with him.

1585
Humour is just another defence against the universe.

1586
Look at Jewish history. Unrelieved lamenting would be intolerable. So, for every ten Jews beating their breasts, God designated one to be crazy and amuse the breast-beaters. By the time I was five I knew I was that one.

BROOKS Thomas 1608-1680
1587
No good deed ever goes unpunished.

BROOKS Van Wyck 1886-1963
1588
Nothing is so soothing to our self-esteem as to find our bad traits in our forebears. It seems to absolve us.

BROUGHAM Lord 1778-1868
1589 *(attributed)*
Education makes a people easy to lead, but difficult to drive; easy to govern, but impossible to enslave.

BROUN Heywood 1888-1939
1590
Men build bridges and throw railroads across deserts, and yet they contend successfully that the job of sewing on a button is beyond them. Accordingly, they don't have to sew buttons.

1591
Sports do not build character. They reveal it.

BROWN Arthur
1592
Music is only sound expressing certain patterns, so to what extent is that sound architecture and to what extent theatre?

BROWN Bob
1593
Behind every successful man there's a lot of unsuccessful years.

BROWN H. Rap 1943-
1594
I say violence is necessary. It is as American as cherry pie.

BROWN Jerry 1938-
1595
The government is becoming the family of last resort.

1596
Prisons don't rehabilitate, they don't punish, they don't protect, so what the hell do they do?

BROWN John Mason 1900-
1597
It is in the hard rockpile labour of seeking to win, hold, or deserve a reader's interest that the pleasant agony of writing comes in.

1598
To many people dramatic criticism must seem like an attempt to tattoo soap bubbles.

BROWN Lew 1893-1958
1599
Life is just a bowl of cherries.

BROWN Thomas 1663-1704
1600
I do not love thee, Doctor Fell,
The reason why I cannot tell;
But this alone I know full well,

I do not love thee, Doctor Fell.

1601 *Letters from the Dead to the Living*
A little before you made a leap into the dark.

BROWNE Cecil 1932-
1602 *(reply to verse by William Norman Ewer)*
But not so odd
As those who choose
A Jewish God,
But spurn the Jews.

BROWNE Sir Thomas 1605-1682
1603 *The Garden of Cyrus*
The quincunx of heaven runs low, and 'tis time to close the five ports of knowledge.

1604 *Hydriotaphia*
Men have lost their reason in nothing so much as their religion, wherein stones and clouts make martyrs.

1605 *Hydriotaphia*
The long habit of living indisposeth us for dying.

1606 *Hydriotaphia*
Generations pass while some trees stand, and old families last not three oaks.

1607 *Hydriotaphia*
Man is a noble animal, splendid in ashes, and pompous in the grave.

1608 *Religio Medici*
Who can speak of eternity without a solecism, or think thereof without an ecstasy? Time we may comprehend, 'tis but five days elder than ourselves.

1609 *Religio Medici*
I have often admired the mystical way of Pythagoras, and the secret magic of numbers.

1610 *Religio Medici*
All things are artificial, for nature is the art of God.

1611 *Religio Medici*
Obstinacy in a bad cause, is but constancy in a good.

1612 *Religio Medici*
Persecution is a bad and indirect way to plant religion.

1613 *Religio Medici*
All places, all airs make unto me one country: I am in England, everywhere, and under any meridian.

1614 *Religio Medici*
This trivial and vulgar way of coition; it is the foolishest act a wise man commits in all his life, nor is there any thing that will more deject his cooled imagination, when he shall consider what an odd and unworthy piece of folly he

hath committed.

1615 *Religio Medici*
We all labour against our own cure, for death is the cure of all diseases.

1616 *Religio Medici*
For the world, I count it not an inn, but an hospital, and a place, not to live, but to die in.

1617 *Religio Medici*
There is surely a piece of divinity in us, something that was before the elements, and owes no homage unto the sun.

1618 *Religio Medici*
We term sleep a death, and yet it is waking that kills us, and destroys those spirits which are the house of life.

1619
The vices we scoff at in others, laugh at us within ourselves.

BROWNE Sir William 1692-1774
1620 *Literary Anecdotes Reply to Trapp's epigram*
The King to Oxford sent a troop of horse,
For Tories own no argument but force:
With equal skill to Cambridge books he sent,
For Whigs admit no force but argument.

BROWNING Elizabeth Barrett 1806-1861
1621 *Aurora Leigh*
The works of women are symbolical.
We sew, sew, prick our fingers, dull our sight,
Producing what? A pair of slippers, sir,
To put on when you're weary.

1622 *Aurora Leigh*
Since when was genius found respectable?

1623 *Aurora Leigh*
The devil's most devilish when respectable.

1624 *'To George Sand - A Desire'*
Thou large-brained woman and large-hearted man.

1625 *'Grief'*
I tell you, hopeless grief is passionless.

1626
Light tomorrow with today!

1627 *Sonnets from the Portuguese*
I love thee with the breath,
Smiles, tears, of all my life! - and if God choose,
I shall but love thee better after death.

1628 *Sonnets from the Portuguese*
How do I love thee? Let me count the ways.

1629 *Sonnets from the Portuguese*
If thou must love me, let it be for naught
Except for love's sake only.

BROWNING Robert 1812-1889
1630 *Aristophanes' Apology*
But, thanks to wine-lees and democracy,
We've still our stage where truth calls spade a spade!

1631 *'In a Balcony'*
A man can have but one life and one death,
One heaven, one hell.

1632 *'In a Balcony'*
I count life just a stuff
To try the soul's strength on, educe the man.

1633 *'Bishop Blougram's Apology'*
All we have gained then by our unbelief
Is a life of doubt diversified by faith,
For one of faith diversified by doubt:
We called the chess-board white - we call it black.

1634 *'Bishop Blougram's Apology'*
No, when the fight begins within himself,
A man's worth something.

1635 *'Bishop Blougram's Apology'*
He said true things, but called them by wrong names.

1636 *'A Blot in the 'Scutcheon'*
I was so young, I loved him so, I had
No mother, God forgot me, and I fell.

1637
Your children are not dead. They are just waiting until the world deserves them.

1638 *'Christmas-Eve'*
In the natural fog of the good man's mind.

1639 *'Confessions'*
What is he buzzing in my ears?
'Now that I come to die,
Do I view the world as a vale of tears?'
Ah, reverend sir, not I!

1640 *'Confessions'*
We loved, sir - used to meet:
How sad and bad and mad it was -
But then, how it was sweet!

1641 *'Cristina'*
She should never have looked at me,
If she meant I should not love her!

1642 *'A Death in the Desert'*
Stung by the splendour of a sudden thought.

1643 *'A Death in the Desert'*
... Progress, man's distinctive mark alone,
Not God's, and not the beasts': God is, they are,
Man partly is and wholly hopes to be.

1644 *A Death in the Desert*
Such ever was love's way; to rise, it stoops.

1645 *'Easter-Day'*
'Tis well averred,
A scientific faith's absurd.

1646 *'Fifine at the Fair'*
So absolutely good is truth, truth never hurts
The teller.

1647 *'By the Fireside'*
How well I know what I mean to do
When the long dark autumn-evenings come.

1648 *'By the Fireside'*
Oh, the little more, and how much it is!
And the little less, and what worlds away!

1649 *'By the Fireside'*
If two lives join, there is oft a scar,
They are one and one, with a shadowy third;
One near one is too far.

1650
Fit for the sunshine, so, it followed him
A happy-tempered bringer of the best
Out of the worst.

1651 *'Home-Thoughts, from Abroad'*
Oh, to be in England
Now that April's there.

1652 *'Home-Thoughts, from the Sea'*
Nobly, nobly Cape Saint Vincent to the North-
west died away:
Sunset ran, one glorious blood-red, reeking into
Cadiz Bay.

1653 *'How they brought the Good News from
Ghent to Aix'*
I sprang to the stirrup, and Joris, and he;
I galloped, Dirk galloped, we galloped all three.

1654 *The Inn Album*
Ignorance is not innocence but sin.

1655 *La Saisiaz [prologue]*
Good, to forgive;
Best, to forget!
Living, we fret;
Dying, we live.

1656 *'My Last Duchess'*
She had
A heart - how shall I say? - too soon made glad,
Too easily impressed: she liked whate'er
She looked on, and her looks went everywhere.

1657 *'The Last Ride Together'*
Who knows but the world may end tonight?

1658
Less is more.

1659 *'The Lost Leader'*
Never glad confident morning again!

1660 *Luria*
Oppression makes the wise man mad.

1661 *'Never the Time and the Place'*
Never the time and the place
And the loved one all together.

1662 *'Old Pictures in Florence'*
Works done least rapidly, Art most cherishes.

1663 *'The Patriot'*
It was roses, roses, all'the way.

1664 *'The Patriot'*
The air broke into a mist with bells.

1665 *'Pictor Ignotus'*
Ah, thought which saddens while it soothes!

1666 *'The Pied Piper of Hamelin'*
Rats!
They fought the dogs and killed the cats,
And bit the babies in the cradles,
And ate the cheeses out of the vats,
And licked the soup from the cooks' own ladles,
Slit open the kegs of salted sprats,
Made nests inside men's Sunday hats,
And even spoiled the women's chats
By drowning their speaking
With shrieking and squeaking
In fifty different sharps and flats.

1667 *Pippa Passes*
The year's at the spring
And day's at the morn;
Morning's at seven;
The hill-side's dew-pearled;
The lark's on the wing;
The snail's on the thorn:
God's in his heaven -
All's right with the world!

1668 *'Rabbi Ben Ezra'*
Grow old along with me!
The best is yet to be.

1669 *'Rabbi Ben Ezra'*
Fancies that broke through language and
escaped.

1670 *The Ring and the Book*
Youth means love,
Vows can't change nature, priests are only men.

1671 *The Ring and the Book*
Faultless to a fault.

1672 *The Ring and the Book*
There's a new tribunal now
higher than God's - the educated man's!

1673 *'Saul'*
'Tis not what man Does which exalts him, but
what man Would do!

1674 *Sordello*
Any nose
May ravage with impunity a rose.

1675
When pain ends, gain ends too.

1676
Who hears music, feels his solitude peopled at once.

1677 *'Any Wife to any Husband'*
Why need the other women know so much?

BRUCE Lenny 1925-1966
1678
The role of a comedian is to make the audience laugh, at a minimum of once every fifteen seconds.

1679
The whole motivation for any performer is 'Look at me, Ma.'

BRUMMELL Beau 1778-1840
1680 *(of the Prince of Wales)*
Who's your fat friend?

1681 *Reminiscences of a Literary Life*
[Brummell] used to say that, whether it was summer or winter, he always liked to have the morning well-aired before he got up.

BRUYERE Jean de la 1645-1696
1682
It is a great misfortune neither to have enough wit to talk well nor enough judgement to be silent.

1683 *Les Caractères ou les moeurs de ce siècle*
The onset and the waning of love make themselves felt in the uneasiness experienced at being alone together.

1684 *Les Caractères ou les moeurs de ce siècle*
The people have little intelligence, the great no heart ... if I had to choose I should have no hesitation: I would be of the people.

1685 *Les Caractères ou les moeurs de ce siècle*
Man has but three events in his life: to be born, to live, and to die. He is not conscious of his birth, he suffers at his death and he forgets to live.

1686 *Les Caractères ou les moeurs de ce siècle*
Between good sense and good taste there is the same difference as between cause and effect.

1687 *Les Caractères ou les moeurs de ce siècle*
Everything has been said, and we are more than seven thousand years of human thought too late.

1688 *Les Caractères ou les moeurs de ce siècle*
Making a book is a craft, as is making a clock; it takes more than wit to become an author.

1689
As long as men are liable to die and are desirous to live, a physician will be made fun of, but he will be well paid.

1690
A man must have very eminent qualities to hold his own without being polite.

1691
A man often runs the risk of throwing away a witticism if he admits that it is his own.

BRYAN Willian Jennings 1860-1925
1692
The humblest citizen of all the land, when clad in the armour of a righteous cause, is stronger than all the hosts of error.

BRZEZINSKI Zbigniew 1928-
1693 *Foreign Affairs*
Russia can be an empire or a democracy, but it cannot be both.

BUCHAN John 1875-1940
1694
An atheist is a man who has no invisible means of support.

1695
He disliked emotion, not because he felt lightly, but because he felt deeply.

1696
We can pay our debt to the past by putting the future in debt to ourselves.

1697 *Mr. Standfast*
Its a great life if you don't weaken.

1698
The true definition of a snob is one who craves for what separates men rather than for what unites them.

1699
'What would you call the highest happiness?' Wratislaw was asked. 'The sense of competence,' was the answer, given without hesitation.

BUCHANAN James 1791-1868
1700 *(to Abraham Lincoln)*
If you are as happy, my dear sir, on entering this house as I am in leaving it and returning home, you are the happiest man in the country.

BUCHANAN Robert 1841-1901
1701 *'White Rose and Red'*
She just wore
Enough for modesty - no more.

BUCHMAN Frank 1878-1961
1702 *Remaking the World*
Suppose everybody cared enough, everybody shared enough, wouldn't everybody have enough? There is enough in the world for everyone's need, but not enough for everyone's greed.

BÜCHNER Georg 1813-1837
1703
Man is an abyss, and I turn giddy when I look down into it.

BUCHWALD Art
1704
Television has a real problem. They have no page two.

1705
When it came to writing about wine, I did what everyone else did - faked it.

BUCK Pearl 1892-1973
1706 *The Good Earth*
It is better to be first with an ugly woman than the hundredth with a beauty.

1707
It is not healthy when a nation lives within a nation, as coloured Americans are living inside America. A nation cannot live confident of its tomorrow if its refugees are among its own citizens.

BUCKLEY Jr. William F. 1925-
1708
A Conservative is a fellow who is standing athwart history yelling 'Stop!'

BUCKOLL H. J. 1803-1871
1709 *Psalms and Hymns for Use of Rugby School Chapel*
Lord, dismiss us with Thy blessing,
Thanks for mercies past received.
Pardon all, their faults confessing;
Time that's lost may all retrieve.

BUCKROSE J.E.
1710
Happiness comes more from loving than being loved; and often when our affection seems wounded it is only our vanity bleeding. To love, and to be hurt often, and to love again - this is the brave and happy life.

BUFFON Comte de 1707-1788
1711
Never think that God's delays are God's denials. Hold on; hold fast; hold out. Patience is genius.

BULLER Arthur 1874-1944
1712 *'Relativity'*
There was a young lady named Bright,
Whose speed was far faster than light;
She set out one day
In a relative way
And returned on the previous night.

BULLOCK Lord
1713
Democracy is not about giving speeches; it is about making committees work.

BULMER-THOMAS Ivor 1905-
1714 *(of Harold Wilson)*
If he ever went to school without any boots it was because he was too big for them.

BÜLOW Prince Bernhard von 1849-1929
1715
We also demand our own place in the sun.

BULWER-LYTTON Edward 1803-1873
1716
Genius does what it must, and talent does what it can.

1717
A good cigar is as great a comfort to a man as a good cry is to a woman.

1718
A good heart is better than all the heads in the world.

1719
Laws die, books never.

1720
In life it is difficult to say who do you the most mischief, enemies with the worst intentions, or friends with the best.

1721
Life would be tolerably agreeable if it were not for its amusements.

1722
Master books, but do not let them master you. Read to live, not live to read.

1723 *The Parisians*
Revolutions are not made with rosewater.

1724 *Richelieu*
Beneath the rule of men entirely great,
The pen is mightier than the sword.

1725 *Richelieu*
In the lexicon of youth, which fate reserves
For a bright manhood, there is no such word
As - *fail*.

1726 *(of Tennyson)*
Out-babying Wordsworth and out-glittering Keats.

1727 *What will he do with it?*
There is no man so friendless but what he can find a friend sincere enough to tell him disagreeable truths.

BUNN Alfred 'Poet' c.1796-1860
1728 *The Bohemian Girl*
I dreamed that I dwelt in marble halls.

BUÑUEL Luis 1900-1983
1729
Thanks to God, I am still an atheist.

The Wordsworth Dictionary of Quotations

BUNYAN John 1628-1888
1730 *The Pilgrim's Progress*
As I walked through the wilderness of this world.

1731 *The Pilgrim's Progress*
The name of the slough was Despond.

1732 *The Pilgrim's Progress*
It is an hard matter for a man to go down into the valley of Humiliation ... and to catch no slip by the way.

1733 *The Pilgrim's Progress*
Hanging is too good for him, said Mr Cruelty.

1734 *The Pilgrim's Progress*
Sleep is sweet to the labouring man.

1735 *The Pilgrim's Progress*
Then I saw that there was a way to Hell, even from the gates of Heaven.

1736 *The Pilgrim's Progress*
So I awoke, and behold it was a dream.

1737 *The Pilgrim's Progress*
One leak will sink a ship, and one sin will destroy a sinner.

1738 *The Pilgrim's Progress*
A man there was, tho' some did count him mad, The more he cast away, the more he had.

1739 *The Pilgrim's Progress*
Mercy ... laboured much for the poor ... an ornament to her profession.

1740 *The Pilgrim's Progress*
Who would true valour see,
Let him come hither;
One here will constant be,
Come wind, come weather
There's no discouragement
Shall make him once relent
His first avowed intent
To be a pilgrim.

BURBANK Luther 1849-1926
1741
Heredity is nothing but stored environment.

BURCHFIELD Charles 1893-1967
1742
As an artist grows older, he has to fight disillusionment and learn to establish the same relation to nature as an adult as he had when a child.

BURGESS Anthony 1917-1993
1743
A clockwork orange.

1744
The downtrodden, who are the great creators of slang, hurl pithiness and colour at poverty and oppression.

BURGON John William 1813-1888
1745 *Petra*
Match me such marvel, save in Eastern clime - A rose-red city - 'half as old as Time'!

BURKE Billie
1746
I am constantly amazed when I talk to young people to learn how much they know about sex and how little about soap.

1747
A woman past forty should make up her mind to be young - not her face.

BURKE Edmund 1729-1797
1748 *(attributed)*
It is necessary only for the good man to do nothing for evil to triumph.

1749 *On American Taxation*
To tax and to please, no more than to love and to be wise, is not given to men.

1750
Bad laws are the worst sort of tyranny.

1751 *On Conciliation with America*
The concessions of the weak are the concessions of fear.

1752 *On Conciliation with America*
The use of force alone is but temporary. It may subdue for a moment; but it does not remove the necessity of subduing again; and a nation is not governed, which is perpetually to be conquered.

1753 *On Conciliation with America*
Abstract liberty, like other mere abstractions, is not to be found.

1754 *On Conciliation with America*
I do not know the method of drawing up an indictment against an whole people.

1755 *On Conciliation with America*
Parties must ever exist in a free country.

1756
Dangers by being despised grow great.

1757
A disposition to preserve, and an ability to improve, taken together, would be my standard of a statesman.

1758
The effect of liberty on individuals is that they may do what they please: we ought to see what it will please them to do, before we risk congratulations.

1759
By gnawing through a dyke, even a rat may drown a nation.

1760
The greater the power, the more dangerous the abuse.

1761
History is a pact between the dead, the living, and the yet unborn.

1762 *Letter to a Member of the National Assembly*
Those who have been once intoxicated with power, and have derived any kind of emolument from it, even though for but one year, can never willingly abandon it.

1763 *Letter to a Member of the National Assembly*
Tyrants seldom want pretexts.

1764 *Letter to a Member of the National Assembly*
You can never plan the future by the past.

1765 *A Letter to a Noble Lord*
To innovate is not to reform.

1766 *Letter to the Sheriffs of Bristol*
Liberty too must be limited in order to be possessed.

1767 *Letter to the Sheriffs of Bristol*
Among a people generally corrupt, liberty cannot long exist.

1768 *Letter to William Smith*
Somebody has said, that a king may make a nobleman but he cannot make a gentleman.

1769 *Observations ... on the Present State of Nation*
There is, however, a limit at which forbearance ceases to be a virtue.

1770
The people are the masters.

1771
The people never give up their liberties but under some delusion.

1772 *Reflections on the Revolution in France*
A state without the means of some change is without the means of its conservation.

1773 *Reflections on the Revolution in France*
Make the Revolution a parent of settlement, and not a nursery of future revolutions.

1774 *Reflections on the Revolution in France*
People will not look forward to posterity, who never look backward to their ancestors.

1775 *Reflections on the Revolution in France*
Those who attempt to level never equalize.

1776 *Reflections on the Revolution in France*
The age of chivalry is gone. That of sophisters, economists, and calculators, has succeeded;

and the glory of Europe is extinguished for ever.

1777 *Reflections on the Revolution in France*
In the groves of their academy, at the end of every vista, you see nothing but the gallows.

1778 *Reflections on the Revolution in France*
Kings will be tyrants from policy when subjects are rebels from principle.

1779 *Reflections on the Revolution in France*
Man is by his constitution a religious animal; atheism is against not only our reason, but our instincts.

1780 *Reflections on the Revolution in France*
A perfect democracy is therefore the most shameless thing in the world.

1781 *Reflections on the Revolution in France*
Superstition is the religion of feeble minds.

1782 *Reflections on the Revolution in France*
Good order is the foundation of all good things.

1783
Your representative owes you, not his industry only, but his judgement; and he betrays, instead of serving you, if he sacrifices it to your opinion.

1784 *On the Sublime and Beautiful*
No passion so effectually robs the mind of all its powers of acting and reasoning as fear.

1785 *On the Sublime and Beautiful*
Custom reconciles us to everything.

1786 *Third Letter...on the Proposals for Peace*
Well is it known that ambition can creep as well as soar.

1787 *Thoughts on the Cause of the Present Discontents*
To complain of the age we live in, to murmur at the present possessors of power, to lament the past, to conceive extravagant hopes of the future, are the common dispositions of the greatest part of mankind.

1788 *Thoughts on the Cause of the Present Discontents*
When bad men combine, the good must associate; else they will fall, one by one, an unpitied sacrifice in a contemptible struggle.

1789 *Thoughts and Details on Scarcity*
And having looked to government for bread, on the very first scarcity they will turn and bite the hand that fed them.

1790 *A Tract on the Popery Laws*
Laws, like houses, lean on one another.

1791 *A Tract on the Popery Laws*
In all forms of Government the people is the true legislator.

1792 *Two Letters on the Proposals for Peace*
All men that are ruined are ruined on the side of their natural propensities.

1793 *(on the younger Pitt's maiden Speech)*
Not merely a chip of the old 'block', but the old block itself.

BURNET Dana
1794
I'd rather have an inch of dog than miles of pedigree.

BURNETT Carol 1934-
1795
Comedy is tragedy - plus time.

BURNEY Fanny (Mme D'Arblay) 1752-1840
1796 *Camilla*
A little alarm now and then keeps life from stagnation.

1797 *Camilla*
It's a delightful thing to think of perfection; but it's vastly more amusing to talk of errors and absurdities.

1798 *Camilla*
No man is in love when he marries. He may have loved before; I have even heard he has sometimes loved after: but at the time never. There is something in the formalities of the matrimonial preparations that drive away all the little cupidons.

1799 *Cecilia*
Travelling is the ruin of all happiness! There's no looking at a building here after seeing Italy.

BURNHAM Daniel H. 1846-1912
1800
Make no little plans; they have no magic to stir men's blood ... Make big plans, aim high in hope and work.

BURNS George 1896-1996
1801
Too bad that all the people who know how to run the country are busy driving taxicabs and cutting hair.

1802
With the collapse of vaudeville new talent has no place to stink.

1803
I must be getting absent-minded. Whenever I complain that things aren't what they used to be, I always forget to include myself.

1804
Happiness? A good cigar, a good meal, and a good woman - or a bad woman; it depends on how much happiness you can handle.

BURNS John 1858-1943
1805
The Thames is liquid history.

BURNS Robert 1759-1796
1806 *'Ae Fond Kiss'*
Ae fond kiss, and then we sever;
Ae fareweel, and then for ever!

1807 *'Ae Fond Kiss'*
Had we never lov'd sae kindly,
Had we never lov'd sae blindly,
Never met - or never parted,
We had ne'er been broken-hearted.

1808 *'For a'that and a'that'*
The rank is but the guinea's stamp,
The man's the gowd for a' that!

1809 *'Auld Lang Syne'*
Should auld acquaintance be forgot
And never brought to mind?

1810 *'Auld Lang Syne'*
We'll tak a cup o' kindness yet,
For auld lang syne.

1811 *'Auld Lang Syne'*
And there's a hand, my trusty fiere!
And gie's a hand o'thine!

1812 *'The Author's Earnest Cry and Prayer'*
Freedom and Whisky gan thegither!

1813 *'Bonnie Lesley'*
To see her is to love her,
And love but her for ever,
For Nature made her what she is,
And ne'er made anither!

1814 *'Comin thro' the rye'*
Gin a body meet a body
Comin thro' the rye,
Gin a body kiss a body
Need a body cry?

1815 *'Death and Dr Hornbook'*
I wasna fou, but just had plenty.

1816 *'The Deil's awa wi' th'Exciseman'*
There's threesome reels, there's foursome reels,
There's hornpipes and strathspeys, man,
But the ae best dance e'er cam to the land
Was, the deil's awa wi' th'Exciseman.

1817 *'Epistle to a Young Friend'*
I waive the quantum o' the sin;
The hazard of concealing;
But och! it hardens a' within,
And petrifies the feeling!

1818 *'Epistle to a Young Friend'*
An atheist-laugh's a poor exchange
For Deity offended!

1819
Gie me a spark o' nature's fire,
That's a' the learning I desire.

1820
God knows, I'm no the thing I should be,
Nor am I even the thing I could be.

1821 *'Green Grow the Rashes'*
Green grow the rashes, O,
Green grow the rashes, O;
The sweetest hours that e're I spend,
Are spent among the lasses, O.

1822 *'My Heart's in the Highlands'*
My heart's in the Highlands, my heart is not
here;
My heart's in the Highlands a-chasing the deer;
Chasing the wild deer, and following the roe,
My heart's in the Highlands, wherever I go.

1823 *'Hey for a Lass wi' a Tocher'*
O, gie me the lass that has acres o' charms,
O, gie me the lass wi' the weel-stockit farms.

1824 *'The Jolly Beggars'*
Life is all a VARIORUM,
We regard not how it goes;
Let them cant about DECORUM,
Who have characters to lose.

1825 *'The Kirkudbright Grace'*
Some have meat and cannot eat,
Some cannot eat that want it:
But we have meat and we can eat,
Sae let the Lord be thankit.

1826 *'There was a Lass'*
A man may drink and no be drunk;
A man may fight and no be slain;
A man may kiss a bonnie lass,
And aye be welcome back again.

1827
O Life! thou art a galling load,
Along a rough, a weary road,
To wretches such as I.

1828 *'To a Louse'*
O wad some Pow'r the giftie gie us
To see oursels as others see us!
It wad frae mony a blunder free us,
And foolish notion.

1829 *'Man was made to Mourn'*
Man's inhumanity to man
Makes countless thousands mourn!

1830 *'Man was made to Mourn'*
O Death! the poor man's dearest friend,
The kindest and the best!

1831 *'To a Mouse'*
Wee, sleekit, cow'rin, tim'rous beastie,
O what a panic's in thy breastie!
Thou need na start awa sae hasty,

Wi' bickering brattle!

1832 *'To a Mouse'*
The best laid schemes o'mice an' men
Gang aft a-gley.

1833 *'A Red Red Rose'*
O, my Luve's like a red, red rose
That's newly sprung in June;
O my Luve's like the melodie
That's sweetly play'd in tune.

1834 *'Robert Bruce's March to Bannockburn'*
Liberty's in every blow!
Let us do - or die!!!

1835 *(said shortly before his death)*
Don't let the awkward squad fire over me.

1836 *'Tam o' Shanter'*
Nae man can tether time or tide.

BURROUGHS John 1837-1921
1837
How beautifully the leaves grow old. How full of
light and colour are their last days.

BURROUGHS William 1914-1997
1838
Americans have a special horror of letting
things happen their own way, without
interference. They would like to jump down
their stomachs, digest the food, and shovel the
shit out.

BURROWS Sir Fred 1887-1973
1839 *(speech as last Governor of undivided
Bengal)*
Unlike my predecessors I have devoted more of
my life to shunting and hooting than to hunting
and shooting.

BURTON Nat
1840 *'The White Cliffs of Dover'*
There'll be bluebirds over the white cliffs of
Dover,
Tomorrow, just you wait and see.

BURTON Sir Richard 1821-1890
1841 *(note to his wife)*
Pay, pack, and follow at convenience.

BURTON Robert 1577-1640
1842 *The Anatomy of Melancholy*
All my joys to this are folly,
Naught so sweet as Melancholy.

1843 *The Anatomy of Melancholy*
A loose, plain, rude writer ... I call a spade a
spade.

1844 *The Anatomy of Melancholy*
All poets are mad.

1845 *The Anatomy of Melancholy*
I may not here omit those two main plagues,
and common dotages of human kind, wine and

women, which have infatuated and besotted myriads of people.

1846 *The Anatomy of Melancholy*
From this it is clear how much the pen is worse than the sword.

1847 *The Anatomy of Melancholy*
One was never married, and that's his hell: another is, and that's his plague.

1848 *The Anatomy of Melancholy*
The gods are well pleased when they see great men contending with adversity.

1849 *The Anatomy of Melancholy*
What is a ship but a prison?

1850 *The Anatomy of Melancholy*
To enlarge or illustrate this power and effect of love is to set a candle in the sun.

1851 *The Anatomy of Melancholy*
England is a paradise for women, and hell for horses: Italy a paradise for horses, hell for women, as the diverb goes.

1852 *The Anatomy of Melancholy*
One religion is as true as another.

1853 *The Anatomy of Melancholy*
Be not solitary, be not idle.

1854
Set a beggar on horseback, and he will ride a gallop.

1855
Diogenes struck the father when the son swore.

1856
If the world will be gulled, let it be gulled.

BUSCH Wilhelm 1832-1908
1857
To become a father is not hard,
To be a father is, however.

BUSENBAUM Hermann 1600-1668
1858 *Medulla Theologiae Moralis*
The end justifies the means.

BUSH Barbara 1925-
1859
Good education is the essential foundation of a strong democracy.

1860
Somewhere out in this audience may even be someone who will one day follow in my footsteps, and preside over the White House as the President's spouse. I wish him well.

BUSH Douglas 1896-1983
1861
The great humorist forgets himself in his delighted contemplation of other people.

BUSH George 1924-
1862 *(campaign pledge on taxation)*
Read my lips: no new taxes.

BUSSY-RABUTIN Comte de 1618-1693
1863
God is usually on the side of big squadrons and against little ones.

1864 *Histoire Amoureuse des Gaules: Maximes d'Amour*
Love comes from blindness,
Friendship from knowledge.

1865 *Histoire Amoureuse des Gaules: Maximes d'Amour*
Absence is to love what wind is to fire;
It extinguishes the small, it kindles the great.

BUSTON Charles
1866
To make pleasure pleasant, shorten.

BUTLER Nicholas Murray 1862-1947
1867 *(attributed)*
An expert is one who knows more and more about less and less.

BUTLER Samuel 1835-1902
1868 *(attributed)*
Brigands demand your money or your life; women require both.

1869
All philosophies, if you ride them home, are nonsense, but some are greater nonsense than others.

1870
An apology for the Devil - it must be remembered that we have only heard one side of the case. God has written all the books.

1871
Books should be tried by a judge and jury as though they were crimes.

1872
I do not mind lying, but I hate inaccuracy.

1873 *Further Extracts from Notebooks*
The three most important things a man has are, briefly, his private parts, his money, and his religious opinions.

1874 *Further Extracts from Notebooks*
Jesus! with all thy faults I love thee still.

1875 *Further Extracts from Notebooks*
Conscience is thoroughly well-bred and soon leaves off talking to those who do not wish to hear it.

1876
It is the function of vice to keep virtue within reasonable grounds.

1877
I can generally bear the separation, but I don't like the leave-taking.

1878
It has been said that though God cannot alter the past, historians can; it is perhaps because they can be useful to Him in this respect that He tolerates their existence.

1879
The great pleasure of a dog is that you may make a fool of yourself with him and not only will he not scold you, but he will make a fool of himself too.

1880
It is hard to come down the social ladder without tumbling off.

1881
A hen is only an egg's way of making another egg.

1882
A lawyer's dream of heaven - every man reclaimed his property at the resurrection, and each tried to recover it from all his forefathers.

1883 *Letters between Samuel Butler and Miss E.M.Savage*
It was very good of God to let Carlyle and Mrs Carlyle marry one another and so make only two people miserable instead of four.

1884
Life is like playing a violin solo in public and learning the instrument as one goes on.

1885
If life must not be taken too seriously - then so neither must death.

1886
It does not matter much what a man hates, provided he hates something.

1887 *Notebooks*
Life is one long process of getting tired.

1888 *Notebooks*
All progress is based upon a universal innate desire on the part of every organism to live beyond its income.

1889 *Notebooks*
The history of art is the history of revivals.

1890 *Notebooks*
Our ideas. They are for the most part like bad sixpences and we spend our lives in trying to pass them on one another.

1891 *Notebooks*
To live is like to love - all reason is against it, and all healthy instinct for it.

1892
The oldest books are still only just out to those who have not read them.

1893
To put one's trust in God is only a longer way of saying that one will chance it.

1894
We pay a person the compliment of acknowledging his superiority whenever we lie to him.

1895
People care more about being thought to have good taste than about being thought either good, clever or amiable.

1896
People in general are equally horrified at hearing the Christian religion doubted, and at seeing it practised.

1897
I reckon being ill is one of the greatest pleasures of life, provided one is not too ill and is not obliged to work till one is better.

1898
Silence is not always tact, and it is tact that is golden, not silence.

1899
The test of a good critic is whether he knows when and how to believe on insufficient evidence.

1900
A virtue to be serviceable must, like gold, be alloyed with some commoner but more durable metal.

1901 *The Way of All Flesh*
Adversity, if a man is set down to it by degrees, is more supportable with equanimity by most people than any great prosperity arrived at in a single lifetime.

1902 *The Way of All Flesh*
All animals, except man, know that the principal business of life is to enjoy it.

1903 *The Way of All Flesh*
The advantage of doing one's praising for oneself is that one can lay it on so thick and exactly in the right places.

1904 *The Way of All Flesh*
Young as he was, his instinct told him that the best liar is he who makes the smallest amount of lying go the longest way.

1905
Whatso'er we perpetrate
We do but row, we are steered by fate.

1906
When you have told anyone you have left him a legacy, the only decent thing to do is to die at once.

BUTLER Samuel 'Hudibras' 1612-1680
1907 *Genuine Remains 'Miscellaneous Thoughts'*
All love at first, like generous wine,
Ferments and frets, until 'tis fine;
But when 'tis settled on the lee,
And from th'impurer matter free,
Becomes the richer still, the older,
And proves the pleasanter, the colder.

1908 *Hudibras*
He'd run in debt by disputation,
And pay with ratiocination.

1909 *Hudibras*
For all a rhetorician's rules
Teach nothing but to name his tools.

1910 *Hudibras*
He knew what's what, and that's as high
As metaphysic wit can fly.

1911 *Hudibras*
Compound for sins, they are inclined to,
By damning those they have no mind to.

1912 *Hudibras*
Great actions are not always true sons
Of great and mighty resolutions.

1913 *Hudibras*
She that with poetry is won,
Is but a desk to write upon.

1914 *Hudibras*
Love is a boy, by poets styled,
Then spare the rod, and spoil the child.

1915 *Hudibras*
Oaths are but words, and words but wind.

1916 *Hudibras*
What makes all doctrines plain and clear?
About two hundred pounds a year.
And that which was proved true before,
Prove false again? Two hundred more.

1917 *Hudibras*
He that complies against his will,
Is of his own opinion still.

1918 *Hudibras*
For Justice, though she's painted blind,
Is to the weaker side inclined.

BUXTON Charles
1919
Pounds are the sons, not of pounds, but of pence.

BYRNE Frankie
1920
Respect is love in plain clothes.

BYROM John 1692-1763
1921
Christians, awake! Salute the happy morn,
Whereon the Saviour of the world was born.

1922
God bless the King, I mean the Faith's Defender;
God bless - no harm in blessing - the Pretender;
But who Pretender is, or who is King,
God bless us all - that's quite another thing.

BYRON Lord 1788-1824
1923
Admire, exult, despise, laugh, weep - for here
There is such matter for all feelings: - Man!
Thou pendulum betwixt a smile and tear.

1924 *'The Age of Bronze'*
For what were all these country patriots born?
To hunt, and vote, and raise the price of corn?

1925 *Beppo*
Our cloudy climate, and our chilly women.

1926 *Beppo*
A pretty woman as was ever seen,
Fresh as the Angel o'er a new inn door.

1927 *The Bride of Abydos*
Where the virgins are soft as the roses they twine,
And all, save the spirit of man, is divine.

1928 *Childe Harold's Pilgrimage*
Here all were noble, save Nobility.

1929 *Childe Harold's Pilgrimage*
On with the dance! let joy be unconfined;
No sleep till morn, when Youth and Pleasure meet
To chase the glowing Hours with flying feet.

1930 *Childe Harold's Pilgrimage*
He rushed into the field, and, foremost fighting, fell.

1931 *Childe Harold's Pilgrimage*
Quiet to quick bosoms is a hell.

1932 *Childe Harold's Pilgrimage*
To fly from, need not be to hate, mankind.

1933 *Childe Harold's Pilgrimage*
I live not in myself, but I become
Portion of that around me; and to me,
High mountains are a feeling, but the hum
Of human cities torture.

1934 *Childe Harold's Pilgrimage*
Of its own beauty is the mind diseased.

1935 *Childe Harold's Pilgrimage*
Dark-heaving - boundless, endless, and sublime
The image of eternity.

1936
Christians have burned each other, quite
persuaded
That all the apostles would have done as they
did.

1937 *'Churchill's Grave'*
The glory and the nothing of a name.

1938 *The Corsair*
Oh! too convincing - dangerously dear -
In woman's eye the unanswerable tear!

1939 *'The Curse of Minerva'(of Scotland)*
A land of meanness, sophistry, and mist.

1940 *'On This Day I Complete my Thirty-Sixth
Year'*
My days are in the yellow leaf;
The flowers and fruits of love are gone;
The worm, the canker, and the grief
Are mine alone!

1941 *'The Destruction of Sennacherib'*
The Assyrian came down like the wolf on the
fold,
And his cohorts were gleaming in purple and
gold;
And the sheen of their spears was like stars on
the sea,
When the blue wave rolls nightly on deep
Galilee.

1942 *'The Destruction of Sennacherib'*
For the Angel of Death spread his wings on the
blast,
And breathed in the face of the foe as he
passed.

1943 *'To Eliza'*
Still I can't contradict, what so oft has been said,
'Though women are angels, yet wedlock's the
devil.'

1944 *English Bards and Scotch Reviewers*
A man must serve his time to every trade
Save censure - critics all are ready made.
Take hackneyed jokes from Miller, got by rote,
With just enough of learning to misquote.

1945 *English Bards and Scotch Reviewers*
Let simple Wordsworth chime his childish verse,
And brother Coleridge lull the babe at nurse.

1946 *English Bards and Scotch Reviewers*
And glory, like the phoenix midst her fires,
Exhales her odours, blazes, and expires.

1947 *English Bards and Scotch Reviewers*
Be warm but pure: be amorous but chaste.

1948
The great art of life is sensation, to feel that we
exist, even in pain.

1949 *(on the instantaneous success of Childe
Harold)*
I awoke one morning and found myself famous.

1950 *Journal, 1813*
The more I see of men, the less I like them. If I
could but say so of women too, all would be
well.

1951 *Don Juan*
And Coleridge, too, has lately taken wing,
But, like a hawk encumbered with his hood,
Explaining metaphysics to the nation -
I wish he would explain his explanation.

1952 *Don Juan*
Married, charming, chaste, and twenty-three.

1953 *Don Juan*
'Twas stange that one so young should thus
concern
His brain about the action of the sky;
If you think 'twas philosophy that this did,
I can't help thinking puberty assisted.

1954 *Don Juan*
Sweet is revenge - especially to women.

1955 *Don Juan*
Pleasure's a sin, and sometimes sin's a pleasure.

1956 *Don Juan*
There's nought, no doubt, so much the spirit
calms
As rum and true religion.

1957 *Don Juan*
And thus they form a group that's quite antique,
Half naked, loving, natural, and Greek.

1958 *Don Juan*
Alas! the love of women! It is known
To be a lovely and a fearful thing!

1959 *Don Juan*
In her first passion woman loves her lover,
In all the others all she loves is love.

1960 *Don Juan*
'Tis melancholy, and a fearful sign
Of human frailty, folly, also crime,
That love and marriage rarely can combine,
Although they both are born in the same clime;
Marriage from love, like vinegar from wine -
A sad, sour, sober beverage - by time
Is sharpened from its high celestial flavour,
Down to a very homely household savour.

1961 *Don Juan*
All tragedies are finished by a death,
All comedies are ended by a marriage;
The future states of both are left to faith.

1962 *Don Juan*
Dreading that climax of all human ills,
The inflammation of his weekly bills.

The Wordsworth Dictionary of Quotations

1963 *Don Juan*
But Shakespeare also says, 'tis very silly
'To gild refinèd gold, or paint the lily.'

1964 *Don Juan*
The mountains look on Marathon -
And Marathon looks on the sea;
And musing there an hour alone,
I dreamed that Greece might still be free.

1965 *Don Juan*
... That all-softening, overpowering knell,
The tocsin of the soul - the dinner bell.

1966 *Don Juan*
There is a tide in the affairs of women,
Which, taken at the flood, leads - God knows
where.

1967 *Don Juan*
A lady of a 'certain age', which means
Certainly aged.

1968 *Don Juan*
Of all the horrid, hideous notes of woe,
Sadder than owl-songs or the midnight blast,
Is that portentous phrase, 'I told you so.'

1969 *Don Juan*
'Tis strange - but true; for truth is always
strange;
Stranger than fiction.

1970 *Don Juan*
Let us have Wine and Women, Mirth and
Laughter
Sermons and soda-water the day after.

1971 *Don Juan*
Society is now one polished horde,
Formed of two mighty tribes,
The Bores and the Bored.

1972 *Don Juan*
What men call gallantry, and gods adultery,
Is much more common where the climate's
sultry.

1973 *Don Juan*
A little still she strove, and much repented,
And whispering 'I will ne'er consent' -
consented.

1974 *Don Juan*
Man's love is of man's life a thing apart,
'Tis woman's whole existence.

1975 *Don Juan*
Merely innocent flirtation.
Not quite adultery, but adulteration.

1976 *Don Juan*
Now hatred is by far the longest pleasure;
Men love in haste, but they detest at leisure.

1977 *Don Juan*
The English winter - ending in July,
To recommence in August.

1978 *(of Keats)*
Such writing is a sort of mental masturbation -
he is always f-gg-g his imagination. I don't mean
that he is indecent but viciously soliciting his
own ideas into a state which is neither poetry
nor any thing else but a Bedlam vision
produced by raw pork and opium.

1979 *'L'Amitié est l'amour sans ailes'*
Friendship is Love without his wings!

1980 *Letter to Annabella Milbanke*
I by no means rank poetry high in the scale of
intelligence - this may look like affectation - but
it is my real opinion - it is the lava of the
imagination whose eruption prevents an
earthquake.

1981 *Letter to James Hogg*
Wordsworth - stupendous genius! damned fool!

1982 *Letter to John Murray*
Pure invention is but the talent of a liar.

1983 *Letter to Lady Melbourne*
The seal is not yet fixed though the wax is
preparing for the impression.

1984 *Letter to Richard Hoppner*
The reading or non-reading a book - will never
keep down a single petticoat.

1985 *Letter to Thomas Moore*
What is hope? nothing but the paint on the face
of Existence; the least touch of truth rubs it off,
and then we see what a hollow cheeked harlot
we have got hold of.

1986 *Letter to Thomas Moore*
Like other parties of the kind, it was first silent,
then talky, then argumentative, then
disputatious, then unintelligible, then
altogethery, then inarticulate, and then drunk.

1987
Though I love my country, I do not love my
countrymen.

1988 *Manfred*
Sorrow is knowledge: they who know the most
Must mourn the deepest o'er the fatal truth,
The Tree of Knowledge is not that of Life.

1989 *Manfred*
Old man! 'tis not so difficult to die.

1990 *Marino Faliero*
You have deeply ventured;
But all must do so who would greatly win.

1991
Roll on, thou deep and dark blue ocean - roll!
Ten thousand fleets sweep over thee in vain;

Man marks the earth with ruin - his control
Stops with the shore.

1992
If from Society we learn to live,
'Tis Solitude should teach us how to die;
It hath no flatterers.

1993 *'So, we'll go no more a-roving'*
So, we'll go no more a-roving
So late into the night,
Though the heart be still as loving,
And the moon be still as bright.

1994 *'So, we'll go no more a-roving'*
Though the night was made for loving,
And the day returns too soon,
Yet we'll go no more a-roving
By the light of the moon.

1995 *'Stanzas for Music'*
There's not a joy the world can give like that it
takes away.

1996 *The Two Foscari*
And when we think we lead, we are most led.

1997 *The Vision of Judgement*
Of course his perspiration was but ichor,
Or some such other spiritual liquor.

1998 *The Vision of Judgement*
Yet still between his Darkness and his
Brightness
There passed a mutual glance of great
politeness.

1999 *The Vision of Judgement*
And when the tumult dwindled to a calm,
I left him practising the hundredth psalm.

2000 *'She Walks in Beauty'*
She walks in beauty, like the night
Of cloudless climes and starry skies;
And all that's best of dark and bright
Meet in her aspect and her eyes:
Thus mellowed to that tender light
Which heaven to gaudy day denies.

CABELL James Branch 1879-1958
2001 *Jurgen*
A man possesses nothing certainly save a brief
loan of his own body.

2002 *The Silver Stallion*
The optimist proclaims that we live in the best
of all possible worlds; and the pessimist fears
this is true.

CAESAR Irving 1895-
2003 *'Tea for Two'*
Picture you upon my knee,
Just tea for two and two for tea.

CAESAR Julius 100-44 BC
2004 *(at the crossing of the Rubicon)*
The die is cast.

2005
Et tu, Brute?
You too, Brutus?

2006 *(inscription)*
Veni, vidi, vici
I came, I saw, I conquered.

2007 *(oral tradition)*
Caesar's wife must be above suspicion.

CAHIER Charles
2008 *(taken from a french cabaret song)*
Tout passe, tout casse, tout lasse
Everthing passes, everything perishes,
everything palls.

CAHN Peggy
2009
I believe that the sign of maturity is accepting
deferred gratification.

CAIN James M. 1892-1977
2010
The postman always rings twice.

CAINE Marti 1945-1995
2011 *(when told she had malignant limphoma)*
Does that mean I'm a lymphomaniac?

CAINE Michael 1933-
2012 *in Alfie*
"My understanding of Women goes only as far
as the pleasure."

2013
The British Film Industry is alive and well and
living in Los Angeles.

CAIRNS Sir Joseph 1920-1981
2014 *(on retiring as Lord Mayor of Belfast)*
The betrayal of Ulster, the cynical and entirely
undemocratic banishment of its properly
elected Parliament and a relegation to the
status of a fuzzy-wuzzy colony is, I hope, a last
betrayal contemplated by Downing Street
because it is the last that Ulster will
countenance.

CAJAL Santiago Ramon y
2015
That which enters the mind through reason can
be corrected. That which is admitted through
faith, hardly ever.

CALISHER Hortense 1911-
2016
First publication is a pure, carnal leap into that
dark which one dreams is life.

CALLIMACHUS c.305-c.240 BC
2017
A great book is like great evil.

2018
I loathe all things held in common.

CALLWOOD June
2019
The central fact of North American history is that there were fifteen British Colonies before 1776. Thirteen rebelled and two did not.

CALVERLEY C.S. 1831-1884
2020 *'Contentment'*
Life is with such all beer and skittles;
They are not difficult to please
About their victuals.

CAMBRONNE Pierre, Baron de 1770-1842
2021 *(attributed, when called upon to surrender)*
The Guards die but do not surrender.

CAMDEN William 1551-1623
2022 *Remains concerning Britain 'Epitaphs'*
Betwixt the stirrup and the ground
Mercy I asked, mercy I found.

CAMERON Simon
2023
An honest politician is one who when he is bought will stay bought.

CAMPBELL Bushrod H.
2024
If I've learned anything in my seventy years it's that nothing's as good or as bad as it appears.

CAMPBELL Jane Montgomery 1817-1878
2025 *'We plough the fields, and scatter'*
We plough the fields, and scatter
The good seed on the land,
But it is fed and watered
By God's almighty hand;
He sends the snow in winter,
The warmth to swell the grain,
The breezes and the sunshine,
And soft refreshing rain.

CAMPBELL Patrick
2026
It seems to me that you can go sauntering along for a certain period, telling the English some interesting things about themselves, and then all at once it feels as if you had stepped on the prongs of a rake.

CAMPBELL Mrs Patrick 1865-1940
2027
Do you know why God withheld the sense of humour from women? So that we might love men instead of laugh at them.

2028
It doesn't matter what you do in the bedroom as long as you don't do it in the street and frighten the horses.

2029 *(on her recent marriage)*
The deep, deep peace of the double-bed after the hurly-burly of the chaise-longue.

CAMPBELL Roy 1901-1957
2030
You praise the firm restraint with which they write -
I'm with you, there, of course:
They use the snaffle and the curb all right,
But where's the bloody horse?

CAMPBELL Thomas 1777-1844
2031 *(attributed)*
Now Barabbas was a publisher.

2032 *'Gertrude of Wyoming'*
Tomorrow let us do or die!

2033 *'The Jilted Nymph'*
Better be courted and jilted
Than never be courted at all.

CAMUS Albert 1913-1960
2034
Every artist preserves deep within him a single source from which, throughout his lifetime, he draws what he is and what he says and when the source dries up the work withers and crumbles.

2035
Beauty is unbearable, drives us to despair, offering us for a minute the glimpse of an eternity that we should like to stretch out over the whole of time.

2036
We call first truths those we discover after all the others.

2037
Charm is a way of getting the answer yes without having asked any clear question.

2038
Without culture, and the relative freedom it presumes, society, even when perfect, is no more than a jungle. This is why every authentic creation is a gift to the future.

2039
We always deceive ourselves twice about the people we love - first to their advantage, then to their disadvantage.

2040
There is dignity in work only when it is work freely accepted.

2041 *The Fall*
We seldom confide in those who are better than ourselves.

2042 *The Fall*
I'll tell you a great secret, my friend. Don't wait for the last judgement. It happens every day.

2043 *The Fall*
A single sentence will suffice for modern man: he fornicated and read the papers.

2044
To be happy, we must not be too concerned with others.

2045
The innocent is the person who explains nothing.

2046
An intense feeling carries with it its own universe, magnificent or wretched as the case may be.

2047
I know myself too well to believe in pure virtue.

2048 *Notebooks*
An intellectual is someone whose mind watches itself.

2049
Nothing is more despicable than respect based on fear.

2050
A novel is never anything but a philosophy put into images.

2051
To know oneself, one should assert oneself.

2052
Politics, and the fate of mankind, are shaped by men without ideals and without greatness.

2053 *The Rebel*
What is a rebel? A man who says no.

2054 *The Rebel*
All modern revolutions have ended in a reinforcement of the State.

2055
As a remedy to life in society, I would suggest the big city. Nowadays it is the only desert within our reach.

2056
If there is a sin against life, it consists perhaps not so much in despairing of life as in hoping for another, and in eluding the implacable grandeur of this life.

2057
The slave begins by demanding justice and ends by wanting to wear a crown. He must

dominate in his turn.

2058
He who despairs of the human condition is a coward, but he who has hope for it is a fool.

CANNING George 1770-1827
2059
Give me the avowed, the erect, and manly foe,
Bold I can meet, perhaps may turn the blow;
But of all plagues, good Heaven, thy wrath can send,
Save, save, oh save me from the candid friend!

2060
In matters of commerce the fault of the Dutch
Is offering too little and asking too much.
The French are with equal advantage content,
So we clap on Dutch bottoms just 20%.

2061 *'The Oracle'*
Pitt is to Addington
As London is to Paddington.

CAPOTE Truman 1924-1984
2062
In California everyone goes to a therapist, is a therapist, or is a therapist going to a therapist.

2063 *(of Jack Kerouac)*
That's not writing, that's typing.

2064
Venice is like eating an entire box of chocolate liqueurs in one go.

CAPP Al 1907-1979
2065 *(on abstract art)*
A product of the untalented, sold by the unprincipled to the utterly bewildered.

CAPRA Frank 1897-1991
2066
Automatic simply means that you can't repair it yourself.

2067
A hunch is creativity trying to tell you something.

CAPRIATI Jennifer
2068
I don't care about being No. 1, but I'm ready and willing to give battle, and that's what sport is all about.

CARDES Liane
2069
Continuous effort - not strength or intelligence - is the key to unlocking our potential.

CARDOZO Benjamin N. 1870-1938
2070
There is an accuracy that defeats itself by the overemphasis of details. I often say that one must permit oneself, and quite advisedly and

deliberately, a certain margin of misstatement.

CAREW Thomas c.1595-1640
2071 *'Inscription on Tomb of Lady Mary Wentworth'*
Good to the poor, to kindred dear,
To servants kind, to friendship clear,
To nothing but herself severe.

2072 *'Mediocrity in Love Rejected'*
Give me more love or more disdain;
The torrid or the frozen zone.
Bring equal ease unto my pain,
The temperate affords me none;
Either extreme of love or hate,
Is sweeter than a calm estate.

2073 *A Pastoral Dialogue*
Love's flames will shine in every tear.

2074 *'A Song'*
Ask me no more where Jove bestows.
When June is past, the fading rose;

CAREY George (Archbishop of Canterbury)
1935-
2075
I am not in the business of alloting sins.

CAREY Henry c.1687-1743
2076 *'Sally in our Alley'*
Of all the girls that are so smart
There's none like pretty Sally,
She is the darling of my heart,
And she lives in our alley.

CARLYLE Jane 1801-1866
2077 *Letter to Thomas Carlyle*
I am not at all the sort of person you and I took me for.

CARLYLE Thomas 1795-1881
2078
All reform except a moral one will prove unavailing.

2079
Burke said there were three Estates in Parliament; but in the reporters' gallery yonder, there sat a fourth Estate more important than them all.

2080
The courage we desire and prize is not the courage to die decently, but to live manfully.

2081
The crash of the whole solar and stellar systems could only kill you once.

2082 *Critical and Miscellaneous Essays*
History is the essence of innumerable biographies.

2083 *Critical and Miscellaneous Essays*
A well-written Life is almost as rare as a well-spent one.

2084 *Critical and Miscellaneous Essays*
Under all speech that is good for anything there lies a silence that is better. Silence is deep as Eternity; speech is shallow as Time.

2085 *Critical and Miscellaneous Essays*
The three great elements of modern civilization, Gunpowder, Printing, and the Protestant Religion.

2086 *Critical and Miscellaneous Essays*
A poet without love were a physical and metaphysical impossibility.

2087
There is endless merit in a man's knowing when to have done.

2088
God Almighty never created a man half as wise as he looks.

2089
A good book is the purest essence of a human soul.

2090 *History of the French Revolution*
A whiff of grapeshot.

2091 *History of French Revolution (of Robespierre)*
The seagreen Incorruptible.

2092 *History of the French Revolution*
France was long a despotism tempered by epigrams.

2093
If Jesus Christ were to come to-day, people would not even crucify him. They would ask him to dinner, and hear what he had to say, and make fun of it.

2094
In the long run every government is the exact symbol of its people, with their wisdom and unwisdom.

2095
Nine-tenths of the miseries and vices of mankind proceed from idleness.

2096 *Past and Present*
Captains of industry.

2097 *On political economy, Latter-Day Pamphlets*
The Dismal Science.

2098
No sadder proof can be given by a man of his own littleness, than disbelief in great men.

2099
The tragedy of life is not so much what men suffer, but rather what they miss.

2100
The true university of these days is a collection of books.

2101
What an enormous magnifier is tradition! How a thing grows in the human memory and in the human imagination, when love, worship, and all that lies in the human heart, is there to encourage it.

2102
When the oak is felled the whole forest echoes with its fall, but a hundred acorns are sown in silence by an unnoticed breeze.

2103
He that can work is a born king of something.

CARMAN Bliss 1861-1929
2104
Whether it be to failure or success, the first need of being is endurance - to endure with gladness if we can, with fortitude in any event.

2105
The greatest joy in nature is the absence of man.

2106
Indifference may not wreck a man's life at any one turn, but it will destroy him with a kind of dryrot in the long run.

2107
There is a passion for perfection which you will rarely see fully developed; but you may note this fact, that in successful lives it is never wholly lacking.

CARNEGIE Dale 1888-1955
2108
How to win friends and influence people.

CARR E.H. 1892-1982
2109
Change is certain, progress is not.

CARREL Alexis 1873-1944
2110
A few observations and much reasoning lead to error; many observations and a little reasoning to truth.

CARROLL Lewis (Charles L. Dodgson) 1832-1898
2111 *Alice's Adventures in Wonderland*
'What is the use of a book' thought Alice, 'without pictures or conversations?'

2112 *Alice's Adventures in Wonderland*
'Curiouser and curiouser!' cried Alice.

2113 *Alice's Adventures in Wonderland*
How cheerfully he seems to grin,
How neatly spreads his claws,
And welcomes little fishes in
With gently smiling jaws!

2114 *Alice's Adventures in Wonderland*
'You are old, Father William,' the young man said,
'And your hair has become very white;
And yet you incessantly stand on your head-
Do you think, at your age, it is right?'

2115 *Alice's Adventures in Wonderland*
Speak roughly to your little boy,
And beat him when he sneezes;
He only does it to annoy,
Because he knows it teases.

2116 *Alice's Adventures in Wonderland*
Everything's got a moral, if you can only find it.

2117 *Alice's Adventures in Wonderland*
'Will you walk a little faster?' said a whiting to a snail,
'There's a porpoise close behind us, and he's treading on my tail.'

2118 *Alice's Adventures in Wonderland*
Will you, won't you, will you, won't you, will you join the dance?

2119 *Alice's Adventures in Wonderland*
'Where shall I begin, please your Majesty?' he asked.
'Begin at the beginning,' the King said, gravely, 'and go on till you come to the end: then stop.'

2120 *Through the Looking-Glass*
'Twas brillig, and the slithy toves
Did gyre and gimble in the wabe;
All mimsy were the borogoves,
And the mome raths outgrabe.'

'Beware the Jabberwock, my son!
The jaws that bite, the claws that catch!'

2121 *Through the Looking-Glass*
'The time has come,' the Walrus said,
'To talk of many things:
Of shoes - and ships - and sealing wax -
Of cabbages - and kings -
And why the sea is boiling hot -
And whether pigs have wings.'

2122 *Through the Looking-Glass*
But answer came there none -

2123 *Through the Looking-Glass*
The rule is, jam tomorrow and jam yesterday - but never jam today.

2124 *Through the Looking-Glass*
It's as large as life and twice as natural!

2125 *Through the Looking-Glass*
'The horror of that moment,' the King went on,
'I shall never, never forget!' 'You will, though,'
the Queen said, 'if you don't make a
memorandum of it.'

2126 *Through the Looking-Glass*
Now here, you see, it takes all the running you
can do to keep in the same place. If you want to
get somewhere else, you must run at least twice
as fast as that!

2127 *Through the Looking-Glass*
What I tell you three times is true.

2128 *Through the Looking-Glass*
It's one of the most serious things that can
possibly happen to one in a battle - to get one's
head cut off.

2129 *Through the Looking-Glass*
Take care of the sense and the sounds will take
of themselves.

CARRUTH William Herbert 1859-1924
2130 *'Each In His Own Tongue'*
Some call it evolution,
And others call it God.

CARRUTHERS Charles Edwin
2131
In judging others, folks will work overtime for
no pay.

CARSON Jack
2132
A fan club is a group of people who tell an actor
he is not alone in the way he feels about
himself.

CARSON Lord 1854-1935
2133
My only great qualification for being put at the
head of the Navy is that I am very much at sea.

CARSON Marco
2134
And by my grave you'd pray to have me back
So I could see how well you look in black.

CARSON Rachael 1907-1964
2135
If a child is to keep alive his inborn sense of
wonder without any such gift from the fairies,
he needs the companionship of at least one
adult who can share it, rediscovering with him
the joy, excitement and mystery of the world we
live in.

2136
For the first time in the history of the world,
every human being is now subjected to contact
with dangerous chemicals, from the moment of
conception until death.

2137
For the sense of smell, almost more than any
other, has the power to recall memories and it is
a pity that we use it so little.

CARTER Boake
2138
In time of war the first casualty is truth.

CARTER Dyson
2139
I feel age like an icicle down my back.

CARTER Hodding
2140
There are only two lasting bequests we can
hope to give our children. One of these is roots,
the other, wings.

CARTER Jimmy 1924-
2141
I've looked on a lot of women with lust. I've
committed adultery in my heart many times.
This is something God recognizes I will do - and
I have done it - and God forgives me for it.

CARTLAND Barbara 1901-
2142
A historical romance is the only kind of book
where chastity really counts.

CARY Joyce 1888-1957
2143 *The Horse's Mouth*
Sara could commit adultery at one end and
weep for her sins at the other, and enjoy both
operations at once.

2144
A man of eighty has outlived probably three
new schools of painting, two of architecture and
poetry, and a hundred in dress.

2145
My novels point out that the world consists
entirely of exceptions.

CASSAVETES John
2146
No matter how old you get, if you can keep the
desire to be creative, you're keeping the man-
child alive.

CASSON Herbert
2147
Net - the biggest word in the language of
business.

CASSON Hugh 1910-
2148
The British love permanence more than they
love beauty.

CASTRO Fidel 1926-
2149 *(on battledress)*
Practical, simple, cheap and does not go out of
fashion.

2150
I am not a great fan of capitalism. But I am a realist.

2151 *(title of pamphlet)*
History will absolve me.

CATLIN Wynn
2152
Diplomacy; the art of saying 'nice doggie' till you can find a rock.

CATO The Elder 234-149 BC
2153
After I am dead, I would rather have men ask why Cato has no monument than why he had one.

CATULLUS c.84-c.54 BC
2154 *Carmina*
For there is nothing sillier than a silly laugh.

2155 *Carmina*
But what a woman says to her lusting lover it is best to write in wind and swift-flowing water.

2156 *Carmina*
Give up wanting to deserve any thanks from anyone, or thinking that anybody can be grateful.

CÉLINE Louis-Ferdinand 1894-1961
2157
If you aren't rich, you should always look useful.

2158
History doesn't pass the dishes again.

CENTLIVRE Susannah c.1667-1723
2159
'Tis my opinion every man cheats in his way, and he is only honest who is not discovered.

CERVANTES Miguel de 1547-1616
2160
God bears with the wicked, but not forever.

2161
Every one is as God made him and oftentimes a good deal worse.

2162
The guts carry the feet, not the feet the guts.

2163
Man appoints, and God disappoints.

2164 *Don Quixote*
Let them eat the lie and swallow it with their bread. Whether the two were lovers or no, they'll have accounted to God for it by now. I have my own fish to fry.

2165
You must not think, sir, to catch old birds with chaff.

2166
Valour lies just halfway between rashness and cowardice.

CHAGALL Marc 1889-1985
2167
All colours are the friends of their neighbours and the lovers of their opposites.

2168
All our interior world is reality - and that perhaps more so than our apparent world.

2169
The fingers must be educated, the thumb is born knowing.

2170
In our lives there is a simple colour, as on an artist's palette, which provides the meaning of life and art. It is the colour of love.

CHAMFORT Sebastien c.1741-1794
2171
Society is composed of two great classes: those who have more dinners than appetite, and those who have more appetite than dinners.

CHANDLER Raymond 1888-1959
2172 *Farewell My Lovely*
She gave me a smile I could feel in my hip pocket.

2173
A good title is the title of a successful book.

2174
At least half the mystery novels published violate the law that the solution, once revealed, must seem to be inevitable.

2175 *The Long Good-Bye*
Alcohol is like love: the first kiss is magic, the second is intimate, the third is routine. After that you just take the girl's clothes off.

CHANEL Coco 1883-1971
2176
Jump out the window if you are the object of passion. Flee it if you feel it. Passion goes, boredom remains.

2177
There is time for work. And time for love. That leaves no other time.

2178 *(on being asked where one should wear perfume)*
Wherever one wants to be kissed.

CHANNING William Ellery 1780-1842
2179
It is a greater work to educate a child, in the true and larger sense of the word, than to rule a state.

2180
Most joyful let the Poet be,
It is through him that all men see.

CHAPIN E.H.
2181
At the bottom of a good deal of the bravery that
appears in the world there lurks a miserable
cowardice. Men will face powder and steel
because they cannot face public opinion.

CHAPMAN John Jay 1774-1845
2182
Every generation is a secret society and has
incommunicable enthusiasms, tastes, and
interests which are a mystery both to its
predecessors and to posterity.

CHAR René 1907-
2183
In action, be primitive; in foresight, a strategist.

2184
That which comes into the world to disturb
nothing deserves neither respect nor patience.

2185
For an inheritance to be really great, the hand of
the defunct must not be seen.

CHARCOT Jean-Martin
2186
Symptoms, then, are in reality nothing but the
cry from suffering organs.

CHARLEMAGNE 742-814
2187
To have another language is to possess a second
soul.

CHARLES, Prince of Wales 1948-
2188
Do you seriously expect me to be the first
Prince of Wales in history not to have a
mistress?

2189 *Letter to a friend*
We've had such a lovely Christmas, the two of
us. It has been extraordinarily happy and cosy
being able to share it together. Next year will be
even nicer with a small one to join us as well.

2190
How awful incompatibility is, and how
dreadfully destructive it can be for the players
in this extraordinary drama. It has all the
ingredients of a Greek tragedy. I never thought
it would end up like this. How could I have got
it all so wrong?

2191 *(of the proposed extension to National
Gallery)*
A monstrous carbuncle on the face of a much-
loved and elegant friend.

CHASE Alexander
2192
The banalities of a great man pass for wit.

2193
Memory is the thing you forget with.

2194
The peak of tolerance is most readily achieved
by those who are not burdened with
convictions.

CHASE Edna Woolman
2195
Fashion can be bought. Style one must possess.

CHAUCER Geoffrey c.1343-1400
2196 *The Canterbury Tales*
He was a verray, parfit gentil knyght.

2197 *The Canterbury Tales*
And gladly wolde he lerne and gladly teche.

2198 *The Canterbury Tales*
Wel loved he garleek, oynons, and eek lekes,
And for to drynken strong wyn, reed as blood.

2199 *The Canterbury Tales*
Trouthe is the hyeste thyng that man may kepe.

2200 *The Canterbury Tales*
And therefore, at the kynges court, my brother,
Ech man for hymself, ther is noon oother.

2201 *The Canterbury Tales*
Kepe wel thy tonge, and thenk upon the crowe.

2202 *The Canterbury Tales*
Derk was the nyght as pich, or as the cole,
And at the wyndow out she putte hir hole,
And Absolon, hym fil no bet ne wers,
But with his mouth he kiste hir naked ers.

2203 *The Canterbury Tales*
'By God,' quod he, 'for pleynly, at a word,
Thy drasty rymyng is nat worth a toord!'

2204 *The Canterbury Tales*
'My lige lady, generally,' quod he,
'Wommen desiren to have sovereynetee
As wel over hir housbond as hir love.'

2205 *The Canterbury Tales*
That he is gentil that dooth gentil dedis.

2206 *The Romaunt of the Rose*
Thou shalt make castels thanne in Spayne
And dreme of joye, all but in vayne.

2207 *Tale of Melibee*
What is bettre than wisedoom? Womman. And
what is bettre than a good womman? Nothyng.

2208 *Troilus and Criseyde*
It is nought good a slepyng hound to wake.

CHAUSSÉE Nivelle de la 1692-1754
2209 *La Gouvernante*
When everyone is wrong, everyone is right.

CHAVEZ Cesar 1927-1993
2210
Is some cases non-violence requires more militancy than violence.

CHAYEFSKY Paddy 1923-1981
2211
Television is not the truth. Television is a god-damned amusement park. Television is a circus, a carnival, a travelling troupe of acrobats, storytellers, dancers, singers, jugglers, sideshow freaks, lion tamers and football players. We're in the boredom-killing business.

CHAZAI
2212
A woman knows how to keep quiet when she is in the right, whereas a man, when he is in the right, will keep on talking.

CHEKHOV Anton 1860-1904
2213
If you are afraid of loneliness, don't marry.

2214
Any idiot can face a crisis - it's this day-to-day living that wears you out.

2215 *Letter to Alexander Chekhov*
Brevity is the sister of talent.

2216
A man and a woman marry because both of them don't know what to do with themselves.

2217
Medicine is my lawful wife. Literature is my mistress.

2218 *The Seagull*
Women can't forgive failure.

2219 *Uncle Vanya*
Man has been endowed with reason, with the power to create, so that he can add to what he's been given. But up to now he hasn't been a creator, only a destroyer. Forests keep disappearing, rivers dry up, wild life's become extinct, the climate's ruined and the land grows poorer and uglier every day.

2220 *Uncle Vanya*
A woman can become a man's friend only in the following stages - first an acquaintance, next a mistress, and only then a friend.

2221 *Uncle Vanya*
When a woman isn't beautiful, people always say, 'You have lovely eyes, you have lovely hair.'

CHENEY Dick 1941-
2222
It is easy to take liberty for granted, when you have never had it taken from you.

CHENNAULT Anna
2223
Equal opportunity is good, but special privilege even better.

CHEPIK Nikolai 1966-1985
2224 *(from his diary)*
Believing that a girl will wait is just like jumping with a parachute packed by someone else.

CHER 1946-
2225
The trouble with some women is they get all excited about nothing - and then they marry him!

CHESTERFIELD Lord 1694-1773
2226
If you would convince others, seem open to conviction yourself.

2227
Without some dissimulation no business can be carried on at all.

2228 *Letters to his Son*
An injury is much sooner forgotten than an insult.

2229 *Letters to his son*
Women are much more like each other than men: they have, in truth, but two passions - var ity and love; these are their universal characteristics.

2230
Patience is a most necessary quality for business; many a man would rather you heard his story than grant his request.

2231
Many people enjoy the inferiority of their best friends.

2232
When a man is once in fashion, all he does is right.

CHESTER Henry
2233
Enthusiasm is the greatest asset in the world. It beats money and power and influence.

CHESTERTON G.K. 1874-1936
2234
I am not absent-minded. It is the presence of mind that makes me unaware of everything else.

2235
Angels fly because they take themselves lightly.

2236 *The Ballad of the White Horse*
I tell you naught for your comfort,
Yea, naught for your desire,
Save that the sky grows darker yet
And the sea rises higher.

2237
The classes that wash most are those that work least.

2238 *The Defendant*
There is a road from the eye to the heart that does not go through the intellect.

2239 *The Defendant 'A Defence of Penny Dreadfuls'*
Literature is a luxury; fiction is a necessity.

2240
Democracy means government by the uneducated, while aristocracy means government by the badly educated.

2241 *'English Graves'*
They died to save their country and they only saved the world.

2242
Facts as facts do not always create a spirit of reality, because reality is a spirit.

2243 *The Flying Inn*
The rich are the scum of the earth in every country.

2244
We make our friends; we make our enemies; but God makes our next-door neighbour.

2245 *Heretics*
Bigotry may be roughly defined as the anger of men who have no opinions.

2246 *'A Hymn'*
From all that terror teaches,
From lies of tongue and pen,
From all the easy speeches
That comfort cruel men,
From sale and profanation
Of honour and the sword,
From sleep and from damnation,
Deliver us, good Lord!

2247
Large organization is loose organization. Nay, it would be almost as true to say that organization is always disorganization.

2248 *'Lepanto'*
Strong gongs groaning as the guns boom far,
Don John of Austria is going to the war.

2249
A man must love a thing very much if he not only practises it without any hope of fame and money, but even practises it without any hope

of doing it well.

2250 *The Man who was Thursday*
Thieves respect property. They merely wish the property to become their property that they may more perfectly respect it.

2251
One may understand the cosmos, but never the ego; the self is more distant than any star.

2252
Men always talk about the most important things to perfect strangers.

2253
Merely having an open mind is nothing. The object of opening the mind, as of opening the mouth, is to shut it again on something solid.

2254
There is nothing the matter with Americans except their ideals. The real American is all right; it is the ideal American who is all wrong.

2255 *Orthodoxy*
All conservatism is based upon the idea that if you leave things alone you leave them as they are. But you do not. If you leave a thing alone you leave it to a torrent of change.

2256
The paradox of courage is that a man must be a little careless of his life even in order to keep it.

2257
Psychoanalysis is confession without absolution.

2258 *'The Rolling English Road'*
Before the Roman came to Rye or out to Severn strode,
The rolling English drunkard made the rolling English road.
A reeling road, a rolling road, that rambles round the shire,
And after him the parson ran, the sexton and the squire;
A merry road, a mazy road, and such as we did tread
The night we went to Birmingham by way of Beachy Head.

2259 *'The Secret People'*
Smile at us, pay us, pass us; but do not quite forget.
For we are the people of England, that never have spoken yet.

2260
Silence is the unbearable repartee.

2261
Tradition means giving votes to the most obscure of all classes - our ancestors. It is the democracy of the dead. Tradition refuses to

submit to the small and arrogant oligarchy of those who merely happen to be walking around.

2262
The way to love anything is to realize that it might be lost.

2263 *What's Wrong with the World*
The Christian ideal has not been tried and found wanting. It has been found difficult; and left untried.

2264 *What's Wrong with the World*
The prime truth of woman, the universal mother ... that if a thing is worth doing, it is worth doing badly.

2265
The word 'good' has many meanings. For example, if a man were to shoot his grandmother at a range of five hundred yards, I should call him a good shot, but not *necessarily* a good man.

CHEVALIER Maurice 1888-1972
2266 *(attributed)*
Many a man has fallen in love with a girl in a light so dim he would not have chosen a suit by it.

2267
The crime of loving is forgetting.

2268
Old age is not so bad when you consider the alternatives.

CHIAROMENTE Nicola
2269
It is only through fiction and the dimension of the imaginary that we can learn something real about individual experience. Any other approach is bound to be general and abstract.

CHILDERS Erskine 1870-1922
2270
Come closer, boys. It will be easier for you.

2271
The riddle of the sands.

CHILDS Richard S.
2272
A reformer is one who sets forth cheerfully towards sure defeat.

CHING Cyrus
2273
I learned long ago never to wrestle with a pig. You get dirty, and besides, the pig likes it.

CHISHOLM Shirley
2274
Of my two 'handicaps', being female put many more obstacles in my path than being black.

CHOPIN Frédéric 1810-1849
2275
Every difficulty slurred over will be a ghost to disturb your repose later on.

CHRISTIE Dame Agatha 1890-1976
2276 *An Autobiography*
War settles nothing ... to win a war is as disastrous as to lose one!

2277 *At Bertram's Hotel*
I learned ... that one can never go back, that one should not ever try to go back - that the essence of life is going forward. Life is really a One Way Street.

2278 *(of her own marriage)*
An archaeologist is the best husband any woman can have. The older she gets, the more interested he is in her.

2279 *The Mysterious Affair at Styles*
He [Hercule Poirot] tapped his forehead. 'These little grey cells. It is "up to them".'

CHRISTINA Queen of Sweden
2280
I love men, not because they are men, but because they are not women.

CHURCH Richard Thomas 1893-1972
2281 *Be Frugal*
Be frugal in the gift of love,
Lest you should kindle in return
Love like your own, that may survive
Long after yours has ceased to burn.

CHURCHILL Charles 1731-1764
2282 *The Conference*
The only difference, after all their rout,
Is, that the one is in, the other out.

2283 *An Epistle to William Hogarth*
The danger chiefly lies in acting well;
No crime's so great as daring to excel.

2284 *The Ghost*
Just to the windward of the law.

2285 *The Ghost*
A joke's a very serious thing.

2286 *Night*
Keep up appearances; there lies the test;
The world wil give thee credit for the rest.

2287 *The Rosciad*
So much they talked, so very little said.

2288 *The Rosciad*
The two extremes appear like man and wife,
Coupled together for the sake of strife.

CHURCHILL Lord Randolph 1849-1894
2289 *(of Gladstone)*
An old man in a hurry.

2290
Ulster will fight; Ulster will be right.

2291
Whenever by an unfortunate occurrence of circumstances an opposition is compelled to support the government, the support should be given with a kick and not a caress and should be withdrawn at the first available moment.

CHURCHILL Sir Winston 1874-1965
2292
He has all of the virtues I dislike and none of the vices I admire.

2293
We are all worms, but I do believe that I am a glow-worm.

2294 *(attributed)*
An appeaser is one who feeds a crocodile - hoping it will eat him last.

2295 *(of the Battle of Britain pilots)*
Never in the field of human conflict was so much owed by so many to so few.

2296 *(of the Battle of Egypt)*
Now this is not the end. It is not even the beginning of the end. But it is, perhaps, the end of the beginning.

2297 *(on becoming Prime Minister)*
I have nothing to offer but blood, toil, tears and sweat.

2298 *(of Clement Attlee)*
A sheep in sheep's clothing.

2299
Courage is rightly esteemed the first of human qualities because it is the quality which guarantees all others.

2300 *My Darling Clementine*
My most brilliant achievement was my ability to be able to persuade my wife to marry me.

2301
It has been said that Democracy is the worst form of government except all those other forms that have been tried from time to time.

2302 *(of the Dunkirk evacuation)*
Let us therefore brace ourselves to our duty, and so bear ourselves that, if the British Commonwealth and its Empire lasts for a thousand years, men will still say, 'This was their finest hour.'

2303 *My Early Life*
Headmasters have powers at their disposal with which Prime Ministers have never yet been invested.

2304 *My Early Life*
It is a good thing for an uneducated man to read books of quotations.

2305
I am easily satisfied with the very best.

2306
The empires of the future are the empires of the mind.

2307 *While England Slept*
Dictators ride to and fro on tigers from which they dare not dismount. And the tigers are getting hungry.

2308
The English never draw a line without blurring it.

2309
A fanatic is one who can't change his mind and won't change the subject.

2310 *Their Finest Hour*
No one can guarantee success in war, but only deserve it.

2311
We shall not flag or fail. We shall go on to the end. We shall fight in France, we shall fight on the seas and oceans, we shall fight with growing confidence and growing strength in the air, we shall defend our island, whatever the cost may be. We shall fight on the beaches, we shall fight on the landing grounds, we shall fight in the fields and in the streets, we shall fight in the hills; we shall never surrender.

2312
I cannot forecast to you the action of Russia. It is a riddle wrapped in a mystery inside an enigma.

2313 *The Gathering Storm*
When you have to kill a man it costs nothing to be polite.

2314
Give us the tools and we will finish the job.

2315
So they [the Government] go on in strange paradox, decided only to be undecided, resolved to be irresolute, adamant for drift, solid for fluidity, all-powerful to be impotent.

2316
If you have an important point to make, don't try to be subtle or clever. Use a pile-driver. Hit the point once. Then come back and hit it again. Then hit it a third time - a tremendous whack!

2317
India is a geographical term. It is no more a united nation than the Equator.

2318
Out of intense complexities intense simplicities emerge.

2319
To jaw-jaw is always better than to war-war.

2320
Labour is not fit to govern.

2321
Without a measureless and perpetual uncertainty, the drama of human life would be destroyed.

2322
It is a mistake to look too far ahead. Only one link in the chain of destiny can be handled at a time.

2323
National compulsory insurance for all classes for all purposes from the cradle to the grave.

2324
I have never accepted what many people have kindly said, namely that I have inspired the nation. It was the nation and the race dwelling all around the globe that had the lion heart. I had the luck to be called upon to give the roar.

2325
Never give in, never give in, never, never, never, never - in nothing great or small, large or petty - never give in except to convictions of honour and good sense.

2326
Politics is more dangerous than war, for in war you are only killed once.

2327
I cannot pretend to feel impartial about colours. I rejoice with the brilliant ones and am genuinely sorry for the poor browns.

2328
Say what you have to say and the first time you come to a sentence with a grammatical ending - sit down.

2329 *The Second World War*
All I wanted was compliance with my wishes after reasonable discussion.

2330
We shape our buildings; thereafter they shape us.

2331
This is the sort of English up with which I will not put.

2332
From Stettin in the Baltic to Trieste in the Adriatic an iron curtain has descended across the Continent.

2333
It is no use saying 'we are doing our best'. You have got to succeed in doing what is necessary.

2334
Victory, victory at all costs, victory in spite of all terror; victory, however long and hard the road may be; for without victory, there is no survival.

2335
In war, as in life, it is often necessary, when some cherished scheme has failed, to take up the best alternative open, and if so, it is folly not to work for it with all your might.

2336
War is mainly a catalogue of blunders.

2337
When I am abroad, I always make it a rule never to criticize or attack the government of my own country. I make up for lost time when I come home.

2338
When I warned them [the French Government] that Britain would fight on alone whatever they did, their generals told their Prime Minister and his divided Cabinet, 'In three weeks England will have her neck wrung like a chicken.' Some chicken! Some neck!

2339
Where does the family start? It starts with a young man falling in love with a girl - no superior alternative has yet been found.

2340
The whole history of the world is summed up in the fact that, when nations are strong, they are not always just, and when they wish to be just, they are no longer strong.

CIANO Count Galeazzo 1903-1944
2341 *Diary*
Victory has a hundred fathers, but defeat is an orphan.

CIARDI John 1916-
2342
Boys are the cash of war. Whoever said: we're not free spenders - doesn't know our like.

2343
Gentility is what is left over from rich ancestors after the money is gone.

2344
Modern art is what happens when painters stop looking at girls and persuade themselves they have a better idea.

2345
Every parent is at some time the father of the unreturned prodigal, with nothing to do but keep his house open to hope.

2346
A savage is simply a human organism that has not received enough news from the human race.

2347
A university is what a college becomes when the faculty loses interest in students.

CIBBER Colley 1671-1757
2348 *The Double Gallant*
Oh! how many torments lie in the small circle of a wedding-ring!

2349 *Richard III*
Perish the thought!

CICERO Marcus Tullius 106-43 BC
2350
I am not ashamed to confess that I am ignorant of what I do not know.

2351
We are in bondage to the law in order that we may be free.

2352 *In Catilinam Speech*
Oh, the times! Oh, the manners!

2353
Certain signs precede certain events.

2354
For it is commonly said: accomplished labours are pleasant.

2355 *De Divinatione*
There is nothing so absurd but some philosopher has said it.

2356
Hatred is settled anger.

2357
I never admired another's fortune so much that I became dissatisfied with my own.

2358
Old age, especially an honoured old age, has so great authority, that this is of more value than all the pleasures of youth.

2359
Old age is by nature rather talkative.

2360
It has seemed to be more necessary to have regard to the weight of words rather than to their number.

2361
There is something pleasurable in calm remembrance of a past sorrow.

2362 *In Verrem Speech 5*
I am a Roman citizen.

2363
When you have no basis for an argument, abuse the plaintiff.

2364
The authority of those who profess to teach is often a positive hindrance to those who desire to learn.

CIORAN E.M.
2365
Democracy is a festival of mediocrity.

2366
No one can keep his griefs in their prime; they use themselves up.

CLAPHAM Lady Elisabeth 1911-1994
2367
I never drink gin. It makes me, by turns, bellicose, lachrymose and comatose.

CLARE John 1793-1864
2368 *(attributed)*
Language has not the power to speak what love indites:
The soul lies buried in the ink that writes.

2369 *'Child Harold'*
My life hath been one chain of contradictions,
Madhouses, prisons, whore-shops.

2370 *'Child Harold'*
They took me from my wife, and to save trouble
I wed again, and made the error double.

2371 *'Child Harold'*
Pale death, the grand physician, cures all pain;
The dead rest well who lived for joys in vain.

2372 *'Child Harold'*
Hopeless hope hopes on and meets no end,
Wastes without springs and homes without a friend.

2373 *'First Love'*
I never saw so sweet a face
As that I stood before.
My heart has left its dwelling place
And can return no more.

2374 *'To Mary'*
I sleep with thee, and wake with thee,
And yet thou are not there.

2375 *'The present is the funeral of the past'*
The present is the funeral of the past,
And man the living sepulchre of life.

CLARENDON Edward, Earl of 1609-1674
2376 *The History of the Rebellion (of Hampden)*
Without question, when he first drew the sword, he threw away the scabbard.

2377 *The History of the Rebellion (of Falkland)*
So enamoured on peace that he would have
been glad the King should have bought it at any
price.

2378 *The History of the Rebellion (of Cromwell)*
He will be looked upon by posterity as a brave
bad man.

CLARK Alan 1928-
2379
The only solution for dealing with the IRA is to
kill 600 people in one night, let the UN and
everyone else make a great scene, and it's over
for 20 years.

CLARK Jane
2380
All girlfriends are like bluebottles. Some are just
a bit harder to swat.

CLARK Kenneth 1903-1983
2381 *Civilisation*
Medieval marriages were entirely a matter of
property, and, as everyone knows, marriage
without love means love without marriage.

2382
We can destroy ourselves by cynicism and
disillusion just as effectively as by bombs.

2383
True perfection is achieved only by those who
are prepared to destroy it. It is a by-product of
greatness.

CLARK Ramsay 1927-
2384
Turbulence is life force. It is opportunity. Let's
love turbulence and use it for change.

CLARKE Arthur C. 1917-
2385
Any sufficiently advanced technology is
indistinguishable from magic.

CLARKE John d. 1658
2386 *Paraemiologia Anglo-Latina 'Diligentia'*
He that would thrive
Must rise at five;
He that hath thriven
May lie till seven.

CLARK Joe 1939-
2387
One of the luxuries of a politician's life is that
you see yourself as others see you.

CLAUDIAN 4th Century AD
2388
The vices of monarchs can never remain
hidden.

CLAUSEWITZ Karl von 1780-1831
2389 *Vom Kriege*
War is nothing but a continuation of politics

with the admixture of other means.

CLAY Henry 1777-1852
2390 *(to Senator Preston of South Carolina)*
I had rather be right than be President.

2391
Statistics are no substitute for judgement.

CLEAVER Eldridge 1935-
2392
Too much agreement kills a chat.

CLEMENCEAU Georges 1841-1929
2393 *(attributed)*
War is too serious a matter to entrust to military
men.

2394
All the great pleasures in life are silent.

2395
All that I know I learned after I was thirty.

2396
It is easier to make war than to make peace.

2397
There is no passion like that of a functionary for
his function.

2398
War is a series of catastrophes which result in
victory.

CLEVELAND John 1613-1658
2399 *'Epitaph on the Earl of Strafford'*
Here lies wise and valiant dust,
Huddled up, 'twixt fit and just:
Strafford, who was hurried hence
'Twixt treason and convenience.
He spent his time here in a mist,
A Papist, yet a Calvinist ...
Riddles lie here, or in a word,
Here lies blood; and let it lie
Speechless still, and never cry.

CLIFT Montgomery 1920-1966
2400
I have enough money to get by. I'm not
independently wealthy, just independently lazy,
I suppose.

CLINTON Bill (William Jefferson) 1946-
2401
I experimented with Marijuana a time or two.
And I didn't like it, and I didn't inhale.

2402
There is nothing wrong with America that
cannot be cured by what is right in America.

2403 *(to Tony Blair, in 1998)*
Ours is a twenty-first century partnership.

2404
The urgent question of our time is whether we can make change our friend and not our enemy.

CLINTON Hillary
2405
We've been accused of everything, including murder. The best thing to do is to be patient and the truth will come out.

CLIVE Lord 1725-1774
2406 *(when his pistol twice failed to fire)*
I feel that I am reserved for some end or other.

CLOUGH Arthur Hugh 1819-1861
2407 *The Bothie of Tober-na-Vuolich*
Grace is given of God, but knowledge is bought in the market.

2408 *Dipsychus*
And almost everyone when age,
Disease, or sorrows strike him,
Inclines to think there is a God,
Or something very like Him.

2409 *'The Latest Decalogue'*
Thou shalt not kill; but need'st not strive
Officiously to keep alive.

2410 *'The Latest Decalogue'*
Do not adultery commit;
Advantage rarely comes of it.

2411 *'The Latest Decalogue'*
Thou shalt not steal; an empty feat,
When it's so lucrative to cheat.

2412 *'The Latest Decalogue'*
Thou shalt not covet; but tradition
Approves all forms of competition.

2413 *'Say not the struggle naught availeth'*
In front the sun climbs slow, how slowly,
But westward, look, the land is bright.

COBAIN Curt 1967-1994
2414 *(suicide note)*
The worst crime is faking it.

COBB Irvin S.
2415
If a woman likes another woman, she's cordial. If she doesn't like her, she's very cordial.

COBBETT William 1762-1835
2416
From a very early age, I had imbibed the opinion, that it was every man's duty to do all that lay in his power to leave his country as good as he had found it.

COCKER Joe
2417
England to me was always the 3 o'clock break - that endless gap between lunch and the pub opening again.

COCTEAU Jean 1889-1963
2418
Art produces ugly things which frequently become beautiful with time. Fashion, on the other hand, produces beautiful things which always become ugly with time.

2419
The greatest masterpiece in literature is only a dictionary out of order.

2420 *Journal d'un inconnu*
Poetry is a religion with no hope.

2421
The joy of the young is to disobey - but the trouble is that there are no longer any orders.

2422 *Le Coq et l'Arlequin*
The essential in daring is to know how far one can go too far.

2423 *Opium*
Life is a horizontal fall.

2424 *Opium*
Victor Hugo was a madman who thought he was Victor Hugo.

2425
Style is a simple way of saying complicated things.

COFFIN Harold
2426
A consumer is a shopper who is sore about something.

COFFIN Rev. William Sloane 1924-
2427
I'm not ok - you're not ok, and that's ok.

2428
The world is too dangerous for anything but truth, and too small for anything but love.

COKE Sir Edward 1552-1634
2429
Corporations cannot commit treason, nor be outlawed, nor excommunicated, for they have no souls.

2430 *Institutes of Laws of England*
How long soever it hath continued, if it be against reason, it is of no force in law.

2431 *Institutes of Laws of England*
For a man's house is his castle.

COLBERT Jean Baptiste 1619-1683
2432
The art of taxation consists in so plucking the goose as to get the most feathers with the least hissing.

COLBY Frank Moore

2433
Many people lose their tempers merely from seeing you keep yours.

COLEMAN John S.

2434
The point to remember is that what the government gives, it must first take away.

COLERIDGE Samuel Taylor 1772-1834

2435
Advice is like snow; the softer it falls, the longer it dwells upon, and the deeper it sinks into, the mind.

2436 *'Epitaph on an Infant'*
Ere sin could blight or sorrow fade,
Death came with friendly care:
The opening bud to Heaven conveyed
And bade it blossom there.

2437
The most happy marriage I can imagine to myself would be the union of a deaf man to a blind woman.

2438 *'Kubla Khan'*
In Xanadu did Kubla Khan
A stately pleasure-dome decree:
Where Alph, the sacred river, ran
Through caverns measureless to man
Down to a sunless sea.
So twice five miles of fertile ground
With walls and towers were girdled round.

2439 *'Kubla Khan'*
It was a miracle of rare device,
A sunny pleasure-dome with caves of ice.

2440 *'Kubla Khan'*
And 'mid this tumult Kubla heard from far
Ancestral voices prophesying war!

2441
So lonely 'twas that God himself
Scarce seemed there to be.

2442
As long as there are readers to be delighted with calumny, there will be found reviewers to calumniate.

2443
To most men, experience is like the stern lights of a ship, which illumine only the track it has passed.

2444
Only the wise possess ideas; the greater part of mankind are possessed by them.

2445 *'The Rime of the Ancient Mariner'*
'God save thee, ancient Mariner!
From the fiends that plague thee thus! -
Why look'st thou so?' - With my cross-bow
I shot the Albatross.

2446 *'The Rime of the Ancient Mariner'*
Water, water, everywhere,
And all the boards did shrink;
Water, water, everywhere,
Nor any drop to drink.
The very deep did rot: O Christ!
That ever this should be!
Yes, slimy things did crawl with legs
Upon the slimy sea.

2447 *'The Rime of the Ancient Mariner'*
The Sun's rim dips; the stars rush out;
At one stride comes the dark.

2448 *'The Rime of the Ancient Mariner'*
Like one, that on a lonesome road
Doth walk in fear and dread,
And having once turned round walks on,
And turns no more his head;
Because he knows, a frightful fiend
Doth close behind him tread.

2449 *'The Rime of the Ancient Mariner'*
No voice; but oh! the silence sank
Like music on my heart.

2450 *'The Rime of the Ancient Mariner'*
He prayeth well, who loveth well
Both man and bird and beast.
He prayeth best, who loveth best
All things both great and small.

2451 *'The Rime of the Ancient Mariner'*
He went like one that hath been stunned,
And is of sense forlorn:
A sadder and a wiser man,
He rose the morrow morn.

2452 *Seven Lectures on Shakespeare and Milton*
Reviewers are usually people who would have been poets, historians, biographers, &c., if they could; they have tried their talents at one or at the other, and have failed; therefore they turn critics.

2453 *Table Talk*
You abuse snuff! Perhaps it is the final cause of the human nose.

2454 *Table Talk*
Prose = words in their best order; - poetry = the best words in the best order.

2455 *Table Talk*
The man's desire is for the woman; but the woman's desire is rarely other than for the desire of the man.

2456 *Table Talk*
In politics, what begins in fear usually ends in folly.

2457
What is an epigram? A dwarfish whole,
Its body brevity, and wit its soul.

2458 *'Work without Hope'*
Work without hope draws nectar in a sieve,
And hope without an object cannot live.

COLES D.L.
2459
The age of strong belief is over, the good is no
longer always very good.

COLETTE (Sidonie-Gabrielle) 1873-1954
2460 *Claudine and Annie*
When she raises her eyelids it's as though she
were taking off all her clothes.

2461
It takes time for the absent to assume their true
shape in our thoughts. After death they take on
a firmer outline and then cease to change.

2462
The woman who thinks she is intelligent
demands equal rights with men. A woman who
is intelligent does not.

COLLIE G. Norman
2463
To make certain that crime does not pay, the
government should take it over and try to run it.

COLLINGBOURNE William d.1484
2464 *The Concordance of Chronicles*
The Cat, the Rat, and Lovell our dog
Rule all England under a hog.

COLLINGWOOD Admiral Lord 1748-1810
2465 *(before the Battle of Trafalgar)*
Now, gentlemen, let us do something today
which the world may talk of hereafter.

COLLINS John Churton 1848-1908
2466
To ask advice is in nine cases out of ten to tout
for flattery.

2467
The world, like an accomplished hostess, pays
most attention to those whom it will soonest
forget.

COLLINS Mortimer 1827-1876
2468 *The Unknown Quantity*
A man is as old as he's feeling.
A woman as old as she looks.

COLLINS William 1721-1759
2469 *'Ode Written in the Year 1746'*
How sleep the brave, who sink to rest,
By all their country's wishes blest!

2470 *'The Passions, an Ode for Music'*
Love of peace, and lonely musing,
In hollow murmurs died away.

2471 *'Verses addressed to Sir Thomas Hanmer'*
Too nicely Jonson knew the critic's part,
Nature in him was almost lost in Art.

COLMAN The Younger, George 1762-1836
2472 *The Heir at Law*
Oh, London is a fine town,
A very famous city,
Where all the streets are paved with gold,
And all the maidens pretty.

COLTON Charles Caleb c.1780-1832
2473
Applause is the spur of noble minds, the end
and aim of weak ones.

2474
Body and mind, like man and wife, do not
always agree to die together.

2475
To dare to live alone is the rarest courage; since
there are many who had rather meet their
bitterest enemy in the field, than their own
hearts in their closet.

2476
Ennui has made more gamblers than avarice,
more drunkards than thirst, and perhaps as
many suicides as despair.

2477
I have found by experience that they who have
spent all their lives in cities, improve their
talents but impair their virtues; and strengthen
their minds but weaken their morals.

2478
We hate some persons because we do not know
them; and will not know them because we hate
them.

2479
If you cannot inspire a woman with love of you,
fill her above the brim with love of herself; all
that runs over will be yours.

2480 *Lacon*
When you have nothing to say, say nothing.

2481 *Lacon*
Examinations are formidable even to the best
prepared, for the greatest fool may ask more
than the wisest man can answer.

2482 *Lacon*
If you would be known, and not know, vegetate
in a village; if you would know, and not be
known, live in a city.

2483 *Lacon*
Friendship often ends in love; but love in
friendship - never.

2484
Men will wrangle for religion, write for it, fight for it, die for it, anything but live for it.

2485
Never join with your friend when he abuses his horse or his wife unless the one is to be sold, and the other to be buried.

2486
We owe almost all our knowledge not to those who have agreed, but to those who have differed.

2487
There is a paradox in pride: it makes some men ridiculous, but prevents others from becoming so.

COMDEN Betty and GREEN Adolph 1919- and 1915-
2488 *'New York, New York'*
New York, New York, a helluva town,
The Bronx is up but the Battery's down,
And people ride in a hole in the ground:
New York, New York, It's a helluva town.

2489 *'The Party's Over'*
The party's over, it's time to call it a day.

COMFORT Alex 1920-
2490
Sex ought to be a wholly satisfying link between two affectionate people from which they emerge unanxious, rewarded, and ready for more.

2491
The telephone is the most important single technological resource of later life.

2492
Two weeks is about the ideal length of time to retire.

COMMONER Barry
2493
The first law of ecology is that everything is related to everything else.

COMPTON-BURNETT Dame Ivy 1884-1969
2494
There is more difference within the sexes than between them.

2495 *A Family and a Fortune*
Well, of course, people are only human ... But it really does not seem much for them to be.

2496 *A Family and a Fortune*
People don't resent having nothing nearly as much as too little.

2497 *The Mighty and their Fall*
There are different kinds of wrong. The people sinned against are not always the best.

2498 *Orion*
My point is that it [wickedness] is not punished, and that is why it is natural to be guilty of it. When it is likely to be punished, most of us avoid it.

2499
There is probably nothing like living together for blinding people to each other.

2500
Real life seems to have no plots.

CONANT James Bryant 1898-1978
2501
Democracy is a small hard core of common agreement, surrounded by a rich variety of individual differences.

2502
Each honest calling, each walk of life, has its own elite, its own aristocracy based on excellence of performance.

2503
Behold the turtle. He makes progress only when he sticks his neck out.

CONE Fairfax
2504
Advertising is what you do when you can't go to see somebody. That's all it is.

CONFUCIUS 551-479 BC
2505
Music produces a kind of pleasure which human nature cannot do without.

CONGREVE William 1670-1729
2506 *The Double Dealer*
There is nothing more unbecoming a man of quality than to laugh; Jesu, 'tis such a vulgar expression of the passion!

2507 *The Double Dealer*
She lays it on with a trowel.

2508 *The Double Dealer*
See how love and murder will out.

2509 *'Hymn to Harmony'*
Music alone with sudden charms can bind
The wand'ring sense, and calm the troubled mind.

2510 *Love for Love*
He that first cries out stop thief, is often he that has stolen the treasure.

2511 *Love for Love*
Women are like tricks by slight of hand,
Which, to admire, we should not understand.

2512 *The Mourning Bride*
Music has charms to soothe a savage breast.

2513 *The Mourning Bride*
Heaven has no rage, like love to hatred turned,
Nor Hell a fury, like a woman scorned.

2514 *The Way of the World*
These articles subscribed, if I continue to
endure you a little longer, I may by degrees
dwindle into a wife.

2515 *The Way of the World*
Courtship to marriage, as a very witty prologue
to a very dull Play.

CONNELL James M. 1852-1929
2516 *'The Red Flag'*
The people's flag is deepest red;
It shrouded oft our martyred dead,
And ere their limbs grew stiff and cold,
Their heart's blood dyed its every fold.
Then raise the scarlet standard high!
Within its shade we'll live or die.
Tho' cowards flinch and traitors sneer,
We'll keep the red flag flying here.

CONNOLLY Cyril 1903-1974
2517
All charming people have something to conceal,
usually their total dependence on the
appreciation of others.

2518
We are all serving a life sentence in the dungeon
of self.

2519
It is closing time in the gardens of the West and
from now on an artist will be judged only by the
resonance of his solitude or the quality of his
despair.

2520 *Enemies of Promise*
Whom the gods wish to destroy they first call
promising.

2521 *Enemies of Promise*
There is no more sombre enemy of good art
than the pram in the hall.

2522
Hate is the consequence of fear; we fear
something before we hate it; a child who fears
noises becomes a man who hates noise.

2523
The man who is master of his passions is
Reason's slave.

2524
It is only in the country that we can get to know
a person or a book.

2525
Most people do not believe in anything very
much and our greatest poetry is given to us by
those that do.

2526 *The Unquiet Grave*
Life is a maze in which we take the wrong
turning before we have learnt to walk.

2527 *The Unquiet Grave*
Imprisoned in every fat man a thin one is wildly
signalling to be let out.

2528 *The Unquiet Grave*
There is no fury like an ex-wife searching for a
new lover.

2529
The one way to get thin is to re-establish a
purpose in life.

2530
Better to write for yourself and have no public,
than to write for the public and have no self.

CONNOR Ralph 1860-1937
2531
I would often be a coward, but for the shame of
it.

2532
Love, you know, seeks to make happy rather
than to be happy.

CONRAD Joseph 1857-1924
2533
Action is consolatory. It is the enemy of
thought and the friend of flattering illusions.

2534 *The Arrow of Gold*
In plucking the fruit of memory one runs the
risk of spoiling its bloom.

2535
Caricature: putting the face of a joke upon the
body of a truth.

2536 *Heart of Darkness*
The conquest of the earth, which mostly means
the taking it away from those who have a
different complexion or slightly flatter noses
than ourselves, is not a pretty thing when you
look into it.

2537 *Heart of Darkness*
We live, as we dream - alone.

2538
History repeats itself, but the special call of an
art which has passed away is never reproduced.
It is utterly gone out of the world as the song of
a destroyed wild bird.

2539
How does one kill fear, I wonder? How do you
shoot a spectre through the heart, slash off its
spectral head, take it by the spectral throat?

2540
The last thing a woman will consent to discover
in a man whom she loves, or on whom she
simply depends, is want of courage.

2541
To have his path made clear for him is the aspiration of every human being in our beclouded and tempestuous existence.

2542
As in political, so in literary action, a man wins friends for himself mostly by the passion of his prejudices.

2543
The sea - the truth must be confessed - has no generosity. No display of manly qualities - courage, hardihood, endurance, faithfulness - has ever been known to touch its irresponsible consciousness of power.

2544
Who knows what true loneliness is - not the conventional word but the naked terror? To the lonely themselves it wears a mask. The most miserable outcast hugs some memory or some illusion.

CONRAN Shirley 1932-
2545 *Superwoman*
Life's too short to stuff a mushroom.

CONSTABLE John 1776-1837
2546
I never saw an ugly thing in my life.

CONSTANT Benjamin 1767-1834
2547
Art for art's sake, ... perverts art.

COOK Dan
2548
The opera ain't over 'til the fat lady sings.

COOK Joe
2549
Of all my wife's relations I like myself the best.

COOLIDGE Calvin 1872-1933
2550
The chief business of the American people is business.

2551
If you don't say anything, you won't be called on to repeat it.

2552
I have noticed that nothing I never said ever did me any harm.

2553
The presidency does not yield to definition. Like the glory of a morning sunrise, it can be experienced - it can not be told.

2554
I think the American public wants a solemn ass as a president, and I think I'll go along with them.

2555
When more and more people are thrown out of work, unemployment results.

COOLIDGE Susan 1845-1905
2556 *What Katy Did*
Blessings brighten as they take their flight.

COOPER Alice 1948-
2557
We've been so bombarded with sex that sex isn't sexy any more. Romance is much sexier now. I think that in the 1990's, we're going to start seeing people dating again.

COOPER Henry 1934-
2558 *(on women's boxing)*
Women are made for loving and not hitting.

COPLAND Aaron 1900-1990
2559
If a literary man puts together two words about music, one of them will be wrong.

CORELLI Marie 1855-1924
2560
I never married because I have three pets at home that answer the same purpose as a husband. I have a dog that growls every morning, a parrot that swears all afternoon, and a cat that comes home late at night.

COREY Professor Irwin
2561
Marriage is like a bank account. You put it in, you take it out, you lose interest.

CORNEILLE Pierre 1606-1684
2562 *Le Cid*
When there is no peril in the fight, there is no glory in the triumph.

2563
Violence is just, where kindness is vain.

CORNFORD Frances 1886-1960
2564 *All Soul's Night*
My love came back to me
Under the November tree
Shelterless and dim.
He put his hand upon my shoulder,
He did not think me strange or older,
Nor I, him.

2565 *'Youth' (of Rupert Brooke)*
A young Apollo, golden-haired,
Stands dreaming on the verge of strife,
Magnificently unprepared
For the long littleness of life.

CORNFORD Francis M. 1874-1943
2566 *Microcosmographia Academica*
University printing presses exist, and are subsidised by the Government for the purpose of producing books which no one can read; and

they are true to their high calling.

2567 *Microcosmographia Academica*
The Principle of Unripe Time is that people should not do at the present moment what they think right at that moment, because the moment at which they think it right has not yet arrived.

COROT Jean Baptiste 1796-1875
2568
I hope with all my heart there will be painting in heaven.

CORT David
2569
Sex is the great amateur art.

CORY William 1823-1892
2570 *'Heraclitus' (translation of Callimachus)*
I wept as I remembered how often you and I
Had tired the sun with talking and sent him down the sky.

COSBY Bill 1937-
2571
Human beings are the only creatures on earth that allow their children to come back home.

COSSMAN Joseph E.
2572
The best way to remember your wife's birthday is to forget it once.

2573
Middle age is when your broad mind and narrow waist begin to change places.

2574
Obstacles are things a person sees when he takes his eyes off his goal.

COTGRAVE Randle
2575
Eat bread at pleasure, drink wine by measure.

COTY René 1882-1962
2576
It's taken me all my life to understand that it is not necessary to understand everything.

COURTELINE Georges
2577
A woman never sees what we do for her, she only sees what we don't do.

COURTENAY Walter R.
2578
God gave man work, not to burden him, but to bless him, and useful work, willingly, cheerfully, effectively done, has always been the finest expression of the human spirit.

COUSINS Norman 1915-1990
2579
The most costly disease is not cancer or coronaries. The most costly disease is boredom - costly for both individual and society.

2580
The eternal quest of the individual human being is to shatter his loneliness.

2581
The human body experiences a powerful gravitational pull in the direction of hope. That is why the patient's hopes are the physician's secret weapon. They are the hidden ingredients in any prescription.

2582
The possibility of war increases in direct proportion to the effectiveness of the instruments of war.

COUTELI
2583
We are dying of accuracy.

COWARD Noël 1899-1973
2584
My body has certainly wandered a good deal, but I have an uneasy suspicion that my mind has not wandered enough.

2585 *'Don't Let's Be Beastly to the Germans'*
Don't let's be beastly to the Germans
When our victory is ultimately won.

2586
As one gets older, one discovers everything is going to be exactly the same with different hats on.

2587
Good heavens, television is something you appear on, you don't watch.

2588
I've sometimes thought of marrying - and then I've thought again.

2589 *'If Love Were All'*
I believe that since my life began
The most I've had is just
A talent to amuse.

2590 *'Mad about the Boy'*
Mad about the boy,
It's pretty funny but I'm mad about the boy.
He has a gay appeal
That makes me feel
There may be something sad about the boy.

2591 *'Mad Dogs and Englishmen'*
Mad dogs and Englishmen
Go out in the midday sun.

2592 *Private Lives*
Very flat, Norfolk.

2593 *Private Lives*
Extraordinary how potent cheap music is.

2594 *(of Randolph Churchill)*
Dear Randolph, utterly unspoiled by failure!

2595 *(attributed - of the retreat from Dunkirk)*
The noise, my dear! And the people!

2596
Work is more fun than fun.

2597 *'Mrs Worthington'*
Don't put your daughter on the stage, Mrs
Worthington.

COWLEY Abraham 1618-1667
2598 *'To Dr Scarborough'*
Life is an incurable disease.

2599
Enjoy the present hour,
Be thankful for the past,
And neither fear nor wish
Th' approaches of the last.

2600
Hope! of all ills that men endure
The only cheap and universal cure.

2601 *'The Wish'*
The crowd, and buzz, and murmurings
Of this great hive, the city.

COWLEY Hannah 1743-1809
2602 *Who's the Dupe?*
But what is woman? - only one of Nature's
agreeable blunders.

COWLEY Malcolm 1898-1989
2603 *(of old age)*
It is the fear of being as dependent as a young
child, while not being loved as a child is loved,
but merely being kept alive against one's will.

2604
They tell you that you'll lose your mind when
you grow older. What they don't tell you is that
you won't miss it very much.

COWPER William 1731-1800
2605
Absence of occupation is not rest,
A mind quite vacant is a mind distress'd.

2606 *'Conversation' (on tobacco)*
Pernicious weed! whose scent the fair annoys.

2607
Existence is a strange bargain. Life owes us
little; we owe it everything. The only true
happiness comes from squandering ourselves
for a purpose.

2608
A fool must now and then be right by chance.

2609
Happiness depends, as Nature shows,
Less on exterior things than most suppose.

2610 *'Hope'*
Men deal with life, as children with their play,
Who first misuse, then cast their toys away.

2611 *'Hope'*
And differing judgements serve but to declare
That truth lies somewhere, if we knew but
where.

2612
How much a dunce that has been sent to roam
Excels a dunce that has been kept at home!

2613 *'John Gilpin'*
John Gilpin was a citizen
Of credit and renown,
A train-band captain eke was he
Of famous London Town.

2614 *'Light Shining out of Darkness'*
God moves in a mysterious way
His wonders to perform;
He plants his footsteps in the sea
And rides upon the storm.

2615
I am monarch of all I survey.

2616 *'The Progress of Error'*
Remorse, the fatal egg by pleasure laid.

2617
He that has seen both sides of fifty has lived to
little purpose if he has no other views of the
world than he had when he was much younger.

2618 *'Table Talk'*
Freedom has a thousand charms to show,
That slaves, howe'er contented, never know.

2619 *'Table Talk' (of Perjury)*
To turn a penny in the way of trade.

2620 *The Task*
But war's a game, which, were their subjects
wise,
Kings would not play at.

2621 *The Task*
Knowledge is proud that he has learned so
much;
Wisdom is humble that he knows no more.

2622 *The Task (of hunting)*
Detested sport,
That owes its pleasures to another's pain.

2623 *The Task 'The Sofa'*
Thus first necessity invented stools,
Convenience next suggested elbow-chairs,
And luxury the accomplished sofa last.

2624 *The Task 'The Sofa'*
God made the country, and man made the
town.

2625 *The Task 'The Timepiece'*
There is a pleasure in poetic pains
Which only poets know.

2626 *The Task 'The Timepiece'*
Variety's the very spice of life,
That gives it all its flavour.

2627 *'Tirocinium'*
The parson knows enough who knows a duke.

2628 *'Truth'*
He has no hope that never had a fear.

2629 *'Walking with God'*
Oh! for a closer walk with God.

CRABBE George 1754-1832
2630 *'The Library'*
Fashion, though Folly's child, and guide of fools,
Rules e'en the wisest, and in learning rules.

2631 *Tales of the Hall*
Secrets with girls, like loaded guns with boys,
Are never valued till they make a noise.

2632 *The Village*
I grant indeed that fields and flocks have charms,
For him that gazes or for him that farms.

CRAIG Cal
2633
Trouble is, kids feel they have to shock their
elders and each generation grows up into
something harder to shock.

CRANE Stephen 1871-1900
2634
Tradition, thou art for suckling children
Thou are the enlivening milk for babes,
But no meat for men is in thee.

CREIGHTON Bishop
2635
Never laugh feebly at what you know is wrong.

CREWS Harry
2636
Survival is triumph enough.

CRICHTON Michael
2637
Abuse of power is not a male monopoly.

CRIPPS Agnes
2638
Educate a man and you educate an individual -
educate a woman and you educate a family.

CRISP Quentin
2639
The young always have the same problem - how
to rebel and conform at the same time. They
have now solved this by defying their parents
and copying one another.

CRITCHLEY Julian 1930-
2640
The only safe pleasure for a parliamentarian is a
bag of boiled sweets.

CROMWELL Oliver 1599-1658
2641 *(addressing the Rump Parliament)*
You have sat too long here for any good you
have been doing. Depart, I say, and let us have
done with you. In the name of God, go!

2642 *(addressing the Rump Parliament)*
Take away that fool's bauble, the mace.

2643 *(of the execution of Charles I)*
Cruel necessity.

2644 *(from which has derived the phrase 'warts and all')*
Mr Lely, I desire you would use all your skill to
paint my picture truly like me, and not flatter
me at all; but remark all these roughnesses,
pimples, warts, and everything as you see me;
otherwise I will never pay a farthing for it.

2645 *(last words)*
My design is to make what haste I can to be
gone.

2646 *Letter to General Assembly of Kirk of Scotland*
I beseech you, in the bowels of Christ, think it
possible you may be mistaken.

2647 *(to Parliament)*
You have accounted yourselves happy on being
environed with a great ditch from all the world
besides.

CRONKITE Walter 1916-
2648
Justice was born outside the home and a long
way from it; and it has never been adopted
there.

CROSBY Bing 1904-1977
2649
I think popular music in this country is one of
the few things in the twentieth century that
have made giant strides in reverse.

CROSSMAN R.H.S. 1907-1974
2650
The main task of a free society is to civilize the
struggle for power. Slavery of the acquiescent
majority to the ruthless few is the hereditary
state of mankind; freedom, a rarely-acquired
characteristic.

CRYSTAL Billy
2651
Women need a reason to have sex - men just
need a place.

CUDLIPP Hugh 1913-
2652 *(of William Randolph Hearst)*
Truth for him was a moving target; he never aimed for the bull and rarely pierced the outer ring.

CULBERTSON Ely 1891-1955
2653
Politics. The diplomatic name for the law of the jungle.

CUMMING R.D.
2654
A good book has no ending.

CUMMINGS E. E. 1894-1962
2655
all ignorance toboggans into know and trudges up to ignorance again.

2656 *Collected Poems*
a pretty girl who naked is
is worth a million statues.

2657 *'since feeling is first'*
who pays any attention
to the syntax of things
will never wholly kiss you.

2658
Be of love (a little) more careful than of anything.

2659
to be nobody but yourself - in a world which is doing its best, night and day, to make you everybody else - means to fight the hardest battle which any human being can fight, and never stop fighting.

2660
a politician is an arse upon which everyone has sat except a man.

2661
unlove's the heavenless hell and homeless home ... lovers alone wear sunlight.

CUMMINGS Fr. Jerome
2662
A friend is one who knows us, but loves us anyway.

CUMMINGS William Thomas
2663
There are no atheists in the foxholes.

CUNNINGHAM James Vincent 1911-1985
2664 *Epigrams*
I married in my youth a wife.
She was my own, my very first.
She gave the best years of her life.
I hope nobody gets the worst.

CUPPY Will
2665
Etiquette means behaving yourself a little better than is absolutely essential.

2666
Henry VIII had so many wives because his dynastic sense was very strong whenever he saw a maid of honour.

CURIE Marie 1867-1934
2667
Nothing in life is to be feared. It is only to be understood.

CURTIS Tony
2668
I wouldn't be caught dead marrying a woman old enough to be my wife.

CUSHMAN Charlotte 1816-1876
2669
Goethe said there would be little left of him if you were to discard what he owed to others.

DAACON George
2670
If absolute power corrupts absolutely, where does that leave God?

DACRE Henry
2671 *Daisy Bell*
Daisy, Daisy, give me your answer do!
I'm half crazy, all for the love of you!
It won't be a stylish marriage,
I can't afford a carriage,
But you'll look sweet upon the seat
Of a bicycle made for two!

DALEY Cass
2672
Marriage is a matter of give and take, but so far I haven't been able to find anybody who'll take what I have to give.

DALI Salvador 1904-1989
2673
I do not paint a portrait to look like the subject, rather does the person grow to look like his portrait.

2674
It is good taste, and good taste alone, that possesses the power to sterilize and is always the first handicap to any creative functioning.

DANGERFIELD Rodney 1921-
2675
I am at the age where food has taken the place of sex in my life. In fact, I've just had a mirror put over my kitchen table.

DANTE Alighieri 1265-1321
2676
The hottest places in hell are reserved for those

who, in time of great moral crisis, maintain their neutrality.

DARROW Clarence 1857-1938
2677
I do not pretend to know what many ignorant men are sure of.

2678
The first half of our lives is ruined by our parents and the second half by our children.

2679
There is no such thing as justice - in or out of court.

2680
True patriotism hates injustice in its own land more than anywhere else.

DARWIN Charles 1809-1882
2681
As for a future life, every man must judge for himself between conflicting vague possibilities.

2682
The mystery of the beginning of all things is insoluble by us; and I for one must be content to remain agnostic.

DARWIN Sir Francis 1848-1925
2683
In science the credit goes to the man who convinces the world, not to the man to whom the idea first occurs.

D'AUREVILLY Barbey
2684
Next to the wound, what women makes best is the bandage.

D'AVENANT Charles 1656-1714
2685 *Circe*
Custom, that unwritten law,
By which the people keep even kings in awe.

D'AVENANT Sir William 1606-1668
2686
Had laws not been, we never had been blam'd;
For not to know we sinn'd is innocence.

DAVIDSON John 1857-1909
2687 *'War Song'*
And blood in torrents pour
In vain - always in vain,
For war breeds war again.

DAVIDSON Sara
2688
The ability to laugh at life is right at the top, with love and communication, in the hierarchy of our needs. Humour has much to do with pain; it exaggerates the anxieties and absurdities we feel, so that we gain distance and through laughter, relief.

DAVIES Paul
2689
It may be bizarre, but in my opinion, science offers a sure path to God and religion.

DAVIES Robertson 1913-1995
2690
The critic is the duenna in the passionate affair between playwrights, actors and audiences - a figure dreaded, and occasionally comic, but never welcome, never loved.

2691
The eye sees only what the mind is prepared to comprehend.

2692
Female beauty is an important minor sacrament ... I am not at all sure that neglect of it does not constitute a sin of some kind.

2693
As a general thing, people marry most happily with their own kind. The trouble lies in the fact that people usually marry at an age when they do not really know what their own kind is.

2694
The love of truth lies at the root of much humour.

2695
If a man wants to be of the greatest possible value to his fellow-creatures, let him begin the long, solitary task of perfecting himself.

2696 *(on a biography of himself)*
It's an exellent life of somebody else. But I've really lived inside myself, and she can't get in there.

2697
The most original thing a writer can do is write like himself. It is also his most difficult task.

2698
Whether you are really right or not doesn't matter; it's the belief that counts.

2699
The world is full of people whose notion of a satisfactory future is, in fact, a return to the idealized past.

DAVIES Sir John 1569-1626
2700 *'Nosce Teipsum'*
Skill comes so slow, and life so fast doth fly,
We learn so little and forget so much.

2701 *'Orchestra, or a Poem of Dancing'*
This wondrous miracle did Love devise,
For dancing is love's proper exercise.

2702 *'Orchestra, or a Poem of Dancing'*
Kind nature first doth cause all things to love;
Love makes them dance, and in just order

The Wordsworth Dictionary of Quotations

move.

DAVIES W.H. 1871-1940
2703 *'April's Charms'*
And hear the pleasant cuckoo, loud and long -
The simple bird that thinks two notes a song.

2704 *'Leisure'*
What is this life if, full of care,
We have no time to stand and stare.

2705 *Sweet Stay-at-Home*
I love thee for a heart that's kind -
Not for the knowledge in thy mind.

DAVIS Bette 1908-1989
2706 *in All About Eve*
"Fasten your seatbelts. It's going to be a bumpy
night."

2707 *in The Cabin in the Cotton*
"I'd luv to kiss ya, but I just washed my hair."

2708
The person who wants to make it has to sweat.
There are no short cuts. And you've got to have
the guts to be hated.

2709
The real actor - like any real artist - has a direct
line to the collective heart.

DAVIS Jr. Sammy 1925-1990
2710 *Yes I Can*
Being a star has made it possible for me to get
insulted in places where the average negro
could never hope to go and get insulted.

DAVIS William T.
2711
Only a few human beings should grow to the
square mile; they are commonly planted too
close.

DAVY Sir Humphrey 1778-1829
2712
The most important of my discoveries have
been suggested to me by my failures.

DAWKINS Richard 1941-
2713 *The Blind Watchmaker*
[Natural selection] has no vision, no foresight,
no sight at all. If it can be said to play the role
of watchmaker in nature, it is the blind
watchmaker.

2714 *The Blind Watchmaker*
The essence of life is statistical improbability on
a colossal scale.

2715 *The Selfish Gene*
They are in you and in me; they created us,
body and mind; and their preservation is the
ultimate rationale for our existence ... they go
by the name of genes, and we are their survival
machines.

DAWSON of Penn, Lord 1864-1945
2716 *(on eve of King George V's death)*
The King's life is moving peacefully towards its
close.

DAY Clarence 1874-1935
2717
Father expected a good deal of God. He didn't
actually accuse God of inefficiency, but when he
prayed his tone was loud and angry, like that of
a dissatisfied guest in a carelessly managed
hotel.

DAY-LEWIS Cecil 1904-1972
2718 *'Hornpipe'*
Now the peak of summer's past, the sky is
overcast
And the love we swore would last for an age
seems deceit.

2719
There's a kind of release
And a kind of torment in every goodbye for
every man.

2720 *'Where are the War Poets?'*
It is the logic of our times,
No subject for immortal verse -
That we who lived by honest dreams
Defend the bad against the worse.

DAY-LEWIS Tamasin
2721
I haven't yet been able to find a happy adulterer.

DEARMER Percy 1867-1936
2722
Jesu, good above all other,
Gentle Child of gentle Mother,
In a stable born our Brother,
Give us grace to persevere.

DE BEAUVOIR Simone 1908-1986
2723
The role of a retired person is no longer to
possess one.

DE BELLOY 1725-1775
2724 *Le Siège de Calais*
The more foreigners I saw, the more I loved my
homeland.

DE BONO Edward 1933-
2725
Many highly intelligent people are poor
thinkers. Many people of average intelligence
are skilled thinkers. The power of a car is
separate from the way the car is driven.

2726
Removing the faults in a stagecoach may
produce a perfect stagecoach, but it is unlikely
to produce the first motor car.

2727
The solid wealth of insurance companies and the success of those who organize gambling are some indication of the profits to be derived from the efficient use of chance.

2728
Think sideways!

2729 *The Use of Lateral Thinking [foreword]*
Some people are aware of another sort of thinking which ... leads to those simple ideas that are obvious only after they have been thought of ... the term 'lateral thinking' has been coined to describe this other sort of thinking; 'vertical thinking' is used to denote the conventional logical process.

DEBS Eugene Victor 1855-1926
2730 *(at his trial for sedition)*
When great changes occur in history, when great principles are involved, as a rule the majority are wrong.

DECATUR Stephen 1779-1820
2731 *(toast)*
Our country! In her intercourse with foreign nations, may she always be in the right; but our country, right or wrong.

DEDDOES Dick
2732
Horses and jockeys mature earlier than people - which is why horses are admitted to race tracks at the age of two, and jockeys before they are old enough to shave.

DEFOE Daniel 1660-1731
2733 *'Character of the late Dr S. Annesley'*
The best of men cannot suspend their fate:
The good die early, and the bad die late.

2734 *The Complete English Tradesman*
Pleasure is a thief to business.

2735 *An Essay Upon Projects*
The soul is placed in the body like a rough diamond, and must be polished, or the lustre of it will never appear.

2736 *The Farther Adventures of Robinson Crusoe*
In trouble to be troubled
Is to have your trouble doubled.

2737 *The History of the Kentish Petition*
Nature has left this tincture in the blood,
That all men would be tyrants if they could.

2738 *A Hymn to the Pillory*
Actions receive their tincture from the times,
And as they change are virtues made or crimes.

2739
It is better to have a lion at the head of an army of sheep, than a sheep at the head of an army of lions.

2740
Middle age is youth without its levity,
And age without decay.

2741 *Moll Flanders*
Vice came in always at the door of necessity, not at the door of inclination.

2742 *Robinson Crusoe*
My man Friday.

2743 *The Serious Reflections of Robinson Crusoe*
Necessity makes an honest man a knave.

2744 *The True-Born Englishman*
Fools out of favour grudge at knaves in place.

2745 *The True-Born Englishman*
Wherever God erects a house of prayer,
The Devil always builds a chapel there;
And 'twill be found, upon examination,
The latter has the largest congregation.

2746 *The True-Born Englishman*
In their religion they are so uneven,
That each one goes his own by-way to heaven.

2747 *The True-Born Englishman*
From this amphibious ill-born mob began
That vain, ill-natured thing, an Englishman.

2748 *The True-Born Englishman*
When kings the sword of justice first lay down,
They are no kings, though they possess the crown.
Titles are shadows, crowns are empty things,
The good of subjects is the end of kings.

2749 *(of writing)*
Voyages in a paper boat.

DEGAS Edgar 1834-1917
2750
Art is vice. You don't marry it legitimately, you rape it.

2751 *Degas, by himself*
There are some women who should barely be spoken to; they should be caressed.

DE GAULLE Charles 1890-1970
2752
Diplomats are useful only in fair weather. As soon as it rains, they drown in every drop.

2753
It will not be any European statesman who will unite Europe: Europe will be united by the Chinese.

2754
France has lost a battle. But France has not lost the war!

2755
Greatness is a road leading towards the unknown.

2756
It so happens that the world is undergoing a transformation to which no change that has yet occurred can be compared, either in scope or in rapidity.

2757
How can you govern a country which has 246 varieties of cheese?

2758
Every man of action has a strong dose of egotism, pride, hardness and cunning. But all those things will be forgiven him, indeed, they will be regarded as high qualities, if he can make them the means to achieve great ends.

2759 *(of Napoleon)*
Before such a prodigious career, judgement is torn between blame and admiration.

2760
In order to become the master, the politician poses as the servant.

2761 *(to the people of Strasbourg)*
Yes, it is Europe, from the Atlantic to the Urals, it is Europe, it is the whole of Europe, that will decide the fate of the world.

2762
Since a politician never believes what he says, he is quite surprised to be taken at his word.

2763 *(replying to Clement Attlee)*
Politics are too serious a matter to be left to the politicians.

2764
A true leader always keeps an element of surprise up his sleeve, which others cannot grasp but which keeps his public excited and breathless.

2765
What we think about death only matters for what death makes us think about life.

2766
Authority doesn't work without prestige, or prestige without distance.

DEKKER Thomas 1570-1641
2767 *Patient Grissill*
Golden slumbers kiss your eyes,
Smiles awake you when you rise.

DE KLERK F.W. 1936-
2768 *(of Nelson Mandela)*
A man of destiny knows that beyond the hill lies another and another. The journey is never complete.

DE LA MARE Walter 1873-1956
2769 *Autumn*
Sad winds where your voice was;

Tears, tears where my heart was;
And ever with me,
Child, ever with me,
Silence where hope was.

DELANEY Shelagh 1939-
2770 *A Taste of Honey*
Women never have young minds. They are born three thousand years old.

DELANO Anthony
2771
She was not a woman likely to settle for equality when sex gave her an advantage.

DELILLE Jacques 1738-1813
2772
Chance makes our parents, but choice makes our friends.

DELORIA Jr. Vine
2773
When asked by an anthropologist what the Indians called America before the white man came, and Indian said simply 'Ours'.

DELORS Jacques 1925-
2774
Socialism is liberty, solidarity, responsibility.

DEMOSTHENES 384-322 BC
2775
It is not possible to found a lasting power upon injustice.

DEMPSEY Jack 1895-1983
2776 *(on losing World Heavyweight title)*
Honey, I just forgot to duck.

DENHAM Sir John 1615-1669
2777 *'Of Prudence'*
Youth, what man's age is like to be doth show;
We may our ends by our beginnings know.

2778 *'To Richard Fanshaw'*
Such is our pride, our folly, or our fate,
That few, but such as cannot write, translate.

DE NIRO Robert 1943-
2779 *in The King of Comedy*
"Better to be king for a night than a schmuck for a lifetime."

DEPEW Chauncey 1834-1928
2780
It's pleasant to hear these nice words while I'm still alive. I'd rather have the taffy than the epitaphy.

DE QUINCEY Thomas 1785-1859
2781 *Confessions of an English Opium Eater*
... a duller spectacle this earth of ours has not to show than a rainy Sunday in London.

2782 *Confessions of an English Opium Eater*
Thou hast the keys of Paradise, oh just, subtle,
and mighty opium!

2783 *'On Murder Considered as One of the Fine
Arts'*
If once a man indulges himself in murder, very
soon he comes to think little of robbing; and
from robbing he comes next to drinking and
sabbath-breaking, and from that to incivility
and procrastination.

DERBY Lord 1799-1869
2784
The duty of an Opposition [is] very simple ... to
oppose everything, and propose nothing.

DESCARTES René 1596-1650
2785 *Discourse on Method*
Common sense is the best distributed
commodity in the world, for every man is
convinced that he is well supplied with it.

2786 *Discourse on Method*
I think, therefore I am.

DESTOUCHES Philippe Néricault 1680-1754
2787 *L'Obstacle imprévu*
The absent are always in the wrong.

DE VOTO Bernard 1897-1955
2788
The proper union of gin and vermouth is a great
and sudden glory; it is one of the happiest
marriages on earth, and one of the shortest
lived.

DE VRIES Peter 1910-1993
2789
Celibacy is the worst form of self-abuse.

2790 *The Mackerel Plaza*
It is the final proof of God's omnipotence that
he need not exist in order to save us.

2791
If there's anything I hate it's the word humorist -
I feel like countering with the word seriousist.

2792
The universe is like a safe to which there is a
combination, but the combination is locked up
in the safe.

2793
Who of us is mature enough for offspring before
the offspring themselves arrive? The value of
marriage is not that adults produce children but
that children produce adults.

DEWAR Lord 1864-1930
2794
Love is an ocean of emotions entirely
surrounded by expenses.

2795
[There are] only two classes of pedestrians in
these days of reckless motor traffic - the quick,
and the dead.

DEWAR Sir James 1842-1923
2796 *(attributed)*
Minds are like parachutes. They only function
when they are open.

DEWEL Duane
2797
Any married man should forget his mistakes -
no use two people remembering the same
thing.

DEWEY John 1859-1952
2798
We only think when we are confronted with a
problem.

DEWEY Thomas E. 1902-1971
2799
No man should be in public office who can't
make more money in private life.

DEWING Thomas W.
2800
Why, if you're not in New York you are camping
out.

DIANA Princess of Wales 1961-1997
2801
I'd like to be a queen in people's hearts but I
don't see myself being Queen of this country.

2802 *(not long before her death in a car
accident)*
You are going to get a big surprise with the next
thing I do.

2803
There were three of us in this marriage, so it was
a bit crowded.

DIANE Comtesse (Marie de Beausacq)
2804
Of all feats of skill, the most difficult is that of
being honest.

2805
The power of habit and the charm of novelty are
the two adverse forces which explain the follies
of mankind.

2806
Wealth makes everything easy - honesty most of
all.

DIAZ Porfirio 1830-1915
2807 *(attributed)*
Poor Mexico, so far from God and so close to
the United States.

DIBDIN Charles 1745-1814
2808 *'The Lass that Loves a Sailor'*
But the standing toast that pleased the most
Was - The wind that blows, the ship that goes,
And the lass that loves a sailor!

DIBDIN Thomas 1771-1841
2809 *'The Snug Little Island'*
Oh! what a snug little Island,
A right little, tight little Island!

DICKENS Charles 1812-1870
2810
If there were no bad people, there would be no good lawyers.

2811 *Barnaby Rudge*
These are strings ... in the human heart that had better not be wibrated.

2812 *Bleak House*
This is a London particular ... A fog, miss.

2813 *Bleak House*
The one great principle of the English law is, to make business for itself.

2814 *The Chimes 'The Second Quarter'*
O let us love our occupations,
Bless tne squire and his relations,
Live upon our daily rations,
And always know our proper stations.

2815 *A Christmas Carol*
'Bah,' said Scrooge. 'Humbug!'

2816 *David Copperfield*
Barkis is willin'.

2817 *Great Expectations*
It is a most miserable thing to feel ashamed of home.

2818 *Hard Times*
Now, what I want is, Facts ... Facts alone are wanted in life.

2819
I have known a vast quantity of nonsense talked about bad men not looking you in the face. Don't trust that conventional idea. Dishonesty will stare honesty out of countenance, any day in the week, if there is anything to be got by it.

2820 *Pickwick Papers*
Never sign a walentine with your own name.

2821
Secret, and self-contained, and solitary as an oyster.

DICKEY James 1923-
2822
Flight is the only true sensation that men have achieved in modern history.

DICKINSON Angie
2823
I dress for women - and I undress for men.

DICKINSON Emily 1830-1886
2824
Anger as soon as fed is dead -
'Tis starving makes it fat.

2825 *'The Bustle in a House'*
The Bustle in a House
The Morning after Death
Is solemnest of industries
Enacted upon Earth -

The Sweeping up the Heart
And putting Love away
We shall not want to use again
Until Eternity.

2826
Dying is a wild night and a new road.

2827
For each ecstatic instant
We must an anguish pay
In keen and quivering ratio
To the ecstasy.

2828 *'Elysium is as far as to'*
What fortitude the Soul contains,
That it can so endure
The accent of a coming Foot -
The opening of a Door.

2829
Fame is a bee
It has a song -
It has a sting -
Ah, too, it has a wing.

2830 *'After great pain, a formal feeling comes'*
This is the Hour of Lead -
Remembered, if outlived,
As Freezing persons, recollect the Snow -
First - Chill - then Stupor - then the letting go.

2831
'Hope' is the thing with feathers
That perches in the soul -
And sings the tune without words
And never stops - at all.

2832 *'My life closed twice before its close'*
Parting is all we know of heaven,
And all we need of hell.

2833
The pedigree of honey
Does not concern the bee;
A clover, anytime, to him
Is aristocracy.

2834 *'They shut me up in prose'*
They shut me up in prose -
As when a little girl
They put me in the closet -
Because they liked me 'still'.

2835 *'Because I could not stop for Death'*
Because I could not stop for Death -
He kindly stopped for me -
The Carriage held but just Ourselves -
And Immortality.

2836 *'Success is counted sweetest'*
Success is counted sweetest
By those who ne'er succeed.
To comprehend a nectar
Requires sorest need.

2837
Where thou art, that, is Home.

DICKINSON Goldsworthy Lowes 1862-1932
2838 *The Greek View of Life*
Dissatisfaction with the world in which we live
and determination to realise one that shall be
better, are the prevailing characteristics of the
modern spirit.

DICKINSON John 1732-1808
2839 *'The Liberty Song'*
Then join hand in hand, brave Americans all.
By uniting we stand, by dividing we fall.

2840 *Reasons for taking up arms against England*
Our cause is just, our union is perfect.

DICKMAN Franklin J.
2841
The glittering generalities of the speaker have
left an impression more delightful than
permanent.

DICKSON Paul 1939-
2842
Rowe's Rule: the odds are five to six that the
light at the end of the tunnel is the headlight of
an oncoming train.

DIDEROT Denis 1713-1784
2843 *Paradoxe sur le comédien*
It has been said that love robs those who have it
of their wit, and gives it to those who have
none.

DIDION Joan 1934-
2844
There is one last thing to remember: writers are
always selling somebody out.

DIEFENBAKER John G. 1895-1979
2845
That one never asks a question unless he knows
the answer is basic to parliamentary
questioning.

2846
A question which can be answered without
prejudice to the government is not a fit
question to ask.

DIEM Ngo Dinh
2847 *(on becoming President of Vietnam)*
Follow me, if I advance; kill me if I retreat;
revenge me if I die!

DIETRICH Marlene 1901-1991
2848 *(attributed)*
Most women set out to try to change a man -
and when they have changed him, they do not
like him.

2849
The average man is more interested in a woman
who is interested in him than he is in a woman
- any woman - with beautiful legs.

2850
How do you know when love is gone? If you
said that you would be there at seven and get
there by nine, and he or she has not called the
police - it's gone.

DILLARD Annie
2851
I read about an Eskimo hunter who asked the
local missionary priest, 'If I did not know about
God and sin, would I go to hell?' 'No,' said the
priest, 'not if you did not know.' 'Then why,'
asked the Eskimo earnestly, 'did you tell me?'

2852
In literary history, generation follows generation
in a rage.

DILLER Phyllis 1917-
2853 *Phyllis Diller's Housekeeping Hints*
Never go to bed mad. Stay up and fight.

DILLON Wentworth c.1633-1685
2854 *Art of Poetry*
But words once spoke can never be recalled.

DIMNET Ernest 1866-1954
2855
Too often we forget that genius ... depends
upon the data within its reach, that Archimedes
could not have devised Edison's inventions.

2856 *What We Live By*
Architecture, of all the arts, is the one which
acts the most slowly, but the most surely, on the
soul.

DIOGENES c.400-c.325 BC
2857
Calumny is only the noise of madmen.

2858 *Plutarch Parallel Lives 'Alexander'*
Alexander ... asked him if he lacked any thing.
'Yes,' said he, 'that I do. that you stand out of my
sun a little.'

DIONYSIUS of Halicarnassus 30-7 BC
2859 *Ars Rhetorica*
History is philosophy learned from examples.

DIRKSEN Everett 1896-1969
2860
The U.S. Senate - an old scow which doesn't
move very fast, but never sinks.

2861
Three Laws of Politics:
1. Get elected.
2. Get re-elected
3. Don't get mad, get even.

DISRAELI Benjamin 1804-1881
2862 *(attributed)*
Damn your principles! Stick to your party.

2863 *(attributed)*
There are three kinds of lies: lies, damned lies
and statistics.

2864 *(advice to a young man)*
Talk as much as possible to women. They ask so
many questions.

2865
Anybody amuses me for once. A new
acquaintance is like a new book. I prefer it,
even if bad, to a classic.

2866
Assassination has never changed the history of
the world.

2867
An author who speaks about his own books is
almost as bad as a mother who talks about her
own children.

2868 *(on becoming Prime Minister)*
I have climbed to the top of the greasy pole.

2869
Colonies do not cease to be colonies because
they are independent.

2870 *Coningsby*
No Government can be long secure without a
formidable Opposition.

2871 *Coningsby*
Youth is a blunder; Manhood a struggle; Old
Age a regret.

2872 *Coningsby*
It seems to me a barren thing this Conservatism
- an unhappy cross-breed, the mule of politics
that engenders nothing.

2873
A Conservative Government is an organized
hypocrisy.

2874 *Contarini Fleming*
Read no history: nothing but biography, for that
is life without theory.

2875
The Continent will [not] suffer England to be
the workshop of the world.

2876 *(on death bed, declining a visit from the
Queen)*
'No, it is better not, she would only ask me to
take a message to Albert.'

2877
Departure should be sudden.

2878
Upon the education of the people of this
country the fate of this country depends.

2879 *(on his elevation to the House of Lords)*
I am dead; dead, but in the Elysian fields.

2880 *Endymion*
His Christianity was muscular.

2881 *Endymion*
Said Waldershare, 'Sensible men are all of the
same religion.' ' And pray what is that?' ...
'Sensible men never tell.'

2882
England does not love coalitions.

2883 *(of Gladstone)*
A sophistical rhetorician, inebriated with the
exuberance of his own verbosity.

2884
Great services are not cancelled by one act or by
one single error.

2885 *Henrietta Temple*
Time is the great physician.

2886
You are not going, I hope, to leave the destinies
of the British Empire to prigs and pedants.

2887
My idea of an agreeable person is a person who
agrees with me.

2888
Increased means and increased leisure are the
two civilizers of man.

2889
An insular country, subject to fogs and with a
powerful middle class, requires grave
statesmen.

2890
Yes, I am a Jew, and when the ancestors of the
right honourable gentlemen were brutal
savages in an unknown land, mine were priests
in the Temple of Solomon.

2891
He has to learn that petulance is not sarcasm, and that insolence is not invective.

2892
We have legalized confiscation, consecrated sacrilege, and condoned high treason.

2893 *Letter to Lord Malmesbury*
These wretched colonies will all be independent, too, in a few years, and are a millstone round our necks.

2894 *Lothair*
Every day when he looked into the glass, and gave the last touch to his consummate toilette, he offered his grateful thanks to Providence that his family was not unworthy of him.

2895 *Lothair*
A Protestant, if he wants aid or advice on any matter can only go to his solicitor.

2896 *Lothair*
London: a nation, not a city.

2897 *Lothair*
When a man fell into his anecdotage it was a sign for him to retire from the world.

2898 *Lothair*
You know who the critics are? The men who have failed in literature and art.

2899 *Lothair*
Every woman should marry - and no man.

2900
The magic of first love is our ignorance that it can ever end.

2901 *(Maiden speech)*
Though I sit down now, the time will come when you will hear me.

2902
Is man an ape or an angel? Now I am on the side of the angels.

2903
Man, my Lord, is a being born to believe.

2904
No man is regular in his attendance at the House of Commons until he is married.

2905 *(to Matthew Arnold)*
Everyone likes flattery; and when you come to Royalty you should lay it on with a trowel.

2906
Never complain and never explain.

2907
Party is organized opinion.

2908
I will not go down to posterity talking bad grammar.

2909
Pray remember, Mr. Dean, no dogma, no Dean.

2910
Predominant opinions are generally the opinions of the generation that is vanishing.

2911
Protection is not only dead, but damned.

2912
Protection is not a principle, but an expedient.

2913 *(on return from Congress of Berlin)*
[We] have brought you back peace - but a peace I hope with honour.

2914
The right hon. Gentleman caught the Whigs bathing, and walked away with their clothes.

2915
Thus you have a starving population, an absentee aristocracy, and an alien Church, and in addition the weakest executive in the world. That is the Irish Question.

2916 *Sybil*
To do nothing and get something, formed a boy's ideal of a manly career.

2917 *Sybil*
I was told that the Priviledged and the People formed Two Nations.

2918 *(of the Treasury Bench)*
You behold a range of exhausted volcanoes.

2919
A University should be a place of light, of liberty, and of learning.

2920 *Vivian Grey*
Experience is the child of Thought, and Thought is the child of Action. We cannot learn men from books.

D'ISRAELI Isaac 1766-1848
2921 *The Literary Character*
There is an art of reading, as well as an art of thinking, and an art of writing.

DIX William Chatterton 1837-1898
2922
As with gladness men of old
Did the guiding star behold,
As with joy they hailed its light,
Leading onward, beaming bright,
So, most gracious Lord, may we
Evermore be led to thee.

DOBIE J. Frank
2923
Luck is being ready for the chance.

2924
The only way a man can get civilized is to become a contemporary of himself.

DOBSON Henry Austin 1840-1921
2925 *'Fame is a Food'*
Fame is a food that dead men eat, -
I have no stomach for such meat.

2926 *'The Paradox of Time'*
Time goes, you say? Ah no!
Alas, Time stays, we go.

DOCTOROW E.L. 1931-
2927
History needs to be rewritten or it becomes mythology and then it can be used destructively.

DODD Ken 1931-
2928
Freud's theory was that when a joke opens a window ... you get a marvellous feeling of relief and elation. The trouble with Freud is that he never had to play the old Glasgow Empire on a Saturday night after Rangers and Celtic had both lost.

DONATUS Aelius c.300-399
2929
Confound those who have said our remarks before us.

DONLEAVY J.P. 1926-
2930 *The Ginger Man*
When you don't have any money, the problem is food. When you have money, it's sex. When you have both it's health.

DONNE John 1572-1631
2931 *'Air and Angels'*
Just such disparity
As is 'twixt air and angels' purity,
'Twixt women's love, and men's will ever be.

2932 *'The Anagram'*
Love built on beauty, soon as beauty, dies.

2933 *An Anatomy of the World: The First Anniversary*
She, she is dead; she's dead; when thou know'st this,
Thou know'st how dry a cinder this world is.

2934 *'The Anniversary'*
Only our love hath no decay;
This, no tomorrow hath, nor yesterday,
Running it never runs from us away,
But truly keeps his first, last, everlasting day.

2935 *'The Autumnal'*
No spring, nor summer beauty hath such grace,
As I have seen in one autumnal face.

2936 *'The Bait'*
Come live with me, and be my love,
And we will some new pleasures prove
Of golden sands, and crystal brooks,
With silken lines, and silver hooks.

2937 *'Going to Bed'*
Full nakedness! All joys are due to thee,
As souls unbodied, bodies uncloth'd must be.

2938 *'Break of Day'*
The day breaks not, it is my heart.

2939 *'The Canonization'*
For God's sake hold your tongue and let me love.

2940 *Death's Duel*
We have a winding sheet in our mother's womb, which grows with us from our conception, and we come into the world, wound up in that winding sheet, for we come to seek a grave.

2941 *Devotions upon Emergent Occasions*
But I do nothing upon my self, and yet I am mine own Executioner.

2942 *Devotions upon Emergent Occasions*
No man is an Island, entire of itself; every man is a piece of the Continent, a part of the main; if a clod be washed away by the sea, Europe is the less.

2943 *Devotions upon Emergent Occasions*
Any man's death diminishes me, because I am involved in mankind; and therefore never send to know for whom the bell tolls; it tolls for thee.

2944
The difference between the reason of man and the instinct of the beast is this, that the beast does but know, but the man knows that he knows.

2945 *'The Good Morrow'*
I wonder by my troth, what thou, and I
Did, till we loved, were we not weaned till then?
But sucked on country pleasures, childishly?
Or snorted we in the seven sleepers den?

2946 *'To Sir Henry Wotton'*
More than kisses, letters mingle souls.

2947 *Holy Sonnets*
Death be not proud, though some have called thee
Mighty and dreadful, for thou art not so.

2948 *Holy Sonnets*
One short sleep past, we wake eternally,
And death shall be no more; Death thou shalt die.

2949 *Holy Sonnets*
Take me to you, imprison me, for I
Except you enthral me, never shall be free,
Nor ever chaste, except you ravish me.

2950 *Holy Sonnets*
What if this present were the world's last night?

2951 *'A Lecture in the Shadow'*
Love is a growing or full constant light;
And his first minute, after noon, is night.

2952
Love, all love of other sights controls.
And makes one little room an everywhere.

2953 *'Love's Deity'*
I long to talk with some old lover's ghost,
Who died before the god of Love was born.

2954 *'To His Mistress Going to Bed'*
Licence my roving hands, and let them go,
Behind, before, above, between, below.
O my America, my new found land,
My kingdom, safeliest when with one man
manned.

2955
I observe the physician with the same diligence
as the disease.

2956 *'The Progress of the Soul'*
Nature's great masterpiece, an elephant,
The only harmless great thing.

2957 *Sermons*
[Death] comes equally to us all, and makes us
all equal when it comes.

2958 *Sermons*
So certainly is there nothing, nothing in
spiritual things, perfect in this world.

2959 *'Song'*
Go, and catch a falling star,
Get with child a mandrake root,
Tell me, where all past years are,
Or who cleft the Devil's foot.

2960 *'The Sun Rising'*
Love, all alike, no season knows, nor clime,
Nor hours, days, months, which are the rags of
time.

2961
Be thine own palace, or the world's thy jail.

2962 *'The Triple Fool'*
I am two fools, I know,
For loving, and for saying so
In whining poetry.

2963 *(to his wife on being dismissed from
service)*
John Donne, Anne Donne, Un-done.

DOREN Carl Van 1885-1950
2964
The race of man, while sheep in credulity, are
wolves for conformity.

DOREN Mark Van 1894-1972
2965
Wit is the only wall
Between us and the dark.

DORMAN-SMITH Sir Reginald 1899-1977
2966
Let 'Dig for Victory' be the motto of every one
with a garden and of every able-bodied man
and woman capable of digging an allotment in
their spare time.

DOSTOEVSKY Fedor 1821-1881
2967
Beauty will save the world.

2968 *The Brothers Karamazov*
If you were to destroy in mankind the belief in
immortality, not only love but every living force
maintaining the life of the world would at once
be dried up.

2969 *The Brothers Karamazov*
The awful thing is that beauty is mysterious as
well as terrible. God and devil are fighting
there, and the battlefield is the heart of man.

2970 *The Brothers Karamazov*
Men reject the prophets and slay them, but they
love their martyrs and honour those whom they
have slain.

2971 *Crime and Punishment*
All people seem to be divided into 'ordinary'
and 'extraordinary'. The ordinary people must
lead a life of strict obedience and have no right
to transgress the law because ... they are
ordinary. Whereas the extraordinary people
have the right to commit any crime they like
and transgress the law in any way just because
they happen to be extraordinary.

2972 *Crime and Punishment*
Power is given only to him who dares to stoop
and take it ... one must have the courage to
dare.

2973 *House of the Dead*
To crush, to annihilate a man utterly, to inflict
on him the most terrible punishment so that
the most ferocious murderer would shudder at
it beforehand, one need only give him work of
an absolutely, completely useless and irrational
character.

2974
It seems, in fact, as though the second half of a
man's life is made up of nothing but the habits
he has accumulated during the first half.

2975
What is hell? I maintain that it is the suffering of being unable to love.

2976
Who doesn't desire his father's death?

DOUGLAS Keith 1920-1944
2977 *'Simplify me when I'm Dead'*
Remember me when I am dead
And simplify me when I'm dead.

2978 *'Vergissmeinnicht, 1943'*
But she would weep to see today
how on his skin the swart flies move;
the dust upon the paper eye
and the burst stomach like a cave.
For here the lover and killer are mingled
who had one body and one heart.
And death, who had the soldier singled
has done the lover mortal hurt.

DOUGLAS Lord Alfred 1870-1945
2979 *'Two Loves'*
I am the Love that dare not speak its name.

DOUGLAS Norman 1868-1952
2980 *Almanac*
To find a friend one must close one eye. To keep him - two.

2981
Justice is too good for some people, and not good enough for the rest.

2982
A man can believe in a considerable deal of rubbish, and yet go about his daily work in a rational and cheerful manner.

2983 *South Wind*
Many a man who thinks to found a home discovers that he has merely opened a tavern for his friends.

2984
It takes a wise man to handle a lie. A fool had better remain honest.

DOWNES Donald
2985
Fear can be headier than whisky, once man has acquired a taste for it.

DOWSON Ernest 1867-1900
2986 *'Non Sum Qualis Eram'*
I have forgot much, Cynara! gone with the wind,
Flung roses, roses, riotously, with the throng,
Dancing, to put thy pale, lost lilies out of mind;
But I was desolate and sick of an old passion,
Yea, all the time, because the dance was long:
I have been faithful to thee, Cynara! in my fashion.

2987 *'Vitae Summa Brevis'*
They are not long, the days of wine and roses:
Out of a misty dream
Our path emerges for a while, then closes
Within a dream.

DOYLE Sir Arthur Conan 1859-1930
2988 *The Adventures of Sherlock Holmes*
Singularity is almost invariably a clue.

2989 *The Adventures of Sherlock Holmes*
It is my belief, Watson, founded upon my experience, that the lowest and vilest alleys in London do not present a more dreadful record of sin than does the smiling and beautiful countryside.

2990 *The Adventures of Sherlock Holmes*
A man should keep his little brain attic stocked with all the furniture that he is likely to use, and the rest he can put away in the lumber room of his library, where he can get it if he wants it.

2991 *The Adventures of Sherlock Holmes*
It is quite a three-pipe problem, ...

2992 *The Adventures of Sherlock Holmes*
You see, but you do not observe.

2993 *His Last Bow* 'The Dying Detective'
Of all ruins that of a noble mind is the most deplorable.

2994 *The Memoirs of Sherlock Holmes*
'Excellent,' I cried. 'Elementary,' said he.

2995 *The Memoirs of Sherlock Holmes*
'Ex-Professor Moriarty of mathematical celebrity ... is the Napoleon of Crime, Watson.'

2996 *A Study in Scarlet*
London, that great cesspool into which all the loungers and idlers of the Empire are irresistibly drained.

2997 *A Study in Scarlet*
It is a capital mistake to theorize before you have all the evidence. It biases the judgement.

2998 *A Study in Scarlet*
Where there is no imagination there is no horror.

2999 *The Sign of Four*
You know my methods. Apply them.

3000 *The Sign of Four*
It is the unofficial force - the Baker Street irregulars.

3001 *The Valley of Fear*
Mediocrity knows nothing higher than itself, but talent instantly recognizes genius.

DOYLE Sir Francis 1810-1888
3002 *'The Unobstrusive Christian'*
His creed no parson ever knew,

For this was still his 'simple plan',
To have with clergymen to do
As little as a Christian can.

DRABBLE Margaret 1939-
3003 *A Natural Curiosity*
England's not a bad country ... It's just a mean,
cold, ugly, divided, tired, clapped-out, post-
imperial, post-industrial slag-heap covered in
polystyrene hamburger cartons.

3004 *A Summer Bird-Cage*
Perhaps the rare and simple pleasure of being
seen for what one is compensates for the misery
of being it.

DRAKE Sir Francis c.1540-1596
3005 *(attributed)*
There is plenty of time to win this game, and to
thrash the Spaniards too.

3006 *(dispatch to Sir Francis Walsingham)*
There must be a beginning of any great matter,
but the continuing unto the end until it be
thoroughly finished yields the true glory.

3007 *(of the expedition to Cadiz)*
The singeing of the King of Spain's Beard.

DRAYTON Michael 1563-1631
3008 *The Barons' Wars*
Ill news hath wings, and with the wind doth go,
Comfort's a cripple and comes ever slow.

3009 *The Barons' Wars*
Thus when we fondly flatter our desires,
Our best conceits do prove the greatest liars.

3010 *To the Cambro-Britons*
Fair stood the wind for France.

3011 *Poly-Olbion*
That shire which we the Heart of England well
may call.

DREW Elizabeth
3012
The world is not run by thought, nor by
imagination, but by opinion.

DRUCKER Peter 1909-
3013
There is nothing so useless as doing efficiently
that which should not be done at all.

3014
Profitability is the sovereign criterion of the
enterprise.

3015
The really important things are said over
cocktails and are never done.

3016
Along this tree
From root to crown
Ideas flow up

And vetoes down.

3017
Whenever you see a successful business,
someone once made a courageous decision.

DRUMMOND Thomas 1797-1840
3018 *Letter to the Earl of Donoughmore*
Property has its duties as well as its rights

DRYDEN John 1631-1700
3019 *Absalom and Achitophel*
In pious times, ere priestcraft did begin,
Before polygamy was made a sin.

3020 *Absalom and Achitophel*
Plots, true or false, are necessary things,
To raise up commonwealths and ruin kings.

3021 *Absalom and Achitophel*
Why should he, with wealth and honour blest,
Refuse his age the needful hours of rest?
Punish a body which he could not please;
Bankrupt of life, yet prodigal of ease?
And all to leave what with his toil he won
To that unfeathered two-legged thing, a son.

3022 *Absalom and Achitophel*
In friendship false, implacable in hate:
Resolved to ruin or to rule the state.

3023 *Absalom and Achitophel*
All empire is no more than power in trust.

3024 *Absalom and Achitophel*
Better one suffer, than a nation grieve,

3025 *Absalom and Achitophel*
But far more numerous was the herd of such
Who think too little and who talk too much.

3026 *Absalom and Achitophel*
A man so various that he seemed to be
Not one, but all mankind's epitome.
Stiff in opinions, always in the wrong;
Was everything by starts, and nothing long:
But, in the course of one revolving moon,
Was chemist, fiddler, statesman, and buffoon.

3027 *Absalom and Achitophel*
In squandering wealth was his peculiar art:
Nothing went unrewarded, but desert.
Beggared by fools, whom still he found too late:
He had his jest, and they had his estate.

3028 *Absalom and Achitophel*
Youth, beauty, graceful action seldom fail:
But common interest always will prevail:
And pity never ceases to be shown
To him, who makes the people's wrongs his
own.

3029 *Absalom and Achitophel*
Never was patriot yet, but was a fool.

3030 *Absalom and Achitophel*
Beware the fury of a patient man.

3031 *Alexander's Feast*
None but the brave deserves the fair.

3032 *Alexander's Feast*
War, he sung, is toil and trouble;
Honour but an empty bubble.

3033 *All for Love*
Errors, like straws, upon the surface flow;
He who would search for pearls must dive
below.

3034 *Aureng-Zebe*
Death, in itself, is nothing; but we fear,
To be we know not what, we know not where.

3035 'The Character of a Good Parson'
Refined himself to soul, to curb the sense
And made almost a sin of abstinence.

3036 *The Conquest of Granada*
I am as free as nature first made man,
Ere the base laws of servitude began,
When wild in woods the noble savage ran.

3037 *The Conquest of Granada*
Thou strong seducer, opportunity!

3038 *Cymon and Iphigenia*
He trudged along unknowing what he sought,
And whistled as he went, for want of thought.

3039 *Cymon and Iphigenia*
She hugged the offender, and forgave the
offence.

3040 *Epistle 'To my honoured kinsman John
Driden'*
The wise, for cure, on exercise depend;
God never made his work, for man to mend.

3041 *An Essay of Dramatic Poesy (of
Shakespeare)*
He was the man who of all modern, and
perhaps ancient poets, had the largest and most
comprehensive soul ... he is always great.

3042
Fight on, my merry men all,
I'm a little wounded, but I am not slain;
I will lay me down for to bleed a while,
Then I'll rise and fight with you again.

3043 *Heroic Stanzas (death of Oliver Cromwell)*
For he was great, ere fortune made him so.

3044 *The Hind and the Panther*
For present joys are more to flesh and blood
Than a dull prospect of a distant good.

3045 *The Hind and the Panther*
By education most have been misled;
So they believe, because they so were bred.
The priest continues what the nurse began,
And thus the child imposes on the man.

3046
Ill habits gather by unseen degrees,
As brooks make rivers, rivers run to seas.

3047
Every inch that is not fool is rogue.

3048 *The Indian Emperor*
And love's the noblest frailty of the mind.

3049 *The Indian Emperor*
Repentance is the virtue of weak minds.

3050 *The Indian Emperor*
For all the happiness mankind can gain
Is not in pleasure, but in rest from pain.

3051 *King Arthur*
War is the trade of kings.

3052 *MacFleknoe*
All human things are subject to decay,
And, when fate summons, monarchs must obey.

3053 *The Maiden Queen*
I am resolved to grow fat and look young till
forty, and then slip out of the world with the
first wrinkle and the reputation of five-and-
twenty.

3054 *Sir Martin Mar-All*
For secrets are edged tools,
And must be kept from children and from fools.

3055 *The Medal*
We loathe our manna, and we long for quails.

3056 *The Medal*
But treason is not owned when 'tis descried;
Successful crimes alone are justified.

3057 *Mithridates*
For, Heaven be thanked, we live in such an age,
When no man dies for love, but on the stage.

3058 *Palamon and Arcite*
But love's a malady without a cure.

3059 *Palamon and Arcite*
Repentance is but want of power to sin.

3060 *Palamon and Arcite*
Since every man who lives is born to die,
And none can boast sincere felicity,
With equal mind, what happens, let us bear,
Nor joy nor grieve too much for things beyond
our care.

3061
There is a pleasure sure,
In being mad, which none but madmen know!

3062 'The Prologue at Oxford, 1680'
But 'tis the talent of our English nation,
Still to be plotting some new reformation.

3063 *'Prologue to the University of Oxon'*
So poetry, which is in Oxford made
An art, in London only is a trade.

3064 *Religio Laici*
A man is to be cheated into passion, but to be
reasoned into truth.

3065 *The Secular Masque*
A very merry, dancing, drinking,
Laughing, quaffing, and unthinking time.

3066 *The Secular Masque*
Joy ruled the day, and Love the night.

3067 *A Song for St Cecilia's Day*
What passion cannot Music raise and quell?

3068 *A Song for St Cecilia's Day*
The soft complaining flute.

3069 *A Song for St Cecilia's Day*
The trumpet shall be heard on high,
The dead shall live, the living die,
And Music shall untune the sky.

3070 *(translation of Horace: Odes)*
Happy the man, and happy he alone,
He, who can call to-day his own:
He who, secure within, can say,
To-morrow do thy worst, for I have lived to-day.

3071 *(translation of Juvenal: Satires)*
Look round the habitable world! how few
Know their own good; or knowing it, pursue.

3072 *(translation of Ovid: The Art of Love)*
To see and be seen, in heaps they run;
Some to undo, and some to be undone.

3073 *(translation of Virgil: Aeneid)*
Arms, and the man I sing ...

3074 *Tyrannic Love*
All delays are dangerous in war.

DU MAURIER Daphne 1907-
3075
Writers should be read - but neither seen nor
heard.

DUBCEK Alexander 1921-1992
3076
... we followed such a policy that socialism
would not lose its human face.

DUBUFFET Jean 1901-1985
3077
Unless one says goodbye to what one loves, and
unless one travels to completely new territories,
one can expect merely a long wearing away of
oneself.

DUCHAMP Marcel 1887-1968
3078
It's not what you see that is art, art is the gap.

DUDEK Louis
3079
A critic at best is a waiter at the great table of
literature.

3080
There are two kinds of people: those who are
always well and those who are always sick.
Most of the evils of the world come from the
first sort and most of the achievements from the
second.

3081
What is forgiven is usually well-remembered.

DUELL Charles H.
3082 *(US Office of Patents 1899)*
Everything that can be invented has been
invented.

DULLES John Foster 1888-1959
3083
You have to take chances for peace, just as you
must take chances in war.

3084
The world will never have lasting peace so long
as men reserve for war the finest human
qualities.

DUMAS Alexandre ('Pere') 1802-1870
3085
All human wisdom is summed up in two words
- wait and hope.

3086 *The Three Musketeers*
All for one, one for all.

DUMAS Alexandre ('Fils') 1824-1895
3087 *(attributed)*
It is only rarely that one can see in a little boy
the promise of a man, but one can almost
always see in a little girl the threat of a woman.

3088
Business? It's quite simple. It's other people's
money.

DUMBRILLE Douglas
3089 *in The Lives of A Bengal Lancer*
"We have ways of making men talk."

DUNBAR Paul Lawrence 1872-1906
3090 *'Sympathy'*
I know why the caged bird sings!

DUNCAN Sara Jeannette
3091
If you have anything to tell me of importance,
for God's sake begin at the end.

3092
Clothes and courage have much to do with each
other.

3093
A human being isn't an orchid, he must draw something from the soil he grows in.

3094
One loses so many laughs by not laughing at oneself.

3095
Why is it that when people have no capacity for private usefulness they should be so anxious to serve the public?

DUNLOP Ian 1925-
3096
The shock of the new: seven historic exhibitions of modern art.

DUNNE Dominick
3097
Let me tell you something about silence: The bullshit stops.

DUNNE Finley Peter 1867-1936
3098
An appeal is when ye ask wan court to show its contempt for another court.

3099
Comfort the afflicted and afflict the comfortable.

3100
You can lead a man up to the university, but you can't make him think.

3101
Many a man that couldn't direct ye to th' drug store on th' corner when he was thirty will get a respectful hearin' when age has further impaired his mind.

3102
A man's idee in a card game is war - crool, devastatin' and pitiless. A lady's idee iv it is a combynation iv larceny, embezzlement an' burglary.

3103
No matter whether the Constitution follows the flag or not, the Supreme Court follows the election return.

3104
I see gr-reat changes takin' place ivry day, but no change at all ivry fifty years.

3105
Th' prisidincy is th' highest office in th' gift iv th' people. Th' vice-prisidincy is th' next highest an' the lowest. It isn't a crime exactly. Ye can't be sint to jail f'r it, but it's a kind iv a disgrace.

3106
Vice goes a long way tow'rd makin' life bearable. A little vice now an' thin is relished by th' best iv men.

3107
Whin a man gets to be my age, he ducks political meetin's, an' reads th' papers an' weighs th' ividence an' th' argymints - pro-argymints an' con-argymints, an' makes up his mind ca'mly, an' votes th' Dimmycratic Ticket.

DUNNING John (Baron Ashburton) 1731-1783
3108 *(motion in the House of Commons)*
The power of the Crown has increased, is increasing, and ought to be diminished.

DUNSANY Lord 1906-
3109
It is very seldom that the same man knows much of science, and about the things that were known before science came.

DURANT Will 1885-1981
3110 *(on his 90th Birthday)*
The love we have in our youth is superficial compared to the love that an old man has for his old wife.

3111
The individual succumbs, but he does not die if he has left something to mankind.

3112
Our knowledge is a receding mirage in an expanding desert of ignorance.

3113
One of the lessons of history is that nothing is often a good thing to do and always a clever thing to say.

3114
So I should say that civilizations begin with religion and stoicism: they end with scepticism and unbelief, and the undisciplined pursuit of individual pleasure. A civilization is born stoic and dies epicurean.

3115
Most of us spend too much time on the last twenty-four hours and too little on the last six thousand years.

3116
Tired mothers find that spanking takes less time than reasoning and penetrates sooner to the seat of the memory.

3117
When liberty destroys order, the hunger for order will destroy liberty.

DURANTY Edmond
3118
It takes immense genius to represent, simply and sincerely, what we see in front of us.

DUROCHER Leo 1906-1991
3119
Nice guys. Finish last.

DURRELL Lawrence 1912-1990
3120 *Justine*
There are only three things to be done with a
woman. You can love her, you can suffer for
her, or you can turn her into literature.

DÜRRENMATT Friedrich 1921-1990
3121
What was once thought can never be
unthought.

DURY Ian 1942-
3122
Sex and drugs and rock and roll.

3123 *'What a Waste'*
I could be the catalyst that sparks the
revolution.
I could be an inmate in a long term institution
I could lean to wild extremes I could do or die,
I could yawn and be withdrawn and watch
them gallop by,
What a waste, what a waste, what a waste, what
a waste.

DUVALL Robert
3124 *Apocalypse Now*
"I love the smell of napalm in the morning...it
smells like victory."

DYER Sir Edward 1545-1607
3125 *The Lowest Trees*
Seas have their source, and so have shallow
springs:
And love is love, in beggars and in kings ...
True hearts have ears and eyes, no tongues to
speak:
They hear and see, and sigh, and then they
break.

3126 *'In praise of a contented mind'*
Some have too much, yet still do crave;
I little have, and seek no more.
They are but poor, though much they have,
And I am rich with little store.
They poor, I rich; they beg, I give;
They lack, I leave; they pine, I live.

DYER John 1700-1758
3127 *Grongar Hill*
But transient is the smile of fate:
A little rule, a little sway,
A sunbeam in a winter's day,
Is all the proud and mighty have
Between the cradle and the grave.

DYLAN Bob 1941-
3128 *'All I Really Want To Do'*
I ain't lookin' to block you up,
Shock or knock or lock you up,
Analyze you, categorize you,

Finalize you or advertise you.

3129 *'It's Alright, Ma (I'm Only Bleeding)'*
Money doesn't talk, it swears.

3130 *'Blowin' in the wind'*
The answer is blowin' in the wind.

3131 *'A Hard Rain's A Gonna Fall'*
... It's a hard rain's a gonna fall.

3132
I'm just glad to be feeling better. I really thought
I'd be seeing Elvis soon.

3133 *'Mr Tambourine Man'*
Hey! Mr Tambourine man, play a song for me.

EAGLETON Professor Terry 1943-
3134
Philosophy, Wittgenstein considered, could say
something, but nothing that was really
important.

EASTWOOD Clint 1930-
3135 *in Sudden Impact*
"Go ahead. Make my day."

EBAN Abba 1915-
3136
History teaches us that men and nations behave
wisely once they have exhausted all other
alternatives.

EDDINGTON Sir Arthur 1882-1944
3137 *The Nature of the Physical World*
... if your theory is found to be against the
second law of thermodynamics I give you no
hope; there is nothing for it but to collapse in
deepest humiliation.

3138 *(attributed)*
Science is an edged tool, with which men play
like children, and cut their own fingers.

EDEN Sir Anthony 1897-1977
3139 *(on the Suez Crisis)*
We are in an armed conflict; that is the phrase I
have used. There has been no declaration of
war.

EDGEWORTH Maria 1768-1849
3140
Artifical manners vanish the moment the
natural passions are touched.

3141 *Leonora*
What a misfortune it is to be born a woman! ...
Why seek for knowledge, which can prove only
that our wretchedness is irremediable?

EDISON Thomas Alva 1847-1931
3142
Everything comes to him who hustles while he
waits.

3143
Genius is one per cent inspiration, ninety-nine per cent perspiration.

3144
I am long on ideas, but short on time. I expect to live only about a hundred years.

3145
Results! Why, man, I have gotten a lot of results. I know several thousand things that won't work.

EDMESTON James 1791-1867
3146
Lead us, Heavenly Father, lead us
O'er the world's tempestuous sea;

EDMONDS John Maxwell 1875-1958
3147
When you go home, tell them of us and say,
'For your tomorrows these gave their today.'

EDWARD VIII (Duke of Windsor) 1894-1972
3148 *(after abdication)*
At long last I am able to say a few words of my own ... you must believe me when I tell you that I have found it impossible to carry the heavy burden of responsibility and to discharge my duties as King as I would wish to do without the help and support of the woman I love.

3149
The thing that impresses me most about America is the way parents obey their children.

3150 *(speaking at derelict Iron and Steel Works)*
Something should be done to get them at work again.

EDWARDS Murray D.
3151
Men of genius are the worst possible models for men of talent.

EDWARDS Oliver 1711-1791
3152
For my part not, I consider supper as a turnpike through which one must pass, in order to get to bed.

3153
I have tried too in my time to be a philosopher; but, I don't know how, cheerfulness was always breaking in.

EDWARDS Richard 1523-1566
3154 *The Paradise of Dainty Devices*
The falling out of faithful friends, renewing is of love.

EDWARDS Robert C.
3155
Never exaggerate your faults; your friends will attend to that.

3156
Whisky drowns some troubles and floats a lot more.

EDWARDS Tryon
3157
Thoroughly to teach another is the best way to learn for yourself.

EGERTON Sarah 1670-1723
3158 *'The Emulation'*
We will our rights in learning's world maintain;
Wit's empire now shall know a female reign.

EHRLICH Paul R. 1932-
3159
The first rule of intelligent tinkering is to save all the parts.

EICHMANN Adolf 1906-1962
3160
Repentance is for little children.

EINSTEIN Albert 1879-1955
3161
All space is slightly curved.

3162
I can't believe that God plays dice with the universe.

3163
If you are out to describe the truth, leave elegance to the tailor.

3164
The environment is everything that isn't me.

3165
No amount of experimentation can ever prove me right; a single experiment can prove me wrong.

3166
God is subtle but he is not malicious.

3167
How do I work? I grope.

3168
A hundred times every day I remind myself that my inner and outer life depend on the labours of other men, living and dead, and that I must exert myself in order to give in the same measure as I have received.

3169
Nationalism is an infantile sickness. It is the measles of the human race.

3170
I never think of the future. It comes soon enough.

3171
Reading after a certain (time) diverts the mind too much from its creative pursuits. Any man

who reads too much and uses his own brain too little falls into lazy habits of thinking.

3172 *(of Relativity)*
I simply ignored axiom.

3173
Science is the attempt to make the chaotic diversity of our sense-experience correspond to a logically uniform system of thought.

3174 *Science, Philosophy and Religion*
Science without religion is lame, religion without science is blind.

3175
If A is a success in life, then A equals x plus y plus z. Work is x; y is play; and z is keeping your mouth shut.

3176
A successful man is he who receives a great deal from his fellow men, usually incomparably more than corresponds to his service to them. The value of a man, however, should be seen in what he gives and not in what he is able to receive.

3177
We should take care not to make the intellect our god; it has, of course, powerful muscles, but no personality.

3178
If my theory of relativity is proven correct, Germany will claim me as a German and France will declare that I am a citizen of the world. Should my theory prove untrue, France will say that I am a German and Germany will declare that I am a Jew.

3179
I think and think for months and years. Ninety-nine times, the conclusion is false. The hundredth time I am right.

3180
The unleashed power of the atom has changed everything save our modes of thinking and we thus drift toward unparalleled catastrophe.

3181
When you sit with a nice girl for two hours, you think it's only a minute. But when you sit on a hot stove for a minute, you think it's two hours. That's relativity.

EISELEY Loren 1907-1977
3182
I no longer cared about survival - I merely loved.

3183
From the solitude of the wood, (Man) has passed to the more dreadful solitude of the heart.

3184
When the human mind exists in the light of reason and no more than reason, we may say with absolute certainty that Man and all that made him will be in that instant gone.

EISENBERG Leon
3185
The university is the last remaining platform for national dissent.

EISENHOWER Dwight D. 1890-1969
3186
You have broader considerations that might follow what you might call the 'falling domino' principle.

3187
Every gun that is made, every warship launched, every rocket fired signifies, in the final sense, a theft from those who hunger and are not fed, those who are cold and are not clothed.

3188
An intellectual is a man who takes more words than necessary to tell more than he knows.

3189
I think that people want peace so much that one of these days governments had better get out of the way and let them have it.

3190
What counts is not necessarily the size of the dog in the fight - it's the size of the fight in the dog.

3191
When you appeal to force, there's one thing you must never do - lose.

ELBRIDGE Gerry
3192
A standing army is like a standing member: an excellent assurance of domestic tranquillity but a dangerous temptation to foreign adventure.

ELGAR Sir Edward 1857-1934
3193
There is music in the air.

ELIOT Charles W. 1834-1926
3194
All business proceeds on beliefs, on judgements of probabilities, and not on certainties.

ELIOT George 1819-1880
3195 *Adam Bede*
Deep, unspeakable suffering may well be called a baptism, a regeneration, the initiation into a new state.

3196 *Adam Bede*
We hand folks over to God's mercy, and show none ourselves.

3197
It's them that takes advantage that gets advantage i' this world.

3198
Animals are such agreeable friends - they ask no questions, they pass no criticisms.

3199
Blessed is the man who, having nothing to say, abstains from giving us wordy evidence of the fact.

3200 *Daniel Deronda*
Gossip is a sort of smoke that comes from the dirty tobacco-pipes of those who diffuse it: it proves nothing but the bad taste of the smoker.

3201 *Daniel Deronda*
A difference of taste in jokes is a great strain on the affections.

3202 *Daniel Deronda*
Friendships begin with liking or gratitude - roots that can be pulled up.

3203 *Felix Holt*
An election is coming. Universal peace is declared, and the foxes have a sincere interest in prolonging the lives of the poultry.

3204 *Felix Holt*
'Abroad', that large home of ruined reputations.

3205
You must either give people what they are used to, or what they don't understand.

3206
Men's men: be they gentle or simple, they're much of a muchness.

3207 *Middlemarch*
A woman dictates before marriage in order that she may have an appetite for submission afterwards.

3208 *Middlemarch*
Among all forms of mistake, prophecy is the most gratuitous.

3209 *Middlemarch*
Plain women he regarded as he did the other severe facts of life, to be faced with philosophy and investigated by science.

3210 *Middlemarch*
A woman, let her be as good as she may, has got to put up with the life her husband makes for her.

3211 *The Mill on the Floss*
Anger and jealousy can no more bear to lose sight of their objects than love.

3212 *The Mill on the Floss*
The dead level of provincial existence.

3213 *The Mill on the Floss*
The happiest women, like the happiest nations, have no history.

3214 *The Mill on the Floss*
I should like to know what is the proper function of women, if it is not to make reasons for husbands to stay at home, and still stronger reasons for bachelors to go out.

3215
Necessity does the work of courage.

3216
There is nothing will kill a man so soon as having nobody to find fault with but himself.

3217
To be right in great and memorable moments is perhaps the thing we should most desire for ourselves.

3218 *Scenes of Clerical Life*
In every parting there is an image of death.

3219 *Scenes of Clerical Life*
Errors look so very ugly in persons of small means - one feels they are taking quite a liberty in going astray; whereas people of fortune may naturally indulge in a few delinquencies.

3220
Speech may be barren; but it is ridiculous to suppose that silence is always brooding on a nestful of eggs.

3221
What makes life dreary is want of motive.

ELIOT T.S. 1888-1965
3222
All cases are unique and very similar to others.

3223 *Ash-Wednesday*
Teach us to care and not to care
Teach us to sit still.

3224
No one can become really educated without having pursued some study in which he took no interest. For it is part of education to interest ourselves in subjects for which we have no aptitude.

3225 *The Cocktail Party*
What is hell?
Hell is oneself,
Hell is alone, the other figures in it
Merely projections. There is nothing to escape from
And nothing to escape to. One is always alone.

3226
An editor should tell the author his writing is better than it is. Not a lot better, a little better.

3227
It is in fact a part of the function of education to help us to escape, not from our own time - for we are bound by that - but from the intellectual and emotional limitations of our time.

3228 *The Family Reunion*
Success is relative:
It is what we can make of the mess we have made of things.

3229
Half of the harm that is done in this world
Is due to people who want to feel important.
They don't mean to do harm - but the harm does not interest them.

3230
The historical sense involves a perception, not only of the pastness of the past, but of its presence.

3231 *'The Hollow Men'*
We are the hollow men ...

3232 *'The Hollow Men'*
Between the idea
And the reality
Between the motion
And the act
Falls the Shadow.

3233
No honest poet can ever feel quite sure of the permanent value of what he has written: he may have wasted his time and messed up his life for nothing.

3234
Human kind cannot bear very much reality.

3235 *'Journey of the Magi' (lines quoted from Andrewes 'Of the Nativity')*
A cold coming we had of it,
Just the worst time of the year
For a journey, and such a long journey:
The ways deep and the weather sharp,
The very dead of winter.

3236
In the last few years everything I'd done up to sixty or so has seemed very childish.

3237
You have now learned to see
That cats are much like you and me
And other people whom we find
Possessed of various types of mind.

3238 *'The Love Song of J. Alfred Prufrock'*
Let us go then, you and I,
When the evening is spread out against the sky
Like a patient etherized upon a table.

3239 *'The Love Song of J. Alfred Prufrock'*
I have measured out my life with coffee spoons.

3240 *Murder in the Cathedral*
Yet we have gone on living,
Living and partly living.

3241 *Murder in the Cathedral*
The last temptation is the greatest treason:
To do the right deed for the wrong reason.

3242 *Murder in the Cathedral*
Clean the air! clean the sky! wash the wind! take the stone from stone, take the skin from the arm, take the muscle from bone, and wash them.

3243 *Old Possum's Book of Practical Cats*
Macavity, Macavity, there's no one like Macavity,
There never was a Cat of such deceitfulness and suavity.
He always has an alibi, and one or two to spare:
At whatever time the deed took place -
MACAVITY WASN'T THERE!

3244
The overwhelming pressure of mediocrity, sluggish and indomitable as a glacier, will mitigate the most violent, and depress the most exalted revolution.

3245
A play should give you something to think about. When I see a play and understand it the first time, then I know it can't be much good.

3246
Poetry is a mug's game.

3247
The poet's mind is ... a receptacle for seizing and storing up numberless feelings, phrases, images, which remain there until all the particles which can unite to form a new compound are present together.

3248 *'Preludes'*
The winter evening settles down
With smell of steaks in passageways.
Six o'clock.
The burnt-out ends of smoky days.

3249 *Four Quartets 'Burnt Norton'*
Footfalls echo in the memory
Down the passage which we did not take
Towards the door we never opened ...

3250 *Four Quartets 'East Coker'*
In my beginning is my end.

3251 *Four Quartets 'Little Gidding'*
What we call the beginning is often the end
And to make an end is to make a beginning.

3252 *Four Quartets 'Little Gidding'*
So, while the light fails
On a winter's afternoon, in a secluded chapel
History is now and England.

3253 *The Rock*
Where is the wisdom we have lost in
knowledge?
Where is the knowledge we have lost in
information?

3254 *The Rock*
And the wind shall say: 'Here were decent
godless people:
Their only monument the asphalt road
And a thousand lost golf balls.'

3255 *The Sacred Wood*
Immature poets imitate; mature poets steal.

3256 *Selected Essays*
We know too much and are convinced of too
little.

3257 *Selected Essays*
Poets in our civilization, as it exists at present,
must be difficult.

3258
I will show you fear in a handful of dust.

3259
I suppose some editors are failed writers - but
so are most writers.

3260 *Sweeney Agonistes*
Birth, and copulation, and death.
That's all the facts when you come to brass
tacks:

3261 'The Hollow Men'
This is the way the world ends
Not with a bang but a whimper.

3262 *The Waste Land*
April is the cruellest month, breeding
Lilacs out of the dead land, mixing
Memory and desire, stirring
Dull roots with spring rain.
Winter kept us warm, covering
Earth in forgetful snow, feeding
A little life with dried tubers.

3263 *The Waste Land*
The typist home at teatime, clears her breakfast,
lights
Her stove, and lays out food in tins.

3264 *The Waste Land*
When lovely woman stoops to folly and
Paces about her room again, alone,
She smoothes her hair with automatic hand,
And puts a record on the gramophone.

3265 *The Waste Land*
To me ... [The Waste Land] was only the relief of
a personal and wholly insignificant grouse
against life; it is just a piece of rhythmical
grumbling.

3266
What is actual is actual only for one time.
And only for one place.

3267
When a great poet has lived certain things have
been done once for all, and cannot be achieved
again.

3268 'Whispers of Immortality'
Webster was much possessed by death
And saw the skull beneath the skin;
And breastless creatures underground
Leaned backward with a lipless grin.

3269 'Whispers of Immortality'
Grishkin is nice: her Russian eye
Is underlined for emphasis;
Uncorseted, her friendly bust
Gives promise of pneumatic bliss.

3270
The young feel tired at the end of an action;
The old at the beginning.

ELIZABETH I Queen 1533-1603
3271 *(attributed)*
I would not open windows into men's souls.

3272 *(to the dying Countess of Nottingham)*
God may pardon you, but I never can.

3273 *(to Edward de Vere)*
My Lord, I had forgot the fart.

3274 *The Golden Speech*
Though God hath raised me high, yet this I
count the glory of my crown: that I have reigned
with your loves.

3275
I have had good experience and trial of this
world. I know what it is to be a subject, what to
be a Sovereign, what to have good neighbours,
and sometimes meet evil-willers.

3276 *(to leaders of her Council)*
I will make you shorter by the head.

3277 *(of Mary Queen of Scots)*
The daughter of debate, that eke discord doth
sow.

3278
I will never be by violence constrained to do
anything.

3279
The queen of Scots is this day leichter of a fair
son, and I am but a barren stock.

3280 *(to troops at Tilbury on approach of
Armada)*
I know I have the body of a weak and feeble
woman, but I have the heart and stomach of a
king, and of a king of England too; and think
foul scorn that Parma or Spain, or any prince of

Europe, should dare to invade the borders of my realm.

3281 *(after Sir Walter Raleigh)*
If thy heart fails thee, climb not at all.

3282 *(to William Cecil on his death-bed)*
I do entreat heaven daily for your longer life, else will my people and myself stand in need of cordials too. My comfort hath been in my people's happiness and their happiness in thy discretion.

3283 *(to William Cecil, who suffered from gout)*
My lord, we make use of you, not for your bad legs, but for your good head.

ELIZABETH II Queen 1926-
3284
In the words of one of my more sympathetic correspondents, it has turned out to be an 'annus horribilis'.

3285 *(on her 25th Wedding Anniversary)*
I think everybody really will concede that on this, of all days, I should begin my speech with the words 'My husband and I'.

ELIZABETH, The Queen Mother 1900-
3286 *Letter to Edith Sitwell (after death of George VI)*
How small and selfish is sorrow. But it bangs one about until one is senseless.

3287 *(to a London policeman)*
I'm glad we've been bombed. It makes me feel I can look the East End in the face.

ELLERTON Alf
3288
Belgium put the kibosh on the Kaiser.

ELLERTON John 1826-1893
3289
The day Thou gavest, Lord, is ended,
The darkness falls at Thy behest.

ELLIOT Henry Rutherford
3290
It it's sanity you're after
There's no recipe like
Laughter.
Laugh it off.

ELLIOTT Ebenezer 1781-1849
3291 *'Epigram'*
What is a communist? One who hath yearnings
For equal division of unequal earnings.

ELLIOTT Jr. John
3292
Big ideas are so hard to recognize, so fragile, so easy to kill. Don't forget that, all of you who don't have them.

ELLIS George 1753-1815
3293 *'The Twelve Months'*
Snowy, Flowy, Blowy,
Showery, Flowery, Bowery,
Hoppy, Croppy, Droppy,
Breezy, Sneezy, Freezy.

ELLIS Havelock 1859-1939
3294
Imagination is a poor substitute for experience.

3295 *Impressions and Comments*
What we call 'progress' is the exchange of one nuisance for another nuisance.

3296
Life is livable because we know that wherever we go most of the people we meet will be restrained in their actions toward us by an almost instinctive network of taboos.

3297 *Little Essays of Love and Virtue*
All civilization has from time to time become a thin crust over a volcano of revolution.

3298
If men and women are to understand each other, to enter into each other's nature with mutual sympathy, and to become capable of genuine comradeship, the foundation must be laid in youth.

3299
The sun, moon and stars would have disappeared long ago had they been within the reach of predatory human hands.

ELSTOW Friar
3300 *(when threated with drowning by Henry VIII)*
With thanks to God we know the way to heaven, to be as ready by water as by land, and therefore we care not which way we go.

EMERSON Ralph Waldo 1803-1882
3301 *(attributed)*
If a man write a better book, preach a better sermon, or make a better mouse-trap than his neighbour, tho' he build his house in the woods, the world will make a beaten path to his door.

3302
Accept the place the divine providence has found for you, the society of your contemporaries, the connection of events.

3303
All the great speakers were bad speakers at first.

3304
All history is but the lengthened shadow of a great man.

3305
Can anything be so elegant as to have few wants, and to serve them one's self?

3306 *(of architecture)*
The flowering of geometry.

3307
We ascribe beauty to that which is simple; which has no superfluous parts; which exactly answers its ends.

3308
The beautiful rests on the foundations of the necessary.

3309
To believe your own thought, to believe that what is true for you in your private heart is true for all men - that is genius.

3310
There is always a best way of doing everything, if it be only to boil an egg. Manners are the happy ways of doing things.

3311
There is a certain satisfaction in coming down to the lowest ground of politics, for then we get rid of cant and hypocrisy.

3312
Character is that which can do without success.

3313
Cities force growth and make men talkative and entertaining, but they make them artificial.

3314 *'Concord Hymn'*
By the rude bridge that arched the flood,
Their flag to April's breeze unfurled,
Here once the embattled farmers stood,
And fired the shot heard round the world.

3315 *The Conduct of Life*
Make yourself necessary to someone.

3316 *The Conduct of Life*
Art is a jealous mistress.

3317 *The Conduct of Life*
The louder he talked of his honour, the faster we counted our spoons.

3318
There is a crack in everything God has made.

3319
The creation of a thousand forests is in one acorn.

3320
A cynic can chill and dishearten with a single word.

3321
The end of the human race will be that it will eventually die of civilization.

3322
I find the Englishman to be him of all men who stands firmest in his shoes.

3323 *Essays*
A friend is a person with whom I may be sincere.
Before him I may think aloud.

3324 *Essays*
The only reward of virtue is virtue; the only way to have a friend is to be one.

3325 *Essays*
There is properly no history; only biography.

3326 *Essays*
The faith that stands on authority is not faith.

3327 *Essays*
In skating over thin ice, our safety is in our speed.

3328 *Essays*
It is so bad, then, to be misunderstood? Pythagoras was misunderstood, and Socrates, and Jesus, and Luther, and Copernicus, and Galileo, and Newton, and every pure and wise spirit that ever took flesh. To be great is to be misunderstood.

3329 *Essays*
To fill the hour - that is happiness.

3330 *Essays*
The years teach much which the days never know.

3331 *Essays*
Men are conservatives when they are least vigorous, or when they are most luxurious. They are conservatives after dinner.

3332 *Essays*
All mankind love a lover.

3333 *Essays*
Every man is wanted, and no man is wanted much.

3334
Extremes meet, and there is no better example than the naughtiness of humility.

3335
The eyes indicate the antiquity of the soul.

3336 *Fortune of the Republic*
What is a weed? A plant whose virtues have not been discovered.

3337
A friend may well be reckoned to be a masterpiece of nature.

3338
God offers to every mind its choice between truth and repose. Take which you please; you can never have both.

3339
A good indignation brings out all one's powers.

3340
Good manners are made up of petty sacrifices.

3341
A great part of courage is the courage of having done the thing before.

3342
It makes a great difference in the force of a sentence whether a man be behind it or no.

3343
I hate the giving of the hand unless the whole man accompanies it.

3344
I hate quotations.

3345
I have heard with admiring submission the experience of the lady who declared that the sense of being well-dressed gives a feeling of inward tranquillity, which religion is powerless to bestow.

3346
Every hero becomes a bore at last.

3347
A hero is no braver than an ordinary man, but he is brave five minutes longer.

3348
We are as much informed of a writer's genius by what he selects as by what he originates.

3349
An institution is the lengthening shadow of one man.

3350 *Journal*
Old age brings along with its uglinesses the comfort that you will soon be out of it.

3351
Shall we judge a country by the majority, or by the minority? By the minority, surely.

3352
Life consists in what a man is thinking of all day.

3353
Every man is a borrower and a mimic; life is theatrical and literature a quotation.

3354
A man builds a fine house; and now he has a master, and a task for life; he is to furnish, watch, show it, and keep it in repair the rest of his life.

3355
Every man is a consumer and ought to be a producer.

3356
Every man is an impossibility until he is born.

3357
No man should travel until he has learned the language of the country he visits, otherwise he voluntarily makes himself a great baby - so helpless and ridiculous.

3358
Men are what their mothers made them.

3359
The merit claimed for the Anglican Church is that, if you let it alone, it will let you alone.

3360
Nature is reckless of the individual. When she has points to carry, she carries them.

3361
Some natures are too good to be spoiled by praise.

3362
The only gift is a portion of thyself.

3363
Outside, among your fellows, among strangers, you must preserve appearances, a hundred things you cannot do; but inside, the terrible freedom!

3364
The peace of the man who has foresworn the use of the bullet seems to me not quite peace, but a canting impotence.

3365
People only see what they are prepared to see.

3366
Perpetual modernness is the measure of merit in every work of art.

3367
A person seldom falls sick but the bystanders are animated with a faint hope that he will die.

3368
It has come to be practically a sort of rule in literature that a man, having once shown himself capable of original writing, is entitled thenceforth to steal from the writings of others at discretion.

3369
It is the privilege of any human work which is well done to invest the doer with a certain haughtiness. He can well afford not to conciliate, whose faithful work will answer for him.

3370 *Representative Men*
Is not marriage an open question, when it is alleged, from the beginning of the world, that such as are in the institution wish to get out; and such as are out wish to get in.

3371
The reward of a thing well done, is to have done it.

3372
Sanity is very rare; every man almost, and every woman, has a dash of madness.

3373
Self-command is the main elegance.

3374
No sensible person ever made an apology.

3375
If you shoot at a king you must kill him.

3376
The sky is the daily bread of the eyes.

3377
Speak what you think today in words as hard as cannon balls, and tomorrow speak what tomorrow thinks in hard words again, though it contradict everything you said today.

3378
Take egotism out, and you would castrate the benefactor.

3379
The things taught in schools are not an education but the means of an education.

3380
It is time to be old,
To take in sail.

3381
'Tis the good reader that makes the good book.

3382
Though we travel the world over to find the beautiful, we must carry it with us or we find it not.

3383
What is the city in which we sit here, but an aggregate of incongrous materials, which have obeyed the will of some man?

3384
Whatever limits us we call Fate.

3385
When we quarrel, how we wish we had been blameless.

3386
The whole of what we know is a system of compensations. Each suffering is rewarded; each sacrifice is made up; every debt is paid.

3387
In every work of genius we recognize our own rejected thoughts; they come back to us with a certain alienated majesty.

3388
The world is all gates, all opportunities, strings of tension waiting to be struck.

ENGELS Friedrich 1820-1895
3339 *Anti-Dühring*
The State is not 'abolished', it withers away.

EN-LAI Chou
3390
China has no income tax, no unemployed and not a single soldier outside its own territory.

EPHELIA
3391 *Female Poems*
And yet I love this false, this worthless man,
With all the passion that a woman can;
Dote on his imperfections, though I spy
Nothing to love; I love, and know not why.

EPICTETUS AD c.50-130
3392
All philosophy lies in two words, sustain and abstain.

3393
Here is the beginning of philosophy: a recognition of the conflicts between men, a search for their cause, a condemnation of mere opinion ... and the discovery of a standard of judgement.

3394
First learn the meaning of what you say, and then speak.

3395
Nature has given to men one tongue, but two ears, that we may hear from others twice as much as we speak.

3396
Nothing great is created suddenly, any more than a bunch of grapes or a fig. If you tell me that you desire a fig, I answer you that there must be time. Let it first blossom, then bear fruit, then ripen.

3397
There is only one way to happiness and that is to cease worrying about things which are beyond the power of our will.

3398
Practice yourself, for heaven's sake, in little things; and thence proceed to greater.

3399
If you would be a reader, read; if a writer, write.

EPICURUS c.310-270 BC
3400
The time when, most of all, you should withdraw into yourself is when you are forced to be in a crowd.

EPSTEIN Sir Jacob 1880-1959
3401 *(attributed)*
Why don't they stick to murder and leave art to us?

EPSTEIN Joseph
3402
There is no word equivalent to 'cuckold' for women.

ERASMUS c.1469-1536
3403 *Adages*
In the country of the blind the one-eyed man is king.

3404
He who shuns the millstone, shuns the meal.

ERICKSEN Sir John Eric
3405 *(in 1873)*
The abdomen, the chest, and the brain will forever be shut from the intrusion of the wise and humane surgeon.

ERICKSON Arthur 1924-
3406
Life is rich, always changing, always challenging, and we architects have the task of transmitting into wood, concrete, glass and steel, of transforming human aspirations into habitable and meaningful space.

ERIKSON Erik
3407
Do not mistake a child for his symptom.

3408
Genius as such can neither be explained nor treated away; only, at times, its delay and inhibition and its perversion to destructive or self-destructive ends.

3409
Healthy children will not fear life if their elders have integrity enough not to fear death.

ERSKINE John 1879-1951
3410
Temperance is the control of all the functions of our bodies. The man who refuses liquor, goes in for apple pie and develops a paunch, is no ethical leader for me.

ERTZ Susan 1894-1985
3411
He talked with more claret than clarity.

ESAR Evan
3412
Housework is what woman does that nobody notices unless she hasn't done it.

3413
The quizzical expression of the monkey at the zoo comes from his wondering whether he is his brother's keeper, or his keeper's brother.

ESCHENBACH Marie Ebner von 1830-1916
3414 *Aphorism*
We don't believe in rheumatism and true love until after the first attack.

ESSLIN Martin
3415
The dignity of man lies in his ability to face reality in all its meaninglessness.

ESTIENNE Henri 1531-1598
3416 *Les Prémices*
If youth knew; if age was able.

EUCLID c.300 BC
3417 *Elementa*
A line is length without breadth.

EURIPIDES c.485-406 BC
3418
We know the good, we apprehend it clearly. But we can't bring it to achievement.

3419
Happiness is brief
It will not stay.
God batters at its sails.

3420
I hate the philosopher who is not wise for himself.

3421
Man's most valuable trait
Is a judicious sense of what not to believe.

3422
Men are men, they needs must err.

3423
Money is the wise man's religion.

3424
There's nothing like the sight of an old enemy down on his luck.

3425
What we look for does not come to pass.
God finds a way for what none foresaw.

3426
The worst, the least curable hatred is that which has superseded deep love.

EUWER Anthony
3427
As a beauty I am not a star,
There are others more handsome by far,
But my face - I don't mind it
For I am behind it.
It's the people in front get the jar.

EVANS Edith 1888-1976
3428
I seem to have an awful lot of people inside me.

EVANS Very Rev Eric (Dean of St Pauls) 1928-3429
Deaneries and crown canonries are the last bastions of the eccentric.

EVERETT David 1769-1813
3430 *'Lines Written for a School Declamation'* *(aged 7)*
Large streams from little fountains flow,
Tall oaks from little acorns grow.

EWART Gavin 1916-1995
3431 *Love Song*
But the heart line on my hand
foretold you;
in your army of lovers
I am a private soldier.

EWER William Norman 1885-1976
3432 *Week-End Book*
How odd
Of God
To choose
The Jews.

EYRE Ivan
3433
When I look at a painting it isn't only the painting that I see but the thing that I am. If there is more in the painting than I am, then I won't see it.

EYRE Richard 1943-
3434
Nobody warns you that when your parents die, you have to be an adult because you are no longer anybody's child.

FADIMAN Clifton
3435
Cheese - milk's leap toward immortality.

3436
One newspaper a day ought to be enough for anyone who still prefers to retain a little mental balance.

3437
One's first book, kiss, home run is always the best.

3438
There are two kinds of writers - the great ones who can give you truths, and the lesser ones, who can only give you themselves.

3439
When you read a classic you do not see in the book more than you did before. You see more in *you* than there was before.

3440
When you travel, remember that a foreign country is not designed to make you comfortable. It is designed to make its own people comfortable.

FAGUET Émile 1847-1916
3441 *(of Voltaire's philosophy)*
A chaos of clear ideas.

FARJEON Eleanor 1881-1965
3442 *Children's Bells*
Morning has broken
Like the first morning,
Blackbird has spoken
Like the first bird.
Praise for the singing!
Praise for the morning!
Praise for them, springing
Fresh from the Lord!

3443
The events of childhood do not pass but repeat themselves like seasons of the year.

FARMER Edward c.1809-1876
3444 *'The Collier's Dying Child'*
I have no pain, dear mother, now;
But oh! I am so dry:
Just moisten poor Jim's lips once more;
And, mother, do not cry!

FAROUK (ex-King) 1920-1965
3445
The whole world is in revolt. Soon there will be only five Kings left - the King of England, the King of Spades, the King of Clubs, the King of Hearts and the King of Diamonds.

FARQUHAR George 1678-1707
3446 *The Beaux' Stratagem*
There is no scandal like rags, nor any crime so shameful as poverty.

3447 *The Beaux' Stratagem*
No woman can be a beauty without a fortune.

3448 *The Inconstant*
Crimes, like virtues, are their own rewards.

3449 *The Recruiting Officer*
Hanging and marriage, you know, go by Destiny.

FARRELL Warren
3450
When women hold off from marrying men, we call it independence. When men hold off from marrying women, we call it fear of commitment.

FAULKNER William 1897-1962
3451
An artist is a creature driven by demons. He doesn't know why they choose him and he's usually too busy to wonder why.

3452
I believe that man will not merely endure: he will prevail. He is immortal, not because he alone among creatures has an inexhaustible

voice, but because he has a soul, a spirit capable of compassion and sacrifice and endurance.

3453
Too much happens ... Man performs, engenders so much more than he can or should have to bear. That's how he finds that he can bear anything.

3454
A man shouldn't fool with booze until he's fifty; then he's a damn fool if he doesn't.

3455
The Swiss are not a people so much as a neat, clean, quite solvent business.

FAWCETT Chris
3456
A building is a string of events belonging together.

FAWKES Guy 1570-1606
3457
A desperate disease requires a dangerous remedy.

FEATHER William
3458
A man of fifty looks as old as Santa Claus to a girl of twenty.

3459
That they may have a little peace, even the best dogs are compelled to snarl occasionally.

3460
The petty economies of the rich are just as amazing as the silly extravagances of the poor.

3461
The philosophy behind much advertising is based on the old observation that every man is really two men - the man he is and the man he wants to be.

3462
If you're naturally kind, you attract a lot of people you don't like.

FEMINA Jerry Della
3463
Advertising is the most fun you can have with your clothes on.

FENTON James 1949-
3464 *German Requiem*
It is not what they built. It is what they knocked down.
It is not the houses. It is the spaces between the houses.
It is not the streets that exist. It is the streets that no longer exist.

FERBER Edna 1887-1968
3465
Life cannot defeat a writer who is in love with writing - for life itself is a writer's love until death.

3466
Being an old maid is like death by drowning, a really delightful sensation after you cease to struggle.

FERDINAND I Emperor 1503-1564
3467 *(motto)*
Let justice be done, though the world perish.

FERGUSON David
3468
Show me the man and I'll show you the law.

FERRE Nels F.S.
3469
A man who exeriences no genuine satisfaction in life does not want peace. People court war to escape meaninglessness and boredom, to be relieved of fear and frustration.

FICHTE Immanuel Hermann von
3470
If we cannot live so as to be happy, let us at least live so as to deserve it.

FICKE Arthur Davison
3471
A man must learn to forgive himself.

FIELDING Henry 1707-1754
3472 *Amelia*
It hath been often said, that it is not death, but dying, which is terrible.

3473
His designs were strictly honourable, as the phrase is: that is, to rob a lady of her fortune by way of marriage.

3474
There is no greater folly than to seek to correct the natural infirmities of those we love.

3475 *Joseph Andrews*
To whom nothing is given, of him can nothing be required.

3476 *Joseph Andrews*
Public schools are the nurseries of all vice and immorality.

3477 *Love in Several Masques*
Love and scandal are the best sweeteners of tea.

3478 *Don Quixote in England*
... a-hunting we will go.

3479
It requires a penetrating eye to discern a fool through the disguise of gaiety and good breeding.

3480
Thwackum was for doing justice, and leaving
mercy to heaven.

3481 *Tom Jones*
That monstrous animal, a husband and wife.

3482 *Tom Jones*
What is commonly called love, namely the
desire of satisfying a voracious appetite with a
certain quantity of delicate white human flesh.

FIELDS Dorothy 1905-1974
3483 *'On the Sunny Side of the Street'*
Grab your coat, and get your hat,
Leave your worries on the doorstep,
Just direct your feet
To the sunny side of the street.

FIELDS W.C. 1880-1946
3484 *You Can't Cheat an Honest Man*
Some weasel took the cork out of my lunch.

3485
We frequently hear of people dying from too
much drinking. That this happens is a matter of
record. But the blame almost always is placed
on whisky. Why this should be I never could
understand. You can die from drinking too
much of anything - coffee, water, milk, soft
drinks and all such stuff as that. And so long as
the presence of death lurks with anyone who
goes through the simple act of swallowing, I will
make mine whisky.

3486
Hell, I never vote for anybody. I always vote
against.

3487
Last week I went to Philadelphia, but it was
closed.

3488
Never give a sucker an even break.

3489
I always keep a supply of stimulant handy in
case I see a snake - which I also keep handy.

3490 *(when caught reading the Bible)*
I'm looking for loopholes.

3491
It was a woman who drove me to drink - and,
you know, I never even thanked her.

3492
Women are like elephants. They are interesting
to look at, but I wouldn't like to own one.

3493 *in You're Telling Me*
"It's a funny old world - a man's lucky if he gets
out of it alive."

FINLEY John
3494
Maturity is the capacity to endure uncertainty.

FIRBANK Ronald 1886-1926
3495 *The Flower Beneath the Foot*
I remember the average curate at home as
something between a eunuch and a snigger.

3496 *Vainglory*
All millionaires love a baked apple.

3497 *Valmouth*
'I know of no joy,' she airily began, 'greater than
a cool white dress after the sweetness of
confession.'

FISCHER Louis
3498
Biography is history seen through the prism of a
person.

FISHER H.A.L. 1856-1940
3499 *A History of Europe*
Purity of race does not exist. Europe is a
continent of energetic mongrels.

FISHER Irving 1857-1947
3500 *(in 1929)*
Stocks have reached what looks like a
permanently high plateau.

FISHER John Arbuthnot 1841-1920
3501 *Memories*
The best scale for an experiment is 12 inches to
a foot.

3502
Never contradict
Never explain
Never apologize.

FISHER Martin H.
3503
Knowledge is a process of piling up facts;
wisdom lies in their simplification.

3504
The practice of medicine is a thinker's art, the
practice of surgery a plumber's.

3505
The specialist is a man who fears the other
subjects.

FISHER Marve
3506 *'An Old-Fashioned Girl'*
I want an old-fashioned house
With an old-fashioned fence
And an old-fashioned millionaire.

FITZGERALD Edward 1809-1883
3507 *The Rubáiyát of Omar Khayyám*
Ah, take the cash in hand and waive the rest;
Oh, the brave music of a distant drum!

3508 *The Rubáiyát of Omar Khayyám*
Ah, make the most of what we yet may spend,
Before we too into the dust descend;
Dust into dust, and under dust, to lie,
Sans wine, sans song, sans singer, and - sans
End!

3509 *The Rubáiyát of Omar Khayyám*
The moving finger writes; and, having writ,
Moves on: nor all thy piety nor wit
Shall lure it back to cancel half a line,
Nor all thy tears wash out a word of it.

3510 *The Rubáiyát of Omar Khayyám*
And that inverted bowl we call The Sky,
Whereunder crawling cooped we live and die.

3511 *The Rubáiyát of Omar Khayyám*
Indeed the idols I have loved so long
Have done my credit in this world much wrong:
Have drowned my glory in a shallow cup
And sold my reputation for a song.

3512
Taste is the feminine of genius.

FITZGERALD F. Scott 1896-1940
3513 *All the Sad Young Men*
Let me tell you about the very rich. They are
different from you and me.

3514
America is a willingness of the heart.

3515
The beautiful and damned.

3516 *The Crack-Up*
Show me a hero and I will write you a tragedy.

3517
No grand idea was ever born in a conference,
but a lot of foolish ideas have died there.

3518 *The Great Gatsby*
In his blue gardens, men and girls came and
went like moths among the whisperings and the
champagne and the stars.

3519 *The Great Gatsby*
Her voice is full of money.

3520 *The Great Gatsby*
They were careless people, Tom and Daisy -
they smashed up things and creatures and then
retreated back into their money or their vast
carelessness, or whatever it was that kept them
together, and let other people clean up the mess
they had made.

3521
Grown up, and that is a terribly hard thing to
do. It is much easier to skip it and go from one
childhood to another.

3522 *'Handle with Care'*
In a real dark night of the soul it is always three
o'clock in the morning.

3523 *The Last Tycoon*
There are no second acts in American lives.

3524 *The Last Tycoon*
One girl can be pretty - but a dozen are only a
chorus.

FITZGERALD Zelda 1900-1948
3525
Nobody has ever measured, even poets, how
much a heart can hold.

FITZHENRY R.I.
3526
The adversary system is a kind of warfare in
mufti.

3527
Timing, degree and conviction are the three
wise men in this life.

3528
The Englishman loves to roll his tongue around
the word, 'extraordinary'. It so pleases him that
he is reluctant to finish the sound which goes
on into harmonics and overtones. The
American publisher is likewise inclined.

3529
Soon after a hard decision something inevitably
occurs to cast doubt. Holding steady against
that doubt usually proves that decision.

3530
Uncertainty and mystery are energies of life.
Don't let them scare you unduly, for they keep
boredom at bay and spark creativity.

3531
The voice is a second signature.

FITZWATER Marlin
3532 *(on inexperience at the White House)*
A few more fat, old bald men wouldn't hurt the
place.

FLANDERS Michael and SWANN Donald 1922-
1975 and 1923-1994
3533
Have some madeira, M'dear.

FLATMAN Thomas 1637-1688
3534 *The Defiance*
There's an experienced rebel, Time,
And in his squadrons Poverty;
There's Age that brings along with him
A terrible artillery:
And if against all these thou keep'st thy crown,
Th'usurper Death will make thee lay it down.

FLAUBERT Gustave 1821-1880
3535 *(letter to Ernest Feydeau)*
Books are made not like children but like pyramids ... and are just as useless! ... Jackals piss at their foot and the bourgeois climb up on them.

3536 *(letter to Louis Bouilhet)*
Things seem to be going at a dizzy rate. We are dancing not on a volcano, but on the rotten seat of a latrine.

3537
Be regular and orderly in your life like a bourgeois, so that you may be violent and original in your work.

FLECKER James Elroy 1884-1915
3538 *The Dying Patriot*
Noon strikes on England, noon on Oxford town, Beauty she was statue cold - there's blood upon her gown.

3539 *The Golden Journey to Samarkand*
When the great markets by the sea shut fast
All that calm Sunday that goes on and on:
When even lovers find their peace at last,
And earth is but a star, that once had shone.

3540 *The Golden Journey to Samarkand*
For lust of knowing what should not be known,
We take the Golden Road to Samarkand.

3541 *To a Poet a Thousand Years Hence*
O friend unseen, unborn, unknown,
Student of our sweet English tongue,
Read out my words at night, alone;
I was a poet, I was young.

FLEMING Alexander D. 1881-1955
3542
A good gulp of hot whisky at bedtime - it's not very scientific, but it helps.

FLEMING Ian 1908-1964
3543 *Dr. No*
A medium Vodka dry Martini - with a slice of lemon peel. Shaken and not stirred.

FLETCHER John 1579-1625
3544 *The Bloody Brother*
Best while you have it use your breath,
There is no drinking after death.

3545 *The Bloody Brother*
And he that will go to bed sober,
Falls with the leaf still in October.

3546 *The Island Princess*
Let's meet, and either do, or die.

3547 *The Knight of Malta*
Of all the paths lead to a woman's love
Pity's the straightest.

FLETCHER Phineas 1582-1650
3548 *Sicelides*
Love is like linen often changed, the sweeter.

3549 *Sicelides*
The coward's weapon, poison.

FLORIAN Jean-Pierre Claris de 1755-1794
3550 *Célestine*
Love's pleasure lasts but a moment; love's sorrow lasts all through life.

FLORIO John c.1553-1625
3551 *Second Frutes*
England is the paradise of women, the purgatory of men, and the hell of horses.

FOCH Ferdinand 1851-1929
3552
Airplanes are interesting toys but of no military value.

3553 *(message sent during Battle of the Marne)*
My centre is giving way, my right is retreating, situation excellent, I am attacking.

3554 *(at the signing of the Treaty of Versailles)*
This is not a peace treaty, it is an armistice for twenty years.

FOLEY J. 1906-1970
3555
Old soldiers never die,
They simply fade away.

FONDA Henry 1905-1982
3556
The best actors do not let the wheels show.

FOOT Michael 1913-
3557 *(of Norman Tebbit)*
It is not necessary that every time he rises he should give his famous imitation of a semi-house-trained polecat.

3558
Think of it! A second Chamber selected by the Whips. A seraglio of eunuchs.

FOOTE Samuel 1720-1777
3559 *(of a dull law lord)*
He is not only dull in himself, but the cause of dullness in others.

3560 *Letter to the Lord Chamberlain*
Between the muse and the magistrate there is a natural confederacy; what the last cannot punish the first often corrects.

FOOTE Shelby
3561
Longevity conquers scandal every time.

FORBES Malcolm S. 1919-1990
3562
Ability will never catch up with the demand for it.

FORD Gerald 1909-

3563
If the Government is big enough to give you everything you want, it is big enough to take away everything you have.

3564
I've had a lot of experience with people smarter than I am.

3565
When a man is asked to make a speech, the first thing he has to decide is what to say.

FORD Henry 1863-1947

3566
Anyone who stops learning is old, whether at twenty or eighty. Anyone who keeps learning stays young. The greatest thing in life is to keep your mind young.

3567
Capital punishment is as fundamentally wrong as a cure for crime as charity is wrong as a cure for poverty.

3568 *(on choice of colour for the Model T Ford)*
Any colour - so long as it's black.

3569
It is not the employer who pays wages - he only handles the money. It is the product that pays wages.

3570
Before everything else, getting ready is the secret of success.

3571
History is more or less bunk.

FORD Lena Guilbert 1870-1916

3572 *Till the Boys Come Home!*
Keep the Home-fires burning,
While your hearts are yearning,
Though your lads are far away
They dream of Home.
There's a silver lining
Through the dark cloud shining;
Turn the dark cloud inside out,
Till the boys come Home.

FORGY Howell 1908-1983

3573 *(at Pearl Harbor)*
Praise the Lord and pass the ammunition.

FORSTER E.M. 1879-1970

3574 *Abinger Harvest*
(Public schoolboys) go forth into a world that is not entirely composed of public-school men or even of Anglo-Saxons.

3575 *Abinger Harvest*
It is not that the Englishman can't feel - it is that he is afraid to feel.

3576
Chicago - a facade of skyscrapers facing a lake and behind the facade every type of dubiousness.

3577
In the creative state a man is taken out of himself. He lets down as it were a bucket into his subconscious, and draws up something which is normally beyond his reach. He mixes this thing with his normal experiences and out of the mixture he makes a work of art.

3578
An efficiency-regime cannot be run without a few heroes stuck about it to carry off the dullness - much as plums have to be put into a bad pudding to make it palatable.

3579
How can I know what I think till I see what I say?

3580 *Howards End*
To trust people is a luxury in which only the wealthy can indulge; the poor cannot afford it.

3581 *Howards End*
Only connect! ... Only connect the prose and the passion, and both will be exalted, and human love will be seen at its height.

3582 *Howards End*
Death destroys a man: the idea of death saves him.

3583
Our life on earth is, and ought to be, material and carnal. But we have not yet learned to manage our materialism and carnality properly; they are still entangled with the desire for ownership.

3584 *The Longest Journey*
There is much good luck in the world, but it is luck. We are none of us safe.

3585 *A Passage to India*
The so-called white races are really pinko-grey.

3586 *A Passage to India*
Where there is officialism every human relationship suffers.

3587
It is pleasant to be transferred from an office where one is afraid of a sergeant-major into an office where one can intimidate generals, and perhaps this is why history is so attractive to the more timid among us.

3588 *Two cheers for Democracy 'What I Believe'*
If I had to choose between betraying my country and betraying my friend, I hope I should have the guts to betray my country.

3589 *Two cheers for Democracy 'What I Believe'*
So Two cheers for Democracy: one because it admits variety and two because it permits criticism.

FORSTER W.E. 1878-1969
3590
What is the use of lying when truth, well distributed, serves the same purpose?

FOSDICK Harry Emerson 1878-1969
3591
Democracy is based upon the conviction that there are extraordinary possibilities in ordinary people.

3592
God is not a cosmic bellboy for whom we can press a button to get things done.

3593
Liberty is always dangerous - but it is the safest thing we have.

3594
Nothing in human life, least of all in religion, is ever right until it is beautiful.

3595
Watch what people are cynical about, and one can often discover what they lack.

FOSDICK Raymond B. 1883-1969
3596
It is always the minorities that hold the key of progress; it is always through those who are unafraid to be different that advance comes to human society.

FOSTER Stephen Collins 1826-1864
3597 *'Jeanie with the Light Brown Hair'*
I dream of Jeanie with the light brown hair,
Floating, like a vapour, on the soft summer air.

3598 *'The Old Folks at Home'*
Way down upon the Swanee River,
Far, far, away,
There's where my heart is turning ever;
There's where the old folks stay.

FOWLER Gene
3599
Writing is easy: all you do is sit staring at the blank sheet of paper until the drops of blood form on your forehead.

FOWLES John Robert 1926-
3600 *The Aristos*
Passion destroys passion; we want what puts an end to wanting what we want.

3601
Men love war because it allows them to look serious; because it is the only thing that stops women laughing at them.

FRANCE Anatole 1844-1924
3602
All changes, even the most longed for, have their melancholy, for what we leave behind us is a part of ourselves; we must die to one life before we can enter into another.

3603
Chance is the pseudonym of God when he did not want to sign.

3604
I do not know any reading more easy, more fascinating, more delightful than a catalogue.

3605
If fifty million people say a foolish thing, it is still a foolish thing.

3606
The good critic is he who narrates the adventures of his soul among masterpieces.

3607
It is human nature to think wisely and to act in an absurd fashion.

3608
The law, in its majestic equality, forbids the rich as well as the poor to sleep under bridges, to beg in the streets, and to steal bread.

3609
Never lend books - nobody ever returns them; the only books I have in my library are those which people have lent me.

3610
I prefer the errors of enthusiasm to the indifference of wisdom.

FRANCIS Brendan
3611
The big difference between sex for money and sex for free is that sex for money usually costs a lot less.

FRANCIS of Sales, Saint 1567-1622
3612
While I am busy with little things, I am not required to do greater things.

3613
Do not wish to be anything but what you are, and try to be that perfectly.

3614
Nothing is more like a wise man than a fool who holds his tongue.

3615
Have patience with all things, but chiefly have patience with yourself. Do not lose courage in considering your own imperfections, but instantly set about remedying them - every day begin the task anew.

3616
If someone below us does not treat us politely, we don't like anything he does. If, instead, we take a liking to someone, we forgive him anything he does.

FRANCIS Xavier, Saint 1506-1552
3617
Give me the children until they are seven and anyone may have them afterwards.

FRANK Lawrence K.
3618
Don't quote me; that's what you heard, not what I said.

FRANKENBERG Lloyd
3619
The apparent serenity of the past is an oil spread by time.

FRANKFURTER Felix 1882-1965
3620
The Court's authority - possessed of neither the purse nor the sword - ultimately rests on substantial public confidence in its moral sanctions.

3621
It is a fair summary of history to say that the safeguards of liberty have frequently been forged in cases involving not very nice people.

3622
Fragile as reason is and limited as law is as the institutionalized medium of reason, that's all we have standing between us and the tyranny of mere will and the cruelty of unbridled, undisciplined feeling.

3623
It simply is not true that war never settles anything.

FRANKLIN Benjamin 1706-1790
3624 *Advice to a Young Tradesman*
Remember that time is money.

3625
A child thinks twenty shillings and twenty years can scarce ever be spent.

3626
There is a difference between imitating a good man and counterfeiting him.

3627
God heals, and the doctor takes the fees.

3628
The greatest monarch on the proudest throne is obliged to sit upon his own arse.

3629 *(letter to Georgiana Shipley)*
Here Skugg
Lies snug

As a bug
In as rug.

3630 *(letter to Jean Baptiste Le Roy)*
In this world nothing can be said to be certain, except death and taxes.

3631 *(letter to Josiah Quincy)*
There never was a good war, or a bad peace.

3632
If a man empties his purse into his head, no one can take it from him.

3633
Ne'er take a wife till though hast a house (and a fire) to put her in.

3634
Were the offer made true, I would engage to run again, from beginning to end, the same career of life. All I would ask should be the privilege of an author, to correct, in a second edition, certain errors of the first.

3635 *Poor Richard's Almanac*
Necessity never made a good bargain.

3636 *Poor Richard's Almanac*
He that lives upon hope will die fasting.

3637 *Poor Richard's Almanac*
Where there's marriage without love, there will be love without marriage.

3638
Praise to the undeserving is severe satire.

3639 *(at the Signing of Declaration of Independence)*
We must indeed all hang together, or, most assuredly, we shall all hang separately.

3640
There are three faithful friends: an old wife, and old dog, and ready money.

3641
If you want a thing done, go - if not, send.

3642
Who is wise? He that learns from everyone.
Who is powerful? He that governs his passions.
Who is rich? He that is content.
Who is that? Nobody.

3643
Nothing is more fatal to health than an overcare of it.

FRANKS Baron 1905-
3644
A secret in the Oxford sense: you may tell it to only one person at a time.

FRAYN Michael 1933-
3645
I feel bad that I don't feel worse.

FRAZER Sir James 1854-1941
3646 *The Golden Bough*
The awe and dread with which the untutored savage contemplates his mother-in-law are amongst the most familiar facts of anthropology.

FREDERICK The Great 1712-1786
3647
I love an opposition that has convictions.

FREUD Anna 1895-1982
3648
Creative minds have always been known to survive any kind of bad training.

FREUD Clement 1924-
3649
If you resolve to give up smoking, drinking and loving, you don't actually live longer; it just seems longer.

FREUD Martin 1895-1982
3650
I didn't know the full facts of life until I was 17. My father [Sigmund Freud] never talked about his work.

FREUD Sigmund 1856-1939
3651
Being entirely honest with oneself is a good exercise.

3652
From error to error one discovers the entire truth.

3653
Hatred of Judaism is at bottom hatred of Christianity.

3654
A hero is a man who stands up manfully against his father and in the end victoriously overcomes him.

3655 *The Interpretation of Dreams*
The interpretation of dreams is the royal road to a knowledge of the unconscious activities of the mind.

3656 *(letter to Marie Bonaparte)*
The great question that has never been answered and which I have not yet been able to answer, despite my thirty years of research into the feminine soul, is 'What does a woman want?'

3657
Life as we find it is too hard for us; it entails too much pain, too many disappointments, impossible tasks. We cannot do without palliative remedies.

3658
Love and work are the cornerstones of our humanness.

3659
Man should not strive to eliminate his complexes, but to get in accord with them; they are legitimately what directs his contact in the world.

3660
A man who has been the indisputable favourite of his mother keeps for life the feeling of a conqueror.

3661
The only unnatural sexual behaviour is none at all.

3662
Toward the person who has died we adopt a special attitude: something like admiration for someone who has accomplished a very difficult task.

3663
It is unavoidable that if we learn more about a great man's life, we shall also hear of occasions on which he has done no better than we, and has in fact come nearer to us as a human being.

3664
When a man is freed of religion, he has a better chance to live a normal and wholesome life.

FRIEDENBERG Edgar Z.
3665
Part of the American dream is to live long and die young.

3666
The 'teenager' seems to have replaced the Communist as the appropriate target for public controversy and foreboding.

FRIEDLANDER Rabbi Albert
3667
Every generation harvests the dragon seeds of hatred sown by the previous generation.

FRIEDMAN Milton 1912-
3668
Inflation is one form of taxation that can be imposed without legislation.

3669
What kind of society isn't structured on greed? The problem of social organization is how to set up an arrangement under which greed will do the least harm; capitalism is that kind of a system.

FRIEDRICH Otto
3670
Madness is part of all of us, all the time, and it comes and goes, waxes and wanes.

FRIENDLY Fred

3671

Today's reporter is forced to become an educator more concerned with explaining the news than with being first on the scene.

FRISCH Max 1911-1991

3672

Technology - the knack of so arranging the world that we don't have to experience it.

FROMM Erich 1900-1980

3673 *The Art of Loving*

Love is the only sane and satisfactory answer to the problem of human existence.

3674

Giving is the highest expression of potency.

3675

Integrity simply means a willingness not to violate one's identity.

3676

The mother-child relationship is paradoxical and, in a sense, tragic. It requires the most intense love on the mother's side, yet this very love must help the child grow away from the mother and to become fully independent.

3677

Only the person who has faith in himself is able to be faithful to others.

3678

I think if you ask people what their concept of heaven is, they would say, if they are honest, that it is a big department store, with new things every week - all the money to buy them, and maybe a little more than the neighbours.

FROST David 1939-

3679

Television is an invention that permits you to be entertained in your living room by people you wouldn't have in your home.

FROST Robert 1874 1963

3680

All thought is a feat of association; having what's in front of you bring up something in your mind that you almost didn't know you knew.

3681

Americans are like a rich father who wishes he knew how to give his son the hardships that made him rich.

3682

Belief is better than anything else, and it is best when rapt - above paying its respects to anybody's doubt whatsoever.

3683

The best things and best people rise out of their separateness; I'm against a homogenized society because I want the cream to rise.

3684

At bottom the world isn't a joke. We only joke about it to avoid an issue with someone, to let someone know that we know he's there with his questions; to disarm him by seeming to have heard and done justice to his side of the standing argument.

3685 *'Cluster of Faith'*

Forgive, O Lord, my little jokes on Thee
And I'll forgive Thy great big one on me.

3686 *'The Death of the Hired Man'*

Home is the place where, when you have to go there,
They have to take you in.

3687

Don't be agnostic - be something.

3688

You don't have to deserve your mother's love. You have to deserve your father's. He's more particular.

3689

Don't ever take a fence down until you know why it was put up.

3690

Education is the ability to listen to almost anything without losing your temper or your self-confidence.

3691 *'Fire and Ice'*

Some say the world will end in fire,
Some say in ice.
From what I've tasted of desire
I hold with those who favour fire.
But if it had to perish twice,
I think I know enough of hate
To say that for destruction ice
Is also great
And would suffice.

3692

Happiness makes up in height for what it lacks in length.

3693 *'The Hardship of Accounting'*

Never ask of money spent
Where the spender thinks it went.
Nobody was ever meant
To remember or invent
What he did with every cent.

3694

Humour is the most engaging cowardice. With it myself I have been able to hold some of my enemy in play far out of gunshot.

3695
An idea is a feat of association, and the height of it is a good metaphor.

3696
A jury consists of twelve persons chosen to decide who has the better lawyer.

3697
A Liberal is a man too broadminded to take his own side in a quarrel.

3698
There may be little or much beyond the grave, But the strong are saying nothing until they see.

3699 *'Mending Wall'*
Good fences make good neighbours.

3700
The only way round is through.

3701
A poem begins with a lump in the throat; a homesickness or a lovesickness. It is a reaching-out toward expression; an effort to find fulfilment. A complete poem is one where an emotion has found its thought and the thought has found words.

3702
Poetry should be common in experience but uncommon in books.

3703
Poetry is a way of taking life by the throat.

3704 *'Precaution'*
I never dared be radical when young
For fear it would make me conservative when old.

3705
To be social is to be forgiving.

3706
A successful lawsuit is the one worn by a policeman.

3707
There's nothing I'm afraid of like scared people.

3708
In three words I can sum up everything I've learned about life. It goes on.

3709
Writing free verse is like playing tennis with the net down.

3710
You've got to be brave and you've got to be bold. Brave enough to take your chance on your own discrimination - what's right and what's wrong, what's good and what's bad.

3711
You've got to love what's lovable, and hate what's hateable. It takes brains to see the difference.

FROUDE James A. 1818-1894
3712
You cannot dream yourself into a character; you must hammer and forge yourself one.

FRY Christopher 1907-
3713
The dark is light enough.

3714
Who, apart
From ourselves, can see any difference between
Our victories and our defeats?

FRYE Northrop 1912-1991
3715
Beauty and truth may be attributes of good writing, but if the writer deliberately aims at truth, he is likely to find that what he has hit is the didactic.

3716
The bible should be taught so early and so thoroughly that it sinks straight to the bottom of the mind where everything that comes along can settle on it.

3717
Historically, a Canadian is an American who rejects the Revolution.

3718
The human landscape of the New World shows a conquest of nature by an intelligence that does not love it.

3719
There is only one way to degrade mankind permanently and that is to destroy language.

3720
We must reject that most dismal and fatuous notion that education is a preparation for life.

3721
Separatism is a very healthy movement within culture. It's a disastrous movement within politics and economics.

3722
The simplest questions are the hardest to answer.

3723
We are being swallowed up by the popular culture of the United States, but then the Americans are being swallowed up by it too. It's just as much a threat to American culture as it is to ours.

3724
The most technologically efficient machine that man has ever invented is the book.

3725
War appeals to young men because it is fundamentally auto-eroticism.

3726
Writing: I certainly do rewrite my central myth in every book, and would never read or trust any writer who did not also do so.

FUCIK Julius
3727
To be a man will continue to demand a heroic heart as long as mankind is not quite human.

FULFORD Robert 1923-
3728
My generation of Canadians grew up believing that, if we were very good or very smart, or both, we would some day graduate from Canada.

FULLER Buckminster 1895-1983
3729
Don't fight forces; use them.

3730 *Operating Manual for Spaceship Earth*
Now there is one outstandingly important fact regarding Spaceship Earth, and that is that no instruction book came with it.

3731
Pollution is nothing but resources we're not harvesting.

3732
Either war is obsolete or men are.

FULLER Margaret 1810-1850
3733
Would that ... a sense of the true aim of life might elevate the tone of politics and trade till public and private honour become identical.

FULLER Thomas 1608-1661
3734
If an ass goes travelling, he'll not come back a horse.

3735
That which is bitter to endure may be sweet to remember.

3736
Cheat me in the price but not in the goods.

3737
We could be cowards, if we had courage enough.

3738
The Devil himself is good when he is pleased.

3739
Don't let your will roar when your power only whispers.

3740
Even doubtful accusations leave a stain behind them.

3741
He that flings dirt at another dirtieth himself most.

3742
A fox should not be on the jury at a goose's trial.

3743
Good is not good, where better is expected.

3744
The great end of life is not knowledge, but action.

3745
Great and good are seldom the same man.

3746
He that has a great nose thinks everybody is speaking of it.

3747
He is idle that might be better employed.

3748
Light, God's eldest daughter, is a principal beauty in a building.

3749
The number of malefactors authorizes not the crime.

3750
Old foxes want no tutors.

3751
Pride, perceiving humility honourable, often borrows her cloak.

3752
Pride had rather go out of the way than go behind.

3753
He that resolves to deal with none but honest men, must leave off dealing.

3754
Riches enlarge, rather than satisfy appetites.

3755
The scalded cat fears even cold water.

3756
Seeing's believing, but feeling's the truth.

3757
Today is yesterday's pupil.

3758
Trust thyself only, and another shall not betray thee.

3759
What a day may bring, a day may take away.

GABIROL Solomon Ibn c.1020-1070
3760
The space in a needle's eye is sufficient for two friends, but the whole world is scarcely big enough to hold two enemies.

3761
What is the test of good manners? Being able to bear patiently with bad ones.

GABLE Clark 1901-1960
3762 *in Gone With the Wind*
"Frankly, my dear, I don't **give** a damn."

GABOR Zsa Zsa 1919-
3763 *(attributed)*
Never despise what it says in the women's magazines. It may not be subtle, but neither are men.

3764 *(asked which of the Gabor women was the oldest)*
She'll never admit it, but I believe it is Mama.

3765
Husbands are like fires. They go out when unattended.

3766
I'm an excellent housekeeper. Everytime I get a divorce, I keep the house.

3767
Macho does not prove mucho.

3768
A man is incomplete until he has married. Then he's finished.

3769
I never hated a man enough to give him his diamonds back.

3770
I know nothing about sex, because I was always married.

GABOURY Étienne
3771
Architecture is space structured to serve man and to move him.

GADDIS William 1922-
3772
What's an artist, but the dregs of his work - the human shambles that follows it around?

GAISFORD Thomas 1779-1855
3773 *Christmas Day Sermon*
Nor can I do better, in conclusion, than impress upon you the study of Greek literature, which not only elevates above the vulgar herd, but leads not infrequently to positions of considerable emolument.

GAITSKELL Hugh 1906-1963
3774 *(at Labour Party Conference)*
There are some of us ... who will fight and fight and fight again to save the Party we love.

GALBRAITH J.K. 1908-
3775 *The Affluent Society*
It is a far, far better thing to have a firm anchor in nonsense than to put out on the troubled seas of thought.

3776 *The Affluent Society*
The greater the wealth, the thicker will be the dirt.

3777
In all modern depressions, recessions, or growth-correction, as variously they are called, we never miss the goods that are not produced. We miss only the opportunities for the labour - for the jobs - that are not provided.

3778
The conspicuously wealthy turn up urging the character-building value of privation for the poor.

3779
More die in the United States of too much food than of too little.

3780
In economics, the majority is always wrong.

3781
One of the greatest pieces of economic wisdom is to know what you do not know.

3782
Humour is richly rewarding to the person who employs it. It has some value in gaining and holding attention. But it has no persuasive value at all.

3783
No intel'igence system can predict what a government will do if it doesn't know itself.

3784
Meetings are indispensable when you don't want to do anything.

3785
Few people at the beginning of the nineteenth century needed an adman to tell them what they wanted.

3786
People of privilege will always risk their complete destruction rather than surrender any material part of their advantage.

3787
Technology means the systematic application of scientific or other organized knowledge to practical tasks.

3788
The more underdeveloped the country, the more overdeveloped the women.

3789
Washington is a place where men praise courage and act on elaborate personal cost-benefit calculations.

GALEN c AD 130-201
3790
Employment is nature's physician, and is essential to human happiness.

GALLANT Mavis 1922-
3791
There are a great many opinions in this world, and a good half of them are professed by people who have never been in trouble.

GALLICO Paul 1897-1976
3792
No one can be as calculatedly rude as the British, which amazes Americans, who do not understand studied insult and can only offer abuse as a substitute.

GALLUP George 1901-1984
3793
I could prove God statistically.

GALSWORTHY John 1867-1933
3794
A man of action forced into a state of thought is unhappy until he can get out of it.

3795
One's eyes are what one is, one's mouth what one becomes.

3796
The value of a sentiment is the amount of sacrifice you are prepared to make for it.

GANDHI Indira 1917-1984
3797
I suppose leadership at one time meant muscles; but today it means getting along with people.

GANDHI Mahatma 1869-1948
3798
I am not built for academic writings. Action is my domain.

3799
I consider myself a Hindu, Christian, Moslem, Jew, Buddhist, and Confucian.

3800
There are limits to self-indulgence, none to self-restraint.

3801
To a man with an empty stomach food is god.

3802
Monotony is the law of nature. Look at the monotonous manner in which the sun rises. The monotony of necessary occupations is exhilarating and life-giving.

3803
Non-violence is the first article of my faith. It is also the last article of my creed.

3804 *Non-Violence in Peace and War*
What difference does it make to the dead, the orphans and the homeless, whether the mad destruction is wrought under the name of totalitarianism or the holy name of liberty or democracy?

3805 *Non-Violence in Peace and War*
The moment the slave resolves that he will no longer be a slave, his fetters fall. He frees himself and shows the way to others. Freedom and slavery are mental states.

3806
It is possible for a single individual to defy the whole might of an unjust empire to save his honour, his religion, his soul and lay the foundation for that empire's fall or its regeneration.

GARBETT Archbishop C. 1875-1955
3807
Any fool can criticize, and many of them do.

GARCIA Jerry d.1995
3808
Truth is something you stumble into when you think you're going some place else.

GARDNER Ed 1901-1963
3809 *Duffy's Tavern*
Opera is when a guy gets stabbed in the back and, instead of bleeding, he sings.

GARDNER Herbert
3810
Once you get people laughing, they're listening and you can tell them almost anything.

GARDNER Dr Howard
3811
It isn't necessary to be a bastard to be a genius, but a disregard for others does seem necessary.

GARDNER John W. 1912-
3812
Art gropes, it stalks like a hunter lost in the woods, listening to itself and to everything around it, unsure of itself, waiting to pounce.

3813
If one defines the term 'dropout' to mean a person who has given up serious effort to meet his responsibilities, then every business office, government agency, golf club and university faculty would yield its quota.

3814
History never looks like history when you are living through it. It always looks confusing and messy, and it always feels uncomfortable.

3815
The ultimate goal of the educational system is to shift to the individual the burden of pursuing his education.

GARIBALDI Giuseppe 1807-1882
3816
Bacchus has drowned more men than Neptune.

3817
I can offer you neither honours nor wages; I offer you hunger, thirst, forced marches, battles and death. Anyone who loves his country, follow me.

GARLAND Judy 1922-1969
3818
If I'm such a legend, then why am I so lonely? Let me tell you, legends are all very well if you've got somebody around who loves you.

GARNER John Nance 1868-1967
3819
The vice-presidency isn't worth a pitcher of warm piss.

GARRICK David 1717-1779
3820 *'Heart of Oak'*
Heart of oak are our ships,
Heart of oak are our men:
We always are ready;
Steady, boys, steady;
We'll fight and we'll conquer again and again.

GARRISON William Lloyd 1805-1879
3821 *The Liberator*
I am in earnest - I will not equivocate - I will not excuse - I will not retreat a single inch - and I will be heard!

3822 *Massachusetts Anti-Slavery Society Resolution*
The compact which exists between the North and the South is 'a covenant with death and an agreement with hell'.

GARY Romain 1914-1990
3823
Humour is an affirmation of dignity, a declaration of man's superiority to all that befalls him.

GASCOIGNE George c.1534-1577
3824 *'Gascoigne's Good Morrow'*
The carrion crow, that loathsome beast,
Which cries against the rain,
Both for her hue and for the rest,
The Devil resembleth plain:
And as with guns we kill the crow,
For spoiling our relief,
The Devil so must we overthrow,
With gunshot of belief.

GASKELL Elizabeth 1810-1865
3825 *Cranford*
A man ... is *so* in the way in the house!

3826 *Cranford*
I'll not listen to reason ... Reason always means what someone else has got to say.

3827 *Sylvia's Lovers*
That kind of patriotism which consists in hating all other nations.

GASSET José Ortega y 1883-1955
3828
All life is the struggle, the effort to be itself. The difficulties which I meet with in order to realize my existence are precisely what awaken and mobilize my activities, my capacities.

3829
I am I plus my circumstances.

3830
Today violence is the rhetoric of the period.

3831
What makes a nation great is not primarily its great men, but the stature of its innumerable mediocre ones.

GATES Bill 1955-
3832 *(of computer memory - in 1981)*
640K ought to be enough for anybody.

GATEWOOD W. Boyd
3833
Very few people go to the doctor when they have a cold, they go to the theatre instead.

GAUGUIN Paul 1848-1903
3834
Art is either plagiarist or revolutionist.

GAVARNI Paul 1801-1866
3835
Les enfants terribles.
The little terrors.

GAY John 1685-1732
3836 *The Beggar's Opera*
How, like a moth, the simple maid
Still plays about the flame!

3837 *The Beggar's Opera*
Our Polly is a sad slut! nor heeds what we have
taught her.
I wonder any man alive will ever rear a
daughter!

3838 *The Beggar's Opera*
Do you think your mother and I should have
lived comfortably so long together, if ever we
had been married?

3839 *The Beggar's Opera*
The comfortable estate of widowhood, is the
only hope that keeps up a wife's spirits.

3840 *The Beggar's Opera*
If with me you'd fondly stray.
Over the hills and far away.

3841 *The Beggar's Opera*
Fill ev'ry glass, for wine inspires us,
And fires us
With courage, love and joy.
Women and wine should life employ.
Is there ought else on earth desirous?

3842 *The Beggar's Opera*
I must have women. There is nothing unbends
the mind like them.

3843 *The Beggar's Opera*
To cheat a man is nothing; but the woman must
have fine parts indeed who cheats a woman!

3844 *The Beggar's Opera*
I am ready, my dear Lucy, to give you
satisfaction - if you think there is any in
marriage?

3845 *The Beggar's Opera*
In one respect indeed, our employment may be
reckoned dishonest, because, like great
Statesmen, we encourage those who betray
their friends.

3846 *The Beggar's Opera*
How happy could I be with either,
Were t'other dear charmer away!

3847 *The Captives*
She who has never loved, has never lived.

3848 *Dione*
Behold the victim of Parthenia's pride!
He saw, he sighed, he loved, was scorned and
died.

3849 *Dione*
A woman's friendship ever ends in love.

3850 *'My Own Epitaph'*
Life is a jest; and all things show it.
I thought so once; but now I know it.

3851 *Fables 'The Dog and the Fox'*
I know you lawyers can, with ease,
Twist words and meanings as you please;

That language, by your skill made pliant,
Will bend to favour ev'ry client.

3852 *Fables (introduction)*
Whence is thy learning? Hath thy toil
O'er books consumed the midnight oil?

3853 *Fables 'The Man, the Cat, the Dog and Fly'*
Studious of elegance and ease,
Myself alone I seek to please.

3854 *Fables 'The Mastiffs'*
Those who in quarrels interpose,
Must often wipe a bloody nose.

3855 *Fables 'The Shepherd's Dog and the Wolf'*
An open foe may prove a curse,
But a pretended friend is worse.

3856 *Fables 'The Squire and his Cur'*
That politician tops his part,
Who readily can lie with art.

3857 *Fables 'The Vulture, the Sparrow,... Birds'*
Give me, kind heaven, a private station,
A mind serene for contemplation.

3858 *'A Letter to a Lady'*
Praising all alike, is praising none.

3859
We only part to meet again.

3860 *'Polly'*
Whether we can afford it or no, we must have
superfluities.

3861 *'Polly'*
No, sir, tho' I was born and bred in England, I
can dare to be poor, which is the only thing
now-a-days men are ashamed of.

3862 *'Polly'*
An inconstant woman, tho' she has no chance
to be very happy, can never be very unhappy.

3863 *'Sweet William's Farewell to Black-Eyed
Susan'*
All in the Downs the fleet was moored,
The streamers waving in the wind,
When black-eyed Susan came aboard.

3864 *'The Toilette'*
A miss for pleasure, and a wife for breed.

3865
Who friendship with a knave hath made,
Is judged a partner in the trade.

GAY Noel 1898-1954
3866 *'Leaning on a Lamp-Post'*
I'm leaning on a lamp-post at the corner of the
street,
In case a certain little lady comes by.

GAYLEN Willard
3867
Shame and guilt are noble emotions essential in

the maintenance of civilized society, and vital for the development of some of the most refined and elegant qualities of human potential - generosity, service, self-sacrifice, unselfishness and duty.

GEAYE Henry
3868
Motives and purposes are in the brain and heart of man. Consequences are in the world of fact.

GEDDES Sir Auckland
3869
So many come to the sickroom thinking of themselves as men of science fighting disease and not as healers with a little knowledge helping nature to get a sick man well.

GEDDES Sir Eric 1875-1937
3870
The Germans, if this Government is returned, are going to pay every penny; they are going to be squeezed as a lemon is squeezed - until the pips squeak.

GELMAN Daniel C.
3871
Where secrecy reigns, carelessness and ignorance delight to hide - skill loves the light.

GENEEN Harold 1910-
3872
I don't believe in just ordering people to do things. You have to sort of grab an oar and row with them.

GEORGE Chief Dan
3873
When the white man came, we had the land and they had the bibles. Now they have the land and we have the bibles.

GEORGE Daniel
3874 *The Perpetual Pessimist*
O Freedom, what liberties are taken in thy name!

GEORGE Henry 1839-1897
3875
Man is the only animal whose desires increase as they are fed; the only animal that is never satisfied.

3876
The state, it cannot too often be repeated, does nothing, and can give nothing, which it does not take from somebody.

GEORGE I King 1660-1727
3877
I hate all Boets and Bainters.

GEORGE II King 1683-1760
3878 *(of General Wolfe)*
Mad, is he? Then I hope he will *bite* some of my other generals.

3879
We are come for your good, for all your goods.

GEORGE III King 1738-1820
3880
Born and educated in this country, I glory in the name of Briton.

3881 *(to Fanny Burney)*
Was there ever such stuff as great part of Shakespeare? Only one must not say so! But what think you? - what? - Is there not sad stuff? what? - what?

GEORGE IV King 1762-1830
3882 *(on first meeting his wife to be)*
Harris, I am not well; pray get me a glass of brandy.

GEORGE V King 1865-1936
3883 *(of his son)*
After I am dead, the boy will ruin himself in twelve months.

3884 *(to Anthony Eden)*
I said to your predecessor: 'You know what they're all saying, no more coals to Newcastle, no more Hoares to Paris.' The fellow didn't even laugh.

3885
Bugger Bognor.

3886
I have many times asked myself whether there can be more potent advocates of peace upon earth through the years to come than this massed multitude of silent witnesses to the desolation of war.

3887 *(to his private secretary on the morning he died)*
How's the Empire?

3888
I venture to allude to the impression which seemed generally to prevail among their brethren across the seas, that the Old Country must wake up if she intends to maintain her old position of pre-eminence in her Colonial trade against foreign competitors.

GEORGE VI King 1895-1952
3889
Abroad is bloody.

3890 *(to Queen Mary)*
Personally I feel happier now that we have no allies to be polite to and to pamper.

GEORGE W.L. 1882-1926
3891
The true America is the Middle West, and Columbus discovered nothing at all except

another Europe.

GERSHWIN Ira 1896-1983
3892 *Damsel in Distress*
A foggy day in London Town
Had me low and had me down.
I viewed the morning with alarm,
The British Museum had lost its charm.
How long, I wondered, could this thing last?
But the age of miracles hadn't passed,
For, suddenly, I saw you there
And through foggy London town the sun was
shining everywhere.

3893 *Damsel in Distress*
Holding hands at midnight
'Neath a starry sky,
Nice work if you can get it,
And you can get it if you try.

3894 *Shall We Dance?*
The way you wear your hat,
The way you sip your tea,
The mem'ry of all that -
No, no! They can't take that away from me!

3895 *Funny Face*
You've made my life so glamorous,
You can't blame me for feeling amorous.

3896 *Girl Crazy*
Embrace me, my sweet embraceable you!
Embrace me, you irreplaceable you!
Just one look at you, my heart grew tipsy in me;
You and you alone bring out the gypsy in me!

3897 *The Goldwyn Follies*
In time the Rockies may crumble,
Gibraltar may tumble,
They're only made of clay,
But our love is here to stay.

GETTY Paul 1892-1976
3898
I have no complex about wealth. I have worked
hard for my money, producing things people
need. I believe that the able industrial leader
who creates wealth and employment is more
worthy of historical notice than politicians or
soldiers.

3899
Going to work for a large company is like
getting on a train. Are you going sixty miles an
hour or is the train going sixty miles an hour
and you're just sitting still?

GIACOSA Giuseppe and ILLICA Luigi 1847-
1906 and 1857-1919
3900 *La Bohème*
Che gelida manina.
Your tiny hand is frozen.

GIBBON Edward 1737-1794
3901 *The Decline and Fall of the Roman Empire*
The various modes of worship, which prevailed
in the Roman world, were all considered by the
people as equally true: by the philosopher, as
equally false; and by the magistrate, as equally
useful. And thus toleration produced not only
mutual indulgence, but even religious concord.

3902 *The Decline and Fall of the Roman Empire*
The principles of a free constitution are
irrecoverably lost, when the legislative power is
nominated by the executive.

3903 *The Decline and Fall of the Roman Empire*
History ... is, indeed, little more than the
register of the crimes, follies, and misfortunes of
mankind.

3904 *The Decline and Fall of the Roman Empire*
In every age and country, the wiser, or at least
the stronger, of the two sexes, has usurped the
powers of the state, and confined the other to
the cares and pleasures of domestic life.

3905 *The Decline and Fall of the Roman Empire*
Corruption, the most infallible symptom of
constitutional liberty.

3906 *The Decline and Fall of the Roman Empire*
In every deed of mischief he had a heart to
resolve, a head to contrive, and a hand to
execute.

3907 *The Decline and Fall of the Roman Empire*
Our sympathy is cold to the relation of distant
misery.

3908 *The Decline and Fall of the Roman Empire*
Persuasion is the resource of the feeble; and the
feeble can seldom persuade.

3909 *The Decline and Fall of the Roman Empire*
All that is human must retrograde if it does not
advance.

3910 *Memoirs of My Life*
The satirist may laugh, the philosopher may
preach, but Reason herself will respect the
prejudices and habits which have been
consecrated by the experience of mankind.

3911 *Memoirs of My Life*
To the University of Oxford I acknowledge no
obligation; and she will as cheerfully renounce
me for a son, as I am willing to disclaim her for
a mother. I spent fourteen months at Magdalen
College: they proved the fourteen months the
most idle and unprofitable of my whole life.

3912 *Memoirs of My Life*
Dr - well remembered that he had a salary to
receive, and only forgot that he had a duty to
perform.

3913 *Memoirs of My Life*
It was here that I suspended my religious inquiries (aged 17).

3914 *Memoirs of My Life*
I saw and loved.

3915 *Memoirs of My Life*
I sighed as a lover, I obeyed as a son.

3916 *Memoirs of My Life*
Crowds without company, and dissipation without pleasure.

3917 *Memoirs of My Life*
My English text is chaste, and all licentious passages are left in the obscurity of a learned language.

3918 *Memoirs of My Life*
The abbreviation of time, and the failure of hope, will always tinge with a browner shade the evening of life.

3919 *Memoirs of My Life (of his own army service)*
The captain of the Hampshire grenadiers ... has not been useless to the historian of the Roman empire.

3920 *Memoirs of My Life (of the dons at Oxford)*
Their dull and deep potations excused the brisk intemperance of youth.

3921
I was never less alone than when by myself.

3922
Many a sober Christian would rather admit that a wafer is God than that God is a cruel and capricious tyrant.

3923
The winds and waves are always on the side of the ablest navigators.

GIBBON John Murray
3924
I always suspect an artist who is successful before he is dead.

GIBBONS Orlando 1583-1625
3925
The silver swan, who, living had no note, When death approached unlocked her silent throat.

GIBBONS Stella 1902-1989
3926 *Cold Comfort Farm*
Every year, in the fulness o' summer, when the sukebind hangs heavy from the wains ... 'tes the same. And when the spring comes her hour is upon her again. 'Tes the hand of Nature and we women cannot escape it.

3927 *Cold Comfort Farm*
Something nasty in the woodshed.

3928 *Cold Comfort Farm*
By god, D.H. Lawrence was right when he had said there must be a dumb, dark, dull, bitter belly-tension between a man and a woman, and how else could this be achieved save in the long monotony of marriage?

GIBLIN II Frank J
3929
Be yourself. Who else is better qualified?

GIBRAN Kahlil 1883-1931
3930
No man can reveal to you aught but that which already lies half asleep in the dawning of your knowledge.

3931 *The New Frontier*
Are you a politician who says to himself: 'I will use my country for my own benefit'? ... Or are you a devoted patriot, who whispers in the ear of his inner self: 'I love to serve my country as a faithful servant.'?

3932 *The Prophet 'On Children'*
Your children are not your children.
They are the sons and daughters of Life's longing for itself.
They came through you but not from you
And though they are with you yet they belong not to you.
You may give them your love but not your thoughts,
For they have their own thoughts.
You may house their bodies but not their souls,
For their souls dwell in the house of tomorrow, which you cannot visit, not even in your dreams.
You may strive to be like them, but seek not to make them like you,
For life goes not backward nor tarries with yesterday.
You are the bows from which your children as living arrows are sent forth.

3933 *The Prophet 'On Marriage'*
But let there be spaces in your togetherness.
And let the winds of the heavens dance between you.

3934 *The Prophet 'On Work'*
Work is love made visible. And if you cannot work with love but only with distaste, it is better that you should leave your work and sit at the gate of the temple and take alms of those who work with joy.

3935 *Sand and Foam*
An exaggeration is a truth that has lost its temper.

3936
The significance of a man is not what he attains but rather in what he longs to attain.

GIBSON Wilfrid 1878-1962

3937 *All Being Well*
I read your letter through and through,
And dreamt of all we'd say and do,
Till in my heart the thought of you
Rang like a bell.

3938 *'Lament'*
But we, how shall we turn to little things
And listen to the birds and winds and streams
Made holy by their dreams,
Nor feel the heart-break in the heart of things?

GIDE André 1869-1951

3939
One doesn't discover new lands without
consenting to lose sight of the shore for a very
long time.

3940 *Journal*
The great secret of Stendhal, his great
shrewdness, consisted in writing *at once ...*
thought charged with emotion.

3941
Our judgements about things vary according to
the time left us to live - that we think is left us to
live.

3942 *Les Caves du Vatican*
I believe ... that profit is not always what
motivates man; that there are disinterested
actions ... By *disinterested* I mean: gratuitous.
And that evil acts, what people call evil, can be
as gratuitous as good acts.

3943 *Les Faux Monnayeurs*
The whole effect of Christianity was to transfer
the drama onto the moral plane.

3944
If one could recover the uncompromising spirit
of one's youth, one's greatest indignation would
be for what one has become.

3945
A work of art is an exaggeration.

3946
The world will be saved by one or two people.

GIESE W.

3947
Contemporary literature can be classified under
three headings: the neurotic, the erotic and the
tommy-rotic.

GIFFORD Frank

3948
Pro football is like nuclear warfare. There are
no winners, only survivors.

GILBERT Sir Humphrey c.1537-1583

3949 *Third and Last Volume of the Voyages*
We are as near to heaven by sea as by land!

GILBERT W.S. 1836-1911

3950
Darwinian Man, though well-behaved,
At best is only a monkey shaved!

3951 *The Gondoliers*
That celebrated,
Cultivated,
Underrated
Nobleman,
The Duke of Plaza Toro!

3952 *The Gondoliers*
Of that there is no manner of doubt -
No probable, possible shadow of doubt -
No possible doubt whatever.

3953 *The Gondoliers*
All shall equal be,
The Earl, the Marquis, and the Dook,
The Groom, the Butler, and the Cook,
The Aristocrat who banks with Coutts,
The Aristocrat who cleans the boots.

3954 *The Gondoliers*
But the privilege and pleasure
That we treasure beyond measure
Is to run on little errands for the Ministers of
State.

3955 *The Gondoliers*
Take a pair of sparkling eyes,
Hidden, ever and anon,
In a merciful eclipse.

3956 *The Gondoliers*
Ambassadors cropped up like hay,
Prime Ministers and such as they
Grew like asparagus in May,
And dukes were three a penny.

3957 *The Gondoliers*
When every one is somebodee,
Then no one's anybody.

3958 *HMS Pinafore*
I'm called Little Buttercup - dear Little
Buttercup,
Though I could never tell why.

3959 *HMS Pinafore*
What, never?
No, never!
What, *never*?
Hardly ever!

3960 *HMS Pinafore*
Though 'Bother it' I may
Occasionally say,
I never use a big, big D -

3961 *HMS Pinafore*
And so do his sisters, and his cousins and his
aunts!
His sisters and his cousins,

Whom he reckons up by dozens,
And his aunts!

3962 *HMS Pinafore*
When I was a lad I served a term
As office boy to an Attorney's firm.
I cleaned the windows and I swept the floor,
And I polished up the handle of the big front door.
I polished up that handle so carefullee
That now I am the Ruler of the Queen's Navee!

3963 *HMS Pinafore*
I always voted at my party's call,
And I never thought of thinking for myself at all.

3964 *HMS Pinafore*
Stick close to your desks and never go to sea,
And you all may be Rulers of the Queen's Navee!

3965 *HMS Pinafore*
Things are seldom what they seem,
Skim milk masquerades as cream.

3966 *HMS Pinafore*
He is an Englishman!
For he himself has said it,
And it's greatly to his credit,
That he is an Englishman!

3967 *HMS Pinafore*
For he might have been a Roosian,
A French, or Turk, or Proosian,
Or perhaps Ital-ian!
But in spite of all temptations
To belong to other nations,
He remains an Englishman!

3968 *HMS Pinafore*
The other, upper crust,
A regular patrician.

3969
As innocent as a new-laid egg.

3970 *Iolanthe*
Bow, bow, ye lower middle classes!
Bow, bow, ye tradesmen, bow, ye masses.

3971 *Iolanthe*
The Law is the true embodiment
Of everything that's excellent.
It has no kind of fault or flaw,
And I, my Lords, embody the Law.

3972 *Iolanthe*
Spurn not the nobly born
With love affected,
Nor treat with virtuous scorn
The well-connected.

3973 *Iolanthe*
Hearts just as pure and fair
May beat in Belgrave Square
As in the lowly air
Of Seven Dials.

3974 *Iolanthe*
I often think it's comical
How Nature always does contrive
That every boy and every gal,
That's born into the world alive,
Is either a little Liberal,
Or else a little Conservative!

3975 *Iolanthe*
When in that House MPs divide,
If they've a brain and cerebellum too,
They have to leave that brain outside,
And vote just as their leaders tell 'em to.

3976 *Iolanthe*
The prospect of a lot
Of dull MPs in close proximity,
All thinking for themselves is what
No man can face with equanimity.

3977 *Iolanthe*
The House of Peers, throughout the war,
Did nothing in particular,
And did it very well.

3978 *Iolanthe*
When you're lying awake with a dismal
headache, and repose is taboo'd by anxiety,
I conceive you may use any language you
choose to indulge in, without impropriety.

3979 *Iolanthe*
For you dream you are crossing the Channel,
and tossing about in a steamer from Harwich -
Which is something between a large bathing
machine and a very small second class carriage.

3980 *Iolanthe*
And bound on that journey you find your
attorney (who started that morning from
Devon);
He's a bit undersized, and you don't feel
surprised when he tells you he's only eleven.

3981 *Iolanthe*
In your shirt and your socks (the black silk with
gold clocks), crossing Salisbury Plain on a
bicycle.

3982 *Iolanthe*
The shares are a penny, and ever so many are
taken by Rothschild and Baring,
And just as a few are allotted to you, you awake
with a shudder despairing.

3983 *The Mikado*
A wandering minstrel I -
A thing of shreds and patches.
Of ballads, songs and snatches,
And dreamy lullaby!

3984 *The Mikado*
I can trace my ancestry back to a protoplasmal
primordial atomic globule. Consequently, my
family pride is something in-conceivable. I

can't help it. I was born sneering.

3985 *The Mikado*
As some day it may happen that a victim must
be found,
I've got a little list - I've got a little list
Of society offenders who might well be under
ground
And who never would be missed - who never
would be missed!

3986 *The Mikado*
The idiot who praises, with enthusiastic tone,
All centuries but this, and every country but his
own.

3987 *The Mikado*
Three little maids from school are we,
Pert as a schoolgirl well can be,
Filled to the brim with girlish glee.

3988 *The Mikado*
Life is a joke that's just begun.

3989 *The Mikado*
Three little maids who, all unwary,
Come from a ladies' seminary.

3990 *The Mikado*
Modified rapture!

3991 *The Mikado*
Awaiting the sensation of a short, sharp shock,
From a cheap and chippy chopper on a big
black block.

3992 *The Mikado*
Here's a how-de-doo!

3993 *The Mikado*
Here's a state of things!

3994 *The Mikado*
Matrimonial devotion
Doesn't seem to suit her notion.

3995 *The Mikado*
My object all sublime
I shall achieve in time -
To let the punishment fit the crime -
The punishment fit the crime.

3996 *The Mikado*
The music-hall singer attends a series
Of masses and fugues and 'ops'
By Bach, interwoven
With Spohr and Beethoven,
At classical Monday Pops.

3997 *The Mikado*
The billiard sharp whom any one catches,
His doom's extremely hard -
He's made to dwell -
In a dungeon cell
On a spot that's always barred.
And there he plays extravagant matches

In fitless finger-stalls
On a cloth untrue
With a twisted cue
And elliptical billiard balls.

3998 *The Mikado*
I have a left shoulder-blade that is a miracle of
loveliness. People come miles to see it. My
right elbow has a fascination that few can resist.

3999 *The Mikado*
Something lingering, with boiling oil in it, I
fancy.

4000 *The Mikado*
Merely corroborative detail, intended to give
artistic verisimiltude to an otherwise bald and
unconvincing narrative.

4001 *The Mikado*
The flowers that bloom in the spring,
Tra la,
Have nothing to do with the case.

4002 *The Mikado*
I've got to take under my wing,
Tra la,
A most unattractive old thing,
Tra la,
With a caricature of a face.

4003 *The Mikado*
'Is it weakness of intellect, birdie?' I cried,
'Or a rather tough worm in your little inside?'
With a shake of his poor little head he replied,
'Oh, Willow, titwillow, titwillow!'

4004 *The Mikado*
He sobbed and he sighed, and a gurgle he gave,
Then he plunged himself into the billowy wave,
And an echo arose from the suicide's grave
'Oh willow, titwillow, titwillow!'

4005 *The Mikado*
There's a fascination frantic
In a ruin that's romantic;
Do you think you are sufficiently decayed?

4006 *Patience*
If you're anxious for to shine in the high
aesthetic line as a man of culture rare.

4007 *Patience*
You must lie upon the daisies and discourse in
novel phrases of your complicated state of
mind,
The meaning doesn't matter if it's only idle
chatter of a transcendental kind.

4008 *Patience*
Then a sentimental passion of a vegetable
fashion must excite your languid spleen,
An attachment à la Plato for a bashful young
potato, or a not too French French bean!
Though the Philistines may jostle, you will rank

as an apostle in the high aesthetic band,
If you walk down Piccadilly with a poppy or a
lily in your medieval hand.

4009 *Patience*
While this magnetic,
Peripatetic
Lover, he lived to learn,
By no endeavour
Can magnet ever
Attract a Silver Churn!

4010 *Patience*
'High diddle diddle'
Will rank as an idyll,
If I pronounce it chaste!

4011 *Patience*
Francesca di Rimini, miminy, piminy,
Je-ne-sais-quoi young man!

4012 *Patience*
A greenery-yallery, Grosvenor Gallery,
Foot-in-the-grave young man!

4013 *The Pirates of Penzance*
It is, it is a glorious thing
To be a Pirate King.

4014 *The Pirates of Penzance*
The question is, had he not been
A thing of beauty,
Would she be swayed by quite as keen
A sense of duty?

4015 *The Pirates of Penzance*
I'm very good at integral and differential
calculus,
I know the scientific names of beings
animalculous;
In short, in matters vegetable, animal, and
mineral,
I am the very model of a modern Major-
General.

4016 *The Pirates of Penzance*
About binomial theorem I'm teeming with a lot
of news,
With many cheerful facts about the square on
the hypotenuse.

4017 *The Pirates of Penzance*
When constabulary duty's to be done,
A policeman's lot is not a happy one.

4018 *The Pirates of Penzance*
They are no members of the common throng;
They are all noblemen who have gone wrong!

4019 *The Pirates of Penzance*
No Englishman unmoved that statement hears,
Because, with all our faults, we love our House
of Peers.

4020 *Princess Ida*
To everybody's prejudice I know a thing or two;
I can tell a woman's age in half a minute - and I
do!

4021 *Princess Ida*
Man is Nature's sole mistake!

4022 *Ruddigore*
You must stir it and stump it,
And blow your own trumpet,
Or trust me, you haven't a chance.

4023 *Ruddigore*
He combines the manners of a Marquis with
the morals of a Methodist.

4024 *Ruddigore*
If a man can't forge his own will, whose will can
he forge?

4025 *Ruddigore*
Some word that teems with hidden meaning -
like Basingstoke.

4026 *Ruddigore*
This particularly rapid, unintelligible patter
Isn't generally heard, and if it is it doesn't
matter.

4027
See how the Fates their gifts allot.
For A is happy - B is not.
Yet B is worthy, I dare say,
Of more prosperity than A.

4028 *The Sorcerer*
I was a pale young curate then.

4029 *Trial by Jury*
So I fell in love with a rich attorney's
Elderly ugly daughter.

4030 *Trial by Jury*
She may very well pass for forty-three
In the dusk with a light behind her!

4031 *The Yeoman of the Guard*
It's a song of a merryman, moping mum,
Whose soul was sad, and whose glance was
glum,
Who sipped no sup, and who craved no crumb,
As he sighed for the love of a ladye.

4032 *The Yeoman of the Guard*
'Tis ever thus with simple folk - an accepted wit
has but to say 'Pass the mustard', and they roar
their ribs out!

4033
And whether you're an honest man, or whether
you're a thief,
Depends on whose solicitor has given me my
brief.

4034
You've no idea what a poor opinion I have of myself - and how little I deserve it.

GILDER George
4035
Poverty is less a matter of income than of prospects. While the incomes of the poor have steadily risen through Great Society largesse, their prospects have plummeted as families have broken into dependent fragments.

GILL Eric 1882-1940
4036 *Art-nonsense and Other Essays*
That state is a state of slavery in which a man does what he likes to do in his spare time and in his working time that which is required of him.

GILMAN Charlotte Perkins 1860-1935
4037
The people people work with best are often very queer.

GINGRICH Newton 1943-
4038
No society can survive, no civilization can survive, with 12-year-olds having babies, with 15-year-olds killing each other, with 17-year-olds dying of Aids, with 18-year-olds getting diplomas they can't read.

GINSBERG Allen 1926-1997
4039 'A *Supermarket in California*'
What peaches and what penumbras! Whole families shopping at night! Aisles full of husbands! Wives in the avocados, babies in the tomatoes! - and you, Garcia Lorca what were you doing down by the watermelons?

4040 '*Graffiti*'
What if someone gave a war & Nobody came? Life would ring the bells of Ecstasy and Forever be Itself again.

4041 *Howl*
I saw the best minds of my generation destroyed by madness, starving hysterical naked,
dragging themselves through the negro streets at dawn looking for an angry fix,
angelheaded hipsters burning for the ancient heavenly connection to the starry dynamo in the machinery of the night.

GINSBERG Louis
4042
Life is ever
Since man was born,
Licking honey
From a thorn.

GIORDANO Bruno
4043
With luck on your side you can do without brains.

GIRAUDOUX Jean 1882-1944
4044 *La Guerre de Troie n'aura pas lieu*
As soon as war is declared it will be impossible to hold the poets back. Rhyme is still the most effective drum.

4045 *La Guerre de Troie n'aura pas lieu*
All of us here know there's no better way of exercising the imagination than the study of law. No poet ever interpreted nature as freely as a lawyer interprets the truth.

GISSING George 1857-1903
4046
This is one of the bitter curses of poverty: it leaves no right to be generous.

GLADSTONE W.E. 1809-1898
4047
We look forward to the time when the power to love will replace the love of power. Then will our world know the blessings of peace.

4048
We have been borne down in a torrent of gin and beer.

4049
We are bound to lose Ireland in consequence of years of cruelty, stupidity and misgovernment and I would rather lose her as a friend than as a foe.

4050
You cannot fight against the future. Time is on our side.

4051
Finance is, as it were, the stomach of the country, from which all the other organs take their tone.

4052
Ideal perfection is not the true basis of English legislation. We look at the attainable; we look at the practical; and we have too much English sense to be drawn away by those sanguine delineations of what might possibly be attained in Utopia, from a path which promises to enable us to effect great good for the people of England.

4053 *(of the Irish Land League)*
It is perfectly true that these gentlemen wish to march through rapine to disintegration and dismemberment of the Empire, and, I am sorry to say, even to the placing of different parts of the Empire in direct hostility one with the other.

4054
My mission is to pacify Ireland.

4055
This is the negation of God erected into a system of Government.

4056 *(on public speaking)*
I absorb the vapour and return it as a flood.

4057 *(on relations with Queen Victoria)*
What that Sicilian mule was to me, I have been
to the Queen.

4058
The resources of civilization against its enemies
are not yet exhausted.

4059
Swimming for his life, a man does not see much
of the country through which the river winds.

4060
I would tell them of my own intention to keep
my counsel ... and I will venture to recommend
them, as an old parliamentary hand, to do the
same.

4061
Let the Turks now carry away their abuses in the
only possible manner, namely by carrying off
themselves ... one and all, bag and baggage,
shall I hope clear out from the province they
have desolated and profaned.

4062
This, if I understand it, is one of those golden
moments of our history, one of those
opportunities which may come and may go, but
which rarely returns.

4063
I will venture to say, that upon the one great
class of subjects, the largest and the most
weighty of them all, where the leading and
determining considerations that ought to lead
to a conclusion are truth, justice, and humanity
- upon these, gentlemen, all the world over, I
will back the masses against the classes.

GLASS Montague
4064
She was an aging singer who had to take every
note above 'A' with her eyebrows.

GLEASON Jackie
4065
Thin people are beautiful but fat people are
adorable.

GLENN Jr. John H. 1921-
4066
People are afraid of the future, of the unknown.
If a man faces up to it, and takes the dare of the
future, he can have some control over his
destiny. That's an exciting idea to me, better
than waiting with everybody else to see what's
going to happen.

GLINKA Mikhail 1804-1857
4067
A nation creates music - the composer only
arranges it.

GODARD Jean-Luc 1930-
4068 *Le Petit Soldat*
Photography is truth. The cinema is truth 24
times per second.

4069
'Movies should have a beginning, a middle and
an end,' harrumphed French film maker
Georges Franju ... 'Certainly,' replied Jean-Luc
Godard. 'But not necessarily in that order.'

GODLEY A.D. 1856-1925
4070 *'The Megalopsychiad'*
Great and good is the typical Don, and of evil
and wrong the foe,
Good, and great, I'm a Don myself, and
therefore I ought to know.

4071
What is this that roareth thus?
Can it be a Motor Bus?
Yes, the smell and hideous hum
Indicat Motorem Bum!...
How shall wretches live like us
Cincti Bis Motoribus?
Domine, defende nos
Contra hos Motores Bos!

GODOLPHIN Sidney 1610-1643
4072 *'Song'*
Or love me less, or love me more
And play not with my liberty;
Either take all, or all restore,
Bind me at least, or set me free.

GODWIN William 1756-1836
4073 *An Enquiry...*
Perfectibility is one of the most unequivocal
characteristics of the human species.

4074 *An Enquiry...*
Love of our country is another of those specious
illusions, which have been invented by
impostors in order to render the multitude the
blind instruments of their crooked designs.

4075 *An Enquiry... (of the penal laws)*
What ... can be more shameless than for society
to make an example of those whom she has
goaded to the breach or order, instead of
amending her own institutions which, by
straining order into tyranny, produce the
mischief?

4076 *An Enquiry... (of war)*
It is a most mistaken way of teaching men to
feel they are brothers, by imbuing their mind
with perpetual hatred.

GOEBBELS Joseph 1897-1945
4077
We can manage without butter but not, for
example, without guns. If we are attacked we

can only defend ourselves with guns not with butter.

GOERING Hermann 1893-1946

4078
We have no butter ... but I ask you - would you rather have butter or guns? ... preparedness makes us powerful. Butter merely makes us fat.

4079 *(instructions to Heydrich)*
I herewith commission you to carry out all preparations with regard to ... a *total solution* of the Jewish question in those territories of Europe which are under German influence.

GOETHE Johann von 1749-1832

4080
We accept every person in the world as that for which he gives himself out only he must give himself out for something. We can put up with the unpleasant more easily than we can endure the insignificant.

4081
He alone deserves liberty and life who daily must win them anew.

4082
Art is called art because it is not nature.

4083
I call architecture 'petrified music'.

4084
Character, in great and little things, means carrying through what you feel able to do.

4085
If children grew up according to early indications, we should have nothing but geniuses.

4086
A clever man commits no minor blunders.

4087
There is no crime of which I do not deem myself capable.

4088
Daring ideas are like chessmen moved forward. They may be beaten, but they may start a winning game.

4089
Every day look at a beautiful picture, read a beautiful poem, listen to some beautiful music, and if possible, say some reasonable thing.

4090
It is better to be deceived by one's friends than to deceive them.

4091 *Der Gross-Cophta*
You must be master and win, or serve and lose, grieve or triumph, be the anvil or the hammer.

4092
From desire I plunge to its fulfilment, where I long once more for desire.

4093
I do not know myself, and God forbid that I should.

4094 *(attributed dying words)*
Mehr Licht!
More light!

4095
Everyone believes in his youth that the world really began with him, and that all merely exists for his sake.

4096 *Faust*
Man will err while yet he strives.

4097 *Faust*
Two souls dwell, alas! in my breast.

4098 *Faust*
I am the spirit that always denies.

4099 *Faust*
Deny yourself! You must deny yourself! That is the song that never ends.

4100 *Faust*
All theory, dear friend, is grey, but the golden tree of actual life springs ever green.

4101 *Faust*
My peace is gone,
My heart is heavy.

4102 *Faust*
The deed is all, the glory nothing.

4103 *Faust*
Eternal Woman draws us upward.

4104 *Italienische Reise*
Since it is a joy to have the benefit of what is good, it is a greater one to experience what is better, and in art the best is good enough.

4105
So, lively brisk old fellow, don't let age get you down. White hairs or not, you can still be a lover.

4106
Love is the ideal thing, marriage the real thing; a confusion of the real with the ideal never goes unpunished.

4107
For a man to achieve all that is demanded of him he must regard himself as greater than he is.

4108
It is said that no man is a hero to his valet. That is because a hero can be recognized only by a hero.

4109
If a man thinks about his physical or moral state, he usually discovers that he is ill.

4110
A man can stand almost anything except a succession of ordinary days.

4111
Mastery often passes for egotism.

4112 *Maximen und Reflexionen*
Superstition is the poetry of life.

4113 *Meher Baba*
Friendships are precious
Hugging friendships are very precious
On-going hugging friendships are the most precious of all.

4114
Mozart is the human incarnation of the divine force of creation.

4115
We are never deceived; we deceive ourselves.

4116
There is nothing more frightening than ignorance in action.

4117
Ordinary people know little of the time and effort it takes to learn to read. I have been eighty years at it, and have not reached my goal.

4118
And here, poor fool, with all my lore,
I stand no wiser than before.

4119
We can always redeem the man who aspires and strives.

4120
For the rest of it, the last and greatest art is to limit and isolate oneself.

4121
The right man is the one that seizes the moment.

4122
There is not a single outward mark of courtesy that does not have a deep moral basis.

4123 *Torquato Tasso*
Talent develops in quiet places, character in the full current of human life.

4124
If you treat men the way they are you never improve them. If you treat them the way you want them to be, you do.

4125
Unlike grownups, children have little need to deceive themselves.

4126
When an idea is wanting, a word can always be found to take its place.

4127
Let him who believes in immortality enjoy his happiness in silence without giving himself airs about it.

4128
Who does not know another language, does not know his own.

4129 *Wilhelm Meisters Lehrjahre*
Who never ate his bread in sorrow,
Who never spent the darksome hours
Weeping and watching for the morrow
He knows ye not, ye heavenly powers.

4130 *Wilhelm Meisters Lehrjahre*
Know you the land where the lemon-trees bloom? In the dark foliage the gold oranges glow; a soft wind hovers from the sky, the myrtle is still and the laurel stands tall - do you know it well? There, there, I would go, O my beloved, with thee!

GOFFIN Harold
4131
Behind every successful man you'll find a woman who has nothing to wear.

GOGOL Nikolai 1809-1852
4132 *Dead Souls*
As you pass from the tender years of youth into harsh and embittered manhood, make sure you take with you on your journey all the human emotions! Don't leave them on the road, for you will not pick them up afterwards!

4133 *Dead Souls*
I am destined by the mysterious powers to walk hand in hand with my strange heroes, viewing life in all its immensity as it rushes past me, viewing it through laughter seen by the world and tears unseen and unknown by it.

4134 *Dead Souls*
[Are not] you too, Russia, speeding along like a spirited *troika* that nothing can overtake? ... Everything on earth is flying past, and looking askance, other nations and states draw aside and make way.

4135
Don't blame the mirror if your face is faulty.

GOLAS Thaddeus
4136
When you first learn to love hell, you will be in heaven.

GOLDBERG Justice Arthur 1908-1990
4137
If Columbus had had an advisory committee he

would probably still be at the dock.

4138
I am surprised nothing has been made of the fact that astronaut Neil Armstrong carried no sidearms when he landed on the moon.

GOLDBERG Isaac 1887-1938
4139 *The Reflex*
Diplomacy is to do and say
The nastiest thing in the nicest way.

GOLDEN Harry 1896-1976
4140
A tablecloth restaurant is still one of the great rewards of civilization.

GOLDMAN Albert
4141
The Jews have always been students, and their greatest study is themselves.

GOLDMAN Emma 1869-1940
4142 *Anarchism and Other Essays*
Anarchism, then, really, stands for the liberation of the human mind from the dominion of religion; the liberation of the human body from the dominion of property; liberation from the shackles and restraints of government.

GOLDSMITH Sir James 1933-1997
4143
The custom is that if you divorce you abandon your wife. That is pure moral turpitude. I do not agree with it and I never have. For me, marriage is having children, not a piece of paper.

4144
I cannot envisage going into business for any other purpose than to make money. There is no vocation about business. The purpose is to make money.

4145
Tolerance is a tremendous virtue, but the immediate neighbours of tolerance are apathy and weakness.

GOLDSMITH Oliver 1730-1774
4146
There is no arguing with Johnson; for when his pistol misses fire, he knocks you down with the butt end of it.

4147 *The Bee no. 3*
The true use of speech is not so much to express our wants as to conceal them.

4148
Conscience is a coward, and those faults it has not strength enough to prevent, it seldom has justice enough to accuse.

4149 *The Deserted Village*
Sweet Auburn, loveliest village of the plain,
Where health and plenty cheered the labouring swain.

4150 *The Deserted Village*
Ill fares the land, to hast'ning ills a prey,
Where wealth accumulates, and men decay;
Princes and lords may flourish, or may fade;
A breath can make them, as a breath has made;
But a bold peasantry, their country's pride,
When once destroyed, can never be supplied.

4151 *The Deserted Village*
How happy he who crowns in shades like these,
A youth of labour with an age of ease.

4152 *The Deserted Village*
The watchdog's voice that bayed the whisp'ring wind,
And the loud laugh that spoke the vacant mind.

4153 *The Deserted Village*
A man he was to all the country dear,
And passing rich with forty pounds a year;
Remote from towns he ran his godly race,
Nor e'er had changed nor wished to change his place.

4154 *The Deserted Village*
He chid their wand'rings, but relieved their pain.

4155 *The Deserted Village*
Truth from his lips prevailed with double sway,
And fools, who came to scoff, remained to pray.

4156 *The Deserted Village*
A man severe he was, and stern to view,
I knew him well, and every truant knew;
Well had the boding tremblers learned to trace
The day's disasters in his morning face;
Full well they laughed with counterfeited glee,
At all his jokes, for many a joke had he.

4157 *The Deserted Village*
The village all declared how much he knew;
'Twas certain he could write and cypher too.

4158 *The Deserted Village*
In arguing too, the parson owned his skill,
For e'en though vanquished, he could argue still;
While words of learned length, and thund'ring sound
Amazed the gazing rustics ranged around,
And still they gazed, and still the wonder grew,
That one small head could carry all he knew.

4159 *The Deserted Village*
The whitewashed wall, the nicely sanded floor,
The varnished clock that clicked behind the door;
The chest contrived a double debt to pay,
A bed at night, a chest of drawers by day.

4160 *The Deserted Village*
In all the silent manliness of grief.

4161 *The Deserted Village*
Thou source of all my bliss, and all my woe,
That found'st me poor at first, and keep'st me
so.

4162 *'Edwin and Angelina, or the Hermit'*
Man wants but little here below,
Nor wants that little long.

4163 *'Elegy on the Death of a Mad Dog'*
The naked every day he clad,
When he put on his clothes.

4164 *'Elegy on the Death of a Mad Dog'*
The dog, to gain some private ends,
Went mad and bit the man.

4165 *'Elegy on the Death of a Mad Dog'*
The man recovered of the bite,
The dog it was that died.

4166 *'Elegy on Mrs. Mary Blaize'*
The doctor found, when she was dead,
Her last disorder mortal.

4167 *The Good-Natured Man*
This same philosophy is a good horse in the
stable, but an arrant jade on a journey.

4168 *The Good-Natured Man*
We must touch his weaknesses with a delicate
hand. There are some faults so nearly allied to
excellence, that we can scarce weed out the
fault without eradicating the virtue.

4169 *The Good-Natured Man*
All his faults are such that one loves him still the
better for them.

4170 *The Good-Natured Man*
Friendship is a disinterested commerce
between equals; love, an abject intercourse
between tyrants and slaves.

4171 *The Good-Natured Man*
Silence is become his mother tongue.

4172 *The Good-Natured Man*
You, that are going to be married, think things
can never be done too fast; but we, that are old,
and know what we are about, must elope
methodically, madam.

4173 *'Logicians Refuted'*
Brutes never meet in bloody fray,
Nor cut each other's throats, for pay.

4174
A modest woman, dressed out in all her finery,
is the most tremendous object of the whole
creation.

4175 *Retaliation*
Our Garrick's a salad; for in him we see
Oil, vinegar, sugar, and saltness agree.

4176 *Retaliation*
Here lies David Garrick, describe me, who can,
An abridgement of all that was pleasant in man.

4177 *Retaliation (of Edmund Burke)*
Who, too deep for his hearers, still went on
refining,
And thought of convincing, while they thought
of dining;
Though equal to all things, for all things unfit,
Too nice for a statesman, too proud for a wit.

4178 *Retaliation (of Garrick)*
On the stage he was natural, simple, affecting;
'Twas only that when he was off he was acting.

4179 *Retaliation (of Reynolds)*
When they talked of their Raphaels, Correggios,
and stuff,
He shifted his trumpet, and only took snuff.

4180 *She Stoops to Conquer*
Is it one of my well-looking days, child? Am I in
face to-day?

4181 *She Stoops to Conquer*
The very pink of perfection.

4182 *She Stoops to Conquer*
I'll be with you in the squeezing of a lemon.

4183 *She Stoops to Conquer*
It's a damned long, dark, boggy, dirty, dangerous
way.

4184 *She Stoops to Conquer*
This is Liberty-Hall, gentlemen.

4185 *She Stoops to Conquer*
The first blow is half the battle.

4186 *She Stoops to Conquer*
Was there ever such a cross-grained brute?

4187 *She Stoops to Conquer 'Song'*
Let schoolmasters puzzle their brain,
With grammar, and nonsense, and learning,
Good liquor, I stoutly maintain,
Gives genius a better discerning.

4188
As I take my shoes from the shoemaker, and my
coat from the tailor, so I take my religion from
the priest.

4189 *The Traveller*
Where'er I roam, whatever realms to see,
My heart untravelled fondly turns to thee;
Still to my brother turns with ceaseless pain,
And drags at each remove a lengthening chain.

4190 *The Traveller*
Such is the patriot's boast, where'er we roam,
His first, best country ever is, at home.

4191 *The Traveller*
Pride in their port, defiance in their eye,
I see the lords of human kind pass by.

4192 *The Traveller*
Laws grind the poor, and rich men rule the law.

4193 *The Traveller*
How small, of all that human hearts endure,
That part which laws or kings can cause or cure!

4194 *The Vicar of Wakefield*
I was ever of opinion, that the honest man who
married and brought up a large family, did more
service than he who continued single and only
talked of population.

4195 *The Vicar of Wakefield*
I ... chose my wife, as she did her wedding
gown, not for a fine glossy surface, but such
qualities as would wear well.

4196 *The Vicar of Wakefield*
All our adventures were by the fire-side, and all
our migrations from the blue bed to the brown.

4197 *The Vicar of Wakefield*
The virtue which requires to be ever guarded is
scarce worth the sentinel.

4198 *The Vicar of Wakefield*
It seemed to me pretty plain, that they had
more of love than matrimony in them.

4199 *The Vicar of Wakefield*
When lovely woman stoops to folly
And finds too late that men betray,
What charm can soothe her melancholy,
What art can wash her guilt away?

GOLDWATER Barry 1909-
4200 *(accepting the presidential nomination)*
I would remind you that extremism in the
defence of liberty is no vice! And let me remind
you also that moderation in the pursuit of
justice is no virtue!

4201
We shall return to proven ways - not because
they are old, but because they are true.

GOLDWYN Sam 1882-1974
4202
I read part of it all the way through.

4203
Chaplin is no businessman - all he knows is that
he can't take anything less.

4204
I'm exhausted from not talking.

4205
Any man who goes to a psychiatrist should have
his head examined.

4206
Pictures are for entertainment, messages should
be delivered by Western Union.

4207 *(on resigning from Motion Picture
Producers)*
Gentlemen, include me out.

4208
If Roosevelt were alive he'd turn in his grave.

4209
From success you get a lot of things, but not
that great inside thing that love brings you.

4210
That's the way with these directors, they're
always biting the hand that lays the golden egg.

4211
A verbal contract isn't worth the paper it is
written on.

4212
Why should people pay good money to go out
and see bad films when they can stay at home
and see bad television for nothing?

GOMBRICH Ernst 1909-
4213
There is no such thing as art. There are only
artists.

GOMPERS Samuel 1850-1924
4214
The worst crime against working people is a
company which fails to operate at a profit.

GONCHAROV Ivan 1812-1891
4215 *Obolomov*
All his anxiety resolved itself into a sigh and
dissolved into apathy and drowsiness.

4216 *Obolomov*
The trouble is that no devastating or redeeming
fires have ever burnt in my life ... My life began
by flickering out.

4217 *Obolomov*
You lost your ability for doing things in
childhood, in Oblomovka ... It all began with
your inability to put on your socks and ended
by your inability to live.

4218
It is a trick among the dishonest to offer
sacrifices that are not needed, or not possible,
to avoid making those that are required.

GONDOLA Paul
4219
Every minute starts an hour.

GOODMAN Al
4220
The perfect computer has been developed. You
just feed in your problems, and they never

come out again.

GOODMAN Paul

4221
Enjoyment is not a goal, it is a feeling that accompanies important ongoing activity.

4222
The family is the American fascism.

4223
Few great men could pass Personnel.

4224
I have learned to have very modest goals for society and myself; things like clean air, green grass, children with bright eyes, not being pushed around, useful work that suits one's abilities, plain tasty food, and occasional satisfying nookie.

GOODMAN Roy M.

4225
Remember that happiness is a way of travel - not a destination.

GOODRICH Rt. Rev. Philip 1929-

4226 *(opening conference on future of marriage)*
If you will excuse me using this expression, the attitude today is too often one of find it, fuck it, and forget it.

GORDON Adam Lindsay 1833-1870

4227 *Ye Wearie Wayfarer 'Fytte 8'*
Life is mostly froth and bubble,
Two things stand like stone,
Kindness in another's trouble,
Courage in your own.

GORDON Mack 1904-1959

4228 *'Chattanooga Choo-choo'*
Pardon me boy is that the Chattanooga Choo-choo,
Track twenty nine,
Boy you can gimme a shine.
I can afford to board a Chattanooga Choo-choo,
I've got my fare and just a trifle to spare.
You leave the Pennsylvania station 'bout a quarter to four,
Read a magazine and then you're in Baltimore,
Dinner in the diner nothing could be finer
Than to have your ham'n eggs in Carolina.

GORDON Ruth

4229
To be somebody you must last.

GORKY Maxim 1868-1936

4230
Every new time will give its law.

4231
To an old man any place that's warm is homeland.

GORMAN Teresa 1931-

4232
The Prime Minister has got the Parliamentary Party by the goolies.

GORRELL Stuart 1902-1963

4233 *'Georgia on my Mind'*
Georgia, Georgia, no peace I find,
Just an old sweet song keeps Georgia on my mind.

GOULBURN Edward Meyrick 1818-1897

4234 *(sermon at Rugby School)*
Let the scintillations of your wit be like the coruscations of summer lightning, lambent but innocuous.

GOULD Bruce

4235
In England I would rather be a man, a horse, a dog or a woman, in that order. In America I think the order would be reversed.

GOULD Gerald 1885-1936

4236 *Monogamy*
And you were very much in love with me,
And half I lured it on, and half I fled it,
Till honour turned its foolish face on mine
Taking for allies music and good wine -
And told me what I ought to say: I said it.

GOURMONT Rémy de 1858-1915

4237
Women still remember the first kiss after men have forgotten the last.

4238
Of all sexual aberrations, perhaps the most peculiar is chastity.

4239
It is fairly obvious that those who are in favour of the death penalty have more affinity with assassins than those who are not.

4240
Very simple ideas lie within the reach only of complex minds.

GOWANS Alan

4241
By the laws of probability, North America ought to speak French, not English, today.

GOWER John c.1330-1408

4242 *Confessio Amantis*
It hath and schal ben evermor
That love is maister wher he wile.

GOWERS Sir Ernest 1880-1966

4243
We are all esquires now, and we are none of us gentlemen any more.

4244 *Plain Words*
It is not easy nowadays to remember anything so contrary to all appearances as that officials are the servants of the public; and the official must try not to foster the illusion that it is the other way round.

GOWRIE Lord 1939-
4245
Quality of life is an industry.

GOYA (Francisco Joseé de Goya y Lucientes) 1746-1828
4246 *Los Caprichos*
The dream of reason produces monsters.

GRACIAN Baltasar 1601-1658
4247
A beautiful woman should break her mirror early.

4248
Do not show your wounded finger, for everything will knock up against it.

4249
Words are feminine; deeds are masculine.

4250
Even knowledge has to be in fashion and where it is not it is wise to affect ignorance.

4251
'No' and 'Yes' are words quickly said, but they need a great amount of thought before you utter them.

4252
Time and I against any two.

4253
At twenty a man is a peacock, at thirty a lion, at forty a camel, at fifty a serpent, at sixty a dog, at seventy an ape, at eighty, nothing at all.

4254
A wise man gets more use from his enemies than a fool from his friends.

4255
Wise men appreciate all men, for they see the good in each and know how hard it is to make anything good.

4256
The wise have a solid sense of silence and the ability to keep a storehouse of secrets. Their capacity and character are respected.

GRAHAM Billy 1918-
4257
Everybody has a little bit of Watergate in him.

GRAHAM Clementina Stirling 1782-1877
4258 *Mystifications*
The best way to get the better of temptation is just to yield to it.

GRAHAM D.M. 1911-
4259 *(motion for debate at Oxford Union)*
That this House will in no circumstances fight for its King and Country.

GRAHAM Harry 1874-1936
4260 *More Ruthless Rhymes for Heartless Homes*
Weep not for little Léonie
Abducted by a French Marquis!
Though loss of honour was a wrench
Just think how it's improved her French.

4261 *Ruthless Rhymes for Heartless Homes*
O'er the rugged mountain's brow
Clara threw the twins she nursed,
And remarked, 'I wonder now
Which will reach the bottom first?'

4262 *Ruthless Rhymes for Heartless Homes*
Aunt Jane observed, the second time
She tumbled off a bus,
'The step is short from the Sublime
To the Ridiculous.'

4263 *Ruthless Rhymes for Heartless Homes*
'There's been an accident,' they said,
'Your servant's cut in half; he's dead!'
'Indeed!' said Mr Jones, 'and please,
Send me the half that's got my keys.'

4264 *Ruthless Rhymes for Heartless Homes*
Billy, in one of his nice new sashes,
Fell in the fire and was burnt to ashes;
Now, although the room grows chilly,
I haven't the heart to poke poor Billy.

GRAHAM James 1612-1650
4265 *'My Dear and Only Love'*
He either fears his fate too much,
Or his deserts are small,
That puts it not unto the touch
To win or lose it all.

4266
Love is blind and marriage is the institution of the blind.

GRAHAM Martha 1893-1991
4267
No artist is ahead of his time. He is his time. It is just that others are behind the time.

4268
The body never lies.

GRAHAME Kenneth 1859-1932
4269
The clever men at Oxford
Know all there is to be knowed -
But they none of them know as half as much
As intelligent Mr. Toad.

4270 *The Golden Age*
Monkeys ... very sensibly refrain from speech, lest they should be set to earn their livings.

4271
The strongest human instinct is to impart information, the second strongest is to resist it.

4272 *The Wind in the Willows*
There is *nothing* - absolutely nothing - half so much worth doing as simply messing about in boats.

GRANT Ulysses S. 1822-1885
4273 *(inaugural address)*
I know no method to secure the repeal of bad or obnoxious laws so effective as their stringent execution.

4274
No terms except unconditional and immediate surrender can be accepted.

GRASS Günter 1927-
4275
The job of a citizen is to keep his mouth open.

GRAVCHEV General Pavel
4276
The Armed forces are the only well-organised and reliable force in society.

GRAVES John Woodcock 1795-1886
4277 *'John Peel'*
D'ye ken John Peel with his coat so grey?
D'ye ken John Peel at the break of the day?
D'ye ken John Peel when he's far far away
With his hounds and his horn in the morning?

GRAVES Robert 1895-1985
4278
I don't really feel my poems are mine at all. I didn't create them out of nothing. I owe them to my relations with other people.

4279 *'To Evoke Posterity'*
To evoke posterity
Is to weep on your own grave,
Ventriloquizing for the unborn.

4280
If I were a girl, I'd despair. The supply of good women far exceeds that of the men who deserve them.

4281
Goodbye to all that.

4282 *Hedges Freaked With Snow*
No argument, no anger, no remorse,
No dividing of blame.
There was poison in the cup - why should we ask
From whose hand it came?

4283 *Occupation: Writer*
In love as in sport, the amateur status must be strictly maintained.

4284 *'The Persian Version'*
Truth-loving Persians do not dwell upon
The trivial skirmish fought near Marathon.

4285
There's no money in poetry, but then there's no poetry in money either.

GRAVINA Gian Vinvenzo
4286
A bore is a man who deprives you of solitude without providing you with company.

GRAY G.L.
4287
The television commercial is the most efficient power-packed capsule of education that appears anywhere on TV.

GRAY John Chipman 1839-1915
4288 *Restraints on the Alienation of Property*
Dirt is only matter out of place.

GRAY Lord d.1612
4289 *(attributed)*
A dead woman bites not.

GRAY Thomas 1716-1771
4290 *Elegy Written in a Country Churchyard*
The curfew tolls the knell of parting day,
The lowing herd wind slowly o'er the lea,
The ploughman homeward plods his weary way,
And leaves the world to darkness and to me.

Now fades the glimmering landscape on the sight,
And all the air a solemn stillness holds,
Save where the beetle wheels his droning flight,
And drowsy tinklings lull the distant folds.

4291 *Elegy Written in a Country Churchyard*
Let not ambition mock their useful toil,
Their homely joys, and destiny obscure;
Nor grandeur hear with a disdainful smile,
The short and simple annals of the poor.

The boast of heraldry, the pomp of pow'r,
And all that beauty, all that wealth e'er gave,
Awaits alike th' inevitable hour,
The paths of glory lead but to the grave.

4292 *Elegy Written in a Country Churchyard*
Can storied urn or animated bust
Back to its mansion call the fleeting breath?
Can honour's voice provoke the silent dust,
Or flatt'ry soothe the dull cold ear of death?

4293 *Elegy Written in a Country Churchyard*
Full many a gem of purest ray serene,
The dark unfathomed caves of ocean bear:
Full many a flower is born to blush unseen,
And waste its sweetness on the desert air.

4294 *Elegy Written in a Country Churchyard*
Far from the madding crowd's ignoble strife,
Their sober wishes never learned to stray;
Along the cool sequestered vale of life
They kept the noiseless tenor of their way.

4295 *Elegy Written in a Country Churchyard*
Here rests his head upon the lap of Earth
A youth to fortune and to fame unknown.
Fair Science frowned not on his humble birth,
And Melancholy marked him for her own.

4296 *'Ode on the Death of a Favourite Cat'*
Not all that tempts your wand'ring eyes
And heedless hearts, is lawful prize;
Nor all, that glisters, gold.

4297 *Ode on a Distant Prospect of Eton College*
Alas, regardless of their doom,
The little victims play!
No sense have they of ills to come,
Nor care beyond to-day.

4298 *'Sketch of his own Character'*
Too poor for a bribe, and too proud to
importune,
He had not the method of making a fortune.

4299
Where ignorance is bliss
'Tis folly to be wise.

GREELEY Horace 1811-1872
4300
The darkest hour of any man's life is when he
sits down to plan how to get money without
earning it.

4301 *Hints toward Reforms*
Go West, young man, and grow up with the
country.

GREEN Benny 1927-
4302
A jazz musician is a juggler who uses harmonies
instead of oranges.

GREEN Matthew 1696-1737
4303 *The Grotto*
They politics like ours profess,
The greater prey upon the less.

GREEN Russell
4304
Heaven is the place where the donkey finally
catches up with his carrot: hell is the eternity
while he waits for it.

4305
A wife encourages her husband's egoism in
order to exercise her own.

GREENAWAY Peter 1942-
4306
Ultimately the best way to understand a highly
charged situation is to take a step back.

GREENBERG Clement
4307
All profoundly original art looks ugly at first.

GREENBURG Martin
4308
The terror of art lies in the representation of the
hidden reality with its shattering effect.

GREENE Graham 1904-1991
4309 *The Comedians*
Communists have committed great crimes, but
at least they have not stood aside, like an
established society, and been indifferent. I
would rather have blood on my hands than
water, like Pilate.

4310
At the end of what is called the 'sexual life' the
only love which has lasted is the love which has
everything, every disappointment, every failure
and every betrayal, which has accepted even
the sad fact that in the end there is no desire so
deep as the simple desire for companionship.

4311
Fame is a powerful aphrodisiac.

4312
Hatred seems to operate on the same glands as
love; it even produces the same actions. If we
had not been taught how to interpret the story
of the Passion, would we have been able to say
from their actions alone whether it was the
jealous Judas or the cowardly Peter who loved
Christ?

4313 *The Heart of the Matter*
Nothing was ever lost by delay.

4314 *The Heart of the Matter*
Against the beautiful and the clever and the
successful, one can wage a pitiless war, but not
against the unattractive.

4315 *The Power and the Glory*
There is always one moment in childhood when
the door opens and lets the future in.

4316 *The Quiet American*
If only it were possible to love without injury -
fidelity isn't enough ... The hurt is in the act of
possession: we are too small in mind and body
to posses another person without pride or to be
possessed without humiliation.

GREENE Robert c.1560-1592
4317 *Perimedes*
Men, when they lust, can many fancies feign.

4318 *'The Shepherd's Wife's Song'*
Ah! what is love! It is a pretty thing,
As sweet unto a shepherd as a king,
And sweeter too;
For kings have cares that wait upon a crown,

And cares can make the sweetest love to frown.
Ah then, ah then,
If country loves such sweet desires do gain,
What lady would not love a shepherd swain?

GREER Germaine 1939-
4319 *The Female Eunuch*
You can now see the Female Eunuch the world over.

4320 *The Female Eunuch*
Love, love, love - all the wretched cant of it, masking egotism, lust, masochism, fantasy under a mythology of sentimental postures.

4321
I didn't fight to get women out from behind the vacuum cleaner to get them onto the board of Hoover.

4322
Women must learn to lighten up if we are to survive.

4323
Most women still need a room of their own and the only way to find it may be outside their own home.

GREGG Alan
4324
A good education should leave much to be desired.

4325
The human race has had long experience and a find tradition in surviving adversity. But we now face a task for which we have little experience, the task of surviving prosperity.

4326
A thousand goodbyes come after death - the first six months of bereavement.

GRELLET Stephen 1773-1855
4327 *(attributed)*
I expect to pass through this world but once; any good thing therefore that I can do, or any kindness that I can show to any fellow-creature, let me do it now; let me not defer or neglect it, for I shall not pass this way again.

GREY Sir Edward 1862-1933
4328 *25 Years*
The lamps are going out all over Europe; we shall not see them lit again in our lifetime.

GREY John
4329
And what's a butterfly? At best,
He's but a caterpillar, drest.

GRICE Glenn le
4330
Florida: God's waiting room.

GROPIUS Walter 1883-1969
4331
How can we expect our students to become bold and fearless in thought and action if we encase them in sentimental shrines feigning a culture which has long since disappeared?

4332
Society needs a good image of itself. That is the job of the architect.

GROSSMITH George and Weedon 1847-1912 and 1854-1919
4333 *The Diary of a Nobody*
What's the good of a home if you are never in it?

4334 *The Diary of a Nobody*
I left the room with silent dignity, but caught my foot in the mat.

4335 *The Diary of a Nobody*
I am a poor man, but I would gladly give ten shillings to find out who sent me the insulting Christmas card I received this morning.

GROTIUS Hugo 1583-1645
4336
Not to know certain things is a great part of wisdom.

GROVE Phillip B.
4337
A dictionary should be descriptive, not prescriptive.

GUEDALLA Philip 1889-1944
4338
I had always assumed that cliché was a suburb of Paris, until I discovered it to be a street in Oxford.

4339 *Mr Churchill*
... the little ships of England brought the Army home.

4340
The Lord Chief Justice of England recently said that the greater part of his judicial time was spent investigating collisions between propelled vehicles, each on its own side of the road, each sounding its horn and each stationary.

4341 *Masters and Men*
Any stigma, as the old saying is, will serve to beat a dogma.

4342 *(of The Duke of Wellington and Sir Robert Peel in 1836)*
Their relations sometimes resembled an exchange of signals between passing icebergs.

4343 *Supers and Supermen*
The cheerful clatter of Sir James Barrie's cans as he went round with the milk of human kindness.

The Wordsworth Dictionary of Quotations

4344 *Supers and Supermen*
History repeats itself. Historians repeat each other.

GUÉRARD Albert
4345
Chivalry is the most delicate form of contempt.

GUINNESS Sir Alec 1914-
4346
Acting is happy agony.

GUITERMAN Arthur
4347
Amoebas at the start were not complex;
They tore themselves apart and started sex.

4348
The porcupine, whom one must handle gloved,
May be respected, but is never loved.

GUITRY Sacha 1885-1957
4349
Honest women are inconsolable for the mistakes they haven't made.

4350
An ideal wife is one who remains faithful to you but tries to be just as if she weren't.

4351
The little I know, I owe to my ignorance.

4352
You can pretend to be serious, but you can't pretend to be witty.

4353 *(attributed remark to his fifth wife)*
The others were only my wives. But you, my dear, will be my widow.

4354
Even the most respectable woman has a complete set of clothes in her wardrobe ready for a possible abduction.

4355
When a man marries his mistress, he creates a job vacancy.

4356
When a man steals your wife, there is no better revenge than to let him keep her.

GULBENKIAN Nubar 1896-1972
4357
The best number for a dinner party is two - myself and a dam' good head waiter.

GUNN Thom 1929-
4358 *Carnal Knowledge*
You know I know you know I know you know.

GUNTHER John 1901-1970
4359
All happiness depends on a leisurely breakfast.

4360
The first essence of journalism is to know what you want to know; the second, is to find out who will tell you.

GUTHRIE Woody 1912-1967
4361
Now as through this world I ramble,
I see lots of funny men,
Some rob you with a six gun
Some with a fountain pen.

GWYN Nell 1650-1687
4362 *(during the Popish Terror)*
Pray, good people, be civil. I am the Protestant whore.

HABERMAN Jr. Philip W.
4363
A gourmet is just a glutton with brains.

HABGOOD John (Archbishop of York) 1927-
4364
The desire to be spoonfed, to have our problems solved for us by someone else, to be given the short, snappy answer, has sunk deep into our culture.

4365 *(of teenage marriage)*
I think under 21 is almost always disastrous.

HAGGARD Sir Henry Rider 1856-1925
4366 *She*
She who must be obeyed.

HAGUE Sir Douglas 1926-
4367
Our state schools were established to produce clerks and book-keepers.

HAIG Earl 1861-1928
4368 *(of the 17th Earl of Derby)*
A very weak-minded fellow I am afraid, and, like the feather pillow, bears the marks of the last person who has sat on him!

4369 *(order to British troops)*
Every position must be held to the last man: there must be no retirement. With our backs to the wall, and believing in the justice of our cause, each one of us must fight on to the end.

HAIGH Kenneth
4370
You need three things in the theatre - the play, the actors and the audience, and each must give something.

HAILSHAM Lord (Quintin Hogg) 1907-
4371 *The Case of Conservatism*
Conservatives do not believe that the political struggle is the most important thing in life ... The simplest of them prefer fox-hunting - the wisest religion.

HALDANE J.B.S. 1892-1964
4372
I have never yet met a healthy person who worries very much about his health, or a really good person who worries much about his own soul.

4373 *Possible Worlds and Other Essays*
Now, my own suspicion is that the universe is not only queerer than we suppose, but queerer than we *can* suppose ... I suspect that there are more things in heaven and earth than are dreamed of, or can be dreamed of, in any philosophy.

HALDEMAN H.R. 1929-
4374 *(of the Watergate affair)*
Once the toothpaste is out of the tube, it is awfully hard to get it back in.

HALE Harlan
4375 *(of Care International in Rwanda)*
We've got 3 categories of refugees: the living dead, the dying dead and the dead dead.

HALE Nathan 1755-1776
4376 *(prior to his execution for spying)*
I only regret that I have but one life to lose for my country.

HALIBURTON Thomas Chandler 1796-1865
4377
I have learnt a good deal from my own talk.

HALIFAX Lord George 1633-1695
4378
Anger raiseth invention, but it overheateth the oven.

4379
A busy fool is fitter to be shut up than a downright madman.

4380
He that leaveth nothing to Chance will do few things ill, but he will do very few things.

4381
Men are not hanged for stealing horses, but that horses may not be stolen.

4382
Nothing has an uglier look to us than Reason, when it is not of our side.

4383
Weak men are apt to be cruel because they stick at nothing that may repair the ill effect of their mistakes.

HALL Joseph 1574-1656
4384 *Works*
Perfection is the child of Time.

HALL Radclyffe 1883-1943
4385 *The Well of Loneliness*
You're neither unnatural, nor abominable, nor mad; you're as much a part of what people call nature as anyone else; only you're unexplained as yet.

HALLA Sven
4386
The good should be grateful to the bad - for providing the world with a basis for comparison.

HALM Friedrich 1806-1871
4387
Two souls with but a single thought,
Two hearts that beat as one.

HALSER Professor A.H.
4388
The project as understood by feminists is making women more like men, but it ought to be making men more like women.

HALSEY Margaret 1910-
4389 *With Malice Toward Some*
The English never smash in a face. They merely refrain from asking it to dinner.

4390
Some persons talk simply because they think sound is more manageable than silence.

4391
Whatever the rest of the world thinks of the English gentleman, the English lady regards him apprehensively as something between God and a goat and equally formidable on both scores.

HAMAKER L.S.
4392
Always remember that the soundest way to progress in any organization is to help the man ahead of you to get promoted.

HAMILTON Alex 1936-
4393
Those who stand for nothing fall for anything.

HAMILTON Alexander 1757-1804
4394
Power over a man's subsistence amounts to a power over his will.

HAMILTON Eleanor
4395
A compliment is a gift, not to be thrown away carelessly unless you want to hurt the giver.

HAMILTON Robert B.
4396
Man is a reasoning, rather than a reasonable animal.

HAMMARSKJÖLD Dag 1905-1961

4397
God does not die on the day when we cease to believe in a personal deity, but we die on the day when our lives cease to be illuminated by the steady radiance, renewed daily, of a wonder, the source of which is beyond all reason.

4398
Life only demands from the strength you possess. Only one feat is possible - not to have run away.

4399
Never look down to test the ground before taking your next step; only he who keeps his eye fixed on the far horizon will find his right road.

4400
A task becomes a duty from the moment you suspect it to be an essential part of that integrity which alone entitles a man to assume responsibility.

4401
Time goes by: reputation increases, ability declines.

HAMMERSTEIN II Oscar 1895-1960

4402
Do you love me because I'm beautiful, or am I beautiful because you love me?

4403 *Lady Be Good*
The last time I saw Paris
Her heart was warm and gay

4404 *Showboat*
Ol' man river, dat ol' man river,
He must know sumpin', but don't say nothin',
He jus' keeps rollin',
He jus' keeps rollin' along.

4405 *South Pacific*
You've got to be taught to be afraid
Of people whose eyes are oddly made,
Of people whose skin is a different shade.
You've got to be carefully taught.

You've got to be taught before it's too late,
Before you are six or seven or eight,
To hate all the people your relatives hate.
You've got to be carefully taught.

HAMPTON Christopher 1946-

4406 *Savages*
A definition of capitalism ... the process whereby American girls turn into American women.

HAND Learned 1872-1961

4407
We accept the verdict of the past until the need for change cries out loudly enough to force upon us a choice between the comforts of further inertia and the irksomeness of action.

4408
The aim of law is the maximum gratification of the nervous system of man.

4409
The art of publicity is a black art.

4410 *(of Samuel Goldwyn)*
A self-made man may prefer a self-made name.

4411
The spirit of liberty is the spirit which is not too sure that it is right.

4412
We shall succeed only so far as we continue that most distasteful of all activity, the intolerable labour of thought.

HANDS Terry 1941-

4413
It is said that Hamlet is the first modern man - so obviously he must be insane.

HANNIBAL 247-182 BC

4414
We will either find a way, or make one.

HANRAHAN Brian 1949-

4415
I counted them all out and I counted them all back.

HARBACH Otto 1873-1963

4416
Smoke gets in your eyes.

4417 *The Wizard of Oz*
Somewhere over the rainbow.

HARBURG E.Y. 1898-1981

4418
Brother can you spare a dime?

4419
The World would be a safer place,
If someone had a plan,
Before exploring Outer Space,
To find the Inner man.

HARDING Warren G. 1865-1923

4420
My God, this is a hell of a job. I have no trouble with my enemies. I can take care of my enemies all right. But my damn friends, my goddamn friends. They're the ones that keep me walking the floor nights.

HARDWICKE Sir Cedric 1893-1964

4421
I regard England as my wife and America as my mistress.

HARDY Oliver 1892-1957
4422 *in The Laurel and Hardy Murder Case*
"Here's another fine mess you've gotten me into."

HARDY Thomas 1840-1928
4423
Aspects are within us, and who seems most kingly is king.

4424
The business of the poet and novelist is to show the sorriness underlying the grandest things, and the grandeur underlying the sorriest things.

4425 *'On the Departure Platform'*
We kissed at the barrier; and passing through
She left me, and moment by moment got
Smaller and smaller, until to my view
She was but a spot.

4426 *The Dynasts*
War makes rattling good history; but Peace is poor reading.

4427 *The Hand of Ethelberta*
A lover without indiscretion is no lover at all.

4428
Love lives on propinquity, but dies on contact.

4429 *'The Man he Killed'*
Yes; quaint and curious war is!
You shoot a fellow down
You'd treat if met where any bar is,
Or help to half-a-crown.

4430
That man's silence is wonderful to listen to.

4431
Measurement of life should be proportioned rather to the intensity of the experience than to its actual length.

4432 *Tess of the D'Urbervilles - preface*
A novel is an impression, not an argument.

HARE Julius and HARE Augustus 1795-1855 and 1792-1834
4433
The greatest truths are the simplest, and so are the greatest men.

4434 *Guesses at Truth*
Half the failures in life arise from pulling in one's horse as he is leaping.

HARINGTON Sir John 1561-1612
4435
Books give not wisdom where none was before.
But where some is, there reading makes it more.

4436 *Epigrams*
Treason doth never prosper, what's the reason?
For if it prosper, none dare call it treason.

HARKNESS Richard
4437
What is a committee? A group of the unwilling, picked from the unfit, to do the unnecessary.

HARLECH Lord (David Ormsby Gore) 1918-1985
4438
Britain will be honoured by historians more for the way she disposed of an empire than for the way in which she acquired it.

4439
It would indeed be a tragedy if the history of the human race proved to be nothing more than the story of an ape playing with a box of matches on a petrol dump.

HARLOW Jean 1911-1937
4440 *in Hell's Angels*
"Excuse me while I slip into something more comfortable."

HARRIS Harwell Hamilton
4441
The house does not frame the view: it projects the beholder into it.

HARRIS Janet
4442
At its most basic root, the death or disintegration of one's parents is a harsh reminder of one's own mortality.

HARRIS Joel Chandler 1848-1908
4443
You k'n hide de fier, but what you guine do wid de smoke?

HARRIS Lawren
4444
A picture can become for us a highway between a particular thing and a universal feeling.

HARRIS Sydney J.
4445
The true test of independent judgement is being able to dislike someone who admires us.

4446
The two words 'information' and 'communication' are often used interchangeably, but they signify quite different things. Information is giving out; communication is getting through.

HART Josephine
4447
Poetry contains almost all you need to know about life.

HART Lorenz 1895-1943
4448 *Babes in Arms*
That's why the lady is a tramp.

4449 *'Mountain Greenery'*
Just two crazy people together.

HARTE Bret 1836-1902
4450
One big vice in a man is apt to keep out a great many smaller ones.

HARTLEY L.P. 1895-1972
4451 *The Go-Between*
The past is a foreign country: they do things differently there.

HASKINS Henry S.
4452
Disappointments should be cremated, not embalmed.

4453
If a man hears much that a woman says, she is not beautiful.

HASKINS Minnie Louise 1875-1957
4454 *Desert 'God Knows'*
And I said to the man who stood at the gate of the year: 'Give me a light that I may tread safely into the unknown.'
And he replied:
'Go out into the darkness and put your hand into the Hand of God. That shall be to you better than light and safer than a known way.'

HASTINGS Lewis
4455
The fact is that the possession of a highly social conscience about large-scale issues is no guarantee whatever of reasonable conduct in private relations.

HAVENS Leston L.
4456
The slow compromise, or even surrender, of our fondest hopes is a regular feature of normal human life.

HAVOC June
4457
You are all you will ever have for certain.

HAWKER R.S. 1803-1875
4458 *'The Song of the Western Men'*
And have they fixed the where and when?
And shall Trelawny die?
Here's twenty thousand Cornish men
Will know the reason why!

HAWKING Stephen 1942-
4459
The behaviour of the universe on a very large scale seems to be simple and not chaotic.

4460 *A Brief History of Time*
Each equation ... in the book would halve the sales.

4461 *A Brief History of Time*
If we find the answer to that [why it is that we and the universe exist], it would be the ultimate triumph of human reason - for then we would know the mind of God.

HAWTHORNE Nathaniel 1804-1864
4462
Selfishness is one of the qualities apt to inspire love.

4463
The world owes all its onward impulses to men ill at ease. The happy man inevitably confines himself within ancient limits.

HAY Ian 1876-1952
4464 *The Housemaster*
What do you mean, funny? Funny-peculiar or funny ha-ha?

HAY John 1838-1905
4465
The best-loved man or maid in the town would perish with anguish could they hear all that their friends say in the course of a day.

HAYAKAWA S.I.
4466
In the age of television, image becomes more important than substance.

4467
We should keep the Panama Canal. After all we stole it fair and square.

HAYDON A. Eustace
4468
Fortunately for serious minds, a bias recognized is a bias sterilized.

HAYEK Friedrich 1899-1992
4469
Competition means decentralized planning by many separate persons.

HAYES J. Milton 1884-1940
4470 *The Green Eye of the Yellow God*
There's a one-eyed yellow idol to the north of Khatmandu,
There's a little marble cross below the town,
There's a broken-hearted woman tends the grave of Mad Carew,
And the Yellow God forever gazes down.

HAYS Brooks
4471
Back of every achievement is a proud wife and a surprised mother-in-law.

HAZLITT William 1778-1830
4472
Actors are the only honest hypocrites.

4473
Without the aid of prejudice and custom, I should not be able to find my way across the room.

4474
All that men really understand is confined to a very small compass; to their daily affairs and experience; to what they have an opportunity to know; and motives to study or practise. The rest is affectation and imposture.

4475
Calumny requires no proof. The throwing out of malicious imputations against any character leaves a stain which no after-refutation can wipe out. To create an unfavourable impression, it is not necessary that cetain things should be true, but that they have been said.

4476
It is essential to the triumph of reform that it shall never succeed.

4477
Grace is the absence of everything that indicates pain or difficulty, hesitation or incongruity.

4478
We are not hypocrites in our sleep.

4479
Indolence is a delightful but distressing state. We must be doing something to be happy.

4480
Landscape painting is the obvious resource of misanthropy.

4481
Learning is the knowledge of that which none but the learned know.

4482
Man is a make-believe animal - he is never so truly himself as when he is acting a part.

4483
Man is the only animal that laughs and weeps; for he is the only animal that is struck by the difference between what things are and what they might have been.

4484
There is nothing good to be had in the country, or, if there be, they will not let you have it.

4485
If a person has no delicacy, he has you in his power.

4486
Persons who undertake to pry into, or cleanse out all the filth of a common sewer, either cannot have very nice noses, or will soon lose them.

4487
Prejudice is the child of ignorance.

4488 *The Round Table*
The art of pleasing consists in being pleased.

4489
The most silent people are generally those who think most highly of themselves.

4490 *Sketches and Essays*
But of all footmen the lowest class is *literary footmen*.

4491 *Sketches and Essays*
A nickname is the heaviest stone that the devil can throw at a man.

4492 *The Spirit of the Age*
Mr Wordsworth's genius is a pure emanation of the Spirit of the Age. Had he lived in any other period of the world, he would never have been heard of.

4493 *Table Talk*
You will hear more good things on the outside of a stagecoach from London to Oxford than if you were to pass a twelvemonth with the undergraduates, or heads of colleges, of that famous university.

4494
The truly proud man is satisfied with his own good opinion, and does not seek to make converts to it.

4495
One truth discovered, one pang of regret at not being able to express it, is better than all the fluency and flippancy in the world.

4496
Those who are fond of setting things to rights have no great objection to setting them wrong.

4497
If we wish to know the force of human genius, we should read Shakespeare. If we wish to see the insignificance of human learning, we may study his commentators.

4498
Wit is the salt of conversation, not the food.

HAZZARD Shirley 1931-
4499 *The Transit of Venus*
The tragedy is not that love doesn't last. The tragedy is the love that lasts.

HEALEY Denis 1917-
4500 *(on being criticized by Sir Geoffrey Howe)*
Like being savaged by a dead sheep.

4501
NATO is now a biological monstrosity - an organ without a function.

HEARST William Randolph 1863-1951
4502
Don't be afraid to make a mistake, your readers might like it.

HEATH Edward 1916-
4503 *(on the Lonrho affair)*
The unpleasant and unacceptable face of capitalism.

HECHT Ben 1893-1964
4504 *Think, February 1963*
A man nearly always loves for other reasons than he thinks. A lover is apt to be as full of secrets from himself as is the object of his love from him.

HEGEL G.W.F. 1770-1831
4505 *Lectures on the Philosphy of World History*
Only in the state does man have a rational existence ... Man owes his entire existence to the state, and has his being within it alone. Whatever worth and spiritual reality he possesses are his solely by virtue of the state.

HEIN Piet
4506
If no thought
your mind does visit
make your speech
not too explicit.

HEINE Heinrich 1797-1856
4507 *Almansor*
Wherever books will be burned, men also, in the end, are burned.

4508 *(as he died)*
God will pardon me. It's his business.

4509
It must require an inordinate share of vanity and presumption after enjoying so much that is good and beautiful on earth, to ask the Lord for immortality in addition to it all.

4510
The Romans would never have had time to conquer the world if they had been obliged to learn Latin first of all.

4511
When the heroes go off the stage, the clowns come on.

4512
On wings of song.

4513
Woman is at once apple and serpent.

HELLER Joseph 1923-
4514 *Catch-22*
Some men are born mediocre, some men achieve mediocrity, and some men have mediocrity thrust upon them. With Major Major it had been all three.

4515
Frankly I'd like to see the government get out of war altogether and leave the whole field to private industry.

4516 *Something Happened*
The company has a policy about getting laid. It's okay ... Talking about getting laid is even more okay than doing it, but doing it is okay too, although talking about getting laid with your own wife is never okay.

4517
When I read something saying I've not done anything as good as *Catch-22*, I'm tempted to reply, 'Who has?'

HELLMAN Lillian 1907-1984
4518
Cynicism is an unpleasant way of saying the truth.

4519
They're fancy talkers about themselves, writers. If I had to give young writers advice, I would say don't listen to writers talking about writing or themselves.

4520 *Toys in the Attic*
People change and forget to tell each other.

4521
If you are willing to take the punishment, you're halfway through the battle. That the issues may be trivial, the battle ugly, is another point.

HELPS Sir Arthur 1813-1875
4522
Men of much depth of mind can bear a great deal of counsel; for it does not easily deface their own character, nor render their purposes indistinct.

4523
Reading is sometimes an ingenious device for avoiding thought.

4524
If you would understand your own age, read the works of fiction produced in it. People in disguise speak freely.

HELVETIUS Claude-Adrien 1715-1771
4525
To limit the press is to insult a nation; to prohibit reading of certain books is to declare the inhabitants to be either fools or slaves.

HEMANS Felicia 1793-1835
4526 *'Casabianca'*
The boy stood on the burning deck
Whence all but he had fled;
The flame that lit the battle's wreck
Shone round him o'er the dead.

4527 *'The Homes of England'*
The stately homes of England,
How beautiful they stand!

HEMINGWAY Ernest 1899-1961
4528 *For Whom the Bell Tolls*
But did thee feel the earth move?

4529
The most essential gift for a good writer is a
built-in, shockproof shit detector. This is the
writer's radar and all great writers have had it.

4530
You lose it if you talk about it.

4531
If you are lucky enough to have lived in Paris as
a young man, then wherever you go for the rest
of your life, it stays with you, for Paris is a
movable feast.

4532
Nobody knows what's in him until he tries to
pull it out. If there's nothing, or very little, the
shock can kill a man.

4533
The writer must write what he has to say, not
speak it.

4534
His (the writer's) standard of fidelity to the truth
should be so high that his invention, out of his
experience, should produce a truer account
than anything factual can be.

HENDERSON Nelson
4535
The true meaning of life is to plant trees, under
whose shade you do not expect to sit.

HENDREN L.L.
4536
Fathers send their sons to college either
because they went to college, or because they
didn't.

HENDRIX Jimi 1942-1970
4537 *'Purple Haze'*
Purple haze is in my brain
Lately things don't seem the same.

HENLEY W.E. 1849-1903
4538
Bland as a Jesuit, sober as a hymn.

4539 *'Invictus. In Memoriam R.T.H.B.'*
In the fell clutch of circumstance,
I have not winced nor cried aloud:
Under the bludgeonings of chance
My head is bloody, but unbowed.

4540 *'Invictus. In Memoriam R.T.H.B.'*
It matters not how strait the gate,
How charged with punishments the scroll,
I am the master of my fate:
I am the captain of my soul.

HENRI IV (King of Navarre) 1553-1610
4541 *(attributed)*
Paris is well worth a mass.

4542 *(of James I of England, attributed)*
The wisest fool in Christendom.

HENRICH Tommy
4543
Catching a fly ball is a pleasure, but knowing
what to do with it is a business.

HENRY II King 1133-1189
4544 *(of Thomas Becket)*
Will no one rid me of this turbulent priest?

HENRY O. 1862-1910
4545 *Gentle Grafter 'Octopus Marooned'*
It was beautiful and simple as all truly great
swindles are.

4546 *(last words)*
Turn up the lights; I don't want to go home in
the dark.

4547 *Memoirs of a Yellow Dog*
If men knew how women pass the time when
they are alone, they'd never marry.

HENRY Patrick 1736-1799
4548
I know not what course others may take; but as
for me, give me liberty, or give me death!

4549
For my part, whatever anguish of spirit it may
cost, I am willing to know the whole truth - to
know the worst and provide for it.

HENRY Will
4550
What is research, but a blind date with
knowledge?

HENRY William (Duke of Gloucester) 1743-
1805
4551
Another damned, thick, square book! Always
scribble, scribble, scribble! Eh! Mr. Gibbon?

HEPBURN Katharine 1909-
4552 *in The African Queen*
"Nature, Mr Allnutt, is what we are put into this
world to rise above."

4553
If you give audiences a chance they'll do half your acting for you.

4554
Only the really plain people know about love - the very fascinating ones try so hard to create an impression that they soon exhaust their talents.

4555
If you're given a choice between money and sex appeal, take the money. As you get older, the money will become your sex appeal.

HERACLITUS c.544-483 BC
4556
All things flow, nothing abides.

HERBERT A.P. 1890-1971
4557
A dull speaker, like a plain woman, is credited with all the virtues, for we charitably suppose that a surface so unattractive must be compensated by interior blessings.

4558 *'The Farmer'*
The Farmer will never be happy again;
He carries his heart in his boots;
For either the rain is destroying his grain
Or the drought is destroying his roots.

4559
A highbrow is the kind of person who looks at a sausage and thinks of Picasso.

4560 *'The President of the Board of Trade'*
This high official, all allow,
Is grossly overpaid;
There wasn't any Board, and now
There isn't any Trade.

4561 *Tough at the Top*
Nothing is wasted, nothing is in vain:
The seas roll over but the rocks remain.

4562 *Uncommon Law*
The critical period in matrimony is breakfast-time.

4563 *Uncommon Law*
The Common Law of England has been laboriously built about a mythical figure - the figure of 'The Reasonable Man'.

HERBERT George 1593-1633
4564 *'The 23rd Psalm'*
The God of love my Shepherd is,
And He that doth me feed:
While He is mine, and I am His,
What can I want or need?

4565 *'Affliction (1)'*
Ah, my dear God! though I am clean forgot,
Let me not love Thee, if I love Thee not.

4566
Let all the world in ev'ry corner sing
My God and King.

4567
The chicken is the country's, but the city eats it.

4568
Deceive not thy physician, confessor, nor lawyer.

4569
Drink not the third glass - which thou can'st not tame when once it is within thee.

4570
He that makes a good war makes a good peace.

4571
A great ship asks deep water.

4572
Hope is the poor man's bread.

4573
You must lose a fly to catch a trout.

4574
A man that looks on glass,
On it may stay his eye;
Or if he pleaseth, through it pass,
And then the heaven espy.

4575
One sword keeps another in the sheath.

4576
Teach me, my God and King,
In all things Thee to see,
And what I do in any thing
To do it as for Thee.

HERBERT Jack
4577
A comedian is a fellow who finds other comedians too humorous to mention.

HERFORD Oliver
4578
Actresses will happen in the best regulated families.

4579
Bigamy is one way of avoiding the painful publicity of divorce and the expense of alimony.

4580
Only the young die good.

HERODOTUS c.485-425 BC
4581
Very few things happen at the right time, and the rest do not happen at all; the conscientious historian will correct these defects.

4582
In peace, sons bury their fathers; in war, fathers bury their sons.

4583
This is the worst pain a man can suffer: to have insight into much and power over nothing.

HEROLD Don
4584
Babies are such a nice way to start people.

4585
A humorist is a man who feels bad but who feels good about it.

4586
There's one thing about baldness - it's neat.

HEROLD J. Christopher
4587
Those who mistake their good luck for their merit are inevitably bound for disaster.

HERRICK Robert 1591-1674
4588
Fain would I kiss my Julia's dainty leg,
Which is as white and hairless as an egg.

4589 *'Upon Julia's Clothes'*
Whenas in silks my Julia goes,
Then, then (methinks) how sweetly flows
That liquefaction of her clothes.
Next, when I cast mine eyes and see
That brave vibration each way free;
O how that glittering taketh me!

4590
If a little labour, little are our gains.
Man's fortunes are according to his pains.

4591 *'An Ode for him' [Ben Jonson]*
And yet each verse of thine
Out-did the meat, out-did the frolic wine.

4592 *'To the Virgins, to Make Much of Time'*
Gather ye rosebuds while ye may,
Old Time is still a-flying:
And this same flower that smiles to-day,
To-morrow will be dying.

4593 *'To the Virgins, to Make Much of Time'*
Then be not coy, but use your time;
And while ye may, go marry:
For having lost but once your prime,
You may for ever tarry.

HERSCHENSOHN Bruce
4594
Boredom turns a man to sex, a woman to shopping, and it drives newscasters berserk.

HERSEY John 1914-1993
4595
Journalism allows it's readers to witness history. Fiction gives its readers an opportunity to live it.

HERSHEY Lenore
4596
Do give books - religious or otherwise - for Christmas. They're never fattening, seldom sinful, and permanently personal.

HERZOG Roman 1934-
4597
One cannot cancel out Hitler through Beethoven.

HESBURGH Rev. Theodore
4598
The most important thing a father can do for his children is to love their mother.

HESCHEL Abraham J.
4599
Our concern is not how to worship in the catacombs but how to remain human in the skyscrapers.

4600
Self-respect is the root of discipline: the sense of dignity grows with the ability to say no to oneself.

HESIOD fl.8th Century BC
4601
The Gods rank work above virtues.

4602
No gossip ever dies away entirely, if many people voice it: it, too, is a kind of divinity.

HESS Stephen
4603 *(of John Major)*
The other European leaders actually **ARE** old: he just acts old.

HESSE Hermann 1877-1962
4604
If you hate a person, you hate something in him that is part of yourself. What isn't part of ourselves doesn't disturb us.

4605
Every man is more than just himself; he also represents the unique, the very special and always significant and remarkable point at which the world's phenomena intersect, only once in this way, and never again.

4606
There is no reality except the one contained within us. That is why so many people live such an unreal life. They take the images outside them for reality and never allow the world within to assert itself.

4607
Those who are too lazy and comfortable to think for themselves and be their own judges obey the laws. Others sense their own laws within them.

HEWART Gordon 1870-1943
4608 *(Rex v Sussex Justices)*
A long line of cases shows that it is not merely of some importance, but is of fundamental importance that justice should not only be done, but should manifestly and undoubtedly be seen to be done.

HEWES Henry
4609
To be reborn is a constantly recurring human need.

HEYWARD Du Bose 1885-1940
4610 *Porgy and Bess 'Summertime'*
Summer time an' the livin' is easy,
Fish are jumpin' an' the cotton is high.
Oh, yo' daddy's rich, and yo' ma' is good lookin',
So hush, little baby, don't yo' cry.

HEYWOOD John c.1497 1580
4611
The more haste, the less speed.

4612
Wedding is destiny, and hanging likewise.

HICKS Sir John 1904-1989
4613 *Econometrica 'The Theory of Monopoly'*
The best of all monopoly profits is a quiet life.

HILL Rowland 1744-1833
4614
He did not see any reason why the devil should have all the good tunes.

HILLARY Sir Edmund 1919-
4615 *(on conquering Mount Everest)*
Well, we knocked the bastard off!

HILLEBRAND Fred 1893-
4616
Home James, and don't spare the horses.

HILLINGDON Lady 1857-1940
4617 *The Rise and Fall of the British Nanny*
I am happy now that Charles calls on my bedchamber less frequently than of old. As it is, I now endure but two calls a week and when I hear his steps outside my door I lie down on my bed, close my eyes, open my legs, and think of England.

HILLMAN Sidney 1887-1946
4618
Politics is the science of how who gets what, when and why.

HILTON James 1900-1954
4619 *Goodbye, Mr Chips*
Nothing really wrong with him - only anno domini, but that's the most fatal complaint of all, in the end.

HIMMEL Sam
4620
A dictatorship is a country where they have taken the politics out of politics.

HINCKS Clarence H.
4621
Nothing succeeds like one's own successor.

HINES James
4622
A gentle Quaker, hearing a strange noise in his house one night, got up and discovered a burglar busily at work. He went and got his gun, came back and stood quietly in the doorway. 'Friend' he said, 'I would do thee no harm for the world, but thou standest where I am about to shoot.'

HIPPOCRATES c.460-377 BC
4623
Wherever a doctor cannot do good, he must be kept from doing harm.

HISLOP Ian 1960-
4624
What satirist ever toppled the government? Swift managed to get one small tax changed in his whole career.

HITCHCOCK Alfred 1899-1980
4625
Drama is life with the dull bits cut out.

4626
The only way to get rid of my fears is to make films about them.

4627
Television has brought back murder into the home - where it belongs.

HITCHCOCK R.D.
4628
In a truly heroic life there is no peradventure. It is always doing or dying.

HITLER Adolf 1889-1945
4629
Belief is harder to shake than knowledge.

4630 *(of massacre of Roehm and associates)*
The night of the long knives.

4631 *Mein Kampf*
The broad mass of a nation ... will more easily fall victim to a big lie than to a small one.

4632
Is Paris burning?

4633
With regard to the problem of the Sudeten Germans, my patience is now at an end!

HO Tao
4634
Good architecture is like a piece of beautifully composed music crystallized in space that elevates our spirits beyond the limitation of time.

HOBBES Thomas 1588-1679
4635
If I had read as much as other men, I should have known no more than they.

4636 *(last words)*
I am about to take my last voyage, a great leap in the dark.

4637 *Leviathan*
No arts; no letters; no society; and which is worst of all, continual fear and danger of violent death; and the life of man, solitary, poor, nasty, brutish, and short.

4638 *Leviathan*
Force, and fraud, are in war the two cardinal virtues.

4639 *Leviathan*
The papacy is not other than the ghost of the deceased Roman Empire, sitting crowned upon the grave thereof.

4640 *Leviathan*
The praise of ancient authors proceeds not from the reverence of the dead, but from the competition, and mutual envy of the living.

4641
Understanding is nothing else than conception caused by speech.

4642
Words are wise men's counters, they do but reckon by them; but they are the money of fools.

HOCHHUTH Rolf 1931-
4643
Men may be linked in friendship. Nations are linked only by interests.

HOCKNEY David 1937-
4644
The thing with high-tech is that you always end up using scissors.

4645
Life doesn't have clear edges.

HODGSON Ralph 1871-1962
4646
Did anyone ever have a boring dream?

4647 *'Bells of Heaven'*
'Twould ring the bells of Heaven
The wildest peal for years,
If Parson lost his senses

And people came to theirs,
And he and they together
Knelt down with angry prayers
For tamed and shabby tigers
And dancing dogs and bears,
And wretched, blind, pit ponies,
And little hunted hares.

HOFFA Jimmy c.1913-1975
4648
I may have faults but being wrong ain't one of them.

HOFFENSTEIN Samuel
4649
Breathes there a man with hide so tough
Who says two sexes aren't enough?

HOFFER Eric 1902-1983
4650
Our credulity is greatest concerning the things we know least about. And since we know least about ourselves, we are ready to believe all that is said about us. Hence the mysterious power of both flattery and calumny.

4651
You can discover what your enemy fears most by observing the means he uses to frighten you.

4652
The end comes when we no longer talk with ourselves. It is the end of genuine thinking and the beginning of the final loneliness.

4653
Fear comes from uncertainty. When we are absolutely certain, whether of our worth or worthlessness, we are almost impervious to fear. Thus a feeling of utter unworthiness can be a source of courage.

4654
It is the malady of our age that the young are so busy teaching us that they have no time left to learn.

4655
Every new adjustment is a crisis in self-esteem.

4656
Passionate hatred can give meaning and purpose to an empty life.

4657
People in a hurry cannot think, cannot grow, nor can they decay. They are preserved in a state of perpetual puerility.

4658
It is a perplexing and unpleasant truth that when men already have 'something worth fighting for', they do not feel like fighting.

4659
The poor on the borderline of starvation live purposeful lives. To be engaged in a desperate struggle for food and shelter is to be wholly free from a sense of futility.

4660
Power corrupts the few, while weakness corrupts the many.

4661
There is a radicalism in all getting, and a conservatism in all keeping. Lovemaking is radical, while marriage is conservative.

4662
There can be no real freedom without the freedom to fail.

4663
Rudeness is the weak man's imitation of strength.

4664
It is always safe to assume that people are more subtle and less sensitive than they seem.

4665
When people are bored, it is primarily with their own selves.

4666
When people are free to do as they please, they usually imitate each other. Originality is deliberate and forced, and partakes of the nature of a protest.

HOFFMAN August Heinrich 1798-1874
4667
Deutschland über alles
Germany above all.

HOFFMANN Heinrich 1809-1894
4668 *Struwwelpeter*
Look at little Johnny there,
Little Johnny Head-In-Air!

HOGG James 1770-1835
4669 *'O'er the Water to Charlie'*
We'll o'er the water, we'll o'er the sea,
We'll o'er the water to Charlie;
Come weel, come wo, we'll gather and go,
And live or die wi' Charlie.

HÖLDERLIN Friedrich 1770-1843
4670
I am mortal, born to love and to suffer.

HOLLAND Agnieszka
4671
In Hollywood they don't feel guilt.

HOLLAND Henry Scott 1847-1918
4672
Death is nothing at all; it does not count. I have only slipped away into the next room.

HOLLAND James
4673
The Middle East is a region where oil is thicker than blood.

HOLLAND J.G. 1819-1881
4674
God gives every bird its food, but he does not throw it into the nest.

4675
There is no royal road to anything. One thing at a time, and all things in succession. That which grows slowly endures.

HOLLWEG Theobald von Bethmann 1856-1921
4676
Just for a word 'neutrality' - a word which in wartime has so often been disregarded - just for a scrap of paper, Great Britain is going to make war on a kindred nation who desires nothing better than to be friends with her.

HOLMAN Libby
4677
I suppose you've heard all those wicked stories about me. Well, I've lived my life as it came and I've done bloody marvels with a bad hand.

HOLMES John Andrew
4678
It is well to remember that the entire population of the universe, with one trifling exception, is composed of others.

HOLMES John Hughes
4679
The universe is not hostile, nor yet is it friendly. It is simply indifferent.

HOLMES Oliver Wendell 1809-1894
4680
Apology - a desperate habit, and one that is rarely cured.

4681
Apology is only egotism wrong side out.

4682 *The Autocrat of the Breakfast Table*
Man has his will - but woman has her way.

4683
The axis of the earth sticks out visibly through the centre of each and every town or city.

4684
Don't be consistent, but be simply true.

4685
A general flavour of mild decay,
But nothing local, as one may say.

4686
The great thing in this world is not so much where we stand, as in what direction we are moving.

4687
Heredity is an omnibus in which all our
ancestors ride, and every now and then one of
them puts his head out and embarrasses us.

4688
Husband and wife come to look alike at last.

4689
So long as the body is affected through the
mind, no audacious device, even of the most
manifestly dishonest character, can fail of
producing occasional good to those who yield
to it an implicit or even a partial faith.

4690
A man must get a thing before he can forget it.

4691
A man is a kind of inverted thermometer, the
bulb uppermost, and the column of self-
valuation is all the time going up and down.

4692
Man's mind stretched to a new idea never goes
back to its original dimensions.

4693
Men are idolaters, and want something to look
at and kiss and hug, or throw themselves down
before; they always did, they always will, and if
you don't make it of wood, you must make it of
words.

4694
Nature is in earnest when she makes a woman.

4695
Nature, when she invented, manufactured and
patented her authors, contrived to make critics
out of the chips that were left.

4696
It is the province of knowledge to speak and it is
the privilege of wisdom to listen.

4697
Every real thought on every real subject knocks
the wind out of somebody or other.

4698
Rough work, iconoclasm, but the only way to
get at the truth.

4699 *(of Samuel Francis Smith)*
Fate tried to conceal him by naming him Smith.

4700
After sixty years the stern sentence of the burial
service seems to have a meaning that one did
not notice in former years. There begins to be
something personal about it.

4701
Sweet is the scene where genial friendship plays
The pleasing game of interchanging praise.

4702
He (Turgenev) had the air of his own statue
erected by national subscription.

4703
A weak mind does not accumulate force enough
to hurt itself; stupidity often saves a man from
going mad.

4704
When the style is fully formed, if it has a sweet
undersong, we call it beautiful, and the writer
may do what he likes in words or syntax.

4705
When you write in prose you say what you
mean. When you write in rhyme you say what
you must.

4706
The young man knows the rules but the old
man knows the exceptions.

HOLMES Oliver Wendell Jr. 1841-1935
4707
The advice of the elders to young men is very
apt to be as unreal as a list of the hundred best
books.

4708
This is a court of law, young man, not a court of
justice.

4709
Fame usually comes to those who are thinking
about something else.

4710
Every calling is great when greatly pursued.

4711
Historic continuity with the past is not a duty, it
is only a necessity.

4712
Life is action and passion; therefore, it is
required of a man that he should share the
passion and action of the time, at peril of being
judged not to have lived.

4713
The life of the law has not been logic, it has
been experience.

4714
Life is painting a picture, not doing a sum.

4715
Longevity is having a chronic disease and taking
care of it.

4716
A man over ninety is a great comfort to all his
elderly neighbours: he is a picket-guard at the
extreme outpost: and the young folks of sixty
and seventy feel that the enemy must get by
him before he can come near their camp.

4717
The mind of a bigot is like the pupil of the eye; the more light you pour upon it, the more it will contract.

4718
A person is always startled when he hears himself seriously called an old man for the first time.

4719
The reward of a general is not a bigger tent - but command.

4720
A sense of wrongdoing is an enhancement of pleasure.

4721
To be seventy years young is sometimes far more cheerful and hopeful than to be forty years old.

4722
If you think that I am going to bother myself again before I die about social improvement, or read any of those stinking upward and onwarders - you err - I mean to have some good out of being old.

4723
The trombone age (moving the page back and forth).

4724
I am on the side of the unregenerate who affirm the worth of life as an end in itself, as against the saints who deny it.

HOLT John
4725
People should be free to find or make for themselves the kinds of educational experiences they want their children to have.

HOLYDAY Barten
4726
A man may as well open an oyster without a knife, as a lawyer's mouth without a fee.

HOME Lord (Sir Alec Douglas-Home) 1903-1995
4727
There are two problems in my life. The political ones are insoluble and the economic ones are incomprehensible.

HOMER fl.8th Century BC
4728
Achilles absent, was Achilles still.

4729
All strangers and beggars are from Zeus, and a gift, though small, is precious.

4730
A councillor ought not to sleep the whole night through - a man to whom the populace is entrusted, and who has many responsibilities.

4731
A decent boldness ever meets with friends.

4732 *The Iliad*
It lies in the lap of the gods.

4733
Men grow tired of sleep, love, singing and dancing sooner than of war.

HOMOLKA Oscar
4734
To really enjoy the better things in life, one must first have experienced the things they are better than.

HONEGGER Arthur 1892-1955
4735
The first requirement for a composer is to be dead.

HOOD Hugh
4736
Nothing ever tasted any better than a cold beer on a beautiful afternoon with nothing to look forward to but more of the same.

HOOD Thomas 1799-1845
4737 *Faithless Nelly Gray*
The love that loves a scarlet coat
Should be more uniform.

4738 'Faithless Sally Brown'
His death, which happened in his berth,
At forty-odd befell:
They went and told the sexton, and
The sexton tolled the bell.

4739 'A Reflection'
When Eve upon the first of Men
The apple pressed with specious cant,
Oh! what a thousand pities then
That Adam was not Adamant!

4740 'I Remember'
I remember, I remember,
The house where I was born,
The little window where the sun
Came peeping in at morn.

4741 *Up the Rhine*
Holland ... lies so low they're only saved by being dammed.

4742 'The Song of the Shirt'
O! men with sisters dear,
O! men with mothers and wives!
It is not linen you're wearing out,
But human creatures' lives!

4743 *'The Song of the Shirt'*
Oh! God! that bread should be so dear,
And flesh and blood so cheap!

HOOKER Richard c.1554-1600
4744 *Of the Laws of Ecclesiastical Polity*
He that goeth about to persuade a multitude,
that they are not so well governed as they ought
to be, shall never want attentive and favourable
hearers.

HOOPER Ellen Sturgis 1816-1841
4745 *'Beauty and Duty'*
I slept, and dreamed that life was beauty;
I woke, and found that life was duty.

HOOVER Herbert 1874-1964
4746
Once upon a time my political opponents
honored me as possessing the fabulous
intellectual and economic power by which I
created a worldwide depression all by myself.

HOPE Anthony 1863-1933
4747 *The Dolly Dialogues*
Economy is going without something you do
want in case you should, some day, want
something you probably won't want.

4748 *The Dolly Dialogues*
Bourgeois ... is an epithet which the riff-raff
apply to what is respectable, and the aristocracy
to what is decent.

HOPE Bob 1903-
4749 *(attributed)*
A bank is a place that will lend you money if
you can prove that you don't need it.

4750
If you haven't any charity in your heart, you
have the worst kind of heart trouble.

4751
The good news is that Jesus is coming back.
The bad news is that he's really pissed off.

4752 *(on receiving honorary knighthood)*
I am literally speechless. Where are my writers
when I need them?

4753
People who throw kisses are hopelessly lazy.

4754
If you watch a game, it's fun. If you play it, it's
recreation. If you work at it, it's golf.

HOPKINS Anthony 1937-
4755 *in The Silence of the Lambs*
"I have to go now, Clarice, I'm having an old
friend for dinner."

HOPKINS Gerard Manley 1844-1889
4756 *'Duns Scotus's Oxford'*
Towery city and branchy between towers;

Cuckoo-echoing, bell-swarmèd, lark-charmèd,
rook-racked, river-rounded.

4757 *'Inversnaid'*
What would the world be, once bereft
Of wet and wildness? Let them be left,
O let them be left, wildness and wet;
Long live the weeds and the wilderness yet.

4758
To lift up the hands in prayer gives God glory,
but a man with a dungfork in his hand, a
woman with a slop-pail, give him glory too.

HOPKINS Harry 1890-1946
4759
Hunger is not debatable.

HOPPER Edward 1882-1967
4760
If you could say it in words there would be no
reason to paint.

HORACE 65-8 BC
4761
Acquittal of the guilty damns the judge.

4762 *Ars Poetica*
It is hard to utter common notions in an
individual way.

4763 *Ars Poetica*
Not gods, nor men, nor even booksellers have
put up with poets being second-rate.

4764
The changing year's progressive plan
Proclaims mortality to man.

4765
Dismiss the old horse in good time, lest he fail
in the lists and the spectators laugh.

4766 *Epistles*
If possible honestly, if not, somehow, make
money.

4767 *Epistles*
We are just statistics, born to consume
resources.

4768 *Epistles*
Anger is a short madness.

4769 *Epistles*
Believe each day that has dawned is your last.
Some hour to which you have not been looking
forward will prove lovely.

4770 *Epistles*
And once sent out a word takes wing beyond
recall.

4771 *Epistles*
No verse can give pleasure for long, nor last,
that is written by drinkers of water.

4772
He has half the deed done who has made a beginning.

4773 *Odes*
Never despair.

4774 *Odes*
Drop the question what tomorrow may bring, and count as profit every day that Fate allows you.

4775 *Odes*
When the going gets rough, remember to keep calm.

4776 *Odes*
Dulce et decorum est pro patria mori.
Sweet and honourable it is to die for one's country.

4777 *Odes*
Force, unaided by judgement, collapses through its own weight.

4778 *Odes*
Mix a little foolishness with your prudence: it's good to be silly at the right moment.

4779
Sport begets tumultuous strife and wrath, and wrath begets fierce quarrels and war to the death.

HORDER Lord Thomas 1910-
4780
It is the duty of a doctor to prolong life and it is not his duty to prolong the act of dying.

HORNER Marina
4781
What is important is to keep learning, to enjoy challenge, and to tolerate ambiguity. In the end there are no certain answers.

HORNEY Karen 1885-1952
4782
Fortunately, analysis is not the only way to resolve inner conflicts. Life itself remains a very effective therapist.

HOUSMAN A.E. 1859-1936
4783 *Last Poems*
These, in the day when heaven was falling,
The hour when earth's foundations fled,
Followed their mercenary calling
And took their wages and are dead.

Their shoulders held the sky suspended;
They stood, and earth's foundations stay;
What God abandoned, these defended,
And saved the sum of things for pay.

4784
Malt does more than Milton can
To justify God's ways to man.

4785
Nature, not content with denying him the ability to think, has endowed him with the ability to write.

4786 *More Poems*
Life, to be sure, is nothing much to lose;
But young men think it is, and we were young.

4787 *A Shropshire Lad*
Loveliest of trees, the cherry now
Is hung with bloom along the bough,
And stands about the woodland ride
Wearing white for Eastertide.

4788 *A Shropshire Lad*
And since to look at things in bloom
Fifty springs are little room,
About the woodlands I will go
To see the cherry hung with snow.

4789 *A Shropshire Lad*
When I was one-and-twenty
I heard a wise man say,
'Give crowns and pounds and guineas
But not your heart away;
Give pearls away and rubies,
But keep your fancy free.'
But I was one-and-twenty,
No use to talk to me.

4790
I, a stranger and afraid
In a world I never made.

HOWARD Elizabeth Jane 1923-
4791
Sex is like petrol. It's a galvaniser, a wonderful fuel for starting a relationship.

HOWARD Philip 1933-
4792
Most history is a record of the triumphs, disasters and follies of top people. The black hole in it is the way of life of mute, inglorious men and women who made no nuisance of themselves in the world.

HOWE Edgar Watson
4793
Abuse a man unjustly, and you will make friends for him.

4794
About all some men accomplish in life is to send a son to Harvard.

4795
If you go to church, and like the singing better than the preaching, that's not orthodox.

4796
Even if a farmer intends to loaf, he gets up in time to get an early start.

4797
Farmers worry only during the growing season, but town people worry all the time.

4798
If a friend is in trouble, don't annoy him by asking if there is anything you can do. Think up something appropriate and do it.

4799
A good scare is worth more to a man than good advice.

4800
A man should be taller, older, heavier, uglier and hoarser than his wife.

4801
A modest man is usually admired - if people ever hear of him.

4802
What people say behind your back is your standing in the community.

4803
When people hear good music, it makes them homesick for something they never had, and never will have.

HOWE Irving
4804 *(of Thomas Hardy)*
He claimed his modest share of the general foolishness of the human race.

HOWE Joseph 1804-1873
4805
Poetry was the maiden I loved, but politics was the harridan I married.

HOWE Julia Ward 1819-1910
4806 *'Battle Hymn of the Republic'*
Mine eyes have seen the glory of the coming of the Lord:
He is trampling out the vintage where the grapes of wrath are stored;
He hath loosed the fateful lightning of his terrible swift sword:
His truth is marching on.

HOWELL James
4807
He that hath the name to be an early riser may sleep till noon.

HOWELLS William Dean 1837-1920
4808
Does it afflict you to find your books wearing out? I mean literally ... the mortality of all inanimate things is terrible to me, but that of books most of all.

4809
Some people can stay longer in an hour than others can in a week.

HOWITT Mary 1799-1888
4810 *'The Spider and the Fly'*
'Will you walk into my parlour?' said a spider to a fly:
''Tis the prettiest little parlour that ever you did spy.'

HOYLE Sir Fred 1915-
4811
Space isn't remote at all. It's only an hour's drive away if your car could go straight upwards.

HSIEH Tehyi
4812
If ignorance is indeed bliss, it is a very low grade of the article.

HUBBARD Elbert 1859-1915
4813
To escape criticism - do nothing, say nothing, be nothing.

4814
God will not look you over for medals, degrees or diplomas, but for scars.

4815
Every man is a damn fool for at least five minutes every day; wisdom consists in not exceeding the limit.

4816
The man who is anybody and who does anything is surely going to be criticized, vilified, and misunderstood. This is part of the penalty for greatness, and every man understands, too, that it is no proof of greatness.

4817 *The Motto Book*
Never explain - your friends do not need it and your enemies will not believe you anyway.

4818
Mystic: a person who is puzzled before the obvious, but who understands the non-existent.

4819
Pessimism is only the name that men of weak nerves give to wisdom.

4820
A pessimist is one who has been compelled to live with an optimist.

4821 *Philistine*
Life is just one damned thing after another.

4822
Polygamy: an endeavour to get more out of life than there is in it.

4823 *The Roycroft Dictionary*
An editor - a person employed on a newspaper, whose business it is to separate the wheat from the chaff, and to see that the chaff is printed.

The Wordsworth Dictionary of Quotations

4824
Victory - a matter of staying power.

4825
We work to become, not to acquire.

HUBBARD Kin 1868-1930
4826
I don't know of anything better than a woman if you want to spend money where it will show.

4827
The fellow that owns his own home is always just coming out of a hardware store.

4828
Some fellows pay a compliment like they expected a receipt.

4829
Folks that blurt out just what they think wouldn't be so bad if they thought.

4830
Some folks can look so busy doing nothin' that they seem indispensable.

4831
A friend that ain't in need is a friend indeed.

4832
Gossip is vice enjoyed vicariously - the sweet, subtle satisfaction without the risk.

4833
I haven't heard of anybody who wants to stop living on account of the cost.

4834
Kindness goes a long way lots o' times when it ought t' stay at home.

4835
The only way to entertain some folks is to listen to them.

4836
An optimist is a fellow who believes what's going to be will be postponed.

4837
It's pretty hard to be efficient without being obnoxious.

4838
The world gets better every day - then worse again in the evening.

HUBBARD L. Ron 1911-1986
4839
If you really want to make a million ... the quickest way is to start your own religion.

HUDSON William Henry 1841-1922
4840
You cannot fly like an eagle with the wings of a wren.

HUGHES Charles Evans 1862-1948
4841
We are under a Constitution, but the Constitution is what the judges say it is.

HUGHES J.B.
4842
If Moses had been a committee, the Israelites would still be in Egypt.

HUGHES Langston 1902-1967
4843 *'Children's Rhymes'*
Lies written down
For white folks
Ain't for us a-tall:
Liberty and Justice-
Huh!- *For All?*

4844 *'I, Too'*
I, too, sing America.
I am the darker brother.

HUGHES Richard 1900-1976
4845
All that non-fiction can do is answer questions. It's fiction's business to ask them.

HUGHES Rupert
4846
Her face was her chaperone.

HUGHES Thomas 1822-1896
4847 *Tom Brown's Schooldays*
It's more than a game. It's an institution.

HUGO Victor 1802-1885
4848
No army can withstand the strength of an idea whose time has come.

4849
If you would civilize a man, begin with his grandmother.

4850
Everything bows to success, even grammar.

4851
There are fathers who do not love their children; there is no grandfather who does not adore his grandson.

4852
Forty is the old age of youth; fifty is the youth of old age.

4853
Sorrow is a fruit; God does not allow it to grow on a branch that is too weak to bear it.

4854
A stand can be made against invasion by an army; no stand can be made against invasion by an idea.

4855
The supreme happiness of life is the conviction that we are loved.

4856
Those who live are those who fight.

HULBERT Harold S.
4857
Children need love, especially when they do not deserve it.

HULBERT James
4858
A company is judged by the president it keeps.

HULL Josephine
4859
Playing Shakespeare is very tiring. You never get to sit down, unless you're a king.

HUME Cardinal Basil 1923-
4860 *(asked how he plans to celebrate the Millennium)*
I'll be splashing around in the fountains of Trafalgar Square with everyone else.

4861 *(on homophobia and Catholicsm)*
To love one another, whether of the same sex or of a different sex, is to have entered the area of richest human experience.

4862
Just as we are not in the numbers game, so we are not in the power game.

HUME David 1711-1776
4863 *Essays, Moral, Political, and Literary*
In all ages of the world, priests have been enemies of liberty.

4864 *Essays, Moral, Political, and Literary*
The heart of man is made to reconcile the most glaring contradictions.

4865
Be a philosopher but, amid all your philosophy be still a man.

4866 *A Treatise upon Human Nature*
Poets ... though liars by profession, always endeavour to give an air of truth to their fictions.

HUME John 1937-
4867
Every party in Ireland was founded on the gun.

HUMPHREY Hubert 1911-1978
4868
The impersonal hand of government can never replace the helping hand of a neighbour.

4869
I've never thought my speeches were too long; I've rather enjoyed them.

4870
The right to be heard does not automatically include the right to be taken seriously.

HUNGERFORD Margaret Wolfe 1855-1897
4871 *Molly Bawn*
Beauty is altogether in the eye of the beholder.

HUNT Leigh 1784-1859
4872 *The Examiner 1808*
Never lay yourself open to what is called conviction: you might as well open your waist-coat to receive a knock-down blow.

4873
If you are ever at a loss to support a flagging conversation, introduce the subject of eating.

4874 *Song of Fairies Robbing an Orchard*
Stolen kisses are always sweeter,
Stolen kisses much completer,
Stolen looks are nice in chapels,
Stolen, stolen, be your apples.

4875 *'The Story of Rimini' (1816)*
The two divinest things this world has got,
A lovely woman in a rural spot!

HUNTINGTON Collis P. 1821-1900
4876
Whatever is not nailed down is mine. Whatever I can pry loose is not nailed down.

HUPFELD Herman 1894-1951
4877 *'As Time Goes By'*
You must remember this, a kiss is still a kiss,
A sigh is just a sigh;
The fundamental things apply,
As time goes by.

HURD Douglas 1930-
4878 *(to cheers)*
This is the last speech, on the last debate on the Maastricht treaty.

4879 *(in Gaza)*
A military occupation is a denial of human rights.

4880
Reality is always ahead of theory.

4881
No substitute has been found for the energy which wells up through the nation state.

4882
Summits are odd creatures.

HUROK Sol 1888-1974
4883
When people don't want to come, nothing will stop them.

HUSSEIN Saddam 1937-
4884
The mother of battles.

HUTCHENS John K.

4885
A writer and nothing else: a man alone in a room with the English language, trying to get human feelings right.

HUTCHINSON Bruce

4886
Our sons, who so easily recognize our errors, and rightly denounce them, will have to confess their own, later on, and they may be as bad as ours, perhaps worse.

HUTCHINSON Sir Robert

4887
Vegetarianism is harmless enough, though it is apt to fill a man with wind and self-righteousness.

HUXLEY Aldous 1894-1963

4888
The advertisement is one of the most interesting and difficult of modern literary forms.

4889 *Antic Hay*
There are few who would not rather be taken in adultery than in provincialism.

4890
A belief in hell and the knowledge that every ambition is doomed to frustration at the hands of a skeleton have never prevented the majority of human beings from behaving as though death were no more than an unfounded rumour, and survival a thing not beyond the bounds of possibility.

4891 *Beyond the Mexique Bay*
Official dignity tends to increase in inverse ratio to the importance of the country in which the office is held.

4892
Every ceiling, when reached, becomes a floor, upon which one walks as a matter of course and prescriptive right.

4893
Children are remarkable for their intelligence and ardour, for their curiosity, their intolerance of shams, the clarity and ruthlessness of their vision.

4894 *Chrome Yellow*
The proper study of mankind is books.

4895
To his dog, every man is Napoleon; hence the constant popularity of dogs.

4896 *Do What you Will*
Too much consistency is as bad for the mind as it is for the body. Consistency is contrary to nature, contrary to life. The only completely consistent people are the dead.

4897
The essay is a literary device for saying almost everything about almost anything.

4898
Experience teaches only the teachable.

4899
Experience is not what happens to a man. It is what a man does with what happens to him.

4900 *Eyeless in Gaza*
Chastity - the most unnatural of all the sexual perversions.

4901
Every gain made by individuals or society is almost instantly taken for granted.

4902
One of the great attractions of patriotism - it fulfills our worst wishes. In the person of our nation we are able, vicariously, to bully and cheat. Bully and cheat, what's more, with a feeling that we are profoundly virtuous.

4903
The greatest triumphs of propaganda have been accomplished, not by doing something, but by refraining from doing. Great is truth, but still greater, from a practical point of view, is silence about truth.

4904 *Heaven and Hell*
'Bed,' as the Italian proverb succinctly puts it, 'is the poor man's opera.'

4905
They intoxicate themselves with work so they won't see how they really are.

4906 *Limbo*
I can sympathize with people's pains, but not with their pleasures. There is something curiously boring about somebody else's happiness.

4907 *Ends and Means*
The end cannot justify the means, for the simple and obvious reason that the means employed determine the nature of the ends produced.

4908
At any given moment, life is completely senseless. But viewed over a period, it seems to reveal itself as an organism existing in time, having a purpose, tending in a certain direction.

4909
The natural rhythm of human life is routine punctuated by orgies.

4910
Nonsense is an assertion of man's spiritual freedom in spite of all the oppressions of circumstance.

4911
An old codger, rampant, and still learning.

4912 *'Fifth Philosopher's Song'*
A million million Spermatozoa,
All of them alive:
Out of their cataclysm but one poor Noah
Dare hope to survive.
And among that billion minus one
Might have chanced to be
Shakespeare, another Newton, a new Donne -
But the One was me.

4913 *'Ninth Philosopher's Song'*
Beauty for some provides escape,
Who gain a happiness in eyeing
The gorgeous buttocks of the ape
Or Autumn sunsets exquisitely dying.

4914 *Point Counter Point*
Several excuses are always less convincing than one.

4915
That we are not much sicker and much madder than we are is due exclusively to that most blessed and blessing of all natural graces, sleep.

4916
After silence, that which comes nearest to expressing the inexpressible is music.

4917
Speed provides the one genuinely modern pleasure.

4918
There is no substitute for talent. Industry and all the virtues are of no avail.

4919
There's only one corner of the universe you can be certain of improving and that's your own self.

4920
The traveller's eye view of men and women is not satisfying. A man might spend his life in trains and restaurants and know nothing of humanity at the end. To know, one must be an actor as well as a spectator.

4921
What we think and feel and are is to a great extent determined by the state of our ductless glands and our viscera.

4922
Why should human females become sterile in their forties, while female crocodiles continue to lay eggs into their third century?

4923
Writers write to influence their readers, their preachers, their auditors, but always, at bottom, to be more themselves.

HUXLEY Sir Julian 1887-1975
4924 *Religion without Revelation*
Operationally, God is beginning to resemble not a ruler but the last fading smile of a cosmic Cheshire cat.

HUXLEY Thomas 1825-1895
4925 *Collected Essays*
If a little knowledge is dangerous, where is the man who has so much as to be out of danger?

4926
Every great advance in natural knowledge has involved the absolute rejection of authority.

4927
The great end of life is not knowledge, but action.

4928
If some great power would agree to make me always think what is true and do what is right, on condition of being some sort of clock and wound up every morning before I got out of bed, I should close instantly with the offer.

4929
The great tragedy of Science: the slaying of a beautiful hypothesis by an ugly fact.

4930
Perhaps the most valuable result of all education is the ability to make yourself do the thing you have to do, when it ought to be done, whether you like it or not; it is the first lesson that ought to be learned, and however early a man's training begins, it is probably the last lesson that he learns thoroughly.

4931
I am too much of a sceptic to deny the possibility of anything.

4932 *Science and Culture and Other Essays*
Irrationally held truths may be more harmful than reasoned errors.

4933
Sit down before fact as a little child, be prepared to give up every preconceived notion, follow humbly wherever and to whatever abyss nature leads, or you shall learn nothing.

4934
Tolerably early in life I discovered that one of the unpardonable sins, in the eyes of most people, is for a man to go about unlabelled. The world regards such a person as the police do an unmuzzled dog.

HUXTABLE Ada Louise
4935
Washington is an endless series of mock palaces clearly built for clerks.

IBARRURI Dolores ('La Pasionaria') 1895-1989
4936
It is better to die on your feet than to live on your knees.

IBSEN Henrik 1828-1906
4937
A minority may be right, and a majority is always wrong.

4938
One should never put on one's best trousers to go out to battle for freedom and truth.

4939
The sea possesses a power over one's moods that has the effect of a will. The sea can hypnotize. Nature in general can do so.

ILES Francis 1893-1970
4940 *Malice Aforethought*
Murder is a serious business.

INGALLS Brian
4941
Grass is the forgiveness of nature - her constant benediction. Forests decay, harvests perish, flowers vanish, but grass is immortal.

INGE Charles 1868-1957
4942 *'On Monsieur Coué'*
This very remarkable man
Commends a most practical plan:
You can do what you want
If you don't think you can't,
So don't think you can't think you can.

INGE William R. 1860-1954
4943
Of all tyrannies a country can suffer, the worst is the tyranny of the majority.

4944
Anxiety is the interest paid on trouble before it is due.

4945
Christianity is good news; not good advice.

4946 *End of an Age*
The enemies of Freedom do not argue; they shout and they shoot.

4947 *End of an Age*
The effect of boredom on a large scale in history is underestimated. It is a main cause of revolutions, and would soon bring to an end all the static Utopias and the farmyard civilization of the Fabians.

4948 *Idea of Progress*
To become a popular religion, it is only necessary for a superstition to enslave a philosophy.

4949
Literature flourishes best when it is half a trade and half an art.

4950
A man usually does his best work just before he is found out.

4951
Middle-aged people are often happier than the young: but it by no means follows that they ought to be...

4952
Let none of us delude himself by supposing that honesty is always the best policy. It is not.

4953 *Outspoken Essays*
It takes in reality only one to make a quarrel. It is useless for the sheep to pass resolutions in favour of vegetarianism, while the wolf remains of a different opinion.

4954 *Outspoken Essays*
The nations which have put mankind and posterity most in their debt have been small states - Israel, Athens, Florence, Elizabethan England.

4955
Public opinion: a vulgar, impertinent, anonymous tyrant who deliberately makes life unpleasant for any one of us who is not content to be the average man.

4956
Religion is a way of walking, not a way of talking.

4957
Because most of the saints were poor, it does not follow that most of the poor are saints.

4958
There are two kinds of fools: one says, 'This is old, therefore it is good'; the other says, 'This is new, therefore it is better.'

4959
What is originality? Undetected plagiarism.

4960
The whole of nature is a conjugation of the verb to eat, in the active and passive.

INGELOW Jean 1820-1897
4961
I have lived to thank God that all my prayers have not been answered.

INGERSOLL Robert G. 1833-1899
4962
My creed is that:
Happiness is the only good.
The place to be happy is here.
The time to be happy is now.
The way to be happy is to make others so.

4963
An honest God is the noblest work of man.

4964
By physical liberty I mean the right to do
anything which does not interfere with the
happiness of another. By intellectual liberty I
mean the right to think wrong.

4965 *Some Reasons Why*
In nature there are neither rewards nor
punishments - there are consequences.

4966
In the republic of mediocrity, genius is
dangerous.

4967
With soap baptism is a good thing.

4968
I suppose it can be truthfully said that hope is
the only universal liar who never loses his
reputation for veracity.

IONESCO Eugene 1912-1994
4969
You can only predict things after they've
happened.

4970
Theatre is simply what cannot be expressed by
any other means; a complexity of words,
movements, gestures that convey a vision of the
world inexpressible in any other way.

IRVING John
4971
The object of war is to survive it.

IRVING Washington 1783-1859
4972
I am always at a loss to know how much to
believe of my own stories.

4973 *The Sketch Book*
A tart temper never mellows with age, and a
sharp tongue is the only edged tool that grows
keener with constant use.

ISHERWOOD Christopher 1904-1986
4974 *'The Common Cormorant'*
The common cormorant (or shag)
Lays eggs inside a paper bag,
You follow the idea, no doubt?
It's to keep the lightning out.

But what these unobservant birds

Have never thought of, is that herds
Of wandering bears might come with buns
And steal the bags to hold the crumbs.

ITAMINI Juzo
4975
If you imagine life as a book, the last page
should be the best, not the blackest.

IZETBEGOVIC Alija 1925-
4976 *(after signing accord between Serbia and
Croatia)*
And to my people I say, this may not be a just
peace, but it is more just than a continuation of
war.

JACKSON Andrew 1767-1845
4977
One man with courage makes a majority.

4978
There goes a man made by the Lord Almighty
and not by his tailor.

4979
Take time to deliberate; but when the time for
action arrives, stop thinking and go in.

JACKSON George
4980
Only one-fourth of the sorrow in each man's life
is caused by outside uncontrollable elements,
the rest is self-imposed by failing to analyze and
act with calmness.

4981
Patience has its limits. Take it too far, and it's
cowardice.

JACKSON Holbrook 1874-1948
4982 *Platitudes in the Making*
As soon as an idea is accepted it is time to reject
it.

JACKSON Jesse 1941-
4983
The Bible is nothing but a succession of civil
rights struggles by the Jewish people against the
oppressors.

4984
Your children need your presence more than
your presents.

JACKSON Robert H. 1892-1954
4985
Men are more often bribed by their loyalties
and ambitions than by money.

JACKSON Thomas (Stonewall) 1824-1863
4986
I like liquor - its taste and its effects - and that is
just the reason why I never drink it.

JACOB Fred
4987
A good husband should always bore his wife.

JACOBS Jane
4988
In small settlements everyone knows your affairs. In the big city, everyone does not - only those you choose to tell will know about you. This is one of the attributes of cities that is precious to most city people.

JAFFREY Saeed
4989 *in My Beautiful Launderette*
"Take my advice, there's money in muck."

JAMES Baroness 1920-
4990 *(of English teaching)*
We cannot aspire to a classless society ... if some children are disadvantaged the moment they open their mouths.

JAMES Cyril 1901-1989
4991
A free man is as jealous of his responsibilities as he is of his liberties.

JAMES Edmund Storer
4992
The interests of childhood and youth are the interests of mankind.

JAMES Henry 1843-1916
4993 *'The Given Case'*
Women never dine alone. When they dine alone they don't dine.

4994
Deep experience is never peaceful.

4995 *Hawthorne*
It takes a great deal of history to produce a little literature.

4996 *Hawthorne*
He was imperfect, unfinished, inartistic; he was worse than provincial - he was parochial.

4997
The real offence, as she ultimately perceived, was her having a mind of her own at all. Her mind was to be his - attached to his own like a small garden plot to a deer park.

JAMES I King (JAMES VI of Scotland) 1566-1625
4998 *A Counterblast to Tobacco*
A branch of the sin of drunkenness, which is the root of all sins.

4999 *A Counterblast to Tobacco*
A custom loathsome to the eye, hateful to the nose, harmful to the brain, dangerous to the lungs, and in the black, stinking fume thereof, nearest resembling the horrible Stygian smoke of the pit that is bottomless.

5000 *(recorded by Archdeacon Plume)*
Dr Donne's verses are like the peace of God; they pass all understanding.

JAMES William 1842-1910
5001
As Charles Lamb says, there is nothing so nice as doing good by stealth and being found out by accident, so I now say it is even nicer to make heroic decisions and to be prevented by 'circumstances beyond your control' from ever trying to execute them.

5002
Footnotes, the little dogs yapping at the heels of the text.

5003
Genius, in truth, means little more than the faculty of perceiving in an unhabitual way.

5004
The great use of life is to spend it for something that will outlast it.

5005
Lives based on having are less free than lives based either on doing or on being.

5006
Man, biologically considered, and whatever else he may be into the bargain, is simply the most formidable of all the beasts of prey, and, indeed, the only one that preys systematically on its own species.

5007 *The Principles of Psychology*
The art of being wise is the art of knowing what to overlook.

5008
An unlearned carpenter of my acquaintance once said in my hearing: 'There is very little difference between one man and another, but what there is is *very important.'*

5009 *The Varieties of Religious Experience*
There is no worse lie than a truth misunderstood by those who hear it.

5010
So far war has been the only force that can discipline a whole community, and until an equivalent discipline is organized, I believe that war must have its way.

5011
Be willing to have it so; acceptance of what has happened is the first step to overcoming the consequences of any misfortune.

JARRELL Randall 1914-1965
5012
The dark, uneasy world of family life - where the greatest can fail and the humblest succeed.

5013
Ezra Pound - idiosyncrasy on a monument.

5014
A good poet is someone who manages, in a lifetime of standing out in thunderstorms, to be struck by lightning five or six times.

5015
The novel is a prose narrative of some length that has something wrong with it.

5016
More and more people think of the critic as an indispensable middle man between writer and reader, and would no more read a book alone, if they could help it, than have a baby alone.

5017 *Pictures from an Institution*
To Americans, English manners are far more frightening than none at all.

JAY Douglas 1907-1996
5018 *(slogan for North Battersea by-election)*
Fair shares for all, is Labour's call.

JEANS Sir James 1877-1946
5019 *The Mysterious Universe*
Life exists in the universe only because the carbon atom possesses certain exceptional properties.

JEANS Ronald d.1973
5020
Actor-manager - one to whom the part is greater than the whole.

JEFFERIES Richard
5021
When I look in the glass I see that every line in my face means pessimism, but in spite of my face - that is my experience - I remain an optimist.

JEFFERSON Thomas 1743-1826
5022 *American Declaration of Independence*
We hold these truths to be sacred and undeniable; that all men are created equal and independent, that from that equal creation they derive rights inherent and inalienable, among which are the preservation of life, and liberty, and the pursuit of happiness.

5023
That government is best which governs the least, because its people discipline themselves.

5024
No government ought to be without censors; and where the press is free, no one ever will.

5025
I hold it, that a little rebellion now and then is a good thing, and as necessary in the political world as storms in the physical.

5026
The man who fears no truths has nothing to fear from lies.

5027
Every man wishes to pursue his occupation and to enjoy the fruits of his labours and the produce of his property in peace and safety, and with the least possible expense. When these things are accomplished, all the objects for which government ought to be established are answered.

5028
The mobs of great cities add just so much to the support of pure government as sores do to the strength of the human body.

5029
Taste cannot be controlled by law.

5030
Walking is the best possible exercise. Habituate yourself to walk very far.

5031
Whenever a man has cast a longing eye on office, a rottenness begins in his conduct.

JEFFREY Peter
5032 *If...*
"Education in Britain is a nubile Cinderella, sparsely clad and often interfered with."

JENKINS Dr David (Bishop of Durham) 1925-
5033
There is no doubting my belief in God, but the Church has driven me close to it.

5034
God is the surprise of the universe, not its answer.

JENKS Earlene Larson
5035
Have the courage to act instead of react.

JEROME Jerome K. 1859-1927
5036 *They and I*
I want a house that has got over all its troubles; I don't want to spend the rest of my life bringing up a young and inexperienced house.

5037
It is easy enough to say that poverty is no crime. No, if it were men wouldn't be ashamed of it. It's a blunder, though, and is punished as such.

5038
Idleness, like kisses, to be sweet must be stolen.

5039 *Idle Thoughts of an Idle Fellow*
It is impossible to enjoy idling thoroughly unless one has plenty of work to do.

5040 *Idle Thoughts of an Idle Fellow*
Love is like the measles; we all have to go through it.

JEROME St. c.340-420
5041
You censure this with difficulty because you have allowed it to become customary.

JERROLD Douglas 1803-1857
5042
Australia is so kind that, just tickle her with a hoe, and she laughs with a harvest.

5043
A Conservative is a man who will not look at the new moon, out of respect for that ancient institution, the old one.

5044 *The Life and Remains of Douglas Jerrold*
If an earthquake were to engulf England to-morrow, the English would manage to meet and dine somewhere among the rubbish, just to celebrate the event.

5045
Love the sea? I dote upon it - from the beach.

5046
The ugliest of trades have their moments of pleasure. Now, if I was a grave digger, or even a hangman, there are some people I could work for with a great deal of enjoyment.

5047 *The Wit and Opinions of Douglas Jerrold*
The best thing I know between France and England is - the sea.

5048 *The Wit and Opinions of Douglas Jerrold*
Love's like the measles - all the worse when it comes late in life.

JIPCHO Ben
5049
Running for money doesn't make you run fast. It makes you run first.

JOACHIM Lord 1831-1907
5050
I have the courage of my opinions, but I have not the temerity to give a political blank cheque to Lord Salisbury.

JOAD C.E.M. 1891-1953
5051
My life is spent in a perpetual alternation between two rhythms, the rhythm of attracting people for fear I may be lonely, and the rhythm of trying to get rid of them because I know that I am bored.

JOBS Steve 1955-
5052 *(of attempts to get interest in the Apple PC)*
We went to Atari and said "We've got this amazing thing..." They said "No". Then we went to Hewlett-Packard; they said, "We don't need you. You haven't got through college yet."

JOHN PAUL II Pope 1920-
5053
In contrast with its original vocation of peace, the family is sadly seen to be the scene of tension and oppression.

5054
To be perfect as a woman does not mean to be like a man.

5055
Religion and peace go together, to wage war in the name of religion is a contradiction.

JOHN XXIII Pope 1881-1963
5056
Italians come to ruin most generally in three ways - women, gambling and farming. My family chose the slowest one.

5057
See everything; overlook a great deal; correct a little.

JOHNSON Gerald
5058
Heroes are created by popular demand, sometimes out of the scantiest materials ... such as the apple that William Tell never shot, the ride that Paul Revere never finished, the flag that Barbara Frietchie never waved.

JOHNSON Lionel 1867-1902
5059 *'The Precept of Silence'*
I know you: solitary griefs,
Desolate passions, aching hours.

JOHNSON Lyndon B. 1908-1973
5060
I may not know much, but I know chicken shit from chicken salad.

5061
What's the difference between a cactus and a caucus>? A cactus has the pricks on the outside.

5062
Doing what's right isn't the problem. It's knowing what's right.

5063
I don't want loyalty. I want *loyalty*. I want him to kiss my ass in Macy's window at high noon and tell me it smells like roses.

5064
I am a free man, an American, a United States Senator, and a Democrat, in that order.

5065 *(of Gerald Ford)*
So dumb he can't fart and chew gum at the same time.

5066
We hope that the world will not narrow into a neighbourhood before it has broadened into a brotherhood.

5067
Only two things are necessary to keep one's wife happy. One is to let her think she is having her own way, and the other, to let her have it.

5068
We are not about to send American boys 9 or 10,000 miles away from home to do what Asian boys ought to be doing for themselves.

5069
There is but one way for a president to deal with the Congress, and that is continuously, incessantly, and without interruption. If it's really going to work, the relationship between the president and the Congress has got to be almost incestuous.

5070
While you're saving your face you're losing your ass. Never trust a man whose eyes are too close to his nose. I never trust a man unless I've got his pecker in my pocket. Better inside the tent pissing out than outside the tent pissing in.

JOHNSON Paul 1928-
5071
Tories, in short, are atrophied Englishmen, lacking certain moral and intellectual reflexes. They are recognizable, homely - even, on occasions, endearing - but liable to turn very nasty at short notice.

JOHNSON Samuel 1709-1784
5072
Abstinence is as easy for me as temperance would be difficult.

5073
(Adversity is) the state in which a man most easily becomes acquainted with himself, being especially free from admirers then.

5074
I would advise no man to marry, who is not likely to propagate understanding.

5075
Almost all absurdity of conduct arises from the imitation of those whom we cannot resemble.

5076
Among the calamities of wars may be justly numbered the diminution of the love of truth by the falsehoods which interest dictates and credulity encourages.

5077
Was there ever yet anything written by mere man that was wished longer by its readers, excepting *Don Quixote, Robinson Crusoe,* and the *Pilgrim's Progress?*

5078
The best part of every author is in general to be found in his book, I assure you.

5079 *Boswell - Life*
A man may write at any time, if he will set himself doggedly to it.

5080 *Boswell - Life*
If a man does not make new acquaintance as he advances through life, he will soon find himself left alone. A man, Sir, should keep his friendship in constant repair.

5081 *Boswell - Life*
Norway, too, has noble wild prospects; and Lapland is remarkable for prodigious noble wild prospects. But, Sir, let me tell you, the noblest prospect which a Scotchman ever sees, is the high road that leads him to England.

5082 *Boswell - Life*
A woman's preaching is like a dog's walking on his hinder legs. It is not done well; but you are surprised to find it done at all.

5083 *Boswell - Life*
Happiness consists in the multiplicity of agreeable consciousness.

5084 *Boswell - Life*
Every man has a lurking wish to appear considerable in his native place.

5085 *Boswell - Life*
All intellectual improvement arises from leisure.

5086 *Boswell - Life*
Patriotism is the last refuge of a scoundrel.

5087 *Boswell - Life*
There is now less flogging in our great schools than formerly, but then less is learned there; so that what the boys get at one end they lose at the other.

5088 *Boswell - Life*
There is nothing which has yet been contrived by man, by which so much happiness is produced as by a good tavern or inn.

5089 *Boswell - Life*
Marriages would in general be as happy, and often more so, if they were all made by the Lord Chancellor, upon a due consideration of characters and circumstances, without the parties having any choice in the matter.

5090 *Boswell - Life*
We would all be idle if we could.

5091 *Boswell - Life*
No man but a blockhead ever wrote, except for money.

5092 *Boswell - Life*
It is better that some should be unhappy than that none should be happy, which would be the case in a general state of equality.

5093 *Boswell - Life*
A man who has not been in Italy, is always conscious of an inferiority, from his not having seen what it is expected a man should see.

5094 *Boswell - Life*
When a man is tired of London, he is tired of life; for there is in London all that life can afford.

5095 *Boswell - Life*
All argument is against it [ghosts]; but all belief is for it.

5096 *Boswell - Life*
Every man thinks meanly of himself for not having been a soldier, or not having been at sea.

5097 *Boswell - Life*
A mere antiquarian is a rugged being.

5098 *Boswell - Life*
Were it not for imagination, Sir, a man would be as happy in the arms of a chambermaid as of a Duchess.

5099 *Boswell - Life*
Claret is the liquor for boys; port, for men; but he who aspires to be a hero (smiling) must drink brandy.

5100 *Boswell - Life*
A man who exposes himself when he is intoxicated, has not the art of getting drunk.

5101 *Boswell - Life*
Every man has a right to utter what he thinks truth, and every other man has a right to knock him down for it. Martyrdom is the test.

5102 *Boswell - Life*
A Frenchman must be always talking, whether he knows anything of the matter or not; an Englishman is content to say nothing, when he has nothing to say.

5103 *Boswell - Life*
Depend upon it, said he, that if a man talks of his misfortunes there is something in them that is not disagreeable to him; for where there is nothing but pure misery, there never is any recourse to the mention of it.

5104 *Boswell - Life*
Now, Sir, there are people whom one should like very well to drop, but would not wish to be dropped by.

5105 *Boswell - Life*
This merriment of parsons is mighty offensive.

5106 *Boswell - Life*
Classical quotation is the *parole* of literary men all over the world.

5107 *Boswell - Life*
Sir, I have two very cogent reasons for not printing any list of subscribers; one, that I have lost all the names; the other, that I have spent all the money.

5108 *Boswell - Life*
Always, Sir, set a high value on spontaneous kindness. He whose inclination prompts him to cultivate your friendship of his own accord, will love you more than one whom you have been at pains to attach to you.

5109 *Boswell - Life*
A wise Tory and a wise Whig, I believe, will agree. Their principles are the same, though their modes of thinking are different.

5110 *Boswell - Life*
How few of his friends' houses would a man choose to be at when he is sick.

5111 *Boswell - Life*
If a young or middle-aged man, when leaving a company, does not recollect where he laid his hat, it is nothing; but if the same inattention is discovered in an old man, people will shrug up their shoulders, and say, 'His memory is going'.

5112 *Boswell - Life*
My dear friend, clear your *mind* of cant ... You may *talk* in this manner, it is a mode of talking in Society: but don't *think* foolishly.

5113 *Boswell - Life*
As I know more of mankind I expect less of them, and am ready now to call a man *a good man*, upon easier terms than I was formerly.

5114 *Boswell - Life*
Sir, I have found you an argument; but I am not obliged to find you an understanding.

5115 *Boswell - Life*
Who can run the race with Death?

5116 *Boswell - Life*
Sir, I look upon every day to be lost, in which I do not make a new acquaintance.

5117 *Boswell - Life*
An odd thought stikes me: we shall receive no letters in the grave.

5118 *Boswell - Life (on biography writing)*
The dogs don't know how to write trifles with dignity.

5119 *Boswell - Life (on the death of Mr Levett)*
Officious, innocent, sincere,
Of every friendless name the friend.
Yet still he fills affection's eye,

Obscurely wise, and coarsely kind.

5120 Boswell - Life (on the death of Mr Levett)
Then, with no throbs of fiery pain,
No cold gradations of decay,
Death broke at once the vital chain,
And freed his soul the nearest way.

5121 Boswell - Life (of Mr Dudley Long)
Mr Long's character is very *short*. It is nothing.
He fills a chair.

5122 Boswell - Life (on the Giant's Causeway)
Worth seeing, yes; but not worth going to see.

5123 Boswell - Life (on his illness)
I will be conquered; I will not capitulate.

5124 Boswell - Life (of Jeremiah Markland)
I hate a fellow whom pride, or cowardice, or
laziness drives into a corner, and who does
nothing when he is there but sit and *growl*; let
him come out as I do, and *bark*.

5125 Boswell - Life (letter to Boswell)
Remember that all tricks are either knavish or
childish.

5126 Boswell - Life (letter to Boswell)
If you are idle, be not solitary; if you are solitary,
be not idle.

5127 Boswell - Life (letter to Boswell)
Resolve not to be poor; whatever you have,
spend less. Poverty is a great enemy to human
happiness; it certainly destroys liberty, and it
makes some virtues impracticable, and others
extremely difficult.

5128 Boswell - Life (of a man who remarried)
A triumph of hope over experience.

**5129 Boswell - Life (on the merits of two minor
poets)**
Sir, there is no settling the point of precedency
between a louse and a flea.

5130 Boswell - Life (of Milton's sonnets)
Milton, Madam, was a genius that could cut a
Colossus from a rock; but could not carve heads
upon cherry-stones.

5131 Boswell - Life (of Oliver Goldsmith)
No man was more foolish when he had not a
pen in his hand, or more wise when he had.

5132 Boswell - Life (of Ossian)
A man might write such stuff for ever, if he
would *abandon* his mind to it.

5133 Boswell - Life (parodying Henry Brooke)
It might as well be said 'Who drives fat oxen
should himself be fat.'

**5134 Boswell - Life (on roast mutton served at an
inn)**
It is as bad as bad can be; it is ill-fed, ill-killed,
ill-kept, and ill-drest.

5135 Boswell - Life (of Thomas Gray's Odes)
They are forced plants, raised in a hot-bed; and
they are poor plants; they are but cucumbers
after all.

5136
The chains of habit are too weak to be felt until
they are too strong to be broken.

5137
Read over your compositions, and when you
meet a passage which you think is particularly
fine, strike it out.

5138
Corneille is to Shakespeare ... as a clipped
hedge is to a forest.

5139
Courage is a quality so necessary for
maintaining virtue that it is always respected,
even when it is associated with vice.

5140
I deny the lawfulness of telling a lie to a sick
man for fear of alarming him; you have no
business with consequences, you are to tell the
truth.

5141 Diary and Letters of Madame D'Arblay
Before you flatter a man so grossly to his face,
you should consider whether or not your
flattery is worth his having.

5142
Dictionaries are like watches. The worst is
better than none at all and even the best cannot
be expected to run quite true.

5143 A Dictionary of the English Language
Every quotation contributes something to the
stability or enlargement of the language.

5144 A Dictionary of the English Language
Dull. To make dictionaries is dull work.

5145 A Dictionary of the English Language
Lexicographer. A writer of dictionaries, a
harmless drudge.

5146 A Dictionary of the English Language
Network. Anything reticulated or decussated at
equal distances, with interstices between the
intersections.

5147
One of the disadvantages of wine is that it
makes a man mistake words for thoughts.

5148
I dogmatise and am contradicted, and in this
conflict of opinions and sentiments I find
delight.

5149
Don't think of retiring from the world until the world will be sorry that you retire.

5150
As the faculty of writing has chiefly been a masculine endowment, the reproach of making the world miserable has always been thrown upon the women.

5151
A fly, Sir, may sting a stately horse and make him wince; but one is but an insect, and the other a horse still.

5152
I have found men more kind than I expected, and less just.

5153 *A Free Enquiry*
The only end of writing is to enable the readers better to enjoy life, or better to endure it.

5154
While grief is fresh, every attempt to divert it only irritates.

5155
That is the happiest conversation where there is no competition, no vanity, but a calm quiet interchange of sentiments.

5156
Hope is itself a species of happiness, and, perhaps, the chief happiness which this world affords.

5157 *The Idler*
When two Englishmen meet, their first talk is of the weather.

5158 *The Idler*
Nothing is more hopeless than a scheme of merriment.

5159 *(attributed, in Instructions to Young Sportsmen)*
Fly fishing may be a very pleasant amusement; but angling or float fishing I can only compare to a stick and a string, with a worm at one end and a fool at the other.

5160
John Wesley's conversation is good, but he is never at leisure. He is always obliged to go at a certain hour. This is very disagreeable to a man who loves to fold his legs and have his talk out as I do.

5161
The joy of life is variety; the tenderest love requires to be renewed by intervals of absence.

5162
It is the just doom of laziness and gluttony to be inactive without ease, and drowsy without tranquillity.

5163
Knowledge is of two kinds; we know a subject ourselves, or we know where we can find information upon it.

5164
Had I learned to fiddle, I should have done nothing else.

5165
Life is a progress from want to want, not from enjoyment to enjoyment.

5166
I live in the crowds of jollity, not so much to enjoy company as to shun myself.

5167
It is better to live rich than to die rich.

5168 *Lives of the English Poets*
A man, doubtful of his dinner, or trembling at a creditor, is not much disposed to abstracted meditation, or remote enquiries.

5169 *London*
Of all the griefs that harrass the distressed,
Sure the most bitter is a scornful jest;
Fate never wounds more deep the gen'rous heart,
Than when a blockhead's insult points the dart.

5170
Love is the wisdom of the fool and the folly of the wise.

5171
A man should be careful never to tell tales of himself to his own disadvantage. People may be amused at the time, but they will be remembered, and brought out against him upon some subsequent occasion.

5172
A man must carry knowledge with him, if he would bring home knowledge.

5173
A man is in general better pleased when he has a good dinner upon his table, than when his wife talks Greek.

5174
No man is a hypocrite in his pleasures.

5175
Every man has, some time in his life, an ambition to be a wag.

5176
Man is not weak - knowledge is more than equivalent to force. The master of mechanics laughs at strength.

5177
Every man who attacks my belief diminishes in some degree my confidence in it, and therefore makes me uneasy, and I am angry with him who makes me uneasy.

5178
The man who is asked by an author what he thinks of his work is put to the torture and is not obliged to speak the truth.

5179
If the man who turnips cries,
Cry not when his father dies,
'Tis a proof that he had rather
Have a turnip than his father.

5180
Your manuscript is both good and original; but the parts that are good are not original, and the parts that are original are not good.

5181
Much may be made of a Scotchman if he be caught young.

5182
No member of a society has a right to teach any doctrine contrary to what society holds to be true.

5183
Men know that women are an overmatch for them, and therefore they choose the weakest or the most ignorant. If they did not think so, they never could be afraid of women knowing as much as themselves.

5184
Moderation is commonly firm, and firmness is commonly successful.

5185
Music ... the only sensual pleasure without vice.

5186
Never be afraid to think yourself fit for anything for which your friends think you fit.

5187
None but a fool worries about things he cannot influence.

5188
Nothing flatters a man as much as the happiness of his wife; he is always proud of himself as the source of it.

5189
Oats: A grain which in England is generally given to horses, but in Scotland supports the people.

5190
Is not a patron one who looks with unconcern on a man struggling for life in the water, and,

when he has reached ground, encumbers him with help?

5191
The poor and the busy have no leisure for sentimental sorrow.

5192
Pride is seldom delicate: it will please itself with very mean advantages.

5193
Promise, large promise, is the soul of an advertisement.

5194
Questioning is not the mode of conversation among gentlemen.

5195 *The Rambler*
No place affords a more striking conviction of the vanity of human hopes, than a public library.

5196 *Rasselas*
Human life is everywhere a state in which much is to be endured, and little to be enjoyed.

5197 *Rasselas*
Marriage has many pains, but celibacy has no pleasures.

5198
Self-confidence is the first requisite to great undertakings.

5199
Shame arises from the fear of man; conscience from the fear of God.

5200
Being in a ship is being in a jail, with the chance of being drowned.

5201 *(shortly before he died)*
Iam moriturus.
I who am about to die.

5202
Silence propagates itself, and the longer talk has been suspended, the more difficult it is to find anything to say.

5203
It is very strange, and very melancholy, that the paucity of human pleasures should persuade us ever to call hunting one of them.

5204
It is better to suffer wrong than to do it, and happier to be sometimes cheated than not to trust.

5205
The true art of memory is the art of attention.

5206
The true genius is a mind of large general powers, accidentaly determined to some particular direction.

5207
It is unjust to claim the privileges of age and retain the playthings of childhood.

5208
What is written without effort is in general read without pleasure.

5209
When an author is yet living, we estimate his powers by his worst performance; and when he is dead, we rate them by his best.

5210
When a man knows he is to be hanged in a fortnight, it concentrates his mind wonderfully.

JOHNSON Vera

5211
There's such a thing as moderation, even in telling the truth.

JOHNSTON Eric

5212
The dinosaur's eloquent lesson is that if some bigness is good, an overabundance of bigness is not necessarily better.

JOHNSTON Jennifer 1930-

5213
We are constantly at risk from the people we love most. They are, after all, the only people who can do us serious damage.

5214
People who haven't created a present for themselves, as the Irish haven't, cannot create a future, so the past assumes a great importance.

5215
Perhaps I take the state of innocence very seriously because it is a state of magic. The loss of that state is what turns us into adults.

JOLSON Al 1886-1950

5216 *in The Jazz Singer (first words spoken on screen)*
"Wait a minute, wait a minute. You ain't heard nuttin' yet."

JONES Clinton 1848-1936

5217
I never been in no situation where havin' money made it any worse.

JONES Franklin P.

5218
Bargain: something you can't use at a price you can't resist.

5219
Experience enables you to recognize a mistake when you make it again.

5220
An extravagance is anything you buy that is of no earthly use to your wife.

5221
Most people like hard work, particularly when they're paying for it.

JONES Henry Arthur and HERMAN Henry
1851-1929 and 1832-1894
5222 *The Silver King*
O God! Put back Thy universe and give me yesterday.

JONES Le Roi
5223
The landscape should belong to the people who see it all the time.

JONES Paul 1747-1792
5224 *(as his ship was sinking)*
I have not yet begun to fight.

JONES Spike
5225
When the audience knows you know better, it's satire, but when they think you can't do any better, it's corn.

JONES Sir William 1746-1794
5226 *(lines substituted in 'Six hours in sleep')*
Seven hours to law, to soothing slumber seven,
Ten to the world allot, and *all* to Heaven.

5227
Power should always be distrusted, in whatever hands it is placed.

JONG Erica 1942-
5228
Everyone has a talent. What is rare is the courage to follow the talent to the dark places where it leads.

5229 *Fear of Flying*
The zipless fuck is absolutely pure. It is free of ulterior motives. There is no power game. The man is not 'taking' and the woman is not 'giving' ... The zipless fuck is the purest thing there is. And it is rarer than the unicorn.

5230 *Fear of Flying*
Jealousy is all the fun you think they had.

JONSON Ben c.1573-1637
5231 *The Alchemist*
Fortune, that favours fools.

5232 *The Alchemist*
The children of perdition are oft-times
Made instruments even of the greatest works.

5233 *The Alchemist*
If I have outstripped
An old man's gravity, or stict canon, think
What a young wife and a good brain may do:
Stretch age's truth sometimes, and crack it too.

5234
All men are Philosophers, to their inches.

5235 *Bartholomew Fair*
The lungs of the tobacconist are rotted, the liver
spotted, the brain smoked like the backside of
the pig-woman's booth here, and the whole
body within, black as her pan you saw e'en now
without.

5236 *Bartholomew Fair*
Neither do thou lust after that tawney weed
tobacco.

5237 *Bartholomew Fair (of Ursula, the pig
woman)*
The very womb and bed of enormity.

5238 *Catiline his Conspiracy*
PEOPLE: The Voice of Cato is the voice of
Rome.
CATO: The voice of Rome is the consent of
heaven!

5239 *Catiline his Conspiracy*
Where it concerns himself,
Who's angry at a slander makes it true.

5240 '*A Celebration of Charis*'
And it is not always face,
Clothes, or fortune gives the grace,
Or the feature, or the youth;
But the language, and the truth,
With the ardour and the passion,
Gives the lover weight and fashion.

5241 '*To Celia*'
Drink to me only with thine eyes
And I will pledge with mine;
Or leave a kiss but in the cup,
And I'll not look for wine.

5242 *Cynthia's Revels*
Slow, slow, fresh fount, keep time with my salt
tears:
Yet, slower, yet; O faintly, gentle springs.

5243 *Cynthia's Revels*
Queen and huntress, chaste and fair,
Now the sun is laid to sleep,
Seated in thy silver chair,
State in wonted manner keep:
Hesperus entreats thy light,
Goddess, excellently bright.

5244
Donne, for not keeping of accent, deserved
hanging ... Shakespeare wanted art.

5245 *The Entertainment at Althrope*
This is Mab, the Mistress-Fairy
That doth nightly rob the dairy.

5246 *Epicene*
Give me a look, give me a face,
That makes simplicity a grace;
Robes loosely flowing, hair as free:
Such sweet neglect more taketh me,
Than all the adulteries of art;
They strike mine eyes, but not my heart.

5247 '*Eupheme*'
The voice so sweet, the words so fair,
As some soft chime had stroked the air;
And though the sound were parted thence,
Still left an echo in the sense.

5248 '*To ... Sir Lucius Carey and Sir H. Morison*'
In small proportions we just beauty see,
And in short measures life may perfect be.

5249 *Every Man in His Humour*
I do honour the very flea of his dog.

5250 *Every Man out of His Humour*
My strict hand
Was made to seize on vice, and with a gripe
Squeeze out the humour of such spongy souls,
As lick up every idle vanity.

5251 *Every Man out of His Humour*
Blind Fortune still
Bestows her gifts on such as cannot use them.

5252
Memory, of all the powers of the mind, is the
most delicate and frail.

5253 '*To the Memory of...William Shakespeare*'
He was not of an age, but for all time!

5254 '*To the Memory of... William Shakespeare*'
Thou hadst small Latin, and less Greek.

5255 '*To Penshurst*'
The blushing apricot and woolly peach
Hang on thy walls, that every child may reach.

5256 *The Poetaster*
Ramp up my genius, be not retrograde;
But boldly nominate a spade a spade.

5257 *The Poetaster*
Detraction is but baseness' varlet;
And apes are apes, though clothed in scarlet. ·

5258 '*On the Portrait of Shakespeare*'
Reader, look
Not on his picture, but his book.

5259 *Sejanus*
Tell proud Jove,
Between his power and thine there is no odds:
'Twas only fear first in the world made gods.

5260 *Timber, or Discoveries made upon Men and Matter*
The players have often mentioned it as an honour to Shakespeare that in his writing, whatsoever he penned, he never blotted out a line. My answer hath been 'Would he had blotted a thousand'.

5261 *Timber, or Discoveries made upon Men and Matter*
The fear of every man that heard him was, lest he should make an end.

5262 *Timber, or Discoveries made upon Men and Matter*
Talking and eloquence are not the same: to speak, and to speak well, are two things.

5263
Underneath this stone doth lie
As much beauty as could die.

5264 *Volpone*
I glory
More in the cunning purchase of my wealth
Than in the glad possession.

5265 *Volpone*
Give 'em words;
Pour oil into their ears, and send them hence.

5266 *Volpone*
What a rare punishment
Is avarice to itself!

5267 *Volpone*
Whilst others have been at the balloo, I have been at my book, and am now past the craggy paths of study, and come to the flowery plains of honour and reputation.

5268 *Volpone*
Calumnies are answered best with silence.

5269 *Volpone*
Almost
All the wise world is little else in nature
But parasites or sub-parasites.

5270 *Volpone*
Suns, that set, may rise again;
But if once we lose this light,
'Tis with us perpetual night.

5271 *Volpone*
Our drink shall be prepared gold and amber;
Which we will take, until my roof whirl around
With the *vertigo*: and my dwarf shall dance.

5272 *Volpone*
Come, my Celia, let us prove,
While we can, the sports of love.

5273 *Volpone*
Honour! tut, a breath,
There's no such thing in nature; a mere term
Invented to awe fools.

5274 *Volpone*
You have a gift, sir, (thank your education),
Will never let you want, while there are men,
And malice, to breed causes.

5275 *Volpone*
Mischiefs feed
Like beasts, till they be fat, and then they bleed.

5276 *'To William Shakespeare'*
Soul of the Age!
The applause, delight, the wonder of our stage!

5277 *'That Women are but Men's Shadows'*
Follow a shadow, it still flies you;
Seem to fly it, it will pursue:
So court a mistress, she denies you;
Let her alone, she will court you.
Say, are not women truly then
Styled but the shadows of us men?

JOPLIN Janis 1943-1970
5278
On stage I make love to twenty-five thousand people; then I go home alone.

5279 *(when Eisenhower's death replaced her in Newsweek)*
Fourteen heart attacks and he had to die in my week. In MY week.

JORDAN David Starr
5280
The world stands aside to let anyone pass who knows where he is going.

JORDAN Thomas c.1612-1685
5281 *'How the War began'*
They plucked communion tables down
And broke our painted glasses;
They threw our altars to the ground
And tumbled down the crosses.
They set up Cromwell and his heir -
The Lord and Lady Claypole -
Because they hated Common Prayer,
The organ and the maypole.

JORTIN John 1698-1770
5282 *(adopted by Lord Nelson as his motto)*
Let him who has won it bear the palm.

JOSEPH Jenny
5283
I was raised to feel that doing nothing was a sin. I had to learn to do nothing.

JOSEPH Sir Keith 1918-1994
5284 *(of national euphoria on the outcome of World War 2)*
We [the Conservative Party] found it hard to avoid the feeling that somehow the lean and tight-lipped mufflered men in the 1930s dole queue were at least partly our fault.

5285
Problems reproduce themselves from
generation to generation ... I refer to this as a
'cycle of deprivation'.

JOUBERT Joseph 1754-1824
5286
Ambition is pitiless. Any merit that it cannot
use it finds despicable.

5287
Be charitable and indulgent to every one but
thyself.

5288
Children have more need of models than of
critics.

5289
Drawing is speaking to the eye; talking is
painting to the ear.

5290
Education should be gentle and stern, not cold
and lax.

5291
Words, like eyeglasses, blur everything that they
do not make clear.

5292
Imagination is the eye of the soul.

5293
Never cut what you can untie.

5294
To teach is to learn twice.

5295
When my friends lack an eye, I look at them in
profile.

JOVANOVICH William
5296
Some words are like the old Roman galleys;
large-scaled and ponderous. They sit low in the
water even when their cargo is light.

5297
Reading, like prayer, remains one of our few
private acts.

JOWETT Benjamin 1817-1893
5298
Don't expect too much: and don't attempt too
little.

5299
There is a great deal of hard lying in the world:
especially among people whose characters are
above suspicion.

5300
The lie in the soul is a true lie.

5301
One man is as good as another until he has
written a book.

5302
No married clergyman should refuse a
bishopric.

5303
Men get lazy, and substitute quantity of work
for quality.

5304
Never explain: never apologize: never repeat the
mistake.

5305
Nowhere probably is there more true feeling,
and nowhere worse taste, than in a churchyard.

5306
'Research' is a mere excuse for idleness.

5307
We have sought truth, and sometimes perhaps
found it. But have we had any fun?

5308
No one who has a great deal of energy will long
be popular in Oxford.

JOYCE James 1882-1941
5309
[on being asked by an admirer whether he
might kiss the hand that wrote *Ulysses*] No, it
did lots of other things too.

5310 *Dubliners*
His soul swooned slowly as he heard the snow
falling faintly through the universe and faintly
falling, like the descent of their last end, upon
all the living and the dead.

5311 *Finnegans Wake*
That ideal reader suffering from an ideal
insomnia.

5312 *Finnegans Wake*
The flushpots of Euston and the hanging
garments of Marylebone.

5313 *Finnegans Wake*
Tell me, tell me, tell me, elm! Night night!
Telmetale of stem or stone. Beside the rivering
waters of hitherandthithering waters of. Night!

5314 *Finnegans Wake*
All moanday, tearsday, wailsday, thumpsday,
frightday, shatterday till the fear of the Law.

5315 *Finnegans Wake*
Three quarks for Muster Mark!

5316 *Finnegans Wake*
The Gracehoper was always jigging ajog, hoppy
on akkant of his joyicity.

5317 *Finnegans Wake*
If I seen him bearing down on me now under whitespread wings like he'd come from Arkangels, I sink I'd die down over his feet, humbly dumbly, only to washup.

5318 *'The Holy Office'*
My little love in light attire
Knows the soft flame that is desire.

5319 *A Portrait of the Artist as a Young Man*
When the soul of a man is born in this country, there are nets flung at it to hold it back from flight. You talk to me of nationality, language, religion. I shall try to fly by those nets.

5320 *A Portrait of the Artist as a Young Man*
Ireland is the old sow that eats her farrow.

5321 *A Portrait of the Artist as a Young Man*
Pity is the feeling which arrests the mind in the presence of whatsoever is grave and constant in human sufferings and unites it with the human sufferer. Terror is the feeling which arrests the mind in the presence of whatsoever is grave and constant in human sufferings and unites it with the secret cause.

5322 *A Portrait of the Artist as a Young Man*
The artist, like the God of the creation, remains within or behind or beyond or above his handiwork, invisible, refined out of existence, indifferent, paring his fingernails.

5323 *A Portrait of the Artist as a Young Man*
I will not serve that in which I no longer believe whether it call itself my home, my fatherland or my church: and I will try to express myself in some mode of life or art as freely as I can and as wholly as I can, using for my defence the only arms I allow myself to use, silence, exile, and cunning.

5324 *A Portrait of the Artist as a Young Man*
Welcome, O life! I go to encounter for the millionth time the reality of experience and to forge in the smithy of my soul the uncreated conscience of my race ... Old father, old artificer, stand me now and ever in good stead.

5325 *'Sleep now, O sleep now'*
My kiss will give peace now
And quiet to your heart -
Sleep on in peace now,
O you unquiet heart!

5326 *Ulysses*
The snotgreen sea. The scrotumtightening sea.

5327 *Ulysses*
It is a symbol of Irish art. The cracked looking-glass of a servant.

5328 *Ulysses*
When I makes tea I makes tea. And when I makes water I makes water ... *Begob, ma'am*, says Mrs Cahill, *God send you don't make them in the one pot.*

5329 *Ulysses*
I fear those big words, Stephen said, which make us so unhappy.

5330 *Ulysses*
History, Stephen said, is a nightmare from which I am trying to awake.

5331 *Ulysses*
Lawn Tennyson, gentleman poet.

5332 *Ulysses*
He ... saw the dark tangled curls of his bush floating, floating hair of the stream around the limp father of thousands, a languid floating flower.

5333 *Ulysses*
Come forth, Lazarus! And he came fifth and lost the job.

5334 *Ulysses*
Plenty to see and hear and feel yet. Feel live warm beings near you. They aren't going to get me this innings. Warm beds; warm full blooded life.

5335 *Ulysses*
A man of genius makes no mistakes. His errors are volitional and are the portals of discovery

5336 *Ulysses*
But it's no use, says he. Force, hatred, history, all that. That's not life for men and women, insult and hatred. And everybody knows that it's the very opposite of that that is really life.

5337 *Ulysses*
Greater love than this, he said, no man hath that a man lay down his wife for his friend. Go thou and do likewise. Thus, or words to that effect, saith Zarathustra, sometime regius professor of French letters to the university of Oxtail.

5338 *Ulysses*
The heaventree of stars hung with humid nightblue fruit.

5339 *Ulysses*
He kissed me under the Moorish wall and I thought well as well him as another and then I asked him with my eyes to ask again yes and then he asked me would I yes to say yes my mountain flower and first I put my arms around him yes and drew him down to me so he could feel my breasts all perfume yes and his heart was going like mad and yes I said yes I will Yes.

JOYCE Major Eric
5340 *(in a pamphlet on the army)*
We are suffering from a debilitating failure to
attract young men and women, yet remain
obsessed with the defence of the very social
order and attitudes which repel them.

JOYCE Peggy
5341
It takes all the fun out of a bracelet if you have
to buy it yourself.

JUDD Walter H.
5342
People often say that, in a democracy, decisions
are made by a majority of the people. Of
course, that is not true. Decisions are made by
a majority of those who make themselves heard
and who vote - a very different thing.

JUDGE Jack and WILLIAMS Harry 1878-1938
and 1874-1924
5343 *'It's a Long Way to Tipperary'*
It's a long way to Tipperary,
It's a long way to go;
It's a long way to Tipperary,
To the sweetest girl I know!
Goodbye, Piccadilly,
Farewell, Leicester Square,
It's a long, long way to Tipperary,
But my heart's right there!

JULIAN of Norwich 1343-after 1416
5344 *Revelations of Divine Love*
Sin is behovely, but all shall be well and all shall
be well and all manner of thing shall be well.

5345 *Revelations of Divine Love*
Wouldest thou wit thy Lord's meaning in this
thing? Wit it well: Love was his meaning. Who
shewed it thee? Love. What shewed He thee?
Love. Wherefore shewed it He? for Love ... Thus
was I learned that Love is our Lord's meaning.

JUNG Carl 1875-1961
5346
If there is anything that we wish to change in
the child, we should first examine it and see
whether it is not something that could better be
changed in ourselves.

5347
As far as we can discern, the sole purpose of
human existence is to kindle a light in the
darkness of mere being.

5348
Every form of addiction is bad, no matter
whether the narcotic be alcohol or morphine or
idealism.

5349
Great talents are the most lovely and often the
most dangerous fruits on the tree of humanity.
They hang upon the most slender twigs that are
easily snapped off.

5350
A man who has not passed through the inferno
of his passions has never overcome them.

5351
Nothing has a stronger influence
psychologically on their environment, and
especially on their children, than the unlived
lives of the parents.

5352
Seldom, or perhaps never, does a marriage
develop into an individual relationship
smoothly and without crises; there is no coming
to consciousness without pain.

5353
Where love rules, there is no will to power, and
where power predominates, there love is
lacking. The one is the shadow of the other.

JUNIUS
5354
If individuals have no virtues, their vices may be
of use to us.

5355 *The Letters of Junius*
The liberty of the press is the *Palladium* of all
the civil, political, and religious rights of an
Englishman.

5356 *Public Advertiser*
There is a holy mistaken zeal in politics as well
as in religion. By persuading others, we
convince ourselves.

5357 *Public Advertiser*
However distinguished by rank or property, in
the rights of freedom we are all equal.

5358 *Public Advertiser*
The injustice done to an individual is
sometimes of service to the public.

5359
The right of election is the very essence of the
constitution.

JUSTINIAN AD 483-565
5360 *Institutes*
Justice is the constant and perpetual wish to
render to every one his due.

JUVENAL AD c.60-c.130
5361
Honesty's praised, then left to freeze.

5362
Luxury is more deadly than any foe.

5363 *Satires*
No one ever suddenly became depraved.

5364 *Satires*
The misfortunes of poverty carry with them nothing harder to bear than that it makes men ridiculous.

5365 *Satires*
They do not easily rise out of obscurity whose talents obstruct at home.

5366 *Satires*
Everything in Rome has its price.

5367 *Satires*
A rare bird on this earth, like nothing so much as a black swan.

5368 *Satires*
Panem et circenses.
Bread and the big match.
[usually misquoted as 'bread and circuses']

5369 *Satires*
Orandum est ut sit mens sana in corpore sano.
You should pray to have a sound mind in a sound body.

5370 *Satires*
No guilty man is acquitted if judged by himself.

5371 *Satires*
Revenge is always the pleasure of a paltry, feeble, tiny mind.

5372 *Satires (on Hannibal)*
Death alone reveals how small are men's poor bodies.

KAEL Pauline 1919-
5373
One of the surest signs of the Philistine is his reverence for the superior tastes of those who put him down.

KAFKA Franz 1883-1924
5374
One must not cheat anybody, not even the world of one's triumph.

5375 *The Trial*
You may object that it is not a trial at all; you are quite right, for it is only a trial if I recognize it as such.

5376 *The Trial*
It's often better to be in chains than to be free.

KAHN Gus and EGAN Raymond 1886-1941 and 1890-1952
5377 *'Ain't We Got Fun'*
There's nothing surer,
The rich get rich and the poor get children.
In the meantime, in between time,
Ain't we got fun.

KAISER Henry J. 1882-1967
5378
Trouble is only opportunity in work clothes.

5379
When your work speaks for itself, don't interrupt.

KAN Alphonse
5380
Every man has three characters - that which he exhibits, that which he has, and that which he thinks he has.

KANE Marie Elizabeth
5381 *(when thirteen years old)*
I feel when people say 'bigger and better' they should say 'bigger and badder'.

KANIN Garson
5382
Amateurs hope. Professionals work.

5383
In a professional once engaged, the performance of the job comes first.

5384
Whenever I'm asked what college I attended, I'm tempted to reply, 'Thornton Wilder'.

KANT Immanuel 1724-1804
5385 *Critique of Practical Reason*
Two things fill the mind with ever new and increasing wonder and awe, the more often and the more seriously reflection concentrates upon them: the starry heaven above me and the moral law within me.

5386
Out of the crooked timber of humanity no straight thing can ever be made.

5387
The desire of a man for a woman is not directed at her because she is a human being, but because she is a woman. That she is a human being is of no concern to him.

5388 *Foundation of the Metaphysics of Morals*
Nothing in the world - indeed nothing even beyond the world - can possibly be conceived which could be called good without qualification except a *good will.*

5389 *Foundation of the Metaphysics of Ethics*
Happiness is not an ideal of reason but of imagination.

5390
Every man is to be respected as an absolute end in himself: and it is a crime against the dignity that belongs to him as a human being, to use him as a mere means for some external purpose.

KAPP K. William
5391
Had there been a computer a hundred years ago, it would probably have predicted that by

now there would be so many horse-drawn vehicles it would be impossible to clear up all the manure.

KAPPEL Frederick
5392
The Bell system is like a damn big dragon. You kick it in the tail, and two years later, it feels it in its head.

KARR Alphonse 1808-1890
5393
If we are to abolish the death penalty, let the murderers take the first step.

5394
Plus ça change, plus c'est la même chose.
The more things change, the more they are the same.

KASLUCK Lady
5395
The worst thing about work in the house or home is that whatever you do is destroyed, laid waste or eaten within twenty-four hours.

KASSAK Lajos
5396
The father of every good work is discontent, and its mother is diligence.

KAUFMAN George S. 1889-1961
5397
Satire is what closes Saturday night.

5398
I like terra firma - the more firma, the less terra.

KAUFMAN Gerald 1930-
5399 *(on the Labour Party's New Hope for Britain)*
The longest suicide note in history.

KAUFMAN Paul and ANTHONY Mike
5400
Poetry in motion.

KAUFMANN Christoph 1753-1795
5401 *(of a period of literary ferment)*
Storm and stress.

KAUFMANN Walter
5402
Faith means intense, usually confident, belief that is not based on evidence sufficient to command assent from every reasonable person.

KAVANAGH Patrick 1905-1967
5403 *'The Great Hunger'*
Clay is the word and clay is the flesh
Where the potato-gatherers like mechanized scarecrows move
Along the side-fall of the hill - Maguire and his men.

5404 *'The Great Hunger'*
That was how his life happened.
No mad hooves galloping in the sky,
But the weak, washy way of true tragedy -
A sick horse nosing around the meadow for a clean place to die.

5405 *'Inniskeen Road: July Evening'*
I hate what every poet hates in spite
Of all the solemn talk of contemplation.
Oh, Alexander Selkirk knew the plight
Of being king and government and nation.
A road, a mile of kingdom, I am king
Of banks and stones and every blooming thing.

KAZAN Elia 1909-
5406
You've got to keep fighting - you've got to risk your life every six months to stay alive.

KAZANTZAKIS Nikos 1883-1957
5407
Every perfect traveller always creates the country where he travels.

KEATE Stuart
5408
Canada reminds me of vichyssoise - it's cold, half-French and difficult to stir.

KEATS John 1795-1821
5409 *'Addressed to [Haydon]'*
... Other spirits there are standing apart
Upon the forehead of the age to come.

5410 *'To Autumn'*
Season of mists and mellow fruitfulness,
Close bosom-friend of the maturing sun;
Conspiring with him how to load and bless
With fruit the vines that round the thatch-eaves run.

5411 *'To Autumn'*
Then in a wailful choir the small gnats mourn
Among the river sallows, borne aloft
Or sinking as the light wind lives or dies.

5412 *'To Autumn'*
The red-breast whistles from a garden-croft;
And gathering swallows twitter in the skies.

5413 *'Bards of Passion and of Mirth'*
Where the nightingale doth sing
Not a senseless, trancèd thing,
But diving melodious truth.

5414 *'Bright star, would I were steadfast as thou art'*
Still, still to hear her tender-taken breath,
And so live ever - or else swoon to death.

5415
In disease Medical Men guess: if they cannot ascertain a disease, they call it nervous.

5416 *'In drear nighted December'*
In drear nighted December
Too happy, happy tree
Thy branches ne'er remember
Their green felicity.

5417 *Endymion*
A thing of beauty is a joy for ever:
Its loveliness increases; it will never
Pass into nothingness; but still will keep
A bower quiet for us, and a sleep
Full of sweet dreams, and health, and quiet
breathing.

5418 *Endymion*
Here is wine,
Alive with sparkles.

5419 *Endymion*
Their smiles,
Wan as primroses gathered at midnight
By chilly fingered spring.

5420 *Endymion (preface)*
The imagination of a boy is healthy, and the
mature imagination of a man is healthy; but
there is a space of life between, in which the
soul is in a ferment, the character undecided,
the way of life uncertain, the ambition thick-
sighted: thence proceeds mawkishness.

5421 *(epitaph for himself)*
Here lies one whose name was writ in water.

5422 *'The Eve of St Agnes'*
St Agnes' Eve - Ah, bitter chill it was!
The owl, for all his feathers, was a-cold;
The hare limped trembling through the frozen
grass,
And silent was the flock in woolly fold.

5423 *'The Eve of St Agnes'*
The silver, snarling trumpets 'gan to chide.

5424 *'The Eve of St Agnes'*
And soft adorings from their loves receive
Upon the honey'd middle of the night.

5425 *'The Eve of St Agnes'*
The music, yearning like a God in pain.

5426 *'The Eve of St Agnes'*
A poor, weak, palsy-stricken, churchyard thing.

5427 *'The Eve of St Agnes'*
Out went the taper as she hurried in;
Its little smoke, in pallid moonshine, died.

5428 *'The Eve of St Agnes'*
By degrees
Her rich attire creeps rustling to her knees.

5429 *'The Eve of St Agnes'*
Trembling in her soft and chilly nest.

5430 *'The Eve of St Agnes'*
As though a rose should shut, and be a bud
again.

5431 *'The Eve of St Agnes'*
He played an ancient ditty, long since mute,
In Provence called, 'La belle dame sans mercy.'

5432 *'The Eve of St Agnes'*
And the long carpets rose along the gusty floor.

5433 *'The Eve of St Agnes'*
And they are gone: aye, ages long ago
These lovers fled away into the storm.

5434 *'The Fall of Hyperion'*
Fanatics have their dreams, wherewith they
weave
A paradise for a sect.

5435 *'The Fall of Hyperion'*
The poet and the dreamer are distinct,
Diverse, sheet opposite, antipodes.
The one pours out a balm upon the world,
The other vexes it.

5436 *'Fancy'*
Ever let the fancy roam,
Pleasure never is at home.

5437 *'Fancy'*
Where's the face
One would meet in every place?

5438 *'On First Looking into Chapman's Homer'*
Much have I travelled in the realms of gold,
And many goodly states and kingdoms seen.

5439 *'On First Looking into Chapman's Homer'*
Then felt I like some watcher of the skies
When a new planet swims into his ken;
Or like stout Cortez when with eagle eyes
He stared at the Pacific - and all his men
Looked at each other with a wild surmise -
Silent, upon a peak in Darien.

5440 *'To George Felton Mayhew'*
Sweet are the pleasures that to verse belong,
And doubly sweet a brotherhood in song.

5441 *'To Homer'*
Aye on the shores of darkness there is light,
And precipices show untrodden green,
There is a budding morrow in midnight,
There is a triple sight in blindness keen.

5442 *'The Human Seasons'*
Four seasons fill the measure of the year;
There are four seasons in the mind of man.

5443 *'Hyperion: A Fragment'*
That large utterance of the early gods!

5444 *'Hyperion: A Fragment'*
O aching time! O moments big as years!

5445 *'Hyperion: A Fragment'*
As when, upon a trancèd summer-night,
Those green-robed senators of mighty woods,
Tall oaks, branch-charmèd by the earnest stars,
Dream, and so dream all night without a stir.

5446 *'Hyperion: A Fragment'*
Sometimes eagle's wings,
Unseen before by gods or wondering men,
Darkened the place.

5447 *'Hyperion: A Fragment'*
And still they were the same bright, patient
stars.

5448 *'Hyperion: A Fragment'*
Knowledge enormous makes a god of me.

5449 *'Isabella; or, The Pot of Basil'*
Why were they proud? again we ask aloud,
Why in the name of Glory were they proud?

5450 *'Isabella; or, The Pot of Basil'*
And she forgot the stars, the moon, and sun,
And she forgot the blue above the trees,
And she forgot the dells where waters run,
And she forgot the chilly autumn breeze;
She had no knowledge when the day was done,
And the new morn she saw not; but in peace
Hung over her sweet Basil evermore,
And moistened it with tears unto the core.

5451 *'Isabella; or, The Pot of Basil'*
'For cruel 'tis,' said she,
'To steal my Basil-pot away from me'

5452 *'To J.H. Reynolds, Esq.'*
It is a flaw
In happiness, to see beyond our bourn -
It forces us in summer skies to mourn:
It spoils the singing of the nightingale.

5453 *'La belle dame sans merci'*
Oh, what can ail thee knight at arms
Alone and palely loitering?
The sedge has withered from the lake
And no birds sing!

5454 *'La belle dame sans merci'*
I see a lily on thy brow
With anguish moist and fever dew,
And on thy cheeks a fading rose
Fast withereth too.

5455 *'La belle dame sans merci'*
I met a lady in the meads
Full beautiful, a faery's child
Her hair was long, her foot was light
And her eyes were wild.

5456 *'La belle dame sans merci'*
She looked at me as she did love
And made sweet moan.

5457 *'La belle dame sans merci'*
I set her on my pacing steed
And nothing else saw all day long
For sidelong would she bend and sing
A faery's song.

5458 *'La belle dame sans merci'*
... La belle dame sans merci
Thee hath in thrall.

5459 *'La belle dame sans merci'*
I saw their starved lips in the gloam
With horrid warning gapèd wide
And I awoke and found me here
On the cold hill's side.

5460 *'Lamia'*
Philosophy will clip an Angel's wings,
Conquer all mysteries by rule and line,
Empty the haunted air, the gnomed mine -
Unweave a rainbow.

5461 *'Lamia'*
She was a gordian shape of dazzling hue,
Vermillion-spotted, golden, green, and blue;
Striped like a zebra, freckled like a pard,
Eyed like a peacock, and all crimson barred.

5462 *'Lamia'*
Love in a hut, with water and a crust,
Is - Love, forgive us! - cinders, ashes, dust;
Love in a palace is perhaps at last
More grievous torment than a hermit's fast.

5463 *'Lamia'*
That purple-linèd palace of sweet sin.

5464 *'Lamia'*
In pale contented sort of discontent.

5465 *'To Leigh Hunt, Esq.'*
Glory and loveliness have passed away.

5466 *Letter to Benjamin Bailey*
A long poem is a test of invention which I take
to be the polar star of poetry, as fancy is the
sails, and imagination the rudder.

5467 *Letter to Benjamin Bailey*
I am certain of nothing but the holiness of the
heart's affections and the truth of imagination -
what the imagination seizes as beauty must be
truth - whether it existed before or not.

5468 *Letter to Benjamin Bailey*
I have never yet been able to perceive how
anything can be known for truth by consecutive
reasoning - and yet it must be.

5469 *Letter to Benjamin Bailey*
O for a life of sensations rather than of
thoughts!

5470 *Letter to Benjamin Bailey*
Scenery is fine - but human nature is finer.

5471 *Letter to Benjamin Bailey*
I am in a temper that if I were under water I would scarcely kick to come to the top.

5472 *Letter to Fanny Brawne*
I have met with women whom I really think would like to be married to a poem and to be given away by a novel.

5473 *Letter to Fanny Brawne*
I wish you could invent some means to make me at all happy without you. Every hour I am more and more concentrated in you; every thing else tastes like chaff in my mouth.

5474 *Letter to George and Georgiana Keats*
The roaring of the wind is my wife and the stars through the window pane are my children.

5475 *Letter to George and Georgiana Keats*
A man's life of any worth is a continual allegory.

5476 *Letter to George and Georgiana Keats*
All clean and comfortable I sit down to write.

5477 *Letter to George and Georgiana Keats*
The only means of strengthening one's intellect is to make up one's mind about nothing - to let the mind be a thoroughfare for all thoughts. Not a select party.

5478 *Letter to George and Thomas Keats*
The excellence of every art is its intensity, capable of making all disagreeables evaporate, from their being in close relationship with beauty and truth.

5479 *Letter to George and Thomas Keats*
There is nothing stable in the world - uproar's your only music.

5480 *Letter to J.H. Reynolds*
A man should have the fine point of his soul taken off to become fit for this world.

5481 *Letter to J.H. Reynolds*
Poetry should be great and unobtrusive, a thing which enters into one's soul, and does not startle it or amaze it with itself, but with its subject.

5482 *Letter to J.H. Reynolds*
It is impossible to live in a country which is continually under hatches ... Rain! Rain! Rain!

5483 *Letter to J.H. Reynolds*
There is an awful warmth about my heart like a load of immortality.

5484 *Letter to John Taylor*
Poetry should surprise by a fine excess, and not by singularity - it should strike the reader as a wording of his own highest thoughts, and appear almost a remembrance.

5485 *Letter to John Taylor*
If poetry comes not as naturally as the leaves to a tree it had better not come at all.

5486 *Letter to B. R. Haydon*
It is true that in the height of enthusiasm I have been cheated into some fine passages but that is nothing.

5487 *'Lines on the Mermaid Tavern'*
Souls of poets dead and gone,
What Elysium have ye known
Happy field or mossy cavern
Choicer than the Mermaid Tavern?

5488 *'Ode on a Grecian Urn'*
Thou still unravished bride of quietness,
Thou foster-child of silence and slow time.

5489 *'Ode on a Grecian Urn'*
Heard melodies are sweet, but those unheard
Are sweeter; therefore, ye soft pipes, play on;
Not to the sensual ear, but, more endeared,
Pipe to the spirit ditties of no tone.

5490 *'Ode on a Grecian Urn'*
For ever piping songs for ever new.

5491 *'Ode on a Grecian Urn'*
For ever warm and still to be enjoyed,
For ever panting, and for ever young;
All breathing human passion far above,
That leaves a heart high-sorrowful and cloyed,
A burning forehead, and a parching tongue.

5492 *'Ode on a Grecian Urn'*
O Attic shape! Fair attitude!

5493 *'Ode on a Grecian Urn'*
'Beauty is truth, truth beauty,' - that is all
Ye know on earth, and all ye need to know.

5494 *'Ode on Melancholy'*
No, no, go not to Lethe, neither twist
Wolf's-bane, tight-rooted, for its poisonous wine.

5495 *'Ode on Melancholy'*
Nor let the beetle, nor the death-moth be
Your mournful Psyche.

5496 *'Ode on Melancholy'*
But when the melancholy fit shall fall
Sudden from heaven like a weeping cloud,
That fosters the droop-headed flowers all,
And hides the green hill in an April shroud;
Then glut thy sorrow on a morning rose.

5497 *'Ode on Melancholy'*
She dwells with Beauty - Beauty that must die;
And Joy, whose hand is ever at his lips
Bidding adieu; and aching Pleasure nigh,
Turning to poison while the bee-mouth sips.

5498 *'Ode to a Nightingale'*
Fade far away, dissolve, and quite forget
What thou among the leaves hast never known,
The weariness, the fever, and the fret
Here, where men sit and hear each other groan;
Where palsy shakes a few, sad, last grey hairs,
Where youth grows pale, and spectre-thin, and
dies;
Where but to think is to be full of sorrow
And leaden-eyed despairs.

5499 *'Ode to a Nightingale'*
Away! away! for I will fly to thee,
Not charioted by Bacchus and his pards,
But on the viewless wings of Poesy,
Though the dull brain perplexes and retards:
Already with thee! tender is the night.

5500 *'Ode to a Nightingale'*
I cannot see what flowers are at my feet,
Nor what soft incense hangs upon the boughs.

5501 *'Ode to a Nightingale'*
Now more than ever seems it rich to die,
To cease upon the midnight with no pain.

5502 *'Ode to a Nightingale'*
Thou wast not born for death, immortal bird!
No hungry generations tread thee down;
The voice I hear this passing night was heard
In ancient days by emperor and clown:

5503 *'Ode to a Nightingale'*
Was it a vision, or a waking dream?
Fled is that music: do I wake or sleep?

5504 *'Ode to Psyche'*
Nor virgin-choir to make delicious moan
Upon the midnight hours.

5505 *'Ode to Psyche'*
A bright torch, and a casement ope at night,
To let the warm Love in!

5506
A proverb is no proverb to you till life has
illustrated it.

5507 *'On Seeing the Elgin Marbles'*
Mortality
Weighs heavily on me like unwilling sleep.

5508 *'Shed no tear - O shed no tear'*
Dry your eyes - O dry your eyes
For I was taught in Paradise
To ease my breast of melodies.

5509 *'Sleep and Poetry'*
Stop and consider! life is but a day;
A fragile dew-drop on its perilous way
From a tree's summit;

5510 *'Sleep and Poetry'*
O for ten years, that I may overwhelm
Myself in poesy; so I may do the deed
That my own soul has to itself decreed.

5511 *'Sleep and Poetry'*
They swayed about upon a rocking horse,
And thought it Pegasus.

5512 *'Sleep and Poetry'*
And they shall be accounted poet kings
Who simply tell the most heart-easing things.

5513 *'O Solitude! if I must with thee dwell'*
Yet the sweet converse of an innocent mind,
Whose words are images of thoughts refined,
Is my soul's pleasure; and it sure must be
Almost the highest bliss of human-kind,
When to thy haunts two kindred spirits flee.

5514 *'Sonnet to Sleep'*
O soft embalmer of the still midnight,
Shutting, with careful fingers and benign
Our gloom-pleased eyes.

5515 *'Sonnet to Sleep'*
Turn the key deftly in the oilèd wards,
And seal the hushèd casket of my soul.

5516 *'I stood tip-toe upon a little hill'*
And then there crept
A little noiseless noise among the leaves,
Born of the very sigh that silence heaves.

5517 *'I stood tip-toe upon a little hill'*
Here are sweet peas, on tip-toe for a flight.

5518 *'When I have fears that I may cease to be'*
When I behold, upon the night's starred face
Huge cloudy symbols of a high romance.

5519 *'To one who has been long in city pent'*
To one who has been long in city pent,
'Tis very sweet to look into the fair
And open face of heaven.

5520 *'Woman! when I behold thee flippant, vain'*
Woman! when I behold thee flippant, vain,
Inconstant, childish, proud, and full of fancies.

KEBLE John 1792-1866
5521 *The Christian Year 'Blessed are the pure...'*
Blessed are the pure in heart,
For they shall see our God,
The secret of the Lord is theirs,
Their soul is Christ's abode.

5522 *The Christian Year 'Morning'*
The trivial round, the common task,
Would furnish all we ought to ask;
Room to deny ourselves; a road
To bring us, daily, nearer God.

5523 *The Christian Year 'Septuagesima'*
There is a book, who runs may read,
Which heavenly truth imparts,
And all the lore its scholars need,
Pure eyes and Christian hearts.

5524
If the Church of England were to fail, it would be found in my parish.

5525 *'Holy Matrimony'*
The voice that breathed o'er Eden,
That earliest wedding-day,
The primal marriage blessing,
It hath not passed away.

KEILLOR Garrison 1942-
5526 *The Book of Guys*
Years ago, manhood was an opportunity for achievement, and now it is a problem to be overcome.

KELLER Helen 1880-1968
5527
It is not possible for civilization to flow backward while there is youth in the world. Youth may be headstrong, but it will advance its allotted length.

5528
Many persons have a wrong idea of what constitutes true happiness. It is not attained through self-gratification but through fidelity to a worthy purpose.

5529
Science may have found a cure for most evils: but it has found no remedy for the worst of them all - the apathy of human beings.

5530
When one door of happiness closes, another opens; but often we look so long at the closed door that we do not see the one which has been opened for us.

KELLY Bishop Francis
5531
Convictions are the mainsprings of action, the driving powers of life. What a man lives are his convictions.

KELLY Hugh 1739-1777
5532 *False Delicacy*
Your people of refined sentiments are the most troublesome creatures in the world to deal with.

5533 *Memoirs of a Magdalen*
Of all the stages in a woman's life, none is so dangerous as the period between her acknowledgement of a passion for a man, and the day set apart for her nuptials.

KELLY Vesta M.
5534
Snowflakes are one of nature's most fragile things, but just look what they can do when they stick together.

KELLY Walt 1913-1973
5535
We have met the enemy, and he is us.

KELLY William M. 1811-1888
5536
Man is a slow, sloppy and brilliant thinker; the machine is fast, accurate and stupid.

KELVIN Lord 1824-1907
5537 *(whilst President of the Royal Society, 1895)*
Heavier-than-air flying machines are impossible.

KEMPIS Thomas à 1379-1471
5538 *De Imitatione Christi*
Seek not to know who said this or that, but take note of what has been said.

5539 *De Imitatione Christi*
It is much safer to be in a subordinate position than in authority.

5540 *De Imitatione Christi*
Today the man is here; tomorrow he is gone. And when he is 'out of sight', quickly also is he out of mind.

5541 *De Imitatione Christi*
We are sometimes stirred by emotion and take it for zeal.

5542 *De Imitatione Christi*
If you bear the cross gladly, it will bear you.

5543
Intelligence must follow faith, never precede it, and never destroy it.

5544
Man proposes; God disposes.

KEMPTON Murray
5545
America ... an economic system prouder of the distribution of its products than of the products themselves.

5546
To say that an idea is fashionable is to say, I think, that it has been adulterated to a point where it is hardly an idea at all.

KEMPTON Sally
5547
It is hard to fight an enemy who has outposts in your head.

5548
Women are the true maintenance class. Society is built upon their acquiescence and upon their small and necessary labours.

KEN Thomas 1637-1711
5549 *'Evening Hymn'*
All praise to thee, my God, this night,
For all the blessings of the light;

Keep me, O keep me, King of Kings,
Beneath thy own almighty wings.

5550 *'Evening Hymn'*
Teach me to live, that I may dread
The grave as little as my bed.

5551 *'Morning Hymn'*
Redeem thy mis-spent time that's past,
And live this day as if thy last.

KENDALL Paul Murray
5552
On the trail of another man, the biographer
must put up with finding himself at every turn:
any biography uneasily shelters an
autobiography within it.

KENEALLY Thomas 1935-
5553 *(talking of his book, Schindlers Ark)*
The Holocaust is a Gentile problem not a Jewish
one.

KENNEDY Florynce
5554
If men could get pregnant, abortion would be a
sacrament.

KENNEDY John F. 1917-1963
5555
Too often we ... enjoy the comfort of opinion
without the discomfort of thought.

5556 *(accepting the Democratic nomination)*
We stand today on the edge of a new frontier ...
But the New Frontier of which I speak is not a
set of promises - it is a set of challenges. It
sums up not what I intend to offer the
American people, but what I intend to ask of
them.

5557
All free men, wherever they may live, are
citizens of Berlin. And therefore, as a free man,
I take pride in the words 'Ich bin ein Berliner'.

5558
Anyone who is honestly seeking a job and can't
find it, deserves the attention of the United
States government, and the people.

5559 *(after appointing his brother Attorney
General)*
I don't see what's wrong with giving Bobby a
little experience before he starts to practise law.

5560
The complacent, the self-indulgent, the soft
societies are about to be swept away with the
debris of history.

5561
The courage of life is often a less dramatic
spectacle that the courage of a final moment;
but it is no less a magnificent mixture of
triumph and tragedy. A man does what he must

- in spite of personal consequences, in spite of
obstacles and dangers and pressures - and that
is the basis of all morality.

5562
Everything changes but change itself.

5563
The Family of Man is more than three billion
strong. It lives in more than one hundred
nations. Most of its members are not white.
Most of them are not Christians. Most of them
know nothing about free enterprise, or due
process of law, or the Australian ballot.

5564
In free society art is not a weapon ... Artists are
not engineers of the soul.

5565 *(asked how he became a war hero)*
It was involuntary. They sank my boat.

5566 *(inaugural address)*
Let the word go forth from this time and place,
to friend and foe alike, that the torch has been
passed to a new generation of Americans - born
in this century, tempered by war, disciplined by
a hard and bitter peace, proud of our ancient
heritage - and unwilling to witness or permit
the slow undoing of those human rights to
which this nation has always been committed,
and to which we are committed today at home
and around the world.

5567 *(Inaugural address)*
Let every nation know, whether it wishes us well
or ill, that we shall pay any price, bear any
burden, meet any hardship, support any friend,
oppose any foe to assure the survival and the
success of liberty.

5568 *(Inaugural address)*
If a free society cannot help the many who are
poor, it cannot save the few who are rich.

5569 *(Inaugural address)*
Let us never negotiate out of fear. But let us
never fear to negotiate.

5570 *(Inaugural address)*
All this will not be finished in the first 100 days.
Nor will it be finished in the first 1,000 days, nor
in the life of this Administration, nor even
perhaps in our lifetime on this planet. But let
us begin.

5571 *(Inaugural address)*
Now the trumpet summons us again - not as a
call to bear arms, though arms we need - not as
a call to battle, though embattled we are - but a
call to bear the burden of a long twilight
struggle, year in and year out, 'rejoicing in hope,
patient in tribulation' - a struggle against the
common enemies of man: tyranny, poverty,
disease and war itself.

5572 *(Inaugural address)*
And so, my fellow Americans: ask not what your country can do for you - ask what you can do for your country.

5573
We will neglect our cities to our peril, for in neglecting them we neglect the nation.

5574 *(on proposed Civil Rights Bill)*
No one has been barred on account of his race from fighting or dying for America - there are no 'white' or 'coloured' signs on the foxholes or graveyards of battle.

5575
There are risks and costs to a program of action. But they are far less than the long-range risks and costs of comfortable inaction.

5576
Once you say you're going to settle for second, that's what happens to you in life, I find.

5577
If we are strong, our strength will speak for itself. If we are weak, words will be no help.

5578 *(to United Nations General Assembly)*
Mankind must put an end to war or war will put an end to mankind.

5579
War will exist until that distant day when the conscientious objector enjoys the same reputation and prestige that the warrior does today.

5580
When we got into office, the thing that surprised me most was to find that things were just as bad as we'd been saying they were.

5581
When power leads man toward arrogance, poetry reminds him of his limitations. When power narrows the areas of man's concern, poetry reminds him of the richness and diversity of his existence. When power corrupts, poetry cleanses. For art establishes the basic human truths which must serve as the touchstone of our judgement.

5582
Those who make peaceful revolution impossible will make violent revolution inevitable.

KENNEDY Joseph P. 1888-1969
5583 *(telegraphed message to J F Kennedy)*
Don't buy a single vote more than necessary. I'll be damned if I'm going to pay for a landslide.

5584
When the going gets tough, the tough get going.

KENNEDY Robert F. 1925-1968
5585
One fifth of the people are against everything all the time.

5586
Moral courage is a more rare commodity than bravery in battle or great intelligence.

5587
Only those who dare to fail greatly can ever achieve greatly.

KEPES Gyorgy
5588
The really great visual experience today is to fly over a huge city and look down into the night. It's like a tremendous jubilant Christmas tree. You just feel life is worth living - when you come down you may have some doubts.

KEROUAC Jack 1922-1969
5589
The beat generation.

KERR Clark 1911-
5590 *(whilst President, University of California)*
I find the three major administrative problems on a campus are sex for the students, athletics for the alumni and parking for the faculty.

KERR Jean 1923-
5591
The thing about having a baby is that thereafter you have it.

5592
Marrying a man is like buying something you've been admiring for a long time in a shop window. You may love it when you get it home, but it doesn't always go with everything in the house.

5593 *Mary, Mary*
Being divorced is like being hit by a truck - if you survive, you start looking very carefully to the left and right.

KETTERING Charles F. 1876-1958
5594
It is easy to build a philosophy. It doesn't have to run.

5595
My interest is in the future because I am going to spend the rest of my life there.

KEY Ellen 1849-1926
5596 *The Morality of Women and Other Essays*
Love is moral even without legal marriage, but marriage is immoral without love.

KEY Francis Scott 1779-1843
5597 *'The Star-Spangled Banner'*
'Tis the star-spangled banner; O long may it wave

O'er the land of the free, and the home of the brave.

KEYES Jr. Ken
5598
A loving person lives in a loving world. A hostile person lives in a hostile world: everyone you meet is your mirror.

KEYNES John Maynard 1883-1946
5599 *The Economic Consequences of the Peace*
Like Odysseus, the President [Woodrow Wilson] looked wiser when he was seated.

5600 *The Economic Consequences of the Peace*
Lenin was right. There is no subtler, no surer means of overturning the existing basis of society than to debauch the currency. The process engages all the hidden forces of economic law on the side of destruction, and does it in a manner which not one man in a million is able to diagnose.

5601 *The End of Laissez-Faire*
I do not know which makes a man more conservative - to know nothing but the present, or nothing but the past.

5602 *The End of Laissez-Faire*
The important thing for Government is not to do things which individuals are doing already, and to do them a little better or a little worse; but to do those things which at present are not done at all.

5603 *Essays in Biography 'Mr Lloyd George'*
This extraordinary figure of our time, this syren, this goat-footed bard, this half-human visitor to our age from the hag-ridden magic and enchanted woods of Celtic antiquity.

5604 *General Theory*
We take it as a fundamental psychological rule of any modern community that, when its real income is increased, it will not increase its consumption by an equal *absolute* amount.

5605 *General Theory*
If the Treasury were to fill old bottles with banknotes, bury them at suitable depths in disused coalmines which are then filled up to the surface with town rubbish, and leave it to private enterprise on well-tried principles of *laissez-faire* to dig the notes up again (the right to do so being obtained, of course, by tendering for leases of the note-bearing territory) there need be no more unemployment and, with the help of the repercussions, the real income of the community, and its capital wealth also, would probably become a good deal greater than it actually is.

5606 *General Theory*
Practical men, who believe themselves to be quite exempt from any intellectual influences, are usually the slaves of some defunct economist. Madmen in authority, who hear voices in the air, are distilling their frenzy from some academic scribbler of a few years back.

5607 *(of his poor results in the Civil Service exams)*
I evidently knew more about economics than my examiners.

5608 *A Tract on Monetary Reform*
In the long run we are all dead.

5609
I work for a Government I despise for ends I think criminal.

KEYNES John Neville 1852-1949
5610 *The Scope and Method of Political Economy*
A *positive science* may be defined as a body of systematized knowledge concerning what is; a *normative* or *regular science* a body of systematized knowledge relating to criteria of what ought to be, and concerned therefore with the ideal as distinguished from the actual.

KEYSERLING Hermann 1880-1946
5611
The greatest American superstition is belief in facts.

KHRUSHCHEV Nikita 1894-1971
5612
If anyone believes that our smiles involve abandonment of the teaching of Marx, Engels and Lenin he deceives himself. Those who wait for that must wait until a shrimp learns to whistle.

5613
Anyone who believes that the worker can be lulled by fine revolutionary phrases is mistaken ... If no concern is shown for the growth of material and spiritual riches, the people will listen today, they will listen tomorrow, and then they may say: 'Why do you promise us everything for the future? You are talking, so to speak, about life beyond the grave. The priest has already told us about this.'

5614
About the capitalist States, it doesn't depend on you whether or not we exist. If you don't like us, don't accept our invitations and don't invite us to come to see you. Whether you like it or not, history is on our side. We will bury you.

5615
If one cannot catch the bird of paradise, better take a wet hen.

5616
You do not know, you cannot know, the difficulty of life of a politician. It means every

minute of the day or night, every ounce of your energy. There is no rest, no relaxation. Enjoyment? A politician does not know the meaning of the word.

5617
I don't like the life here in New York. There is no greenery. It would make a stone sick.

5618
Politicians are the same all over. They promise to build a bridge even when there is no river.

5619
If we should promise people nothing better than only revolution, they would scratch their heads and say, 'Isn't it better to have good goulash?'

5620
If you start throwing hedgehogs under me, I shall throw a couple of porcupines under you.

KIERAN John
5621
I am a part of all I have read.

KIERKEGAARD Sören 1813-1855
5622
Anxiety is the dizziness of freedom.

5623
Life can only be understood backwards; but it must be lived forwards.

5624
Most people believe that the Christian commandments are intentionally a little too severe - like setting a clock half an hour ahead to make sure of not being late in the morning.

5625
People hardly ever make use of the freedom they have, for example, freedom of thought; instead they demand freedom of speech as a compensation.

5626
The sadness in legitimate humour consists in the fact that honestly, and without deceit, it reflects in a purely human way upon what it is to be a child.

5627
What our age lacks is not reflection but passion.

5628
Wherever there is a crowd there is untruth.

KILMER Joyce 1886-1918
5629
Things have a terrible permanence when people die.

5630 *'Trees'*
I think that I shall never see
A poem lovely as a tree.

5631 *'Trees'*
Poems are made by fools like me,
But only God can make a tree.

KILMUIR Lord (Sir David Maxwell Fyfe) 1900-1967
5632
Loyalty is the Tory's secret weapon.

KILVERT Francis 1840-1879
5633 *Diary*
Of all noxious animals, too, the most noxious is a tourist. And of all tourists the most vulgar, ill-bred, offensive and loathsome is the British tourist.

5634 *Diary*
The Vicar of St Ives says the smell of fish there is sometimes so terrific as to stop the church clock.

5635 *Diary*
It is a fine thing to be out on the hills alone. A man can hardly be a beast or a fool alone on a great mountain.

KING Benjamin Franklin 1857-1894
5636 *'The Pessimist'*
Nothing to do but work,
Nothing to eat but food,
Nothing to wear but clothes
To keep one from going nude.

Nothing to breathe but air,
Quick as a flash 't is gone,
Nowhere to fall but off,
Nowhere to stand but on.

5637 *'The Pessimist'*
Nowhere to go but out,
Nowhere to come but back.

KING Henry 1592-1669
5638 *'An Exequy'*
My last Good night! Thou wilt not wake
Till I thy fate shall overtake:
Till age, or grief, or sickness must
Marry my body to that dust
It so much loves.

5639 *'The Surrender'*
We that did nothing study but the way
To love each other, ...
Must learn the hateful art, how to forget.

KING Martin Luther 1929-1968
5640 *(day before assassination)*
I just want to do God's will. And he's allowed me to go up to the mountain. And I've looked over, and I've seen the promised land ... So I'm happy tonight. I'm not worried about anything. I'm not fearing any man.

5641
Don't hate, it's too big a burden to bear.

5642
I have a dream that one day on the red hills of
Georgia the sons of former slaves and the sons
of former slave owners will be able to sit down
together at the table of brotherhood ...
I have a dream that my four little children will
one day live in a nation where they will not be
judged by the colour of their skin but by the
content of their character.

5643
Human Salvation lies in the hands of the
creatively maladjusted.

5644
Injustice anywhere is a threat to justice
everywhere.

5645
We must learn to live together as brothers or
perish together as fools.

5646
Man must evolve for all human conflict a
method which rejects revenge, aggression and
retaliation. The foundation of such a method is
love.

5647
The Negro's great stumbling block in the stride
toward freedom is not the White Citizens
Councillor or the Ku Klux Klanner but the white
moderate who is more devoted to order than to
justice; who prefers a negative peace which is
the absence of tension to a positive peace
which is the presence of justice.

5648
Non-violence is a powerful and just weapon. It
is a weapon unique in history, which cuts
without wounding and enobles the man who
wields it. It is a sword that heals.

5649 *Strength to Love*
The means by which we live have outdistanced
the ends for which we live. Our scientific power
has outrun our spiritual power. We have guided
missiles and misguided men.

5650
I submit to you that if a man hasn't discovered
something he will die for, he isn't fit to live.

5651
The ultimate measure of a man is not where he
stands in moments of comfort and
convenience, but where he stands at times of
challenge and controversy.

5652
I want to be the white man's brother, not his
brother-in-law.

5653 *Where Do We Go From Here?*
A riot is at bottom the language of the unheard.

KING Stoddard 1889-1933
5654 *'There's a Long, Long Trail'*
There's a long, long trail awinding
Into the land of my dreams.

KING William Lyon Mackenzie 1874-1950
5655
Government in the last analysis is organized
opinion. Where there is little or no public
opinion, there is likely to be bad government,
which sooner or later becomes autocratic
government.

5656
Not necessarily conscription, but conscription if
necessary.

5657
The promises of yesterday are the taxes of
today.

5658
I really believe my greatest service is in the
many unwise steps I prevent.

KINGSLEY Charles 1819-1875
5659
We act as though comfort and luxury were the
chief requirements of life, when all that we need
to make us really happy is something to be
enthusiastic about.

5660 *'Airly Beacon'*
Airly Beacon, Airly Beacon;
Oh the pleasant sight to see
Shires and towns from Airly Beacon,
While my love climbed up to me!

5661 *'A Farewell'*
Be good, sweet maid, and let who will be clever;
Do noble things, not dream them, all day long:
And so make life, death, and that vast for-ever
One grand, sweet song.

5662 *Health and Education*
To be discontented with the divine discontent,
and to be ashamed with the noble shame, is the
very germ and first upgrowth of all virtue.

5663 *'The Invitation. To Tom Hughes'*
What we can we will be,
Honest Englishmen.
Do the work that's nearest,
Though it's dull at whiles,
Helping, when we meet them,
Lame dogs over stiles.

5664 *Letters to the Chartists*
We have used the Bible as if it was a constable's
handbook - an opium-dose for keeping beasts
of burden patient while they are being
overloaded.

5665
He was one of those men who possess almost
every gift, except the gift of the power to use
them.

5666 *'Ode to the North-East Wind'*
'Tis the hard grey weather
Breeds hard English men.

5667 *'Ode to the North-East Wind'*
Come; and strong within us
Stir the Vikings' blood;
Bracing brain and sinew;
Blow, thou wind of God!

5668 *'The Sands of Dee'*
'O Mary, go and call the cattle home,
And call the cattle home,
And call the cattle home,
Across the sands of Dee.'
The western wind was wild and dank with
foam,
And all alone went she.

5669 *'The Three Fishers'*
Three fishers went sailing away to the west,
Away to the west as the sun went down;
Each thought on the woman who loved him the
best,
And the children stood watching them out of
the town.

5670 *'The Three Fishers'*
For men must work, and women must weep,
And there's little to earn, and many to keep,
Though the harbour bar be moaning.

5671
Truth, for its own sake, had never been a virtue
with the Roman clergy.

5672 *The Water Babies*
As thorough an Englishman as ever coveted his
neighbour's goods.

5673 *The Water Babies 'Young and Old'*
When all the world is young, lad,
And all the trees are green;
And every goose a swan, lad,
And every lass a queen;
Then hey for boot and horse, lad,
And round the world away:
Young blood must have its course, lad,
And every dog his day.

5674 *Westward Ho!*
Eustace is a man no longer; he is become a
thing, a tool, a Jesuit.

KINGSMILL Hugh 1889-1949
5675 *(on friends)*
God's apology for relations.

5676
Society is based on the assumption that
everyone is alike and no one is alive.

5677 *'Two Poems, after A.E. Housman'*
What still alive at twenty-two,
A clean upstanding chap like you?
Sure, if your throat 'tis hard to slit,
Slit your girl's and swing for it.

Like enough, you won't be glad,
When they come to hang you, lad:
But bacon's not the only thing
That's cured by hanging from a string.

KINNOCK Neil 1942-
5678
I will regret to my dying day that I failed to lead
you to the victory you deserved.

5679 *(on Tory re-election)*
I warn you not to be ordinary, I warn you not to
be young, I warn you not to fall ill, and I warn
you not to grow old.

KIPLING Rudyard 1865-1936
5680 *'The Absent-Minded Beggar'*
When you've shouted 'Rule Britannia', when
you've sung 'God save the Queen' -
When you've finished killing Kruger with your
mouth.

5681 *For All We Have and Are*
There is but one task for all -
For each one life to give,
What stands if freedom fall?
Who dies if England live?

5682
All the people like us are We,
And everyone else is They.

5683 *'The Anvil'*
England's on the anvil - hear the hammers ring
-
Clanging from the Severn to the Tyne!
Never was a blacksmith like our Norman King -
England's being hammered, hammered,
hammered into line!

5684 *'The Ballad of East and West'*
Oh, East is East, and West is West, and never the
twain shall meet,
Till Earth and Sky stand presently at God's great
Judgement Seat;
But there is neither East nor West, Border, nor
Breed, nor Birth,
When two strong men stand face to face, tho'
they come from the ends of earth!

5685 *'The Ballad of the King's Jest'*
And the talk slid north, and the talk slid south,
With the sliding puffs from the hookah-mouth.
Four things greater than all things are,
Women and Horses and Power and War.

5686 *Barrack-Room Ballads*
There be triple ways to take, of the eagle or the snake,
Or the way of a man with a maid;
But the sweetest way to me is a ship's upon the sea
In the heel of the North-East Trade.

5687 *The Betrothed*
And a woman is only a woman but a good cigar is a Smoke.

5688 *'Boots'*
Foot - foot - foot - foot - sloggin' over Africa -
(Boots - boots - boots - boots - movin' up and down again!)

5689 *'Common Form'*
If any question why we died,
Tell them, because our fathers lied.

5690 *'The Conundrum of the Workshops'*
We know that the tail must wag the dog, for the horse is drawn by the cart;
But the Devil whoops, as he whooped of old:
'It's clever, but is it Art?'

5691 *'Danny Deever'*
For they're hangin' Danny Deever, you can hear the Dead March play,
The regiment's in 'ollow square - they're hanging him to-day;
They've taken of his buttons off an' cut his stripes away,
An' they're hangin' Danny Deever in the mornin'.

5692 *'The 'Eathen'*
The 'eathen in 'is blindness bows down to wood an' stone;
'E don't obey no orders unless they is 'is own;

5693 *'The 'Eathen'*
The 'eathen in 'is blindness must end where 'e began.
But the backbone of the Army is the non-commissioned man!

5694 *'The English Flag'*
Winds of the World, give answer! They are whimpering to and fro -
And what should they know of England who only England know?

5695 *'The Female of the Species'*
The female of the species is more deadly than the male.

5696 *'Fuzzy-Wuzzy'*
So 'ere's *to* you, Fuzzy-Wuzzy, at your 'ome in the Soudan;
You're a pore benighted 'eathen but a first-class fightin' man;
An' 'ere's *to* you, Fuzzy-Wuzzy, with your 'ayrick 'ead of 'air -

You big black boundin' beggar - for you broke a British square!

5697 *'Gentlemen-Rankers'*
We're poor little lambs who've lost our way,
Baa! Baa! Baa!
We're little black sheep who've gone astray,
Baa-aa-aa!
Gentlemen-rankers out on the spree,
Damned from here to Eternity,
God ha' mercy on such as we,
Baa! Yah! Bah!

5698 *'The Glory of the Garden'*
Our England is a garden, and such gardens are not made
By singing:- 'Oh, how beautiful!' and sitting in the shade,
While better men than we go out and start their working lives
At grubbing weeds from gravel paths with broken dinner-knives.

5699 *'The Gods of the Copybook Headings'*
As it will be in the future, it was at the birth of Man -
There are only four things certain since Social Progress began:-
That the Dog returns to his Vomit and the Sow returns to her Mire,
And the burnt Fool's bandaged finger goes wabbling back to the Fire.

5700 *'Gunga Din'*
The uniform 'e wore
Was nothin' much before,
An' rather less than 'arf o' that be'ind.

5701 *'Gunga Din'*
Though I've belted you and flayed you,
By the livin' Gawd that made you,
You're a better man than I am, Gunga Din!

5702 *'The Islanders'*
Then ye returned to your trinkets; then ye contented your souls
With the flannelled fools at the wicket or the muddied oafs at the goals.

5703 *The Jungle Book 'Road Song of the BandarLog'*
Brother, thy tail hangs down behind!

5704 *Just So Stories 'The Cat that Walked ...'*
He walked by himself, and all places were alike to him.

5705 *Just So Stories 'The Cat that Walked ...'*
And he went back through the Wet Wild Woods, waving his wild tail and walking by his wild lone. But he never told anybody.

5706 *Just So Stories 'The Elephant's Child'*
Then the Elephant's Child put his head down close to the Crocodile's musky, tusky mouth,

and the Crocodile caught him by his little nose
... 'Led go! You are hurtig be!'

5707 *Just So Stories 'The Elephant's Child'*
I keep six honest serving-men
(They taught me all I knew);
Their names are What and Why and When
And How and Where and Who.

5708 *Just So Stories 'How the Camel got his Hump'*
The cure for this ill is not to sit still,
Or frowst with a book by the fire;
But to take a large hoe and a shovel also,
And dig till you gently perspire.

5709 *Just So Stories 'How the Whale ...'*
And the small 'Stute Fish said in a small 'stute
voice, 'Noble and generous Cetacean, have you
ever tasted Man?' 'No,' said the Whale. 'What is
it like?' 'Nice,' said the small 'Stute Fish. 'Nice
but nubbly.'

5710 *Just So Stories 'How the Whale ...'*
He had his Mummy's leave to paddle, or else he
would never have done it, because he was a
man of infinite-resource-and-sagacity.

5711 *Kim*
The mad all are in God's keeping.

5712 *'The Ladies'*
I've taken my fun where I've found it,
An' now I must pay for my fun,
For the more you 'ave known o' the others
The less will you settle to one.

5713 *'The Ladies'*
When you get to a man in the case,
They're like as a row of pins -
For the Colonel's Lady an' Judy O'Grady
Are sisters under their skins!

5714 *'Our Lady of the Snows'*
A Nation spoke to a Nation,
A Throne sent word to a Throne:
'Daughter am I in my mother's house,
But mistress in my own.
The gates are mine to open,
As the gates are mine to close,
And I abide by my Mother's House.'
Said our Lady of the Snows.

5715 *'The Last Chantey'*
And Ye take mine honour from me if Ye take
away the sea!

5716 *'The Liner She's a Lady'*
The Liner she's a lady, an' she never looks nor
'eeds -
The Man-o'-War's 'er 'usband, an' 'e gives 'er all
she needs;
But, oh, the little cargo boats that sail the wet
seas roun',
They're just the same as you an' me a-plyin' up

and down!

5717
The man who would be king.

5718 *'Mandalay'*
On the road to Mandalay,
Where the flyin'-fishes play,
An' the dawn comes up like thunder outer
China 'crost the Bay!

5719 *'Mandalay'*
An' I seed her first a-smokin' of a whackin' white
cheroot,
An' a-wastin' Christian kisses on an 'eathen
idol's foot.

5720 *'Mandalay'*
Ship me somewheres east of Suez, where the
best is like the worst,
Where there aren't no Ten Commandments an'
a man can raise a thirst.

5721 *(of Max Aitken's political standpoint)*
Power without responsibility: the prerogative of
the harlot throughout the ages.

5722
Nations have passed away and left no traces,
And history gives the naked cause of it -
One single simple reason in all cases;
They fell because their peoples were not fit.

5723 *The Naulahka*
And the end of the fight is a tombstone white,
with the name of the late deceased,
And the epitaph drear: 'A fool lies here who tried
to hustle the East'.

5724 *'In the Neolithic Age'*
There are nine and sixty ways of constructing
tribal lays,
And - every - single - one - of - them - is - right!

5725 *'Pagett, MP'*
The toad beneath the harrow knows
Exactly where each tooth-point goes;
The butterfly upon the road
Preaches contentment to that toad.

5726 *'In Partibus'*
But I consort with long-haired things
In velvet collar-rolls,
Who talk about the Aims of Art,
And 'theories' and 'goals',
And moo and coo with women-folk
About their blessed souls.

5727 *Plain Tales from the Hills*
Every one is more or less mad on one point.

5728 *Plain Tales from the Hills*
Take my word for it, the silliest woman can
manage a clever man; but it takes a very clever
woman to manage a fool.

5729 *'The Power of the Dog'*
There is sorrow enough in the natural way
From men and women to fill our day;
But when we are certain of sorrow in store,
Why do we always arrange for more?
Brothers and Sisters, I bid you beware
Of giving your heart to a dog to tear.

5730 *Puck of Pook's Hill 'Harp Song...'*
What is a woman that you forsake her,
And the hearth-fire and the home-acre,
To go with the old grey Widow-maker?

5731 *Puck of Pook's Hill 'A Smuggler's Song'*
Five and twenty ponies,
Trotting through the dark-
Brandy for the parson,
'Baccy for the Clerk;
Laces for a lady, letters for a spy,
Watch the wall, my darling, while the
Gentlemen go by!

5732 *Puck of Pook's Hill 'A Tree Song'*
Of all the trees that grow so fair,
Old England to adorn,
Greater are none beneath the Sun,
Than Oak, and Ash, and Thorn.

5733 *'Recessional'*
The tumult and the shouting dies -
The captains and the kings depart -
Still stands Thine ancient Sacrifice,
An humble and a contrite heart.
Lord God of Hosts, be with us yet,
Lest we forget - lest we forget!

5734 *'Recessional'*
Far-called our navies melt away -
On dune and headland sinks the fire -
Lo, all our pomp of yesterday
Is one with Nineveh, and Tyre!

5735 *'Recessional'*
If, drunk with sight of power, we loose
Wild tongues that have not Thee in awe -
Such boasting as the Gentiles use,
Or lesser breeds without the Law.

5736 *Rewards and Fairies 'If -'*
If you can keep your head when all about you
Are losing theirs and blaming it on you;

5737 *Rewards and Fairies 'If -'*
If you can trust yourself when all men doubt
you,
But make allowance for their doubting too;
If you can wait and not be tired by waiting,
Or being lied about, don't deal in lies,
Or being hated, don't give way to hating,
And yet don't look too good, nor talk too wise;

5738 *Rewards and Fairies 'If -'*
If you can dream - and not make dreams your
master;
If you can think - and not make thoughts your

aim,
If you can meet with triumph and disaster
And treat those two imposters just the same ...

5739 *Rewards and Fairies 'If -'*
If you can talk with crowds and keep your
virtue,
Or walk with Kings - nor lose the common
touch,
If neither foes nor loving friends can hurt you,
If all men count with you, but none too much;

5740 *Rewards and Fairies 'If -'*
If you can fill the unforgiving minute
With sixty seconds' worth of distance run,
Yours is the Earth and everything that's in it,
And - which is more - you'll be a Man, my son!

5741 *Rewards and Fairies 'The Thousandth Man'*
One man in a thousand, Solomon says,
Will stick more close than a brother.

5742 *Rewards and Fairies 'The Way through...'*
They shut the road through the woods
Seventy years ago.
Weather and rain have undone it again,
And now you would never know
There was once a road through the woods.

5743 *The Second Jungle Book 'Law of the Jungle'*
Now this is the Law of the Jungle - as old and as
true as the sky;
And the Wolf that shall keep it may prosper, but
the Wolf that shall break it must die.

5744
There was a small boy of Quebec
Who was buried in snow to the neck:
When they said 'Are you friz?'
He replied 'Yes, I is -
But we don't call this cold in Quebec!'

5745 *'The Song of the Dead'*
We have fed our sea for a thousand years
And she calls us, still unfed,
Though there's never a wave of all her waves
But marks our English dead:

5746 *'The Song of the Dead'*
We have strawed our best to the weed's unrest
To the shark and sheering gull.
If blood be the price of admiralty,
Lord God, we ha' paid in full!

5747 *The Story of the Gadsbys*
Down to Gehenna or up to the Throne,
He travels the fastest who travels alone.

5748 *The Story of the Gadsbys 'Poor Dear*
Mamma'
Being kissed by a man who *didn't* wax his
moustache was - like eating an egg without salt.

5749 *'Tomlinson'*
For the sin ye do by two and two ye must pay
for one by one!

5750 *'Tommy'*
For it's Tommy this, an' Tommy that, an' 'Chuck
him out, the brute!'
But it's 'Saviour of 'is country' when the guns
begin to shoot.

5751 *Traffics and Discoveries 'Mrs Bathurst'*
'Tisn't beauty, so to speak, nor good talk
necessarily. It's just It. Some women'll stay in a
man's memory if they once walked down a
street.

5752 *'The Vampire'*
A fool there was and he made his prayer
(Even as you and I!)
To a rag and a bone and a hank of hair
(We called her the woman who did not care)
But the fool he called her his lady fair -
(Even as you and I!)

5753 *'What Dane-geld means'*
It is always a temptation to a rich and lazy
nation,
To puff and look important and to say:-
'Though we know we should defeat you, we
have not the time to meet you,
We will therefore pay you cash to go away.

5754 *'When Earth's Last Picture is Painted'*
And only the Master shall praise us, and only
the Master shall blame;
And no one shall work for money, and no one
shall work for fame,
But each for the joy of the working, and each, in
his separate star,
Shall draw the Thing as he sees It for the God of
Things as They are!

5755 *'The White Man's Burden'*
Take up the White Man's burden -
Send forth the best ye breed -
Go, bind your sons to exile
To serve your captives' need.

5756 *'The Young British Soldier'*
When you're wounded and left on Afghanistan's
plains
And the women come out to cut up what
remains
Just roll on your rifle and blow out your brains
An' go to your Gawd like a soldier.

KISSINGER Henry 1923-
5757
The history of things that didn't happen has
never been written.

5758
The illegal we do immediately. The
unconstitutional takes a little longer.

5759
Intelligence is not all that important in the
exercise of power and is often, in point of fact,
useless. Just as a leader doesn't need
intelligence, a man in my job doesn't need too
much of it either.

5760
Power is the ultimate aphrodisiac.

5761
We are the President's men.

5762
Now when I bore people at a party, they think
it's their fault.

KITCHENER Lord 1850-1916
5763 *(to the Prince of Wales during First World
War)*
I don't mind your being killed, but I object to
your being taken prisoner.

5764 *(to soldiers of British Expeditionary Force)*
You are ordered abroad as a soldier of the King
to help our French comrades against the
invasion of a common enemy ... In this new
experience you may find temptations both in
wine and women. You must entirely resist both
temptations, and, while treating all women with
perfect courtesy, you should avoid any intimacy.
Do your duty bravely. Fear God. Honour the
king.

KLEE Paul 1879-1940
5765
Art does not reproduce the visible; rather, it
makes visible.

5766
The more horrifying this world becomes, the
more art becomes abstract.

KLOPSTOCK Friedrich 1724-1803
5767 *(of a passage in one of his poems)*
God and I both knew what it meant once; now
God alone knows.

KNIGHT Charles and LYLE Kenneth
5768 *'Here we are! Here we are again!!'*
When there's trouble brewing,
When there's something doing,
Are we downhearted?
No! Let 'em all come!

KNIGHT Frank H. 1885-1973
5769 *Risk, Uncertainty and Profit*
Costs merely register competing attractions.

KNOWLES Mary 1733-1807
5770 *(of Samuel Johnson)*
He gets at the substance of a book directly; he
tears out the heart of it.

KNOX John c.1505-1572
5771
The First Blast of the Trumpet Against the
Monstrous Regiment of Women.

5772
A man with God is always in the majority.

5773
As the world is wearie of me so am I of it.

KNOX Ronald 1888-1957
5774 *'Absolute and Abitofhell'*
When suave politeness, tempering bigot zeal,
Corrected *I believe to One does feel.*

5775 *(advertisement placed in a newspaper)*
Evangelical vicar, in want of a portable, second-
hand font, would dispose, for the same, of a
portrait, in frame, of the Bishop, elect, of
Vermont.

5776 *(definition of a baby, attributed)*
A loud noise at one end and no sense of
responsibility at the other.

5777
O God, for as much as without Thee
We are not enabled to doubt Thee,
Help us all by Thy grace
To convince the whole race
It knows nothing whatever about Thee.

5778 *'Magister Reformator'*
Hail him like Etonians, without a single word,
Absolutely silent and indefinitely bored.

5779
There once was a man who said, 'God
Must think it exceedingly odd
If he finds that this tree
Continues to be
When there's no one about in the Quad.'

5780 *'After the party'*
The tumult and the shouting dies,
The captains and the kings depart,
And we are left with large supplies
Of cold blancmange and rhubarb tart.

5781 *(on being asked to perform a baptism in English)*
The baby doesn't understand English and the
Devil knows Latin.

5782
The room smelt of not having been smoked in.

5783 *A Spiritual Aeneid*
After all, what was a paradox but a statement of
the obvious so as to make it sound untrue?

5784
It's not the taste of water I object to. It's the
after-effects.

KNOX Vicesimus 1752-1821
5785 *Essays Moral and Literary*
That learning belongs not to the female
character, and that the female mind is not
capable of a degree of improvement equal to
that of the other sex, are narrow and
unphilosophical prejudices.

5786 *In A Vindication of the Rights of Women*
Can anything be more absurd than keeping
women in a state of ignorance, and yet so
vehemently to insist on their resisting
temptation?

KOCH Kenneth
5787
One trouble with a kind of falsely therapeutic
and always reassuring attitude that it is easy to
fall into with old people, is the tendency to be
satisfied with too little.

KOCH William
5788
Frontal attack never works, sneak attack is
always the best.

KOEHLER Ted
5789 *'Stormy Weather'*
Stormy weather,
Since my man and I ain't together.

KOESTLER Arthur 1905-1983
5790 *Darkness at Noon*
One may not regard the world as a sort of
metaphysical brothel for emotions.

5791 *Darkness at Noon*
The definition of the individual was: a
multitude of one million divided by one million.

5792 *The Ghost in the Machine*
Behaviourism is indeed a kind of flat-earth view
of the mind ... it has substituted for the
erstwhile anthropomorphic view of the rat, a
ratomorphic view of man.

5793 *The Ghost in the Machine*
God seems to have left the receiver off the hook,
and time is running out.

5794
Nothing is more sad than the death of an
illusion.

5795
The more original a discovery, the more obvious
it seems afterwards.

5796
Wars are not fought for territory, but for words.
Man's deadliest weapon is language. He is
susceptible to being hypnotized by slogans as
he is to infectious diseases. And where there is
an epidemic, the group-mind takes over.

5797
A writer's ambition should be ... to trade a hundred contemporary readers for ten readers in ten years' time and for one reader in a hundred years.

KOHL Helmut 1930-
5798
We all need Europe, but Germans need it most of all.

5799
We Germans now have the historic chance to realize the unity of our fatherland.

5800
The policy of European integration is in reality a question of war and peace in the 21st century.

The KORAN
5801
He deserves paradise who makes his companions laugh.

5802
Give God time.

5803
That which God writes on thy forehead, thou wilt come to it.

KORZYBSKI Alfred 1879-1950
5804
There are two ways to slide easily through life; to believe everything or doubt everything. Both ways save us from thinking.

KOSINSKI Jerzy 1933-1991
5805
You don't die in the United States, you underachieve.

KRAUS Karl
5806
Stupidity is an elemental force for which no earthquake is a match.

5807
He who gladly does without the praise of the crowd will not miss the opportunity of becoming his own fan.

5808
A writer is someone who can make a riddle out of an answer.

KRISHNAMURTI Jiddu 1895-1986
5809
Discipline does not mean suppression and control, nor is it adjustment to a pattern or ideology. It means a mind that sees 'what is' and learns from 'what was'.

5810
Religion is the frozen thought of men out of which they build temples.

5811
Truth is a pathless land, and you cannot approach it by any path whatsoever, by any religion, by any sect.

KRISTOFFERSON Kris 1936-
5812 *'Me and Bobby McGee'*
Freedom's just another word for nothin' left to lose,
Nothin' ain't worth nothin', but it's free.

KRISTOL Irving
5813
Even if we can't be happy, we must always be cheerful.

KRONENBERGER Louis
5814
Individualism is rather like innocence; there must be something unconscious about it.

KRONSBERG Jeremy Joe
5815
Every which way but loose.

KRUSE Scott M.
5816
As a matter of biology, if something bites you it is probably female.

KRUTCH Joseph Wood 1893-1970
5817
It is from the artist that society gains its loftier images of itself.

5818
Cats seem to go on the principle that it never does any harm to ask for what you want.

5819
Civilizations die from philosophical calm, irony, and the sense of fair play quite as surely as they die of debauchery.

5820
A humanist is anyone who rejects the attempt to describe or account for man wholly on the basis of physics, chemistry or animal behaviour.

5821
Though many have tried, no one has ever yet explained away the decisive fact that science, which can do so much, cannot decide what it ought to do.

5822
True tragedy may be defined as a dramatic work in which the outward failure of the principal personage is compensated for by the dignity and greatness of his character.

5823 *The Twelve Seasons 'February'*
The most serious charge which can be brought against New England is not Puritanism but February.

5824
When a man wantonly destroys a work of man we call him a vandal; when a man destroys one of the works of God, we call him a sportsman.

KRYLOV Ivan
5825
The weak against the strong,
Is always in the wrong.

KUBRICK Stanley 1928-
5826
The great nations have always acted like gangsters, and the small nations like prostitutes.

KUMAR Satish 1937-
5827 *'Prayer for Peace'*
Lead me from death to life, from falsehood to truth.
Lead me from despair to hope, from fear to trust.
Lead me from hate to love, from war to peace.
Let peace fill our heart, our world, our universe.

KUNDERA Milan 1929-
5828
The unbearable lightness of being.

KUPCINET Irv
5829
Air pollution is turning Mother Nature prematurely grey.

KUSMENKO Mika
5830
Female empowerment is such vague terminology that I doubt it exists in any language but English.

KYD Thomas 1558-1594
5831 *The Spanish Tragedy*
Oh eyes, no eyes, but fountains fraught with tears;
Oh life, no life, but lively form of death;
Oh world, no world, but mass of public wrongs.

5832 *The Spanish Tragedy*
Thus must we toil in other men's extremes,
That know not how to remedy our own.

5833 *The Spanish Tragedy*
I am never better than when I am mad. Then methinks I am a brave fellow; then I do wonders. But reason abuseth me, and there's the torment, there's the hell.

5834 *The Spanish Tragedy*
For what's a play without a woman in it?

LA BRUYERE Jean de 1645-1696
5835 *Les Caractères, 'De la société et la conversation'*
There are some who speak one moment before they think.

5836 *Les Caractères, 'De l'homme'*
The majority of men devote the greater part of their lives to making their remaining years unhappy.

5837 *Les Caractères, 'De quelques usages'*
The punishment of a criminal is an example to the rabble; but every decent man is concerned if an innocent person is condemned.

5838 *Les Caractères, 'Des femmes'*
Women run to extremes; they are either better or worse than men.

5839 *Les Caractères, 'Des ouvrages de l'esprit'*
The pleasure of criticizing robs us of the pleasure of being moved by some very fine things.

5840 *Les Caractères, 'Du coeur'*
Liberality lies less in giving liberally than in the timeliness of the gift.

5841 *Les Caractères, 'Du coeur'*
One must laugh before one is happy, or one may die without ever laughing at all.

LA FONTAINE Jean de 1621-1695
5842
Everyone has his faults which he continually repeats; neither fear nor shame can cure them.

5843 *Fables 'Démocrite et les Abdéritains'*
He knows the universe and does not know himself.

5844 *Fables 'L'Alouette et ... Maître d'un Champ'*
Rely only on yourself; it is a common proverb.

5845 *Fables 'La Mort et le Bûcheron'*
Rather suffer than die is man's motto.

5846 *Fables 'La Mort et le Mourant'*
Death never takes the wise man by surprise; he is always ready to go.

5847 *Fables 'L'Ane et le Chien'*
People must help one another; it is nature's law.

5848 *Fables 'Le Chartier Embourbé'*
Aide-toi, le ciel t'aidera.
Help yourself, and heaven will help you.

5849 *Fables 'Le Chêne et le Roseau'*
I bend and I break not.

5850 *Fables 'Le Coq et le Renard'*
It is doubly pleasing to trick the trickster.

5851 *Fables 'Le Corbeau et le Renard'*
Be advised that all flatterers live at the expense of those who listen to them.

5852 *Fables 'Le Lion et le Rat'*
Patience and passage of time do more than strength and fury.

5853 *Fables 'Le Loup et l'Agneau'*
The reason of the strongest is always the best.

5854 *Fables 'Le Meunier, son Fils et l'Ane'*
The greatest ass of the three is not the one you would think.

5855 *Fables 'Le Milan et le Rossignol'*
A hungry stomach has no ears.

5856 *Fables 'L'Enfant et le Maître d'École'*
My friend, get me out of danger. You can make your speech afterwards.

5857 *Fables 'Le Rat de Ville et le Rat des Champs'*
But someone disturbed the feast.

5858 *Fables 'Le Renard et le Bouc'*
This fellow did not see further than his own nose.

5859 *Fables 'Le Renard et le Bouc'*
In all matters one must consider the end.

5860 *Fables 'L'Ours et les deux Compagnons'*
Never sell the bear's skin before one has killed the beast.

5861 *Fables 'Parole de Socrate'*
Everyone calls himself a friend, but only a fool relies on it; nothing is commoner than the name, nothing rarer than the thing.

5862
One returns to the place one came from.

5863
By the work one knows the workman.

LA MANCE Thomas
5864
Life is what happens to us while we are making other plans.

LA ROCHEFOUCAULD François Duc de 1613-1680
5865
Of all our faults, the one that we excuse most easily is idleness.

5866
There are bad people who would be less dangerous if they were quite devoid of goodness.

5867
There are few chaste women who are not tired of their trade.

5868
We often forgive those who bore us, but can't forgive those whom we bore.

5869
Generosity is the vanity of giving.

5870
Before we set our hearts too much upon anything, let us examine how happy they are, who already possess it.

5871
Hope, deceitful as it is, serves at least to lead us to the end of life along an agreeable road.

5872
We are lazier in our minds than in our bodies.

5873
No man deserves to be praised for his goodness unless he has the strength of character to be wicked. All other goodness is generally nothing but indolence or impotence of will.

5874 *Maxims*
Absence diminishes little passions and increases great ones just as the wind blows out a candle and fans a fire.

5875 *Maxims*
We are all strong enough to bear the misfortunes of others.

5876 *Maxims*
There are good marriages, but no delightful ones.

5877 *Maxims*
Hypocrisy is a tribute which vice pays to virtue.

5878 *Maxims*
The height of cleverness is to be able to conceal it.

5879 *Maxims*
There is scarcely a single man sufficiently aware to know all the evil he does.

5880 *Maxims*
In most of mankind gratitude is merely a secret hope for greater favours.

5881 *Maxims*
The accent of one's birthplace lingers in the mind and in the heart as it does in one's speech.

5882 *Maxims*
We need greater virtues to bear good fortune than bad.

5883 *Maxims*
If we had no faults we should not take so much pleasure in noticing them in others.

5884 *Maxims*
If one judges love by the majority of its effects, it is more like hatred than like friendship.

5885 *Maxims*
Love of justice in most men is no more than the fear of suffering injustice.

5886 *Maxims*
It is more shameful to distrust one's friends than to be deceived by them.

5887 *Maxims*
Everyone complains of his memory, but no one complains of his judgement.

5888 *Maxims*
The intellect is always fooled by the heart.

5889 *Maxims*
One gives nothing so freely as advice.

5890 *Maxims*
One had rather malign oneself than not speak of oneself at all.

5891 *Maxims*
To refuse praise reveals a desire to be praised twice over.

5892 *Maxims*
Flattery is false coin that is only current thanks to our vanity.

5893 *Maxims*
We only confess our little faults to persuade people that we have no large ones.

5894 *Maxims*
We seldom attribute common sense except to those who agree with us.

5895 *Maxims*
One can find women who have never had a love affair, but it is rare to find a woman who has had only one.

5896 *Maxims*
There are very few people who are not ashamed of having been in love when they no longer love each other.

5897
Moderation is an ostentatious proof of our strength of character.

5898
We are oftener treacherous through weakness than through calculation.

5899
Few people know how to be old.

5900
We promise according to our hopes, and perform according to our fears.

5901
Quarrels would not last long if the fault was only on one side.

5902 *Réflexions ou Maximes Morales*
In the misfortune of our best friends, we always find something which is not displeasing to us.

5903
If we resist our passions, it is more due to their weakness than to our strength.

5904 *Sentences et Maximes de Morale*
One is never as unhappy as one thinks, nor as happy as one hopes.

5905
It is not enough to succeed, a friend must fail.

5906
Weak people cannot be sincere.

5907
What is perfectly true is perfectly witty.

5908
When our vices leave us, we flatter ourselves with the credit of having left them.

5909
He who lives without folly is not as wise as he thinks.

LACKINGTON James 1746-1815
5910 *Memoirs*
At last, by singing and repeating enthusiastic amorous hymns, and ignorantly applying particular texts of scripture, I got my imagination to the proper pitch, and thus was I born again in an instant.

LACTANTIUS c.240-320
5911
Nobody is poor unless he stand in need of justice.

LAFORGUE Jules 1860-1887
5912
Ah! que la vie est quotidienne.
Oh, what a day-to-day business life is.

LAING R.D. 1927-1989
5913 *The Politics of Experience*
The brotherhood of man is evoked by particular men according to their circumstances ... In the name of our freedom and our brotherhood we are prepared to blow up the other half of mankind and to be blown up in turn.

5914 *The Politics of Experience*
Madness need not be all breakdown. It may also be break-through.

5915
The psychiatrist must become a fellow traveller with his patient.

5916 *(of schizophrenia)*
The divided self.

5917 *Self and Others*
True guilt is guilt at the obligation one owes to oneself to be oneself. False guilt is guilt felt at not being what other people feel one ought to be or assume that one is.

5918
When family relations are no longer harmonious, we have filial children and devoted parents.

LAMARTINE Alphonse de 1790-1869
5919 *Le Lac*
O time, suspend your flight, and you, happy hours, stay your feet! Let us savour the swift delights of our life's loveliest days!

5920
Limited in his nature, infinite in his desires, man is a fallen god who remembers heaven.

5921 *'L'Isolement'*
Sometimes, when one person is missing, the whole world seems depopulated.

5922
If one had but a single glance to give the world, one should gaze on Istanbul.

LAMB A.J. 1870-1928
5923
She's a bird in gilded cage.

LAMB Lady Caroline 1785-1828
5924 *(on first meeting Lord Byron)*
Mad, bad, and dangerous to know.

LAMB Charles 1775-1834
5925
Here cometh April again, and as far as I can see the world hath more fools in it than ever.

5926 *(on the death of his mother)*
I have something more to do than feel.

5927
If dirt were trumps, what hands you would hold!

5928
We do not go (to the theatre) like our ancestors, to escape from the pressure of reality, so much as to confirm our experience of it.

5929 *Essays of Elia 'A Bachelor's Complaint'*
I know that a sweet child is the sweetest thing in nature ... but the prettier the kind of a thing is, the more desirable it is that it should be pretty of its kind.

5930 *Essays of Elia 'Mrs Battle's Opinions'*
She unbent her mind afterwards - over a book.

5931 *Essays of Elia 'Mrs Battle's Opinions on Whist'*
They do not play at cards, but only play at playing at them.

5932 *Essays of Elia 'Mrs Battle's Opinions on Whist'*
Man is a gaming animal. He must always be trying to get the better in something or other.

5933 *Essays of Elia 'A Chapter on Ears'*
Sentimentally I am disposed to harmony. But organically I am incapable of a tune.

5934 *Essays of Elia 'A Dissertation upon Roast Pig'*
Presents, I often say, endear Absents.

5935 *Essays of Elia 'Dream Children'*
We are nothing; less than nothing, and dreams. We are only what might have been, and must wait upon the tedious shores of Lethe millions of ages before we have existence, and a name.

5936 *Essays of Elia 'Imperfect Sympathies'*
I am, in plainer words, a bundle of prejudices - made up of likings and dis-likings.

5937 *Essays of Elia 'Imperfect Sympathies'*
I have been trying all my life to like Scotchmen, and am obliged to desist from the experiment of despair.

5938 *Essays of Elia 'The Old and the New Schoolmaster'*
Boys are capital fellows in their own way, among their mates; but they are un-wholesome companions for grown people.

5939 *Essays of Elia 'Oxford in the Vacation'*
A votary of the desk - a notched and cropt scrivener - one that sucks his substance, as certain sick people are said to do, through a quill.

5940 *Essays of Elia 'Quakers' Meeting'*
The uncommunicating muteness of fishes.

5941 *Essays of Elia 'The Two Races of Men'*
The human species, according to the best theory I can form of it, is composed of two distinct races, *the men who borrow*, and *the men who lend*.

5942 *Essays of Elia 'The Two Races of Men'*
Your *borrowers of books* - those mutilators of collections, spoilers of the symmetry of shelves, and creators of odd volumes.

5943 *Essays of Elia 'Valentine's Day'*
Not many sounds in life, and I include all urban and all rural sounds, exceed in interest a knock at the door.

5944 *Essays of Elia 'Witches, and Other...'*
Credulity is the man's weakness, but the child's strength.

5945 *'A Farewell to Tobacco'*
For thy sake, Tobacco, I
Would do any thing but die.

5946 *'Hester'*
Gone before
To that unknown and silent shore.

5947 *'On an Infant Dying as soon as Born'*
Riddle of destiny, who can show
What thy short visit meant, or know
What thy errand here below?

5948 *'The Jovial Crew'*
What a lass that were to go a-gipsying through
the world with.

5949 *Last Essays of Elia 'The Convalescent'*
How sickness enlarges the dimensions of a
man's self to himself.

5950 *Last Essays of Elia 'Detached Thoughts'*
Books think for me.

5951 *Last Essays of Elia 'Detached Thoughts'*
Things in books' clothing.

5952 *Last Essays of Elia 'Detached Thoughts'*
Newspapers always excite curiosity. No one
ever lays one down without a feeling of
disappointment.

5953 *Last Essays of Elia 'Poor Relations'*
A poor relation - is the most irrelevant thing in
nature.

5954 *Last Essays of Elia 'Popular Fallacies'*
[A pun] is a pistol let off at the ear; not a feather
to tickle the intellect.

5955 *Letter to B.W. Proctor*
When my sonnet was rejected, I exclaimed,
'Damn the age; I will write for Antiquity!'

5956 *Letter to Dorothy Wordsworth*
How I like to be liked, and what I do to be liked!

5957 *Letter to Southey*
Anything awful makes me laugh. I mis-behaved
once at a funeral.

5958 *Letter to S.T. Coleridge*
Cultivate simplicity, Coleridge.

5959 *Letter to Thomas Manning*
The man must have a rare recipe for
melancholy, who can be dull in Fleet Street.

5960 *Letter to Thomas Manning*
Nothing puzzles me more than time and space;
and yet nothing troubles me less, as I never
think about them.

5961 *Letter to Thomas Manning*
This very night I am going to leave off tobacco!
Surely there must be some other world in which
this unconquerable purpose shall be realized.

5962 *Letter to Wordsworth (of Coleridge)*
An Archangel a little damaged.

5963
New Year's Day is every man's birthday.

5964 *'The Old Familiar Faces'*
I have had playmates, I have had companions,
In my days of childhood, in my youthful school-
days,
All, all are gone, the old familiar faces.

5965
The only true time which a man can properly
call his own, is that which he has all to himself;
the rest, though in some sense he may be said
to live it, is other people's time, not his.

5966 *'Parental Recollections'*
A child's a plaything for an hour.

5967
To be sick is to enjoy monarchial prerogatives.

5968 *'Table Talk by the late Elia'*
The greatest pleasure I know, is to do a good
action by stealth, and to have it found out by
accident.

LAMBERT Constant 1905-1951
5969 *(written in a copy of Coeleb's In Search of a
Wife)*
If ever I marry a wife,
I'll marry a landlord's daughter,
For then I may sit in the bar,
And drink cold brandy and water.

5970
The average English critic is a don *manqué*,
hopelessly parochial when not exaggeratedly
teutonophile, over whose desk must surely hang
the motto (presumably in Gothic lettering)
'Above all no enthusiasm'.

5971 *Music Ho!*
The whole trouble with a folk song is that once
you have played it through there is nothing
much you can do except play it over again and
play it rather louder.

LAMBTON John George 1792-1840
5972
£40,000 a year a moderate income - such a one
as a man *might jog on with*.

LAMMING George 1927-
5973
In the castle of my skin.

LAMONT Norman 1942-
5974
We give the impression of being in office but
not in power.

5975
The green shoots of economic spring are
appearing once again.

5976
Politics is like surfing. You are bound to fall off
from time to time.

LAMPEDUSA Prince Giuseppe di 1896-1957
5977 *The Leopard*
If we want things to stay as they are, things will
have to change.

LAMPTON William James 1859-1917
5978 *June Weddings*
Same old slippers,
Same old rice,
Same old glimpse of
Paradise.

LANCE Bert 1931-
5979 *Nation's Business*
If it ain't broke, don't fix it.

LANDERS Ann 1918-
5980
Class is an aura of confidence that is being sure
without being cocky. Class has nothing to do
with money. Class never runs scared. It is self-
discipline and self-knowledge. It's the sure-
footedness that comes with having proved you
can meet life.

5981
Television has proved that people will look at
anything rather than each other.

5982
Trouble is the common denominator of living.
It is the great equalizer.

5983
If you want your children to listen, try talking
softly - to someone else.

5984
We wouldn't worry so much about what people
thought of us if we knew how seldom they did.

LANDON Letitia Elizabeth (L.E.L.) 1802-1838
5985 *Apple Blossoms*
As beautiful as woman's blush,
As evanescent too.

5986 *'The Poor'*
Few, save the poor, feel for the poor.

LANDOR Walter Savage 1775-1864
5987 *'Death stands above me'*
Death stands above me, whispering low
I know not what into my ear;
Of his strange language all I know
Is, there is not a word of fear.

5988 *Deceive Me Once Again*
You smiled, you spoke, and I believed,
By every word and smile deceived.
Another man would hope no more;
Nor hope I what I hoped before:
But let not this last wish be vain:
Deceive, deceive me once again!

5989 *'Dying Speech of an Old Philosopher'*
I strove with none; for none was worth my
strife;
Nature I loved, and, next to Nature, Art.

5990 *Epigram in The Atlas*
George the First was always reckoned
Vile, but viler George the Second;
And what mortal ever heard
Any good of George the Third?
When from earth the Fourth descended
God be praised the Georges ended!

5991
Great men too often have greater faults than
little men can find room for.

5992 *'To Ianthe'*
'Tis verse that gives
Immortal youth to mortal maids.

5993 *Imaginary Conversations 'Aesop and
Rhodope'*
There are no fields of amaranth on this side of
the grave.

5994 *Imaginary Conversations*
Prose on certain occasions can bear a great deal
of poetry: on the other hand, poetry sinks and
swoons under a moderate weight of prose.

5995 *Imaginary Conversations 'Pollio and
Calvus'*
States, like men, have their growth, their
manhood, their decrepitude, their decay.

5996 *Imaginary Conversations*
Clear writers, like clear fountains, do not seem
so deep as they are; the turbid look the most
profound.

5997 *Imaginary Conversations*
Fleas know not whether they are upon the body
of a giant or upon one of ordinary size.

5998
An ingenuous mind feels in unmerited praise
the bitterest reproof.

5999 *'Ireland never was contented'*
Ireland never was contented ...
Say you so? You are demented.
Ireland was contented when
All could use the sword and pen.

6000
Literature is the effort of man to indemnify
himself for the wrongs of his condition.

6001
A man's vanity tells him what is honour; a man's
conscience what is justice.

6002 *'To Robert Browning'*
There is delight in singing, tho' none hear
Beside the singer.

6003 *'Rose Aylmer'*
Ah, what avails the sceptred race!
Ah, what the form divine!

6004 *'To Wordsworth: Those Who Have Laid the Harp ...'*
Thee gentle Spenser fondly led;
But me he mostly sent to bed.

LANE George Martin 1823-1897
6005 *One Fish-Ball*
The waiter roars it through the hall:
'We don't give bread with one fish-ball!'

LANG Andrew 1844-1912
6006 *'Almae Matres'*
St Andrews by the Northern sea,
A haunted town it is to me!

6007 *'Brahma'*
If the wild bowler thinks he bowls,
Or if the batsman thinks he's bowled,
They know not, poor misguided souls,
They too shall perish unconsoled.
I am the batsman and the bat,
I am the bowler and the ball,
The umpire, the pavilion cat,
The roller, pitch and stumps, and all.

6008 *'The Odyssey'*
They hear like ocean on a western beach
The surge and thunder of the Odyssey.

6009
He uses statistics as a drunken man uses lamp-posts - for support rather than illumination.

LANG Julia 1921-
6010 *on Listen with Mother*
"Are you sitting comfortably? Then I'll begin."

LANGBRIDGE Frederick 1849-1923
6011 *Cluster of Quiet Thoughts*
Two men look out through the same bars:
One sees the mud, and one the stars.

LANGER Susanne 1895-1985
6012 *Mind*
Art is the objectification of feeling, and the subjectification of nature.

LANGLAND William c.1330-1400
6013 *The Vision of Piers Plowman*
In a somer seson, whan softe was the sonne.

6014 *The Vision of Piers Plowman*
A faire feeld ful of folk fond I ther bitwene
Of alle manere of men, the meene and the riche,
Werchynge and wandrynge as the world asketh.

6015 *The Vision of Piers Plowman*
A gloton of wordes.

6016 *The Vision of Piers Plowman*
Whan alle tresors arn tried, Truthe is the beste.

6017 *The Vision of Piers Plowman*
Brewesters and baksters, bochiers and cokes -
For thise are men on this molde that moost harm wercheth
To the povere peple.

6018 *The Vision of Piers Plowman*
For if hevene be on this erthe, and ese to any soule,
It is in cloistre or in scole.

6019 *The Vision of Piers Plowman*
Suffraunce is a soverayn vertue, and a swift vengeaunce.
Who suffreth moore than God?

6020 *The Vision of Piers Plowman*
Grammer, the ground of al.

6021 *The Vision of Piers Plowman*
Innocence is next God, and nyght and day it crieth
'Vengeaunce! Vengeaunce! Forgyve be it nevere
That shente us and shedde oure blood!

6022 *The Vision of Piers Plowman*
'After sharpest shoures,' quath Pees 'most shene is the sonne;
Is no weder warmer than after watry cloudes.'

6023 *The Vision of Piers Plowman*
Forthi be noght abasshed to bide and to be nedy,
Since he that wroghte al the world was wilfulliche nedy.

LANGTON Stephen c.1150-1228
6024 *The 'Golden Sequence' for Whit Sunday*
Come, Holy Spirit, and send out from heaven the beam of your light.

LAO-TSU c.604-c.531 BC
6025
As for the best leaders, the people do not notice their existence. The next best, the people honour and praise. The next, the people fear, and the next the people hate. When the best leader's work is done, the people say, 'we did it ourselves!'

6026
To lead the people, walk behind them.

6027
The reality of the building does not consist in the roof and walls, but in the space within to be lived in.

6028 *Tao-Tê-Ching*
Heaven and Earth are not ruthful;
To them the Ten Thousand Things are but as straw dogs.

6029 *Tao-Tê-Ching*
The Way is like an empty vessel that yet may be drawn from.

LAPHAM Lewis H.

6030
The supply of government exceeds the demand.

LARDNER Ring 1885-1933

6031
How can you write if you can't cry?

6032
They gave each other a smile with a future in it.

6033 *The Young Immigrunts*
Are you lost daddy I arsked tenderly.
Shut up he explained.

LARKIN Philip 1922-1985

6034 *'Annus Mirabilis'*
Sexual intercourse began
In nineteen sixty-three
(Which was rather late for me) -
Between the end of the *Chatterley* ban
And the Beatles' first LP.

6035 *'An Arundel Tomb'*
Time has transfigured them into
Untruth. The stone fidelity
They hardly meant has come to be
Their final blazon, and to prove
Our almost-instinct almost true:
What will survive of us is love.

6036 *'Church Going'*
Hatless, I take off
My cycle-clips in awkward reverence.

6037 *'Church Going'*
A serious house on serious earth it is,
In whose blent air all our compulsions meet,
Are recognised, and robed as destinies.

6038 *'Days'*
What are days for?
Days are where we live.
They come, they wake us
Time and time over.
They are to be happy in:
Where can we live but days?

6039 *'Dockery & Son'*
Life is first boredom, then fear.
Whether or not we use it, it goes,
And leaves what something hidden from us
chose,
And age, and then the only end of age.

6040 *'High Windows'*
Rather than words comes the thought of high
windows:
The sun-comprehending glass,
And beyond it, the deep blue air, that shows
Nothing, and is nowhere, and is endless.

6041 *'Homage to a Government'*
Next year we shall be living in a country
That brought its soldiers home for lack of
money.
The statues will be standing in the same
Tree-muffled squares, and look nearly the same.
Our children will not know it's a different
country.
All we can hope to leave them now is money.

6042 *'MCMXIV'*
Never such innocence,
Never before or since,
As changed itself to past
Without a word - the men
Leaving the gardens tidy,
The thousands of marriages
Lasting a little while longer:
Never such innocence again.

6043 *(novel formula)*
A beginning, a muddle, and an end.

6044 *'The Old Fools'*
Perhaps being old is having lighted rooms
Inside your head, and people in them, acting.
People you know, yet can't quite name.

6045 *'Study of Reading Habits'*
Don't read too much now: the dude
Who lets the girl down before
The hero arrives, the chap
Who's yellow and keeps the store,
Seem far too familiar. Get stewed:
Books are a load of crap.

6046 *'I Remember, I Remember'*
Nothing, like something, happens anywhere

6047 *Required Writing*
Deprivation is for me what daffodils were for
Wordsworth.

6048 *'Toads'*
Why should I let the toad *work*
Squat on my life?
Can't I use my wit as a pitchfork
And drive the brute off?

Six days of the week it soils
With its sickening poison -
Just for paying a few bills!
That's out of proportion.

6049 *'Toads Revisited'*
Give me your arm, old toad;
Help me down Cemetery Road.

6050 *'This Be The Verse'*
They fuck you up, your mum and dad.
They may not mean to, but they do.
They fill you with the faults they had
And add some extra, just for you.

6051 *'This Be The Verse'*
Man hands on misery to man.
It deepens like a coastal shelf.
Get out as early as you can,

And don't have any kids yourself.

6052 *'The Whitsun Weddings'*
I thought of London spread out in the sun,
Its postal districts packed like squares of wheat.

LATHAM Peter
6053
Common sense is in medicine the master
workman.

LATIMER Hugh c.1485-1555
6054 *(prior to being burned for heresy)*
Be of good comfort Master Ridley, and play the
man. We shall this day light such a candle by
God's grace in England, as (I trust) shall never
be put out.

6055 *The Second Sermon preached ...*
The drop of rain maketh a hole in the stone, not
by violence, but by oft falling.

LAUDER Sir Harry 1870-1950
6056 *'The End of the Road'*
Keep right on to the end of the road,
Keep right on to the end.
Tho' the way be long, let your heart be strong,
Keep right on round the bend.
Tho' you're tired and weary,
Still journey on
Till you come to your happy abode,
Where all you love you've been dreaming of
Will be there at the end of the road.

6057
The future is not a gift - it is an achievement.

6058 *'I Love a Lassie'*
I love a lassie, a bonnie, bonnie lassie,
She's as pure as the lily in the dell.
She's as sweet as the heather, the bonnie
bloomin' heather -
Mary, ma Scotch Bluebell.

6059
O! it's nice to get up in the mornin',
But it's nicer to stay in bed.

6060 *'Roamin' in the Gloamin''*
Roamin' in the gloamin',
On the bonnie banks o' Clyde.
Roamin' in the gloamin'
Wae my lassie by my side.

6061
If y'can say
It's a braw brecht moonlecht necht,
Yer a' recht, ye ken.

LAURENCE Margaret
6062
Follow your heart, and you perish.

LAURENCE William L. 1888-1977
6063 *(of first atomic explosion)*
At first it was a giant column that soon took the

shape of a supramundane mushroom.

LAURIER Rt. Hon. Sir Wilfrid 1841-1919
6064
The Englishman respects your opinions, but he
never thinks of your feelings.

LAVATER Johann Kaspar
6065
He who, when called upon to speak a
disagreeable truth, tells it boldly and has done,
is both bolder and milder than he who nibbles
in a low voice and never ceases nibbling.

LAVER James 1899-1975
6066
Clothes are nothing less than the furniture of
the mind made visible.

6067 *Taste and Fashion*
The same costume will be
Indecent ... 10 years before its time
Shameless ... 5 years before its time
Outré (daring) 1 year before its time
Smart
Dowdy ... 1 year after its time
Hideous ... 10 years after its time
Ridiculous ... 20 years after its time
Amusing ... 30 years after its time
Quaint ... 50 years after its time
Charming ... 70 years after its time
Romantic ... 100 years after its time
Beautiful ... 150 years after its time

LAW Andrew Bonar 1858-1923
6068
If I am a great man, then a good many of the
great men of history are frauds.

6069
There is no such thing as inevitable war. If war
comes it will be from failure of human wisdom.

LAW Vernon
6070
Experience is the worst teacher; it gives the test
before presenting the lesson.

LAW William
6071
Be intent upon the perfection of the present
day.

LAWRENCE D.H. 1885-1930
6072
Art-speech is the only truth. An artist is usually
a damned liar but his art, if it be art, will tell you
the truth of his day. And that is all that matters.
Away with eternal truth. The truth lives from
day to day, and the marvellous Plato of
yesterday is chiefly bosh today.

6073 *'Don'ts'*
Don't be sucked in by the su-superior,
don't swallow the culture bait,

don't drink, don't drink and get beerier and beerier,
do learn to discriminate.

6074 *Dull London*
The English people on the whole are surely the *nicest* people in the world, and everyone makes everything so easy for everybody else, that there is almost nothing to resist at all.

6075 *Etruscan Places 'Cerveteri'*
To the Puritan all things are impure, as somebody says.

6076 *Now It's Happened*
Too much of the humble Willy wet-leg
And the holy can't-help-it touch.

6077 *'How Beastly the Bourgeois Is'*
How beastly the bourgeois is
Especially the male of the species.

6078 *Lady Chatterley's Lover*
Ours is essentially a tragic age, so we refuse to take it tragically.

6079 *Lady Chatterley's Lover*
And here lies the vast importance of the novel, properly handled. It can inform and lead into new places the flow of our sympathetic consciousness and it can lead our sympathy away in recoil from things gone dead.

6080 *Lady Chatterley's Lover*
John Thomas says good-night to Lady Jane, a little droopingly, but with a hopeful heart.

6081 *'Leave Sex Alone'*
... While we think of it, and talk of it
Let us leave it alone, physically, keep apart.
For while we have sex in the mind, we truly have none in the body.

6082 *Letter to A.W. McLeod*
Tragedy ought really to be a great kick at misery.

6083 *Letter to Edward Garnett*
Curse the blasted, jelly-boned swines, the slimy, the belly-wriggling invertebrates, the miserable sodding rotters, the flaming sods, the snivelling, dribbling, dithering, palsied, pulse-less lot that make up England today. They've got white of egg in their veins, and their spunk is that watery it's a marvel they can breed. They *can* nothing but frog-spawn - the gibberers! God, how I hate them!

6084 *Letter to J. Middleton Murry*
The dead don't die. They look on and help.

6085 *Letter to J. Middleton Murry*
I want to go south, where there is no autumn, where the cold doesn't crouch over one like a snow-leopard waiting to pounce. The heart of the North is dead, and the fingers of cold are corpse fingers.

6086 *Letter to Lady Cynthia Asquith*
I like to write when I feel spiteful; it's like having a good sneeze.

6087
Life is ours to be spent, not to be saved.

6088 *'Mountain Lion'*
Men! The only animal in the world to fear!

6089
Never trust the artist. Trust the tale. The proper function of a critic is to save the tale from the artist who created it.

6090 *Phoenix*
The English ... are paralysed by fear. That is what thwarts and distorts the Anglo-Saxon existence ... Nothing could be more lovely and fearless than Chaucer. But already Shakespeare is morbid with fear, fear of consequences. That is the strange phenomenon of the English Renaissance: this mystic terror of the consequences, the consequences of action.

6091 *Phoenix*
If you try to nail anything down in the novel, either it kills the novel, or the novel gets up and walks away with the nail.

6092 *Phoenix*
Morality in the novel is the trembling instability of the balance. When the novelist puts his thumb in the scale, to pull down the balance to his own predilection, that is immorality.

6093 *Phoenix*
Pornography is the attempt to insult sex, to do dirt on it.

6094 *Phoenix*
In life ... no new thing has ever arisen, or can arise, save out of the impulse of the male upon the female, the female upon the male. The interaction of the male and female spirit begot the wheel, the plough, and the first utterance that was made on the face of the earth.

6095 *Phoenix*
The novel is the one bright book of life.

6096 *'Piano'*
So now it is vain for the singer to burst into clamour
With the great black piano appassionato. The glamour
Of Childish days is upon me, my manhood is cast
Down in the flood of remembrance, I weep like a child for the past.

6097 *'Self-Pity'*
I never saw a wild thing
Sorry for itself.

6098 *'Snake'*
A snake came to my water-trough
On a hot, hot day, and I in pyjamas for the heat,
To drink there.

6099 *'Snake'*
And so, I missed my chance with one of the lords
Of life.
And I have something to expiate:
A pettiness.

6100 *'Song of a Man who has Come Through'*
Not I, not I, but the wind that blows through me!
A fine wind is blowing the new direction of Time.

6101 *'When I Read Shakespeare'*
When I read Shakespeare I am struck with wonder
That such trivial people should muse and thunder
In such lovely language.

6102 *The White Peacock*
Be a good animal, true to your instincts.

6103 *Women in Love*
Don't you find it a beautiful clean thought, a world empty of people, just uninterrupted grass, and a hare sitting up?

LAWRENCE T.E. 1888-1935
6104 *The Mint*
Many men would take the death-sentence without a whimper to escape the life-sentence which fate carries in her other hand.

6105 *The Mint*
The trumpets came out brazenly with the last post. We all swallowed our spittle, chokingly, while our eyes smarted against our wills. A man hates to be moved to folly by a noise.

6106 *The Seven Pillars of Wisdom*
I loved you, so I drew these tides of men into my hands and wrote my will across the sky in stars
To earn you freedom, the seven pillared worthy house, that your eyes might be shining for me
When we came.

LAWRENSON Helen
6107
You have to go back to the Children's Crusade in 1212 AD to find as unfortunate and fatuous an attempt at manipulated hysteria as the Women's Liberation Movement.

6108
Whatever else can be said about sex, it cannot be called a dignified performance.

LAWSON Sonia 1934-
6109
You're not meant to understand - They're bloody works of art.

LAZARUS Arnold and FAY Alan
6110
We firmly believe that therapy is education rather than healing; that it is growth rather than treatment.

LAZARUS Emma 1849-1887
6111 *'The New Colossus' (inscribed on Statue of Liberty)*
Give me your tired, your poor,
Your huddled masses yearning to breathe free,
The wretched refuse of your teeming shore,
Send these, the homeless, tempest-tossed, to me:
I lift my lamp beside the golden door.

LE CARRÉ John 1931-
6112
He has the gift of quiet.

6113 *A Perfect Spy*
Love is whatever you can still betray ... Betrayal can only happen if you love.

6114
The spy who came in from the cold.

LE CORBUSIER 1887-1965
6115
This frightful word [function] was born under other skies than those I have loved - those where the sun reigns supreme.

6116
Genius is personal, decided by fate, but it expresses itself by means of system. There is no work of art without system.

6117
A house is a machine for living in.

6118
The materials of city planning are sky, space, trees, steel and cement in that order and in that hierarchy.

LE GALLIENNE Richard 1866-1947
6119 *'The Cry of the Little Peoples'*
The cry of the Little People goes up to God in vain,
For the world is given over to the cruel sons of Cain.

6120 *Song*
She's somewhere in the sunlight strong,
Her tears are in the falling rain,
She calls me in the wind's soft song,
And with the flowers she comes again.

LEACH Jim

6121
Patriotism is when you risk your life not when you risk your wallet.

6122 *(Reith Lectures)*
Far from being the basis of the good society, the family, with its narrow privacy and tawdry secrets, is the source of all our discontents.

LEACH Reggie

6123
Success is not the result of spontaneous combustion. You must set yourself on fire.

LEACOCK Stephen 1869-1944

6124
Advertising may be described as the science of arresting the human intelligence long enough to get money from it.

6125
The best definition of humour I know is: humour may be defined as the kindly contemplation of the incongruities of life, and the artistic expression thereof. I think this is the best I know because I wrote it myself.

6126
The British are terribly lazy about fighting. They like to get it over and done with and then set up a game of cricket.

6127
The classics are only primitive literature. They belong to the same class as primitive machinery and primitive music and primitive medicine.

6128
You encourage a comic man too much, and he gets silly.

6129
A half truth, like half a brick, is always more forcible as an argument than a whole one. It carries better.

6130
I'm a great believer in luck. I find the harder I work, the more I have of it.

6131 *Here are my Lectures*
I am what is called a *professor emeritus* from the Latin *e*, 'out', and *meritus*, 'so he ought to be'.

6132
Life, we learn too late, is in the living, in the tissue of every day and hour.

6133 *Literary Lapses 'Boarding-House Geometry'*
The landlady of a boarding-house is a parallelogram - that is, an oblong figure, which cannot be described, but which is equal to anything.

6134 *Literary Lapses 'A Manual of Education'*
Electricity is of two kinds, positive and negative. The difference is, I presume, that one comes a little more expensive, but is more durable; the other is a cheaper thing, but the moths get into it.

6135 *Literary Lapses 'Reflections on Riding'*
There are no handles to a horse, but the 1910 model has a string to each side of its face for turning its head when there is anything you want it to see.

6136
The Lord said 'let there be wheat' and Saskatchewan was born.

6137
Any man will admit if need be that his sight is not good, or that he cannot swim or shoots badly with a rifle, but to touch upon his sense of humour is to give him mortal affront.

6138
Many a man in love with a dimple makes the mistake of marrying the whole girl.

6139 *Nonsense Novels 'Gertrude the Governess'*
He flung himself from the room, flung himself upon his horse and rode madly off in all directions.

6140 *My Remarkable Uncle*
A sportsman is a man who, every now and then, simply has to get out and kill something. Not that he's cruel. He wouldn't hurt a fly. It's not big enough.

6141
The sorrows and disasters of Europe always brought fortune to America.

6142
When actors begin to think, it is time for a change. They are not fitted for it.

6143
Writing is no trouble: you just jot down ideas as they occur to you. The jotting is simplicity itself - it is the occurring which is difficult.

LEAPOR Mary 1722-1746
6144 *'An Essay on Woman'*
Woman, a pleasing but a short-lived flower,
Too soft for business and too weak for power:
A wife in bondage, or neglected maid:
Despised, if ugly; if she's fair, betrayed.

6145 *'Mira to Octavia'*
In spite of all romantic poets sing,
This gold, my dearest, is an useful thing.

LEAR Edward 1812-1888
6146 *A Book of Nonsense*
There was an Old Man with a beard,
Who said, 'It is just as I feared! -

Two Owls and a Hen,
Four Larks and a Wren,
Have all built their nests in my beard!'

6147 *Book of Nonsense*
There was an Old Man in a tree,
Who was horribly bored by a bee;
When they said, 'Does it buzz?'
He replied, 'Yes, it does!
It's a regular brute of a bee!'

6148 *'The Courtship of the Yonghy-Bonghy-Bó*
On the coast of Coromandel
Where the early pumpkins blow,
In the middle of the woods,
Lived the Yonghy-Bonghy-Bó.
Two old chairs, and half a candle;
One old jug without a handle,
These were all his worldly goods.

6149 *'The Dong with a Luminous Nose'*
'The Dong! - the Dong!
The wandering Dong through the forest goes!
The Dong! - the Dong!
The Dong with a Luminous Nose!'

6150 *'The Jumblies'*
Far and few, far and few,
Are the lands were the Jumblies live;
Their heads are green, and their hands are blue,
And they went to sea in a Sieve.

6151 *'The Jumblies'*
They called aloud 'Our Sieve ain't big,
But we don't care a button! We don't care a fig!'

6152 *Nonsense Songs (preface)*
'How pleasant to know Mr Lear!'
Who has written such volumes of stuff!
Some think him ill-tempered and queer,
But a few think him pleasant enough.

6153 *Nonsense Songs (preface)*
He has many friends, laymen and clerical.
Old Foss is the name of his cat:
His body is perfectly spherical,
He weareth a runcible hat.

6154 *'The Owl and the Pussy-Cat'*
The Owl and the Pussy-Cat went to sea
In a beautiful pea-green boat.
They took some honey, and plenty of money,
Wrapped up in a five-pound note.
The Owl looked up to the Stars above
And sang to a small guitar,
'Oh lovely Pussy! O Pussy, my love,
What a beautiful Pussy you are.'

6155 *'The Owl and the Pussy-Cat'*
'Dear Pig, are you willing to sell for one shilling
Your ring?' Said the Piggy, 'I will.'

6156 *'The Owl and the Pussy-Cat'*
They dined on mince, and slices of quince,
Which they ate with a runcible spoon;

And hand in hand, on the edge of the sand,
They danced by the light of the moon.

6157 *'The Pobble Who Has No Toes'*
The Pobble who has no toes
Had once as many as we;
When they said, 'Some day you may lose them all';
He replied, 'Fish fiddle de-dee!'

6158 *'The Pobble Who Has No Toes'*
When boats or ships came near him
He tinkledy-binkledy-winkled a bell.

6159 *'The Quangle-Wangle's Hat'*
'But the longer I live on this Crumpetty Tree
The plainer than ever it seems to me
That very few people come this way
And that life on the whole is far from gay!'
Said the Quangle-Wangle Quee.

6160 *'The Two Old Bachelors'*
And what can we expect if we haven't any dinner,
But to lose our teeth and eyelashes and keep on growing thinner.

LEARY Timothy 1920-1996
6161
If you take the game of life seriously, if you take your nervous system seriously, if you take your sense organs seriously, if you take the energy process seriously, you must turn on, tune in and drop out.

LEAVIS F.R. 1895-1978
6162
The common pursuit.

6163 *The Great Tradition*
The few really great - the major novelists ... are significant in terms of the human awareness they promote; awareness of the possibilities of life.

6164 *New Bearings in English Poetry*
The Sitwells belong to the history of publicity rather than of poetry.

LEAVITT Robert Keith
6165
People don't ask for facts in making up their minds. They would rather have one good, soul-satisfying emotion than a dozen facts.

LEBOWITZ Fran 1946-
6166
The best fame is a writer's fame; it's enough to get a table at a good restaurant, but not enough that you get interrupted when you eat.

6167
Ask your child what he wants for dinner only if he is buying.

6168 *Metropolitan Life*
There is no such thing as inner peace. There is only nervousness or death.

6169 *Metropolitan Life*
Life is something to do when you can't sleep.

LEC Stanislaw 1909-1966
6170
I give you bitter pills in sugar coating. The pills are harmless: the poison is in the sugar.

6171 *Unkempt Thoughts*
Is it progress if a cannibal uses knife and fork?

6172
In a war of ideas it is people who get killed.

LEDRU-ROLLIN Alexandre
6173
I've got to follow them - I am their leader.

LEE Gypsy Rose 1914-1970
6174 *(attributed)*
God is love, but get it in writing.

LEE Harper 1926-
6175 *To Kill a Mockingbird*
Shoot all the bluejays you want, if you can hit 'em, but remember it's a sin to kill a mockingbird.

LEE Henry ('Light-Horse Harry') 1756-1818
6176 *(funeral Oration for George Washington)*
A citizen, first in war, first in peace, and first in the hearts of his countrymen.

LEE Laurie 1914-1997
6177 *Cider with Rosie*
I was set down from the carrier's cart at the age of three; and there with a sense of bewilderment and terror my life in the village began.

6178 *'Day of these Days'*
Such a morning it is when love
leans through geranium windows
and calls with a cockerel's tongue.
When red-haired girls scamper like roses
over the rain-green grass,
and the sun drips honey.

6179
The urge to write is also the fear of death - the need to leave messages saying 'I was here, I saw it too.'

LEE Nathaniel c.1653-1692
6180 *Oedipus (with John Dryden)*
When the sun sets, shadows, that showed at noon
But small, appear most long and terrible.

6181 *The Rival Queens*
He speaks the kindest words, and looks such things,

Vows with so much passion, swears with so much grace.
That 'tis a kind of heaven to be deluded by him.

6182 *The Rival Queens*
'Tis beauty calls and glory leads the way.

6183 *The Rival Queens*
When Greeks joined Greeks, then was the tug of war!

6184 *The Rival Queens*
Philip fought men, but Alexander women.

6185 *Theodosius*
Man, false man, smiling, destructive man.

LEE Robert E. 1807-1870
6186 *(after the battle of Fredericksburg, attributed)*
It is well that war is so terrible. We should grow too fond of it.

6187
The devil's name is Dullness.

6188
We have fought this fight as long, and as well as we know how. We have been defeated. For us, as a Christian people, there is now but one course to pursue. We must accept the situation.

6189 *(last words)*
Let the tent be struck.

LEES-MILNE James
6190
Seven years is about the limit for passion.

LEHMAN Ernest 1920-
6191
Sweet smell of success.

LEHRER Tom 1928-
6192 *'We Will All Go Together When We Go'*
Life is like a sewer. What you get out of it depends on what you put into it.

6193 *'Lobachevski'*
Plagiarize! Let no one else's work evade your eyes,
Remember why the good Lord made your eyes.

6194
It is a sobering thought, that when Mozart was my age, he had been dead for two years.

LEIBNIZ Gottfried Wilhelm 1646-1716
6195 *Letter to S. Clarke*
We should like Nature to go no further; we should like it to be finite, like our mind; but this is to ignore the greatness and majesty of the Author of things.

6196 *Letter on a General Principle ... Laws of Nature*
It is God who is the ultimate reason of things,

and the knowledge of God is no less the beginning of science than his essence and will are the beginning of beings.

6197 *Letter to Magnus Wedderkopf*
God wills the things which he understands to be the best and most harmonious and selects them, as it were, from an infinite number of all possibilities.

6198 *The Monadology*
It is the knowledge of necessary and eternal truths which distinguishes us from mere animals, and gives us *Reason* and the sciences, raising us to knowledge of ourselves and of God. It is this in us which we call the rational soul or *Mind*.

6199 *Studies in Physics and the Nature of Body*
There is nothing without a reason.

6200
Two things are identical if one can be substituted for the other without affecting the truth.

LEIGH Fred W. d.1924
6201 *'Waiting at the Church'*
Here's the very note,
This is what he wrote -
'Can't get away to marry you today,
My wife won't let me!'

6202 *'Waiting At The Church'*
There was I, waiting at the church,
Waiting at the church, waiting at the church,
When I found he'd left me in the lurch,
Lor' how it did upset me!...

6203 *'Why Am I Always the Bridesmaid?'*
Why am I always the bridesmaid,
Never the blushing bride?

LEIGH H.S. 1837-1883
6204 *'An Allegory, written in Deep Dejection'*
That loathsome centipede, Remorse,
Invaded with a stealthy tread
My nasal organ.

6205 *Carols of Cockayne*
The rapturous, wild, and ineffable pleasure
Of drinking at somebody else's expense.

6206 *'Only Seven'*
I wondered hugely what she meant,
And said, 'I'm bad at riddles;
But I know where little girls are sent
For telling taradiddles.'

6207 *'The Twins'*
In form and feature, face and limb,
I grew so like my brother
That folks got taking me for him
And each for one another.

6208 *'The Twins'*
For one of us was born a twin
And not a soul knew which.

6209
If you wish to grow thinner, diminish your dinner.

LEIGH Vivien 1913-1967
6210 *in A Streetcar Named Desire*
"I don't want realism - I want magic."

LEMAY Curtis E. 1906-1990
6211 *(of the North Vietnamese)*
They've got to draw in their horns and stop their aggression, or we're going to bomb them back into the Stone Age.

LEMM Leesa
6212 *(testifying before an industrial tribunal)*
Two slow dances do not constitute a love affair.

LENCLOS Ninon de 1620-1705
6213 *(attributed)*
Old age is woman's hell.

LENIN 1870-1924
6214
Communism is Soviet power plus the electrification of the whole country.

6215 *(of George Bernard Shaw)*
A good man fallen among Fabians.

6216
Imperialism is the monopoly stage of capitalism.

6217
Liberty is precious - so precious that it must be rationed.

6218 *State and Revolution*
Democracy is *not* identical with majority rule. Democracy is a *State* which recognizes the subjection of the minority to the majority, that is, an organization for the systematic use of *force* by one class against the other, by one part of the population against another.

6219 *State and Revolution*
While the State exists, there can be no freedom. When there is freedom there will be no State.

LENNON John 1940-1980
6220 *(of The Beatles in 1966)*
We're more popular than Jesus now; I don't know which will go first - rock'n'roll or Christianity.

6221 *'Imagine'*
Imagine there's no heaven,
It's easy if you try,
No hell below us,
Above us only sky,
Imagine all the people

Living for today.

6222 *(at Royal Variety Performance)*
Will those in the cheap seats clap their hands?
All the rest of you, just rattle your jewellery.

LENNON John and McCARTNEY Paul 1940-
1980 and 1942-
6223
All we are saying is
Give peace a chance.

6224 *'Can't Buy Me Love'*
I don't care too much for money,
For money can't buy me love.

6225 *'A Day in the Life'*
I heard the news today, oh boy.
Four thousand holes in Blackburn Lancashire.
And though the holes were rather small,
They had to count them all.
Now they know how many holes it takes to fill
the Albert Hall.
I'd love to turn you on.

6226 *'Eleanor Rigby'*
Eleanor Rigby picks up the rice in the church
where a wedding has been
Lives in a dream.
Waits at the window, wearing the face that she
keeps in a jar by the door,
Who is it for?
All the lonely people, where do they all come
from?

6227 *'A Hard Day's Night'*
It's been a hard day's night,
And I've been working like a dog.

6228 *'With a Little Help From My Friends'*
Oh I get by with a little help from my friends,
Mm, I get high with a little help from my
friends.

6229 *'I am the Walrus'*
I am he
As you are me
And we are all together.

6230 *'When I'm Sixty-Four'*
Will you still need me, will you still feed me,
When I'm sixty four?

6231 *'Happiness is a Warm Gun'*
I know no one can do me no harm
because happiness is a warm gun.

6232 *'In my Life'*
There are places I'll remember
all my life, though some have changed,
some forever, not for better,
some have gone and some remain.

6233 *'Yesterday'*
Yesterday
all my troubles seemed so far away,

now it looks as though they're here to stay,
oh I believe in yesterday.

LENO Dan 1860-1904
6234 *Dan Leno Hys Booke*
Ah! What is man? Wherefore does he why?
Whence did he whence? Whither is he
withering?

LENT Edwin
6235
Cats are living adornments.

LENTHALL William 1591-1662
6236 *(while Speaker of the House of Commons,
to Charles I)*
I have neither eye to see, nor tongue to speak
here, but as the house is pleased to direct me.

LEONARDO DA VINCI 1452-1519
6237
The common sense is that which judges the
things given to it by other senses.

6238
A good painter is to paint two main things,
namely men and the working of man's mind.

6239
Human subtlety ... will never devise an
invention more beautiful, more simple or more
direct than does Nature, because in her
inventions nothing is lacking, and nothing is
superfluous.

6240
Iron rusts from disuse; stagnant water loses it
purity and in cold weather becomes frozen;
even so does inaction sap the vigour of the
mind.

6241
Just as courage imperils life, fear protects it.

6242
Life well spent is long.

6243
Every man at three years old is half his height.

6244 *Notebooks*
While I thought that I was learning how to live, I
have been learning how to die.

6245
The poet ranks far below the painter in the
representation of visible things, and far below
the musician in that of invisible things.

LERMONTOV Mikhail 1814-1841
6246 *A Hero of our Time*
Happy people are ignoramuses and glory is
nothing else but success, and to achieve it one
only has to be cunning.

6247 *A Hero of our Time*
The love of savages isn't much better than the love of noble ladies; ignorance and simpleheartedness can be as tiresome as coquetry.

6248 *A Hero of our Time*
Of two close friends, one is always the slave of the other.

6249 *A Hero of our Time*
I am like a man yawning at a ball; the only reason he does not go home to bed is that his carriage has not arrived yet.

6250 *A Hero of our Time*
I have always been the essential character of the fifth act.

6251 *'I'm lonely and sad'*
What is passion? That sickness so sweet, either early or late,
Will vanish at reason's protesting;
And life, if you ever, attentive and cool, contemplate,
Is but empty and meaningless jesting.

LERNER Alan Jay 1918-1986
6252 *'Camelot'*
Don't let it be forgot,
That once there was a spot -
For one brief shining moment
That was known as Camelot.

6253 *My Fair Lady 'You Did It'*
Oozing charm from every pore,
He oiled his way around the floor.

6254 *My Fair Lady 'A Hymn to Him'*
Why can't a woman be more like a man?
Men are so honest, so thoroughly square;
Eternally noble, historically fair;
Who, when you win, will always give your back a pat.
Why can't a woman be like that?

6255 *My Fair Lady 'I've Grown Accustomed to her Face'*
I've grown accustomed to the trace
Of something in the air;
Accustomed to her face.

6256 *My Fair Lady 'The Rain in Spain'*
The rain in Spain stays mainly in the plain.

6257 *My Fair Lady 'The Rain in Spain'*
In Hertford, Hereford, and Hampshire,
Hurricanes hardly happen.

6258 *Gigi 'I Remember it Well'*
We met at nine.
We met at eight.
I was on time.
No, you were late.
Ah yes! I remember it well.

LERNER Max
6259
I have a simple principle for the conduct of life - never to resist an adequate temptation.

6260
What is dangerous about tranquillizers is that whatever peace of mind they bring is packaged peace of mind. Where you buy a pill and buy peace with it, you get conditioned to cheap solutions instead of deep ones.

LESAGE Alain René 1668-1747
6261 *Crispin rival de son maître*
Justice is such a fine thing that we cannot pay too dearly for it.

6262 *Le Diable boîteux*
They made peace between us; we embraced, and we have been mortal enemies ever since.

LESPINASSE Julie de
6263
The logic of the heart is absurd.

LESSING Doris 1919-
6264 *The Grass is Singing*
When old settlers say 'One has to understand the country,' what they mean is, 'You have to get used to our ideas about the native.'

6265
Growing up is after all only the understanding that one's unique and incredible experience is what everyone shares.

6266 *The Habit of Loving*
Pleasure resorts are like film stars and royalty ... embarrassed by the figures they cut in the fantasies of people who have never met them.

6267 *Particularly Cats*
What is charm then? The free giving of a grace, the spending of something given by nature in her role of spendthrift ... something extra, superfluous, unnecessary, essentially a power thrown away.

6268
Think wrongly, if you please, but in all cases think for yourself.

6269
Women are the cowards they are because they have been semi-slaves for so long. The number of women prepared to stand up for what they really think, feel, experience, with a man they are in love with is still very small.

LESSING G.E. 1729-1781
6270 *Eine Duplik*
If God were to hold out enclosed in His right hand all Truth, and in His left hand just the active search for Truth, though with the condition that I should always err therein, and

He should say to me: Choose! I should humbly take His left hand and say: Father! Give me this one; absolute Truth belongs to Thee alone.

6271 *Emilia Galotti*
A man who does not lose his reason over certain things has none to lose.

6272 *'Lied aus dem Spanischen'*
Yesterday I loved, today I suffer, tomorrow I die: but I still think fondly, today and tomorrow, of yesterday.

6273 *Minna von Barnhelm*
One single grateful thought raised to heaven is the most perfect prayer.

LESTER Richard 1932-
6274
Film-making has become a kind of hysterical pregnancy.

L'ESTRANGE Sir Roger 1616-1704
6275 *Aesop's Fables*
It is with our passions as it is with fire and water, they are good servants, but bad masters.

6276 *Aesop's Fables*
Though this may be play to you, 'tis death to us.

LETTE Kathy
6277
As a breastfeeding mother you are basically just meals on heels.

LETTS Winifred Mary 1882-1972
6278 *'The Spires of Oxford'*
I saw the spires of Oxford
As I was passing by,
The grey spires of Oxford
Against a pearl-grey sky;
My heart was with the Oxford men
Who went abroad to die.

LEVANT Oscar
6279
Epigram: a wisecrack that has played Carnegie Hall.

6280
There is a thin line between genius and insanity. I have erased this line.

LEVERSON Ada 1865-1936
6281 *Letters to the Sphinx (of Oscar Wilde)*
He seemed at ease and to have the look of the last gentleman in Europe.

6282 *Tenterhooks*
You don't know a woman until you have had a letter from her.

6283 *The Twelfth Hour*
'No hurry, no hurry,' said Sir James, with that air of self-denial that conveys the urgent necessity of intense speed.

LEVIN Bernard 1928-
6284 *(of Mao Tse-tung)*
Whom the mad would destroy, they first make gods.

6285 *The Pendulum Years*
Paul Getty ... had always been vastly, immeasurably wealthy, and yet went about looking like a man who cannot quite remember whether he remembered to turn the gas off before leaving home.

6286 *The Pendulum Years*
In every age of transition men are never so firmly bound to one way of life as when they are about to abandon it, so that fanaticism and intolerance reach their most intense forms just before tolerance and mutual acceptance come to be the natural order of things.

6287 *The Pendulum Years (of Macmillan and Wilson)*
Between them, then, Walrus and Carpenter, they divided up the Sixties.

6288 *The Pendulum Years (of Macmillan)*
The Stag at Bay with the mentality of a fox at large.

LEVINE Ellen
6289
Sexual revolution has allowed us an equal opportunity to ogle.

LEVINSON Sam
6290
Insanity is hereditary - you can get it from your children.

LÉVIS Duc de 1764-1830
6291 *Maximes et Réflexions*
Noblesse oblige.
Nobility has its obligations.

6292 *Maximes et Réflexions*
Gouverner, c'est choisir.
To govern is to choose.

LÉVI-STRAUSS Claude 1908-1990
6293 *La Pensée sauvage*
Language is a form of human reason, and has its reasons which are unknown to man.

LEWES G.H. 1817-1878
6294 *The Physiology of Common Life*
Murder, like talent, seems occasionally to run in families.

6295 *Ranthorpe*
The pen, in our age, weighs heavier in the social scale than the sword of a Norman Baron.

6296 *The Spanish Drama*
Many a genius has been slow of growth. Oaks that flourish for a thousand years do not spring up into beauty like a reed.

LEWIN Kurt
6297
A successful individual typically sets his next goal somewhat but not too much above his last achievement. In this way he steadily raises his level of aspiration.

LEWIS C.S. 1898-1963
6298
Pain is God's megaphone to rouse a deaf world.

LEWIS Alun 1915-1944
6299 *Goodbye*
So we must say Goodbye, my darling,
And go, as lovers go, for ever;
Tonight remains, to pack and fix on labels
And make an end of lying down together.

LEWIS C.S. 1898-1963
6300
I believe in Christianity as I believe that the sun has risen. Not only because I see it, but because I see everything by it.

6301
Courage is not simply *one* of the virtues but the form of every virtue at the testing point.

6302
The safest road to Hell is the gradual one - the gentle slope, soft underfoot, without sudden turnings, without milestones, without signposts.

6303 *The Screwtape Letters*
We have trained them [men] to think of the Future as a promised land which favoured heroes attain - not as something which everyone reaches at the rate of sixty minutes an hour, whatever he does, whoever he is.

6304 *The Screwtape Letters*
She's the sort of woman who lives for others - you can always tell the others by their hunted expression.

6305 *'Unreal Estates'*
I'd sooner live among people who don't cheat at cards than among people who are earnest about not cheating at cards.

6306
Unsatisfied desire is in itself more desirable than any other satisfaction.

6307
A woman means by unselfishness chiefly taking trouble for others; a man means not giving trouble to others. Thus each sex regards the other as basically selfish.

LEWIS Esther c.1747-1789
6308 *'A Mirror for Detractors'*
Are simple women only fit
To dress, to darn, to flower, or knit,

To mind the distaff, or the spit?
Why are the needle and the pen
Thought incompatible by men?

LEWIS Sir George Cornewall 1806-1863
6309
Life would be tolerable but for its amusements.

LEWIS Joe E.
6310
You only live once - but if you work it right, once is enough.

LEWIS John Spedan 1885-1963
6311 *(motto of the John Lewis Partnership)*
Never knowingly undersold.

LEWIS Sinclair 1885-1951
6312 *The American Fear of Literature*
Our American professors like their literature clear and cold and pure and very dead.

6313 *Babbitt*
His motor car was poetry and tragedy, love and heroism. The office was his pirate ship but the car his perilous excursion ashore.

6314 *Babbitt*
In other countries, art and literature are left to a lot of shabby bums living in attics and feeding on booze and spaghetti, but in America the successful writer or picture-painter is indistinguishable from any other decent business man.

6315 *Babbitt*
She did her work with the thoroughness of a mind which reveres detail and never quite understands them.

6316
It can't happen here.

LEWIS Stephen
6317 *(to Morton Shulman)*
How do you make a million?
You start with $900,000.

LEWIS Wyndham 1882-1957
6318 *The Apes of God*
Those prosperous mountebanks who alternately imitate and mock at and traduce those figures they at once admire and hate.

6319
Art is the expression of an enormous preference.

6320
People are so overwhelmed with the prestige of their instruments that they consider their personal judgement of hardly any account.

LEWISOHN Lewis L.
6321
His shortcoming is his long staying.

LEY Robert 1890-1945
6322 *(German Labour Front slogan from 1933)*
Kraft durch Freude.
Strength through joy.

LEYBOURNE George d.1884
6323 *'The Flying Trapese'*
He'd fly through the air with the greatest of ease,
A daring young man on the flying trapeze.

LIBERACE Wladziu Valentino 1919-1987
6324 *Autobiography*
When the reviews are bad I tell my staff that
they can join me as I cry all the way to the bank.

LICHTENBERG G.C. 1742-1799
6325
Barbaric accuracy - whimpering humility.

6326
A book is a mirror: if an ass peers into it, you
can't expect an apostle to look out.

6327
Everyone is a genius at least once a year; a real
genius has his original ideas closer together.

6328
One can live in this world on soothsaying but
not on truth saying.

6329
Most men of education are more superstitious
than they admit - nay, than they think.

6330
Never undertake anything for which you
wouldn't have the courage to ask the blessings
of heaven.

6331
Sometimes men come by the name of genius in
the same way that certain insects come by the
name of centipede - not because they have a
hundred feet, but because most people can't
count above fourteen.

LICHTENBERG Joseph
6332
If moderation is a fault, then indifference is a
crime.

LIDDON H.P. 1829-1890
6333
What we do upon some great occasion will
probably depend on what we already are: and
what we are will be the result of previous years
of self-discipline.

LIEBLING A.J. 1904-1963
6334
Freedom of the press is guaranteed only to
those who own one.

6335
I can write better than anyone who can write
faster, and I can write faster than anyone who
can write better.

LILIENTHAL David
6336 *1899-1981*
Big business is basic to the very life of this
country; and yet many - perhaps most -
Americans have a deep-seated fear and an
emotional repugnance to it. Here is
monumental contradiction.

LILLIE Beatrice 1894-1989
6337 *(to a waiter who had spilled soup down her
neck)*
Never darken my Dior again!

LILLO George 1693-1739
6338 *The Fatal Curiosity*
There's sure no passion in the human soul,
But finds its food in music.

LINCOLN Abraham 1809-1865
6339 *(attributed)*
You may fool all the people some of the time;
you can even fool some of the people all the
time; but you can't fool all of the people all the
time.

6340 *(attributed)*
The Lord prefers common looking people. That
is why he makes so many of them.

6341
This country, with its institutions, belongs to
the people who inhabit it. Whenever they shall
grow weary of the existing government, they
can exercise their constitutional right of
amending it, or their revolutionary right to
dismember or overthrow it.

6342
I desire to so conduct the affairs of this
administration that if, at the end ... I have lost
every friend on earth, I shall have one friend
left, and that friend shall be down inside me.

6343
The dogmas of the quiet past are inadequate to
the stormy present. As our case is new, so we
must think anew and act anew. We must
disenthrall ourselves, and then we shall save
our country.

6344
I have been driven many times to my knees by
the overwhelming conviction that I had
nowhere else to go. My own wisdom, and that
of all about me seemed insufficient for the day.

6345
Let us have faith that right makes might, and in
that faith, let us, to the end, dare to do our duty
as we understand it.

6346
Our fathers brought forth upon this continent a new nation, conceived in liberty, and dedicated to the proposition that all men are created equal.

6347
I feel like the man who was tarred and feathered and ridden out of town on a rail. To the man who asked how he liked it he said: 'If it wasn't for the honour of the thing, I'd rather walk.'

6348
Fellow citizens, we cannot escape history ... The fiery trial through which we pass will light us down in honour or dishonour to the last generation.

6349
Fondly do we hope, fervently do we pray, that this mighty scourge of war may speedily pass away.

6350
To give victory to the right, not bloody bullets, but peaceful ballots only, are necessary.
[popularly quoted as: The ballot is stronger than the bullet.]

6351
In giving freedom to the slave, we assure freedom to the free - honourable alike in what we give and what we preserve. We shall nobly save, or meanly lose, the last, best hope of earth.

6352
Must a government of necessity be too strong for the liberties of its people or too weak to maintain its own existence?

6353
With high hope for the future, no prediction is ventured.

6354
We here highly resolve that the dead shall not have died in vain, that this nation, under God, shall have a new birth of freedom; and that government of the people, by the people, and for the people, shall not perish from the earth.

6355
We hold the power and bear the responsibility.

6356
Honest statemanship is the wise employment of individual meannesses for the public good.

6357
'A house divided against itself cannot stand.' I believe this government cannot endure permanently, half slave and half free.

6358
I'm a slow walker, but I never walk back.

6359 *(judgement of a book)*
People who like this sort of thing will find this the sort of thing they like.

6360
The legitimate object of government is to do for a community of people, whatever they need to have done, but cannot do at all, or cannot so well do for themselves, in their separate and individual capacities.

6361 *Letter to A.G. Hodges*
I claim not to have controlled events, but confess plainly that events have controlled me.

6362 *Letter to Horace Greeley*
I have here stated my purpose according to my views of official duty and I intend no modification of my oft-expressed personal wish that all men everywhere could be free.

6363
With malice toward none; with charity for all; with firmness in the right, as God gives us to see the right, let us strive on to finish the work we are in.

6364
Every man over forty is responsible for his face.

6365
Every man is said to have his peculiar ambition.

6366
Marriage is neither heaven nor hell; it is simply purgatory.

6367
Any people anywhere, being inclined and having the power, have the right to rise up and shake off the existing government and form a new one. This is a most valuable and sacred right - a right which we hope and believe is to liberate the world.

6368 *(reply to National Union League)*
It is not best to swap horses when crossing streams.

6369
He has a right to criticize, who has a heart to help.

6370
Seriously, I do not think I am fit for the presidency.

6371
As I would not be a slave, so I would not be a master. This expresses my idea of democracy.

6372
I take the official oath to-day with no mental reservations, and with no purpose to construe the Constitution or laws by any hypercritical rules.

6373
We trust, sir, that God is on our side. It is more important to know that we are on God's side.

6374
What is conservatism? Is it not adherence to the old and tried, against the new and untried?

6375
What kills a skunk is the publicity it gives itself.

6376
When you have got an elephant by the hind leg, and he is trying to run away, it is best to let him run.

6377
A woman is the only thing I am afraid of that I know will not hurt me.

LINDBERGH Anne Morrow 1906-
6378
The fundamental magic of flying is a miracle that has nothing to do with any of its practical purposes - purposes of speed, accessibility and convenience - and will not change as they change.

6379
A simple enough pleasure, surely, to have breakfast alone with one's husband, but how seldom married people in the midst of life achieve it.

6380
Woman's normal occupations in general run counter to creative life, or contemplative life, or saintly life.

LINDNER R.M. 1914-1956
6381
Rebel without a cause.

LINDSAY Vachel 1879-1931
6382 *'The Congo'*
Then I saw the Congo, creeping through the black,
Cutting through the forest with a golden track.

6383 *'The Congo'*
Mumbo-Jumbo is dead in the jungle.

6384 *'General William Booth Enters into Heaven'*
Booth died blind and still by faith he trod,
Eyes still dazzled by the ways of God.

LINDSEY Ben
6385
I demand for the unmarried mother, as a sacred channel of life, the same reverence and respect as for the married mother; for Maternity is a cosmic thing and once it has come to pass, our conventions must not be permitted to blaspheme it.

6386
I do beseech you to direct your efforts more to preparing youth for the path and less to preparing the path for the youth.

LINKLATER Eric 1899-1974
6387 *Juan in America*
The people [in America] are all too clean. They spend all their time changing their shirts and washing themselves. You can't feel fierce and revolutionary in a bathroom.

LINKLETTER Art 1912-
6388 *A Child's Garden of Misinformation*
The four stages of man are infancy, childhood, adolescence and obsolescence.

LINLEY George 1798 1865
6389 *'God Bless the Prince of Wales'*
Among our ancient mountains,
And from our lovely vales,
Oh, let the prayer re-echo:
'God bless the Prince of Wales!'

LIPPMANN Walter 1899-1974
6390
In a democracy, the opposition is not only tolerated as constitutional, but must be maintained because it is indispensable.

6391
The final test of a leader is that he leaves behind in other men the conviction and the will to carry on.

6392
The first principle of a civilized state is that the power is legitimate only when it is under contract.

6393
Life is an irreversible process and for that reason its future can never be a repetition of the past.

6394
A man has honour if he holds himself to an ideal of conduct though it is inconvenient, unprofitable or dangerous to do so.

6395
While the right to talk may be the beginning of freedom, the necessity of listening is what makes the right important.

6396
Many a time I have wanted to stop talking and find out what I really believed.

LIPSIUS Justus 1547-1606
6397
He who does not desire or fear the uncertain day or capricious fate, is equal to the gods above and loftier than mortals.

LITTLER William 1908-
6398
The cheap, no matter how charming, how immediate, does not wear so well. It has a way of telling its whole story the first time through.

LITTLEWOOD Joan and CHILTON Charles
1914-1991 and 1914-
6399
Oh what a lovely war.

LITVINOV Maxim 1876-1951
6400 *Note to the Allies*
Peace is indivisible.

LIVINGSTONE Ken 1945-
6401
If voting changed anything they'd abolish it.

LIVY (Titus Livius) 59 BC-AD 17
6402 *(battle cry)*
Vae victis.
Down with the defeated!

6403
A gentleman is mindful no less of the freedom of others than of his own dignity.

6404 *(of Hannibal's ambush of the Romans)*
Pugna magna victi sumus.
We were defeated in a great battle.

LLEWELLYN Karl
6405
Law ... begins when someone takes to doing something someone else does not like.

LLEWELLYN Richard 1907-1983
6406
How green was my valley.

LLOYD C.F.
6407
God made me on a morning when he had nothing else to do.

LLOYD GEORGE David 1863-1945
6408
[Clemenceau] knows that the finest eloquence is that which gets things done and the worst is that which delays them.

6409
Don't be afraid to take a big step if one is indicated. You can't cross a chasm in two small jumps.

6410
A fully-equipped duke costs as much to keep up as two Dreadnoughts; and dukes are just as great a terror and they last longer.

6411
The great peaks of honour we had forgotten - Duty, Patriotism, and - clad in glittering white - the great pinnacle of Sacrifice, pointing like a rugged finger to Heaven.

6412
Negotiating with de Valera ... is like trying to pick up mercury with a fork.

6413
A politician was a person with whose politics you did not agree. When you did agree, he was a statesman.

6414 *(of Ramsay MacDonald)*
Sufficient conscience to bother him, but not sufficient to keep him straight.

6415
What is our task? To make Britain a fit country for heroes to live in.

6416
Whenever the Germans found the Canadian Corps coming into the line, they prepared for the worst.

6417
The world is becoming like a lunatic asylum run by lunatics.

6418 *(of World War I)*
At eleven o'clock this morning came to an end the cruellest and most terrible war that has ever scourged mankind. I hope we may say that thus, this fateful morning, came to an end all wars.

LLOYD Marie 1870-1922
6419
I'm a bit of a ruin that Cromwell knocked about a bit.

6420
A little of what you fancy does you good.

LLOYD Robert 1733-1764
6421 *'The Hare and the Tortoise'*
Slow and steady wins the race.

6422 *'The Law-Student'*
Turn parson, Colman, that's the way to thrive;
Your parsons are the happiest men alive.

6423 *'The Law-Student' (of Lord Mansfield)*
Alone from Jargon born to rescue Law,
From precedent, grave hum, and formal saw!
To strip chicanery of its vain pretence,
And marry Common Law to Common Sense!

6424 *'Shakespeare'*
True Genius, like Armida's wand,
Can raise the spring from barren land.
While all the art of Imitation,
Is pilf'ring from the first creation.

LOCKE John 1632-1704
6425 *An Essay concerning Human Understanding*
New opinions are always suspected, and usually

opposed, without any other reason but because they are not already common.

6426 *An Essay concerning Human Understanding*
The commonwealth of learning is not at this time without master-builders, whose mighty designs, in advancing the sciences, will leave lasting monuments to the admiration of posterity ... 'tis ambition enough to be employed as an under-labourer in clearing ground a little, and removing some of the rubbish that lies in the way of knowledge.

6427 *An Essay concerning Human Understanding*
General propositions are seldom mentioned in the huts of Indians: much less are they to be found in the thoughts of children.

6428 *An Essay concerning Human Understanding*
Nature never makes excellent things for mean or no uses.

6429 *An Essay concerning Human Understanding*
No man's knowledge here can go beyond his experience.

6430 *An Essay concerning Human Understanding*
It is one thing to show a man that he is in error, and another to put him in possession of truth.

6431 *An Essay concerning Human Understanding*
Reason is natural revelation, whereby the eternal Father of light, and fountain of all knowledge communicates to mankind that portion of truth which he has laid within the reach of their natural faculties.

6432 *An Essay concerning Human Understanding*
Crooked things may be as stiff and unflexible as straight: and men may be as positive in error as in truth.

6433 *An Essay concerning Human Understanding*
All men are liable to error; and most men are, in many points, by passion or interest, under temptation to it.

6434 *Second Treatise of Civil Government*
[That] ill deserves the name of confinement which hedges us in only from bogs and precipices. So that, however it may be mistaken, the end of law is, not to abolish or restrain, but to preserve and enlarge freedom.

6435 *Second Treatise of Civil Government*
Man ... hath by nature a power ... to preserve his property - that is, his life, liberty, and estate -

against the injuries and attempts of other men.

6436 *Second Treatise of Civil Government*
Man being ... by nature all free, equal, and independent, no one can be put out of this estate, and subjected to the political power of another, without his own consent.

6437 *Second Treatise of Civil Government*
The only way by which any one divests himself of his natural liberty and puts on the bonds of civil society is by agreeing with other men to join and unite into a community.

6438 *Second Treatise of Civil Government*
This power to act according to discretion for the public good, without the prescription of the law, and sometimes even against it, is that which is called prerogative.

6439
The thoughts that come often unsought, and, as it were, drop into the mind, are commonly the most valuable of any we have.

6440 *Some Thoughts Concerning Education*
The rod, which is the only instrument of government that tutors generally know, or ever think of, is the most unfit of any to be used in education.

6441 *Some Thoughts Concerning Education*
You would think him a very foolish fellow, that should not value a virtuous, or a wise man, infinitely before a great scholar.

LOCKER-LAMPSON Frederick 1821-1895
6442 *'The Jester's Plea'*
The world's as ugly, ay, as sin,
And almost as delightful.

6443 *'The Jester's Plea'*
And many are afraid of God -
And more of Mrs Grundy.

6444 *'The Jester's Plea'*
Some men are good for righting wrongs,
And some for writing verses.

LOCKHART John Gibson 1794-1854
6445 *Epitaph for Patrick ('Peter'), Lord Robertson*
Here lies that peerless paper peer Lord Peter,
Who broke the laws of God and man and metre.

LODGE David 1935-
6446 *The British Museum is Falling Down*
Literature is mostly about having sex and not much about having children. Life is the other way round.

6447 *Changing Places*
Four times, under our educational rules, the human pack is shuffled and cut - at eleven-plus, sixteen-plus, eighteen-plus and twenty-plus - and happy is he who comes top of the deck on each occasion, but especially the last. This is

called Finals, the very name of which implies that nothing of importance can happen after it.

6448 *Small World*
I gave up screwing around a long time ago. I came to the conclusion that sex is a sublimation of the work instinct.

6449 *Small World*
Another law of academic life: *it is impossible to be excessive in flattery of one's peers.*

LODGE George Cabot 1873-1909
6450
When you are accustomed to anything, you are estranged from it.

LODGE Jr. Henry Cabot 1850-1924
6451
This organization (United Nations) is created to prevent you from going to hell. It isn't created to take you to heaven.

LODGE Thomas 1558-1625
6452 *'Love in my bosom like a bee'*
Love in my bosom like a bee
Doth suck his sweet.

6453 *'Love guards the roses of thy lips'*
Love guards the roses of thy lips
And flies about them like a bee;
If I approach he forward skips,
And if I kiss he stingeth me.

6454 *'Margarite of America'*
Devils are not so black as they are painted.

LOESSER Frank 1910-1969
6455 *'Boys in the Back Room'*
See what the boys in the back room will have
And tell them I'm having the same.

6456 *'The King's New Clothes'*
Isn't it grand! Isn't it fine! Look at the cut, the style, the line!
The suit of clothes is altogether, but altogether it's altogether
The most remarkable suit of clothes that I have ever seen.

LOEVINGER Lee
6457
Television is a gold goose that lays scrambled eggs; and it is futile and probably fatal to beat it for not laying caviar.

6458
Television is the literature of the illiterate, the culture of the low-brow, the wealth of the poor, the privilege of the underprivileged, the exclusive club of the excluded masses.

LOGAN John 1748-1788
6459 *To the Cuckoo (attributed)*
Thou hast no sorrow in thy song,
No winter in thy year.

LOGAU Friedrich von 1604-1655
6460 *(translated by Longfellow)*
Though the mills of God grind slowly, yet they grind exceeding small;
Though with patience He stands waiting, with exactness grinds He all.

LOGUE Christopher 1926-
6461 *Christopher Logues ABC 'M'*
Said Marx: 'Don't be snobbish, we seek to abolish
The 3rd Class, not the 1st.'

LOLLABRIGIDA Gina
6462
The light is better than a plastic surgeon.

LOMBARDI Vince 1913-1970
6463
If you aren't fired with enthusiasm, you'll be fired with enthusiasm.

6464
Fatigue makes cowards of us all.

6465
Winning isn't everything. It is the only thing.

LOMBROSO Cesare 1836-1909
6466 *The Man of Genius*
The ignorant man always adores what he cannot understand.

LONERGAN Bernard 1904-1985
6467
In philosophy an individual is becoming himself.

LONG Huey 1893-1935
6468 *(attributed)*
The time has come for all good men to rise above principle.

6469
Bible's the greatest book ever written. But I sure don't need anybody I can buy for six bits and a chew of tobacco to explain it to me. When I need preachers I buy 'em cheap.

6470 *(to journalists on his political personality)*
Oh hell, say that I am *sui generis* and let it go at that.

LONGFELLOW Henry Wadsworth 1807-1882
6471
All things must change to something new, to something strange.

6472 *'The Arrow and the Song'*
I shot an arrow into the air,
It fell to earth, I knew not where.

6473 *'The Arrow and the Song'*
And the song, from beginning to end,
I found again in the heart of a friend.

6474 *'The Bridge'*
I stood on the bridge at midnight,
As the clocks were striking the hour.

6475 *'The Building of the Ship'*
Thou, too, sail on, O Ship of State!
Sail on, O Union, strong and great!
Humanity with all its fears,
With all the hopes of future years,
Is hanging breathless on thy fate!

6476 *'Children'*
Ye are better than all the ballads
That ever were sung or said;
For ye are living poems,
And all the rest are dead.

6477 *'The Children's Hour'*
Between the dark and the daylight,
When the night is beginning to lower,
Comes a pause in the day's occupations,
That is known as the Children's Hour.

6478 *(composed for his second daughter)*
There was a little girl
Who had a little curl
Right in the middle of her forehead,
When she was good
She was very, very good,
But when she was bad she was horrid.

6479 *'The Day is Done'*
The cares that infest the day
Shall fold their tents, like the Arabs,
And as silently steal away.

6480 *'The Day is Done'*
The bards sublime,
Whose distant footsteps echo
Through the corridors of Time.

6481 *'Elegiac Verse'*
If you would hit the mark, you must aim a little
above it;
Every arrow that flies feels the attraction of
earth.

6482 *Evangeline*
This is the forest primeval.

6483 *Evangeline*
Sorrow and silence are strong, and patient
endurance is godlike.

6484 *Evangeline, 'Prelude'*
Silently one by one, in the infinite meadows of
heaven
Blossomed the lovely stars, the forget-me-nots
of the angels.

6485 *'Excelsior'*
The shades of night were falling fast,
As through an Alpine village passed
A youth, who bore, 'mid snow and ice,
A banner with the strange device,

Excelsior!

6486 *'Excelsior'*
'Try not the Pass!' the old man said;
'Dark lowers the tempest overhead.'

6487 *'Excelsior'*
A traveller, by the faithful hound,
Half-buried in the snow was found.

6488 *'Giotto's Tower'*
Giotto's tower,
The lily of Florence blossoming in stone.

6489 *'God's-Acre'*
I like that ancient Saxon phrase, which calls
The burial-ground God's-Acre!

6490 *Hiawatha's Childhood 'The Song of
Hiawatha'*
By the shore of Gitche Gumee,
By the shining Big-Sea-Water,
Stood the wigwam of Nokomis.

6491 *'Holidays'*
The holiest of all holidays are those
Kept by ourselves in silence and apart;
The secret anniversaries of the heart.

6492
We judge ourselves by what we feel capable of
doing, while others judge us by what we have
already done.

6493 *'The Ladder of Saint Augustine'*
The heights by great men reached and kept
Were not attained by sudden flight,
But they, while their companions slept,
Were toiling upward in the night.

6494 *'My Lost Youth'*
A boy's will is the wind's will
And the thoughts of youth are long, long
thoughts.

6495 *'Maidenhood'*
Standing, with reluctant feet,
Where the brook and river meet,
Womanhood and childhood fleet!

6496 *'Michael Angelo'*
The men that women marry,
And why they marry them, will always be
A marvel and a mystery to the world.

6497
Each morning sees some task begun,
Each evening sees it close.
Something attempted, something done,
Has earned a night's repose.

6498 *'Nuremberg' (on Albrecht Dürer)*
Emigravit is the inscription on the tombstone
where he lies;
Dead he is not, but departed - for the artist
never dies.

6499 *'The Poets'*
Not in the clamour of the crowded street,
Not in the shouts and plaudits of the throng,
But in ourselves, are triumph and defeat.

6500 *'A Psalm of Life'*
Tell me not, in mournful numbers,
Life is but an empty dream!
For the soul is dead that slumbers,
And things are not what they seem.
Life is real! Life is earnest!
And the grave is not its goal;
Dust thou art, to dust returnest,
Was not spoken of the soul.

6501 *'A Psalm of Life'*
Art is long, and Time is fleeting,
And our hearts, though stout and brave,
Still, like muffled drums, are beating
Funeral marches to the grave.

6502 *'A Psalm of Life'*
Trust no Future, howe'er pleasant!
Let the dead Past bury its dead!
Act - act in the living Present!
Heart within, and God o'erhead!

6503 *'A Psalm of Life'*
Lives of great men all remind us
We can make our lives sublime,
And, departing, leave behind us
Footprints on the sands of time.

6504 *'A Psalm of Life'*
Let us, then, be up and doing,
With a heart for any fate;
Still achieving, still pursuing,
Learn to labour and to wait.

6505 *'A Psalm of Life'*
There is no flock, however watched and tended,
But one dead lamb is there!
There is no fireside, howsoe'er defended,
But has one vacant chair!

6506 *'The Reaper and the Flowers'*
There is a Reaper whose name is Death,
And, with his sickle keen,
He reaps the bearded grain at a breath,
And the flowers that grow between.

6507 *'Santa Filomena' (on Florence Nightingale)*
A Lady with a Lamp shall stand
In the great history of the land,
A noble type of good,
Heroic womanhood.

6508
To say the least, a town life makes one more
tolerant and liberal in one's judgement of
others.

6509
If we could read the secret history of our
enemies, we should find in each man's life,

sorrow and suffering enough to disarm all
hostility.

6510 *'The Secret of the Sea'*
'Wouldst thou' - so the helmsman answered,
'Learn the secret of the sea?
Only those who brave its dangers
Comprehend its mystery!'

6511 *'The Slave's Dream'*
The forests, with their myriad tongues,
Shouted of liberty;
And the Blast of the Desert cried aloud,
With a voice so wild and free,
That he started in his sleep and smiled
At their tempestuous glee.

6512 *'The Song of Hiawatha'*
From the waterfall he named her,
Minnehaha, Laughing Water.

6513 *Tales of a Wayside Inn 'Elizabeth'*
Ships that pass in the night, and speak each
other in passing;
Only a signal shown and a distant voice in the
darkness;
So on the ocean of life we pass and speak one
another,
Only a look and a voice; then darkness again
and a silence.

6514 *Tales of A Wayside Inn 'The Student's Tale'*
Our ingress into the world
Was naked and bare;
Our progress through the world
Is trouble and care.

6515 *'The Village Blacksmith'*
Under a spreading chestnut tree
The village smithy stands;
The smith, a mighty man is he,
With large and sinewy hands;
And the muscles of his brawny arms
Are strong as iron bands.

6516
In this world, a man must either be anvil or
hammer.

6517 *'The Wreck of the Hesperus'*
But the father answered never a word,
A frozen corpse was he.

LONGWORTH Alice Roosevelt
6518 *(attributed)*
If you can't say something good about someone,
sit right here by me.

6519
I have a simple philosophy. Fill what's empty.
Empty what's full. And scratch where it itches.

6520
My speciality is detached malevolence.

LOON Hendrick Willem van 1882-1944
6521
The history of the world is the record of a man in quest of his daily bread and butter.

LOOS Anita 1893-1981
6522 *Gentlemen Prefer Blondes*
This gentleman said a girl with brains ought to do something with them besides think.

6523 *Gentlemen Prefer Blondes*
She always believed in the old adage, 'Leave them while you're looking good.'

6524 *Gentlemen Prefer Blondes*
Fun is fun but no girl wants to laugh all of the time.

6525 *Gentlemen Prefer Blondes*
Kissing your hand may make you feel very, very good but a diamond and safire bracelet lasts for ever.

6526
I'm furious about Women's Liberationists. They keep getting up on soapboxes and proclaiming that women are brighter than men. That's true, but it should be kept very quiet or it ruins the whole racket.

LORD Peter
6527
Nobody does nothing for nobody for naught.

LORENZ Konrad 1903-1989
6528 *On Agression*
It is a good morning exercise for a research scientist to discard a pet hypothesis every day before breakfast. It keeps him young.

6529
I believe I've found the missing link between animal and civilized man. It is us.

LOUIS Joe 1914-1981
6530
I don't like money actually, but it quiets my nerves.

LOUIS XIV King 1638-1715
6531 *(attributed)*
Ah, if I were not king, I should lose my temper.

6532 *(on accession of his grandson to Spanish throne)*
The Pyrenees are no more.

6533
First feelings are always the most natural.

6534
J'ai failli attendre.
I was nearly kept waiting.

6535
L'État c'est moi.
I am the State.

6536
Every time I create an appointment, I create a hundred malcontents and one ingrate.

LOUIS XVIII King 1755-1824
6537 *(attributed)*
Punctuality is the politeness of kings.

LOVELACE Richard 1618-1658
6538 *'To Althea, From Prison'*
When I lie tangled in her hair,
And fettered to her eye;
The Gods, that wanton in the air
Know no such liberty.

6539 *'To Althea, From Prison'*
When thirsty grief in wine we steep,
When healths and draughts go free,
Fishes, that tipple in the deep,
Know no such liberty.

6540 *'To Althea, From Prison'*
Stone walls do not a prison make,
Nor iron bars a cage;
Minds innocent and quiet take
That for an hermitage;
If I have freedom in my love,
And in my soul am free;
Angels alone, that soar above,
Enjoy such liberty.

6541 *'The Ant'*
Forbear, thou great good husband, little ant.

6542 *'Gratiana Dancing and Singing'*
And when she ceased, we sighing saw
The floor lay paved with broken hearts.

6543 *'To Lucasta, Going Beyond the Seas'*
If to be absent were to be
Away from thee;
Or that when I am gone,
You or I were alone;
Then my Lucasta might I crave
Pity from blust'ring wind, or swallowing wave.

6544 *'To Lucasta, Going to the Wars'*
True; a new mistress now I chase,
The first foe in the field;
And with a stronger faith embrace
A sword, a horse, a shield.

Yet this inconstancy is such,
As you too shall adore;
I could not love thee, Dear, so much,
Loved I not honour more.

6545 *'The Scrutiny'*
Lady, it is already morn,
And 'twas last night I swore to thee
That fond impossibility.

LOVELL Sir Bernard 1913-
6546
Youth is vivid rather than happy.

LOVELL Maria 1803-1877
6547 *'Ingomar the Barbarian'*
Two souls with but a single thought,
Two hearts that beat as one.

LOVEMAN Robert 1864-1923
6548 *April Rain*
It is not raining rain to me,
It's raining violets.

LOVER Samuel 1797-1868
6549 *Handy Andy*
When once the itch of literature comes over a
man, nothing can cure it but the scratching of a
pen.

LOW Sir David 1891-1963
6550
I have never met anyone who wasn't against
war. Even Hitler and Mussolini were, according
to themselves.

LOWE Robert (Viscount Sherbrooke) 1811-
1892
6551
The Chancellor of the Exchequer is a man
whose duties make him more or less of a taxing
machine. He is intrusted with a certain amount
of misery which it is his duty to distribute as
fairly as he can.

6552 *(on the passing of the Reform Bill)*
I believe it will be absolutely necessary that you
should prevail on our future masters to learn
their letters.

LOWELL A.L. 1856-1943
6553 *(while President of Harvard)*
The freshmen bring a little knowledge in and
the seniors take none out, so it accumulates
through the years.

LOWELL Amy 1874-1925
6554 *'Patterns'*
And the softness of my body will be guarded by
embrace
By each button, hook, and lace.
For the man who should loose me is dead,
Fighting with the Duke in Flanders,
In a pattern called a war.
Christ! What are patterns for?

6555 *'Sheppy'*
I [Death] was astonished to see him in Baghdad,
for
I had an appointment with him tonight in
Samarra.

6556 *'Sword Blades and Poppy Seed'*
All books are either dreams or swords,
You can cut, or you can drug, with words.

LOWELL James Russell 1819-1891
6557 *Among My Books 'Shakespeare Once More'*
A wise scepticism is the first attribute of a good
critic.

6558 *The Biglow Papers*
An' you've gut to git up airly
Ef you want to take in God.

6559 *The Biglow Papers*
It ain't by princerples nor men
My preudunt course is steadied, -
I scent wich pays the best, an' then
Go into it baldheaded.

6560 *The Biglow Papers*
We've a war, an' a debt, an' a flag; an' ef this
Ain't to be inderpendunt, why, wut on airth is?

6561 *The Biglow Papers*
He's been true to *one* party - an' thet is himself.

6562 *The Biglow Papers*
But libbaty's a kind o'thing
That don't agree with niggers.

6563 *The Biglow Papers*
An' in convartin' public trusts
To very privit uses.

6564 *The Biglow Papers*
I *don't* believe in princerple,
But oh, I *du* in interest.

6565 *The Biglow Papers*
God makes sech nights, all white and still,
Fur'z you can look or listen.

6566 *The Biglow Papers*
All kin' o' smily round the lips,
An' teary round the lashes.

6567 *The Biglow Papers*
My gran'ther's rule was safer 'n 't is to crow:
Don't never prophesy - onless ye know.

6568 *'On the Capture of Fugitive Slaves'*
Before Man made us citizens, great Nature
made us men.

6569
In creating, the only hard thing's to begin;
A grass-blade's no easier to make than an oak.

6570 *Democracy and other Addresses*
'Democracy'
There is no good in arguing with the inevitable.
The only argument available with an east wind
is to put on your overcoat.

6571 *Democracy and other Addresses*
'Democracy'
The misfortunes hardest to bear are those
which never come.

6572 *'A Fable for Critics'*
There comes Poe with his raven like Barnaby
Rudge,
Three-fifths of him genius, and two-fifths sheer
fudge.

6573
The foolish and the dead alone never change their opinions.

6574
A ginooine statesman should be on his guard, if he must hev beliefs, not to b'lieve 'em too hard.

6575 *'A Glance Behind the Curtain'*
No man is born into the world, whose work
Is not born with him; there is always work,
And tools to work withal, for those who will:
And blessèd are the horny hands of toil!

6576
God'll send the bill to you.

6577
May is a pious fraud of the almanac
A ghastly parody of real Spring
Shaped out of snow and breathed with eastern wind.

6578
Ah, men do not know how much strength is in poise,
That he goes the farthest who goes far enough.

6579
Nature fits all her children with something to do,
He who would write and can't write, can surely review.

6580 *'The Present Crisis'*
Once to every man and nation comes the moment to decide,
In the strife of Truth with Falsehood, for the good or evil side.

6581 *'The Present Crisis'*
Truth forever on the scaffold, Wrong forever on the throne, -
Yet that scaffold sways the future, and, behind the dim unknown,
Standeth God within the shadow, keeping watch above his own.

6582 *'The Present Crisis'*
New occasions teach new duties: Time makes ancient good uncouth;
They must upward still, and onward, who would keep abreast of Truth.

6583
The pressure of public opinion is like the pressure of the atmosphere; you can't see it - but all the same, it is sixteen pounds to the square inch.

6584
Solitude is as needful to the imagination as society is wholesome for the character.

6585
Take a winter as you find him and he turns out to be a thoroughly honest fellow with no nonsense in him: and tolerating none in you, which is a great comfort in the long run.

6586
Talent is that which is in a man's power; genius is that in whose power a man is.

6587
What a sense of security in an old book which time has criticized for us!

6588
Whatever you may be sure of, be sure of this - that you are dreadfully like other people.

LOWELL Robert 1917-1977
6589 *'Since 1939'*
We feel the machine slipping from our hands
As if someone else were steering;
If we see light at the end of the tunnel,
It's the light of the oncoming train.

6590 *'Our Afterlife I'*
After fifty
the clock can't stop,
each saving breath
takes something.

6591 *'The Day'*
It's amazing
the day is still here
like lightning on an open field,
terra firma and transient
swimming on variation,
fresh as when man first broke
like the crocus all over the earth.

6592 *'During Fever'*
Terrible that old life of decency
without unseemly intimacy
or quarrels, when the unemancipated woman
still had her Freudian papa and maids!

6593 *'Memories of West Street and Lepke'*
These are the tranquillized *Fifties*,
and I am forty. Ought I to regret my seed-time?

6594 *'Middle Age'*
At forty-five,
What next, what next?
At every corner,
I meet my Father,
my age, still alive.

6595 *'We Took Our Paradise'*
Folly comes from something -
the present, yes,
we are in it,
it's the infection
of things gone.

6596 *'The Quaker Graveyard in Nantucket'*
The Lord survives the rainbow of His will.

6597 *'Skunk Hour'*
My mind's not right.

A car radio bleats,
'Love, O careless Love ...' I hear
my ill-spirit sob in each blood cell,
as if my hand were at its throat ...
I myself am hell,
nobody's here.

6598 *'Tenth Muse'*
But I suppose even God was born
too late to trust the old religion -
all those settings out
that never left the ground,
beginning in wisdom, dying in doubt.

6599 *'For the Union Dead'*
The aquarium is gone. Everywhere,
giant finned cars nose forward like fish;
a savage servility
slides by on grease.

6600 *'For the Union Dead'*
Their monument sticks like a fishbone
in the city's throat.

6601 *'Waking Early Sunday Morning'*
Pity the planet, all joy gone
from this sweet volcanic cone;
peace to our children when they fall
in small war on the heels of small war - until the
end of time
to police the earth, a ghost
orbiting forever lost
in our monotonous sublime.

LOWER Arthur R.M.
6602
All zeal runs down. What replaces it?
Intellectualism.

LOWNDES William 1652-1724
6603
Take care of the pence, and the pounds will take
care of themselves.

LOWRY Malcolm 1909-1957
6604
Fear ringed by doubt is my eternal moon.

6605
I like prefaces. I read them. Sometimes I do not
read any further.

6606 *Under the Volcano*
How alike are the groans of love to those of the
dying.

LOYOLA St Ignatius 1491-1556
6607 *'Prayer for Generosity'*
Teach us, good Lord, to serve Thee as Thou
deservest:
To give and not to count the cost;
To fight and not to heed the wounds;
To toil and not to seek for rest;
To labour and not to ask for any reward
Save that of knowing that we do Thy will.

LUBBOCK John
6608
A poor woman from Manchester, on being
taken to the seaside, is said to have expressed
her delight on seeing for the first time
something of which there was enough for
everybody.

LUCAN 39-65 AD
6609 *Pharsalia*
Thinking nothing done while anything
remained to be done.

6610 *Pharsalia*
Jupiter is whatever you see, whichever way you
move.

6611 *Pharsalia*
The victorious cause pleased the Gods, but the
conquered one pleased Cato.

6612 *Pharsalia*
Caesar lives after his battles, but his fortune has
perished.

6613 *Pharsalia (of Pompey)*
There stands the ghost of a great name.

LUCAS Charles L.
6614
Civilization is just a slow process of learning to
be kind.

LUCAS E.V. 1868-1938
6615
One of the most adventurous things left is to go
to bed, for no one can lay a hand on our
dreams.

LUCAS George 1944-
6616 *Star Wars*
Man your ships, and may the force be with you.

LUCE Clare Booth 1903-1987
6617
Censorship, like charity, should begin at home;
but unlike charity, it should end there.

6618
Technological man can't believe in anything
that can't be measured, taped, or put into a
computer.

LUCIUS Cary 1610-1643
6619 *Discourses of Infallibility*
When it is not necessary to change, it is
necessary not to change.

LUCKMAN Charles
6620
Success is that old A B C - ability, breaks and courage.

LUCRETIUS 99-55 BC
6621 *De Rerum Natura*
So much wrong could religion induce.

6622 *De Rerum Natura*
Nothing can be created out of nothing.

6623 *De Rerum Natura*
Some races increase, others are reduced, and in a short while the generations of living creatures are changed and like runners relay the torch of life.

6624 *De Rerum Natura*
Death therefore is nothing to us nor does it concern us a scrap, seeing that the nature of the spirit we possess is something mortal.

6625 *De Rerum Natura*
And life is given to none freehold, but it is leasehold for all.

6626 *De Rerum Natura*
From the midst of the fountain of delights rises something bitter that chokes them all amongst the flowers.

6627 *De Rerum Natura*
What is food to one man is bitter poison to others.

6628
Sweet is it, when on the high seas the winds are lashing the waters, to gaze from the land on another's struggles.

LUMLEY Joanna
6629
What sustains the human spirit is gorgeousness.

LUND Robert S.
6630
Every man of genius is considerably helped by being dead.

LUTHER Martin 1483-1546
6631 *(attributed)*
Who loves not women, wine and song,
Remains a fool his whole life long.

6632
Every thing that is done in the world is done by hope.

6633
I am more afraid of my own heart than of the Pope and all his cardinals. I have within me the great Pope, Self.

6634
Christian life consists of faith and charity.

6635 *Colloquia Mensalia*
For, where God built a church, there the devil would also build a chapel ... In such sort is the devil always God's ape.

6636 *(attributed, at the Diet of Worms)*
Hier stehe ich. Ich kann nicht anders. Gott helfe mir. Amen.
Here stand I. I can do no other. God help me. Amen.

6637 *'Eine feste Burg ist unser Gott'*
A safe stronghold our God is still,
A trusty shield and weapon.

6638
The fewer the words, the better the prayer.

6639
If I had heard that as many devils would set on me in Worms as there are tiles on the roofs, I should none the less have ridden there.

6640 *Large Catechism*
The confidence and faith of the heart alone make both God and an idol.

6641 *Large Catechism 'The First Commandment'*
Whatever your heart clings to and confides in, that is really your God.

6642 *Letter to Melanchthon*
Be a sinner and sin strongly, but more strongly have faith and rejoice in Christ.

6643
I never work better than when I am inspired by anger; for when I am angry, I can write, pray, and preach well, for then my whole temperament is quickened, my understanding sharpened, and all mundane vexations and temptations depart.

6644
Peace if possible, but truth at any rate.

6645 *Tischreden oder Colloquia*
So our Lord God commonly gives riches to those gross asses to whom He vouchsafes nothing else.

LUTOSLAWSKI Witold 1913-
6646
Our role is to offer a message from an ideal world.

LUXEMBURG Rosa 1871-1919
6647 *Die Russische Revolution*
Freedom is always and exclusively freedom for the one who thinks differently.

LYDGATE John c.1370-c.1451
6648 *The Fall of Princes*
Sithe he off Inglissh in makyng was the beste,
Preie onto God to yiue his soule good reste.

6649 *The Fall of Princes*
Comparisouns doon offte gret greuaunce.

6650 *The Fall of Princes (of Chaucer)*
Sithe off oure language he was the lodesterre.

6651 *Secrets of Old Philosophers*
Woord is but wynd; leff woord and tak the dede.

6652 *The Story of Thebes*
Love is mor than gold or gret richesse.

LYLY John c.1554-1606
6653
If all the earth were paper white
And all the sea were ink
'Twere not enough for me to write
As my poor heart doth think.

6654
It is a blind goose that cometh to the fox's
sermon.

6655 *Campaspe*
Cupid and my Campaspe played
At cards for kisses, Cupid paid.

6656 *Campaspe*
What bird so sings, yet so does wail?
O 'tis the ravished nightingale.
Jug, jug, jug, jug, tereu, she cries,
And still her woes at midnight rise.

6657 *Euphues*
It seems to me (said she) that you are in some
brown study.

6658
Marriages are made in heaven and
consummated on earth.

6659 *The Maydes Metamorphosis*
Night hath a thousand eyes.

6660
Where the mind is past hope, the heart is past
shame.

LYND Robert 1879-1949
6661
It is in games that many men discover their
paradise.

6662
One of the greatest joys known to man is to take
a flight into ignorance in search of knowledge.

6663
It may be the games are silly. But, then, so are
human beings.

6664
There is nothing in which the birds differ more
from man than the way in which they can build
and yet leave a landscape as it was before.

LYNES Russell
6665
Cynicism - the intellectual cripple's substitute
for intelligence.

6666
The true snob never rests; there is always a
higher goal to attain, and there are, by the same
token, always more and more people to look
down upon.

LYONS Lord
6667
If you're given champagne at lunch, there's a
catch somewhere.

LYSANDER d.395 BC
6668
Deceive boys with toys, but men with oaths.

LYTE Henry Francis 1793-1847
6669 *'Abide with Me'*
Abide with me: fast falls the eventide;
The darkness deepens; Lord, with me abide:
When other helpers fail, and comforts flee,
Help of the helpless, O abide with me.
Swift to its close ebbs out life's little day;
Earth's joys grow dim, its glories pass away;
Change and decay in all around I see;
O Thou, who changest not, abide with me.

6670 *'Praise, my soul, the King of heaven'*
Father-like, he tends and spares us;
Well our feeble frame he knows ...
Praise him! Praise him!
Widely as his mercy flows.

LYTTELTON George 1709-1773
6671 *'Advice to a Lady'*
Seek to be good, but aim not to be great;
A woman's noblest station is retreat.

McALPINE Lord 1942-
6672
The party needs a good scrub with a hard
brush.

McARTHUR Alexander and LONG H. Kingley
6673 *'Advice to a Lady'*
Battles and sex are the only free diversions in
slum life. Couple them with drink, which costs
money, and you have the three principal outlets
for that escape complex which is for ever
working in the tenement dweller's subconscious
mind.

MacARTHUR Douglas 1880-1964
6674
In war, indeed, there can be no substitute for
victory.

McARTHUR Peter
6675
A satirist is a man who discovers unpleasant
things about himself and then says them about

other people.

MacCAIG Norman 1910-
6676 *Sounds of the Day*
When the door
Scraped shut, it was the end
Of all the sounds there are.
You left me
Beside the quietest fire in the world.

McCARTHY Eugene 1916-
6677
He's like a football coach who's smart enough to
win the game, and dumb enough to think it's
important.

6678
The Senate is the last primitive society in the
world. We still worship the elders of the tribe
and honour the territorial imperative.

McCARTHY Joseph 19087-1957
6679
McCarthyism is Americanism with its sleeves
rolled.

McCARTHY Mary 1912-1989
6680
Bureaucracy, the rule of no one, has become the
modern form of despotism.

6681 *On the Contrary*
The immense popularity of American movies
abroad demonstrates that Europe is the
unfinished negative of which America is the
proof.

6682 *On the Contrary*
If someone tells you he is going to make a
'realistic decision', you immediately understand
that he has resolved to do something bad.

6683 *On the Contrary*
In violence, we forget who we are.

6684 *On the Contrary*
There are no new truths, but only truths that
have not been recognized by those who have
perceived them without noticing.

6685
Liberty, as it is conceived by current opinion,
has nothing inherent about it; it is a sort of gift
or trust bestowed on the individual by the state
pending good behaviour.

6686 *(of Lillian Hellmann)*
Every word she writes is a lie, including 'and'
and 'the'.

McCARTNEY Paul 1942-
6687 *(on reaching the age of 50)*
Ballads and babies. That's what happened to
me.

McCLENAHAN John L.
6688
It requires a great deal of faith for a man to be
cured by his own placebos.

McCLUNG Nellie 1873-1951
6689
Chivalry is a poor substitute for justice, if one
cannot have both. Chivalry is something like
the icing on cake, sweet, but not nourishing.

6690
The economic dependence of women is
perhaps the greatest injustice that has been
done to us, and has worked the greatest injury
to the race.

6691 *(to a heckler about women being elected)*
This proves what a purifying effect women
would have on politics.

6692
Never retract, never explain, never apologize -
get the thing done and let them howl.

6693
By nice women ... you probably mean selfish
women who have no more thought for the
underpriviledged, overworked women than a
pussycat in a sunny window for the starving
kitten in the street. Now in that sense I am not
a nice woman, for I do care.

6694
Women who set a low value on themselves
make life hard for all women.

McCLURE Robert 1807-1873
6695
A = r + p (or Adventure equals risk plus
purpose)

McCORD David 1897-
6696 *'Remainders' (epitaph for a waiter)*
By and by
God caught his eye.

McCORMICK Anne O'Hare d.1954
6697
Today the real test of power is not capacity to
make war but capacity to prevent it.

McCRAE John 1872-1918
6698 *'In Flanders Fields'*
In Flanders fields the poppies blow
Between the crosses, row on row.

6699 *'In Flanders Fields'*
To you from failing hands we throw
The torch; be yours to hold it high.
If ye break faith with us who die
We shall not sleep, though poppies grow.

MacDIARMID Hugh 1892-1978
6700 *A Drunk Man Looks at the Thistle*
I'll ha'e nae hauf-way hoose, but aye be whaur

Extremes meet - it's the only way I ken
To dodge the curst conceit o' bein' richt
That damns the vast majority o' men.

6701 *A Drunk Man Looks at the Thistle*
He's no a man ava',
And lacks a proper pride,
Gin less than a' the world
Can ser' him for a bride!

6702 *The International Brigade*
It is very rarely that a man loves
And when he does it is nearly always fatal.

MacDONALD George 1824-1905
6703 *David Elginbrod*
Here lie I, Martin Elginbrodde:
Hae mercy o' my soul, Lord God;
As I wad do, were I Lord God,
And ye were Martin Elginbrodde.

6704
It is not by driving away our brother that we can be alone with God.

6705 *'That Holy Thing'*
They all were looking for a king
To slay their foes, and lift them high;
Thou cam'st, a little baby thing,
That made a woman cry.

6706 *At the Back of the North Wind*
Where did you come from, baby dear?
Out of the everywhere into here.

6707
To be trusted is a greater compliment than to be loved.

MacDONALD Sir John A. 1815-1891
6708
Confederation is only yet in the gristle, and it will require five years more before it hardens into bone.

6709
Macdonald's Law: Never write a letter if you can help it, and never destroy one.

6710
A new Member requires the experience of his first session in the House to teach him how to hang up his overcoat and take his seat in a manner befitting a gentleman.

6711
When Fortune empties her chamberpot on your head, smile and say 'We are going to have a summer shower'.

MacDONALD Ramsay 1866-1937
6712 *(after forming the National Government)*
Tomorrow every Duchess in London will be wanting to kiss me!

6713
We hear war called murder. It is not: it is suicide.

MacDONALD Ross 1888-1964
6714
The walls of books around him, dense with the past, formed a kind of insulation against the present world and its disasters.

McEWAN Ian 1948-
6715 *The Child in Time*
Shakespeare would have grasped wave functions, Donne would have understood complementarity and relative time. They would have been excited. What richness! They would have plundered this new science for their imagery. And they would have educated their audiences too. But you 'arts' people, you're not only ignorant of these magnificent things, you're rather proud of knowing nothing.

McFEE William 1881-1966
6716
One must choose between Obscurity with Efficiency, and Fame with its inevitable collateral of Bluff.

6717
The world belongs to the enthusiast who keeps cool.

McGEACHY J.B.
6718
We sing about the North, but live as far south as possible.

McGINLEY Phyllis 1905-
6719
Nothing fails like success; nothing is so defeated as yesterday's triumphant cause.

6720
Not reading poetry amounts to a national pastime here.

McGOUGH Roger 1937-
6721 *'Comeclose and Sleepnow'*
You will put on a dress of guilt
and shoes with broken high ideals.

6722 *'Let Me Die a Youngman's Death'*
Let me die a youngman's death
Not a clean & in-between-
The-sheets, holy-water death,
Not a famous-last-words
Peaceful out-of-breath death.

6723 *'A lot of Water has Flown under your Bridge'*
i remember how
when we lay together for the first time
the room smiled,
said 'excuse me',
and tiptoed away.

McGREGOR Douglas 1906-1964
6724
Man is a wanting animal - as soon as one of his needs is satisfied, another appears in its place. This process is unending. It continues from birth to death.

McGREGOR Jimmy
6725 *'Football Crazy'*
Oh, he's football crazy, he's football mad
And the football it has robbed him o' the wee bit sense he had.

MacGREGOR Sir Ian 1912-
6726 *(during the coal-miners' strike)*
People are now discovering the price of insubordination and insurrection. And boy, are we going to make it stick!

McHUGH Vincent
6727
Self-expression is for babies and seals, where it can be charming. A writer's business is to affect the reader.

MacINNES Colm
6728
At rare moments in history, by a series of accidents never to be repeated, arise flower societies in which the cult of happiness is paramount, hedonistic, mindless, intent upon the glorious physical instant.

McINTYRE Leslie M.
6729
Nobody objects to a woman being a good writer or sculptor or geneticist if at the same time she manages to be a good wife, good mother, good looking, good tempered, well groomed and unaggressive.

MACKAY Charles 1814-1889
6730
There is no such thing as death,
In nature, nothing dies:
From each sad moment of decay
Some forms of life arise.

McKAY Claude 1890-1948
6731 *'If We Must Die'*
If we must die, let it not be like hogs
Hunted and penned in an inglorious spot,
While round us bark the mad and hungry dogs,
Making their mock at our accursed lot.

MACKENZIE Sir Compton 1883-1972
6732 *The Adventures of Sylvia Scarlett*
Prostitution. Selling one's body to keep one's soul: this is the meaning of the sins that were forgiven to the woman because she loved much: one might say of most marriages that they were selling one's soul to keep one's body.

6733 *Literature in My Time*
Women do not find it difficult nowadays to behave like men, but they often find it extremely difficult to behave like gentlemen.

6734 *Vestal Fire*
You are offered a piece of bread and butter that feels like a damp handkerchief and sometimes, when cucumber is added to it, like a wet one.

MACKENZIE William Lyon 1795-1861
6735
He is ... like many other geniuses, a greater friend to the bottle, than the bottle is to him.

MACKINTOSH Sir James 1765-1832
6736 *The Causes of the Revolution*
Disciplined inaction.

6737 *Dissertation on the Progress of Ethical Philosophy*
Men are never so good or so bad as their opinions.

6738 *Vindiciae Gallicae*
The Commons, faithful to their system, remained in a wise and masterly inactivity.

MACLAINE Shirley 1934-
6739
The best way to get husbands to do something is to suggest that perhaps they are too old to do it.

6740
When you look back ... on your love affairs ... what you really find out is that the only person you really go to bed with is yourself.

MACLAREN Alexander 1826-1910
6741 *Expositions of Holy Scripture: Acts of the Apostles*
'The Church is an anvil which has worn out many hammers', and the story of the first collision is, in essentials, the story of all.

McLAUGHLIN Mignon
6742
It's important to our friends to believe that we are unreservedly frank with them, and important to friendship that we are not.

6743
No one has ever loved anyone the way everyone wants to be loved.

6744
Every society honours its live conformists and its dead troublemakers.

6745
Our strength is often composed of the weakness that we're damned if we are going to show.

6746
We'd all like a reputation for generosity and we'd all like to buy it cheap.

McLEAN Don 1945-
6747 *'American Pie' (on death of Buddy Holly)*
I can't remember if I cried
When I read about his widowed bride.
Something touched me deep inside
The day the music died.

MacLEISH Archibald 1892-1982
6748 *'Ars Poetica'*
A Poem should be palpable and mute
As a globed fruit

Dumb
As old medallions to the thumb

Silent as the sleeve-worn stone
Of casement ledges where the moss has grown -
A poem should be wordless
As the flight of birds.

6749 *'Ars Poetica'*
A poem should not mean
But be.

6750
We have no choice but to be guilty,
God is unthinkable if we are innocent.

6751
The perversion of the mind is only possible when those who should be heard in its defence are silent.

6752
Around, around the sun we go:
The moon goes round the earth.
We do not die of death:
We die of vertigo.

MACLENNAN Hugh 1907-1990
6753
An artist has to take life as he finds it. Life by itself is formless wherever it is. Art must give it form.

6754
The farmer's way of saving money: to be owed by someone he trusted.

6755
A novel must be exceptionally good to live as long as the average cat.

McLEOD Fiona 1855-1905
6756 *'The Lonely Hunter'*
My heart is a lonely hunter that hunts on a lonely hill.

McLUHAN Marshall 1911-1980
6757
Ads are the cave art of the twentieth century.

6758
Art at its most significant is a Distant Early Warning System that can always be relied on to tell the old culture what is beginning to happen to it.

6759
Good taste is the first refuge of the non-creative. It is the last ditch stand of the artist.

6760 *The Gutenberg Galaxy*
The new electronic interdependence recreates the world in the image of a global village.

6761
One matter Englishmen don't think in the least funny is their happy consciousness of possessing a deep sense of humour.

6762
Money is the poor people's credit card.

6763
Publication is a self-invasion of privacy.

6764
Our sense of identity is our sense of density.

6765
A successful book cannot afford to be more than ten per cent new.

6766 *Understanding Media*
The medium is the message.

6767 *Understanding Media*
The name of a man is a numbing blow from which he never recovers.

6768 *Understanding Media*
The car has become an article of dress without which we feel uncertain, unclad and incomplete in the urban compound.

6769
Violence is the quest for identity. When identity disappears with technological innovation, violence is the natural recourse.

MACMAHON Comte de 1808-1893
6770 *(at taking of Malakoff fortress, Crimean War)*
J'y suis, j'y reste.
Here I am, and here I stay.

MACMILLAN Sir Harold 1894-1986
6771 *(on privatization, summarized as 'Selling off the family silver'*
First of all the Georgian silver goes, and then all that nice furniture that used to be in the saloon. Then the Canalettos go.

6772
You will find the Americans much as the Greeks found the Romans: great, big, vulgar, bustling people more vigorous than we are and also more idle, with more unspoiled virtues but also

more corrupt.

6773 *(of Aneurin Bevan)*
He enjoys prophesying the imminent fall of the capitalist system and is prepared to play a part, any part, in its burial, except that of mute.

6774 *(at Cape Town)*
The wind of change is blowing through this continent, and, whether we like it or not, this growth of [African] national consciousness is a political fact.

6775
Let us be frank about it: most of our people have never had it so good.

6776 *(on the life of a Foreign Secretary)*
Forever poised between a cliché and an indiscretion.

6777
I have never found, in a long experience of politics, that criticism is ever inhibited by ignorance.

6778 *(on the Profumo affair)*
I was determined that no British government should be brought down by the action of two tarts.

6779
It was a storm in a tea cup, but in politics we sail in paper boats.

6780
I thought the best thing to do was to settle up these little local difficulties [resignation of the Chancellor of the Exchequer and others], and then turn to the wider vision of the Commonwealth.

6781
There are three bodies no sensible man directly challenges: the Roman Catholic Church, the Brigade of Guards and the National Union of Mineworkers.

McNABB Vincent
6782
There are no short cuts to Heaven, only the ordinary way of ordinary things.

McNALLY Leonard 1752-1820
6783 *The Lass of Richmond Hill*
On Richmond Hill there lives a lass,
More sweet than May day morn,
Whose charms all other maids surpass,
A rose without a thorn.

MacNEICE Louis 1907-1963
6784 *Autumn Journal*
Better authentic mammon than a bogus god.

6785 *'Bagpipe Music'*
It's no go the merry-go-round, it's no go the rickshaw,
All we want is a limousine and a ticket for the peepshow.

6786 *'Bagpipe Music'*
It's no go the Government grants, it's no go the elections,
Sit on your arse for fifty years and hang your hat on a pension.

6787 *'Bagpipe Music'*
It's no go my honey love, it's no go my poppet;
Work your hands from day to day, the winds will blow the profit.
The glass is falling hour by hour, the glass will fall for ever,
But if you break the bloody glass you won't hold up the weather.

6788 *'The British Museum Reading Room'*
And under the totem poles - the ancient terror -
Between the enormous fluted Ionic columns
There seeps from heavily jowled or hawk-like foreign faces
The guttural sorrow of the refugees.

6789 *'Débâcle'*
Crumbling between the fingers, under the feet,
Crumbling behind the eyes,
Their world gives way and dies
And something twangs and breaks at the end of the street.

6790 *'Les Sylphides'*
So they were married - to be the more together -
And found they were never again so much together,
Divided by the morning tea,
By the evening paper,
By children and tradesmen's bills.

6791 *'Meeting Point'*
Time was away and somewhere else,
There were two glasses and two chairs
And two people with the one pulse
(Somebody stopped the moving stairs):
Time was away and somewhere else.

6792 *'Snow'*
World is crazier and more of it than we think,
Incorrigibly plural. I peel and portion
A tangerine and spit the pips and feel
The drunkenness of things being various.

6793 *'Sunday Morning'*
Down the road someone is practising scales,
The notes like little fishes vanish with a wink of tails,
Man's heart expands to tinker with his car
For this is Sunday morning, Fate's great bazaar.

6794 *'Sunlight on the Garden'*
The sunlight on the garden
Hardens and grows cold,
We cannot cage the minute
Within its net of gold,
When all is told
We cannot beg for pardon.

6795 *'Thalassa'*
By a high star our course is set,
Our end is Life. Put out to sea.

MacPHAIL Agnes 1890-1954
6796
Do not rely completely on any other human
being, however dear. We meet all life's greatest
tests alone.

McPHEE John
6797
Behind every tennis player there is another
tennis player.

McWILLIAM Candia
6798
With the birth of each child you lose two novels.

MACAULAY Baron (Thomas Babington) 1800-
1859
6799 *'The Armada'*
The rugged miners poured to war from
mendip's sunless caves.

6800 *'The Battle of Naseby'*
Obadiah Bind-their-kings-in-chains-and-their-
nobles-with-links-of-iron.

6801 *'The Battle of Naseby'*
Oh, wherefore come ye forth in triumph from
the north,
With your hands, and your feet, and your
raiment all red?
And wherefore doth your rout send forth a
joyous shout?
And whence be the grapes of the wine-press
which ye tread?

6802 *Biographical Essays 'Frederic the Great'*
In order that he might rob a neighbour whom
he had promised to defend, black men fought
on the coast of Coromandel, and red men
scalped each other by the Great Lakes of North
America.

6803
The English Bible, a book which, if everything
else in our language should perish, would alone
suffice to show the whole extent of its beauty
and power.

6804 *'Essay on Athenian Orators'*
The object of oratory alone is not truth, but
persuasion.

6805 *Essays ... 'Gladstone on Church and State'*
The rising hope of those stern and unbending
Tories.

6806 *Essays ... 'Hallam'*
The business of everybody is the business of
nobody.

6807 *Essays ... 'Hallam'*
The gallery in which the reporters sit has
become a fourth estate of the realm.

6808 *Essays ... 'Horace Walpole'*
The conformation of his mind was such that
whatever was little seemed to him great, and
whatever was great seemed to him little.

6809 *Essays ... 'Sir James Mackintosh'*
The highest intellects, like the tops of
mountains, are the first to catch and to reflect
the dawn.

6810 *Essays ... 'Sir James Mackintosh'*
The history of England is emphatically the
history of progress.

6811 *Essays ... 'John Hampden'*
He knew that the essence of war is violence, and
that moderation in war is imbecility.

6812 *Essays ... 'Lord Bacon'*
An acre in Middlesex is better than a
principality in Utopia.

6813 *Essays ... 'Lord Clive'*
Every schoolboy knows who imprisoned
Montezuma, and who strangled Atahualpa.

6814 *Essays ... 'Machiavelli'*
Out of his surname they have coined an epithet
for a knave, and out of his Christian name a
synonym for the Devil.

6815 *Essays ... 'Milton'*
As civilization advances, poetry almost
necessarily declines.

6816 *Essays ... 'Milton'*
If men are to wait for liberty till they become
wise and good in slavery, they may indeed wait
for ever.

6817 *Essays ... 'Milton' (about Puritans)*
Nobles by the right of an earlier creation, and
priests by the imposition of a mightier hand.

6818 *Essays ... 'Moore's - Life of Lord Byron'*
We know no spectacle so ridiculous as the
British public in one of its periodical fits of
morality.

6819 *Essays ... 'Moore's - Life of Lord Byron'*
From the poetry of Lord Byron they drew a
system of ethics, compounded of misanthropy
and voluptuousness, a system in which the two
great commandments were, to hate your
neighbour, and to love your neighbour's wife.

6820 *Essays ... (of Richard Steele)*
A rake among scholars, and a scholar among rakes.

6821 *Essays ... 'Samuel Johnson'*
The gigantic body, the huge massy face, seamed with the scars of disease, the brown coat, the black worsted stockings, the grey wig with the scorched foretop, the dirty hands, the nails bitten and pared to the quick.

6822 *Essays ... 'Samuel Johnson' (of writers)*
They knew luxury; they knew beggary; but they never knew comfort.

6823 *Essays ... 'Southey's Colloquies'*
We have heard it said that five per cent is the natural interest of money.

6824 *Essays ... 'Von Ranke'*
She [the Roman Catholic Church] may still exist in undiminished vigour when some traveller from New Zealand shall, in the midst of a vast solitude, take his stand on a broken arch of London Bridge to sketch the ruins of St Paul's.

6825 *Essays ... 'Von Ranke'*
She [the Church of Rome] thoroughly understands what no other church has ever understood, how to deal with enthusiasts.

6826 *Essays ... 'Warren Hastings'*
The Chief Justice was rich, quiet, and infamous.

6827 *Essays ... 'Warren Hastings'*
That temple of silence and reconciliation [Westminster Abbey] where the enmities of twenty generations lie buried.

6828 *Essays ... 'The War of Succession in Spain'*
The reluctant obedience of distant provinces generally costs more than it [the territory] is worth.

6829 *History of England*
I shall cheerfully bear the reproach of having descended below the dignity of history.

6830 *History of England*
Thus our democracy was, from an early period, the most aristocratic, and our aristocracy the most democratic in the world.

6831 *History of England*
The Puritan hated bear-baiting, not because it gave pain to the bear, but because it gave pleasure to the spectators.

6832 *History of England*
There were gentlemen and there were seamen in the navy of Charles the Second. But the seamen were not gentlemen; and the gentlemen were not seamen.

6833
An intellectual is someone whose mind watches itself.

6834 *'A Jacobite's Epitaph'*
To my true king I offered free from stain
Courage and faith; vain faith, and courage vain.

6835 *'A Jacobite's Epitaph'*
By those white cliffs I never more must see,
By that dear language which I spake like thee,
Forget all feuds, and shed one English tear
O'er English dust. A broken heart lies here.

6836 *(of John Dryden)*
His imagination resembled the wings of an ostrich. It enabled him to run, though not to soar.

6837
Knowledge advances by steps, and not by leaps.

6838 *Lays of Ancient Rome*
Let no man stop to plunder,
But slay, and slay, and slay;
The Gods who live for ever
Are on our side to-day.

6839 *Lays of Ancient Rome 'Horatius'*
Then out spake brave Horatius,
The Captain of the Gate:
'To every man upon this earth
Death cometh soon or late.
And how can man die better
Than facing fearful odds,
For the ashes of his fathers,
And the temples of his Gods?'

6840 *Lays of Ancient Rome 'Horatius'*
Now who will stand on either hand,
And keep the bridge with me?

6841 *Lays of Ancient Rome 'Horatius'*
Then none was for a party;
Then all were for the state;
The the great man helped the poor,
And the poor man loved the great:
Then lands were fairly portioned;
The spoils were fairly sold:
The Romans were like brothers
In the brave days of old.

6842 *Lays of Ancient Rome 'Horatius'*
Was none who would be foremost
To lead such dire attack;
But those behind cried 'Forward!'
And those before cried 'Back!'

6843 *Lays of Ancient Rome 'Horatius'*
Oh, Tiber! father Tiber
To whom the Romans pray,
A Roman's life, a Roman's arms,
Take thou in charge this day!

6844 *Lays of Ancient Rome 'Horatius'*
And even the ranks of Tuscany
Could scarce forbear to cheer.

6845 *Lays of Ancient Rome 'Horatius'*
With weeping and with laughter
Still is the story told,
How well Horatius kept the bridge
In the brave days of old.

6846 *Literary Essays 'Milton'*
Perhaps no person can be a poet, or can even
enjoy poetry, without a certain unsoundness of
mind.

6847
It seems that the creative faculty and the critical
faculty cannot exist together in their highest
perfection.

MACAULAY Dame Rose 1889-1958
6848
It was a book to kill time for those who like it
better dead.

6849 *Crewe Train*
Gentlemen know that fresh *air* should be kept
in its proper place - out of doors - and that, God
having given us indoors and out-of-doors, we
should not attempt to do away with this
distinction.

6850 *Poetry Review*
Poem me no poems.

6851 *The Towers of Trebizond*
'Take my camel, dear,' said my aunt Dot, as she
climbed down from this animal on her return
from High Mass.

6852
Women have one great advantage over men. It
is commonly thought that if they marry they
have done enough, and need career no further.
If a man marries, on the other hand, public
opinion is all against him if he takes this view.

MACHIAVELLI Niccolo 1469-1527
6853 *'Advice to Raffaello Girolami'*
And if, to be sure, sometimes you need to
conceal a fact with words, do it in such a way
that it does not become known, or, if it does
become known, that you have a ready and
quick defence.

6854 *(during the coal-miners' strike)*
Benefits should be granted little by little, so that
they may be better enjoyed.

6855 *Discourse - Livy*
It is necessary for him who lays out a state and
arranges laws for it to presuppose that all men
are evil and that they are always going to act
according to the wickedness of their spirits
whenever they have free scope.

6856
Men hesitate less to injure a man who makes
himself loved than to injure one who makes
himself feared, for their love is held by a chain
of obligation which, because of men's
wickedness, is broken on every occasion for the
sake of selfish profit; but their fear is secured by
a dread of punishment.

6857
Men are always wicked at bottom unless they
are made good by some compulsion.

6858 *The Prince*
Men should be either treated generously or
destroyed, because they take revenge for slight
injuries - for heavy ones they cannot.

6859 *The Prince*
It is much safer for a prince to be feared than
loved, if he is to fail in one of the two.

6860 *The Prince*
Let no one oppose this belief of mine with that
well-worn proverb: 'He who builds on the
people builds on mud'.

6861 *The Prince*
So long as the great majority of men are not
deprived of either property or honour, they are
satisfied.

6862 *The Prince*
There is no other way for securing yourself
against flatteries except that men understand
that they do not offend you by telling you the
truth; but when everybody can tell you the
truth, you fail to get respect.

6863
Where the willingness is great, the difficulties
cannot be great.

MACHLOWITZ Marilyn
6864
Because it is less structured than work, leisure
time leaves workaholics at a loss for what to do.
Workaholics practically climb the wall when
they can't work.

6865
Workaholics are energized rather than
enervated by their work - their energy
paradoxically expands as it is expended.

MACHLUP Fritz 1902-1983
6866
Let us remember the unfortunate
econometrician who, in one of the major
functions of his system, had to use a proxy for
risk and a dummy for sex.

MADAN Geoffrey 1895-1947
6867
Attractive Etonians who go straight onto the

Stock Exchange missing University on their fathers' advice: the raw material of the great bores.

6868
The cat which isn't let out of the bag often becomes a skeleton in the cupboard.

6869
Conservative ideal of freedom and progress: everyone to have an unfettered opportunity of remaining exactly where they are.

6870
The great tragedy of the classical languages is to have been born twins.

6871
King George, passing slowly in a closed car, looking like a big, rather worn *penny* in the window.

6872 *Livre sans nom: Twelve Reflections*
The dust of exploded beliefs may make a fine sunset.

6873
I love drink, so long as it isn't in moderation.

6874
A marquis is a sort of four-move chess problem.

6875
Peers: a kind of eye-shade or smoked glass, to protect us from the full glare of Royalty.

6876
To say you should treat a duke as an ordinary man is like telling you to read the Bible like an ordinary book.

MADARIAGA Salvador de 1886-1978
6877 *Morning Without Noon*
Since, in the main, it is not armaments that cause wars but wars (or the fears thereof) that cause armaments, it follows that every nation will at every moment strive to keep its armament in an efficient state as required by its fear, otherwise styled security.

MADDEN Samuel 1686-1765
6878 *Boulter's Monument*
Words are men's daughters, but God's sons are things.

MADISON James 1751-1836
6879 *The Federalist*
Liberty is to faction what air is to fire, an ailment without which it instantly expires. But it could not be less folly to abolish liberty, which is essential to political life, because it nourishes faction than it would be to wish the annihilation of air, which is essential to animal life, because it imparts to fire its destructive agency.

MADONNA 1959-
6880
The definition of S & M is letting someone hurt you that you know would never hurt you.

MAETERLINCK Maurice 1862-1949
6881
What man is there that does not laboriously, though all unconsciously, himself fashion the sorrow that is to be the pivot of his life.

MAGARY James
6882
Computers can figure out all kinds of problems, except the things in the world that just don't add up.

MAGEE William Connor 1821-1891
6883 *(on the Intoxicating Liquor Bill)*
It would be better that England should be free than that England should be compulsorily sober.

MAGNA CARTA 1215
6884 *Clause 1*
That the English Church shall be free.

6885 *Clause 39*
No free man shall be taken or imprisoned or dispossessed, or outlawed or exiled, or in any way destroyed, nor will we go upon him, nor will we send against him except by the lawful judgement of his peers or by the law of the land.

6886 *Clause 40*
To no man will we sell, or deny, or delay, right or justice.

MAHAN Alfred Thayer 1840-1914
6887
Force is never more operative than when it is known to exist but is not brandished.

MAHBUBANI Kishore
6888
To have good Government you often need less, not more, democracy.

MAHLER Gustav 1860-1911
6889 *(on seeing Niagara Falls)*
Fortissimo at last!

MAHON Derek 1941-
6890 *Antarctica (title poem)*
'I am just going outside and may be some time.'
The others nod, pretending not to know.
At the heart of the ridiculous, the sublime.

MAILER Norman 1923-
6891 *A Fire on the Moon*
The horror of the Twentieth Century was the size of each event, and the paucity of its reverberation.

6892
The highest prize in a world of men is the most beautiful woman available on your arm and living there in her heart loyal to you.

6893 *Marilyn*
Marilyn who was every man's love affair with America, Marilyn Monroe who was blonde and beautiful and had a sweet little rinky-dink of a voice and all the cleanliness of all the clean American backyards.

6894 *The Presidential Papers*
Ultimately a hero is a man who would argue with the Gods, and so awakens devils to contest his vision.

6895
With the pride of the artist, you must blow against the walls of every power that exists, the small trumpet of your defiance.

6896
The private terror of the liberal spirit is invariably suicide, not murder.

6897
I think it's bad to talk about one's present work, for it spoils something at the root of the creative act. It discharges the tension.

6898 *Voices of Dissent*
Hip is the sophistication of the wise primitive in a giant jungle.

MAINE Sir Henry 1822-1888
6899 *Ancient Law*
The movement of the progressive societies has hitherto been a movement *from Status to Contract.*

6900 *Village Communities*
Except the blind forces of Nature, nothing moves in this world which is not Greek in its origin.

MAISTRE Josephe de 1753-1821
6901 *Lettres et Opuscules Inédits*
Every country has the government it deserves.

MAJOR John 1943-
6902
I am a coalition government on my own.

6903
I am more a European in my head than in my heart.

6904
I am fit, I am well, I am here - I am staying.

6905
Good order brings good learning.

6906
Society needs to condemn a little more and understand a little less.

6907
It is time to get back to basics; to self-discipline and respect for the law, to consideration for others, to accepting responsibility for yourself and your family, and not shuffling it off on the state.

6908
My trade has never been in adjectives.

MALAMUD Bernard 1914-1986
6909 *Dublin's Lives*
The past exudes legend: one can't make pure clay of time's mud. There is no life that can be recaptured wholly; as it was. Which is to say that all biography is ultimately fiction.

MALCOLM Janet
6910
If you scratch a great photograph, you find two things: a painting and a photograph.

MALHERBE François de 1555-1628
6911 *(on his death bed, to a priest)*
Stop, Sir, stop - go away: I cannot bear your style.

MALLARMÉ Stéphane 1842-1898
6912 *'Brise Marin'*
The flesh, alas, is wearied; and I have read all the books there are.

6913 *Plusieurs Sonnets*
That virgin, vital, fine day: today.

6914
Prélude à l'après-midi d'un faune.
Prelude to the afternoon of a fawn.

6915
A throw of the dice will never eliminate chance.

MALLET (or MALLOCH) David c.1705-1765
6916 *'Imitation of Horace'*
O grant me, Heaven, a middle state,
Neither too humble nor too great;
More than enough, for nature's ends,
With something left to treat my friends.

MALLORY George Leigh 1886-1924
6917 *(on being asked why he wanted to climb Everest)*
Because it's there.

MALONE Dudley Field
6918
I have never in my life learned anything from any man who agreed with me.

MALONEY Martin
6919
If anything is poisoning our lives and weakening our society, it is reality - and not the fabrication of television writers and producers.

MALORY Sir Thomas d.1471
6920 *Le Morte D'Arthur*
Whoso pulleth out this sword of this stone and
anvil is rightwise King born of all England.

6921 *Le Morte D'Arthur*
God defend me, said Dinadan, for the joy of
love is too short, and the sorrow thereof, and
what cometh thereof, dureth over long.

6922 *Le Morte D'Arthur*
Through this man and me hath all this war been
wrought, and the death of the most noblest
knights of the world; for through our love that
we have loved together is my most noble lord
slain.

6923 *Le Morte D'Arthur*
This beast went to the well and drank, and the
noise was in the beast's belly like unto the
questing of thirty couple hounds, but all the
while the beast drank there was no noise in the
beast's belly.

6924 *Le Morte D'Arthur*
So they rode till they came to a lake that was a
fair water and broad. And in the midst Arthur
was ware of an arm clothed in white samite,
that held a fair sword in that hand.

6925 *Le Morte D'Arthur*
The month of May was come, when every lusty
heart beginneth to blossom, and to bring forth
fruit.

6926 *Le Morte D'Arthur*
For love that time was not as love is nowadays.

6927 *Le Morte D'Arthur*
And much more am I sorrier for my good
knights' loss than for the loss of my fair queen;
for queens I might have enough, but such a
fellowship of good knights shall never be
together in no company.

6928 *Le Morte D'Arthur*
For as well as I have loved thee heretofore, mine
heart will not serve now to see thee; for through
thee and me is the flower of kings and knights
destroyed.

MALRAUX André 1901-1976
6929
All art is a revolt against man's fate.

6930
La Condition humaine.
The human condition.

6931 *Les Noyers d'Altenburg*
Man knows that the world is not made on a
human scale; and he wishes that it were.

6932 *L'Espoir*
There are not fifty ways of fighting, there's only
one, and that's to win. Neither revolution nor
war consists in doing what one pleases.

6933 *Les Voix du silence*
Art is a revolt against fate.

6934
Man is a dog's ideal of what God should be.

6935
The mind supplies the idea of a nation, but
what gives this idea its sentimental force is a
community of dreams.

MALTHUS Thomas Robert 1766-1834
6936 *Essay on the Principle of Population*
Population, when unchecked, increases in a
geometrical ratio. Subsistence only increases in
an arithmetical ratio.

6937 *Essay on the Principle of Population*
The perpetual struggle for room and food.

MAMET David 1947-
6938
Writing is not a political tool. Drama never
changed anybody's mind.

MANCROFT Lord 1957-
6939 *Bees in Some Bonnets*
Cricket - a game which the English, not being a
spiritual people, have invented in order to give
themselves some conception of eternity.

MANDALE W.R.
6940 *'Pop Goes the Weasel'*
Up and down the City Road,
In and out the Eagle,
That's the way the money goes -
Pop goes the weasel!

MANDELA Winnie 1934-
6941
With that stick of matches, with our necklace,
we shall liberate this country.

MANDELSON Peter 1953-
6942
Defeat brings its own humility, which is not a
bad thing for everyone to taste, especially a
politician.

MANDELSTAM Osip 1892-1938
6943 *'The Age'(translated by C.M. Bowra)*
The age is rocking the wave
with human grief
to a golden beat, and an adder
is breathing in time with it in the grass.

The buds will go on swelling,
the rush of green will explode,
but your spine has been shattered,
my splendid derelict, my age.
Cruel and feeble, you'll look back
with the smile of a half-wit:
an animal that could run once,

staring at its own tracks.

6944 *Selected Poems (translated by D. McDuff)*
Perhaps my whisper was already born before
my lips.

6945 *'Tristia'(translated by C.M. Bowra)*
I've studied all the lore of separation
From grievances bare-headed in the night.

6946 *'Tristia'(translated by C.M. Bowra)*
Only in war our fate has consummation,
And divination too will perish them.

MANET Edouard 1832-1883
6947
The country has charms only for those not
obliged to stay there.

MANION Clarence C.
6948
The average man that I encounter all over the
country regards government as a sort of great
milk cow, with its head in the clouds eating air,
and growing a full teat for everybody on earth.

MANLEY Mrs 1663-1724
6949 *The Lost Lover*
No time like the present.

MANN Horace 1796-1859
6950
Character is what God and the angels know of
us; reputation is what men and women think of
us.

6951 *'Lost, Two Golden Hours'*
Lost, yesterday, somewhere between Sunrise
and Sunset, two golden hours, each set with
sixty diamond minutes. No reward is offered,
for they are gone forever.

6952
We put things in order - God does the rest. Lay
an iron bar east and west, it is not magnetized.
Lay it north and south and it is.

MANN Thomas 1875-1955
6953 *The Confessions of Felix Krull*
Our capacity for disgust, let me observe, is in
proportion of our desires; that is in proportion
to the intensity of our attachment to the things
of this world.

6954
Habituation is a falling asleep or fatiguing of the
sense of time; which explains why young years
pass slowly, while later life flings itself faster and
faster upon its course.

6955
Human reason needs only to will more strongly
than fate, and she *is* fate.

6956
A human being who is first of all an invalid is all
body; therein lies his inhumanity and his
debasement.

6957 *The Magic Mountain*
Time has no divisions to mark its passage, there
is never a thunderstorm or blare of trumpets to
announce the beginning of a new month or
year. Even when a new century begins it is only
we mortals who ring bells and fire off pistols.

6958 *The Magic Mountain*
Waiting we say is long. We might just as well -
or more accurately - say it is short, since it
consumes whole spaces of time without our
living them or making any use of them as such.

6959 *The Magic Mountain*
We come out of the dark and go into the dark
again, and in between lie the experiences of our
life. But the beginning and end, birth and
death, we do not experience; they have no
subjective character, they fall entirely in the
category of objective events, and that's that.

6960 *The Magic Mountain*
A man's dying is more the survivors' affair than
his own.

6961
Opinions cannot survive if one has no chance
to fight for them.

6962
Speech is civilization itself. The word, even the
most contradictory word, preserves contact - it
is silence which isolates.

6963
Time cools, time clarifies; no mood can be
maintained quite unaltered through the course
of hours.

6964
He who loves the more is the inferior and must
suffer.

MANNERS Lord John 1818-1906
6965 *England's Trust*
Let wealth and commerce, laws and learning
die,
But leave us still our old nobility!

MANNES Marya
6966
To lead means to direct and to exact, and no
man dares do either - he might be unpopular.
What authority we are given now is a trinity: the
grin, the generality, and God (the Word).

6967
The sign of an intelligent people is their ability
to control emotions by the application of
reason.

MANSFIELD Katherine 1888-1923
6968 *Journal*
E.M. Forster never gets any further than
warming the teapot. He's a rare fine hand at
that. Feel this teapot. Is it not beautifully
warm? Yes, but there ain't going to be no tea.

6969 *Journal*
Whenever I prepare for a journey I prepare as
though for death. Should I never return, all is in
order.

6970 *Letter to John Middleton Murray*
I hate the sort of licence that English people
give themselves ... to spread over and flop and
roll about. I feel as fastidious as though I wrote
with acid.

6971
Make it a rule of life never to regret and never
look back. Regret is an appalling waste of
energy; you can't build on it; it's good only for
wallowing in.

MAO TSE-TUNG 1893-1976
6972
The atom bomb is a paper tiger which the
United States reactionaries use to scare people.
It looks terrible, but in fact it isn't ... All
reactionaries are paper tigers.

6973
Every Communist must grasp the truth,
'Political power grows out of the barrel of a gun'.

6974
The guerilla must live amongst the people as
the fish lives in the water.

6975
Letting a hundred flowers blossom and a
hundred schools of thought contend is the
policy for promoting progress in the arts and
the sciences and a flourishing socialist culture
in our land.

6976
Politics is war without bloodshed while war is
politics with bloodshed.

MARCEAU Marcel 1923-
6977
Dance is in the air ... Mime is on the floor.

MARCY William Learned 1786-1857
6978
The politicians of New York ... see nothing
wrong in the rule, that to the victor belong the
spoils of the enemy.

MARGOLYES Miriam 1941-
6979
Life, if you're fat, is a minefield - you have to
pick your way, otherwise you blow up.

MARIE Queen of Rumania
6980
Between husband and wife a shadow of
courtship should always subsist.

6981
When a man loves his children with an excess of
passion, be sure that he is not happy.

6982
A woman's virtue ought indeed to be great:
since it often has to suffice for two.

6983
Fashion exists for women with no taste,
etiquette for people with no breeding.

MARIE-ANTOINETTE Queen 1755-1793
6984 *(on being told that her people had no
bread)*
Qu'ils mangent de la brioche.
Let them eat cake.

MARKEL Lester
6985
What you see is news, what you know is
background, what you feel is opinion.

MARKHAM Edwin 1852-1940
6986 *'The Man with the Hoe'*
Bowed by the weight of centuries he leans
Upon his hoe and gazes on the ground,
The emptiness of ages in his face,
And on his back the burden of the world.
Who made him dead to rapture and despair,
A thing that grieves not and that never hopes,
Stolid and stunned, a brother to the ox?

MARKS Johnny 1909-1985
6987 *'Rudolph, the Red-Nosed Reindeer'*
Rudolph, the Red-Nosed Reindeer
Had a very shiny nose,
And if you ever saw it,
You would even say it glows.

MARLEY Bob 1945-1981
6988 *'I Shot the Sheriff'*
I shot the sheriff
But I swear it was in self-defence
I shot the sheriff
And they say it is a capital offence.

6989 *'Get up, Stand up'*
Get up, stand up
Stand up for your rights
Get up, stand up
Never give up the fight.

MARLOWE Christopher 1564-1593
6990 *Doctor Faustus*
Sweet Analytics, 'tis thou hast ravished me.

6991 *Doctor Faustus*
I'll have them fly to India for gold,
Ransack the ocean for orient pearl.

6992 *Doctor Faustus*
Hell hath no limits nor is circumscribed
In one self place, where we are is Hell,
And to be short, when all the world dissolves,
· And every creature shall be purified,
All places shall be hell that are not heaven.

6993 *Doctor Faustus*
Was this the face that launched a thousand ships,
And burnt the topless towers of Ilium?
Sweet Helen, make me immortal with a kiss!
Her lips suck forth my soul: see, where it flies!
Come Helen, come give me my soul again.
Here will I dwell, for heaven be in these lips,
And all is dross that is not Helena.

6994 *Doctor Faustus*
Now hast thou but one bare hour to live,
And then thou must be damned perpetually.
Stand still, you ever-moving spheres of heaven,
That time may cease, and midnight never come.
Fair nature's eye, rise, rise again and make
Perpetual day; or let this hour be but
A year, a month, a week, a natural day
That Faustus may repent and save his soul.

6995 *Doctor Faustus*
O lente lente currite noctis equi.
The stars move still, time runs, the clock will strike,
The devil will come, and Faustus must be damned.
O I'll leap up to my God: who pulls me down?
See, see, where Christ's blood streams in the firmament.
One drop would save my soul, half a drop, ah my Christ.

6996 *Doctor Faustus*
You stars that reigned at my nativity,
Whose influence hath allotted death and hell,
Now draw up Faustus like a foggy mist ...

6997 *Doctor Faustus*
O soul, be changed into little water drops,
And fall into the ocean, ne'er be found:
My God, my God, look not so fierce on me.

6998 *Doctor Faustus*
Oh, thou art fairer than the evening air
Clad in the beauty of a thousand stars.

6999 *Doctor Faustus*
Ugly hell, gape not! come not, Lucifer!
I'll burn my books!

7000 *Doctor Faustus*
Cut is the branch that might have grown full straight,
And burnèd is Apollo's laurel-bough,
That sometime grew within this learnèd man.

7001 *Edward II*
My men, like satyrs grazing on the lawns,
Shall with their goat feet dance an antic hay.

7002 *Edward II*
Stand still you watches of the element;
All times and seasons, rest you at a stay,
That Edward may be still fair England's king.

7003 *Hero and Leander*
Who ever loved that loved not at first sight?

7004 *Hero and Leander*
And as she wept, her tears to pearl he turned,
And wound them on his arm, and for her mourned.

7005 *Hero and Leander*
Like untun'd golden strings all women are
Which long time lie untouch'd, will harshly jar.

7006 *The Jew of Malta*
I count religion but a childish toy,
And hold there is no sin but ignorance.

7007 *The Jew of Malta*
Thus methinks should men of judgement frame
Their means of traffic from the vulgar trade,
And, as their wealth increaseth, so enclose
Infinite riches in a little room.

7008 *The Jew of Malta*
As for myself, I walk abroad o'nights
And kill sick people groaning under walls:
Sometimes I go about and poison wells.

7009 *The Jew of Malta*
BARNARDINE: Thou hast committed-
BARABAS: Fornication? But that was in another
Country: and besides, the wench is dead.

7010 *The Massacre at Paris*
That like I best, that flies beyond my reach.

7011 *The Passionate Shepherd to his Love*
And I will make thee beds of roses
And a thousand fragrant posies.

7012 *Tamburlaine the Great*
From jigging veins of rhyming mother-wits,
And such conceits as clownage keeps in pay,
We'll lead you to the stately tents of war.

7013 *Tamburlaine the Great*
Our swords shall play the orators for us.

7014 *Tamburlaine the Great*
Accurst be he that first invented war.

7015 *Tamburlaine the Great*
Is it not passing fair to be a king,
And ride in triumph through Persepolis?

7016 *Tamburlaine the Great*
Nature that framed us of four elements,
Warring within our breasts for regiment,

Doth teach us all to have aspiring minds.

7017 *Tamburlaine the Great*
Virtue is the fount whence honour springs.

7018 *Tamburlaine the Great*
Ah fair Zenocrate, divine Zenocrate,
Fair is too foul an epithet for thee.

7019 *Tamburlaine the Great*
Now walk the angels on the walls of heaven,
As sentinels to warn th'immortal souls,
To entertain divine Zenocrate.

7020 *Tamburlaine the Great*
Yet let me kiss my Lord before I die,
And let me die with kissing of my Lord.

7021 *Tamburlaine the Great*
More childish valorous than manly wise.

7022 *Tamburlaine the Great*
Holla, ye pampered jades of Asia!
What, can ye draw but twenty miles a day?

MARQUEZ Gabriel Garcia 1928-
7023
While a person does not give up on sex, sex
does not give up on the person.

MARQUIS Don 1878-1937
7024 *archy does his part*
boss there is always
a comforting thought
in time of trouble when
it is not our trouble.

7025 *archy and mehitabel*
procrastination is the
art of keeping
up with yesterday.

7026 *archy and mehitabel*
an optimist is a guy
that has never had
much experience.

7027 *archy and mehitabel*
but wotthehell wotthehell
oh i should worry and fret
death and I will coquette
there's a dance in the old dame yet
toujours gai toujours gai.

7028 *archys life of mehitabel*
honesty is a good
thing but
it is not profitable to
its possessor
unless it is
kept under control.

7029 *archys life of mehitabel*
did you ever
notice that when
a politician

does get an idea
he usually
gets it all wrong.

7030 *archys life of mehitabel*
now and then
there is a person born
who is so unlucky
that he runs into accidents
which started to happen
to somebody else.

7031
The art of newspaper paragraphing is to stroke
a platitude until it purrs like an epigram.

7032
Happiness comes fleetingly now and then,
To those who have learned to do without it
And to them only.

7033
Happiness is the interval between periods of
unhappiness.

7034
Ours is a world where people don't know what
they want and are willing to go through hell to
get it.

7035
Pity the meek for they shall inherit the earth.

7036
The successful people are the ones who think
up things for the rest of the world to keep busy
at.

7037
Writing a book of poetry is like dropping a rose
petal down the Grand Canyon and waiting for
the echo.

MARRIOT John 1780-1825
7038 *'Thou, whose eternal Word'*
Thou, whose eternal Word
Chaos and darkness heard,
And took their flight,
Hear us, we humbly pray,
And, where the Gospel-day
Sheds not its glorious ray,
Let there be light!

MARRYAT Captain Frederick 1792-1848
7039 *Japhet, in Search of a Father*
There's no getting blood out of a turnip.

7040 *The King's Own*
As savage as a bear with a sore head.

7041 *Mr Midshipman Easy*
All zeal ... all zeal, Mr Easy.

7042 *Mr Midshipman Easy (of an illegitimate baby)*
If you please, ma'am, it was a very little one.

7043 *Settlers in Canada*
Every man paddle his own canoe.

MARSHALL Herbert
7044
There's nothing an economist should fear so much as applause.

MARSHALL John 1755-1835
7045
The power to tax involves the power to destroy.

MARSHALOV Boris
7046
Congress is so strange. A man gets up to speak and says nothing. Nobody listens, then everybody disagrees.

MARSTON John 1576-1634
7047 *Satire VII*
'A man, a man!' 'Peace, Cynic, yon is one:
A complete soul of all perfection.'
'What, mean'st thou him that walks all open-breasted,
Drawn through the ear, with ribands, plumy-crested;
He that doth snort in fat-fed luxury,
And gapes for some grinding monopoly;
He that in effeminate invention,
In beastly source of all pollution,
In riot, lust, and fleshly seeming sweetness,
Sleeps sound, secure, under the shade of greatness?

7048 *The Scourge of Villainy*
Foul canker of fair virtuous action,
Vile blaster of the freshest blooms on earth,
Envy's abhorrèd child, Detraction ...

7049 *The Scourge of Villainy*
My mind disdains the dungy muddy scum
Of abject thoughts and Envy's raging hate.

MARTIAL AD c.40-c.104
7050 *Epigrammata*
Believe me, wise men don't say 'I shall live to do that', tomorrow's life's too late; live today.

7051 *Epigrammata*
I don't love you Sabidius, and I can't tell you why;
All I can tell you is this, that I don't love you.

7052 *Epigrammata*
They praise those works, but read these.

7053 *Epigrammata*
Life's not just being alive, but being well.

7054 *Epigrammata*
Difficult or easy, pleasant or bitter, you are the same you: I cannot live with you - or without you.

7055 *Epigrammata*
Rus in urbe.
Country in the town.

7056
Lawyers are men who hire out their words and anger.

MARTIN Dean 1917-1995
7057
Marriage is not a word but a sentence.

MARTINDELL Jackson
7058
Capital is past savings accumulated for future production.

MARTINEAU Harriet 1802-1876
7059 *Society in America*
Anyone must see at a glance that if men and women marry those whom they do not love, they must love those whom they do not marry.

MARTINEZ Jacinto Benaventey
7060
When one admires an artist it is important not to know him personally.

MARTIN Pete
7061 *(after his Bank's computer had doubled all clients' deposits)*
The hazards of computing are limited only by your imagination.

MARTIN-WIELAND Christoph
7062
An illusion which makes me happy is worth a verity which drags me to the ground.

MARVELL Andrew 1621-1678
7063 *'Upon Appleton House'*
What luckless apple did we taste,
To make us mortal, and thee waste?

7064 *'Upon Appleton House'*
Unhappy birds! what does it boot
To build below the grass's root,
When lowness is unsafe as height,
And chance o'ertakes, what 'scapeth spite?

7065 *'Upon Appleton House'*
'Tis not what once it was, the world,
But a rude heap together hurled.

7066 *'Upon Appleton House'*
But now the salmon-fishers moist
Their leathern boats begin to hoist;
And, like Antipodes in shoes,
Have shod their heads in their canoes.

7067 *'Bermudas'*
Where the remote Bermudas ride
In the ocean's bosom unespied.

7068 *'Bermudas'*
He hangs in shades the orange bright,
Like golden lamps in a green night.

7069 *'Bermudas'*
And makes the hollow seas, that roar,
Proclaim the ambergris on shore.
He cast (of which we rather boast)
The gospel's pearl upon our coast.

7070 *'To His Coy Mistress'*
Had we but world enough, and time,
This coyness, lady, were no crime.

7071 *'To His Coy Mistress'*
I would
Love you ten years before the flood:
And you should, if you please, refuse
Till the conversion of the Jews
My vegetable love should grow
Vaster than empires, and more slow.

7072 *'To His Coy Mistress'*
But at my back I always hear
Time's wingèd chariot hurrying near:
And yonder all before us lie
Deserts of vast eternity.
Thy beauty shall no more be found;
Nor, in thy marble vault, shall sound
My echoing song; then worms shall try
That long preserved virginity:
And your quaint honour turn to dust;
And into ashes all my lust.
The grave's a fine and private place,
But none, I think, do there embrace.

7073 *'To His Coy Mistress'*
Let us roll all our strength, and all
Our sweetness, up into one ball:
And tear our pleasures with rough strife,
Thorough the iron gates of life.
Thus, though we cannot make our sun
Stand still, yet we will make him run.

7074 *'The Definition of Love'*
My love is of a birth as rare
As 'tis for object strange and high:
It was begotten by Despair
Upon Impossibility.

Magnanimous Despair alone
Could show me so divine a thing.
Where feeble Hope could ne'er have flown
But vainly flapped its tinsel wing.

7075 *'The Definition of Love'*
As lines (so loves) oblique may well
Themselves in every angle greet:
But ours so truly parallel,
Though infinite, can never meet.

Therefore the love which us doth bind,
But Fate so enviously debars,
Is the conjunction of the mind,

And opposition of the stars.

7076 *'The First Anniversary of the Government...'*
Choosing each stone, and poising every weight,
Trying the measures of the breadth and height;
Here pulling down, and there erecting new,
Founding a firm state by proportions true.

7077 *'The Garden'*
How vainly men themselves amaze
To win the palm, the oak, or bays,
And their uncessant labours see
Crowned from some single herb or tree.

7078 *'The Garden'*
Fair Quiet, have I found thee here,
And Innocence, thy sister dear!

7079 *'The Garden'*
Society is all but rude,
To this delicious solitude.

7080 *'The Garden'*
Stumbling on melons, as I pass,
Ensnared with flowers, I fall on grass.

7081 *'The Garden'*
Meanwhile the mind, from pleasure less,
Withdraws into its happiness.

7082 *'The Garden'*
Annihilating all that's made
To a green thought in a green shade.

7083 *'The Garden'*
Here at the fountain's sliding foot,
Or at some fruit-tree's mossy root,
Casting the body's vest aside,
My soul into the boughs does glide.

7084 *'The Garden'*
Such was the happy garden-state,
While man there walked without a mate.

7085 *'The Garden'*
But 'twas beyond a mortal's share
To wander solitary there:
Two paradises 'twere in one
To live in paradise alone.

7086 *'An Horatian Ode upon Cromwell's Return from Ireland'*
He nothing common did or mean
Upon that memorable scene:
But with his keener eye
The axe's edge did try.

7087 *'An Horatian Ode upon Cromwell's Return...'*
And now the Irish are ashamed
To see themselves in one year tamed:
So much one man can do,
That does both act and know.

7088 *'The Mower to the Glow-worms'*
Ye country comets, that portend
No war, nor prince's funeral,
Shining unto no higher end
Than to presage the grass's fall.

7089 *'The Nymph Complaining for the Death of her Fawn'*
I have a garden of my own
But so with roses overgrown,
And lilies, that you would it guess
To be a little wilderness.

7090 *'The Nymph Complaining for the Death of her Fawn'*
Had it lived long, it would have been
Lilies without, roses within.

7091 *'The Statue in Stocks-Market' (of Charles II)*
For though the whole world cannot show such another,
Yet we'd better by far have him than his brother.

MARX Chico 1891-1961
7092 *(when discovered by his wife with a chorus girl)*
I wasn't kissing her, I was just whispering in her mouth.

MARX Groucho 1895-1977
7093 *(attributed)*
A man is only as old as the woman he feels.

7094
One of the best hearing aids a man can have is an attentive wife.

7095 *in The Coconuts*
"Your eyes shine like the pants of my blue serge suit."

7096 *in A Day at the Races*
"Either he's dead, or my watch has stopped."

7097 *in A Day at the Races*
"I've never been so insulted in my life..."
" Well, it's early yet."

7098 *in Duck Soup*
"Remember, you're fighting for this woman's honour ... which is probably more than she ever did."

7099 *in Duck Soup*
"If you can't leave in a taxi you can leave in a huff. If that's too soon, you can leave in a minute and a huff."

7100 *Groucho and Me*
Please accept my resignation. I don't want to belong to any club that will accept me as a member.

7101
The husband who wants a happy marriage should learn to keep his mouth shut and his chequebook open.

7102
I never forget a face, but in your case I'll make an exception.

7103 *in A Night in Casablanca*
"Send two dozen roses to Room 424 and put 'Emily, I love you' on the back of the bill."

7104
Politics doesn't make strange bedfellows, marriage does.

7105
There is one way to find out if a man is honest - ask him. If he says 'yes,' you know he is crooked.

MARX Karl 1818-1883
7106 *A Contribution... Hegel's Philosophy of Right*
Religion ... is the opium of the people.

7107 *A Contribution ... of Political Economy*
Mankind always sets itself only such problems as it can solve; since, looking at the matter more closely, it will always be found that the task itself arises only when the material conditions for its solution already exist or are at least in the process of formation.

7108 *A Contribution ... of Political Economy*
It is not the consciousness of men that determines their being, but, on the contrary, their social being that determines their consciousness.

7109 *Critique of the Gotha Programme*
From each according to his abilities, to each according to his needs.

7110 *The Eighteenth Brumaire of Louis Bonaparte*
Hegel says somewhere that all great events and personalities in world history reappear in one fashion or another. He forgot to add: the first time as tragedy, the second as farce.

7111
The more of himself man attributes to God, the less he has left in himself.

7112 *Theses on Feuerbach*
The philosophers have only interpreted the world in various ways; the point is to change it.

7113
What I did that was new was to prove ... that the class struggle necessarily leads to the dictatorship of the proletariat.

MARX Karl and ENGELS Friedrich 1818-1883 and 1820-1895
7114 *The Communist Manifesto*
A spectre is haunting Europe - the spectre of

Communism.

7115 *The Communist Manifesto*
The history of all hitherto existing society is the
history of class struggles.

7116 *The Communist Manifesto*
In place of the old bourgeois society, with its
classes and class antagonists, we shall have an
association, in which the free development of
each is the free development of all.

7117 *The Communist Manifesto*
The proletarians have nothing to lose but their
chains. They have a world to win. WORKING
MEN OF ALL COUNTRIES, UNITE!

MARY I, Queen (Mary Tudor) 1516-1558
7118
When I am dead and opened, you shall find
'Calais' lying in my heart.

MARY Queen 1867-1953
7119 *Letter to the Duke of Windsor*
I do not think you have ever realised the shock,
which the attitude you took up caused your
family and the whole nation. It seemed
inconceivable to those who had made such
sacrifices during the war that you, as their King,
refused a lesser sacrifice.

MARY Princess
7120
Go in in front of Royalty: but never pass in front
of them.

MARY Queen 1867-1953
7121 *(after abdication of her son, King Edward
VIII)*
All *this* thrown away for *that*.

MARY Queen of Scots 1542-1587
7122 *(motto)*
En ma fin git mon commencement.
In my end is my beginning.

MASARYK Jan 1886-1948
7123
Dictators are rulers who always look good until
the last ten minutes.

MASCHWITZ Eric 1901-1969
7124 *'These Foolish Things Remind Me of You'*
A cigarette that bears a lipstick's traces
An airline ticket to romantic places;
And still my heart has wings
These foolish things
Remind me of you.

MASEFIELD John 1878-1967
7125
An art in which the artist by means of rhythm
and great sincerity can convey to others the
sentiment which he feels about life.

7126 *Captain Stratton's Fancy*
Oh some are fond of Spanish wine, and some
are fond of French.

7127 *'Cargoes'*
Quinquireme of Nineveh from distant Ophir
Rowing home to haven in sunny Palestine,
With a cargo of ivory,
And apes and peacocks,
Sandalwood, cedarwood, and sweet white wine.

7128 *'Cargoes'*
Dirty British coaster with a salt-caked smoke
stack,
Butting through the Channel in the mad March
days,
With a cargo of Tyne coal,
Road-rails, pig lead,
Firewood, ironware, and cheap tin trays.

7129
Once in a century a man may be ruined or
made insufferable by praise. But surely once a
minute something generous dies for want of it.

7130 *'C.L.M.'*
In the dark womb where I began
My mother's life made me a man.
Through all the months of human birth
Her beauty fed my common earth.
I cannot see, nor breathe, nor stir,
But through the death of some of her.

7131 *'The Everlasting Mercy'*
The corn that makes the holy bread
By which the soul of man is fed,
The holy bread, the food unpriced,
Thy everlasting mercy, Christ.

7132 *Laugh and Be Merry*
Laugh and be merry, remember, better the
world with a song.
Better the world with a blow in the teeth of a
wrong.

7133 *Pompey The Great*
Death opens unknown doors. It is most grand
to die.

7134 *Roadways*
One road leads to London,
One road runs to Wales,
My road leads me seawards
To the white dipping sails.

7135 *'Sea Fever'*
I must go down to the sea again, to the lonely
sea and the sky,
And all I ask is a tall ship and a star to steer her
by,
And the wheel's kick and the wind's song and
the white sail's shaking,
And a grey mist on the sea's face and a grey
dawn breaking.

7136 *'Sea Fever'*
I must go down to the sea again, for the call of
the running tide
Is a wild call and a clear call that may not be
denied.

7137 *'Sea Fever'*
I must go down to the sea again, to the vagrant
gypsy life,
To the gull's way and the whale's way where the
wind's like a whetted knife;
And all I ask is a merry yarn from a laughing
fellow-rover,
And quiet sleep and a sweet dream when the
long trick's over.

MASLOW Abraham 1908-1970
7138
I can feel guilty about the past, apprehensive
about the future, but only in the present can I
act. The ability to be in the present moment is
a major component of mental wellness.

MASON Donald 1913-
7139 *(radio message)*
Sighted sub, sank same.

MASSE Marcel 1936-
7140
The more the world is specialized the more it
will be run by generalists.

MASSEY Anna 1937-
7141
Optimism is like a spiritual magnet.

MASSINGER Philip 1583-1640
7142 *The Bashful Lover*
Ambition, in a private man a vice,
Is in a prince the virtue.

7143 *The Bondman*
He that would govern others, first should be
The master of himself.

7144 *The City Madam*
Pray enter
You are learned Europeans and we worse
Than ignorant Americans.

7145 *The Duke of Milan*
Now speak,
Or be for ever silent.

7146 *The Great Duke of Florence*
I am driven
Into a desperate strait and cannot steer
A middle course.

7147
Immature poets imitate: mature poets steal.

7148 *A New Way to Pay Old Debts*
The devil turned precisian!

7149 *The Parliament of Love*
Oh that thou hadst like others been all words,
And no performance.

7150 *A Very Woman*
Death hath a thousand doors to let out life:
I shall find one.

MASSON Tom
7151
Hamlet is the tragedy of tackling a family
problem too soon after college.

7152
You can always get someone to love you - even
if you have to do it yourself.

7153
'Be yourself!' is about the worst advice you can
give to some people.

MATHEW Father
7154
Horse-sense is something a horse has that
prevents him betting on people.

MATHEW Sir James 1830-1908
7155
In England, justice is open to all - like the Ritz
Hotel.

MATHEWS Shailer 1863-1941
7156
An epigram is a half-truth so stated as to irritate
the person who believes the other half.

MATISSE Henri 1869-1954
7157
There is nothing more difficult for a truly
creative painter than to paint a rose, because
before he can do so he has first to forget all the
roses that were ever painted.

7158
A work should contain its total meaning within
itself and should impress it on the spectator
before he even knows the subject.

MATTHEWS Brander 1852-1929
7159
A highbrow is a person educated beyond his
intelligence.

MATTHEWS W.
7160
Unless a man has trained himself for his
chance, the chance will only make him
ridiculous.

7161
In the world a man lives in his own age; in
solitude in all ages.

MAUDSLEY Henry 1771-1831
7162
The sorrow which has no vent in tears may

make other organs weep.

MAUGHAM W. Somerset 1874-1965
7163 *(attributed)*
The love that lasts longest is the love that is never returned.

7164
I have not been afraid of excess: excess on occasion is exhilarating. It prevents moderation from acquiring the deadening effect of a habit.

7165
American women expect to find in their husbands a perfection that English women only hope to find in their butlers.

7166
Beauty is an ecstasy; it is as simple as hunger. There is really nothing to be said about it.

7167 *Our Betters*
The degree of a nation's civilization is marked by its disregard for the necessities of existence.

7168 *The Bread-Winner*
You know, of course, that the Tasmanians, who never committed adultery, are now extinct.

7169 *Cakes and Ale*
Hypocrisy is the most difficult and nerve-racking vice that any man can pursue; it needs an unceasing vigilance and a rare detachment of spirit. It cannot, like adultery or gluttony, be practised at spare moments; it is a whole-time job.

7170 *Cakes and Ale*
From the earliest times the old have rubbed it into the young that they are wiser than they, and before the young had discovered what nonsense this was they were old too, and it profited them to carry on the imposture.

7171 *Cakes and Ale*
Poor Henry [James], he's spending eternity wandering round and round a stately park and the fence is just too high for him to peep over and they're having tea just too far away for him to hear what the countess is saying.

7172 *The Circle*
You can't learn too soon that the most useful thing about a principle is that it can always be sacrificed to expediency.

7173 *The Circle*
A woman will always sacrifice herself if you give her the opportunity. It is her favourite form of self-indulgence.

7174 *The Circle*
When married people don't get on they can separate, but if they're not married it's impossible. It's a tie that only death can sever.

7175
It is dangerous to let the public behind the scenes. They are easily disillusioned and then they are angry with you, for it was the illusion they loved.

7176
Dinner, a time when ... one should eat wisely but not too well, and talk well but not too wisely.

7177 *Of Human Bondage*
Like all weak men he laid an exaggerated stress on not changing one's mind.

7178 *Of Human Bondage*
People ask you for criticism, but they only want praise.

7179 *Of Human Bondage*
Money is like a sixth sense without which you cannot make a complete use of the other five.

7180
Imagination grows by exercise, and contrary to common belief, is more powerful in the mature than in the young.

7181 *The Moon and Sixpence*
Impropriety is the soul of wit.

7182 *The Moon and Sixpence*
It is not true that suffering ennobles the character; happiness does that sometimes, but suffering, for the most part, makes men petty and vindictive.

7183 *The Moon and Sixpence*
A woman can forgive a man for the harm he does her, but she can never forgive him for the sacrifices he makes on her account.

7184 *The Moon and Sixpence*
Because women can do nothing except love, they've given it a ridiculous importance.

7185
Something wonderful and strange that the artist fashions out of the chaos of the world in the torment of his soul.

7186 *The Summing Up*
I would sooner read a time-table or a catalogue than nothing at all ... They are much more entertaining than half the novels that are written.

7187
A Unitarian very earnestly disbelieves what everyone else believes.

7188 *A Writer's Notebook*
Few misfortunes can befall a boy which bring worse consequences than to have a really affectionate mother.

7189 *A Writer's Notebook*
Music-hall songs provide the dull with wit, just as proverbs provide them with wisdom.

7190 *A Writer's Notebook*
Men have an extraordinarily erroneous opinion of their position in nature; and the error is ineradicable.

7191 *A Writer's Notebook*
Sentimentality is only sentiment that rubs you up the wrong way.

MAULDIN Bill 1921-
7192 *(cartoon caption)*
I feel like a fugitive from th' law of averages.

MAUPASSANT Guy de 1850-1893
7193
Get black on white.

MAURIAC François 1885-1970
7194
Human love is often but the encounter of two weaknesses.

7195
No love, no friendship can cross the path of our destiny without leaving some mark on it forever.

MAUROIS André 1885-1967
7196
Business is a combination of war and sport.

7197
If you create an act, you create a habit. If you create a habit, you create a character. If you create a character, you create a destiny.

7198
The effectiveness of work increases according to geometric progression if there are no interruptions.

7199
Growing old is no more than a bad habit which a busy man has no time to form.

7200
In literature as in love we are astounded by what is chosen by others.

7201
Men fear silence as they fear solitude, because both give them a glimpse of the terror of life's nothingness.

7202
Style is the hallmark of a temperament stamped upon the material at hand.

MAXTON James 1885-1946
7203 *(opposing disaffiliation of SILP from Labour)*
All I say is, if you cannot ride two horses you have no right in the circus.

MAXWELL William
7204
Happiness is the light on the water. The water is cold and dark and deep.

MAY Rollo
7205
Anxiety is essential to the human condition. The confrontation with anxiety can relieve us from boredom, sharpen the sensitivity and assure the presence of tension that is necessary to preserve human existence.

7206
Anxiety is the experience of Being affirming itself against non-Being.

7207
Depression is the inability to construct a future.

7208
Hate is not the opposite of love; apathy is.

7209
I think Dostoevsky was right, that every human being must have a point at which he stands against the culture, where he says, this is me and the damned world can go to hell.

MAYAKOVSKY Vladimir 1893-1930
7210 *'The Cloud in Trousers'*
If you wish -
... I'll be irreproachably tender;
not a man, but - a cloud in trousers!

7211 *'Conversation with Inspector of Taxes ....'*
In our language rhyme is a barrel. A barrel of dynamite. The line is a fuse. The line smoulders to the end and explodes; and the town is blown sky-high in a stanza.

7212 *'Conversation with Inspector of Taxes....'*
Our duty is to blare like brazen-throated horns in the fog of philistinism and in seething storms. The poet is always indebted to the universe, paying interest and fines on sorrow.

7213 *'Homewards'*
I want to be understood by my country, and if I am not - never mind, I will pass over my native land sideways, as a slanted rain passes.

7214 *'Letter ... to Comrade Kostorov on Nature of Love'*
To us love says humming that the heart's stalled motor has begun working again.

7215 *'Our March' (translated by C.M. Bowra)*
Tramp squares with rebellious treading!
Up heads! As proud peaks be seen!
In the second flood we are spreading
Every city on earth will be clean.

7216 *'At the Top of my Voice' (translated by C.M. Bowra)*
Deploying in a parade

the armies of my pages,
I pass in review
the front of my lines.
Verses stand
lead-heavily,
ready for death
and for immortal fame.

7217 *(from unfinished poem, and in suicide letter)*
The love boat has crashed against the everyday.
You and I, we are quits, and there is no point in listing mutual pains, sorrows, and hurts.

MAYHEW Jonathan 1720-1766
7218 *A Discourse ... to the Higher Powers*
Rulers have no authority from God to do mischief.

7219 *A Discourse ... to the Higher Powers*
As soon as the prince sets himself up above the law, he loses the king in the tyrant; he does to all intents and purpose unking himself ... And in such cases, has no more right to be obeyed, than any inferior officer who acts beyond his commission.

MEAD Margaret 1901-1978
7220
No matter how many communes anybody invents, the family always creeps back.

7221 *Sex and Temperament in Three Primitive Societies*
The knowledge that the personalities of the two sexes are socially produced is congenial to every programme that looks forward towards a planned order of society. It is a two-edged sword.

7222
In almost any society, I think, the quality of the non-conformists is like to be just as good as, and no better than that of the conformists.

7223
Each suburban housewife spends her time presiding over a power plant sufficient to have staffed the palace of a Roman emperor with a hundred slaves.

MEAD Shepherd 1914-
7224
How to succeed in business without really trying.

MEANY George 1894-1980
7225
Anybody who has any doubt about the ingenuity or the resourcefulness of a plumber never got a bill from one.

MEARNS Hughes 1875-1965
7226 *The Psycho-ed*
As I was walking up the stair

I met a man who wasn't there.
He wasn't there again today.
I wish, I wish he'd stay away.

MEDICI Cosimo de 1389-1464
7227
We read that we ought to forgive our enemies; but we do not read that we ought to forgive our friends.

MEIR Golda 1898-1978
7228
Don't be so humble. You're not that great.

7229
We Jews have a secret weapon in our struggle with the Arabs - we have no place to go.

7230
Can we today measure devotion to husband and children by our indifference to everything else?

7231
Whether women are better than men I cannot say - but I can say they are certainly no worse.

MELBOURNE William Lamb 2nd Lord 1779-1848
7232 *(attributed)*
Now, is it to lower the price of corn, or isn't it? It is not much matter which we say, but mind, we must all say *the same*.

7233 *(of the Catholic Emancipation Act)*
What all the wise men promised has not happened, and what all the d-d fools said would happen has come to pass.

7234 *(on being dismissed by William IV)*
I have always thought complaints of ill-usage contemptible, whether from a seduced disappointed girl or a turned-out Prime Minister.

7235
God help the Minister that meddles with art!

7236 *(on hearing an evangelical sermon)*
Things have come to a pretty pass when religion is allowed to invade the sphere of private life.

7237
While I cannot be regarded as a pillar, I must be regarded as a buttress of the church, because I support if from outside.

7238 *(replying to a politician)*
What I want is men who will support me when I am in the wrong.

MELLON Andrew 1855-1937
7239
Gentlemen prefer bonds.

MELVILLE Herman 1819-1891
7240 *Hawthorne and His Mosses*
That Calvinistic sense of innate depravity and
original sin from whose visitations, in some
shape or other, no deeply thinking mind is
always and wholly free.

7241 *Hawthorne and His Mosses*
Genius, all over the world, stands hand in hand,
and one shock of recognition runs the whole
circle round.

7242 *Moby Dick*
But when a man's religion becomes really
frantic; when it is a positive torment to him;
and, in fine, makes this earth of ours an
uncomfortable inn to lodge in; then I think it
high time to take that individual aside and
argue the point with him.

7243 *Moby Dick*
A whaleship was my Yale College and my
Harvard.

7244 *Moby Dick*
Aye, toil as we may, we all sleep at last on the
field. Sleep? Aye, and rust amid greenness; as
last year's scythes flung down, and left in the
half-cut swaths.

7245 *Moby Dick*
Towards thee I roll, thou all-destroying but
unconquering whale ... from hell's heart I stab
at thee.

7246 *Moby Dick*
Better sleep with a sober cannibal than a
drunken Christian.

7247
From without, no wonderful effect is wrought
within ourselves, unless some interior,
responding wonder meets it.

MENANDER 342-c.292 BC
7248 *Dis Exapaton*
Whom the gods love dies young.

7249 *The Lady of Andros in Menander*
We live, not as we wish to, but as we can.

MENCIUS 372-289 BC
7250
There is no greater delight than to be conscious
of sincerity on self-examination.

MENCKEN H.L. 1880-1956
7251
A man loses his sense of direction after four
drinks; a woman loses hers after four kisses.

7252
Bachelors know more about women than
married men; if they didn't, they'd be married
too.

7253
The basic fact about human existence is not
that it is a tragedy, but that it is a bore.

7254
He [Calvin Coolidge] slept more than any other
President, whether by day or by night. Nero
fiddled, but Coolidge only snored.

7255
A celebrity is one who is known to many
persons he is glad he doesn't know.

7256 *Chrestomathy*
Love is the delusion that one woman differs
from another.

7257 *Chrestomathy*
Puritanism. The haunting fear that someone,
somewhere, may be happy.

7258
Conscience is a mother-in-law whose visit
never ends.

7259
A cynic is a man who, when he smells flowers,
looks around for a coffin.

7260
Under democracy, one party always devotes its
chief energies to trying to prove that the other
party is unfit to rule - and both commonly
succeed, and are right.

7261
If, after I depart this vale, you ever remember
me and have thought to please my ghost,
forgive some sinner and wink your eye at some
homely girl.

7262
The double standard of morality will survive in
this world so long as the woman whose
husband has been lured away is favoured with
the sympathetic tears of other women, and a
man whose wife has made off is laughed at by
other men.

7263
God is a comedian whose audience is afraid to
laugh.

7264
I hate all sports as rabidly as a person who likes
sports hates common sense.

7265
Injustice is relatively easy to bear; what stings is
justice.

7266
I've made it a rule never to drink by daylight
and never to refuse a drink after dark.

7267
A judge is a law student who marks his own examination papers.

7268 *A Little Book in C major*
Democracy is the theory that the common people know what they want, and deserve to get it good and hard.

7269 *A Little Book in C major*
Conscience: the inner voice which warns us that someone may be looking.

7270
No matter how happily a woman may be married, it always pleases her to discover that there is a nice man who wishes she were not.

7271
One may no more live in the world without picking up the moral prejudices of the world than one will be able to go to hell without perspiring.

7272
Men have a much better time of it than women. For one thing, they marry later. For another thing, they die earlier.

7273
Nobody ever went broke underestimating the taste of the American public.

7274 *Notebooks*
It is now quite lawful for a Catholic woman to avoid pregnancy by a resort to mathematics, though she is still forbidden to resort to physics and chemistry.

7275
Nothing can come out of an artist that is not in the man.

7276
Opera in English is, in the main, just about as sensible as baseball in Italian.

7277
Penetrating so many secrets, we cease to believe in the unknowable. But there it sits nevertheless, calmly licking its chops.

7278 *Prejudices*
Women hate revolutions and revolutionists. They like men who are docile, and well regarded at the bank, and never late at meals.

7279
We must respect the other fellow's religion, but only in the sense and to the extent that we respect his theory that his wife is beautiful and his children smart.

7280
The saddest life is that of a political aspirant under democracy. His failure is ignominious and his success is disgraceful.

7281
Time is a great legalizer, even in the field of morals.

7282
What men value in the world is not rights, but privileges.

7283
Women have simple tastes. They get pleasure out of the conversation of children in arms and men in love.

MENNINGER Karl
7284
Listening is a magnetic and strange thing, a creative force. The friends who listen to us are the ones we move toward, and we want to sit in their radius. When we are listened to, it creates us, makes us unfold and expand.

7285
Love cures people; both the ones who give it and the ones who receive it.

7286
Neurotic means he is not as sensible as I am, and psychotic means he's even worse than my brother-in-law.

7287
What's done to children, they will do to society.

MENNINGER William 1899-1966
7288
Mental health problems do not affect three or four out of every five persons, but one out of one.

7289
What the world needs is some 'do-give-a-damn' pills.

MERCER David 1928-1980
7290
A suitable case for treatment.

MERCER Johnny 1909-1976
7291 *'Ac-cent-tchu-ate the Positive'*
You've got to ac-cent-tchu-ate the positive
Elim-my-nate the negative
Latch on to the affirmative
Don't mess with Mister In-between.

7292 *'One For My Baby'*
We're drinking my friend,
To the end of a brief episode,
Make it one for my baby
And one more for the road.

7293 *'Jeepers Creepers'*
Jeepers Creepers - where'd you get those peepers?
Jeepers Creepers - where'd get those eyes?

7294
That old black magic.

MEREDITH George 1828-1909
7295 *Beauchamp's Career*
Thoughts of heroes were as good as warming-pans.

7296
Caricature is rough truth.

7297 *One of Our Conquerors*
None of your dam punctilio.

7298
Cultivated men and women who do not skim the cream of life, and are attached to the duties, yet escape the harsher blows, make acute and balanced observers.

7299 *Diana of the Crossways*
A witty woman is a treasure; a witty beauty is a power.

7300 *Diana of the Crossways*
'Tis Ireland gives England her soldiers, her generals too.

7301 *Diana of the Crossways*
There is nothing the body suffers the soul may not profit by.

7302 *Diana of the Crossways*
As we to the brutes, poets are to us.

7303 *The Egoist*
A Phoebus Apollo turned fasting friar.

7304 *The Egoist*
A dainty rogue in porcelain.

7305 *The Egoist*
Cynicism is intellectual dandyism without the coxcomb's feathers.

7306 *The Egoist*
In ... the Book of Egoism it is written: Possession without obligation to the object possessed approaches felicity.

7307
The lark ascending.

7308 'Love in the Valley'
She whom I love is hard to catch and conquer,
Hard, but O the glory of the winning were she won!

7309 'Lucifer in Starlight'
On a starred night Prince Lucifer uprose.
Tired of his dark dominion swung the fiend ...

7310 'Lucifer in Starlight'
Around the ancient track marched, rank on rank,
The army of unalterable law.

7311 *Modern Love*
'I play for Seasons; not Eternities!'
Says Nature.

7312 *Modern Love*
In tragic life, God wot,
No villain need be! Passions spin the plot:
We are betrayed by what is false within.

7313 *Modern Love*
Ah, what a dusty answer gets the soul
When hot for certainties in this our life!

7314 *Modern Love*
Not till the fire is dying in the grate,
Look we for any kinship with the stars.

7315 *Modern Love*
And if I drink oblivion of a day,
So shorten I the stature of my soul.

7316 *Modern Love*
That rarest gift
To Beauty, Common Sense.

7317 *The Ordeal of Richard Feverel*
I expect that Woman will be the last thing civilized by Man.

7318 *The Ordeal of Richard Feverel*
In action Wisdom goes by majorities.

7319 *The Ordeal of Richard Feverel*
Who rises from prayer a better man, his prayer is answered.

7320 *The Ordeal of Richard Feverel*
Kissing don't last: cookery do!

7321 *The Ordeal of Richard Feverel*
Speech is the small change of silence.

7322
Published memoirs indicate the end of a man's activity, and that he acknowledges the end.

7323
The well of true wit is truth itself.

7324 *Vittoria*
Much benevolence of the passive order may be traced to a disinclination to inflict pain upon oneself.

MEREDITH Owen 1831-1891
7325 'Last Words of a Sensitive Second-Rate Poet'
Genius does what it must, and Talent does what it can.

7326 *Lucile*
We may live without poetry, music and art;
We may live without conscience, and live without heart;
We may live without friends; we may live without books;
But civilized man cannot live without cooks.

He may live without books, - what is knowledge
but grieving?
He may live without hope, - what is hope but
deceiving?
He may live without love, - what is passion but
pining?
But where is the man that can live without
dining?

MERRILL James 1926-
7327 *'Museum Piece'*
The good grey guardians of art
Patrol the halls on spongy shoes,
Impartially protective, though
Perhaps suspicious of Toulouse.
Here dozes one against the wall,
Disposed upon a funeral chair.
A Degas dancer pirouettes
Upon the parting of his hair.

7328 *'The Thousand and Second Night'*
Free me, I pray, to go in search of joys
Unembroidered by your high, soft voice,
Along that stony path the senses pave.

MERRITT Dixon Lanier 1879-1972
7329
Oh, a wondrous bird is the pelican!
His beak holds more than his belican.
He takes in his beak
Food enough for a week.
But I'll be darned if I know how the helican.

MERTON Thomas 1915-1968
7330
The truth that many people never understand,
until it is too late, is that the more you try to
avoid suffering the more you suffer because
smaller and more insignificant things begin to
torture you in proportion to your fear of being
hurt.

7331
Violence is essentially wordless, and it can
begin only where thought and rational
communication have broken down.

METTERNICH Prince 1773-1859
7332 *Concessionen und Nichtconcessionen*
The greatest gift of any stateman rests not in
knowing what concessions to make, but
recognizing when to make them.

7333
Error has never approached my spirit.

7334 *Letter to Count Bombelles*
Der Kaiser ist Alles, Wien ist nichts!

The Emperor is everything, Vienna is nothing.

7335 *Mein Politisches Testament*
The word 'freedom' means for me not a point of
departure but a genuine point of arrival. The
point of departure is defined by the word 'order'.

Freedom cannot exist without the concept of
order.

7336 *(to Palmerston)*
Italy is a geographical expression.

MEYER Alan H.
7337
The best ad is a good product.

MEYER Sir Anthony 1920-
7338 *(speaking against the Falklands War)*
I question the right of that great Moloch,
national sovereignty, to burn its children to save
its pride.

MICHAELS Leonard
7339
Reasons are whores.

MICHELANGELO 1474 1564
7340
Beauty is the purgation of superfluities.

7341
It is well with me only when I have a chisel in
my hand.

MICHELET Jules 1798-1874
7342
Women are perfectly well aware that the more
they seem to obey the more they rule.

MICHENER Wendy
7343
The British are just as keen to make money as
the Americans, but they prefer hypocrisy to a
blatantly commercial attitude.

MIDDLETON Thomas c.1580-1627
7344
Anything for a quiet life.

7345 *Blurt, Master-Constable*
I never heard
Of any true affection, but 'twas nipt
With care.

7346 *The Changeling*
Beneath the stars, upon yon meteor
Ever hung my fate, 'mongst things corruptible.

7347 *The Changeling (with William Rowley)*
I could not get the ring without the finger.

7348 *The Changeling (with William Rowley)*
Y'are the deed's creature.

7349 *The Revenger's Tragedy*
Does the silk-worm expend her yellow labours
For thee? for thee does she undo herself?

7350 *The Witch*
There's no hate lost between us.

7351 *The Witch*
Though I be poor, I'm honest.

7352 *No Wit, No Help, Like a Woman's*
By many a happy accident.

MIKES George 1912-1987
7353 *How to be an Alien*
On the Continent people have good food; in England people have good table manners.

7354 *How to be an Alien*
Continental people have sex life; the English have hot-water bottles.

7355 *How to be an Alien*
An Englishman, even if he is alone, forms an orderly queue of one.

MILES Sarah
7356
Isn't it amazing that there's no copyright on your own life?

MILL John Stuart 1806-1873
7357 *Auguste Comte and Positivism*
As often as a study is cultivated by narrow minds, they will draw from it narrow conclusions.

7358 *Autobiography*
Ask yourself whether you are happy, and you cease to be so.

7359 *Autobiography*
No great improvements in the lot of mankind are possible, until a great change takes place in the fundamental constitution of their modes of thought.

7360 *Considerations on Representative Government*
The Conservatives ... being by the law of their existence the stupidest party.

7361 *Dissertations and Discussions*
When society requires to be rebuilt, there is no use in attempting to rebuild it on the old plan.

7362 *Dissertations and Discussions*
If we may be excused the antithesis, we should say that eloquence is *heard,* poetry is *overheard.*

7363 *Dissertations and Discussions*
Detention by the State of the unearned increment of rent.

7364
His eminence was due to the flatness of the surrounding landscape.

7365 *Letter to Alexander Bain*
The most important thing women have to do is to stir up the zeal of women themselves.

7366 *On Liberty*
The sole end for which mankind are warranted, individually or collectively, in interfering with the liberty of action of any of their number, is self-protection.

7367 *On Liberty*
The only purpose for which power can be rightfully exercised over any member of a civilized community, against his will, is to prevent harm to others. His own good, either physical or moral, is not a sufficient warrant.

7368 *On Liberty*
If all mankind minus one were of one opinion, and only one person were of the contrary opinion, mankind would be no more justified in silencing that one person, than he, if he had the power, would be justified in silencing mankind.

7369 *On Liberty*
A party of order or stability, and a party of progress or reform, are both necessary elements of a healthy state of political life.

7370 *On Liberty*
The liberty of the individual must be thus far limited; he must not make himself a nuisance to other people.

7371 *On Liberty*
Liberty consists in doing what one desires.

7372 *On Liberty*
A State which dwarfs its men, in order that they may be more docile instruments in its hands even for beneficial purposes, will find that with small men no great thing can really be accomplished.

7373 *On Liberty*
He who knows only his own side of the case knows little of that.

7374 *On Liberty*
All good things which exist are the fruits of originality.

7375 *On Liberty*
The worth of a State, in the long run, is the worth of the individuals composing it.

7376
We can never be sure that the opinion we are endeavouring to stifle is a false opinion; and if we were sure, stifling it would be an evil still.

7377 *Speech on Perfectibility*
The great majority of those who speak of perfectibility as a dream, do so because they feel that it is one which would afford them no pleasure if it were realized.

7378 *The Subjection of Women*
The principle which regulates the existing social relations between the two sexes - the legal subordination of one sex to the other - is wrong in itself, and now one of the chief hindrances to human improvement.

7379 *The Subjection of Women*
What is now called the nature of women is an
eminently artificial thing - the result of forced
repression in some directions, unnatural
stimulation in others.

7380 *The Subjection of Women*
No slave is a slave to the same lengths, and in so
full a sense of the word, as a wife is.

7381 *The Subjection of Women*
If married life were all that it might be expected
to be, looking to the laws alone, society would
be a hell upon earth.

7382 *The Subjection of Women*
The true virtue of human beings is fitness to live
together as equals; claiming nothing for
themselves but what they as freely concede to
everyone else; regarding command of any kind
as an exceptional necessity, and in all cases a
temporary one.

7383
Unquestionably, it is possible to do without
happiness; it is done involuntarily by nineteen-
twentieths of mankind.

MILLAY Edna St Vincent 1892-1950
7384
April,
Comes like an idiot, babbling, and strowing
flowers.

7385 *'Childhood is the Kingdom where Nobody
dies'*
Childhood is not from birth to a certain age and
at a certain age
The child is grown, and puts away childish
things.
Childhood is the kingdom where nobody dies.
Nobody that matters, that is.

7386 *'Dirge Without Music'*
Down, down, down into the darkness of the
grave
Gently they go, the beautiful, the tender, the
kind;
Quietly they go, the intelligent, the witty, the
brave.
I know. But I do not approve. And I am not
resigned.

7387 *A Few Figs From Thistles 'First Fig'*
My candle burns at both ends;
It will not last the night;
But ah, my foes, and oh, my friends -
It gives a lovely light.

7388 *A Few Figs From Thistles 'Second Fig'*
Safe upon solid rock the ugly houses stand:
Come and see my shining palace built upon the
sand!

7389 *The Harp-Weaver and Other Poems*
I only know that summer sang in me
A little while, that in me sings no more.

7390 *'Passer Mortuus Est'*
After all, my erstwhile dear,
My no longer cherished,
Need we say it was not love,
Now that love is perished?

7391
A person who publishes a book appears willfully
in public with his pants down.

7392
With him for a sire, and her for a dam
What should I be, but just what I am?

7393
Strange how few
After all's said and done, the things that are
Of moment.

7394 *'Thursday'*
And if I loved you Wednesday,
Well what is that to you?
I do not love you Thursday -
So much is true.

7395
It is not true that life is one damn thing after
another - it's one damn thing over and over

7396
Where you used to be, there is a hole in the
world, which I find myself constantly walking
around in the daytime, and falling into at night.
I miss you like hell.

MILLE Agnes de 1905-1993
7397
Living is a form of not being sure, not knowing
what next or how. The moment you know how,
you begin to die a little. The artist never
entirely knows. We guess. We may be wrong,
but we take leap after leap in the dark.

MILLE James de
7398
Horror is a feeling that cannot last long; human
nature is incapable of supporting it.

MILLER Arthur 1915-
7399
If there weren't any anti-semitism, I wouldn't
think of myself as Jewish.

7400 *The Crucible*
All organization is and must be grounded on
the idea of exclusion and prohibition just as two
objects cannot occupy the same space.

7401 *Death of a Salesman*
The world is an oyster, but you don't crack it
open on a mattress.

7402 *Death of a Salesman 'Requiem'*
A salesman is got to dream, boy. It comes with the territory.

7403 *(describing Eastern Europe)*
A theatre where no-one is allowed to walk out and everyone is forced to applause.

7404 *After the Fall*
A suicide kills two people, Maggie, that's what it's for!

7405
A good newspaper is a nation talking to itself.

7406 *The Price*
The car, the furniture, the wife, the children - everything has to be disposable. Because you see the main thing today is - shopping.

7407 *'Shadows of the Gods'*
The structure of a play is always the story of how the birds came home to roost.

7408
The task of the real intellectual consists of analyzing illusions in order to discover their causes.

7409 *A View from the Bridge*
This is Red Hook, not Sicily ... This is the gullet of New York swallowing the tonnage of the world.

MILLER Jr. Frank
7410
The day you write to please everyone you no longer are in journalism. You are in show business.

MILLER H.T. 1873-1948
7411
Give us men to match our mountains,
Give us men to match our plains:
Men with empires in their purpose
And new eras in their brains.

MILLER Harlan
7412
Often the difference between a successful marriage and a mediocre one consists of leaving about three or four things a day unsaid.

MILLER Henry 1891-1980
7413
The study of crime begins with the knowledge of oneself.

7414
Destiny is what you are supposed to do in life. Fate is what kicks you in the ass to make you do it.

7415
Life, as it is called, is for most of us one long postponement.

7416
The one thing we can never get enough of is love. And the one thing we never give enough of is love.

7417
I struggled in the beginning. I said I was going to write the truth, so help me God. And I thought I was. I found I couldn't. Nobody can write the absolute truth.

7418 *Big Sur and the Oranges of Hieronymus Bosch*
Sex is one of the nine reasons for reincarnation ... The other eight are unimportant.

7419 *Tropic of Cancer*
Even before the music begins there is that bored look on people's faces. A polite form of self-imposed torture, the concert.

7420 *Tropic of Cancer*
Every man with a bellyful of the classics is an enemy to the human race.

MILLER Joaquin 1839-1913
7421
The biggest dog has been a pup.

MILLER Jonathan 1934-
7422 *Beyond the Fringe*
In fact, I'm not really a *Jew*. Just Jew-*ish*. Not the whole hog, you know.

MILLER Max 1895-1963
7423 *The Max Miller Blue Book*
There was a little girl who had a little curl,
Right in the middle of her forehead;
When she was good she was very very good,
And when she was bad she was very very popular.

MILLER Olin
7424
One of the best things people could do for their decendants would be to sharply limit the number of them.

MILLER William 1810-1872
7425 *'Willie Winkie'*
Wee Willie Winkie rins through the town,
Up stairs and down stairs in his nicht-gown,
Tirling at the window, crying at the lock,
Are the weans in their bed, for it's now ten o'clock?

MILLIGAN Spike 1918-
7426 *The Goon Show 'Only in the mating season'*
'Do you come here often?'

7427 *The Last Goon Show of All*
Contraceptives should be used on every conceivable occasion.

7428 *Puckoon*
Money couldn't buy friends but you got a better class of enemy.

MILLS Hugh
7429
Nothing unites the English like war. Nothing divides them like Picasso.

MILLSTEIN Gilbert
7430
He speaks English with the flawless imperfection of a New Yorker.

MILMAN Henry Hart 1791-1868
7431 *The Belvedere Apollo*
And the cold marble leapt to life a god.

7432 *'Ride On! ride on in majesty!'*
Ride on, ride on in majesty!
In lowly pomp ride on to die.

7433 *'Ride on! ride on in majesty!'*
Ride on, ride on in majesty!
The wingèd squadrons of the sky
Look down with sad and wond'ring eyes
To see the approaching sacrifice.

MILNE A.A. 1882-1956
7434
One of the advantages of being disorderly is that one is constantly making exciting discoveries.

7435 *The House at Pooh Corner*
The more he looked inside the more Piglet wasn't there.

7436 *The House at Pooh Corner*
'I don't *want* him,' said Rabbit. 'But it's always useful to know where a friend-and-relation *is*, whether you want him or whether you don't.'

7437 *The House at Pooh Corner*
He respects Owl, because you can't help respecting anybody who can spell TUESDAY, even if he doesn't spell it right; but spelling isn't everything. There are days when spelling Tuesday simply doesn't count.

7438 *The House at Pooh Corner*
Pooh began to feel a little more comfortable, because when you are a Bear of Very Little Brain, and you Think of Things, you find sometimes that a Thing which seemed very Thingish inside you is quite different when it gets out into the open and has other people looking at it.

7439 *When We Were Very Young 'Buckingham Palace'*
They're changing guard at Buckingham Palace -
Christopher Robin went down with Alice.
Alice is marrying one of the guard.
'A soldier's life is terrible hard,'
Says Alice.

7440 *When We Were Very Young 'Disobedience'*
James James
Morrison Morrison
Weatherby George Dupree
Took great
Care of his Mother,
Though he was only three.
James James
Said to his Mother,
'Mother,' he said, said he;
'You must never go down to the end of the town, if you don't go down with me.'

7441 *When We Were Very Young 'The Dormouse ...'*
There once was a Dormouse who lived in a bed
Of delphiniums (blue) and geraniums (red),
And all the day long he'd a wonderful view
Of geraniums (red) and delphiniums (blue)

7442 *When We Were Very Young 'King's Breakfast'*
The King asked
The Queen, and
The Queen asked
The Dairymaid:
'Could we have some butter for
The Royal slice of bread?'

7443 *When We Were Very Young 'Rice Pudding'*
What is the matter with Mary Jane?
She's perfectly well and she hasn't a pain,
And it's lovely rice pudding for dinner again!
What *is* the matter with Mary Jane.

7444 *When We Were Very Young 'Vespers'*
Hush! Hush! Whisper who dares!
Christopher Robin is saying his prayers.

7445 *Winnie-the-Pooh*
Isn't it funny
How a bear likes honey?
Buzz! Buzz! Buzz!
I wonder why he does?

7446 *Winnie-the-Pooh*
How sweet to be a Cloud
Floating in the Blue!
It makes him very proud
To be a little cloud.

7447 *Winnie-the-Pooh*
Time for a little something.

7448 *Winnie-the-Pooh*
My spelling is Wobbly. It's good spelling but it Wobbles, and the letters get in the wrong places.

7449 *Winnie-the-Pooh*
Owl hasn't exactly got Brain, but he Knows Things.

7450 *Winnie-the-Pooh*
I am a Bear of Very Little Brain and long words
Bother me.

7451 *Winnie-the-Pooh*
I have decided to catch a Heffalump.

7452 *Winnie-the-Pooh*
'Pathetic,' he said. 'That's what it is. Pathetic.'

MILNER Alfred 1854-1925
7453
If we believe a thing to be bad, and if we have a
right to prevent it, it is our duty to try to prevent
it and to damn the consequences.

MILTON John 1608-1674
7454 *An Apology for Smectymnuus*
He who would not be frustrate of his hope to
write well hereafter in laudable things, ought
himself to be a true poem.

7455 *An Apology for Smectymnuus*
His words ... like so many nimble and airy
servitors trip about him at command.

7456 *'Arcades'*
Such sweet compulsion doth in music lie.

7457 *Areopagitica*
Books are not absolutely dead things, but do
contain a potency of life in them to be as active
as that soul was whose progeny they are.

7458 *Areopagitica*
As good almost kill a man as kill a good book:
who kills a man kills a reasonable creature,
God's image; but he who destroys a good book,
kills reason itself, kills the image of God, as it
were in the eye.

7459 *Areopagitica*
It was from out the rind of one apple tasted that
the knowledge of good and evil as two twins
cleaving together leaped forth into the world.
And perhaps this is that doom that Adam fell
into of knowing good and evil, that is to say, of
knowing good by evil.

7460 *Areopagitica*
Assuredly we bring not innocence into the
world, we bring impurity much rather: that
which purifies us is trial, and trial is by what is
contrary.

7461 *Areopagitica*
If we think to regulate printing, thereby to
rectify manners, we must regulate all
recreations and pastimes, all that is delightful to
man.

7462 *Areopagitica*
And who shall silence all the airs and madrigals,
that whisper softness in chambers?

7463 *Areopagitica*
Where there is much desire to learn, there of
necessity will be much arguing, much writing,
many opinions; for opinion in good men is but
knowledge in the making.

7464 *Areopagitica*
Methinks I see in my mind a noble and puissant
nation rousing herself like a strong man after
sleep, and shaking her invincible locks.
Methinks I see her as an eagle mewing her
mighty youth, and kindling her undazzled eyes
at the full midday beam.

7465 *Areopagitica*
Give me the liberty to know, to utter, and to
argue freely according to conscience, above all
liberties.

7466 *Areopagitica*
Let her [Truth] and Falsehood grapple; who ever
knew Truth put to the worse, in a free and open
encounter?

7467 *Areopagitica (of London)*
Behold now this vast city; a city of refuge, the
mansion-house of liberty, encompassed and
surrounded with his protection.

7468 *Comus*
Before the starry threshold of Jove's Court
My mansion is.

7469 *Comus*
Above the smoke and stir of this dim spot,
Which men call earth.

7470 *Comus*
Yet some there be that by due steps aspire
To lay their just hands on that golden key
That opes the palace of eternity.

7471 *Comus*
That like to rich and various gems inlay
The unadornèd bosom of the deep.

7472 *Comus*
An old and haughty nation proud in arms.

7473 *Comus*
And the gilded car of day
His glowing axle doth allay
In the steep Atlantic stream.

7474 *Comus*
What hath night to do with sleep?

7475 *Comus*
Come, knit hands, and beat the ground,
In a light fantastic round.

7476 *Comus*
Was I deceived, or did a sable cloud
Turn forth her silver lining on the night?

7477 *Comus*
Can any mortal mixture of earth's mould
Breathe such divine enchanting ravishment?

7478 *Comus*
Such sober certainty of waking bliss
I never heard till now.

7479 *Comus*
Virtue could see to do what Virtue would
By her own radiant light, though sun and moon
Were in the flat sea sunk ...

7480 *Comus*
But he that hides a dark soul, and foul thoughts
Benighted walks under the midday sun;
Himself is his own dungeon.

7481 *Comus*
'Tis chastity, my brother, chastity:
She that has that, is clad in complete steel.

7482 *Comus*
And filled the air with barbarous dissonance.

7483 *Comus*
I was all ear,
And took in strains that might create a soul
Under the ribs of death.

7484 *Comus*
Against the threats
Of malice or of sorcery, or that power
Which erring men call chance, this I hold firm,
Virtue may be assailed, but never hurt,
Surprised by unjust force, but not enthralled.

7485 *Comus*
Beauty is Nature's coin, must not be hoarded,
But must be current, and the good thereof
Consists in mutual and partaken bliss.

7486 *Comus*
Obtruding false rules pranked in reason's garb.

7487 *Comus*
Sabrina fair,
Listen where thou art sitting
Under the glassy, cool, translucent wave,
In twisted braids of lilies knitting
The loose train of thy amber-dropping hair.

7488 *Comus*
Thus I set my printless feet
O'er the cowslip's velvet head,
That bends not as I tread.

7489 *'On the Death of a Fair Infant Dying of a Cough'*
O fairest flower no sooner blown but blasted,
Soft silken primrose fading timelessly.

7490 *The Doctrine and Discipline of Divorce*
Let not England forget her precedence of
teaching nations how to live.

7491 *Of Education*
I call therefore a complete and generous
education that which fits a man to perform
justly, skilfully and magnanimously all the
offices both private and public of peace and
war.

7492 *Of Education 'Their Exercise'*
In those vernal seasons of the year, when the air
is calm and pleasant, It were an injury and
sullenness against nature not to go out, and see
her riches, and partake in her rejoicing with
heaven and earth.

7493 *'Let us with a gladsome mind'*
Let us with a gladsome mind
Praise the Lord, for he is kind,
For his mercies ay endure,
Ever faithful, ever sure.

7494 *'Il Penseroso'*
Hence, vain deluding joys,
The brood of folly without father bred.

7495 *'Il Penseroso'*
As thick and numberless
As the gay motes that people the sunbeams.

7496 *'Il Penseroso'*
Hail, divinest Melancholy,
Whose saintly visage is too bright
To hit the sense of human sight;
And therefore to our weaker view,
O'erlaid with black staid wisdom's hue.

7497 *'Il Penseroso'*
Come, pensive nun, devout and pure,
Sober, steadfast, and demure.

7498 *'Il Penseroso'*
And join with thee calm Peace, and Quiet,
Spare Fast, that oft with gods doth diet.

7499 *'Il Penseroso'*
And add to these retirèd Leisure,
That in trim gardens takes his pleasure.

7500 *'Il Penseroso'*
Sweet bird that shunn'st the noise of folly,
Most musical, most melancholy!

7501 *'Il Penseroso'*
And missing thee, I walk unseen
On the dry smooth-shaven green,
To behold the wandering moon,
Riding near her highest noon.

7502 *'Il Penseroso'*
Where glowing embers through the room
Teach light to counterfeit a gloom,
Far from all resort of mirth,
Save the cricket on the hearth.

7503 *'Il Penseroso'*
Or bid the soul of Orpheus sing
Such notes as warbled to the string,

Drew iron tears down Pluto's cheeck.

7504 *'Il Penseroso'*
Where more is meant than meets the ear.

7505 *'Il Penseroso'*
Hide me from day's garish eye.

7506 *'Il Penseroso'*
But let my due feet never fail
To walk the studious cloister's pale.

7507 *'Il Penseroso'*
There let the pealing organ blow
To the full-voiced quire below,
In service high, and anthems clear,
As may with sweetness, through mine ear,
Dissolve me into ecstasies,
And bring all heaven before mine eyes.

7508 *'Il Penseroso'*
Till old experience do attain
To something like prophetic strain.

7509 *The Judgement of Martin Bucer*
I owe no light or leading received from any man
in the discovery of this truth.

7510 *'L'Allegro'*
Hence, loathèd Melancholy,
Of Cerberus, and blackest Midnight born,
In Stygian cave forlorn
'Mongst horrid shapes, and shrieks, and sights
unholy.

7511 *'L'Allegro'*
Haste thee nymph, and bring with thee
Jest and youthful jollity,
Quips and cranks, and wanton wiles,
Nods, and becks, and wreathèd smiles.

7512 *'L'Allegro'*
Come, and trip it as ye go
On the light fantastic toe,
And in thy right hand lead with thee,
The mountain nymph, sweet Liberty.

7513 *'L'Allegro'*
Mirth, admit me of thy crew
To live with her, and live with thee,
In unreprovèd pleasures free.

7514 *'L'Allegro'*
While the cock with lively din
Scatters the rear of darkness thin,
And to the stack, or the barn door,
Stoutly struts his dames before.

7515 *'L'Allegro'*
Right against the eastern gate,
Where the great sun begins his state.

7516 *'L'Allegro'*
Of herbs, and other country messes,
Which the neat-handed Phyllis dresses.

7517 *'L'Allegro'*
And young and old come forth to play
On a sunshine holiday.

7518 *'L'Allegro'*
Then to the spicy nut-brown ale.

7519 *'L'Allegro'*
Towered cities please us then,
And the busy hum of men.

7520 *'L'Allegro'*
With store of ladies, whose bright eyes
Rain influence, and judge the prize
Of wit or arms.

7521 *'L'Allegro'* (of Mirth, one of three Graces)
So buxom, blithe, and debonair.

7522 *'To the Lord General Cromwell'*
... Peace hath her victories
No less renowned than war.

7523 *'On Lord General Fairfax ... Siege of
Colchester'*
For what can war, but endless war still breed?

7524 *'Lycidas'*
Hence with denial vain, and coy excuse.

7525 *'Lycidas'*
For we were nursed upon the self-same hill.

7526 *'Lycidas'*
But O the heavy change, now thou art gone,
Now thou art gone, and never must return!

7527 *'Lycidas'*
The woods, and desert caves,
With wild thyme and the gadding vine
o'ergrown.

7528 *'Lycidas'*
Alas! What boots it with uncessant care
To tend the homely slighted shepherd's trade,
And strictly meditate the thankless muse;
Were it not better done as others use,
To sport with Amaryllis in the shade,
Or with the tangles of Neaera's hair?

7529 *'Lycidas'*
Fame is the spur that the clear spirit doth raise
(That last infirmity of noble mind)
To scorn delights, and live laborious days;
But the fair guerdon when we hope to find,
And think to burst out into sudden blaze,
Comes the blind Fury with th'abhorrèd shears,
And slits the thin-spun life.

7530 *'Lycidas'*
Fame is no plant that grows on mortal soil.

7531 *'Lycidas'*
At last he rose, and twitched his mantle blue:
Tomorrow to fresh woods, and pastures new.

7532 *'On the Morning of Christ's Nativity'*
This is the month, and this the happy morn
Wherein the son of heaven's eternal king,
Of wedded maid, and virgin mother born,
Our great redemption from above did bring.

7533 *'On the Morning of Christ's Nativity'*
The star-led wizards haste with odours sweet.

7534 *'On the Morning of Christ's Nativity'*
It was the winter wild,
While the heaven-born-child
All meanly wrapped in the rude manger lies;
Nature in awe to him
Had doffed her gaudy trim,
With her great master so to sympathize.

7535 *'On the Morning of Christ's Nativity'*
No war, or battle's sound
Was heard the world around,
The idle spear and shield were high up hung.

7536 *'On the Morning of Christ's Nativity'*
Perhaps their loves, or else their sheep,
Was all that did their silly thoughts so busy
keep.

7537 *'On the Morning of Christ's Nativity'*
The helmèd cherubim
And sworded seraphim
Are seen in glittering ranks with wings
displayed.

7538 *'On the Morning of Christ's Nativity'*
For if such holy song
Enwrap our fancy long,
Time will run back, and fetch the age of gold,
And speckled vanity
Will sicken soon and die.

7539 *'On the Morning of Christ's Nativity'*
And hell itself will pass away,
And leave her dolorous mansions to the peering
day.

7540 *'On the Morning of Christ's Nativity'*
Swinges the scaly horror of his folded tail.

7541 *'On the Morning of Christ's Nativity'*
The oracles are dumb,
No voice or hideous hum
Runs through the archèd roof in words
deceiving.
Apollo from his shrine
Can no more divine,
With hollow shriek the steep of Delphos leaving.

7542 *'On the Morning of Christ's Nativity'*
So when the sun in bed,
Curtained with cloudy red,
Pillows his chin upon an orient wave.

7543 *'On the Morning of Christ's Nativity'*
But see the virgin blest,
Hath laid her babe to rest.

Time is our tedious song should here have
ending.

7544 *Paradise Lost*
Of man's first disobedience, and the fruit
Of that forbidden tree, whose mortal taste
Brought death into the world, and all our woe,
With loss of Eden.

7545 *Paradise Lost*
Things unattempted yet in prose or rhyme.

7546 *Paradise Lost*
What in me is dark
Illumine, what is low raise and support;
That to the height of this great argument
I may assert eternal providence,
And justify the ways of God to men.

7547 *Paradise Lost*
The infernal serpent; he it was, whose guile
Stirred up with envy and revenge, deceived
The mother of mankind.

7548 *Paradise Lost*
Him the almighty power
Hurled headlong flaming from the ethereal sky
With hideous ruin and combustion down
To bottomless perdition, there to dwell
In adamantine chains and penal fire,
Who durst defy the omnipotent to arms.

7549 *Paradise Lost*
A dungeon horrible, on all sides round
As one great furnace flamed, yet from those
flames
No light, but rather darkness visible
Served only to discover sights of woe,
Regions of sorrow, doleful shades, where peace
And rest can never dwell, hope never comes
That comes to all.

7550 *Paradise Lost*
... What though the field be lost?
All is not lost; the unconquerable will,
And study of revenge, immortal hate,
And courage never to submit or yield:
And what is else not to be overcome?

7551 *Paradise Lost*
Vaunting aloud, but racked with deep despair.

7552 *Paradise Lost*
Fallen cherub, to be weak is miserable,
Doing or suffering: but of this be sure,
To do aught good never will be our task,
But ever to do ill our sole delight.

7553 *Paradise Lost*
And out of good still to find means of evil.

7554 *Paradise Lost*
What reinforcement we may gain from hope;
If not, what resolution from despair. ❦

7555 *Paradise Lost*
The will
And high permission of all-ruling heaven
Left him at large to his own dark designs,
That with reiterated crimes he might
Heap on himself damnation.

7556 *Paradise Lost*
Is this the region, this the soil, the clime,
Said then the lost archangel, this the seat
That we must change for heaven, this mournful gloom
For that celestial light?

7557 *Paradise Lost*
Farewell, happy fields
Where joy for ever dwells: hail horrors, hail
Infernal world, and thou profoundest hell
Receive thy new possessor: one who brings
A mind not to be changed by place or time.
The mind is its own place, and in itself
Can make a heaven of hell, a hell of heaven.

7558 *Paradise Lost*
To reign is worth ambition though in hell:
Better to reign in hell, than serve in heaven.

7559 *Paradise Lost*
First Moloch, horrid king besmeared with blood
Of human sacrifice, and parents' tears.

7560 *Paradise Lost*
Who overcomes
By force, hath overcome but half his foe.

7561 *Paradise Lost*
Let none admire
That riches grow in hell; that soil may best
Deserve the precious bane.

7562 *Paradise Lost*
Anon out of the earth a fabric huge
Rose like an exhalation.

7563 *Paradise Lost*
From morn
To noon he fell, from noon to dewy eve,
A summer's day; and with the setting sun
Dropped from the zenith like a falling star.

7564 *Paradise Lost*
Nor aught availed him now
To have built in heaven high towers; nor did he scape
By all his engines, but was headlong sent
With his industrious crew to build in hell.

7565 *Paradise Lost*
... Pandemonium, the high capital
Of Satan and his peers.

7566 *Paradise Lost*
... The strongest and the fiercest spirit
That fought in heaven; now fiercer by despair:
His trust was with the eternal to be deemed

Equal in strength, and rather than be less
Cared not to be at all.

7567 *Paradise Lost*
My sentence is for open war: of wiles
More unexpert, I boast not.

7568 *Paradise Lost*
For who would lose,
Though full of pain, this intellectual being.

7569 *Paradise Lost*
There to converse with everlasting groans,
Unrespited, unpitied, unreprieved,
Ages of hopeless end.

7570 *Paradise Lost*
Our torments also may in length of time
Become our elements.

7571 *Paradise Lost*
To sit in darkness here
Hatching vain empires.

7572 *Paradise Lost*
... Who shall tempt with wandering feet
The dark unbottomed infinite abyss
And through the palpable obscure find out
His uncouth way.

7573 *Paradise Lost*
Long is the way
And hard, that out of hell leads up to light.

7574 *Paradise Lost*
O shame to men! Devil with devil damned
Firm concord holds, men only disagree
Of creatures rational.

7575 *Paradise Lost*
Whence and what art thou, execrable shape?

7576 *Paradise Lost*
Incensed with indignation Satan stood
Unterrified, and like a comet burned
That fires the length of Ophiuchus huge
In the Artic sky, and from his horrid hair
Shakes pestilence and war.

7577 *Paradise Lost*
... Their fatal hands
No second stroke intend.

7578 *Paradise Lost*
I fled, and cried out Death!
Hell trembled at the hideous name, and sighed
From all her caves, and back resounded Death.

7579 *Paradise Lost*
On a sudden open fly
With impetuous recoil and jarring sound
The infernal doors, and on their hinges grate
Harsh thunder.

7580 *Paradise Lost*
Chaos umpire sits,
And by decision more embroils the fray

By which he reigns; next him high arbiter
Chance governs all.

7581 *Paradise Lost*
Sable-vested Night, eldest of things.

7582 *Paradise Lost*
With ruin upon ruin, rout on rout,
Confusion worse confounded.

7583 *Paradise Lost*
Die he or justice must.

7584 *Paradise Lost*
Dark with excessive bright.

7585 *Paradise Lost*
So on this windy sea of land, the fiend
Walked up and down alone bent on his prey.

7586 *Paradise Lost*
Into a limbo large and broad, since called
The Paradise of Fools, to few unknown.

7587 *Paradise Lost*
For neither man nor angel can discern
Hypocrisy, the only evil that walks
Invisible, except to God alone.

7588 *Paradise Lost*
At whose sight all the stars
Hide their diminished heads.

7589 *Paradise Lost*
Warring in heaven against heaven's matchless
king.

7590 *Paradise Lost*
A grateful mind
By owing owes not, but still pays, at once
Indebted and discharged.

7591 *Paradise Lost*
So farewell hope, and with hope farewell fear,
Farewell remorse! All good to me is lost;
Evil, be thou my good.

7592 *Paradise Lost*
Flowers of all hue, and without thorn the rose.

7593 *Paradise Lost*
Not that fair field
Of Enna, where Proserpine gathering flowers
Herself a fairer flower by gloomy Dis
Was gathered, which cost Ceres all that pain.

7594 *Paradise Lost*
For contemplation he and valour formed,
For softness she and sweet attractive grace,
He for God only, she for God in him:
His fair large front and eye sublime declared
Absolute rule.

7595 *Paradise Lost*
And by her yielded, by him best received,
Yielded with coy submission, modest pride,
And sweet reluctant amorous delay.

7596 *Paradise Lost*
Adam, the goodliest man of men since born
His sons, the fairest of her daughters Eve.

7597 *Paradise Lost*
The unwieldy elephant
To make them mirth used all his might, and
wreathed
His lithe proboscis.

7598 *Paradise Lost*
These two
Emparadised in one another's arms
The happier Eden, shall enjoy their fill
Of bliss on bliss.

7599 *Paradise Lost*
God is thy law, thou mine: to know no more
Is woman's happiest knowledge and her praise.
With thee conversing I forget all time.

7600 *Paradise Lost*
Millions of spiritual creatures walk the earth
Unseen, both when we wake, and when we
sleep.

7601 *Paradise Lost*
Hail, wedded love, mysterious law, true source
Of human offspring, sole propriety
In Paradise of all things common else.

7602 *Paradise Lost*
Sleep on
Blest pair; and O yet happiest if ye seek
No happier state, and know to know no more.

7603 *Paradise Lost*
Him there they found
Squat like a toad, close at the ear of Eve.

7604 *Paradise Lost*
But wherefore thou alone? Wherefore with thee
Came not all hell broke loose?

7605 *Paradise Lost*
His sleep
Was airy light from pure digestion bred.

7606 *Paradise Lost*
My fairest, my espoused, my latest found,
Heaven's last best gift, my ever new delight.

7607 *Paradise Lost*
Best image of myself and dearer half.

7608 *Paradise Lost*
So saying, with dispatchful looks in haste
She turns, on hospitable thoughts intent.

7609 *Paradise Lost*
Nor jealousy
Was understood, the injured lover's hell.

7610 *Paradise Lost*
Freely we serve,
Because we freely love, as in our will
To love or not; in this we stand or fall.

7611 *Paradise Lost*
What if earth
Be but the shadow of heaven, and things
therein
Each to other like, more than on earth is
thought?

7612 *Paradise Lost*
All seemed well pleased, all seemed, but were
not all.

7613 *Paradise Lost*
Satan, so call him now, his former name
Is heard no more in heaven.

7614 *Paradise Lost*
Servant of God, well done, well hast thou fought
The better fight, who single has maintained
Against revolted multitudes the cause
Of truth, in word mightier than they in arms.

7615 *Paradise Lost*
Necessity and chance
Approach not me, and what I will is fate.

7616 *Paradise Lost*
The planets in their stations listening stood,
While the bright pomp ascended jubilant.
Open, ye everlasting gates, they sung,
Open, ye heavens, your living doors; let in
The great creator from his work returned
Magnificent, his six days' work, a world.

7617 *Paradise Lost*
Heaven is for thee too high
To know what passes there; be lowly wise:
Think only what concerns thee and thy being.

7618 *Paradise Lost*
In solitude
What happiness? who can enjoy alone,
Or all enjoying, what contentment find?

7619 *Paradise Lost*
Oft-times nothing profits more
Than self esteem, grounded on just and right
Well managed.

7620 *Paradise Lost*
The serpent subtlest beast of all the field.

7621 *Paradise Lost*
For solitude sometimes is best society,
And short retirement urges sweet return.

7622 *Paradise Lost*
As one who long in populous city pent,
Where houses thick and sewers annoy the air,
Forth issuing on a summer's morn to breathe
Among the pleasant villages and farms
Adjoined, from each thing met conceives
delight.

7623 *Paradise Lost*
She fair, divinely fair, fit love for gods.

7624 *Paradise Lost*
Law to our selves, our reason is our law.

7625 *Paradise Lost*
Her rash hand in evil hour
Forth reaching to the fruit, she plucked, she ate:
Earth felt the wound, and Nature from her seat
Sighing through all her works gave signs of woe
That all was lost.

7626 *Paradise Lost*
O fairest of creation, last and best
Of all God's works.

7627 *Paradise Lost*
For with thee
Certain my resolution is to die;
How can I live without thee, how forgo
Thy sweet converse and love so dearly joined,
To live again in these wild woods forlorn?

7628 *Paradise Lost*
Flesh of flesh,
Bone of my bone thou art, and from thy state
Mine never shall be parted, bliss or woe.

7629 *Paradise Lost*
What thou art is mine;
Our state cannot be severed, we are one,
One flesh; to lose thee were to lose my self.

7630 *Paradise Lost*
... Yet I shall temper so
Justice with mercy.

7631 *Paradise Lost*
He hears
On all sides, from innumerable tongues
A dismal universal hiss, the sound
Of public scorn.

7632 *Paradise Lost*
O why did God,
Creator wise, that peopled highest heaven
With spirits masculine, create at last
This novelty on earth, this fair defect
Of nature?

7633 *Paradise Lost*
Demoniac frenzy, moping melancholy
And moon-struck madness.

7634 *Paradise Lost*
Nor love thy life, nor hate; but what thou liv'st
Live well, how long or short permit to heaven.

7635 *Paradise Lost*
... The evening star,
Love's harbinger.

7636 *Paradise Lost*
For now I see
Peace to corrupt no less than war to waste.

7637 *Paradise Lost*
Light out of darkness! full of doubt I stand,
Whether I should repent me now of sin
By me done and occasioned, or rejoice
Much more, that much more good thereof shall
spring.

7638 *Paradise Lost*
In me is no delay; with thee to go,
Is to stay here; without thee here to stay,
Is to go hence unwilling; thou to me
Art all things under heaven, all places thou,
Who for my wilful crime art banished hence.

7639 *Paradise Lost*
They hand in hand, with wandering steps and
slow,
Through Eden took their solitary way.

7640 *Paradise Lost (the Pygmies)*
... That small infantry
Warred on by cranes.

7641 *Paradise Lost 'The Verse'*
Rhyme being no necessary adjunct or true
ornament of poem or good verse, in longer
works especially, but the invention of a
barbarous age, to set off wretched matter and
lame metre.

7642 *Paradise Regained*
Skilled to retire, and in retiring draw
Hearts after them tangled in amorous nets.

7643 *Paradise Regained*
Of whom to be dispraised were no small praise.

7644 *Paradise Regained*
But on occasion's forelock watchful wait.

7645 *Paradise Regained*
... The childhood shows the man,
As morning shows the day. Be famous then
By wisdom; as thy empire must extend,
So let extend thy mind o'er all the world.

7646 *Paradise Regained*
Athens, the eye of Greece, mother of arts
And eloquence, native to famous wits
Or hospitable, in her sweet recess,
City or suburban, studious walks and shades;
See there the olive grove of Acadame,
Plato's retirement, where the Attic bird
Trills her thick-warbled notes the summer long.

7647 *Paradise Regained*
The first and wisest of them all professed
To know this only, that he nothing knew.

7648 *Paradise Regained*
Who reads
Incessantly, and to his reading brings not
A spirit and judgement equal or superior
(And what he brings, what needs he elsewhere
seek?)

Uncertain and unsettled still remains,
Deep-versed in books and shallow in himself.

7649 *Paradise Regained (of the prophets)*
In them is plainest taught, and easiest learnt,
What makes a nation happy, and keeps it so.

7650 *Paradise Regained (of Saul)*
He who seeking asses found a kingdom.

7651 *'The Passion'*
But headlong joy is ever on the wing.

7652
Reason is also choice.

7653 *The Reason of Church Government*
The land had once enfranchised herself from
this impertinent yoke of prelaty, under whose
inquisitorious and tyrannical duncery no free
and splendid wit can flourish.

7654 *The Reason of Church Government*
Beholding the bright countenance of truth in
the quiet and still air of delightful studies.

7655 *Samson Agonistes*
Ask for this great deliverer now, and find him
Eyeless in Gaza at the mill with slaves.

7656 *Samson Agonistes*
O dark, dark, dark, amid the blaze of noon,
Irrecoverably dark, total eclipse
Without all hope of day!

7657 *Samson Agonistes*
The sun to me is dark
And silent as the moon,
When she deserts the night
Hid in her vacant interlunar cave.

7658 *Samson Agonistes*
To live a life half dead, a living death.

7659 *Samson Agonistes*
Ran on embattled armies clad in iron,
And, weaponless himself,
Made arms ridiculous.

7660 *Samson Agonistes*
Wisest men
Have erred, and by bad women been deceived;
And shall again, pretend they ne'er so wise.

7661 *Samson Agonistes*
Just are the ways of God,
And justifiable to men;
Unless there be who think not God at all.

7662 *Samson Agonistes*
... Of such doctrine never was there school,
But the heart of the fool,
And no man therein doctor but himself.

7663 *Samson Agonistes*
But what availed this temperance, not complete
Against another object more enticing?

What boots it at one gate to make defence,
And at another to let in the foe?

7664 *Samson Agonistes*
That grounded maxim
So rife and celebrated in the mouths
Of wisest men; that to the public good
Private respects must yield.

7665 *Samson Agonistes*
Yet beauty, though injurious, hath strange
power,
After offence returning, to regain
Love once possessed.

7666 *Samson Agonistes*
Love-quarrels oft in pleasing concord end.

7667 *Samson Agonistes*
Lords are lordliest in their wine.

7668 *Samson Agonistes*
For evil news rides post, while good news baits.

7669 *Samson Agonistes*
And though her body die, her fame survives,
A secular bird ages of lives.

7670 *Samson Agonistes*
Samson hath quit himself
Like Samson, and heroically hath finished
A life heroic.

7671 *Samson Agonistes*
Nothing is here for tears, nothing to wail
Or knock the breast, no weakness, no contempt,
Dispraise, or blame, nothing but well and fair,
And what may quiet us in a death so noble.

7672 *Samson Agonistes*
And calm of mind, all passion spent.

7673 *(of his school, Christ College)*
A stony-hearted step-mother.

7674 *'On Shakespeare'*
What needs my Shakespeare for his honoured
bones,
The labour of an age in pilèd stones,
Or that his hallowed relics should be hid
Under a star-ypointing pyramid?

7675 *Sonnet 12 'I did but prompt the age'*
I did but prompt the age to quit their clogs
By the known rules of ancient liberty,
When straight a barbarous noise environs me
Of owls and cuckoos, asses, apes, and dogs.

7676 *Sonnet 12 'I did but prompt the age'*
Licence they mean when they cry liberty;
For who loves that, must first be wise and good.

7677 *Sonnet 16 'When I consider how my light is
spent'*
When I consider how my light is spent,
E're half my days, in this dark world and wide,
And that one talent which is death to hide

Lodged with me useless.

7678 *Sonnet 16 'When I consider how my light is
spent'*
Thousands at his bidding speed
And post o'er land and ocean without rest:
They also serve who only stand and wait.

7679 *Sonnet 19 'Methought I saw my late
espousèd saint'*
Methought I saw my late espousèd saint
Brought to me like Alcestis from the grave.

7680 *Sonnet 19 'Methought I saw my late
espousèd saint'*
But oh as to embrace me she inclined
I waked, she fled, and day brought back my
night.

7681 *Sonnet 7 'How soon hath time'*
How soon hath time the subtle thief of youth,
Stol'n on his wing my three and twentieth year!

7682 *The Tenure of Kings and Magistrates*
None can love freedom heartily, but good men;
the rest love not freedom, but licence.

7683 *The Tenure of Kings and Magistrates*
No man who knows aught, can be so stupid to
deny that all men naturally were born free.

7684 *The...Way to Establish a Free
Commonwealth*
What I have spoken, is the language of that
which is not called amiss *The good old Cause.*

7685 *'On Time'*
Fly envious Time, till thou run out thy race,
Call on the lazy leaden-stepping hours.

7686
Where no hope is left, is left no fear.

MILVERTON Lord 1930-
7687
The ideal committee is one with me as
chairman, and two other members in bed with
flu.

MIRABEAU Comte de 1749-1791
7688 *(attributed)*
La guerre est l'industrie nationale de la Prusse.
War is the national industry of Prussia.

MIRO Joán 1893-1983
7689
The painting rises from the brushstrokes as a
poem rises from the words. The meaning
comes later.

MISTINGUETT 1874-1956
7690
A kiss can be a comma, a question mark, or an
exclamation point. That's basic spelling that
every woman ought to know.

MITCHELL Adrian 1932-
7691 *Poems*
Most people ignore most poetry
because
most poetry ignores most people.

MITCHELL Joni 1945-
7692 *'Both Sides Now'*
I've looked at life from both sides now,
From win and lose and still somehow
It's life's illusions I recall;
I really don't know life at all.

7693 *'Woodstock'*
We are stardust,
We are golden,
And we got to get ourselves
Back to the garden.

7694 *'Big Yellow Taxi'*
They paved paradise
And put up a parking lot,
With a pink hotel,
A boutique, and a swinging hot spot.

MITCHELL Langdon
7695
Marriage is three parts love and seven parts
forgiveness of sins.

MITCHELL Margaret 1900-1949
7696 *Gone with the Wind*
Death and taxes and childbirth! There's never
any convenient time for any of them.

7697 *Gone with the Wind*
I wish I could care what you do or where you go
but I can't ... My dear, I don't give a damn.

7698 *Gone with the Wind*
After all, tomorrow is another day.

MITCHELL S. Weir 1829-1914
7699
The arctic loneliness of age.

MITFORD Mary Russell 1787-1855
7700 *(of Jane Austen)*
Perpendicular, precise and taciturn.

MITFORD Nancy 1904-1973
7701 *Love in a Cold Climate*
'Always be civil to the girls, you never know who
they may marry' is an aphorism which has
saved many an English spinster from being
treated like an Indian widow.

7702 *Noblesse Oblige*
An aristocracy in a republic is like a chicken
whose head has been cut off: it may run about
in a lively way, but in fact it is dead.

7703 *The Pursuit of Love*
Wooing, so tiring.

7704 *The Pursuit of Love*
Frogs ... are slightly better than Huns or Wops,
but abroad is unutterably bloody and foreigners
are fiends.

MITTERAND President François 1916-1996
7705
Nothing is won forever in human affairs, but
everything is always possible.

7706 *(to his adviser)*
You, Attali, are a mere chapter. I am the entire
volume.

MIZNER Wilson 1876-1933
7707
The cuckoo who is on to himself is halfway out
of the clock.

7708
A fellow who is always declaring he's no fool
usually has his suspicions.

7709 *(of Hollywood)*
A trip through a sewer in a glass-bottomed boat.

7710
I've had several years in Hollywood and I still
think the movie heroes are in the audience.

7711
Be nice to people on your way up because you'll
meet 'em on your way down.

7712
If you steal from one author, it's plagiarism; if
you steal from many, it's research.

MOLIÉRE 1622-1673
7713
A doctor wastes no time with patients; and if
you have to die, he will put the business
through quicker than anybody else.

7714 *Don Juan*
He who lives without tobacco is not worthy to
live.

7715 *La Critique de l'école des femmes*
It's an odd job, making decent people laugh.

7716 *La Critique de l'école des femmes*
I shouldn't be surprised if the greatest rule of all
weren't to give pleasure.

7717 *Le Dépit amoureux*
One dies only once, and it's for such a long
time!

7718 *Les Femmes savantes*
It's good food and not fine words that keeps me
alive.

7719 *Les Femmes savantes*
Rags and tatters, if you like: I am fond of my
rags and tatters.

7720 *Les Femmes savantes*
A knowledgeable fool is a greater fool than an ignorant fool.

7721 *Les Femmes savantes*
Reading and marriage don't go well together.

7722 *Les Précieuses Ridicules*
People of quality know everything without ever having been taught anything.

7723
Long is the road from conception to completion.

7724
The more we love our friends, the less we flatter them; it is by excusing nothing that pure love shows itself.

7725 *The Misanthrope*
What's needed in this world is an accommodating sort of virtue.

7726 *The Misanthrope*
Of all human follies there's none could be greater
Than trying to render our fellow-men better.

7727 *The Misanthrope*
One should look long and carefully at oneself before one considers judging others.

7728 *The Miser*
Always present your front to the world.

7729 *The Miser*
One should eat to live, and not live to eat.

7730 *Monsieur de Pourceaugnac*
Here [in Paris] they hang a man first, and try him afterwards.

7731
You never see the old austerity
That was the essence of civility;
Young people hereabouts, unbridled, now
Just want.

7732
It is permitted me to take good fortune where I find it.

7733 *The Sicilian*
Assassination is the quickest way.

7734 *Tartuffe*
I am not the less human for being devout.

7735 *Tartuffe*
God it is true, does some delights condemn,
But 'tis not hard to come to terms with Him.

7736 *Tartuffe*
It is public scandal that constitutes offence, and to sin in secret is not to sin at all.

7737 *Tartuffe*
Man, I can assure you, is a nasty creature.

7738 *The Would-be Gentleman*
All that is not prose is verse; and all that is not verse is prose.

7739 *The Would-be Gentleman*
Ah, it's a lovely thing, to know a thing or two.

MOLLINEUX Mary 1651-1695
7740 *'Solitude'*
How sweet is harmless solitude!
What can its joys control?
Tumults and noise may not intrude,
To interrupt the soul.

MOLTKE Helmuth Von 1800-1891
7741 *Letter to Dr. J.K. Bluntschli*
Everlasting peace is a dream, and not even a pleasant one; and war is a necessary part of God's arrangement of the world ... Without war the world would deteriorate into materialism.

MONDALE Walter 1928-
7742
There will be no veterans of World War III.

MONKHOUSE William Cosmo 1840-1901
7743 *Nonsense Rhymes*
There once was an old man of Lyme
Who married three wives at a time,
When asked 'Why a third?'
He replied, 'One's absurd!
And bigamy, Sir, is a crime!'

MONMOUTH Duke of 1649-1685
7744 *(to his executioner)*
Do not hack me as you did my Lord Russell.

MONRO Harold 1879-1932
7745 *Milk for the Cat*
When the tea is brought at five o'clock,
And all the neat curtains are drawn with care,
The little black cat with bright green eys
Is suddenly purring there.

7746 *Milk for the Cat*
The white saucer like some full moon descends
At last from the clouds of the table above.

MONROE Marilyn 1926-1962
7747 *in Gentlemen Prefer Blondes*
"I always say a kiss on the hand might feel very good, but a diamond tiara lasts forever."

7748 *(on posing nude)*
It's not true I had nothing on. I had the radio on.

MONSELL John Samuel Bewley 1811-1875
7749 *'Fight the good fight with all thy might'*
Fight the good fight with all thy might,
Christ is thy strength and Christ thy right;
Lay hold on life, and it shall be
Thy joy and crown eternally.

7750 *'O worship the Lord in the beauty of holiness'*
O worship the Lord in the beauty of holiness,
Bow down before him, his glory proclaim;
With gold of obedience and incense of lowliness,
Kneel and adore him: the Lord is his name.

MONTAGU Ashley 1905-
7751
Today, while the titular head of the family may still be the father, everyone knows that he is little more than chairman, at most, of the entertainment committee.

7752
In Victorian times the purpose of life was to develop a personality once and for all and then stand on it.

MONTAGU Lady Mary Wortley 1689-1762
7753 *(attributed)*
This world consists of men, women, and Herveys.

7754 *'Answered, for Lord William Hamilton'*
But the fruit that can fall without shaking,
Indeed is too mellow for me.

7755
I give myself, sometimes, admirable advice, but I am incapable of taking it.

7756 *To the Imitator of the First Satire of Horace*
Satire should, like a polished razor keen,
Wound with a touch that's scarcely felt or seen.

7757 *Letter to daughter Mary, Countess of Bute*
Civility costs nothing and buys everything.

7758 *Letter to husband, Edward Wortley Montagu*
General notions are generally wrong.

7759
People wish their enemies dead - but I do not; I say give them the gout, give them the stone!

7760 *The Plain Dealer*
Let this great maxim be my virtue's guide:
In part she is to blame, who has been tried,
He comes too near, that comes to be denied.

7761 *Six Town Eclogues 'The Lover'*
And we meet with champagne and a chicken at last.

7762 *Six Town Eclogues 'The Lover'*
As Ovid has sweetly in parable told,
We harden like trees, and like rivers grow cold.

7763 *Summary of Lord Lyttelton's Advice*
Be plain in dress, and sober in your diet;
In short, my deary! kiss me, and be quiet.

7764 *'Verses on Self-Murder'*
In chains and darkness, wherefore should I stay,
And mourn in prison, while I keep the key?

MONTAGUE C.E. 1867-1928
7765 *Disenchantment*
War hath no fury like a non-combatant.

7766 *Fiery Particles*
I was born below par to th' extent of two whiskies.

MONTAIGNE Michel de 1533-1592
7767
All the fame I look for in life is to have lived it quietly.

7768
The Ancient Mariner said to Neptune during a great storm, 'O God, you will save me if you wish, but I am going to go on holding my tiller straight.'

7769
The beauty of stature is the only beauty of men.

7770
It is commonly seen by experience that excellent memories do often accompany weak judgements.

7771
Once conform, once do what others do because they do it, and a kind of lethargy steals over all the finer senses of the soul.

7772
There is no course of life so weak and sottish as that which is managed by order, method and discipline.

7773
No doctor takes pleasure in the health even of his friends.

7774 *Essays*
One should be ever booted and spurred and ready to depart.

7775 *Essays*
To make judgements about great and lofty things, a soul of the same stature is needed; otherwise we ascribe to them that vice which is our own.

7776 *Essays*
The ceaseless labour of your life is to build the house of death.

7777 *Essays*
The value of life lies not in the length of days but in the use you make of them; he has lived for a long time who has little lived. Whether you have lived enough depends not on the number of your years but on your will.

7778 *Essays*
It should be noted that children at play are not playing about; their games should be seen as their most serious-minded activity.

7779 *Essays*
There is scarcely any less bother in the running of a family than in that of an entire state. And domestic business is no less importunate for being less important.

7780 *Essays*
The greatest thing in the world is to know how to be oneself.

7781 *Essays*
Fame and tranquility can never be bedfellows.

7782 *Essays*
Living is my job and my art.

7783 *Essays*
Virtue shuns ease as a companion ... It demands a rough and thorny path.

7784 *Essays*
Our religion is made so as to wipe out vices; it covers them up, nourishes them, incites them.

7785 *Essays*
When I play with my cat, who knows whether she isn't amusing herself with me more than I am with her?

7786 *Essays*
Unless a man feels he has a good enough memory, he should never venture to lie.

7787 *Essays*
A woman who goes to bed with a man ought to lay aside her modesty with her skirt, and put it on again with her petticoat.

7788 *Essays*
A little of everything and nothing thoroughly.

7789 *Essays*
Life is a dream; when we sleep we are awake, and when awake we sleep.

7790 *Essays*
Que sais-je?
What do I know?

7791 *Essays*
It [marriage] is like a cage; one sees the birds outside desperate to get in, and those inside equally desperate to get out.

7792 *Essays*
The world is but a school of inquiry.

7793 *Essays*
Poverty of goods is easily cured; poverty of soul, impossible.

7794 *Essays*
It might well be said of me that here I have merely made up a bunch of other men's flowers, and provided nothing of my own but the string to bind them.

7795 *Essays*
A man who fears suffering is already suffering from what he fears.

7796
There is no man so good, who, were he to submit all his thoughts and actions to the laws, would not deserve hanging ten times in his life.

7797
I have never seen a greater monster or miracle in the world than myself.

7798
There never were two opinions alike in all the world, no more than two hours or two grains: the most universal quality is diversity.

7799
There is no passion so much transports the sincerity of judgement as doth anger.

7800
Philosophy is doubt.

7801
If you press me to say why I loved him, I can say no more than it was because he was he, and I was I.

7802
I quote others in order to better express my own self.

7803
I speak the truth, not so much as I would, but as much as I dare; and I dare a little more, as I grow older.

7804
Whatever is enforced by command is more imputed to him who exacts than to him who performs.

7805
When I religiously confess myself to myself, I find that the best virtue I have has in it some tincture of vice.

7806
A wise man sees as much as he ought, not as much as he can.

7807
The word is half his that speaks, and half his that hears it.

MONTALE Eugenio 1896-1981
7808 *'Felicità raggiunta'*
Happiness, for you we walk on a knife edge. To the eyes you are a flickering light, to the feet,

thin ice that cracks; and so may no one touch you who loves you.

MONTALVO Juan 1832-1889
7809
There is nothing harder than the softness of indifference.

7810
Old age is an island surrounded by death.

MONTESQUIEU Charles Baron de 1689-1755
7811
An empire founded by war has to maintain itself by war.

7812 *L'Esprit de lois, XI*
Liberty is the right to do everything which the laws allow.

7813 *Lettres Persanes*
Men should be bewailed at their birth, and not at their death.

7814 *Lettres Persanes*
There is a very good saying that if triangles invented a god, they would make him three-sided.

7815 *Pensées diverses 'Portrait de Montesquieu'*
I suffer from the disease of writing books and being ashamed of them when they are finished.

7816 *Pensées et fragments inédits*
Great lords have their pleasures, but the people have fun.

7817
Republics are brought to their ends by luxury; monarchies by poverty.

MONTGOMERY Lucy Maud 1874-1942
7818
Worrying helps you some. It seems as if you are doing something when you're worrying.

MONTGOMERY Robert 1807-1855
7819 *Luther: a Poem 'Man's Need and God's Supply'*
The solitary monk who shook the world.

7820 *The Omnipresence of the Deity*
And thou, vast ocean! on whose awful face
Time's iron feet can print no ruin-trace.

MONTHERLANT Henri de 1896-1972
7821
Great ideas are not charitable.

MONTROND Casimir Comte de 1768-1843
7822 *(attributed)*
Have no truck with first impulses for they are always generous ones.

7823 *(attributed)*
If something pleasant happens to you, don't forget to tell it to your friends, to make them feel bad.

MONTROSE Percy
7824 *'Clementine'*
In a cavern, in a canyon,
Excavating for a mine,
Dwelt a miner, Forty-niner,
And his daughter, Clementine.
Oh, my darling, oh my darling, oh my darling Clementine!
Thou art lost and gone for ever, dreadful sorry,
Clementine.

7825 *'Clementine'*
Light she was and like a fairy,
And her shoes were number nine;
Herring boxes without topses,
Sandals were for Clementine.

7826 *'Clementine'*
But I kissed her little sister,
And forgot my Clementine.

MOODIE Susanna 1803-1885
7827
When things come to the worst, they generally mend.

MOODY D.L. 1837-1899
7828
If I take care of my character, my reputation will take care of itself.

MOORE Brian 1921-
7829
We also serve who only punctuate.

MOORE Clement C. 1779-1863
7830 *'A Visit from St Nicholas'*
'Twas the night before Christmas, when all through the house
Not a creature was stirring, not even a mouse;
The stockings were hung by the chimney with care,
In hopes that St Nicholas soon would be there.

MOORE Edward 1712-1757
7831 *The Foundling*
This is adding insult to injuries.

7832 *The Foundling*
I am rich beyond the dreams of avarice.

MOORE George 1852-1933
7833 *The Bending of the Bough*
All reformers are bachelors.

7834 *The Brook Kerith*
A man travels the world in search of what he needs and returns home to find it.

7835
No place in England where everyone can go is considered respectable.

7836 *Hail and Farewell: Ave*
Art must be parochial in the beginning to
become cosmopolitan in the end.

7837 *Impressions and Opinions 'Balzac'*
The lot of critics is to be remembered by what
they failed to understand.

7838
Ireland is a fatal disease; fatal to Englishmen
and doubly fatal to Irishmen.

7839
A literary movement consists of five or six
people who live in the same town and hate each
other cordially.

MOORE Henry 1831-1895
7840
Now I really make the little idea from clay, and I
hold it in my hand. I can turn it, look at it from
underneath, see if from one view, hold it against
the sky, imagine it any size I like, and really be
in control, almost like God creating something.

MOORE Marianne 1887-1972
7841
Beauty is everlasting
And dust is for a time.

7842
I'm troubled. I'm dissatisfied. I'm Irish.

7843 *'Poetry'*
I, too, dislike it: there are things that are
important beyond all this fiddle.
Reading it, however, with a perfect contempt for
it, one discovers in it, after all, a place for the
genuine.

7844 *'Poetry'*
Nor till the poets among us can be
'literalists of
the imagination' - above
insolence and triviality and can present
for inspection, imaginary gardens with real
toads in them, shall we have
it.

7845
Poetry is all nouns and verbs.

7846 *'Silence'*
My father used to say,
'Superior people never make long visits,
have to be shown Longfellow's grave
or the glass flowers at Harvard'.

7847 *'Silence'*
Nor was he insincere in saying, 'Make my house
your inn'.
Inns are not residences.

MOORE Mavor
7848
Vice is as much a part of human nature as folly,

and pornography may be as necessary to vent
vice as satire is to vent folly.

MOORE Sparkle
7849
The Strip Club is another form of safe sex.

MOORE Sturge 1870-1944
7850 *'The Gazelles'*
Then, cleaving the grass, gazelles appear
(The gentler dolphins of kindlier waves)
With sensitive heads alert of ear;
Frail crowds that a delicate hearing saves.

MOORE Thomas 1779-1852
7851 *'Believe me, if all those endearing young charms'*
Believe me, if all those endearing young
charms,
Which I gaze on so fondly today,
Were to change by tomorrow, and fleet in my
arms,
Like fairy gifts fading away!
Thou wouldst still be adored as this moment
thou art.

7852 *'Believe me, if all those endearing young charms'*
No, the heart that has truly loved never forgets,
But as truly loves on to the close,
As the sun-flower turns on her god, when he
sets,
The same look which she turned when he rose.

7853 *'Farewell! - but whenever'*
You may break, you may shatter the vase, if you
will,
But the scent of the roses will hang round it still.

7854 *The Fudge Family in Paris*
Who can help loving the land that has taught us
Six hundred and eighty-five ways to dress eggs?

7855 *The Fudge Family in Paris*
I may, without vanity, hint -
Though an angel should write, still 'tis *devils*
must print.

7856 *'The harp that once through Tara's halls'*
The harp that once through Tara's halls
The soul of music shed,
Now hangs as mute on Tara's walls
As if that soul were fled.
So sleeps the pride of former days,
So glory's thrill is o'er;
And hearts, that once beat high for praise,
Now feel that pulse no more.

7857 *Lalla Rookh 'The Fire-Worshippers'*
Like Dead Sea fruits, that tempt the eye,
But turn to ashes on the lips!

7858 *'Love's Young Dream'*
No, there's nothing half so sweet in life
As love's young dream.

7859 *'The Minstrel Boy'*
The Minstrel Boy to the war is gone,
In the ranks of death you'll find him;
His father's sword he has girded on,
And his wild harp slung behind him.

7860 *'Oft in the Stilly Night'*
Oft, in the stilly night,
Ere Slumber's chain has bound me,
Fond Memory brings the light
Of other days around me.

7861 *'Oh! blame not the bard'*
Oh! blame not the bard, if he fly to the bowers,
Where Pleasure lies, carelessly smiling at Fame.

7862 *'Oh! breathe not his name'*
Oh! breathe not his name, let it sleep in the
shade,
Where cold and unhonoured his relics are laid.

7863 *'Rich and rare were the gems she wore'*
Rich and rare were the gems she wore,
And a bright gold ring on her wand she bore.

7864 *'The time I've lost in wooing'*
My only books
Were woman's looks,
And folly's all they've taught me.

7865 *''Tis the last rose of summer'*
'Tis the last rose of summer
Left blooming alone;
All her lovely companions
Are faded and gone.

7866 *'The young May moon'*
Then awake! the heavens look bright, my dear;
'Tis never too late for delight, my dear;
And the best of all ways
To lengthen our days
Is to steal a few hours from the night, my dear!

MORDAUNT Thomas Osbert 1730-1809
7867
Sound, sound the clarion, fill the fife,
Throughout the sensual world proclaim,
One crowded hour of glorious life
Is worth an age without a name.

MORDDEN Ethan
7868
For most singers the first half of the career
involves extending one's repertoire, the second
half trimming it.

MORE Hannah 1745-1833
7869 *'An Address to the Meeting in Spa Fields'*
For you'll ne'er mend your fortunes, nor help
the just cause,
By breaking of windows, or breaking of laws.

7870 *Christian Morals*
Man cannot be safely trusted with a life of
leisure.

7871 *Essays ... for Young Ladies 'On Dissipation'*
The prevailing manners of an age depend more
than we are aware, or are willing to allow, on the
conduct of the women; this is one of the
principal hinges on which the great machine of
human society turns.

7872 *Florio*
Small habits, well pursued betimes,
May reach the dignity of crimes.

7873 *Florio*
He liked those literary cooks
Who skim the cream of others' books;
And ruin half an author's graces
By plucking bon-mots from their places.

7874
In grief we know the worst of what we feel,
But who can tell the end of what we fear?

7875
Imagination frames events unknown,
In wild, fantastic shapes of hideous ruin,
And what it fears, creates.

7876 *Moses in the Bulrushes*
Did not God
Sometimes withhold in mercy what we ask,
We should be ruined at our own request.

7877
Going to the opera, like getting drunk, is a sin
that carries its own punishment with it and that
a very severe one.

MORE Sir Thomas 1478-1535
7878 *(to his executioner)*
Pluck up thy spirits, man, and be not afraid to
do thine office; my neck is very short; take heed
therefore thou strike not awry, for saving of
thine honesty.

7879 *(to his executioner, pulling his beard aside)*
This hath not offended the king.

7880 *(to a friend who had versified a mediocre
book)*
Yea, marry, now it is somewhat, for now it is
rhyme; before, it was neither rhyme nor reason.

7881
Is not this house [the Tower of London] as nigh
heaven as my own?

7882
We may not look at our pleasure to go to heaven
in feather-beds; it is not the way.

7883 *(on mounting the scaffold)*
I pray you, master Lieutenant, see me safe up,
and my coming down let me shift for my self.

7884 *Utopia*
Your sheep, that were wont to be so meek and
tame, and so small eaters, now, as I hear say, be

become so great devourers, and so wild, that they eat up and swallow down the very men themselves.

MOREAU Jean
7885
Age does not protect you from love but love to some extent protects you from age.

MORELL Thomas 1703-1784
7886 *Judas Maccabeus*
See the conquering hero comes!
Sound the trumpets, beat the drums!

MORGAN Arthur E. 1886-1956
7887
Lack of something to feel important about is almost the greatest tragedy a man may have.

MORGAN Augustus de 1806-1871
7888 *A Budget of Paradoxes*
Great fleas have little fleas upon their backs to bite 'em,
And little fleas have lesser fleas, and so *ad infinitum*.

MORGAN Charles Langbridge 1894-1958
7889 *(attributed)*
There is no surprise more magical than the surprise of being loved: It is God's finger on man's shoulder.

MORGAN J.P. 1837-1913
7890
Well, I don't know as I want a lawyer to tell me what I cannot do. I hire him to tell me how to do what I want to do.

MORGAN Robin 1941-
7891
Sisterhood is powerful.

MORGENSTERN Christian
7892
Home is not where you live but where they understand you.

7893
Humour is the contemplation of the finite from the point of view of the infinite.

7894
To me, the term 'middle-class' connotes a safe, comfortable, middle-of-the-road policy. Above all, our language is 'middle-class' in the middle of our road. To drive it to one side or the other or even off the road, is the noblest task of the future.

MORLEY Christopher 1890-1957
7895
All cities are mad: but the madness is gallant.
All cities are beautiful: but the beauty is grim.

7896
The courage of the poet is to keep ajar the door that leads into madness.

7897
The enemies of the future are always the very nicest people.

7898
No man is lonely while eating spaghetti - it requires so much attention.

7899
Any man worth his salt has by the time he is forty-five accumulated a crown of thorns, and the problem is to learn to wear it over one ear.

7900
New York, the nation's thyroid gland.

7901
We are only cave men who have lost their cave.

7902
There is only one success - to be able to spend your life in your own way.

7903
My theology, briefly,
Is that the universe
Was dictated
But not signed.

7904
There are three ingredients in the good life; learning, earning and yearning.

7905 *Thunder on the Left*
Life is a foreign language: all men mispronounce it.

7906
A town that has no ceiling price,
A town of double-talk;
A town so big men name her twice,
Like so; 'N'Yawk, N'Yawk.'

7907
It is unfair to blame man too fiercely for being pugnacious; he learned the habit from nature.

7908
We've had bad luck with our kids - they've all grown up.

MORLEY Lord John 1838-1923
7909
It makes all the difference in the world whether we put truth in the first place, or in the second place.

7910 *On Compromise*
You have not converted a man simply because you have silenced him.

7911 *Critical Miscellanies*
The golden Gospel of Silence is effectively compressed in thirty fine volumes.

7912
Politics is a field where action is one long second best and where the choice constantly lies between two blunders.

7913
He who hates vice hates men.

MORLEY Robert 1908-1992
7914
We are articulate, but we are not particularly conversational. An Englishman won't talk for the sake of talking. He doesn't mind silence. But after the silence, he sometimes says something.

MORNAY Suzanne
7915
In extreme youth, in our most humiliating sorrow, we think we are alone. When we are older we find that others have suffered too.

MORPHY Countess
7916 *English Recipes*
The tragedy of English cooking is that 'plain' cooking cannot be entrusted to 'plain' cooks.

MORRIS Charles 1745-1838
7917 *The Contrast*
If one must have a villa in summer to dwell,
Oh give me the sweet shady side of Pall Mall!

7918 *'Country and Town'*
But a house is much more to my mind than a tree,
And for groves, O! a good grove of chimneys for me.

MORRIS Desmond 1928-
7919 *The Human Zoo*
The city is not a concrete jungle, it is a human zoo.

7920
Life is like a very short visit to a toyshop between birth and death.

7921 *The Naked Ape*
There are one hundred and ninety-three living species of monkeys and apes. One hundred and ninety-two of them are covered with hair. The exception is a naked ape self-named *Homo sapiens.*

MORRIS George Pope 1802-1864
7922 *'Woodman, Spare That Tree'*
Woodman, spare that tree!
Touch not a single bough!
In youth it sheltered me,
And I'll protect it now.

MORRIS Robert T.
7923
I hate funerals, and would not attend my own if it could be avoided, but it is well for every man to stop once in a while to think of what sort of a collection of mourners he is training for his final event.

MORRIS William 1834-1896
7924 *Chants for Socialists 'March of the Workers'*
What is this, the sound and rumour? What is this that all men hear,
Like the wind in hollow valleys when the storm is drawing near,
Like the rolling on of ocean in the eventide of fear?
'Tis the people marching on.

7925 *A Dream of John Ball*
Fellowship is heaven, and lack of fellowship is hell: fellowship is life, and lack of fellowship is death: and the deeds that ye do upon the earth, it is for fellowship's sake that ye do them.

7926 *The Earthly Paradise*
Forget six counties overhung with smoke,
Forget the snorting steam and piston stroke,
Forget the spreading of the hideous town;
Think rather of the pack-horse on the down,
And dream of London, small and white and clean,
The clear Thames bordered by its gardens green.

7927 *The Earthly Paradise 'An Apology'*
The idle singer of an empty day.

7928 *The Earthly Paradise 'An Apology'*
Dreamer of dreams, born out of my due time,
Why should I strive to set the crooked straight?
Let it suffice me that my murmuring rhyme
Beats with light wing against the ivory gate,
Telling a tale not too importunate.

7929 *'The Haystack in the Floods'*
Had she come all the way for this,
To part at last without a kiss?

7930 *Hopes and Fears for Art*
Have nothing in your houses that you do not know to be useful, or believe to be beautiful.

7931 *News from Nowhere*
The reward of labour is life.

MORRISON Edmund
7932
Like stones, words are laborious and unforgiving, and the fitting of them together, like the fitting of stones, demands great patience and strength of purpose and particular skill.

MORRISON Jim 1943-1971
7933 *'Five to One'*
Five to one, baby, one in five,
No one here gets out alive ...
They got the guns but we got the numbers
Gonna win, yeah, we're taking over.

7934 *'Light My Fire'*
C'mon, baby, light my fire.

MORRISON Toni 1931-
7935
We die. That may be the meaning of our lives.
But we do language. That may be the measure
of our lives.

MORROW Dwight 1873-1931
7936
We judge ourselves by our motives and others
by their actions.

7937 *Letter to his son*
The world is divided into people who do things
and people who get the credit. Try, if you can,
to belong to the first class. There's far less
competition.

7938
As I get older ... I become more convinced that
good government is not a substitute for self-
government.

MORTIMER John 1923-
7939 *(attributed, of himself)*
Champagne socialist.

7940 *Clinging to the Wreckage*
The law seems like a sort of maze through
which a client must be led to safety, a collection
of reefs, rocks, and underwater hazards through
which he or she must be piloted.

7941
[Irritable judges] suffer from a bad case of
premature adjudication.

7942 *Paradise Postponed*
They do you a decent death on the hunting-
field.

7943
Being successful in England is a dangerous
occupation.

7944
The virtue of much literature is that it is
dangerous and may do you extreme harm.

7945 *A Voyage Round My Father*
At school I never minded the lessons. I just
resented having to work terribly hard at playing.

7946 *A Voyage Round My Father*
No brilliance is needed in the law. Nothing but
common sense, and relatively clean finger nails.

MORTON Rogers 1914-1979
7947 *(after losing primaries as Ford's campaign
manager)*
I'm not going to rearrange the furniture on the
deck of the Titanic.

MOSELY Sir Oswald 1896-1980
7948
Vote Labour: Sleep Tory.

MOSES Grandma 1860-1961
7949
I paint from the top down. First the sky, then
the mountains, then the hills, then the houses,
then the cattle, and then the people.

MOSES Ludwig van
7950
Government is the only institution that can take
a valuable commodity like paper, and make it
worthless by applying ink.

MOSES Robert 1888-1981
7951
Once you sink that first stake, they'll never
make you pull it up.

MOSLEY Sir Oswald 1896-1980
7952
I am not, and never have been, a man of the
right. My position was on the left and is now in
the centre of politics.

MOSTEL Zero 1915-1977
7953
I wanted to say something about the universe.
There's God, angels, plants ... and horseshit.

MOTHERWELL Robert 1915-1991
7954
Abstract art is uniquely modern. It is a
fundamentally romantic response to modern
life - rebellious, individualistic, unconventional,
sensitive, irritable.

MOTION Andrew 1952-
7955 *'Leaving Belfast'*
Each sudden gust of light explains itself
as flames, but neither they, nor even

bombs redoubled on the hills tonight
can quite include me in their fear.
What does remains invisible, is lost
in curt societies whose deaths become

revenge by morning, and whose homes
are nothing more than all they pity most.

MOTLEY John Lothrop 1814-1877
7956
Give us the luxuries of life, and we will dispense
with its necessities.

7957 *(of William of Orange)*
As long as he lived, he was the guiding star of a whole brave nation, and when he died the little children cried in the streets.

MOTTOES and SLOGANS
7958
Ad majorem Dei gloriam.
To the greater glory of God.

7959 *(advertising slogan)*
Access, your flexible friend.

7960 *(advertising slogan)*
Beanz meanz Heinz.

7961 *(advertising slogan)*
Guinness is good for you.

7962 *(advertising slogan)*
Things go better with Coke.

7963 *(advertising slogan)*
A Mars a day, helps you work, rest and play.

7964 *(advertising slogan, Audi motors)*
Vorsprung durch Technik.
Progress through Technology.

7965 *(advertising slogan, British Egg Marketing Bord)*
Go to work on an egg.

7966 *(advertising slogan, British Telecom)*
It's for you-hoo!

7967 *(advertising slogan, Castelmaine lager)*
Australians wouldn't give a XXXX for anything else.

7968 *(advertising slogan, Doan's Backache Kidney Pills)*
Every picture tells a story.

7969 *(advertising slogan, Double Diamond beer)*
I'm only here for the beer.

7970 *(advertising slogan, Esso)*
Put a tiger in your tank.

7971 *(advertising slogan, the Hat Council)*
If you want to get ahead, get a hat.

7972 *(advertising slogan, Heineken beer)*
Refreshes the parts other beers cannot reach.

7973 *(advertising slogan, Milk Marketing Board)*
Drinka Pinta Milka Day.

7974 *(advertising slogan, Yellow Pages)*
Let your fingers do the walking.

7975 *(government health warning)*
Smoking can seriously damage your health.

7976 *(health slogan, World War II)*
Coughs and sneezes spread diseases. Trap the germs in your handkerchief.

7977 *(issued by Central Office of Information, 1950s)*
Keep Britain Tidy.

7978 *(motto, US Air Force test base)*
Ad Inexplorate.
Toward the Unknown.

7979 *(motto, Boy Scouts)*
Be Prepared.

7980 *(motto, British SAS regiment)*
Who dares wins.

7981 *(motto, the Crown of Scotland)*
Nemo me impune lacessit.
No one provokes me with impunity.

7982 *(motto, the French Revolution)*
Liberté! Égalité! Fraternité!
Freedom! Equality! Brotherhood!

7983 *(motto, the Olympic Games)*
Citius, altius, fortius.
Swifter, higher, stronger.

7984 *(motto, the Order of the Garter)*
Honi soit qui mal y pense.
Evil be to him who evil thinks.

7985 *(motto, the RAF)*
Per ardua ad astra.
Through struggle to the stars.

7986 *(motto, Volunteers Movement)*
Defence, not defiance.

7987 *(on the construction of Dreadnoughts)*
We want eight, and we won't wait.

7988 *(pacifist slogan)*
A bayonet is a weapon with a worker at each end.

7989 *(pacifist slogan)*
War will cease when men refuse to fight.

7990 *(recruiting advertisement, World War I)*
What did you do in the Great War, daddy?

7991 *(safety slogan, USA)*
Stop-look-listen.

7992 *(security slogan, World War II)*
Careless talk costs lives.

7993 *(slogan, 1968)*
Je suis Marxiste - tendance Groucho.
I am a Marxist - of the Groucho tendency.

7994 *(slogan, AIDS awareness)*
Don't die of ignorance.

7995 *(slogan, American civil rights campaigners)*
Black is beautiful.

7996 *(slogan, American life insurance)*
Death [is] nature's way of telling you to slow down.

7997 *(slogan, US Armed Forces)*
The difficult we do immediately - the impossible takes a little longer.

7998 *(slogan, Black Extremists)*
Burn, Baby, Burn.

7999 *(slogan, Black Panther movement)*
Power to the people.

8000 *(slogan, British Rail)*
Let the train take the strain.

8001 *(slogan, British Telecom)*
It's good to talk.

8002 *(slogan, Campaign for Nuclear Disarmament)*
Ban the Bomb.

8003 *(slogan, Conservative Party, 1978)*
Labour isn't working.

8004 *(slogan, Democratic Party, 1960)*
All the way, with LBJ.

8005 *(slogan, Democratic Party, 1952)*
You never had it so good.

8006 *(slogan, FBI)*
Crime doesn't pay.

8007 *(slogan, national campaign in 1968)*
I'm backing Britain.

8008 *(slogan, Nazi party)*
Ein reich, ein volk, ein Führer.
One realm, one people, one leader.

8009 *(slogan, nuclear disarmament campaigners)*
Better red than dead.

8010 *(slogan, road safety)*
Don't ask a man to drink and drive.

8011 *(slogan, road safety campaign)*
Clunk, click, *every* trip.

8012 *(slogan, Tesco stores)*
Pile it high, sell it cheap.

8013 *(slogan, Woolworth stores)*
Nothing over sixpence.

8014 *(slogan, World Whores Congress)*
Good girls go to heaven. Bad girls go everywhere.

8015 *(student slogan, 1960s)*
Make love, not war.

MOULTON Lord 1844-1921
8016
Tyranny is yielding to the lust of governing.

MOUNTBATTEN Louis, Earl 1900-1979
8017
The nuclear arms race has no military purpose.
Wars cannot be fought with nuclear weapons. Their existence only adds to our perils.

MOZART Wolfgang Amadeus 1756-1791
8018
Neither a lofty degree of intelligence nor imagination nor both together go to the making of genius. Love, love, love, that is the soul of genius.

8019
I write as a sow piddles.

MUGABE Robert 1924-
8020
Cricket civilizes people and creates good gentlemen. I want everyone to play cricket in Zimbabwe; I want ours to be a nation of gentlemen.

MUGGERIDGE Malcolm 1903-1990
8021
Good taste and humour are a contradiction in terms, like a chaste whore.

8022 *The Infernal Grove*
To succeed pre-eminently in English public life it is necessary to conform either to the popular image of a bookie or of a clergyman; Churchill being a perfect example of the former, Halifax of the latter.

8023
Few men of action have been able to make a graceful exit at the appropriate time.

8024
An orgy looks particularly alluring seen through the mists of righteous indignation.

8025 *Tread Softly*
The orgasm has replaced the Cross as the focus of longing and the image of fulfilment.

8026 *Tread Softly (of Sir Anthony Eden)*
He was not only a bore; he bored for England.

8027
When you reach your sixties, you have to decide whether you're going to be a sot or an ascetic. In other words if you want to go on working after you're sixty, some degree of asceticism is inevitable.

MUIR Edwin 1887-1959
8028 *Journeys and Places 'Hölderlin's Journey'*
And without fear the lawless roads
Ran wrong through all the land.

MULLER Herbert J.
8029
Few have heard of Fra Luca Parioli, the inventor of double entry bookkeeping, but he has probably had more influence on human life than has Dante or Michelangelo.

The Wordsworth Dictionary of Quotations

MUMFORD Ethel Watts
8030
O wad some power the giftie gie us to see some people before they see us.

MUMFORD Lewis 1895-1990
8031 *The Brown Decades*
Every generation revolts against its fathers and makes friends with its grandfathers.

8032
One of the functions of intelligence is to take account of the dangers that come from trusting solely to the intelligence.

8033
Our national flower is the concrete cloverleaf.

MUNTHE Axel 1857-1949
8034
Christ - an anarchist who succeeded.

8035
A man can stand a lot as long as he can stand himself. He can live without hope, without friends, without books, even without music, as long as he can listen to his own thoughts.

MURDOCH Dame Iris 1919-
8036
The absolute yearning of one human body for another particular body and its indifference to substitutes is one of life's major mysteries.

8037 *The Bell*
Dora Greenfield left her husband because she was afraid of him. She decided six months later to return to him for the same reason.

8038
We live in a fantasy world, a world of illusion. The great task in life is to find reality.

8039 *Metaphysics as a Guide to Morals*
Insight into the truth is the flash which in live conversation upon serious matters, carries one beyond words.

8040 *Nuns and Soldiers*
Only in our virtues are we original, because virtue is difficult ... Vices are general, virtues are particular.

8041 *'The Sublime and the Beautiful Revisited'*
Freedom is not choosing; that is merely the move that we make when all is already lost. Freedom is knowing and understanding and respecting things quite other than ourselves.

8042 *'The Sublime and the Good'*
Love is the extremely difficult realization that something other than oneself is real.

MURRAY Jim
8043 *(on the death of Casey Stengel)*
Well, God is certainly getting an earful tonight.

MURRAY Lord William 1705-1793
8044 *(advice to newly appointed colonial governor)*
Consider what you think justice requires, and decide accordingly. But never give your reasons; for your judgement will probably be right, but your reasons will certainly be wrong.

MURROW Edward R. 1908-1965
8045
Everyone is a prisoner of his own experiences. No one can eliminate prejudices - just recognize them.

8046 *(of the Vietnam War)*
Anyone who isn't confused doesn't really understand the situation.

8047
He [Winston Churchill] mobilized the English language and sent it into battle to steady his fellow countrymen and hearten those Europeans upon whom the long dark night of tyranny had descended.

MURRY John Middleton 1889-1957
8048
There is nothing more dangerous to the formation of a prose style than the endeavour to make it poetic.

MUSSELMAN M.M.
8049
One of the best things about marriage is that it gets young people to bed at a decent hour.

MUSSET Alfred de 1810-1857
8050 *La Coupe et les lèvres*
I hate like death the situation of the plagiarist; the glass I drink from is not large, but at least it is my own.

8051 *'L'Espoir en Dieu'*
I can't help it, the idea of the infinite torments me.

8052 *Lorenzaccio*
Great artists have no country.

8053 *Rollo*
I have come too late into a world too old.

MUSSOLINI Benito 1883-1945
8054
If I advance, follow me! If I retreat, cut me down! If I die, avenge me!

8055 *(to a station-master)*
We must leave exactly on time ... From now on everything must function to perfection.

8056
You know what I think about violence. For me it is profoundly moral - more moral than compromises and transactions.

MUSSORGSKY Modeste Petrovich 1839-1881
8057
Art is not an end in itself, but a means of addressing humanity.

MUSTE A.J. 1885-1967
8058
There is no way to peace. Peace is the way.

NABOKOV Vladimir 1899-1977
8059
Genius is an African who dreams up snow.

8060
No one can any longer write in the fat style of Strauss. That was killed by Stravinsky. He stripped the body of much of its clothes. Music is the craft of building structures with sound and that is what Stravinsky represents.

8061 *Pale Fire*
Life is a great surprise. I do not see why death should not be an even greater one.

8062 *Speak, Memory*
The cradle rocks above an abyss, and common sense tells us that our existence is but a brief crack of light between two eternities of darkness.

8063 *Strong Opinions*
I think like a genius, I write like a distinguished author, and I speak like a child.

8064 *Strong Opinions*
A work of art has no importance whatever to society. It is only important to the individual, and only the individual reader is important to me.

NADER Ralph 1934-
8065
Unsafe at any speed.

NAIPAUL V.S. 1932-
8066
One always writes comedy at the moment of deepest hysteria.

NAIRN Ian 1930-
8067
If what is called development is allowed to multiply at the present rate, then by the end of the century Great Britain will consist of isolated oases of preserved monuments in a desert of wire, concrete roads, cosy plots and bungalows ... Upon this new Britain the *Review* bestows a name in the hope that it will stick - SUBTOPIA.

NAITO Fern
8068
When you've got them by their wallets, their hearts and minds will follow.

NAMATH Joe 1943-
8069
When you win, nothing hurts.

NANSEN Fridtjof 1861-1930
8070
Never stop because you are afraid - you are never so likely to be wrong. Never keep a line of retreat: it is a wretched invention. The difficult is what takes a little time; the impossible is what takes a little longer.

NAPOLÉON I (Bonaparte) 1769-1821
8071 *(attributed)*
An army marches on its stomach.

8072 *(on the introduction of the metric system)*
Nothing is more contrary to the organization of the mind, of the memory, and of the imagination ... The new system of weights and measures will be a stumbling block and the source of difficulties for several generations ... It's just tormenting the people with trivia!!!

8073
L'Angleterre est une nation de boutiquiers.
England is a nation of shopkeepers.

8074
Le courage de l'improviste.
Spontaneous courage.

8075 *Letter to Consul Cambacérès (of the Channel)*
It is a mere ditch, and will be crossed as soon as someone has the courage to attempt it.

8076 *Letter to Empress Josephine (justifying divorce)*
I still love you, but ...

8077 *Letter to J. Finckenstein*
It is easier to put up with unpleasantness from a man of one's own way of thinking than from one who takes an entirely different point of view.

8078 *Letter to the King of Holland*
A prince who gets a reputation for good nature in the first year of his reign, is laughed at in the second.

8079 *(attributed, but probably apocryphal)*
Not tonight, Josephine.

8080 *(reply to Spanish king)*
The bullet that is to kill me has not yet been moulded.

8081 *(after the retreat from Moscow)*
There is only one step from the sublime to the ridiculous.

8082
Soldiers, consider that from the summit of these pyramids, forty centuries look down upon you.

8083
In war, three-quarters turns on personal
character and relations; the balance of
manpower and materials counts only for the
remaining quarter.

8084 *(when asked how to deal with the Pope)*
As though he had 200,000 men.

NASH Ogden 1902-1971
8085 *The Canary*
The song of canaries
Never varies,
And when they're moulting
They're pretty revolting.

8086 'The Cow'
The cow is of the bovine ilk;
One end is moo, the other, milk.

8087
Ask Daddy, He Won't Know.

8088 *England Expects*
Children aren't happy with nothing to ignore,
And that's what parents were created for.

8089 'Family Court'
One would be in less danger
From the wiles of the stranger
If one's own kin and kith
Were more fun to be with.

8090
Another good thing about gossip is that it is
within everybody's reach,
And it is much more interesting than any other
form of speech.

8091 'Lather as You Go'
Beneath this slab
John Brown is stowed.
He watched the ads,
And not the road.

8092 'Lines on Facing Forty'
I have a bone to pick with Fate.
Come here and tell me, girlie,
Do you think my mind is maturing late,
Or simply rotted early?

8093
Middle age: when you're sitting at home on
Saturday night and the telephone rings and you
hope it isn't for you.

8094
Parsley
is gharsley.

8095 'The Perfect Husband'
He tells you when you've got on too much
lipstick,
And helps you with your girdle when your hips
stick.

8096 'Plea for Less Malice Toward None'
Any kiddie in school can love like a fool,
But hating, my boy, is an art.

8097
Poets aren't very useful,
Because they aren't consumeful or very
produceful.

8098
Progress might have been all right once, but it's
gone on too long.

8099
Purity is obscurity.

8100 'Reflections on Ice-breaking'
Candy
Is dandy
But liquor
Is quicker.

8101 'Samson Agonistes'
I test my bath before I sit,
And I'm always moved to wonderment
That what chills the finger not a bit
Is so frigid upon the fundament.

8102
Senescence begins
And middle age ends,
The day your descendants
Outnumber your friends.

8103 'Song of the Open Road'
I think that I shall never see
A billboard lovely as a tree.
Perhaps, unless the billboards fall,
I'll never see a tree at all.

8104 'What's the Use?'
Sure, deck your lower limbs in pants;
Yours are the limbs, my sweeting.
You look divine as you advance -
Have you seen yourself retreating?

8105
In the world of mules there are no rules.

NASHE Thomas 1567-1601
8106 *Summer's Last Will and Testament*
Beauty is but a flower
Which wrinkles will devour;
Brightness falls from the air;
Dust hath closed Helen's eye.
I am sick, I must die.
Lord have mercy on us.

8107 *Summer's Last Will and Testament*
From winter, plague and pestilence, good lord,
deliver us!

NATHAN George Jean 1882-1958
8108
I drink to make other people interesting.

8109
Love demands infinitely less than friendship.

8110
Love is an emotion experienced by the many and enjoyed by the few.

8111
Opening night is the night before the play is ready to open.

NAVRATILOVA Martina 1956-
8112
The moment of victory is much too short to live for that and nothing else.

NAYLOR James Ball 1860-1945
8113 *'King David and King Solomon'*
King David and King Solomon
Led merry, merry lives,
With many, many lady friends,
And many, many wives;
But when old age crept over them -
With many, many qualms! -
King Solomon wrote the Proverbs
And King David wrote the Psalms.

NEALE John Mason 1818-1866
8114
Good King Wenceslas looked out,
On the Feast of Stephen;
When the snow lay round about,
Deep and crisp and even.

8115
Jesusalem the golden,
With milk and honey blest,
Beneath thy contemplation
Sink heart and voice opprest.

8116
In his master's steps he trod,
Where the snow lay dinted.

NEEDHAM Richard J.
8117
God punishes us mildly by ignoring our prayers and severely by answering them.

8118
Love is a fever which marriage puts to bed and cures.

8119
People are like birds - from a distance, beautiful: from close up, those sharp beaks, those beady little eyes.

8120
People who are brutally honest get more satisfaction out of the brutality than out of the honesty.

8121
Power is a drug on which the politicians are hooked. They buy it from the voters, using the voters' own money.

8122
When a man tells me he's run out of steam in the sex department, I'll tell him, 'Count your blessings; you've escaped from the clutches of a cruel tyrant. Enjoy!'

NEHRU Jawaharlal 1889-1964
8123 *'Basic Approach'*
Democracy and socialism are means to an end, not the end itself.

8124 *'Basic Approach'*
Normally speaking, it may be said that the forces of a capitalist society, if left unchecked, tend to make the rich richer and the poor poorer and thus increase the gap between them.

8125
Democracy is good. I say this because other systems are worse.

8126 *(following Gandhi's assassination)*
The light has gone out of our lives and there is darkness everywhere.

NELLIST Dave 1952-
8127
The quickest way to become a left winger in the Labour Party today is to stand still for six months.

NELSON Horatio Lord 1758-1805
8128 *(before the battle of the Nile)*
Before this time to-morrow I shall have gained a peerage, or Westminster Abbey.

8129 *(at the battle of Trafalgar)*
England expects that every man will do his duty.

8130 *(at the battle of Trafalgar)*
This is too warm work, Hardy, to last long.

8131 *(at the battle of Trafalgar)*
Thank God, I have done my duty.

8132 *(at the battle of Trafalgar)*
Kiss me, Hardy.

8133
In case signals can neither be seen nor perfectly understood, no captain can do very wrong if he places his ship alongside the enemy.

8134
Close with a Frenchman, but out-manoeuvre a Russian.

8135
You must consider every man your enemy who speaks ill of your king: and ... you must hate a Frenchman as you hate the devil.

8136 *(putting telescope to his blind eye)*
I have a right to be blind sometimes ... I really do not see the signal!

8137
Something must be left to chance; nothing is sure in a sea fight beyond all others.

8138 *(when asked to cover the stars on his uniform)*
In honour I gained them, and in honour I will die with them.

NELSON John Kirk
8139
More and more these days I find myself pondering on how to reconcile my net income with my gross habits.

NERO AD 37-68
8140
What an artist dies with me!

NERVAL Gérard de 1808-1855
8141 *Les Chimères 'El Desdichado'*
I am the darkly shaded, the bereaved, the inconsolate, the prince of Aquitaine, with the blasted tower. My only *star* is dead, and my star-strewn lute carries on it the black *sun* of *melancholy*.

8142 *Les Chimères 'Le Christ aux Oliviers'*
God is dead! Heaven is empty - Weep, children, you no longer have a father.

NEURATH Otto 1882-1945
8143 *Logical Positivism 'Protocal Sentences'*
We are like sailors who must rebuild their ship on the open sea, never able to dismantle it in dry-dock and to reconstruct it there out of the best materials.

NEVILL Dorothy d.1913
8144
The real art of conversation is not only to say the right thing in the right place but to leave unsaid the wrong thing at the tempting moment.

NEWBOLT Sir Henry 1862-1938
8145 *'Clifton Chapel'*
To set the cause above renown,
To love the game beyond the prize,
To honour, while you strike him down,
The foe that comes with fearless eyes.

8146 *'Drake's Drum'*
'Take my drum to England, hang et by the shore,
Strike et when your powder's runnin' low;
If the Dons sight Devon, I'll quit the port o' Heaven,
An' drum them up the Channel as we drummed them long ago.'

8147 *'Drake's Drum'*
Drake he's in his hammock till the great Armadas come.
(Capten, art tha sleepin' there below?)

8148 *'Drake's Drum'*
Call him on the deep sea, call him up the Sound,
Call him when ye sail to meet the foe;
Where the old trade's plyin' an' the old flag flyin'
They shall find him ware an' wakin', as they found him long ago!

8149 *'He Fell Among Thieves'*
'Ye have robbed,' said he, 'ye have slaughtered and made an end,
Take your ill-got plunder, and bury the dead.'

8150 *'The Fighting Téméraire'*
Now the sunset breezes shiver,
And she's fading down the river,
But in England's song for ever
She's the Fighting Téméraire.

8151 *'Vitaï Lampada'*
There's a breathless hush in the Close to-night -
Ten to make and the match to win -
A bumping pitch and a blinding light,
An hour to play and the last man in.
And it's not for the sake of a ribboned coat,
Or the selfish hope of a season's fame,
But his Captain's hand on his shoulder smote -
'Play up! play up! and play the game'.

8152 *'Vitaï Lampada'*
The river of death has brimmed its banks
And England's far and honour a name,
But the voice of a schoolboy rallies the ranks:
'Play up! play up! and play the game!'

NEWLEY Anthony and BRICUSSE Leslie 1931- and 1931-
8153
Stop the world, I want to get off.

NEWLOVE John
8154
If you know nothing, be pleased to know nothing.

NEWMAN Andrea
8155
Toothache doesn't stop hurting because someone else has cancer.

NEWMAN Ernest 1868-1959
8156
The good composer is slowly discovered, the bad composer is slowly found out.

NEWMAN John Henry, Cardinal 1801-1890
8157
Let us act on what we have, since we have not what we wish.

8158 *Apologia pro Vita Sua*
It is very difficult to get up resentment towards persons whom one has never seen.

8159 *Apologia pro Vita Sua*
There is such a thing as legitimate warfare: war has its laws; there are things which may fairly be done, and things which may not be done ... He has attempted (as I may call it) to *poison the wells*.

8160 *Apologia pro Vita Sua*
I will vanquish, not my Accuser, but my judges.

8161 *Apologia pro Vita Sua*
Two and two only supreme and luminously self-evident beings, myself and my Creator.

8162 *Apologia pro Vita Sua*
Ten thousand difficulties do not make one doubt.

8163 *Apologia pro Vita Sua*
The all-corroding, all-dissolving scepticism of the intellect in religious enquiries.

8164
We should ever conduct ourselves towards our enemy as if he were one day to be our friend.

8165 *The Dream of Gerontius*
Praise to the Holiest in the height,
And in the depth be praise;
In all his words most wonderful,
Most sure in all His ways.

8166 *'Faith and Reason, ...'*
When men understand what each other mean, they see, for the most part, that controversy is either superfluous or hopeless.

8167
Growth is the only evidence of life.

8168 *The Idea of a University*
It is almost a definition of a gentleman to say that he is one who never inflicts pain.

8169 *'Lead, kindly Light'*
Lead, kindly Light, amid the encircling gloom,
Lead thou me on;
The night is dark, and I am far from home.

8170 *'Lead, kindly Light'*
I loved the garish day, and spite of fears,
Pride ruled my will: remember not past years.

8171 *Letter to Mrs William Froude*
We can believe what we choose. We are answerable for what we choose to believe.

8172
Reason is God's gift, but so are the passions. Reason is as guilty as passion.

8173 *Sermons Bearing on Subjects of the Day*
May He support us all the day long, till the shades lengthen, and the evening comes, and the busy world is hushed, and the fever of life is over, and our work is done! Then in His mercy may he give us a safe lodging, and a holy rest, and peace at the last.

8174 *'The Usurpations of Reason'*
It is as absurd to argue men, as to torture them, into believing.

NEWMAN Paul 1925-
8175 *in Butch Cassidy and the Sundance Kid*
"He'll feel a lot better once we've robbed a couple of banks."

NEWMAN Peter
8176
Power tends to connect; absolute power connects absolutely.

NEWTON A. Edward
8177
The formula for complete happiness is to be very busy with the unimportant.

NEWTON Sir Isaac 1642-1727
8178 *(to a dog who destroyed some of his work)*
O Diamond! Diamond! thou little knowest the mischief done!

8179
I don't know what I may seem to the world, but as to myself, I seem to have been only like a boy playing on the sea-shore and diverting myself in now and then finding a smoother pebble or a prettier shell than ordinary, whilst the great ocean of truth lay all undiscovered before me.

8180 *Letter to Edmond Halley*
Philosophy is such an impertinently litigious lady that a man has as good be engaged in law suits as have to do with her.

8181 *Letter to Robert Hooke*
If I have seen further it is by standing on the shoulders of giants.

8182 *Opticks*
Whence is it that Nature does nothing in vain: and whence arises all that order and beauty which we see in the world? ... does it not appear from phenomena that there is a Being incorporeal, living, intelligent, omnipresent, who in infinite space, as it were in his Sensory, sees the things themselves intimately, and thoroughly perceives them, and comprehends them wholly.

8183 *Opticks*
The changing of bodies into light, and light into bodies, is very comfortable to the course of Nature, which seems delighted with transmutations.

8184 *Principia Mathematica*
Every body continues in its state of rest, or of uniform motion in a right line, unless it is compelled to change that state by forces impressed upon it.

8185 *Principia Mathematica*
The alteration of motion is ever proportional to the motive force impressed; and is made in the direction of the right line in which that force is impressed.

8186 *Principia Mathematica*
To every action there is always opposed an equal reaction: or the mutual actions of two bodies upon each other are always equal, and directed to contrary parts.

8187 *Principia Mathematica*
Hypotheses non fingo.
I do not feign hypotheses.

NEWTON John 1725-1807
8188 *'Amazing grace'*
Amazing grace! how sweet the sound
That saved a wretch like me!
I once was lost, but now am found,
Was blind, but now I see.

8189 *'How sweet the name of Jesus sounds'*
How sweet the name of Jesus sounds
In a believer's ear!
It soothes his sorrows, heals his wounds,
And drives away his fear.

NICHOLAS I 1796-1855
8190 *(attributed)*
Russia has two generals in whom she can confide - Generals Janvier [January] and Février [February].

8191
Turkey is a dying man. We may endeavour to keep him alive, but we shall not succeed. He will, he must die.

NICHOLSON Jack 1937-
8192
You only lie to two people; your girlfriend and the police. Everyone else you tell the truth to.

NICHOLSON William
8193 *Shadowlands*
We read to know we are not alone.

8194 *Shadowlands (words spoken by C. S. Lewis)*
Happiness is not wanting to be anywhere else, not waiting for anything new to happen, not looking round the next corner or over the next hill.

NICIAS c.470-413 BC
8195
For a city consists in men, and not in walls nor in ships empty of men.

NICOLLE Charles 1866-1936
8196
Chance favours only those who know how to court her.

NICOLSON Sir Harold 1886-1968
8197 *(anticipating the aftermath of World War 2)*
We shall have to walk and live a Woolworth life hereafter.

8198 *Diaries and Letters*
I am haunted by mental decay such as I saw creeping over Ramsay MacDonald. A gradual dimming of the lights.

8199
To be a good diarist, one must have a little snouty, sneaky mind.

8200 *(of King George V)*
For seventeen years he did nothing at all but kill animals and stick in stamps.

8201 *Public Faces*
Ponderous and uncertain is that relation between pressure and resistance which constitutes the balance of power. The arch of peace is morticed by no iron tendons ... One night a handful of dust will patter from the vaulting: the bats will squeak and wheel in sudden panic: nor can the fragile fingers of man then stay the rush and rumble of destruction.

8202
The worst thing, I fear, about being no longer young, is that one is no longer young.

NIEBUHR Reinhold 1892-1971
8203 *Children of Light and Children of Darkness*
Man's capacity for justice makes democracy possible, but man's inclination to injustice makes democracy necessary.

8204
O God, give us serenity to accept what cannot be changed; courage to change what should be changed, and wisdom to distinguish the one from the other.

8205
The mastery of nature is vainly believed to be an adequate substitute for self-mastery.

8206
The sad duty of politics is to establish justice in a sinful world.

NIEMÖLLER Martin 1892-1984
8207
When Hitler attacked the Jews I was not a Jew, therefore, I was not concerned. And when Hitler attacked the Catholics, I was not a Catholic, and therefore, I was not concerned. And when Hitler attacked the unions and the industrialists, I was not a member of the unions

and I was not concerned. Then, Hitler attacked me and the Protestant church - and there was nobody left to be concerned.

NIETZSCHE Friedrich 1844-1900

8208
The abdomen is the reason why man does not easily take himself for a god.

8209
The advantage of a bad memory is that one enjoys several times the same good thing for the first time.

8210 *The Antichrist*
Woman was God's second blunder.

8211 *The Antichrist*
When a man is in love he endures more than at other times; he submits to everything.

8212
In architecture the pride of man, his triumph over gravitation, his will to power, assume a visible form. Architecture is a sort of oratory of power by means of forms.

8213
Ascetic: one who makes a necessity of virtue.

8214
Our destiny rules over us, even when we are not yet aware of it; it is the future that makes laws for our today.

8215 *Die fröhliche Wissenschaft*
God is dead: but considering the state the species Man is in, there will perhaps be caves, for ages yet, in which his shadow will be shown.

8216 *Die fröhliche Wissenschaft*
Morality is the herd-instinct in the individual.

8217 *Die fröhliche Wissenschaft*
The Christian resolution to find the world ugly and bad has made the world ugly and bad.

8218 *Die fröhliche Wissenschaft*
Believe me! The secret of reaping the greatest fruitfulness and the greatest enjoyment from life is *to live dangerously!*

8219
To do great things is difficult, but to command great things is more difficult.

8220 *Ecce Homo*
As an artist, a man has no home in Europe save in Paris.

8221 *Ecce Homo*
My time has not yet come either; some are born posthumously.

8222
There are no facts, only interpretations.

8223
Should not the giver be thankful that the receiver received? Is not giving a need? Is not receiving, mercy?

8224
One is healthy when one can laugh at the earnestness and zeal with which one has been hypnotized by any single detail of one's life.

8225
The historian looks backward. In the end he also believes backward.

8226
Insanity in individuals is rare - but in groups, parties, nations, and epochs, it is the rule.

8227 *Jenseits von Gut und Böse*
He who fights with monsters might take care lest he thereby become a monster. And if you gaze for long into an abyss, the abyss gazes also into you.

8228 *Jenseits von Gut und Böse*
The thought of suicide is a great source of comfort: with it a calm passage is to be made across many a bad night.

8229 *Jenseits von Gut und Böse*
Herren-Moral und Sklaven-Moral.
Master-morality and slave-morality.

8230 *Jenseits von Gut und Böse*
Is not life a hundred times too short for us to bore ourselves?

8231
A joke is an epigram on the death of a feeling.

8232
The lie is a condition of life.

8233
The lonely one offers his hand too quickly to whomever he encounters.

8234 *Menschliches, Allzumenschliches*
Wit is the epitaph of an emotion.

8235
Without music, life would be a mistake.

8236
Never to talk of oneself is a form of hypocrisy.

8237
A politician divides mankind into two classes: tools and enemies.

8238
Profundity of thought belongs to youth, clarity of thought to old age.

8239
Sleeping is no mean art. For its sake one must stay awake all day.

8240
Speaking generally, punishment hardens and
numbs, it produces concentration, it sharpens
the consciousness of alienation, it strengthens
the power of resistance.

8241 *Thus spoke Zarathustra*
I teach you the superman. Man is something to
be surpassed.

8242
It is not the strength, but the duration, of great
sentiments that makes great men.

8243
I understand by 'freedom of spirit' something
quite definite - the unconditional will to say No,
where it is dangerous to say No.

8244
The most unendurable thing, to be sure, the
really terrible thing, would be a life without
habits, a life which continually required
improvisation.

8245
What does not destroy me, makes me strong.

8246
Of what is great, one must either be silent, or
speak with greatness - that means cynically and
with innocence.

8247
When one has not had a good father, one must
create one.

8248
When a hundred men stand together, each of
them loses his mind and gets another one.

8249
When thou goest to woman, take thy whip.

8250
Not to he who is offensive to us are we most
unfair, but to he who does not concern us at all.

8251
He who has a why to live can bear with almost
anyhow.

8252
A woman may very well form a friendship with
a man, but for this to endure, it must be
assisted by a little physical antipathy.

8253
Has a woman who knew that she was well
dressed ever caught a cold?

8254
The more you let yourself go, the less others let
you go.

NIGHTINGALE Earl
8255
Success is the progressive realization of a
worthy ideal.

NIGHTINGALE Florence 1820-1910
8256
The very first requirement in a hospital is that it
should do the sick no harm.

8257 *Notes on Nursing*
No *man*, not even a doctor, ever gives any other
definition of what a nurse should be than this -
'devoted and obedient'. This definition would
do just as well for a porter. It might even do for
a horse. It would not do for a policeman.

8258 *(on the Order of Merit being brought to her
home)*
Too kind, too kind.

NIN Anaïs 1903-1977
8259
It is the function of art to renew our perception.
What we are familiar with we cease to see. The
writer shakes up the familiar scene, and as if by
magic, we see a new meaning in it.

8260
A war regarded as inevitable or even probable,
and therefore much prepared for, has a very
good chance of eventually being fought.

NIXON Richard 1913-1994
8261
Sometimes at the end of the day when I'm
smiling and shaking hands, I want to kick them.

8262
You know very well that whether you are on
page one or page thirty depends on whether
they fear you. It is just as simple as that.

8263
I let the American people down, and I have to
carry that burden for the rest of my life. My
political life is over. I will never again have an
opportunity to serve in any official position.
Maybe I can give a little advice from time to
time.

8264
I brought myself down. I gave them a sword.
And they stuck it in.

8265 *(farewell address)*
This country needs good farmers, good
businessmen, good plumbers, good carpenters.

8266
The great silent majority.

8267 *(on Watergate)*
There can be no whitewash at the White House.

8268
The people's right to change what does not work is one of the greatest principles of our system of government.

8269
I welcome this kind of examination because people have got to know whether or not their President is a crook. Well, I'm not a crook.

8270
When the President does it, that means that it is not illegal.

8271
Those who hate you don't win unless you hate them - and then you destroy yourself.

NIZER Louis 1902-
8272
In cross-examination, as in fishing, nothing is more ungainly than a fisherman pulled into the water by his catch.

NOCHLIN Linda
8273
Safe taste is bad taste.

NOEL Thomas 1799-1861
8274 *'The Pauper's Drive'*
Rattle his bones over the stones;
He's only a pauper, whom nobody owns!

NOLTE Dorothy Law
8275
If a child lives with approval, he learns to live with himself.

NORDEN Dennis
8276 *(dictum on television scripts)*
We don't want it good - we want it Tuesday.

NORFOLK Charles Howard, Duke of 1746-1815
8277
If a man is to go to the devil, he may as well go thither from the House of Lords as from any other place on earth.

NORRIS Kathleen 1880-
8278
Just the knowledge that a good book is awaiting one at the end of a long day makes that day happier.

8279
Marriage; a job. Happiness or unhappiness has nothing to do with it.

8280
There is no solitude in the world like that of the big city.

NORTH Christopher 1785-1854
8281
Such accidents will happen in the best-regulated families.

8282
Animosities are mortal, but the Humanities live for ever.

8283
Insultin the sun, and quarrellin wi' the equator.

8284
Laws were made to be broken.

8285
His majesty's dominions, on which the sun ever sets.

8286
I cannot sit still, James, and hear you abuse the shopocracy.

NORTHCLIFFE Lord 1865-1922
8287
The power of the press is very great, but not so great as the power of suppress.

8288
When I want a peerage, I shall buy it like an honest man.

NORTON Caroline 1808-1877
8289 *'Not Lost but Gone Before'*
For death and life, in ceaseless strife,
Beat wild on this world's shore,
And all our calm is in that balm -
Not lost but gone before.

NORWORTH Jack 1879-1959
8290 *'Shine On, Harvest Moon'*
Oh, shine on, shine on, harvest moon
Up in the sky.
I ain't had no lovin'
Since April, January, June, or July.

NOVALIS 1772-1801
8291
Character is perfectly educated will.

8292 *Heinrich von Ofterdingen*
I often feel, and ever more deeply I realise, that fate and character are the same conception.

8293
Not only England, but every Englishman is an island.

8294 *(of Spinoza, attributed)*
A God-intoxicated man.

NYE Bill
8295 *Autobiography*
I have been told that Wagner's music is better than it sounds.

NYE Edgar Wilson
8296
There must be at least 500 million rats in the United States; of course, I am speaking only from memory.

OATES Captain Lawrence 1880-1912
8297 *(last words)*
I am just going outside and may be some time.

O'BRIEN Edna 1936-
8298
August is a wicked month.

O'BRIEN Flann 1911-1966
8299 *The Hard Life*
It is not that I half knew my mother. I knew half of her: the lower half - her lap, legs, feet, her hands and wrists as she bent forward.

8300 *At Swim-Two-Birds*
The conclusion of your syllogism, I said lightly, is fallacious, being based upon licensed premises.

8301 *At Swim-Two-Birds*
A pint of plain is your only man.

O'CASEY Sean 1880-1964
8302 *Juno and the Paycock*
The whole worl's in a state o' chassis!

8303 *Juno and the Paycock*
The Polis as Polis, in this city, is Null an' Void!

8304 *(of P.G. Wodehouse)*
English literature's performing flea.

8305 *The Plough and the Stars*
There's no reason to bring religion into it. I think we ought to have as great a regard for religion as we can, so as to keep it out of as many things as possible.

8306 *The Plough and the Stars*
It's my rule never to lose me temper till it would be dethrimental to keep it.

8307
You cannot put a rope around the neck of an idea: you cannot put an idea up against a barrack-square wall and riddle it with bullets: you cannot confine it in the strongest prison cell that your slaves could ever build.

OCHS Adolph S. 1858-1935
8308 *(motto of the New York Times)*
All the news that's fit to print.

O'CONNELL Daniel 1775-1847
8309
The Englishman has all the qualities of a poker except its occasional warmth.

8310
Peel's smile: like the silver plate on a coffin.

8311
Whatever little we have gained, we have gained by agitation, while we have uniformly lost by moderation.

O'CONNOR Frank 1903-1966
8312
No man is as anti-feminist as a really feminine woman.

ODETS Clifford 1906-1963
8313
Sex - the poor man's polo.

O'DONNELL Emmett
8314
Retirement: statutory senility.

O'FAOLAIN Sean 1900-
8315
Celibacy bestows on a man the qualified freedom of a besieged city where one sometimes has to eat rats.

8316
An Irish queer: a fellow who prefers women to drink.

8317
Love lives in sealed bottles of regret.

OGBURN Jr. Charleton
8318
Happiness to a dog is what lies on the other side of a door.

OGILVY David 1911-
8319 *(advice to advertising copywriters)*
The consumer is not a moron; she's your wife.

OGILVY James 1664-1730
8320 *(as he signed the Act of Union)*
Now there's ane end of ane old song.

O'HARA Frank 1926-1966
8321
It is easy to be beautiful; it is difficult to appear so.

O'HARA John 1905-1970
8322 *The Portable F. Scott Fitzgerald*
An artist is his own fault.

O'HARA Neal
8323
We forget that money gives its value - that someone exchanged work for it.

O'HARA Theodore 1820-1867
8324 'The Bivouac of the Dead'
Sons of the dark and bloody ground.

O'KEEFE Patrick 1872-1934
8325 *(slogan for the Society of American Florists)*
Say it with flowers.

O'KEEFFE John 1747-1833
8326 *The Agreeable Surprise*
Amo, amas, I love a lass,
As a cedar tall and slender;
Sweet cowslip's grace
Is her nom'native case,

And she's of the feminine gender.

8327 *The Irish Mimic*
Fat, fair and forty were all the toasts of the young men.

OLIVER Frederick Scott 1864-1934
8328 *The Endless Adventure*
A wise politician will never grudge a genuflexion or a rapture if it is expected of him by prevalent opinion.

OLIVIER Sir Laurence 1907-1989
8329
Acting is a masochistic form of exhibitionism. It is not quite the occupation of an adult.

8330 *(appealing on behalf of the Rose Theatre remains)*
Can a muse of fire exist under a ceiling of commerce?

8331 *(introduction to his screen adaptation of Hamlet)*
The tragedy of a man who could not make up his mind.

8332 *(after a performance as 'Othello')*
I know it was wonderful, but I don't know how I did it.

8333 *in Rebecca*
"I'm asking you to marry me, you little fool"

8334
Shakespeare - the nearest thing in incarnation to the eye of God.

OLSEN Ken 1926-
8335 *(whilst President of Digital Equipment Corp 1977)*
There is no reason why anyone would want to have a computer in their home.

O'MALLEY Austin
8336
The best blood will sometimes get into a fool or a mosquito.

8337
A hole is nothing at all, but you can break your neck in it.

ONASSIS Aristotle 1906-1975
8338
The secret of business is to know something that nobody else knows.

ONASSIS Jacqueline 1929-1994
8339 *The Fitzgeralds and the Kennedys*
It was a very spasmodic courtship, conducted mainly at long distance with a great clanking of coins in dozens of phone booths.

O'NEIL Max
8340
Flirtation - attention without intention.

O'NEILL Eugene 1888-1953
8341
The child was diseased at birth - stricken with an hereditary ill that only the most vital men are able to shake off. I mean poverty - the most deadly and prevalent of all diseases.

8342
The iceman cometh.

8343
A long day's journey into night.

8344
Man's loneliness is but his fear of life.

8345 *Marco Millions*
Life is perhaps most wisely regarded as a bad dream between two awakenings, and every day is a life in miniature.

8346 *Mourning becomes Electra*
The sea hates a coward!

ONO Yoko 1933-
8347
Woman is the nigger of the world.

OPIE John 1761-1807
8348 *(asked with what he mixed his colours)*
I mix them with my brains, sir.

OPPENHEIMER J. Robert 1904-1967
8349 *(of Albert Einstein)*
Any man whose errors take ten years to correct, is quite a man.

8350 *Open Mind*
In some sort of crude sense which no vulgarity, no humour, no overstatement can quite extinguish, the physicists have known sin; and this is a knowledge which they cannot lose.

ORBACH Susie 1946-
8351
Fat is a feminist issue.

ORCZY Baroness 1865-1947
8352 *The Scarlet Pimpernel*
We seek him here, we seek him there,
Those Frenchies seek him everywhere.
Is he in heaven? - Is he in hell?
That demmed, elusive Pimpernel?

O'REILLY J.B. 1844-1890
8353 *In Bohemia*
The organized charity, scrimped and iced,
In the name of a cautious, statistical Christ.

ORTEGA y GASSET José 1883-1955
8354 *La Rebelión de las Masas*
Civilization is nothing more than the effort to reduce the use of force to the last resort.

8355 *Meditaciones del Quijote*
I am I plus my surroundings, and if I do not preserve the latter I do not preserve myself.

ORTON Joe 1933-1967
8356 *Entertaining Mr Sloane*
I'd the upbringing a nun would envy ... Until I
was fifteen I was more familiar with Africa than
my own body.

8357 *Entertaining Mr. Sloane*
Even if he thee worshipped with his body, his
mind would be elsewhere.

8358 *Loot*
Every luxury was lavished on you - atheism,
breast-feeding, circumcision.

8359 *Loot*
Policemen, like red squirrels, must be
protected.

8360 *Loot*
Reading isn't an occupation we encourage
among police officers. We try to keep the paper
work down to a minimum.

8361 *Prick Up Your Ears*
I'm from the gutter and don't you forget it,
because I won't.

8362 *What the Butler Saw*
You were born with your legs apart. They'll
send you to the grave in a Y-shaped coffin.

ORTON William A.
8363
If you keep your mind sufficiently open, people
will throw a lot of rubbish into it.

ORWELL George 1903-1950
8364 *(attributed)*
Advertising is the rattling of a stick inside a swill
bucket.

8365
In our age there is no such thing as 'keeping out
of politics'. All issues are political issues.

8366 *Animal Farm*
Man is the only creature that consumes without
producing.

8367 *Animal Farm*
Four legs good, two legs bad.

8368 *Animal Farm*
All animals are equal but some animals are
more equal than others.

8369
Keep the aspidistra flying.

8370 *Collected Essays*
Good prose is like a window-pane.

8371 *Coming up For Air*
I'm fat, but I'm thin inside. Has it ever struck
you that there's a thin man inside every fat man,
just as they say there's a statue inside every
block of stone?

8372
No doubt alcohol, tobacco, and so forth, are
things that a saint must avoid, but sainthood is
also a thing that human beings must avoid.

8373
The great enemy of clear language is insincerity.
When there is a gap between one's real and
one's declared aims, one turns as if it were
instinctively to long words and exhausted
idioms, like a cuttlefish squirting out ink.

8374
International sport is war without shooting.

8375 *(last words in his notebook)*
At 50, everyone has the face he deserves.

8376
Liberal - a power worshipper without power.

8377 *The Lion and the Unicorn*
Probably the battle of Waterloo *was* won on the
playing-fields of Eton, but the opening battles
of all subsequent wars have been lost there.

8378 *Nineteen Eighty-Four*
BIG BROTHER IS WATCHING YOU.

8379 *Nineteen Eighty-Four*
War is peace. Freedom is slavery. Ignorance is
strength.

8380 *Nineteen Eighty-Four*
Doublethink means the power of holding two
contradictory beliefs in one's mind
simultaneously, and accepting both of them.

8381 *Nineteen Eighty-Four*
Power is not a means, it is an end. One does
not establish a dictatorship in order to
safeguard a revolution; one makes the
revolution in order to establish the dictatorship.

8382 *Nineteen Eighty-Four*
If you want a picture of the future, imagine a
boot stamping on a human face - for ever.

8383
Most people get a fair amount of fun out of
their lives, but on balance life is suffering and
only the very sound or the very foolish imagine
otherwise.

8384 *Polemic, May*
The quickest way of ending a war is to lose it.

8385 *The Road to Wigan Pier*
A person of bourgeois origin goes through life
with some expectation of getting what he
wants, within reasonable limits. Hence the fact
that in times of stress 'educated' people tend to
come to the front.

8386 *The Road to Wigan Pier*
In a Lancashire cotton-town you could probably
go for months on end without once hearing an

'educated' accent, whereas there can hardly be a town in the South of England where you could throw a brick without hitting the niece of a bishop.

8387 *The Road to Wigan Pier*
The typical Socialist is ... a prim little man with a white-collar job, usually a secret teetotaller and often with vegetarian leanings, with a history of Nonconformity behind him, and, above all, with a social position which he has no intention of forfeiting.

8388 *The Road to Wigan Pier*
To the ordinary working man, the sort you would meet in any pub on Saturday night, Socialism does not mean much more than better wages and shorter hours and nobody bossing you about.

8389 *The Road to Wigan Pier*
The high-water mark, so to speak, of Socialist literature is W.H. Auden, a sort of gutless Kipling.

8390 *The Road to Wigan Pier*
We of the sinking middle class ... may sink without further struggles into the working class where we belong, and probably when we get there it will not be so dreadful as we feared, for, after all, we have nothing to lose but our aitches.

8391 *Shooting an Elephant*
Serious sport has nothing to do with fair play. It is bound up with hatred, jealousy, boastfulness, and disregard of all the rules.

8392 *Shooting an Elephant*
In our time, political speech and writing are largely the defence of the indefensible.

8393 *Shooting an Elephant*
Political language ... is designed to make lies sound truthful and murder respectable, and to give an appearance of solidity to pure wind.

8394 *Shooting an Elephant*
Saints should always be judged guilty until they are proved innocent.

8395
Whatever is funny is subversive, every joke is ultimately a custard pie ... A dirty joke is a sort of mental rebellion.

OSBORN Robert
8396
America once had the clarity of a pioneer axe.

OSBORNE John 1929-
8397 *The Entertainer*
Don't clap too hard - it's a very old building.

8398 *The Entertainer*
Thank God we're normal,
Yes, this is our finest shower!

8399 *The Entertainer*
But I have a go, lady, don't I? I'ave a go. I do.

8400 *Look Back in Anger*
His knowledge of life and ordinary human beings is so hazy, he really deserves some sort of decoration for it - a medal inscribed 'For Vaguery in the Field'.

8401 *Look Back in Anger*
Slamming their doors, stamping their high heels, banging their irons and saucepans - the eternal flaming racket of the female.

8402 *Look Back in Anger*
I don't think one 'comes down' from Jimmy's university. According to him, it's not even red brick, but white tile.

8403 *Look Back in Anger*
They spend their time mostly looking forward to the past.

8404 *Look Back in Anger*
There aren't any good, brave causes left. If the big bang does come, and we all get killed off, it won't be in aid of the old-fashioned, grand design. It'll just be for the Brave New Nothing-very-much-thank-you. About as pointless and inglorious as stepping in front of a bus.

8405
Monarchy is the gold filling in the mouth of decay.

8406 *Time Present*
She's like the old line about justice - not only must be done, but must be seen to be done.

O'SHAUGHNESSY Arthur 1844-1881
8407 *'Ode'*
We are the music makers,
We are the dreamers of dreams ...
We are the movers and shakers
Of the world for ever, it seems.

8408 *'Ode'*
For each age is a dream that is dying,
Or one that is coming to birth.

OSLER Sir William 1849-1919
8409 *Aphorisms from his Bedside Teachings*
That man can interrogate as well as observe nature, was a lesson slowly learned in his evolution.

8410 *Aphorisms from his Bedside Teachings*
One finger in the throat and one in the rectum makes a good diagnostician.

8411
The desire to take medicine is perhaps the greatest feature which distinguishes man from animals.

8412
One of the first duties of the physician is to educate the masses not to take medicine.

8413
It is much more important to know what sort of a patient has a disease than what sort of a disease a patient has.

8414
Look wise, say nothing, and grunt. Speech was given to conceal thought.

8415
In science the credit goes to the man who convinces the world, not to the man to whom the idea first occurs.

8416 *Science and Immortality*
The natural man has only two primal passions, to get and beget.

8417
The Scots are the backbone of Canada. They are all right in their three vital parts - head, heart and haggis.

8418
It is strange how the memory of a man may float to posterity on what he would have himself regarded as the most trifling of his works.

OTIS James 1725-1783
8419 *(Watchword of the American Revolution)*
Taxation without representation is tyranny.

O'TOOLE Peter 1932-
8420
Relationships get more difficult as you get older. The idea now of beginning to go through all that again is unsupportable, so I don't bother.

OTWAY Thomas 1652-1685
8421 *Venice Preserved*
No praying, it spoils business.

OUIDA 1839-1908
8422
The longest absence is less perilous to love than the terrible trials of incessant proximity.

OVERBURY Thomas 1581-1613
8423
The man who has not anything to boast of but his illustrious ancestors is like a potato - the only good belonging to him is underground.

OVERSTREET Bonaro
8424
Psychiatrists today ... see the irrational hostility

that people everywhere vent upon one another as chiefly projected self-hate.

OVERSTREET Harry A. 1876-1970
8425
The immature mind hops from one thing to another; the mature mind seeks to follow through.

8426
Newspapers have developed what might be called a vested interest in catastrophe. If they can spot a fight, they play up that fight. If they can uncover a tragedy, they will headline that tragedy.

OVID 43 BC-AD c.17
8427 *Ars Amatoria*
It is convenient that there be gods, and, as it is convenient, let us believe that there are.

8428 *Ars Amatoria*
Perhaps my name too will be linked with theirs.

8429
Chance is always powerful. Let your hook be always cast. In the pool where you least expect it, will be a fish.

8430
In an easy cause any man may be eloquent.

8431 *Epistulae Ex Ponto*
Though the strength is lacking, yet the willingness is commendable.

8432 *Epistulae Ex Ponto*
Dripping water hollows out a stone, a ring is worn away by use.

8433
Whether they give or refuse, women are glad to have been asked.

8434
Judgement of beauty can err, what with the wine and the dark.

8435 *Metamorphoses*
You will go most safely by the middle way.

8436 *Metamorphoses*
Plenty has made me poor.

8437 *Metamorphoses*
I see the better things, and approve; I follow the worse.

8438 *Metamorphoses*
Time the devourer of everything.

8439 *Remedia Amoris*
You who seek an end of love, love will yield to business: be busy, and you will be safe.

8440
If you want to be loved, be lovable.

8441
A woman is always buying something.

OWEN David 1938-
8442
Very few wars are brought to an end tidily.

OWEN John c.1563-1622
8443 *Epigrams*
God and the doctor we alike adore
But only when in danger, not before;
The danger o'er, both are alike requited,
God is forgotten, and the Doctor slighted.

OWEN Robert 1771-1858
8444 *(to W. Allen)*
All the world is queer save thee and me, and
even thou art a little queer.

OWEN Wilfred 1893-1918
8445
All a poet can do today is warn.

8446 *'Anthem for Doomed Youth'*
What passing-bells for these who die as cattle?
Only the monstrous anger of the guns.
Only the stuttering rifles' rapid rattle
Can patter out their hasty orisons.
No mockeries now for them; no prayers nor
bells,
Nor any voice of mourning save the choirs
The shrill, demented choirs of wailing shells;
And bugles calling for them from sad shires.

8447 *'Anthem for Doomed Youth'*
The pallor of girls' brows shall be their pall;
Their flowers the tenderness of patient minds,
And each slow dusk a drawing-down of blinds.

8448 *'Futility'*
Move him into the sun -
Gently its touch awoke him once,
At home, whispering of fields half-sown.

8449 *'Greater Lover'*
Red lips are not so red
As the stained stones kissed by the English
dead.

8450 *'Strange Meeting'*
'Strange friend,' I said, 'here is no cause to
mourn.'
'None,' said that other, 'save the undone years,
The hopelessness. Whatever hope is yours,
Was my life also.'

8451
My subject is War, and the pity of War.
The Poetry is in the pity.

OXENSTIERNA Count 1583-1654
8452 *Letter to his son*
Dost thou not know, my son, with how little
wisdom the world is governed?

OZ Amos 1939-
8453
The death of a parent makes you ready for the
call 'Next please'.

PACAUD George W.
8454
Why inflict pain on oneself, when so many
others are ready to save us the trouble?

PACHET Pierre
8455
Louis Pasteur's theory of germs is ridiculous
fiction.

PACKARD Vance 1914-
8456 *(study of the advertising industry)*
The hidden persuaders.

PADEREWSKI Ignacy Jan 1860-1941
8457
Before I was a genius I was a drudge.

PAGE Irvine H.
8458
I came, I saw, I concurred.

PAGE Shebly
8459
The number of agency people required to shoot
a commercial on location is in direct proportion
to the mean temperature of the location.

PAGE William Tyler 1868-1942
8460 *American's Creed*
A government of the people, by the people, for
the people, whose just powers are derived from
the consent of the governed.

8461 *American's Creed*
A perfect Union, one and inseparable,
established upon those principles of freedom,
equality, justice, and humanity for which
American patriots sacrificed their lives and
fortunes.

PAGNOL Marcel 1895-1974
8462 *Marius*
Honour is like a match, you can only use it
once.

8463 *Topaze*
It's better to choose the culprits than to seek
them out.

PAIGE Satchel 1906-1982
8464
(Airplanes) may kill you, but they ain't likely to
hurt you.

8465
Never let your head hang down. Never give up
and sit down and grieve. Find another way.
And don't pray when it rains if you don't pray
when the sun shines.

8466
Never look behind you. Something may be gaining on you.

8467
If your stomach disputes you, lie down and pacify it with cool thoughts.

PAINE Thomas 1737-1809
8468 *The Age of Reason*
Infidelity does not consist in believing, or in disbelieving, it consists in professing to believe what one does not believe.

8469 *The Age of Reason*
Any system of religion that has any thing in it that shocks the mind of a child cannot be a true system.

8470 *The Age of Reason*
The sublime and the ridiculous are often so nearly related, that it is difficult to class them separately. One step above the sublime, makes the ridiculous; and one step above the ridiculous, makes the sublime again.

8471 *Common Sense*
Government, even in its best state, is but a necessary evil; in its worst state, an intolerable one.

8472 *The Crisis*
These are the times that try men's souls. The summer soldier and the sunshine patriot will, in this crisis, shrink from the service of their country.

8473 *(of Edmund Burke)*
As he rose like a rocket, he fell like the stick.

8474 *Letter ... on the Invasion of England*
The religion of humanity.

8475 *The Rights of Man*
Lay then the axe to the root, and teach governments humanity. It is their sanguinary punishments which corrupt mankind.

8476 *The Rights of Man*
Titles are but nicknames, and every nickname is a title.

8477 *The Rights of Man*
When, in countries that are called civilized, we see age going to the workhouse and youth to the gallows, something must be wrong in the system of government.

8478 *The Rights of Man*
My country is the world, and my religion is to do good.

8479
Those who expect to reap the blessings of freedom must, like men, undergo the fatigue of supporting it.

PALAFOX José de 1780-1847
8480 *(at the siege of Saragossa)*
Guerra a cuchillo.
War by the knife.

PALEY Grace
8481
All that is really necessary for survival of the fittest, it seems, is an interest in life, good, bad or peculiar.

PALEY William 1743-1805
8482 *Principles of Moral and Political Philosophy*
Who can refute a sneer?

PALMA Brian de
8483
No Art has a shorter life than Political Art.

PALMER Lilli
8484
I sweat. If anything comes easy to me, I mistrust it.

PALMER Samuel 1805-1881
8485
A picture has been said to be something between a thing and a thought.

PALMERSTON Lord 1784-1865
8486
We have no eternal allies and we have no perpetual enemies. Our interests are eternal and perpetual, and those interests it is our duty to follow.

8487 *(of Foreign Office handwriting)*
Iron railings leaning out of the perpendicular.

8488
The function of a government is to calm, rather than to excite agitation.

8489 *(last words)*
Die, my dear Doctor, that's the last thing I shall do!

8490 *(of a projected Palmerston-Disraeli coalition)*
You may call it combination, you may call it the accidental and fortuitous concurrence of atoms.

8491
What is merit? The opinion one man entertains of another.

8492 *(attributed, when asked whether English has a word for sensibilité)*
Yes we have. Humbug.

PANCHATANTRA
8493
A great man does not lose his self-possession when he is afflicted; the ocean is not made muddy by the falling in of its banks.

8494
One should seek for the salutary in the unpleasant: if it is there, it is after all nectar. One should seek for the deceitful in the pleasant: if it is there it is after all poison.

PANKHURST Dame Christabel 1880-1958
8495 *Unshackled*
Never lose your temper with the Press or the public is a major rule of political life.

8496 *Votes for Women*
We are here to claim our right as women, not only to be free, but to fight for freedom. That it is our right as well as our duty.

PARISH Mitchell
8497 *'Deep Purple'*
When the deep purple falls over sleepy garden walls,
And the stars begin to flicker in the sky,
Thru' the mist of a memory you wander back to me,
Breathing my name with a sigh.

PARKER Charlie 1920-1955
8498
Music is your own experience, your thoughts, your wisdom. If you don't live it it won't come out of your horn.

PARKER Dorothy 1893-1967
8499 *(attributed)*
If all the girls attending the Yale Prom were laid end to end, I wouldn't be at all surprised.

8500 *'Ballade of a Great Weariness'*
Scratch a lover, and find a foe.

8501 *'Comment'*
Oh, life is a glorious cycle of song,
A medley of extemporanea;
And love is a thing that can never go wrong;
And I am Marie of Roumania.

8502
It cost me never a stab nor squirm
To tread by chance upon a worm.
'Aha, my little dear' I say,
'Your clan will pay me back one day.'

8503 *'Inventory'*
Four be the things I'd been better without:
Love, curiosity, freckles, and doubt.

8504 *(of Katherine Hepburn)*
She ran the whole gamut of the emotions from A to B.

8505 *'Here Lies'*
And I'll stay off Verlaine too; he was always chasing Rimbauds.

8506 *'Here Lies'*
Sorrow is tranquillity remembered in emotion.

8507 *'News Item'*
Men seldom make passes
At girls who wear glasses.

8508
He and I had an office so tiny that an inch smaller and it would have been adultery.

8509 *'Résumé'*
Poisons pain you;
Rivers are damp;
Acid stains you;
And drugs cause cramp.
Guns aren't lawful;
Nooses give;
Gas smells awful;
You might as well live.

8510
They sicken of the calm that know the storm.

8511
I shall stay the way I am
Because I do not give a damn.

8512 *(suggested epitaph for herself)*
Excuse My Dust.

8513
There's a hell of a distance between wisecracking and wit. Wit has truth in it; wisecracking is simply callisthenics with words.

8514 *'Unfortunate Coincidence'*
By the time you say you're his,
Shivering and sighing
And he vows his passion is
Infinite, undying -
Lady, make a note of this:
One of you is lying.

8515
Where, unwilling, dies the rose,
Buds the new, another year.

8516
Where's the man could ease the heart
Like a satin gown?

PARKER Martin 1600-1656
8517 *'The Valiant Sailors'*
You gentlemen of England
Who live at home at ease,
How little do you think
On the dangers of the seas.

PARKER Ross and CHARLES Hugh 1914-1974 and 1907-
8518 *'There'll always be an England'*
There'll always be an England
While there's a country lane,
Wherever there's a cottage small
Beside a field of grain.

PARKINSON Northcote 1909-1993

8519
Expansion means complexity and complexity decay.

8520 *The Law and the Profits*
Expenditure rises to meet income.

8521 *Parkinson's Law*
Work expands so as to fill the time available for its completion.

8522 *Parkinson's Law*
Time spent on any item of the agenda will be in inverse proportion to the sum involved.

8523 *Parkinson's Law*
The man who is denied the opportunity of taking decisions of importance begins to regard as important the decisions he is allowed to take.

8524 *Parkinson's Law*
Men enter local politics solely as a result of being unhappily married.

PARNELL Charles Stewart 1846-1891

8525
No man has a right to fix the boundary of the march of a nation; no man has a right to say to his country - thus far shalt thou go and no further.

PARNELL Thomas 1679-1718

8526
Let time that makes you homely, make you sage

PARR Samuel 1747-1825

8527 *(of Dr Johnson)*
Now that the old lion is dead, every ass thinks he may kick at him.

PARRIS Matthew 1949-

8528
Being an MP feeds your vanity and starves your self respect.

PARTRIDGE Marianne

8529
As a woman, to be competitive is to be passive.

PASCAL Blaise 1623-1662

8530
Let is not be said that I have said nothing new. The arrangement of the material is new.

8531
All our reasoning ends in surrender to feeling.

8532
No animal admires another animal.

8533
Our own interests are still an exquisite means for dazzling our eyes agreeably.

8534
The last advance of reason is to recognize that it is surpassed by innumerable things; it is feeble if it cannot realize that.

8535
The majority is the best way, because it is visible, and has strength to make itself obeyed. Yet it is the opinion of the least able.

8536 *Pensées*
The last thing one knows in constructing a work is what to put first.

8537 *Pensées*
When we see a natural style, we are quite surprised and delighted, for we expected to see an author and we find a man.

8538 *Pensées*
How vain painting is, exciting admiration by its resemblance to things of which we do not admire the originals.

8539 *Pensées*
Had Cleopatra's nose been shorter, the whole face of the world would have changed.

8540 *Pensées*
The eternal silence of these infinite spaces [the heavens] terrifies me.

8541 *Pensées*
On mourra seul.
We shall die alone.

8542 *Pensées*
The heart has its reasons which reason knows nothing of.

8543 *Pensées*
Man is only a reed, the weakest thing in nature; but he is a thinking reed.

8544 *Pensées*
Continual eloquence is tedious.

8545 *Pensées*
The *self* is hateful.

8546 *Pensées*
Comfort yourself, you would not seek me if you had not found me.

8547 *Pensées*
Not to care for philosophy is to be a true philosopher.

8548 *Pensées*
The more intelligence one has the more people one finds original. Commonplace people see no difference between men.

8549 *The Provincial Letters*
I have made this [letter] longer than usual, only because I have not had the time to make it shorter.

8550
If a soldier or labourer complains of the
hardship of his lot, set him to do nothing.

8551
Two things control man's nature: instinct and
experience.

PASQUA Charles 1927-
8552
Fear of the policeman is the beginning of
wisdom.

PASTERNAK Boris 1890-1960
8553 *Doctor Zhivago*
Man is born to live, not to prepare for life.

8554 *Doctor Zhivago*
Most people experience love, without noticing
that there is anything remarkable about it.

8555 *Doctor Zhivago*
I don't like people who have never fallen or
stumbled. Their virtue is lifeless and it isn't of
much value. Life hasn't revealed its beauty to
them.

8556 *Doctor Zhivago*
Art always serves beauty, and beauty is the joy
of possessing form, and form is the key to
organic life since no living thing can exist
without it.

8557 *Doctor Zhivago*
Yet the order of the acts is planned
And the end of the way inescapable.
I am alone; all drowns in the Pharisees'
hyprocrisy.
To live your life is not as simple as to cross a
field.

8558 *Doctor Zhivago*
Love is not weakness. It is strong. Only the
sacrament of marriage can contain it.

8559
In every generation there has to be some fool
who will speak the truth as he sees it.

8560 *'My Sister Life'*
My sister life's in flood today, she's broken
her waves over us all in the spring rain.

8561 *'When It Clears Up'*
World, nature, Universe's Essence,
With secret trembling, to the end,
I will thy long and moving service
In tears of happiness attend.

8562 *'When I Grow Weary'*
In time to come, I tell them, we'll be equal
to any living now. If cripples, then
no matter; we shall just have been run over
by 'New Man' in the wagon of his 'Plan'.

8563 *(to the woman who inspired 'Lara' in Dr.
Zhivago)*
Let me lock your beauty
In the dark tower of a poem.

PASTEUR Louis 1822-1895
8564
There are no such things as applied sciences,
only applications of science.

8565
Blessed is he who carries within himself a god
and an ideal and who obeys it - an ideal of art,
of science, or gospel virtues. Therein lie the
springs of great thoughts and great actions.

8566
In the field of observation, chance favours the
prepared mind.

8567
Let me tell you the secret that has led me to my
goal. My strength lies solely in my tenacity.

PATER Walter 1839-1894
8568
All art constantly aspires towards the condition
of music.

8569 *(of the Mona Lisa)*
She is older than the rocks among which she
sits; like the vampire, she has been dead many
times, and learned the secrets of the grave.

8570 *Studies in the History of the Renaissance*
To burn always with this hard, gemlike flame, to
maintain this ecstasy, is success in life.

PATERSON 'Banjo' 1864-1941
8571 *'Waltzing Matilda'*
Once a jolly swagman camped by a billabong,
Under the shade of a coolibah tree;
And he sang as he watched and waited till his
'Billy' boiled:
'You'll come a waltzing, Matilda, with me.'

PATMORE Coventry 1823-1896
8572 *The Angel in the House*
We love, Fool, for the good we do,
Not that which unto us is done!

8573 *The Angel in the House*
'I saw you take his kiss!' ''Tis true.'
'O modesty!' ''Twas strictly kept:
He thought me asleep; at least, I knew
He thought I thought he thought I slept.'

8574 *The Angel in the House*
A woman is a foreign land,
Of which, though there he settle young,
A man will ne'er quite understand
The customs, politics and tongue.

8575 *'Olympus'*
Some dish more sharply spiced than this
Milk-soup men call domestic bliss.

8576 *The Victories of Love*
He that but once too nearly hears
The music of forfended spheres
Is thenceforth lonely, and for all
His days as one who treads the Wall
Of China, and, on this hand, sees
Cities and their civilities
And, on the other, lions.

PATTON George S. 1885-1945
8577
Courage is fear holding on a minute longer.

8578
Never tell people how to do things. Tell them
what to do and they will surprise you with their
ingenuity.

PAUL Elliot 1891-1958
8579
Patience makes a woman beautiful in middle
age.

PAUL Leslie 1905-1985
8580
Angry young man.

PAUL Saint AD 3-68
8581
Faith is the substance of things hoped for, the
evidence of things not seen.

PAVESE Cesare
8582
Every luxury must be paid for, and everything is
a luxury, starting with being in the world.

8583
Whatever people may say, the fastidious formal
manner of the upper classes is preferable to the
slovenly easygoing behaviour of the common
middle class. In moments of crisis, the former
know how to act, the latter become uncouth
brutes.

8584
No woman marries for money; they are all
clever enough, before marrying a millionaire, to
fall in love with him first.

PAXMAN Jeremy 1950-
8585
It's very difficult to remain calm when you're
listening to someone talking complete bollocks.

PAYN James 1830-1898
8586
I had never had a piece of toast
Particularly long and wide,
But fell upon the sanded floor,
And always on the buttered side.

PAYNE J.H. 1791-1852
8587 *Clari, or, The Maid of Milan 'Home, Sweet
Home'*

Mid pleasures and palaces though we may
roam,
Be it ever so humble, there's no place like home.

PAZ Octavio 1914-
8588
Our democratic capitalist society has converted
Eros into an employee of Mammon.

8589
Solitude is the profoundest fact of the human
condition. Man is the only being who knows he
is alone.

PEACOCK Thomas Love 1785-1866
8590 *Gryll Grange*
A Sympathizer would seem to imply a certain
degree of benevolent feeling. Nothing of the
kind. It signifies a ready-made accomplice in
any species of political villainy.

8591 *'Love and Age'*
But though first love's impassioned blindness
Has passed away in colder light,
I still have thought of you with kindness,
And shall do, till our last good-night.

8592 *Melincourt*
Marriage may often be a stormy lake, but
celibacy is almost always a muddy horsepond.

8593 *'The Misfortunes of Elphin'*
Not drunk is he who from the floor
Can rise alone and still drink more;
But drunk is he, who prostrate lies,
Without the power to drink or rise.

8594 *'The Misfortunes of Elphin'*
The mountain sheep are sweeter,
But the valley sheep are fatter;
We therefore deemed it meeter
To carry off the latter.

8595 *Nightmare Abbey*
Laughter is pleasant, but the exertion is too
much for me.

8596 *Nightmare Abbey*
He was sent, as usual, to a public school, where
a little learning was painfully beaten into him,
and from thence to the university, where it was
carefully taken out of him.

PEARSON Hesketh 1887-1964
8597 *Common Misquotations*
Misquotation is, in fact, the pride and privilege
of the learned. A widely-read man never quotes
accurately, for the rather obvious reason that he
has read too widely.

8598 *The Pilgrim Daughters*
There is no stronger craving in the world than
that of the rich for titles, except perhaps that of
the titled for riches.

PEARSON Lester 1897-1972
8599 *(defining attitude toward U.S.)*
The situation is one something like living with
your wife. Sometimes it is difficult and even
irritating to live with her, but it is always
impossible to live without her.

8600
The strongest pressure in the world can be
friendly pressure.

PEARSON Maryon
8601
Behind every great man there is a surprised
woman.

PEEL Paul
8602
It is no rest to be idle.

PEEL Robert 1788-1850
8603
Public opinion is a compound of folly,
weakness, prejudice, wrong feeling, right
feeling, obstinacy, and newspaper paragraphs.

PEELE George c.1556-1596
8604 *The Hunting of Cupid*
What thing is love for (well I wot) love is a thing.
It is a prick, it is a sting,
It is a pretty, pretty thing;
It is a fire, it is a coal
Whose flame creeps in at every hole.

8605 *The Old Wive's Tale*
When as the rye reach to the chin,
And chopcherry, chopcherry ripe within,
Strawberries swimming in the cream,
And schoolboys playing in the stream,
Then O, then O, then O, my true love said,
Till that time come again,
She could not live a maid.

8606 *Polyhymnia*
Goddess, allow this aged man his right,
To be your beadsman now that was your knight.

PÉGUY Charles 1873-1914
8607 *Basic Verities*
He who does not bellow the truth when he
knows the truth makes himself the accomplice
of liars and forgers.

8608 *Basic Verities*
Tyranny is always better organised than
freedom.

8609 *Basic Verities*
The sinner is at the heart of Christianity ... No
one is as competent as the sinner in matters of
Christianity. No one, except a saint.

8610
It has never been given to a man to attain at
once his happiness and his salvation.

8611
Short of genius, a rich man cannot imagine
poverty.

8612
One must always tell what one sees. Above all,
which is more difficult, one must always see
what one sees.

8613
When a man dies, he does not just die of the
disease he has: he dies of his whole life.

PEI Mario 1901-1978
8614
Good architecture lets nature in.

PEMBROKE Henry Herbert, 2nd Earl of c.1534-
1601
8615
A parliament can do any thing but make a man
a woman, and a woman a man.

PEMBROKE Henry Herbert, 10th Earl of 1734-
1794
8616
Dr Johnson's sayings would not appear so
extraordinary, were it not for his bow-wow way.

PENDENYS Arthur 1865-1946
8617
A good meal makes a man feel more charitable
toward the whole world than any sermon.

PENN William 1644-1718
8618
Avoid popularity; it has many snares, and no
real benefit.

8619 *No Cross, No Crown*
No pain, no palm; no thorns, no throne; no gall,
no glory; no cross, no crown.

8620 *Some Fruits of Solitude*
It is a reproach to religion and government to
suffer so much poverty and excess.

8621 *Some Fruits of Solitude*
Men are generally more careful of the breed of
their horses and dogs than of their children.

PENROSE Roger 1931-
8622 *The Emperor's New Mind*
Consciousness ... is the phenomenon whereby
the universe's very existence is made known.

PEPYS Samuel 1633-1703
8623 *Diary*
Strange the difference of men's talk!

8624 *Diary*
And so to bed.

8625 *Diary*
I went out to Charing Cross, to see Major-
general Harrison hanged, drawn, and
quartered; which was done there, he looking as

cheerful as any man could do in that condition.

8626 *Diary*
A good honest and painful sermon.

8627 *Diary*
If ever I was foxed it was now.

8628 *Diary*
But methought it lessened my esteem of a king, that he should not be able to command the rain.

8629 *Diary*
I see it is impossible for the King to have things done as cheap as other men.

8630 *Diary*
But Lord! to see the absurd nature of Englishmen, that cannot forbear laughing and jeering at everything that looks strange.

8631 *Diary*
My wife, who, poor wretch, is troubled with her lonely life.

8632 *Diary*
A woman sober, and no high flyer, as he calls it.

8633 *Diary*
Most of their discourse was about hunting, in a dialect I understand very little.

8634 *Diary*
While we were talking came by several poor creatures carried by, by constables, for being at a conventicle ... I would to God they would either conform, or be more wise, and not be catched!

8635 *Diary*
Strange to see how a good dinner and feasting reconciles everybody.

8636 *Diary*
Strange to say what delight we married people have to see these poor fools decoyed into our condition.

8637 *Diary*
Music and women I cannot but give way to, whatever my business is.

8638 *Diary*
But it is pretty to see what money will do.

8639 *Diary*
Home, and, being washing-day, dined upon cold meat.

8640 *Diary (ad fin)*
And so I betake myself to that course, which is almost as much as to see myself go into my grave - for which, and all the discomforts that will accompany my being blind, the good God prepare me!

8641 *Diary (of Nell Gwynne)*
Pretty witty Nell.

PERCIVAL Lloyd
8642
The physically fit can enjoy their vices.

PERELMAN S.J. 1904-1979
8643
Crazy like a fox.

8644
There is such a thing as too much couth.

8645 *Quotations for Speakers and Writers*
Love is not the dying moan of a distant violin - it's the triumphant twang of a bedspring.

PERES Shimon 1923-
8646
A leader who rides to war is always having applause; a leader who rides to peace is always being criticized.

8647
Peace is made with yesterday's enemies. What is the alternative?

8648
The peace process is like a wedding night in a minefield.

PERICLES c 495-429 BC
8649
We do not imitate, but are a model to others.

8650
For famous men have the whole earth as their memorial.

8651 *(funeral oration)*
Our love of what is beautiful does not lead to extravagance; our love of the things of the mind does not make us soft.

PERKINS Anthony 1932-1992
8652 *in Psycho*
"A boy's best friend is his mother."

PERKINS Maxwell 1884-1947
8653 *(advice to Marcia Davenport)*
Just get it down on paper, and then we'll see what to do with it.

8654
I believe the writer ... should always be the final judge. I have always held to that position and have sometimes seen books hurt thereby, but at least as often helped. The book belongs to the author.

8655
Every good thing that comes is accompanied by trouble.

8656
You have to throw yourself away when you write.

PERLMAN Itzhak 1945-
8657
Ask many of us who are disabled what we would like in life and you would be surprised how few would say, 'Not to be disabled'. We accept our limitations.

PERRONET Edward 1726-1792
8658 *'All hail the power of Jesus' Name'*
All hail the power of Jesus' Name;
Let Angels prostrate fall;
Bring forth the royal diadem
To crown Him Lord of all.

PERRY Jimmy
8659 *'Who do you think you are kidding, Mister Hitler'*
Who do you think you are kidding, Mister Hitler?
If you think we're on the run?
We are the boys who will stop your little game
We are the boys who will make you think again.

PERSE St. John 1887-1975
8660
The only menace is inertia.

PERSIUS AD 34-62
8661 *Satires*
And don't consult anyone's opinions but your own.

8662 *Satires*
Let them recognize virtue and rot for having lost it.

8663 *Satires*
Confront disease at its onset.

8664 *Satires*
Live with yourself: get to know how poorly furnished you are.

PERSONS Ted
8665
Things ain't what they used to be.

PÉTAIN Henri Philippe 1856-1951
8666
To write one's memoirs is to speak ill of everybody except oneself.

PETER Irene
8667
Ignorance is no excuse, it's the real thing.

PETER Laurence 1910-1990
8668
The cave-dweller's wife complained that he hadn't dragged her anywhere in months.

8669
Early to bed, early to rise, work like hell, and advertise.

8670
If we lacked imagination enough to foresee something better, life would indeed be a tragedy.

8671 *The Peter Principle*
In a hierarchy every employee tends to rise to his level of incompetence.

8672
Psychiatry enables us to correct our faults by confessing our parents' shortcomings.

8673
When I want your opinion I'll give it to you.

8674
Work is accomplished by those employees who have not yet reached their level of incompetence.

PETRONIUS d. AD 65
8675
Delight of lust is gross and brief
And weariness treads on desire.

8676 *Satyricon*
He's gone to join the majority [the dead].

8677 *Satyricon*
Horace's careful felicity.

8678
We trained hard, but it seemed that every time we were beginning to form up into teams we would be re-organised. I was to learn later in life that we tend to meet any new situation by re-organising, and a wonderful method it can be for creating the illusion of progress while producing confusion, inefficiency and demoralisation.

PETROWSKY Christina
8679
Autumn is the bite of a harvest apple.

PETTITO Anthony J.
8680
The best way to bring up some children is short.

PFIZER Beryl
8681
All the movies used to be 'colossal'. Now they're all 'frank'. I think I liked 'colossal' better.

8682
A little public scandal is good once in a while - takes the tension out of the news.

8683
I wonder what language truck drivers are using, now that everyone is using theirs?

PHAEDRUS fl.c.AD 8
8684
Everyone ought to bear patiently the results of his own conduct.

PHELPS Edward John 1822-1900
8685
The man who makes no mistakes does not usually make anything.

PHELPS William Lyon
8686
The belief that youth is the happiest time of life is founded upon a fallacy. The happiest person is the person who thinks the most interesting thoughts, and we grow happier as we grow older.

8687
This is the final test of a gentleman: his respect for those who can be of no possible service to him.

PHILBY Kim 1912-1988
8688
To betray, you must first belong.

PHILIP 'Jack' 1840-1900
8689 *(at the battle of Santiago)*
Don't cheer, men; those poor devils are dying.

PHILIP Prince, Duke of Edinburgh 1921-
8690
I think our children have all done rather well under very demanding circumstances.

8691
When a man opens the car door for his wife, it's either a new car or a new wife.

PHILIPS Ambrose c.1675-1749
8692 *The First Pastoral*
The flowers anew, returning seasons bring;
But beauty faded has no second spring.

8693 *'A Winter-Piece'*
There solid billows of enormous size,
Alps of green ice, in wild disorder rise.

PHILLIPS H.I. 1887-1965
8694
Oratory: the art of making deep noises from the chest sound like important messages from the brain.

PHILLIPS Morgan 1902-1963
8695
The Labour Party owes more to Methodism than to Marxism.

PHILLIPS Stephen 1864-1915
8696 *Ulysses*
Behold me now
A man not old, but mellow, like good wine.
Not over-jealous, yet an eager husband.

PHILLIPS Wendell 1811-1884
8697
One on God's side is a majority.

8698
Governments exist to protect the rights of minorities. The loved and the rich need no protection - they have many friends and few enemies.

8699
Law is nothing unless close behind it stands a warm, living public opinion.

8700
We live under a government of men and morning newspapers.

8701
Every man meets his Waterloo at last.

8702
Politics is but the common pulse beat.

8703
Every step of progress the world has made has been from scaffold to scaffold, and from stake to stake.

8704
What is defeat? Nothing but education, nothing but the first step toward something better.

PIAZZOLLA Aslor
8705
Good music is everything that swings. Mozart also swings.

PICASSO Pablo 1881-1973
8706
We all know that Art is not truth. Art is a lie that makes us realize truth.

8707
Art washes away from the soul the dust of everyday life.

8708
Every child is an artist. The problem is how to remain an artist once he grows up.

8709
I do not seek. I find.

8710
Everyone wants to understand painting. Why don't they try to understand the singing of birds? People love the night, a flower, everything that surrounds them without trying to understand them. But painting - that they *must* understand.

8711
God is really only another artist. He invented the giraffe, the elephant, and the cat. He has no real style. He just goes on trying other things.

8712
It takes a long time to become young.

8713
I paint objects as I think them, not as I see them.

8714
Painting is a blind man's profession. He paints not what he sees, but what he feels, what he tells himself about what he has seen.

8715
Painting is just another way of keeping a diary.

8716
Photographers, along with dentists, are the two professions never satisfied with what they do. Every dentist would like to be a doctor and inside every photographer is a painter trying to get out.

8717
Every positive value has its price in negative terms ... The genius of Einstein leads to Hiroshima.

8718
Taste is the enemy of creativeness.

PIERCE Lorne
8719
A publisher is somebody looking for someone who has something to say.

PINDAR 518-438 BC
8720
Learn what you are, and be such.

8721 *Olympian Odes*
Water is best. But gold shines like fire blazing in the night, supreme of lordly wealth.

8722 *Pythian Odes*
My soul, do not seek immortal life, but exhaust the realm of the possible.

PINDAR Peter 1738-1819
8723 *Expostulatory Odes*
Care to our coffin adds a nail no doubt;
And ev're grin, so merry, draws one out.

8724 *(to the Royal Academicians)*
What rage for fame attends both great and small!
Better be damned than mentioned not at all!

PINERO Sir Arthur Wing 1855-1934
8725
I believe the future is only the past again, entered through another gate.

8726
How many 'coming men' has one known? Where on earth do they all go to?

8727 *Second Mrs Tanqueray*
From forty to fifty a man is at heart either a stoic or a satyr.

8728 *Second Mrs Tanqueray*
I love fruit, when it is expensive.

PINOCHET Augusto 1915-
8729
There have never been dictatorships here. I am a democrat.

PINTER Harold 1930-
8730 *The Caretaker*
Them bastards at the monastery let me down again.

8731 *The Homecoming*
Apart from the known and the unknown, what else is there?

8732
One way of looking at speech is to say it is a constant stratagem to cover nakedness.

8733 *(on being asked what his plays were about)*
The weasel under the cocktail cabinet.

PIRANDELLO Luigi 1867-1936
8734
You too must not count overmuch on your reality as you feel it today, since, like that of yesterday, it may prove an illusion for you tomorrow.

PIRSIG Robert M. 1928-
8735 *Zen and the Art of Motorcycle Maintenance*
That's the classical mind at work, runs fine inside but looks dingy on the surface.

PITT William (The Elder) 1708-1778
8736 *(attributed)*
Our watchword is security.

8737
The atrocious crime of being a young man ... I shall neither attempt to palliate nor deny.

8738
We have a Calvinistic creed, a Popish liturgy, and an Arminian clergy.

8739
Confidence is a plant of slow growth in an aged bosom: youth is the season of credulity.

8740
You cannot conquer America.

8741
I invoke the genius of the Constitution!

8742
The parks are the lungs of London.

8743
The poorest man may in his cottage bid defiance to all the forces of the Crown. It may

be frail - its roof may shake - the wind may blow through it - the storm may enter - the rain may enter - but the King of England cannot enter!

8744
There is something behind the throne greater than the King himself.

8745
Unlimited power is apt to corrupt the minds of those who possess it.

PITT William (The Younger) 1759-1806
8746 *(on hearing of Napleon's victory at Austerlitz)*
Roll up that map; it will not be wanted these ten years.

8747
Necessity is the plea for every infringement of human freedom: it is the argument of tyrants; it is the creed of slaves.

8748 *(replying to a toast, as saviour of his country)*
England has saved herself by her exertions, and will, as I trust, save Europe by her example.

PITTER Ruth 1897-1992
8749 *But for Lust*
But for lust we could be friends,
On each other's necks could weep:
In each other's arms could sleep
In the calm the cradle lends.

PIUS VII Pope 1742-1823
8750 *(attempting to reach an agreement with Napoleon)*
We are prepared to go to the gates of Hell - but no further.

PLANCK Max 1858-1947
8751 *A Scientific Autobiography*
A new scientific truth does not triumph by convincing its opponents and making them see the light, but rather because its opponents eventually die, and a new generation grows up that is familiar with it.

PLATH Sylvia 1932-1963
8752 *'The Applicant'*
A living doll, everywhere you look.
It can sew, it can cook,
It can talk, talk, talk.

It works, there is nothing wrong with it.
You have a hole, it's a poultice.
You have an eye, it's an image.
My boy, it's your last resort.
Will you marry it, marry it, marry it.

8753 *'Apprehensions'*
Is there no way out of the mind?

8754 *'Daddy'*
I have always been scared of *you*,
With your Luftwaffe, your gobbledygoo.
And your neat moustache
And your Aryan eye, bright blue.
Panzer-man, panzer-man, O You -

8755 *'Daddy'*
Every woman adores a Fascist,
The boot in the face, the brute
Brute heart of a brute like you.

8756 *'Lady Lazarus'*
Dying,
Is an art, like everything else.

8757 *'Morning Song'*
Love set you going like a fat gold watch.
The midwife slapped your footsoles, and your bald cry
Took its place among the elements.

8758
For me, poetry is an evasion of the real job of writing prose.

8759 *'Widow'*
Widow. The word consumes itself.

PLATO 429-347 BC
8760
All learning has an emotional base.

8761 *Apology*
Socrates is guilty of corrupting the minds of the young, and of believing in deities of his own invention instead of the gods recognized by the State.

8762
Boys should abstain from all use of wine until their eighteenth year, for it is wrong to add fire to fire.

8763
The most effective kind of education is that a child should play amongst lovely things.

8764 *Euthyphro 10*
Is that which is holy loved by the gods because it is holy, or is it holy because it is loved by the gods?

8765
Everything that deceives may be said to enchant.

8766
I have hardly ever known a mathematician who was capable of reasoning.

8767 *The Republic*
The blame is his who chooses: God is blameless.

8768 *Republic*
I wonder if we could contrive ... some magnificent myth that would in itself carry conviction to our whole community.

8769 *Republic*
There will be no end to the troubles of states, or indeed, my dear Glaucon, of humanity itself, till philosophers become kings in this world, or till those we now call kings and rulers really and truly become philosophers.

8770 *Republic*
Democracy passes into despotism.

8771
The spiritual eyesight improves as the physical eyesight declines.

8772
There are three classes of men - lovers of wisdom, lovers of honour, lovers of gain.

8773
When the mind is thinking, it is talking to itself.

PLAUTUS c.250-184 BC
8774 *Asinaria*
A man is a wolf rather than a man to another man, when he hasn't yet found out what he's like.

8775 *Bacchides*
He whom the gods favour dies young.

8776
The bell never rings of itself; unless someone handles or moves it, it is dumb.

8777
Always bring money along with your complaints.

8778
It is customary these days to ignore what should be done in favour of what pleases us.

8779 *Persa*
A sentence is enough for a sensible man.

PLAYER Gary 1935-
8780
The harder you work, the luckier you get.

PLINY (The Elder) AD 23-79
8781
The brain is the citadel of sense perception.

8782 *Natural History*
Harmless thunderbolts.

8783 *Natural History*
Africa always brings [us] something new.

8784 *Natural History*
Addito salis grano.
With the addition of a grain of salt.

8785 *Natural History*
In vino veritas.
Truth comes out in wine.

8786 *Natural History*
Sal Atticum.
Attic salt.

8787 *Natural History*
Nulla dies sine linea.
Not a day without a line.

PLINY (The Younger) AD 62-c.114
8788
Prosperity tries the fortunate; adversity the great.

PLOMER William 1903-1973
8789 *'The Boer War'*
Out of that bungled, unwise war
An alp of unforgiveness grew.

8790 *'Father and Son: 1939'*
With first-rate sherry flowing into second-rate whores,
And third-rate conversation without one single pause:
Just like a young couple
Between the wars.

8791 *'Mews Flat Mona'*
On a sofa upholstered in panther skin
Mona did researches in original sin.

8792 *'Playboy of the Demi-World: 1938'*
A rose-red sissy half as old as time.

PLOMIN Professor Robert
8793 *(on how to have gifted children)*
Marry an intelligent person.

PLOTINUS 205-270
8794 *Enneads III*
And here we have, incidentally, lighted upon the cause of the Circuit of the All; it is a movement which seeks perpetuity by way of futurity.

PLUNKETT Joseph 1887-1916
8795 *I see His Blood*
I see His blood upon the rose
And in the stars the glory of His eyes.

PLUTARCH AD c.46-c.120
8796
Character is long-standing habit.

8797
It is a hard matter, my fellow citizens, to argue with the belly, since it has no ears.

8798
It is indeed a desirable thing to be well descended, but the glory belongs to our ancestors.

8799 *Parallel Lives 'Lysander'*
He who cheats with an oath acknowledges that he is afraid of his enemy, but that he thinks little of God.

8800
Rest is the sweet sauce of labour.

8801
Those who aim at great deeds must also suffer greatly.

POCOCK R.
8802
The land too poor for any other crop, is best for raising men.

POE Edgar Allan 1809-1849
8803 *'Annabel Lee'*
This maiden she lived with no other thought
Than to love and be loved by me.

8804 *'Annabel Lee'*
I was a child and she was a child,
In this kingdom by the sea;
But we loved with a love which was more than love -
I and my Annabel Lee.

8805 *'For Annie'*
The fever called 'Living'
Is conquered at last.

8806 *'The Bells'*
Keeping time, time, time,
In a sort of Runic rhyme,
To the tintinnabulation that so musically wells
From the bells, bells, bells, bells.

8807 *'A Dream within a Dream'*
All that we see or seem
Is but a dream within a dream.

8808 *'To Helen'*
Helen, thy beauty is to me
Like those Nicean barks of yore, ...

...Thy Naiad airs have brought me home,
To the glory that was Greece
And the grandeur that was Rome.

8809
Man's real life is happy, chiefly because he is ever expecting that it soon will be so.

8810 *'The Raven'*
Once upon a midnight dreary, while I pondered, weak and weary,
Over many a quaint and curious volume of forgotten lore,
While I nodded, nearly napping, suddenly there came a tapping,
As of someone gently rapping, rapping at my chamber door.

8811 *'The Raven'*
Take thy beak from out my heart, and take thy form from off my door!
Quoth the Raven, 'Nevermore'.

POGREBIN Letty Cottin
8812
Boys don't make passes at female smart-asses.

8813
No labourer in the world is expected to work for room, board, and love - except the housewife.

POINCARÉ Henri 1854-1912
8814 *Science and Hypothesis*
Science is built up of facts, as a house is built of stones; but an accumulation of facts is no more a science than a heap of stones is a house.

POITIERS Diane de 1499-1566
8815
We only make a dupe of the friend whose advice we ask, for we never tell him all; and it is usually what we have left unsaid that decides our conduct.

POLLARD J.G.
8816
Executive ability is deciding quickly and getting somebody else to do the work.

POLLOCK Channing
8817
A critic is a legless man who teaches running.

8818
Marriage is a great institution, and no family should be without it.

POLLOCK Frances
8819
I have learned little from the years that fly; but I have wrung the colour from the years.

POMERANTZ Hart
8820
To some lawyers, all facts are created equal.

POMFRET John 1667-1702
8821 *'Reason'*
We live and learn, but not the wiser grow.

POMPADOUR Madame de 1721-1764
8822
Après nous le déluge.
After us the deluge.

POMPIDOU Georges 1911-1974
8823
A statesman is a politician who places himself at the service of the nation. A politician is a statesman who places the nation at his service.

POPE Alexander 1688-1744
8824
Alive, ridiculous, and dead forgot?

8825 *The Dunciad*
Poetic Justice, with her lifted scale,
Where, in nice balance, truth with gold she weighs,
And solid pudding against empty praise.

8826 *The Dunciad*
While pensive poets painful vigils keep,
Sleepless themselves, to give their readers sleep.

8827 *The Dunciad*
Gentle Dullness ever loves a joke.

8828 *The Dunciad*
A brain of feathers, and a heart of lead.

8829 *The Dunciad*
How little, mark! that portion of the ball,
Where, faint at best, the beams of science fall.

8830 *The Dunciad*
All crowd, who foremost shall be damned to Fame.

8831 *The Dunciad*
A wit with dunces, and a dunce with wits.

8832 *The Dunciad*
Whate'er the talents, or howe'er designed,
We hang one jingling padlock on the mind.

8833 *The Dunciad*
The Right Divine of Kings to govern wrong.

8834 *The Dunciad*
For thee explain a thing till all men doubt it,
And write about it, Goddess, and about it.

8835 *The Dunciad*
With the same cement, ever sure to bind,
We bring to one dead level ev'ry mind.
Then take him to develop, if you can,
And hew the block off, and get out the man.

8836 *The Dunciad*
She marked thee there,
Stretched on the rack of a too easy chair,
And heard thy everlasting yawn confess
The pains and penalties of idleness.

8837 *The Dunciad*
Religion blushing veils her sacred fires,
And unawares Morality expires.

8838 *The Dunciad*
Lo! thy dread empire, Chaos! is restored;
Light dies before thy uncreating word:
Thy hand, great Anarch! lets the curtain fall;
And universal darkness buries all.

8839 *The Dunciad*
Vital spark of heav'nly flame!
Quit, oh quit this mortal frame:
Trembling, hoping, ling'ring, flying,
Oh the pain, the bliss of dying!

8840 *'Elegy to the Memory of an Unfortunate Lady'*
Is it, in heav'n, a crime to love too well?

8841 *'Elegy to the Memory of an Unfortunate Lady'*
Is there no bright reversion in the sky,
For those who greatly think, or bravely die?

8842 *'Elegy to the Memory of an Unfortunate Lady'*
Ambition first sprung from your blest abodes;
The glorious fault of angels and of gods.

8843 *'Elegy to the Memory of an Unfortunate Lady'*
A heap of dust alone remains of thee;
'Tis all thou art, and all the proud shall be!

8844 *Eloisa to Abelard*
Oh happy state! when souls each other draw,
When love is liberty, and nature, law:
All then is full, possessing, and possessed,
No craving void left aching in the breast.

8845 *Eloisa to Abelard*
How happy is the blameless Vestal's lot!
The world forgetting, by the world forgot.

8846 *Eloisa to Abelard*
One thought of thee puts all the pomp to flight,
Priests, tapers, temples, swim before my sight.

8847 *Eloisa to Abelard*
See my lips tremble, and my eyeballs roll,
Suck my last breath, and catch my flying soul!

8848 *'Epigram: You beat your pate'*
You beat your pate, and fancy wit will come:
Knock as you please, there's nobody at home.

8849 *'Epigram from the French'*
Sir, I admit your gen'ral rule
That every poet is a fool:
But you yourself may serve to show it,
That every fool is not a poet.

8850 *'An Epistle to Dr Arbuthnot'*
Shut, shut the door, good John! fatigued I said,
Tie up the knocker, say I'm sick, I'm dead,
The dog-star rages!

8851 *'An Epistle to Dr Arbuthnot'*
You think this cruel? take it for a rule,
No creature smarts so little as a fool.

8852 *'An Epistle to Dr Arbuthnot'*
Destroy his fib, or sophistry; in vain,
The creature's at his dirty work again.

8853 *'An Epistle to Dr Arbuthnot'*
As yet a child, nor yet a fool to fame,
I lisped in numbers, for the numbers came.

8854 *'An Epistle to Dr Arbuthnot'*
To help me through this long disease, my life.

8855 *'An Epistle to Dr Arbuthnot'*
And he, whose fustian's so sublimely bad,
It is not poetry, but prose run mad.

8856 *'An Epistle to Dr Arbuthnot'*
Who breaks a butterfly upon a wheel?

8857 *'An Epistle to Dr Arbuthnot'*
Yet let me flap this bug with gilded wings,
This painted child of dirt that stinks and stings.

8858 *'An Epistle to Dr Arbuthnot'*
Eternal smiles his emptiness betray,
As shallow streams run dimpling all the way.

8859 *'An Epistle to Dr Arbuthnot'*
And he himself one vile antithesis.

8860 *'An Epistle to Dr Arbuthnot'*
A cherub's face, a reptile all the rest.

8861 *'Epistle to Dr Arbuthnot'*
Curst be the verse, how well soe'er it flow,
That tends to make one worthy man my foe.

8862 *'An Epistle to Dr Arbuthnot' (of his own father)*
Unlearn'd, he knew no schoolman's subtle art,
No language, but the language of the heart.

8863 *Epistles to Several Persons 'To a Lady'*
Chaste to her husband, frank to all beside,
A teeming mistress, but a barren bride.

8864 *Epistles to Several Persons 'To a Lady'*
Virtue she finds too painful an endeavour,
Content to dwell in decencies for ever.

8865 *Epistles to Several Persons 'To a Lady'*
Still round and round the ghosts of Beauty glide,
And haunt the places where their honour died.
See how the world its veterans rewards!
A youth of frolics, and old age of cards.

8866 *Epistles to Several Persons 'To a Lady'*
And mistress of herself, though china fall.

8867 *Epistles to Several Persons 'To a Lady'*
Woman's at best a contradiction still.

8868 *Epistles to Several Persons 'To Lord Bathurst'*
Who shall decide, when doctors disagree.

8869 *Epistles to Several Persons 'To Lord Bathurst'*
But thousands die, without or this or that,
Die, and endow a college, or a cat.

8870 *Epistles to Several Persons 'To Lord Bathurst'*
The ruling passion, be it what it will,
The ruling passion conquers reason still.

8871 *Epistles to Several Persons 'To Lord Cobham'*
'Tis education forms the common mind,

Just as the twig is bent, the tree's inclined.

8872 *'Epitaph: On Mr Gay in Westminster Abbey'*
Of manners gentle, of affections mild;
In wit, a man; simplicity, a child;
With native humour temp'ring virtuous rage,
Formed to delight at once and lash the age.

8873 *'Epitaph: Intended for Sir Isaac Newton'*
Nature, and Nature's laws lay hid in night.
God said, *Let Newton be!* and all was light.

8874 *An Essay on Criticism*
A little learning is a dangerous thing;
Drink deep, or taste not the Pierian spring:
There shallow draughts intoxicate the brain,
And drinking largely sobers us again.

8875 *An Essay on Criticism*
Whoever thinks a faultless piece to see,
Thinks what ne'er was, nor is, nor e'er shall be.

8876 *An Essay on Criticism*
Poets like painters, thus unskilled to trace
The naked nature and the living grace,
With gold and jewels cover ev'ry part,
And hide with ornaments their want of art.

8877 *An Essay on Criticism*
Expression is the dress of thought.

8878 *An Essay on Criticism*
As some to church repair,
Not for the doctrine, but the music there.

8879 *An Essay on Criticism*
True ease in writing comes from art, not chance,
As those move easiest who have learned to dance.
'Tis not enough no harshness gives offence,
The sound must seem an echo to the sense.

8880 *An Essay on Criticism*
Yet let not each gay turn thy rapture move,
For fools admire, but men of sense approve.

8881 *An Essay on Criticism*
Some praise at morning what they blame at night;
But always think the last opinion right.

8882 *An Essay on Criticism*
To err is human; to forgive, divine.

8883 *An Essay on Criticism*
All seems infected that th'infected spy,
As all looks yellow to the jaundiced eye.

8884 *An Essay on Criticism*
Men must be taught as if you taught them not,
And things unknown proposed as things forgot.

8885 *An Essay on Criticism*
The bookful blockhead, ignorantly read,
With loads of learned lumber in his head.

8886 *An Essay on Criticism*
For fools rush in where angels fear to tread.

8887 *An Essay on Criticism*
True wit is nature to advantage dressed,
What oft was thought but ne'er so well
expressed.

8888 *An Essay on Criticism*
While expletives their feeble aid do join,
And ten low words oft creep in one dull line.

8889 *An Essay on Man*
Awake, my St John! leave all meaner things
To low ambition, and the pride of kings.
Let us (since Life can little more supply
Than just to look about us and to die)
Expatiate free o'er all this scene of man;
A mighty maze! but not without a plan.

8890 *An Essay on Man*
Eye Nature's walks, shoot Folly as it flies,
And catch the Manners living as they rise.
Laugh where we must, be candid where we can;
But vindicate the ways of God to man.

8891 *An Essay on Man*
Observe how system into system runs,
What other planets circle other suns.

8892 *An Essay on Man*
Who sees with equal eye, as God of all,
A hero perish, or a sparrow fall,
Atoms or systems into ruin hurled,
And now a bubble burst, and now a world.

8893 *An Essay on Man*
Pride still is aiming at the blest abodes,
Men would be angels, angels would be gods.

8894 *An Essay on Man*
Why has not man a microscopic eye?
For this plain reason, man is not a fly.

8895 *An Essay on Man*
The spider's touch, how exquisitely fine!
Feels at each thread, and lives along the line.

8896 *An Essay on Man*
All are but parts of one stupendous whole,
Whose body, Nature is, and God the soul.

8897 *An Essay on Man*
All nature is but art, unknown to thee;
All chance, direction, which thou canst not see;
All discord, harmony, not understood;
All partial evil, universal good:
And, spite of Pride, in erring Reason's spite,
One truth is clear, 'Whatever IS, IS RIGHT'.

8898 *An Essay on Man*
Created half to rise, and half to fall;
Great lord of all things, yet a prey to all;
Sole judge of truth, in endless error hurled;
The glory, jest, and riddle of the world!

8899 *An Essay on Man*
Go, teach Eternal Wisdom how to rule -
Then drop into thyself, and be a fool!

8900 *An Essay on Man*
Fixed like a plant on his peculiar spot,
To draw nutrition, propagate, and rot.

8901 *An Essay on Man*
Vice is a monster of so frightful mien,
As, to be hated, needs but to be seen;
Yet seen too oft, familiar with her face,
We first endure, then pity, then embrace.

8902 *An Essay on Man*
The learn'd is happy nature to explore,
The fool is happy that he knows no more.

8903 *An Essay on Man*
Behold the child, by Nature's kindly law
Pleased with a rattle, tickled with a straw.

8904 *An Essay on Man*
Scarfs, garters, gold, amuse his riper stage;
And beads and pray'r-books are the toys of age:
Pleased with this bauble still, as that before;
Till tired he sleeps, and life's poor play is o'er!

8905 *An Essay on Man*
For forms of government let fools contest;
Whate'er is best administered is best.

8906 *An Essay on Man*
Thus God and nature linked the gen'ral frame,
And bade self-love and social be the same.

8907 *An Essay on Man*
Oh Happiness! our being's end and aim!
Good, pleasure, ease, content! whate'er thy
name:
That something still which prompts th'eternal
sigh,
For which we bear to live, or dare to die.

8908 *An Essay on Man*
A wit's a feather, and a chief a rod;
An honest man's the noblest work of God.

8909 *An Essay on Man*
Slave to no sect, who takes no private road,
But looks thro' Nature, up to Nature's God.

8910 *An Essay on Man*
All our knowledge is, ourselves to know.

8911 *An Essay on Man*
Hope springs eternal in the human breast
Man never is, but always to be blest.

8912
Be not the first by whom the new are tried
Nor yet the last to lay the old aside.

8913 *To George, Lord Lyttelton*
Here am I, dying of a hundred good symptoms.

8914
The hungry judges soon the sentence sign,
And wretches hang that jurymen may dine.

8915 *Imitations of Horace*
Our Gen'rals now, retired to their estates,
Hang their old trophies o'er the garden gates,
In life's cool ev'ning satiate of applause.

8916 *Imitations of Horace*
Not to go back, is somewhat to advance,
And men must walk at least before they dance.

8917 *Imitations of Horace*
Get place and wealth, if possible, with grace;
If not, by any means get wealth and place.

8918 *Imitations of Horace*
Not to admire, is all the art I know,
To make men happy, and to keep them so.

8919 *Imitations of Horace*
The worst of madmen is a saint run mad.

8920 *Imitations of Horace*
Shakespeare (whom you and ev'ry play-house bill
Style the divine, the matchless, what you will)
For gain, not glory, winged his roving flight,
And grew immortal in his own despite.

8921 *Imitations of Horace*
The people's voice is odd,
It is, and it is not, the voice of God.

8922 *Imitations of Horace*
But those who cannot write, and those who can,
All rhyme, and scrawl, and scribble, to a man.

8923 *Imitations of Horace*
There still remains, to mortify a wit,
The many-headed monster of the pit.

8924 *Imitations of Horace*
Ask you what provocation I have had?
The strong antipathy of good to bad.

8925 *Imitations of Horace*
Yes, I am proud; I must be proud to see
Men not afraid of God, afraid of me.

8926
Light quirks of music, broken and uneven,
Make the soul dance upon a jig of heaven.

8927
A man of business may talk of philosophy; a
man who has none may practise it.

8928 *Martinus Scriblerus ...*
Ye gods! annihilate but space and time,
And make two lovers happy.

8929 *Miscellanies*
To endeavour to work upon the vulgar with fine
sense, is like attempting to hew blocks with a
razor.

8930 *Miscellanies*
A man should never be ashamed to own he has
been in the wrong, which is but saying, in other
words, that he is wiser to-day than he was
yesterday.

8931 *Miscellanies*
It is with narrow-souled people as with narrow-
necked bottles: the less they have in them, the
more noise they make in pouring it out.

8932
I never knew any man in my life who could not
bear another's misfortunes perfectly like a
Christian.

8933 *'Ode on Solitude' (written when aged about 12)*
Happy the man, whose wish and care
A few paternal acres bound,
Content to breathe his native air,
In his own ground.

8934 *'Ode on Solitude' (written when aged about 12)*
Thus let me live, unseen, unknown;
Thus unlamented let me die;
Steal from the world, and not a stone
Tell where I lie.

8935
Party-spirit ... which at best is but the madness
of many for the gain of a few.

8936
A perfect judge will read each word of wit with
the same spirit that its author writ.

8937 *The Rape of the Lock*
What dire offence from am'rous causes springs,
What mighty contests rise from trivial things.

8938 *The Rape of the Lock*
If to her share some female errors fall,
Look on her face, and you'll forget 'em all.

8939 *The Rape of the Lock*
Coffee, (which makes the politician wise,
And see thro' all things with his half-shut eyes).

8940 *The Rape of the Lock*
Not louder shrieks to pitying heav'n are cast,
When husbands or when lapdogs breathe their
last.

8941 *The Rape of the Lock*
Beauties in vain their pretty eyes may roll;
Charms strike the sight, but merit wins the soul.

8942
Sickness is a sort of early old age; it teaches us a
diffidence in our earthly state.

8943
Know then thyself, presume not God to scan:
The proper study of mankind is man.

8944 *'The Universal Prayer'*
Teach me to feel another's woe;
To hide the fault I see;
That mercy I to others show,
That mercy show to me.

8945 *The Rape of the Lock*
Fair tresses man's imperial race ensnare,
And beauty draws us with a single hair.

POPPER Sir Karl 1902-1994
8946 *The Open Society and its Enemies*
We may become the makers of our fate when
we have ceased to pose as its prophets.

8947 *The Open Society and its Enemies*
We must plan for freedom, and not only for
security, if for no other reason than that only
freedom can make security secure.

8948 *The Open Society and its Enemies*
There is no history of mankind, there are only
many histories of all kinds of aspects of human
life. And one of these is the history of political
power. This is elevated into the history of the
world.

8949 *'The Philosophy of Science'*
Science must begin with myths, and with the
criticism of myths.

8950 *The Poverty of Historicism*
Piecemeal social engineering resembles
physical engineering in regarding the *ends* as
beyond the province of technology.

PORCHIA Antonio
8951
One lives in the hope of becoming a memory.

PORTER Cole 1891-1964
8952 *'Anything Goes'*
In olden days a glimpse of stocking
Was looked on as something shocking
Now, heaven knows,
Anything goes.

8953 *'Begin the Beguine'*
When they begin the Beguine
It brings back the sound of music so tender,
It brings back a night of tropical splendour,
It brings back a memory ever green.

8954 *'Well, Did You Evah?*
Have you heard it's in the stars,
Next July we collide with Mars?
Well, did your evah! What a swell party this is.

8955
My heart belongs to Daddy.

8956 *'Just One of Those Things'*
So goodbye dear, and Amen,
Here's hoping we meet now and then,
It was great fun,
But it was just one of those things.

8957 *'I Get a Kick Out of You'*
I get no kick from champagne,
Mere alcohol doesn't thrill me at all,
So tell my why should it be true
That I get a kick out of you?

8958 *'Let's Do It'*
Birds do it, bees do it,
Even educated fleas do it.
Let's do it, let's fall in love.

8959
Miss Otis regrets (she's unable to lunch today).

8960 *'Night and Day'*
Night and day, you are the one,
Only you beneath the moon and under the sun.

8961 *'Every Time We Say Goodbye'*
When you're near there's such an air of spring
about it;
I can hear a lark somewhere begin to sing about
it;
There's no love song finer,
But how strange the change from major to
minor
Every time we say goodbye.

8962 *'You're the Top'*
You're the top! You're the Coliseum,
You're the top! You're the Louvre Museum,
You're a melody
From a symphony by Strauss,
You're a Bendel bonnet,
A Shakespeare sonnet,
You're Mickey Mouse!

PORTEUS Beilby 1731-1808
8963 *Death*
... One murder made a villain,
Millions a hero.

8964 *Death*
War its thousands slays, Peace its ten
thousands.

8965 *Death*
Teach him how to live,
And, oh! still harder lesson! how to die.

PORTILLO Michael 1953-
8966
Conservatives are not xenophobic - we are
patriotic.

POST Emily 1872-1960
8967
The attributes of a great lady may still be found
in the rule of the four S's: Sincerity, Simplicity,
Sympathy, and Serenity.

POTTER Beatrix 1866-1943
8968 *The Tailor of Gloucester*
I am worn to a ravelling ... I am undone and
worn to a thread-paper, for I have NO MORE

TWIST.

8969 *The Tale of the Flopsy Bunnies*
It is said that the effect of eating too much lettuce is 'soporific'.

8970 *The Tale of Peter Rabbit*
Don't go into Mr McGregor's garden: your father had an accident there, he was put into a pie by Mrs McGregor.

POTTER Dennis 1935-1994
8971
Religion to me has always been the wound, not the bandage.

8972
Things are both more trivial than they ever were, and more important than they ever were, and the difference between them doesn't seem to matter. But the nowness of everything is absolutely wondrous.

POTTER Henry Codman 1835-1908
8973 *Bishop Potter's Address*
We have exchanged the Washingtonian dignity for the Jeffersonian simplicity, which was, in truth, only another name for the Jacksonian vulgarity.

POTTER Stephen 1900-1969
8974 *Lifemanship*
How to be one up - how to make the other man feel that something has gone wrong, however slightly.

8975 *Lifemanship*
Each of us can, by ploy or gambit, most naturally gain the advantage.

8976 *One-Upmanship (on wine-tasting)*
A good general rule is to state that the bouquet is better than the taste, and vice versa.

8977
The theory and practice of gamesmanship or the art of winning games without actually cheating.

POTTER David E. 1943-
8978
Human beings are not born with a chair stuck to their backsides, and the afterbirth isn't a PC. It is a condition of the human being that he is mobile.

POTTIER Eugene 1816-1887
8979 *'L'Internationale'*
C'est la lutte finale
Groupons-nous, et, demain,
L'Internationale
Sera le genre humain.
This is the final conflict: let us form up and, tomorrow, the International will encompass the human race.

POUND Ezra 1885-1972
8980 *The ABC of Reading*
Any general statement is like a cheque drawn on a bank. Its value depends on what is there to meet it.

8981 *The ABC of Reading*
Literature is news that STAYS news.

8982 *The ABC of Reading*
Real education must ultimately be limited to one who INSISTS on knowing, the rest is mere sheep-herding.

8983 *'Ancient Music'*
Winter is icummen in,
Lhude sing Goddamm,
Raineth drop and staineth slop,
And how the wind doth ramm!
Sing: Goddamm.

8984 *'Cino'*
Bah! I have sung women in three cities,
But it is all the same;
And I will sing of the sun.

8985 *Draft of XXX Cantos*
Hang it all, Robert Browning,
There can be but the one 'Sordello'.

8986 *Draft of XXX Cantos*
In the gloom, the gold gathers the light against it.

8987 *Draft of XXX Cantos*
And even I can remember
A day when the historians left blanks in their writings,
I mean for things they didn't know.

8988 *'The Garden'*
And she is dying piece-meal
of a sort of emotional anaemia.

And round about there is a rabble
of the filthy, sturdy, unkillable infants of the very poor.

8989 *'Mr Housman's Message'*
O woe, woe,
People are born and die,
We also shall be dead pretty soon
Therefore let us act as if we were dead already.

8990 *How to Read*
Great literature is simply language charged with meaning to the utmost possible degree.

8991 *Hugh Selwyn Mauberley*
For three years, out of key with his time,
He strove to resuscitate the dead art
Of poetry; to maintain 'the sublime'
In the old sense. Wrong from the start -

8992 *Hugh Selwyn Mauberley*
The age demanded an image
Of its accelerated grimace,
Something for the modern stage,
Not, at any rate, an Attic grace;
Not, not certainly, the obscure reveries
Of the inward gaze;
Better mendacities
Than the classics in paraphrase!

8993 *Hugh Selwyn Mauberley*
Died some, pro patria,
non 'dulce' non 'et decor' ...
walked eye-deep in hell
believing in old men's lies, the unbelieving
came home, home to a lie.

8994 *Hugh Selwyn Mauberley*
hysterias, trench confessions,
laughter out of dead bellies.

8995 *Literary Essays*
Artists are the antennae of the race, but the
bullet-headed many will never learn to trust
their great artists.

8996
No man understands a deep book until he has
seen and lived at least part of its contents.

8997
Properly we should read for power. Man
reading should be man intensely alive. The
book should be a ball of light in one's hand.

8998 *'In a Station of the Metro'*
The apparition of these faces in the crowd;
Petals on a wet, black bough.

8999 *'Villanelle; the psychological hour'*
I had over-prepared the event,
that much was ominous.
With middle-ageing care
I had laid out just the right books.
I had almost turned down the pages.

POUND Roscoe 1870-1964
9000
The law must be stable and yet is must not
stand still.

POWELL Anthony 1905-
9001 *The Acceptance World*
He fell in love with himself at first sight and it is
a passion to which he has always remained
faithful.

9002 *The Acceptance World*
Dinner at the Huntercombes' possessed only
two dramatic features - the wine was a farce
and the food a tragedy.

9003 *(after the painting by Nicolas Poussin)*
A dance to the music of time.

9004
Books do furnish a room.

9005
One hears about life all the time from different
people with very different narrative gifts.

9006 *A Question of Upbringing*
He's so wet you could shoot snipe off him.

9007 *Temporary Kings*
Growing old is like being increasingly penalised
for a crime you haven't committed.

POWELL Enoch 1912-1998
9008
All political careers end in failure.

9009
The amateur in politics is the person who is
always sure he knows the result of the next
general election.

9010
History is littered with the wars which
everybody knew would never happen.

9011
A little nonsense now and then is not a bad
thing. Where would we politicians be if we were
not allowed to talk it sometimes?

9012
A plumber who has Latin is a better plumber
than one who does not.

9013
For a politician to complain about the press is
like a ship's captain complaining about the sea.

9014
A politician crystallises what most people
mean, even if they don't know it.

9015
To pretend that you cannot exchange food and
services freely with a Frenchman or an Italian
unless there is an identical standard of bathing
beaches or tap water in the different countries
is not logic. It is naked aggression.

9016
It is like watching a nation busily engaged in
heaping up its own funeral pyre. As I look
ahead, I am filled with foreboding. Like the
Roman, I seem to see 'the River Tiber foaming
with much blood'.

POWELL Sir John 1645-1713
9017 *Lord Raymond's Reports*
Let us consider the reason of the case. For
nothing is law that is not reason.

POWELL Laurence Clark
9018
Writing is a solitary occupation. Family, friends
and society are the natural enemies of a writer.

He must be alone, uninterrupted and slightly savage if he is to sustain and complete an undertaking.

POWER John O'Connor 1846-
9019 *(of the Liberal Unionists)*
The mules of politics: without pride of ancestry, or hope of posterity.

PRAED W.M. 1802-1839
9020 *The Chant of the Brazen Head*
I think that nought is worth a thought,
And I'm a fool for thinking.

9021 *Goodnight to the Season*
The ice of her Ladyship's manners,
The ice of his Lordship's champagne.

9022 *'The Talented Man'*
Of science and logic he chatters
As fine and as fast as he can;
Though I am no judge of such matters,
I'm sure he's a talented man.

PRESTON Keith 1884-1927
9023 *'The Liberators'*
Of all the literary scenes
Saddest this sight to me:
The graves of little magazines
Who died to make verse free.

PRÉVERT Jacques 1900-1977
9024 *Les Enfants du Paradis*
Love is so simple.

9025 *'Pater Noster'*
Our Father which art in heaven
Stay there
And we will stay on earth
Which is sometimes so pretty.

PRIESTLEY J.B. 1894-1984
9026
One of the delights known to age, and beyond the grasp of youth, is that of 'not going'.

9027
I don't like baths. I don't enjoy them in the slightest and, if I could, I'd prefer to go around dirty.

9028
Any fool can be fussy and rid himself of energy all over the place, but a man has to have something in him before he can settle down to do nothing.

9029
God can stand being told by Professor Ayer and Marghanita Laski that He doesn't exist.

9030 *Good Companions*
To say that these men paid their shillings to watch twenty-two hirelings kick a ball is merely to say that a violin is wood and catgut, that *Hamlet* is so much paper and ink. For a shilling the Bruddersford United AFC offered you Conflict and Art.

9031 *Saturn Over the Water*
I can't help feeling wary when I hear anything said about the masses. First you take their faces from 'em by calling 'em the masses and then you accuse 'em of not having any faces.

9032
I sometimes wish they would swagger more now, buy bigger overcoats and wilder hats, and retain those traces of make-up that put them outside respectability and keep them rogues and vagabonds, which is what, at heart - bless 'em - they are.

PRIESTLEY Joseph 1733-1804
9033 *An Essay on the First Principles of Government*
Every man, when he comes to be sensible of his natural rights, and to feel his own importance, will consider himself as fully equal to any other person whatever.

PRIOR Matthew 1664-1721
9034 *'A Better Answer'*
I court others in verse: but I love thee in prose:
And they have my whimsies, but thou hast my heart.

9035 *'To a Child of Quality of Five Years Old'*
For, as our different ages move,
'Tis so ordained (would Fate but mend it!)
That I shall be past making love,
When she begins to comprehend it.

9036 *'An English Padlock'*
Be to her virtues very kind;
Be to her faults a little blind;
Let all her ways be unconfined;
And clap your padlock - on her mind.

9037 *'Epitaph'*
Nobles and heralds, by your leave,
Here lies what once was Matthew Prior,
The son of Adam and of Eve,
Can Stuart or Nassau go higher?

9038
He's half absolv'd
Who has confess'd.

9039 *'To the Hon. Charles Montague'*
From ignorance our comfort flows,
The only wretched are the wise.

9040 *'Jinny the Just'*
For the idiom of words very little she heeded,
Provided the matter she drove at succeeded,
She took and gave languages just as she needed.

9041 *'Paolo Purganti and his Wife'*
The doctor understood the call;
But had not always wherewithal.

9042 *'Upon this Passage in Scaligerana'*
They never taste who always drink;
They always talk, who never think.

9043 *'The Remedy Worse than the Disease'*
Cured yesterday of my disease,
I died last night of my physician.

9044
Similies are like songs of love:
They much describe, they nothing prove.

9045 *'Solomon'*
What is a King? - a man condemned to bear
The public burden of the nation's care.

9046 *'A True Maid'*
No, no; for my virginity,
When I lose that, says Rose, I'll die:
Behind the elms last night, cried Dick,
Rose, were you not extremely sick?

PRITCHETT V.S. 1900-1997
9047 *The Living Novel*
The principle of procrastinated rape is said to
be the ruling one in all the great best-sellers.

9048
The mark of genius is an incessant activity of
mind. Genius is a spiritual greed.

9049
Those mausoleums of inactive masculinity are
places for men who prefer armchairs to women.

9050
A natural New Yorker is a native of the present
tense.

9051
Queen Victoria - a mixture of national landlady
and actress.

9052
The State, that cawing rookery of committees
and subcommittees.

9053
The word for New York is activity.

PROCTER Adelaide Ann 1825-1864
9054 *'A Lost Chord'*
Seated one day at the organ,
I was weary and ill at ease,
And my fingers wandered idly
Over the noisy keys.

9055 *'A Lost Chord'*
But I struck one chord of music,
Like the sound of a great Amen.

PROCTER J.J.
9056
There are things of deadly earnest that can only
be safely mentioned under cover of a joke.

PROPERTIUS c.50-16 BC
9057 *Elegies*
Even if strength fail, boldness at least will
deserve praise: in great endeavours even to
have had the will is enough.

9058
Give the historians something to write about.

PROTAGORAS 490-421 BC
9059
[That] man is the measure of all things.

PROUDHON Pierre-Jospeh 1809-1865
9060 *Qu'est-ce que la propriété?*
La propriété c'est le vol.
Property is theft.

PROUST Marcel 1871-1922
9061
Until I saw Chardin's painting, I never realized
how much beauty lay around me in my parents'
house, in the half-cleared table, in the corner of
a tablecloth left awry, in the knife beside the
empty oyster shell.

9062 *Cities of the Plain*
'Anyhow,' Mme de Cambremer went on, 'I have
a horror of sunsets, they're so romantic, so
operatic.'

9063
The one thing more difficult than following a
regimen is not imposing it on others.

9064 *Guermantes Way*
Everything we think of as great has come to us
from neurotics. It is they and they alone who
found religions and create great works of art.
The world will never realise how much it owes
to them and what they have suffered in order to
bestow their gifts on it.

9065 *Guermantes Way*
There is nothing like desire for preventing the
things one says from bearing any resemblance
to what one has in one's mind.

9066
At the heart of our friendly or purely social
relations, there lurks a hostility momentarily
cured but recurring in fits and starts.

9067
A la recherche du temps perdu.
In search of lost time.

9068
Let us leave pretty women to men without
imagination.

9069 *A l'ombre des jeunes filles en fleurs*
One becomes moral as soon as one is unhappy.

9070
There can be no peace of mind in love, since the advantage one has secured is never anything but a fresh starting-point for further desires.

9071
There are perhaps no days of our childhood we lived so fully as those we believe we left without having lived them: those we spent with a favourite book.

9072
That which we remember of our conduct is ignored by our closest neighbour; but that which we have forgotten having said, or even what we never said, will cause laughter even into the next world.

9073 *Swann's Way*
For a long time I used to go to bed early.

9074 *Swann's Way*
To think that I've wasted years of my life, that I've longed to die, that I've experienced my greatest love for a woman who didn't appeal to me, who wasn't even my type.

9075 *Time Regained*
One of those telegrams of which M. de Guermantes had wittily fixed the formula: 'Cannot come, lie follows'.

9076 *Time Regained*
The true paradises are the paradises that we have lost.

9077 *Time Regained*
For if unhappiness develops the forces of the mind, happiness alone is salutary to the body.

PROVERBS and SAYINGS
9078 *African*
Indecision is like a stepchild: if he doesn't wash his hands, he is called dirty; if he does, he is wasting the water.

9079 *African*
When elephants fight it is the grass that suffers.

9080
All would live long, but none would be old.

9081 *American Indian*
Listen or thy tongue will keep thee deaf.

9082 *American Indian*
Never criticize a man until you've walked a mile in his moccasins.

9083 *Arab*
Throw a lucky man into the sea, and he will come up with a fish in his mouth.

9084 *Arab*
The enemy of my enemy is my friend.

9085 *Arab*
God sells knowledge for labour - honour for risk.

9086 *Arab*
After dinner, rest a while, after supper walk a mile.

9087 *Arab*
The sinning is the best part of repentance.

9088 *Arab*
It is a good thing to speak the truth: but it is a better thing to know the truth and to talk about date stones.

9089 *Asidic*
For the unlearned, old age is winter; for the learned, it is the season of the harvest.

9090 *Australian Aboriginal*
Hypocrite - mouth one way, belly 'nother way.

9091 *Australian Aboriginal*
Those who lose dreaming are lost.

9092 *Belgian*
Experience is the comb that Nature gives us when we are bald.

9093 *Bosnian*
Who lies for you, will lie against you.

9094 *Canadian Indian*
Love Canada or give it back.

9095 *Chinese*
A book is like a garden carried in the pocket.

9096 *Chinese*
Make happy those who are near, and those who are far will come.

9097 *Chinese*
If heaven made him, earth can find some use for him.

9098 *Chinese*
People in the West are always getting ready to live.

9099 *Chinese*
Married couples who love each other tell each other a thousand things without talking.

9100 *Chinese*
The palest ink is better than the best memory.

9101 *Chinese*
One dog barks at something, the rest bark at him.

9102 *Chinese*
With time and patience the mulberry leaf becomes a silk gown.

9103 *Chinese*
When you have only two pennies left in the world, buy a loaf of bread with one, and a lily

with the other.

9104 *Chinese*
I hear and I forget. I see and I remember. I do and I understand.

9105 *Chinese*
To be uncertain is to be uncomfortable, but to be certain is to be ridiculous.

9106 *Chinese*
If you don't want anyone to know it, don't do it.

9107 *Colombian*
He who must die must die in the dark, even though he sells candles.

9108 *Congolese*
The teeth are smiling, but is the heart?

9109 *Cree Indian*
There is no chance for old fools.

9110 *Czechoslovakian*
When you buy, use your eyes and your mind, not your ears.

9111 *Danish*
Lawyers and painters can soon change white to black.

9112 *Dutch*
He who is outside his door already has a hard part of his journey behind him.

9113 *Dutch*
God does not pay weekly, but he pays at the end.

9114 *Dutch*
A handful of patience is worth more than a bushel of brains.

9115 *Dutch*
God made the ocean, but the Dutch made Holland.

9116 *English*
Everyone must row with the oars he has.

9117 *English*
The absent are always wrong.

9118 *English*
The shortest answer is doing.

9119 *English*
A Scotch mist may wet an Englishman to the skin.

9120 *English*
Danger and delight grow on one stalk.

9121 *English*
Affectation is a greater enemy to the face than smallpox.

9122 *English*
We are usually the best men when in the worst health.

9123 *English*
There's none so blind as those who won't see.

9124 *English*
When a proud man hears another praised, he feels himself injured.

9125 *English*
As old as the itch.

9126 *English*
A man of words and not of deeds,
Is like a garden full of weeds.

9127 *English*
One of these days is none of these days.

9128 *English*
Don't fall before you're pushed.

9129 *English*
There is but an hour a day between a good housewife and a bad one.

9130
That which is escaped now is pain to come.

9131 *Ethiopian*
When spider webs unite, they can tie up a lion.

9132
Fire tries gold, misfortune men.

9133 *French*
He who can lick can bite.

9134 *French*
The price spoils the pleasure.

9135 *French*
Tout passe, tout lasse, tout casse.
Everything passes; everything wears out; everything breaks.

9136 *French*
The worst is not always certain but it's very likely.

9137 *French*
A good meal ought to begin with hunger.

9138 *French*
There is no such thing as a pretty good omelette.

9139 *French*
Only great men may have great faults.

9140 *French*
There's a pinch of the madman in every great man.

9141 *French*
With enough 'ifs' we could put Paris into a bottle.

9142 *French*
There is one who kisses, and the other who offers·a cheek.

9143 *French*
Gratitude is the heart's memory.

9144 *French*
To want to forget something is to think of it.

9145 *French*
A father is a banker provided by nature.

9146 *French*
Nothing is so burdensome as a secret.

9147 *French*
L'amour est aveugle; l'amitié ferme les yeux
Love is blind: friendship closes its eyes.

9148 *German*
It's the whole, not the detail, that matters.

9149 *German*
God gives the nuts, but he does not crack them.

9150 *German*
Old birds are hard to pluck.

9151 *German*
Whose bread I eat, his song I sing.

9152 *German*
Good things are not done in a hurry.

9153 *German*
When the fox preaches, look to your geese.

9154 *German*
Invalids live longest.

9155 *German*
The eyes believe themselves; the ears believe other people.

9156 *German*
Who takes the child by the hand takes the mother by the heart.

9157 *German*
Better silent than stupid.

9158 *German*
Truth has a handsome countenance but torn garments.

9159
A great city, a great solitude.

9160 *Greek*
Whatever is good to know is difficult to learn.

9161 *Greek*
It is easier to talk than to hold one's tongue.

9162 *Hindu*
An arch never sleeps.

9163 *Hindu*
If you ask the hungry man how much is two and two, he replies four loaves.

9164 *Hindu*
Dictators ride to and fro upon tigers from which they dare not dismount.

9165 *Hindu*
Fatigue is the best pillow.

9166 *Hindu*
There is nothing noble about being superior to some other man. The true nobility is in being superior to your previous self.

9167 *Hottentot*
Good is when I steal other people's wives and cattle; bad is when they steal mine.

9168
Hunger is the best sauce.

9169
An indecent mind is a perpetual feast.

9170 *Irish*
Better be quarrelling than lonesome.

9171 *Irish*
Every invalid is a physician.

9172 *Irish*
Money swore an oath that nobody who did not love it should ever have it.

9173 *Irish*
A dimple in the chin; a devil within.

9174 *Irish*
Trust me, but look to thyself.

9175 *Irish*
Seeing's believing - but feeling is God's own truth.

9176 *Italian*
He that jokes confesses.

9177 *Italian*
Below the navel there is neither religion nor truth.

9178 *Italian*
Since the house is on fire let us warm ourselves.

9179 *Italian*
Summer is the mother of the poor.

9180 *Italian*
If it is not true, it is a happy invention.

9181 *Japanese*
The go-between wears out a thousand sandals.

9182 *Japanese*
The crow that mimics a cormorant gets drowned.

9183 *Japanese*
The nail that sticks out is hammered down.

9184 *Japanese*
Fall seven times, stand up eight.

9185 *Jewish*
What you don't see with your eyes, don't invent with your tongue.

9186 *Jewish*
Worries go down better with soup than without.

9187 *Jewish*
Make sure to send a lazy man for the Angel of Death.

9188 *Jewish*
The innkeeper loves the drunkard, but not for a son-in-law.

9189 *Jewish*
The poor schlemiel is a man who falls on his back and breaks his nose.

9190 *Jewish*
Good men need no recommendation and bad men it wouldn't help.

9191 *Jewish*
The hardest work is to go idle.

9192 *Jewish*
Truth is the safest lie.

9193 *Jewish*
A half-truth is a whole lie.

9194 *Jewish*
You can't force anyone to love you or to lend you money.

9195 *Jewish*
With money in your pocket, you are wise, and you are handsome, and you sing well too.

9196 *Jewish*
If the rich could hire other people to die for them, the poor would make a wonderful living.

9197 *Jewish*
God could not be everywhere and therefore he made mothers.

9198 *Jewish*
Pride is the mask of one's own faults.

9199 *Jewish*
'For example' is not proof.

9200 *Jewish*
Do not make yourself so big. You are not so small.

9201 *Jewish*
Sleep faster, we need the pillows.

9202 *Jewish*
A wise man hears one word and understands two.

9203 *Korean*
Where there are no tigers, a wildcat is very self-important.

9204 *Lancashire*
Shake a bridle over a Yorkshireman's grave, and he'll rise and steal a horse.

9205 *Latin*
By learning you will teach; by teaching you will learn.

9206 *Latin*
Fortune is fickle and soon asks back what he has given.

9207 *Latin*
God will be present, whether asked or not.

9208 *Latin*
To spur a willing horse.

9209 *Latin*
Vox populi, vox dei.
The voice of the people is the voice of God.

9210 *Latin*
Sweet is war to those who have never experienced it.

9211 *Latin*
Deliberate often - decide once.

9212 *Latin*
Nature abhors a vacuum.

9213 *Latvian*
A smiling face is half the meal.

9214 *Malay*
Don't think there are no crocodiles because the water is calm.

9215 *Malay*
Though a tree grow ever so high, the falling leaves return to the root.

9216 *Maltese*
Time gives good advice.

9217 *Medieval*
Habit is second nature.

9218 *Medieval*
You cannot argue with someone who denies the first principles.

9219 *Medieval*
Ignorance excuses from sin.

9220 *Medieval*
It is better to be than not to be.

9221 *Medieval*
Nature gives to each what is appropriate.

9222 *Medieval*
Nature always desires what is better.

9223 *Medieval*
A good man and a good citizen are not the same thing.

9224 *Medieval*
All men naturally desire to know.

9225 *Medieval*
There should be no enmity among seekers after the truth.

9226 *Medieval*
Parents love their children more than children love their parents.

9227 *Medieval*
The touchstone of knowledge is the ability to teach.

9228 *Medieval*
Silence is a woman's finest ornament.

9229 *Medieval*
Time is the measure of movement.

9230 *Moroccan*
None but a mule deserves his family.

9231
Nature, time and patience are the three great physicians.

9232 *Nigerian*
When the mouse laughs at the cat there's a hole nearby.

9233 *Norwegian*
Many become brave when brought to bay.

9234 *(old bookseller)*
It fell dead from the Press.

9235 *Persian*
If fortune turns against you, even jelly breaks your tooth.

9236 *Persian*
When its time has come, the prey goes to the hunter.

9237 *Persian*
He who wants a rose must respect the thorn.

9238 *Persian*
The man who speaks the truth is always at ease.

9239 *Polish*
Even were a cook to cook a fly, he would keep the breast for himself.

9240 *Polish*
Fish, to taste right, must swim three times - in water, in butter and in wine.

9241 *Polish*
The greater love is a mother's; then comes a dog's; then a sweetheart's.

9242 *Portuguese*
Visits always give pleasure - if not the arrival, the departure.

9243 *Post-classical*
Post coitum omne animal triste.
After coition every animal is sad.

9244 *Rabbinical*
Don't limit a child to your own learning, for he was born in another time.

9245 *Rhodesian*
A bull does not enjoy fame in two herds.

9246 *Russian*
Don't buy the house; buy the neighbourhood.

9247 *Russian*
If you were born lucky, even your rooster will lay eggs.

9248 *Russian*
No matter how much you feed a wolf, he will always return to the forest.

9249 *Russian*
Believe not your own brother - believe, instead, your own blind eye.

9250 *Russian*
Gossip needs no carriage.

9251 *Russian*
If the thunder is not loud, the peasant forgets to cross himself.

9252 *Russian*
The rich would have to eat money, but luckily the poor provide food.

9253 *Scottish*
The Devil's boots don't creak.

9254 *Scottish*
What may be done at any time will be done at no time.

9255 *Siberian*
June's too soon, July's too late - for summer.

9256 *Sioux*
A people without history is like wind on the buffalo grass.

9257 *Spanish*
From a fallen tree, all making kindling.

9258 *Spanish*
You can't have more bugs than a blanketful.

9259 *Spanish*
Don't offer me advice, give me money.

9260 *Spanish*
Drink nothing without seeing it; sign nothing without reading it.

9261 *Spanish*
Whoever gossips to you will gossip of you.

9262 *Spanish*
No revenge is more honourable than the one not taken.

9263 *Spanish*
How beautiful it is to do nothing, and then rest afterward.

9264 *Spanish*
Laws, like the spider's web, catch the fly and let the hawk go free.

9265 *Spanish*
Tomorrow is often the busiest day of the year.

9266 *Spanish*
Woe to the house where the hen crows and the rooster keeps still.

9267 *Spanish*
An ounce of mother is worth a pound of clergy.

9268 *Spanish*
If I die, I forgive you: if I recover, we shall see.

9269 *Spanish*
When three people call you an ass, put on a bridle.

9270 *Spanish*
Speaking without thinking is shooting without taking aim.

9271 *Swedish*
The afternoon knows what the morning never suspected.

9272 *Swedish*
When a blind man carries the lame man, both go forward.

9273
The tongue ever turns to the aching tooth.

9274
Trouble will rain on those who are already wet.

9275 *Turkish*
If you speak the truth you have a foot in the stirrup.

9276
What was hard to endure is sweet to recall.

9277 *Yiddish*
The world is more exacting that God himself.

9278 *Yiddish*
If you can't bite, don't show your teeth.

9279 *Zen*
A beautiful woman who is pleasing to men is good only for frightening fish when she falls into the water.

PUBLILIUS Syrus 1st century BC
9280 *Sententiae*
A beautiful face is a mute recommendation.

9281 *Sententiae*
He gives the poor man twice as much good who gives quickly.

9282 *Sententiae*
The judge is condemned when the guilty party is acquitted.

9283 *Sententiae*
Necessity gives the law without itself acknowledging one.

PUCCINI Giacomo 1858-1924
9284
Art is a kind of illness.

PULTENEY William 1684-1764
9285 *'The Honest Jury'*
For Sir Ph-p well knows
That innuendos
Will serve him no longer in verse or in prose,
Since twelve honest men have decided the cause,
And were judges of fact, tho' not judges of laws.

PUNCH 1841-1992
9286
Advice to persons about to marry - 'Don't'.

9287
It ain't the 'unting as 'urts 'im, it's the 'ammer, 'ammer, 'ammer along the 'ard 'igh road.

9288
It appears the Americans have taken umbrage.
The deuce they have!
Whereabouts is that?

9289
Botticelli isn't a wine, you Juggins! Botticelli's a *cheese*!

9290
Go directly - see what she's doing, and tell her she mustn't.

9291
The Half-Way House to Rome, Oxford.

9292
I am not hungry; but thank goodness, I am greedy.

9293
I'm afraid you've got a bad egg, Mr Jones.
Oh no, my Lord, I assure you! Parts of it are excellent!

9294
Look here, Steward, if this is coffee, I want tea;
but if this is tea, then I wish for coffee.

9295
Nearly all our best men are dead! Carlyle,
Tennyson, Browning, George Eliot! - I'm not
feeling very well myself.

9296
I never read books - I *write* them.

9297
Never do today what you can put off till
tomorrow.

9298
Nothink for nothink 'ere, and precious little for
sixpence.

9299
There was an old owl lived in an oak
The more he heard, the less he spoke;
The less he spoke, the more he heard
O, if men were all like that wise bird!

9300
You pays your money and you takes your
choice.

9301
I used your soap two years ago; since then I
have used no other.

9302
Sometimes I sits and thinks, and then again I
just sits.

9303
What is Matter? - Never mind.
What is Mind? - No matter.

9304
What is better than presence of mind in a
railway accident? Absence of body.

9305
What sort of a doctor is he?
Oh well, I don't know very much about his
ability; but he's got a very good bedside manner!

9306
It's worse than wicked, my dear, it's vulgar.

PURSUIT Dan
9307
All children wear the sign: 'I want to be
important NOW'. Many of our juvenile
delinquency problems arise because nobody
reads the sign.

PUSHKIN Alexander 1799-1837
9308 *Eugene Onegin*
From early youth his dedication
Was to a single occupation ...
The science of the tender passion.

9309 *Eugene Onegin*
A man of sense, I am conceding,
Can pay attention to his nails;
Why should one quarrel with good breeding?
With some folk, custom's rule prevails.

9310 *Eugene Onegin*
A woman's love for us increases
The less we love her, sooth to say -
She stoops, she falls, her struggling ceases;
Caught fast, she cannot get away.

9311 *Eugene Onegin*
The sky breathed autumn, sombre, shrouded;
Shorter and shorter grew the days;
Sad murmurs filled the woodland ways
As the dark coverts were denuded;

9312 *Eugene Onegin*
Moscow: those syllables can start
A tumult in the Russian heart.

9313
Please, never despise the translator. He's the
mailman of human civilization.

9314 *'The Poet'*
No sooner does the divine word touch his keen
hearing than the poet's soul starts like an eagle
that has been roused.

9315 *'Remembrances'*
When trade and traffic and all the noise of town
Is dimmed, and on the streets and squares
The filmy curtain of the night sinks down
With sleep, the recompense of cares,
To me the darkness brings not sleep nor rest.

9316 *'It's Time'*
It's time, my dear, it's time! The heart demands
its quittance -
As day flies after day and each bears off its
pittance
Withdrawn from living's store and meanwhile
you and I
Draw up our plans to live ... And then, why
then, we'll die.

PUTNAM Israel 1718-1790
9317 *(at Bunker Hill)*
Men, you are all marksmen - don't one of you
fire until you see the white of their eyes.

PUTNAM VI
9318
The entire sum of existence is the magic of
being needed by just one person.

PUZO Mario 1920-
9319 *The Godfather*
I'll make him an offer he can't refuse.

9320 *The Godfather*
A lawyer with his briefcase can steal more than
a hundred men with guns.

PYM Barbara 1913-1980
9321 *Jane and Prudence*
It is better taste somehow that a man should be
unfaithful to his wife away from home.

9322 *Less than Angels*
She experienced all the cosiness and irritation
which can come from living with thoroughly
nice people with whom one has nothing in
common.

QUARLES Francis 1592-1644
9323 *Divine Fancies*
Our God and soldiers we alike adore
Ev'n at the brink of danger; not before:
After deliverance, both alike requited,
Our God's forgotten, and our soldiers slighted.

9324 *Emblems*
I wish thee as much pleasure in the reading, as I
had in the writing.

9325 *Emblems*
My soul, sit thou a patient looker-on;
Judge not the play before the play is done:
Her plot hath many changes; every day
Speaks a new scene; the last act crowns the play.

9326 *Emblems*
We spend our midday sweat, our midnight oil;
We tire the night in thought, the day in toil.

9327 *Emblems*
Be wisely worldly, be not worldly wise.

9328 *Emblems*
Man is Heaven's masterpiece.

9329 *Emblems*
Thou art my way; I wander, if thou fly;
Thou art my light; if hid, how blind am I!
Thou art my life; if thou withdraw, I die.

9330 *Hieroglyphics of the Life of Man*
He that begins to live, begins to die.

9331 *The Shepherd's Oracles*
We'll cry both arts and learning down,
And hey! then up go we!

QUENEAU Raymond 1903-1976
9332
Learning to learn is to know how to navigate in
a forest of facts, ideas and theories, a
proliferation of constantly changing items of
knowledge. Learning to learn is to know what
to ignore but at the same time not rejecting
innovation and research.

9333
Man's usual routine is to work and to dream and
work and dream.

QUENNELL Peter 1905-
9334 *The Sign of the Fish*
An elderly fallen angel travelling incognito.

QUILLER-COUCH Sir Arthur (Q) 1863-1944
9335
The best is the best, though a hundred judges
have declared it so.

9336 *'Lady Jane. Sapphics'*
Simple this tale! - but delicately perfumed
As the sweet roadside honeysuckle. That's why,
Difficult though its metre was to tackle,
I'm glad I wrote it.

QUINAULT Philippe 1635-1688
9337
It is not wise to be wiser than is necessary.

QUINCY Josiah 1772-1864
9338 *Abridgement of Debates of Congress*
As it will be the right of all, so it will be the duty
of some, definitely to prepare for a separation,
amicably if they can, violently if they must.

QUINE W.V.O. 1908-
9339 *Quiddities*
It is the tension between the scientist's laws and
his own attempted breaches of them that
powers the engines of science and makes it
forge ahead.

9340 *Theories and Things*
Students of the heavens are separable into
astronomers and astrologers as readily as are
the minor domestic ruminants into sheep and
goats, but the separation of philosophers into
sages and cranks seems to be more sensitive to
frames of reference.

QUINTILIAN AD 42-118
9341
A liar should have a good memory.

9342
The obscurity of a writer is generally in
proportion to his incapacity.

RABELAIS François c.1494-c.1553
9343 *Gargantua*
The appetite grows by eating.

9344 *Gargantua*
I drink for the thirst to come.

9345 *(attributed last words)*
I am going to seek a great perhaps ... Bring
down the curtain, the farce is played out.

9346
I never sleep in comfort save when I am hearing
a sermon or praying to God.

9347
There are more old drunkards than old
physicians.

RABIN Yitzhak 1922-1995
9348 *(on signing of Israel-Palestine Declaration, 1993)*

We say to you today in a loud and a clear voice;
enough of blood and tears. Enough.

RACINE Jean 1639-1699
9349 *Andromaque*
I have loved him too much not to feel any
hatred for him.

9350 *Andromaque*
I loved you when you were inconsistent. What
should I have done if you had been faithful.

9351 *Athalie*
It was during the horror of a deep night.

9352 *Athalie*
She wavers, she hesitates. In a word, she is a
woman.

9353 *Les Plaideurs*
Honour, without money, is just a disease.

9354 *Phèdre*
Crime, like virtue, has its degrees.

9355
A single word often betrays a great design.

RADDALL Thomas H.
9356
Don't brood on what's past, but never forget it
either.

RADFORD Arthur William 1896-1973
9357
A decision is the action an executive must take
when he has information so incomplete that
the answer does not suggest itself.

RADNER Gilda
9358
I can always be distracted by love, but
eventually I get horny for my creativity.

RAE Bob
9359
Forgiving is all; forgetting is another thing.

RAE John 1931-
9360 *The Custard Boys*
War is, after all, the universal perversion ... war
stories, the pornography of war.

RAINBOROWE Thomas d.1648
9361 *(army debates at Putney)*
The poorest he that is in England hath a life to
live as the greatest he.

RAINE Craig 1944-
9362
Reality is prodigal, but fiction must be laconic.

RAINE Kathleen 1908-
9363
The work of the artist is to heal the soul.

RAKOFF Aman Vivian
9364
Communication is and should be hell fire and
sparks as well as sweetness and light.

RALEGH Sir Walter 1552-1618
9365 *'Conceit begotten by the Eyes'*
Desire, nor reason hath, nor rest,
And blind doth seldom choose the best.

9366 *(on feeling the edge of the axe at his
execution)*
'Tis a sharp remedy, but a sure one for all ills.

9367
Hatreds are the cinders of affection.

9368 *The History of the World*
[History] hath triumphed over time, which
besides it, nothing but eternity hath triumphed
over.

9369 *The History of the World*
Whosoever, in writing a modern history, shall
follow truth too near the heels, it may happily
strike out his teeth.

9370 *The History of the World*
O eloquent, just, and mighty Death! ... thou hast
drawn together all the far-stretched greatness,
all the pride, cruelty, and ambition of man, and
covered it all over with these two narrow words,
Hic jacet [Here lies].

9371 *'As You came From the Holy Land'*
Love is a durable fire,
In the mind ever burning:
Never sick, never old, never dead,
From itself never turning.

9372 *'On the Life of Man'*
We die in earnest, that's no jest.

9373 *Line written on a window-pane*
Fain would I climb, yet fear I to fall.

9374 *'The Passionate Man's Pilgrimage'*
Give me my scallop-shell of quiet,
My staff of faith to walk upon,
My scrip of joy, immortal diet,
My bottle of salvation,
My gown of glory, hope's true gage,
And thus I'll take my pilgrimage.

9375 *(returning to prison from his trial)*
The world itself is but a large prison, out of
which some are daily led to execution.

9376
Tell zeal it wants devotion;
Tell love it is but lust;
Tell time it metes but motion;
Tell flesh it is but dust;
And wish them not reply,
For thou must give the lie.

9377
It is not truth, but opinion that can travel the world without a passport.

9378 *'Sir Walter Ralegh to the Queen'*
Our passions are most like to floods and streams;
The shallow murmur, but the deep are dumb.

RALEIGH Sir Walter Alexander 1861-1922
9379 *'Stans Puer ad Mensam'*
Eat slowly: only men in rags
And gluttons old in sin
Mistake themselves for carpet bags
And tumble victuals in.

9380 *'Wishes of an Elderly Man'*
I wish I loved the Human Race;
I wish I loved its silly face;
I wish I liked the way it walks;
I wish I liked the way it talks;
And when I'm introduced to one
I wish I thought *What Jolly Fun!*

RAND Ayn 1905-1982
9381
To demand 'sense' is the hallmark of nonsense. Nature does not make sense. Nothing makes sense.

9382
The skyline of New York is a monument of a splendour that no pyramids or palaces will ever equal or approach.

9383
Upper classes are a nation's past; the middle class is its future.

9384
What is a demanding pleasure? A pleasure that demands the use of one's mind; not in the sense of problem solving, but in the sense of exercising discrimination, judgement, awareness.

RANDALL Clarence
9385
Every man who has lived his life to the full should, by the time his senior years are reached, have established a reserve inventory of unfinished thinking.

RANDALL Stanley J.
9386
The closest to perfection a person ever comes is when he fills out a job application form.

RANKIN Ruth
9387
The government is concerned about the population explosion, and the population is concerned about the government explosion.

RANSOM John Crowe 1888-1974
9388 *'Here Lies a Lady'*
Here lies a lady of beauty and high degree.
Of chills and fever she died, of fever and chills,
The delight of her husband, her aunts, an infant of three,
And of medicos marvelling sweetly on her ills.

9389 *'Winter Remembered'*
Two evils, monstrous either one apart,
Possessed me, and were long and loath at going:
A cry of Absence, Absence, in the heart,
And in the wood the furious winter blowing.

RAPHAEL Frederic 1931-
9390 *Darling*
Your idea of fidelity is not having more than one man in bed at the same time.

9391 *The Glittering Prizes, 'A Sex Life'*
I come from suburbia ... and I don't ever want to go back. It's the one place in the world that's further away from anywhere else.

9392
Truth may be stranger than fiction, but fiction is truer.

RAPSON Ralph
9393
Develop an infallible technique and then place yourself at the mercy of inspiration.

RATH Dorothy H.
9394
I have come back again to where I belong; not an enchanted place, but the walls are strong.

RATNER Gerald 1949-
9395
We even sell a pair of earrings for under £1, which is cheaper than a prawn sandwich from Marks & Spencers. But I have to say the earrings probably won't last as long.

RATNER Herbert
9396
The doctor, if he forgets he is only the assistant to nature and zealously takes over the stage, may so add to what nature is already doing well that he actually throws the patient into shock by the vigour he adds to nature's forces.

RATTIGAN Terence 1911-1977
9397 *In Praise of Love*
Do you know what 'le vice Anglais' - the English vice - really is? ... It's our refusal to admit our emotions. We think they demean us, I suppose.

9398 *Separate Tables*
You can be in the Horseguards and still be common, dear.

RAVERAT Gwen 1885-1957
9399 *Period Piece*
Ladies were ladies in those days; they did not do things themselves.

RAY John 1628-1705
9400
The honester the man, the worse luck.

9401
Many without punishment, none without sin.

RAYBURN Sam 1882-1961
9402
Any jackass can kick down a barn, but it takes a good carpenter to build one.

RAYMOND F.J.
9403
Next to being shot at and missed, nothing is quite as satisfying as an income tax refund.

RAYNER Clare 1931-
9404
I always say I don't think everyone has the right to happiness or to be loved. Even the Americans have written into their constitution that you have the right to the 'pursuit of happiness'. You have the right to try but that's all.

READ Sir Herbert 1893-1968
9405 *International Surrealist Exhibition Catalogue*
Do not judge this movement kindly. It is not just another amusing stunt. It is defiant - the desperate act of men too profoundly convinced of the rottenness of our civilization to want to save a shred of its respectability.

9406 *The Meaning of Art*
Art is ... pattern informed by sensibility.

READE Charles 1814-1884
9407 *(attributed)*
Sow an act, and you reap a habit. Sow a habit and you reap a character. Sow a character, and you reap a destiny.

9408 *The Cloister and the Hearth*
Courage, mon ami, le diable est mort!
Take courage, my friend, the devil is dead!

9409
Not a day passes over the earth, but men and women of no note do great deeds, speak great words and suffer noble sorrows.

REAGAN Ronald 1911-
9410
Abortion is advocated only by persons who have themselves been born.

9411 *(after assassination attempt)*
Nothing in life is so exhilarating as to be shot at without result.

9412 *(of Col. Gadaffi of Libya)*
This mad dog of the Middle East.

9413 *(following hijack of a US plane)*
We are especially not going to tolerate these attacks from outlaw states run by the strangest collection of misfits, Looney Tunes, and squalid criminals since the advent of the Third Reich.

9414
Middle age is when you're faced with two temptations and you choose the one that will get you home by nine o'clock.

9415
Politics is supposed to be the second oldest profession. I have come to realize that it bears a very close resemblance to the first.

9416 *(revealing that he had Alzheimer's disease)*
I now begin the journey that will lead me into the sunset of my life.

9417
You can tell a lot about a fellow's character by his way of eating jellybeans.

REED Henry 1914-1986
9418 *Not a Drum was Heard:...*
In a civil war, a general must know ... exactly when to move over to the other side.

9419 *Emily Butler*
I think it may justly be said that English women in general are very common diatonic little numbers.

9420 *A Very Great Man Indeed*
Modest? My word no ... He was an all-the-lights-on man.

9421 *A Very Great Man Indeed*
I have known her pass the whole evening without mentioning a single book, or *in fact anything unpleasant*, at all.

9422 *Private Life of Hilda Tablet*
And the sooner the tea's out of the way, the sooner we can get out the gin, eh?

REED John 1887-1920
9423
Ten days that shook the world.

REED Rex
9424
In Hollywood, if you don't have happiness, you send out for it.

REEVE Christopher
9425 *in Superman*
"I never drink when I fly."

REGER Max 1873-1916
9426
I am sitting in the smallest room in my house. I have your review in front of me. Soon it will be

behind me.

REGNARD Jean François
9427
We love without reason, and without reason we hate.

REICHMANN Paul
9428
You build on cost and you borrow on value.

REID Kate
9429
Acting is not being emotional, but being able to express emotion.

REIK Theodor 1888-1969
9430
In our civilization, men are afraid that they will not be men enough and women are afraid that they might be considered only women.

9431
Even the wisest men make fools of themselves about women, and even the most foolish women are wise about men.

9432
Work and love - these are the basics. Without them there is neurosis.

REINHARDT Adina
9433
Art disease is caused by a hardening of the categories.

REINHARDT Gottfried
9434
Money is good for bribing yourself through the inconveniences of life.

REMARQUE Erich Maria 1898-1970
9435
Im Westen nichts Neues.
All Quiet on the Western Front.

RENAN Ernest 1823-1892
9436
Man makes holy what he believes, as he makes beautiful what he loves.

9437
A nation is a body of people who have done great things together.

RENARD Jules 1864-1910
9438
I am afraid I shall not find Him, but I shall still look for Him. If He exists, He may be appreciative of my efforts.

9439
A cold in the head causes less suffering than an idea.

9440
Failure is not our only punishment for laziness: there is also the success of others.

9441
Les bourgeois, ce sont les autres.
The bourgeois are other people.

9442
I have a remarkable memory; I forget everything. It is wonderfully convenient. It is as though the world were constantly renewing itself for me.

RENDALL Montague John 1862-1950
9443 *(motto of the BBC)*
Nation shall speak peace unto nation.

RENOIR Jean 1894-1979
9444 *My Life and My Films*
Is it possible to succeed without any act of betrayal?

RENOIR Pierre Auguste 1841-1919
9445 *(attributed)*
I paint with my prick. (possibly an inversion of 'It's with my brush, that I make love')

9446 *(of the men of the French Commune)*
They were madmen; but they had in them that little flame which is not to be snuffed out.

9447
A painter who has the feel of breasts and buttocks is saved.

REPPLIER Agnes 1858-1950
9448
It is not easy to find happiness in ourselves, and it is not possible to find it elsewhere.

9449
A man who listens because he has nothing to say can hardly be a source of inspiration. The only listening that counts is that of the talker who alternately absorbs and expresses ideas.

9450
It has been wisely said that we cannot really love anybody at whom we never laugh.

REYNOLD Gillian
9451
Art is life rearranged until it makes sense.

REYNOLDS Sir Joshua 1723-1792
9452 *Discourses on Art*
If you have great talents, industry will improve them: if you have but moderate abilities, industry will supply their deficiency.

9453 *Discourses on Art*
A mere copier of nature can never produce anything great.

9454 *Discourses on Art*
Could we teach taste or genius by rules, they
would be no longer taste and genius.

9455 *Discourses on Art*
The value and rank of every art is in proportion
to the mental labour employed in it, or the
mental pleasure produced by it.

REYNOLDS Malvina 1900-1978
9456 *'Little Boxes'*
Little boxes on the hillside ...
And they're all made out of ticky-tacky
And they all look just the same.

RHODES Cecil 1853-1902
9457 *(on the day of his death)*
So little done, so much to do.

9458
Ask any man what nationality he would prefer
to be, and ninety-nine out of a hundred will tell
you that they would prefer to be Englishmen.

RHYS Jean 1894-1979
9459 *The Left Bank 'Illusion'*
The perpetual hunger to be beautiful and that
thirst to be loved which is the real curse of Eve.

9460 *The Left Bank 'In the Rue de l'Arrivée'*
Only the hopeless are starkly sincere and ... only
the unhappy can either give or take sympathy.

9461 *(describing herself)*
A doormat in a world of boots.

9462 *Good Morning, Midnight*
Some must cry so that others may be able to
laugh the more heartily.

9463 *Voyage in the Dark*
The feeling of Sunday is the same everywhere,
heavy, melancholy, standing still. Like when
they say 'As it was in the beginning, is now, and
ever shall be, world without end'.

RICE Grantland 1880-1954
9464 *'Alumnus Football'*
For when the One Great Scorer comes to mark
against your name,
He writes - not that you won or lost - but how
you played the Game.

9465 *'The Two Sides of War'*
All wars are planned by old men
In council rooms apart.

RICE Tim 1944-
9466 *Jesus Christ Superstar 'Herod's Song'*
Prove to me that you're no fool,
Walk across my swimming pool.

RICHARDS Rebecca
9467
Oh, to be only half as wonderful as my child
thought I was when he was small, and only half

as stupid as my teenager now thinks I am.

RICHARDSON Justin
9468
If only I hadn't had sisters
How much more romantic I'd be
But my sisters were such little blisters
That all women are sisters to me.

RICHARDSON Samuel 1689-1761
9469 *Clarissa*
It is more difficult to catch a bird than a lady.

9470 *Clarissa*
Mine is the most plotting heart in the world.

9471 *History of Sir Charles Grandison*
A feeling heart is a blessing that no one, who
has it, would be without; and it is a moral
security of innocence.

RICHLER Mordecai 1931-
9472
Fundamentally, all writing is about the same
thing; it's about dying, about the brief flicker of
time we have here, and the frustrations that it
creates.

9473
Listen your Lordship, I'm a respecter of
institutions. Even in Paris, I remained a
Canadian. I puffed hashish, but I didn't inhale.

9474
There are ten commandments, right? Well, it's
like an exam. You get eight out of ten, you're
just about top of the class.

9475
Wherever I travel, I'm too late. The orgy has
moved elsewhere.

9476
I work every day - or at least I force myself into
office or room. I may get nothing done, but you
don't earn bonuses without putting in time.
Nothing may come for three months, but you
don't earn the fourth without it.

RICHTER Hans 1843-1916
9477 *(attributed)*
Up with your damned nonsense will I put twice,
or perhaps once, but sometimes always, by
God, never.

RICHTER Jean Paul 1763-1825
9478
There is a certain noble pride, through which
merits shine brighter than through modesty.

9479
Man's feelings are always purest and most
glowing in the hour of meeting and of farewell.

9480
No one is more profoundly sad than he who laughs too much.

9481
Providence has given to the French the empire of the land, to the English that of the sea, and to the Germans that of - the air!

9482
It is simpler and easier to flatter men than to praise them.

9483
Sleep, riches and health to be truly enjoyed must be interrupted.

9484
A variety of nothing is superior to a monotony of something.

9485
What makes old age so sad is not that our joys but our hopes cease.

RICKENBACKER Eddie 1890-1973
9486
Courage is doing what you're afraid to do. There can be no courage unless you're scared.

RIDDING George 1828-1904
9487
I feel a feeling which I feel you all feel.

RIDER Mike
9488
Designers and freelance artists and editors can set their hourly rates by dividing their annual income needs by 1000.

RIDLEY Nicholas 1929-1993
9489
This is all a German racket, designed to take over the whole of Europe.

RIIS Sharon
9490
Basically, I'm interested in friendship, sex and death.

RILKE Rainer Maria 1875-1926
9491
Do continue to believe that with your feeling and your work you are taking part in the greatest; the more strongly you cultivate in yourself this belief, the more will reality and the world go forth from it.

9492
Fame is the sum of the misunderstanding that gathers about a new name.

9493
The gnarled fidelity of an old habit.

9494 *Letter to Paula Modersohn-Becker*
I hold this to be the highest task for a bond between two people: that each protects the solitude of the other.

9495
Love consists in this, that two solitudes protect and touch and greet each other.

9496
Nothing in the world can one imagine beforehand, not the least thing. Everything is made up of so many unique particulars that cannot be foreseen.

9497
Oh longing for places that were not
Cherished enough in that fleeting hour
How I long to make good from afar
The forgotten gesture, the additional act.

RIMBAUD Arthur 1854-1891
9498 *'Ma Bohème'*
I was walking along, hands in holey pockets; my overcoat also was entering the realms of the ideal.

9499 *'Le Bâteau ivre'*
Sweeter than the flesh of tart apples to children, the green water penetrates my wooden hull.

9500 *'Le Bâteau ivre'*
I have bathed in the Poem of the Sea, steeped in stars, and milky, devouring the green azures.

9501 *'Le Bâteau ivre'*
I pine for Europe of the ancient parapets!

9502 *'Voyelles'*
A black, E white, I red, U green, O blue: vowels, some day I will tell of the births that may be yours.

RINEY Hal 1932-
9503 *(slogan for Ronald Reagan's election campaign)*
It's morning again in America.

RITZ César 1850-1918
9504
Le client n'a jamais tort.
The customer is never wrong.

RIVAROL Antoine de 1753-1801
9505
What is not clear is not French.

ROADE W. Winwood
9506
Men prefer to believe that they are degenerated angels, rather than elevated apes.

ROBBINS Leonard H.
9507
How a minority,
Reaching majority,

Seizing authority,
Hates a minority!

ROBBINS Lord 1898-1984
9508 *Essay on the Nature ... of Economic Science*
Economics is the science which studies human
behaviour as a relationship between ends and
scarce means which have alternative uses.

ROBESPIERRE Maximilien 1758-1794
9509 *Déclaration des droits de l'homme*
Any law which violates the inalienable rights of
man is essentially unjust and tyrannical; it is
not a law at all.

9510 *Lettres à ses commettans*
The general will rules in society as the private
will governs each separate individual.

9511
Wickedness is the root of despotism as virtue is
the essence of the Republic.

ROBIN Leo 1900-
9512 *Gentlemen Prefer Blondes 'Diamonds...'*
A kiss on the hand may be quite continental,
But diamonds are a girl's best friend ...

9513 *Gentlemen Prefer Blondes 'Diamonds...'*
Men grow cold as girls grow old
And we all lose our charms in the end.
But square cut or pear shape,
These rocks won't lose their shape,
Diamonds are a girl's best friend.

9514 *(with Ralph Rainger)*
Thanks for the memory.

ROBINSON Edwin Arlington 1869-1935
9515 *'John Brown'*
I shall have more to say when I am dead.

9516 *Literature in the Making*
The world is not a 'prison house', but a kind of
kindergarten, where millions of bewildered
infants are trying to spell God with the wrong
blocks.

ROBINSON James Harvey 1863-1935
9517
We find it hard to believe that other people's
thoughts are as silly as our own, but they
probably are.

ROCHE Arthur Somers
9518
Anxiety is a thin stream of fear trickling through
the mind. If encouraged, it cuts a channel into
which all other thoughts are drained.

ROCHE Sir Boyle 1743-1807
9519 *(attributed)*
Mr Speaker, I smell a rat; I see him forming in
the air and darkening the sky; but I'll nip him in
the bud.

ROCHE John P.
9520
In politics, a straight line is the shortest distance
to disaster.

ROCHESTER John Wilmot, Earl of 1647-1680
9521 *'Against Constancy'*
Tell me no more of constancy,
that frivolous pretence,
Of cold age, narrow jealousy,
disease and want of sense.

9522 *'The King's Epitaph' (Charles II)*
Here lies a great and mighty king
Whose promise none relies on;
He never said a foolish thing,
Nor ever did a wise one.

9523 *'A Letter from Artemisia in the Town to Chloe...'*
Love ...
That cordial drop heaven in our cup has thrown
To make the nauseous draught of life go down.

9524 *'Upon Nothing'*
Nothing, thou elder brother even to shade
Thou hadst a being ere the world was made,
And, well fixed, art alone of ending not afraid.

9525 *'A Ramble in St James' Park'*
... Natural freedoms are but just:
There's something generous in mere lust.

9526 *'A Satire against Mankind'*
Reason, an *ignis fatuus* of the mind,
Which leaves the light of nature, sense, behind.

9527 *'A Satire against Mankind'*
For all men would be cowards if they durst.

9528 *'Song'*
Love a woman? You're an ass!
'Tis a most insipid passion
To choose out for your happiness
The silliest part of God's creation.

ROCKEFELLER 2nd John D. 1874-1960
9529
I was born into it and there was nothing I could
do about it. It was there, like air or food, or any
other element. The only question with wealth is
what you do with it.

ROCKEFELLER 3rd John D. 1906-1978
9530
Everyone likes to think that he has done
reasonably well in life, so that it comes as a
shock to find our children believing differently.
The temptation is to tune them out; it takes
much more courage to listen.

ROCKEFELLER John D. 1839-1937
9531
The ability to deal with people is as purchasable
a commodity as sugar or coffee. And I pay more

for that ability than for any other under the sun.

9532
Good management consists of showing average people how to do the work of superior people.

ROCKEFELLER Nelson 1908-1979
9533
It is essential that we enable young people to see themselves as participants in one of the most exciting eras in history, and to have a sense of purpose in relation to it.

ROCKNE Knute 1888-1931
9534
Show me a good and gracious loser, and I'll show you a failure.

RODDENBERRY Gene 1921-1991
9535 *Star Trek*
These are the voyages of the starship *Enterprise*. Its five-year mission ... to boldly go where no man has gone before.

9536 *Star Trek*
Beam us up, Mr Scott.
(usually quoted as "Beam me up, Scotty")

RODGERS Richard 1902-1979
9537 *No Strings 'The Sweetest Sounds'*
The sweetest sounds I'll ever hear
Are still inside my head.
The kindest words I'll ever know
Are waiting to be said.

RODIN Auguste 1840-1917
9538
I invent nothing. I rediscover.

9539
One must work, nothing but work, and one must have patience.

ROETHKE Theodore 1908-1963
9540 *'The Adamant'*
Truth never is undone;
Its shafts remain.

9541
Deep in their roots,
All flowers keep the light.

9542 *'Dolour'*
I have known the inexorable sadness of pencils,
Neat in their boxes, dolour of pad and paper-weight,
All the misery of manilla folders and mucilage,
Desolation in immaculate public places.

9543 *'The Exorcism'*
In a dark wood I saw -
I saw my several selves
Come running from the leaves,
Lewd, tiny, careless lives
That scuttled under stones,
Or broke, but would not go.

9544
I learn by going where I have to go.

9545 *'Open House'*
My secrets cry aloud.
I have no need for tongue.
My heart keeps open house,
My doors are widely flung.
An epic of the eyes
My love with no disguise.

ROGERS Samuel 1763-1855
9546 *(attributed)*
A man who attempts to read all the new productions must do as the fleas do - skip.

9547 *'To -, 1814'*
There's such a charm in melancholy,
I would not, if I could, be gay.

9548 *'Human Life'*
Think nothing done while aught remains to do.

9549 *'Human Life'*
Then, never less alone than when alone,
Those whom he loved so long and sees no more,
Loved and still loves - not dead - but gone before,
He gathers round him.

9550 *Jacqueline*
To know her was to love her.

9551 *Table Talk*
Sheridan was listened to with such attention that you might have heard a pin drop.

9552 *Table Talk*
It doesn't much signify whom one marries, for one is sure to find next morning that it was someone else.

ROGERS Thorold 1823-1890
9553
See, ladling butter from alternate tubs
Stubbs butters Freeman, Freeman butters Stubbs.

ROGERS Will 1879-1935
9554
We are all here for a spell, get all the good laughs you can.

9555
Well, all I know is what I read in the papers.

9556 *Autobiography*
There is only one thing that can kill the movies, and that is education.

9557
You can't say civilization don't advance, however, for in every war they kill you in a new way.

9558
A difference of opinion is what makes horse racing and missionaries.

9559
Don't gamble; take all your savings and buy some good stock and hold it till it goes up, then sell it. If it don't go up, don't buy it.

9560
Everybody is ignorant, only on different subjects.

9561
Half our life is spent trying to find something to do with the time we have rushed through life trying to save.

9562
This thing of being a hero, about the main thing to it is to know when to die.

9563
Being a hero is about the shortest-lived profession on earth.

9564
A holding company is the people you give your money to while you're being searched.

9565 *The Illiterate Digest*
The more you read and observe about this Politics thing, you got to admit that each party is worse than the other.

9566 *The Illiterate Digest*
Everthing is funny as long as it is happening to Somebody Else.

9567
I'm not a member of any organized party, I'm a Democrat.

9568
The income tax has made more liars out of the American people than golf has. Even when you make a tax form out on the level, you don't know when it's through, if you are a crook or a martyr.

9569
If you ever injected truth into politics you would have no politics.

9570
Invest in inflation. It's the only thing going up.

9571
More men have been elected between Sundown and Sun-up than ever were elected between Sun-up and Sundown.

9572
Politics has got so expensive that it takes lots of money to even get beat with.

9573
One revolution is like one cocktail, it just gets you organized for the next.

9574
The schools ain't what they used to be and never was.

9575
Be thankful we're not getting all the government we're paying for.

9576 *Weekly Articles*
Communism is like prohibition, it's a good idea but it won't work.

9577
It isn't what we don't know that gives us trouble, it's what we know that ain't so.

9578
When you put down the good things you ought to have done, and leave out the bad things you did do - well, that's memoirs.

ROGOW Arnold A.
9579
Ultimately politics in a democracy reflects values much more than it shapes them.

ROHE Mies Van der 1886-1969
9580
Architecture begins when you place two bricks *carefully* together.

ROLAND Madame 1754-1793
9581
O liberty! O liberty! what crimes are committed in thy name!

ROLFE Frederick William ('Baron Corvo') 1860-1913
9582 *Hadrian VII*
That cold, white, candent voice which was more caustic than silver nitrate and more thrilling than a scream.

9583 *Hadrian VII*
Pray for the repose of His soul. He was so tired.

ROLLIN Charles 1661-1741
9584
The highest and most lofty trees have the most reason to dread the thunder.

RONSARD Pierre de 1524-1585
9585 *Odes, à Cassandre (translated by Andrew Lang)*
See, Mignonne, hath not the rose
That this morning did unclose
Her purple mantle to the light,
Lost, before the day be dead,
The glory of her raiment red,
Her colour, bright as yours is bright?

ROONEY Mickey

9586
You always pass failure on the way to success.

ROOSEVELT Eleanor 1884-1962

9587
Character building begins in our infancy, and continues until death.

9588
No one can make you feel inferior without your consent.

9589
Life has got to be lived - that's all there is to it. At seventy, I would say the advantage is that you take life more calmly. You know that 'this, too, shall pass!'

9590
I think somehow we learn who we really are and then live with that decision.

9591
What one has to do usually can be done.

9592
When you cease to make a contribution you begin to die.

ROOSEVELT Franklin D. 1882-1945

9593
I have said this before, but I shall say it again and again and again: Your boys are not going to be sent into any foreign wars.

9594 *(accepting Presidential nomination)*
I pledge you, I pledge myself, to a new deal for the American people. Let us all here assembled constitute ourselves prophets of a new order of competence and courage. This is a call to arms.

9595
Books can not be killed by fire. People die, but books never die. No man and no force can abolish memory.

9596
It is common sense to take a method and try it. If it fails, admit it frankly and try another, but above all, try something.

9597
I have no expectation of making a hit every time I come to bat.

9598 *'Fireside Chat'*
We have the men - the skill - the wealth - and above all, the will ... We must be the great arsenal of democracy.

9599 *(inaugural address)*
The only thing we have to fear is fear itself.

9600 *(inaugural address)*
In the field of world policy I would dedicate this Nation to the policy of the good neighbour.

9601
We look forward to a world founded upon four essential human freedoms. The first is freedom of speech and expression - everywhere in the world. The second is freedom of every person to worship God in his own way - everywhere in the world. The third is freedom from want ... everywhere in the world. The fourth is freedom from fear ... anywhere in the world.

9602 *(second inaugural address)*
I see one-third of a nation ill-housed, ill-clad, ill-nourished.

9603
If I were starting life over again, I am inclined to think that I would go into the advertising business in preference to almost any other. The general raising of standards of modern civilization among all groups of people during the past half-century would have been impossible without that spreading of the knowledge of higher standards by means of advertising.

9604
I think we consider too much the good luck of the early bird, and not enough the bad luck of the early worm.

9605
These unhappy times call for the building of plans that ... build from the bottom up and not from the top down, that put their faith once more in the forgotten man at the bottom of the economic pyramid.

ROOSEVELT Theodore 1858-1919

9606 *Autobiography*
Foolish fanatics ... the men who form the lunatic fringe in all reform movements.

9607
Do what you can, with what you have, where you are.

9608
No man is above the law and no man is below it: nor do we ask any man's permission when we ask him to obey it.

9609
A man who is good enough to shed his blood for the country is good enough to be given a square deal afterwards. More than that no man is entitled to, and less than that no man shall have.

9610
The men with the muck-rakes are often indispensable to the well-being of society; but only if they know when to stop raking the muck.

9611
Nine-tenths of wisdom consists in being wise in time.

9612
I am only an average man, but, by George, I work harder at it than the average man.

9613
There is no room in this country for hyphenated Americanism.

9614
The most successful politician is he who says what everybody is thinking most often and in the loudest voice.

9615
I wish to preach, not the doctrine of ignoble ease, but the doctrine of the strenuous life.

ROREM Ned 1923-
9616 *The Paris Diary of Ned Rorem*
Quarrels in France strengthen a love affair. In America they end it.

ROSCOMMON Earl of 1637-1685
9617 *Essay on Translated Verse*
Choose an author as you choose a friend.

9618 *Essay on Translated Verse*
Immodest words admit of no defence,
For want of decency is want of sense.

9619 *Essay on Translated Verse*
The multitude is always in the wrong.

ROSE Billy 1899-1966
9620
Never invest your money in anything that eats or needs repairing.

ROSEBERY Lord 1847-1929
9621
It is beginning to be hinted that we are a nation of amateurs.

9622
The Empire is a Commonwealth of Nations.

9623 *(on remaining outside Liberal Party leadership)*
I must plough my furrow alone.

ROSENBERG Ethel and ROSENBERG Julius
1916-1953 and 1918-1953
9624 *(letter from Julius before their execution)*
We are the first victims of American Fascism.

ROSENBERG John D.
9625
New York is notoriously inhospitable to the past, disowning it whenever it can.

ROSENBERG Leo
9626
First you forget names, then you forget faces,

then you forget to pull your zipper up, then you forget to pull your zipper down.

ROSS Alan S.C. 1907-1980
9627
U and Non-U, An Essay in Sociological Linguistics.

ROSSELLINI Roberto 1906-1977
9628
Noble acts and momentous events happen in the same way and produce the same impression as the ordinary facts.

ROSSETTI Christina 1830-1894
9629 *'A Birthday'*
Because the birthday of my life
Is come, my love is come to me.

9630 *'Mid-Winter'*
In the bleak mid-winter
Frosty wind made moan,
Earth stood hard as iron,
Water like a stone.

9631 *'Oh roses for the flush of youth'*
Oh roses for the flush of youth,
And laurel for the perfect prime;
But pluck an ivy branch for me
Grown old before my time.

9632 *'Remember'*
Remember me when I am gone away,
Gone far away into the silent land.
Better by far you should forget and smile
Than you should remember and be sad.

9633 *'Rest'*
O Earth, lie heavily upon her eyes;
Seal her sweet eyes weary of watching, Earth.

9634 *'Rest'*
Silence more musical than any song.

9635 *'When I am dead'*
When I am dead, my dearest,
Sing no sad songs for me.

ROSSETTI Dante Gabriel 1828-1882
9636 *'The Blessed Damozel'*
The blessed damozel leaned out
From the gold bar of Heaven;
Her eyes were deeper than the depth
Of waters stilled at even;
She had three lilies in her hand,
And the stars in her hair were seven.

9637 *'The Blessed Damozel'*
Her hair that lay along her back
Was yellow like ripe corn.

9638 *'The Blessed Damozel'*
As low as where this earth
Spins like a fretful midge.

9639 *'The Blessed Damozel'*
And the souls mounting up to God
Went by her like thin flames.

9640
Conception, my boy, fundamental brainwork, is
what makes the difference in all art.

9641 *The House of Life*
A sonnet is a moment's monument -
Memorial from the Soul's eternity
To one dead deathless hour.

9642 *The House of Life 'Body's Beauty'*
And round his heart one strangling golden hair.

9643 *The House of Life 'Lost Days'*
I do not see them here; but after death
God knows I know the faces I shall see,
Each one a murdered self, with low last breath.

9644 *The House of Life 'Silent Noon'*
'Tis visible silence, still as the hour-glass.

9645 *The House of Life 'Silent Noon'*
Oh! clasp we to our hearts, for deathless dower,
This close-companioned inarticulate hour
When twofold silence was the song of love.

9646 *The House of Life 'A Superscription'*
Look in my face; my name is Might-have-been;
I am also called No-more, Too-late, Farewell.

9647 *The House of Life 'A Superscription'*
Sleepless with cold commemorative eyes.

9648 *'Soothsay'*
Unto the man of yearning thought
And aspiration, to do nought
Is in itself almost an act.

9649 *'Sudden Light'*
I have been here before,
But when or how I cannot tell:
I know the grass beyond the door,
The sweet keen smell,
The sighing sound, the lights around the shore.

9650
The worst moment for the atheist is when he is
really thankful, and has nobody to thank.

ROSSINI Gioacchino 1792-1868
9651
Give me a laundry-list and I'll set it to music.

9652
How wonderful opera would be if there were no
singers.

9653
One cannot judge 'Lohengrin' from a first
hearing, and I certainly do not intend to hear it
a second time.

9654
Wagner has lovely moments but awful quarters
of an hour.

ROSSITER Clinton
9655
The final greatness of the presidency lies in the
truth that it is not just an office of incredible
power but a breeding ground of indestructible
myth.

ROSTAND Edmond 1868-1918
9656 *Cyrano de Bergerac*
A large nose is in fact the sign of an affable man,
good, courteous, witty, liberal, courageous, such
as I am.

9657 *La Princesse Lointaine*
The dream, alone, is of interest. What is life,
without a dream?

ROSTAND Jean 1894-1977
9658 *Le Mariage*
A married couple are well suited when both
partners usually feel the need for a quarrel at
the same time.

9659 *Pensées d'un biologiste*
Kill a man, and you are an assassin. Kill
millions of men, and you are a conqueror. Kill
everyone, and you are a god.

9660
My pessimism goes to the point of suspecting
the sincerity of the pessimists.

ROSTEN Leo 1908-
9661 *(of W.C. Fields)*
Any man who hates dogs and babies can't be all
bad.

ROTH Philip 1933-
9662 *Portnoy's Complaint*
A Jewish man with parents alive is a fifteen-
year-old boy, and will remain a fifteen-year-old
boy until *they die!*

9663 *Portnoy's Complaint*
Doctor, my doctor, what do you say, LET'S PUT
THE ID BACK IN YID!

ROTHSCHILD Baron 1840-1915
9664
It isn't enough for you to love money - it's also
necessary that money should love you.

ROTSTEIN Abraham
9665
Every dogma has its day.

9666
Power is the recognition of necessity.

ROTTEN Johnny
9667
Love is two minutes and fifty seconds of

squelching.

ROUAULT Georges 1871-1958
9668
For me, painting is a way to forget life. It is a cry in the night, a strangled laugh.

ROUGET DE LISLE Claude-Joseph 1760-1836
9669 *'La Marseillaise'*
Come, children of our country, the day of glory has arrived ... To arms, citizens! Form your battalions!

ROUPELL Charles
9670 *(attributed)*
To play billiards well is a sign of an ill-spent youth.

ROUSSEAU Jean-Jacques 1712-1778
9671
Everything is good when it leaves the Creator's hands; everything degenerates in the hands of man.

9672
Happiness: a good bank account, a good cook and a good digestion.

9673
I hate books; they teach us only to talk about what we do not know.

9674
Little privations are easily endured when the heart is better treated than the body.

9675
Man was born free, and everywhere he is in shackles.

9676
Whoever blushes is already guilty; true innocence is ashamed of nothing.

ROUTH Martin Joseph 1755-1854
9677 *(attributed)*
You will find it a very good practice always to verify your references, sir!

ROUX Joseph
9678
Science is for those who learn; poetry for those who know.

ROWAN Carl T. 1925-
9679
A minority group has 'arrived' only when it has the right to produce some fools and scoundrels without the entire group paying for it.

ROWE Nicholas 1674-1718
9680 *The Fair Penitent*
Is this that haughty, gallant, gay Lothario?

9681 *The Fair Penitent*
Like Helen, in the night when Troy was sacked.

9682 *The Fair Penitent*
Death is the privilege of human nature,
And life without it were not worth our taking.

9683
The joys of meeting pay the pangs of absence;
Else who could bear it?

ROWLAND Helen 1875-1950
9684
Failing to be there when a man wants her is a woman's greatest sin, except to be there when he doesn't want her.

9685 *A Guide to Men*
A husband is what is left of a lover, after the nerve has been extracted.

9686 *A Guide to Men*
Somehow a bachelor never quite gets over the idea that he is a thing of beauty and a boy forever.

9687 *A Guide to Men*
The follies which a man regrets most in his life, are those which he didn't commit when he had the opportunity.

9688
In olden times, sacrifices were made at the altar, a practice which is still very much practised.

9689 *Reflections of a Bachelor Girl*
When you see what some girls marry, you realize how much they must hate to work for a living.

9690 *The Rubaiyat of a Bachelor*
Never trust a husband too far, nor a bachelor too near.

9691
When a girl marries, she exchanges the attentions of many men for the inattention of one.

9692 *The Wit of Women*
Before marriage, a man will lie awake thinking about something you said; after marriage, he'll fall asleep before you finish saying it.

ROWLAND Richard c.1881-1947
9693 *(of the take-over of United Artists)*
The lunatics have taken charge of the asylum.

ROXBOROUGH Henry
9694
Sport is one area where no participant is worried about another's race, religion or wealth: and where the only concern is 'Have you come to play?'

ROY Gabrielle 1909-
9695
The life of a writer is tragic: the more we advance, the farther there is to go and the more

there is to say, the less time there is to say it.

ROYCE Josiah
9696
Thinking is like loving and dying - each of us
must do it for himself.

9697
Unless you can find some sort of loyalty, you
cannot find unity and peace in your active
living.

ROYDEN Maude 1876-1956
9698
The Church should go forward along the path of
progress and be no longer satisfied only to
represent the Conservative Party at prayer.

ROYDE-SMITH Naomi c.1875-1964
9699 *Weekend Book*
I know two things about the horse
And one of them is rather coarse.

RUBENS Paul Alfred 1875-1917
9700 *'Your King and Country Want You'*
Oh! we don't want to lose you but we think you
ought to go
For your King and your Country both need you
so.

RUBENS Peter Paul 1577-1640
9701
Sir, when their backsides look good enough to
slap, there's nothing more to do.

RUBIN Theodore Isaac
9702
Compassion for myself is the most powerful
healer of them all.

RUBINSTEIN Artur 1888-1982
9703
Of course there is no formula for success
except, perhaps, an unconditional acceptance
of life and what it brings.

9704
I am tired before the concert, not afterward.

9705
When I was young, I used to have successes
with women because I was young. Now I have
successes with women because I am old.
Middle age was the hardest part.

RUBINSTEIN Helena 1871-1965
9706
There are no ugly women, only lazy ones.

RUNES Dagobert
9707
Happy the man who gains sagacity in youth, but
thrice happy he who retains the fervour of
youth in age.

9708
If tomorrow were never to come, it would not
be worth living today.

9709
Work is man's most natural form of relaxation.

RUNYON Damon 1884-1946
9710
Guys and dolls.

9711 *'A Very Honourable Guy'*
Always try to rub up against money, for if you
rub up against money long enough, some of it
may rub off on you.

9712 *'The Idyll of Miss Sarah Brown'*
At such an hour the sinners are still in bed
resting up from their sinning of the night
before, so they will be in good shape for more
sinning a little later on.

9713 *'A Nice Price'*
I long ago came to the conclusion that all life is
6 to 5 against.

9714
Much as he is opposed to lawbreaking, he is not
bigoted about it.

9715
The race is not always to the swift nor the battle
to the strong - but that's the way to bet.

RUSHTON Willie 1937-1996
9716 *(to a guest who had spilt red wine on his
white dinner jacket)*
I always dress to match the colour of the food.

RUSK Dean 1909-1994
9717
One of the best ways to persuade others is with
your ears.

9718 *(of the Cuban missile crisis)*
We're eyeball to eyeball, and I think the other
fellow just blinked.

9719
One third of the people of the world are asleep
at any given moment. The other two thirds are
awake and probably stirring up trouble
somewhere.

RUSKIN John 1819-1900
9720 *(attributed)*
A single villa can mar a landscape, and
dethrone a dynasty of hills.

9721
The beauty of the animal form is in exact
proportion to the amount of moral and
intellectual virtue expressed by it.

9722
If a book is worth reading, it is worth buying.

9723
To make your children capable of honesty is the beginning of education.

9724
No one can do me any good by loving me; I have more love than I need, or could do any good with; but people do me good by making me love them - which isn't easy.

9725
There is hardly anything in the world that some man can't make a little worse and sell a little cheaper, and the people who consider price only are this man's lawful prey.

9726 *Unto this Last*
Soldiers of the ploughshare as well as soldiers of the sword.

9727 *Unto this Last*
Government and co-operation are in all things the laws of life; anarchy and competition the laws of death.

9728 *Unto this Last*
There is no wealth but life.

9729 *Lectures on Architecture and Painting*
No person who is not a great sculptor or painter can be an architect. If he is not a sculptor or painter, he can only be a *builder*

9730 *Modern Painters*
All violent feelings ... produce in us a falseness in all our impressions of external things, which I would generally characterize as the 'Pathetic Fallacy'.

9731 *Modern Painters*
Mountains are the beginning and the end of all natural scenery.

9732
The purest and most thoughtful minds are those which love colour the most.

9733 *Sesame and Lilies*
All books are divisible into two classes, the books of the hour, and the books of all time.

9734 *Sesame and Lilies*
Be sure that you go to the author to get at his meaning, not to find yours.

9735 *Sesame and Lilies*
Which of us ... is to do the hard and dirty work for the rest - and for what pay? Who is to do the pleasant and clean work, and for what pay?

9736 *Sesame and Lilies*
We call ourselves a rich nation, and we are filthy and foolish enough to thumb each other's books out of circulating libraries!

9737 *Seven Lamps of Architecture*
When we build, let us think that we build for ever.

9738 *Stones of Venice*
Remember that the most beautiful things in the world are the most useless; peacocks and lilies for instance.

9739 *Time and Tide*
Your honesty is *not* to be based either on religion or policy. Both your religion and policy must be based on *it.*

9740 *The Two Paths*
Fine art is that in which the hand, the head, and the heart of man go together.

9741 *The Two Paths*
Not only is there but one way of *doing* things rightly, but there is only one way of *seeing* them, and that is, seeing the whole of them.

9742
When love and skill work together expect a masterpiece.

9743 *On Whistler's Nocturne in Black and Gold*
I have seen, and heard, much of Cockney impudence before now; but never expected to hear a coxcomb ask two hundred guineas for flinging a pot of paint in the public's face.

RUSSELL Bertrand 1872-1970
9744
To be without some of the things you want is an indispensable part of happiness.

9745
In all affairs, love, religion, politics or business, it's a healthy idea, now and then, to hang a question mark on things you have long taken for granted.

9746
If we were all given by magic the power to read each other's thoughts, I suppose the first effect would be to dissolve all friendships.

9747 *(of Sir Anthony Eden)*
Not a gentleman; dresses too well.

9748
Anything you're good at contributes to happiness.

9749 *Autobiography*
Three passions, simple but overwhelmingly strong, have governed my life: the longing for love, the search for knowledge and unbearable pity for the suffering of mankind.

9750
The average man's opinions are much less foolish than they would be if he thought for himself.

9751
One must care about a world one will not see.

9752
'Change' is scientific, 'progress' is ethical; change is indubitable, whereas progress is a matter of controversy.

9753 *The Conquest of Happiness*
To be able to use leisure intelligently will be the last product of an intelligent civilization.

9754 *The Conquest of Happiness*
Men who are unhappy, like men who sleep badly, are always proud of the fact.

9755 *The Conquest of Happiness*
Boredom is ... a vital problem for the moralist, since half the sins of mankind are caused by the fear of it.

9756 *The Conquest of Happiness*
One of the symptoms of approaching nervous breakdown is the belief that one's work is terribly important, and that to take a holiday would bring all kinds of disaster.

9757 *The Conquest of Happiness*
One should as a rule respect public opinion in so far as is necessary to avoid starvation and to keep out of prison, but anything that goes beyond this is voluntary submission to an unnecessary tyranny.

9758 *The Conquest of Happiness*
A sense of duty is useful in work, but offensive in personal relations. People wish to be liked, not to be endured with patient resignation.

9759 *The Conquest of Happiness*
Of all forms of caution, caution in love is perhaps the most fatal to true happiness.

9760
Cynicism such as one finds very frequently among the most highly educated young men and women of the West, results from the combination of comfort and powerlessness.

9761
I do not believe that any peacock envies another peacock his tail, because every peacock is persuaded that his own tail is the finest in the world. The consequence of this is that peacocks are peaceable birds.

9762
Drunkenness is temporary suicide: the happiness that it brings is merely negative, a momentary cessation of unhappiness.

9763
The fundamental defect of fathers is that they want their children to be a credit to them.

9764
The good life, as I conceive it, is a happy life. I do not mean that if you are good you will be happy - I mean that if you are happy you will be good.

9765
Every man is encompassed by a cloud of comforting convictions, which move with him like flies on a summer day.

9766 *Marriage and Morals*
To fear love is to fear life, and those who fear life are already three parts dead.

9767
Men fear thought more than they fear anything else on earth - more than ruin, more even than death. Thought is subversive and revolutionary, destructive and terrible; thought is merciless to priviledge, established institutions, and comfortable habits; thought is anarchic and lawless, indifferent to authority, careless of the well-tried wisdom of ages.

9768 *Mysticism and Logic*
The law of causality, I believe, ... is a relic of a bygone age, surviving, like the monarchy, only because it is erroneously supposed to do no harm.

9769 *Mysticism and Logic*
Brief and Powerless is Man's life; on him and all his race the slow, sure doom falls pitiless and dark.

9770
There was never any reason to believe in any innate superiority of the male, except his superior muscle.

9771
It is only in marriage with the world that our ideals can bear fruit; divorced from it they remain barren.

9772
Many people would die sooner than think; in fact, they do.

9773
There is much pleasure to be gained from useless knowledge.

9774
It is preoccupation with possession, more than anything else, that prevents men from living freely and nobly.

9775
The more we realize our minuteness and our impotence in the face of cosmic forces, the more astonishing becomes what human beings have achieved.

9776
The reformative effect of punishment is a belief that dies hard, chiefly, I think, because it is so satisfying to our sadistic impulses.

9777
The most savage controversies are those about matters as to which there is no good evidence either way.

9778 *Sceptical Essays*
We have two kinds of morality side by side: one which we preach but do not practice, and the other which we practice but seldom preach.

9779 *Sceptical Essays*
It is obvious that 'obscenity' is not a term capable of exact legal definition; in the practice of the Courts, it means 'anything that shocks the magistrate'.

9780
Science is what you know, philosophy is what you don't know.

9781 *The Scientific Outlook*
When I come to die I shall not feel I have lived in vain. I have seen the earth run red at evening, the dew sparkling in the morning, and the snow shining under a frosty sun.

9782
Simpson succeeded in proving that there was no harm in giving anaesthetics to men, because God put Adam into a deep sleep when He extracted his rib. But male ecclesiastics remained unconvinced as regards the sufferings of women, at any rate in childbirth.

9783
To teach how to live with uncertainty, and yet without being paralyzed by hesitation, is perhaps the chief thing that philosophy in our age can still do for those who study it.

9784
Thought looks into the pit of hell and is not afraid. It sees man, a feeble speck, surrounded by unfathomable depths of silence; yet bears itself proudly, as unmoved as if it were the lord of the universe. Thought is great and swift and free, the light of the world, and the chief glory of man.

9785
What men want is not knowledge, but certainty.

RUSSELL Dora 1894-1986
9786 *Hypatia*
We want better reasons for having children than not knowing how to prevent them.

RUSSELL Foster Meharny
9787
Every story has three sides to it - yours, mine

and the facts.

RUSSELL George W. 1867-1935
9788
Our hearts were drunk with a beauty
Our eyes could never see.

RUSSELL Lord John 1792-1878
9789 *(attributed)*
A proverb is one man's wit and all men's wisdom.

9790
Among the defects of the Bill, which were numerous, one provision was conspicuous by its presence and another by its absence.

9791 *(on defeat of the second Reform Bill)*
It is impossible that the whisper of a faction should prevail against the voice of a nation.

9792
If peace cannot be maintained with honour, it is no longer peace.

RUSSELL Sir William Howard 1820-1907
9793 *(of the Russians charging the British at Crimea)*
They dashed on towards that thin red line tipped with steel.

RUTHERFORD Lord 1871-1937
9794 *(attributed)*
All science is either physics or stamp collecting.

9795 *(attributed)*
We haven't got the money, so we've got to think!

9796 *(in 1937)*
The energy produced by the breaking down of the atom is a very poor kind of thing. Anyone who expects a source of power from the transformation of these atoms is talking moonshine.

RUTHERFORD Mark 1831-1913
9797
Most of us have no real loves and no real hatreds. Blessed is love, less blessed is hatred, but thrice accursed is that indifference which is neither one nor the other.

RYAN Joe
9798
A committee of one gets things done.

RYLE Gilbert 1900-1976
9799 *The Concept of Mind*
Philosophy is the replacement of category-habits by category-disciplines.

9800 *The Concept of Mind*
The dogma of the Ghost in the Machine.

SAADI c.1184-c.1292
9801
Whoever has his foe at his mercy, and does not

kill him, is his own enemy.

SACKLER Howard 1929-
9802 *Good-bye Fidel*
Affairs, like revolutions, should only have
beginnings.

SACKS Dr. Oliver
9803
People can be consumed by creativity as they
are by tuberculosis.

SACKVILLE-WEST Vita 1892-1962
9804 *The King's Daughter*
The greater cats with golden eyes
Stare out between the bars.
Deserts are there, and different skies,
And night with different stars.

9805 *The Land 'Winter'*
The country habit has me by the heart,
For he's bewitched for ever who has seen,
Not with his eyes but with his vision, Spring
Flow down the woods and stipple leaves with
sun.

SAGAN Carl 1934-1996
9806
It is of interest to note that while some dolphins
are reported to have learned English - up to fifty
words used in correct context - no human being
has been reported to have learned dolphinese.

9807
Who are we? We find that we live on an
insignificant planet of a humdrum star lost in a
galaxy tucked away in some forgotten corner of
a universe in which there are far more galaxies
than people.

SAGAN Françoise 1935-1994
9808 *La Chamade*
To jealousy, nothing is more frightful than
laughter.

9809
Every little girl knows about love. It is only her
capacity to suffer because of it that increases.

9810
I like men to behave like men. I like them
strong and childish.

SAID Edward
9811
The intellectual should be a disrupter or a
dissenter - a nay sayer.

ST LAURENT Yves 1936-
9812
Fashions fade - style is eternal.

SAINT-EXUPÉRY Antoine de 1900-1944
9813
A chief is a man who assumes responsibility. He
says, 'I was beaten', he does not say 'My men

were beaten'.

9814
The field of consciousness is tiny. It accepts
only one problem at a time. Get into a fist fight,
put your mind on the strategy of the fight, and
you will not feel the other fellow's punches.

9815 *Le Petit Prince*
Grownups never understand anything for
themselves, and it is tiresome for children to be
always and forever explaining things to them.

9816 *Le Petit Prince*
It is only with the heart that one can see rightly;
what is essential is invisible to the eye.

9817
To be a man is to feel that one's own stone
contributes to building the edifice of the world.

9818
Night, when words fade and things come alive,
when the destructive analysis of day is done,
and all that is truly important becomes whole
and sound again. When man reassembles his
fragmentary self and grows with the calm of a
tree.

9819
A single event can awaken within us a stranger
totally unknown to us. To live is to be slowly
born.

9820
What saves a man is to take a step. Then
another step. It is always the same step, but you
have to take it.

9821 *Wind, Sand and Stars*
Experience shows us that love does not consist
in gazing at each other but in looking together
in the same direction.

SAKI (Hector Hugh Monro) 1870-1916
9822 *Chronicles of Clovis*
The people of Crete unfortunately make more
history than they can consume locally.

9823 *Chronicles of Clovis*
All decent people live beyond their incomes
nowadays, and those who aren't respectable live
beyond other peoples'.

9824
The clock struck eleven with the respectful
unobtrusiveness of one whose mission in life is
to be ignored.

9825
Hating anything in the way of ill-natured gossip
ourselves, we are always grateful to those who
do it for us and do it well.

9826
Oysters are more beautiful than any religion ...
there's nothing in Christianity or Buddhism that
quite matches the sympathetic unselfishness of
an oyster.

9827 *Reginald*
The cook was a good cook, as cooks go; and as
good cooks go, she went.

9828 *Reginald*
I always say beauty is only sin deep.

9829 *Reginald in Russia*
Good gracious, you've got to educate him first.
You can't expect a boy to be vicious till he's been
to a good school.

9830 *Reginald in Russia*
Addresses are given to us to conceal our
whereabouts.

9831 *The Square Egg*
A little inaccuracy sometimes saves tons of
explanation.

9832 *Toys of Peace and Other Papers*
Children with Hyacinth's temperament don't
know better as they grow older; they merely
know more.

9833 *The Unbearable Bassington*
We all know that Prime Ministers are wedded to
the truth, but like other married couples they
sometimes live apart.

SALINGER J.D. 1919-
9834 *The Catcher in the Rye*
Sex is something I really don't understand too
hot. You never know *where* the hell you are. I
keep making up these sex rules for myself, and
then I break them right away.

9835
A confessional passage has probably never been
written that didn't stink a little bit of the writer's
pride in having given up his pride.

SALISBURY Lord 1893-1972
9836 *(of Iain Macleod, Colonial Secretary)*
Too clever by half.

SALISBURY Lord 1830-1903
9837
We are part of the community of Europe and we
must do our duty as such.

9838 *(comparing his role with that of Gladstone)*
I rank myself no higher in the scheme of things
than a policeman - whose utility would
disappear if there were no criminals.

9839 *(of the Daily Mail)*
By office boys for office boys.

9840
Horny-handed sons of toil.

9841 *Letter to Lord Lytton*
English policy is to float lazily downstream,
occasionally putting out a diplomatic boathook
to avoid collisions.

9842 *Letter to Lord Lytton*
No lesson seems to be so deeply inculcated by
the experience of life as that you never should
trust experts. If you believe the doctors,
nothing is wholesome: if you believe the
theologians, nothing is innocent: if you believe
the soldiers, nothing is safe.

SALLUST 86-34 BC
9843 *Catiline*
Coveting other men's property, and squandering
his own.

9844 *Catiline*
To like and dislike the same things, that is
indeed true friendship.

SALMON Andrew
9845
There is only one truth, steadfast, healing,
salutary, and that is the absurd.

SALVANDY Comte de 1795-1856
9846 *(just before the revolution)*
We are dancing on a volcano.

SAMPSON Anthony 1926-
9847 *Anatomy of Britain*
Members [of civil service orders] rise from CMG
(known sometimes in Whitehall as 'Call Me
God') to the KCMG ('Kindly Call Me God') to
for a select few governors and super-
ambassadors - the GCMG ('God Calls Me God').

SAMUEL Lord 1870-1963
9848 *A Book of Quotations*
A library is thought in cold storage.

9849 *Book of Quotations*
It takes two to make a marriage a success and
only one to make it a failure.

9850
Equality of opportunity is an equal opportunity
to prove unequal talents.

9851 *Romanes Lecture*
Without doubt the greatest injury of all was
done by basing morals on myth. For, sooner or
later, myth is recognized for what it is, and
disappears. Then morality loses the foundation
on which it has been built.

SAMUELSON Paul A. 1915-
9852 *Economics*
The consumer, so it is said, is the king ... each is
a voter who uses his money as votes to get the
things done that he wants done.

SAND George 1804-1876
9853
Work is not man's punishment. It is his reward and his strength, his glory and his pleasure.

SANDBURG Carl 1878-1967
9854 *'Chicago'*
Stormy, husky, brawling,
City of the Big Shoulders.

9855 *'Cool Tombs'*
When Abraham Lincoln was shovelled into the tombs,
he forgot the copperheads and the assassin...
In the dust, in the cool tombs.

9856 *'Fog'*
The fog comes
on little cat feet.
It sits looking
over harbour and city
on silent haunches
and then moves on.

9857 *'Grass'*
Pile the bodies high at Austerlitz and Waterloo.
Shovel them under and let me work -
I am the grass; I cover all.

9858
One of the greatest necessities in America is to discover creative solitude.

9859
Hope is an echo, hope ties itself yonder, yonder.

9860 *Incidentals*
I am an idealist. I don't know where I'm going but I'm on the way.

9861
Poetry is the journal of a sea animal living on land, wanting to fly in the air.

9862 *'Poetry Considered'*
Poetry is the opening and closing of a door, leaving those who look through to guess about what is seen during a moment.

9863 *'Prairie'*
I tell you the past is a bucket of ashes.

9864
Slang is a language that rolls up its sleeves, spits on its hands and goes to work.

9865
Sometime they'll give a war and nobody will come.

SANDERS Henry 'Red'
9866
Sure, winning isn't everything. It's the only thing.

SANGER Margaret 1883-1966
9867
No woman can call herself free who does not own and control her body. No woman can call herself free until she can choose consciously whether she will or will not be a mother.

SANTAYANA George 1863-1952
9868
Art is a delayed echo.

9869
An artist may visit a museum but only a pedant can live there.

9870
My atheism, like that of Spinoza, is true piety towards the universe and denies only gods fashioned by men in their own image, to be servants of their human interest.

9871
Since barbarism has its pleasures it naturally has its apologists.

9872
I believe in the possibility of happiness, if one cultivates intuition and outlives the grosser passions, including optimism.

9873
A child educated only at school is an uneducated child.

9874
Before you contradict an old man, my fair friend, you should endeavour to understand him.

9875
Friendship is almost always the union of a part of one mind with a part of another; people are friends in spots.

9876
Government is the political representative of a natural equilibrium, of custom, or inertia; it is by no means a representative of reason.

9877
Habit is stronger than reason.

9878
Happiness is the only sanction of life; where happiness fails, existence remains a mad and lamentable experiment.

9879
It would hardly be possible to exaggerate man's wretchedness if it were not so easy to overestimate his sensibility.

9880
For an idea ever to be fashionable is ominous, since it must afterwards be always old-fashioned.

9881
Intelligence is quickness in seeing things as they
are.

9882 *Introduction to the Ethics of Spinoza*
The Bible is literature, not dogma.

9883
Knowledge of what is possible is the beginning
of happiness.

9884 *The Life of Reason*
Fanaticism consists in redoubling your effort
when you have forgotten your aim.

9885 *The Life of Reason*
Those who cannot remember the past are
condemned to repeat it.

9886 *The Life of Reason*
It takes patience to appreciate domestic bliss;
volatile spirits prefer unhappiness.

9887 *The Life of Reason*
An artist is a dreamer consenting to dream of
the actual world.

9888
Man is as full of potentiality as he is of
impotence.

9889
If a man really knew himself he would utterly
despise the ignorant notions others might form
on a subject in which he had such matchless
opportunities for observation.

9890
By nature's kindly disposition, most questions
which it is beyond man's power to answer do
not occur to him at all.

9891
Nothing you can lose by dying is half so
precious as the readiness to die, which is man's
charter of nobility.

9892
There is nothing to which men, while they have
food and drink, cannot reconcile themselves.

9893
Popular poets are the parish priests of the Muse,
retailing her ancient divinations to a long since
converted public.

9894
Every real object must cease to be what it
seemed and none could ever be what the whole
soul desired.

9895
Real unselfishness consists in sharing the
interests of others.

9896
Each religion, by the help of more or less myth
which it takes more or less seriously, proposes
some method of fortifying the human soul and
enabling it to make its peace with destiny.

9897 *Soliloquies in England*
There is no cure for birth and death save to
enjoy the interval.

9898 *Soliloquies in England, 'The British
Character'*
England is the paradise of individuality,
eccentricity, heresy, anomalies, hobbies, and
humours.

9899
The truth is cruel, but it can be loved, and it
makes free those who have loved it.

9900 *The Unknowable*
It is a great advantage for a system of
philosophy to be substantially true.

9901
Almost every wise saying has an opposite one,
no less wise, to balance it.

9902
Work and love - these are the basics; waking life
is a dream controlled.

SAPHIR Moritz G.
9903
Love makes of the wisest man a fool, and of the
most foolish woman, a sage.

9904
The mirror is the conscience of women; they
never do a thing without first consulting it.

SAPHIR Morty
9905
Man's attitude toward great qualities in others is
often the same as toward high mountains - he
admires them but he prefers to walk around
them.

SAPIRSTEIN Milton R.
9906
Our unconsciousness is like a vast subterranean
factory with intricate machinery that is never
idle, where work goes on day and night from the
time we are born until the moment of our
death.

SARAH 1st Duchess of Marlborough 1660-1744
9907
The Duke returned from the wars today and did
pleasure me in his top-boots.

9908 *(refusing marriage offer from Duke of
Somerset)*
If I were young and handsome as I was, instead
of old and faded as I am, and you could lay the
empire of the world at my feet, you should

never share the heart and hand that once belonged to John, Duke of Marlborough.

SARAH Duchess of York 1959-
9909 *(as spokesperson for US Weightwatchers)*
Free your mind and your bottom will follow.

9910
I don't know where the money went - it just went. I don't even like shopping.

SARGENT John Singer 1856-1925
9911
A portrait is a painting with something wrong with the mouth.

9912
Every time I paint a portrait I lose a friend.

SARONY Leslie 1897-1985
9913
Ain't it grand to be blooming well dead?

SAROYAN William 1908-1981
9914
The greatest happiness you can have is knowing that you do not necessarily require happiness.

9915
Every man in the world is better than someone else. And not as good as some one else.

SARRAUTE Nathalie 1902-
9916
Radio and television ... have succeeded in lifting the manufacture of banality out of the sphere of handicraft and placed it in that of a major industry.

SARTRE Jean-Paul 1905-1980
9917 *Words*
Like all dreamers, I mistook disenchantment for truth.

9918 *Words*
I confused things with their names: that is belief.

9919 *Words*
There is no good father, that's the rule. Don't lay the blame on men but on the bond of paternity, which is rotten. To beget children, nothing better; to *have* them, what iniquity!

9920 *Words*
The poor don't know that their function in life is to exercise our generosity.

9921 *Words*
She believed in nothing; only her scepticism kept her from being an atheist.

9922 *The Flies*
Human life begins on the far side of despair.

9923
Once freedom lights its beacon in a man's heart, the gods are powerless against him.

9924
Once you hear the details of victory, it is heard to distinguish it from a defeat.

9925 *Huis Clos*
Hell is other people.

9926 *Lucifer and the Lord*
When the rich wage war it's the poor who die.

9927 *Being and Nothingness*
Existence precedes and rules essence.

9928 *Being and Nothingness*
I am condemned to be free.

9929 *Being and Nothingness*
Man is a useless passion.

9930 *(refusing the Nobel Prize in Stockholm)*
A writer must refuse ... to allow himself to be transformed into an institution.

9931
The writer is committed when he plunges to the very depths of himself with the intent to disclose, not his individuality, but his person in the complex society that conditions and supports him.

SASSOON Siegfried 1886-1967
9932 *'Dreamers'*
Soldiers are citizens of death's grey land,
Drawing no dividend from time's tomorrows.

9933 *'Everyone Sang'*
Everyone suddenly burst out singing;
And I was filled with such delight
As prisoned birds must find in freedom.

9934 *'Everyone Sang'*
The song was wordless; the singing will never be done.

9935 *'The General'*
But he did for them both by his plan of attack.

9936 *'Does it Matter?'*
Does it matter? - losing your sight? ...
There's such splendid work for the blind;
And people will always be kind,
As you sit on the terrace remembering
And turning your face to the light.

SASSOON Vidal
9937
Hair is another name for sex.

SAVILE George 1633-1695
9938 *Political, Moral, and Miscellaneous Thoughts and Reflections*
Anger is never without an argument, but seldom with a good one.

9939 *Political, Moral, and Miscellaneous Thoughts and Reflections*
Malice is of a low stature, but it hath very long arms.

9940 *Political, Moral, and Miscellaneous Thoughts and Reflections*
When the people contend for their liberty, they seldom get anything by their victory but new masters.

9941 *Political, Moral, and Miscellaneous Thoughts and Reflections*
Men are not hanged for stealing horses, but that horses may not be stolen.

SAY Jean Baptiste
9942
It is the aim of good government to stimulate production, of bad government to encourage consumption.

SAYERS Dorothy L. 1893-1957
9943 *Creed or Chaos?*
A society in which consumption has to be artificially stimulated in order to keep production going is a society founded on trash and waste, and such a society is a house built upon sand.

9944 *That's Why I Never Read Modern Novels*
As I grow older and older,
And totter towards the tomb,
I find that I care less and less
Whom goes to bed with whom.

SCALPONE Al
9945 *(motto for Roman Catholic Family Rosary Crusade)*
The family that prays together stays together.

SCANLON Hugh 1913-
9946
Of course liberty is not licence. Liberty in my view is conforming to majority opinion.

SCARGILL Arthur 1938-
9947 *(evidence to House of Commons Select Committee)*
Parliament itself would not exist in its present form had people not defied the law.

SCHARPING Rudolf 1947-
9948
Remembrance is the secret of reconciliation.

SCHAUBLE Wolfgang 1942-
9949
The soul of Germany is Europe, it is not the D. Mark.

SCHELLING Friedrich von 1775-1854
9950 *Philosophie der Kunst*
Architecture in general is frozen music.

SCHERER Paul 1933-
9951
Love is a spendthrift, leaves its arithmetic at home, is always 'in the red'.

SCHICK Béla 1877-1967
9952
It is very difficult to slow down. The practice of medicine is like the heart muscle's contraction - it's all or none.

SCHIFF Leonard
9953
Electric clocks reveal to you
Precisely when your fuses blew.

SCHILLER Friedrich von 1759-1805
9954 *Don Carlos*
The sun does not set in my dominions.

9955 *'An Die Freude'*
All men become brothers under your tender wing.

9956 *Die Jungfrau von Orleans*
With stupidity the gods themselves struggle in vain.

9957
The will of man is his happiness.

9958
I am better than my reputation.

9959 *'Resignation'*
The world's history is the world's judgement.

9960
The world is ruled only by consideration of advantages.

9961
The world's history is constant, like the laws of nature, and simple, like the souls of men. The same conditions continually produce the same results.

SCHLAGGENBERG Kajetan von
9962
Maturity consists of no longer being taken in by oneself.

SCHLESINGER Jr. Arthur 1917-
9963
Almost all important questions are important precisely because they are not susceptible to quantitative answer.

9964
What we need is a rebirth of satire, of dissent, of irreverence, of an uncompromising insistance that phoniness is phony and platitudes are platitudinous.

SCHNABEL Artur 1882-1951
9965 *My Life and Music*
I know two kinds of audiences only - one

coughing, and one not coughing.

9966 *(of Mozart's sonatas)*
Too easy for children, and too difficult for artists.

9967
The notes I handle no better than many pianists. But the pauses between the notes - ah, that is where the art resides!

SCHNITZLER Arthur 1862-1931
9968
Martyrdom has always been a proof of the intensity, never of the correctness of a belief.

SCHOPENHAUER Arthur 1788-1860
9969
Any book which is at all important should be re-read immediately.

9970
We should comport ourselves with the masterpieces of art as with exalted personages - stand quietly before them and wait till they speak to us.

9971
In early youth, as we contemplate our coming life, we are like children in a theatre before the curtain is raised, sitting there in high spirits and eagerly waiting for the play to begin.

9972
Fame is something which must be won; honour is something which must not be lost.

9973
The fly ought to be used as the symbol of impertinence and audacity; for whilst all other animals shun man more than anything else, and run away even before he comes near them, the fly lights upon his very nose.

9974
The fundamental fault of the female character is that it has no sense of justice.

9975
Every parting gives a foretaste of death; every coming together again a foretaste of the resurrection.

9976
Hatred comes from the heart; contempt from the head; and neither feeling is quite within our control.

9977
Intellect is invisible to the man who has none.

9978
A man never feels the want of what it never occurs to him to ask for.

9979
Money is human happiness in the abstract.

9980
Necessity is the constant scourge of the lower classes, ennui of the higher ones.

9981
Obstinacy is the result of the will forcing itself into the place of the intellect.

9982
(Politeness is) a tacit agreement that people's miserable defects, whether moral or intellectual, shall on either side be ignored and not be made the subject of reproach.

9983
Pride is the direct appreciation of oneself.

9984
Reason deserves to be called a prophet; for in showing up the consequence and effect of our actions in the present, does it not tell us what the future will be?

9985
The will is the strong blind man who carries on his shoulders the lame man who can see.

9986
Not to go to the theatre is like making one's toilet without a mirror.

9987
Every truth passes through three stages before it is recognized. In the first it is ridiculed, in the second it is opposed, in the third it is regarded as self-evident.

9988
If you want to know your true opinion of someone, watch the effect produced in you by the first sight of a letter from him.

SCHUDSON Michael
9989
Buy me and you will overcome the anxieties I have just reminded you of.

SCHULLER Robert
9990
Someone once said to me, 'Reverend Schuller, I hope you live to see all your dreams fulfilled'. I replied, 'I hope not, because if I live and all my dreams are fulfilled, I'm dead'. It's unfulfilled dreams that keep you alive.

SCHULZ Charles M. 1922-
9991
I've developed a new philosophy - I only dread one day at a time.

9992
Jogging is very beneficial. It's good for your legs and your feet. It's also very good for the ground. It makes it feel needed.

9993
My life has no purpose, no direction, no aim, no meaning, and yet I'm happy. I can't figure it out. What am I doing right?

SCHURZ Carl 1829-1906
9994
My country, right or wrong; if right, to be kept right; and if wrong, to be set right!

SCHWEITZER Albert 1875-1965
9995
As we acquire more knowledge, things do not become more comprehensible, but more mysterious.

9996
A great secret of success is to go through life as a man who never gets used up.

9997
Happiness? That's nothing more than health and a poor memory.

9998
A man does not have to be an angel in order to be a saint.

9999
Man can hardly even recognize the devils of his own creation.

10000
One thing I know: the only ones among you who will be really happy are those who will have sought and found how to serve.

10001
Thought is the strongest thing we have. Work done by true and profound thought - that is a real force.

SCIPIO Africanus 236-104 BC
10002
Never less idle than when unoccupied, nor less alone than when without company.

SCOTT C.P. 1846-1932
10003
Comment is free, but facts are sacred.

10004
Television? The word is half Latin and half Greek. No good can come of it.

SCOTT F.R.
10005
An arena
large as Europe
Silent
waiting the contest.

10006
The world is my country,
The human race is my race.
The spirit of man is my god,

The future of man is my heaven.

SCOTT Howard
10007
A criminal is a person with predatory instincts who has not sufficient capital to form a corporation.

SCOTT Paul 1920-1978
10008
The truth did not come to me suddenly,
It came quietly, cicumspectly, snuffling and whimpering
Looking to be let in many times before.

SCOTT Robert 1868-1912
10009 *(last journal entry)*
For God's sake look after our people.

10010 *(last letter to his wife)*
Make the boy interested in natural history if you can; it is better than games.

10011 *'Message to the Public'*
Had we lived, I should have had a tale to tell of the hardihood, endurance, and courage of my companions which would have stirred the heart of every Englishman. These rough notes and our dead bodies must tell the tale.

10012 *(of the South Pole)*
Great God! this is an awful place.

SCOTT Sir Walter 1771-1832
10013 *The Antiquary*
It's no fish ye're buying - it's men's lives.

10014 *The Bride of Lammermoor*
Vacant heart and hand, and eye -
Easy live and quiet die.

10015 *The Bride of Lammermoor*
I live by twa trades fiddle, sir, and spade;
filling the world, and emptying of it.

10016 *The Heart of Midlothian*
The hour is come, but not the man.

10017
One hour of life, crowded to the full with glorious action, and filled with noble risks, is worth whole years of those mean observances of paltry decorum.

10018 *The Lady of the Lake*
His ready speech flowed fair and free,
In phrase of gentlest courtesy;
Yet seemed that tone, and gesture bland,
Less used to sue than to command.

10019 *The Lady of the Lake*
He is gone on the mountain,
He is lost to the forest,
Like a summer-dried fountain,
When our need was the sorest.

10020 *The Lady of the Lake*
Hail to the chief who in triumph advances!

10021 *The Lady of the Lake*
And the stern joy which warriors feel
In foemen worthy of their steel.

10022 *The Lay of the Last Minstrel*
If thou would'st view fair Melrose aright,
Go visit it by the pale moonlight.

10023 *The Lay of the Last Minstrel*
They waste their toil
For the vain tribute of a smile.

10024 *The Lay of the Last Minstrel*
The unpremeditated lay.

10025 *The Lay of the Last Minstrel*
Love rules the court, the camp, the grove,
And men below, and saints above;
For love is heaven, and heaven is love.

10026 *The Lay of the Last Minstrel*
True love's the gift which God has given
To man alone beneath the heaven.

10027 *The Lay of the Last Minstrel*
Breathes there the man, with soul so dead,
Who never to himself hath said,
This is my own, my native land!

10028 *The Lay of the Last Minstrel*
The wretch, concentred all in self,
Living, shall forfeit fair renown,
And, doubly dying, shall go down
To the vile dust, from whence he sprung,
Unwept, unhonoured, and unsung.

10029 *Letter to J.G. Lockhart, 1830*
All men who have turned out worth anything
have had the chief hand in their own education.

10030 *The Lord of the Isles*
O! many a shaft, at random sent,
Finds mark the archer little meant!
And many a word, at random spoken,
May soothe or wound a heart that's broken.

10031 *Marmion*
Had'st thou but lived, though stripped of power,
A watchman on the lonely tower.

10032 *Marmion*
And come he slow, or come he fast,
It is but Death who comes at last.

10033 *Marmion*
O what a tangled web we weave,
When first we practise to deceive!

10034 *Marmion*
O Woman! in our hours of ease,
Uncertain, coy, and hard to please,
And variable as the shade
By the light quivering aspen made;
When pain and anguish wring the brow,

A ministering angel thou!

10035 *Redgauntlet*
The ae half of the warld thinks the tither daft.

10036 *Rob Roy*
But with the morning cool repentance came.

10037 *Rob Roy*
There's a gude time coming.

10038 *The Talisman*
Rouse the lion from his lair.

SCOTT William 1745-1836
10039
A dinner lubricates business.

10040 *(attributed opinion, while Advocate-General)*
A precedent embalms a principle.

SCOTT-MAXWELL Florida
10041
No matter how old a mother is, she watches her
middle-aged children for signs of improvement.

SEDLEY Sir Charles c.1639-1701
10042 *'Love still has something'*
Love still has something of the sea
From whence his mother rose.

10043 *'Phyllis Knotting'*
Phyllis, without frown or smile,
Sat and knotted all the while.

10044 *'Song'*
Phyllis is my only joy,
Faithless as the winds or seas;
Sometimes coming, sometimes coy,
Yet she never fails to please.

10045 *'Song'*
She deceiving,
I believing;
What need lovers wish for more?

SEEGER Alan 1888-1916
10046 *'I Have a Rendezvous with Death'*
I have a rendezvous with Death
At some disputed barricade.

SEEGER Pete 1919-
10047
Where have all the flowers gone?

SEELEY Sir John 1834-1895
10048 *The Expansion of England*
We [the English] seem, as it were, to have
conquered and peopled half the world in a fit of
absence of mind.

10049
History is past politics; and politics present
history.

SEGAL Erich 1937-
10050 *Love Story*
Love means never having to say you're sorry.

SÉGUR Sophie Rostopchine
10051
God keeps the wicked to give them time to repent.

SELDEN John 1584-1654
10052 *Table Talk 'Friends'*
Old friends are best. King James used to call for his old shoes; they were easiest for his feet.

10053 *Table Talk 'Humility'*
'Tis not the drinking that is to be blamed, but the excess.

10054 *Table Talk 'Of a King'*
A king is a thing men have made for their own sakes, for quietness' sake. Just as in a family one man is appointed to buy the meat.

10055 *Table Talk 'Law'*
Ignorance of the law excuses no man; not that all men know the law, but because 'tis an excuse every man will plead, and no man can tell how to confute him.

10056 *Table Talk 'Libels'*
Take a straw and throw it up into the air, you shall see by that which way the wind is.

10057 *Table Talk 'Marriage'*
Marriage is nothing but a civil contract.

10058 *Table Talk 'Parson'*
There never was a merry world since the fairies left off dancing, and the Parson left conjuring.

10059 *Table Talk 'Pleasure'*
Pleasure is nothing else but the intermission of pain.

10060 *Table Talk 'Preaching'*
Preachers say, Do as I say, not as I do.

SELDON Arthur 1584-1654
10061 *Capitalism*
Government of the busy by the bossy for the bully.

SELLAR W.C. and YEATMAN R.J. 1898-1951 and 1898-1968
10062 *1066 and All That*
The Roman Conquest was, however, a *Good Thing*, since the Britons were only natives at the time.

10063 *1066 and All That*
The Cavaliers (Wrong but Wromantic) and the Roundheads (Right but Repulsive).

10064 *1066 and All That*
The National Debt is a very Good Thing and it would be dangerous to pay it off, for fear of Political Economy.

10065 *1066 and All That*
Napoleon's armies always used to march on their stomachs shouting: 'Vive l'Intérieur!'

10066 *1066 and All That 'Compulsory Preface'*
History is not what you thought. *It is what you can remember.*

10067 *And Now All This*
For every person who wants to teach there are approximately thirty who don't want to learn - much.

SENDAK Maurice 1928-
10068
William Blake really is important, my cornerstone. Nobody ever told me before he did that childhood was such a damned serious business.

SENECA c.4 BC-AD 65
10069
All cruelty springs from weakness.

10070
Anyone can stop a man's life, but no one his death.

10071
Constant exposure to dangers will breed contempt for them.

10072
Drunkenness is nothing but voluntary madness.

10073
Eternal law has arranged nothing better than this, that it has given us one way in to life, but many ways out.

10074
Failure changes for the better, success for the worse.

10075
Fate rules the affairs of mankind with no recognizable order.

10076
The foremost art of kings is the power to endure hatred.

10077
A good mind possesses a kingdom: a great fortune is a great slavery.

10078
A great step toward independence is a good-humoured stomach.

10079
Whom they have injured, they also hate.

10080
Injustice never rules forever.

10081
Love of bustle is not industry.

10082
Night brings our troubles to the light rather than banishes them.

10083
There is nothing so bitter, that a patient mind cannot find some solace for it.

10084
It is often better not to see an insult, than to avenge it.

10085
Even while they teach, men learn.

10086
Time discovered truth.

10087
No untroubled day has ever dawned for me.

10088
Vices can be learnt, even without a teacher.

10089
When I think over what I have said, I envy dumb people.

SENN J.P.
10090
Let us respect grey hairs, especially our own.

SERVICE Robert 1874-1958
10091 *'The Cremation of Sam McGee'*
A promise made is a debt unpaid, and the trail has its own stern code.

10092
The happy man is he who knows his limitations, yet bows to no false gods.

10093 *'It is Later Thank You Think'*
Ah! the clock is always slow;
It is later than you think.

10094 *'The Law of the Yukon'*
This is the law of the Yukon, that only the Strong shall thrive;
That surely the Weak shall perish, and only the Fit survive.

10095 *'Michael'*
When we, the Workers, all demand: 'What are WE fighting for?' ...
Then, then we'll end that stupid crime, that devil's madness - War.

10096
It isn't the mountain ahead that wears you out - it's the grain of sand in your shoe.

SETH Vikram
10097
Boredom provides a stronger inclination to write than anything.

SÉVIGNÉ Mme de 1626-1692
10098 *(attributed)*
The more I see of men, the more I admire dogs.

SEWARD William 1801-1872
10099
I know, and all the world knows, that revolutions never go backward.

SEXTON Anne 1928-1974
10100 *'Old'*
In a dream you are never eighty.

SEYMOUR Horatio
10101
After listening to thousands of pleas for pardon to offenders, I can hardly recall a case where I did not feel that I might have fallen as my fellow man had done, if I had been subjected to the same demoralizing influences and pressed by the same temptations.

SHADWELL Thomas 1642-1692
10102 *Psyche*
Words may be false and full of art,
Sighs are the natural language of the heart.

10103 *A True Widow*
And wit's the noblest frailty of the mind.

10104 *A True Widow*
The haste of a fool is the slowest thing in the world.

10105 *A True Widow*
Every man loves what he is good at.

SHAFFER Ivan
10106
A man isn't a man until he has to meet a payroll.

SHAFFER Peter 1926-
10107 *Equus*
All my wife has ever taken from the Mediterranean - from that whole vast intuitive culture - are four bottles of Chianti to make into lamps.

10108 *Equus*
The Ordinary made beautiful; ... the Average made lethal.

SHAKESPEARE William 1564-1616
10109 *As You Like It*
When I was at home, I was in a better place; but travellers must be content.

10110 *As You Like It*
Sir, you have wrestled well, and overthrown
More than your enemies.

10111 *As You Like It*
O, how full of briers is this working-day world!

10112 *As You Like It*
Sweet are the uses of adversity,
Which like the toad, ugly and venomous,

Wears yet a precious jewel in his head;
And this our life, exempt from public haunt,
Finds tongues in trees, books in the running
brooks,
Sermons in stones, and good in everything.

10113 *As You Like It*
If thou remember'st not the slightest folly
That ever love did make thee run into
Thou has not loved.

10114 *As You Like It*
Under the greenwood tree
Who loves to lie with me.

10115 *As You Like It*
Who doth ambition shun
And loves to live i' the sun,
Seeking the food he eats,
And pleased with what he gets.

10116 *As You Like It*
And so, from hour to hour, we ripe and ripe,
And then from hour to hour, we rot and rot:
And thereby hangs a tale.

10117 *As You Like It*
All the world's a stage,
And all the men and women merely players:
They have their exits and their entrances;
And one man in his time plays many parts,
His acts being seven ages.

10118 *As You Like It*
Last scene of all,
That ends this strange eventful history,
Is second childishness, and mere oblivion,
Sans teeth, sans eyes, sans taste, sans
everything.

10119 *As You Like It*
Blow, blow, thou winter wind,
Thou art not so unkind
As man's ingratitude.

10120 *As You Like It*
Most friendship is feigning, most loving mere
folly.

10121 *As You Like It*
He that wants money, means, and content is
without three good friends.

10122 *As You Like It*
Do you not know I am a woman? when I think, I
must speak.

10123 *As You Like It*
I do desire we may be better strangers.

10124 *As You Like It*
I pray you, do not fall in love with me,
For I am falser than vows made in wine.

10125 *As You Like It*
Men have died from time to time, and worms
have eaten them, but not for love.

10126 *As You Like It*
Men are April when they woo, December when
they wed: maids are May when they are maids,
but the sky changes when they are wives.

10127 *As You Like It*
Your 'if' is the only peace-maker; much virtue in
'if'.

10128 *Much Ado About Nothing*
How much better is it to weep at joy than to joy
at weeping.

10129 *Much Ado About Nothing*
Speak low, if you speak love.

10130 *Much Ado About Nothing*
Friendship is constant in all other things
Save in the office and affairs of love.

10131 *Much Ado About Nothing*
Sigh no more, ladies, sigh no more,
Men were deceivers ever;
One foot in sea, and one on shore,
To one thing constant never.

10132 *Much Ado About Nothing*
Doth not the appetite alter? A man loves the
meat in his youth that he cannot endure in his
age.

10133 *Much Ado About Nothing*
When I said I would die a bachelor, I did not
think I should live till I were married.

10134 *Much Ado About Nothing*
Everyone can master a grief but he that has it.

10135 *Much Ado About Nothing*
To be a well-favoured man is the gift of fortune;
but to write and read comes by nature.

10136 *Much Ado About Nothing*
I thank God, I am as honest as any man living,
that is an old man and no honester than I.

10137 *Much Ado About Nothing*
Comparisons are odorous.

10138 *Much Ado About Nothing*
There was never yet philosopher
That could endure the toothache patiently.

10139 *All's Well that Ends Well*
It were all one
That I should love a bright particular star
And think to wed it, he is so above me.

10140 *All's Well that Ends Well*
The hind that would be mated with the lion
Must die of love.

10141 *All's Well that Ends Well*
Our remedies oft in ourselves do lie
Which we ascribed to heaven.

10142 *All's Well that Ends Well*
A young man married is a man that's marred.

10143 *All's Well that Ends Well*
The web of our life is of a mingled yarn, good
and ill together.

10144 *Antony and Cleopatra*
The stroke of death is as a lover's pinch,
Which hurts and is desired.

10145 *Antony and Cleopatra*
The triple pillar of the world transformed
Into a strumpet's fool.

10146 *Antony and Cleopatra*
There's beggary in the love that can be
reckoned.

10147 *Antony and Cleopatra*
Let Rome in Tiber melt, and the wide arch
Of the ranged empire fall. Here is my space.

10148 *Antony and Cleopatra*
O excellent! I love long life better than figs.

10149 *Antony and Cleopatra*
A Roman thought hath struck him.

10150 *Antony and Cleopatra*
Indeed the tears live in an onion that should
water this sorrow.

10151 *Antony and Cleopatra*
In time we hate that which we often fear.

10152 *Antony and Cleopatra*
Eternity was in our lips and eyes,
Bliss in our brows bent.

10153 *Antony and Cleopatra*
The demi-Atlas of this earth, the arm
And burgonet of men. He's speaking now,
Or murmuring, 'Where's my serpent of old
Nile?'

10154 *Antony and Cleopatra*
My salad days,
When I was green in judgment, cold in blood,
To say as I said then!

10155 *Antony and Cleopatra*
The barge she sat in, like a burnished throne,
Burned on the water; the poop was beaten gold,
Purple the sails, and so perfumed, that
The winds were love-sick with them.

10156 *Antony and Cleopatra*
The city cast
Her people out upon her, and Antony,
Enthroned i' the market-place, did sit alone,
Whistling to the air; which, but for vacancy,
Had gone to gaze on Cleopatra too

And made a gap in nature.

10157 *Antony and Cleopatra*
Age cannot wither her, nor custom stale
Her infinite variety; other women cloy
The appetites they feed, but she makes hungry
Where most she satisfied.

10158 *Antony and Cleopatra*
Give me some music - music, moody food
Of us that trade in love.

10159 *Antony and Cleopatra*
I will praise any man that will praise me.

10160 *Antony and Cleopatra*
Against the blown rose may they stop their
nose,
That kneeled unto the buds.

10161 *Antony and Cleopatra*
Let's have one other gaudy night: ...
Let's mock the midnight bell.

10162 *Antony and Cleopatra*
To business that we love we rise betime,
And go to 't with delight.

10163 *Antony and Cleopatra*
Unarm, Eros; the long day's task is done,
And we must sleep.

10164 *Antony and Cleopatra*
I am dying, Egypt, dying; only
I here importune death awhile, until
Of many thousand kisses the poor last
I lay upon thy lips.

10165 *Antony and Cleopatra*
The crown o' the earth doth melt. My lord!
O! withered is the garland of the war,
The soldier's pole is fall'n; young boys and girls
Are level now with men; the odds is gone,
And there is nothing left remarkable
Beneath the visiting moon.

10166 *Antony and Cleopatra*
A rarer spirit never
Did steer humanity; but you, gods, will give us
Some faults to make us men.

10167 *Antony and Cleopatra*
The bright day is done,
And we are for the dark.

10168 *Antony and Cleopatra*
My resolution's placed, and I have nothing
Of woman in me; now from head to foot
I am marble-constant, now the fleeting moon
No planet is of mine.

10169 *Antony and Cleopatra*
Give me my robe, put on my crown; I have
Immortal longings in me.

10170 *Antony and Cleopatra*
Dost thou not see my baby at my breast,
That sucks the nurse asleep?

10171 *Antony and Cleopatra*
No grave upon the earth shall clip in it
A pair so famous.

10172 *The Comedy of Errors*
I to the world am like a drop of water
That in the ocean seeks another drop,
Who, falling there to find his fellow forth,
Unseen, inquisitive, confounds himself.

10173 *Coriolanus*
Action is eloquence.

10174 *Coriolanus*
Custom calls me to 't:
What custom wills, in all things should we do't,
The dust on antique time would lie unswept,
And mountainous error be too highly heaped
For truth to o'erpeer.

10175 *Coriolanus*
What is the city but the people?

10176 *Coriolanus*
Like a dull actor now,
I have forgot my part, and I am out,
Even to a full disgrace.

10177 *Cymbeline*
Fortune brings in some boats that are not
steered.

10178 *Cymbeline*
Weariness
Can snore upon the flint, when resty sloth
Finds the down pillow hard.

10179 *Cymbeline*
How hard it is to hide the sparks of nature!

10180 *Cymbeline*
Fear no more the heat o' the sun,
Nor the furious winter's rages;
Thou thy wordly task hast done,
Home art gone and ta'en thy wages:
Golden lads and girls all must,
As chimney-sweepers, come to dust.

10181 *Cymbeline*
Every good servant does not all commands.

10182 *Cymbeline*
He that sleeps feels not the toothache.

10183 *Hamlet*
The undiscovered country from whose bourn
no traveller returns.

10184 *Hamlet*
God has given you one face, and you make
yourselves another.

10185 *Hamlet*
A politician ... one that would circumvent God.

10186 *Hamlet*
For some must watch, while some must sleep;
thus runs the world away.

10187 *Hamlet*
A little more than kin, and less than kind.

10188 *Hamlet*
But I have that within which passeth show;
These but the trappings and the suits of woe.

10189 *Hamlet*
O! that this too too solid flesh would melt,
Thaw, and resolve itself into a dew;
Or that the Everlasting had not fixed
His canon 'gainst self-slaughter! O God! O God!
How weary, stale, flat, and unprofitable
Seem to me all the uses of this world.

10190 *Hamlet*
Frailty, thy name is woman!

10191 *Hamlet*
It is not, nor it cannot come to good;
But break, my heart, for I must hold my tongue.

10192 *Hamlet*
He was a man, take him for all in all,
I shall not look upon his like again.

10193 *Hamlet*
Foul deeds will rise,
Though all the earth o'erwhelm them, to men's
eyes.

10194 *Hamlet*
Do not, as some ungracious pastors do,
Show me the steep and thorny way to heaven,
Whiles, like a puffed and reckless libertine,
Himself the primrose path of dalliance treads,
And recks not his own rede.

10195 *Hamlet*
Give every man thine ear, but few thy voice;
Take each man's censure, but reserve thy
judgement.
Costly thy habit as thy purse can buy,
But not expressed in fancy; rich, not gaudy;
For the apparel oft proclaims the man ...
Neither a borrower, nor a lender be;
For loan oft loses both itself and friend,
And borrowing dulls the edge of husbandry,
This above all: to thine own self be true,
And it must follow, as the night the day,
Thou canst not then be false to any man.

10196 *Hamlet*
But to my mind - though I am native here,
And to the manner born - it is a custom
More honoured in the breach than the
observance.

10197 *Hamlet*
Something is rotten in the state of Denmark.

10198 *Hamlet*
Murder most foul, as in the best it is;
But this most foul, strange, and unnatural.

10199 *Hamlet*
These are but wild and whirling words, my lord.

10200 *Hamlet*
There are more things in heaven and earth, Horatio,
Than are dreamt of in your philosophy.

10201 *Hamlet*
The time is out of joint; O cursèd spite,
That ever I was born to set it right!

10202 *Hamlet*
Brevity is the soul of wit.

10203 *Hamlet*
Doubt thou the stars are fire;
Doubt that the sun doth move;
Doubt truth to be a liar;
But never doubt I love.

10204 *Hamlet*
Ay, sir; to be honest, as this world goes, is to be one man picked out of ten thousand.

10205 *Hamlet*
Though this be madness, yet there is method in't.

10206 *Hamlet*
There is nothing either good or bad, but thinking makes it so.

10207 *Hamlet*
What a piece of work is a man! How noble in reason! how infinite in faculty! in form, in moving, how express and admirable! in action how like an angel! in apprehension how like a god! the beauty of the world! the paragon of animals! And yet, to me, what is this quintessence of dust? man delights not me; no, nor woman neither, though, by your smiling, you seem to say so.

10208 *Hamlet*
I am but mad north-north-west; when the wind is southerly, I know a hawk from a handsaw.

10209 *Hamlet*
Use every man after his desert, and who should 'scape whipping?

10210 *Hamlet*
The play's the thing
Wherein I'll catch the conscience of the king.

10211 *Hamlet*
To be, or not to be: that is the question:
Whether 'tis nobler in the mind to suffer
The slings and arrows of outrageous fortune,
Or to take arms against a sea of troubles,
And by opposing end them?

10212 *Hamlet*
To sleep: perchance to dream: ay, there's the rub;
For in that sleep of death what dreams may come
When we have shuffled off this mortal coil,
Must give us pause.

10213 *Hamlet*
Thus conscience doth make cowards of us all;
And thus the native hue of resolution
Is sicklied o'er with the pale cast of thought.

10214 *Hamlet*
Get thee to a nunnery: why wouldst thou be a breeder of sinners?

10215 *Hamlet*
Suit the action to the word, the word to the action.

10216 *Hamlet*
The lady doth protest too much, methinks.

10217 *Hamlet*
Let me be cruel, not unnatural;
I will speak daggers to her, but use none.

10218 *Hamlet*
My words fly up, my thoughts remain below:
Words without thoughts never to heaven go.

10219 *Hamlet*
A king of shreds and patches.

10220 *Hamlet*
I must be cruel only to be kind.

10221 *Hamlet*
Diseases desperate grown,
By desperate appliances are relieved,
Or not at all.

10222 *Hamlet*
We go to gain a little patch of ground,
That hath in it no profit but the name.

10223 *Hamlet*
How all occasions do inform against me,
And spur my dull revenge! What is a man,
If his chief good and market of his time
Be but to sleep and feed? a beast, no more.

10224 *Hamlet*
Some craven scruple
Of thinking too precisely on the event.

10225 *Hamlet*
When sorrows come, they come not single spies,
But in battalions.

10226 *Hamlet*
There's such divinity doth hedge a king,
That treason can but peep to what it would.

10227 *Hamlet*
There's rosemary, that's for remembrance; pray,
love, remember: and there is pansies, that's for
thoughts.

10228 *Hamlet*
Too much of water hast thou, poor Ophelia,
And therefore I forbid my tears; but yet
It is our trick, nature her custom holds,
Let shame say what it will.

10229 *Hamlet*
Alas, poor Yorick. I knew him, Horatio; a fellow
of infinite jest, of most excellent fancy.

10230 *Hamlet*
There's a divinity that shapes our ends,
Rough-hew them how we will.

10231 *Hamlet*
If thou didst ever hold me in thy heart,
Absent thee from felicity awhile,
And in this harsh world draw thy breath in pain,
To tell my story.

10232 *Hamlet*
The rest is silence.

10233 *Henry IV, Part 1*
Thou hast the most unsavoury similies.

10234 *Henry IV, Part 1*
If all the year were playing holidays,
To sport would be as tedious as to work;
But when they seldom come, they wished to
come.

10235 *Henry IV, Part 1*
Go hang thyself in thine own heir-apparent
garters!

10236 *Henry IV, Part 1*
Falstaff sweats to death
And lards the lean earth as he walks along.

10237 *Henry IV, Part 1*
Out of this nettle, danger, we pluck this flower,
safety.

10238 *Henry IV, Part 1*
If sack and sugar be a fault, God help the
wicked!

10239 *Henry IV, Part 1*
For my part, I may speak it to my shame,
I have a truant been to chivalry.

10240 *Henry IV, Part 1*
Honour pricks me on. Yea, but how if honour
prick me off when I come on? how then? Can
honour set-to a leg? No. Or an arm? No. Or
take away the grief of a wound? No. Honour
hath no skill in surgery, then? No. What is

honour? A word. What is that word, honour?
Air.

10241 *Henry IV, Part 1*
O gentlemen! the time of life is short;
To spend that shortness basely were too long.

10242 *Henry IV, Part 2*
I am as poor as Job, my lord, but not so patient.

10243 *Henry IV, Part 2*
It was always yet the trick of our English nation,
if they have a good thing, to make it too
common.

10244 *Henry IV, Part 2*
Doth it not show vilely in me to desire small
beer?

10245 *Henry IV, Part 2*
Let the end try the man.

10246 *Henry IV, Part 2*
He was indeed the glass
Wherein the noble youth did dress themselves.

10247 *Henry IV, Part 2*
Is it not strange that desire should so many
years outlive performance?

10248 *Henry IV, Part 2*
Uneasy lies the head that wears the crown.

10249 *Henry IV, Part 2*
There is a history in all men's lives,
Figuring the nature of the times deceased,
The which observed, a man my prophesy,
With a near aim, of the main chance of things
As yet not come to life, which in their seeds
And weak beginnings lie intreasurèd.

10250 *Henry IV, Part 2*
We have heard the chimes at midnight.

10251 *Henry IV, Part 2*
I care not; a man can die but once; we owe God
a death.

10252 *Henry IV, Part 2*
Thy wish was father, Harry, to that thought.

10253 *Henry IV, Part 2*
Commit
The oldest sins the newest kind of ways.

10254 *Henry V*
O! for a Muse of fire, that would ascend
The brightest heaven of invention;
A kingdom for a stage, princes to act
And monarchs to behold the swelling scene.

10255 *Henry V*
I dare not fight; but I will wink and hold out
mine iron.

10256 *Henry V*
Once more unto the breach, dear friends, once
more;

Or close the wall up with our English dead!
In peace there's nothing so becomes a man
As modest stillness and humility:
But when the blast of war blows in our ears,
Then imitate the action of the tiger;
Stiffen the sinews, summon up the blood,
Disguise fair nature with hard-favoured rage;
Then lend the eye a terrible aspect.

10257 *Henry V*
I see you stand like greyhounds in the slips,
Straining upon the start. The game's afoot:
Follow your spirit; and, upon this charge
Cry 'God for Harry! England and Saint George!'

10258 *Henry V*
Would I were in an alehouse in London! I would
give all my fame for a pot of ale, and safety.

10259 *Henry V*
Men of few words are the best men.

10260 *Henry V*
A little touch of Harry in the night.

10261 *Henry V*
I think the king is but a man, as I am: the violet
smells to him as it doth to me.

10262 *Henry V*
Every subject's duty is the king's; but every
subject's soul is his own.

10263 *Henry V*
Old men forget: yet all shall be forgot,
But he'll remember with advantages
What feats he did that day.

10264 *Henry V*
And gentlemen in England, now a-bed
Shall think themsleves accursed they were not
here,
And hold their manhoods cheap whiles any
speaks
That fought with us upon Saint Crispin's day.

10265 *Henry VI, Part 1*
Unbidden guests
Are often welcomest when they are gone.

10266 *Henry VI, Part 2*
Could I come near your beauty with my nails
I'd set my ten commandments in your face.

10267 *Henry VI, Part 2*
What stronger breastplate than a heart
untainted!
Thrice is he armed that hath his quarrel just,
And he but naked, though locked up in steel,
Whose conscience with injustice is corrupted.

10268 *Henry VI, Part 3*
Suspicion always haunts the guilty mind;
The thief doth fear each bush an officer.

10269 *Henry VIII*
Heat not a furnace for your foe so hot
That it do singe yourself.

10270 *Henry VIII*
I would not be a queen
For all the world.

10271 *Henry VIII*
A peace above all earthly dignities,
A still and quiet conscience.

10272 *Henry VIII*
Had I but served my God with half the zeal
I served my king, he would not in mine age
Have left me naked to mine enemies.

10273 *Henry VIII*
Men's evil manners live in brass; their virtues
We write in water.

10274 *Henry VIII*
Some come to take their ease
And sleep an act or two.

10275 *Julius Caesar*
Why, man, he doth bestride the narrow world
Like a Colossus; and we petty men
Walk under his huge legs, and peep about
To find ourselves dishonourable graves.
Men at some time are masters of their fates:
The fault, dear Brutus, is not in our stars,
But in ourselves, that we are underlings.

10276 *Julius Caesar*
Let me have men about me that are fat;
Sleek-headed men and such as sleep o'nights;
Yond' Cassius has a lean and hungry look;
He thinks too much: such men are dangerous.

10277 *Julius Caesar*
Those that understood him smiled at one
another and shook their heads; but, for mine
own part, it was Greek to me.

10278 *Julius Caesar*
Nor stony tower, nor walls of beaten brass,
Nor airless dungeon, nor strong links of iron,
Can be retentive to the strength of spirit;
But life, being weary of these worldly bars,
Never lacks power to dismiss itself.

10279 *Julius Caesar*
Let's carve him as a dish fit for the gods,
Not hew him as a carcass fit for hounds.

10280 *Julius Caesar*
Cowards die many times before their deaths;
The valiant never taste of death but once.

10281 *Julius Caesar*
Et tu, Brute? Then fall, Caesar!

10282 *Julius Caesar*
That we shall die, we know; 'tis but the time
And drawing days out, that men stand upon.

10283 *Julius Caesar*
He that cuts off twenty years of life
Cuts off so many years of fearing death.

10284 *Julius Caesar*
O mighty Caesar! dost thou lie so low?
Are all thy conquests, glories, triumphs, spoils,
Shrunk to this little measure?

10285 *Julius Caesar*
O! pardon me, thou bleeding piece of earth,
That I am meek and gentle with these butchers;
Thou art the ruins of the noblest man
That ever livèd in the tide of times.

10286 *Julius Caesar*
Cry, 'Havoc!' and let slip the dogs of war.

10287 *Julius Caesar*
Passion, I see, is catching.

10288 *Julius Caesar*
Not that I loved Caesar less, but that I loved
Rome more.

10289 *Julius Caesar*
Friends, Romans, countrymen, lend me your
ears;
I come to bury Caesar, not to praise him.
The evil that men do lives after them,
The good is oft interrèd with their bones;
So let it be with Caesar.

10290 *Julius Caesar*
He was my friend, faithful and just to me:
But Brutus says he was ambitious;
And Brutus is an honourable man.

10291 *Julius Caesar*
Ambition should be made of sterner stuff.

10292 *Julius Caesar*
You are not wood, you are not stones, but men;
And, being men, hearing the will of Caesar,
It will inflame you, it will make you mad.

10293 *Julius Caesar*
If you have tears, prepare to shed them now.

10294 *Julius Caesar*
This was the most unkindest cut of all;
For when the noble Caesar saw him stab,
Ingratitude, more strong than traitors' arms,
Quite vanquished him: then burst his mighty
heart.

10295 *Julius Caesar*
For I have neither wit, nor words, nor worth,
Action, nor utterance, nor power of speech,
To stir men's blood; I only speak right on;
I tell you that which you yourselves do know.

10296 *Julius Caesar*
I had rather be a dog, and bay the moon,
Than such a Roman.

10297 *Julius Caesar*
Do not presume too much upon my love;
I may do that I shall be sorry for.

10298 *Julius Caesar*
A friend should bear his friend's infirmities,
But Brutus makes mine greater than they are.

10299 *Julius Caesar*
There is a tide in the affairs of men,
Which, taken at the flood, leads on to fortune;
Omitted, all the voyage of their life
Is bound in shallows and in miseries.

10300 *Julius Caesar*
The deep of night is crept upon our talk,
And nature must obey necessity.

10301 *King John*
Well, whiles I am a beggar, I will rail,
And say there is no sin, but to be rich;
And, being rich, my virtue then shall be,
To say there is no vice, but beggary.

10302 *King John*
Old Time the clock-setter.

10303 *King John*
Bell, book, and candle shall not drive me back,
When gold and silver becks me to come on.

10304 *King John*
Life is as tedious as a twice-told tale,
Vexing the dull ear of a drowsy man.

10305 *King John*
To gild refinèd gold, to paint the lily,
To throw a perfume on the violet,
To smooth the ice, or add another hue
Unto the rainbow, or with taper light
To seek the beauteous eye of heaven to garnish,
Is wasteful and ridiculous excess.

10306 *King John*
How oft the sight of means to do ill deeds
Make ill deeds done!

10307 *King John*
Heaven take my soul, and England keep my
bones!

10308 *King John*
I beg cold comfort; and you are so strait
And so ingrateful, you deny me that.

10309 *King Lear*
Mend your speech a little,
Lest it may mar your fortunes.

10310 *King Lear*
Nothing will come of nothing: speak again.

10311 *King Lear*
Come not between the dragon and his wrath.

10312 *King Lear*
Love is not love
When it is mingled with regards that stand
Aloof from the entire point.

10313 *King Lear*
This is the excellent foppery of the world, that,
when we are sick in fortune - often the surfeit of
our own behaviour - we make guilty of our own
disasters the sun, the moon, and the stars.

10314 *King Lear*
Have more than thou showest,
Speak less than thou knowest,
Lend less than thou owest.

10315 *King Lear*
Ingratitude, thou marble-hearted fiend,
More hideous, when thou show'st thee in a
child,
Than the sea-monster.

10316 *King Lear*
How sharper than a serpent's tooth it is
To have a thankless child!

10317 *King Lear*
O! let me not be mad, not mad, sweet heaven;
Keep me in temper; I would not be mad!

10318 *King Lear*
Thou whoreson zed! thou unnecessary letter!

10319 *King Lear*
Down, thou climbing sorrow!
Thy element's below.

10320 *King Lear*
O reason not the need! Our basest beggars
Are in the poorest thing superfluous.
Allow not nature more than nature needs,
Man's life is cheap as beast's.

10321 *King Lear*
Blow, winds, and crack your cheeks! rage! blow!
You cataracts and hurricanoes, spout
Till you have drenched our steeples, drowned
the cocks!

10322 *King Lear*
There was never yet fair woman but she made
mouths in a glass.

10323 *King Lear*
The art of our necessities is strange,
That can make vile things precious.

10324 *King Lear*
O! that way madness lies; let me shun that.

10325 *King Lear*
I have no way, and therefore want no eyes;
I stumbled when I saw.

10326 *King Lear*
The worst is not,
So long as we can say, 'This is the worst.'

10327 *King Lear*
As flies to wanton boys, are we to the gods;
They kill us for their sport.

10328 *King Lear*
Every inch a king.

10329 *King Lear*
The wren goes to't, and the small gilded fly
Does lecher in my sight.
Let copulation thrive.

10330 *King Lear*
Get thee glass eyes;
And, like a scurvy politician, seem
To see the things thou dost not.

10331 *King Lear*
When we are born we cry that we are come
To this great stage of fools.

10332 *King Lear*
Men must endure
Their going hence, even as their coming hither:
Ripeness is all.

10333 *King Lear*
The gods are just, and of our pleasant vices
Make instruments to plague us.

10334 *King Lear*
The wheel is come full circle.

10335 *Love's Labour's Lost*
At Christmas I no more desire a rose
Than wish a snow in May's new-fangled mirth;
But like of each thing that in season grows.

10336 *Love's Labour's Lost*
He hath not fed of the dainties that are bred in a
book; he hath not eat paper, as it were; he hath
not drunk ink.

10337 *Love's Labour's Lost*
He draweth out the thread of his verbosity finer
than the staple of his argument.

10338 *Love's Labour's Lost*
A jest's prosperity lies in the ear
Of him that hears it, never in the tongue
Of him that makes it.

10339 *Macbeth*
FIRST WITCH: When shall we three meet again
In thunder, lightning, or in rain?
SECOND WITCH: When the hurly-burly's done,
When the battle's lost and won.

10340 *Macbeth*
So foul and fair a day I have not seen.

10341 *Macbeth*
Were such things here as we do speak about?
Or have we eaten on the insane root
That takes the reason prisoner?

10342 *Macbeth*
This supernatural soliciting
Cannot be ill, cannot be good.

10343 *Macbeth*
Come what come may,
Time and the hour runs through the roughest
day.

10344 *Macbeth*
Nothing in his life
Became him like the leaving it: he died
As one that had been studied in his death
To throw away the dearest thing he owed
As 'twere a careless trifle.

10345 *Macbeth*
Yet I do fear thy nature;
It is too full o' the milk of human kindness
To catch the nearest way.

10346 *Macbeth*
The raven himself is hoarse
That croaks the fatal entrance of Duncan
Under my battlements.

10347 *Macbeth*
If it were done when 'tis done, then 'twere well
It were done quickly.

10348 *Macbeth*
I have no spur
To prick the sides of my intent, but only
Vaulting ambition, which o'erleaps itself,
And falls on the other.

10349 *Macbeth*
I dare do all that may become a man;
Who dares do more is none.

10350 *Macbeth*
False face must hide what the false heart doth
know.

10351 *Macbeth*
Is this a dagger which I see before me,
The handle toward my hand?

10352 *Macbeth*
The attempt and not the deed,
Confounds us.

10353 *Macbeth*
Methought I heard a voice cry, 'Sleep no more!
Macbeth does murder sleep.'

10354 *Macbeth*
The sleeping and the dead
Are but as pictures; 'tis the eye of childhood
That fears a painted devil.

10355 *Macbeth*
A little water clears us of this deed.

10356 *Macbeth*
The wine of life is drawn, and the mere lees
Is left this vault to brag of.

10357 *Macbeth*
Come, seeling night,
Scarf up the tender eye of pitiful day,
And with thy bloody and invisible hand,
Cancel and tear to pieces that great bond
Which keeps me pale!

10358 *Macbeth*
... Now I am cabined, cribbed, confined, bound
in
To saucy doubts and fears.

10359 *Macbeth*
Stand not upon the order of your going.

10360 *Macbeth*
I am in blood
Stepped in so far that, should I wade no more,
Returning were as tedious as go o'er.

10361 *Macbeth*
Double, double toil and trouble;
Fire burn and cauldron bubble.

10362 *Macbeth*
Eye of newt, and toe of frog,
Wool of bat, and tongue of dog,
Adder's fork, and blind-worm's sting,
Lizard's leg, and howlet's wing,
For a charm of powerful trouble,
Like a hell-broth boil and bubble.

10363 *Macbeth*
By the pricking of my thumbs,
Something wicked this way comes.

10364 *Macbeth*
Be bloody, bold, and resolute; laugh to scorn
The power of man, for none of woman born
Shall harm Macbeth.

10365 *Macbeth*
When our actions do not,
Our fears do make us traitors.

10366 *Macbeth*
Out, damned spot! out, I say!

10367 *Macbeth*
Yet who would have thought the old man to
have had so much blood in him?

10368 *Macbeth*
Here's the smell of the blood still: all the
perfumes of Arabia will not sweeten this little
hand.

10369 *Macbeth*
What's done cannot be undone.

10370 *Macbeth*
Foul whisperings are abroad. Unnatural deeds
Do breed unnatural troubles; infected minds
To their deaf pillows will discharge their secrets.

10371 *Macbeth*
I have lived long enough: my way of life
Is fall'n into the sear, the yellow leaf;
And that which should accompany old age,
As honour, love, obedience, troops of friends,
I must not look to have.

10372 *Macbeth*
I have supped full with horrors;
Direness, familiar to my slaughterous thoughts,
Cannot once start me.

10373 *Macbeth*
To-morrow, and to-morrow, and to-morrow,
Creeps in this petty pace from day to day,
To the last syllable of recorded time;
And all our yesterdays have lighted fools
The way to dusty death. Out, out, brief candle!
Life's but a walking shadow, a poor player,
That struts and frets his hour upon the stage
And then is heard no more; it is a tale
Told by an idiot, full of sound and fury,
Signifying nothing.

10374 *Macbeth*
I 'gin to be aweary of the sun,
And wish the estate o' the world were now
undone.

10375 *Measure for Measure*
We must not make a scarecrow of the law,
Setting it up to fear the birds of prey,
And let it keep one shape, till custom make it
Their perch and not their terror.

10376 *Measure for Measure*
Man, proud man,
Drest in a little brief authority,
Most ignorant of what he's most assured,
His glassy essence, like an angry ape,
Plays such fantastic tricks before high heaven,
As make the angels weep.

10377 *Measure for Measure*
That in the captain's but a choleric word,
Which in the soldier is flat blasphemy.

10378 *Measure for Measure*
Is this her fault or mine?
The tempter or the tempted, who sins most?

10379 *Measure for Measure*
The miserable have no other medicine
But only hope:
I have hope to live and am prepared to die.

10380 *Measure for Measure*
Thou hast nor youth nor age;
But, as it were, an after-dinner's sleep,
Dreaming on both.

10381 *Measure for Measure*
Ay, but to die, and go we know not where;
To lie in cold obstruction and to rot.

10382 *Measure for Measure*
The hand that hath made you fair hath made
you good.

10383 *Measure for Measure*
I am a kind of burr; I shall stick.

10384 *Measure for Measure*
Haste still pays haste, and leisure answers
leisure;
Like doth quit like, and Measure still for
Measure.

10385 *Measure for Measure*
They say best men are moulded out of faults,
And, for the most, become much more the
better
For being a little bad.

10386 *The Merchant of Venice*
God made him, and therefore let him pass for a
man.

10387 *The Merchant of Venice*
They are as sick that surfeit with too much, as
they that starve with nothing. It is no mean
happiness, therefore, to be seated in the mean.

10388 *The Merchant of Venice*
If to do were as easy as to know what were good
to do, chapels had been churches, and poor
men's cottages princes' palaces.

10389 *The Merchant of Venice*
There is not one among them but I dote on his
very absence.

10390 *The Merchant of Venice*
How like a fawning publican he looks!

10391 *The Merchant of Venice*
The devil can cite Scripture for his purpose.
An evil soul, producing holy witness,
Is like a villain with a smiling cheek,
A goodly apple rotten at the heart.

10392 *The Merchant of Venice*
You call me misbeliever, cut-throat dog,
And spit upon my Jewish gabardine,
And all for use of that which is mine own.

10393 *The Merchant of Venice*
It is a wise father that knows his own child.

10394 *The Merchant of Venice*
Truth will come to light; murder cannot be hid
long.

10395 *The Merchant of Venice*
Love is blind, and lovers cannot see
The pretty follies that themselves commit.

10396 *The Merchant of Venice*
My daughter! O my ducats! O my daughter!
Fled with a Christian! O my Christian ducats!
Justice! the law! my ducats, and my daughter!

10397 *The Merchant of Venice*
I will not choose what many men desire,
Because I will not jump with common spirits
And rank me with the barbarous multitude.

10398 *The Merchant of Venice*
Let him look to his bond.

10399 *The Merchant of Venice*
Hath not a Jew eyes? hath not a Jew hands,
organs, dimensions, senses, affections,
passions? fed with the same food, hurt with the
same weapons, subject to the same diseases,
healed by the same means, warmed and cooled
by the same winter and summer, as a Christian
is? If you prick us, do we not bleed? if you tickle
us, do we not laugh? if you poison us, do we not
die? and if you wrong us, shall we not revenge?
If we are like you in the rest, we will resemble
you in that.

10400 *The Merchant of Venice*
Tell me, where is fancy bred,
Or in the heart, or in the head?
How begot, how nourishèd ...?

It is engendered in the eyes,
With gazing fed; and fancy dies
In the cradle where it lies.

10401 *The Merchant of Venice*
There is no vice so simple but assumes
Some mark of virtue on his outward parts.

10402 *The Merchant of Venice*
The quality of mercy is not strained,
It droppeth as the gentle rain from heaven
Upon the place beneath: it is twice blessed;
It blesseth him that gives and him that takes.

10403 *The Merchant of Venice*
A Daniel come to judgement! yea, a Daniel!

10404 *The Merchant of Venice*
How sweet the moonlight sleeps upon this
bank!
Here will we sit, and let the sounds of music
Creep in our ears.

10405 *The Merchant of Venice*
I am never merry when I hear sweet music.

10406 *The Merchant of Venice*
The man that hath no music in himself,
Nor is not moved with concord of sweet sounds,
Is fit for treasons, stratagems, and spoils.

10407 *The Merchant of Venice*
How far that little candle throws his beams!
So shines a good deed in a naughty world.

10408 *The Merchant of Venice*
This night methinks is but the daylight sick.

10409 *The Merchant of Venice*
A light wife doth make a heavy husband.

10410 *The Merry Wives of Windsor*
Why, then the world's mine oyster,
Which I with sword will open.

10411 *The Merry Wives of Windsor*
O, what a world of vile ill-favoured faults
Looks handsome in three hundred pounds a
year!

10412 *The Merry Wives of Windsor*
There is divinity in odd numbers, either in
nativity, chance or death.

10413 *A Midsummer Night's Dream*
For aught that ever I could read,
Could ever hear by tale or history,
The course of true love never did run smooth.

10414 *A Midsummer Night's Dream*
Love looks not with the eyes, but with the mind,
And therefore is winged Cupid painted blind.

10415 *A Midsummer Night's Dream*
I must go seek some dew-drops here,
And hang a pearl in every cowslip's ear.

10416 *A Midsummer Night's Dream*
Ill met by moonlight, proud Titania.

10417 *A Midsummer Night's Dream*
I know a bank whereon the wild thyme blows,
Where oxlips and the nodding violet grows
Quite over-canopied with luscious woodbine.

10418 *A Midsummer Night's Dream*
A lion among ladies, is a most dreadful thing;
for there is not a more fearful wild-fowl than
your lion living.

10419 *A Midsummer Night's Dream*
What angel wakes me from my flowery bed?

10420 *A Midsummer Night's Dream*
Lord, what fools these mortals be!

10421 *A Midsummer Night's Dream*
The lunatic, the lover, and the poet,
Are of imagination all compact.

10422 *A Midsummer Night's Dream*
And, as imagination bodies forth
The forms of things unknown, the poet's pen
Turns them to shapes, and gives to airy nothing
A local habitation and a name.

10423 *A Midsummer Night's Dream*
If we shadows have offended,
Think but this, and all is mended,
That you have but slumbered here
While these visions did appear.

10424 *Othello*
Reputation is an idle and most false imposition;
oft got without merit, and lost without
deserving.

10425 *Othello*
There are many events in the womb of time
which will be delivered.

10426 *Othello*
Do not put me to't,
For I am nothing if not critical.

10427 *Othello*
To suckle fools and chronicle small beer.

10428 *Othello*
'Tis pride that pulls the country down.

10429 *Othello*
O! I have lost my reputation. I have lost the
immortal part of myself, and what remains is
bestial.

10430 *Othello*
Who steals my purse steals trash; 'tis something,
nothing;
'Twas mine, 'tis his, and has been slave to
thousands;
But he that filches from me my good name
Robs me of that which not enriches him,
And makes me poor indeed.

10431 *Othello*
O! beware, my lord, of jealousy;
It is the green-eyed monster which doth mock
The meat it feeds on.

10432 *Othello*
O curse of marriage!
That we can call these delicate creatures ours,
And not their appetites. I had rather be a toad,
And live upon the vapour of a dungeon,
Than keep a corner in the thing I love
For others' uses.

10433 *Othello*
Trifles light as air
Are to the jealous confirmations strong
As proofs of holy writ.

10434 *Othello*
Farewell the neighing steed and the shrill
trump,
The spirit-stirring drum, the ear-piercing fife,
The royal banner, and all quality,
Pride, pomp, and circumstance of glorious war!

10435 *Othello*
Unkindness may do much;
And his unkindness may defeat my life,
But never taint my love.

10436 *Othello*
Let husbands know
Their wives have sense like them. They see, and
smell,
And have their palates both for sweet and sour,
As husbands have.

10437 *Othello*
Put out the light, and then put out the light:
If I quench thee, thou flaming minister,
I can again thy former light restore,
Should I repent me; but once put out thy light,
Thou cunning'st pattern of excelling nature,
I know not where is that Promethean heat
That can thy light relume.

10438 *Othello*
Speak of me as I am; nothing extenuate,
Nor set down aught in malice: then, must you
speak
Of one that loved not wisely but too well;
Of one not easily jealous, but being wrought,
Perplexed in the extreme; of one whose hand,
Like the base Indian, threw a pearl away
Richer than all his tribe.

10439 *Pericles*
Few love to hear the sins they love to act.

10440 *Pericles*
O you gods!
Why do you make us love your goodly gifts,
And snatch them straight away?

10441 *Pericles*
This world to me is but a ceaseless storm
Whirring me from my friends.

10442 *Richard II*
The purest treasure mortal times afford
Is spotless reputation; that away,
Men are but gilded loam or painted clay.

10443 *Richard II*
Take honour from me, and my life is done.

10444 *Richard II*
Things sweet to taste prove in digestion sour.

10445 *Richard II*
Teach thy necessity to reason thus;
There is no virtue like necessity.

10446 *Richard II*
This royal throne of kings, this sceptered isle,
This earth of majesty, this seat of Mars,
This other Eden, demi-paradise,
This fortress built by Nature for herself
Against infection and the hand of war,
This happy breed of men, this little world,
This precious stone set in the silver sea,
Which serves it in the office of a wall,
Or as a moat defensive to a house,
Against the envy of less happier lands,
This blessèd plot, this earth, this realm, this
England,
This nurse, this teeming womb of royal kings,
Feared by their breed and famous by their birth.

10447 *Richard II*
Grace me no grace, nor uncle me no uncle.

10448 *Richard II*
Not all the water in the rough rude sea
Can wash the balm from an anointed king;
The breath of worldly men cannot depose
The deputy elected by the Lord.

10449 *Richard II*
The worst is death, and death will have his day.

10450 *Richard II*
For God's sake, let us sit upon the ground
And tell sad stories of the death of kings:
How some have been deposed; some slain in
war;
Some haunted by the ghosts they have deposed;
Some poisoned by their wives, some sleeping
killed;
All murdered: for within the hollow crown
That rounds the mortal temples of a king
Keeps Death his court.

10451 *Richard II*
The purple testament of bleeding war.

10452 *Richard II*
What must the king do now? Must he submit?
The king shall do it; must he be deposed?
The king shall be contented: must he lose
The name of king? o' God's name, let it go.

10453 *Richard II*
You may my glories and my state depose,
But not my griefs; still am I king of those.

10454 *Richard II*
How sour sweet music is,
When time is broke, and no proportion kept!
So is it in the music of men's lives.

10455 *Richard II*
I wasted time, and now doth time waste me.

10456 *Richard II*
Mount, mount, my soul! thy seat is up on high;
Whilst my gross flesh sinks downwards, here to
die.

10457 *Richard III*
Now is the winter of our discontent
Made glorious summer by this sun of York.

10458 *Richard III*
Sent before my time
Into this breathing world, scarce half made up.

10459 *Richard III*
And therefore, since I cannot prove a lover,
To entertain these fair well-spoken days,
I am determinèd to prove a villain,
And hate the idle pleasures of these days.

10460 *Richard III*
No beast so fierce but knows some touch of pity.

10461 *Richard III*
Lord, Lord! methought what pain it was to
drown:
What dreadful noise of water in mine ears!
What sights of ugly death within mine eyes!

10462 *Richard III*
Woe to the land that's governed by a child!

10463 *Richard III*
So wise so young, they say, do never live long.

10464 *Richard III*
I am not in the giving vein to-day.

10465 *Richard III*
Conscience is but a word that cowards use,
Devised at first to keep the strong in awe.

10466 *Richard III*
A horse! a horse! my kingdom for a horse!

10467 *Romeo and Juliet*
Adversity's sweet milk, philosophy.

10468 *Romeo and Juliet*
From forth the fatal loins of these two foes
A pair of star-crossed lovers take their life.

10469 *Romeo and Juliet*
You and I are past our dancing days.

10470 *Romeo and Juliet*
O! she doth teach the torches to burn bright.
It seems she hangs upon the cheek of night
Like a rich jewel in an Ethiop's ear;
Beauty too rich for use, for earth too dear.

10471 *Romeo and Juliet*
My only love sprung from my only hate!
Too early seen unknown, and known too late!

10472 *Romeo and Juliet*
He jests at scars, that never felt a wound.
But, soft! what light through yonder window
breaks?
It is the east, and Juliet is the sun.

10473 *Romeo and Juliet*
O Romeo, Romeo! wherefore art thou Romeo?

10474 *Romeo and Juliet*
What's in a name? that which we call a rose
By any other name would smell as sweet.

10475 *Romeo and Juliet*
What love can do that dares love attempt.

10476 *Romeo and Juliet*
O! swear not by the moon, the inconstant
moon,
That monthly changes in her circled orb,
Lest that thy love prove likewise variable.

10477 *Romeo and Juliet*
My bounty is as boundless as the sea,
My love as deep; the more I give to thee,
The more I have, for both are infinite.

10478 *Romeo and Juliet*
Good-night, good-night! parting is such sweet
sorrow
That I shall say good-night till it be morrow.

10479 *Romeo and Juliet*
A plague o' both your houses!

10480 *Romeo and Juliet*
Thank me no thankings, nor proud me no
prouds.

10481 *Romeo and Juliet*
Death lies on her like an untimely frost
Upon the sweetest flower of all the field.

10482 *The Taming of the Shrew*
There's a small choice in rotten apples.

10483 *The Taming of the Shrew*
Nothing comes amiss, so money comes withal.

10484 *The Taming of the Shrew*
O! this learning, what a thing it is.

10485 *The Taming of the Shrew*
I am ashamed that women are so simple
To offer war where they should kneel for peace.

10486 *The Tempest*
Full fathom five thy father lies;
Of his bones are coral made:
Those are pearls that were his eyes:
Nothing of him that doth fade,
But doth suffer a sea-change
Into something rich and strange.

10487 *The Tempest*
Misery acquaints a man with strange
bedfellows.

10488 *The Tempest*
He that dies pays all debts.

10489 *The Tempest*
We are such stuff
As dreams are made on, and our little life
Is rounded with a sleep.

10490 *The Tempest*
But this rough magic
I here abjure ...
...I'll break my staff,
Bury it certain fathoms in the earth,
And, deeper than did ever plummet sound,
I'll drown my book.

10491 *The Tempest*
How beauteous mankind is! O brave new world,
That has such people in't.

10492 *Timon of Athens*
Every man has his fault, and honesty is his.

10493 *Timon of Athens*
'Tis not enough to help the feeble up,
But to support him after.

10494 *Timon of Athens*
I wonder men dare trust themselves with men.

10495 *Timon of Athens*
Like madness is the glory of this life.

10496 *Timon of Athens*
Men shut their doors against a setting sun.

10497 *Timon of Athens*
Nothing emboldens sin so much as mercy.

10498 *Troilus and Cressida*
Modest doubt is call'd
The beacon of the wise.

10499 *Troilus and Cressida*
Women are angels, wooing:
Things won are done; joy's soul lies in the
doing;
That she beloved knows nought that knows not
this:
Men prize the thing ungained more than it is.

10500 *Troilus and Cressida*
O! when degree is shaked,
Which is the ladder to all high designs,
The enterprise is sick.

10501 *Troilus and Cressida*
To be wise, and love,
Exceeds man's might.

10502 *Troilus and Cressida*
Time hath, my lord, a wallet at his back,
Wherein he puts alms for oblivion,
A great-sized monster of ingratitudes.

10503 *Troilus and Cressida*
Perseverance, dear my lord,
Keeps honour bright: to have done, is to hang
Quite out of fashion, like a rusty mail
In monumental mockery.

10504 *Troilus and Cressida*
One touch of nature makes the whole world kin.

10505 *Troilus and Cressida*
The end crowns all,
And that old common arbitrator, Time,
Will one day end it.

10506 *Troilus and Cressida*
Lechery, lechery; still, wars and lechery: nothing
else holds fashion.

10507 *Troilus and Cressida*
Hector is dead; there is no more to say.

10508 *Twelfth Night*
If music be the food of love, play on;
Give me excess of it, that, surfeiting,
The appetite may sicken, and so die.

10509 *Twelfth Night*
Is it a world to hide virtues in?

10510 *Twelfth Night*
Many a good hanging prevents a bad marriage.

10511 *Twelfth Night*
Not to be a-bed after midnight is to be up betimes.

10512 *Twelfth Night*
What is love? 'tis not hereafter;
Present mirth hath present laughter;
What's to come is still unsure:
In delay there lies no plenty;
Then come kiss me, sweet and twenty,
Youth's a stuff will not endure.

10513 *Twelfth Night*
Dost thou think, because thou art virtuous, there shall be no more cakes and ale?

10514 *Twelfth Night*
My purpose is, indeed, a horse of that colour.

10515 *Twelfth Night*
Let thy love be younger than thyself,
Or thy affection cannot hold the bent.

10516 *Twelfth Night*
She never told her love,
But let concealment, like a worm i' the bud,
Feed on her damask cheek: she pined in thought;
And with a green and yellow melancholy,
She sat like patience on a monument,
Smiling at grief.

10517 *Twelfth Night*
Some men are born great, some achieve greatness, and some have greatness thrust upon them.

10518 *Twelfth Night*
Love sought is good, but giv'n unsought is better.

10519 *Twelfth Night*
Go, hang yourselves all! you are idle shallow things: I am not of your element.

10520 *Twelfth Night*
If this were played upon a stage now, I could condemn it as an improbable fiction.

10521 *Twelfth Night*
Still you keep o' the windy side of the law.

10522 *Twelfth Night*
I hate ingratitude more in a man
Than lying, vainness, babbling drunkenness,
Or any taint of vice whose strong corruption
Inhabits our frail blood.

10523 *The Two Gentlemen of Verona*
Home-keeping youth have ever homely wits.

10524 *The Two Gentlemen of Verona*
He was more than over shoes in love.

10525 *The Two Gentlemen of Verona*
I have no other but a woman's reason:
I think him so, because I think him so.

10526 *The Two Gentlemen of Verona*
O heaven! were man
But constant, he were perfect.

10527 *The Winter's Tale*
It is a heretic that makes the fire,
Not she which burns in 't.

10528 *The Winter's Tale*
I am a feather for each wind that blows.

10529 *The Winter's Tale*
What's gone and what's past help
Should be past grief.

10530 *The Winter's Tale*
A snapper-up of unconsidered trifles.

10531 *The Winter's Tale*
She is
The queen of curds and cream.

10532 *The Winter's Tale*
This dream of mine,
Being now awake, I'll queen it no inch further,
But milk my ewes and weep.

10533 *The Winter's Tale*
Though I am not naturally honest, I am so sometimes by chance.

10534 *The Winter's Tale (stage direction)*
Exit, pursued by a bear.

10535 *The Passionate Pilgrim (attribution doubtful)*
Crabbed age and youth cannot live together:
Youth is full of pleasance, age is full of care.

10536 *The Passionate Pilgrim (attribution doubtful)*
Age, I do abhor thee, youth, I do adore thee.

10537 *The Rape of Lucrece*
Beauty itself doth of itself persuade
The eyes of men without an orator.

10538 *The Rape of Lucrece*
Who buys a minute's mirth to wail a week?
Or sells eternity to get a toy?
For one sweet grape who will the vine destroy?

10539 *The Rape of Lucrece*
Time's glory is to calm contending kings,
To unmask falsehood, and bring truth to light.

10540 *Sonnet 2*
When forty winters shall besiege thy brow,
And dig deep trenches in thy beauty's field.

10541 *Sonnet 3*
Thou art thy mother's glass, and she in thee
Calls back the lovely April of her prime.

10542 *Sonnet 8*
Music to hear, why hear'st thou music sadly?
Sweets with sweets war not, joy delights in joy:
Why lov'st thou that which thou receiv'st not
gladly,
Or else receiv'st with pleasure thine annoy?
If the true concord of well-tunèd sounds,
By unions married, do offend thine ear,
They do but sweetly chide thee.

10543 *Sonnet 12*
When lofty trees I see barren of leaves,
Which erst from heat did canopy the herd,
And summer's green all girded up in sheaves,
Borne on the bier with white and bristly beard.

10544 *Sonnet 17*
If I could write the beauty of your eyes
And in fresh numbers number all your graces,
The age to come would say, 'This poet lies.'

10545 *Sonnet 18*
Shall I compare thee to a summer's day?
Thou art more lovely and more temperate:
Rough winds do shake the darling buds of May,
And summer's lease hath all too short a date.

10546 *Sonnet 29*
When in disgrace with fortune and men's eyes
I all alone beweep my outcast state,
And trouble deaf heaven with my bootless cries,
And look upon myself and curse my fate.

10547 *Sonnet 29*
Haply I think on thee - and then my state,
Like to the lark at break of day arising
From sullen earth, sings hymns at heaven's gate;
For thy sweet love remembered such wealth
brings
That then I scorn to change my state with kings.

10548 *Sonnet 30*
When to the sessions of sweet silent thought
I summon up remembrance of things past,
I sigh the lack of many a thing I sought,
And with old woes new wail my dear times'
waste.

10549 *Sonnet 55*
Not marble, nor the gilded monuments
Of princes, shall outlive this powerful rhyme;
But you shall shine more bright in these
contents
Than unswept stone, besmeared with sluttish
time.

10550 *Sonnet 57*
So true a fool is love that in your will,
Though you do anything, he thinks no ill.

10551 *Sonnet 60*
Like as the waves make towards the pebbled
shore,
So do our minutes hasten to their end.

10552 *Sonnet 64*
When I have seen the hungry ocean gain
Advantage on the kingdom of the shore.

10553 *Sonnet 73*
That time of year thou mayst in me behold
When yellow leaves, or none, or few, do hang
Upon those boughs which shake against the
cold.

10554 *Sonnet 87*
Farewell! thou art too dear for my possessing,
And like enough thou know'st thy estimate:
The charter of thy worth gives thee releasing;
My bonds in thee are all determinate.

10555 *Sonnet 87*
Thus have I had thee, as a dream doth flatter,
In sleep a king, but, waking, no such matter.

10556 *Sonnet 94*
For sweetest things turn sourest by their deeds;
Lilies that fester smell far worse than weeds.

10557 *Sonnet 97*
How like a winter hath my absence been
From thee, the pleasure of the fleeting year!
What freezings have I felt, what dark days seen!
What old December's bareness everywhere!

10558 *Sonnet 106*
When in the chronicle of wasted time
I see descriptions of the fairest wights.

10559 *Sonnet 106*
For we, which now behold these present days,
Have eyes to wonder, but lack tongues to praise.

10560 *Sonnet 116*
Let me not to the marriage of true minds
Admit impediments. Love is not love
Which alters when it alteration finds,
Or bends with the remover to remove:
O, no! it is an ever-fixèd mark,
That looks on tempests and is never shaken.

10561 *Sonnet 116*
Love alters not with his brief hours and weeks,
But bears it out even to the edge of doom.
If this be error, and upon me proved,
I never writ, nor no man ever loved.

10562 *Sonnet 129*
The expense of spirit in a waste of shame
Is lust in action; and till action, lust
Is perjured, murderous, bloody, full of blame,
Savage, extreme, rude, cruel, not to trust;
Enjoyed no sooner but despisèd straight.

10563 *Sonnet 130*
And yet, by heaven, I think my love as rare
As any she belied with false compare.

10564 *Sonnet 138*
When my love swears that she is made of truth,
I do believe her, though I know she lies.

10565 *Sonnet 144*
Two loves I have of comfort and despair,
Which like two spirits do suggest me still:
The better angel is a man right fair,
The worser spirit a woman, coloured ill.

10566 *Venus and Adonis*
Love is a spirit all compact of fire,
Not gross to sink, but light, and will aspire.

10567 *Venus and Adonis*
Love comforteth like sunshine after rain.

10568 *(epitaph on his tomb, probably self-composed)*
Good friend, for Jesu's sake forbear
To dig the dust enclosed here.
Blest be the man that spares these stones,
And curst be he that moves my bones.

SHAMGAR Judge Meir
10569
The complete truth is not the prerogative of the human judge.

SHANKLY Bill 1914-1981
10570
Some people think football is a matter of life and death ... I can assure them it is much more serious than that.

SHARPE Tom 1928-
10571 *Indecent Exposure*
The South African police would leave no stone unturned to see that nothing disturbed the even terror of their lives.

SHAW George Bernard 1856-1950
10572 *(attributed)*
England and America are two countries divided by a common language.

10573 *Annajanska*
All great truths begin as blasphemies.

10574 *The Apple Cart*
One man that has a mind and knows it can always beat ten men who haven't and don't.

10575 *The Apple Cart*
I never resist temptation, because I have found that things that are bad for me do not tempt me.

10576 *Arms and the Man*
You're not a man, you're a machine.

10577
The art of government is the organization of idolatry.

10578
I believe in the discipline of silence and could talk for hours about it.

10579
The best brought-up children are those who have seen their parents as they are. Hypocrisy is not the parents' first duty.

10580
Beware of the man whose God is in the skies.

10581 *Caesar and Cleopatra*
When a stupid man is doing something he is ashamed of, he always declares that it is his duty.

10582 *Candida*
We have no more right to consume happiness without producing it than to consume wealth without producing it.

10583 *Candida*
It is easy - terribly easy - to shake a man's faith in himself. To take advantage of that to break a man's spirit is devil's work.

10584 *Candida*
I'm only a beer teetotaller, not a champagne teetotaller.

10585
Christianity might be a good thing if anyone ever tried it.

10586
[Dancing is] a perpendicular expression of a horizontal desire.

10587 *The Devil's Disciple*
The worst sin towards our fellow creatures is not to hate them, but to be indifferent to them: that's the essence of inhumanity.

10588 *The Devil's Disciple*
Martyrdom ... the only way in which a man can become famous without ability.

10589 *The Devil's Disciple*
I never expect a soldier to think.

10590 *The Devil's Disciple*
SWINDON: What will history say?
BURGOYNE: History, sir, will tell lies as usual.

10591 *The Devil's Disciple*
The British soldier can stand up to anything except the British War Office.

10592
Do not do unto others as you would that they should do unto you. Their tastes may not be the same.

10593 *The Doctor's Dilemma*
All professions are conspiracies against the laity.

10594
You don't learn to hold your own by standing on guard, but by attacking, and getting well hammered yourself.

10595 *Everybody's Political What's What?*
A government which robs Peter to pay Paul can always depend on the support of Paul.

10596
Everything happens to everybody sooner or later if there is time enough.

10597 *Fanny's First Play*
It's all that the young can do for the old, to shock them and keep them up to date.

10598
Fashions, after all, are only induced epidemics.

10599 *Getting Married*
What God hath joined together no man ever shall put asunder: God will take care of that.

10600 *Getting Married 'The Right to Motherhood'*
The one point on which all women are in furious secret rebellion against the existing law is the saddling of the right to a child with the obligation to become the servant of a man.

10601
A great devotee of the gospel of getting on.

10602
Hatred is the coward's revenge for being intimidated.

10603 *John Bull's Other Island*
An Irishman's heart is nothing but his imagination.

10604 *John Bull's Other Island*
What really flatters a man is that you think him worth flattering.

10605 *John Bull's Other Island*
There are only two qualities in the world: efficiency and inefficiency, and only two sorts of people: the efficient and the inefficient.

10606
She had lost the art of conversation, but not, unfortunately, the power of speech.

10607
Love is a gross exaggeration of the difference between one person and everybody else.

10608 *Major Barbara*
I am a Millionaire. That is my religion.

10609 *Major Barbara*
Wot prawce Selvytion nah?

10610 *Major Barbara*
Alcohol is a very necessary article ... It enables Parliament to do things at eleven at night that no sane person would do at eleven in the morning.

10611 *Major Barbara*
He knows nothing; and he thinks he knows everything. That points clearly to a political career.

10612 *Major Barbara*
Nothing is ever done in this world until men are prepared to kill one another if it is not done.

10613 *Man and Superman*
But a lifetime of happiness! No man alive could bear it: it would be hell on earth.

10614 *Man and Superman*
An Englishman thinks he is moral when he is only uncomfortable.

10615 *Man and Superman*
When the military man approaches, the world locks up its spoons and packs off its womankind.

10616 *Man and Superman*
What is virtue but the Trade Unionism of the married?

10617 *Man and Superman*
It is a woman's business to get married as soon as possible, and a man's to keep unmarried as long as he can.

10618 *Man and Superman*
There are two tragedies in life. One is to lose your heart's desire. The other is to gain it.

10619 *Man and Superman 'Maxims: Democracy'*
Democracy substitutes election by the incompetent many for appointment by the corrupt few.

10620 *Man and Superman 'Maxims: Education'*
He who can, does. He who cannot, teaches.

10621 *Man and Superman 'Maxims: How to Beat Children'*
If you strike a child take care that you strike it in anger, even at the risk of maiming it for life. A blow in cold blood neither can nor should be forgiven.

10622 *Man and Superman 'Maxims: Liberty and Equality'*
Liberty means responsibility. That is why most men dread it.

10623 *Man and Superman 'Maxims: Marriage'*
Marriage is popular because it combines the maximum of temptation with the maximum of opportunity.

10624 *Man and Superman 'Maxims: Reason'*
The reasonable man adapts himself to the world: the unreasonable one persists in trying to adapt the world to himself. Therefore all progress depends on the unreasonable man.

10625 *Man and Superman 'Maxims: Stray Sayings'*
Every man over forty is a scoundrel.

10626 *Man and Superman 'Maxims: Stray Sayings'*
Youth, which is forgiven everything, forgives itself nothing: age, which forgives itself everything, is forgiven nothing.

10627 *Man and Superman 'Maxims: Stray Sayings'*
Take care to get what you like or you will be forced to like what you get.

10628 *Man and Superman 'The Revolutionist's Handbook'*
Revolutions have never lightened the burden of tyranny: they have only shifted it to another shoulder.

10629
Men are wise in proportion, not to their experience, but to their capacity for experience.

10630
My method is to take the utmost trouble to find the right thing to say, and then to say it with the utmost levity.

10631 *Back to Methuselah*
I enjoy convalescence. It is the part that makes illness worthwhile.

10632 *Misalliance*
Anarchism is a game at which the police can beat you.

10633
Modern poverty is not the poverty that was blest in the Sermon on the Mount.

10634
Morality is not respectability.

10635
Never believe anything a writer tells you about himself. A man comes to believe in the end the lies he tells himself about himself.

10636 *O'Flaherty V.C.*
You'll never have a quiet world till you knock the patriotism out of the human race.

10637
My only policy is to profess evil and do good.

10638
My opportunities were still there; nay, they multiplied tenfold; but the strength and youth to cope with them began to fail, and to need eking out with the shifty cunning of experience.

10639
A perpetual holiday is a good working definition of hell.

10640 *The Philanderer*
The fickleness of the women I love is only equalled by the infernal constancy of the women who love me.

10641
The philosopher is Nature's pilot - and there you have our difference; to be in hell is to drift: to be in heaven is to steer.

10642 *Plays Pleasant and Unpleasant*
There is only one religion, though there are a hundred versions of it.

10643 *Pygmalion*
PICKERING: Have you no morals, man?
DOOLITTLE: Can't afford them, Governor.

10644
I often quote myself. It adds spice to my conversation.

10645
Reformers have the idea that change can be achieved by brute sanity.

10646
Religion is a great force - the only real motive force in the world; but you must get a man through his own religion, not through yours.

10647 *Saint Joan*
If ever I utter an oath again may my soul be blasted to eternal damnation!

10648 *Saint Joan*
How can what an Englishman believes be heresy? It is a contradiction in terms.

10649
The savage bows down to idols of wood and stone, the civilized man to idols of flesh and blood.

10650
The secret of being miserable is to have leisure to bother about whether you are happy or not. The cure for it is occupation.

10651 *The Showing-Up of Blanco Posnet*
Assassination is the extreme form of censorship.

10652
Silence is the most perfect expression of scorn.

10653
I was taught when I was young that if people would only love one another, all would be well with the world. This seemed simple and very nice; but I found when I tried to put it in practice not only that other people were seldom lovable, but that I was not very lovable myself.

10654
The test of a man or woman's breeding is how they behave in a quarrel.

10655
What is life but a series of inspired follies? The difficulty is to find them to do.

10656
When I was a young man I observed that nine out of ten things I did were failures. I didn't want to be a failure, so I did ten times more work.

10657 *(of William Morris)*
You can lose a man like that by your own death, but not by his.

10658
I work as my father drank.

SHAW Henry Wheeler (Josh Billings) 1818-1885
10659 *Josh Billings, his Sayings*
Thrice is he armed that hath his quarrel just,
But four times he who gets his blow in fust.

10660 *Proverb*
It is better to know nothing than to know what ain't so.

SHAWN Ted 1891-1972
10661
Dance is the only art of which we ourselves are the stuff of which it is made.

SHAY R.E.
10662
Depend on the rabbit's foot if you will, but remember it didn't work for the rabbit!

SHEEHY Gail
10663
When men reach their sixties and retire, they go to pieces. Women just go right on cooking.

SHELDON William H.
10664
Happiness is essentially a state of going somewhere, wholeheartedly, one-directionally, without regret or reservation.

SHELLEY Mary 1797-1851
10665 *Frankenstein*
You seek for knowledge and wisdom as I once did; and I ardently hope that the gratification of your wishes may not be a serpent to sting you, as mine has been.

10666
Nothing contributes so much to tranquilize the mind as a steady purpose - a point on which the soul may fix its intellectual eye.

10667 *(of her son's education)*
Teach him to think for himself? Oh, my God, teach him rather to think like other people.

SHELLEY Percy Bysshe 1792-1822
10668 *Adonais*
To that high Capital, where kingly Death
Keeps his pale court in beauty and decay,
He came.

10669 *Adonais*
She faded, like a cloud which had outwept its rain.

10670 *Adonais*
Winter is come and gone,
But grief returns with the revolving year.

10671 *Adonais*
From the great morning of the world when first
God dawned on Chaos.

10672 *Adonais*
Dust to the dust! but the pure spirit shall flow
Back to the burning fountain whence it came,
A portion of the Eternal.

10673 *Adonais*
He hath awakened from the dream of life -
'Tis we, who lost in stormy visions, keep
With phantoms an unprofitable strife,
And in mad trance, strike with our spirit's knife
Invulnerable nothings.

10674 *Adonais*
From the contagion of the world's slow stain
He is secure, and now can never mourn
A heart grown cold, a head grown grey in vain.

10675 *Adonais*
He is a portion of the loveliness
Which once he made more lovely.

10676 *Adonais*
Life, like a dome of many-coloured glass,
Stains the white radiance of Eternity,
Until Death tramples it to fragments.

10677 *'The Cloud'*
I am the daughter of Earth and Water,
And the nursling of the Sky;
I pass through the pores of the ocean and shores;
I change, but I cannot die.

10678 *'The Cloud'*
I silently laugh at my own cenotaph,
And out of the caverns of rain,
Like a child from the womb, like a ghost from the tomb,
I arise and unbuild it again.

10679 *Declaration of Rights*
Titles are tinsel, power a corrupter, glory a bubble, and excessive wealth a libel on its possessor.

10680 *Defence of Poetry*
Poetry is the record of the best and happiest moments of the happiest and best minds.

10681 *'Epipsychidion'*
I never was attached to that great sect,
Whose doctrine is that each one should select
Out of the crowd a mistress or a friend,
And all the rest, though fair and wise, commend
To cold oblivion.

10682 *'An Exhortation'*
Chameleons feed on light and air:
Poets' food is love and fame.

10683 *'Good Night'*
Good-night? ah! no; the hour is ill
Which severs those it should unite;
Let us remain together still,
Then it will be *good* night.

10684 *Hellas*
The world's great age begins anew,
The golden years return,
The earth doth like a snake renew
Her winter weeds outworn;
Heaven smiles, and faiths and empires gleam,
Like wrecks of a dissolving dream.

10685 *Hellas*
The world is weary of the past,
Oh, might it die or rest at last!

10686 *'Letter to Maria Gisborne'*
Have you not heard
When a man marries, dies or turns Hindoo,
His best friends hear no more of him?

10687 *'Letter to Maria Gisborne'(of Thomas Love Peacock)*
His fine wit
Makes such a wound, the knife is lost in it.

10688 *'Lines: When the lamp'*
When the lamp is shattered
The light in the dust lies dead -
When the cloud is scattered
The rainbow's glory is shed.
When the lute is broken,
Sweet tones are remembered not;
When the lips have spoken,
Loved accents are soon forgot.

10689 *'Lines written amongst the Euganean Hills'(Venice)*
Sun-girt city, thou hast been
Ocean's child, and then his queen;
Now is come a darker day,
And thou soon must be his prey.

10690 *'The Mask of Anarchy'*
I met Murder on the way -
He had a mask like Castlereagh.

10691 *'Mutability'*
Nought may endure but Mutability.

10692 *'Ode to the West Wind'*
O wild West Wind, thou breath of Autumn's being,
Thou, from whose unseen presence the leaves dead
Are driven, like ghosts from an enchanter fleeing,

Yellow, and black, and pale, and hectic red,
Pestilence-striken multitudes.

10693 *'Ode to the West Wind'*
Oh, lift me as a wave, a leaf, a cloud!
I fall upon the thorns of life! I bleed!

10694 *'Ode to the West Wind'*
Make me thy lyre, even as the forest is:
What if my leaves are falling like its own!

10695 *'Ode to the West Wind'*
Scatter, as from an unextinguished hearth
Ashes and sparks, my words among mankind!
Be through my lips to unawakened earth

The trumpet of a prophecy! O, Wind,
If Winter comes, can Spring be far behind?

10696 *'Ozymandias'*
I met a traveller from an antique land
Who said: Two vast and trunkless legs of stone
Stand in the desert.

10697 *'Ozymandias'*
'My name is Ozymandias, king of kings;
Look on my works, ye Mighty, and despair!'

10698 *'Peter Bell the Third'*
Hell is a city much like London -
A populous and smoky city.

10699 *'Prometheus Unbound'*
It doth repent me; words are quick and vain;
Grief for awhile is blind, and so was mine.

10700 *'Prometheus Unbound'*
The dust of creeds outworn.

10701 *'Prometheus Unbound'*
On a poet's lips I slept
Dreaming like a love-adept
In the sound his breathing kept.

10702 *'Prometheus Unbound'*
He gave man speech, and speech created thought,
Which is the measure of the universe.

10703 *'Prometheus Unbound'*
A traveller from the cradle to the grave
Through the dim night of this immortal day.

10704 *'Prometheus Unbound'*
Familiar acts are beautiful through love.

10705
Reason respects the differences, and
imagination the similitudes of things.

10706 *'The Revolt of Islam'*
With hue like that when some great painter dips
His pencil in the gloom of earthquake and
eclipse.

10707 *'To a Skylark'*
Hail to thee, blithe Spirit!
Bird thou never wert,
That from Heaven, or near it,
Pourest thy full heart
In profuse strains of unpremeditated art.

10708 *'To a Skylark'*
And singing still dost soar, and soaring ever
singest.

10709 *'To a Skylark'*
Like an unbodied joy whose race is just begun.

10710 *'To a Skylark'*
We look before and after,
And pine for what is not:
Our sincerest laughter
With some pain is fraught;
Our sweetest songs are those that tell of saddest
thought.

10711 *'To a Skylark'*
Teach me half the gladness
That thy brain must know,
Such harmonious madness
From my lips would flow
The world should listen then - as I am listening
now.

10712 *'Song to the Men of England'*
Men of England, wherefore plough
For the lords who lay ye low?

10713 *'Song to the Men of England'*
The seed ye sow, another reaps;
The wealth ye find, another keeps;
The robes ye weave, another wears;
The arms ye forge, another bears.

10714 *'Sonnet'*
Lift not the painted veil which those who live
Call Life.

10715 *'Sonnet: England in 1819'*
An old, mad, blind, despised, and dying king.

SHENSTONE William 1714-1763
10716 *Works in Verse and Prose*
Laws are generally found to be nets of such a
texture, as the little creep through, the great
break through, and the middle-sized are alone
entangled in.

10717 *'Written at an Inn at Henley'*
Whoe'er has travelled life's dull round,
Where'er his stages may have been,

May sigh to think he still has found
The warmest welcome, at an inn.

SHERIDAN Philip Henry 1831-1888
10718 *(attributed)*
The only good Indian is a dead Indian.

SHERIDAN Richard Brinsley 1751-1816
10719 *'Clio's Protest'*
You write with ease, to show your breeding,
But easy writing's vile hard reading.

10720 *The Critic*
If it is abuse - why one is always sure to hear of
it from one damned goodnatured friend or
another!

10721 *The Critic*
I wish sir, you would practise this without me. I
can't stay dying here all night.

10722 *The Critic*
An oyster may be crossed in love!

10723 *The Duenna*
I was struck all of a heap.

10724 *The Duenna*
Conscience has no more to do with gallantry
than it has with politics.

10725
Our memories are independent of our wills. It
is not so easy to forget.

10726
The Right Honourable gentleman is indebted to
his memory for his jests and to his imagination
for his facts.

10727 *The Rivals*
Illiterate him, I say, quite from your memory.

10728 *The Rivals*
'Tis safest in matrimony to begin with a little
aversion.

10729 *The Rivals*
He is the very pineapple of politeness!

10730 *The Rivals*
An aspersion upon my parts of speech! was ever
such a brute! Sure, if I reprehend anything in
this world, it is the use of my oracular tongue,
and a nice derangement of epitaphs!

10731 *The School for Scandal*
You had no taste when you married me.

10732 *The School for Scandal*
Here is the whole set! a character dead at every
word.

10733 *The School for Scandal*
An unforgiving eye, and a damned disinheriting
countenance!

SHERMAN William 1820-1891
10734
There is many a boy here to-day who looks on war as all glory, but, boys, it is all hell.

10735 *(defining courage)*
A perfect sensibility of the measure of danger, and a mental willingness to endure it.

SHINN Florence Scovel
10736
Intuition is a spiritual faculty and does not explain, but simply points the way.

SHINWELL Emanuel 1884-1986
10737
We know that the organised workers of the country are our friends. As for the rest, they don't matter a tinker's cuss.

SHIPLEY Sir Arthur 1861-1927
10738 *Life 'Ere you were Queen of Sheba'*
When we were a soft amoeba, in ages past and gone,
Ere you were Queen of Sheba, or I King Solomon,
Alone and undivided, we lived a life of sloth,
Whatever you did, I did; one dinner served for both.
Anon came separation, by fission and divorce,
A lonely pseudopodium I wandered on my course.

SHIRLEY James 1596-1666
10739 *The Contention of Ajax and Ulysses*
There is no armour against fate;
Death lays his icy hand on kings.

10740 *The Contention of Ajax and Ulysses*
Only the actions of the just
Smell sweet, and blossom in their dust.

10741 *The Wedding*
How little room
Do we take up in death, that, living know
No bounds?

SHORE Dinah
10742
Trouble is a part of your life, and if you don't share it, you don't give the person who loves you a chance to love you enough.

SHORT Clare 1946-
10743
I am amazed how many vultures there are out there trying to peck my eyes out.

10744
I fear I will carry on irritating some people because some people are very irritable.

SHRINER Herb
10745
Our doctor would never really operate unless it was necessary. He was just that way. If he didn't need the money, he wouldn't lay a hand on you.

SHULTZ George P. 1920-
10746
Nothing ever gets settled in this town (Washington). It's not like running a company or even a university. It's a seething debating society, in which the debate never stops; in which people never give up, including me, and that's the atmosphere in which you administer.

SHUTE Evan
10747
Change must be measured from a known base line.

SICKERT Walter 1860-1942
10748 *'The Language of Art'*
Nothing knits man to man, ... like the frequent passage from hand to hand of cash.

SIDNEY Algernon 1622-1683
10749 *Discourses concerning Government*
Liars ought to have good memories.

10750 *Discourses concerning Government*
Men lived like fishes; the great ones devoured the small.

10751 *Discourses concerning Government*
'Tis not necessary to light a candle to the sun.

SIDNEY Sir Philip 1554-1586
10752 *Arcadia*
Who shoots at the mid-day sun, though he be sure he shall never hit the mark; yet as sure he is he shall shoot higher than who aims but at a bush.

10753 *Arcadia*
My true love hath my heart and I have his,
By just exchange one for the other giv'n;
I hold his dear, and mine he cannot miss,
There never was a better bargain driv'n.

10754 *Astrophel and Stella*
They love indeed who quake to say they love.

10755 *Astrophel and Stella, Sonnet 1*
'Fool,' said my Muse to me, 'look in thy heart and write.'

10756 *Certain Sonnets*
Leave me, O Love which reachest but to dust,
And thou, my mind, aspire to higher things;
Grow rich in that which never taketh rust;
Whatever fades, but fading pleasure brings.

10757 *The Defence of Poetry*
Comedy is an imitation of the common errors of our life.

SIEYES Emmanuel Joseph 1748-1836
10758 *(attributed, voting for the death of Louis XVI)*
La mort, sans phrases.
Death, without rhetoric.

10759 *(asked what he had done during the French Revolution)*
J'ai vécu.
I survived.

SIFTON Clifford Sir 1861-1929
10760
I think a stalwart peasant in a sheepskin coat, born on the soil, whose forefathers have been farmers for ten generations, with a stout wife and a half-dozen chickens, is good quality.

SIGISMUND Emperor 1361-1437
10761 *(to prelate who had criticized his Latin)*
I am the Roman Emperor, and am above grammar.

SIGNORET Simone 1921-1985
10762
Pains do not hold a marriage together. It is threads, hundreds of tiny threads which sew people together through the years. That's what makes a marriage last - more than passion or even sex.

SIGOURNEY Lydia 1791-1865
10763
The strength of a nation, especially of a republican nation, is in the intelligent and well-ordered homes of the people.

10764
Whatever you would have your children become, strive to exhibit in your own lives and conversation.

SILLITOE Alan 1928-
10765
The loneliness of the long-distance runner.

SILLS Beverly 1929-
10766
You may be disappointed if you fail, but you are doomed if you don't try.

SIMENON Georges 1903-1989
10767
Writing is not a profession but a vocation of unhappiness.

SIMON Paul 1942-
10768 *'Bridge over Troubled Water'*
Like a bridge over troubled water
I will lay me down.

10769 *'Mrs Robinson' The Graduate*
And here's to you, Mrs Robinson
Jesus loves you more than you will know.

10770 *'Sound of Silence'*
People talking without speaking
People hearing without listening ...
'Fools,' said I, 'You do not know
Silence like a cancer grows.'

SIMONIDES c.556-486 BC
10771 *(attributed)*
Go, tell the Spartans, thou who passest by,
That here obedient to their laws we lie.

10772 *In Plutarch*
Painting is silent poetry, poetry is eloquent painting.

SIMONSON Lee 1888-1967
10773
An artist has been defined as a neurotic who continually cures himself with his art.

10774
Any event, once it has occurred, can be made to appear inevitable by a competent historian.

SIMPSON N.F. 1919-
10775 *A Resounding Tinkle*
A problem left to itself dries up or goes rotten. But fertilize a problem with a solution - you'll hatch out dozens.

SIMPSON O.J. 1947-
10776
Fear of losing is what makes competitors so great. Show me a gracious loser and I'll show you a perennial loser.

SIMPSON Wallis 1896-1986
10777
I don't remember any love affairs. One must keep love affairs quiet.

10778 *Letter to Edward VIII*
I look a hundred and weigh 110 - you won't love me when you see the wreck that England has made of me.

SIMS Sylvia
10779
You can have your face lifted but there comes a time when you are still going to be offered the Nurse, not Juliet.

SINCLAIR Gordon John
10780 *in Gregory's Girl*
"It doesn't look nice. If women were meant to play football they'd have their tits somewhere else."

SINGER Isaac Bashevis 1904-1991
10781
A good writer is basically a story-teller, not a scholar or a redeemer of mankind.

10782
The waste basket is a writer's best friend.

10783
Writing has power, but its power has no vector. Writers can stir the mind, but they can't direct it. Time changes things, God changes things, the dictators change things, but writers can't change anything.

SISSON C.H. 1914-
10784 *In The London Zoo*
Here lies a civil servant. He was civil
To everyone, and servant to the devil.

SITWELL Dame Edith 1887-1964
10785 *Façade 'Aubade'*
Jane, Jane,
Tall as a crane,
The morning light creaks down again.

10786 *Façade 'Dark Song'*
The fire was furry as a bear.

10787 *Façade 'Lullaby for Jumbo'*
Jumbo asleep!
Grey leaves thick-furred
As his ears, keep
Conversation blurred.

10788 *'Still Falls the Rain'*
Still falls the Rain -
Dark as the world of man, black as our loss
Blind as the nineteen hundred and forty nails
Upon the Cross.

10789
A great many people now reading and writing would be better employed in keeping rabbits.

10790 *'The Sleeping Beauty'*
Forget-me-nots, whose eyes of childish blue,
Gold-starred like heaven, speak of love still true.

10791
I have often wished I had time to cultivate modesty ... But I am too busy thinking about myself.

SITWELL Sir Osbert 1892-1969
10792
The artist, like the idiot, or clown, sits on the edge of the world, and a push may send him over it.

10793 *'On the Coast of Coromandel'*
On the coast of Coromandel
Dance they to the tunes of Handel.

10794 *At the House of Mrs Kinfoot*
The British Bourgeoisie
Is not born,
And does not die,
But, if it is ill,
It has a frightened look in its eyes.

10795 *'Milordo Inglese'*
In reality, killing time
Is only the name for another of the multifarious

ways
By which Time kills us.

SKELTON John c.1460-1529
10796 *The Bouge of Court*
The sovereign'st thing that any man may have
Is little to say, and much to hear and see.

10797 *The Garland of Laurel' To Mistress Margaret Hussey'*
With solace and gladness,
Much mirth and no madness,
All good and no badness;
So joyously,
So maidenly,
So womanly,
Her demeaning.

10798 *Magnificence*
I blunder, I bluster, I blow, and I blother,
I make on the one day, and I mar on the other.
Busy, busy, and ever busy,
I dance up and down till I am dizzy.

SKELTON Robin
10799
I have no history but the length of my bones.

SKINNER B.F. 1904-1990
10800 *Contingencies of Reinforcement*
The real question is not whether machines think but whether men do.

10801
Education is what survives when what has been learnt has been forgotten.

SKINNER Cornelia Otis 1901-1979
10802
Women keep a special corner of their hearts for sins they have never committed.

SMART Christopher 1722-1771
10803 *Hymns and Spiritual Songs 'The Nativity ...'*
God all-bounteous, all-creative,
Whom no ills from good dissuade,
Is incarnate, and a native
Of the very world he made.

10804 *Jubilate Agno*
For in my nature I quested for beauty, but God, God hath sent me to sea for pearls.

10805 *Jubilate Agno*
For sincerity is a jewel which is pure and transparent, eternal and inestimable.

10806 *Jubilate Agno*
For Charity is cold in the multitude of possessions, and the rich are covetous of their crumbs.

10807 *Jubilate Agno*
I will consider my Cat Jeoffrey.
For he is the servant of the Living God duly and

daily serving him.

10808 *A Song to David*
Strong is the lion - like a coal
His eye-ball - like a bastion's mole
His chest against his foes:

10809 *A Song to David*
Glorious the northern lights astream;
Glorious the song, when God's the theme;
Glorious the thunder's roar.

SMILES Samuel 1812-1904
10810 *Duty*
We each day dig our graves with our teeth.

10811 *Self-Help*
The spirit of self-help is the root of all genuine
growth in the individual.

10812 *Self-Help*
The shortest way to do many things is to do
only one thing at once.

10813 *Self-Help*
Cheerfulness gives elasticity to the spirit.
Spectres fly before it.

10814 *Self-Help*
We often discover what *will* do, by finding out
what will not do; and probably he who never
made a mistake never made a discovery.

10815 *Thrift*
A place for everything, and everything in its
place.

SMITH Adam 1723-1790
10816
Man, an animal that makes bargains.

10817 *Theory of Moral Sentiments*
Though our brother is on the rack, as long as we
ourselves are at ease, our senses will never
inform us of what he suffers.

10818 *Wealth of Nations*
It is not from the benevolence of the butcher,
the brewer, or the baker, that we expect our
dinner, but from their regard to their own
interest. We address ourselves not to their
humanity but their self love.

10819 *Wealth of Nations*
People of the same trade seldom meet together,
even for merriment and diversion, but the
conversation ends in a conspiracy against the
public, or in some contrivance to raise prices.

10820 *Wealth of Nations*
Consumption is the sole end and purpose of
production; and the interest of the producer
ought to be attended to only so far as it may be
necessary for promoting that of the consumer.

10821 *Wealth of Nations*
There is no art which one government sooner
learns of another than that of draining money
from the pockets of the people.

SMITH Alexander 1830-1867
10822
If you wish to preserve your secret, wrap it up in
frankness.

SMITH A.W. 1937-
10823
Where there is one Englishman there is a
garden. Where there are two Englishmen there
will be a club. But this does not mean any
falling off in the number of gardens. There will
be three. The club will have one too.

SMITH Charles Merrill
10824
The cocktail party - a device for paying off
obligations to people you don't want to invite to
dinner.

SMITH Sir Cyril 1928-
10825 *(of the House of Commons)*
The longest running farce in the West End.

SMITH Dodie 1896-1990
10826 *Dear Octopus*
The family - that dear octopus from whose
tentacles we never quite escape.

SMITH Edgar 1857-1938
10827 *'Heaven Will Protect the Working-Girl'*
You may tempt the upper classes
With your villainous demi-tasses,
But; Heaven will protect a working-girl!

SMITH F.E. 1872-1930
10828 *Contemporary Personalities*
We have the highest authority for believing that
the meek shall inherit the earth; though I have
never found any particular corroboration of this
aphorism in the records of Somerset House.

10829 *Law, Life and Letters*
Nature has no cure for this sort of madness
[Bolshevism], though I have known a legacy
from a rich relative work wonders.

10830
The world continues to offer glittering prizes to
those who have stout hearts and sharp swords.

SMITH Goldwin 1823-1910
10831
The father of confederation is deadlock.

SMITH Hannah Whitall
10832
The true secret of giving advice is, after you
have honestly given it, to be perfectly
indifferent whether it is taken or not and never
persist in trying to set people right.

SMITH Horace 1779-1849
10833
Inconsistency is the only thing in which men are consistent.

SMITH Ian 1919-
10834
I don't believe in black majority rule in Rhodesia - not in a thousand years.

SMITH James and Horace 1775-1839 and 1779-1849
10835 *Rejected Addresses 'Cui Bono?'*
Sated with home, of wife, of children tired.
The restless soul is driven abroad to roam;
Sated abroad, all seen and all admired,
The restless soul is driven to ramble home.

10836 *Rejected Addresses, 'Loyal Effusion'*
Who makes the quartern loaf and Luddites rise?
Who fills the butchers' shops with large blue flies?

10837 *Rejected Addresses, 'Loyal Effusion'*
God bless the Army, bless their coats of scarlet,
God bless the Navy, bless the Princess Charlotte.

SMITH John 1938-1995
10838 *(of John Major)*
I sometimes think that when the Prime Minister tries to select a weapon it is the boomerang he finds most effective.

SMITH Logan Pearsall 1865-1946
10839 *Afterthoughts*
There are two things to aim at in life: first, to get what you want; and, after that, to enjoy it. Only the wisest of mankind achieve the second.

10840 *Afterthoughts 'Age and Death'*
There is more felicity on the far side of baldness than young men can possibly imagine.

10841 *Afterthoughts 'Age and Death'*
The denunciation of the young is a necessary part of the hygiene of older people, and greatly assists the circulation of their blood.

10842 *Afterthoughts 'All Trivia'*
What I like in a good author is not what he says, but what he whispers.

10843 *Afterthoughts 'Art and Letters'*
The test of a vocation is the love of the drudgery it involves.

10844 *Afterthoughts 'Art and Letters'*
A best-seller is the gilded tomb of a mediocre talent.

10845 *Afterthoughts 'Life and Human Nature'*
An improper mind is a perpetual feast.

10846 *Afterthoughts 'Myself'*
People say that life is the thing, but I prefer reading.

10847 *Afterthoughts 'Other People'*
Those who set out to serve both God and Mammon soon discover that there is no God.

10848 *Afterthoughts 'Other People'*
Most people sell their souls, and live with a good conscience on the proceeds.

10849 *Afterthoughts 'In the World'*
To suppose, as we all suppose, that we could be rich and not behave as the rich behave, is like supposing that we could drink all day and keep absolutely sober.

10850
Every author, however modest, keeps a most outrageous vanity chained like a madman in the padded cell of his breast.

10851
Charming people live up to the very edge of their charm, and behave as outrageously as the world will let them.

10852
Don't laugh at a youth for his affectations; he's only trying on one face after another till he finds his own.

10853
Don't tell your friends their social faults; they will cure the fault and never forgive you.

10854
I cannot forgive my friends for dying: I do not find these vanishing acts of theirs at all amusing.

10855
How it infuriates a bigot, when he is forced to drag out his dark convictions!

10856
How can they say my life isn't a success? Have I not for more than sixty years got enough to eat and escaped being eaten?

10857
We need new friends. Some of us are cannibals who have eaten their old friends up; others must have ever-renewed audiences before whom to re-enact an ideal version of their lives.

10858
Self-respecting people do not care to peep at their reflections in unexpected mirrors, or to see themselves as others see them.

10859
There are few sorrows, however poignant, in which a good income is of no avail.

SMITH Minnie
10860
I am as my Creator made me, and since He is satisfied, so am I.

SMITH Ray

10861
The Americans believe they answered all first questions in 1776: since then they've just been hammering out the practical details.

SMITH Samuel Francis 1808-1895
10862 *'America'*
My country, 'tis of thee,
Sweet land of liberty,
Of thee I sing.

SMITH Stevie 1902-1971
10863 *'This Englishwoman'*
This Englishwoman is so refined
She has no bosom and no behind.

10864 *'The Galloping Cat'*
Oh I am a cat that likes to
Gallop about doing good.

10865
A good time was had by all.

10866 *Novel on Yellow Paper*
If you cannot have your dear husband for a comfort and a delight, for a breadwinner and a crosspatch, for a sofa, chair or a hot-water bottle, one can use him as a Cross to be Borne.

10867 *'The Past'*
People who are always praising the past
And especially the times of faith as best
Ought to go and live in the Middle Ages
And be burnt at the stake as witches and sages.

10868
If there wasn't death, I think you couldn't go on.

10869 *'Not Waving but Drowning'*
Oh, no no no, it was too cold always
(Still the dead one lay moaning)
I was much too far out all my life
And not waving but drowning.

SMITH Sydney 1771-1845
10870
Among the smaller duties in life, I hardly know any one more important than that of not praising when praise is not due.

10871
It is always considered a piece of impertinence in England if a man of less than two or three thousand a year has any opinions at all upon important subjects.

10872
Death must be distinguished from dying, with which it is often confused.

10873
My definition of marriage ... it resembles a pair of shears, so joined that they cannot be separated; often moving in opposite directions, yet always punishing anyone who comes

between them.

10874
As the French say, there are three sexes - men, women, and clergymen.

10875
No furniture so charming as books.

10876
Great men hallow a whole people, and lift up all who live in their time.

10877
Heat, ma'am! It was so dreadful here that I found there was nothing left for it but to take off my flesh and sit in my bones.

10878
How can a bishop marry? How can he flirt? The most he can say is, 'I will see you in the vestry after service.'

10879
I am just going to pray for you at St Paul's, but with no very lively hope of success.

10880 *Letter to Miss G. Harcourt*
I have no relish for the country; it is a kind of healthy grave.

10881 *Letters of Peter Plymley*
The moment the very name of Ireland is mentioned, the English seem to bid adieu to common feeling, common prudence, and common sense, and to act with the barbarity of tyrants, and the fatuity of idiots.

10882 *(of Macaulay)*
He not only overflowed with learning, but stood in the slop.

10883 *(of Macauley)*
He has occasional flashes of silence, that make his conversation perfectly delightful.

10884
I never read a book before reviewing it; it prejudices a man so.

10885
You never say a word of yourself, dear Lady Grey. You have that dreadful sin of anti-egotism.

10886
Never try to reason the prejudice out of a man. It was not reasoned into him, and cannot be reasoned out.

10887
Oh, don't tell me of facts - I never believe in facts; you know Canning said nothing was so fallacious as facts, except figures.

10888
Politeness is good nature regulated by good sense.

10889
Poverty is no disgrace to a man, but it is confoundedly inconvenient.

10890 *'Receipt for a Salad'*
Let onion atoms lurk within the bowl,
And, scarce-suspected, animate the whole.

10891 *'Receipt for a Salad'*
Serenely full, the epicure would say,
Fate cannot harm me, I have dined to-day.

10892
It requires a surgical operation to get a joke well into a Scotch understanding.

10893
He has returned from Italy a greater bore than ever; he bores on architecture, painting, statuary and music.

10894 *Sketches of Moral Philosophy*
I never could find any man who could think for two minutes together.

10895
What you don't know would make a great book.

10896
What a pity it is that we have no amusements in England but vice and religion!

10897
What two ideas are more inseparable than Beer and Britannia?

10898 *(of Whewell)*
Science is his forte, and omniscience his foible.

SMITH Walter Chalmers 1824-1908
10899 *'Immortal, invisible, God only wise'*
We blossom and flourish as leaves on the tree,
And wither and perish; but naught changeth thee.

SMITH Willie ('The Lion') 1897-
10900
Romance without finance is no good.

SMOLLETT Tobias 1721-1771
10901 *The Adventures of Sir Launcelot Greaves*
I think for my part one half of the nation is mad - and the other not very sound.

10902 *Humphry Clinker*
I am pent up in frowzy lodgings, where there is not room enough to swing a cat.

SMYTH Harley S.
10903 *(medical maxim)*
When you hear hoofbeats, think of horses before zebras.

SNOW C.P. 1905-1980
10904 *Homecomings*
The official world, the corridors of power.

SNOWDEN Philip 1864-1937
10905 *(on Labour Party's election programme)*
This is not Socialism. It is Bolshevism run mad.

SOCRATES 469-399 BC
10906 *(looking at multitude of wares exposed for sale)*
How many things I can do without!

10907
I know nothing except the fact of my ignorance.

10908 *In Plato - Apology*
Virtue does not come from money, but from virtue comes money and all other good things to man, both to the individual and to the state.

10909 *In Plato - Crito*
It is never right to do wrong or to requite wrong with wrong; or when we suffer evil to defend ourselves by doing evil in return.

10910 *In Plato - Phaedo*
It is perfectly certain that the soul is immortal and imperishable, and our souls will actually exist in another world.

10911 *Plutarch, De Exilio*
I am a citizen, not of Athens or Greece, but of the world.

10912 *Plutarch, Moralia, 'How a Young Man Ought to ...'*
Bad men live to eat and drink, whereas good men eat and drink in order to live.

SOLON c.640-c.556 BC
10913
If all our misfortunes were laid in one common heap, whence everyone must take an equal portion, most people would be content to take their own and depart.

10914
Call no man happy before he dies, he is at best but fortunate.

10915
I grow old ever learning many things.

SOLZHENITSYN Aleksandr 1918-
10916
All revolutions unleash the most elemental barbarism.

10917
No one can bar the road to truth, and to advance its cause I'm ready to accept even death.

10918
One can build the Empire State Building, discipline the Prussian army, make a state

hierarchy mightier than God, yet fail to overcome the unaccountable superiority of certain human beings.

10919
For a country to have a great writer is to have another government.

10920 *One Day in the Life of Ivan Denisovich*
Work was like a stick. It had two ends. When you worked for the knowing you gave them quality; when you worked for a fool you simply gave him eye-wash.

10921 *One Day in the Life of Ivan Denisovich*
The thoughts of a prisoner - they're not free either. They keep returning to the same things.

10922 *The First Circle*
When you've robbed a man of *everything* he's no longer in your power - he's free again.

10923
If one is forever cautious, can one remain a human being?

10924
If only there were evil people somewhere, insidiously committing evil deeds, and it were necessary only to separate them from the rest of us and destroy them. But the line dividing good and evil cuts through the heart of every human being. And who is willing to destroy a piece of his own heart?

10925
Talent is always conscious of its own abundance, and does not object to sharing.

SOMERVILLE William 1675-1742
10926 *The Chase*
The chase, the sport of kings;
Image of war, without its guilt.

10927 *The Chase*
Hail, happy Britain! highly favoured isle,
And Heaven's peculiar care!

SOMOZA Anastasio 1925-1980
10928 *(replying to an accusation of ballot-rigging)*
You won the elections, but I won the count.

SONDHEIM Stephen 1930-
10929 *Gypsy*
Everything's coming up roses.

10930 *A Little Night Music 'Every Day a Little ..'*
Ev'ry day a little death
On the lips and in the eyes,
In the murmurs, in the pauses,
In the gestures, in the sighs.
Ev'ry day a little dies.

10931 *A Little Night Music 'Send in the Clowns'*
Isn't it rich?
Are we a pair?
Me here at last on the ground, you in mid-air ...

Isn't it bliss?
Don't you approve?
One who keeps tearing around, one who can't move ...

Where are the clowns?
Send in the clowns.

10932 *West Side Story*
I like to be in America!
O.K. by me in America!
Ev'rything free in America
For a small fee in America!

SONTAG Susan 1933-
10933
The camera makes everyone a tourist in other people's reality, and eventually in one's own.

10934
Illness is the night-side of life, a more onerous citizenship. Everyone who is born holds dual citizenship, in the kingdom of the well and in the kingdom of the sick.

10935
Instead of just recording reality, photographs have become the norm for the way things appear to us, thereby changing the very idea of reality and of realism.

10936
Interpretation is the revenge of the intellect upon art.

10937
Life is not about significant details, illuminated in a flash, fixed forever. Photographs are.

10938
What is most beautiful in virile men is something feminine; what is most beautiful in feminine women is something masculine.

10939
What pornography is really about, ultimately, isn't sex but death.

SOPER Baron 1903-
10940 *(on the quality of debate in the House of Lords)*
It is, I think, good evidence of life after death.

SOPHOCLES c.496-406
10941 *Ajax*
Enemies' gifts are no gifts and do no good.

10942 *Antigone*
There are many wonderful things, and nothing is more wonderful than man.

10943
Most gladly indeed am I rid of it all [sex], as
though I had escaped from a mad and savage
master.

10944
The keenest sorrow is to recognize ourselves as
the sole cause of all our adversities.

10945
It is terrible to speak well and be wrong.

10946
Time is a kindly god.

10947
One word frees us of all the weight and pain of
life; that word is love.

SORLEY Charles Hamilton 1895-1915
10948 *'To Poets'*
We have a dumb spirit within:
The exceeding bitter agony
But not the exceeding bitter cry.

SOUTH Robert 1634-1716
10949 *Twelve Sermons ...*
An Aristotle was but the rubbish of an Adam,
and Athens but the rudiments of Paradise.

SOUTHERNE Thomas 1660-1746
10950 *Sir Anthony Love*
Love is but discovery:
When that is made, the pleasure's done.

10951 *The Loyal Brother*
When we're worn,
Hacked hewn with constant service, thrown
aside
To rust in peace, or rot in hospitals.

SOUTHEY Robert 1774-1843
10952 *'The Battle of Blenheim'*
'And everybody praise the Duke,
Who this great fight did win.'
'But what good came of it at last?'
Quoth little Peterkin.
'Why that I cannot tell,' said he,
'But 'twas a famous victory.'

10953 *'The Battle of Blenheim'*
He came to ask what he had found,
That was so large, and smooth, and round.

10954 *'The Battle of Blenheim'*
But what they fought each other for,
I could not well make out.

10955 *Colloquies on the Progress ... of Society*
The arts babblative and scribblative.

10956 *Colloquies on the Progress ... of Society*
The march of intellect.

10957 *The Curse of Kehama*
Thou hast been called, O Sleep! the friend of
Woe,

But 'tis the happy who have called thee so.

10958 *The Curse of Kehama (motto)*
Curses are like young chickens, they always
come home to roost.

10959 *'The Devil's Walk' (written with Coleridge)*
From his brimstone bed, at break of day
A walking the Devil is gone,
To look at his little snug farm of the World,
And see how his stock went on.

10960 *The Doctor*
Your true lover of literature is never fastidious.

10961 *The Doctor*
Beware of those who are homeless by choice.

10962 *The Doctor*
Live as long as you may, the first twenty years
are the longest half of your life.

10963 *'The Lay of the Laureate'*
My name is Death: the last best friend am I.

10964 *Madoc*
Blue, darkly, deeply, beautifully blue.

10965 *Madoc*
We wage no war with women nor with priests.

10966 *'The March to Moscow'*
And last of all an Admiral came,
A terrible man with a terrible name -
A name which you all know by sight very well,
But which no one can speak, and no one can
spell.

10967 *'The Old Man's Comforts'*
In the days of my youth I remembered my God!
And He hath not forgotten my age.

10968
What will not woman, gentle woman dare
When strong affection stirs her spirit up?

10969
It has been more wittily than charitably said
that hell is paved with good intentions. They
have their place in heaven also.

SOUTHWELL Robert c.1561-1595
10970 *'Content and Rich'*
To rise by other's fall
I deem a losing gain;
All states with others' ruins built
To ruin run amain.

10971 *'Loss in Delays'*
Good is best when soonest wrought,
Lingered labours come to naught.

10972 *'Times go by Turns'*
Times go by turns, and chances change by
course,
From foul to fair, from better hap to worse.

SPARK Muriel 1918-
10973 *The Comforters*
The one certain way for a woman to hold a man is to leave him for religion.

10974
It is impossible to repent of love. The sin of love does not exist.

10975 *The Prime of Miss Jean Brodie*
I am putting old heads on your young shoulders ... all my pupils are the crème de la crème.

10976 *The Prime of Miss Jean Brodie*
Give me a girl at an impressionable age, and she is mine for life.

10977 *The Prime of Miss Jean Brodie*
One's prime is elusive. You little girls, when you grow up, must be on the alert to recognize your prime at whatever time of your life it may occur.

10978 *The Prime of Miss Jean Brodie*
To me education is a leading out of what is already there in the pupil's soul. To Miss Mackay it is a putting in of something that is not there, and that is not what I call education, I call it intrusion.

10979 *The Wit of Women*
Do you think it pleases a man when he looks into a woman's eyes and sees a reflection of the British Museum Reading Room?

SPARROW John 1906-1992
10980 *Epitaph for Maurice Bowra*
Without you, Heaven would be too dull to bear, And Hell would not be Hell if you are there.

10981
That indefatigable and unsavoury engine of pollution, the dog.

SPENCER Herbert 1820-1903
10982 *Definitions*
Time: That which man is always trying to kill, but which ends in killing him.

10983 *Education*
Science is organized knowledge.

10984 *Education*
People are beginning to see that the first requisite to success in life is to be a good animal.

10985 *Essays 'The Americans'*
The Republican form of Government is the highest form of government; but because of this it requires the highest type of human nature - a type nowhere at present existing.

10986 *Essays 'Prison Ethics'*
Absolute morality is the regulation of conduct in such a way that pain shall not be inflicted.

10987 *First Principles*
Evolution ... is - a change from an indefinite, incoherent homogeneity, to a definite coherent heterogeneity.

10988 *Principles of Biology*
This survival of the fittest implies multiplication of the fittest.

10989 *Principles of Ethics*
How often misused words generate misleading thoughts.

10990
It was remarked to me ... that to play billiards was the sign of an ill-spent youth.

10991 *Social Statics*
Progress, therefore, is not an accident, but a necessity ... It is a part of nature.

10992 *Social Statics*
Education has for its object the formation of character.

10993 *Social Statics*
Opinion is ultimately determined by the feelings, and not by the intellect.

SPENCER Countess Raine 1929-
10994 *The Spencers on Spas*
Alas, for our towns and cities. Monstrous carbuncles of concrete have erupted in gentle Georgian Squares.

SPENDER Sir Stephen 1909-1995
10995
Born of the sun they travelled a short while towards the sun
And left the vivid air signed with their honour.

10996 *'The Express'*
After the first powerful plain manifesto
The black statement of pistons, without more fuss
But gliding like a queen, she leaves the station.

10997
I must have love enough to run a factory on, Or give a city power, or drive a train.

10998
Never being, but always at the edge of Being.

10999 *'My parents kept me from children who were rough'*
My parents kept me from children who were rough
And who threw words like stones and who wore torn clothes.

11000 *'What I expected, was'*
What I had not foreseen
Was the gradual day
Weakening the will
Leaking the brightness away.

11001 *'Who live under the shadow of a war'*
Who live under the shadow of a war,
What can I do that matters?

SPENGLER Oswald 1880-1936
11002
The secret of all victory lies in the organization
of the non-obvious.

SPENSER Edmund c.1552-1599
11003 *Amoretti*
The merry cuckoo, messenger of Spring,
His trumpet shrill hath thrice already sounded.

11004 *Amoretti*
So let us love, dear Love, like as we ought,
- Love is the lesson which the Lord us taught.

11005 *'Epithalamion'*
Ah! when will this long weary day have end,
And lend me leave to come unto my love?

11006 *The Faerie Queen*
A gentle knight was pricking on the plain.

11007 *The Faerie Queen*
Her angel's face
As the great eye of heaven shinèd bright,
And made a sunshine in the shady place.

11008 *The Faerie Queen*
Still as he fled, his eye was backward cast,
As if his fear still followed him behind.

11009 *The Faerie Queen*
That darksome cave they enter, there they find
That cursèd man, low sitting on the ground,
Musing full sadly in his sullen mind.

11010 *The Faerie Queen*
Sleep after toil, port after stormy seas,
Ease after war, death after life does greatly
please.

11011 *The Faerie Queen*
So double was his pains, so double be his
praise.

11012 *The Faerie Queen*
Upon her eyelids many Graces sate,
Under the shadow of her even brows.

11013 *The Faerie Queen*
And all for love, and nothing for reward.

11014 *The Faerie Queen*
Gather therefore the rose, whilst yet is prime,
For soon comes age, that will her pride
deflower.

11015 *The Faerie Queen*
And painful pleasure turns to pleasing pain.

11016 *The Faerie Queen*
The gentle mind by gentle deeds is known.
For a man by nothing is so well bewrayed,
As by his manners.

11017 *The Shepherd's Calendar 'July'*
And he that strives to touch the stars,
Oft stumbles at a straw.

11018 *The Shepherd's Calendar 'Letter to Gabriel
Harvey'*
So now they have made our English tongue a
gallimaufry or hodgepodge of all other
speeches.

11019 *The Shepherd's Calendar 'March. Willy's
Emblem'*
To be wise and eke to love,
Is granted scarce to God above.

SPETTIGUE Doug
11020
Husbands don't really count ... in the miracle of
birth.

SPINOZA Baruch 1632-1677
11021 *Ethics*
By *God* I mean a being absolutely infinite - that
is, a substance consisting in infinite attributes,
of which each expresses eternal and infinite
essentiality.

11022 *Ethics*
Man is a social animal.

11023 *Ethics*
We feel and know that we are eternal.

11024
Will and intellect are one and the same thing.

11025
Peace is not an absence of war, it is a virtue, a
state of mind, a disposition for benevolence,
confidence, justice.

11026 *Tractatus Politicus*
I have striven not to laugh at human actions,
not to weep at them, nor to hate them, but to
understand them.

SPOCK Dr. Benjamin 1903-1998
11027
There are only two things a child will share
willingly - communicable diseases and his
mother's age.

11028 *(of Vietnamese War)*
To win in Vietnam, we will have to exterminate
a nation.

SPOONER Rev. W.A. 1844-1930
11029 *(attributed)*
I remember your name perfectly, but I just can't
think of your face.

11030 *(attributed)*
Let us drink to the queer old Dean.

11031 *(attributed)*
Sir, you have tasted two whole worms; you have
hissed all my mystery lectures and been caught

The Wordsworth Dictionary of Quotations

fighting a liar in the quad; you will leave Oxford by the next town drain.

11032 *(announcing the hymn in New College Chapel)*
Kinquering Congs their titles take.

11033
You will find as you grow older that the weight of rages will press harder and harder upon the employer.

SPRING Dick 1950-
11034
The real Ireland is walking in spirit behind the coffins of your sons.

SPRING-RICE Sir Cecil 1859-1918
11035 *(of American politics)*
Dullness, occasionally relieved by rascality.

11036 *The Masque of Balliol*
I am the Dean of Christ Church, Sir:
There's my wife; look well at her.
She's the Broad and I'm the High;
We are the University.

11037 *'I Vow to Thee, My Country'*
I vow to thee, my country - all earthly things above -
Entire and whole and perfect, the service of my love.

11038 *'I Vow to Thee, My Country'*
Here ways are ways of gentleness and all her paths are Peace.

SPRINGSTEEN Bruce 1949-
11039 *'Born to Run'*
We gotta get out while we're young,
'Cause tramps like us, baby, we were born to run.

11040 *'Born in the USA'*
Born down in a dead man's town
The first kick I took was when I hit the ground.

11041 *'The River'*
Is a dream a lie if it don't come true,
Or is it something worse?

SPURGEON Charles Haddon 1834-1992
11042
Learn to say 'No'; it will be of more use to you than to be able to read Latin.

SQUIRE Sir J.C. 1884-1958
11043 *'Ballade of Soporific Absorption'*
But I'm not so think as you drunk I am.

11044 *'In continuation of Pope on Newton'*
It did not last: the Devil howling 'Ho!
Let Einstein be!' restored the status quo.

STACKMAN Elvin
11045
Science cannot stop while ethics catches up -

and nobody should expect scientists to do all the thinking for the country.

STALIN Joseph 1879-1953
11046 *Foundations of Leninism*
The State is an instrument in the hands of the ruling class, used to break the resistance of the adversaries of that class.

11047
The rich experience of history teaches that up to now not a single class has vountarily made way for another class.

11048 *(when asked to encourage Catholicism in Russia)*
The Pope! How many divisions has *he* got?

11049
Writers are the engineers of human souls.

STANFIELD Robert
11050
He is a pragmatist. He is not right wing, nor left wing nor any wing.

STANISLAW II King 1764-1795
11051
To believe with certainty we must begin with doubting.

STANLEY Sir Henry Morton 1841-1904
11052
Dr Livingstone, I presume?

STANTON Edwin McMasters 1814-1869
11053 *(of Abraham Lincoln, following his assassination)*
Now he belongs to the ages.

STANTON Elizabeth Cady 1815-1902
11054 *Letter to Susan B. Anthony*
Woman's degradation is a man's idea of his sexual rights. Our religion, laws, customs, are all founded on the belief that woman was made for man.

11055
Social science affirms that a woman's place in society marks the level of civilization.

STARK Freya 1893-1993
11056
Absence is one of the most useful ingredients of family life, and to do it rightly is an art like any other.

STARK John 1728-1822
11057
We beat them to-day or Molly Stark's a widow.

STARR Roger
11058
Money is the most egalitarian force in society. It confers power on whoever holds it.

STAËL Mme de 1766-1817
11059
One must choose in life between boredom and suffering.

11060 *Corinne*
To be totally understanding makes one very indulgent.

11061 *Delphine*
A man can brave opinion, a woman must submit to it.

11062 *(attributed, asked what she talked of with lover)*
Speech happens not to be his language.

11063
Wit consists in knowing the resemblance of things which differ and the difference of things which are alike.

STEAD Christina 1902-1983
11064 *House of All Nations*
A self-made man is one who believes in luck and sends his son to Oxford.

STEELE Sir Richard 1672-1729
11065
The insupportable labour of doing nothing.

11066 *(of Lady E. Hastings)*
To love her is a liberal education.

11067 *The Lover*
Women dissemble their Passions better than Men, but Men subdue their Passions better than Women.

11068
Reading is to the mind what exercise is to the body.

11069 *(of The Tatler)*
It is to be noted that when any part of this paper appears dull there is a design in it.

11070
When one has no design but to speak plain truth, he may say a great deal in a very narrow compass.

11071
There are so few who can grow old with a good grace.

11072
A woman seldom writes her mind but in her postscript.

STEFFENS Lincoln 1866-1936
11073 *(following a visit to the Soviet Union in 1919)*
I have seen the future; and it works.

STEICHEN Edward 1879-1973
11074
Photography records the gamut of feelings written on the human face; the beauty of the earth and skies that man has inherited; and the wealth and confusion man has created. It is a major force in explaining man to man.

STEIN Gertrude 1874-1946
11075 *Autobiography of Alice B. Toklas*
Remarks are not literature.

11076
The central theme of the novel is that they were glad to see each other.

11077
Everybody gets so much common information all day long that they lose their common sense.

11078 *The Geographical History of America*
In the United States there is more space where nobody is than where anybody is. That is what makes America what it is.

11079
One of the laws of paleontology is that an animal which must protect itself with thick armour is degenerate. It is usually a sign that the species is on the road to extinction.

11080
You have to learn to do everything, even to die.

11081
Money is always there but the pockets change: it is not in the same pockets after a change, and that is all there is to say about money.

11082 *Sacred Emily*
Rose is a rose is a rose is a rose, is a rose.

11083 *Four Saints in Three Acts*
Pigeons on the grass alas.

11084
I understand you undertake to overthrow my undertaking.

11085
When you get there, there isn't any there there.

11086
I write for myself and strangers. The strangers, dear Readers, are an afterthought.

11087 *(of the young who served in the First World War)*
You are all a lost generation.

STEINBECK John 1902-1968
11088 *The Grapes of Wrath*
Man, unlike any other thing organic or inorganic in the universe, grows beyond his work, walks up the stairs of his concepts, emerges ahead of his accomplishments.

STEINBERG Saul
11089
Doodling is the brooding of the hand.

11090
The life of the creative man is led, directed and controlled by boredom. Avoiding boredom is one of our most important purposes.

STEINEM Gloria 1934-
11091
We are becoming the men we wanted to marry.

11092
The first problem for all of us, men and women, is not to learn, but to unlearn.

11093
Outrageous acts and everyday rebellions.

11094
A woman without a man is like a fish without a bicycle.

STEKEL Wilhelm
11095
Anxiety is fear of one's self.

STENDHAL 1783-1842
11096
One can acquire everything in solitude except character.

11097
The first qualification for a historian is to have no ability to invent.

11098 *Le Rouge et le noir*
A novel is a mirror which passes over a highway. Sometimes it reflects to your eyes the blue of the skies, at others the churned-up mud of the road.

11099
If you want to be witty, work on your character and say what you think on every occasion.

STENGEL Casey 1889-1975
11100
Going to bed with a woman never hurt a ball player. It's staying up all night looking for them that does you in.

STEPHEN J.K. 1859-1892
11101 *'To R.K.'*
Will there never come a season
Which shall rid us from the curse
Of a prose which knows no reason
And an unmelodious verse ...

11102 *'To R.K.'*
When the Rudyards cease from kipling
And the Haggards ride no more.

11103 *'A Sonnet' (parodying Wordsworth)*
.. an old half-witted sheep
Which bleats articulate monotony,

And indicates that two and one are three.

STEPHEN Leslie 1832-1904
11104
Every man who says frankly and fully what he thinks is doing a public service.

STEPHEN Sir James Fitzjames 1829-1894
11105 *Liberty, Equality and Fraternity*
The way in which the man of genius rules is by persuading an efficient minority to coerce an indifferent and self-indulgent majority.

STEPHENS James 1882-1950
11106 *The Crock of Gold*
Finality is death. Perfection is finality. Nothing is perfect. There are lumps in it.

11107
Originality does not consist in saying what no one has ever said before, but in saying exactly what you think yourself.

11108 *'The Snare'*
I hear a sudden cry of pain!
There is a rabbit in a snare.

STERN Gil
11109
Man is a complex being: he makes deserts bloom and lakes die.

STERNE Laurence 1713-1768
11110
God tempers the wind to the shorn lamb.

11111
A man cannot dress, without his ideas get clothed at the same time.

11112
Philosophy has a fine saying for everything - for Death it has an entire set.

11113 *A Sentimental Journey*
They order, said I, this matter better in France.

11114 *A Sentimental Journey*
As an Englishman does not travel to see Englishmen, I retired to my room.

11115 *A Sentimental Journey*
If ever I do a mean action, it must be in some interval betwixt one passion and another.

11116 *A Sentimental Journey*
There are worse occupations in this world than feeling a woman's pulse.

11117 *Sermons*
This sad vicissitude of things.

11118 *Tristram Shandy*
I wish either my father or my mother, or indeed both of them, as they were in duty both equally bound to it, had minded what they were about when they begot me.

11119 *Tristram Shandy*
As we jog on, either laugh with me, or at me, or in short do anything - only keep your temper.

11120 *Tristram Shandy*
'Tis known by the name of perseverance in a good cause - and of obstinacy in a bad one.

11121 *Tristram Shandy*
Digressions, incontestably, are the sunshine; they are the life, the soul of reading; take them out of this book for instance, you might as well take the book along with them.

11122 *Tristram Shandy*
Writing, when properly managed (as you may be sure I think mine is) is but a different name for conversation.

11123 *Tristram Shandy*
Whenever a man talks loudly against religion, always suspect that it is not his reason, but his passions which have got the better of his creed.

11124 *Tristram Shandy*
'Our armies swore terribly in Flanders,' cried my uncle Toby, 'but nothing to this.'

11125 *Tristram Shandy*
Of all the cants which are canted in this canting world, though the cant of hypocrites may be the worst, the cant of criticism is the most tormenting!

11126 *Tristram Shandy*
There is a North-west passage to the intellectual World.

11127 *Tristram Shandy*
My brother Toby, quoth she, is going to be married to Mrs Wadman.
Then he will never, quoth my father, lie *diagonally* in his bed again as long as he lives.

11128 *Tristram Shandy*
A man should know something of his own country too, before he goes abroad.

11129 *Tristram Shandy*
And who are you? said he. Don't puzzle me, said I.

11130 *Tristram Shandy*
'-d!' said my mother, 'what is all this story about?'
'A Cock and a Bull', said Yorick.

11131 *Tristram Shandy*
The nonsense of the old women (of both sexes).

STEUBEN Baron von 1730-1794
11132
You say to your soldier, 'Do this' and he does it. But I am obliged to say to the American, 'This is why you ought to do this' and then he does it.

STEVENS Brooks
11133
Our whole economy is based on planned obsolescence ... we make good products, we induce people to buy them, and then the next year we deliberately introduce something that will make these products old-fashioned, out of date, obsolete.

STEVENS Wallace 1879-1955
11134 *'Adagia'*
The poet is the priest of the invisible.

11135 *'Bantams in Pine Woods'*
Chieftain Iffucan of Azcan in caftan
Of tan with henna hackles, halt!

11136 *'Disillusionment of Ten O'Clock'*
Only, here and there, an old sailor,
Drunk and asleep in his boots,
Catches tigers
In red weather.

11137 *'The Emperor of Ice-Cream'*
Let be be finale of seem.
The only emperor is the emperor of ice-cream.

11138
Frogs Eat Butterflies. Snakes Eat Frogs. Hogs Eat Snakes. Men Eat Hogs.

11139 *'A High-Toned old Christian Woman'*
Poetry is the supreme fiction, madame.

11140 *'The Man with the Blue Guitar'*
They said, 'You have a blue guitar,
You do not play things as they are.'
The man replied, 'Things as they are
Are changed upon the blue guitar.'

11141 *'Of Mere Being'*
The palm at the end of the mind,
Beyond the last thought, rises ...
A gold-feathered bird
Sings in the palm.

11142 *The Noble Rider and the Sound of Words*
What makes the poet the potent figure that he is, or was, or ought to be, is that he creates the world to which we turn incessantly and without knowing it and that he gives to life the supreme fictions without which we are unable to conceive of it.

11143 *Notes Toward a Supreme Fiction*
They will get it straight one day at the Sorbonne.
We shall return at twilight from the lecture Pleased that the irrational is rational.

11144 *'An Ordinary Evening in New Haven'*
We keep coming back and coming back
To the real: to the hotel instead of the hymns
That fall upon it out of the wind.

11145 *'Thirteen Ways of Looking at a Blackbird'*
I do not know which to prefer,
The beauty of inflections
Or the beauty of innuendos,
The blackbird whistling
Or just after.

STEVENSON Adlai 1900-1965
11146
Every age needs men who will redeem the time
by living with a vision of things that are to be.

11147
In America, any boy may become president,
and I suppose it's just one of the risks he takes.

11148
My definition of a free society is a society where
it is safe to be unpopular.

11149
It is often easier to fight for principles than to
live up to them.

11150
There is no evil in the atom; only in men's souls.

11151
A funny thing happened to me on the way to
the White House.

11152
We hear the Secretary of State [John Foster
Dulles] boasting of his brinkmanship - the art of
bringing us to the edge of the abyss.

11153
A hungry man is not a free man.

11154
I'm not an old, experienced hand at politics.
But I am now seasoned enough to have learned
that the hardest thing about any political
campaign is how to win without proving that
your are unworthy of winning.

11155
Laws are never as effective as habits.

11156 *(on learning of Eleanor Roosevelt's death)*
She would rather light a candle than curse the
darkness, and her glow has warmed the world.

11157
Let's talk sense to the American people. Let's
tell them the truth, that there are no gains
without pains.

11158
It is not the years in your life but the life in your
years that counts.

11159
Patriotism is not short, frenzied outbursts of
emotion, but the tranquil and steady dedication
of a lifetime.

11160
Some people approach every problem with an
open mouth.

11161
If they [the Republicans] will stop telling lies
about the Democrats, we will stop telling the
truth about them.

11162
I suppose flattery hurts no one, that is, if you
don't inhale.

11163
What a man knows at fifty that he did not know
at twenty is for the most part incommunicable.

11164
I have said what I meant and meant what I said.
I have not done as well as I should like to have
done, but I have done my best, frankly and
forthrightly; no man can do more, and you are
entitled to no less.

11165
It is said that a wise man who stands firm is a
statesman, and a foolish man who stands firm
is a catastrophe.

STEVENSON Anne 1933-
11166 *'Green Mountain, Black Mountain'*
Blackbirds are the cellos of the deep farms.

STEVENSON Robert Louis 1850-1894
11167
Absences are a good influence in love and keep
it bright and delicate.

11168 *Across the Plains 'Beggars'*
Everyone lives by selling something.

11169 *Across the Plains 'A Christmas Sermon'*
A mortified appetite is never a wise companion.

11170
Is there anything in life so disenchanting as
attainment?

11171
There is but one art, to omit.

11172 *Ballads 'Christmas at Sea'*
But all that I could think of, in the darkness and
the cold,
Was that I was leaving home and my folks were
growing old.

11173
Keep busy at something. A busy person never
has time to be unhappy.

11174 *A Child's Garden of Verses 'Bed in Summer'*
In winter I get up at night
And dress by yellow candle-light.
In summer, quite the other way -
I have to go to bed by day.

11175 *A Child's Garden of Verses 'Happy Thought'*
The world is so full of a number of things,
I'm sure we should all be as happy as kings.

11176 *A Child's Garden of Verses 'Looking Forward'*
When I am grown to man's estate
I shall be very proud and great,
And tell the other girls and boys
Not to meddle with my toys.

11177 *A Child's Garden of Verses 'System'*
The child that is not clean and neat,
With lots of toys and things to eat,
He is a naughty child, I'm sure -
Or else his dear papa is poor.

11178 *A Child's Garden of Verses 'Whole Duty ...'*
A child should always say what's true,
And speak when he is spoken to,
And behave mannerly at table:
At least as far as he is able.

11179
Extreme busyness, whether at school, or college, kirk or market, is a symptom of deficient vitality; and a faculty for idleness implies a catholic appetite and a strong sense of personal identity.

11180 *Familiar Studies of Men and Books*
Politics is perhaps the only profession for which no preparation is thought necessary.

11181
For God's sake give me the young man who has brains enough to make a fool of himself.

11182 *Kidnapped*
I've a grand memory for forgetting, David.

11183 *Letter to Sidney Colvin*
I believe in an ultimate decency of things.

11184
If a man loves the labour of his trade, apart from any question of success or fame, the gods have called him.

11185
Marriage is one long conversation checkered by disputes.

11186
If your morals make you dreary, depend on it they are wrong.

11187 *New Arabian Nights 'The Rajah's Diamond'*
I regard you with an indifference closely bordering on aversion.

11188 *New Arabian Nights 'The Suicide Club'*
The devil, depend upon it, can sometimes do a very gentlemanly thing.

11189
The Saints are the Sinners who keep on trying.

11190 *Songs of Travel 'The Vagabond'*
Wealth I seek not, hope nor love,
Nor a friend to know me;
All I seek, the heaven above
And the road below me.

11191
By the time a man gets well into his seventies his continued existence is a mere miracle.

11192
For my part, I travel not to go anywhere, but to go. I travel for travel's sake. The great affair is to move.

11193 *Treasure Island*
Fifteen men on the dead man's chest
Yo-ho-ho, and a bottle of rum!
Drink and the devil had done for the rest -
Yo-ho-ho, and a bottle of rum!

11194 *Treasure Island*
Tip me the black spot.

11195 *Treasure Island*
Many's the long night I've dreamed of cheese - toasted, mostly.

11196 *Virginibus Puerisque*
In marriage, a man becomes slack and selfish, and undergoes a fatty degeneration of his moral being.

11197 *Virginibus Puerisque*
Marriage is like life in this - that it is a field of battle, and not a bed of roses.

11198 *Virginibus Puerisque*
To marry is to domesticate the Recording Angel. Once you are married, there is nothing left for you, not even suicide, but to be good.

11199 *Virginibus Puerisque*
The cruellest lies are often told in silence.

11200 *Virginibus Puerisque 'Aes Triplex'*
Even if the doctor does not give you a year, even if he hesitates about a month, make one brave push and see what can be accomplished in a week.

11201 *Virginibus Puerisque 'An Apology for Idlers'*
There is no duty we so much underrate as the duty of being happy.

11202 *Virginibus Puerisque 'An Apology for Idlers'*
He sows hurry and reaps indigestion.

11203 *Virginibus Puerisque 'Crabbed Age and Youth'*
Old and young, we are all on our last cruise.

11204 *Virginibus Puerisque 'El Dorado'*
To travel hopefully is a better thing than to arrive, and the true success is to labour.

11205 *The Wrong Box (with Lloyd Osborne)*
What hangs people ... is the unfortunate circumstance of guilt.

11206 *The Wrong Box (with Lloyd Osborne)*
Nothing like a little judicious levity.

STILL John
11207
The memories of men are too frail a thread to hang history from.

STING
11208
Cocaine is God's way of telling you you've got too much money.

STINNETT Caskie 1911-
11209 *Out of the Red*
A diplomat ... is a person who can tell you to go to hell in such a way that you actually look forward to the trip.

11210
The trouble with being a hypochondriac these days is that antibiotics have cured all the good diseases.

STIPE Michael
11211
I believe in the theory that anyone can get laid, it's just a matter of lowering your standards!

STOCKDALE Edmund
11212
Money isn't everything - but it's a long way ahead of what comes next.

STODDARD Elizabeth Drew 1823-1902
11213 *Two Men*
A woman despises a man for loving her, unless she returns his love.

STODDARD R.H.
11214
We love in others what we lack ourselves, and would be everything but what we are.

STONE I.F. 1907-1989
11215
Every emancipation has in it the seeds of a new slavery, and every truth easily becomes a lie.

11216
Every government is run by liars and nothing they say should be believed.

11217
If you live long enough the venerability factor creeps in; you get accused of things you never did and praised for virtues you never had.

STONE Professor Lawrence
11218 *(of the ingredients of marriage)*
Affection was a late 18th century development.

STONE Samuel John 1839-1900
11219 *Lyra Fidelium 'The Church's one foundation'*
The Church's one foundation
Is Jesus Christ, her Lord;
She is his new creation
By water and the word.

STOPES Marie 1880-1958
11220 *Married Love*
An impersonal and scientific knowledge of the structure of our bodies is the surest safeguard against prurient curiosity and lascivious gloating.

STOPPARD Tom 1937-
11221
Age is a high price to pay for maturity.

11222
Everything has to be taken on trust; truth is only that which is taken to be true. It's the currency of living. There may be nothing behind it, but it doesn't make any difference so long as it is honoured.

11223 *Jumpers*
It's not the voting that's democracy, it's the counting.

11224 *Lord Malquist and Mr Moon (c/f Kipling of Max Aitken)*
The House of Lords, an illusion to which I have never been able to subscribe - responsibility without power, the prerogative of the eunuch throughout the ages.

11225 *Night and Day*
The media. It sounds like a convention of spiritualists.

11226 *Night and Day*
I'm with you on the free press. It's the newspapers I can't stand.

11227 *Night and Day*
Comment is free but facts are on expenses.

11228
It's better to be quotable than to be honest.

11229 *Rosencrantz and Guildenstern are Dead*
You're familiar with the tragedies of antiquity, are you? The great homicidal classics?

11230 *Rosencrantz and Guildenstern are Dead*
All your life you live so close to truth, it becomes a permanent blur in the corner of your eye, and when something nudges it into outline it is like being ambushed by a grotesque.

11231 *Rosencrantz and Guildenstern are Dead*
Eternity's a terrible thought. I mean, where's it all going to end?

11232 *Rosencrantz and Guildenstern are Dead*
The bad end unhappily, the good unluckily. That is what tragedy means.

11233 *Rosencrantz and Guildenstern are Dead*
Life is a gamble at terrible odds - if it was a bet, you wouldn't take it.

11234 *Rosencrantz and Guildenstern are Dead*
Death is not anything ... death is not ... It's the absence of presence, nothing more ... the endless time of never coming back ... a gap you can't see, and when the wind blows through it, it makes no sound.

11235
You could say you'd seen the future after visiting America. I don't think you could add: 'and it works'.

11236 *Travesties*
War is capitalism with the gloves off and many who go to war know it but they go to war because they don't want to be a hero.

STOREY Wilbur F.
11237
It is a newspaper's duty to print the news and raise hell.

STORR Anthony 1920-
11238
That man is an aggressive creature will hardly be disputed. With the exception of certain rodents, no other vertebrate habitually destroys members of its own species.

STORY William Wetmore 1819-1895
11239
Of every noble work the silent part is best,
Of all expression that cannot be expressed.

STOWE Harriet Beecher 1811-1896
11240 *Uncle Tom's Cabin*
'Never was born!' persisted Topsy ... 'never had no father, nor mother, nor nothin'. I was raised by a speculator, with lots of others.'

11241 *Uncle Tom's Cabin*
I s'pect I growed. Don't think nobody never made me.

STRACHEY Lionel
11242
A brilliant epigram is a solemn platitude gone to a masquerade ball.

STRACHEY Lytton 1880-1932
11243 *(on his deathbed)*
If this is dying, then I don't think much of it.

11244
Discretion is not the better part of biography.

11245 *Eminent Victorians*
Ignorance is the first requisite of the historian - ignorance, which simplifies and clarifies, which selects and omits, with a placid perfection unattainable by the highest art.

11246 *Eminent Victorians 'Cardinal Manning'*
The time was out of joint, and he was only too delighted to have been born to set it right.

11247 *Eminent Victorians 'Florence Nightingale'*
Her conception of God was certainly not orthodox. She felt towards Him as she might have felt towards a glorified sanitary engineer; and in some of her speculations she seems hardly to distinguish between the Deity and the Drains.

11248
Happiness is the perpetual possession of being well deceived.

11249 *Pope*
The verses, when they were written, resembled nothing so much as spoonfuls of boiling oil, ladled out by a fiendish monkey at an upstairs window upon such passers-by whom the wretch had a grudge against.

STRAVINSKY Igor 1882-1971
11250 *(attributed)*
Academism results when the reasons for the rule change, but not the rule.

11251
Childhood - a period of waiting for the moment when I could send everyone and everything connected with it to hell.

11252
Conductors' careers are made for the most part with 'romantic' music. 'Classic' music eliminates the conductor; we do not remember him in it.

11253
Conformism is so hot on the heels of the mass-produced avant garde that the 'ins' and the 'outs' change places with the speed of mach 3.

11254
Music is given to us specifically to make order of things, to move from an anarchic, individualistic state to a regulated, perfectly concious one, which alone insures vitality and durability.

11255
Old age is a time of humiliations, the most disagreeable of which, for me, is that I cannot work long at sustained high pressure with no leaks in concentration.

11256
I know that the twelve notes in each octave and the varieties of rhythm offer me oppotunities that all of human genius will never exhaust.

STREETER Edward
11257
Travel is ninety per cent anticipation and ten per cent recollection.

STREISAND Barbra 1942-
11258 *(of Bill Clinton, in 1998)*
We elected a President, not a Pope.

STRINDBERG Johan August 1849-1912
11259
Growing old - it's not nice, but it's interesting.

STRINGER Arthur 1922-
11260
Society, my dear, is like salt water, good to swim in but hard to swallow.

STRUNSKY Simeon 1879-1948
11261
Famous remarks are very seldom quoted correctly.

11262
Once a man would spend a week patiently waiting if he missed a stage coach, but now he rages if he misses the first section of a revolving door.

11263
To renew ties with the past need not always be daydreaming; it may be tapping old sources of strength for new tasks.

11264
If you want to understand democracy, spend less time in the library with Plato, and more time in the buses with people.

STUBBS John Heath 1918-
11265
Its always good to remember that people find it easier to name 10 artists from any century than 10 politicians.

STUDDERT KENNEDY G.A. 1883-1929
11266
It is much easier to do and die than it is to reason why.

11267 *Peace Rhymes of a Padre 'Indifference'*
When Jesus came to Birmingham they simply passed Him by,
They never hurt a hair of Him, they only let Him die.

11268 *More Rough Rhymes of a Padre 'Waste'*
Waste of Blood, and waste of Tears,
Waste of youth's most precious years,
Waste of ways the saints have trod,
Waste of Glory, waste of God,

War!

SUCKLING Sir John 1609-1642
11269 *Aglaura 'Song'*
If of herself she will not love,
Nothing can make her:
The devil take her!

11270 *'A Ballad upon a Wedding'*
Her feet beneath her petticoat,
Like little mice, stole in and out,
As if they feared the light.

11271 *'Against Fruition'*
Women enjoyed (whatsoe'er before they've been)
Are like romances read, or sights once seen: ...
'Tis expectation makes a blessing dear;
It were not heaven, if we knew what it were.

11272 *'Love's Offence'*
Love is the fart
Of every heart:
It pains a man when 'tis kept close,
And others doth offend, when 'tis let loose.

SUETONIUS c.70-c.140
11273 *Augustus*
Festina lente.
Hasten slowly.

11274 *Augustus*
He so improved the city that he justly boasted he had found it brick and left it marble.

11275 *Claudius*
Ave, Imperator, morituri te salutant
Hail, Emperor, those about to die salute you.

SULLIVAN Henry Stack
11276
When the satisfaction or the security of another person becomes as significant to one as one's own satisfaction or security, then the state of love exists.

SULLIVAN Louis Henri 1856-1924
11277 *The Tall Office Building Artistically Considered*
Form follows function.

SULLY Maximilen de Béthune, Duc de 1559-1641
11278 *(attributed)*
The English take their pleasures sadly after the fashion of their country.

11279 *Mémoires*
Tilling and grazing are the two breasts by which France is fed.

SULZBERGER Arthur Hays 1891-1968
11280 *(on journalism)*
We tell the public which way the cat is jumping. The public will take care of the cat.

The Wordsworth Dictionary of Quotations

SUMMERSKILL Edith 1901-1980
11281
The housewife is the Cinderella of the affluent state ... She is wholly dependent on the whim of an individual to give her money for the essentials of life.

SUMNER William Graham 1840-1874
11282
The forgotten man. He is the clean, quiet, virtuous domestic citizen who pays his debts and his taxes and is never heard of outside his little circle.... He works, he votes, generally he prays, but his chief business in life is to pay.

SURTEES R.S. 1805-1864
11283 *The Analysis of the Hunting Field*
More people are flattered into virtue than bullied out of vice.

11284 *Mr Facey Romford's Hounds*
Better be killed than frightened to death.

11285 *Mr Facey Romford's Hounds*
Life would be very pleasant if it were not for its enjoyments.

11286 *Mr Facey Romford's Hounds*
Everyone knows that the real business of a ball is either to look out for a wife, to look after a wife, or to look after somebody else's wife

11287 *Handley Cross*
'Unting is all that's worth living for ... it's the sport of kings, the image of war without its guilt, and only five-and-twenty per cent of its danger.

11288 *Handley Cross*
I'll fill hup the chinks wi' cheese.

11289 *Handley Cross*
It ar'n't that I loves the fox less, but that I loves the 'ound more.

11290 *Hillingdon Hall*
Three things I never lends - my 'oss, my wife, and my name.

11291 *Jorrocks's Jaunts and Jollities*
Champagne certainly gives one werry gentlemanly ideas, but for a continuance, I don't know but I should prefer mild hale.

11292 *Ask Mamma*
The only infallible rule we know is, that the man who is always talking about being a gentleman never is one.

11293 *Mr Sponge's Sporting Tour*
The young ladies entered the drawing-room in the full fervour of sisterly animosity.

11294 *Mr Sponge's Sporting Tour*
He was a gentleman who was generally spoken of as having nothing a-year, paid quarterly.

11295 *Mr Sponge's Sporting Tour*
There is no secret so close as that between a rider and his horse.

SUSSER Dr. Laurence
11296
Workaholics commit slow suicide by refusing to allow the child inside them to play.

SUTHERLAND Graham 1903-1980
11297
I don't think anyone is free - one creates one's own prison.

SUTTON David 1944-
11298 *'Geomancies'*
Sorrow in all lands, and grievous omens.
Great anger in the dragon of the hills,
And silent now the earth's green oracles
That will not speak again of innocence.

SWAFFER Hannen 1879-1962
11299
Freedom of the press in Britain means freedom to print such of the proprietor's prejudices as the advertisers don't object to.

SWANSON Gloria 1897-1983
11300 *(of her passport photo)*
If I look like this, I need the trip.

11301 *in Sunset Boulevard*
"I am big. It is the pictures got small."

SWEET Ben
11302
The greatest success is successful self-acceptance.

SWIFT Jonathan 1667-1745
11303 *The Battle of the Books*
Satire is a sort of glass, wherein beholders do generally discover everybody's face but their own.

11304 *The Battle of the Books*
Instead of dirt and poison we have rather chosen to fill our hives with honey and wax; thus furnishing mankind with the two noblest of things, which are sweetness and light.

11305
He was a bold man that first ate an oyster.

11306 *A Critical Essay upon the Faculties of the Mind*
Laws are like cobwebs, which may catch small flies, but let wasps and hornets break through.

11307 *A Critical Essay upon the Faculties of the Mind*
There is nothing in this world constant, but inconstancy.

11308 *On the Death of Dr Swift*
Some great misfortune to portend,
No enemy can match a friend.

11309 *'To Mr Delany'*
Hated by fools, and fools to hate,
Be that my motto and my fate.

11310
Dignity, high station, or great riches are in some
sort necessary to old men, in order to keep the
younger at a distance, who are otherwise too
apt to insult them upon the score of their age.

11311 *The Drapier's Letters*
I have heard of a man who had a mind to sell
his house, and therefore carried a piece of brick
in his pocket, which he shewed as a pattern to
encourage purchasers.

11312 *(epitaph)*
Where fierce indignation can no longer tear his
heart.

11313 *Gulliver's Travels 'A Voyage to
Brobdingnag'*
I cannot but conclude the bulk of your natives
to be the most pernicious race of little odious
vermin that nature ever suffered to crawl upon
the surface of the earth.

11314 *Gulliver's Travels 'A Voyage to
Houyhnhnms'*
I told him ... that we ate when we were not
hungry, and drank without the provocation of
thirst.

11315 *Gulliver's Travels 'Voyage to Lilliput'*
Big-endians and small-endians.

11316 *'The Journal'*
How haughtily he lifts his nose,
To tell what every schoolboy knows.

11317 *Journal of a Modern Lady*
Convey a libel in a frown,
And wink a reputation down.

11318 *Journal to Stella*
We were to do more business after dinner; but
after dinner is after dinner - an old saying and a
true, 'much drinking, little thinking'.

11319 *Journal to Stella*
We are so fond of one another, because our
ailments are the same.

11320 *Journal to Stella*
I love good creditable acquaintance; I love to be
the worst of the company.

11321 *Letter to Bolingbroke*
Not die here in a rage, like a poisoned rat in a
hole.

11322 *Letter to Miss Vanhomrigh*
If Heaven had looked upon riches to be a
valuable thing, it would not have given them to
such a scoundrel.

11323 *Letter to Pope*
Principally I hate and detest that animal called
man; although I heartily love John, Peter,
Thomas, and so forth.

11324 *Letter to a Young Gentleman ....Holy
Orders*
Proper words in proper places, make the true
definition of a style.

11325
May you live all the days of your life.

11326 *'Ode to Sir W. Temple'*
Philosophy! the lumber of the schools.

11327 *'A Pastoral Dialogue between Richmond
Lodge ...'*
Walls have tongues, and hedges ears.

11328 *'On Poetry'*
As learned commentators view
In Homer more than Homer knew.

11329 *'On Poetry'*
Hobbes clearly proves, that every creature
Lives in a state of war by nature.

11330 *'On Poetry'*
So, naturalists observe, a flea
Hath smaller fleas that on him prey;
And these have smaller fleas to bite 'em,
And so proceed *ad infinitum*.
Thus every poet, in his kind,
Is bit by him that comes behind.

11331 *Polite Conversation*
Faith, that's as well said, as if I had said it
myself.

11332 *Polite Conversation*
Promises and pie-crust are made to be broken.

11333 *Polite Conversation*
Bachelor's fare; bread and cheese, and kisses.

11334 *Polite Conversation*
'Tis happy for him, that his father was before
him.

11335 *Polite Conversation*
Why, everyone one as they like; as the good
woman said when she kissed her cow.

11336
Most sorts of diversion in men, children and
other animals, are in imitation of fighting.

11337 *A Tale of a Tub*
Last week I saw a woman flayed, and you will
hardly believe, how much it altered her person
for the worse.

11338 *Thoughts on Various Subjects*
We have just enough religion to make us hate,
but not enough to make us love one another.

11339 *Thoughts on Various Subjects*
Few are qualified to shine in company; but it is
in most men's power to be agreeable.

11340 *Thoughts on Various Subjects*
Every man desires to live long; but no man
would be old.

11341
'Tis an old maxim in the schools,
That flattery's the food of fools;
Yet now and then your men of wit
Will condescend to take a bit.

11342
I shall be like that tree, I shall die at the top.

11343
Usually speaking, the worst-bred person in
company is a young traveller just returned from
abroad.

11344 *'Verses on the Death of Dr Swift'*
The rest will give a shrug, and cry,
'I'm sorry - but we all must die!'

11345 *'Verses on the Death of Dr Swift'*
Yet malice never was his aim;
He lashed the vice, but spared the name;
No individual could resent,
Where thousands equally were meant.

11346
What some invent, the rest enlarge.

11347
When men grow virtuous in their old age, they
only make a sacrifice to God of the devil's
leavings.

11348
When a true genius appears in the world you
may know him by this sign, that the dunces are
all in confederacy against him.

11349
When the world has once begun to use us ill, it
afterwards continues the same treatment with
less scruple or ceremony, as men do to a whore.

11350
No wise man ever wished to be younger.

SWINBURNE Algernon Charles 1837-1909
11351 *'Anactoria'*
Superflux of pain.

11352 *'Atalanta in Calydon'*
Maiden, and mistress of the months and stars
Now folded in the flowerless fields of heaven.

11353 *'Atalanta in Calydon'*
And in green underwood and cover
Blossom by blossom the spring begins.

11354 *'Atalanta in Calydon'*
Before the beginning of years
There came to the making of man
Time with a gift of tears,
Grief with a glass that ran.

11355 *'Atalanta in Calydon'*
Strength without hands to smite,
Love that endures for a breath;
Night, the shadow of light,
And Life, the shadow of death.

11356 *'Atalanta in Calydon'*
For words divide and rend;
But silence is most noble till the end.

11357 *'Atalanta in Calydon'*
He weaves, and is clothed with derision;
Sows, and he shall not reap;
His life is a watch or a vision
Between a sleep and a sleep.

11358 *'Ballad of François Villon'*
Villon, our sad bad glad mad brother's name.

11359 *'Dolores'*
Change in a trice
The lilies and languors of virtue
For the raptures and roses of vice.

11360 *'Dolores'*
O splendid and sterile Dolores,
Our Lady of Pain.

11361 *'Dolores'*
Ah beautiful passionate body
That never has ached with a heart!

11362 *'Dolores'*
And love is more cruel than lust.
Time turns the old days to derision
Our loves into corpses or wives.

11363 *'Erotion'*
I shall remember while the light lives yet
And in the night time I shall not forget.

11364 *'A Forsaken Garden'*
In a coign of the cliff between lowland and
highland,
At the sea-down's edge between windward and
lee,
Walled round with rocks as an inland island,
The ghost of a garden fronts the sea.

11365 *'A Forsaken Garden'*
As a god self-slain on his own strange altar,
Death lies dead.

11366 *'The Garden of Proserpine'*
Pale, beyond porch and portal,
Crowned with calm leaves, she stands

Who gathers all things mortal
With cold immortal hands.

11367 *The Heptalogia 'The Higher Pantheism ...'*
Fiddle, we know, is diddle: and diddle, we take
it, is dee.

11368 *'Hymn of Man'*
But God, if a God there be, is the substance of
men which is man.

11369 *'Hymn to Proserpine'*
Thou hast conquered, O pale Galilean; the
world has grown grey from thy breath;
We have drunken of things Lethean, and fed on
the fullness of death.

11370 *'An Interlude'*
And the best and the worst of this is
That neither is most to blame,
If you have forgotten my kisses
And I have forgotten your name.

11371 *'Itylus'*
Till life forget and death remember,
Till thou remember and I forget.

11372 *'The Triumph of Time'*
I will go back to the great sweet mother,
Mother and lover of men, the sea.
I will go down to her, I and no other,
Close with her, kiss her and mix her with me.

SWINNERTON Frank 1884-1982
11373
The wisest man I have ever known once said to
me: 'Nine out of every ten people improve on
acquaintance,' and I have found his words true.

SWOPE Herbert Bayard
11374
I cannot give you the formula for success, but I
can give you the formula for failure, which is -
try to please everybody.

SYMONDS John Addington 1840-1893
11375
These things shall be! A loftier race
Than e'er the world hath known shall rise,
With flame of freedom in their souls,
And light of knowledge in their eyes.

SYMONS Arthur 1865-1945
11376
An invitation is the sincerest form of flattery.

11377 *Memory*
As a perfume doth remain
In the folds where it hath lain,
So the thought of you, remaining
Deeply folded in my brain,
Will not leave me: all things leave me:
You remain.

SYMS Rev Richard
11378
An actor and a priest both require similar skills -
dressing up and talking in a loud voice.

SYNGE John Millington 1871-1909
11379 *The Aran Islands*
We do be afraid of the sea, and we do only be
drownded now and again.

11380 *The Aran Islands*
'A translation is no translation,' he said, 'unless
it will give you the music of a poem along with
the words of it.'

11381 *The Playboy of the Western World*
Oh my grief, I've lost him surely. I've lost the
only Playboy of the Western World.

11382
Before verse can be human again it must learn
to be brutal.

SYRUS Publilius 1st Century BC
11383
Everything is worth what its purchaser will pay
for it.

11384
There are some remedies worse than the
disease.

SZASZ Thomas 1920-
11385 *The Second Sin*
Traditionally, sex has been a very private,
secretive activity. Herein perhaps lies its
powerful force for uniting people in a strong
bond. As we make sex less secretive, we may
rob it of its power to hold men and women
together.

11386 *The Second Sin 'Childhood'*
A child becomes an adult when he realizes that
he has a right not only to be right but also to be
wrong.

11387 *The Second Sin 'Education'*
A teacher should have maximal authority and
minimal power.

11388 *The Second Sin 'Emotions'*
Happiness is an imaginary condition, formerly
often attributed by the living to the dead, now
usually attributed by adults to children, and by
children to adults.

11389 *The Second Sin 'Personal Conduct'*
The stupid neither forgive nor forget; the naïve
forgive and forget; the wise forgive but do not
forget.

11390 *The Second Sin 'Science and Scientism'*
Formerly, when religion was strong and science
weak, men mistook magic for medicine; now,
when science is strong and religion weak, men
mistake medicine for magic.

11391 *The Second Sin 'Sex'*
Masturbation: the primary sexual activity of
mankind. In the nineteenth century, it was a
disease; in the twentieth, it's a cure.

11392 *The Second Sin 'Social Relations'*
Two wrongs don't make a right, but they make a
good excuse.

11393
If you talk to God, you are praying; if God talks
to you, you have schizophrenia.

SZELL George 1897-1970
11394
Conductors must give unmistakable and
suggestive signals to the orchestra, not
choreography to the audience.

SZENT-GYÖRGYI Albert von 1893-1986
11395
Discovery consists of seeing what everybody
has seen and thinking what nobody has
thought.

TACITUS AD c.56-c.117
11396 *Agricola*
They make a wilderness and call it peace.

11397 *Agricola*
It is part of human nature to hate the man you
have hurt.

11398 *Annals*
With neither anger nor partiality.

11399 *Annals (of Petronius)*
The arbiter of taste.

11400
Candour and generosity, unless tempered by
due moderation, lead to ruin.

11401
Things forbidden have a secret charm.

11402
Greater things are believed of those who are
absent.

11403 *Histories*
These times having the rare good fortune that
you may think what you like and say what you
think.

11404 *Histories*
The gods are on the side of the stronger.

TAFT William Howard 1857-1930
11405
Some men are graduated from college cum
laude, some are graduated summa cum laude,
and some are graduated mirabile dictu.

TAGORE Sir Rabindranath 1861-1941
11406 *Fireflies*
Bigotry tries to keep truth safe in its hand

With a grip that kills it.

11407
Men are cruel, but man is kind.

11408
The mountain remains unmoved at seeming
defeat by the mist.

11409
He only may chastise who loves.

11410
The soil, in return for her service, keeps the tree
tied to her; the sky asks nothing and leaves it
free.

TAINE Hippolyte 1828-1893
11411
There are four varieties in society; the lovers,
the ambitious, observers, and fools. The fools
are the happiest.

TALBOT Nellie
11412
Jesus wants me for a sunbeam.

TALLENTYRE S.G.
11413
The crowning blessing of life - to be born with a
bias to some pursuit.

TALLEYRAND Charles Maurice de 1754-1838
11414
Above all, gentlemen, not the slightest zeal.

11415 *(announcing Napoleon's defeat at
Borodino)*
This is the beginning of the end.

11416
The art of putting the right men in the right
places is first in the science of government; but
that of finding places for the discontented is the
most difficult.

11417
The art of statemanship is to foresee the
inevitable and to expedite its occurrence.

11418 *(of Mme. de Staël)*
She is such a good friend that she would throw
all her acquaintances into the water for the
pleasure of fishing them out.

The TALMUD
11419
The burden is equal to the horse's strength.

11420
The deeper the sorrow the less tongue it hath.

11421
Would that life were like the shadow cast by a
wall or a tree, but it is like the shadow of a bird
in flight.

11422
The sun will set without thy assistance.

11423
It is not upon thee to finish the work; neither art thou free to abstain from it.

11424
Three things are good in little measure and evil in large: yeast, salt and hesitation.

TANFIELD Elizabeth Lady c.1565-1628
11425 *(epitaph for her husband)*
Love made me poet,
And this I writ;
My heart did do it,
And not my wit.

TARKINGTON Booth 1869-1946
11426 *(attributed)*
An ideal wife is any woman who has an ideal husband.

11427 *Penrod*
There are two things that will be believed of any man whatsoever, and one of them is that he has taken to drink.

TARSHIS Jerome
11428
The history of medicine is a story of amazing foolishness and amazing intelligence.

TATE Nahum 1652-1715
11429 *Dido and Aeneas 'Dido's Lament'*
When I am laid in earth my wrongs create
No trouble in thy breast.
Remember me, but ah! forget my fate.

11430 *'While Shepherds Watched'*
While shepherds watched their flocks by night,
All seated on the ground,
The angel of the Lord came down,
And glory shone around.

TAWNEY R.H. 1880-1962
11431 *The Acquisitive Society*
The characteristic virtue of Englishmen is power of sustained practical activity and their characteristic vice a reluctance to test the quality of that activity by reference to principles.

11432 *The Acquisitive Society*
Militarism ... is fetish worship. It is the prostration of men's souls and the laceration of their bodies to appease an idol.

11433
Clever men are impressed in their differences from their fellows. Wise men are conscious of their resemblance to them.

11434 *(declining the offer of a peerage)*
What harm have I ever done to the Labour Party?

11435
If a man has important work, and enough leisure and income to enable him to do it properly, he is in possession of as much happiness as is good for any of the children of Adam.

11436 *Religion and the Rise of Capitalism*
A reasonable estimate of economic organisation must allow for the fact that, unless industry is to be paralysed by recurrent revolts on the part of outraged human nature, it must satisfy criteria which are not purely economic.

TAYLOR A.J.P. 1906-1990
11437 *English History 1914-45*
History gets thicker as it approaches recent times.

11438
History is not another name for the past, as many people imply. It is the name for stories about the past.

11439 *'Mistaken Lessons from the Past'*
Like most of those who study history, he [Napoleon III] learned from the mistakes of the past how to make new ones.

11440 *The Origins of the Second World War*
Human blunders usually do more to shape history than human wickedness.

11441 *Politicians, Socialism and Historians*
If men are to respect each other for what they are, they must cease to respect each other for what they own.

11442 *Rumours of Wars*
Crimea: The War That Would Not Boil.

TAYLOR Ann and TAYLOR Jane 1782-1866 and 1783-1824
11443 *Hymns for Infant Minds 'A Child's Hymn of Praise'*
I thank the goodness and the grace
Which on my birth have smiled,
And made me, in these Christian days,
A happy English child.

11444 *Original Poems for Infant Minds 'My Mother'*
Who ran to help me when I fell,
And would some pretty story tell,
Or kiss the place to make it well?
My Mother.

11445 *Rhymes for the Nursery 'The Star'*
Twinkle, twinkle, little star,
How I wonder what you are!
Up above the world so high,
Like a diamond in the sky!

11446 *Rhymes for the Nursery 'The Way to be Happy'*
How pleasant it is, at the end of the day,
No follies to have to repent;
But reflect on the past, and be able to say,
That my time has been properly spent.

TAYLOR Bayard 1825-1878
11447 *'Bedouin Song'*
Till the sun grows cold,
And the stars are old,
And the leaves of the Judgement Book unfold.

11448
The loving are the daring.

TAYLOR Bert Leston 1866-1921
11449
A bore is a man who, when you ask him how he is, tells you.

TAYLOR Elizabeth 1932-
11450 *(on her first brief marriage at 19)*
I have a woman's body and a child's emotions.

TAYLOR Henry
11451
Shy and unready men are great betrayers of secrets; for there are few wants more urgent for the moment than the want of something to say.

11452
The world knows nothing of its greatest men.

TAYLOR Bishop Jeremy 1613-1667
11453 *Ductor Dubitantium 'When in Rome, do as the Romans do'*
If you are at Rome, live in the Roman style; if you are elsewhere, live as they live elsewhere.

11454 *The Real Prescence ...*
This thing ... that can be understood and not expressed, may take a neuter gender; and every schoolboy knows it.

11455 *The Rule and Exercise of Holy Dying*
As our life is very short, so it is very miserable, and therefore it is well it is short.

11456 *The Rule and Exercise of Holy Dying*
Desperate by too quick a sense of a constant infelicity.

11457 *Sermons 'The Marriage Ring'*
The union of hands and hearts.

11458 *Sermons 'Married Love'*
He that loves not his wife and children, feeds a lioness at home and broods a nest of sorrows.

TAYLOR Joe
11459
It takes time to save time.

TAYLOR W.M.
11460
Temptation rarely comes in working hours. It is in their leisure time that men are made or marred.

TEALE Edwin Way
11461
In nature, there is less death and destruction than death and transmutation.

TEASDALE Sara 1884-1933
11462
Beauty, more than bitterness
Makes the heart break.

TEBBIT Norman 1931-
11463
I grew up in the Thirties with our unemployed father. He did not riot, he got on his bike and looked for work.

11464
It is a mistake to judge people by their friends. Judge them by their enemies. I am very proud of my enemies.

11465
Youngsters of all races born here should be taught that British history in their history, or they will forever be foreigners holding British passports, and this kingdom will become a Yugoslavia.

TEMPLE William 1881-1944
11466 *(attributed)*
Personally, I have always looked on cricket as organized loafing.

11467
Learning passes for wisdom among those who want both.

11468 *In The Life of the Church and the Order of Society*
Human status ought not to depend upon the changing demands of the economic process.

11469
It is a mistake to suppose that God is only, or even chiefly, concerned with religion.

TENNYSON Alfred Lord 1809-1892
11470
I am a part of all that I have met.

11471 *'The Ancient Sage'*
For nothing worthy of proving can be proven,
Nor yet disproven: wherefore thou be wise,
Cleave ever to the sunnier side of doubt.

11472 *'Break, Break, Break'*
But O for the touch of a vanished hand,
And the sound of a voice that is still!

11473 *'The Brook'*
I come from haunts of coot and hern,
I make a sudden sally
And sparkle out among the fern,

To bicker down a valley.

11474 *'The Brook'*
For men may come and men may go,
But I go on for ever.

11475 *'The Charge of the Light Brigade'*
Half a league, half a league,
Half a league onward,
All in the valley of Death
Rode the six hundred.

11476 *'The Charge of the Light Brigade'*
'Forward, the Light Brigade!'
Was there a man dismayed?
Not though the soldier knew
Some one had blundered:
Their's not to make reply,
Their's not to reason why,
Their's but to do and die:
Into the valley of Death
Rode the six hundred.

Cannon to right of them,
Cannon to left of them,
Cannon in front of them
Volleyed and thundered.

11477 *'The Charge of the Light Brigade'*
Into the jaws of Death,
Into the mouth of Hell.

11478 *(of Churton Collins)*
A louse in the locks of literature.

11479 *'Crossing the Bar'*
Twilight and evening bell,
And after that the dark!
And may there be no sadness of farewell,
When I embark.

11480 *'The Eagle'*
The wrinkled sea beneath him crawls;
He watches from his mountain walls,
And like a thunderbolt he falls.

11481 *'Far-Far-Away'*
The mellow lin-lan-lone of evening bells.

11482 *'Fatima'*
O Love, O fire! once he drew
With one long kiss my whole soul through
My lips, as sunlight drinketh dew.

11483 *'Sir Galahad'*
My strength is as the strength of ten,
Because my heart is pure.

11484 *'The Gardener's Daughter'*
More black than ashbuds in the front of March.

11485 *'The Gardener's Daughter'*
News from the humming city comes to it
In sound of funeral or of marriage bells.

11486 *'The Gardener's Daughter'*
Half light, half shade,
She stood, a sight to make an old man young.

11487 *'Godiva'*
Then she rode forth, clothed only with chastity.

11488 *'The Golden Year'*
Ah! when shall all men's good
Be each man's rule, and universal peace
Lie like a shaft of light across the land?

11489 *'The Golden Year'*
Through all the circle of the golden year.

11490 *'The Grandmother'*
That a lie which is all a lie may be met and
fought with outright,
But a lie which is part a truth is a harder matter
to fight.

11491 *'Hands all Round'*
Pray God our greatness may not fail
Through craven fears of being great.

11492
The happiness of a man in this life does not
consist in the absence but in the mastery of his
passions.

11493 *'The Higher Pantheism'*
Closer is He than breathing, and nearer than
hands and feet.

11494 *Idylls of the King* *'The Coming of Arthur'*
Man's word is God in man.

11495 *Idylls of the King* *'The Coming of Arthur'*
Rain, rain, and sun! a rainbow in the sky!
A young man will be wiser by and by;
An old man's wit may wander ere he die.

11496 *Idylls of the King* *'The Coming of Arthur'*
From the great deep to the great deep he goes.

11497 *Idylls of the King* *'The Coming of Arthur'*
Blow trumpet, for the world is white with May.

11498 *Idylls of the King - Dedication*
Wearing the white flower of a blameless life,
Before a thousand peering littlenesses.

11499 *Idylls of the King* *'Gareth and Lynette'*
Live pure, speak true, right wrong, follow the
King -
Else, wherefore born?

11500 *Idylls of the King* *'The Holy Grail'*
For good ye are and bad, and like to coins,
Some true, some light, but every one of you
Stamped with the image of the King.

11501 *Idylls of the King* *'Lancelot and Elaine'*
He is all fault who hath no fault at all:
For who loves me must have a touch of earth.

11502 *Idylls of the King 'Lancelot and Elaine'*
I know not if I know what true love is,
But if I know, then, if I love not him,
I know there is none other I can love.

11503 *Idylls of the King 'Lancelot and Elaine'*
His honour rooted in dishonour stood,
And faith unfaithful kept him falsely true.

11504 *Idylls of the King 'Lancelot and Elaine'*
He makes no friend who never made a foe.

11505 *Idylls of the King 'The Last Tournament'*
The dirty nurse, Experience, in her kind
Hath fouled me.

11506 *Idylls of the King 'The Marriage of Geraint'*
Our hoard is little, but our hearts are great.

11507 *Idylls of the King 'The Marriage of Geraint'*
For man is man and master of his fate.

11508 *Idylls of the King 'Merlin and Vivien'*
It is the little rift within the lute,
That by and by will make the music mute,
And ever widening slowly silence all.

11509 *Idylls of the King 'Merlin and Vivien'*
And trust me not at all or all in all.

11510 *Idylls of the King 'Merlin and Vivien'*
Man dreams of fame while woman wakes to
love.

11511 *Idylls of the King 'Merlin and Vivien'*
Where blind and naked Ignorance
Delivers brawling judgements, unashamed,
On all things all day long.

11512 *Idylls of the King 'The Passing of Arthur'*
I found Him in the shining of the stars,
I marked Him in the flowering of His fields,
But in His ways with men I find Him not.

11513 *Idylls of the King 'The Passing of Arthur'*
Authority forgets a dying king.

11514 *Idylls of the King 'The Passing of Arthur'*
And the days darken round me, and the years,
Among new men, strange faces, other minds.

11515 *Idylls of the King 'The Passing of Arthur'*
The old order changeth, yielding place to new,
And God fulfils himself in many ways,
Lest one good custom should corrupt the world.

11516 *Idylls of the King 'The Passing of Arthur'*
If thou shouldst never see my face again,
Pray for my soul. More things are wrought by
prayer
Than this world dreams of.

11517 *'Lady Clara Vere de Vere'*
'Tis only noble to be good.
Kind hearts are more than coronets,
And simple faith than Norman blood.

11518 *'Lady Clara Vere de Vere'*
A simple maiden in her flower
Is worth a hundred coats of arms.

11519 *'The Lady of Shalott'*
Willows whiten, aspens quiver,
Little breezes dusk and shiver.

11520 *'The Lady of Shalott'*
Or when the moon was overhead,
Came two young lovers lately wed;
'I am half sick of shadows,' said
The Lady of Shalott.

11521 *'The Lady of Shalott'*
A bow-shot from her bower-eaves,
He rode between the barley-sheaves,
The sun came dazzling through the leaves,
And flamed upon the brazen greaves
Of bold Sir Lancelot.

11522 *'The Lady of Shalott'*
She left the web, she left the loom,
She made three paces through the room,
She saw the water-lily bloom,
She saw the helmet and the plume,
She looked down to Camelot.
Out flew the Web and floated wide;
The mirror cracked from side to side;
'The curse is come upon me,' cried
The Lady of Shalott.

11523 *'Locksley Hall'*
In the spring a young man's fancy lightly turns
to thoughts of love.

11524 *'Locksley Hall'*
And our spirits rushed together at the touching
of the lips.

11525 *'Locksley Hall'*
He will hold thee, when his passion shall have
spent its novel force,
Something better than his dog, a little dearer
than his horse.

11526 *'Locksley Hall'*
This is truth the poet sings,
That a sorrow's crown of sorrow is remembering
happier things.

11527 *'Locksley Hall'*
Like a dog, he hunts in dreams.

11528 *'Locksley Hall'*
But the jingling of the guinea helps the hurt that
Honour feels.

11529 *'Locksley Hall'*
Till the war-drum throbbed no longer, and the
battle-flags were furled
In the Parliament of man, the Federation of the
world.

11530 *'Locksley Hall'*
Science moves, but slowly slowly, creeping on
from point to point.

11531 *'Locksley Hall'*
Yet I doubt not through the ages one increasing
purpose runs,
And the thoughts of men are widened with the
process of the suns.

11532 *'Locksley Hall'*
Knowledge comes, but wisdom lingers.

11533 *'Locksley Hall'*
I will take some savage woman, she shall rear
my dusky race.

11534 *'Locksley Hall'*
I the heir of all the ages, in the foremost files of
time.

11535 *'Locksley Hall'*
Forward, forward let us range,
Let the great world spin for ever down the
ringing grooves of change.

11536 *'Locksley Hall'*
Better fifty years of Europe than a cycle of
Cathay.

11537 *'The Lotos-Eaters'*
All things are taken from us, and become
Portions and parcels of the dreadful Past.

11538 *'The Lotos-Eaters' Choric Song*
Live and lie reclined
On the hills like Gods together, careless of
mankind.

11539 *'Mariana'*
Her tears fell with the dews at even;
Her tears fell ere the dews were dried.

11540 *'Maud'*
Faultily faultless, icily regular, splendidly null,
Dead perfection, no more.

11541 *'Maud'*
One still strong man in a blatant land,
Whatever they call him, what care I,
Aristocrat, democrat, autocrat - one
Who can rule and dare not lie.

11542 *'Maud'*
Gorgonised me from head to foot
With a stony British stare.

11543 *'Maud'*
Come into the garden, Maud,
For the black bat, night, has flown,
Come into the garden, Maud,
I am here at the gate alone;
And the woodbine spices are wafted abroad,
And the musk of the rose is blown.

For a breeze of morning moves,

And the planet of Love is on high,
Beginning to faint in the light that she loves
On a bed of daffodil sky.

11544 *'Maud'*
Queen rose of the rosebud garden of girls.

11545 *'Maud'*
O that 'twere possible
After long grief and pain
To find the arms of my true love
Round me once again!

11546 *'Maud'*
I embrace the purpose of God, and the doom
assigned.

11547 *In Memoriam*
Dark house, by which once more I stand
Here in the long unlovely street.

11548 *In Memoriam*
I hold it true, whate'er befall;
I feel it when I sorrow most;
'Tis better to have loved and lost
Than never to have loved at all.

11549 *In Memoriam*
Nature, red in tooth and claw.

11550 *In Memoriam*
But I was *born* to other things.

11551 *In Memoriam*
There rolls the deep where grew the tree.

11552 *In Memoriam A.H.H.*
Thou madest man, he knows not why,
He thinks he was not made to die.

11553 *In Memoriam A.H.H.*
Our little systems have their day;
They have their day and cease to be:
They are but broken lights of thee,
And thou, O Lord, art more than they.

11554 *In Memoriam A.H.H.*
I held it truth, with him who sings
To one clear harp in divers tones,
That men may rise on stepping-stones
Of their dead selves to higher things.

11555 *In Memoriam A.H.H.*
For words, like Nature, half reveal
And half conceal the Soul within.

11556 *In Memoriam A.H.H.*
The last red leaf is whirled away,
The rooks are blown about the skies.

11557 *In Memoriam A.H.H.*
The Shadow cloaked from head to foot,
Who keeps the keys of all the creeds.

11558 *In Memoriam A.H.H.*
And Thought leapt out to wed with Thought
Ere Thought could wed itself with Speech.

11559 *In Memoriam A.H.H.*
I envy not in any moods
The captive void of noble rage,
The linnet born within the cage,
That never knew the summer woods.

11560 *In Memoriam A.H.H.*
Her eyes are homes of silent prayer.

11561 *In Memoriam A.H.H.*
Be near me when my light is low,
When the blood creeps, and the nerves prick
And tingle; and the heart is sick,
And all the wheels of Being are slow.

11562 *In Memoriam A.H.H.*
Time, a maniac scattering dust,
And Life, a Fury slinging flame

11563 *In Memoriam A.H.H.*
Oh yet we trust that somehow good
Will be the final goal of ill.

11564 *In Memoriam A.H.H.*
But what am I?
An infant crying in the night:
An infant crying for the light:
And with no language but a cry.

11565 *In Memoriam A.H.H.*
The great world's altar-stairs
That slope through darkness up to God.

11566 *In Memoriam A.H.H.*
Peace; come away: we do him wrong
To sing so wildly: let us go.

11567 *In Memoriam A.H.H.*
O Sorrow, wilt thou live with me
No casual mistress, but a wife.

11568 *In Memoriam A.H.H.*
Who breaks his birth's invidious bar,
And graps the skirts of happy chance,
And breasts the blows of circumstance,
And grapples with his evil star.

11569 *In Memoriam A.H.H.*
So many worlds, so much to do,
So little done, such things to be.

11570 *In Memoriam A.H.H.*
And round thee with the breeze of song
To stir a little dust of praise.

11571 *In Memoriam A.H.H.*
God's finger touched him, and he slept.

11572 *In Memoriam A.H.H.*
Fresh from brawling courts
And dusty purlieus of the law.

11573 *In Memoriam A.H.H.*
You tell me, doubt is Devil-born.

11574 *In Memoriam A.H.H.*
There lives more faith in honest doubt,
Believe me, than in half the creeds.

11575 *In Memoriam A.H.H.*
Their meetings made December June,
Their every parting was to die.

11576 *In Memoriam A.H.H.*
He seems so near and yet so far.

11577 *In Memoriam A.H.H.*
Ring out the old, ring in the new,
Ring, happy bells, across the snow:
The year is going, let him go;
Ring out the false, ring in the true.

11578 *In Memoriam A.H.H.*
One God, one law, one element,
And one far-off divine event,
To which the whole creation moves.

11579 *In Memoriam A.H.H. (of Nature)*
So careful of the type she seems,
So careless of the single life.

11580 *'Merlin and The Gleam'*
After it, follow it,
Follow The Gleam.

11581 *'Northern Farmer. New Style'*
'Doänt thou marry for munny, but goä wheer
munny is!'

11582 *'Ode on the Death of the Duke of
Wellington'*
The last great Englishman is low.

11583 *'Ode on the Death of the Duke of
Wellington'*
O good grey head which all men knew!

11584 *'Ode on the Death of the Duke of
Wellington'*
Who never sold the truth to serve the hour,
Nor paltered with Eternal God for power.

11585 *'Ode on the Death of the Duke of
Wellington'*
This is England's greatest son,
He that gained a hundred fights,
Nor ever lost an English gun.

11586 *'Ode on the Death of the Duke of
Wellington'*
In that world-earthquake, Waterloo!

11587 *'The Princess'*
And blessings on the falling out
That all the more endears,
When we fall out with those we love
And kiss again with tears!

11588 *'The Princess'*
Quoted odes, and jewels five-words-long,
That on the stretched forefinger of all Time
Sparkle for ever.

11589 *'The Princess'*
Sweet and low, sweet and low,
Wind of the western sea.

11590 *'The Princess'*
Our echoes roll from soul to soul,
And grow for ever and for ever.

11591 *'The Princess'*
Tears from the depth of some divine despair.

11592 *'The Princess'*
Man is the hunter; woman is his game:
The sleek and shining creatures of the chase,
We hunt them for the beauty of their skins;
They love us for it, and we ride them down.

11593 *'The Princess'*
The woman is so hard
Upon the woman.

11594 *'The Princess'*
Now slides the silent meteor on, and leaves
A shining furrow, as thy thoughts in me.

11595 *'The Princess'*
The moan of doves in immemorial elms,
And murmuring of innumerable bees.

11596 *'The Princess'*
No little lily-handed baronet he,
A great broad-shouldered genial Englishman.

11597 *'The Princess'*
O tell her, brief is life but love is long.

11598 *'The Princess'*
Ask me no more: thy fate and mine are sealed:
I strove against the stream and all in vain:
Let the great river take me to the main:
No more, dear love, for at a touch I yield;
Ask me no more.

11599 *'The Princess'*
The woman's cause is man's: they rise or sink
Together.

11600 *'To the Revd F.D. Maurice'*
You'll have no scandal while you dine,
But honest talk and wholesome wine.

11601 *'The Revenge'*
I should count myself the coward if I left them,
my Lord Howard,
To these Inquisition dogs and the devildoms of
Spain.

11602 *'The Revenge'*
And they blest him in their pain, that they were
not left to Spain,
To the thumbscrew and the stake, for the glory
of the Lord.

11603 *'The Revenge'*
I have fought for Queen and Faith like a valiant
man and true;
I have only done my duty as a man is bound to
do.

11604
Self-reverence, self-knowledge, self-control -
these three alone lead to sovereign power.

11605
Sleep - kinsman thou to death and trance and
madness.

11606 *'Tithonus'*
Here at the quiet limit of the world,
A white-haired shadow roaming like a dream
The ever-silent spaces of the East.

11607 *'The Two Voices'*
No life that breathes with human breath
Has ever truly longed for death.

11608 *'Ulysses'*
How dull it is to pause, to make an end,
To rust unburnished, not to shine in use!
As though to breathe were life.

11609 *'Ulysses'*
This grey spirit yearning in desire
To follow knowledge like a sinking star,
Beyond the utmost bound of human thought.

11610 *'Ulysses'*
The long day wanes: the slow moon climbs: the
deep
Moans round with many voices.

11611 *'To Virgil'*
Wielder of the stateliest measure
ever moulded by the lips of man.

11612 *'The Vision of Sin'*
Every moment dies a man,
Every moment one is born.

11613 *'Will Waterproof's Lyrical Monologue'*
Or that eternal want of pence,
Which vexes public men.

11614 *'Come not, when I am dead'*
Come not, when I am dead,
To drop thy foolish tears upon my grave,
To trample round my fallen head,
And vex the unhappy dust thou wouldst not
save.

TERENCE c.190-159 BC
11615 *Andria*
Hence those tears.

11616 *Andria*
Lovers' rows make love whole.

11617
My closest relation is myself.

11618 *Eunuchus - prologue*
Nothing has yet been said that's not been said
before.

11619
Of my friends I am the only one I have left.

11620 *Heauton Timorumenos*
I am a man, I count nothing human foreign to me.

11621
I know the nature of women;
When you want to, they don't want to;
And when you don't want to, they desire exceedingly.

11622 *Phormio*
Fortune favours the bold.

11623 *Phormio*
There are as many opinions as there are people: each has his own correct way. [each a law unto himself]

TERESA Mother 1910-1997
11624
One filled with joy preaches without preaching.

11625
I have found the paradox that if I love until it hurts, then there is no hurt, but only more love.

11626
Loneliness and the feeling of being unwanted is the most terrible poverty.

TERTULLIAN c.160 c.220
11627 *Apologeticus*
See how these Christians love one another.

11628 *Apologeticus*
The blood of the martyrs is the seed of the Church.

TESSIER Josephine
11629
Anything that comes easy, comes wrong.

TESSIMOND A.S.J. 1902-1962
11630 *'Cats'*
Cats, no less liquid than their shadows,
Offer no angles to the wind.
They slip, diminished, neat, through loopholes
Less than themselves.

THACKERAY William Makepeace 1811-1863
11631
Charlotte, having seen his body borne before her on a shutter, like a well conducted person, went on cutting bread and butter.

11632 *Henry Esmond*
'Tis strange what a man may do, and a woman yet think him an angel.

11633 *The History of Henry Esmond*
We love being in love, that's the truth on't.

11634
Mother is the name of God in the lips and hearts of children.

11635 *The Newcomes*
What money is better bestowed than that of a schoolboy's tip?

11636 *Pendennis*
Yes, I am a fatal man, Madame Frisbi. To inspire hopeless passion is my destiny.

11637 *Pendennis*
Remember, it is as easy to marry a rich woman as a poor woman.

11638 *Pendennis*
For a slashing article, sir, there's nobody like the Capting.

11639 *Pendennis*
The *Pall Mall Gazette* is written by gentlemen for gentlemen.

11640 *The Rose and the Ring*
Business first; pleasure afterwards.

11641 *Vanity Fair*
A woman with fair opportunities and without a positive hump, may marry whom she likes.

11642 *Vanity Fair*
Whenever he met a great man he grovelled before him, and my lorded him as only a free born Briton can do.

11643 *Vanity Fair*
If a man's character is to be abused, say what you will, there's nobody like a relation to do the business.

11644 *Vanity Fair*
Them's my sentiments!

11645 *Vanity Fair*
Nothing like blood, sir, in hosses, dawgs, and men.

11646 *Vanity Fair*
I think I could be a good woman if I had five thousand a year.

11647 *Vanity Fair*
Some cynical Frenchman has said that there are two parties to a love transaction; the one who loves and the other who condescends to be so treated.

11648
The world is a looking glass and gives back to every man the reflection of his own face.

THATCHER Margaret 1925-
11649
The Act of Concensus is the negation of leadership.

11650 *(after John Major's appointment)*
I shan't be pulling the levers there but I shall be a very good back-seat driver.

11651
We have become a grandmother.

11652 *(of Falklands campaign)*
It is exciting to have a real crisis on your hands, when you have spent half your political life dealing with humdrum issues like the environment.

11653
The lady's not for turning.

11654
No one would remember the Good Samaritan if he'd only had good intentions. He had money as well.

11655
There is no such thing as Society. There are individual men and women, and there are families.

11656
I think sometimes the Prime Minister should be intimidating. There's not much point being a weak, floppy thing in the chair, is there?

11657
We must try to find ways to starve the terrorist and the hijacker of the oxygen of publicity on which they depend.

11658
Women are much better at saying no than men.

THEOCRITUS c.310-c.250 BC
11659
Man will ever stand in need of man.

THIRY Paul
11660
Buildings should be good neighbours.

THOMAS Brandon 1856-1914
11661 *Charley's Aunt*
I'm Charley's aunt from Brazil - where the nuts come from.

THOMAS Dylan 1914-1953
11662 *'And death shall have no dominion'*
Though they go mad they shall be sane,
Though they sink through the sea they shall rise again;
Though lovers be lost love shall not;
And death shall have no dominion.

11663 *(defining an alcoholic)*
A man you don't like who drinks as much as you do.

11664 *'Do Not Go Gentle into that Good Night'*
Do not go gentle into that good night,
Old age should burn and rave at close of day;

Rage, rage against the dying of the light.

11665
My education was the liberty I had to read indiscriminately and all the time, with my eyes hanging out.

11666 *'Fern Hill'*
Oh as I was young and easy in the mercy of his means,
Time held me green and dying
Though I sang in my chains like the sea.

11667 *'The force that through the green fuse ...'*
The force that through the green fuse drives the flower
Drives my green age.

11668 *'The force that through the green fuse ...'*
And I am dumb to tell the lover's tomb
How at my sheet goes the same crooked worm.

11669
The function of posterity is to look after itself.

11670 *'Shall Gods be said to Thump the Clouds?'*
Shall gods be said to thump the clouds
When clouds are cursed by thunder?

11671
Hands have not tears to flow.

11672 *'The hand that signed the paper felled ...'*
The hand that signed the treaty bred a fever,
And famine grew, and locusts came;
Great is the hand that holds dominion over
Man by a scribbled name.

11673 *'Light breaks where no sun shines'*
Light breaks where no sun shines;
Where no sea runs, the waters of the heart
Push in their tides.

11674 *Under Milk Wood*
To begin at the beginning: It is spring, moonless night in the small town, starless and bible-black.

11675 *Under Milk Wood*
Chasing the naughty couples down the grassgreen gooseberried double-bed of the wood.

11676 *Under Milk Wood*
Before you let the sun in, mind it wipes its shoes.

11677 *Under Milk Wood*
Oh, isn't life a terrible thing, thank God?

11678 *Under Milk Wood*
The boys are dreaming wicked or of the bucking ranches of the night and the jollyrodgered sea.

11679 *Under Milk Wood*
Sleeping as quiet as death, side by wrinkled side, toothless, salt and brown, like two old

The Wordsworth Dictionary of Quotations

kippers in a box.

11680 *Under Milk Wood*
Straightfaced in his cunning sleep he pulls the
legs of his dreams.

11681 *Under Milk Wood*
Nothing grows in our garden, only washing.
And babies.

11682 *Under Milk Wood*
It is always opening time in the Sailors Arms.

11683 *Under Milk Wood*
Seventeen and never been sweet in the grass ho
ho.

11684 *Under Milk Wood*
Gomer Owen who kissed her once by the pig-
sty when she wasn't looking and never kissed
her again although she was looking all the time.

11685 *Quite Early One Morning*
There is only one position for an artist
anywhere: and that is, upright.

11686 *'A Refusal to Mourn the Death...'*
Deep with the first dead lies London's daughter,
Robed in the long friends,
The grains beyond age, the dark veins of her
mother,
Secret by the unmourning water
Of the riding Thames.
After the first death, there is no other.

11687 *(of Wales)*
The land of my fathers. My fathers can have it.

THOMAS Edith M. 1854-1925
11688
What mighty battles have I seen and heard
waged between the trees and the west wind - an
Iliad fought in the fields of air.

THOMAS Edward 1878-1917
11689 *'Adlestrop'*
Yes; I remember Adlestrop -
The name, because one afternoon
Of heat the express-train drew up there
Unwontedly. It was late June.

11690 *'Out In The Dark'*
How weak and little is the light,
All the universe of sight,
Love and delight,
Before the might,
If you love it not, of night.

11691 *'Early one morning in May I set out'*
The past is the only dead thing that smells
sweet.

11692 *'Lights Out'*
I have come to the borders of sleep,
The unfathomable deep
Forest where all must lose

Their way.

11693 *'The Trumpet'*
Open your eyes to the air
That has washed the eyes of the stars
Through all the dewy night:
Up with the light,
To the old wards:
Arise, arise.

11694 *'The Unknown'*
I have not seen,
I have no news of her;
I can tell only
She is not here, but there
She might have been.

THOMAS Elizabeth 1675-1731
11695 *'A New Litany, ... invitation to a wedding'*
From marrying in haste, and repenting at
leisure;
Not liking the person, yet liking his treasure:
Libera nos.

THOMAS Irene
11696
Protestant women may take the pill. Roman
Catholic women must keep taking The Tablet.

THOMAS Lewis
11697
Cats - a standing rebuke to behavioural
scientists ... least human of all creatures.

11698
Most things get better by themselves. Most
things, in fact, are better by morning.

THOMAS R.S. 1913-
11699 *'They'*
There is no love
For such, only a willed
gentleness.

11700 *'In a Country Church'*
The dry whisper of unseen wings,
Bats not angels, in the high roof.

11701 *'Pietà'*
In the darkness ... the sound of a man
Breathing, testing his faith
On emptiness, nailing his questions
One by one to an untenanted cross.

11702 *'Welsh Landscape'*
Worrying the carcase of an old song.

THOMAS Terry 1911-1990
11703 *in I'm All Right Jack*
"We've got men here who can break into a muck
sweat merely by standing still."

THOMPSON E.P.
11704
For two decades the state has been taking
liberties, and these liberties were once ours.

THOMPSON Francis 1859-1907

11705 *'Daisy'*
Nothing begins, and nothing ends,
That is not paid with moan;
For we are born in other's pain,
And perish in our own.

11706 *'The Hound of Heaven'*
I fled Him, down the nights and down the days;
I fled Him, down the arches of the years;
I fled Him, down the labyrinthine ways
Of my own mind; and in the mist of tears
I hid from Him, and under running laughter.

11707 *'The Hound of Heaven'*
All things betray thee, who betrayest Me.

11708 *'The Hound of Heaven'*
I said to Dawn: Be sudden - to Eve:
Be soon.

11709 *'The Hound of Heaven'*
To all swift things for swiftness did I sue;
Clung to the whistling mane of every wind.

11710 *'A Judgement in Heaven'*
There is no expeditious road
To pack and label men for God,
And save them by the barrel-load.
Some may perchance, with strange surprise,
Have blundered into Paradise.

11711 *'The Kingdom of God'*
O world invisible, we view thee,
O world intangible, we touch thee,
O world unknowable, we know thee,
Inapprehensible, we clutch thee!

11712 *'The Kingdom of God'*
The angels keep their ancient places -
Turn but a stone, and start a wing!
'Tis ye, 'tis your estrangèd faces,
That miss the many-splendoured thing.

11713 *'The Kingdom of God'*
Shall shine the traffic of Jacob's ladder
Pitched betwixt Heaven and Charing Cross.

11714 *'To a Snowflake'*
What heart could have thought you?
Past our devisal
(O filigree petal!)
Fashioned so purely,
Fragilely, surely,
From what Paradisal
Imagineless metal,
Too costly for cost?

11715 *'To a Snowflake'*
Insculped and embossed,
With His hammer of wind,
And His graver of frost.

THOMPSON Kent

11716
If you're on the merry-go-round, you have to go
round.

THOMPSON William Hepworth 1810-1886

11717 *(of Sir Richard Jebb)*
What time he can spare from the adornment of
his person he devotes to the neglect of his
duties.

THOMSON James 1834-1882

11718 *'The City of Dreadful Night'*
The City is of Night; perchance of Death,
But certainly of Night.

11719 *'The City of Dreadful Night'*
The chambers of the mansion of my heart,
In every one whereof thine image dwells,
Are black with grief eternal for thy sake.

11720 *'The City of Dreadful Night'*
I find no hint throughout the universe
Of good or ill, of blessing or of curse;
I find alone Necessity Supreme.

11721 *'Sunday at Hampstead'*
As we rush, as we rush in the train,
The trees and the houses go wheeling back,
But the starry heavens above that plain
Come flying on our track.

11722 *'Sunday up the River'*
Give a man a horse he can ride,
Give a man a boat he can sail.

THOMSON James 1700-1748

11723 *Alfred: a Masque*
When Britain first, at heaven's command,
Arose from out the azure main,
This was the charter of the land,
And guardian angels sung this strain:
'Rule, Britannia, rule the waves;
Britons never will be slaves.'

11724 *The Castle of Indolence*
A little round, fat, oily man of God.

11725 *'Epitaph on Solomon Mendez'*
Here lies a man who never lived,
Yet still from death was flying;
Who, if not sick, was never well;
And died - for fear of dying!

11726 *The Seasons 'Spring'*
Delightful task! to rear the tender thought,
To teach the young idea how to shoot.

11727 *The Seasons 'Spring'*
An elegant sufficiency, content,
Retirement, rural quiet, friendship, books.

11728 *The Seasons 'Summer'*
O'er heaven and earth, far as the ranging eye
Can sweep, a dazzling deluge reigns; and all
From pole to pole is undistinguished blaze.

11729 *The Seasons 'Summer'*
Ships, dim-discovered, dropping from the clouds.

11730 *The Seasons 'Summer'*
Sighed and looked unutterable things.

11731 *The Seasons 'Winter'*
Welcome, kindred glooms!
Congenial horrors, hail!

11732 *The Seasons 'Winter'*
Studious let me sit,
And hold high converse with the mighty dead.

THOMSON Roy (Baron Thomson of Fleet)
1894-1976
11733
I'm frank, brutally frank. And even when I'm not frank, I look frank.

11734
If people knew what they had to do to be successful, most people wouldn't.

11735 *(on the profitability of commercial TV in Britain)*
Like having your own licence to print money.

11736
Socialism has been preached for so long the British people no longer have any sense of personal responsibility.

THOREAU Henry David 1817-1862
11737
If one advances confidently in the direction of his dreams, and endeavours to live the life which he has imagined, he will meet with a success unexpected in common hours.

11738
He is the best sailor who can steer within fewest points of the wind, and exact a motive power out of the greatest obstacles.

11739
Beware all enterprises that require new clothes.

11740
The bluebird carries the sky on his back.

11741
It is characteristic of wisdom not to do desperate things.

11742
Some circumstantial evidence is very strong, as when you find a trout in the milk.

11743
Colour, which is the poet's wealth, is so expensive that most take to mere outline sketches and become men of science.

11744
Do not be too moral. You may cheat yourself out of much life. So aim above morality. Be not simply good; be good for something.

11745
The eye is the jewel of the body.

11746
The frontiers are not east or west, north or south, but wherever a man fronts a fact.

11747
Between whom there is hearty truth, there is love.

11748
How often we find ourselves turning our backs on our actual friends, that we may go and meet their ideal cousins.

11749
How vain it is to sit down to write when you have not stood up to live.

11750
If I knew ... that a man was coming to my house with the conscious design of doing me good, I should run for my life.

11751
Most of the luxuries, and many of the so-called comforts, of life are not only not indispensable, but positive hindrances to the elevation of mankind.

11752
That man is richest whose pleasures are the cheapest.

11753
I never found the companion that was so companionable as solitude.

11754
Politics is the gizzard of society, full of gut and gravel.

11755
You cannot receive a shock unless you have an electric affinity for that which shocks you.

11756
Through our own recovered innocence we discern the innocence of our neighbours.

11757
We like that a sentence should read as if its author, had he held a plough instead of a pen, could have drawn a furrow deep and straight to the end.

11758
As for style of writing, if one has anything to say, it drops from him simply and directly, as a stone falls to the ground.

11759
I think that we may safely trust a good deal
more than we do.

11760
I think that there is nothing, not even crime,
more opposed to poetry, to philosophy, ay, to
life itself than this incessant business.

11761
'Tis healthy to be sick sometimes.

11762
I have travelled a good deal in Concord.

11763
It takes two to speak the truth - one to speak,
and another to hear.

11764 *Walden 'Conclusion'*
If a man does not keep pace with his
companions, perhaps it is because he hears a
different drummer. Let him step to the music
which he hears, however measured or far away.

11765 *Walden 'Conclusion'*
The government of the world I live in was not
framed, like that of Britain, in after-dinner
conversations over the wine.

11766 *Walden 'Economy'*
As if you could kill time without injuring
eternity.

11767 *Walden 'Economy'*
The mass of men lead lives of quiet desperation.

11768 *Walden 'Economy'*
As for Doing-good, that is one of the
professions which are full.

11769 *Walden 'Sounds'*
The three-o'clock in the morning courage,
which Bonaparte thought was the rarest.

11770 *Walden 'Where I Lived, and What I Lived
For'*
Our life is frittered away by detail ... Simplify,
simplify.

11771 *Walden 'Where I Lived, and What I Lived
For'*
Time is but the stream I go a-fishing in.

11772
To know that we know what we know, and that
we do not know what we do not know, that is
true knowledge.

11773
What is morality but immemorial custom?
Conscience is the chief of conservatives.

11774
What recommends commerce to me is its
enterprise and bravery. It does not clasp its
hands and pray to Jupiter.

11775
The youth gets together this material to build a
bridge to the moon, or perchance, a palace or
temple on earth, and at length, the middle-aged
man concludes to build a woodshed with them.

THOREAU Marshall
11776
A man is rich in proportion to the things he can
afford to let alone.

THORPE Jeremy 1929-
11777 *(on Macmillan sacking seven of his
Cabinet)*
Greater love hath no man than this, that he lay
down his friends for his life.

THURBER James 1894-1961
11778
We all have flaws, and mine is being wicked.

11779 *'The Bear Who Let It Alone'*
You might as well fall flat on your face as lean
over too far backward.

11780
The difference between our decadence and the
Russians' is that while theirs is brutal, ours is
apathetic.

11781
I am not a dog-lover. To me, a dog-lover is a dog
who is in love with another dog.

11782
Humour is emotional chaos remembered in
tranquillity.

11783
A lady of forty-seven who has been married
twenty-seven years and has six children knows
what love really is and once described it for me
like this: 'Love is what you've been through with
somebody.'

11784 *My Life and Hard Times*
Her own mother lived the latter years of her life
in the horrible suspicion that electricity was
dripping invisibly all over the house.

11785
Man is flying too fast for a world that is round.
Soon he will catch up with himself in a great
rear-end collision and Man will never know that
what hit him from behind was Man.

11786
It's a naive domestic burgundy without any
breeding, but I think you'll be amused by its
presumption.

11787
Though statisticians in our time
Have never kept the score
Man wants a great deal here below
And Woman even more.

11788
The war between men and women.

11789
Woman's place is in the wrong.

11790
Well, if I called the wrong number, why did you answer the phone?

THURLOW Edward 1731-1806
11791 *(attributed)*
Did you ever expect a corporation to have a conscience, when it has no soul to be damned, and no body to be kicked.

11792
As guardian of His majesty's conscience.

11793
When I forget my sovereign, may God forget me!

TIBBET Paul W.
11794 *(of atomic bomb explosion)*
A mushroom of boiling dust up to 20,000 feet.

TICHNOR Don
11795
To convert an hourly wage to an approximate yearly salary, double the wage and change the decimal to a comma.

TICKELL Thomas 1686-1740
11796
Boredom is rage spread thin.

11797 *Colin and Lucy*
I hear a voice you cannot hear,
Which says I must not stay;
I see a hand you cannot see,
Which beckons me away.

11798 *'To the Earl of Warwick. On the Death of Mr Addison'*
There taught us how to live; and (oh! too high The price for knowledge) taught us how to die.

TILLICH Paul 1886-1965
11799 *(attributed)*
The first duty of love is to listen.

11800 *The Courage To Be*
Neurosis is the way of avoiding non-being by avoiding being.

11801 *Dynamics of Faith*
Faith is the state of being ultimately concerned.

11802
The joy about our work is spoiled when we perform it not because of what we produce but because of the pleasure with which it can provide us, or the pain against which it can protect us.

11803
Language has created the word 'loneliness' to express the pain of being alone, and the word 'solitude' to express the glory of being alone.

11804
The passion for truth is silenced by answers which have the weight of undisputed authority.

TILLOTSON John 1630-1694
11805 *Sermon 93*
If God were not a necessary Being of himself, He might almost seem to be made for the use and benefit of mankind.

TITUS AD 39-81
11806 *(on having done nothing to help anybody all day)*
Friends, I have lost a day.

TOCQUEVILLE Alexis de 1805-1859
11807 *De la Démocratie en Amérique*
Of all nations, those submit to civilization with the most difficulty which habitually live by the chase.

11808 *De la Démocratie en Amérique*
What is understood by republican government in the United States is the slow and quiet action of society upon itself.

11809 *De la Démocratie en Amérique*
The Russians and the Americans ... Their starting point is different, and their courses are not the same; yet each of them seems to be marked out by the will of Heaven to sway the destinies of half the globe.

11810 *L'Ancien régime*
Despots themselves do not deny that freedom is excellent; only they desire it for themselves alone, and they maintain that everyone else is altogether unworthy of it.

11811 *L'Ancien régime*
History is a gallery of pictures in which there are few originals and many copies.

11812 *L'Ancien régime*
He who desires in liberty anything other than itself is born to be a servant.

11813
In politics a community of hatred is almost always the foundation of friendships.

TOFFLER Alvin 1928-
11814 *Future Shock*
'Future shock' ... the shattering stress and disorientation that we induce in individuals by subjecting them to too much change in too short a time.

11815
Parenthood remains the greatest single preserve of the amateur.

11816
Still round the corner there may wait,
A new road, or a secret gate.

TOLKIEN J.R.R. 1892-1973
11817 *The Fellowship of the Ring*
One Ring to rule them all, One Ring to find them
One Ring to bring them all and in the darkness bind them.

11818 *The Hobbit*
Never laugh at live dragons.

TOLSTOY Leo 1828-1910
11819
All art has this characteristic - it unites people.

11820
It is amazing how complete is the delusion that beauty is goodness.

11821 *Anna Karenina*
All happy families resemble one another, but each unhappy family is unhappy in its own way.

11822 *Anna Karenina*
There are no conditions of life to which a man cannot get accustomed, especially if he sees them accepted by everyone about him.

11823 *Anna Karenina*
The candle by which she had been reading the book ... flared up with a brighter light, illuminating for her everything that before had been enshrouded in darkness, flickered, grew dim, and went out for ever.

11824
Art is a human activity, consisting in this, that one man consciously, by means of external signs, hands on to others feelings he has worked through, and other people are infected by these feelings and also experience them.

11825
Government is an association of men who do violence to the rest of us.

11826 *Memoirs of a Madman*
I am always with myself, and it is I who am my tormentor.

11827
Music is the shorthand of emotion.

11828 *War and Peace*
In historical events great men - so-called - are but labels serving to give a name to the event, and like labels they have the least possible connexion with the event itself.

11829 *War and Peace*
Pure and complete sorrow is as impossible as pure and complete joy.

11830 *War and Peace*
The most powerful weapon of ignorance - the diffusion of printed material.

11831 *What Then Must We Do?*
I sit on a man's back, choking him and making him carry me, and yet assure myself and others that I am very sorry for him and wish to ease his lot by all possible means - except by getting off his back.

11832
Work is the inevitable condition of human life, the true source of human welfare.

TOMALIN Claire 1933-
11833
Everybody is vulnerable through love of their children. Hostages to fortune.

TOMLIN Lily
11834
We're all in this together - by ourselves.

11835
If love is the answer, could you rephrase the question?

TOMLINSON H.M. 1873-1958
11836
I do not love the sea. The look of it is disquieting. There is something in the very sound of it that stirs the premonition felt while we listen to noble music; we become inexplicably troubled.

TOPLADY Augustus Montague 1740-1778
11837 *'Rock of Ages, cleft for me'*
Rock of Ages, cleft for me,
Let me hide myself in Thee.

TOSCANINI Arturo 1867-1957
11838
When I was very young, I kissed my first woman, and smoked my first cigarette on the same day. Believe me, never since have I wasted any more time on tobacco.

TOUSSENEL A.
11839 *L'Esprit des bêtes*
The more one gets to know of men, the more one values dogs.

TOWNSHEND Pete 1945-
11840
The critical moment for you as a teenager is when you realise you're on your own.

11841 *'My Generation'*
Hope I die before I get old.

TOYNBEE Arnold 1889-1975
11842
To be able to fill leisure intelligently is the last product of civilization.

11843
Civilization is a movement - not a condition; a voyage - not a harbour.

11844
We are in the first age since the dawn of civilization in which people have dared to think it practicable to make the benefits of civilization available to the whole human race.

11845
We have been God-like in our planned breeding of our domestic plants and animals, but rabbit-like in our unplanned breeding of ourselves.

11846
The history of almost every civilization furnishes examples of geographical expansion coinciding with deterioration in quality.

TRAHERNE Thomas c.1637-1674
11847 *Centuries of Meditations 'First Century'*
An empty book is like an infant's soul, in which anything may be written. It is capable of all things, but containeth nothing.

11848 *Centuries of Meditations 'First Century'*
You never enjoy the world aright, till the sea itself floweth in your veins, till you are clothed with the heavens, and crowned with the stars: and perceive yourself to be the sole heir of the whole world.

11849 *Centuries of Meditations 'Third Century'*
The green trees when I saw them first ... transported and ravished me, their sweetness and unusual beauty made my heart to leap and almost mad with ecstasy, they were such strange and wonderful things.

11850 *'Wonder'*
I within did flow
With seas of life, like wine.
I nothing in this world did know,
But 'twas divine!

TRAILL Henry Duff 1842-1900
11851 *'After Dilettante Concetti'*
Look in my face. My name is Used-to-was;
I am also called Played-out and Done-to-death,
And It-will-wash-no-more.

TRAPP Joseph 1679-1747
11852 *(of George I's donation of Library to Cambridge)*
The King, observing with judicious eyes
The state of both his universities,
To Oxford sent a troop of horse, and why?
That learned body wanted loyalty;
To Cambridge books, as very well discerning
How much that loyal body wanted learning.

TRAVIS Merle 1917-1983
11853 *'Sixteen Tons'*
Sixteen tons, what do you get?

Another day older and deeper in debt.
Say brother, don't you call me 'cause I can't go
I owe my soul to the company store.

TREE Sir Herbert Beerbohm 1852-1917
11854 *(to females assembled to play ladies-in-waiting)*
Ladies, just a little more virginity, if you don't mind.

11855 *(of Israel Zangwill)*
He is an old bore. Even the grave yawns for him.

11856 *(pressed by gramophone company for testimonial)*
Sirs, I have tested your machine. It adds a new terror to life and makes death a long-felt want.

TRENCH Herbert 1865-1923
11857
Come, let us make love deathless.

TRENT Lord 1889-1956
11858
As I learnt very early in my life in Whitehall, the acid test of any political question is: What is the alternative?

TREVELYAN G.M. 1876-1962
11859 *English Social History*
Disinterested intellectual curiosity is the life-blood of real civilization.

11860 *English Social History*
If the French noblesse had been capable of playing cricket with their peasants, their chateaux would never have been burnt.

11861 *English Social History*
It [education] has produced a vast population able to read but unable to distinguish what is worth reading.

TREVOR William 1928-
11862 *(of the troubles in Northern Ireland)*
A disease in the family that is never mentioned.

TRIBE Laurence H.
11863
An excess of law inescapably weakens the rule of law.

TRILLIN Calvin
11864 *(attributed)*
The shelf life of the modern hardback writer is somewhere between the milk and the yoghurt.

TRILLING Lionel 1905-1975
11865
It is now life and not art that requires the willing suspension of disbelief.

TRINDER Tommy 1909-1989
11866 *(of American troops in Britain during World War 2)*

Overpaid, overfed, oversexed, and over here.

TROLLOPE Anthony 1815-1882

11867 *Autobiography*
He must have known me had he seen me as he was wont to see me, for he was in the habit of flogging me constantly. Perhaps he did not recognize me by my face.

11868 *Autobiography*
Take away from English authors their copyrights, and you would very soon take away from England her authors.

11869 *Autobiography*
Three hours a day will produce as much as a man ought to write.

11870 *Ayala's Angel*
A man's mind will very generally refuse to make itself up until it be driven and compelled by emergency.

11871 *Barchester Towers*
... She well knew the great architectural secret of decorating her constructions, and never descended to construct a decoration.

11872 *The Bertrams*
Those who have courage to love should have courage to suffer.

11873 *Doctor Thorne*
There is no road to wealth so easy and respectable as that of matrimony.

11874 *Doctor Thorne*
Let no man boast himself that he has got through the perils of winter till at least the seventh of May.

11875 *Miss Mackenzie*
If you wish to get the sweetest fragrance from the herb at your feet, tread on it and bruise it.

11876 *Orley Farm*
It is because we put up with bad things that hotel-keepers continue to give them to us.

11877 *Orley Farm*
As for conceit, what man will do any good who is not conceited? Nobody holds a good opinion of a man who has a low opinion of himself.

11878 *Phineas Finn*
She knew how to allure by denying, and to make the gift rich by delaying it.

11879 *Phineas Redux*
What man thinks of changing himself so as to suit his wife? And yet men expect that women shall put on altogether new characters when they are married, and girls think that they can do so.

11880 *The Small House at Allington*
I doubt whether any girl would be satisfied with her lover's mind if she knew the whole of it.

11881
There is no villainy to which education cannot reconcile us.

11882 *The Warden*
The tenth Muse, who now governs the periodical press.

11883 *The Way We Live Now*
Love is like any other luxury. You have no right to it unless you can afford it.

TROLLOPE Joanna 1943-
11884
The middle class is the backbone of England. In intellectual circles that's been absolutely unsayable.

TRONCHIN Théodore 1709-1781
11885
In medicine, sins of commission are mortal, sins of omission venial.

TROTSKY Leon 1879-1940
11886
Not believing in force is the same as not believing in gravitation.

11887 *Diary in Exile*
Old age is the most unexpected of all things that happen to a man.

11888 *History of the Russian Revolution*
Civilization has made the peasantry its pack animal. The bourgeoisie in the long run only changed the form of the pack.

11889 *History of the Russian Revolution*
You [the Mensheviks] are pitiful isolated individuals; you are bankrupts; your role is played out. Go where you belong from now on - into the dustbin of history!

11890 *What Next?*
Where force is necessary, there it must be applied boldly, decisively and completely. But one must know the limitations of force; one must know when to blend force with a manoeuvre, a blow with an agreement.

TROTTER Wilfred 1951-
11891
Disease often tells its secrets in a casual parenthesis.

TROUBRIDGE St Vincent 1895-1963
11892
There is an iron curtain across Europe.

TRUDEAU Pierre Elliott 1919-
11893
In academic life you seek to state absolute

truths; in politics you seek to accommodate truth to the facts around you.

11894
Canada is not a country for the cold of heart or the cold of feet.

11895
The democracy which embodies and guarantees our freedom is not powerless, passive or blind, nor is it in retreat. It has no intention of giving way to the savage fantasies of its adversaries. It is not prepared to give advance blessing to its own destruction.

11896
The essential ingredient of politics is timing.

11897
Living next to the United States is in some ways like sleeping with an elephant. No matter how friendly and even-tempered is the beast, one is affected by every twitch and grunt.

11898
Power only tires those who don't exercise it.

TRUDELL Dennis
11899
Sloppy, raggedy-assed old life. I love it. I never want to die.

TRUMAN Harry S 1884-1972
11900 *(attributed)*
Always be sincere, even if you don't mean it.

11901
Democracy is based on the conviction that man has the moral and intellectual capacity, as well as the inalienable right, to govern himself with reason and justice.

11902
Within the first few months I discovered that being a president is like riding a tiger. A man has to keep riding or be swallowed.

11903 *Letter to his sister*
All the President is, is a glorified public relations man who spends his time flattering, kissing and kicking people to get them to do what they are supposed to do anyway.

11904
I never give them [the public] hell. I just tell the truth, and they think it is hell.

11905
A politician is a man who understands government, and it takes a politician to run a government.
A statesman is a politician who's been dead 10 or 15 years.

11906
The president is the representative of the whole nation and he's the only lobbyist that all the one hundred and sixty million people in this country have.

11907
It's a recession when your neighbour loses his job; it's a depression when you lose yours.

11908
Well, I wouldn't say that I was in the 'great' class, but I had a great time while I was trying to be great.

11909
Wherever you have an efficient government you have a dictatorship.

TUCHMAN Barbara W. 1912-1989
11910 *August 1914*
Dead battles, like dead generals, hold the military mind in their dead grip and Germans, no less than other peoples, prepare for the last war.

11911 *August 1914*
No more distressing moment can ever face a British government than that which requires it to come to a hard, fast and specific decision.

11912 *August 1914*
For one August in its history Paris was French - and silent.

11913
War is the unfolding of miscalculations.

TUCKER Antony fl. 1653-1661
11914 *(attributed, whilst Master of St. John's College, Oxford)*
With their godliness they may deceive me, with their learning they cannot.

TUCKER Karla Faye
11915 *(last words before her execution)*
I'm going for a face-to-face with Jesus.

TUCKER Sophie 1884-1966
11916
From birth to 18 a girl needs good parents. From 18 to 35, she needs good looks. From 35 to 55, good personality. From 55 on, she needs good cash.

TUER A.W. 1838-1900
11917 *(title of Portuguese-English conversational guide)*
English as she is Spoke.

TUPPER Martin 1810-1889
11918 *Proverbial Philosophy 'Of Reading'*
A good book is the best of friends, the same to-day and for ever.

TURGENEV Ivan 1818-1823
11919 *Fathers and Sons*
Nature is not a temple, but a workshop, and man's the workman in it.

11920 *Fathers and Sons*
I share no one's ideas. I have my own.

11921 *Fathers and Sons*
Just try and set death aside. It sets you aside, and that's the end of it!

11922 *Fathers and Sons*
Whatever a man prays for, he prays for a miracle. Every prayer reduces itself to this: Great God, grant that twice two be not four.

TURNER Walter James Redfern 1889-1946
11923 *'Romance'*
When I was but thirteen or so
I went into a golden land,
Chimborazo, Cotopaxi
Took me by the hand.

TUSSER Thomas c.1524-1580
11924 *Five Hundred Points of Good Husbandry*
At Christmas play and make good cheer,
For Christmas comes but once a year.

11925 *Five Hundred Points of Good Husbandry*
Who goeth a-borrowing
Goeth a-sorrowing.
Few lend (but fools)
Their working tools.

11926 *Five Hundred Points of Good Husbandry*
In doing of either, let wit bear a stroke,
For buying or selling of pig in a poke.

11927 *Five Hundred Points of Good Husbandry*
Some respite to husbands the weather may send,
But housewives' affairs have never an end.

11928 *Five Hundred Points of Good Husbandry*
Seek home for rest,
For home is best.

TWAIN Mark 1835-1910
11929 *The Adventures of Huckleberry Finn*
There was things which he stretched, but mainly he told the truth.

11930 *The Adventures of Huckleberry Finn*
'Pilgrim's Progress', about a man that left his family, it didn't say why ... The statement was interesting, but tough.

11931 *The Adventures of Huckleberry Finn*
All kings is mostly rapscallions.

11932 *The Adventures of Huckleberry Finn*
Hain't we got all the fools in town on our side? and ain't that a big enough majority in any town.

11933
Put all thine eggs in one basket and - watch that basket.

11934
It isn't so astonishing, the number of things that I can remember, as the number of things I can remember that aren't so.

11935
Biographies are but the clothes and buttons of the man - the biography of the man himself cannot be written.

11936
I was born modest; not all over, but in spots.

11937
We should be careful to get out of an experience only the wisdom that is in it - and stop there, lest we be like the cat that sits down on a hot stove-lid. She will never sit down on a hot stove-lid again - and that is well; but also she will never sit down on a cold one anymore.

11938
In certain trying circumstances, urgent circumstances, desperate circumstances, profanity furnishes a relief denied even to prayer.

11939
We are chameleons, and our partialities and prejudices change places with an easy and blessed facility.

11940
I conceive that the right way to write a story for boys is to write so that it will not only interest boys but strongly interest any man who has ever been a boy. That immensely enlarges the audience.

11941
Consider well the proportion of things. It is better to be a young June bug, than an old bird of paradise.

11942
Courage is resistance to fear, mastery of fear, not absence of fear.

11943
The Creator made Italy with designs by Michelangelo.

11944 *A Curious Dream 'Facts concerning...'*
Soap and education are not as sudden as a massacre, but they are more deadly in the long run.

11945 *A Curious Dream 'A Mysterious Visit'*
Barring that natural expression of villainy which we all have, the man looked honest enough.

11946
It is better to deserve honours and not have them than to have them and not deserve them.

11947
The difference between the right word and the almost right word is the difference between lightning and the lightning bug.

11948 *Following the Equator*
Truth is the most valuable thing we have. Let us economize it.

11949 *Following the Equator*
It is by the goodness of God that in our country we have those three unspeakably precious things: freedom of speech, freedom of conscience, and the prudence never to practise either of them.

11950 *Following the Equator*
Man is the Only Animal that Blushes. Or needs to.

11951 *Following the Equator*
There are several good protections against temptations, but the surest is cowardice.

11952 *Following the Equator*
It takes your enemy and your friend, working together, to hurt you to the heart: the one to slander you and the other to get the news to you.

11953
Ethical man - a Christian holding four aces.

11954
Everyone is a moon and has a dark side which he never shows to anybody.

11955
Get your facts first, and then you can distort 'em as much as you please.

11956
Fame is a vapour, popularity an accident; the only earthly certainty is oblivion.

11957
Fewer things are harder to put up with than the annoyance of a good example.

11958
Golf is a good walk spoiled.

11959
The human race is a race of cowards; and I am not only marching in that procession but carrying a banner.

11960 *The Innocents Abroad*
They spell it Vinci and pronounce it Vinchy; foreigners always spell better than they pronounce.

11961
That kind of so-called housekeeping where they have six Bibles and no cork-screw.

11962
Life would be infinitely happier if we could only be born at the age of eighty and gradually approach eighteen.

11963
I can live for two months on a good compliment.

11964
Each man must for himself alone decide what is right and what is wrong, which course is patriotic and which isn't. You cannot shirk this and be a man.

11965
The man who does not read good books has no advantage over the man who can't read them.

11966
We may not pay Satan reverence, for that would be indiscreet, but we can at least respect his talents.

11967
Make money and the whole world will conspire to call you a gentleman.

11968
Noise proves nothing. Often a hen who has merely laid an egg cackles as if she had laid an asteroid.

11969 *Notebooks*
Familiarity breeds contempt - and children.

11970 *Notebooks*
Good breeding consists in concealing how much we think of ourselves and how little we think of the other person.

11971
I am opposed to millionaires, but it would be dangerous to offer me the position.

11972
In Paris they simply stared when I spoke to them in French; I never did succeed in making those idiots understand their own language.

11973
The pause - that impressive silence, that eloquent silence, that geometrically progressive silence which often achieves a desired effect where no combination of words, howsoever felicitous, could accomplish it.

11974
In prayer we call ourselves 'worms of the dust', but it is only on a sort of tacit understanding that the remark shall not be taken at par.

11975
In his private heart no man much respects himself.

11976 *Pudd'nhead Wilson*
Cauliflower is nothing but cabbage with a college education.

11977 *Pudd'nhead Wilson*
When angry, count four; when very angry, swear.

11978 *Pudd'nhead Wilson*
As to the Adjective: when in doubt, strike it out.

11979
The reports of my death are greatly exaggerated.

11980
Richard Wagner, a musician who wrote music which is better than it sounds.

11981
If I cannot smoke cigars in heaven, I shall not go.

11982
If you tell the truth you don't have to remember anything.

11983
Let us be thankful for the fools. But for them the rest of us could not succeed.

11984
Tomorrow night I appear for the first time before a Boston audience - 4000 critics.

11985
Travel is fatal to prejudice, bigotry and narrow-mindedness.

11986
There is no unhappiness like the misery of sighting land again after a cheerful, careless voyage.

11987
What a good thing Adam had - when he said a good thing, he knew nobody had said it before.

11988
When I was a boy of fourteen, my father was so ignorant I could hardly stand to have the old man around. But when I got to be twenty-one, I was astonished at how much the old man had learned in seven years.

11989
When we remember that we are all mad, the mysteries disappear and life stands explained.

11990
When I was younger, I could remember anything, whether it had happened or not.

11991
There are those who would misteach us that to stick in a rut is consistency - and a virtue, and that to climb out of the rut is inconsistency - and a vice.

11992
I wish to become rich, so that I can instruct the people and glorify honest poverty a little, like those kind-hearted, fat, benevolent people do.

11993
Wit is the sudden marriage of ideas which, before their union, were not perceived to have any relation.

TYNAN Kenneth 1927-1980
11994
All of life is more or less what the French would call *'s'imposer'* - to be able to create one's own terms for what one does.

11995
A critic is a man who knows the way but can't drive the car.

11996 *Curtains (of Noel Coward)*
Forty years ago he was Slightly in *Peter Pan,* and you might say that he has been wholly in *Peter Pan* ever since.

11997
A neurosis is a secret you don't know you're keeping.

11998 *Tynan Right and Left*
Drama criticism ... [is] a self-knowing account of the way in which one's consciousness has been modified during an evening in the theatre.

11999
The unique thing about Margaret Rutherford is that she can act with her chin alone. Among its many moods I especially cherish the chin commanding, the chin in doubt, and the chin at bay.

12000
What, when drunk, one sees in other women, one sees in Garbo sober.

TZU-SUN
12001
If you know the enemy and know yourself you need not fear the results of a hundred battles.

12002
The supreme excellence is not to win a hundred victories in a hundred battles. The supreme excellence is to subdue the armies of your enemies without even having to fight them.

UDALL Steward
12003
Gross National Product is our Holy Grail.

UDKOFF Bob
12004
Hate is such a luxurious emotion, it can only be spent on one we love.

UNDERHILL Frank
12005
A nation is a body of people who have done great things together in the past and hope to do great things together in the future.

UNRUH Jesse
12006
Money is the mother's milk of politics.

UPDIKE John 1932-
12007
The artist brings something into the world that didn't exist before, and ... he does it without destroying something else.

12008 *Assorted Prose 'Confessions of a Wild Bore'*
A healthy male adult bore consumes *each year* one and a half times his own weight in other people's patience.

12009 *Assorted Prose 'More Love ... Western World'*
The heart *prefers* to move against the grain of circumstance; perversity is the soul's very life.

12010
The Englishman is under no constitutional obligation to believe that all men are created equal. The American agony is therefore scarcely intelligible, like a saint's self-flagellation viewed by an atheist.

12011
Every marriage tends to consist of an aristocrat and a peasant, of a teacher and a learner.

12012 *Picked Up Pieces (of England)*
A soggy little island huffing and puffing to keep up with Western Europe.

12013 *Picked Up Pieces 'London Life'*
America is a land whose centre is nowhere; England one whose centre is everywhere.

12014 *Problems 'How to love America ...'*
America is a vast conspiracy to make you happy.

12015
Russia is the only country of the world you can be homesick for while you're still in it.

USTINOV Sir Peter 1921-
12016
If Botticelli were alive today he'd be working for *Vogue*.

12017
Comedy is simply a funny way of being serious.

12018 *Dear Me*
Laughter ... the most civilized music in the world.

12019 *Dear Me*
I do not believe that friends are necessarily the people you like best, they are merely the people who got there first.

12020 *(on imitating Harold Macmillan - attributed)*
Talk as though you have a cathedral in your mouth.

12021
By increasing the size of the keyhole, today's playwrights are in danger of doing away with the door.

12022
Laughter would be bereaved if snobbery died.

12023
Love is an act of endless forgiveness; a tender look that becomes a habit.

12024
Parents are the bones on which children cut their teeth.

12025 *Romanoff and Juliet*
At the age of four with paper hats and wooden swords we're all Generals. Only some of us never grow out of it.

12026 *Romanoff and Juliet*
This is a free country, madam. We have a right to share your privacy in a public place.

VADIM Roger 1928-
12027
Youth has become a class.

VALENTINE Alan
12028
Whenever science makes a discovery, the devil grabs it while the angels are debating the best way to use it.

VALERIUS MAXIMUS fl. AD c.15
12029 *Facta et Dicta Memorabilia*
I appeal from Philip drunk to Philip sober.

VALÉRY Paul 1871-1945
12030
An artist never really finishes his work, he merely abandons it.

12031
A businessman is a hybrid of a dancer and a calculator.

12032
Conscience reigns but it does not govern.

12033
If some great catastrophe is not announced every morning, we feel a certain void. 'Nothing in the paper today,' we sigh.

12034
History is the science of what never happens twice.

12035 *Littérature*
A poem is never finished; it's always an accident that puts a stop to it - that is to say, gives it to the public.

12036 *Moralités*
Science means simply the aggregate of all the recipes that are always successful. The rest is literature.

12037
Peace is a virtual, mute, sustained victory of potential powers against probable greeds.

12038
To penetrate one's being, one must go armed to the teeth.

12039 *Tel Quel 1 'Moralités'*
God created man and, finding him not sufficiently alone, gave him a companion to make him feel his solitude more keenly.

12040 *Tel Quel 2 'Rhumbs'*
Politics is the art of preventing people from taking part in affairs which properly concern them.

VAN GOGH Vincent 1853-1890
12041
I dream my painting, and then I paint my dream.

12042
It's as interesting and as difficult to say a thing well as to paint it. There is the art of lines and colours, but the art of words exists too, and will never be less important.

12043
One may have a blazing hearth in one's soul, and yet no one ever comes to sit by it.

12044
As a painter I shall never signify anything of importance. I feel it absolutely.

VAN HORNE William 1843-1915
12045
The biggest things are always the easiest to do because there is no competition.

VAN MILDERT Bishop
12046
Want of friends argues either want of humility or of courage, or both.

VANBRUGH Sir John 1664-1726
12047 *The Provoked Husband*
Much of a muchness.

12048 *The Relapse*
When once a woman has given you her heart, you can never get rid of the rest of her body.

12049 *The Relapse*
In matters of love men's eyes are always bigger than their bellies. They have violent appetites, 'tis true; but they have soon dined.

12050
The want of a thing is perplexing enough, but the possession of it is intolerable.

VAUGHAN Bill
12051
Occasionally we sigh for an earlier day when we could just look at the stars without worrying whether they were theirs or ours.

12052
One trouble with growing older is that it gets progressively tougher to find a famous historical figure who didn't amount to much when he was your age.

VAUGHAN Harry
12053
If you can't stand the heat, get out of the kitchen.

VAUGHAN Henry 1622-1695
12054
Caesar had perished from the world of men Had not his sword been rescued by his pen.

12055 *Silex Scintillans 'They are all gone'*
They are all gone into the world of light,
And I alone sit lingering here;
Their very memory is fair and bright,
And my sad thoughts doth clear.

12056 *Silex Scintillans 'They are all gone'*
I see them walking in an air of glory,
Whose light doth trample on my days.

12057 *Silex Scintillans 'They are all gone'*
Dear, beauteous death! the jewel of the just,
Shining nowhere but in the dark.

12058 *Silex Scintillans 'Man'*
Man is the shuttle, to whose winding quest
And passage through these looms
God ordered motion, but ordained no rest.

12059 *Silex Scintillans 'Peace'*
My soul, there is a country
Far beyond the stars,
Where stands a wingèd sentry
All skilful in the wars;
There, above noise and danger,
Sweet Peace is crowned with smiles,
And One born in a manger

Commands the beauteous files.

12060 *Silex Scintillans 'The Retreat'*
Happy those early days, when I
Shined in my angel-infancy.
Before I understood this place
Appointed for my second race,
Or taught my soul to fancy aught
But a white, celestial thought.

12061 *Silex Scintillans 'The Retreat'*
And in those weaker glories spy
Some shadows of eternity.

12062 *Silex Scintillans 'The Retreat'*
But felt through all this fleshly dress
Bright shoots of everlastingness.

12063 *Silex Scintillans 'The World'*
I saw Eternity the other night,
Like a great ring of pure and endless light,
All calm, as it was bright.

12064 *Silex Scintillans 'The World'*
And round beneath it, Time in hours, days,
years,
Driv'n by the spheres
Like a vast shadow moved; in which the world
And all her train were hurled.

VAUGHAN Sam
12065
The editorial job has become, unlike the
ancient age when one judged what one read, a
job of making judgements on outlines, ideas,
reputations, previous books, scenarios,
treatments, talk and promises.

VAUVENARGUES Marquis de 1715-1747
12066
The most absurd and reckless aspirations have
sometimes led to extraordinary success.

12067
To achieve great things, we must live as though
we were never going to die.

12068
All men are born truthful, and die liars.

12069
The lazy are always wanting to do something.

12070
The mind reaches great heights only by spurts.

12071
Vice stirs up war; virtue fights.

12072
If virtue were its own reward, it would no longer
be a human quality, but supernatural.

12073
When we are sick our virtues and our vices are
in abeyance.

VAUX Thomas 1510-1556
12074 *'The Aged Lover Renounceth Love'*
For age with stealing steps
Hath clawed me with his clutch,
And lusty life away she leaps,
As there had been none such.

VEBLEN Thorsten 1857-1929
12075
All business sagacity reduces itself in the last
analysis to a judicious use of sabotage.

12076
Conservatism is the maintenance of
conventions already in force.

12077
In order to stand well in the eyes of the
community, it is necessary to come up to a
certain, somewhat indefinite, conventional
standard of wealth.

VEGETIUS AD 379-395
12078
Let him who desires peace, prepare for war.

VERGNIAUD Pierre 1753-1793
12079
There was reason to fear that the Revolution,
like Saturn, might devour in turn each one of
her children.

VERLAINE Paul 1844-1896
12080 *'Art poétique'*
All the rest is mere fine writing.

12081 *'Chanson d'Automne'*
The drawn-out sobs of autumn's violins wound
my heart with a monotonous languor.

12082 *Romances sans paroles 'Ariettes oubliées'*
Tears are shed in my heart like the rain on the
town.

VESPASIAN AD 9-79
12083 *(replying to objection to tax public
lavatories)*
Money has no smell.

12084 *(when fatally ill)*
Woe is me, I think I am becoming a god.

VICTORIA Queen 1819-1901
12085 *(attributed)*
We are not amused.

12086 *(on the Boer War during 'Black Week')*
We are not interested in the possibilities of
defeat; they do not exist.

12087 *(of Gladstone)*
He speaks to me as if I was a public meeting.

12088 *(on Gladstone's last appointment as P.M.)*
The danger to the country, to Europe, to her
vast Empire, which is involved in having all
these great interests entrusted to the shaking

hand of an old, wild, and incomprehensible man of 82, is very great!

12089
The important thing is not what they think of me, it is what I think of them.

12090 *(on being shown a chart of the line of succession)*
I will be good.

12091 *(of St Paul's Cathedral)*
Dirty, dark, and undevotional.

VIDAL Gore 1925-
12092
[Commercialism is] doing well that which should not be done at all.

12093
I'm all for bringing back the birch, but only between consenting adults.

12094 *(of Ronald Regan)*
A triumph of the embalmer's art.

12095
A talent for drama is not a talent for writing, but is an ability to articulate human relationships.

12096
Whenever a friend succeeds, a little something in me dies.

VIERA GALLO José Antonio 1943-
12097
Socialism can only arrive by bicycle.

VIGNY Alfred de 1797-1863
12098 *La Bouteille à la mer*
The true God, the mighty God, is the God of ideas.

12099 *La Maison du Berger*
I love the majesty of human suffering.

12100 *La Mort du loup*
Only silence is great; all else is weakness.

12101 *Moïse*
Alas, Lord, I am powerful but alone. Let me sleep the sleep of the earth.

12102 *Servitude et grandeur militaire*
An army is a nation within a nation; it is one of the vices of our age.

VILLARS Marshall de 1653-1734
12103
God save me from my friends - I can protect myself from my enemies.

VILLIERS George 1628-1687
12104 *The Dramatic Works*
The world is made up for the most part of fools and knaves, both irreconcilable foes to truth.

12105 *The Rehearsal*
Ay, now the plot thickens very much upon us.

VILLIERS DE L'ISLE-ADAM Philippe-Auguste 1838-1889
12106 *Axël*
Living? The servants will do that for us.

VILLON François 1431-c.1465
12107 *Le Grand Testament 'Ballade des dames du temps jadis'*
But where are the snows of yesteryear?

12108 *Le Grand Testament 'Ballade pour prier Nostre Dame'*
In this faith I wish to live and to die.

VINCENT Field Marshall Sir Richard 1931-
12109
The first principle of war is: For God's sake decide what you're trying to achieve before you go out and start doing it.

VIRGIL 70-19 BC
12110 *Aeneid*
Trust one who has tried.

12111 *Aeneid*
I sing of arms and the man.

12112 *Aeneid*
Why such great anger in those heavenly minds?

12113 *Aeneid*
So massive was the effort to found the Roman nation.

12114 *Aeneid*
Odd figures swimming were glimpsed in the waste of waters.

12115 *Aeneid*
O you who have borne even heavier things, God will grant an end to these too.

12116 *Aeneid*
Maybe one day it will be cheering to remember even these things.

12117 *Aeneid*
No stranger to trouble myself I am learning to care for the unhappy.

12118 *Aeneid*
Do not trust the horse, Trojans. Whatever it is, I fear the Greeks even when they bring gifts.

12119 *Aeneid*
From the one crime recognize all as culprits.

12120 *Aeneid*
The only safe course for the defeated is to expect no safety.

12121 *Aeneid*
The gods thought otherwise.

12122 *Aeneid*
To what do you not drive human hearts, cursed craving for gold!

12123 *Aeneid*
Fickle and changeable always is woman.

12124 *Aeneid*
Rise up from my dead bones, avenger!

12125 *Aeneid*
They can because they think they can.

12126 *Aeneid*
I see wars, horrible wars, and the Tiber foaming with much blood.

12127 *Aeneid*
Darkling they went under the lonely night through the shadow and through the empty dwellings and unsubstantial realms of Hades.

12128 *Aeneid*
If I am unable to make the gods above relent, I shall move Hell.

12129 *Aeneid*
Blessings on your young courage, boy; that's the way to the stars.

12130 *Aeneid*
Fortune assists the bold.

12131 *Eclogues no.2*
Don't bank too much on your complexion, lovely boy.

12132 *Eclogues no.3*
There's a snake hidden in the grass.

12133 *Eclogues no.8*
Now I know what Love is.

12134 *Eclogues no.8*
We can't all do everything.

12135 *Eclogues no.10*
Love conquers all things: let us too give in to Love.

12136 *Georgics no.2 (of Lucretius)*
Lucky is he who has been able to understand the causes of things.

12137 *Georgics no.3*
Irretrievable time is flying.

VOLNEY Constantin, Comte de 1757-1820
12138
The first book of the nation is the dictionary of its language.

VOLTAIRE 1694-1778
12139 *(attributed)*
I disapprove of what you say, but I will defend to the death your right to say it.

12140
I advise you to go on living solely to enrage those who are paying your annuities. It is the only pleasure I have left.

12141
All the ancient histories, as one of our wits has said, are but fables that have been agreed upon.

12142
I know I am among civilized men because they are fighting so savagely.

12143
The best government is a benevolent tyranny tempered by an occasional assassination.

12144 *Candide*
In this best of possible worlds ... all is for the best. [usually quoted 'All is for the best in the best of all possible worlds.']

12145 *Candide*
If we do not find anything pleasant, at least we shall find something new.

12146 *Candide*
In this country [England] it is thought well to kill an admiral from time to time to encourage the others.

12147 *Candide*
We must cultivate our garden.

12148 *Candide*
The best is the enemy of the good.

12149 *Dialogues 'Le Chapon et la poularde'*
[Men] use thought only to justify their injustices, and speech only to conceal their thoughts.

12150 *Discours en vers sur l'homme 'De la nature'*
The secret of being a bore ... is to tell everything.

12151
Doubt is not a pleasant condition, but certainty is.

12152
England has forty-two religions and only two sauces.

12153 *Épîtres 'A l'Auteur du livre des trois ...'*
If God did not exist, it would be necessary to invent him.

12154 *Essai sur l'histoire générale...*
This agglomeration which was called and which still calls itself the Holy Roman Empire was neither holy, nor Roman, nor an empire.

12155
Fear succeeds crime - it is its punishment.

12156
If God made us in his image, we have certainly returned the compliment.

12157
It is hard to free fools from the chains they revere.

12158 *Le Mondain*
The superfluous, a very necessary thing.

12159 *L'Enfant prodigue*
All styles are good except the tiresome kind.

12160 *L'Ingénu*
Indeed, history is nothing more than a tableau of crimes and misfortunes.

12161
Men argue, nature acts.

12162
Never having been able to succeed in the world, he took his revenge by speaking ill of it.

12163
We never live, but we are always in the expectation of living.

12164
I never was ruined but twice - once when I lost a lawsuit, and once when I gained one.

12165
We offer up prayers to God only because we have made Him after our own image. We treat Him like a Pasha, or a Sultan, who is capable of being exasperated and appeased.

12166
Originality is nothing but judicious imitation.

12167 *The Piccini Notebooks*
Governments need both shepherds and butchers.

12168 *The Piccini Notebooks*
God is on the side not of the heavy battalions, but of the best shots.

12169 *'Première Lettre sur Oedipe'*
We owe respect to the living; to the dead we owe only truth.

12170 *Thoughts of a Philosopher*
Marriage is the only adventure open to the cowardly.

12171
Ask a toad what is beauty? ... a female with two great round eyes coming out of her little head, a large flat mouth, a yellow belly and a brown back.

12172
There are truths that are not for all men, nor for all times.

12173
Weakness on both sides is, as we know, the motto of all quarrels.

12174
What a heavy burden is a name that has become too famous.

12175
When it is a question of money, everybody is of the same religion.

12176 *(when asked to renounce the Devil, on deathbed)*
This is no time for making new enemies.

12177
Whoever serves his country well has no need of ancestors.

12178
Work banishes those three great evils, boredom, vice, and poverty.

VONNEGUT Kurt 1922-
12179
Educating a beautiful woman is like pouring honey into a fine Swiss watch: everything stops.

VORSE Mary Heaton
12180
(Writing) - the art of applying the seat of the pants to the seat of the chair.

VOZNESENKSY Andrei 1933-
12181
The times spat at me. I spit back at the times.

WAGNER Robert 1930-
12182
As a parent you just hang on for the ride.

WALDEGRAVE William 1946-
12183
In exceptional circumstances it is necessary to say something that is untrue in the House of Commons.

12184
Much of Government's activity is more like poker than chess. You don't put all your cards on the table.

WALKER Alice 1944-
12185 *'We Have a Beautiful Mother'*
We have a beautiful
mother
Her green lap
immense
Her brown embrace
eternal
Her blue body
everything
we know.

12186 *'Expect nothing'*
Expect nothing. Live frugally
on surprise.

12187 *'Did This Happen To Your Mother? ...'*
... Needs grow too fast;
they come up like weeds.
Through cracks in the conversation.
Through silences in the dark.
Through everything you thought was concrete.

12188 *'The QPP'*
The quietly pacifist peaceful
always die
to make room for men
who shout. Who tell lies to
children, and crush the corners
off of old men's dreams.

WALKER James J.
12189
A reformer is a guy who rides through a sewer
in a glass-bottomed boat.

WALL Max 1908-1990
12190
Show business is like sex. When it's wonderful,
it's wonderful. But when it isn't very good, it's
still all right.

WALLACE Edgar 1875-1932
12191
What is a highbrow? He is a man who has
found something more interesting than women.

WALLACE George 1919-
12192 *(inaugural speech as Governor of Alabama)*
Segregation now, segregation tomorrow and
segregation forever!

WALLACE Henry 1888-1965
12193
The century on which we are entering - the
century which will come out of this war - can be
and must be the century of the common man.

WALLACE Joe
12194
Ours is a sovereign nation
Bows to no foreign will
But whenever they cough in Washington
They spit on Parliament Hill.

WALLACE William Ross 1819-1881
12195 *'What rules the world'*
For the hand that rocks the cradle
Is the hand that rules the world.

WALLAS Graham 1858-1932
12196 *The Art of Thought*
The little girl had the making of a poet in her
who, being told to be sure of her meaning
before she spoke, said, 'How can I know what I
think till I see what I say?'

WALLER Edmund 1606-1687
12197 *'Of English Verse'*
Poets that lasting marble seek
Must carve in Latin or in Greek.

12198 *'On a Girdle'*
That which her slender waist confined
Shall now my joyful temples bind;
No monarch but would give his crown
His arms might do what this has done.

12199 *'Of the Last Verses in the Book'*
Leaving the old, both worlds at once they view,
That stand upon the threshold of the new.

12200 *'Go, lovely rose!'*
Go, lovely rose!
Tell her, that wastes her time and me,
That now she knows,
When I resemble her to thee,
How sweet and fair she seems to be.

12201 *'Panegyric to My Lord Protector'*
Rome, though her eagle through the world had
flown,
Could never make this island all her own.

12202
Vexed sailors curse the rain
For which poor shepherds prayed in vain.

12203 *'Of a War with Spain'*
Others may use the ocean as their road,
Only the English make it their abode.

12204 *'To My Young Lady Lucy Sidney'*
Why came I so untimely forth
Into a world which, wanting thee,
Could entertain us with no worth,
Or shadow of felicity?

WALLPORT Gordon
12205
A mark of maturity seems to be the range and
extent of one's feeling of self-involvement in
abstract ideals.

WALPOLE Horace 1717-1797
12206 *Letter to Anne, Countess of Upper Ossory*
This world is a comedy to those that think, a
tragedy to those that feel.

12207 *Letter to Anne, Countess of Upper Ossory*
Tell me, ye divines, which is the most virtuous
man, he who begets twenty bastards, or he who
sacrifices an hundred thousand lives?

12208 *Letter to Caroline, Countess of Ailesbury*
When people will not weed their own minds,
they are apt to be overrun with nettles.

12209 *Letter to Chrisopher Wren*
One of the greatest geniuses that ever existed,
Shakespeare, undoubtedly wanted taste.

12210 *Letter to George Montagu*
Every drop of ink in my pen ran cold.

12211 *Letter to George Montagu*
The best sun we have is made of Newcastle coal.

12212 *Letter to George Selwyn*
It is charming to totter into vogue.

12213 *Letter to Hon. Henry Conway*
But, thank God! the Thames is between me and the Duchess of Queensberry.

12214 *Letter to Sir Horace Mann*
Our supreme governors, the mob.

12215 *Letter to Sir Horace Mann*
When will the world know that peace and propagation are the two most delightful things in it?

12216 *Letter to Revd. William Cole*
The way to ensure summer in England is to have it framed and glazed in a comfortable room.

12217 *Memoirs of the Reign of King George II*
Whoever knows the interior of affairs, must be sensible to how many more events the faults of statesmen give birth, than are produced by their good intentions.

12218
I am in a moment of pretty wellness.

12219
Virtue knows to a farthing what it has lost by not having been vice.

WALPOLE Sir Hugh 1884-1941
12220 *Fortitude*
'Tisn't life that matters! 'Tis the courage you bring to it.

WALPOLE Sir Robert 1676-1745
12221
The balance of power.

12222 *(on the declaration of war with Spain)*
They now *ring* the bells, but they will soon *wring* their hands.

12223 *(of fellow parliamentarians)*
All those men have their price.

12224
I always tell a young man not to use the word `always'.

WALSH William 1663-1708
12225 *'The Despairing Lover'*
A lover forsaken
A new love may get,
But a neck when once broken
Can never be set.

12226 *'Song: Of All the Torments'*
In love alone we hate to find
Companions of our woe.

12227 *'Song: Of All the Torments'*
I can endure my own despair,
But not another's hope.

WALTERS Barbara
12228
I can get a better grasp of what is going on in the world from one good Washington dinner party than from all the background information NBC piles on my desk.

WALTERS Maryanne
12229
The point of therapy is to get unhooked, not to thrash around on how you got hooked.

WALTON Izaak 1593-1683
12230
Of this blest man, let his just praise be given,
Heaven was in him, before he was in Heaven.

12231 *The Compleat Angler*
Good company and good discourse are the very sinews of virtue.

12232 *The Compleat Angler*
An excellent angler, and now with God.

12233 *The Compleat Angler*
I love such mirth as does not make friends ashamed to look upon one another next morning.

12234 *The Compleat Angler*
No man can lose what he never had.

12235 *The Compleat Angler*
Use him as though you loved him.

12236 *The Compleat Angler*
The dish of meat is too good for any but anglers, or very honest men.

12237 *The Compleat Angler 'Epistle to the Reader'*
Angling may be said to be so like the mathematics, that it can never be fully learnt.

12238 *The Compleat Angler 'Epistle to the Reader'*
As no man is born an artist, so no man is born an angler.

WANAMAKER Zöe
12239
Laughter can be an aphrodisiac, yet it can also be a substitute for sex.

WARBURTON William 1698-1779
12240 *(to Lord Sandwich)*
Orthodoxy is my doxy; heterodoxy is another man's doxy.

WARD Artemus 1834-1867
12241 *Artemus Ward His Book 'Fourth of July Oration'*
I'm not a politician and my other habits are good.

12242 *Artemus Ward His Book 'The Showman's Courtship'*
I wish thar was winders to my Sole, sed I, so that you could see some of my feelins.

12243 *Artemus Ward His Book 'A Visit to Brigham Young'*
I girdid up my Lions & fled the Seen.

12244 *Artemus Ward His Book 'Woman's Rights'*
The female woman is one of the greatest institooshuns of which this land can boste.

12245 *Artemus Ward in London*
It is a pity that Chawcer, who had geneyus, was so unedicated. He's the wuss speller I know of.

12246 *Artemus Ward in London*
Let us all be happy, and live within our means, even if we have to borrer the money to do it with.

12247 *Artemus Ward's Lecture*
Why is this thus? What is the reason of this thusness?

12248 *Artemus Ward's Lecture 'Brigham Young's...'*
He is dreadfully married. He's the most married man I ever saw in my life.

12249
Why don't you show us a statesman who can rise up to the emergency, and cave in the emergency's head?

WARD Nathaniel 1578-1652
12250 *Epigram*
The world is full of care, much like unto a bubble;
Woman and care, and care and women, and women and care and trouble.

WARD Thomas 1577-1639
12251 *England's Reformation*
Where to elect there is but one,
'Tis Hobson's choice, - take that or none.

WARE Eugene Fitch 1841-1911
12252
Work brings its own relief;
He who most idle is
Has most of grief.

WARHOL Andy 1927-1987
12253
Some day each of us will be famous for fifteen minutes.

12254
The most exciting thing is *not* doing it. If you fall in love with someone and never do it, it's much more exciting.

WARNER Charles Dudley 1829-1900
12255
It is one of the beautiful compensations of this life that no one can sincerely try to help another without helping himself.

12256
There isn't a wife in the world who has not taken the exact measure of her husband, weighed him and settled him in her own mind, and knows him as well as if she had ordered him after designs and specifications of her own.

WARNER H.M.
12257 *(of talking pictures - in 1927)*
Who the hell wants to hear actors talk?

WARNER Susan 1819-1885
12258 *The Love of Jesus*
Jesus loves me - this I know,
For the Bible tells me so.

WARREN Earl 1891-1974
12259
I'm very pleased with each advancing year. It stems back to when I was forty. I was a bit upset about reaching that milestone, but an older friend consoled me. 'Don't complain about growing old - many people don't have that privilege.'

12260
We are now at the point where we must decide whether we are to honour the concept of a plural society which gains strength through diversity, or whether we are to have bitter fragmentation that will result in perpetual tension and strife.

12261
The sports page records people's accomplishments, the front page usually records nothing but man's failures.

WARREN Robert Penn 1905-1989
12262
For what is a poem but a hazardous attempt at self-understanding: it is the deepest part of autobiography.

WASHINGTON George 1732-1799
12263
I beg leave to assure the Congress that no pecuniary consideration could have tempted me to accept this arduous employment at the expense of my domestic ease and happiness. I do not wish to make any profit from it.

12264
I can't tell a lie, Pa; you know I can't tell a lie. I did cut it with my hatchet.

12265 *General Orders*
The time is now near at hand which must probably determine whether Americans are to be freemen or slaves.

12266 *General Orders*
The fate of unborn millions will now depend, under God, on the courage and conduct of this army. Our cruel and unrelenting enemy leaves us only the choice of brave resistance, or the most abject submission. We have, therefore, to resolve to conquer or die.

12267
Government is not reason, it is not eloquence - it is force.

12268
Few men have virtue to withstand the highest bidder.

12269
My movement to the chair of government will be accompanied by feelings not unlike those of a culprit who is going to the place of execution.

12270
I shall never ask, never refuse, nor ever resign an office.

12271
To persevere in one's duty and be silent, is the best answer to calumny.

12272 *President's Address*
'Tis our true policy to steer clear of permanent alliances, with any portion of the foreign world.

12273 *President's Address*
Let me ... warn you in the most solemn manner against the baneful effects of the spirit of party.

WASHINGTON Ned 1901-1976
12274 *'My Foolish Heart'*
There's a line between love and fascination
That's hard to see on an evening such as this,
For they both give the very same sensation
When you're lost in the magic of a kiss.

12275 *(song from the film Pinocchio)*
Hi diddle dee dee (an actor's life for me).

WATKYNS Richard
12276
When I was born I did lament and cry
And now each day doth shew the reason why.

WATKYNS Rowland c.1616-1664
12277 *'Antipathy'*
I love him not, but show no reason can
Wherefore, but this, *I do not love* the man.

WATSON Arthur K. 1867-1947
12278
Show me a man with both feet on the ground and I'll show you a man who can't put his pants on.

WATSON Thomas
12279 *(whilst Chairman of IBM in 1943)*
I think there's a world market for maybe five computers.

WATSON William c.1559-1603
12280 *A Decacordon of Ten Quodlibeticall Questions*
Let justice be done though the heavens fall.

WATSON Sir William 1858-1936
12281 *April*
April, April
Laugh thy girlish laughter;
Then, the moment after,
Weep thy girlish tears!

12282 *A Study in Contrasts*
The staid, conservative,
Came-over-with-the Conqueror type of mind.

WATTENBERG Ben
12283
Like most successful politicians Clinton has a coalition in his brain.

WATTS Isaac 1674-1748
12284 *Divine Songs for Children 'Against Evil'*
One sickly sheep infects the flock,
And poisons all the rest.

12285 *Divine Songs for Children 'Against Idleness'*
How doth the little busy bee
Improve each shining hour,
And gather honey all the day
From every opening flower!

12286 *Divine Songs for Children 'Against Idleness'*
For Satan finds some mischief still
For idle hands to do.

12287 *Divine Songs for Children 'Against Quarrelling'*
Let dogs delight to bark and bite,
For God hath made them so.

12288 *Divine Songs for Children 'Love between Brothers'*
Birds in their little nests agree
And 'tis a shameful sight,
When children of one family
Fall out, and chide, and fight.

12289 *Divine Songs for Children 'The Sluggard'*
'Tis the voice of the sluggard; I heard him complain,
'You have waked me too soon, I must slumber

again'.
As the door on its hinges, so he on his bed,
Turns his sides and his shoulders and his heavy
head.

12290
Let me be dressed fine as I will,
Flies, worms, and flowers, exceed me still.

12291 *Hymns and Spiritual Songs 'Crucifixion ...'*
When I survey the wondrous cross
On which the prince of glory died,
My richest gain I count but loss,
And pour contempt on all my pride.

12292 *The Psalms of David Imitated Psalm 90*
Our God, our help in ages past
Our hope for years to come,
Our shelter from the stormy blast,
And our eternal home.

WAUGH Evelyn 1903-1966
12293 *Decline and Fall*
I haven't been to sleep for over a year. That's
why I go to bed early. One needs more rest if
one doesn't sleep.

12294 *Decline and Fall*
Very hard for a man with a wig to keep order.

12295 *Decline and Fall*
That's the public-school system all over. They
may kick you out, but they never let you down.

12296 *The Loved One*
You never find an Englishman among the
under dogs - except in England, of course.

12297
Manners are especially the need of the plain.
The pretty can get away with anything.

12298 *'An Open Letter'*
Impotence and sodomy are socially O.K. but
birth control is flagrantly middle-class.

12299
Perhaps host and guest is really the happiest
relation for father and son.

12300
Punctuality is the virtue of the bored.

12301 *Scoop*
News is what a chap who doesn't care much
about anything wants to read. And it's only
news until he's read it. After that it's dead.

12302 *Scoop*
I will not stand for being called a woman in my
own house.

12303 *Scoop*
Other nations use 'force'; we Britons alone use
'Might'.

12304 *Vile Bodies*
All this fuss about sleeping together. For
physical pleasure I'd sooner go to my dentist
any day.

12305 *(asked what he did for his college)*
I drink for it.

12306
Winston Churchill is always expecting rabbits to
come out of an empty hat.

WAVELL Lord 1883-1950
12307 *(attributed)*
(Love) is like a cigar. If it goes out, you can light
it again but it never tastes quite the same.

WAYNE John 1907-1979
12308
Tomorrow is the most important thing in life.
Comes in to us at midnight very clean. It's
perfect when it arrives and it puts itself in our
hands and hopes we've learnt something from
yesterday.

12309 *in She wore a Yellow Ribbon*
"Never apologise and never explain. It's a sign of
weakness."

WEATHERLY Frederick 1848-1929
12310 *'The Old Brigade'*
Where are the boys of the old Brigade,
Who fought with us side by side?

12311 *'Roses of Picardy'*
Roses are flowering in Picardy,
But there's never a rose like you.

WEBB Sidney (Baron Passfield) 1859-1947
12312
The inevitability of gradualness cannot fail to be
appreciated.

12313
Marriage is the waste-paper basket of the
emotions.

WEBER Max 1864-1920
12314 *Archiv für Sozialwissenschaft..*
The protestant ethic and the spirit of
capitalism.

12315 *'Politik als Beruf'*
The State is a relation of men dominating men,
a relation supported by means of legitimate (i.e.
considered to be legitimate) violence.

12316 *'Politik als Beruf'*
The experience of the irrationality of the world
has been the driving force of all religious
revolution.

WEBSTER Daniel 1782-1852
12317
I was born an American; I will live an American;
I shall die an American.

12318 *(on completion of Bunker Hill Monument)*
Thank God, I - I also - am an American!

12319 *(on joining overcrowded legal profession)*
There is always room at the top.

12320
Liberty *and* Union, now and forever, one and
inseparable.

12321
The past, at least, is secure.

12322
The people's government, made for the people,
made by the people, and answerable to the
people.

WEBSTER John c.1580-c.1625
12323 *The Devil's Law-Case*
Vain the ambition of kings,
Who seek by trophies and dead things,
To leave a living name behind,
And weave but nets to catch the wind.

12324 *The Duchess of Malfi*
Unequal nature, to place women's hearts
So far upon the left side.

12325 *The Duchess of Malfi*
Why should only I ...
Be cased up, like a holy relic? I have youth
And a little beauty.

12326 *The Duchess of Malfi*
Raised by that curious engine, your white hand.

12327 *The Duchess of Malfi*
Glories, like glow-worms, afar off shine bright,
But looked to near, have neither heat nor light.

12328 *The Duchess of Malfi*
I know death hath ten thousand several doors
For men to take their exits.

12329 *The Duchess of Malfi*
Cover her face, mine eyes dazzle: she died
young.

12330 *The Duchess of Malfi*
Physicians are like kings - they brook no
contradiction.

12331 *The Duchess of Malfi*
We are merely the stars' tennis-balls, struck and
bandied
Which way please them.

12332 *The White Devil*
Fortune's a right whore:
If she give aught, she deals it in small parcels,
That she may take away all at one swoop.

12333 *The White Devil*
Only the deep sense of some deathless shame.

12334 *The White Devil*
Cowardly dogs bark loudest.

12335 *The White Devil*
But keep the wolf far thence that's foe to men,
For with his nails he'll dig them up again.

12336 *The White Devil*
There's nothing of so infinite vexation
As man's own thoughts.

12337 *The White Devil*
I have caught
An everlasting cold; I have lost my voice
Most irrecoverably.

WEBSTER Noah 1758-1843
12338
Power is always right, weakness always wrong.
Power is always insolent and despotic.

WEDGWOOD Josiah 1730-1795
12339 *(legend on Wedgwood cameo)*
Am I not a man and a brother.

WEEKS Edward
12340
To live with fear and not be afraid is the final
test of maturity.

WEIL Simone 1909-1943
12341
All sins are attempts to fill voids.

12342
A hateful act is the transference to others of the
degradation we bear in ourselves.

12343
The intelligent man who is proud of his
intelligence is like the condemned man who is
proud of his large cell.

12344
What a country calls its vital economic interests
are not the things which enable its citizens to
live, but the things which enable it to make war.

12345
Those who serve a cause are not those who love
that cause. They are those who love the life
which has to be led in order to serve it - except
in the case of the very purest, and they are rare.

WEINBERGER Harry
12346
The greatest right in the world is the right to be
wrong.

WEINREICH Max
12347
A language is a dialect with its own army and
navy.

WEISSMULLER Johnny 1904-1984
12348 *(summing up his role in Tarzan)*
Me Tarzan, you Jane.

WEITZ John
12349
When a woman dresses up for an occasion, the man should become the black velvet pillow for the jewel.

WEIZMANN Chaim 1874-1952
12350
Miracles sometimes occur, but one has to work terribly hard for them.

WELCH Raquel 1940-
12351
The mind can also be an erogenous zone.

WELDON Fay 1931-
12352
Hell is not other people, hell is no other people.

WELLES Orson 1915-1985
12353
Every actor in his heart believes everything bad that's printed about him.

12354
A film is never really good unless the camera is an eye in the head of a poet.

12355 *(of the RKO studios)*
The biggest electric train set any boy ever had!

12356 *in The Third Man*
"In Italy for thirty years under the Borgias they had warfare, terror, murder, bloodshed - they produced Michelangelo, Leonardo da Vinci and the Renaissance. In Switzerland they had brotherly love, five hundred years of democracy and peace and what did that produce ...? The cuckoo clock."

WELLINGTON Duke of 1769-1852
12357 *(attributed)*
The battle of Waterloo was won on the playing fields of Eton.

12358
Possible? Is anything impossible? Read the newspapers.

12359 *(advice to a new MP)*
Don't quote Latin; say what you have to say, and then sit down.

12360 *The Croker Papers*
All the business of war, and indeed all the business of life, is to endeavour to find out what you don't know by what you do; that's what I called 'guessing what was at the other side of the hill'.

12361
Nothing except a battle lost can be half so melancholy as a battle won.

12362
Ours [our army] is composed of the scum of the earth - the mere scum of the earth.

12363 *(replying to a blackmail threat - attributed)*
Publish and be damned.

12364 *(attributed, on reviewing his troops)*
I don't know what effect these men will have on the enemy, but by God, they frighten *me*.

12365
I used to say of him [Napoleon] that his presence on the field made the difference of forty thousand men.

12366 *(on seeing the first Reformed Parliament)*
I never saw so many shocking bad hats in my life.

12367 *(of steam locomotives)*
I see no reason to suppose that these machines will ever force themselves into general use.

WELLS Carolyn 1869-1942
12368
We should live and learn; but by the time we've learned, it's too late to live.

WELLS C.M. 1908-
12369
All port tastes the same after lunch.

WELLS H.G. 1866-1946
12370
Advertising is legalized lying.

12371
Crude classifications and false generalizations are the curse of organized life.

12372 *The History of Mr Polly*
I'll make a gory mess of you. I'll cut bits orf you.

12373
To be honest, one must be inconsistent.

12374 *Kipps*
'I'm a Norfan, both sides,' he would explain, with the air of one who had seen trouble.

12375 *Kipps*
I was thinking jest what a Rum Go everything is.

12376 *The Outline of History*
Human history becomes more and more a race between education and catastrophe.

12377 *Select Conversations with an Uncle*
Bah! the thing is not a nose at all, but a bit of primordial chaos clapped on to my face.

12378
The shape of things to come.

12379
I want to go ahead of Father Time with a scythe of my own.

12380
The war that will end war.

12381 *The Wife of Sir Isaac Harman*
Moral indignation is jealousy with a halo.

WELTY Eudora 1909-
12382
Children, like animals, use all their senses to discover the world. Then artists come along and discover it the same way all over again.

WENDELL Barrett 1855-1921
12383
Words and sentences are subjects of revision; paragraphs and whole compositions are subjects of prevision.

WESKER Arnold 1932-
12384 *Chips with Everything*
It said 'Chips with everything'. Chips with every damn thing. You breed babies and you eat chips with everything.

12385 *Roots*
Education ent only books and music - it's asking questions, all the time. There are millions of us, all over the country, and no one, not one of us, is asking questions, we're all taking the easiest way out.

WESLEY Charles 1707-1788
12386 *'And can it be'*
Amazing love! How can it be
That thou, my God, shouldst die for me?

12387 *'Gentle Jesus ...'*
Gentle Jesus, meek and mild,
Look upon a little child;
Pity my simplicity,
Suffer me to come to thee.

12388 *'Hymn for Christmas'*
Hail, the heaven-born Prince of Peace!
Hail, the Sun of Righteousness!

WESLEY John 1703-1791
12389
Beware you be not swallowed up in books! An ounce of love is worth a pound of knowledge.

12390 *Journal*
I went to America to convert the Indians; but oh, who shall convert me?

12391 *Journal*
I look upon all the world as my parish.

12392 *Journal*
I have this day lived fourscore years ... God grant that I may never live to be useless!

12393 *Letter to Miss March*
Though I am always in haste, I am never in a hurry.

12394
Passion and prejudice govern the world; only under the name of reason.

12395 *Sermons on Several Occasions*
I design plain truth for plain people.

WESLEY Samuel 1662-1735
12396 *'An Epistle to a Friend concerning Poetry'*
Style is the dress of thought; a modest dress,
Neat, but not gaudy, will true critics please.

WEST Jessamyn
12397
It is very easy to forgive others their mistakes. It takes more gut and gumption to forgive them for having witnessed your own.

12398
Fiction reveals truth that reality obscures.

WEST Mae 1892-1980
12399 *(attributed)*
When I'm good, I'm very good, but when I'm bad, I'm better.

12400 *in Belle of the Nineties*
"A man in the house is worth two in the street."

12401 *in Every Day's a Holiday*
"I always say, keep a diary and some day it'll keep you."

12402
I generally avoid temptation unless I can't resist it.

12403
Too much of a good thing can be wonderful.

12404 *in I'm No Angel*
"It's not the men in my life that counts - it's the life in my men."

12405 *in Klondike Annie*
"Give a man a free hand and he'll try to put it all over you."

12406 *in My Little Chickadee*
"Is that a gun in your pocket, or are you just glad to see me?"

12407
Marriage is a great institution, but I am not ready for an institution.

12408
I used to be snow-white ... but I drifted.

12409
When choosing between two evils, I always like to take the one I've never tried before.

The Wordsworth Dictionary of Quotations

12410 *The Wit and Wisdom of Mae West*
When women go wrong, men go right after them.

12411 *in She Done Him Wrong*
"Why don't you come up sometime, and see me?" [usually quoted: 'Why don't you come up and see me sometime?']

WEST Rebecca 1892-1983
12412 *There is No Conversation*
It is queer how it is always one's virtues and not one's vices that precipitate one into disaster.

12413 *(of Michael Arlen)*
Every other inch a gentleman.

12414 *The Salt of the Earth*
The point is that nobody likes having salt rubbed into their wounds, even if it is the salt of the earth.

WEST-MEADS Zelda 1947-
12415
For most people, infidelity feels like the ultimate betrayal. Very few people can cope with the thought of their partner making love to, touching, and having candlelight dinners with somebody else.

WESTCOTT Brooke Foss 1825-1901
12416
Great occasions do not make heroes or cowards; they simply unveil them to the eyes of men. Silently and imperceptibly, as we wake or sleep, we grow strong or weak; and at last some crisis shows what we have become.

12417
What we can do for another is the test of powers; what we can suffer is the test of love.

WESTCOTT Edward Noyes 1846-1898
12418
The only man who can change his mind is the man who's got one.

12419
I reckon there's as much human nature in some folks as there is in others, if not more.

12420
They say a reasonable amount o' fleas is good for a dog - it keeps him from broodin' over bein' a dog mebbe.

WESTON Edward 1996-1958
12421
Art is based on order. The world is full of 'sloppy Bohemians' and their work betrays them.

WESTON R.P. and LEE Bert 1878-1936 and 1880-1947
12422 *'Good-bye-ee!'*
Good-bye-ee! - Good-bye-ee!

Wipe the tear, baby dear, from your eye-ee.
Tho' it's hard to part, I know,
I'll be tickled to death to go.
Don't cry-ee - don't sigh-ee!
There's a silver lining in the sky-ee!
Bonsoir, old thing! cheerio! chin-chin!
Nahpoo! Toodle-oo! Good-bye-ee!

WHARTON Edith 1862-1937
12423 *The Descent of Man 'The Other Two'*
If he paid for each day's comfort with the small change of his illusions, he grew daily to value the comfort more and set less store upon the coin.

12424 *Ethan Frome*
People struggled on for years with 'troubles', but they almost always succumbed to 'complications'.

12425
In any really good subject, one has only to probe deep enough to come to tears.

12426 *Xingu and Other Stories 'Xingu'*
Mrs Ballinger is one of the ladies who pursue Culture in bands, as though it were dangerous to meet it alone.

WHATELY Richard 1787-1863
12427 *Apophthegms*
Preach not because you have to say something, but because you have something to say.

12428 *Apophthegms*
Happiness is no laughing matter

12429 *Apophthegms*
It is a folly to expect men to do all that they may reasonably be expected to do.

12430 *Apophthegms*
Honesty is the best policy; but he who is governed by that maxim is not an honest man.

12431 *(of 'Authorized Version' of The Bible)*
Never forget that this is *not* the Bible. This, gentlemen, is only a *translation* of the Bible.

12432 *Introductory lectures on Political Economy*
It is not that pearls fetch a high price *because* men have dived for them; but on the contrary, men dive for them because they fetch a high price.

WHEWELL William 1794-1866
12433 *Elementary Treatise on Mechanics*
Hence no force however great can stretch a cord however fine into an horizontal line which is accurately straight: there will always be a bending downwards.

12434 *Philosophy of the Inductive Sciences*
Man is the interpreter of nature, science the right interpretation.

WHISTLER James McNeill 1834-1903
12435 *(in his case against Ruskin)*
[Replying to the question 'For two days' labour, you ask two hundred guineas?']
No, I ask it for the knowledge of a lifetime.

12436 *The Gentle Art of Making Enemies*
I am not arguing with you - I am telling you.

12437 *(to a lady reminded of his work by a 'haze')*
Yes madam, Nature is creeping up.

12438
Nature is usually wrong.

12439
To say to the painter that Nature is to be taken as she is, is to say to the player that he may sit on the piano.

12440
Two and two continue to make four, in spite of the whine of the amateur for three, or the cry of the critic for five.

12441 *Mr Whistler's 'Ten O'Clock'*
Art is upon the Town!

WHITE E.B. 1899-1985
12442
Advice to young writers who want to get ahead without any annoying delays: don't write about Man, write about a man.

12443 *'The Commuter'*
Commuter - one who spends his life
In riding to and from his wife;
A man who shaves and takes a train,
And then rides back to shave again.

12444
Commuters give the city its tidal restlessness, natives give it solidity and continuity, but the settlers give it passion.

12445
Democracy is the recurrent suspicion that more than half of the people are right more than half of the time.

12446
The first day of spring was once the time for taking the young virgins into the fields, there in dalliance to set an example in fertility for Nature to follow. Now we just set the clock an hour ahead and change the oil in the crankcase.

12447
Humour can be dissected, as a frog can, but the thing dies in the process.

12448
Humour plays close to the big, hot fire, which is the truth, and the reader feels the heat.

12449
His words leap across rivers and mountains, but his thoughts are still only six inches long.

12450
At present, I am a sojourner in the city again, but here in the green warmth of a city backyard, I see only the countenance of spring in the country.

12451
Reading is the work of the alert mind, is demanding, and under ideal conditions produces finally a sort of ecstasy. This gives the experience of reading a sublimity and power unequalled by any other form of communication.

12452
I liked to sail alone. The sea was the same as a girl to me - I did not want anyone else along.

12453
If the world were merely seductive, that would be easy. If it were merely challenging, that would be no problem. But I rise in the morning torn between a desire to improve (or save) the world and a desire to enjoy (or savour) the world. This makes it hard to plan the day.

WHITE H. Kirke 1785-1806
12454 *'Oft in danger, oft in woe'*
Oft in danger, oft in woe,
Onward, Christians, onward go;
Bear the toil, maintain the strife,
Strengthened with the Bread of Life.

WHITE John
12455
There are three kinds of people in the world: those who can't stand Picasso, those who can't stand Raphael and those who've never heard of either of them.

WHITE Patrick 1912-1990
12456 *The Tree of Man*
Conversation is imperative if gaps are to be filled, and old age, it is the last gap but one.

WHITE Paul Dudley 1886-1973
12457
A vigorous five-mile walk will do more good for an unhappy but otherwise healthy adult than all the medicine and psychology in the world.

WHITE T.H. 1906-1964
12458 *Farewell Victoria*
The Victorians had not been anxious to go away for the weekend. The Edwardians, on the contrary, were nomadic.

12459
The once and future king.

12460 *The Sword in the Stone*
But I unfortunately was born at the wrong end of time, and I have to live *backwards* from in front.

WHITE Theodore
12461
There is no excitement anywhere in the world, short of war, to match the excitement of the American presidential campaign.

12462
Quality - in its classic Greek sense - how to live with grace and intelligence, with bravery and mercy.

WHITE William Allen 1868-1944
12463 *(when Roosevelt retired from Presidential campaign)*
All dressed up, with nowhere to go.

WHITE William Hale 1831-1913
12464
Blessed are they who heal us of self-despisings. Of all services which can be done to man, I know of none more precious.

WHITEFIELD George
12465
It is better to wear out than to rust out.

WHITEHEAD Alfred North 1861-1947
12466 *Adventures of Ideas*
Life is an offensive, directed against the repetitious mechanism of the Universe.

12467
The antithesis between a technical and a liberal education is fallacious. There can be no adequate technical education which is not liberal, and no liberal education which is not technical.

12468
The art of progress is to preserve order amid change, and to preserve change amid order.

12469
A civilized society is one that exhibits the five qualities of truth, beauty, adventure, art and peace.

12470
The deepest definition of youth is life as yet untouched by tragedy.

12471 *Dialogues*
Intelligence is quickness to apprehend as distinct from ability, which is capacity to act wisely on the thing apprehended.

12472 *Dialogues*
What is morality in any given time or place? It is what the majority then and there happen to like, and immorality is what they dislike.

12473 *Dialogues*
Art is the imposing of a pattern on experience, and our aesthetic enjoyment is recognition of the pattern.

12474
Education with inert ideas is not only useless; it is above all things harmful.

12475
The factor in human life provocative of a noble discontent is the gradual emergence of a sense of criticism, founded upon appreciation of beauty, and of intellectual distinction, and of duty.

12476
Ideas won't keep: something must be done about them.

12477
Not ignorance, but ignorance of ignorance is the death of knowledge.

12478 *Introduction to Mathematics*
Civilization advances by extending the number of important operations which we can perform without thinking about them.

12479
The major advances in civilization are processes which all but wreck the societies in which they occur.

12480
A man really writes for an audience of about ten persons. Of course if others like it, that is clear gain. But if those ten are satisfied, he is content.

12481
From the moment of birth we are immersed in action, and can only fitfully guide it by taking thought.

12482
The only justification in the use of force is to reduce the amount of force necessary to be used.

12483 *Process and Reality*
The safest general characterization of the European philosophical tradition is that it consists of a series of footnotes to Plato.

12484
A science which hesitates to forget its founders is lost.

12485 *(of scientific revolution in 16th Century)*
Since a babe was born in a manger, it may be doubted whether so great a thing has happened with so little stir.

12486
Not a sentence or a word is independent of the circumstances under which it is uttered.

12487
The total absence of humour in the Bible is one of the most singular things in all literature.

12488
Vigorous societies harbour a certain extravagance of objectives.

WHITEHORN Katharine 1926-
12489 *Roundabout 'The Office Party'*
Bringing down the mighty from their seats is an agreeable and necessary pastime, but no one supposes that the mighty, having struggled so hard to get seated, will enjoy the dethronement.

12490 *Shouts and Murmurs 'Hats'*
Hats divide generally into three classes: offensive hats, defensive hats, and shrapnel.

12491 *Sunday Best 'Decoding the West'*
I wouldn't say when you've seen one Western you've seen the lot; but when you've seen the lot you get the feeling you've seen one.

WHITMAN Walt 1819-1892
12492
I am as bad as the worst, but, thank God, I am as good as the best.

12493 *'Out of the cradle endlessly rocking'*
Out of the cradle endlessly rocking,
Out of the mockingbird's throat, the musical shuttle ...
A reminiscence sing.

12494
The dirtiest book of all is the expurgated book.

12495
Do I contradict myself?
Very well, then I contradict myself,
I am large, I contain multitudes.

12496
Out of every fruition of success, no matter what, comes forth something to make a new effort necessary.

12497
To have great poets there must be great audiences too.

12498
There is that indescribable freshness and unconsciousness about an illiterate person that humbles and mocks the power of the noblest expressive genius.

12499 *Leaves of Grass - preface*
The United States themselves are essentially the greatest poem.

12500 *'So Long!'*
Camerado, this is no book,
Who touches this touches a man.

12501
It is native personality, and that alone, that endows a man to stand before presidents or generals, or in any distinguished collection, with aplomb - and not culture, or any intellect whatever.

12502
I sing the body electric.

12503 *'Song of the Broad Axe'*
Where the populace rise at once against the never-ending audacity of elected persons.

12504 *'Song of Myself'*
I celebrate myself, and sing myself.

12505 *'Song of Myself'*
Urge and urge and urge,
Always the procreant urge of the world.

12506 *'Song of Myself'*
I also say it is good to fall, battles are lost in the same spirit in which they are won.

12507 *'Song of Myself'*
I believe a leaf of grass is no less than the journey-work of the stars.

12508 *'Song of Myself'*
I think I could turn and live with animals, they are so placid and self-contained.

12509 *'Song of Myself'*
Behold, I do not give lectures or a little charity,
When I give I give myself.

12510 *'Song of Myself'*
I sound my barbaric yawp over the roofs of the world.

WHITTIER John Greenleaf 1807-1892
12511 *'Barbara Frietchie'*
'Shoot, if you must, this old grey head,
But spare your country's flag,' she said.

12512 *'The Brewing of Soma'*
Dear Lord and Father of mankind,
Forgive our foolish ways!

12513 *'Maud Muller'*
For of all sad words of tongue or pen,
The saddest are these: 'It might have been!'

12514 *'Memories'*
The Indian Summer of the heart!

12515 *'Worship'*
O brother man! fold to thy heart thy brother.

WHITTINGTON Robert c.1480-1530
12516 *(of Sir Thomas More)*
A man for all seasons.

WHITTON Charlotte 1896-1975
12517
Whatever women do they must do twice as well as men to be thought half as good. Luckily, this is not difficult.

WHUR Cornelius
12518 *'The Female Friend'*
While lasting joys the man attend
Who has a faithful female friend.

WHYTE Lancelot Law
12519
Thought is born of failure.

WHYTE-MELVILLE George John 1821-1878
12520 *'The Good Grey Mare'*
But I freely admit that the best of my fun
I owe it to horse and hound.

WICKHAM Anna 1884-1947
12521 *'The Affinity'*
It is well within the order of things
That man should listen when his mate sings;
But the true male never yet walked
Who liked to listen when his mate talked.

WIENER Norbert 1894-1964
12522
The simple faith in progress is not a conviction belonging to strength, but one belonging to acquiescence and thence to weakness.

WIESEL Elie 1928-
12523
God of forgiveness, do not forgive those murderers of Jewish children here.

12524
The opposite of love is not hate, it's indifference.

12525
Not to transmit an experience is to betray it.

WIGGAN A.E.
12526
Intelligence appears to be the thing that enables a man to get along without education.
Education appears to be the thing that enables a man to get along without the use of his intelligence.

WIGGLESWORTH E.
12527
Man's happiness springs mainly from moderate troubles, which afford the mind a healthful stimulus, and are followed by a reaction which produces a cheerful flow of spirits.

WILBERFORCE Samuel 1805-1873
12528 *Impromptu verse (attributed)*
If I were a cassowary
On the plains of Timbuctoo,
I would eat a missionary,
Cassock, band, and hymn-book too.

12529 *(to T.H. Huxley)*
Was it through his grandfather or his grandmother that he claimed his descent from a monkey?

WILBUR Richard 1921-
12530 *'Advice to a Prophet'*
Spare us all word of the weapons, their force and range,
The long numbers that rocket the mind;
Our slow, unreckoning hearts will be left behind,
Unable to fear what is too strange.

12531 *'Epistemology'*
We milk the cow of the world, and as we do
We whisper in her ear, 'You are not true'.

12532 *'Mind'*
Mind in its purest play is like some bat
That beats about in caverns all alone,
Contriving by a kind of senseless wit
Not to conclude against a wall of stone.

WILCOX Ella Wheeler 1855-1919
12533
And from the discontent of man
The world's best progress springs.

12534 *'Solitude'*
Laugh and the world laughs with you;
Weep, and you weep alone;
For the sad old earth must borrow its mirth,
But has trouble enough of its own.

12535 *'The World's Need'*
So many gods, so many creeds,
So many paths that wind and wind,
While just the art of being kind
Is all the sad world needs.

WILDE Oscar 1854-1900
12536
Anybody can be good in the country. There are no temptations there.

12537
Arguments are to be avoided - they are always vulgar and often convincing.

12538 *The Ballad of Reading Gaol*
And the wild regrets, and the bloody sweats,
None knew so well as I:
For he who lives more lives than one,
More deaths than one must die.

12539 *The Ballad of Reading Gaol*
I never saw a man who looked
With such a wistful eye
Upon that little tent of blue
Which prisoners call the sky.

12540 *The Ballad of Reading Gaol*
Yet each man kills the thing he loves,
By each let this be heard,

Some do it with a bitter look,
Some with a flattering word.
The coward does it with a kiss,
The brave man with a sword!

12541 *The Ballad of Reading Gaol*
Something was dead in each of us,
And what was dead was Hope.

12542
To become the spectator of one's own life is to
escape the suffering of life.

12543 *(of Bernard Shaw)*
He hasn't an enemy in the world, and none of
his friends like him.

12544
Consistency is the last refuge of the
unimaginative.

12545
It is a dangerous thing to reform anyone.

12546
If England treats her criminals the way she has
treated me, she doesn't deserve to have any.

12547
English conversationalists have a miraculous
power of turning wine into water.

12548
Fashion is that by which the fantastic becomes
for a moment universal.

12549
My great mistake, the fault for which I can't
forgive myself, is that one day I ceased my
obstinate pursuit of my own individuality.

12550
I hope you have not been leading a double life,
pretending to be wicked and being really good
all the time. That would be hypocrisy.

12551 *An Ideal Husband*
Men can be analysed, women ... merely adored.

12552 *An Ideal Husband*
Questions are never indiscreet. Answers
sometimes are.

12553 *An Ideal Husband*
To love oneself is the beginning of a lifelong
romance.

12554 *The Importance of Being Earnest*
Really, if the lower orders don't set us a good
example, what on earth is the use of them?

12555 *The Importance of Being Earnest*
The truth is rarely pure, and never simple.

12556 *The Importance of Being Earnest*
To lose one parent, Mr Worthing, may be
regarded as a misfortune; to lose both looks like
carelessness.

12557 *The Importance of Being Earnest*
In married life three is company and two none.

12558 *The Importance of Being Earnest*
All women become like their mothers. That is
their tragedy. No man does. That's his.

12559 *The Importance of Being Earnest*
The good ended happily, and the bad
unhappily. That is what fiction means.

12560 *The Importance of Being Earnest*
None of us are perfect. I myself am peculiarly
susceptible to draughts.

12561 *The Importance of Being Earnest*
I never travel without my diary. One should
always have something sensational to read in
the train.

12562 *The Importance of Being Earnest*
This suspense is terrible. I hope it will last.

12563 *Impressions of America 'Leadville'*
Please do not shoot the pianist. He is doing his
best.

12564 *Intentions 'The Critic as Artist'*
Every great man nowadays has his disciples,
and it is always Judas who writes the biography.

12565 *Intentions 'The Critic as Artist'*
The one duty we owe to history is to rewrite it.

12566 *Intentions 'The Critic as Artist'*
A little sincerity is a dangerous thing, and a
great deal of it is absolutely fatal.

12567
I've put my genius into my life; I've only put my
talent into my works.

12568 *Lady Windermere's Fan*
I can resist everything except temptation.

12569 *Lady Windermere's Fan*
We are all in the gutter, but some of us are
looking at the stars.

12570 *Lady Windermere's Fan*
What is a cynic?
A man who knows the price of everything and
the value of nothing.

12571 *Lady Windermere's Fan*
Experience is the name every one gives to their
mistakes.

12572 *(to Mrs Leverson on his release from
prison)*
My dear, you're the only woman in the world
who'd have known the right hat to wear on an
occasion like this.

12573
As long as war is regarded as wicked, it will
always have its fascination. When it is looked
upon as vulgar, it will cease to be popular.

12574
There is luxury in self-reproach. When we blame ourselves we feel that no one else has the right to blame us.

12575
Men become old, but they never become good.

12576
Nothing is so dangerous as being too modern; one is apt to grow old-fashioned quite suddenly.

12577
I have nothing to declare except my genius.

12578
Nothing that is worth knowing can be taught.

12579
The only beautiful things are the things that do not concern us.

12580
The only thing to do with good advice is to pass it on. It is never any use to oneself.

12581
It is only shallow people who do not judge by appearances. The true mystery of the world is the visible, not the invisible.

12582
Only the shallow know themselves.

12583
The only way to get rid of a temptation is to yield to it. Resist it, and your soul grows sick with longing for the things it has forbidden to itself.

12584
She is a peacock in everything but beauty.

12585
Pessimist - one who, when he has the choice of two evils, chooses both.

12586 *The Picture of Dorian Gray*
There is no such thing as a moral or an immoral book. Books are well written, or badly written.

12587 *The Picture of Dorian Gray*
There is only one thing in the world worse than being talked about, and that is not being talked about.

12588 *The Picture of Dorian Gray*
A man cannot be too careful in the choice of his enemies.

12589 *The Picture of Dorian Gray*
A cigarette is the perfect type of a perfect pleasure. It is exquisite, and it leaves one unsatisfied. What more can one want?

12590
I played with an idea, and grew wilful; tossed it into the air and transformed it; let it escape and recaptured it; made it iridescent with fancy, and winged it with paradox.

12591
It is not the prisoners who need reformation, it is the prisons.

12592
The public is wonderfully tolerant. It forgives everything except genius.

12593
Punctuality is the thief of time.

12594 *Sebastian Melmoth*
A thing is not necessarily true because a man dies for it.

12595 *Sebastian Melmoth 'The Soul of Man ...'*
Democracy means simply the bludgeoning of the people by the people for the people.

12596
A sentimentalist is simply one who desires to have the luxury of an emotion without paying for it.

12597
Success is a science. If you have the conditions, you get the result.

12598
The tragedy of old age is not that one is old, but that one is young.

12599
A true gentleman is one who is never unintentionally rude.

12600
When critics disagree, the artist is in accord with himself.

12601 *(when told of huge fee for surgical operation)*
Ah, well, then, I suppose that I shall have to die beyond my means.

12602 *A Woman of No Importance*
The English country gentleman galloping after a fox - the unspeakable in full pursuit of the uneatable.

12603 *A Woman of No Importance*
One should never trust a woman who tells one her real age. A woman who would tell one that, would tell one anything.

12604 *A Woman of No Importance*
The Book of Life begins with a man and a woman in a garden.
It ends with Revelations.

12605 *A Woman of No Importance*
Children begin by loving their parents; after a time they judge them; rarely, if ever, do they forgive them.

12606 *A Woman of No Importance*
You should study the Peerage, Gerald ... It is the best thing in fiction the English have ever done.

12607 *A Woman of No Importance*
Twenty years of romance make a woman look like a ruin; but twenty years of marriage make her something like a public building.

12608
Work is the curse of the drinking classes.

WILDER Billy 1906-
12609
Hindsight is always twenty-twenty.

WILDER Thornton 1897-1975
12610
Literature is the orchestration of platitudes.

12611
If a man has no vices, he's in great danger of making vices about his virtues, and there's a spectacle.

12612 *The Merchant of Yonkers*
Marriage is a bribe to make a housekeeper think she's a householder.

12613 *The Merchant of Yonkers*
The fights are the best part of married life. The rest is merely so-so.

12614
Nurse one vice in your bosom. Give it the attention it deserves and let your virtues spring up modestly around it. Then you'll have the miser who's no liar; and the drunkard who's the benefactor of a whole city.

12615
A play visibly represents pure existing.

12616
Many plays, certainly mine, are like blank cheques. The actors and directors put their own signatures on them.

12617
Pride, avarice and envy are in every home.

12618
The unecumbered stage encourages the truth operative in everyone. The less seen, the more heard. The eye is the enemy of the ear in real drama.

12619
For what human ill does not dawn seem to be an alleviation?

WILENSKY Robert
12620
We've all heard that a million monkeys banging on a million typewriters will eventually reproduce the entire works of Shakespeare. Now, thanks to the Internet, we know this is not true.

WILHELM II ('Kaiser Bill') 1859-1941
12621
We have ... fought for our place in the sun and have won it.

WILL George
12622
World War II was the last government program that really worked.

WILLIAM The Silent 1533-1584
12623
One need not hope in order to undertake; nor succeed in order to persevere.

WILLIAM III (William of Orange) 1650-1702
12624
Every bullet has its billet.

12625
There is one way never to see it [my country] lost, and that is to die in the last ditch.

WILLIAMS Charles 1886-1945
12626
Hell is indefinite.

WILLIAMS Harry and JUDGE Jack 1874-1924 and 1878-1938
12627 *'It's a Long Way to Tipperary'*
Good-bye Piccadilly, Farewell Leicester Square;
It's a long, long way to Tipperary, but my heart's right there!

WILLIAMS Heathcote
12628
Reason is an emotion for the sexless.

WILLIAMS Isaac 1802-1865
12629 *'Be thou my Guardian and my Guide'*
Be thou my Guardian and my Guide,
And hear me when I call;
Let not my slippery footsteps slide,
And hold me lest I fall.

WILLIAMS Nigel
12630
This is the BBC - we are not making programmes for the glitterati or the literati of any kindy of arty.

WILLIAMS Tennessee 1911-1983
12631 *Camino Real*
We have to distrust each other. It's our only defence against betrayal.

12632 *Camino Real*
We're all of us guinea pigs in the laboratory of God. Humanity is just a work in progress.

12633
I can't stand a naked light bulb, any more than I can stand a rude remark or a vulgar action.

12634 *Cat on a Hot Tin Roof*
What is the victory of a cat on a hot tin roof? - I wish I knew ... Just staying on it, I guess, as long as she can.

12635 *Cat on a Hot Tin Roof*
Mendacity is a system that we live in. Liquor is one way out an' death's the other.

12636 *Cat on a Hot Tin Roof*
I'm not living with you. We occupy the same cage, that's all.

12637
I don't ask for your pity, but just your understanding - no, not even that - no. Just for your recognition of me in you, and the enemy, time, in us all.

12638 *The Glass Menagerie*
I didn't go to the moon, I went much further - for time is the longest distance between two places.

12639
A high station in life is earned by the gallantry with which appalling experiences are survived with grace.

12640 *Orpheus Descending*
We're all of us sentenced to solitary confinement inside our own skins, for life!

12641 *A Streetcar named Desire*
I have always depended on the kindness of strangers.

12642
A vacuum is a hell of a lot better than some of the stuff that nature replaces it with.

12643
Make voyages. Attempt them. There's nothing else.

WILLIAMS William Carlos 1883-1963
12644 *'To Ford Madox Ford in Heaven'*
Is it any better in heaven, my friend Ford,
Than you found it in Provence?

12645 *'Paterson'*
Minds like beds always made up,
(more stony than a shore)
unwilling or unable.

12646 *'Paterson'*
No woman is virtuous
who does not give herself to her lover
- forthwith.

WILLIAMSON Nicol
12647
Nothing means anything until you're doing it.

12648
If you can make a woman laugh you can do anything with her.

WILLKIE Wendell 1892-1944
12649 *An American Programme*
The constitution does not provide for first and second class citizens.

12650 *One World*
Freedom is an indivisible word. If we want to enjoy it, and fight for it, we must be prepared to extend it to everyone, whether they are rich or poor, whether they agree with us or not, no matter what their race or colour of their skin.

12651 *One World*
There exists in the world today a gigantic reservoir of good will toward us, the American people.

WILLS Garry
12652
Politicians make good company for a while just as children do - their self-enjoyment is contagious. But they soon exhaust their favourite subjects - themselves.

WILSON A.N. 1950-
12653
Twenty years ago the cleverest people did become dons, but not any more. The really clever people now want to be lawyers or journalists.

WILSON Earl
12654
Gossip is when you hear something you like about someone you don't.

WILSON Edmund 1895-1972
12655
I think with my right hand.

WILSON Ethel 1890-
12656
The business of writing is one of the four or five most private things in the world.

12657
Dullness is a misdemeanour.

WILSON Senator Gordon
12658 *(after meeting with IRA)*
They told me that history is on their side.

WILSON Sir Harold 1916-1995
12659
All these financiers, all the little gnomes in Zurich and the other financial centres about whom we keep on hearing.

12660
One man's wage rise is another man's price increase.

12661
The Monarchy is a labour-intensive industry.

12662
The office of president requires the constitution of an athlete, the patience of a mother, the endurance of an early Christian.

12663
This party is a moral crusade or it is nothing.

12664
In politics a week is a very long time.

12665
From now the pound abroad is worth 14 per cent or so less in terms of other currencies. It does not mean, of course, that the pound here in Britain, in your pocket or purse or in your bank, has been devalued.

WILSON Sandy 1924-
12666 *The Boyfriend*
We've got to have
We plot to have
For it's so dreary not to have
That certain thing called the Boy Friend.

12667 *The Boy Friend*
But it's nicer, much nicer in Nice.

12668
It's never too late to have a fling
For autumn is just as nice as spring
And it's never too late to fall in love.

WILSON Woodrow 1856-1924
12669
America is the only idealistic nation in the world.

12670
Armed neutrality is ineffectual enough at best.

12671
It is a fearful thing to lead this great peaceful people into war, into the most terrible and disastrous of all wars, civilization itself seeming to be in the balance. But the right is more precious than peace, and we shall fight for the things which we have always carried nearest our hearts - for democracy.

12672
A friend of mine says that every man who takes office in Washington either grows or swells, and when I give a man an office, I watch him carefully to see whether he is swelling or growing.

12673
You cannot be friends upon any other terms than upon the terms of equality.

12674
The history of liberty is a history of the limitation of governmental power, not the increase of it.

12675
I'm a vague, conjunctured personality, more made up of opinions and academic prepossessions than of human traits and red corpuscles.

12676 *(last words)*
I am a broken machine. I am ready to go.

12677
I used to be a lawyer, but now I am a reformed character.

12678
Once lead this people into war and they will forget there ever was such a thing as tolerance.

12679
There is such a thing as a man being too proud to fight; there is such a thing as a nation being so right that it does not need to convince others by force that it is right.

12680
No man ever saw a government. I live in the midst of the Government of the United States, but I never saw the Government of the United States.

12681
The man who is swimming against the stream knows the strength of it.

12682
A man's rootage is more important than his leafage.

12683
The men who act stand nearer to the mass of man than the men who write; and it is in their hands that new thought gets its translation into the crude language of deeds.

12684
No nation is fit to sit in judgement upon any other nation.

12685
Nothing was ever done so systematically as nothing is being done now.

12686
I not only use all the brains I have, but all I can borrow.

12687
It must be a peace without victory ... Only a peace between equals can last.

12688
We have stood apart, studiously neutral.

12689
If you think about what you ought to do for other people, your character will take care of itself.

12690
When you come into the presence of a leader of men, you know that you have come into the presence of fire - that it is best not uncautiously to touch that man - that there is something that makes it dangerous to cross him.

12691
The world must be made safe for democracy. Its peace must be planted upon the tested foundations of political liberty.

WINCHELL Walter 1897-1972
12692
Gossip is the art of saying nothing in a way that leaves practically nothing unsaid.

WINCHILSEA Lady Anne Finch 1661-1720
12693 *'Enquiry after Peace'*
Thirst of wealth no quiet knows,
But near the deathbed fiercer grows.

12694 *'Enquiry after Peace'*
Love (if such a thing there be)
Is all despair, or ecstasy.
Poetry's the feverish fit,
Th' o'erflowing of unbounded wit.

12695 *'The Spleen'*
We faint beneath the aromatic pain.

WINDHAM William 1750-1810
12696
Those entrusted with arms ... should be persons of some substance and stake in the country.

WINTHROP Robert Charles 1809-1894
12697
A Star for every State, and a State for every Star.

WISE Dennis
12698
We've signed five foreigners over the summer but I'll be on hand to learn them a bit of English.

WITHER George 1588-1667
12699 *A Collection of Emblems*
And when I mind with how much greediness
We seek the present gain in everything,
Not caring (so our lust we may possess)
What damage to posterity we bring ...

12700 *A Description of Love 'I Loved a lass ...'*
I loved a lass, a fair one,
As fair as e'er was seen;
She was indeed a rare one,
Another Sheba queen.

12701 *Sonnet*
Shall I, wasting in despair,
Die because a woman's fair?

12702 *Sonnet*
For, if she be not for me,
What care I how fair she be.

WITTGENSTEIN Ludwig 1889-1951
12703
The limits of my language mean the limits of my world.

12704
The philosopher's treatment of a question is like the treatment of an illness.

12705
Philosophy is a battle against the bewitchment of our intelligence by means of language.

12706
What is your aim in philosophy? - To show the fly the way out of the fly-bottle.

12707
The world of the happy is quite different from that of the unhappy.

WODEHOUSE P.G. 1881-1975
12708 *The Adventures of Sally*
When you marry, Sally, grab a chump. Tap his forehead first, and if it rings solid, don't hesitate. All the unhappy marriages come from the husbands having brains.

12709
The butler entered the room, a solemn procession of one.

12710 *The Code of the Woosters*
He spoke with a certain what-is-it in his voice, and I could see that, if not actually disgruntled, he was far from being gruntled.

12711 *The Code of the Woosters*
Slice him where you like, a hellhound is always a hellhound.

12712 *The Inimitable Jeeves*
It was my Uncle George who discovered that alcohol was a food well in advance of medical thought.

12713 *My Man Jeeves 'Rallying Round Old George'*
What a queer thing Life is! So unlike anything else, don't you know, if you see what I mean.

12714 *The Man Upstairs*
It is a good rule in life never to apologize. The right sort of people do not want apologies, and the wrong sort take a mean advantage of them.

12715
Why don't you get a haircut; you look like a chrysanthemum.

WOLF Marcus
12716 *(at his trial)*
Your honour is not my honour.

WOLFE Charles 1791-1823
12717 *'The Burial of Sir John Moore at Corunna'*
Not a drum was heard, not a funeral note,

As his corse to the rampart we hurried.

12718 *'The Burial of Sir John Moore at Corunna'*
We buried him darkly at dead of night,
The sods with our bayonets turning.

12719 *'The Burial of Sir John Moore at Corunna'*
We carved not a line, and we raised not a stone
But we left him alone with his glory.

WOLFE Humbert 1886-1940
12720 *'Over the Fire'*
You cannot hope
to bribe or twist,
thank God! the
British journalist.
But, seeing what
the man will do
unbribed, there's
no occasion to.

WOLFE Thomas 1900-1938
12721
This is the artist, then - life's hungry man, the
glutton of eternity, beauty's miser, glory's slave.

12722
That enfabled rock, that ship of life, that
swarming, million-footed, tower-masted, sky-
soaring citadel that bears the magic name of the
Island of Manhattan.

12723
Loneliness is and always has been the central
and inevitable experience of every man.

12724 *Look Homeward, Angel*
Most of the time we think we're sick, it's all in
the mind.

12725
The reason a writer writes a book is to forget a
book and the reason a reader reads one is to
remember it.

WOLFE Tom 1931-
12726
The bonfire of the vanities.

12727 *Mauve Gloves and Madmen 'The Me
Decade'*
We are now in the Me Decade - seeing the
upward roll of ... the third great religious wave
in American history ... and this one has the
mightiest, holiest roll of all, the beat that goes ...
Me ... Me ... Me ... Me.

12728
Radical Chic ... is only radical in Style; in its
heart it is part of Society and its tradition -
Politics, like Rock, Pop, and Camp, has its uses.

WOLFENDEN John
12729
Schoolmasters and parents exist to be grown
out of.

WOLLSTONECRAFT Mary 1759-1797
12730 *A Vindication of the Rights of Woman*
A king is always a king - and a woman always a
woman: his authority and her sex ever stand
between them and rational converse.

12731 *A Vindication of the Rights of Woman*
I do not wish them [women] to have power over
men; but over themselves.

12732 *A Vindication of the Rights of Woman*
Taught from infancy that beauty is woman's
sceptre, the mind shapes itself to the body, and
roaming round its gilt cage, only seeks to adorn
its prison.

12733 *A Vindication of the Rights of Woman*
A slavish bondage to parents cramps every
faculty of the mind.

WOLSEY Thomas c.1475-1530
12734
Father Abbot, I am come to lay my bones
amongst you.

12735
Had I but served God as diligently as I have
served the King, he would not have given me
over in my grey hairs.

WOMBAT R.T.
12736
The lazy man gets round the sun as quickly as
the busy one.

WOOD James Mason
12737
Education today, more than ever before, must
see clearly the dual objectives: education for
living and educating for making a living.

WOOD Mrs Henry 1814-1887
12738 *East Lynne*
Dead! and ... never called me mother.

WOODCOCK George 1904-1979
12739
It is not in life but in art that self-fulfillment is
to be found.

12740
Pioneers did not produce original works of art,
because they were creating original human
environments; they did not imagine utopias
because they were shaping them.

WOODFORD Jack
12741
Few human beings are proof against the
implied flattery of rapt attention.

WOODRUFF Julia Louise Matilda 1833-1909
12742
Out of the strain of the Doing
Into the peace of the Done.

WOODS Harry
12743 *'Side by Side'*
Oh we ain't got a barrel of money,
Maybe we're ragged and funny,
But we'll travel along
Singin' a song,
Side by side.

WOOLF Virginia 1882-1941
12744
A biography is considered complete if it merely
accounts for six or seven selves, whereas a
person may well have as many as a thousand.

12745 *The Common Reader 'Lady Dorothy
Nevill'*
In one of those comfortably padded lunatic
asylums which are known, euphemistically, as
the stately homes of England.

12746 *The Common Reader 'The Modern Essay'*
We are nauseated by the sight of trivial
personalities decomposing in the eternity of
print.

12747 *The Common Reader 'Modern Fiction'*
Examine for a moment an ordinary mind on an
ordinary day.

12748 *The Common Reader 'Modern Fiction'*
Life is not a series of gig lamps symmetrically
arranged; life is a luminous halo, a semi-
transparent envelope surrounding us from the
beginning of consciousness to the end.

12749 *(of E.M. Forster)*
He is limp and damp and milder than the
breath of a cow.

12750
The first duty of a lecturer - to hand you after an
hour's discourse a nugget of pure truth to wrap
up between the pages of your notebooks and
keep on the mantelpiece for ever.

12751 *Jacob's Room*
Each had his past shut in him like the leaves of
a book known to him by heart; and his friends
could only read the title.

12752 *To the Lighthouse*
So that is marriage, Lily thought, a man and a
woman looking at a girl throwing a ball.

12753
Money dignifies what is frivolous if unpaid for.

12754
As for my next book, I am going to hold myself
from writing it till I have it impending in me:
grown heavy in my mind like a ripe pear,
pendant, gravid, asking to be cut or it will fall.

12755
Have you any notion how many books are
written about women in the course of one year?

Have you any notion how many are written by
men? Are you aware that you are, perhaps, the
most discussed animal in the universe?

12756 *A Room of One's Own*
A woman must have money and a room of her
own if she is to write fiction.

12757 *A Room of One's Own*
Women have served all these centuries as
looking-glasses possessing the magic and
delicious power of reflecting the figure of a man
at twice its natural size.

12758 *A Room of One's Own*
Literature is strewn with the wreckage of men
who have minded beyond reason the opinions
of others.

12759 *A Room of One's Own*
Why are women ... so much more interesting to
men than men are to women?

12760
One of the signs of passing youth is the birth of
a sense of fellowship with other human beings
as we take our place among them.

WOOLLCOTT Alexander 1887-1943
12761
All the things I really like to do are either
immoral, illegal or fattening.

12762
A broker is a man who takes your fortune and
runs it into a shoestring.

12763
The English have an extraordinary ability for
flying into a great calm.

12764
I must get out of these wet clothes and into a
dry Martini.

WOOTON Sir Henry 1568-1639
12765
An ambassador is an honest man sent to lie
abroad for the good of his country.

12766 *'The Character of a Happy Life'*
Lord of himself, though not of lands,
And having nothing, yet hath all.

12767
Critics are like brushers of noblemen's clothes.

12768 *'Upon the Death of Sir Albertus Moreton's
Wife'*
He first deceased; she for a little tried
To live without him: liked it not, and died.

12769 *'On His Mistress, the Queen of Bohemia'*
You meaner beauties of the night,
That poorly satisfy our eyes,
More by your number, than your light;
You common people of the skies,

What are you when the moon shall rise?

12770 *'Poem written in his youth'*
Untrue she was; yet I believed her eyes,
Instructed spies,
Till I was taught, that love was but a school
To breed a fool.

12771 *'Upon the sudden restraint of Earl of Somerset'*
No man marks the narrow space
'Twixt a prison and a smile.

WORDSWORTH Dorothy 1771-1855
12772 *Journals 'Alfoxden Journal'*
One only leaf upon the top of a tree - the sole remaining leaf - danced round and round like a rag blown by the wind.

WORDSWORTH Dame Elizabeth 1840-1932
12773 *'Good and Clever'*
If all the good people were clever,
And all clever people were good,
The world would be nicer than ever
We thought that it possibly could.

12774 *'The Affliction of Margaret -'*
My apprehensions come in crowds;
I dread the rustling of the grass:
The very shadows of the clouds
Have power to shake me as they pass.

WORDSWORTH William 1770-1850
12775 *'The Borderers'*
Action is transitory - a step, a blow,
The motion of a muscle - this way or that -
'Tis done, and in the after vacancy
We wonder at ourselves like men betrayed:
Suffering is permanent, obscure and dark,
And shares the nature of infinity.

12776 *'To a Butterfly, I've Watched you now'*
Sweet childish days, that were as long
As twenty days are now.

12777 *'Composed upon Westminster Bridge'*
Earth has not anything to show more fair:
Dull would he be of soul who could pass by
A sight so touching in its majesty.

12778 *'Composed upon Westminster Bridge'*
Dear God! the very houses seem asleep;
And all that mighty heart is lying still!

12779 *'To the Cuckoo'*
Thrice welcome, darling of the spring!
Even yet thou art to me
No bird, but an invisible thing,
A voice, a mystery.

12780 *'To the Daisy'*
Oft on the dappled turf at ease
I sit, and play with similies,
Loose types of things through all degrees.

12781 *'She dwelt among the untrodden ways'*
She dwelt among the untrodden ways
Beside the springs of Dove,
A maid whom there were none to praise
And very few to love.

12782 *'She dwelt among the untrodden ways'*
But she is in her grave, and, ho,
The difference to me!

12783 *'Elegiac Stanzas'(on picture of Peele Castle)*
The light that never was, on sea or land,
The consecration, and the Poet's dream.

12784 *'The Excursion'*
Oh! many are the Poets that are sown
By Nature; men endowed with highest gifts,
The vision and the faculty divine;
Yet wanting the accomplishment of verse.

12785 *'The Excursion'*
The good die first,
And they whose hearts are dry as summer dust
Burn to the socket.

12786 *'The Excursion'*
Society became my glittering bride,
And airy hopes my children.

12787 *'The Excursion'*
Strongest minds
Are often those of whom the noisy world
Hears least.

12788 *'The Fountain'*
The wiser mind
Mourns less for what age takes away
Than what it leaves behind.

12789 *'The French Revolution, as it Appeared ...'*
Bliss was it in that dawn to be alive,
But to be young was very heaven!

12790 *'My heart leaps up when I behold'*
My heart leaps up when I behold
A rainbow in the sky.

12791 *'My heart leaps up when I behold'*
The Child is father of the Man.

12792 *'Laodamia'*
The gods approve
The depth, and not the tumult, of the soul.

12793 *Letter to Lady Beaumont*
Every great and original writer, in proportion as he is great and original, must himself create the taste by which he is to be relished.

12794 *'Lines composed ... above Tintern Abbey'*
That best portion of a good man's life,
His little, nameless, unremembered, acts
Of kindness and of love.

12795 *'Lines composed ... above Tintern Abbey'*
That blessed mood
In which the burthen of the mystery,
In which the heavy and the weary weight
Of all this unintelligible world,
Is lightened.

12796 *'Lines composed ... above Tintern Abbey'*
I have learned
To look on nature, not as in the hour
Of thoughtless youth; but hearing oftentimes
The still, sad music of humanity.

12797 *'Lines composed ... above Tintern Abbey'*
And I have felt
A presence that disturbs me with the joy
Of elevated thoughts; a sense sublime
Of something far more deeply interfused,
Whose dwelling is the light of setting suns,
And the round ocean and the living air,
And the blue sky, and in the mind of man;
A motion and a spirit, that impels
All thinking things, all objects of all thoughts,
And rolls through all things.

12798 *'Lines composed ... above Tintern Abbey'*
All the mighty world
Of eye and ear, both what they half-create,
And what perceive.

12799 *'Lines composed ... above Tintern Abbey'*
Nature never did betray
The heart that loved her.

12800 *'Lines Written in Early Spring'*
And much it grieved my heart to think
What man has made of man.

12801 *Lyrical Ballads - Preface*
Poetry is the breath and finer spirit of all
knowledge; it is the impassioned expression
which is in the countenance of all science.

12802 *Lyrical Ballads - Preface*
Poetry is the spontaneous overflow of powerful
feelings: it takes its origin from emotion
recollected in tranquillity.

12803
A man he seems of cheerful yesterdays
And confident tomorrows.

12804 *'Milton! thou shouldst be living ...'*
Milton! thou shouldst be living at this hour:
England hath need of thee.

12805 *National Independence and Liberty
'November 1806'*
Another year! - another deadly blow!
Another mighty empire overthrown!
And we are left, or shall be left, alone.

12806 *'Ode. Intimations of Immortality'*
The rainbow comes and goes,
And lovely is the rose,

The moon doth with delight
Look round her when the heavens are bare;
Waters on a starry night
Are beautiful and fair;
The sunshine is a glorious birth;
But yet I know, where'er I go,
That there hath passed away a glory from the
earth.

12807 *'Ode. Intimations of Immortality'*
A timely utterance gave that thought relief,
And I again am strong.

12808 *'Ode. Intimations of Immortality'*
The winds come to me from the fields of sleep.

12809 *'Ode. Intimations of Immortality'*
Whither is fled the visionary gleam?
Where is it now, the glory and the dream?

12810 *'Ode. Intimations of Immortality'*
Our birth is but a sleep and a forgetting.

12811 *'Ode. Intimations of Immortality'*
And not in utter nakedness,
But trailing clouds of glory do we come
From God, who is our home.

12812 *'Ode. Intimations of Immortality'*
As if his whole vocation
Were endless imitation.

12813 *'Ode. Intimations of Immortality'*
Though nothing can bring back the hour
Of splendour in the grass, of glory in the flower;
We will grieve not, rather find
Strength in what remains behind ...
In the faith that looks through death,
In years that bring the philosophic mind.

12814 *'Ode. Intimations of Immortality'*
To me the meanest flower that blows can give
Thoughts that do often lie too deep for tears.

12815 *Peter Bell*
Some sipping punch, some sipping tea,
But as you by their faces see
All silent, and all damned?

12816 *Peter Bell - prologue*
There's something in a flying horse,
There's something in a huge balloon;
But through the clouds I'll never float
Until I have a little Boat,
Shaped like the crescent-moon.

12817 *'She Was a Phantom of Delight'*
She was a phantom of delight
When first she gleamed upon my sight;
A lovely apparition, sent
To be a moment's ornament.

12818 *'She Was a Phantom of Delight'*
And now I see with eye serene
The very pulse of the machine;
A being breathing thoughtful breath,

A traveller between life and death.

12819 *'She Was a Phantom of Delight'*
A perfect woman, nobly planned,
To warn, to comfort, and command.

12820 *'A Poet's Epitaph'*
One that would peep and botanize
Upon his mother's grave?

12821 *'A Poet's Epitaph'*
A reasoning, self-sufficing thing,
An intellectual All-in-all!

12822 *'A Poet's Epitaph'*
The harvest of a quiet eye
That broods and sleeps on his own heart.

12823 *The Prelude*
Made one long bathing of a summer's day.

12824 *The Prelude*
Dust as we are, the immortal spirit grows
Like harmony in music; there is a dark
Inscrutable workmanship that reconciles
Discordant elements, makes them cling
together
In one society.

12825 *The Prelude*
And I was taught to feel, perhaps too much,
The self-sufficing power of Solitude.

12826 *The Prelude*
Science appears but what in truth she is,
Not as our glory and our absolute boast,
But as a succedaneum, and a prop
To our infirmity.

12827 *The Prelude*
We were brothers all
In honour, as in one community,
Scholars and gentlemen.

12828 *The Prelude*
Through the turnings intricate of verse,
Present themselves as objects recognised,
In flashes, and with glory not their own.

12829 *'Resolution and Independence'*
We poets in our youth begin in gladness;
But thereof comes in the end despondency and
madness.

12830 *'The River Duddon'- 'After-Thought'*
Still glides the Stream, and shall for ever glide;
The Form remains, the Function never dies.

12831 *'The River Duddon'- 'After-Thought'*
Enough, if something from our hands have
power
To live, and act, and serve the future hour.

12832 *'Rob Roy's Grave'*
The good old rule
Sufficeth them, the simple plan,
That they should take who have the power,

And they should keep who can.

12833 *'Scorn not the Sonnet'*
Scorn not the Sonnet; Critic, you have frowned,
Mindless of its just honours; with this key
Shakespeare unlocked his heart.

12834 *'To Sleep'*
A flock of sheep that leisurely pass by,
One after one; the sound of rain, and bees
Murmuring: the fall of rivers, winds and seas,
Smooth fields, white sheets of water, and pure
sky;
I have thought of all by turns, and yet do lie
Sleepless!

12835 *'To Sleep'*
Blessed barrier between day and day.

12836 *'To Sleep'*
Suprised by joy - impatient as the wind
I turned to share the transport.

12837 *'To Sleep'*
The holy time is quiet as a nun
Breathless with adoration.

12838 *'To Sleep'*
The world is too much with us; late and soon,
Getting and spending, we lay waste our powers.

12839 *'A slumber did my spirit seal'*
A slumber did my spirit seal;
I had no human fears:
She seemed a thing that could not feel
The touch of earthly years.

No motion has she now, no force;
She neither hears nor sees;
Rolled round in earth's diurnal course,
With rocks, and stones, and trees.

12840 *'The Tables Turned'*
One impulse from a vernal wood
May teach you more of man,
Of moral evil and of good,
Than all the sages can.

12841 *'The Tables Turned'*
Our meddling intellect
Mis-shapes the beauteous forms of things:-
We murder to dissect.

12842 *'Tis Said that some have Died'*
'Tis said that some have died for love.

12843 *'I travelled among unknown men'*
I travelled among unknown men,
In lands beyond the sea;
Nor England! did I know till then
What love I bore to thee.

12844 *'I wandered lonely as a cloud'*
I wandered lonely as a cloud
That floats on high o'er vales and hills,
When all at once I saw a crowd,

A host, of golden daffodils.

12845 *'I wandered lonely as a cloud'*
And then my heart with pleasure fills,
And dances with the daffodils.

12846 *'Written in March'*
Like an army defeated
The snow hath retreated.

WORK H.C. 1832-1884
12847 *'Grandfather's Clock'*
But it stopped short - never to go again -
When the old man died.

12848 *'Come Home, Father'*
Father, dear father, come home with me now,
The clock in the steeple strikes one.

12849 *'Wake Nicodemus'*
There's a good time coming, it's almost here,
'Twas a long, long time on the way.

WRIGHT Frank Lloyd 1867-1959
12850 *Autobiography*
The necessities were going by default to save
the luxuries until I hardly knew which were
necessities and which luxuries.

12851
A doctor can bury his mistakes, but an architect
can only advise his clients to plant vines.

12852
Early in life I had to choose between arrogance
and hypocritical humility. I chose honest
arrogance and have seen no occasion to
change.

12853
I hate intellectuals. They are from the top
down. I am from the bottom up.

12854
No house should ever be on a hill, or on
anything. It should be of the hill. Hill and
house should live together, each the happier for
the other.

12855
An idea is salvation by imagination.

12856
Pictures deface walls oftener than they decorate
them.

12857
Television is chewing gum for the eyes.

WRIGHT Ronald 1908-
12858
Societies that do not eat people are fascinated
by those that do.

WRIGHT Steven
12859
The older you get, the more you learn to see

what you've been taught to see. When you're a
kid, you see what's there.

WRIGLEY Jr. William 1861-1932
12860
When two men in business always agree, one of
them is unnecessary.

WROTH Lady Mary c.1586-c.1652
12861 *'Love, a child, is ever crying'*
Love, a child, is ever crying:
Please him and he straight is flying.
Give him, he the more is craving,
Never satisfied with having.

WUNDERLICH Paul
12862
I refuse to explain everything, because if you
know too much about yourself, you become
impotent. Better not to know what it is that
makes you tick.

WYATT Sir Thomas c.1503-1542
12863 *'Farewell, Love'*
Farewell, Love, and all thy laws forever.
Thy baited hooks shall tangle me no more.

12864 *'They flee from me'*
They flee from me, that sometime did me seek
With naked foot, stalking in my chamber.

WYBROW Bob
12865
We have three sexes: men, women who are
housewives, and other women.

WYCHERLEY William c.1640-1716
12866 *The Country Wife*
A mistress should be like a little country retreat
near the town, not to dwell in constantly, but
only for a night and away.

12867 *The Country Wife*
Go to your business, I say, pleasure, whilst I go
to my pleasure, business.

12868 *The Country Wife*
Women and fortune are truest still to those that
trust 'em.

WYKEHAM William of 1324-1404
12869 *(motto)*
Manners maketh man.

WYLIE Philip 1902-
12870
If liberty has any meaning it means freedom to
improve.

WYLIE William T.
12871
Your can't automate in the arts. Since the
sixteenth century there has been no change in
the number of people necessary to produce
Hamlet.

X Malcolm 1925-1965
12872
Power never takes a back step - only in the face of more power.

YATES Douglas
12873
No scientific theory achieves public acceptance until it has been thoroughly discredited.

YATES John 1925-
12874
There is a lot to be said in the Decade of Evangelism for believing more and more in less and less.

YBARRA Thomas Russell 1880-
12875 *'The Christian'*
A Christian is a man who feels
Repentance on a Sunday
For what he did on Saturday
And is going to do on Monday.

YEAMES W.F. 1835-1918
12876 *(title of painting)*
And when did you last see your father?

YEATS William Butler 1865-1939
12877
All empty souls tend to extreme opinion.

12878 *'All Things can Tempt Me'*
When I was young,
I had not given a penny for a song
Did not the poet sing it with such airs,
That one believed he had a sword upstairs.

12879 *'Among School Children'*
O body swayed to music, O brightening glance,
How can we know the dancer from the dance?

12880 *'Byzantium'*
A starlit or a moonlit dome distains
All that man is;
All mere complexities,
The fury and the mire of human veins.

12881 *'The Circus Animals' Desertion'*
Now that my ladder's gone
I must lie down where all ladders start
In the foul rag and bone shop of the heart.

12882 *'A Coat'*
For there's more enterprise
In walking naked.

12883 *'The Coming of Wisdom with Time'*
Though leaves are many, the root is one;
Through all the lying days of my youth
I swayed my leaves and flowers in the sun;
Now I may wither into the truth.

12884
Of our conflicts with others we make rhetoric;
of our conflicts with ourselves we make poetry.

12885 *'The Countess Cathleen'*
The years like great black oxen tread the world,
And God the herdsman goads them on behind,
And I am broken by their passing feet.

12886 *A Drinking Song*
Wine comes in at the mouth
And love comes in at the eye;
That's all we shall know for truth
Before we grow old and die.

12887 *'Easter, 1916'*
I have met them at close of day
Coming with vivid faces
From counter or desk among grey
Eighteenth-century houses.
I have passed with a nod of the head
Or polite meaningless words.

12888 *'Easter, 1916'*
Changed, changed utterly:
A terrible beauty is born.

12889
Education is not the filling of a pail, but the lighting of a fire.

12890 *'Ego Dominus Tuus'*
The rhetorician would deceive his neighbours,
The sentimentalist himself; while art
Is but a vision of reality.

12891 *'An Irish Airman Foresees his Death'*
Nor law, nor duty bade me fight,
Nor public men, nor cheering crowds,
A lonely impulse of delight
Drove to this tumult in the clouds.

12892 *Letters on Poetry ... to Dorothy Wellesley*
Think like a wise man but express yourself like the common people.

12893
Life is a long preparation for something that never happens.

12894 *'In Memory of Eva Gore Booth and Con Markiewicz'*
The innocent and the beautiful
Have no enemy but time.

12895 *'The Municipal Gallery Re-visited'*
Think where man's glory most begins and ends
And say my glory was I had such friends.

12896 *'From Oedipus at Colonus'*
The second best's a gay good-night and quickly turn away.

12897
Only that which does not teach, which does not cry out, which does not condescend, which does not explain, is irresistible.

12898 *'The Pity of Love'*
A pity beyond all telling,
Is hid in the heart of love.

12899 *'Politics'*
How can I, that girl standing there,
My attention fix
On Roman or on Russian
Or on Spanish politics?

12900 *'Remorse for Intemperate Speech'*
I carry from my mother's womb
A fanatic heart.

12901 *'Down by the Salley Gardens'*
Down by the salley gardens my love and I did
meet;
She passed the salley gardens with little snow-
white feet.
She bid me take love easy, as the leaves grow on
the tree;
But I, being young and foolish, with her would
not agree.

12902 *'The Second Coming'*
The best lack all conviction, while the worst
Are full of passionate intensity.

12903 *'The Second Coming'*
And what rough beast, its hour come round at
last,
Slouches towards Bethlehem to be born?

12904 *'No Second Troy'*
Why, what could she have done being what she
is?
Was there another Troy for her to burn?

12905
Be secret and exult,
Because of all things known
That is most difficult.

12906 *'The Secret Rose'*
Far-off, most secret and inviolate Rose,
Enfold me in my hour of hours.

12907 *'September, 1913'*
Romantic Ireland's dead and gone,
It's with O'Leary in the grave.

12908 *'Song of Wandering Aengus'*
And pluck till time and times are done,
The silver apples of the moon,
The golden apples of the sun.

12909 *'The Spur'*
You think it horrible that lust and rage
Should dance attendance upon my old age;
They were not such a plague when I was young.

12910
A statesman is an easy man,
He tells his lies by rote;
A journalist makes up his lies
And takes you by the throat;

So stay at home and drink your beer
And let the neighbours vote.

12911
Style, personality - deliberately adopted and
therefore a mask - is the only escape from the
hot-faced bargainers and money-changers.

12912 *'On being asked for a War Poem'*
I think it better that at times like these
We poets keep our mouths shut.

12913 *'When You Are Old'*
When you are old and grey and full of sleep,
And nodding by the fire, take down this book
And slowly read and dream of the soft look
Your eyes had once, and of their shadows deep.

12914 *'He Wishes for the Cloths of Heaven'*
I have spread my dreams under your feet;
Tread softly because you tread on my dreams.

YEATS-BROWN Francis 1888-1944
12915
To me the charm of an encyclopedia is that it
knows - and I needn't.

YELTSIN Boris 1931-
12916
Europe is in danger of plunging into a cold
peace.

12917
It is Russia's mission to be first among equals.

12918
Today is the last day of an era past.

YESENIN Sergei 1895-1925
12919 *(before committing suicide)*
In this life there's nothing new in dying,
But nor, of course, is living any newer.

12920 *'Pleasure's for the Bad'*
It's always the good feel rotten.
Pleasure's for those who are bad.

12921 *'I Have One Remaining Pastime'*
I indulged in obscenities and scandals
In order to burn more bright.

YEVTUSHENKO Yevgeny 1933-
12922 *'No People are Uninteresting'*
No people are uninteresting.
Their fate is like the chronicle of planets.
Nothing in them is not particular,
and planet is dissimilar from planet.

12923
A show of envy is an insult to oneself.

12924
Time has a way of demonstrating ... the most
subborn are the most intelligent.

YOGANANDA Paramahansa

12925
Learn to see God in all persons, of whatever race or creed. You will know what divine love is when you begin to feel your oneness with every human being, not before. In mutual service we forget the little self and glimpse the one measureless self, the spirit that unifies all men.

12926
There is a magnet in your heart that will attract true friends. That magnet is unselfishness, thinking of others first ... when you learn to live for others, they will live for you.

YOST Charles 1907-1981

12927
A leader may symbolize and express what is best in his people, like Pericles, or what is worst, like Hitler, but he cannot successfully express what is only in his heart and not in theirs.

12928
Romanticism is the expression of man's urge to rise above reason and common sense, just as rationalism is the expression of his urge to rise above theology and emotion.

YOUNG Arthur

12929
There is a great difference between a good physician and a bad one; yet very little between a good one and none at all.

YOUNG Edward 1683-1765

12930 *The Love of Fame*
Some for renown on scraps of learning dote,
And think they grow immortal as they quote.

12931 *The Love of Fame*
None think the great unhappy, but the great.

12932 *The Love of Fame*
Be wise with speed;
A fool at forty is a fool indeed.

12933 *The Love of Fame*
With skill she vibrates her eternal tongue,
For ever most divinely in the wrong.

12934 *The Love of Fame*
One to destroy, is murder by the law;
And gibbets keep the lifted hand in awe;
To murder thousands, takes a specious name,
'War's glorious art', and gives immortal fame.

12935 *The Love of Fame*
How commentators each dark passage shun,
And hold their farthing candle to the sun.

12936 *Night Thoughts 'Night 1'*
Tired Nature's sweet restorer, balmy sleep!

12937 *Night Thoughts 'Night 1'*
Be wise to-day; 'tis madness to defer.

12938 *Night Thoughts 'Night 1'*
Procrastination is the thief of time.

12939 *Night Thoughts 'Night 1'*
At thirty a man suspects himself a fool;
Knows it at forty, and reforms his plan;
At fifty chides his infamous delay,
Pushes his prudent purpose to resolve;
In all the magnanimity of thought
Resolves; and re-resolves; then dies the same.

12940 *Night Thoughts 'Night 1'*
All men think all men mortal, but themselves.

12941 *Night Thoughts 'Night 4'*
Man wants but little, nor that little long.

12942 *Night Thoughts 'Night 5'*
By night an atheist half believes in God.

12943 *The Revenge*
Life is the desert, life the solitude;
Death joins us to the great majority.

12944
Tomorrow is a satire on today,
And shows its weakness.

YOUNG G.W. 1846-1919

12945 *'The Lips That Touch Liquor'*
Though in silence, with blighted affection, I pine,
Yet the lips that touch liquor must never touch mine!

YOUNG Jock

12946
The person by far the most likely to kill you is yourself.

YOUNG Michael 1915-

12947 *The Rise of the Meritocracy*
Today we frankly recognize that democracy can be no more than aspiration, and have rule not so much by the people as by the cleverest people; not an aristocracy of birth, not a plutocracy of wealth, but a true meritocracy of talent.

YOUNG Owen D. 1874-1962

12948
I really believe that more harm is done by old men who cling to their influence than by young men who anticipate it.

YOURCENAR Marguerite 1903-1987

12949
He had come to that time in his life (it varies from every man) when a human being gives himself over to his demon or to his genius, according to a mysterious law which orders him either to destroy or to surpass himself.

YUTANG Lin 1895-1976

12950
All women's dresses are merely variations on the

eternal struggle between the admitted desire to dress and the unadmitted desire to undress.

12951
A solemn funeral is inconceivable to the Chinese mind.

12952
Sometimes it is more important to discover what one cannot do, than what one can do.

ZAMYATIN Yevgeny 1884-1937
12953 *Essays 'I am Afraid'*
There can by no bronze literature, there can only be a newspaper literature, which is read today, and used for wrapping soap tomorrow.

12954 *'Literature, Revolution and Entropy'*
Heretics are the only bitter remedy against the entropy of human thought.

ZANGWILL Israel 1864-1926
12955 *Children of the Ghetto*
Scratch the Christian and you find the pagan - spoiled.

12956
In how many lives does Love really play a dominant part? The average taxpayer is no more capable of a 'grand passion' than of a grand opera.

12957 *The Melting Pot*
America is God's Crucible, the great Melting-Pot where all the races of Europe are melting and re-forming!

ZAPATA Emiliano 1879-1919
12958 *(of the maderistas)*
Many of them, so as to curry favour with tyrants, for a fistful of coins, or through bribery or corruption, are shedding the blood of their brothers.

ZAPPA Frank 1940-
12959
Rock journalism is people who can't write interviewing people who can't talk for people who can't read.

ZILBOORG Gregory
12960
There is more than a mere suspicion that the scientist who comes to ask metaphysical questions and turns away from metaphysical answers may be afraid of those answers.

ZINGERS 'Smile'
12961
The first sign of maturity is the discovery that the volume knob also turns to the left.

The ZOHAR
12962
It is the way of a dog that if he is hit by a stone, he bites a fellow dog.

ZOLA Émile 1840-1902
12963 La Bête humaine
Don't go on looking at me like that, because you'll wear your eyes out.

12964 (open letter on the Dreyfus affair)
J'accuse.
I accuse.

12965
If you ask me what I came to do in this world, I, an artist, I will answer you: 'I am here to live out loud.'

12966
A work of art is a corner of creation seen through a temperament.

ZUCKER Carl
12967
What children expect from grownups is not to be 'understood', but only to be loved, even though this love may be expressed clumsily or in sternness. Intimacy does not exist between generations - only trust.

Keyword Index

a b c
6620 is that old A B C - ability,

a-fishing
11771 the stream I go a-fishing in.

a-gipsying
5948 were to go a-gipsying through

a-hunting
3478 .. a-hunting we will go.

a-smokin'
5719 her first a-smokin' of a

abandon
1762 never willingly abandon it.
4143 divorce you abandon your wife.
5132 he would abandon his mind
12030 work, he merely abandons it.

abandonment
5612 involve abandonment of the

abashed
6023 be noght abasshed to bide

abateth
726 commonly abateth industry.

abdomen
3405 The abdomen, the chest, and
8208 The abdomen is the reason why

abducted
4260 Léonie Abducted by a

abduction
4354 ready for a possible abduction.

abeyance
12073 and our vices are in abeyance.

abhor
10536 Age, I do abhor thee,

abide
4556 things flow, nothing abides.
6669 Abide with me: fast falls

abilities
4224 suits one's abilities, plain
7109 to his abilities, to each
9452 moderate abilities, industry

ability
769 man is the ability to give
1757 and an ability to
2688 The ability to laugh at life
3562 Ability will never catch up
4217 lost your ability for doing
4401 increases, ability declines.
4930 is the ability to make
6620 old A B C - ability, breaks
8816 Executive ability is deciding
9305 about his ability, but he's
9531 The ability to deal with
10588 become famous without ability.
12471 from ability, which is

able
4084 what you feel able to do.
11178 at able: At least

abode
12203 English make it their abode.

abolish
6401 anything they'd abolish it.
6461 we seek to abolish The 3rd

abolished
3389 is not abolished', it

abomination
240 An abomination unto the Lord, but

abortion
5554 pregnant, abortion would be a
9410 Abortion is advocated only by

above
4552 this world to rise above."

abridgement
4176 who can, An abridgement of all

abroad
3204 Abroad', that large home of
3889 Abroad is bloody.
6278 men Who went abroad to die.
7704 Wops, but abroad is
10835 is driven abroad to roam;
11128 too, before he goes abroad.
11343 just returned from abroad.
12765 sent to lie abroad for the

absence
199 Absence makes the heart grow

902 Absence makes the heart grow
967 in my absence and
1865 Absence is to love what wind
2105 nature is the absence of man.
4477 is the absence of
5161 by intervals of absence.
5874 Absence diminishes little
8422 The longest absence is less
9304 accident? Absence of body.
9389 A cry of Absence, Absence,
9683 pangs of absence; Else who
9790 and another by its absence.
10389 I dote on his very absence.
10557 hath my absence been From
11056 Absence is one of the most
11167 Absences are a good influence

absent
455 would be absent from the
2461 for the absent to assume
2787 The absent are always in the
4728 Achilles absent, was
6543 If to be absent were to be
9117 The absent are always wrong.
11402 of those who are absent.

absent-minded
1803 be getting absent-minded. Whenever
2234 I am not absent-minded. It is the

absents
5934 I often say, endear Absents.

absolutely
2670 corrupts absolutely, where
12044 I feel it absolutely.

absolutism
298 ours is absolutism moderated

absolve
1588 It seems to absolve us.
2151 History will absolve me.
9038 He's half absolv'd Who has

abstain
3199 to say, abstains from
3302 words, sustain and abstain.
8762 Boys should abstain from all
11423 thou free to abstain from it.

abstinence
608 many, total abstinence is easier
2025 made almost a sin of abstinence
5072 Abstinence is as easy for me as

abstract
5766 the more art becomes abstract.
7954 Abstract art is uniquely
9979 happiness in the abstract.
12205 in abstract ideals.

abstractions
1753 other mere abstractions, is not to

absurd
1645 A scientific faith's absurd.
2355 nothing so absurd but some
7743 'One's absurd! And
8630 to see the absurd nature of
9845 and that is the absurd.

absurdities
1797 to talk of errors and absurdities.

absurdity
5075 Almost all absurdity of conduct

abundance
10925 of its own abundance, and does

abuse
2485 when he abuses his horse
3792 only offer abuse as a
4061 away their abuses in the
4793 Abuse a man unjustly, and
8286 hear you abuse the
10720 If it is abuse - why one is

abused
11643 is to be abused, say what

abyss
1703 Man is an abyss, and I turn
7572 infinite abyss And
8227 into an abyss, the abyss
11152 us to the edge of the abyss.

acadame
7646 grove of Acadame, Plato's

academic
6449 law of academic life: it
11893 In academic life you seek to

academism
11250 Academism results when the

academy
1777 of their academy, at the

accent
5244 keeping of accent, deserved
5881 The accent of one's
8386 'educated' accent, whereas

accept
614 Accept the things to which
3302 Accept the place the divine
4080 We accept every person in
6188 We must accept the

acceptance
5011 have it so; acceptance of what
9703 acceptance of life
12873 public acceptance until it

accepted
4982 an idea is accepted it is time
11822 sees them accepted by

accessible
944 them how accessible men are;

accident
30 Accident counts for much in
431 of an auto accident it makes
670 a profession; it's an accident.
4283 been an accident,' they
5001 out by accident, so I now
5968 have it found out by accident.
7352 By many a happy accident.
8970 had an accident there, he
9304 a railway accident? Absence
10991 is not an accident, but a
12035 always an accident that puts

accidental
8490 call it the accidental and

accidents
1015 of habitual accidents .. is to
7030 runs into accidents which
8281 Such accidents will happen in

accommodating
7725 world is an accommodating sort of

accompanies
3343 the whole man accompanies it.

accomplice
8590 ready-made accomplice in any
8607 himself the accomplice of liars

accomplish
4794 some men accomplish in life is

accomplished
1237 The desire accomplished is sweet
7372 thing can really be accomplished.
11200 what can be accomplished in a week.

accomplishments
11088 emerges ahead of his
accomplishments.
12261 people's accomplishments, the front

accord
12600 is in accord with

account
2561 like a bank account. You put
9672 a good bank account, a good

accounted
2164 have accounted to God for
2647 You have accounted yourselves

accumulated
2974 he has accumulated during the

accuracy
2070 There is an accuracy that
2583 We are dying of accuracy.
6325 Barbaric accuracy - whimpering

accurately
8597 quotes accurately, for the

accursed
7014 Accurst be he that first
10264 themselves accursed they were

accusations
3740 doubtful accusations leave a

accuse
9031 then you accuse 'em of not
12964 J'accuse. I accuse.

accused
2405 We've been accused of
11217 in; you get accused of things

accuser
8160 not my Accuser, but my

accustomed
6255 I've grown accustomed to the
6450 you are accustomed to
11822 cannot get accustomed,

aces
11953 holding four aces.

ached
11361 never has ached with a

achieve
1443 great, some achieve greatness,
2758 means to achieve great
4107 a man to achieve all that
4514 some men achieve
5587 can ever achieve greatly.
10839 of mankind achieve the
12067 To achieve great things, we
12109 trying to achieve before you

achieved
3267 and cannot be achieved again.
9775 human beings have achieved.

achievement
2300 brilliant achievement was my
3418 we can't bring it to achievement.
4471 of every achievement is a proud
6057 not a gift - it is an achievement.
6297 his last achievement. In this

achievements
1255 we pay to achievements that
3080 most of the achievements from the

achieving
6504 fate; Still achieving, still

achilles
4728 Achilles absent, was Achilles

aching
5444 O aching time! O moments

acid
6970 though I wrote with acid.

acorn
3319 forests is in one acorn.

acorns
2102 a hundred acorns are sown
3430 oaks from little acorns grow.

acquaintance
1252 Acquaintance, n: a person whom we
1809 Should auld acquaintance be forgot
2220 - first an acquaintance, next a
2865 A new acquaintance is like a
5080 make new acquaintance as he
5116 I do not make a new acquaintance.
11320 creditable acquaintance; I love to
11373 improve on acquaintance,' and I

acquire
4825 to become, not to acquire.
11096 One can acquire everything in

acquittal
4761 Acquittal of the guilty damns

acquitted
5370 man is acquitted if judged
9282 the guilty party is acquitted.

act
465 easier to act than to
3607 and to act in an
3789 courage and act on
6250 cha acter of the
7087 does both act and know.
8157 Let us act on what we
8989 let us act as if we
9325 the last act crowns the
9648 in itself almost an act.
10439 the sins they love to act.
11999 she can act with her
12683 The men who act stand

acting
863 Acting consists of the
4178 he was off he was acting.
4346 Acting is happy agony.

acting *(continued)*
4482 as when he is acting a part.
4553 do half your acting for you.
8329 Acting is a masochistic form
9429 Acting is not being

action
176 purposes of action nothing is
1561 grasped by action, not by
2183 In action, be primitive; in
2533 Action is consolatory. It
2758 man of action has a
3744 is not knowledge, but action.
3794 A man of action forced into
3798 writings. Action is my
4407 the irksomeness of action.
4927 is not knowledge, but action.
5575 program of action. But they
7912 field where action is one
8023 Few men of action have been
8186 To every action there is
10017 glorious action, and
10173 Action is eloquence.
10215 Suit the action to the word,
11115 I do a mean action, it must
12481 immersed in action, and can
12775 Action is transitory - a

actions
1912 Great actions are not always
2738 Actions receive their
7936 and others by their actions.
8565 thoughts and great actions.
9984 of our actions in the
10365 When our actions do not, Our
10740 Only the actions of the just
11026 at human actions, not to

activity
4221 important ongoing activity.
4412 of all activity, the
7322 of a man's activity, and that
9053 word for New York is activity.
11431 practical activity and their
11824 is a human activity,

actor
433 A good actor must never be
1526 An actor's a guy who, if
2132 who tell an actor he is not
2709 The real actor - like any
10176 Like a dull actor now, I
11378 An actor and a priest both
12275 dee dee (an actor's life for
12353 Every actor in his heart

actor-manager
5020 Actor-manager - one to whom the

actors
3556 The best actors do not let
4370 play, the actors and the
4472 Actors are the only honest
12257 wants to hear actors talk?
12616 The actors and

actress
4578 Actresses will happen in the
9051 national landlady and actress.

acts
1072 first four acts already
3523 no second acts in
9628 Noble acts and momentous
12794 acts Of

actual
3266 What is actual is actual
5610 from the actual.

ad
7337 The best ad is a good

ad infinitum
7888 fleas, and so ad infinitum
11330 so proceed ad infinitum . Thus

adage
6523 in the old adage, 'Leave

adam
330 Adam Had'em.
412 Whilst Adam slept, Eve
828 When Adam delved, and Eve
1474 I wish Adam had died with
1480 When Adam and Eve were
4739 then That Adam was not
7596 Adam, the goodliest man of
11435 of the children of Adam.
11987 good thing Adam had - when

adapt
10624 man adapts himself

added
1170 shall be added unto you.

addiction
5348 form of addiction is bad, no

addictive
574 tends to be addictive, and the

addition
8784 With the addition of a grain

addresses
9830 Addresses are given to us to

adjective
235 as if they were adjectives.
6908 has never been in adjectives.
11978 As to the Adjective: when in

adjudication
7941 bad case of premature adjudication.

adjustment
4655 Every new adjustment is a crisis

adlestrop
11689 I remember Adlestrop - The

adman
3785 needed an adman to tell

administer
8905 is best administered is best.
10746 in which you administer.

administration
5570 of this Administration, nor even
6342 of this administration that if,

administrative
5590 three major administrative problems

admiral
10966 of all an Admiral came, A

admiration
1490 by their admirations, others
3662 like admiration for

admire
104 admire any man
1392 a greater fool to admire him.
1923 Admire, exult, despise,
2511 Which, to admire, we should
6318 they at once admire and hate.
8918 Not to admire, is all the

admired
815 as well as those you admired.
4801 is usually admired - if

admirers
5073 free from admirers then.

admires
7060 When one admires an artist it
8532 No animal admires another
9905 - he admires them but

admiring
5592 you've been admiring for a long

admit
3764 never admit it, but I

adopted
2648 has never been adopted there.

adorable
1458 are most adorable when they

adoration
12837 a nun Breathless with adoration.

adore
4851 does not adore his
6544 too shall adore; I could
7750 Kneel and adore him: the
8443 we alike adore But only
9323 we alike adore Ev'n at
10536 youth, I do adore thee.

adored
7851 still be adored as this
12551 women .. merely adored.

adorings
5424 And soft adorings from their

adornment
6235 Cats are living adornments.
11717 from the adornment of his

ads
6757 Ads are the cave art of
8091 watched the ads, And not

adult
273 in the adult, but to
3434 to be an adult because
8329 the occupation of an adult.
11386 becomes an adult when he

adulterated
5546 it has been adulterated to a point

adulterer
2721 able to find a happy adulterer.

adulteries
5246 all the adulteries of art;

adultery
1972 and gods adultery, Is much
1975 Not quite adultery, but
2141 committed adultery in my
2143 commit adultery at one end
2410 Do not adultery commit;
4889 be taken in adultery than in
7168 committed adultery, are now
8508 it would have been adultery.

adults
2793 is not that adults produce
5215 is what turns us into adults.
11388 by adults to
12093 between consenting adults.

advance
177 things advance, nine
3596 that advance comes to
3909 if it does not advance.
8054 If I advance, follow me! If
9557 don't advance, however,

advances
10020 chief who in triumph advances!
12479 The major advances in

advantage
2039 to their advantage, then to
2410 commit; Advantage rarely
2771 when sex gave her an advantage.
3197 that takes advantage that gets
6852 one great advantage over men.
8209 The advantage of a bad memory
8975 naturally gain the advantage.
10552 ocean gain Advantage on the
11965 has no advantage over the
12714 take a mean advantage of them.

advantages
1472 had your advantages. What
5192 itself with very mean advantages.
9960 by consideration of advantages.

adventure
114 of this unsuccessful adventure.
869 be an awfully big adventure.
3192 temptation to foreign adventure.
6695 = r + p (or Adventure equals
12170 is the only adventure open to

adventures
4196 All our adventures were by the

adventurous
6615 of the most adventurous things

adversary
3526 The adversary system is a kind

adversities
10944 sole cause of all our adversities.

adversity
692 Testament, adversity is the
693 and adversity is not
694 vice, but adversity doth best
1278 Adversity has the same effect
1848 men contending with adversity.
1901 Adversity, if a man is set down
4325 surviving adversity. But we
5073 Adversity is) the state in
8788 fortunate; adversity the great.
10112 the uses of adversity, Which
10467 Adversity's sweet milk,

advertise
8669 work like hell, and advertise.

advertisement
4888 The advertisement is one of the
5193 is the soul of an advertisement.

advertisers
11299 as the advertisers don't

advertising
1444 with advertising come less

2504 Advertising is what you do when
3461 behind much advertising is based
6124 Advertising may be described as
8364 Advertising is the rattling of a
9603 go into the advertising business
12370 Advertising is legalized lying.

advice
68 seldom asks advice until she
1279 My advice to those who are
1296 to me for advice, I find
2435 Advice is like snow; the
2466 To ask advice is in nine
4799 to a man than good advice.
4945 good news; not good advice.
4989 "Take my advice, there's
5889 nothing so freely as advice.
7153 the worst advice you can
7755 admirable advice, but I am
8263 a little advice from time
8815 whose advice we ask,
9216 Time gives good advice.
9259 offer me advice, give me
9286 Advice to persons about to
10832 of giving advice is, after
12442 Advice to young writers who
12580 with good advice to pass

advise
1018 Flooded. Please advise.

aesthetic
4006 in the high aesthetic line as a

aestheticism
277 Aestheticism is the last resort of

affable
9656 sign of an affable man, good,

affair
2690 passionate affair between
5895 had a love affair, but it is
6212 not constitute a love affair.
9616 a love affair. In
11192 The great affair is to

affairs
691 serious affairs and
4988 knows your affairs. In the
6740 your love affairs .. what
9745 In all affairs, love,
9802 Affairs, like revolutions,
10130 office and affairs of love.
10777 any love affairs. One must
12040 part in affairs which
12217 interior of affairs, must be

affect
6727 is to affect the
7288 do not affect three or

affectation
1980 look like affectation - but it
9121 Affectation is a greater enemy to
10852 for his affectations; he's

affecting
6200 without affecting the truth.

affection
640 show more affection than she
1710 when our affection seems
5119 he fills affection's eye,
7345 Of any true affection, but 'twas
9367 are the cinders of affection.
10515 Or thy affection cannot
10968 When strong affection stirs her
11218 Affection was a late 18th
12945 blighted affection, I pine,

affectionate
7188 have a really affectionate mother.

affections
3201 a great strain on the affections.

affinity
11755 an electric affinity for that

afflict
3099 Comfort the afflicted and
4808 Does it afflict you to find

afflicted
8493 when he is afflicted; the ocean

afford
3860 we can afford it or no,
10643 Can't afford them,
11776 he can afford to let
11883 it unless you can afford it.

affronts
72 soon forget affronts. Old age

afghanistan
5756 and left on Afghanistan's plains

afraid
154 I'm not afraid to die. I
1559 We are all afraid - for our
2213 If you are afraid of
3575 is that he is afraid to feel.
3587 one is afraid of a
3707 nothing I'm afraid of like
4066 People are afraid of the
4405 to be afraid Of people
4790 and afraid In a world
5183 could be afraid of women
6443 many are afraid of God -
6633 I am more afraid of my own
8037 she was afraid of him.
8070 you are afraid - you are
8799 that he is afraid of his
8925 see Men not afraid of God,
9524 alone of ending not afraid
9784 and is not afraid. It sees
11379 We do be afraid of the sea,
12340 and not be afraid is the

africa
5688 over Africa - (Boots -
8356 with Africa than my
8783 Africa always brings (us)

african
8059 is an African who dreams

after
1970 soda-water the day after.
8822 le déluge. After us the
12410 men go right after them

after-dinner
10380 it were, an after-dinner's sleep,
11765 Britain, in after-dinner

afternoon
4736 a beautiful afternoon with
9271 The afternoon knows what the

afterthought
11086 dear Readers, are an afterthought.

afterwards
203 together afterwards that is
3617 anyone may have them afterwards.

again
10192 look upon his like again.

against
1179 is not with me is against me.
1863 and against little
4252 Time and I against any two.
5585 people are against everything
9093 for you, will lie against you,

age
730 Age will not be defied.
881 Age is only a number, a
1299 grow old. Age shall not
1430 the time of age: forsake
2114 at your age, it is
2139 I feel age like an icicle
2268 Old age is not so bad
2359 Old age is by nature
2740 Middle age is youth
3057 in such an age, When no
3101 when age has
3350 Old age brings along with
3416 knew; if age was able.
4020 a woman's age in half a
4105 don't let age get you
5253 not of an age, but for
6039 chose, And age, and then
6286 In every age of
6943 The age is rocking the
7161 in his own age; in
7385 a certain age and at a
7675 prompt the age to quit
7699 arctic loneliness of age.
7810 Old age is an island
7867 Is worth an age without a
7885 Age does not protect you
8238 of thought to old age.
8408 For each age is a dream
8477 we see age going to
8904 his riper s age; And beads
8992 The age demanded an image

9026 known to age, and
9707 fervour of youth in age.
10157 Age cannot wither her,
10371 old age, As
10535 Crabbed age and youth
10626 nothing: age, which
10684 great age begins
10967 hath not forgotten my age.
11146 Every age needs men who
11221 Age is a high price to
11664 night, Old age should
11844 the first age since the
12074 For age with stealing
12603 her real age. A woman
12788 for what age takes away

aged
1967 means Certainly aged.

agenda
8522 item of the agenda will be in

ages
9035 different ages move, 'Tis
10117 His acts being seven ages.
11053 Now he belongs to the ages.
11531 through the ages one

agglomeration
12154 This agglomeration which was called

aggravation
32 men is the aggravation of self, a

aggression
86 weapon of aggression. It is
1547 Aggression is showing people you
5646 revenge, aggression and
6211 stop their aggression, or we're
9015 logic. It is naked aggression.

aggressive
11238 man is an aggressive creature

agitation
8311 gained by agitation, while we

agnes
5422 St Agnes' Eve - Ah, bitter

agnostic
2682 be content to remain agnostic.
3687 Don't be agnostic - be

agony
1581 But only agony, and that
4346 Acting is happy agony.
10948 bitter agony But not

agree
12 anxious to agree than to
1308 that you agree to a thing
2474 not always agree to die
2887 idea of an agreeable person
5894 to those who agree with us.
6413 you did not agree. When you
12860 always agree, one of
12901 with her would not agree.

agreeable
639 to be very agreeable, as it
1721 tolerably agreeable if it were
2887 idea of an agreeable person is
5871 of life along an agreeable road.
11339 men's power to be agreeable.

agreed
1193 except they be agreed?
2486 who have agreed, but to
6918 any man who agreed with me.

agreement
2392 Too much agreement kills a
2501 of common agreement,
3822 and an agreement with
9982 is) a tacit agreement that

ahead
2322 too far ahead. Only one
3135 "Go ahead. Make my day."
7971 want to get ahead, get a
11212 a long way ahead of what

aid
4473 Without the aid of

aids
7994

ail
5453 what can ail thee

ailments
11319 because our ailments are the

aim
1800 big plans, aim high in
3733 of the true aim of life
6481 you must aim a little
9884 have forgotten your aim.
10839 things to aim at in
12706 is your aim in

aims
5726 about the Aims of Art,
10752 than who aims but at a

air
66 with the air of a man
1664 The air broke into a mist
3193 There is music in the air.
6040 deep blue air, that
6255 in the air;
6849 that fresh air should be
6879 what air is to
7482 filled the air with
9481 Germans that of - the air!
10056 up into the air, you shall
10240 that word, honour? Air.
11688 in the fields of air.

airline
7124 traces An airline ticket to

airplanes
3552 Airplanes are interesting toys
8464 Airplanes) may kill you, but

airs
4127 himself airs about it.

airy
7605 sleep Was airy light from

aisles
4039 at night! Aisles full of

aitches
8390 to lose but our aitches.

alarm
1796 A little alarm now and then

alas
2926 say? Ah no! Alas, Time
10229 Alas, poor Yorick. I knew

albatross
2445 cross-bow I shot the Albatross.

albert
2876 to take a message to Albert.'

albert hall
6225 to fill the Albert Hall. I'd love

alcohol
361 caused by lack of alcohol.
2175 Alcohol is like love: the
8372 No doubt alcohol, tobacco,
8957 Mere alcohol doesn't
10610 Alcohol is a very necessary
12712 that alcohol was a food

aldershot
1103 by Aldershot sun, What

ale
7518 the spicy nut-brown ale.
10513 be no more cakes and ale?

alehouse
10258 were in an alehouse in London!

alexander
2858 Alexander .. asked him if he

alibi
3243 has an alibi, and one

alice
2112 and curiouser!' cried Alice.
7439 down with Alice. Alice is

alienated
3387 a certain alienated majesty.

alienation
8240 of alienation, it

alike
4688 come to look alike at last.
5676 everyone is alike and no one
5704 places were alike to him.

alimony
201 Alimony: the cash surrender
4579 and the expense of alimony.

alive
1053 no longer alive. There is
1098 Half dead and half alive!
2013 Industry is alive and well

2409 Officiously to keep alive.
2603 being kept alive against
2780 I'm still alive. I'd
4208 were alive he'd turn
5406 six months to stay alive.
5677 What still alive at
6594 Father, my age, still alive.
7053 just being alive, but being
7718 words that keeps me alive.
7933 gets out alive .. They
8191 to keep him alive, but we
8824 Alive, ridiculous, and dead
9990 dreams that keep you alive.
12789 dawn to be alive, But to be

all
107 slum you've seen them all.
128 All things bright and
291 wife, all things to
550 beneath me. All women do.
1146 All things were made by
1663 roses, roses, all the way.
3086 All for one, one for all.
7612 All seemed well pleased,
8004 All the way, with LBJ.
10865 good time was had by all.
11509 me not at all or all in

all-destroying
7245 roll, thou all-destroying but

all-softening
1965 .. That all-softening,

allah
336 no god but Allah alone and

allegiance
804 pledged allegiance, along

allegory
5475 worth is a continual allegory.

alleviation
12619 dawn seem to be an alleviation?

alley
892 of going up alleys to see if
2076 And she lives in our alley.

alliances
12272 permanent alliances, with any

allies
3890 we have no allies to be
4236 Taking for allies music and
8486 no eternal allies and we

allotted
3982 a few are allotted to you,

allowed
8523 he is allowed to take.

alloyed
1900 gold, be alloyed with some

allure
932 should allure and
11878 knew how to allure by

alluring
8024 alluring seen

ally
1305 only one ally: the

almighty
4978 by the Lord Almighty and not by
5549 Beneath thy own almighty wings.
7548 Him the almighty power Hurled

alms
1168 thou doest alms, let not
10502 he puts alms for

alone
506 been, shalt be, art, alone'.
1683 at being alone together.
2537 live, as we dream - alone.
3225 Hell is alone, the other
3359 you let it alone, it will
3921 never less alone than when
4547 they are alone, they'd
4993 never dine alone. When they
5080 left alone. A man,
5278 then I go home alone.
5635 the hills alone. A man
5668 And all alone went she.
5747 fastest who travels alone.
6081 us leave it alone,
6543 or I were alone; Then my
6704 we can be alone with God.

6796 life's greatest tests alone.
7355 if he is alone, forms an
7604 thou alone?
7618 can enjoy alone, Or all
8193 to know we are not alone.
8541 seul. We shall die alone.
8589 being who knows he is alone.
9018 He must be alone,
9549 never less alone than when
9623 must plough my furrow alone.
10002 nor less alone than when
11803 of being alone, and the
12039 alone, gave him
12055 And I alone sit
12452 to sail alone. The sea
12719 we left him alone with his
12805 or shall be left, alone.

along
3797 getting along with

aloof
10312 that stand Aloof from the

alpha
1139 I am Alpha and Omega, the

alpine
6485 through an Alpine village

alps
8693 size, Alps of green

also
7678 rest: They also serve who

altar
1491 A high altar on the move.
5281 threw our altars to the
9688 made at the altar, a

altar-stairs
11565 world's altar-stairs That slope

alter
10132 appetite alter? A man
10561 Love alters not with his

alteration
8185 The alteration of motion is ever
10560 when it alteration finds, Or

altered
11337 how much it altered her person

alternation
5051 a perpetual alternation between

alternative
2335 up the best alternative open, and
2339 no superior alternative has yet
11858 is: What is the alternative?

alternatives
2268 when you consider the alternatives.

altogether
6456 clothes is altogether, but

always
8518 There'll always be an
12224 I always tell a young man

amaranth
5993 fields of amaranth on this

amaryllis
7528 sport with Amaryllis in the

amateur
1512 the excited amateur has to die
4283 sport, the amateur status
9009 The amateur in politics is
11815 preserve of the amateur.
12440 of the amateur for three,

amateurs
5382 Amateurs hope. Professionals
9621 we are a nation of amateurs.

amaze
7077 themselves amaze To win the

amazed
1746 constantly amazed when I

amazing
5052 got this amazing thing.."
6591 It's amazing the day is still
8188 Amazing grace! how sweet the
12386 Amazing love! How can it be

amazon
1367 She was an Amazon. Her

ambassador
3956 Ambassadors cropped up like hay,
12765 An ambassador is an honest man

amber-dropping
7487 train of thy amber-dropping hair.

ambition
1786 known that ambition can creep
4291 Let not ambition mock their
5175 life, an ambition to be a
5286 Ambition is pitiless. Any
6365 to have his peculiar ambition.
6426 .. 'tis ambition enough to
7142 Ambition, in a private man a
7558 is worth ambition though in
8842 Ambition first sprung from
8889 To low ambition, and the
9370 and ambition of man,
10115 Who doth ambition shun And
10291 Ambition should be made of
10348 Vaulting ambition, which
12323 Vain the ambition of kings,

ambitious
10290 says he was ambitious; And

ambushed
11230 like being ambushed by a

amen
9055 the sound of a great Amen.

america
147 America - the best poor man's
793 America, thou half-brother of
889 minds of America had better
1017 In America there are two
1078 God bless America, Land that
1707 as coloured Americans are
2402 wrong with America that
2773 called America before the
2954 below. O my America, my new
3514 America is a willingness of
3891 The true America is the
4235 order. In America I think
4241 North America ought to
4844 too, sing America. I am the
5574 dying for America - there
6141 brought fortune to America
6314 but in America the
6681 of American movies
8396 America once had the clarity
8740 You cannot conquer America.
9503 It's morning again in America.
9858 In America is to
10932 to be in America! O.K. by
11078 what makes America what it
11147 In America, any boy may
11235 visiting America. I don't
12013 America is a land whose
12014 America is a vast conspiracy
12390 I went to America to convert
12669 America is the only
12957 America is God's Crucible,

american
1594 It is as American as cherry
2254 matter with Americans except
2550 of the American people is
3520 The American publisher
3665 Part of the American dream is
5068 to send American boys 9 or
5556 offer the American people,
7165 American women expect to find
7273 taste of the American public.
8263 I let the American people
8461 for which American patriots
9594 for the American people.
11132 say to the American, 'This is
12010 equal. The American agony is
12317 was born an American; I will
12318 I - I also - am an American!
12651 toward us, the American people.

americanism
6679 is Americanism with its
9613 for hyphenated Americanism.

americans
451 Good Americans, when they die,
1838 Americans have a special horror
2839 hand, brave Americans all, By
3792 amazes Americans, who do
5017 To Americans, English manners
5566 of Americans - born in
5572 my fellow Americans: ask not
6336 most - Americans have a
6772 find the Americans much as

7144 worse Than ignorant Americans.
9288 appears the Americans have taken
10861 The Americans believe they
11809 and the Americans .. Their
12265 whether Americans are to be

amiss
10483 comes amiss, so money

ammunition
3573 the Lord and pass the ammunition.

amoeba
4347 Amoebas at the start were
10738 were a soft amoeba, in ages

amorous
271 quite so amorous Over
1947 pure: be amorous but
7595 sweet reluctant amorous delay.
8937 from am'rous causes

amount to
12052 who didn't amount to much when

amour
972 the beginning of an Amour!

amphibious
2747 From this amphibious ill-born

amputation
566 is like an amputation; you

amused
12085 We are not amused.

amusement
2211 god-damned amusement park.

amusements
1721 it were not for its amusements.
6309 tolerable but for its amusements.
10896 we have no amusements in England

amuses
2865 Anybody amuses me for once.

amusing
1797 vastly more amusing to talk of
7785 she isn't amusing herself
10854 acts of theirs at all amusing.

anaemia
8988 emotional anaemia. And

anaesthetics
9782 in giving anaesthetics to men,

analysed
12551 Men can be analysed, women ..

analysis
169 Analysis kills spontaneity.
4782 analysis is not the

analyze
3128 you up, Analyze you,

anarchic
9767 thought is anarchic and
11254 from an anarchic,

anarchism
4142 Anarchism, then, really, stands
10632 Anarchism is a game at which

anarchist
1034 up a small anarchist community,
8034 Christ - an anarchist who

anarchy
948 next to anarchy, is
9727 of life; anarchy and

anatomy
836 has studied anatomy and

ancestors
101 had begotten their ancestors.
1774 backward to their ancestors.
2261 - our ancestors. It is
2343 from rich ancestors after the
2890 when the ancestors of the
4687 all our ancestors ride, and
8423 illustrious ancestors is like a
8798 glory belongs to our ancestors.
12177 well has no need of ancestors.

ancestry
3984 trace my ancestry back to a
9019 pride of ancestry, or hope

anchor
3775 have a firm anchor in

ancient
1348 feet in ancient time Walk
5502 heard In ancient days by

6389 Among our ancient mountains,
7310 Around the ancient track

anecdotage
2897 into his anecdotage it was a

anew
1548 and do, start life anew.
10684 age begins anew, The

angel
1387 "You're an angel. I'll
1926 as the Angel o'er a new
1942 For the Angel of Death
2902 ape or an angel? Now I am
7587 man nor angel can
7855 - Though an angel should
9187 man for the Angel of Death.
9334 fallen angel travelling
9998 to be an angel in order
10034 A ministering angel thou!
10419 What angel wakes me from my
11430 ground, The angel of the
11632 yet think him an angel.

angel-infancy
12060 in my angel-infancy. Before I

angelheaded
4041 angry fix, angelheaded hipsters

angels
92 on, Four angels round my
681 for God and angels to be
6484 forget-me-nots of the angels.
7019 walk the angels on the
8658 Name; Let Angels prostrate
8886 in where angels fear to
8893 would be angels, angels
9506 degenerated angels, rather
10376 As make the angels weep.
11700 Bats not angels, in the
11712 The angels keep their
12028 while the angels are

anger
671 Anger cannot be dishonest.
684 Anger makes dull men witty,
1242 is slow to anger is better
1373 degree of anger, fear and
2356 Hatred is settled anger.
2824 Anger as soon as fed is
3211 Anger and jealousy can no
4378 Anger raiseth invention,
4768 Anger is a short madness.
6643 inspired by anger; for when
7799 of judgement as doth anger.
9938 Anger is never without an
10621 it in anger, even at
11398 neither anger nor
12112 such great anger in those

angler
12232 excellent angler, and now
12236 for any but anglers, or very
12238 so no man is born an angler.

anglican
3359 for the Anglican Church is

angling
5159 but angling or float
12237 Angling may be said to be so

anglo-irishman
966 He was an Anglo-Irishman. MEG: In

anglo-saxon
3574 men or even of Anglo-Saxons.
6090 the Anglo-Saxon existence

angry
943 to you when he is angry.
1133 Be ye angry and sin not:
1361 I was angry with my friend;
8580 Angry young man.
11977 When angry, count four;

anguish
2827 We must an anguish pay In
4465 perish with anguish could they
4549 whatever anguish of spirit
5454 brow With anguish moist and

animal
3875 is the only animal whose
4396 than a reasonable animal.
6102 Be a good animal, true to
6943 an animal that could
8532 No animal admires another

9243 coitum omne animal triste.
9721 of the animal form is in
10816 Man, an animal that makes
11022 Man is a social animal.

animals
907 us from the other animals.
1902 All animals, except man, know
3198 Animals are such agreeable
8200 but kill animals and stick
8368 All animals are equal but
8411 man from animals.
12508 live with animals, they are

animate
10890 animate the whole.

animosities
8282 Animosities are mortal, but the

animosity
11293 fervour of sisterly animosity.

annihilate
2973 crush, to annihilate a man
8928 Ye gods! annihilate but space

annihilating
7082 Annihilating all that's made To a

anno domini
4619 him - only anno domini, but

announce
6957 trumpets to announce the

annoyance
11957 than the annoyance of a good

annoys
2606 whose scent the fair annoys.

annual
9488 their annual income

annuities
12140 paying your annuities. It is

annuity
655 An annuity is a very serious

annulled
1274 universe be annulled in behalf ·

annus
3284 to be an annus

anointed
10448 from an anointed king; The

anomalies
9898 heresy, anomalies, hobbies,

another
1132 We are members one of another.
6207 him And each for one another.
10184 you make yourselves another.
10713 ye sow, another reaps; The

answer
20 The Answer to the great
156 Love is the answer, but while
1240 A soft answer turneth away
1562 way to a pertinent answer.
2037 getting the answer yes
2122 But answer came there none -
2671 me your answer do! I'm
2845 knows the answer is basic
3130 The answer is blowin' in the
3722 are the hardest to answer.
4364 snappy answer, has sunk
4461 we find the answer to that
5034 the universe, not its answer.
5808 a riddle out of an answer.
7313 a dusty answer gets the
9118 The shortest answer is doing.
9357 that the answer does not
9890 power to answer do not
9963 to quantitative answer.
11790 why did you answer the phone?
11835 love is the answer, could you

answerable
8171 We are answerable for what
12322 people, and answerable to the

answered
4961 prayers have not been answered.
6517 the father answered never a
7319 man, his prayer is answered.

answering
8117 and severely by answering them.

answers
565 The answers you get from

4781 there are no certain answers.
12552 Answers sometimes
12960 answers may be

ant
6541 good husband, little ant.

anthropomorphic
5792 erstwhile anthropomorphic view of

anti-egotism
10885 that dreadful sin of anti-egotism.

anti-feminist
8312 man is as anti-feminist as a

anti-semitism
7399 weren't any anti-semitism, I

antibiotics
11210 is that antibiotics have cured

anticipate
12948 by young men who anticipate it.

anticipation
11257 per cent anticipation and ten

antipathy
8252 by a little physical antipathy.
8924 The strong antipathy of good to

antipodes
7066 And, like Antipodes in shoes,

antiquarian
5097 A mere antiquarian is a rugged

antique
958 of that antique station,
10174 The dust on antique time would

antiquities
677 Antiquities are history defaced,

antiquity
3335 the antiquity of the
5955 I will write for Antiquity!'

antithesis
8859 he himself one vile antithesis.
12467 The antithesis between a

anvil
1391 twenty times upon the anvil.
4091 be the anvil or the
5683 on the anvil - hear the
6516 either be anvil or hammer.
6741 is an anvil which has

anxieties
9989 the anxieties I have

anxiety
3978 taboo'd by anxiety, I
4215 All his anxiety resolved
4944 Anxiety is the interest paid
5622 Anxiety is the dizziness of
7205 Anxiety is essential to the
7206 Anxiety is the experience of
9518 Anxiety is a thin stream of
11095 Anxiety is fear of one's

anxious
4006 If you're anxious for to

anybody
2672 to find anybody who'll
3486 vote for anybody. I always
3957 Then no one's anybody.
4816 man who is anybody and who
11078 than where anybody is. That
12536 Anybody can be good in the

anyhow
8251 can bear with almost anyhow.

anyone
10070 Anyone can stop a man's

anything
1572 But is there anything beyond?
3810 can tell them almost anything.
4393 for nothing fall for anything.
7344 Anything for a quiet life.
7967 give a XXXX for anything else.
8952 heaven knows, Anything goes.
9725 is hardly anything in the
12648 you can do anything with her.

anyway
2662 us, but loves us anyway.

anywhere
1124 and go anywhere I damn
1499 belongs anywhere, even the
6046 something, happens anywhere.
8194 to be anywhere else, not

The Wordsworth Dictionary of Quotations

apart
8731 Apart from the known and
9833 they sometimes live apart.
12688 have stood apart,

apathetic
11780 is brutal, ours is apathetic.

apathy
4145 are apathy and
5529 all - the apathy of human

ape
2902 Is man an ape or an
4439 story of an ape playing

apes
5257 varlet; And apes are apes,
7921 monkeys and apes. One
9506 rather than elevated apes.

aphrodisiac
1006 a writer. It's an aphrodisiac.
4311 Fame is a powerful aphrodisiac.
12239 can be an aphrodisiac, yet it

aplomb
12501 with aplomb - and not

apollo
132 Mercury and Apollo programs
2565 A young Apollo,
7541 deceiving. Apollo from his

apologise
12309 "Never apologise and never

apologists
9871 it naturally has its apologists.

apologize
1253 Apologize, v: to lay the
3502 Never explain Never apologize.
5304 never apologize: never
6692 never apologize - get the
12714 never to apologize. The

apology
3374 person ever made an apology.
4680 Apology - a desperate habit,
4681 Apology is only egotism wrong
5675 God's apology for relations.

apostle
4008 rank as an apostle in the

apostles
100 the true apostles of
1936 all the apostles would have

apparel
10195 For the apparel oft

apparent
2168 so than our apparent world.

apparition
8998 The apparition of these faces in
12817 A lovely apparition, sent To

appeal
3090 An appeal is when ye ask wan
9074 who didn't appeal to me, who
12029 I appeal from Philip drunk

appear
192 When I appear in public,
384 rather what you appear to be.
903 make things appear what they
8321 it is difficult to appear so.
11984 night I appear for the

appearances
2286 Keep up appearances; there lies
3363 preserve appearances, a hundred
12581 judge by appearances. The true

appeaser
2294 An appeaser is one who feeds a

appetite
2171 than appetite, and those
3482 a voracious appetite with a
9343 The appetite grows by eating.
10132 not the appetite alter? A
10508 The appetite may
11169 A mortified appetite is never a
11179 a catholic appetite and a

appetites
3754 rather than satisfy appetites.
10157 cloy The appetites they feed,
12049 violent appetites, 'tis

applause
2473 Applause is the spur of noble
5276 Age! The applause, delight,
7044 fear so much as applause.
7403 everyone is forced to applause.
8646 having applause; a leader
8915 ev'ning satiate of applause.

apple
1203 him as the apple of his
3496 love a baked apple.
4739 of Men The apple pressed
7063 luckless apple did we
7459 rind of one apple tasted
8679 the bite of a harvest apple.

apples
4874 stolen, be your apples.
9499 of tart apples to
10482 choice in rotten apples.
12908 The silver apples of the

application
8564 only applications of
9386 fills out a job application form.

apply
2999 my methods. Apply them.

appointed
10054 one man is appointed to buy the
12060 this place Appointed for my

appointment
1369 they had an appointment at the end
6536 I create an appointment, I create
6555 I had an appointment with him

appoints
2163 Man appoints, and God

appreciation
9983 the direct appreciation of

apprehend
12471 to apprehend as

apprehension
12774 My apprehensions come in crowds; I

apprehensive
7138 the past, apprehensive about the

apprenticeship
843 be any apprenticeship for

approach
944 you must approach each man
7615 and chance Approach not me,

appropriate
4798 something appropriate and do it.
8023 exit at the appropriate time.
9221 gives to each what is appropriate.

approval
8275 lives with approval, he learns

approve
8437 things, and approve; I follow
8880 but men of sense approve.
12792 The gods approve The depth,

apricot
5255 blushing apricot and woolly

april
208 Every April, God rewrites
1651 Now that April's there.
3262 April is the cruellest
3314 flag to April's breeze
5925 Here cometh April again, and
7384 April, Comes like an idiot,
10541 the lovely April of her
12281 April, April Laugh thy

aptitude
3224 for which we have no aptitude.

aquarium
6599 The aquarium is gone.

aquitaine
8141 prince of Aquitaine, with the

arabs
7229 with the Arabs - we have

arbiter
11399 The arbiter of taste.

arbitrator
10505 old common arbitrator, Time,

arcadia
395 Et in Arcadia ego. And I

arch
9162 An arch never sleeps.

arch-enemy
437 it has one arch-enemy - and that

arch-flatterer
720 that 'the arch-flatterer with whom

archaeologist
2278 An archaeologist is the best

archangel
5962 An Archangel a little damaged.
7556 the lost archangel, this the

archer
10030 mark the archer little

archimedes
2855 reach, that Archimedes could not

architect
4332 is the job of the architect.
9729 can be an architect. If he is
12851 but an architect can only

architects
3406 and we architects have the

architectural
11871 the great architectural secret of

architecture
1522 Architecture is inhabited
1592 that sound architecture and to
2856 Architecture, of all the arts, is
3771 Architecture is space structured
4083 I call architecture 'petrified
4634 Good architecture is like a piece
8212 In architecture the pride of man,
8614 Good architecture lets nature in.
9580 Architecture begins when you place
9950 Architecture in general is frozen

arctic
7699 The arctic loneliness of

ardour
5240 With the ardour and the

ardua
7985 Per ardua ad astra.

arena
10005 an arena large as Europe

argue
909 in order to argue about
6894 who would argue with the
7242 aside and argue the point
7465 and to argue freely
8174 absurd to argue men, as to
8797 to argue with the
9218 You cannot argue with

arguing
4146 There is no arguing with
4158 In arguing too, the parson
7463 be much arguing, much
12436 I am not arguing with you - I

argument
206 is a rotten argument, but it
1620 own no argument but force:
2363 for an argument, abuse the
3684 side of the standing argument.
4282 No argument, no anger, no
4432 an impression, not an argument.
5095 All argument is against it
5114 you an argument; but I am
6129 as an argument than a
6570 The only argument available
9938 without an argument, but
10337 the staple of his argument.
12537 Arguments are to be avoided -

arguments
3107

arise
11693 the old wards: Arise, arise.

aristocracy
2240 while aristocracy means
2833 anytime, to him Is aristocracy.
2915 an absentee aristocracy, and an
6830 and our aristocracy the most
7702 An aristocracy in a republic is

aristocrat
3953 Cook, The Aristocrat who banks
11541 care I, Aristocrat, democrat,
12011 of an aristocrat and a

aristocratic
500 clearly the aristocratic class from

aristotle
10949 An Aristotle was but the

arithmetic
9951 leaves its arithmetic at home,

arithmetical
6936 increases in an arithmetical ratio.

arm
200 someone you arm them
544 has his arm round your
621 which today arm you
6924 ware of an arm clothed in
9669 .. To arms,

armadas
8147 the great Armadas come.

armaments
6877 it is not armaments that cause

armchairs
9049 who prefer armchairs to women.

armed
4276 The Armed forces are the
10267 is he armed that hath
10659 is he armed that hath
12038 one must go armed to the
12670 Armed neutrality is

armies
381 all the armies in the
7659 embattled armies clad in
11124 'Our armies swore terribly

arminian
8738 and an Arminian clergy.

armistice
3554 it is an armistice for twenty

armour
10739 There is no armour against
11079 with thick armour is

arms
3073 Arms, and the man I sing
7614 mightier than they in arms.
8749 other's arms could
9594 This is a call to arms.
9939 but it hath very long arms.
10713 wears; The arms ye forge,
11545 To find the arms of my true
12111 I sing of arms and the
12696 with arms .. should

armstrong
4138 Neil Armstrong carried no

army
3192 A standing army is like a
3431 in your army of lovers
4339 brought the Army home.
4848 No army can withstand the
4854 by an army; no stand
5340
5693 of the Army is the
7310 rank, The army of
8071 An army marches on its
10837 bless the Army, bless
12102 An army is a nation within
12347 with its own army and navy.
12846 Like an army defeated The

aromatic
12695 beneath the aromatic pain.

arose
11723 command, Arose from out

around
136 while you're still around.
6752 Around, around the sun we

arrangement
8530 new. The arrangement of the

arranging
3672 knack of so arranging the world

arrival
7335 point of arrival. The

arrive
11204 than to arrive, and the

arrived
2567 it right has not yet arrived.
9679 group has arrived' only when

arrogance
12852 between arrogance and

arrow
6472 I shot an arrow into the
6481 it; Every arrow that flies

arrows
1349 Bring me my arrows of desire:
3932 as living arrows are sent

arse
2202 no bet be ers, But with
2660 is an arse upon which
3628 to sit upon his own arse.
6786 Sit on your arse for fifty

arsenal
9598 the great arsenal of

art
210 Art is all that cannot be
573 Art is born of
792 Art is man's nature;
856 that Art is
887 not a lost art, but the
978 Art and Religion are
1011 Art has something to do
1069 Art has no other object
1088 Art is I, science is we.
1304 is the art of the
1335 in minute articulars
1355 are the Great Code of Art.
1528 Art is meant to disturb,
1662 rapidly, Art most
2418 Art produces ugly things
2547 Art for art's sake, ..
2569 is the great amateur art.
2750 Art is vice. You don't
2898 in literature and art.
3063 made An art, in London
3096 exhibitions of modern art.
3316 Art is a jealous
3366 in every work of art.
3401 and leave art to us?
3577 he makes a work of art.
3812 Art gropes, it stalks
3945 A work of art is an
4082 Art is called art because
4104 and in art the best
4120 greatest art is to
4213 thing as art. There
4409 The art of publicity is a
4488 The art of pleasing
4949 a trade and half an art.
5244 Shakespeare wanted art.
5246 of art; They
5690 by the art; But the
5765 Art does not reproduce
6109 bloody works of art.
6314 countries, art and
6319 Art is the expression of
6501 is long, and Time is
6757 the cave art of the
6758 Art at its most
6933 Art is a revolt against
7025 is the art of keeping
7125 An art in which the
7235 that meddles with art!
7327 of art Patrol the
7782 is my job and my art.
7836 Art must be parochial in
7954 Abstract art is uniquely
8057 Art is not an end in
8064 A work of art has no
8239 is no mean art. For its
8259 function of art to renew
8483 No Art has a shorter life
8556 Art always serves beauty,
8568 All art constantly
8706 know that Art is not
8707 Art washes away from the
8756 Is an art, like
8876 ev'ry art, And hide
8879 comes from art, not
8918 is all the art I know, To
9284 Art is a kind of illness.
9406 Art is .. pattern
9433 Art disease is caused by
9451 Art is life rearranged
9455 of every art is in
9640 the difference in all art.
9740 Fine art is that in which
9868 Art is a delayed echo.

10661 is the only art of which
10936 of the intellect upon art.
11056 is an art like any
11171 is but one art, to omit.
11819 All art has this
11824 Art is a human activity,
12421 Art is based on order.
12441 Art is upon the Town!
12473 Art is the imposing of a
12739 life but in art that
12890 while art Is but a
12966 A work of art is a corner

art-speech
6072 Art-speech is the only truth.

arthur
6924 the midst Arthur was ware

articles
2514 These articles subscribed, if

articulate
7914 We are articulate, but we are
12095 ability to articulate human

artificer
5324 father, old artificer, stand me

artificial
1610 things are artificial, for
3313 but they make them artificial.
7379 eminently artificial thing -

artist
557 into an artist, but the
1512 before the artist can be
1742 As an artist grows older, he
2034 Every artist preserves deep
2519 now on an artist will be
3451 An artist is a creature
3772 What's an artist, but the
4267 No artist is ahead of his
5322 The artist, like the God of
5817 is from the artist that
6498 - for the artist never
6753 An artist has to take life
6759 ditch stand of the artist.
7185 that the artist fashions
7275 out of an artist that is
7397 The artist never
8140 What an artist dies with me!
8220 As an artist, a man has no
8322 An artist is his own fault.
8708 child is an artist. The
8711 another artist. He
8995 Artists are the antennae of
9363 work of the artist is to heal
9869 An artist may visit a museum
9887 An artist is a dreamer
10773 An artist has been defined
10792 The artist, like the idiot,
11685 for an artist anywhere:
12007 The artist brings something
12030 An artist never really
12238 is born an artist, so no man
12600 the artist is in
12721 This is the artist, then -
12965 I, an artist, I will

artistic
4000 to give artistic

artists
802 All artists, if they
4213 art. There are only artists.
8052 Great artists have no
11265 to name 10 artists from any
12382 Then artists come along

arts
4637 No arts; no letters; no
7646 mother of arts And
9331 cry both arts and
12871 in the arts. Since

aryan
8754 And your Aryan eye,

ascending
7307 The lark ascending.

ascent
1559 has made the Ascent of Man.

ascetic
8027 a sot or an ascetic. In other
8213 Ascetic: one who makes a

ascribed
10141 Which we ascribed to heaven.

ashamed
2350 I am not ashamed to confess
2817 thing to feel ashamed of home.
3861 now-a-days men are ashamed of.
5037 wouldn't be ashamed of it.
5662 and to be ashamed with the
5896 who are not ashamed of having
7087 Irish are ashamed To see
7815 and being ashamed of them
8930 never be ashamed to own he
10485 I am ashamed that women are
10581 he is ashamed of, he
12233 friends ashamed to look

ashbuds
11484 black than ashbuds in the

ashes
1419 to earth, ashes to ashes,
4264 nice new ashes, Fell in
6839 For the ashes of his
7857 But turn to ashes on the
9863 past is a bucket of ashes.

ashore
6313 perilous excursion ashore.

asia
7022 jades of Asia! What, can

asian
5068 to do what Asian boys ought

aside
5280 stands aside to let
8912 last to lay the old aside.
11921 set death aside. It sets

ask
1172 Ask, and it shall be
4845 business to ask them.
9978 occurs to him to ask for.
11598 Ask me no more: thy fate

asked
5178 man who is asked by an
6330 and then I asked him with
8433 are glad to have been asked.
9207 whether asked or not.

asleep
3930 lies half asleep in the
9602 he'll fall asleep before you
9719 world are asleep at any
12778 houses seem asleep; And all

asparagus
905 this giant asparagus bed of
3956 Grew like asparagus in May,

aspects
4423 Aspects are within us, and
8948 kinds of aspects of human

aspersion
10730 An aspersion upon my parts of

aspidistra
8369 Keep the aspidistra flying.

aspiration
2541 him is the aspiration of every
6297 raises his level of aspiration.
12947 more than aspiration, and have

aspirations
12066 reckless aspirations have

aspire
10566 but light, and will aspire.
10756 my mind, aspire to higher

ass
2554 a solemn ass as a
3734 If an ass goes
5854 greatest ass of the
8527 dead, every ass thinks he
9269 call you an ass, put on a

assassin
4239 with assassins than
9659 you are an assassin. Kill
9855 and the assassin.. In the

assassination
298 moderated by assassination'.
2866 Assassination has never changed the
7733 Assassination is the quickest way.
10651 Assassination is the extreme form
12143 by an occasional assassination.

assemble
801 creates. I assemble, and I

assembly
886 In any assembly the simplest

assert
2051 one should assert oneself.
7546 I may assert eternal

assertions
666 His assertions cannot

asses
6645 those gross asses to whom He
7650 who seeking asses found a

asset
2233 greatest asset in the

assistance
11422 will set without thy assistance.

association
3680 a feat of association; having
7116 have an association, in which
11825 is an association of men who

assumed
4338 had always assumed that

assumption
5676 on the assumption that

assyrian
1941 The Assyrian came down like

asteroid
11968 as if she had laid an asteroid.

astonished
6555 [Death] was astonished to see him

astonishing
11934 It isn't so astonishing, the

astounded
7200 love we are astounded by what is

astra
7985 ardua ad astra. Through

astray
5697 who've gone astray,

astrologers
9340 and astrologers as readily

astute
5709 the small 'Stute Fish said

asunder
1183 let not man put asunder.
1441 let no man put asunder.
10599 shall put asunder: God will

asylum
6417 a lunatic asylum run by
9693 taken charge of the asylum.
12745 lunatic asylums which are

atahualpa
6813 and who strangled Atahualpa.

atari
5052 We went to Atari and said

ate
4129 Who never ate his bread
7625 she ate: Earth
11314 .. that we ate when we

atheism
687 Atheism is rather in the lip
695 mind to atheism, but depth
1779 animal; atheism is against
8358 on you - atheism,
9870 My atheism, like that of

atheist
1694 An atheist is a man who has
1729 to God, I am still an atheist.
1818 An atheist-laugh's a poor
2663 are no atheists in the
9650 for the atheist is when he
9921 her from being an atheist.
12942 By night an atheist half

athens
7646 Athens, the eye of Greece,

atlantic
427 across the Atlantic, and more
7473 In the steep Atlantic stream.

atom
1515 of the atom, and
3180 of the atom has
5019 the carbon atom possesses

9796 down of the atom is a very
11150 evil in the atom; only in

atoms
8490 concurrence of atoms.
8892 fall, Atoms or systems

attachment
6953 of our attachment to the

attack
616 for an unforeseen attack.
3414 until after the first attack.
5788 Frontal attack never works,
9935 both by his plan of attack.

attacking
1112 in attacking the
3553 excellent, I am attacking.
10594 but by attacking, and

attain
3936 not what he attains but

attainment
11170 so disenchanting as attainment?

attempt
5298 and don't attempt too
10352 The attempt and not the deed,
10475 to that dares love attempt.

attend
183 did not attend was

attendance
1319 Attendance at school is
2904 in his attendance at the

attention
479 of serious attention than
1011 arrest of attention in the
1041 their entire attention to it.
2467 pays most attention to those
2657 pays any attention to the
3782 and holding attention. But it
5205 memory is the art of attention.
5558 the attention of the
7898 - it requires so much attention.
8340 - attention without
9200 Can pay attention to his
9551 with such attention that you
12741 flattery of rapt attention.
12899 there, My attention fix On

attentions
9601 the attentions of many

attentive
4744 never want attentive and
7094 can have is an attentive wife.

attic
5492 O Attic shape! Fair
7646 where the Attic bird
8786 Sal Atticum. Attic salt.

attire
5428 Her rich attire creeps

attitude
4226 the attitude today is
5492 O Attic shape! Fair attitude!

attitudes
5340 order and attitudes which

attorney
3962 boy to an Attorney's firm. I
3980 find your attorney (who
4029 with a rich attorney's Elderly

attract
3462 kind, you attract a lot of
4009 magnet ever Attract a Silver

attraction
1337 Attraction and
6481 feels the attraction of earth.

attractions
5769 register competing attractions.

attributed
11388 often attributed by the

attributes
4988 one of the attributes of cities
7111 himself man attributes to God,
8967 The attributes of a great lady
11021 in infinite attributes, of which

auburn
4149 Sweet Auburn, loveliest

audacity
12503 audacity of elected

auden
8389 is W.H. Auden, a sort of

audible
417 Audible at five miles,

audience
863 to keep an audience from
4370 and the audience, and each
7710 heroes are in the audience.
11394 choreography to the audience.
11940 enlarges the audience.
12480 for an audience of about

audiences
4553 If you give audiences a chance
9965 kinds of audiences only - one
10857 audiences before
12497 must be great audiences too.

august
8298 August is a wicked month.
11912 For one August in its

auld
1810 yet, For auld lang syne.

aunt
4262 Aunt Jane observed, the
11661 Charley's aunt from

aunts
3961 and his aunts! His

aura
1397 only an aura of living

austerity
7731 see the old austerity That was

austerlitz
9857 high at Austerlitz and

australia
5042 Australia is so kind that, just

australian
5563 of law, or the Australian ballot.

australians
7967 Australians wouldn't give a XXXX

authentic
6784 Better authentic mammon than a

author
1688 than wit to become an author.
2867 An author who speaks about
3226 tell the author his
3634 of an author, to
5078 of every author is in
5209 When an author is yet
6195 of the Author of things.
8063 author, and I
8537 to see an author and we
8654 book belongs to the author.
8936 spirit that its author writ.
9617 Choose an author as you
9734 go to the author to get at
10842 in a good author is not
10850 Every author, however

authority
667 founded on authority, even if
2364 The authority of those who
2766 Authority doesn't work without
3326 stands on authority is not
4926 absolute rejection of authority.
5539 position than in authority.
6966 What authority we are
7218 have no authority from God
10376 brief authority, Most
10828 the highest authority for
11387 maximal authority and
11513 Authority forgets a dying king.
11804 weight of undisputed authority.
12730 woman: his authority and her

authors
674 let great authors have their
4640 of ancient authors proceeds
4695 her authors, contrived
11868 English authors their

auto-eroticism
3725 it is fundamentally auto-eroticism.

autobiography
995 intolerable, so with autobiography.
5552 shelters an autobiography within it.
12262 the deepest part of autobiography.

autocratic
5655 becomes autocratic

automate
12871 Your can't automate in the

automatic
2066 Automatic simply means that you

autumn
1489 strikes - autumn arrives in
1647 long dark autumn-evenings
4913 the ape Or Autumn sunsets
8679 Autumn is the bite of a
9311 breathed autumn, sombre,
10692 breath of Autumn's being,

autumnal
2935 have seen in one autumnal face.

avail
10859 good income is of no avail.

avant garde
11253 avant garde that the

avarice
5266 Is avarice to itself!
7832 beyond the dreams of avarice.

avenge
8054 down! If I die, avenge me!
10084 an insult, than to avenge it.

avenged
1448 The South is avenged.

avenger
12124 from my dead bones, avenger!

average
2849 The average man is more
4955 content to be the average man.
9532 of showing average people how
9612 am only an average man, but,
10108 .. the Average made

aversion
10728 begin with a little aversion.
11187 closely bordering on aversion.

avoid
741 in avoiding
8372 saint must avoid, but

avoided
83 that could have been avoided.
12537 are to be avoided - they are

avoiding
4579 one way of avoiding the

awake
3982 to you, you awake with a
5330 which I am trying to awake.
7789 we are awake, and when
7866 Then awake! the heavens
8239 one must stay awake all day.
9719 thirds are awake and

awakened
10673 He hath awakened from the

aware
5879 aware to know

awareness
6163 the human awareness they

away
3840 the hills and far away.
9321 to his wife away from home.

awe
2685 keep even kings in awe.
3646 The awe and dread with
5273 Invented to awe fools.

aweary
10374 'gin to be aweary of the

awful
9654 moments but awful quarters
10012 God! this is an awful place.

awkward
1835 let the awkward squad fire

awoke
1736 So I awoke, and behold it
1949 I awoke one morning and
5459 wide And I awoke and found
8448 its touch awoke him once,

axe
319 took an axe And gave
7086 eye The axe's edge did
8396 clarity of a pioneer axe.
8475 then the axe to the

axiom
3172 I simply ignored axiom.

axis
4683 The axis of the earth

axle
7473 His glowing axle doth allay

babblative
10955 The arts babblative and

babe
7543 laid her babe to rest.

babes
2634 milk for babes, But no

babies
1666 And bit the babies in the
4584 Babies are such a nice way
6687 Ballads and babies. That's
9661 dogs and babies can't be
11681 only washing. And babies.
12384 You breed babies and you

baby
213 Baby faced people suffer
867 the first baby laughed
5016 it, than have a baby alone.
5591 having a baby is that
5781 The baby doesn't
6705 a little baby thing,
6706 come from, baby dear? Out
7934 C'mon, baby, light my
7998 Burn, Baby, Burn.
10170 not see my baby at my

babylon
1438 waters of Babylon we sat

bacchus
3816 Bacchus has drowned more men
5499 by Bacchus and his

baccy
5731 parson, Baccy for the

bach
3996 'ops' By Bach,

bachelor
403 Now I am a bachelor, I live by
9686 Somehow a bachelor never quite
9690 far, nor a bachelor too near.
10133 would die a bachelor, I did not
11333 Bachelor's fare; bread and

bachelors
3214 reasons for bachelors to go out.
7252 Bachelors know more about women
7833 All reformers are bachelors.

back
957 put gently back at Oxford
2134 to have me back So I could
2277 never go back, that one
4415 I counted them all back.
4802 behind your back is your
5637 Nowhere to come but back.
6358 but I never walk back.
6842 those before cried Back!'
8916 Not to go back, is
9391 want to go back. It's the
11144 keep coming back and coming
11740 the sky on his back.
11831 on a man's back, choking

back room
6455 boys in the back room will have

back-seat
11650 be a very good back-seat driver.

backbone
5693 But the backbone of the
8417 are the backbone of Canada.
11884 is the backbone of

background
6985 you know is background, what you

backing
8007 I'm backing Britain.

backs
4369 With our backs to the
11748 turning our backs on our

backside
8978 to their backsides, and the
9701 when their backsides look good

backward
8225 looks backward. In the
10099 revolutions never go backward.
11008 his eye was backward cast, As
11779 as lean over too far backward.

backwards
5623 understood backwards; but it
12460 to live backwards from in

backyard
12450 of a city backyard, I see

bad
14 are almost always bad men.
275 and so much bad in the
959 will come to a bad end.
1056 the bad to the
1513 is bad it must be
1788 When bad men combine, the
1890 part like bad sixpences
2024 good or as bad as it
2733 and the bad die late.
2810 were no bad people,
3303 were bad speakers
3645 I feel bad that I don't
4386 to the bad - for
5134 It is as bad as bad can
5580 just as bad as we'd
5866 There are bad people who
6682 to do something bad.
7453 thing to be had, and if we
8014 to heaven. Bad girls go
8273 Safe taste is bad taste.
9167 and cattle; bad is when
9190 and bad men it
9293 got a bad egg, Mr
9661 babies can't be all bad.
10305 For being a little bad.
10575 that are bad for me do
10912 Bad men live to eat and
11876 put up with bad things
12399 when I'm bad, I'm
12492 I am as bad as the worst,
12559 and the bad unhappily.

badder
5381 say 'bigger and badder'.

badly
2264 it is worth doing badly.

bag
4974 a paper bag, You
6868 out of the bag often

baggage
4061 bag and baggage, shall I

baghdad
6555 see him in Baghdad, for I had

bait
6073 the culture bait, don't

baits
7668 post, while good news baits.

balance
1226 the small dust of the balance:
3436 a little mental balance.
6092 of the balance. When the
8201 the balance of power.
8825 in nice balance, truth
9901 no less wise, to balance it.
12221 The balance of power.

bald
771 is either bald or dead or
1454 between two bald men over a
9092 gives us when we are bald.

baldheaded
6559 an' then Go into it baldheaded.

baldness
4586 thing about baldness - it's
10840 far side of baldness than young

balkans
1307 silly thing in the Balkans.

ball
6249 at a ball; the only
8829 of the ball, Where,
11286 of a ball is either

ballads
3983 patches. Of ballads, songs and
6476 all the ballads That ever
6687 Ballads and babies. That's

balliol
982 Balliol made me, Balliol fed

balloo
5267 been at the balloo, I have

ballots
6350 peaceful ballots only, are

balls
874 can hear my balls clank.

balm
5435 pours out a balm upon the
10448 wash the balm from an

baltic
2332 in the Baltic to Trieste

ban
8002 Ban the Bomb.

banalities
2192 The banalities of a great man

banality
1487 from utter banality.
9916 of banality out of the

bandage
2684 makes best is the bandage.
8971 the wound, not the bandage.

bandied
12331 struck and bandied Which way

bane
7561 Deserve the precious bane.

bang
226 A bigger bang for a buck.
3261 Not with a bang but a

banish
7638 crime art banished hence.
10002 rather than banishes them.

bank
158 in my name at a Swiss bank.
2561 is like a bank account.
4749 A bank is a place that
6324 all the way to the bank.
8175 robbed a couple of banks."
10417 I know a bank whereon the
12131 Don't bank too much on

banker
9145 father is a banker provided

bankruptcy
39 Bankruptcy is a legal proceeding

banks
3953 who banks with

banner
6485 and ice, A banner with the
11959 but carrying a banner.

baptism
3195 be called a baptism, a
4967 With soap baptism is a good

baptist
265 John the Baptist pretending

bar
5670 the harbour bar be

barabbas
2031 Now Barabbas was a publisher.

barbarians
500 in my own mind the Barbarians.

barbarism
9871 Since barbarism has its
10916 the most elemental barbarism.

barbarity
10881 with the barbarity of

barbarous
7482 air with barbarous

bard
7861 not the bard, if he fly

bards
6480 The bards sublime, Whose

bargain
3635 never made a good bargain.
5218 Bargain: something you can't
10753 was a better bargain driv'n.

bargains
10816 an animal that makes bargains.

barge
10155 The barge she sat in, like

bark
5124 out as I do, and bark .
9101 One dog barks at

barking
233 you cannot keep from barking.

barn
9402 kick down a barn, but it

barrel
6973 out of the barrel of a gun'.

barrel-load
11710 them by the barrel-load. Some may

barren
3279 and I am but a barren stock.
6424 spring from barren land.
9771 from it they remain barren.

barricade
10046 At some disputed barricade.

barrier
12835 Blessed barrier between day

baseball
424 those of a baseball player.
889 had better learn baseball.
7276 sensible as baseball in

bashfulness
61 particular bashfulness in

basic
4442 At its most basic root, the

basics
6907 get back to basics; to
9902 are the basics; waking

basil
5450 her sweet Basil evermore,
5451 steal my Basil-pot away

basingstoke
4025 hidden meaning - like Basingstoke.

basket
11933 eggs in one basket and -

bastard
3811 to be a bastard to be a
4615 we knocked the bastard off!

bastards
8730 Them bastards at the monastery
12207 twenty bastards, or he who

bastion
3429 the last bastions of the

bat
9597 every time I come to bat.
12532 like some bat That beats

bath
8101 I test my bath before I

bathed
9500 I have bathed in the Poem of

bathing
3979 a large bathing machine
12823 one long bathing of a

bathroom
1379 goes to the bathroom, with the
6387 revolutionary in a bathroom.

baths
9027 don't like baths. I don't

bats
743 are like bats amongst
11700 wings, Bats not

batsman
6007 Or if the batsman thinks

battalions
9669 citizens! Form your battalions!
10225 single spies, But in battalions.
12168 the heavy battalions, but of

battle
1208 nor the battle to the
2068 to give battle, and
2128 to one in a battle - to get
2659 the hardest battle which any
2754 has lost a battle. But
4521 through the battle. That the
4526 lit the battle's wreck
4938 go out to battle for
5571 a call to battle, though
5574 or graveyards of battle.
6404 defeated in a great battle.
8047 it into battle to steady
9715 nor the battle to the
10339 When the battle's lost and
11197 a field of battle, and not a
12361 except a battle lost can

battle-flags
11529 and the battle-flags were

battlefield
2969 and the battlefield is the

battles
4884 The mother of battles.
6673 Battles and sex are the only
8377 the opening battles of all
11688 What mighty battles have I
12001 results of a hundred battles.

bauble
8904 with this bauble still, as

bay
9233 brave when brought to bay.

bayed
4152 voice that bayed the

bayonet
7988 A bayonet is a weapon with a
12718 with our bayonets turning.

bbc
12630 This is the BBC - we are

be
3613 not wish to be anything
6749 should not mean But be.
8720 you are, and be such.
10211 To be, or not to be:

beach
5045 upon it - from the beach.

beaches
2311 on the beaches, we shall

beachy head
2258 Birmingham by way of Beachy Head.

beacon
5660 Airly Beacon, Airly Beacon;
9923 lights its beacon in a man's
10498 call'd The beacon of the

beadsman
8606 To be your beadsman now that

beak
7329 His beak holds more
8811 Take thy beak from out my

beam
9536 Beam us up, Mr Scott.

beans
7960 Beanz meanz Heinz.

bear
1530 For every Bear that ever
3453 have to bear. That's
5542 If you bear the cross
6911 I cannot bear your
7040 savage as a bear with a
7438 you are a Bear of Very
7450 I am a Bear of Very Little
10534 Exit, pursued by a bear.
10613 alive could bear it: it
10786 fire was furry as a bear.

bear-baiting
6831 hated bear-baiting, not

bearable
3106 makin' life bearable. A little

beard
3007 the King of Spain's Beard.
6146 Man with a beard, Who said,
10543 white and bristly beard.

beareth
729 river, that beareth up things

bearing
5317 I seen him bearing down on me

bears
4647 dogs and bears, And
4974 wandering bears might come

beast
482 be either a beast or a god.
5635 hardly be a beast or a fool
6923 This beast went to the well
7620 subtlest beast of all the
10223 and feed? a beast, no more.
10460 No beast so fierce but
11897 is the beast, one is
12903 what rough beast, its hour

beastie
269 beasties And
1831 tim'rous beastie, O what a

beastly
2585 let's be beastly to the

beasts
5275 feed Like beasts, till they

beat
250 his wife can beat him at.
2115 boy, And beat him when
4387 hearts that beat as one.
5589 The beat generation.
7475 hands, and beat the
10574 can always beat ten men
10632 the police can beat you.
11057 We beat them to-day or

beaten
3301 will make a beaten path to
4088 They may be beaten, but they
8596 painfully beaten into him,
9813 'I was beaten', he does

beating
6501 drums, are beating Funeral

beatles
6034 ban And the Beatles' first LP.

beats
2233 world. It beats money and

beauteous
10491 How beauteous mankind is! O

beauties
8941 Beauties in vain their pretty
12769 You meaner beauties of the

beautiful
432 Things are beautiful if you
908 woman: 'Be beautiful if you
2221 woman isn't beautiful, people
2418 become beautiful with time.
2849 any woman - with beautiful legs.
3308 The beautiful rests on the
3382 to find the beautiful, we must
3515 The beautiful and damned.
3594 right until it is beautiful.
4089 look at a beautiful picture,
4247 A beautiful woman should break
4314 Against the beautiful and the
4402 because I'm beautiful, or am I
4453 says, she is not beautiful.
4527 How beautiful they
4545 It was beautiful and simple as
4704 we call it beautiful, and the
5985 As beautiful as woman's blush,
6067 its time Beautiful .. 150
6103 find it a beautiful clean
6892 is the most beautiful woman
7895 cities are beautiful: but the
7930 or believe to be beautiful.
7995 Black is beautiful.
8119 a distance, beautiful: from
8321 easy to be beautiful; it is
8579 a woman beautiful in middle
8651 of what is beautiful does not
9280 A beautiful face is a mute
9738 the most beautiful things in
10704 acts are beautiful through
10938 is most beautiful in virile
12579 The only beautiful things are
12894 and the beautiful Have no

beautifully
10964 darkly, deeply, beautifully blue.

beauty
119 Beauty - the adjustment of
212 rather have beauty than
519 June for beauty's
697 part of beauty, which a
751 excellent beauty that hath
1346 Exuberance is beauty.
1549 Beauty sat with me all the
1706 the hundredth with a beauty.
1934 Of its own beauty is the
2000 walks in beauty, like the
2035 Beauty is unbearable, drives
2148 more than they love beauty.
2692 Female beauty is an
2932 built on beauty, soon as
2935 nor summer beauty hath such
2967 Beauty will save the world.
2969 is that beauty is
3307 We ascribe beauty to that
3427 As a beauty I am not a star,
3447 can be a beauty without a
3538 town, Beauty she was

beauty
3715 Beauty and truth may be
3748 a principal beauty in a
4014 A thing of beauty, Would she
4745 life was beauty; I woke,
4871 Beauty is altogether in the
4913 Beauty for some provides
5263 lie As much beauty as could
5417 A thing of beauty is a joy
5493 Beauty is truth, truth
5497 dwells with Beauty - Beauty
5751 'Tisn't beauty, so to speak,
6182 'Tis beauty calls and glory
6296 up into beauty like a
6803 of its beauty and power.
6998 Clad in the beauty of a
7130 birth Her beauty fed my
7166 Beauty is an ecstasy; it is
7340 Beauty is the purgation of
7485 Beauty is Nature's coin,
7665 Yet beauty, though
7769 The beauty of stature is the
7841 Beauty is everlasting And
8106 Beauty is but a flower Which
8434 of beauty can err,
8556 serves beauty, and
8563 lock your beauty In the
8692 bring; But beauty faded has
8865 ghosts of Beauty glide, And
9061 how much beauty lay around
9686 a thing of beauty and a boy
9721 The beauty of the animal
9788 with a beauty Our eyes
9828 always say beauty is only
10266 near your beauty with my
10470 ear; Beauty too rich
10537 Beauty itself doth of itself
10540 in thy beauty's field.
10544 write the beauty of your
10804 quested for beauty, but God,
11074 face; the beauty of the
11462 Beauty, more than bitterness
11820 that beauty is
11849 and unusual beauty made my
12171 what is beauty? .. a
12325 youth And a little beauty.
12584 in everything but beauty.
12732 that beauty is woman's
12888 A terrible beauty is born.

beaverbrook
563 mind was that of Lord Beaverbrook.

because
377 We're here because we're here
496 we forget because we must
6917 Because it's there.
7801 than it was because he was he,

beckons
11797 see, Which beckons me away.

becoming
1511 Becoming number one is easier
11091 We are becoming the men we
12084 I think I am becoming a god.

bed
103 is not a bed to be made
134 Never go to bed with a
180 get out of bed for it;
187 to stay in bed with
218 never go to bed alone.
1015 to stay in bed all day.
1039 years in bed and over
2853 Never go to bed mad. Stay
4159 to pay, A bed at night,
4904 Bed,' as the Italian
6004 me he mostly sent to bed.
6059 it's nicer to stay in bed.
6249 go home to bed is that
6740 go to bed with is
7425 in their bed, for it's
7787 who goes to bed with a man
8049 people to bed at a
8624 And so to bed.
9073 I used to go to bed early.
9390 one man in bed at the
9944 goes to bed with whom.
11100 Going to bed with a woman
11174 have to go to bed by day.
12289 he on his bed, Turns his
12645 Minds like beds always

bedchamber
4617 calls on my bedchamber less

bedfellows
7104 strange bedfellows, marriage
7781 can never be bedfellows.
10487 a man with strange bedfellows.

bedlam
1978 else but a Bedlam vision

bedroom
2028 do in the bedroom as long as

bedside
9305 a very good bedside manner!

bedspring
8645 triumphant twang of a bedspring.

bee
137 sting like a bee.
2829 Fame is a bee It has a
2833 concern the bee; A clover,
6147 bored by a bee; When
6452 like a bee Doth suck
6453 them like a bee; If I
12285 little busy bee Improve

been
195 Been there, done that, got

beer
2020 such all beer and
4736 than a cold beer on a
7969 I'm only here for the beer.
7972 parts other beers cannot
10244 in me to desire small beer?
10427 and chronicle small beer.
10584 I'm only a beer
10897 than Beer and

bees
8958 do it, bees do it,
11595 of innumerable bees.

beethoven
3996 Spohr and Beethoven, At
4597 out Hitler through Beethoven.

beetle
3433 Nor let the beetle, nor the

befell
4738 forty-odd befell: They went

before
322 never loved before; Let those
3109 were known before science
8289 - Not lost but gone before.
9649 been here before, But when
10351 which I see before me, The
11618 that's not been said before.
11987 nobody had said it before.

beg
6794 We cannot beg for

began
4095 really began with him,

beget
8416 passions, to get and beget.
9919 rotten. To beget children,
12207 man, he who begets twenty

beggar
1854 Set a beggar on horseback,
5696 boundin' beggar - for you
10301 I am a beggar, I will

beggared
3027 but desert. Beggared by fools,

beggars
3125 is love, in beggars and in
10320 Our basest beggars Are in the

beggary
6822 they knew beggary; but they
10146 There's beggary in the love

begin
3091 God's sake begin at the
6010 Then I'll begin."
6569 thirsty's to begin; A
6617 should begin at home;
11674 To begin at the beginning:

beginning
214 The beginning is easy; what
1139 Omega, the beginning and the
1145 In the beginning was the Word,
2119 at the beginning,' the King
2296 even the beginning of the
2682 of the beginning of all

3250 In my beginning is my end.
3251 we call the beginning is often
4069 have a beginning, a middle
4772 done who has made a beginning.
6043 A beginning, a muddle, and an
6196 no less the beginning of science
7122 In my end is my beginning.
9463 was in the beginning, is now,
11354 Before the beginning of years
11415 This is the beginning of the

beginnings
9802 should only have beginnings.
10249 And weak beginnings lie

begins
9035 When she begins to
9330 He that begins to live,
11705 Nothing begins, and nothing

begot
11118 about when they begot me.

begotten
101 if they had begotten their

beguine
8953 begin the Beguine It brings

begun
5224 have not yet begun to fight.

behave
211 who shall behave in a
6733 nowadays to behave like men,
9810 like men to behave like men.
10654 is how they behave in a
10849 and not behave as the
11178 to, And behave mannerly

behaving
2665 means behaving yourself a

behaviour
4459 The behaviour of the universe
5820 chemistry or animal behaviour.
6685 state pending good behaviour.
9508 human behaviour as a

behaviourism
6702 Behaviourism is indeed a kind of

behind
1180 Get thee behind me, Satan.
3752 of the way than go behind.
4030 dusk with a light behind her!
5703 thy tail hangs down behind!
6026 the people, walk behind them.
6797 Behind every tennis player
8466 Never look behind you.
9426 Soon it will be behind me.
10863 has no bosom and no behind.

behold
5518 When I behold, upon the
10559 which now behold these

beholder
4871 in the eye of the beholder.

being
7108 their being, but, on
7206 of Being affirming
7568 this intellectual being.
7617 concerns thee and thy being.
8161 beings, myself
10998 Never being, but always at
11561 wheels of Being are slow.

belgrave
3973 May beat in Belgrave Square As

belief
1400 A belief is not merely an
2459 of strong belief is over,
2698 it's the belief that
3682 Belief is better than
4629 Belief is harder to shake
5033 doubting my belief in God,
5095 but all belief is for it.
5177 attacks my belief diminishes
5402 confident, belief that is
9918 their names: that is belief.
9968 the correctness of a belief.

beliefs
6574 he must hev beliefs, not to
6872 of exploded beliefs may make a

believe
738 nor to believe and take
868 'I don't believe in

979 what we believe is not
1147 wonders, ye will not believe.
2525 do not believe in
2903 is a being born to believe.
2982 A man can believe in a
3309 To believe your own thought,
3421 sense of what not to believe.
4650 ready to believe all that
4972 how much to believe of my own
5804 life; to believe everything
6233 oh I believe in
6300 I believe in Christianity as
7453 If we believe a thing to be
8171 We can believe what we
8427 let us believe that there
9155 The eyes believe themselves;
9249 Believe not your own brother
9491 continue to believe that with
9506 prefer to believe that they
9842 If you believe the
10635 Never believe anything a
11051 To believe with certainty we
11183 I believe in an ultimate

believed
74 young, and believed everything
6396 out what I really believed.
9921 She believed in nothing; only
11216 they say should be believed
11402 things are believed of those
11427 will be believed of any man

believer
8189 sounds in a believer's ear! It

believes
761 that he more readily believes.
9436 what he believes, as he
12353 his heart believes everything
12942 atheist half believes in God.

believing
8174 to torture them, into believing.
8468 consist in believing, or in
8761 and of believing in deities
9175 Seeing's believing - but
10045 I believing; What need
11886 Not believing in force is the
12874 for believing more and

bell
2943 whom the bell tolls; it
4738 The sexton tolled the bell.
5392 The Bell system is like a
6158 a bell.
8776 The bell never rings of
10161 mock the midnight bell.
10303 Bell, book, and candle

bellboy
3592 a cosmic bellboy for whom

belle
5458 .. La belle dame sans

bellicose
2367 by turns, bellicose,

bellies
12049 than their bellies. They

bells
375 The bells of hell go
4647 ring the bells of Heaven
8806 From the bells, bells,
11481 of evening bells.
11485 or of marriage bells.

belly
6923 the beast's belly like unto
8797 with the belly, since it
9090 one way, belly 'nother

belly-tension
3928 bitter belly-tension between a

bellyful
7420 man with a bellyful of the

belong
3932 yet they belong not to
5223 should belong to the
8688 you must first belong.
9394 to where I belong; not an
11889 where you belong from now

belongs
11053 Now he belongs to the ages.

beloved
1327 never be beloved by men He

1327 never be beloved by men He
4130 go, O my beloved, with
10499 That she beloved knows

below
538 without hitting below it.

below par
7766 I was born below par to th'

belt
538 can't see a belt without

belted
5701 Though I've belted you and

bench
309 hard board bench. No more

bend
5849 I bend and I break not.
12433 always be a bending

benefactor
3378 would castrate the benefactor.
12614 who's the benefactor of a whole

beneficial
9992 is very beneficial. It's

benefit
3931 for my own benefit'? .. Or
4104 to have the benefit of what is
8618 snares, and no real benefit.
11805 the use and benefit of

benefits
6854 Benefits should be granted
11844 to make the benefits of

benevolence
7324 Much benevolence of the passive
10818 from the benevolence of the

benevolent
8590 degree of benevolent feeling.
11992 fat, benevolent people do.

bent
7585 down alone bent on his
8299 wrists as she bent forward.

bequests
2140 two lasting bequests we can

bereaved
8141 shaded, the bereaved, the
12022 would be bereaved if

bereavement
4326 first six months of bereavement.

berliner
5557 words 'Ich bin ein Berliner'.

bermudas
7067 the remote Bermudas ride In

besieged
8315 of a besieged city where

besmeared
7559 horrid king besmeared with blood
10549 stone, besmeared with

best
23 now is the best time of
1668 me! The best is yet to
1830 The kindest and the best!
2000 all that's best of dark
2305 with the very best.
2333 doing our best'. You
2450 He prayeth best, who
2664 gave the best years of
3310 is always a best way of
3437 run is always the best.
3683 The best things and best
4975 be the best, not the
6648 was the beste, Preie
9122 usually the best men when
9335 The best is the best,
10259 few words are the best men.
10385 They say best men are
11164 done my best, frankly
11928 for rest, For home is best.
12144 In this best of possible
12148 The best is the enemy of
12168 but of the best shots.
12563 He is doing his best.
12896 The second best's a gay
12902 The best lack all

best friend
9512 are a girl's best friend ..

best man
278 not marrying the best man.

best-loved
4465 The best-loved man or maid in

best-seller
1442 Best-sellerism is the star system
1445 A best-seller was a book which
10844 A best-seller is the gilded tomb

best-sellers
9047 one in all the great best-sellers.

bestial
10429 and what remains is bestial.

bestows
2074 where Jove bestows. When June

bestride
10275 he doth bestride the narrow

bet
9715 but that's the way to bet.
11233 if it was a bet, you

bethlehem
12903 towards Bethlehem to be

betimes
10511 midnight is to be up betimes.

betray
3758 shall not betray thee.
3845 those who betray their
4199 that men betray, What
8688 To betray, you must first
11707 All things betray thee, who
12525 experience is to betray it.
12799 never did betray The heart

betrayal
2014 The betrayal of Ulster, the
6113 betray .. Betrayal can only
9444 without any act of betrayal?
12415 ultimate betrayal. Very few
12631 only defence against betrayal.

betrayed
813 we are most endlessly betrayed.
7312 We are betrayed by what is
12775 like men betrayed: Suffering

betrayers
11451 are great betrayers of

betraying
3588 between betraying my country

betrays
1783 and he betrays, instead
9355 word often betrays a great

better
656 `He is not better, he is
797 knows of a better 'ole, go
934 purpose of becoming better.
1242 to anger is better than the
1569 And a better one than
2041 who are better than
2207 What is bettre than
3132 be feeling better. I really
3226 writing is better than it
3301 man write a better book,
3743 good, where better is
4838 world gets better every day
5602 a little better or a
5701 You're a better man than I
5838 are either better or worse
5932 to get the better in
6335 I can write better than
7091 Yet we'd better by far
7132 remember, better the world
7231 women are better than men I
7319 prayer a better man, his
7558 in hell: Better to reign
7726 render our fellow-men better.
7962 Things go better with Coke.
8175 feel a lot better once we've
8437 I see the better things, and
9220 It is better to be than not
9832 don't know better as they
9915 world is better than
9958 I am better than my
10385 more the better For being
10565 still: The better angel is a
11548 most; 'Tis better to have
11658 are much better at saying
11698 things get better by
12399 but when I'm bad, I'm better.

betting
7154 him betting on people.

between
10873 anyone who comes between them.
12213 Thames is between me and the

bewailed
7813 should be bewailed at their

beware
96 Beware that you do not lose
1173 Beware of false prophets,
10580 Beware of the man whose God
10961 Beware of those who are
11739 Beware all enterprises that

bewildered
602 victims Are equally bewildered.
2065 to the utterly bewildered.

bewitched
9805 For he's bewitched for ever

bewitchment
12705 against the bewitchment of our

bewrayed
11016 is so well bewrayed, As by his

bias
4468 minds, a bias recognized
11413 born with a bias to some

bible
215 The bible tells us to
311 page of the Bible and it's
3716 The bible should be taught
5664 used the Bible as if it
6469 Bible's the greatest book
6803 The English Bible, a book
6876 to read the Bible like an
9882 The Bible is literature,
12258 For the Bible tells me
12431 not the Bible. This,
12487 in the Bible is one of

bible-black
11674 town, starless and bible-black.

bibles
3873 had the bibles. Now they
11961 have six Bibles and no

bicker
11473 fern, To bicker down a

bickering
1831 hasty, Wi' bickering brattle!

bicycle
2671 seat Of a bicycle made for
11094 like a fish without a bicycle.
12097 can only arrive by bicycle.

bidder
12268 withstand the highest bidder.

bidding
7678 at his bidding speed And

big
1714 he was too big for them.
3960 I never use a big, big D -
9200 yourself so big. You are
11301 "I am big. It is the

big bang
8404 If the big bang does come,

big-endians
11315 Big-endians and small-endians.

big-sea-water
6490 the shining Big-Sea-Water, Stood the

bigamy
216 Bigamy is having one husband
4579 Bigamy is one way of
7743 absurd! And bigamy, Sir, is a

bigger
217 The bigger they are, the
5381 people say bigger and

bigness
5212 if some bigness is good,

bigot
4717 mind of a bigot is like
10855 a bigot, when he

bigoted
9714 he is not bigoted about it.

bigotry
2245 Bigotry may be roughly
11406 Bigotry tries to keep truth

bike
11463 got on his bike and looked

bill
6576 send the bill to you.
7103 on the back of the bill."
9790 of the Bill, which

billabong
8571 camped by a billabong, Under the

billboard
8103 never see A billboard lovely as

billet
12624 Every bullet has its billet.

billiard
3997 The billiard sharp whom any

billiards
9670 To play billiards well is a
10990 to play billiards was the

billows
8693 There solid billows of

billowy
4004 into the billowy wave, And

bills
447 she sends in terrific bills.
1962 of his weekly bills.
6048 a few bills! That's
6790 and tradesmen's bills.

billy
4264 Billy, in one of his nice
8571 till his Billy' boiled:

bind
1359 please, To bind another to
6800 Obadiah Bind-their-
11817 in the darkness bind them.
12198 temples bind; No

binds
614 which fate binds you, and

binomial
4016 About binomial theorem I'm

biographer
5552 man, the biographer must put

biographies
2082 of innumerable biographies.
11935 Biographies are but the clothes

biography
460 Biography is one of the new
1054 The Art of Biography Is
2874 nothing but biography, for that
3325 no history; only biography.
3498 Biography is history seen
6909 that all biography is
11244 the better part of biography.
12564 Judas who writes the biography.
12744 A biography is considered

biology
5816 a matter of biology, if

birch
12093 back the birch, but only

bird
1481 like a bird on the
3090 why the caged bird sings!
4674 gives every bird its food,
5923 She's a bird in gilded
6656 What bird so sings, yet so
7500 Sweet bird that shunn'st
9469 to catch a bird than a
9604 the early bird, and not
11141 bird Sings in
11421 shadow of a bird in flight.
12779 to me No bird, but an

bird-haunted
512 some wet bird-haunted English

birds
822 others - birds, wild
4974 unobservant birds Have never
5453 the lake And no birds sing!
6664 which the birds differ
7064 Unhappy birds! what does it
7407 of how the birds came home
7791 sees the birds outside
8119 are like birds - from a
8958 Birds do it, bees do it,
9150 Old birds are hard to
10375 to fear the birds of prey,
12288 Birds in their little nests

birmingham
633 hopes from Birmingham, I always
11267 came to Birmingham they

birth
1685 of his birth, he
3260 Birth, and copulation, and
5699 was at the birth of Man -
6798 With the birth of each
6959 and end, birth and death,
7813 at their birth, and not
8408 one that is coming to birth.
10446 and famous by their birth.
11020 .. in the miracle of birth.
11443 Which on my birth have
11568 breaks his birth's
11916 From birth to 18 a girl
12481 moment of birth we are
12810 Our birth is but a sleep

birth control
12298 O.K. but birth control is

birthday
2572 your wife's birthday is to
5963 Day is every man's birthday.
9629 Because the birthday of my life

birthplace
5881 of one's birthplace lingers in

births
688 As the births of living
9502 tell of the births that may

bishop
1416 The Bishop of Rome hath no
8386 the niece of a bishop.
10878 How can a bishop marry? How

bishopric
5302 should refuse a bishopric.

bit
4164 Went mad and bit the man.

bite
1789 turn and bite the hand
3878 he will bite some of
7000 backs to bite 'em. And
9133 He who can lick can bite.
9278 you can't bite, don't
11330 fleas to bite 'em, And
12287 to bark and bite, For God

bites
4289 A dead woman bites not.
5816 something bites you it is
12962 a stone, he bites a fellow

biting
4210 always biting the hand

bitter
3735 which is bitter to endure
6626 something bitter that
10083 nothing so bitter, that a
10948 exceeding bitter agony But

bitterness
11462 more than bitterness Makes the

bizarre
2689 It may be bizarre, but in my

black
2134 how well you look in black.
2274 in my path than being black.
3568 - so long as it's black.
5235 within, black as her pan
6454 are not so black as they
6802 to defend, black men fought
7193 Get black on white.
7294 That old black magic.
7995 Black is beautiful.
10834 believe in black majority
11194 Tip me the black spot.
11484 More black than ashbuds in

black hole
4792 The black hole in it is

black-eyed
3863 wind, When black-eyed Susan came

blackbird
3442 morning, Blackbird has spoken
11145 The blackbird whistling
11166 Blackbirds are the cellos of

blackburn
6225 holes in Blackburn

blacksmith
5683 Never was a blacksmith like our

blame
1025 wrong to blame Marx for
1583 take the blame for
2759 between blame and
3895 You can't blame me for
4135 Don't blame the mirror if
4282 dividing of blame. There was
7760 she is to blame, who has
7861 Oh! blame not the bard, if
7907 unfair to blame man too
8767 The blame is his who
8881 what they blame at night;
11370 is most to blame, If you
12574 When we blame ourselves

blameless
3385 we wish we had been blameless.
11498 flower of a blameless life,

blaming
5736 theirs and blaming it on you;

blancmange
5780 Of cold blancmange and

bland
4538 Bland as a Jesuit, sober as

blank
3500 at the blank sheet of
8987 left blanks in their

blanketful
9258 have more bugs than a blanketful.

blare
7212 duty is to blare like

blaspheme
6385 be permitted to blaspheme it.

blasphemies
10573 great truths begin as blasphemies.

blasphemy
10377 the soldier is flat blasphemy.

blasted
7489 blown but blasted, Soft

blaster
7048 Vile blaster of the

blaze
11728 is undistinguished blaze.

blazer
790 to make them wear a blazer.

bleak
9630 In the bleak mid-winter

bleed
5275 be fat, and then they bleed.
10399 do we not bleed? if you
10693 the thorns of life! I bleed!

bleeding
10285 me, thou bleeding piece of
10451 testament of bleeding war.

blend
11890 when to blend force with

bless
2578 him, but to bless him, and
10837 God bless the Army, bless

blessed
620 no man so blessed that some
1164 Blessed are the poor in
1230 taken away; blessed be the
3199 Blessed is the man who,
4915 that most blessed and
5521 Blessed are the pure in
10402 it is twice blessed; It

blessing
4 the simple blessing of a
692 is the blessing of the Old
883 greatest blessing of our
9471 heart is a blessing that no
11271 makes a blessing dear; It
11413 crowning blessing of life -

blessings
2556 Blessings brighten as they take
5549 For all the blessings of the
6330 to ask the blessings of heaven.
8122 'Count your blessings; you've
8479 to reap the blessings of freedom
11587 And blessings on the falling

blest
92 The bed be blest that I lie
2469 country's wishes blest!
8911 is, but always to be blest.
10568 here. Blest be the man
10633 that was blest in the

blew
1378 for him And blew his head

blind
339 judge - Too blind the
712 she be blind, yet she
892 to see if they are blind.
1497 of a blind man in a
1918 painted blind, Is to the
2437 a deaf man to a blind woman.
2713 it is the blind
3403 of the blind the
4266 Love is blind and marriage
5251 Blind Fortune still Bestows
8136 right to be blind sometimes
8640 my being blind, the good
8714 is a blind man's
9123 none so blind as those
9147 Love is blind;
9272 When a blind man carries
9365 rest, And blind doth
9936 for the blind; And
10395 Love is blind, and lovers
10699 awhile is blind, and so

blind man
9985 the strong blind man who

blinding
2499 for blinding people to

blindly
1807 lov'd sae blindly, Never

blindness
5441 triple sight in blindness keen.
5692 in 'is blindness bows down

blinds
8447 a drawing-down of blinds.

blinked
9718 the other fellow just blinked.

bliss
3269 promise of pneumatic bliss.
4161 of all my bliss, and all
5513 the highest bliss of
7478 of waking bliss I never
7485 mutual and partaken bliss.
7598 fill Of bliss on bliss.
8575 men call domestic bliss.
9886 domestic bliss; volatile
10152 and eyes, Bliss in our
10931 Isn't it bliss? Don't you
12789 Bliss was it in that dawn

blisters
9468 such little blisters That all

blithe
10707 to thee, blithe Spirit!

block
1793 of the old block', but the
3128 lookin' to block you up,
3991 on a big black block.
8835 And hew the block off, and

blockhead
5091 man but a blockhead ever
5169 Than when a blockhead's insult
8885 The bookful blockhead,

blocks
9516 God with the wrong blocks.

blonde
6893 who was blonde and

blood
1223 man's blood, by man
1303 out through blood and iron.
2198 strong wyn, reed as blood.
2297 offer but blood, toil,
2516 heart's blood dyed its
2687 And blood in torrents pour
3599 drops of blood form on
5746 gull. If blood be the
6021 us and shedde oure blood!
6995 Christ's blood streams in
7039 no getting blood out of a
8336 The best blood will
8795 I see His blood upon the

9016 foaming with much blood'.
9348 enough of blood and tears.
9609 to shed his blood for the
10360 I am in blood Stepped in so
10367 had so much blood in him?
10368 of the blood still: all
11561 When the blood creeps,
11628 The blood of the martyrs is
11645 like blood, sir, in
12958 the blood of their

bloodshed
6976 war without bloodshed while war

bloody
3854 often wipe a bloody nose.
3889 Abroad is bloody.
8324 the dark and bloody ground.
10357 with thy bloody and

bloom
872 a sort of bloom on a
2534 risk of spoiling its bloom.
4788 things in bloom Fifty
11109 deserts bloom and lakes

blooming
7865 summer Left blooming alone; All

blossom
2436 And bade it blossom there.
6925 to blossom, and to
10740 sweet, and blossom in their
10899 We blossom and flourish as
11353 and cover Blossom by blossom

blotted
5260 he never blotted out a

blow
4022 it, And blow your own
5913 prepared to blow up the
6895 you must blow against
6979 way, otherwise you blow up.
10119 Blow, blow, thou winter
10321 Blow, winds, and crack
10659 who gets his blow in fust.
11497 Blow trumpet, for the

blowing
3130 answer is blowin' in the
6100 wind is blowing the new
6774 change is blowing through

blows
349 that nobody blows good.
5874 as the wind blows out a

bludgeoning
12595 simply the bludgeoning of the

bludgeonings
4539 Under the bludgeonings of chance

blue
3518 In his blue gardens, men
10790 of childish blue,
10964 Blue, darkly, deeply,

bluebell
6058 - Mary, ma Scotch Bluebell.

bluebird
1840 There'll be bluebirds over the
11740 The bluebird carries the sky

bluebottles
2380 are like bluebottles. Some are

bluejays
6175 all the bluejays you want,

blunder
1055 At so grotesque a blunder.
1287 than with making a blunder.
1828 frae mony a blunder free us,
8210 was God's second blunder.
10798 I blunder, I bluster, I blow,

blundered
11476 one had blundered: Their's

blunders
1288 makes any blunders; when she
2336 mainly a catalogue of blunders.
2602 of Nature's agreeable blunders.
4086 man commits no minor blunders.
7912 lies between two blunders.
11440 Human blunders usually do more

blur
11230 a permanent blur in the

blurring
2308 a line without blurring it.

blushes
9676 Whoever blushes is already
11950 Animal that Blushes. Or needs

board
4560 wasn't any Board, and now

boast
7567 More unexpert, I boast not.
8423 anything to boast of but his

boasting
5735 awe - Such boasting as the

boat
2749 Voyages in a paper boat.
11722 a man a boat he can
12816 a little Boat, Shaped

boathook
9841 diplomatic boathook to avoid

boats
4272 messing about in boats.
6158 When boats or ships came
10177 in some boats that are

bobby
5559 with giving Bobby a little

bodies
253 it had worn out two bodies.
1071 all those bodies which
5872 our minds than in our bodies.
6781 are three bodies no
8183 changing of bodies into
9857 Pile the bodies high at
10011 our dead bodies must tell
11220 of our bodies is the

body
920 use of my body I would
1419 commit his body to the
1440 with my body I thee
1814 Gin a body meet a body
2457 whole, Its body brevity,
2474 Body and mind, like man
2581 The human body experiences
2584 My body has certainly
3280 I have the body of a weak
4268 The body never lies.
4689 long as the body is
5028 strength of the human body.
5369 sound mind in a sound body.
7301 nothing the body suffers
7669 though her body die, her
8036 one human body for
8184 Every body continues in
8356 Africa than my own body.
8357 with his body, his mind
8896 Whose body, Nature
9077 is salutary to the body.
9674 treated than the body.
9867 control her body. No woman
11068 exercise is to the body.
11631 seen his body borne
11791 and no body to be
12048 of the rest of her body.
12502 I sing the body electric.

bognor
3885 Bugger Bognor.

bogs
6434 only from bogs and

bogus
6784 mammon than a bogus god.

bohemians
12421 of 'sloppy Bohemians' and their

boil
3310 be only to boil an egg.
11442 War That Would Not Boil.

boiling
3999 with boiling oil in it,
11249 of boiling oil,

bold
3710 got to be bold. Brave
11305 He was a bold man that
11622 Fortune favours the bold.
12130 Fortune assists the bold.

boldly
6065 tells it boldly and has
9535 .. to boldly go where

boldness
4731 A decent boldness ever meets
9057 fail, boldness at least

bollocks
8585 talking complete bollocks.

bolshevism
10905 It is Bolshevism run mad.

bomb
6211 going to bomb them back
6972 The atom bomb is a paper
8002 Ban the Bomb.

bombed
821 from being bombed. Whatever
3287 we've been bombed. It makes

bombs
1102 friendly bombs, and fall
2382 as effectively as by bombs.
7955 nor even bombs redoubled

bon-mots
7873 By plucking bon-mots from their

bonaparte
11769 which Bonaparte thought

bond
357 the lonely, bond of the
10398 Let him look to his bond.

bondage
2351 We are in bondage to the law
12733 A slavish bondage to parents

bonds
6437 puts on the bonds of civil
7239 Gentlemen prefer bonds.
10554 My bonds in thee

bone
1218 This is now bone of my
1265 hope of retaining his bone.
6708 it hardens into bone.
7628 of flesh. Bone of my bone
8092 I have a bone to pick with

bones
7674 honoured bones, The
8274 Rattle his bones over the
10307 and England keep my bones!
10486 Of his bones are coral
10568 be he that moves my bones.
10799 but the length of my bones.
10877 flesh and sit in my bones.
12024 are the bones on which
12734 to lay my bones amongst

bonfire
12726 The bonfire of the vanities.

bonnet
8962 a Bendel bonnet, A

bonnie
6060 On the bonnie banks o'

bonsoir
12422 the sky-ee! Bonsoir, old

bonuses
9476 don't earn bonuses without

book
218 Book lovers never go to
1115 when he can read the book?
1442 of the book world. A
1688 Making a book is a craft,
2017 A great book is like great
2089 A good book is the purest
2111 use of a book' thought
2524 to know a person or a book.
2654 A good book has no ending.
2865 like a new book. I prefer
3381 that makes the good book.
3724 ever invented is the book.
4551 square book! Always
5016 more read a book alone, if
5078 in his book, I assure
5258 his picture, but his book.
5267 been at my book, and am
5523 There is a book, who runs
5770 of a book directly;
5930 afterwards - over a book.
6095 one bright book of life.
6765 successful book cannot
6848 It was a book to kill time
7458 kill a good book: who kills
8278 that a good book is

8654 seen books hurt
8996 a deep book until he
8997 alive. The book should be
9071 with a favourite book.
9095 A book is like a garden
9421 a single book, or in
9722 If a book is worth
9969 Any book which is at all
10336 bred in a book; he hath
10884 read a book before
10895 would make a great book.
11121 out of this book for
11047 An empty book is like an
11918 A good book is the best of
12494 dirtiest book of all is
12500 this is no book, Who
12604 The Book of Life begins
12725 writes a book is to
12751 leaves of a book known to
12754 for my next book, I am
12913 down this book And slowly

book-keepers
4367 to produce clerks and book-keepers.

bookie
8022 image of a bookie or of a

bookkeeping
8029 entry bookkeeping, but he

books
88 of good books, the point
578 Some books are undeservedly
690 Some books are to be
700 Books will speak plain when
763 Books must follow sciences,
857 Books say: she did this
1719 Laws die, books never.
1722 Master books, but do not
1871 Books should be tried by a
1892 The oldest books are still
2100 is a collection of books.
2304 man to read books of
2566 producing books which no
2867 his own books is almost
3535 Books are made not like
3609 Never lend books - nobody
3702 but uncommon in books.
3852 toil O'er books consumed
4435 Books give not wisdom where
4507 Wherever books will be
4525 of certain books is to
4596 Do give books - religious
4707 of the hundred best books.
4808 find your books wearing
4894 study of mankind is books.
5942 of books - those
5950 Books think for me.
6045 Get stewed: Books are a load
6556 All books are either dreams
6714 walls of books around
7457 Books are not absolutely
7648 in books and
7815 of writing books and being
7864 My only books Were woman's
8999 the right books. I had
9004 Books do furnish a room.
9595 Books can not be killed by
9673 I hate books; they teach us
9733 All books are divisible
9736 other's books out of
10875 so charming as books.
11965 read good books has no
12389 up in books! An ounce
12586 book. Books are well
12755 how many books are

booksellers
4763 nor even booksellers have put

bookshops
1026 Bookshops are the one

bookstore
947 so weak as in the bookstore?

boomerang
10838 it is the boomerang he finds

boot
8382 imagine a boot stamping
8755 The boot in the

booted
7774 be ever booted and

booth
6384 Booth died blind and still

boots
1714 without any boots it was
3953 who cleans the boots.
4558 in his boots; For
5688 Africa - Boots - boots -
9253 The Devil's boots don't
9461 doormat in a world of boots.

booze
3454 fool with booze until he's

bore
3346 becomes a bore at last.
4286 A bore is a man who
4987 always bore his wife.
5762 Now when I bore people at
5868 those who bore us, but
7253 but that it is a bore.
8026 not only a bore; he bored
8230 for us to bore ourselves?
10893 a greater bore than ever;
11449 A bore is a man who, when
11855 is an old bore. Even the
12008 male adult bore consumes
12150 of being a bore .. is to

bored
4665 people are bored, it is
5051 I know that I am bored.
5778 and indefinitely bored.
7419 is that bored look on
12300 Is the virtue of the bored.

boredom
1465 inexorable boredom that is at
2176 Passion goes, boredom remains.
2579 disease is boredom - costly
3530 they keep boredom at bay and
4594 Boredom turns a man to sex, a
4947 effect of boredom on a large
6039 is first boredom, then
7205 us from boredom, sharpen
9755 Boredom is .. a vital
10097 Boredom provides a stronger
11059 between boredom and
11090 by boredom. Avoiding
11796 Boredom is rage spread thin.

boredom-killing
2211 We're in the boredom-killing business.

bores
6867 material of the great bores.

boring
194 It's a very boring time. I am
4646 ever have a boring dream?

born
125 has yet to be born.
227 are Tories born wicked, or
546 that we are born to eternal
705 as to be born; and to a
1233 Man is born unto trouble,
1330 Some are born to sweet
1386 "I was born when you
1443 Some are born great, some
1512 the artist can be born.
1924 patriots born? To hunt,
2903 is a being born to
3060 lives is born to die,
3141 it is to be born a woman!
3356 until he is born.
3861 tho' I was born and bred
3880 Born and educated in this
4740 where I was born, The
5910 thus was I born again in
6575 No man is born into the
6598 God was born too late
7766 I was born below par to
8221 some are born
8553 Man is born to live, not
9410 have themselves been born.
9529 I was born into it and
9819 live is to be slowly born.
9906 time we are born until the
10201 ever I was born to set it
10331 When we are born we cry
10364 of woman born Shall harm
10517 men are born great,
10794 Is not born, And does
10995 Born of the sun they

11040 Born down in a dead man's
11240 'Never was born!'
11246 have been born to set it
11413 - to be born with a
11499 - Else, wherefore born?
11550 But I was born to other
11612 Every moment one is born.
11962 only be born at the age
12238 no man is born an artist,
12276 When I was born I did
12317 I was born an American; I
12460 was born at the
12485 a babe was born in a
12903 Bethlehem to be born?

borne
4048 have been borne down in a
10866 him as a Cross to be Borne.
12115 who have borne even

borrow
1252 enough to borrow from, but
5941 the men who borrow, and the
9428 cost and you borrow on value.
12246 we have to borrer the money
12686 I have, but all I can borrow.

borrower
3353 man is a borrower and a
10195 Neither a borrower, nor a

borrowing
11925 Who goeth a borrowing Goeth

bosom
10863 She has no bosom and no

boss
7024 boss there is always a

bossing
8388 and nobody bossing you about.

bossy
10061 busy by the bossy for the

boston
220 Boston lady, when
450 A Boston man is the east
1464 is good old Boston, The home
11984 before a Boston audience -

botanize
12820 peep and botanize Upon his

bother
3960 Though Bother it' I may

botticelli
9289 Botticelli isn't a wine, you
12016 If Botticelli were alive today

bottle
898 is a bottle of wine, a
6735 to the bottle, than the
9141 put Paris into a bottle.
11193 and a bottle of rum!

bottles
562 into old bottles without
8317 in sealed bottles of regret.
8931 bottles: the less

bottom
4261 will reach the bottom first?'
9909 and your bottom will
12853 I am from the bottom up.

bough
4787 along the bough, And
10553 Upon those boughs which

bought
2023 when he is bought will stay

bound
11603 as a man is bound to do.

boundary
8525 to fix the boundary of the

bounty
10477 My bounty is as boundless as

bouquet
8976 that the bouquet is better

bourgeois
277 last resort of the bourgeois.
3535 and the bourgeois climb up
3537 life like a bourgeois, so that
4748 Bourgeois .. is an epithet
6077 beastly the bourgeois is
7116 of the old bourgeois society,
8385 A person of bourgeois origin
9441 Les bourgeois, ce sont les

bourgeoisie
10794 The British Bourgeoisie Is not
11888 The bourgeoisie in the

bow
1349 Bring me my bow of burning
3970 Bow, bow, ye lower middle

bow-shot
11521 A bow-shot from her

bow-wow
8616 it not for his bow-wow way.

bowed
6986 Bowed by the weight of

bowels
2646 you, in the bowels of Christ,

bowler
6007 If the wild bowler thinks he

boxes
9456 Little boxes on the

boy
219 One boy's a boy, two boys
2590 about the boy, It's
4228 Pardon me boy is that the
4526 The boy stood on the
8179 only like a boy playing on
8652 "A boy's best friend is
9662 boy, and will
9686 beauty and a boy forever.
10010 Make the boy interested
11147 any boy may become
11940 a story for boys is to
12355 set any boy ever had!

boy friend
12666 thing called the Boy Friend.

boys
2342 Boys are the cash of war.
5938 Boys are capital fellows
6455 what the boys in the
8659 We are the boys who will
8762 Boys should abstain from
9593 again: Your boys are not
11678 The boys are dreaming
12310 are the boys of the old

brace
2302 therefore brace ourselves

bracelet
5341 out of a bracelet if you

braces
1345 Damn braces: Bless relaxes.

braids
7487 In twisted braids of lilies

brain
160 My Brain? It's my second
535 of lightning in the brain.
2990 his little brain attic
3171 his own brain too little
3405 and the brain will
3975 they've a brain and
4537 is in my brain Lately
5233 and a good brain may do:
7449 exactly got Brain, but he
7450 Very Little Brain and long
8694 messages from the brain.
8781 The brain is the citadel of
8828 A brain of feathers, and a

brains
539 his brains go to his
3711 It takes brains to see the
4043 you can do without brains.
6522 a girl with brains ought to
7411 And new eras in their brains.
8348 mix them with my brains, sir.
9114 more than a bushel of brains.
11181 man who has brains enough to
12686 use all the brains I have,
12708 the husbands having brains.

brainwork
9640 fundamental brainwork, is what

branch
4853 grow on a branch that is
4998 A branch of the sin of
5416 tree Thy branches ne'er
7000 Cut is the branch that might

branchy
4756 city and branchy between

brandished
6887 to exist but is not brandished.

brandy
3882 get me a glass of brandy.
5099 (smiling) must drink brandy.
5731 the dark- Brandy for the
5969 drink cold brandy and water.

brassiere
856 is not a brassiere. At

brave
1710 this is the brave and happy
2378 as a brave bad man.
2469 sleep the brave, who sink
3031 but the brave deserves
3710 got to be brave and you've
5597 and the home of the brave.
5833 I am a brave fellow;
8404 any good, brave causes
9233 Many become brave when
10491 is! O brave new world,

bravely
5764 your duty bravely. Fear

bravery
2181 deal of the bravery that
5586 than bravery in battle
11774 and bravery. It does
12462 with bravery and mercy.

braw
6061 say It's a braw brecht

brawling
1245 than with a brawling woman in a

brazil
11661 aunt from Brazil - where

breach
10196 in the breach than the
10256 unto the breach, dear

bread
204 trees were bread and cheese
2575 Eat bread at pleasure,
4572 is the poor man's bread.
4743 God! that bread should be
5368 circenses. Bread and the
6005 don't give bread with one
6521 his daily bread and
6734 a piece of bread and butter
7131 the holy bread By which
7442 The Royal slice of bread?'
9103 a loaf of bread with one,
9151 Whose bread I eat, his song
11333 fare; bread and

breadth
3417 is length without breadth.

breadwinner
10866 for a breadwinner and a

break
1040 on the shoe, but not break.
3125 sigh, and then they break.
3488 give a sucker an even break.
5849 I bend and I break not.
8337 but you can break your neck
9834 and then I break them right
10191 good; But break, my heart,
10583 of that to break a man's

breakdown
5914 not be all breakdown. It may
9756 nervous breakdown is the

breakfast
752 is a good breakfast, but it is
4359 on a leisurely breakfast.
6379 to have breakfast alone with

breakfast-time
4562 in matrimony is breakfast-time.

breaking
7869 cause, By breaking of

breaks
631 every party breaks up the
6789 twangs and breaks at the end
8856 Who breaks a butterfly upon
9135 wears out; everything breaks.
9189 his back and breaks his nose.
11568 Who breaks his birth's

breast
505 beats in every human breast.
4097 dwell, alas! in my breast.

8844 left aching in the breast.
9239 keep the breast for
10170 baby at my breast, That
10850 padded cell of his breast.

breast-beaters
1586 amuse the breast-beaters. By the

breastfeeding
6277 As a breastfeeding mother you are

breastplate
10267 stronger breastplate than a

breasts
5339 feel my breasts all
9447 the feel of breasts and
11279 are the two breasts by which

breath
3544 it use your breath, There is
4150 may fade; A breath can make
4292 fleeting breath? Can
5414 breath, And so
6590 each saving breath takes
8847 my last breath, and catch
9643 self, with low last breath.
12749 than the breath of a cow.

breathe
373 students to breathe for one
5636 Nothing to breathe but air,
7622 morn to breathe Among the
7862 Oh! breathe not his name, let
8940 lapdogs breathe their
11608 though to breathe were life.

breathed
1942 blast, And breathed in the

breathes
10027 Breathes there the man, with
11607 life that breathes with human

breathing
1582 England's, breathing English
10701 In the sound his breathing kept.
11493 is He than breathing, and

breathless
12037 as a nun Breathless with

breed
3864 and a wife for breed.
5755 the best ye breed - Go, bind
7523 but endless war still breed?
8631 of the breed of their
10446 This happy breed of men,

breeding
3479 of gaiety and good breeding.
6983 for people with no breeding.
9309 with good breeding? With some
10654 of woman's breeding is how
10719 show your breeding, But easy
11786 without any breeding, but I
11845 our planned breeding of our
11970 Good breeding consists in

breeze
11570 with the breeze of song To

breezes
11519 Little breezes dusk and

breezy
3293 Droppy, Breezy, Sneezy,

brethren
3888 among their brethren across the

brevity
2215 Brevity is the sister of
10202 Brevity is the soul of wit.

brewery
256 me to a brewery And leave

bribe
4985 more often bribed by their
12612 is a bribe to make a
12720 hope to bribe or twist,

bribery
12958 or through bribery or

bribing
9434 is good for bribing yourself

brick
6129 like half a brick, is always
8386 throw a brick without
9580 place two bricks
11274 found it brick and left
11311 a piece of brick in his

bride
278 day for the bride as she
5488 unravished bride of
6203 always the bridesmaid,
6701 Can ser' him for a bride!
8863 but a barren bride.
12786 glittering bride, And airy

bridesmaid
6203 always the bridesmaid, Never the

bridge
993 and Bridge) Broke -
1099 through the bridge? And
5618 to build a bridge even when
6474 on the bridge at
6840 And keep the bridge with me?
6845 kept the bridge In the
10768 Like a bridge over troubled
11775 to build a bridge to the

bridle
9204 Shake a bridle over a
9269 you an ass, put on a bridle.

brief
9769 Brief and Powerless is
11597 O tell her, brief is life

briefcase
9320 with his briefcase can steal

briers
10111 how full of briers is this

brigade
12310 of the old Brigade, Who

brigands
1868 Brigands demand your money or

bright
128 All things bright and
282 are what makes a man bright.
1362 burning bright, In the
1712 lady named Bright, Whose
2413 look, the land is bright.
9585 Her colour, bright as yours

brighten
2330 Blessings brighten as they

brightness
1550 brightness Of the
11000 will Leaking the brightness away.

brilliance
7946 No brilliance is needed in the

brilliant
545 He has a brilliant mind until

brillig
2120 'Twas brillig, and the slithy

brimstone
10959 From his brimstone bed, at

bring
3759 a day may bring, a day may

bring up
1280 To bring up a child in the way
8680 best way to bring up some

bringer
1650 bringer of the

bringing
592 the Border, Bringing the cheque

brings
8953 Beguine It brings back the

brinkmanship
11152 of his brinkmanship - the art

britain
10 Great Britain has lost an
494 Britain's best bulwarks are
2338 that Britain would
4438 Britain will be honoured by
6415 To make Britain a fit
7977 Keep Britain Tidy.
8007 I'm backing Britain.
10927 Hail, happy Britain! highly

britannia
10897 than Beer and Britannia?

british
562 I think the British have the
855 who aren't British - as they
1461 by the British than these
2148 The British love permanence
2886 of the British Empire to
3792 rude as the British, which

3892 alarm, The British Museum had
5633 is the British tourist.
6126 The British are terribly lazy
6818 as the British public in
7343 The British are just as keen
10591 The British soldier can stand
11465 taught that British history in
11736 so long the British people no

briton
3880 glory in the name of Briton.

britons
10062 , since the Britons were only
11723 the waves; Britons never will

broadminded
3697 a man too broadminded to take

broke
993 and Bridge) Broke - and
5696 - for you broke a British
5979 If it ain't broke, don't fix
6445 Peter, Who broke the laws
7273 ever went broke

broken
1581 Naught broken save this
3442 Morning has broken Like the
5136 are too strong to be broken.
8284 Laws were made to be broken.
11332 are made to be broken.
12676 I am a broken machine. I am
12885 And I am broken by their

broken-hearted
1807 We had ne'er been broken-hearted.
4470 There's a broken-hearted woman

broker
12762 A broker is a man who takes

bronchitis
105 unless he or she has bronchitis.

bronx
2488 town, The Bronx is up but

brood
9356 Don't brood on what's past.
12822 eye That broods and

brooding
3220 is always brooding on a
11089 is the brooding of the

brook
6495 Where the brook and river

brothel
5790 brothel for

brothels
1343 of Law, brothels with

brother
313 it been his brother, Still
994 Strong brother in God and
1419 of our dear brother here
4189 Still to my brother turns with
4418 Brother can you spare a dime?
4844 I am the darker brother.
5741 more close than a brother.
6207 so like my brother That folks
6704 away our brother that we
6986 stunned, a brother to the ox?
7091 far have him than his brother.
8378 BIG BROTHER IS WATCHING YOU.
9249 your own brother - believe,
9524 thou elder brother even to
10817 Though our brother is on the
12339 Am I not a man and a brother.
12515 O brother man! fold to thy

brother-in-law
5652 brother, not his brother-in-law.

brotherhood
5066 has broadened into a brotherhood.
5642 table of brotherhood .. I have
5913 The brotherhood of man is evoked
7982 Freedom! Equality! Brotherhood!

brothers
4076 they are brothers, by
5645 together as brothers or perish
9955 men become brothers under your
12827 We were brothers all In
12958 the blood of their brothers.

brought
1191 For we brought nothing into

brow
10034 wring the brow, A
11012 shadow of her even brows.

brown
6657 you are in some brown study.
11679 salt and brown, like two

bruise
11875 tread on it and bruise it.

brush
6672 scrub with a hard brush.
9445 with my brush, that I

brushers
12767 are like brushers of

brushstrokes
7689 from the brushstrokes as a poem

brutal
11382 it must learn to be brutal.
11780 theirs is brutal, ours is

brutally
8120 who are brutally honest get
11733 I'm frank, brutally frank.

brute
4186 such a cross-grained brute?
5750 out, the brute!' But it's
6147 a regular brute of a bee!'
8755 face, the brute Brute

brutes
4173 Brutes never meet in bloody
7302 we to the brutes, poets are
8583 latter become uncouth brutes.

brutus
2005 tu, Brute? You too, Brutus?
10290 to me: But Brutus says he

bubble
1598 to tattoo soap bubbles.
3032 Honour but an empty bubble.
8892 And now a bubble burst, and
10362 a hell-broth boil and bubble.
12250 like unto a bubble; Woman and

buck
226 A bigger bang for a buck.
372 The buck stops here.

bucket
1226 a drop of a bucket, and are
9863 past is a bucket of ashes.

buckingham
7439 guard at Buckingham Palace -

buckle
678 reason doth buckle and bow

bud
2436 The opening bud to Heaven
5430 shut, and be a bud again.

buddhism
9826 or Buddhism that quite

buds
6943 grass. The buds will go on
8515 the rose, Buds the new,
10160 That kneeled unto the buds.
10545 the darling buds of May,

buffoon
3026 statesman, and buffoon.

bug
3629 snug As a bug In as rug.
8857 flap this bug with

bugles
1570 out, you bugles, over the
8446 shells; And bugles calling

bugs
1022 all the bugs off a
9258 have more bugs than a

build
1590 Men build bridges and throw
6664 they can build and yet
7064 it boot To build below the
7776 life is to build the house
9428 You build on cost and you
9737 When we build, let us think
10918 One can build the Empire

builder
9729 he can only be a builder .

building
3456 A building is a string of

6027 of the building does not
9605 for the building of plans

buildings
2330 shape our buildings;
11660 Buildings should be good

builds
186 what she builds in a man's
1358 ease, And builds a Heaven
3354 A man builds a fine house;
6860 'He who builds on the

built
663 I have built her up.
1247 a house is built and
3464 what they built. It is
6146 Have all built their
7564 now To have built in heaven

bulb
12633 naked light bulb, any more

bull
9245 A bull does not enjoy fame

bullet
3364 use of the bullet seems to
8080 The bullet that is to kill
12624 Every bullet has its billet.

bullets
6350 not bloody bullets, but
8307 it with bullets: you

bullied
11283 virtue than bullied out of

bullshit
3097 silence: The bullshit stops.

bully
4902 to bully and cheat.
10061 by the bossy for the bully.

bulwark
494 best bulwarks are her
1314 floating bulwark of the

bump
269 that go bump in the

bumpy
2706 going to be a bumpy night."

bums
6314 of shabby bums living in

bunch
7794 made up a bunch of other

bungled
8789 Out of that bungled, unwise

bunk
3571 is more or less bunk.

burden
1134 shall bear his own burden.
3148 the heavy burden of
3815 the burden of
5641 too big a burden to bear.
6986 back the burden of the
8263 carry that burden for the
9045 The public burden of the
11419 The burden is equal to the
12174 a heavy burden is a name

burdensome
9146 is so burdensome as a

bureaucracy
833 Bureaucracy is a giant mechanism
6680 Bureaucracy, the rule of no one,

burglar
4622 a burglar busily at

burglary
3102 embezzlement an' burglary.

burgled
438 is never burgled, and the

burgundy
11786 domestic burgundy without

burial
4700 of the burial service

burial-ground
6489 calls The burial-ground

buried
534 should have buried the
2485 and the other to be buried.
5744 Who was buried in snow to
6827 generations lie buried.
12718 We buried him darkly at dead

burke
2079 Burke said there were three

burn
6999 I'll burn my books!
7998 Burn, Baby, Burn.
8570 To burn always with this
12785 summer dust Burn to the
12904 Troy for her to burn?
12921 In order to burn more

burned
990 and the House, were Burned.
4507 will be burned, men also,

burning
1001 A smell of burning fills the
4526 on the burning deck
4632 Is Paris burning?
5491 cloyed, A burning forehead,
9371 mind ever burning: Never

burnished
10155 in, like a burnished throne,

burns
10527 Not she which burns in 't.

burnt
4216 have ever burnt in my life
10867 Ages And be burnt at the

burps
858 just burps, and we

burr
10383 a kind of burr; I shall

burst
513 what a burst! What

bury
1021 You may bury my body in
1175 the dead bury their
4582 peace, sons bury their
5605 banknotes, bury them at
6502 dead Past bury its dead!
8149 and bury the dead.'
10289 I come to bury Caesar,
10490 my staff, Bury it certain

bus
4071 be a Motor Bus? Yes, the
8404 in front of a bus.

buses
11264 time in the buses with

busiest
9265 often the busiest day of the

business
22 over, and Business is
78 had attended business college.
634 Business, you know, may bring
716 fame, and servants of business.
774 Business is really more
914 Business is more exciting than
1003 It is the business of the
1075 There's no business like show
2075 not in the business of
2147 in the language of business.
2227 no business can be
2230 quality for business; many a
2550 The chief business of the
2813 is, to make business for
3017 successful business, someone
3088 Business? It's quite simple.
3194 All business proceeds on
3455 clean, quite solvent business.
4144 going into business for any
4424 The business of the poet and
4508 pardon me. It's his business.
4543 to do with it is a business.
6336 Big business is basic to the
6806 The business of everybody is
7196 Business is a combination of
7224 succeed in business without
8338 secret of business is to know
8421 No praying, it spoils business.
8637 to, whatever my business is.
8927 A man of business may talk of
10039 A dinner lubricates business.
10162 To business that we love we
10617 a woman's business to get
11282 his chief business in life is
11318 to do more business after
11640 Business first; pleasure
11760 than this incessant business.

12075 All business sagacity reduces
12860 two men in business always
12867 Go to your business, I say,

businessman
4203 is no businessman - all he
12031 A businessman is a hybrid of a

bustle
10081 Love of bustle is not

busy
548 knowest how busy I must be
3451 usually too busy to wonder
3612 While I am busy with
4830 can look so busy doing
7036 the world to keep busy at.
7519 And the busy hum of
7536 thoughts so busy keep.
8439 be busy, and you
10061 of the busy by the
10791 I am too busy thinking
10798 the other. Busy, busy, and
11173 Keep busy at something. A
12736 as quickly as the busy one.

busyness
11179 Extreme busyness, whether at

but
941 qualifies it with a but'.
8076 I still love you, but ..

butchers
10285 with these butchers; Thou art
10836 fills the butchers' shops
12167 both shepherds and butchers.

butler
12709 The butler entered the room,

butlers
988 my opinion, Butlers ought To
7165 hope to find in their butlers.

butt
4146 with the butt end of it.

butter
4077 without butter but not,
4078 We have no butter, but I
7442 have some butter for The
9240 water, in butter and in
9553 ladling butter from
11631 on cutting bread and butter.

buttercup
3958 Little Buttercup - dear

buttered
8586 always on the buttered side.

butterfly
137 like a butterfly, sting
4329 what's a butterfly? At best,
8856 breaks a butterfly upon a

buttocks
4913 gorgeous buttocks of the ape
9447 breasts and buttocks is saved,

button
3592 can press a button to get
6151 care a button! We don't
6554 By each button, hook, and

buttons
844 to sew buttons on a
1590 don't have to sew buttons.
5691 of his buttons off an'

buttress
7237 as a buttress of the

buxom
7521 So buxom, blithe, and

buy
5341 you have to buy it
5583 Don't buy a single vote
6469 I can buy for six
8288 I shall buy it like an
9110 When you buy, use your
9246 Don't buy the house; buy
9989 Buy me and you will

buying
6167 dinner only if he is buying.
8441 is always buying something.
9722 reading, it is worth buying.
11926 stroke, For buying or selling

buys
413 Who buys has need of two
10538 Who buys a minute's mirth

buzzing
1639 What is he buzzing in my

by-product
2383 It is a by-product of

bymatter
701 as if it had been a bymatter.

byron
6819 of Lord Byron they drew

bystanders
3367 but the bystanders are

cabbage
2121 wax - Of cabbages - and
11976 nothing but cabbage with a

cabined
10358 Now I am cabined, cribbed,

cabinet
537 mislead the Cabinet, and the
779 A cabinet is a combining

cabots
1464 talk to the Cabots And the

cactus
5061 between a cactus and a

cadiz bay
1652 reeking into Cadiz Bay.

caesar
281 Hail Caesar, those who are
291 Like Caesar's wife, all
1186 unto Caesar the things
1456 Caesar or nothing.
2007 Caesar's wife must be above
6612 Caesar lives after his
10281 Brute? Then fall, Caesar!
10284 O mighty Caesar! dost thou
12054 Caesar had perished from the

caftan
11135 of Azcan in caftan Of tan

cage
1326 breast in a cage Puts all
5923 a bird in gilded cage.
6794 We cannot cage the minute
7791 is like a cage; one sees
11559 within the cage, That
12636 the same cage, that's

caged
3090 why the caged bird

cain
6119 to the cruel sons of Cain.

cajolery
1110 amount of cajolery, and no

cake
542 lies to ice a wedding cake.
6984 Let them eat cake.
10513 be no more cakes and ale?

calais
7118 shall find Calais' lying in

calamities
5076 Among the calamities of wars may

calculation
5898 weakness than through calculation.

calculator
12031 of a dancer and a calculator.

calculus
4015 calculus, I know

california
2062 In California everyone goes to a

call
113 must needs call the tune
517 for they call you,
5571 - not as a call to bear
7136 for the call of the
8148 Call him on the deep sea,
9041 the call; But had
9847 as Call Me God')

called
11790 Well, if I called the wrong
11851 I am also called Played-out

calling
2502 Each honest calling, each walk
4710 Every calling is great when

callisthenics
8513 is simply callisthenics with

calm
18 the still calm of life,
2072 sweeter than a calm estate.
2509 sense, and calm the
4775 remember to keep calm.
7672 And calm of mind, all
8228 with it a calm passage is
8488 is to calm, rather
8510 of the calm that know
8585 to remain calm when
9214 because the water is calm.
9818 with the calm of a tree.
12763 flying into a great calm.

calmly
9589 life more calmly. You know

calories
1019 The extra calories needed for

calumnies
5268 Calumnies are answered best

calumny
2442 with calumny, there
2857 Calumny is only the noise of
4475 Calumny requires no proof.
12271 is the best answer to calumny.

calvinistic
7240 That Calvinistic sense of innate
8738 We have a Calvinistic creed, a

cambridge
770 than Cambridge to the
1578 For Cambridge people rarely
11852 loyalty; To Cambridge books, as

came
2006 vici I came, I saw, I
8458 I came, I saw, I

camel
222 A camel is a horse designed
6851 'Take my camel, dear,' said

camelot
6252 That was known as Camelot.
11522 down to Camelot. Out flew

camera
557 of the camera is not the
10933 The camera makes everyone a
12354 unless the camera is an eye

camping
2800 New York you are camping out.

campus
5590 on a campus are sex

can
9607 Do what you can, with what
10620 He who can, does. He who
12125 They can because they

can't
4942 think you can't, So don't
6201 he wrote - Can't get away
6316 It can't happen here.
12134 We can't all do everything.

can't-help-it
6076 And the holy can't-help-it touch.

canada
1475 Canada has no cultural
3728 day graduate from Canada.
5408 Canada reminds me of
9094 Love Canada or give it back.
11894 Canada is not a country for

canadian
3717 a Canadian is an
9473 remained a Canadian. I puffed

canalettos
6771 saloon. Then the Canalettos go.

canaries
8085 The song of canaries Never

cancel
10357 hand, Cancel and tear

cancer
1 ideology of the cancer cell.
8155 someone else has cancer.
10770 Silence like a cancer grows.'

candid
8890 we must, be candid where we

candle
121 of even one small candle.
1850 is to set a candle in the

6054 such a candle by God's
7387 My candle burns at both
10303 book, and candle shall not
10373 out, brief candle! Life's
10407 that little candle throws his
10751 to light a candle to the
11156 light a candle than curse
11823 The candle by which she had
12935 farthing candle to the

candles
9107 even though he sells candles.

candour
11400 Candour and generosity,

candy
8100 Candy Is dandy But liquor

canker
7048 Foul canker of fair virtuous

cannibal
6171 if a cannibal uses knife
7246 a sober cannibal than a

cannibals
10857 of us are cannibals who have

cannon
1413 that precede cannon shots.
11476 hundred. Cannon to right

canoe
7043 man paddle his own canoe.
7066 their heads in their canoes.

canopy
10543 heat did canopy the herd,

cans
4343 Barrie's cans as he went

cants
11125 Of all the cants which are

capable
181 who are capable of
1407 many really capable men are
4087 I do not deem myself capable.
6492 we feel capable of doing,

capacities
3828 my activities, my capacities.

capital
2997 It is a capital mistake to
6988 say it is a capital offence.
7058 Capital is past savings
7565 the high capital Of Satan
10007 sufficient capital to form a
10668 that high Capital, where

capitalism
1501 thing about capitalism -
2150 fan of capitalism. But I am
3669 least harm; capitalism is that
4406 of capitalism .. the
4503 unacceptable face of capitalism.
6216 the monopoly stage of capitalism.
11236 War is capitalism with the
12314 and the spirit of capitalism.

capitalist
5614 About the capitalist States, it
6773 fall of the capitalist system and
8124 forces of a capitalist society,
8588 democratic capitalist society

capitulate
5123 conquered; I will not capitulate.

captain
2096 Captains of industry.
3919 The captain of the Hampshire
4540 I am the captain of my
8133 no captain can do
8151 But his Captain's hand on
9013 a ship's captain
10377 That in the captain's but a
11638 nobody like the Capting.

captive
5755 To serve your captives' need.

car
2725 power of a car is
2726 the first motor car.
6313 His motor car was poetry
6768 The car has become an
7406 The car, the furniture,
7473 the gilded car of day His
8691 opens the car door for

carborundum
345 Nil carborundum illegitimi (Cod

carbuncle
2191 A monstrous carbuncle on the
10994 Monstrous carbuncles of

carcase
11702 the carcase of an old

card game
3102 idee in a card game is war -

cards
5931 not play at cards, but only
6655 played At cards for
12184 all your cards on the

care
776 at least - care fifty
1324 better care of myself.
1358 hath any care; But for
1702 everybody cared enough,
1895 People care more about
3060 for things beyond our care.
3223 Teach us to care and not to
6603 Take care of the pence,
6693 nice woman, for I do care.
7440 Took great Care of his
7697 I could care what you
7828 If I take care of my
8547 Not to care for philosophy
8723 Care to our coffin adds a
9751 One must care about a
10251 I care not; a man can die
10599 God will take care of that.
12117 learning to care for the
12250 is full of care, much like
12689 will take care of itself.

career
247 in his long career which
2759 prodigious career, judgement
2916 ideal of a manly career.
3634 the same career of life.
6852 and need career no
10611 to a political career.
11252 Conductors' careers are made

careers
9008 political careers end in

careful
2658 more careful than of
8621 more careful of the
11579 So careful of the type she
12588 be too careful in the

carefully
3962 handle so carefullee That now I

careless
2256 be a little careless of his
3520 They were careless people, Tom
11538 together, careless of
11579 seems, So careless of the

carelessness
12556 lose both looks like carelessness.

cares
4318 kings have cares that wait
6479 The cares that infest the

caressed
2751 to; they should be caressed.

cargo
5296 when their cargo is light.
5716 the little cargo boats that
7128 With a cargo of Tyne

caricature
2535 Caricature: putting the face of
4002 la, With a caricature of a face.
7296 Caricature is rough truth.

carlyle
1883 God to let Carlyle and Mrs

carnegie
6279 that has played Carnegie Hall.

carpenter
5008 unlearned carpenter of my
9402 a good carpenter to build

carpet
5432 the long carpets rose
9379 for carpet bags And

carriage
2671 afford a carriage, But
2835 me - The Carriage held but

3979 small second class carriage.
6249 is that his carriage has not
9250 Gossip needs no carriage.

carrion
3824 The carrion crow, that

carry
341 for to carry me home; I
1481 cry; Carry the lad
3360 points to carry, she
3382 we must carry it with us
5172 A man must carry knowledge
8594 meeter To carry off the
11831 making him carry me, and

cars
880 think that cars today are
6599 finned cars nose

cart
6177 carrier's cart at the age

carve
10279 Let's carve him as a dish
12197 seek Must carve in Latin

carved
12719 We carved not a line, and we

case
613 spoken; the case is
4001 to do with the case.
7290 A suitable case for

cash
3507 take the cash in hand
10748 from hand to hand of cash.
11916 55 on, she needs good cash.

casket
5515 the hushèd casket of my

cassowary
12528 If I were a cassowary On the

cast
1430 Cast me not away in the
1738 The more he cast away, the
2004 The die is cast.
7069 shore. He cast (of which

castle
2431 a man's house is his castle.
5973 In the castle of my skin.

castles
2206 shalt make castels thanne in

castrate
3378 you would castrate the

casualty
2138 the first casualty is truth.

cat
2560 and a cat that comes
3243 never was a Cat of such
6153 name of his cat: His body
6755 long as the average cat.
6868 The cat which isn't let
7745 black cat with
7785 with my cat, who knows
9232 at the cat there's a
9856 on little cat feet. It
10807 consider my Cat Jeoffrey.
10864 Oh I am a cat that likes
10902 enough to swing a cat.
11280 way the cat is
12634 of a cat on a hot

cataclysm
4912 of their cataclysm but one

catacombs
4599 in the catacombs but how to

catalogue
2336 is mainly a catalogue of
3604 delightful than a catalogue.

catalyst
3123 be the catalyst that

catastrophe
3180 toward unparalleled catastrophe.
8426 interest in catastrophe. If they
11165 who stands firm is a catastrophe.
12033 some great catastrophe is not

catastrophes
2398 a series of catastrophes which

catch
1732 .. and to catch no slip by
2165 sir, to catch old birds

2959 Go, and catch a falling
6667 there's a catch somewhere.
6809 first to catch and to
7451 decided to catch a
8272 into the water by his catch.
9264 web, catch the fly
9469 to catch a bird
11306 which may catch small

catching
976 Come away; poverty's catching.
4543 Catching a fly ball is a
10287 Passion, I see, is catching.

categories
9433 by a hardening of the categories.

categorize
3128 you, categorize you,

caterpillar
4329 He's but a caterpillar, drest.

cathay
11536 than a cycle of Cathay,

cathedral
880 Gothic cathedrals: I mean
12020 you have a cathedral in your

catholic
183 did not attend was Catholic.
996 I am a Catholic .. If you
6824 [the Roman Catholic Church]
7274 for a Catholic woman to
8207 the Catholics, I was
11696 Roman Catholic women must

cato
237 to Cato, and
2153 men ask why Cato has no

cats
3237 to see That cats are much
5818 Cats seem to go on the
6235 Cats are living
9804 The greater cats with
11630 Cats, no less liquid than
11697 Cats - a standing rebuke

cattle
5668 call the cattle home, And
8446 who die as cattle? Only the
9167 wives and cattle; bad is

caucus
5061 and a caucus? A caucus

caught
2668 wouldn't be caught dead
4334 but caught my foot in
8634 more wise, and not be catched!
9310 ceases; Caught fast, she

cauldron
10361 Fire burn and cauldron bubble.

cauliflower
11976 Cauliflower is nothing but

causality
9768 The law of causality, I

cause
1686 as between cause and
2840 Our cause is just, our
3559 but the cause of
6381 Rebel without a cause.
6719 triumphant cause.
7614 the cause Of truth,
7684 amiss The good old Cause .
7869 the just cause, By
8145 To set the cause above
8430 In an easy cause any man
10917 advance its cause I'm ready
11599 The woman's cause is man's:
12345 who serve a cause are not

causes
7408 to discover their causes.
8404 good, brave causes left. If

caustic
9582 was more caustic than

caution
9759 forms of caution, caution

cautious
10923 is forever cautious, can one

cavaliers
10063 The Cavaliers (Wrong but

cave
7901 We are only cave men who

cave-dweller
8668 The cave-dweller's wife complained

cavern
7824 In a cavern, in a canyon,

caverns
2438 ran Through caverns
12532 about in caverns all alone,

caves
4293 unfathomed caves of ocean
7578 all her caves, and back

caviar
6457 it for not laying caviar.

cease
5501 to die, To cease upon the
7358 and you cease to be so.
11102 Rudyards cease from
11553 day and cease to be:

ceased
6542 when she ceased, we

ceiling
4892 Every ceiling, when reached,

celebrate
5044 just to celebrate the event.
12504 I celebrate myself, and sing

celebrated
1402 All celebrated people lose
3951 That celebrated, Cultivated,
7664 So rife and celebrated in the

celebrity
1446 A sign of a celebrity is often
7255 A celebrity is one who is known

celestial
7556 gloom For that celestial light?

celia
5272 Come, my Celia, let us

celibacy
2789 Celibacy is the worst form of
5197 pains, but celibacy has no
8315 Celibacy bestows on a man the
8592 lake, but celibacy is almost

cell
10850 the padded cell of his

cellos
11166 are the cellos of the

celtic
5603 woods of Celtic antiquity.

cement
8835 the same cement, ever sure

cemetery
6049 Help me down Cemetery Road.

censors
5024 be without censors; and where

censorship
6617 Censorship, like charity, should
10651 the extreme form of censorship.

censure
5041 You censure this with

cent
3693 he did with every cent.

centipede
6204 loathsome centipede, Remorse,

centre
337 which the centre is
3553 My centre is giving way, my
4683 through the centre of each
7952 now in the centre of
12013 land whose centre is

centuries
8082 forty centuries look down

century
2403 century
5800 and peace in the 21st century.
6957 when a new century begins it
12193 The century on which we are

cerberus
7510 Of Cerberus, and

ceres
7593 which cost Ceres all that

certain
682 same, is sufficiently certain.
1967 lady of a certain age',
3630 said to be certain, except

certainties
4457 will ever have for certain.
5699 four things certain since
9136 not always certain but it's

certainties
675 begin with certainties, he shall
3194 and not on certainties.
7313 hot for certainties in this

certainty
3184 absolute certainty that Man
9785 is not knowledge, but certainty.
11051 with certainty we must
11956 earthly certainty is
12151 condition, but certainty is.

cesspool
2996 that great cesspool into which

chaff
2165 catch old birds with chaff.
4823 from the chaff, and to
5473 tastes like chaff in my

chain
4189 remove a lengthening chain.

chains
5136 The chains of habit are too
5376 to be in chains than to be
6800 chains-and-their-
7764 In chains and darkness,
11666 sang in my chains like the
12157 from the chains they

chair
5121 nothing. He fills a chair.
8836 a too easy chair, And heard
8978 born with a chair stuck to
12180 to the seat of the chair.
12269 to the chair of

chairman
7687 with me as chairman, and two
7751 more than chairman, at most,

chaise-longue
2029 hurly-burly of the chaise-longue.

challenges
5550 is a set of challenges. It sums
6781 directly challenges: the Roman

chamber
224 In his chamber, weak and
1484 Chamber music - a
8550 A second Chamber selected

chambermaid
5098 arms of a chambermaid as of a

chamberpot
6711 empties her chamberpot on your

chambers
11719 The chambers of the mansion of

chameleons
10682 Chameleons feed on light and
11939 We are chameleons, and our

champagne
3518 and the champagne and the
6667 given champagne at lunch,
7761 meet with champagne and a
7939 Champagne socialist.
8957 kick from champagne, Mere
9021 ice of his Lordship's champagne.
10584 not a champagne
11291 Champagne certainly gives one

chance
1893 that one will chance it.
2608 and then be right by chance.
2727 the efficient use of chance.
2772 Chance makes our parents,
2923 being ready for the chance.
3603 Chance is the pseudonym of
3710 take your chance on your
4022 me, you haven't a chance.
4380 nothing to Chance will do
6099 I missed my chance with one
6223 is Give peace a chance.
6915 will never eliminate chance.
7064 height, And chance o'ertakes,
7160 for his chance, the
7484 men call chance, this I
7580 arbiter Chance governs
7615 and chance Approach
8137 be left to chance; nothing
8196 Chance favours only those
8429 Chance is always powerful.

8566 chance favours
8897 thee; All chance,
9109 There is no chance for old
10533 I am so sometimes by chance.
10972 turns, and chances change by

chancellor
5089 by the Lord Chancellor, upon a
6551 The Chancellor of the Exchequer

change
106 God cannot change the past.
119 subtract or change without
263 but an abhorrence of change.
387 Times change, and we
549 who want to change everything
617 To change your mind and to
1122 when you want to change him
1772 of some change is without
2109 Change is certain, progress
2255 it to a torrent of change.
2309 who can't change his mind
2404 we can make change our friend
2848 to try to change a man -
4520 People change and forget to
5346 we wish to change in the
5394 Plus ça change, plus c'est
5562 Everything changes but
5977 things will have to change.
6142 time for a change. They are
6378 will not change as they
6471 things must change to
6619 to change, it is
6669 pass away; Change and decay
7112 the point is to change it.
7359 a great change takes
7526 O the heavy change, now thou
8268 right to change what does
9111 can soon change white to
9752 Change' is scientific,
10645 idea that change can be
10677 shores; I change, but I
10747 Change must be measured from
10783 it. Time changes things,
10972 and chances change by course,
11081 the pockets change; it is not
11253 the 'outs' change places
11359 Change in a trice The lilies
11535 ringing grooves of change.
11814 to too much change in too
11939 prejudices change places
12423 the small change of his
12468 order amid change, and to

changed
682 things are changed, and that
6042 since, As changed itself to
6401 If voting changed anything
6623 are changed and like
8204 cannot be changed; courage
11140 are Are changed upon the
12888 Changed, changed utterly: A

changes
595 place - it changes with the
2730 When great changes occur in
3104 see gr-reat changes takin'
3602 All changes, even the most

changeth
10899 but naught changeth thee.
11515 old order changeth, yielding

changing
4764 The changing year's
7177 on not changing one's
8183 The changing of bodies into
11879 thinks of changing himself so

channel
7128 through the Channel in the mad
8146 them up the Channel as we
9518 it cuts a channel into which

chaos
33 Chaos often breeds life,
3441 A chaos of clear ideas.
7185 out of the chaos of the
7580 Chaos umpire sits, And by
8838 empire, Chaos! is
10671 first God dawned on Chaos.
11782 emotional chaos remembered
12377 primordial chaos clapped on

chaotic
3173 to make the chaotic diversity

chapel
925 will build a chapel just by.
6635 build a chapel .. In
10388 good to do, chapels had been

chaperone
4846 Her face was her chaperone.

chaplin
4203 Chaplin is no businessman -

chaps
1054 Biography is about Chaps.

chapter
7706 are a mere chapter. I am the

character
225 Character is like a tree, and
1466 whatever character we choose.
1591 not build character. They
3312 Character is that which can do
3712 into a character; you must
4084 Character, in great and little
4123 places, character in the
4522 their own character, nor
5420 the character undecided,
5642 the content of their character.
5897 of our strength of character.
6250 essential character of the
6584 is wholesome for the character.
6950 Character is what God and the
7828 care of my character, my
8083 on personal character and
8291 Character is perfectly educated
8292 fate and character are the
8796 Character is long-standing
9407 you reap a character. Sow a
9417 a fellow's character by his way
9587 Character building begins in
10732 set! a character dead at
10992 the formation of character.
11096 in solitude except character.
11099 on your character and say
11643 If a man's character is to be
12689 your character will take

characteristic
51 English characteristic for which
11819 has this characteristic - it

characteristics
2229 are their universal characteristics.
4073 unequivocal characteristics of the

characters
18 that great characters are
1584 to other characters living
1824 Who have characters to lose.
5089 of characters and
5299 whose characters are above
5380 has three characters - that
11879 new characters when they

charge
5823 serious charge which can
6843 Take thou in charge this day!

charged
4306 a highly charged situation

charges
709 to begin charges which once

charing cross
8625 went out to Charing Cross, to see

chariot
341 low, sweet chariot Comin' for
1349 Bring me my chariot of fire.
7072 wingèd chariot hurrying

charitable
5287 Be charitable and indulgent to
7821 Great ideas are not charitable.
8617 feel more charitable toward the

charity
495 living need charity more than
604 Charity is no substitute for
1128 up, but charity edifieth.
1129 hope, charity, these
3567 crime as charity is wrong
4750 haven't any charity in your
6363 none; with charity for all;
6617 like charity, should
6634 consists of faith and charity.
8353 organized charity, scrimped

10806 For Charity is cold in the
12509 or a little charity, When I

charlie
4669 water to Charlie; Come

charm
2037 Charm is a way of getting
2805 and the charm of novelty
3892 lost its charm. How long,
4199 What charm can soothe
6253 Oozing charm from every
6267 What is charm then? The
9547 such a charm in
10362 wing, For a charm of
11401 have a secret charm.

charmer
3946 t'other dear charmer away!

charming
2517 All charming people have
10851 Charming people live up to the
12212 It is charming to totter into

charms
1823 acres o' charms, O, gie me
2632 flocks have charms, For him
6783 morn, Whose charms all other
6947 country has charms only for
7851 young charms, Which I
8941 may roll; Charms strike the
9513 lose our charms in the

charter
11723 was the charter of the

chartreuse
333 pot calls the kettle chartreuse.

chase
1929 meet To chase the
11592 of the chase, We hunt
11807 live by the chase.

chassis
8302 worl's in a state o' chassis!

chaste
1952 charming, chaste, and
4010 If I pronounce it chaste!
5867 are few chaste women who
8021 terms, like a chaste whore.
8863 Chaste to her husband, frank

chastise
11409 He only may chastise who loves.

chastity
605 Give me chastity and
2142 book where chastity really
4238 the most peculiar is chastity.
4900 Chastity - the most unnatural
7481 'Tis chastity, my brother,
11487 clothed only with chastity.

chat
2392 agreement kills a chat.

chateaux
11860 their chateaux would

chattanooga
4228 is that the Chattanooga Choo-choo,

chatter
4007 only idle chatter of a

chatterley
6034 end of the Chatterley ban And

chaucer
6090 than Chaucer. But
12245 a pity that Chawcer, who had

cheap
699 maketh himself cheap.
4743 flesh and blood so cheap!
6222 in the cheap seats clap
6398 The cheap, no matter how
6746 all like to buy it cheap.
8012 Pile it high, sell it cheap.
8629 done as cheap as other
10320 life is cheap as

cheaper
6134 other is a cheaper thing, but
9395 which is cheaper than a
9725 a little cheaper, and the

cheapest
11752 pleasures are the cheapest.

cheat
1097 who never cheated, never
1470 he may cheat at cards

2411 it's so lucrative to cheat.
3736 Cheat me in the price but
3843 To cheat a man is nothing;
5374 must not cheat anybody,
6305 who don't cheat at cards
11744 You may cheat yourself

cheated
5204 sometimes cheated than not

cheating
1270 a period of cheating between
8977 without actually cheating.

cheats
2159 every man cheats in his
8799 He who cheats with an oath

cheek
1167 thy right cheek, turn to
9142 other who offers a cheek.

cheek-to-cheek
1080 out together dancing cheek-to-cheek.

cheer
6844 scarce forbear to cheer.
8689 Don't cheer, men; those
11924 make good cheer, For

cheerful
5813 we must always be cheerful.
8625 looking as cheerful as any man

cheerfully
2272 sets forth cheerfully towards
6829 I shall cheerfully bear the

cheerfulness
3153 know how, cheerfulness was always
10813 Cheerfulness gives elasticity to

cheering
12116 it will be cheering to

cheerio
1099 And cheerioh' or
12422 old thing! cheerio!

cheers
3589 So Two cheers for Democracy:

cheese
1543 hole when the cheese is gone?
2757 has 246 varieties of cheese?
3435 Cheese - milk's leap toward
9289 Botticelli's a cheese !
11195 dreamed of cheese - toasted,
11288 hup the chinks wi' cheese.

cheesed
1035 soon had me cheesed off.

chemicals
2136 dangerous chemicals, from the

chemistry
1309 a matter of chemistry. That must

cheque
8980 is like a cheque drawn on a
12616 like blank cheques. The

chequebook
7101 shut and his chequebook open.

cherished
1567 could be cherished,
7390 no longer cherished, Need we

cheroot
5719 white cheroot, An'

cherries
1599 is just a bowl of cherries.

cherry
4787 trees, the cherry now Is
4788 To see the cherry hung with

cherry pie
1594 It is as American as cherry pie.

cherry-stones
5130 not carve heads upon cherry-stones.

cherub
8860 A cherub's face, a reptile

cherubim
7537 The helmèd cherubim And

cheshire
4924 smile of a cosmic Cheshire cat.

chess
6874 of four-move chess problem.

chess-board
1633 called the chess-board white - we

chest
3405 the chest, and the
4159 door; The chest contrived
8694 from the chest sound like
11193 dead man's chest Yo-ho-ho,

chestnut
6515 a spreading chestnut tree The

chew
5065 fart and chew gum at the

chianti
10107 bottles of Chianti to make

chic
12728 Radical Chic .. is only

chicago
3576 Chicago - a facade of

chicken
2338 like a chicken.' Some
4567 The chicken is the country's,
5060 but I know chicken shit from
7702 is like a chicken whose head
7761 and a chicken at last.

chickens
98 count your chickens before
10958 like young chickens, they

chid
4154 He chid their wand'rings,

chide
5423 trumpets 'gan to chide.
10542 do but sweetly chide thee.

chief
9813 A chief is a man who
10020 Hail to the chief who in
10029 had the chief hand in

chieftain
11135 Chieftain Iffucan of Azcan in

child
273 Good children's literature
302 Give me a child for the
321 Love is the child of
1129 I was a child, I spake
1244 Even a child is known by
1246 Train up a child in the way
1280 bring up a child in the way
2135 If a child is to keep alive
2179 educate a child, in the
3434 no longer anybody's child.
3625 A child thinks twenty
4384 is the child of Time.
5346 in the child, we should
5626 what it is to be a child.
5966 A child's a plaything for
6167 Ask your child what he
8063 and I speak like a child.
8275 If a child lives with
8469 mind of a child cannot be
8708 Every child is an artist.
8804 I was a child and she was a
8853 As yet a child, nor yet a
8857 painted child of dirt
8903 Behold the child, by
9156 takes the child by the
9244 limit a child to your
10315 thee in a child, Than the
10316 To have a thankless child!
10393 that knows his own child.
10462 that's governed by a child!
10600 right to a child with the
10621 strike a child take care
10678 Like a child from the
11027 things a child will share
11177 The child that is not clean
11178 A child should always say
11296 allow the child inside
11443 days, A happy English child.
11450 body and a child's
12387 a little child; Pity my
12791 The Child is father of the

childbirth
7696 taxes and childbirth! There's
9782 women, at any rate in childbirth.

childhood
894 Genius is childhood recaptured.
3521 go from one childhood to
4315 moment in childhood when the
5964 my days of childhood, in my
7385 Childhood is not from birth to
7645 .. The childhood shows the
9071 days of our childhood we lived
10068 he did that childhood was such a
11251 Childhood - a period of waiting

childish
250 a silly, childish game, it's
1129 I put away childish things.
3236 or so has seemed very childish.
5125 are either knavish or childish.
7021 More childish valorous than
9810 like them strong and childish.
12776 Sweet childish days, that were

childishness
10118 Is second childishness, and mere

children
2 for their children - clean,
207 now learn from their children.
308 Children are luxuries rather
358 the world is done by children.
703 death as children fear to go
728 Children sweeten labours, but
803 Children have never been very
1017 first class, and with children.
1079 glisten And children listen To
1164 be called the children of God.
1174 But the children of the
1181 as little children, ye shall
1221 shalt bring forth children.
1407 men are children more than
1637 Your children are not dead.
2571 allow their children to come
2610 life, as children with their
2793 produce children but that
2867 talks about her own children.
3054 kept from children and from
3149 parents obey their children.
3160 is for little children.
3409 Healthy children will not fear
3617 Give me the children until they
3932 Your children are not your
4095 If children grew up according
4143 is having children, not a
4725 want their children to have.
4893 Children are remarkable for
5232 The children of perdition are
5288 Children have more need of
5351 on their children, than the
5669 And the children stood
5983 want your children to listen,
6290 can get it from your children.
6427 in the thoughts of children.
6446 having children. Life is
6477 known as the Children's Hour.
7287 done to children, they will
7778 noted that children at play
7957 the little children cried in
8088 Children aren't happy with
8621 dogs than of their children.
8680 up some children is short.
8690 I think our children have all
9226 love their children more than
9307 All children wear the sign: 'I
9530 to find our children believing
9669 Come, children of our country,
9723 make your children capable of
9763 want their children to be a
9786 for having children than not
9815 for children to be
9832 Children with Hyacinth's
10041 middle-aged children for signs
10579 brought-up children are those
10764 have your children become,
11388 adults to children, and by
11634 lips and hearts of children.
11833 of their children. Hostages
11969 breeds contempt - and children.
12024 on which children cut their
12079 turn each one of her children.
12288 sight, When children of one
12382 Children, like animals, use
12605 Children begin by loving their
12786 And airy hopes my children.
12967 What children expect from

chill
2830 - First - Chill - then

3320 A cynic can chill and
5422 Ah, bitter chill it was!

chills
8101 That what chills the finger

chilly
1925 and our chilly women.
4264 room grows chilly, I haven't

chime
5247 some soft chime had

chimes
10250 heard the chimes at

chimneys
7918 good grove of chimneys for me.

chin
9172 in the shin, a devil
11999 with her chin alone.

china
3390 China has no income tax, no
8866 herself, though china fall.

chinese
2753 will be united by the Chinese.
12951 to the Chinese mind.

chintzy
1098 Oh! Chintzy, Chintzy

chip
1793 merely a chip of the old

chips
12384 It said Chips with

chisel
7341 I have a chisel in my

chivalry
1776 The age of chivalry is gone.
4345 Chivalry is the most delicate
6689 Chivalry is a poor substitute
10239 have a truant been to chivalry.

chocolate
2064 box of chocolate liqueurs

choice
3338 mind its choice between
4407 upon us a choice between
5089 having any choice in the
7652 Reason is also choice.
7912 where the choice constantly
9300 and you takes your choice.
10482 a small choice in rotten
12585 he has the choice of two
12588 in the choice of his

choir
1071 All the choir of heaven and
5411 a wailful choir the small

choo-choo
4228 Chattanooga Choo-choo, Track

choose
1504 have to choose between
5183 they choose the
6292 To govern is to choose.
6716 One must choose between
8171 what we choose. We are
8463 better to choose the
10397 I will not choose what many

chooses
435 he wants, of what he chooses.

choosing
8041 is not choosing; that is
12409 When choosing between two

chopper
3991 and chippy chopper on a big

chops
7277 calmly licking its chops.

chord
9055 struck one chord of music,

choreographer
801 I am a choreographer. A

chorus
3524 a dozen are only a chorus.

chose
4195 I .. chose my wife, as she

chosen
1185 called, but few are chosen.
7200 by what is chosen by others.

christ
2093 If Jesus Christ were to come

7749 thy might, Christ is thy
8034 Christ - an anarchist who
8353 cautious, statistical Christ.

christendom
4542 The wisest fool in Christendom.

christian
60 what peace a Christian can die.
524 to form Christian men for
934 A Christian is nothing but a
2263 The Christian ideal has not
3002 do As little as a Christian can.
3922 a sober Christian would
5523 Pure eyes and Christian hearts.
6634 Christian life consists of
6814 out of his Christian name a
7146 than a drunken Christian
8217 The Christian resolution to
8932 perfectly like a Christian.
10396 Fled with a Christian! O my
11443 in these Christian days, A
11953 man - a Christian holding
12875 A Christian is a man who feels
12955 Scratch the Christian and you

christianity
335 Muscular Christianity.
2880 His Christianity was muscular.
3653 at bottom hatred of Christianity.
3943 effect of Christianity was to
4945 Christianity is good news; not
6300 believe in Christianity as I
8609 heart of Christianity .. No
9826 nothing in Christianity or
10585 Christianity might be a good thing

christians
657 like good Christians.
1921 Christians, awake! Salute the
1936 Christians have burned each
11627 how these Christians love one

christmas
22 Christmas is over, and Business
70 well that Christmas should
2189 a lovely Christmas, the two
4335 insulting Christmas card I
4596 - for Christmas. They're
5588 jubilant Christmas tree. You
7830 before Christmas, when all
10335 At Christmas I no more desire a
11924 At Christmas play and make good

chronicle
10427 fools and chronicle small
10558 When in the chronicle of wasted

chrysanthemum
12715 you look like a chrysanthemum.

chump
12708 grab a chump. Tap his

church
190 nearer the Church the
228 The Church of England is the
612 salvation outside the church.
925 buildeth a church, the devil
4795 you go to church, and like
5033 but the Church has driven
5524 If the Church of England
6202 at the church, Waiting
6635 God built a church, there the
6741 'The Church is an anvil
6781 Catholic Church, the
6825 She [the Church of Rome]
6884 the English Church shall be
7237 of the church, because I
8878 As some to church repair,
9698 The Church should go forward
11219 The Church's one foundation

churchill
563 that of Mr. Churchill but the
564 Winston Churchill - fifty per
8022 clergyman; Churchill being a
12306 Winston Churchill is always

churchman
1379 the British churchman, he goes

churchyard
5305 taste, than in a churchyard.
5426 palsy-stricken, churchyard thing.

cicero
237 terrible to Cicero, desirable

cigar
26 five-cent cigars in the
1717 A good cigar is as great a
1804 A good cigar, a good
5687 but a good cigar is a
12307 is like a cigar. If it

cigarette
7124 A cigarette that bears a
12589 A cigarette is the perfect type

cigars
11981 smoke cigars in heaven,

cinder
2933 how dry a cinder this world

cinderella
5032 is a nubile Cinderella, sparsely
11991 is the Cinderella of the

cinema
4068 truth. The cinema is truth

circle
10334 wheel is come full circle.
11489 all the circle of the

circles
615 and come round in circles.

circuit
8794 of the Circuit of the

circulation
10841 assists the circulation of their

circumcision
8358 breast-feeding, circumcision.

circumference
337 and the circumference is

circumstance
4539 clutch of circumstance, I have
11568 blows of circumstance, And
12009 grain of circumstance;

circumstances
3829 I am I plus my circumstances.
5001 by circumstances beyond
8690 under very demanding circumstances.
11938 trying circumstances, urgent
12183 exceptional circumstances it is
12486 of the circumstances under

circumvent
10185 one that would circumvent God.

circus
7203 have no right in the circus.

cistern
1030 loud the cistern, As I read

citadel
8781 is the citadel of sense
12722 sky-soaring citadel that bears

cities
93 hell to men, hell to cities.
3313 Cities force growth and make
5573 neglect our cities to our
7895 All cities are mad: but the
8984 in three cities, But it is

citius
7983 Citius, altius, fortius.

citizen
598 To the citizen or the
1524 is that of private citizen.
2362 I am a Roman citizen.
2613 was a citizen Of credit
4275 job of a citizen is to keep
6176 A citizen, first in war,
9223 and a good citizen are not
10911 I am a citizen, not of Athens
11282 domestic citizen who pays

citizens
1707 are among its own citizens.
6348 Fellow citizens, we cannot
6568 Man made us citizens, great
12344 enable its citizens to live,
12649 and second class citizens.

citizenship
10934 onerous citizenship. Everyone

city
399 to the city in the
519 that sweet City with her
2055 the big city. Nowadays
2896 a nation, not a city.
3383 What is the city in which

4567 but the city eats it.
4683 and every town or city.
4988 In the big city, everyone
5519 long in city pent, 'Tis
6940 down the City Road, In
7467 this vast city; a city of
7622 in populous city pent,
7919 The city is not a concrete
8195 For a city consists in
8280 like that of the big city.
9159 A great city, a great
9854 brawling, City of the Big
10156 The city cast Her people
10175 What is the city but the
10689 Sun-girt city, thou hast
11485 the humming city comes to
11718 The City is of Night;
12450 in the city again, but

civil
4362 people, be civil. I am the
7701 'Always be civil to the
10057 but a civil contract.
10784 Here lies a civil servant.

civil war
9418 In a civil war, a general must

civilities
8576 and their civilities And, on

civility
7731 essence of civility; Young
7757 Civility costs nothing and

civilization
1559 man, every civilization, has gone
3297 All civilization has from time to
3321 eventually die of civilization.
4140 the great rewards of civilization.
5527 for civilization to flow
6614 Civilization is just a slow
6815 As civilization advances, poetry
7167 a nation's civilization is marked
8354 Civilization is nothing more than
9430 In our civilization, men are
9557 can't say civilization don't
9753 of an intelligent civilization.
11055 marks the level of civilization.
11807 submit to civilization with the
11842 the last product of civilization.
11843 Civilization is a movement - not a
11844 the dawn of civilization in which
11846 every civilization furnishes
11859 life-blood of real civilization.
12478 Civilization advances by extending

civilizations
3114 say that civilizations begin with
5819 Civilizations die from

civilize
4849 you would civilize a man,

civilized
2924 man can get civilized is to
6529 animal and civilized man. It
7317 the last thing civilized by Man.
7326 books; But civilized man cannot
8477 are called civilized, we see
10649 stone, the civilized man to
12142 I am among civilized men

civilizers
2888 are the two civilizers of man.

civilizes
8020 Cricket civilizes people and

clad
7481 that, is clad in

clamour
6499 Not in the clamour of the

clan
8502 say, 'Your clan will pay

clanging
5683 ring - Clanging from the

clap
8397 Don't clap too hard - it's

claret
3411 with more claret than
5099 Claret is the liquor for

clarion
7867 sound the clarion, fill the

clarity
8238 to youth, clarity of thought
8396 had the clarity of a

class
1527 coulda had class and been
4063 one great class of
5980 Class is an aura of
6461 The 3rd Class, not the
7113 that the class struggle
7115 history of class struggles.
8583 the upper classes is
11047 a single class has
12027 Youth has become a class.

classes
2171 two great classes: those
2323 for all classes for all
8237 into two classes: tools and
8772 are three classes of men -
10827 the upper classes With your

classic
2865 it, even if bad, to a classic.
3439 you read a classic you do not
11252 music. Classic' music

classical
3996 At classical Monday
5106 Classical quotation is the
8735 That's the classical mind at

classics
6127 The classics are only
7420 of the classics is an
8992 Than the classics in
11229 The great homicidal classics?

classifications
12371 Crude classifications and false

classless
4990 aspire to a classless society

clatter
1009 above the clatter as part of
4343 cheerful clatter of Sir

claw
11549 red in tooth and claw.

clawed
12074 steps Hath clawed me with

claws
2113 spreads his claws, And

clay
3897 made of clay, But our
5403 Clay is the word and clay
7840 idea from clay, and I
10442 loam or painted clay.

clean
3242 Clean the air! clean the
6387 are all too clean. They
6722 death Not a clean &
7215 city on earth will be clean.

cleaned
3962 firm. I cleaned the

cleanliness
6893 and all the cleanliness of all the

cleanness
1580 swimmers into cleanness leaping.

cleansed
1347 were cleansed everything

clear
5291 that they do not make clear.
9505 What is not clear is not

cleave
1219 and shall cleave unto his

clementine
7824 daughter, Clementine. Oh, my
7825 Sandals were for Clementine.

cleopatra
8539 Had Cleopatra's nose been
10156 to gaze on Cleopatra too And

clergy
5671 virtue with the Roman clergy.
9267 is worth a pound of clergy.

clergyman
5302 No married clergyman should
8022 or of a clergyman; Churchill

clergymen
3002 have with clergymen to do As
10874 - men, women, and clergymen.

clerical
1576 On lissom, clerical, printless

clerks
4367 to produce clerks and
4935 clearly built for clerks.

clever
539 He's very clever, but
3113 always a clever thing to
4086 A clever man commits no
5661 who will be clever; Do noble
5728 manage a clever man; but
9836 Too clever by half.
11433 Clever men are impressed in
12773 people were clever, And all

cleverest
229 The cleverest woman finds a
12653 ago the cleverest people did

cleverness
5878 height of cleverness is to be

clich,
4338 that cliché was a

click
8011 Clunk, click, every trip.

client
3851 bend to favour ev'ry client.

cliffs
1840 the white cliffs of Dover,
6835 those white cliffs I never

climate
590 but a whole climate of
1546 the climate, the
1972 where the climate's sultry.

climb
3281 fails thee, climb not at
9373 would I climb, yet fear

climbed
193 curiosity, one climbed on.
2868 I have climbed to the top of

cling
1029 I will cling to the old
12824 makes them cling together

clinton
12283 politicians Clinton has a

clive
1053 like about Clive Is that he

cloak
3751 often borrows her cloak.

clock
544 and his eye on the clock.
1579 the Church clock at ten to
4159 varnished clock that
5624 setting a clock half an
5634 as to stop the church clock
6590 fifty the clock can't
7707 is halfway out of the clock.
9824 The clock struck eleven
10093 Ah! the clock is always
12446 set the clock an hour
12848 me now. The clock in the

clock-setter
10302 Old Time the clock-setter.

clocks
6474 As the clocks were
9953 Electric clocks reveal to

clockwork
1743 A clockwork orange.

clogs
7675 quit their clogs By the

cloister
6018 It is in cloistre or in

close
182 man trying to close in.
662 ugly head, close your eyes,
4617 on my bed, close my eyes,

closed
3487 but it was closed.

closer
1311 Pope be any closer to God
2270 Come closer, boys. It will
2629 Oh! for a closer walk with
6327 ideas closer together.
11493 Closer is He than breathing,

closes
5530 happiness closes, another

closet
2475 own hearts in their closet.
2834 me in the closet - Because

closing
2519 It is closing time in the

cloth
831 wearing a cloth coat. The

clothed
11111 ideas get clothed at the
11487 rode forth, clothed only with

clothes
935 Clothes and manners do not
2175 take the girl's clothes off.
2460 taking off all her clothes.
2914 away with their clothes.
3092 Clothes and courage have much
3463 can have with your clothes on.
4589 of her clothes. Next,
6066 Clothes are nothing less than
6456 The suit of clothes is
11739 that require new clothes.
11935 are but the clothes and
12764 these wet clothes and into a

clothing
99 wolf in the sheep's clothing.
2298 A sheep in sheep's clothing.
5951 Things in books' clothing.

cloud
5496 a weeping cloud, That
7210 but - a cloud in
7446 to be a Cloud Floating
7476 did a sable cloud Turn forth
10669 like a cloud which had
10688 - When the cloud is
12844 lonely as a cloud That

clouds
1550 The clouds blew off
7746 from the clouds of the
11670 thump the clouds When
12811 trailing clouds of glory
12816 through the clouds I'll never

cloudy
1925 Our cloudy climate, and our
7542 with cloudy red,

cloverleaf
8033 is the concrete cloverleaf.

clowns
4511 stage, the clowns come on.
10931 are the clowns? Send in

club
1279 hand and a club in the
6458 exclusive club of the
7100 to any club that will
10823 will be a club. But this

clue
2988 almost invariably a clue.

clunk
8011 Clunk, click, every trip.

clutch
11711 we clutch thee!

clutching
518 hope, still Clutching the

cluttered
230 If a cluttered desk is an

coach
6677 a football coach who's
11262 a stage coach, but now

coal
1116 mainly of coal and
3884 no more coals to
12211 is made of Newcastle coal.

coalition
2882 does not love coalitions.
6902 I am a coalition government on
12283 has a coalition in his

coalmines
5605 in disused coalmines which are

coarse
9699 one of them is rather coarse.

coaster
7128 British coaster with a

coat
423 a mink coat but a
4188 and my coat from the

coats of arms
11518 Is worth a hundred coats of arms.

cobwebs
11306 are like cobwebs, which may

cocaine
11208 Cocaine is God's way of

cock
916 Our cock won't fight.
7514 While the cock with lively
11130 about?' 'A Cock and a

cockerel
6178 with a cockerel's tongue.

cocktail
8733 under the cocktail cabinet.
9573 is like one cocktail, it just
10824 The cocktail party - a device

cocktails
271 over cocktails That

code
10091 has its own stern code.

codfish
1024 out of it. That and codfish.

codger
4911 An old codger, rampant, and

coerce
11105 minority to coerce an

coffee
231 Coffee in England is just
8939 Coffee, (which makes the
9294 if this is coffee, I want

coffin
142 won't fit into my coffin.
946 the way down to the coffin.
7259 looks around for a coffin.
8310 the silver plate on a coffin.
8362 grave in a Y-shaped coffin.
8723 Care to our coffin adds a
11034 behind the coffins of your

cohorts
1941 And his cohorts were

coin
12423 less store upon the coin.

coins
8339 clanking of coins in dozens
11500 and like to coins, Some

coition
1614 way of coition; it is the
9243 After coition every

coke
7962 Things go better with Coke.

cold
191 progress. A cold coming
668 the common cold, And gives
882 in the midst of a cold war.
1566 Cold in the earth - and
3755 cat fears even cold water.
5459 here On the cold hill's
5744 call this cold in
6085 where the cold doesn't
6114 who came in from the cold.
7762 and like rivers grow cold.
8253 dressed ever caught a cold?
9439 A cold in the head causes
10154 judgment, cold in blood,
10869 it was too cold always
11366 mortal With cold immortal
11894 for the cold of heart
12210 of ink in my pen ran cold.
12337 everlasting cold; I have

cold blood
10621 A blow in cold blood neither

cold storage
9848 library is thought in cold storage.

coleridge
1945 And brother Coleridge lull the
1951 And Coleridge, too, has lately
5958 Cultivate simplicity, Coleridge.

coliseum
8962 You're the Coliseum, You're

collections
5942 of collections, spoilers

college
2347 is what a college becomes
4536 sons to college either
5052 got through college yet."
5384 asked what college I
7151 too soon after college.
11405 from college cum laude,

collide
8954 July we collide with Mars?

collision
11785 rear-end collision and Man

collisions
4340 collisions between
9841 boathook to avoid collisions.

colonial
3888 in her Colonial trade

colonies
2019 British Colonies before
2869 Colonies do not cease to be
2893 wretched colonies will all

colossal
8681 used to be colossal'. Now

colossus
5130 could cut a Colossus from a
10275 Like a Colossus; and we

colour
3 I know the colour rose, and
2170 is a simple colour, as on an
3568 Any colour - so long as it's
5642 by the colour of their
8819 wrung the colour from the
9716 match the colour of the
9732 which love colour the most.
11743 Colour, which is the poet's
12650 race or colour of their

coloured
10565 spirit a woman, coloured ill.

colours
2167 All colours are the friends
2327 about colours. I

columbus
3891 West, and Columbus discovered
4137 If Columbus had had an

column
4691 and the column of

comatose
2367 lachrymose and comatose.

comb
1454 two bald men over a comb.
9092 is the comb that

combination
2792 there is a combination, but the
8490 may call it combination, you may

combustion
6123 spontaneous combustion. You must

come
1178 Come unto me, all ye that
3170 future. It comes soon
3879 We are come for your good,
4883 want to come, nothing
5768 No! Let 'em all come!
6706 did you come from, baby
7426 'Do you come here often?'
7929 Had she come all the way
9708 never to come, it would
9865 a war and nobody will come.
12378 shape of things to come.
12411 don't you come up

comedian
1678 role of a comedian is to make
4577 A comedian is a fellow who
7263 God is a comedian whose

comedies
1961 death, All comedies are ended

comedy
1795 Comedy is tragedy - plus
8066 writes comedy at the
10757 Comedy is an imitation of
12017 Comedy is simply a funny way
12206 world is a comedy to those

comet
7576 and like a comet burned

cometh
8342 The iceman cometh.

comets
7088 Ye country comets, that

comfort
645 at home for real comfort.
1426 rod and thy staff comfort me.
1717 as great a comfort to a man
2236 for your comfort, Yea,
3008 doth go, Comfort's a
3099 Comfort the afflicted and
5555 enjoy the comfort of opinion
5651 moments of comfort and
5659 as though comfort and luxury
6054 Be of good comfort Master
6585 is a great comfort in the
6822 but they never knew comfort.
8228 source of comfort: with it a
8546 Comfort yourself, you would
10308 I beg cold comfort; and you
10866 for a comfort and a

comfortable
3440 to make you comfortable. It is
4440 into something more comfortable."
5476 clean and comfortable I sit down

comforting
7024 is always a comforting thought in

comforts
693 not without comforts and hopes.
10567 Love comforteth like sunshine

comic
6128 encourage a comic man too

comical
3974 think it's comical How Nature

coming
341 chariot Comin' for to
8726 How many coming men' has
10037 There's a gude time coming.
12849 a good time coming, it's

command
4719 a bigger tent - but command,
7382 regarding command of any
7455 trip about him at command.
7804 enforced by command is more
8219 but to command great
8628 be able to command the rain.
10010 used to sue than to command.
10181 servant does not all commands.
12819 warn, to comfort, and command.

commandments
5624 Christian commandments are
5720 no Ten Commandments an' a man
9474 are ten commandments, right?
10266 set my ten commandments in your

commemorative
9647 with cold commemorative eyes.

commendable
8431 the willingness is commendable.

commendation
1255 Commendation, n: the tribute that

comment
10003 Comment is free, but facts
11227 Comment is free but facts are

commentators
4497 we may study his commentators.
12935 How commentators each dark passage

commerce
1272 Piracy, n: commerce without
2060 matters of commerce the fault
8330 under a ceiling of commerce?
11774 recommends commerce to me is

commercial
4287 television commercial is the
8459 to shoot a commercial on

commission
4079 I herewith commission you to
7219 who acts beyond his commission.

commit
9687 he didn't commit when he
10253 Commit The oldest sins the

commitment
1559 personal commitment and the
3450 we call it fear of commitment.

committed
7009 Thou hast committed- BARABAS:
9931 writer is committed when he

committee
141 Committee - a group of men who
222 a horse designed by a committee.
4137 an advisory committee he would
4437 What is a committee? A group
4842 had been a committee, the
7687 The ideal committee is one with
7751 of the entertainment committee.
9798 A committee of one gets things

committees
1713 is about making committees work.
9052 rookery of committees and

commodity
9531 a commodity as sugar

common
310 off the common, But lets
576 can find no common
1125 .. The common man, I
2018 all things held in common.
3028 fail: But common interest
4018 of the common throng,
4762 to utter common notions in
5739 lose the common touch, If
6423 And marry Common Law to
6425 they are not already common.
7086 He nothing common did or
7268 that the common people
7601 of all things common else.
9398 and still be common, dear.
9419 are very common diatonic
10243 thing, to make it too common.
10881 adieu to common feeling,
11077 so much common
12193 century of the common man.
12769 light; You common people of
12892 like the common people.

common sense
6237 The common sense is that which
9063 abyss, and common sense tells us

common-looking
6340 prefers common-looking people.

commoner
5861 nothing is commoner than the

commonplace
8548 original. Commonplace people see

commons
2904 House of Commons until he
6738 The Commons, faithful to
12183 in the House of Commons

commonwealth
2302 the British Commonwealth and its
6780 wider vision of the Commonwealth.
9622 Empire is a Commonwealth of

communes
7220 how many communes anybody

communication
405 a means of communication. The
4446 and communication' are often
7331 rational communication have
9364 Communication is and should be hell
12451 by any other form of communication.

communism
561 [Russian Communism is] the
6214 Communism is Soviet power plus
7114 - the spectre of Communism.
9576 Communism is like prohibition,

communist
3291 What is a communist? One who
3666 the Communist as the
6973 Every Communist must grasp the

communists
4309 Communists have committed great

community
1268 of a community consisting
5010 a whole community, and until
6360 to do for a community of people,
7367 a civilized community, against
9837 part of the community of Europe
12827 as in one community, Scholars

commuter
12443 Commuter - one who spends his
12444 Commuters give the city its

compact
3822 The compact which exists

companion
994 in God and last companion, Wine.
7783 ease as a companion .. It
11753 found the companion that was

companions
722 mistresses, companions for middle
1065 the best companions.
6493 while their companions slept,
12226 to find Companions of our

companionship
30 for much in companionship as in
4310 the simple desire for companionship.

company
4214 people is a company which
4286 providing you with company.
4516 The company has a policy
4858 A company is judged by the
5166 to enjoy company as to shun
11320 be the worst of the company.
11339 to shine in company; but it is
12231 Good company and good
12557 three is company and two

compare
10545 Shall I compare thee to a
10563 she belied with false compare.

compared
2756 can be compared, either in

comparison
4386 with a basis for comparison.

comparisons
6649 Comparisouns doon ofte gret
10137 Comparisons are odorous.

compass
11070 deal in a very narrow compass.

compassion
9702 Compassion for myself is the

compelled
11070 driven and compelled by

compensations
3386 a system of compensations. Each
12255 beautiful compensations of this

competence
1699 sense of competence,' was the

competition
2412 Approves all forms of competition.
4469 Competition means decentralized
4640 from the competition, and
5155 there is no competition, no
7937 There's far less competition.
12045 because there is no competition,

competitive
8529 to be competitive is to be

competitors
10776 what makes competitors so great.

complacent
5560 The complacent, the

complain
1787 To complain of the age we live
2906 Never complain and never
9013 to complain about the

complaining
3068 The soft complaining flute.

complaint
4619 most fatal complaint of all, in

complaints
7234 thought complaints of
8777 money along with your complaints.

completion
7723 from conception to completion.
8521 available for its completion.

complex
4347 were not complex; They tore
11109 Man is a complex being: he

complexes
3659 his complexes, but to

complexion
569 hair. His complexion exceeding
12131 on your complexion, lovely

complexities
2318 of intense complexities intense
12880 All mere complexities, The fury

complexity
8519 means complexity and

compliance
2329 wanted was compliance with my

complicated
2425 way of saying complicated things.

complications
12424 always succumbed to complications'.

complies
1917 He that complies against his

compliment
1894 person the compliment of
4395 A compliment is a gift, not to
4828 pay a compliment like they
11963 two months on a good compliment.
12156 returned the compliment.

composed
4678 is composed of others.

composer
4067 music - the composer only
4735 for a composer is to be
8156 The good composer is slowly

composers
1557 of a few composers, a very

compound
1911 Compound for sins, they are

comprehend
2691 mind is prepared to comprehend.
8182 them, and comprehends them

comprehensible
9995 become more comprehensible, but more

compressed
7911 effectively compressed in thirty

compromise
4456 The slow compromise, or even
8056 moral than compromises and

compulsion
7456 Such sweet compulsion doth in

compulsorily
6883 should be compulsorily sober.

computer
4220 The perfect computer has been
5391 been a computer a hundred
6618 taped, or put into a computer.
8335 to have a computer in their

computers
261 Computers in the future will
6882 Computers can figure out all
12279 market for maybe five computers.

computing
7061 hazards of computing are

comradeship
3298 of genuine comradeship, the

conceal
2517 to conceal, usually
5878 is to be able to conceal it.
6853 you need to conceal a fact
9830 to us to conceal our

concealing
11970 consists in concealing how much

concealment
10516 But let concealment, like a

concede
7382 as freely concede to

conceit
11877 As for conceit, what man will

conceits
7012 And such conceits as

conceivable
7427 on every conceivable occasion.

conceived
880 of an era, conceived with

concensus
11649 The Act of Concensus is the

concentrated
5473 and more concentrated in you;

concentrates
5210 it concentrates his mind

concentration
8240 it produces concentration, it
11255 with no leaks in concentration.

conception
2940 us from our conception, and we
4641 else than conception caused by
7723 road from conception to
8292 are the same conception.
9640 Conception, my boy, fundamental
11247 Her conception of God was

concepts
11088 of his concepts, emerges

concern
497 life and its largest concern.
8250 does not concern us at all.
12040 which properly concern them.
12579 things that do not concern us.

concerned
2044 not be too concerned with
8207 I was not concerned. And when
11801 of being ultimately concerned.

concert
7419 torture, the concert.
9704 before the concert, not

concessions
1751 The concessions of the weak are
7332 what concessions to make,

conciliate
3369 not to conciliate, whose

conclusion
1372 A conclusion is the place where
7357 draw from it narrow conclusions.
9713 came to the conclusion that all

concord
7666 oft in pleasing concord end.
10406 moved with concord of sweet
10542 If the true concord of
11762 a good deal in Concord.

concrete
8033 is the concrete
10994 of concrete have
12187 you thought was concrete.

concrete jungle
7919 is not a concrete jungle, it is a

concurred
8458 I came, I saw, I concurred.

concurrence
8490 fortuitous concurrence of atoms.

condemn
1299 the years condemn. At the
6906 needs to condemn a little
7735 delights condemn, But 'tis
10520 I could condemn it as an

condemned
5837 an innocent person is condemned.
9282 judge is condemned when the
9928 I am condemned to be free.
12343 is like the condemned man who is

condescend
11341 of wit Will condescend to take a
11647 other who condescends to be so
12897 does not condescend, which

condition
2058 the human condition is a
6000 for the wrongs of his condition.
6930 La Condition humaine. The
8636 decoyed into our condition.

conditions
9961 The same conditions
11822 are no conditions of life to
12597 have the conditions, you get

conduct
497 Conduct is three-fourths of
6342 to so conduct the
6394 an ideal of conduct though it
7871 on the conduct of the
8684 results of his own conduct.
8815 that decides our conduct.
9072 of our conduct is ignored
10986 of conduct in such a

conductors
933 foreign conductors around -
11252 Conductors' careers are made for
11394 Conductors must give

confederacy
11348 are all in confederacy against

confederation
6708 Confederation is only yet in the
10831 father of confederation is

conference
739 a full man; conference a ready
3517 born in a conference, but a lot

confess
4886 have to confess their own,
5893 We only confess our little
7805 religiously confess myself to
9038 absolv'd Who has confess'd.
9176 He that jokes confesses.

confessing
8672 faults by confessing our

confession
401 a confession of
802 a kind of confession, more or
2257 is confession without
3497 the sweetness of confession.'
8994 trench confessions, laughter

confessional
9835 A confessional passage has

confide
2041 We seldom confide in those

confidence
3620 public confidence in its
6640 The confidence and faith of the
8739 Confidence is a plant of slow

confidently
11737 advances confidently in the

confides
6641 to and confides in, that

confine
8307 you cannot confine it in the

confinement
6434 the name of confinement which
12640 to solitary confinement inside our

confirmation
232 Confirmation at Eton: like a huge
10433 the jealous confirmations strong As

conflict
2295 of human conflict was so
3139 in an armed conflict; that is
5148 and in this conflict of
5646 all human conflict a method
8979 the final conflict: let us
9030 offered you Conflict and Art.

conflicts
4782 inner conflicts. Life
12884 Of our conflicts with others we

conform
7771 Once conform, once do what
8022 to conform either to
8634 either conform, or be

conformation
6808 The conformation of his mind was

conforming
9946 my view is conforming to

conformism
11253 Conformism is so hot on the

conformists
6744 is live conformists and its
7222 of the non conformists is like to

confound
2929 Confound those who have said
10352 and not the deed, Confounds us.

confront
8663 Confront disease at its onset.

confused
8046 who isn't confused doesn't
9918 I confused things with their
10872 which it is often confused.

confusing
3814 looks confusing and messy,

confusion
764 from error than from confusion.
7582 on rout, Confusion worse
8678 producing confusion,

congenial
7221 produced is congenial to every

congo
6382 I saw the Congo, creeping

congratulations
1758 to do, before we risk congratulations.

congregation
2745 has the largest congregation.

congress
5069 with the Congress, and that
7046 Congress is so strange. A man
12263 assure the Congress that no

congressman
185 Our Congressman are the finest

conjugation
4960 nature is a conjugation of the

connect
3581 Only connect! .. Only
8176 tends to connect; absolute

conquer
3820 and we'll conquer again and
4510 had time to conquer the world
5460 wings, Conquer all
7308 catch and conquer, Hard, but
8740 You cannot conquer America.
12266 to resolve to conquer or die.

conquered
1752 is perpetually to be conquered.
2006 I came, I saw, I conquered.
5123 I will be conquered; I will not
6611 but the conquered one
8805 'Living' Is conquered at last.
10048 to have conquered and
11369 Thou hast conquered, O pale

conquering
7886 See the conquering hero comes!

conqueror
3660 life the feeling of a conqueror.
9659 you are a conqueror. Kill
12282 Conqueror type of

conquers
8870 passion conquers reason
12135 Love conquers all things: let

conquest
2536 The conquest of the earth
3718 shows a conquest of nature
10284 Are all thy conquests, glories,

conscience
233 Conscience is a cur that will
1083 happiness or a quiet conscience.
1516 without conscience. Ours is
1875 Conscience is thoroughly
4148 Conscience is a coward, and
4455 social conscience about
5199 of man; conscience from the
5324 uncreated conscience of my race
6001 a man's conscience what is
6414 Sufficient conscience to bother
7250 Conscience is a mother-in-law
7269 Conscience: the inner voice
7465 to conscience, above all
9904 is the conscience of women;
10210 catch the conscience of the
10213 Thus conscience doth make
10267 Whose conscience with
10271 A still and quiet conscience.
10465 Conscience is but a word that
10724 Conscience has no more to do
10848 with a good conscience on the
11773 custom? Conscience is the
11791 to have a conscience, when it
11792 of His majesty's conscience.
12032 Conscience reigns but it does

conscientious
5579 when the conscientious objector

consciousness
6079 sympathetic consciousness and it can
7108 is not the consciousness of men
8622 Consciousness .. is the phenomenon
11998 which one's consciousness has been

conscription
5656 necessarily conscription, but

consecration
12783 land, The consecration, and the

consent
1973 will ne'er consent' -
6436 without his own consent.
9588 inferior without your consent.

consenting
12093 only between consenting adults.

consequence
780 is the consequence of cabinet

consequences
110 to take all the consequences.
3868 of man. Consequences are in the
4965 - there are consequences.
5011 the consequences of any
6090 fear of consequences. That is
7453 it and to damn the consequences.

conservation
1772 the means of its conservation.

conservatism
2255 All conservatism is based upon the
2872 thing this Conservatism - an
6374 What is conservatism? Is it not
12076 Conservatism is the maintenance of

conservative
468 become a conservative on the day
1122 The most conservative man in this
1708 A Conservative is a fellow who is
2873 A Conservative Government is an
3704 make me conservative when old.
3974 Or else a little Conservative!
4661 while marriage is conservative.
5043 A Conservative is a man who will
5601 a man more conservative - to know
6869 Conservative ideal of freedom and
9698 the Conservative Party at
12282 The staid, conservative,

conservatives
3331 Men are conservatives when they are
4371 Conservatives do not believe that
7360 The Conservatives .. being by the
8966 Conservatives are not xenophobic -

consider
52 Pray consider what a figure a
62 always consider how much
3799 I consider myself a Hindu,
5141 you should consider whether or
5060 one must consider the end.
7677 When I consider how my light
9017 Let us consider the reason of

considerable
1468 into a considerable portion.
5084 to appear considerable in his

considerate
354 Being considerate,

consideration
1415 with a due consideration of

considerations
4063 determining considerations that ought

consistency
1063 Consistency requires you to be as
4896 Too much consistency is as bad
12544 Consistency is the last refuge of

consistent
4684 Don't be consistent, but be
10833 in which men are consistent.

consists
7753 This world consists of men,

console
546 seek To be consoled as to
1505 will all console themselves

consoler
357 friends, consoler of the

consort
5726 But I consort with

conspicuous
9790 was conspicuous by its

conspiracies
10593 are conspiracies against

conspiracy
10819 ends in a conspiracy against
12014 is a vast conspiracy to make

constabulary
4017 When constabulary duty's to be

constancy
1611 is but constancy in a good.
9521 no more of constancy, that
10640 infernal constancy of the

constant
1740 here will constant be, Come
9961 history is constant, like the
10131 To one thing constant never.
10526 man But constant, he were
11307 this world constant, but
11456 sense of a constant

constantinople
1264 in Constantinople, one who

constitute
9594 assembled constitute ourselves

constitution
221 the British Constitution is in
298 has its own constitution; ours is
778 In such constitutions [as
1315 of the English constitution.
3103 whether the Constitution follows
3902 of a free constitution are
4841 are under a Constitution, but the
5359 very essence of the constitution.
6372 the Constitution or laws by
8741 the genius of the Constitution!
12649 The constitution does not provide
12662 the constitution of an

constitutional
6390 as constitutional, but must

constrained
3278 by violence constrained to do

construct
7207 inability to construct a future.

constructing
8536 knows in constructing a work is

constructions
11871 her constructions, and never

consult
8661 And don't consult anyone's

consulting
9904 without first consulting it.

consume
9822 than they can consume locally
10382 right to consume happiness

consumed
1478 of pop music is to be consumed
9803 can be consumed by

consumer
2426 A consumer is a shopper who is
3355 man is a consumer and ought
8319 The consumer is not a moron;
9852 The consumer, so it is said,
10820 promoting that of the consumer.

consumes
6958 since it consumes whole
8366 that consumes without
8759 The word consumes itself.
12008 adult bore consumes each year

consummated
6658 heaven and consummated on earth.

consumption
5604 its consumption by an
9942 to encourage consumption.
10820 Consumption is the sole end and

contagion
10674 From the contagion of the

contemplation
1561 by action, not by contemplation.
1861 delighted contemplation of other
3857 A mind serene for contemplation.
5405 talk of contemplation. Oh,
7594 For contemplation he and valour

contemporaries
3302 of your contemporaries, the

contemporary
2924 to become a contemporary of
5797 a hundred contemporary readers

contempt
3098 to show its contempt for
4345 most delicate form of contempt.
7843 a perfect contempt for it,
9976 the heart; contempt from the
10071 will breed contempt for them.
11969 breeds contempt - and
12291 And pour contempt on all my

contemptible
63 appear so contemptible and little

941 most contemptible kind of
7234 ill-usage contemptible, whether

contend
9940 the people contend for their

contender
1527 been a contender. I coulda

content
675 he will be content to begin
10913 would be content to take

contented
5464 In pale contented sort of
5999 never was contented .. Say
10452 shall be contented: must he

contentment
5725 Preaches contentment to that
7618 enjoying, what contentment find?

contest
8905 let fools contest; Whate'er
10005 Silent waiting the contest.

continent
2875 The Continent will [not] suffer
6346 upon this continent a new
7353 On the Continent people have

continental
9512 be quite continental, But

continuation
4976 just than a continuation of war.

continue
709 which once begun will continue.

continuity
4711 Historic continuity with the

contraception
152 story about contraception. I asked

contraceptives
7427 Contraceptives should be used on

contract
4211 A verbal contract isn't worth
4717 it, the more it will contract.
6392 only when it is under contract.

contradict
738 Read not to contradict and
1943 I can't contradict, what so
3377 though it contradict everything
3502 Never contradict Never explain
9874 Before you contradict an old
12495 Do I contradict myself? Very

contradiction
5055 name of religion is a contradiction.
6336 Here is monumental contradiction.
8021 are a contradiction in terms,
8867 at best a contradiction still.
10648 It is a contradiction in terms.
12330 kings - they brook no contradiction.

contradictions
2369 chain of contradictions,
4864 the most glaring contradictions.

contradictory
8380 holding two contradictory beliefs in

contraries
1337 Without contraries is no

contrary
8186 and directed to contrary parts.

contribution
9592 to make a contribution you begin

contrivance
10819 or in some contrivance to raise

contrive
8768 if we could contrive .. some

contrived
5088 yet been contrived by man, by

control
510 Sees man control the wind,
1547 people you are out of control.
1991 ruin - his control Stops with
2952 sights controls. And
7028 it is kept under control.
8551 Two things control man's
9976 is quite within our control.

controlled
6361 not to have controlled events,

controversies
9777 most savage controversies are those

controversy
3666 for public controversy and
5651 of challenge and controversy.
8166 part, that controversy is either
9752 is a matter of controversy.

convalescence
10631 I enjoy convalescence. It is the

convenient
7696 never any convenient time for
8427 It is convenient that there be

conventicle
8634 being at a conventicle .. I

convention
1556 the first convention of the
11225 like a convention of
12076 of conventions already

conversation
1484 music - a conversation between
4498 the salt of conversation, not the
4873 a flagging conversation, introduce
5155 happiest conversation where
5160 Wesley's conversation is good,
5194 the mode of conversation among
8039 in live conversation upon
8144 real art of conversation is not
8790 third-rate conversation without
10606 the art of conversation, but not,
10644 It adds spice to my conversation.
10787 ears, keep Conversation blurred.
10819 but the conversation ends in a
10883 make his conversation perfectly
11122 a different name for conversation.
11185 is one long conversation checkered
12456 Conversation is imperative if gaps

conversational
7914 conversational. An

converse
7569 There to converse with
7627 Thy sweet converse and love
11732 hold high converse with the

conversion
7071 Till the conversion of the

convert
4494 seek to make converts to it.
12390 America to convert the

converted
1181 ye be converted, and
7910 have not converted a man

converting
6563 An' in convartin' public trusts

conviction
2226 seem open to conviction yourself.
3527 degree and conviction are the
4872 is called conviction: you might
6344 conviction that I had
6391 men the conviction and the
8768 carry conviction to our
12902 lack all conviction, while the

convictions
2194 are not burdened with convictions.
2325 except to convictions of honour
3647 opposition that has convictions.
5531 Convictions are the mainsprings
9765 comforting convictions, which
10855 to drag out his dark convictions!

convince
2226 you would convince others,
5777 grace To convince the whole

convinces
8415 the man who convinces the world,

convincing
1938 Oh! too convincing - dangerously
4914 always less convincing than one.
8751 triumph by convincing its

cook
1045 intelligent cook can play
1100 Norman As Cook is a
8752 sew, it can cook, It can
9239 Even were a cook to cook a
9827 The cook was a good cook,

cookery
7320 don't last: cookery do!

cooking
7916 of English cooking is that
10663 just go right on cooking.

cooks
7326 without cooks. He may
7873 literary cooks Who skim
7916 entrusted to 'plain' cooks.

coolibah
8571 shade of a coolibah tree; And

copier
9453 A mere copier of nature can

copies
11811 originals and many copies.

copulation
3260 Birth, and copulation, and
10329 my sight. Let copulation thrive.

copyright
7356 there's no copyright on your
11868 their copyrights, and you

coquetry
6247 can be as tiresome as coquetry.

cordial
2415 she's cordial. If she
9523 .. That cordial drop

cordially
7839 and hate each other cordially.

core
1465 is at the core of life.

cork-screw
11961 six Bibles and no cork-screw.

cormorant
4974 The common cormorant (or shag)
9182 mimics a cormorant gets

corn
1924 raise the price of corn?
5225 do any better, it's corn.
7131 The corn that makes the
7232 price of corn, or isn't
9637 Was yellow like ripe corn.

corneille
5138 Corneille is to Shakespeare ..

corner
1036 bit in the corner you can't
1582 some corner of a
3866 at the corner of the
5124 into a corner, and who
6594 At every corner, I meet my
8194 the next corner or over
11816 round the corner there may

cornerstone
10068 my cornerstone. Nobody

cornerstones
3658 are the cornerstones of our

cornish
4458 thousand Cornish men Will

coromandel
6148 coast of Coromandel Where the
6802 coast of Coromandel, and red
10793 coast of Coromandel Dance they

coronets
11517 more than coronets, And

corporation
10007 capital to form a corporation.
11791 expect a corporation to have a

corporations
2429 Corporations cannot commit

corps
6416 Canadian Corps coming

corpse
6085 of cold are corpse fingers.
6517 word, A frozen corpse was he.
11362 loves into corpses or wives.

corpuscles
12675 human traits and red corpuscles.

correct
306 All present and correct.
3474 to seek to correct the
4581 will correct these
5057 great deal: correct a little.
8349 years to correct, is quite
11623 has his own correct way. [each

correction
879 infinite correction to

corridors
6480 Through the corridors of Time.
10904 world, the corridors of power.

corroboration
10828 particular corroboration of this

corroborative
4000 Merely corroborative detail,

corrugated
928 on a corrugated tin roof.

corrupt
1767 generally corrupt, liberty
6772 virtues but also more corrupt.
7636 Peace to corrupt no less
8745 is apt to corrupt the minds
10619 by the corrupt few.

corrupter
10679 power a corrupter, glory a

corruptible
7346 fate, 'mongst things corruptible.

corrupting
1476 for novelty becomes corrupting,
8761 guilty of corrupting the minds

corruption
3905 Corruption, the most infallible

corrupts
14 power corrupts
2670 power corrupts
4660 Power corrupts the few, while
5581 When power corrupts, poetry

cortez
5439 like stout Cortez when with

cosiness
9322 all the cosiness and

cosmic
9775 the face of cosmic forces,

cosmopolitan
7836 to become cosmopolitan in the

cosmos
2251 the cosmos, but never

cost
4833 on account of the cost.

costly
1095 at least as costly as the
11714 metal, Too costly for cost?

costs
407 What costs nothing is worth
439 you get free costs too much.
2334 at all costs, victory
5575 risks and costs to a
5769 Costs merely register
7757 Civility costs nothing and

costume
6067 The same costume will be

cottage
8743 may in his cottage bid
10388 poor men's cottages princes'

cotton
329 to' don't pick no cotton.
4610 an' the cotton is high.

cough
12194 they cough in

coughing
863 keep an audience from coughing.
9965 only - one coughing, and one

coughs
7976 Coughs and sneezes spread

council
9465 old men In council rooms

councillor
4730 A councillor ought not to sleep

counsel
4060 to keep my counsel .. and I
4522 deal of counsel; for it

counsellors
700 plain when counsellors blanch.

count
98 Don't count your chickens
1628 Let me count the ways.
1632 I count life just a stuff
6225 They had to count them all.

6331 can't count above
8734 must not count overmuch
10928 but I won the count.
11977 When angry, count four; when

counted
1226 and are counted as the
4415 I counted them all out and I

countenance
939 of countenance as much as
7654 the bright countenance of truth
12801 is in the countenance of all

counterfeiting
3626 a good man and counterfeiting him.

countess
7171 what the countess is saying.

counting
11223 democracy, it's the counting.

countries
1461 are no countries in the
10572 are two countries divided by

country
399 born in the country and moved
1189 save in his own country.
1377 This was my country and it may
1613 unto me one country: I am in
1700 happiest man in the country,
1801 to run the country are busy
2416 leave his country as good as
2524 only in the country that we
2624 made the country, and man
2731 Our country! In her
2801 being Queen of this country.
2878 of this country the fate
3003 not a bad country .. It's
3588 my country and
3986 and every country but his
4059 much of the country through
4074 Love of our country is another
4484 had in the country, or, if
4620 is a country where they
4776 is to die for one's country.
5319 in this country, there are
5572 what your country can do for
6341 This country, with its
6343 we shall save our country.
6901 Every country has the
6947 The country has charms only
7055 in urbe. Country in the
8052 Great artists have no country.
8265 This country needs good
8472 the service of their country.
8478 My country is the world, and
8518 there's a country lane,
9609 for the country is good
9700 and your Country both need
9805 The country habit has me by
9994 My country, right or wrong;
10183 country from whose
10428 that pulls the country down.
10862 My country, 'tis of thee,
10880 for the country; it is a
11037 to thee, my country - all
11128 of his own country too,
12450 of spring in the country.
12536 good in the country. There
12765 for the good of his country.

countrymen
1987 I do not love my countrymen.
10289 Romans, countrymen, lend me

countryside
2989 smiling and beautiful countryside.

counts
3190 What counts is not

coupled
2288 and wife, Coupled together

couples
11675 the naughty couples down the

courage
446 Courage! I have shown it for
832 depends on courage and work.
1089 Courage - fear that has said
1406 of fatigue; courage is only
1409 As to moral courage, I have
2080 The courage we desire and
2256 paradox of courage is that a
2299 Courage is rightly esteemed

2475 the rarest courage; since
2540 depends, is want of courage.
2972 must have the courage to dare.
3092 Clothes and courage have much
3215 does the work of courage.
3341 part of courage is the
3737 if we had courage enough.
3841 us With courage, love and
4227 trouble, Courage in your
4653 can be a source of courage.
4977 man with courage makes a
5035 Have the courage to act
5050 I have the courage of my
5139 Courage is a quality so
5228 rare is the courage to follow
5561 The courage of life is often
5586 Moral courage is a more rare
6241 Just as courage imperils
6301 Courage is not simply one
6834 from stain Courage and faith;
7550 hate, And courage never to
7896 The courage of the poet is to
8074 Le courage de l'improviste.
8075 has the courage to attempt
8204 be changed; courage to change
8577 Courage is fear holding on a
9408 Courage, mon ami, le diable
9486 Courage is doing what you're
10011 and courage of my
11769 the morning courage, which
11872 who have courage to love
11942 Courage is resistance to
12046 or of courage, or both.
12129 your young courage, boy;
12220 'Tis the courage you bring
12266 God, on the courage and

courageous
9656 liberal, courageous, such as I

course
4548 not what course others may
6559 My preudunt course is
6706 star our course is set,
7146 cannot steer A middle course.
8640 to that course, which is
10413 The course of true
11809 and their courses are not

court
2200 the kynges court, my
2679 - in or out of court.
3103 the Supreme Court follows
3620 The Court's authority -
5277 pursue: So court a
8196 who know how to court her.
9034 I court others in verse:
10668 his pale court in beauty

courted
2033 Better be courted and jilted

courtesy
4122 mark of courtesy that does
5764 perfect courtesy, you
10018 of gentlest courtesy; Yet

courts
9779 of the Courts, it means
11572 brawling courts And dusty

courtship
2515 Courtship to marriage, as a
6980 a shadow of courtship should
8339 spasmodic courtship, conducted

cousins
3961 and his cousins and his
11748 and meet their ideal cousins.

couth
8644 a thing as too much couth.

covenant
3822 South is 'a covenant with death

cover
12329 Cover her face, mine eyes

covet
5672 as ever coveted his

coveting
9843 Coveting other men's property,

covetous
10806 rich are covetous of their

cow
912 till the cow comes

6948 great milk cow, with its
8086 The cow is of the bovine
11335 when she kissed her cow.
12531 We milk the cow of the

coward
2058 is a coward, but he
2531 often be a coward, but for
3549 The coward's weapon, poison.
4148 is a coward, and those
8346 The sea hates a coward!
10602 is the coward's revenge
11601 myself the coward if I left

cowardice
2166 between rashness and cowardice.
2181 a miserable cowardice. Men will
3694 engaging cowardice. With it
4981 it too far, and it's cowardice.
11951 but the surest is cowardice.

cowardly
12170 adventure open to the cowardly.
12334 Cowardly dogs bark loudest.

cowards
2516 die. Tho' cowards flinch and
3737 We could be cowards, if we had
6269 are the cowards they are
6464 makes cowards of us all.
9527 would be cowards if they
10213 doth make cowards of us all;
10280 Cowards die many times before
10465 a word that cowards use,
11959 a race of cowards; and I am
12416 heroes or cowards; they

cowslip
7488 O'er the cowslip's velvet

coxcomb
7305 without the coxcomb's
9743 to hear a coxcomb ask two

coy
4593 Then be not coy, but use
7524 vain, and coy excuse.
10044 sometimes coy, Yet she

coyness
7070 time, This coyness, lady,

crabbed
10535 Crabbed age and youth cannot

crack
3318 There is a crack in
9149 but he does not crack them.

cradle
946 to the cradle goes all
2323 from the cradle to the
3127 Between the cradle and the
8062 The cradle rocks above an
8749 In the calm the cradle lends.
10400 dies In the cradle where it
10703 from the cradle to the
12195 rocks the cradle Is the
12493 Out of the cradle endlessly

cramps
12733 to parents cramps every

crane
10785 Tall as a crane, The

crash
2081 The crash of the whole

craved
4031 and who craved no crumb,

craving
8598 no stronger craving in the
12122 cursed craving for gold!
12861 the more is craving, Never

crawl
11313 suffered to crawl upon the

crazy
258 to have a crazy person
350 and find oil? You're crazy.
1586 one to be crazy and amuse
2671 I'm half crazy, all for
4449 Just two crazy people
8643 Crazy like a fox.

creak
9253 Devil's boots don't creak.

cream
3683 I want the cream to rise.
3965 milk masquerades as cream.

7298 skim the cream of life,
7873 skim the cream of others'

create
1548 need to create, as it
4278 I didn't create them out
7197 If you create an act, you
8247 father, one must create one.
11994 be able to create one's own
12793 himself create the taste

created
2088 never created a man half
2715 in me; they created us, body
3396 great is created suddenly,
6451 Nations) is created to prevent
6622 can be created out of
8898 Created half to rise, and

creates
5407 always creates the
7875 And what it fears, creates.
11142 is that he creates the world

creating
6569 In creating, the only hard
7840 like God creating something.

creation
2038 authentic creation is a gift
4114 the divine force of creation.
6424 from the first creation.
7626 fairest of creation, last and
9528 part of God's creation.
9999 the devils of his own creation.
11219 is his new creation By water
11578 which the whole creation moves.
12966 a corner of creation seen

creative
2146 to be creative, you're
3577 In the creative state a man is
3648 Creative minds have always
6847 that the creative faculty
11090 life of the creative man is

creativeness
8718 Taste is the enemy of creativeness.

creativity
2067 A hunch is creativity trying to
3530 at bay and spark creativity.
9358 I get horny for my creativity.
9803 consumed by creativity as they

creator
7616 The great creator from his
7632 did God, Creator wise, that
8161 beings, myself and my Creator.
9671 leaves the Creator's hands;
10860 I am as my Creator made me,
11943 The Creator made Italy with

creature
7348 Y'are the deed's creature.
7830 house Not a creature was
8366 is the only creature that
8852 vain, The creature's at his
11329 that every creature Lives in a

creatures
67 all other creatures by the
128 All creatures great and
198 the earth as other creatures do.
2571 the only creatures on earth
4882 Summits are odd creatures.
7600 spiritual creatures walk the
8634 poor creatures carried

credit
3966 to his credit, That he
6762 poor people's credit card.
7937 who get the credit. Try, if
9763 to be a credit to them.

creditors
39 your coat to your creditors.

credulity
4650 Our credulity is greatest
5944 Credulity is the man's
8739 is the season of credulity.

creed
3002 His creed no parson ever
3803 last article of my creed.
11123 got the better of his creed.

creeds
10700 The dust of creeds outworn.

11557 the keys of all the creeds.
11574 me, than in half the creeds.

creep
10373 to-morrow, Creeps in this

creeping
11530 slowly, creeping on from
12437 madam, Nature is creeping up.

cremated
4452 should be cremated, not

crept
5516 then there crept A little

crescent-moon
12816 Boat, Shaped like the crescent-moon.

crete
9822 people of Crete

cricket
6126 then set up a game of cricket.
6939 Cricket - a game which the
7502 Save the cricket on the
8020 Cricket civilizes people and
11466 looked on cricket as
11860 of playing cricket with their

cried
6747 if I cried When I

cries
10546 my bootless cries, And look

crime
63 not a real crime makes a
1321 Tough on crime and tough
2283 well; No crime's so great
2414 The worst crime is faking
2463 that crime does not
2995 Napoleon of Crime, Watson.'
3105 It isn't a crime exactly.
3567 a cure for crime as charity
3749 authorizes not the crime.
3995 fit the crime - The
4087 There is no crime of which I
4214 The worst crime against
5037 is no crime. No, if
7070 lady, were no crime.
7413 study of crime begins
8006 Crime doesn't pay.
8737 atrocious crime of being a
8840 heav'n, a crime to love
9007 for a crime you
9354 Crime, like virtue, has its
10095 that stupid crime, that
11760 not even crime, more
12119 the one crime recognize
12155 succeeds crime - it is

crimea
11442 Crimea: The War That Would

crimes
2738 are virtues made or crimes.
3056 Successful crimes alone are
3448 Crimes, like virtues, are
7555 reiterated crimes he might
7872 reach the dignity of crimes.
9581 what crimes are
12160 tableau of crimes and

criminal
5609 for ends I think criminal.
10007 A criminal is a person with

criminals
9838 if there were no criminals.
12546 treats her criminals the way

cripples
8562 now. If cripples, then no

crisis
2676 great moral crisis, maintain
8472 in this crisis, shrink
8583 moments of crisis, the
11652 have a real crisis on your
12416 last some crisis shows what

crisp
8114 Deep and crisp and even.

criteria
5610 relating to criteria of what

critic
1899 of a good critic is whether
2471 knew the critic's part,
2690 The critic is the duenna in
3079 A critic at best is a waiter

3606 The good critic is he who
5016 of the critic as an
5970 English critic is a don
6089 of a critic is to save
6557 attribute of a good critic.
8817 A critic is a legless man
11995 A critic is a man who knows
12440 cry of the critic for five.
12833 the Sonnet; Critic, you have

critical
6847 and the critical faculty
10426 I am nothing if not critical.
11840 The critical moment for you as

criticism
504 at bottom a criticism of life.
780 made a criticism of
1373 of anger, fear and criticism.
1598 dramatic criticism must seem
3589 because it permits criticism.
4813 To escape criticism - do
6777 that criticism is ever
7178 ask you for criticism, but they
8949 and with the criticism of myths.
11125 the cant of criticism is the
11998 Drama criticism .. [is] a
12475 a sense of criticism, founded

criticize
2337 never to criticize or attack
3807 fool can criticize, and many
6369 a right to criticize, who has a
9082 Never criticize a man until

criticized
4816 going to be criticized, vilified,
6587 which time has criticized for us!
8646 peace is always being criticized.

criticizing
5839 pleasure of criticizing robs us of

critics
964 Critics are like eunuchs in a
1944 censure - critics all are
2452 therefore they turn critics.
7999 who the critics are? The
4695 to make critics out of the
5288 of models than of critics.
7837 The lot of critics is to be
11984 audience - 4000 critics.
12396 will true critics please.
12600 When critics disagree, the
12767 Critics are like brushers of

croaks
10346 hoarse That croaks the fatal

crocodile
2294 who feeds a crocodile - hoping
5706 to the Crocodile's musky,

crocodiles
749 of the crocodiles, that shed
4922 female crocodiles continue
9214 are no crocodiles because

crocus
6591 like the crocus all over

cromwell
926 a ruin that Cromwell knocked
5281 They set up Cromwell and his
6419 a ruin that Cromwell knocked

crook
8269 is a crook. Well,
9568 you are a crook or a

crooked
1333 but the crooked roads
4074 of their crooked designs.
5386 Out of the crooked timber of
6432 Crooked things may be as
7105 'yes,' you know he is crooked.

crop
8802 any other crop, is best

cross
848 With the cross of Jesus
5542 bear the cross gladly, it
8025 the Cross as the
9251 forgets to cross himself.
10788 forty nails Upon the Cross.
11701 one to an untenanted cross.
12291 wondrous cross On which
12690 it dangerous to cross him.

cross-bow
2445 - With my cross-bow I shot the

cross-grained
4186 ever such a cross-grained brute?

crossed
647 likes to be crossed in love a
8075 and will be crossed as soon as

crosses
5281 down the crosses. They set
6698 Between the crosses, row on

crossing
6368 horses when crossing streams.

crow
2201 and thenk upon the crowe
3824 The carrion crow, that
6567 'n 't is to crow: Don't
9182 The crow that mimics a

crowd
713 A crowd is not company, and
862 Every crowd has a silver
953 you can make a crowd of men.
2601 The crowd, and buzz, and
3400 are forced to be in a crowd.
5628 there is a crowd there is
5807 of the crowd will not
8830 All crowd, who foremost
12844 I saw a crowd, A host,

crowded
2803 so it was a bit crowded.

crowds
3916 Crowds without company, and
5166 live in the crowds of
7850 ear; Frail crowds that a
12774 come in crowds; I dread

crowing
122 silly cock crowing on its own

crown
1109 have the crown of thorns
1236 woman is a crown to her
2057 to wear a crown. He must
2710 possess the crown. Titles
3108 of the Crown has
3274 glory of my crown: that I
7899 a crown of thorns,
8619 glory; no cross, no crown.
8658 diadem To crown Him Lord
10165 The crown o' the earth doth
10169 put on my crown; I have
10248 head that wears the crown.
10450 the hollow crown That
11526 a sorrow's crown of sorrow

crowned
7077 labours see Crowned from some

crowns
10505 The end crowns all, And that

crucified
130 Lord was crucified, Who died

crucify
2093 not even crucify him. They

cruel
2643 Cruel necessity.
4383 apt to be cruel because
5451 'For cruel 'tis,' said she,
8851 think this cruel? take it
9899 truth is cruel, but it
10217 Let me be cruel, not
10220 I must be cruel only to be
11407 Men are cruel, but man is

cruellest
3262 is the cruellest month,
11199 The cruellest lies are often

cruelty
1331 Cruelty has a human heart,
10069 All cruelty springs from

cruise
11203 are all on our last cruise.

crumbling
6789 Crumbling between the fingers,

crumbs
4974 the bags to hold the crumbs.

crumpetty
6159 on this Crumpetty Tree The

crusade
6107 Children's Crusade in 1212 AD
12663 is a moral crusade or it is

crush
2973 To crush, to annihilate a
12188 and crush the

crusoe
5077 Robinson Crusoe, and the

cry
1717 as a good cry is to a
1814 a body Need a body cry?
3444 And, mother, do not cry!
5179 cries, Cry not when
6031 write if you can't cry?
6119 The cry of the Little
6324 me as I cry all the
8757 your bald cry Took its
9331 We'll cry both arts and
9462 Some must cry so that
9668 It is a cry in the
10257 this charge Cry 'God for
10331 are born we cry that we
11108 a sudden cry of pain!
12276 lament and cry And now

crying
11564 An infant crying in the

crystal
1115 read the crystal when he

crystallises
9014 politician crystallises what most

cuckold
3402 to cuckold' for

cuckoo
2703 pleasant cuckoo, loud and
7707 The cuckoo who is on to
11003 The merry cuckoo, messenger

cuckoo clock
12356 produce ..? The cuckoo clock."

cuckoo-echoing
4756 towers; Cuckoo-echoing,

cucumber
5135 are but cucumbers after
6734 when cucumber is added

cue
3997 a twisted cue And

culprit
12269 those of a culprit who is

culprits
8463 choose the culprits than to
12119 recognize all as culprits.

cult
163 What's a cult? It just
6728 which the cult of

cultivate
5108 him to cultivate your
5958 Cultivate simplicity,
12147 We must cultivate our garden.

cultivated
3951 celebrated, Cultivated,
7298 Cultivated men and women who do

culture
498 Culture is the passion for
499 The men of culture are the
970 who leaves culture to his
2038 Without culture, and the
3723 the popular culture of the
4006 line as a man of culture rare.
4331 feigning a culture which has
4364 sunk deep into our culture.
6458 the culture of the
6758 the old culture what is
7209 against the culture, where he
12426 who pursue Culture in bands,
12501 - and not culture, or any

cunning
702 than that cunning men pass
5323 silence, exile, and cunning.
6246 it one only has to be cunning.

cup
1188 let this cup pass from
1810 We'll tak a cup o'

cupid
6655 Cupid and my Campaspe
10414 is winged Cupid painted

cupidons
1798 away all the little cupidons.

cur
233 is a cur that will

curable
1266 often curable by

curate
3495 the average curate at home as
4028 was a pale young curate then.

curates
1564 shower of curates has fallen
1576 Curates, long dust, will come

curds
10531 queen of curds and cream.

cure
5 The best cure for
986 is no Cure for this
2600 cheap and universal cure.
3058 a malady without a cure.
5708 The cure for this ill is
5842 nor shame can cure them.
9897 There is no cure for birth
10650 not. The cure for it is
10829 has no cure for this
11391 the twentieth, it's a cure.

cured
2402 cannot be cured by what is
4680 one that is rarely cured.
5677 That's cured by hanging
6688 a man to be cured by his own
7793 is easily cured; poverty
9043 Cured yesterday of my

cures
7285 Love cures people; both the
8118 puts to bed and cures.
10773 continually cures himself

curfew
4290 The curfew tolls the knell

curiosity
193 of general curiosity, one
4893 for their curiosity, their
5952 excite curiosity. No one
11220 prurient curiosity and
11859 curiosity is the

curiouser
2112 Curiouser and curiouser!'

curl
6478 a little curl Right in
7423 a little curl, Right in

currencies
12665 of other currencies. It does

currency
11222 It's the currency of living.

current
7485 But must be current, and the

curse
6083 Curse the blasted,
9459 is the real curse of Eve.
10546 myself and curse my fate.
11101 us from the curse Of a prose
11522 side; 'The curse is come
12608 Work is the curse of the

curses
4046 the bitter curses of
10958 Curses are like young

curst
10568 stones, And curst be he that

curtain
8838 lets the curtain fall; And
9345 down the curtain, the farce

curtains
7745 the neat curtains are drawn

curve
374 smile is a curve that can

curved
3161 All space is slightly curved.

custard pie
8395 a custard pie .. A

custom
1785 Custom reconciles us to
2685 Custom, that unwritten law,
4999 A custom loathsome to the
9309 some folk, custom's rule
10174 Custom calls me to 't: What
10196 - it is a custom More
11515 one good custom should
11773 immemorial custom?

customary
5041 allowed it to become customary.
8778 It is customary these days to

customer
9504 tort. The customer is never

cut
5293 Never cut what you can
6456 Look at the cut, the
10294 unkindest cut of all;
12264 lie. I did cut it with my
12372 you. I'll cut bits orf

cuts
10283 He that cuts off twenty

cutting
981 pleasure Of cutting all the

cuttlefish
8373 like a cuttlefish squirting

cycle
5285 this as a cycle of

cycle-clips
6036 take off My cycle-clips in awkward

cynic
1256 Cynic, n: a blackguard
3320 A cynic can chill and
7259 A cynic is a man who, when
12570 What is a cynic? A man who

cynical
969 Irish are cynical. It's
3595 people are cynical about, and

cynically
8246 that means cynically and with

cynicism
2382 by cynicism and
4518 Cynicism is an unpleasant way
6665 Cynicism - the intellectual
7305 Cynicism is intellectual
9760 Cynicism such as one finds

daddy
7990 do in the Great War, daddy?
8087 Ask Daddy, He Won't Know.
8955 My heart belongs to Daddy.

daffodil
11543 loves On a bed of daffodil sky.

daffodils
6047 for me what daffodils were for
12844 A host, of golden daffodils.
12845 And dances with the daffodils.

daft
10035 thinks the tither daft.

dagger
10351 Is this a dagger which I see

daggers
10217 will speak daggers to her,

daintily
1100 have things daintily served.
1522 Pardon's Daintily alights

dainty
4588 my Julia's dainty leg, Which

dairy
5245 doth nightly rob the dairy.

dairymaid
7442 asked The Dairymaid: 'Could we

daisies
4007 upon the daisies and

daisy
2671 Daisy, Daisy, give me your

dalliance
10194 path of dalliance treads,

dam
7392 her for a dam What

damage
5213 who can do us serious damage.
7975 seriously damage your
12699 What damage to

dames
7514 struts his dames before.

dammed
4741 only saved by being dammed.

damn
369 give a damn, I wish I
3762 I don't give a damn."
5955 exclaimed, Damn the age; I
7395 life is one damn thing
7697 dear, I don't give a damn.
8511 I do not give a damn.

damnation
574 is what is called damnation.
1420 everlasting damnation, Good
7555 might Heap on himself damnation.
10647 be blasted to eternal damnation!

damned
2911 is not only dead, but damned.
3515 The beautiful and damned.
4183 It's a damned long, dark,
4821 is just one damned thing
5697 the spree, Damned from here
6994 must be damned
7574 with devil damned Firm
8724 Better be damned than
8830 shall be damned to Fame.
12363 Publish and be damned.
12815 All silent, and all damned?

damning
1911 to, By damning those they

damns
6700 richt That damns the vast

damozel
9636 The blessed damozel leaned out

dance
1076 Must you dance ev'ry dance
1816 the ae best dance e'er cam
1929 On with the dance! let joy
2986 because the dance was long:
6977 Dance is in the air ..
7027 there's a dance in the old
8879 learned to dance. 'Tis not
8916 at least before they dance.
9003 A dance to the music of
10661 Dance is the only art of
10793 Coromandel Dance they to
12909 rage Should dance attendance

danced
6156 sand, They danced by the

dancer
7327 A Degas dancer pirouettes
12031 hybrid of a dancer and a
12879 we know the dancer from the

dances
6212 Two slow dances do not
12845 fills, And dances with the

dancing
1080 together dancing
2701 devise, For dancing is love's
9846 We are dancing on a volcano.
10469 I are past our dancing days.
10586 Dancing is] a perpendicular

dandyism
7305 dandyism without

danger
40 There is a danger from all
1423 run into any kind of danger.
2283 The danger chiefly lies in
4925 is dangerous, where
5856 me out of danger. You can
8089 be in less danger From the
8443 when in danger, not
9120 Danger and delight grow on
9323 brink of danger; not
10237 nettle, danger, we pluck
10735 measure of danger, and a
11287 per cent of its danger.
12088 The danger to the country,
12454 Oft in danger, oft in woe,
12916 is in danger of

dangerous
112 is more dangerous than an
1760 the more dangerous the abuse.
4183 boggy, dirty, dangerous way.
4925 is dangerous, where is
4999 the brain, dangerous to the
5533 none is so dangerous as the
5866 be less dangerous if they
5924 Mad, bad, and dangerous to know.
7943 is a dangerous

7944 that it is dangerous and may do
8048 more dangerous to the
8874 is a dangerous thing;
10276 much: such men are dangerous.
12426 it were dangerous to meet it
12545 It is a dangerous thing to
12566 is a dangerous thing, and
12576 is so dangerous as being

dangerously
8218 life is to live dangerously !

dangers
549 The main dangers in this life
1756 Dangers by being despised
6510 brave its dangers Comprehend
8032 of the dangers that come
8517 On the dangers of the
10071 exposure to dangers will breed

daniel
10403 A Daniel come to judgement!

dare
7803 much as I dare; and I
10349 I dare do all that may
10968 woman dare When

dares
2972 to him who dares to stoop
7980 Who dares wins.
10475 can do that dares love

daring
202 comes from daring to begin.
2422 in daring is to know
11448 The loving are the daring.

dark
904 When it is dark enough,
1601 made a leap into the dark.
2202 Derk was the nyght as
2447 one stride comes the dark.
2965 Between us and the dark.
3713 The dark is light enough.
4546 to go home in the dark.
4636 a great leap in the dark.
5228 to the dark places
6486 man said; Dark lowers the
6959 out of the dark and go
7555 to his own dark designs,
7584 Dark with excessive
7656 O dark, dark, dark, amid
9107 die in the dark, even
10167 And we are for the dark.
10788 the Rain - Dark as the
11954 and has a dark side which
12057 nowhere but in the dark.

dark-heaving
1935 Dark-heaving - boundless, endless,

darken
5446 men, Darkened the
6337 Never darken my Dior again!

darker
4844 I am the darker brother.

darkest
4300 The darkest hour of any man's

darkling
12127 Darkling they went under the

darkness
121 not enough darkness in all the
1174 into outer darkness; there
1998 between his Darkness and his
3289 ended, The darkness falls at
4454 into the darkness and put
5347 in the darkness of mere
5441 shores of darkness there is
6669 The darkness deepens;
7549 but rather darkness visible
7637 out of darkness! full of
8062 two eternities of darkness.
8126 there is darkness
8838 universal darkness buries
9315 To me the darkness brings not
11701 In the darkness .. the sound

darksome
4129 spent the darksome hours
11009 That darksome cave they enter,

darling
859 to call you darling after sex.
2076 She is the darling of my

7824 Oh, my darling, oh my
10545 shake the darling buds of

darwinian
3950 Darwinian Man, though

date
1033 out of date.

dating
2557 seeing people dating again.

daughter
2597 put your daughter on the
3277 The daughter of debate, that
3837 will ever rear a daughter!
5714 a Throne: Daughter am I in my
10396 My daughter! O my ducats! O my
10677 I am the daughter of Earth and

daughters
487 one of her daughters - any one
6878 are men's daughters, but God's

david
8113 King David and King Solomon

dawn
5718 An' the dawn comes up
6809 and to reflect the dawn.
7135 and a grey dawn breaking.
11708 I said to Dawn: Be sudden
12619 does not dawn seem to be

dawned
10087 day has ever dawned for me.
10671 first God dawned on Chaos.

day
9 comes one day at a time.
1460 dog has his day, and mine
2042 It happens every day.
2938 The day breaks not, it is
3104 place ivry day, but no
3135 "Go ahead. Make my day."
3289 The day Thou gavest,
3759 What a day may bring, a
4769 each day that has
4774 every day that Fate
6071 of the present day.
6591 amazing the day is still
6747 inside The day the music
7698 tomorrow is another day.
8170 the garish day, and spite
9279 of a long day makes that
8787 Not a day without a
9316 - As day flies
9409 Not a day passes over the
9665 Every dogma has its day.
10087 untroubled day has ever
10167 The bright day is done,
10340 and fair a day I have not
10449 death will have his day.
11000 the gradual day Weakening
11446 end of the day, No
11553 have their day; They have
11610 The long day wanes: the
12835 between day and day.

day-to-day
2214 - it's this day-to-day living
5912 Oh, what a day-to-day business

daydreaming
11263 always be daydreaming; it may be

daylight
10408 is but the daylight sick.

days
168 the bad old days, there
1432 number our days: that we
1940 My days are in the yellow
2987 long, the days of wine
3248 ends of smoky days.
3330 which the days never
6038 What are days for? Days
7777 length of days but in the
7866 our days Is to
9127 of these days is none of
11325 all the days of your
11514 And the days darken round
12776 childish days, that were

dazzle
12329 mine eyes dazzle: she died

dazzling
8533 means for dazzling our eyes
11728 sweep, a dazzling deluge

dead
236 A dead man Who never
313 and is dead: Had it
495 charity more than the dead.
823 end if the dead could
868 that falls down dead.
985 When I am dead, I hope it
1003 struck him dead: And serve
1053 to be said For being dead.
1175 Let the dead bury their
1574 die. It's dead. Alone,
1637 are not dead. They are
2795 - the quick, and the dead.
2879 I am dead; dead, but in
2933 She, she is dead; she's
2977 when I am dead And
3069 high, The dead shall
3883 After I am dead, the boy
3924 before he is dead.
4166 she was dead, Her last
4289 A dead woman bites not.
4375 the living dead, the dying
4526 round him o'er the dead.
4735 a composer is to be dead
4896 people are the dead.
5608 long run we are all dead.
5745 But marks our English dead:
6084 The dead don't die. They
6194 he had been dead for two
6312 and pure and very dead.
6476 And all the rest are dead.
6498 he lies; Dead he is not,
6502 Let the dead Past bury
6554 loose me is dead, Fighting
6573 and the dead alone
6630 helped by being dead.
6848 who like it better dead.
7009 besides, the wench is dead.
7096 he's dead, or my
7118 When I am dead and opened,
7702 but in fact it is dead.
8009 Better red than dead.
8142 God is dead! Heaven is
8215 God is dead: but
8449 kissed by the English dead.
8989 shall be dead pretty
9234 It fell dead from the
9293 men are dead! Carlyle,
9515 more to say when I am dead.
9635 When I am dead, my
9766 already three parts dead.
9913 to be blooming well dead?
10507 Hector is dead; there is
10718 Indian is a dead Indian.
10869 (Still the dead one lay
11614 when I am dead, To drop
11686 the first dead lies
11691 is the only dead thing that
11732 with the mighty dead.
11905 who's been dead 10 or 15
11910 Dead battles, like dead
12169 to the dead we owe
12301 it. After that it's dead.
12541 was dead in each of
12738 Dead! and .. never

deadlock
10831 of confederation is deadlock.

deadly
5695 is more deadly than the
11944 are more deadly in the
12805 - another deadly blow!

deaf
2437 union of a deaf man to a
6298 to rouse a deaf world.
9081 tongue will keep thee deaf.

deal
6825 how to deal with
9609 a square deal

dealing
3753 men, must leave off dealing.

dean
1576 sly shade of a Rural Dean.
2909 Mr. Dean, no dogma,
11030 to the queer old Dean.
11036 I am the Dean of Christ

deaneries
3429 Deaneries and crown canonries

dear
3762 my dear, I don't
7697 .. My dear, I don't
10554 art too dear for my

dearer
7607 of myself and dearer half.
11525 a little dearer than his

dearest
10344 away the dearest thing he

death
4 visible, Death's artifact
114 to die, death will
180 Death has got something to
237 Death is terrible to
338 thing to death in life Is
375 O Death, where is thy
460 of the new terrors of death.
703 Men fear death as children
704 the fear of death. And
706 Death hath this
785 for the death of a
918 personal victory over death.
1102 a cow. Swarm over, Death!
1130 shall be destroyed is death.
1131 O death, where is thy
1141 be no more death, neither
1143 The wages of sin is death.
1418 of life we are in death.
1426 shadow of death, I will
1581 and enemy is but Death.
1615 cure, for death is the
1627 thee better after death.
1830 O Death! the poor man's
1885 then so neither must death.
2136 of conception until death.
2371 Pale death, the grand
2461 After death they take
2765 think about death only
2825 after Death Is
2835 stop for Death - He
2943 Any man's death diminishes
2947 Death be not proud, though
2948 And death shall be
2957 Death] comes equally to us
2976 desire his father's death?
2978 heart. And death, who had
3034 Death, in itself, is
3218 there is an image of death.
3260 and death. That's
3268 by death And saw
3409 enough not to fear death.
3472 it is not death, but
3485 presence of death lurks with
3534 Th'usurper Death will make
3582 Death destroys a man: the
3630 except death and taxes.
3925 note, When death approached
4239 of the death penalty
4292 the dull cold ear of death?
4326 come after death - the
4442 root, the death or
4548 liberty, or give me death!
4672 Death is nothing at all; it
4738 His death, which happened
4779 and war to the death.
4890 as though death were no
5115 can run the race with Death?
5120 of decay, Death broke at
5372 Death alone reveals how
5393 abolish the death penalty,
5414 - or else swoon to death.
5831 form of death; Oh world,
5846 Death never takes the wise
5987 Death stands above me,
6168 only nervousness or death.
6276 to you, 'tis death to us.
6624 Death therefore is nothing
6724 from birth to death.
6730 thing as death, In
6752 not die of death: We die of
6839 this earth Death cometh
6922 and the death of the
6969 though for death. Should I
6996 allotted death and hell,
7130 through the death of some of
7133 Death opens unknown doors.
7150 Death hath a thousand doors
7544 Brought death into the

7578 cried out Death! Hell
7658 half dead, a living death.
7671 us in a death so noble.
7696 Death and taxes and
7776 to build the house of death.
7810 island surrounded by death.
7813 and not at their death.
7859 ranks of death you'll
7942 a decent death on the
7996 Death [is] nature's way of
8061 not see why death should not
8152 river of death has
8453 The death of a parent makes
9187 man for the Angel of Death.
9370 and mighty Death! .. thou
9490 friendship, sex and death.
9587 and continues until death.
9682 Death is the privilege of
9727 the laws of death.
9906 the moment of our death.
9932 citizens of death's grey
9975 of death; every
10032 It is but Death who comes
10070 life, but no one his death.
10144 stroke of death is as a
10212 sleep of death what
10280 their deaths; The
10283 many years of fearing death.
10449 worst is death, and death
10450 of the death of kings:
10461 of ugly death within
10481 Death lies on her like an
10657 by your own death, but not
10668 kingly Death Keeps his
10676 Until Death tramples
10739 fate; Death lays his
10741 take up in death, that,
10758 phrases. Death, without
10868 wasn't death, I think
10872 Death must be distinguished
10917 ready to accept even death.
10930 a little death On the
10939 isn't sex but death.
10963 My name is Death: the last
11010 after war, death after life
11106 Finality is death.
11112 - for Death it has an
11234 Death is not anything ..
11284 than frightened to death.
11365 altar, Death lies dead.
11461 is less death and
11475 valley of Death Rode the
11477 the jaws of Death, Into the
11605 thou to death and trance
11607 ever truly longed for death.
11662 not; And death shall have
11718 of Death, But
11725 still from death was
11856 and makes death a
11921 try and set death aside. It
11979 of my death are
12057 beauteous death! the jewel
12328 I know death hath ten
12635 way out an' death's the
12943 solitude; Death joins us

death-moth
5495 nor the death-moth be Your

death-sentence
6104 take the death-sentence without a

deathbed
620 by his deathbed won't hail
12693 near the deathbed fiercer

deathless
9641 To one dead deathless hour.
11857 let us make love deathless.

deaths
7955 whose deaths become
12538 one, More deaths than one

debasement
6956 inhumanity and his debasement.

debatable
4759 Hunger is not debatable.

debate
3277 daughter of debate, that eke
4878 on the last debate on the
10746 which the debate never

debauch
1470 a man may debauch his
5600 than to debauch the

debauche
1258 Debauche, n: one who has so

debauchery
5819 surely as they die of debauchery.

debonair
7521 So buxom, blithe, and debonair.

debris
5560 with the debris of

debt
1696 can pay our debt to the
1908 He'd run in debt by
4159 a double debt to pay, A
4954 in their debt have been
10064 National Debt is a very
10091 made is a debt unpaid,
11853 deeper in debt. Say

debtor
689 every man a debtor to his

debts
10488 He that dies pays all debts.

decade
12727 in the Me Decade - seeing

decadence
11780 between our decadence and the

decay
2934 hath no decay; This, no
3052 subject to decay, And, when
4685 of mild decay, But
5995 decrepitude, their decay.
6730 moment of decay Some forms
8198 by mental decay such as I
8405 in the mouth of decay.
8519 and complexity decay.

decayed
4005 you are sufficiently decayed?

deceased
5723 of the late deceased, And the
10249 the times deceased, The which
12768 He first deceased; she for a

deceit
1357 a Smile of Deceit, And there
2718 last for an age seems deceit.

deceitful
8494 for the deceitful in the

deceitfulness
3243 Cat of such deceitfulness and

deceive
2039 We always deceive ourselves
4125 need to deceive
4568 Deceive not thy physician,
6668 Deceive boys with toys, but
10033 first we practise to deceive!
11914 they may deceive me, with
12890 would deceive his

deceived
882 us not be deceived - we are
4090 to be deceived by one's
4115 are never deceived; we
5886 than to be deceived by them.
5988 and smile deceived. Another
7547 revenge, deceived The mother
7660 women been deceived; And shall
11248 of being well deceived.

deceivers
1444 of our deceivers' than from
10131 Men were deceivers ever; One

deceives
8765 that deceives may be

deceiving
10045 She deceiving, I believing;

december
865 might have roses in December.
5416 nighted December Too happy,

decembers
1566 wild Decembers, From

decencies
8864 to dwell in decencies for ever.

decency
6592 old life of decency without

9618 For want of decency is want of
11183 an ultimate decency of things.

decendants
7424 for their decendants would be

decent
4748 to what is decent.
6314 any other decent business
7942 do you a decent death on
9823 All decent people live

decently
2080 to die decently, but to

decentralized
4469 means decentralized planning

decide
5821 cannot decide what it
6580 moment to decide, In the
8868 Who shall decide, when
9211 often - decide once.
12109 God's sake decide what

decision
3017 made a courageous decision.
3529 a hard decision something
8523 of taking decisions of
9357 A decision is the action an
9590 then live with that decision.
11911 fast and specific decision.

declare
12577 nothing to declare except my

declaring
7708 is always declaring he's no

declines
6815 almost necessarily declines.

declining
747 in the declining age of a

decomposing
12746 decomposing in the

decorate
12856 than they decorate them.

decorating
11871 secret of decorating her

decoration
8400 sort of decoration for it - a

decorum
1824 cant about DECORUM, Who have
10017 observances of paltry decorum.

decreed
5510 soul has to itself decreed.

dedication
9308 youth his dedication Was to a
11159 and steady dedication of a

dee
5668 sands of Dee.' The
11367 we take it, is dee.

deed
876 prize the deed and
1587 No good deed ever goes
3241 the right deed for the
4102 The deed is all, the glory
4772 half the deed done who
5510 may do the deed That my
6651 woord and tak the dede.
7348 Y'are the deed's creature.
10352 and not the deed, Confounds
10355 clears us of this deed.
10407 a good deed in a

deeds
2205 that dooth gentil dedis.
4249 feminine; deeds are
7925 and the deeds that ye do
8801 at great deeds must also
9126 and not of deeds, Is like a
9409 do great deeds, speak
10193 Foul deeds will rise,
10306 to do ill deeds Make ill
12683 the crude language of deeds.

deep
239 Deep down he is shallow.
2084 Silence is deep as
4177 Who, too deep for his
5996 not seem so deep as they
11496 the great deep to the
11551 rolls the deep where grew
11610 climbs: the deep Moans

12333 Only the deep sense of
12814 lie too deep for tears.

deep-versed
7648 remains, Deep-versed in books

deer
1822 the deer; Chasing

deface
12856 Pictures deface walls

defeat
937 afraid of defeat. You are
2272 towards sure defeat.
2341 but defeat is an
3714 victories and our defeats?
5753 we should defeat you, we
6499 are triumph and defeat.
6942 Defeat brings its own
8704 What is defeat? Nothing but
9924 distinguish it from a defeat.
10435 may defeat my life,
11408 at seeming defeat by the
12086 of defeat; they do

defeated
264 were never defeated, they were
6100 have been defeated. For us,
6402 Down with the defeated!
6404 We were defeated in a great
6719 is so defeated as
12120 for the defeated is to

defect
1370 a hidden physical defect.
7632 this fair defect Of
9763 fundamental defect of fathers

defects
9790 Among the defects of the
9982 miserable defects, whether

defence
816 of the defence of England
821 The only defence is in
1314 greatest defence and
1551 no adequate defence, except
1505 another defence against
5323 for my defence the only
6853 a ready and quick defence.
7663 to make defence, And at
7986 Defence, not defiance.
8392 largely the defence of the
12631 our only defence against

defend
815 you had to defend people you
2311 we shall defend our
2720 dreams Defend the bad
4077 we can only defend ourselves
6802 promised to defend, black men
10909 evil to defend ourselves
12139 but I will defend to the

defended
6505 howsoe'er defended, But has

defender
1922 the Faith's Defender; God bless

defiance
4191 their port, defiance in their
7986 Defence, not defiance.
8743 cottage bid defiance to all the

defiant
9405 It is defiant the

deficiencies
470 also completes its deficiencies.

defied
730 Age will not be defied.
9947 people not defied the law.

definition
2553 yield to definition. Like the
6880 The definition of S & M is
8257 any other definition of what a
9779 exact legal definition; in the
10639 good working definition of hell.

deflower
11014 that will her pride deflower.

deformity
540 modesty amounts to deformity.

defunct
2185 hand of the defunct must not

defy
3806 to defy the whole

defying
2639 this by defying their

degenerate
9671 everything degenerates in the
11079 armour is degenerate. It is

degeneration
11196 a fatty degeneration of his

degradation
11054 Woman's degradation is a man's
12342 of the degradation we bear in

degrade
3719 one way to degrade mankind

degree
1466 be in some degree whatever
10500 O! when degree is shaked,

degrees
5428 By degrees Her rich attire
9354 like virtue, has its degrees.

deity
1818 exchange For Deity offended!
4397 a personal deity, but we
11247 between the Deity and the

delay
348 To avoid delay, please have
7638 In me is no delay; with thee

delaying
11878 the gift rich by delaying it.

delays
1711 that God's delays are God's
3074 All delays are dangerous in
6408 is that which delays them.
12442 annoying delays: don't

delegate
1450 in trouble, delegate. (3) When

deleted
383 Expletive deleted.

deliberate
4979 time to deliberate; but when
9211 Deliberate often - decide once.

deliberates
57 woman that deliberates is lost.

delicacy
4485 has no delicacy, he has

delicate
5192 is seldom delicate: it will

delight
279 was my delight,
620 the occasion with delight.
1330 to sweet delight, Some are
1338 Energy is Eternal Delight.
5148 and sentiments I find delight.
6608 her delight on seeing
7250 no greater delight than to be
7606 gift, my ever new delight.
7622 thing met conceives delight.
7866 late for delight, my dear;
8872 Formed to delight at once
9120 Danger and delight grow on
9388 chills, The delight of her
9933 with such delight As
10162 And go to 't with delight.
12817 phantom of delight When first
12891 impulse of delight Drove to

delightful
5876 but no delightful ones.
6442 as sin, And almost as delightful.
7461 all that is delightful to man.
12215 two most delightful things in

delights
5919 the swift delights of our
6626 fountain of delights rises
7735 does some delights condemn,
10207 dust? man delights not me;

delinquencies
3219 indulge in a few delinquencies.

delinquency
9307 juvenile delinquency problems

deliver
269 night, Good Lord, deliver us!
1420 Good Lord, deliver us.
2246 damnation, Deliver us, good
8107 good lord, deliver us!

deliverance
9323 After deliverance, both

delivered
10425 of time which will be delivered.

deliverer
7655 this great deliverer now, and

delivers
11511 Ignorance Delivers brawling

delphiniums
7441 in a bed Of delphiniums (blue) and

delphos
7541 the steep of Delphos leaving.

deluge
8822 déluge. After us the deluge.

delusion
181 The delusion that there are
1771 but under some delusion.
7256 Love is the delusion that one
11820 is the delusion that

demand
1293 been in excess of the demand.
3562 up with the demand for it.
5058 by popular demand, sometimes
6030 exceeds the demand.
9384 What is a demanding

demands
4398 Life only demands from the

demean
9397 think they demean us, I

demeaning
10797 So womanly, Her demeaning.

demi-atlas
10153 The demi-Atlas of this earth,

democracy
484 extreme democracy or
555 a little less democracy to save.
560 Democracy means government by
1523 We can have democracy in this
1630 and democracy, We've
1693 empire or a democracy, but it
1713 Democracy is not about giving
1780 A perfect democracy is
1859 of a strong democracy.
2240 Democracy means government by
2301 said that Democracy is the
2365 Democracy is a festival of
2501 Democracy is a small hard core
3589 cheers for Democracy: one
3591 Democracy is based upon the
5342 that, in a democracy, decisions
6218 Democracy is not identical
6371 expresses my idea of democracy.
6390 In a democracy, the opposition
6830 Thus our democracy was, from an
6888 need less, not more, democracy.
7260 Under democracy, one party
7268 Democracy is the theory that
8123 Democracy and socialism are
8125 Democracy is good. I say this
8203 makes democracy possible,
8770 Democracy passes into
9579 in a democracy reflects
9598 the great arsenal of democracy.
10619 Democracy substitutes election
11223 that's democracy, it's the
11264 understand democracy, spend
11895 The democracy which embodies
11901 Democracy is based on the
12445 Democracy is the recurrent
12595 Democracy means simply the
12671 our hearts - for democracy.
12691 safe for democracy. Its
12947 that democracy can be no

democrat
5064 and a Democrat, in that
8729 here. I am a democrat.
9567 party, I'm a Democrat.

democratic
853 first truly democratic culture -
3107 an' votes th' Dimmycratic Ticket.

democrats
11161 about the Democrats, we will

demolished
1061 No man is demolished but by

demon
12949 over to his demon or to his

demoniac
7633 Demoniac frenzy, moping

demons
3451 driven by demons. He

denial
7524 Hence with denial vain, and

denied
7760 that comes to be denied.
8523 man who is denied the

denies
4098 spirit that always denies.
9218 someone who denies the first

denmark
10197 in the state of Denmark.

denominator
5982 the common denominator of living.

denounce
4886 and rightly denounce them, will

density
6764 is our sense of density.

dentist
8716 along with dentists, are the
12304 go to my dentist any day.

denuded
9311 the dark coverts were denuded;

denunciation
10841 The denunciation of the young is a

deny
696 They that deny a God
4099 Deny yourself! You must
5522 Room to deny ourselves;
10308 you deny me that.

denying
11878 allure by denying, and to

depart
1246 he will not depart from it.
2641 doing. Depart, I say,
5780 the kings depart, And we
7261 If, after I depart this vale,

departed
6498 is not, but departed - for the

department
3678 it is a big department store,

departure
2877 Departure should be sudden.
7335 a point of departure but a
9242 not the arrival, the departure.

depend
10662 Depend on the rabbit's foot
11468 not to depend upon the

depended
12641 have always depended on the

dependence
813 through our dependence on this
2517 their total dependence on the
6690 economic dependence of women

dependent
2603 of being as dependent as a young
11281 is wholly dependent on the

deplorable
2993 mind is the most deplorable.

deploying
7216 Deploying in a parade the

depopulated
5921 the whole world seems depopulated.

deposed
10452 must he be deposed? The king

deposit
158 a large deposit in my name

depraved
5363 ever suddenly became depraved.

depravity
7240 of innate depravity and

depress
3244 and depress the most

depression
3777 all modern depressions,
4746 a worldwide depression all by
7207 Depression is the inability to
11907 job; it's a depression when you

deprivation
6047 Deprivation is for me what

deprived
674 be not deprived of his
6861 men are not deprived of either

derision
11362 old days to derision Our loves

descendants
8102 day your descendants Outnumber

descended
2332 curtain has descended across the
5990 the Fourth descended God be
6829 of having descended below the
8798 to be well descended, but the

descending
679 some descending from

descent
5310 like the descent of their

describe
5820 attempt to describe or account
9044 They much describe, they

descriptions
10558 time I see descriptions of the

descriptive
4337 should be descriptive, not

desert
2055 is the only desert within our
6511 of the Desert cried
8067 in a desert of wire,
10209 after his desert, and who
10696 of stone Stand in the desert.

deserts
585 In the deserts of the heart
4265 Or his deserts are small,
9804 the bars. Deserts are there,

deserve
2310 in war, but only deserve it.
3470 live so as to deserve it.
3688 have to deserve your
4034 - and how little I deserve it.
4280 of the men who deserve them.
4857 when they do not deserve it.
7268 want, and deserve to get it
9230 but a mule deserves his
11946 better to deserve honours
12546 she doesn't deserve to have

deserves
1637 until the world deserves them.
6901 has the government it deserves.
8375 has the face he deserves.

design
2645 My design is to make what
9355 often betrays a great design.
11069 dull there is a design in it.
11070 one has no design but to
11750 conscious design of doing

designers
9488 Designers and freelance artists

designing
1052 Say I am designing St.

desirable
5929 the more desirable it is that

desire
1237 The desire accomplished is
1349 arrows of desire: Bring me
1354 gratified desire. What is
1444 from the desire to seduce
1449 My desire to get here
1525 man, the desire for
1819 a' the learning I desire.
1888 innate desire on the
2236 for your desire, Save that
2455 The man's desire is for the
2976 Who doesn't desire his
3217 should most desire for
3482 namely the desire of
4092 From desire I plunge to its
5318 soft flame that is desire.
5387 The desire of a man for a
6306 Unsatisfied desire is in
8675 weariness treads on desire.
9065 like desire for
9224 men naturally desire to know.
9365 Desire, nor reason hath, nor

desire
10123 I do desire we may be better
10244 in me to desire small
10247 that desire should so
10618 heart's desire. The
11621 to, they desire
11810 only they desire it for
12950 admitted desire to dress

desired
4324 leave much to be desired.
9894 what the whole soul desired.
10144 Which hurts and is desired.

desires
1366 He who desires, but acts not,
1421 devices and desires of our own
3009 flatter our desires, Our best
3875 whose desires increase
4318 such sweet desires do gain,
5920 in his desires, man is a
6953 of our desires; that is
7371 in doing what one desires.
9070 for further desires.
9222 always desires what is

desirous
3841 ought else on earth desirous?

desk
1913 is but a desk to write
3964 to your desks and never

desolation
9542 mucilage, Desolation in

despair
1567 And even Despair was
2035 us to despair, offering
2476 as many suicides as despair.
4280 a girl, I'd despair. The
4773 Never despair.
5937 the experiment of despair.
7074 begotten by Despair Upon
7551 but racked with deep despair.
7554 what resolution from despair.
7566 fiercer by despair: His trust
9922 on the far side of despair.
11591 depth of some divine despair.
12227 my own despair, But not
12694 be) Is all despair, or
12701 wasting in despair, Die

despairing
2056 so much in despairing of life as
3982 awake with a shudder despairing

desperate
7791 outside desperate to get in,
10221 Diseases desperate grown, By
11456 Desperate by too quick a sense
11741 not to do desperate things.

desperation
11767 lead lives of quiet desperation.

despicable
2049 is more despicable than
5286 cannot use it finds despicable.

despise
3763 Never despise what it says in
9889 utterly despise the
11213 A woman despises a man for

despised
1756 by being despised grow
6144 maid: Despised, if ugly;

despond
1731 of the slough was Despond.

despotic
12338 always insolent and despotic.

despotism
484 or despotism will come
2092 was long a despotism tempered
6680 the modern form of despotism.
8770 Democracy passes into despotism.
9511 the root of despotism as virtue

despots
11810 Despots themselves do not

dessert
223 uncertain - eat dessert first

destination
4225 way of travel - not a destination.

destined
4133 I am destined by the

destinies
2886 leave the destinies of the
6037 and robed as destinies.
11809 to sway the destinies of half

destiny
1257 Destiny, n: a tyrant's
2322 chain of destiny can be
2768 A man of destiny knows that
3449 you know, go by Destiny.
4066 over his destiny. That's
4612 Wedding is destiny, and
5947 Riddle of destiny, who can
7195 path of our destiny without
7197 you create a destiny.
7414 Destiny is what you are
8214 Our destiny rules over us,
9407 and you reap a destiny.
11636 passion is my destiny.

destroy
696 deny a God destroy man's
2106 but it will destroy him with a
2382 We can destroy ourselves by
2383 prepared to destroy it. It is
2520 wish to destroy they first
3719 that is to destroy language.
5543 it, and never destroy it.
6284 mad would destroy, they
6709 it, and never destroy one.
7045 involves the power to destroy.
8245 does not destroy me, makes
8271 and then you destroy yourself.
8852 Destroy his fib, or
10924 of us and destroy them. But
12934 One to destroy, is murder by

destroyed
1130 shall be destroyed is death.
1521 What's not destroyed by Time's
2321 human life would be destroyed.
2538 song of a destroyed wild bird.
4041 generation destroyed by
4150 When once destroyed, can never
5395 you do is destroyed, laid
6928 of kings and knights destroyed.

destroyer
2219 only a destroyer. Forests

destroying
4669 the rain is destroying his grain
12007 it without destroying something

destroys
1368 which destroys, into
1618 us, and destroys those
5127 certainly destroys liberty,
5824 wantonly destroys a work of
11238 habitually destroys members of

destruction
1241 before destruction, and an
3691 that for destruction ice Is
3786 complete destruction rather
3804 the mad destruction is wrought
8201 rush and rumble of destruction.
11895 blessing to its own destruction.

destructive
2190 dreadfully destructive it can be
3408 to destructive or
6185 man, smiling, destructive man.
6879 to fire its destructive agency.
9818 when the destructive analysis

destructively
2927 then it can be used destructively.

detail
6315 reveres detail and never
9148 not the detail, that
11770 away by detail ..

details
2070 of details. I often
10861 out the practical details.
10937 significant details,

detention
7363 Detention by the State of the

determination
2838 we live and determination to realise

determined
4921 extent determined by the

detest
1976 but they detest at

dethrone
9720 and dethrone a dynasty

dethronement
12489 will enjoy the dethronement.

detraction
7048 abhorrèd child, Detraction ..

detrimental
8306 it would be dethrimental to keep

devalued
12665 your bank, has been devalued.

develop
8835 take him to develop, if you

developed
2107 see fully developed; but you

development
8067 is called development is allowed
11218 a late 18th century development.

device
4689 audacious device, even of

devices
1421 much the devices and

devil
284 He'd give the devil ulcers.
925 church, the devil will build
1420 of the devil; from thy
1623 The devil's most devilish
1816 Was, the deil's awa wi'
1870 for the Devil - it must
2745 prayer, The Devil always
3738 The Devil himself is good
3824 rest, The Devil resembleth
4491 that the devil can throw
4614 why the devil should
5690 But the Devil whoops, as
5781 and the Devil knows
6187 The devil's name is
6635 there the devil would also
6814 a synonym for the Devil.
6995 strike, The devil will come,
7148 The devil turned precisian!
7574 to men! Devil with devil
8135 as you hate the devil.
8277 go to the devil, he may as
9173 in the chin; a devil within.
9253 The Devil's boots don't
0100 friend, the devil is dead!
10354 That fears a painted devil.
10391 The devil can cite
10583 spirit is devil's work.
10784 and servant to the devil.
10959 walking the Devil is gone,
11044 last: the Devil howling
11188 The devil, depend upon it,
11269 her: The devil take her!
12028 the devil grabs it

devil-born
11573 You tell me, doubt is Devil-born.

devils
6454 Devils are not so black as
6639 as many devils would set
6894 so awakens devils to contest
7855 still 'tis devils must
9999 the devils of his own

devon
1480 west, 'Twas Devon, glorious
8146 Dons sight Devon, I'll quit

devoted
8257 this - devoted and

devotee
10601 A great devotee of the gospel

devotion
3994 Matrimonial devotion Doesn't
7230 measure devotion to husband

devour
12079 might devour in turn

devoured
10750 great ones devoured the small.

devourer
7884 so great devourers, and so
8438 Time the devourer of

devouring
9500 and milky, devouring the green

devout
7734 less human for being devout.

dew
403 from the foggy, foggy dew.
9781 the dew sparkling
11482 as sunlight drinketh dew.
11539 with the dews at even;

dew-drops
10415 seek some dew-drops here, And

dewy
11693 all the dewy night: Up

diagnose
5600 a million is able to diagnose.

diagnostician
8410 rectum makes a good diagnostician.

diagonally
11127 lie diagonally in his

dialect
8633 in a dialect I
12347 is a dialect with its

diamond
2735 a rough diamond, and must
6525 good but a diamond and safire
7747 good, but a diamond tiara
8178 O Diamond! Diamond! thou
11445 Like a diamond in the

diamonds
3769 to give him his diamonds back.
9512 But diamonds are a
9513 shape, Diamonds are a

diarist
8199 be a good diarist, one must

diary
8715 way of keeping a diary.
12401 say, keep a diary and some
12561 without my diary. One

diatonic
9419 very common diatonic little

dice
3162 God plays dice with the
6915 of the dice will never

dickens
1035 were put to Dickens as

dictated
7903 Was dictated But not

dictators
2307 Dictators ride to and fro on
7123 Dictators are rulers who always
9164 Dictators ride to and fro upon

dictatorship
4620 A dictatorship is a country where
7113 to the dictatorship of the
8381 establish a dictatorship in order
8729 never been dictatorships here. I
11909 government you have a dictatorship.

dictionaries
5142 Dictionaries are like watches.
5144 To make dictionaries is dull
5145 A writer of dictionaries is

dictionary
2419 is only a dictionary out of
4337 A dictionary should be
12138 is the dictionary of its

didactic
3715 he has hit is the didactic.

diddle
4010 'High diddle diddle' Will
11367 we know, is diddle: and

die
42 not to die before we
55 That we can die but once
60 peace a Christian can die.
136 when you die. You want
236 others to die Seldom
256 And leave me there to die.
281 about to die salute
451 when they die, go to
532 in case you don't die.
580 this man to die: Would
834 and die young is
869 To die will be an awfully
1062 is no self left to die.
1225 for tomorrow we shall die.
1573 And when we die All's over
1582 If I should die, think
1616 to live, but to die in.

1639 I come to die, Do I view
1685 and to die. He is
1689 liable to die and are
1834 Let us do - or die!!!
1906 to do is to die at once.
1989 not so difficult to die.
2004 The die is cast.
2032 Tomorrow let us do or die!
2474 agree to die together.
3060 is born to die, And none
3111 he does not die if he has
3367 hope that he will die.
3546 and either do, or die.
3602 we must die to one
3665 live long and die young.
3779 More die in the United
4397 does not die on the day
4580 Only the young die good.
4722 before I die about
4776 it is to die for one's
4936 better to die on your
5167 rich than to die rich.
5201 I who am about to die.
5263 much beauty as could die.
5279 he had to die in my
5497 that must die; And Joy,
5501 it rich to die, To cease
5629 when people die.
5650 he will die for, he
5743 shall break it must die.
5841 or one may die without
5845 suffer than die is man's
5945 do any thing but die.
6244 been learning how to die.
6722 Let me die a youngman's
6731 If we must die, let it
6965 learning, But leave
7020 before I die, And let
7133 It is most grand to the
7248 the gods love dies young.
7272 thing, they die earlier.
7397 begin to die a little.
7583 Die he or justice must.
7627 is to die; How can I
7713 you have to die, he will
7935 We die. That may be the
7994 Don't die of ignorance.
8054 down! If I die, avenge
8106 I must die. Lord have
8138 I will die with them.
8191 He will, he must die.
8446 these who die as cattle?
8489 Die, my dear Doctor,
8541 seul. We shall die alone.
8841 think, or bravely die?
8869 thousands die, without
8965 harder lesson! how to die.
9046 Rose, I'll die: Behind
9107 He who must die must die
9196 people to die for them,
9268 If I die, I forgive you:
9329 if thou withdraw, I die.
9330 to live, begins to die.
9372 We die in earnest, that's
9562 it is to know when to die.
9592 you begin to die.
9662 boy until they die!
9772 would die sooner
9781 I come to die I shall
10140 lion Must die of love.
10251 a man can die but once;
10282 we shall die, we know;
10381 Ay, but to die, and go we
10456 downwards, here to die.
10677 change, but I cannot die.
11080 everything, even to die.
11109 bloom and lakes die.
11266 to do and die than it is
11267 they only let Him die.
11275 about to die salute
11321 Not die here in a rage,
11342 I shall die at the
11344 - but we all must die!'
11476 the so dier knew Some
11552 he was not made to die.
11798 taught us how to die.
11841 Hope I die before I get
11899 it. I never want to die.

12067 were never going to die.
12317 I shall die an
12386 God, shouldst die for me?
12538 deaths than one must die.
12601 have to die beyond my
12701 in despair, Die because a
12785 The good die first, And
12886 we grow old and die.

died
130 Who died to save us
1386 me. I died when you
2241 They died to save their
3662 who has died we adopt a
3848 was scorned and died.
4165 The dog it was that died.
5427 in pallid moonshine, died.
5689 why we died, Tell
8993 Died some, pro patria, non
9043 disease. I died last night
9388 fever she died, of fever
10125 Men have died from time to
12329 dazzle: she died young.
12768 liked it not, and died.
12842 some have died for love.
12847 - When the old man died.

dies
435 Man dies when he wants, as
1313 The king never dies.
2932 soon as beauty, dies.
4428 but dies on
4602 gossip ever dies away
5681 fall? Who dies if England
7385 nobody dies. Nobody
7717 One dies only once, and
8140 an artist dies with not.
8613 When a man dies, he does
8775 the gods favour dies young.
10488 He that dies pays all
10930 Ev'ry day a little dies.
11612 moment dies a man,
12096 something in me dies.
12447 the thing dies in the
12594 because a man dies for it.
12939 then dies the same.

diet
7498 oft with gods doth diet.
7763 in your diet; In short,

differed
2486 but to those who have differed.

difference
971 the hell difference does it
1686 is the same difference as between
2282 The only difference, after all
2494 is more difference within the
3342 a great difference in the
3714 can see any difference between
3804 What difference does it make to
4483 by the difference between
5008 very little difference between
5061 What's the difference between a
7909 all the difference in the
8548 see no difference between
8623 Strange the difference of men's
10607 of the difference between
11063 and the difference of things
11947 The difference between the right
12365 made the difference of forty
12782 and, ho, The difference to me!
12929 is a great difference between a

differences
2501 variety of individual differences.
10705 the differences, and
11433 in their differences from their

different
353 How different, how very
2586 the same with different hats on.
3513 They are different from you
6041 know it's a different country.
7438 is quite different when it
8077 an entirely different point of

differently
4451 they do things differently there.

differs
7256 one woman differs from

difficult
203 afterwards that is difficult.

1289 the most difficult thing to
2263 been found difficult; and left
3257 at present, must be difficult.
6733 not find it difficult nowadays
7054 Difficult or easy, pleasant or
7997 The difficult we do immediately
8070 The difficult is what
8219 things is difficult, but to
8420 get more difficult as you get
9063 thing more difficult than
9966 and too difficult for
12517 Luckily, this is not difficult.
12905 known That is most difficult.

difficulties
3828 The difficulties which I
6780 local difficulties
6863 great, the difficulties cannot be
8162 thousand difficulties do not

difficulty
2275 Every difficulty slurred over
5616 know, the difficulty of life of
10655 The difficulty is to find

dig
2900 Let Dig for Victory' be
5708 also, And dig till you
10568 forbear To dig the dust
10810 We each day dig our graves
12335 nails he'll dig them up

digest
246 is human, to digest, divine,

digested
690 few to be chewed and digested.

digestion
7605 light from pure digestion bred.
9672 good cook and a good digestion.
10444 taste prove in digestion sour.

diggeth
1209 He that diggeth a pit shall

dignified
778 - the dignified parts ..
6100 be called a dignified

dignifies
12753 Money dignifies what is

dignity
15 that gives dignity and worth
400 equal in dignity and
471 Dignity does not consist in
1402 people lose dignity on a close
2040 There is dignity in work only
3415 The dignity of man lies in
4334 with silent dignity, but
4891 Official dignity tends to
5118 to write trifles with dignity.
5390 against the dignity that
6403 than of his own dignity.
8973 dignity for the
11310 Dignity, high station, or

digressions
11121 Digressions, incontestably, are

dime
4418 can you spare a dime?

dimensions
4692 back to its original dimensions.
5949 the dimensions of a man's

diminished
3108 and ought to be diminished.
7588 Hide their diminished heads.

dimmed
9315 of town Is dimmed, and on

dimming
8198 A gradual dimming of the

dimple
6138 love with a dimple makes the
9173 A dimple in the chin; a

dine
428 her to dine; Private
1052 am going to dine with some
4993 Women never dine alone.
5044 to meet and dine somewhere
11600 while you dine, But

dined
1503 a man more dined against
10891 me, I have dined to-day.

diner
4228 in the diner nothing

dingy
8735 but looks dingy on the

dining
4177 thought of dining; Though
7326 that can live without dining?

dinner
334 to get your dinner, and you
1965 the soul - the dinner bell.
2093 ask him to dinner, and hear
4357 for a dinner party is
4755 an old friend for dinner."
5173 has a good dinner upon his
6160 haven't any dinner, But to
6167 wants for dinner only if he
6209 diminish your dinner.
7176 Dinner, a time when .. one
8635 how a good dinner and
9002 Dinner at the Huntercombes'
9086 After dinner, rest a while,
10039 A dinner lubricates
10818 expect our dinner, but from
10824 want to invite to dinner.
11318 after dinner; but after

dinner party
12228 Washington dinner party than from

dinner-knives
5698 paths with broken dinner-knives.

dinners
2171 have more dinners than

dinosaur
5212 The dinosaur's eloquent lesson

dior
6337 Never darken my Dior again!

diplomacy
2152 Diplomacy; the art of saying
4139 Diplomacy is to do and say The

diplomat
242 diplomat could hold
2752 Diplomats are useful only in
11209 A diplomat .. is a person who

diplomatic
12 the classic diplomatic sense
2653 The diplomatic name for

direction
4908 tending in a certain direction.
5206 to some particular direction.
6139 madly off in all directions.
7251 sense of direction after four
8185 made in the direction of the

director
4210 with these directors, they're

directs
3659 what directs his

direful
633 something direful in the

dirt
3741 that flings dirt at another
3776 thicker will be the dirt.
4288 Dirt is only matter out of
11304 Instead of dirt and poison

dirtiest
12494 The dirtiest book of all is

dirty
9027 prefer to go around dirty.
9078 is called dirty; if he
12091 Dirty, dark, and

dirty joke
8395 pie .. A dirty joke is a sort

dirty work
8852 at his dirty work again.

disabled
8657 us who are disabled what we

disadvantage
2039 then to their disadvantage.
5147 One of the disadvantages of wine
5171 to his own disadvantage. People

disadvantaged
4990 are disadvantaged the moment

disagree
7574 men only disagree Of

disagreeable
5103 that is not disagreeable to him;
5160 is very disagreeable to a man

disagreeables
5478 making all disagreeables evaporate,

disagrees
7046 then everybody disagrees.

disappear
9838 would disappear if there

disappeared
3299 would have disappeared long ago

disappointed
989 you have disappointed us! We had

disappointing
885 he'll be the least disappointing.

disappointment
4452 Disappointments should be cremated,
5952 without a feeling of disappointment.

disappoints
2163 Man appoints, and God disappoints.

disapprove
12139 I disapprove of what you say,

disarm
6509 enough to disarm all

disaster
4156 The day's disasters in his
4587 inevitably bound for disaster.
9520 shortest distance to disaster.
9756 bring all kinds of disaster.
12412 precipitate one into disaster.
12412 precipitate one into disaster.

disastrous
4365 21 is almost always disastrous.

disbelief
2098 than disbelief in great
11865 willing suspension of disbelief.

disbelieves
7187 earnestly disbelieves what

discharges
6897 act. It discharges the

disciples
12564 has his disciples, and it is

discipline
883 freedom to discipline ourselves.
4600 the root of discipline: the sense
5010 that can discipline a whole
5023 its people discipline
5809 Discipline does not mean
9799 by category disciplines.
10578 in the discipline of silence

disciplined
6736 Disciplined inaction.

disclose
9931 intent to disclose, not his

discomforts
8640 and all the discomforts that will

discontent
521 and age in common - discontent.
5464 contented sort of discontent.
10457 of our discontent Made
12475 of a noble discontent is the
12533 from the discontent of man The

discontented
5662 To be discontented with the divine
11416 for the discontented is the

discontents
6122 the source of all our discontents.

discord
56 from civil discord flow.

discouragement
1740 There's no discouragement Shall make

discourse
8633 of their discourse was about

discover
2036 those we discover after all
2540 consent to discover in a man
3939 One doesn't discover new lands
10814 We often discover what will
12382 senses to discover the world.
12952 to discover what one

discovered
24 ago we discovered the exact
8156 is slowly discovered, the bad

discoverers
680 are ill discoverers that think

discoveries
2712 of my discoveries have been
7434 making exciting discoveries.

discovery
3393 .. and the discovery of a
7509 man in the discovery of this
10950 Love is but discovery: When that
11395 Discovery consists of seeing
12028 makes a discovery, the devil

discredited
12873 has been thoroughly discredited.

discretion
3282 happiness in thy discretion.
6438 to discretion for the
11244 Discretion is not the better

discriminate
6073 beerier, do learn to discriminate.

discrimination
213 suffer job discrimination like other
9384 exercising discrimination,

discussed
12755 the most discussed animal in

discussion
560 by discussion, but it is
2329 after reasonable discussion.

disease
276 sexually transmitted disease.
430 youth is a disease from which
516 strange disease of modern
734 is worse than the disease.
2579 most costly disease is not
2955 same diligence as the disease.
3457 A desperate disease requires a
4715 a chronic disease and taking
5415 In disease Medical Men guess:
7815 from the disease of writing
7838 is a fatal disease; fatal to
8413 has a disease than what
8854 this long disease, my life.
9353 money, is just a disease.
11384 worse than the disease.
11391 it was a disease; in the
11862 A disease in the family that
11891 Disease often tells its

diseased
8341 child was diseased at birth -

diseases
1615 is the cure of all diseases.
5796 infectious diseases. And
7976 spread diseases. Trap the
10221 Diseases desperate grown, By
11027 diseases and his
11210 cured all the good diseases.

disenchanting
11170 in life so disenchanting as

disenchantment
9917 I mistook disenchantment for truth.

disgrace
360 life is a disgrace. I really
3105 but it's a kind iv a disgrace.
10176 out, Even to a full disgrace.
10546 When in disgrace with fortune
10889 is no disgrace to a man,

disgruntled
12710 actually disgruntled, he was

disguise
775 is a disguised republic
1530 go in disguise For every
3479 through the disguise of gaiety
9545 eyes My love with no disguise.

disgust
6953 for disgust, let me

dish
8575 Some dish more sharply
10279 him as a dish fit for

dishes
2158 pass the dishes again.

dishonest
671 Anger cannot be dishonest.

3845 be reckoned dishonest, because,
4218 among the dishonest to offer

dishonesty
2819 idea. Dishonesty will stare

disillusioned
7175 are easily disillusioned and then

disillusionment
1742 to fight disillusionment and learn

disinclination
7324 traced to a disinclination to inflict

disinheriting
10733 a damned disinheriting

disinterested
3942 there are disinterested actions

dislike
815 people you disliked and
4445 able to dislike someone
7843 I, too, dislike it: there are

dismal
2097 The Dismal Science.

dismay
1332 left his parents in dismay.

dismemberment
4053 and dismemberment of the

dismiss
4765 Dismiss the old horse in good

dismount
2307 dare not dismount. And the
9164 which they dare not dismount.

disobedience
7544 man's first disobedience, and the

disobey
2421 young is to disobey - but the

disorder
8693 ice, in wild disorder rise.

disorderly
7434 of being disorderly is that

disorganization
2247 is always disorganization.

disparity
2931 Just such disparity As is

dispatch
59 in business than dispatch.

dispatchful
7608 with dispatchful looks in

displeasing
5902 which is not displeasing to us.

disposable
7406 has to be disposable. Because

disposed
4438 the way she disposed of an

disposes
5544 Man proposes; God disposes.

disposition
1757 A disposition to preserve, and an
1787 the common dispositions of the

dispossessed
1480 Eve were dispossessed Of the

dispraise
7671 contempt, Dispraise, or blame,

disputes
11185 checkered by disputes.

disquieting
11836 of it is disquieting. There is

disregard
3811 but a disregard for others
7167 by its disregard for the

disrupter
9811 should be a disrupter or a

dissatisfaction
2838 Dissatisfaction with the world in

dissatisfied
2357 I became dissatisfied with my

dissected
836 anatomy and dissected at least
12447 can be dissected, as a frog

dissent
3185 platform for national dissent.

dissenter
9811 or a dissenter - a nay

dissimulation
2227 some dissimulation no

dissipation
3916 and dissipation without

dissolve
9746 would be to dissolve all

dissolved
4215 a sigh and dissolved into

dissolves
6992 the world dissolves, And every

distance
1451 shortest distance between
8339 at long distance with a
12638 the longest distance between

distinctive
1643 man's distinctive mark

distinguish
907 there is to distinguish us from
11861 unable to distinguish what is

distinguished
67 man is distinguished from all
8063 like a distinguished author,

distinguishes
6198 which distinguishes us from
8411 which distinguishes man from

distort
11955 you can distort 'em as

distracted
9358 always be distracted by love,

distress'd
2605 vacant is a mind distress'd.

distressing
11911 No more distressing moment can

distribute
6551 his duty to distribute as fairly

distribution
5545 of the distribution of its

distrust
12631 We have to distrust each

disturb
1528 is meant to disturb, science
2184 world to disturb nothing

disturbed
5637 But someone disturbed the feast.

ditch
2647 a great ditch from all
8075 is a mere ditch, and will
12625 is to die in the last ditch.

ditty
5431 an ancient ditty, long

dive
12432 men have dived for them;

diversion
6673 only free diversions in slum
11336 sorts of diversion in men,

diversity
7798 universal quality is diversity.
12260 through diversity, or

divided
1160 a house be divided against
5791 one million divided by one
5916 The divided self.
6287 they divided up the
6790 together, Divided by the
7937 world is divided into
10572 countries divided by a

dividend
9932 Drawing no dividend from

dividing
2839 we stand, by dividing we fall.

divination
6946 And divination too will

divinations
9893 her ancient divinations to a long

divine
65 The hand that makes us divine
246 is human, to digest, divine.
6003 Ah, what the form divine!
7074 show me so divine a thing.
8104 You look divine as you
8920 Style the divine, the
11578 one far-off divine event, To

11850 did know, But 'twas divine!
12925 know what divine love is

divine service
363 it being Sunday, had Divine Service.

divineness
678 of divineness, because

divinest
4875 The two divinest things this

divinity
1617 a piece of divinity in us,
4602 it, too, is a kind of divinity.
10226 such divinity doth hedge
10230 There's a divinity that shapes
10412 There is divinity in odd

divisions
11048 How many divisions has he

divorce
566 A divorce is like an
3766 I get a divorce, I keep
4143 that if you divorce you
4579 of divorce and the
8076

divorced
5593 Being divorced is like being
9771 bear fruit; divorced from it

dizziness
5622 is the dizziness of

dizzy
3536 going at a dizzy rate. We
10798 up and down till I am dizzy.

do
829 you cannot do is more
1834 Let us do - or
2032 let us do or die!
3546 and either do, or die.
5956 and what I do to be
8578 how to do things.
9399 did not do things
9561 to do with the
9591 one has to do usually
10060 say, Do as I say,
10388 If to do were as easy as
10592 Do not do unto others as
11132 soldier, Do this' and
11266 easier to do and die
11476 but to do and die:
12952 one cannot do, than what

dock
4137 still be at the dock.

doctor
6 Doctor, feel my purse.
452 training to become a doctor.
1107 in front of the doctor.
3627 and the doctor takes the
3833 go to the doctor when they
4166 The doctor found, when she
4623 Wherever a doctor cannot do
7662 man therein doctor but
7713 A doctor wastes no time with
7773 No doctor takes pleasure in
8257 not even a doctor, ever
8443 God and the doctor we alike
9041 The doctor understood the
9305 sort of a doctor is he? Oh
9396 The doctor, if he forgets he
9663 Doctor, my doctor, what do
10745 Our doctor would never
11200 Even if the doctor does not
12851 A doctor can bury his

doctors
8868 decide, when doctors disagree.

doctrine
1916 makes all doctrines plain and
5182 teach any doctrine contrary
7662 .. Of such doctrine never was
8878 Not for the doctrine, but the
9615 not the doctrine of ignoble
10681 sect, Whose doctrine is that

does
841 A gentleman does things no

dog
938 The dog is the god of
1460 every dog has his
1879 of a dog is that
2560 I have a dog that

3190 size of the dog in the
3640 and old dog, and ready
4164 The dog, to gain some
4165 bite, The dog it was
4895 To his dog, every man is
5249 the very flea of his dog.
5673 And every dog his day.
5699 That the Dog returns to
5729 heart to a dog to tear.
6934 Man is a dog's ideal of
7421 The biggest dog has been a
8318 to a dog is what
9101 One dog barks at
9241 comes a dog's; then a
10296 rather be a dog, and bay
10981 of pollution, the dog.
11525 than his dog, a little
11527 Like a dog, he hunts in
11781 I am not a dog-lover. To
12420 good for a dog - it keeps
12962 way of a dog that if he

dog-star
8850 I'm dead, The dog-star rages!

doggedly
5079 set himself doggedly to it.

dogma
2909 Mr. Dean, no dogma, no Dean.
4341 will serve to beat a dogma.
9665 Every dogma has its day.
9800 The dogma of the Ghost in
9882 is literature, not dogma.

dogmas
6343 The dogmas of the quiet past

dogmatise
5148 I dogmatise and am

dogs
2591 Mad dogs and Englishmen Go
5663 them, Lame dogs over
6731 and hungry dogs, Making
7675 asses, apes, and dogs.
9661 who hates dogs and babies
10090 the more I admire dogs.
10286 let slip the dogs of war.
11839 the more one values dogs.
12287 Let dogs delight to bark
12334 Cowardly dogs bark

doing
170 Doing easily what others
788 in life is doing what
1014 to be doing at that
1531 is when I'm doing what I
4628 It is always doing or dying.
5005 either on doing or on
5062 Doing what's right isn't
6504 be up and doing, With a
7818 if you are doing something
9290 what she's doing, and tell
9741 one way of doing things
12092 is doing well that
12254 is not doing it. If
12647 until you're doing it.
12742 of the Doing Into the

doing-good
11768 As for Doing-good, that is one

doings
1244 child is known by his doings.

dole
5284 the 1930s dole queue were

doleful
7549 of sorrow, doleful shades,

doll
8752 A living doll, everywhere

dollar
1283 of a dollar with a

dolls
9710 Guys and dolls.

dolores
11360 and sterile Dolores, Our Lady

dolphinese
9806 to have learned dolphinese.

dolphins
7850 gentler dolphins of

domestic
3904 and pleasures of domestic life.

7779 state. And domestic business
8575 men call domestic bliss.

domesticate
11198 marry is to domesticate the

dominant
1262 always been dominant and

dominate
2057 He must dominate in his

dominating
12315 of men dominating men, a

dominion
4142 from the dominion of
7309 of his dark dominion swung the
11662 death shall have no dominion.
11672 that holds dominion over Man

dominions
8285 majesty's dominions, on which
9954 does not set in my dominions.

domino
3186 'falling domino'

don
4070 the typical Don, and of

done
964 how it's done, they've
3015 and are never done.
3267 have been done once for
3341 of having done the thing
3371 thing well done, is to
3641 a thing done, go - if
4608 not only be done, but
6408 gets things done and the
6609 nothing done while
6632 that is done in the
8406 must be done, but must
8572 that which unto us is done!
9254 What may be done at any
9457 So little done, so much to
9476 get nothing done, but you
9591 to do usually can be done.
9798 of one gets things done.
10180 task hast done, Home art
10347 If it were done when 'tis
10369 What's done cannot be
10612 is ever done in this
12092 should not be done at all.
12476 must be done about
12685 was ever done so
12742 Into the peace of the Done.
12904 she have done being what

dong
6149 'The Dong! the Dong! The

donkey
4304 where the donkey finally

donne
2963 John Donne, Anne Donne,
5000 Dr Donne's verses are like
5244 Donne, for not keeping of
6715 functions, Donne would have

dons
12653 did become dons, but not

doodling
11089 Doodling is the brooding of

doom
4297 of their doom, The
7459 is that doom that Adam
9769 slow, sure doom falls
10561 the edge of doom. If this
11546 God, and the doom assigned.

doomed
10766 but you are doomed if you

door
944 each man by the right door.
2828 - The opening of a Door.
3249 Towards the door we never
3301 a beaten path to his door.
4315 when the door opens and
5530 When one door of happiness
6676 When the door Scraped
8318 the other side of a door.
8811 from off my door! Quoth the
8850 shut the door, good
9112 outside his door already
9862 of a door, leaving
11262 of a revolving door.
12021 doing away with the door.

doormat
9461 A doormat in a world of

doors
7150 a thousand doors to let out
7579 infernal doors, and on
9545 house, My doors are widely
10496 shut their doors against a
12328 several doors For men to

dormouse
7441 once was a Dormouse who lived

dotages
1845 and common dotages of human

dote
10389 them but I dote on his

double
10361 Double, double toil and
11011 So double was his pains, so

double life
12550 leading a double life,

double-bed
2029 of the double-bed after the
11675 double-bed of the

doubled
2736 to have your trouble doubled.

doublethink
8380 Doublethink means the power of

doubt
984 never doubt What
1633 a life of doubt
3529 to cast doubt. Holding
3682 anybody's doubt
3952 manner of doubt - No
5737 all men doubt you, But
5777 enabled to doubt Thee, Help
5804 or doubt
7637 full of doubt I stand,
7800 Philosophy is doubt.
8162 do not make one doubt.
10203 Doubt thou the stars are
10498 Modest doubt is call'd The
11471 the sunnier side of doubt.
11573 tell me, doubt is
11574 in honest doubt, Believe
11978 when in doubt, strike it
12151 Doubt is not a pleasant

doubtful
5168 A man, doubtful of his dinner,

doubting
11051 we must begin with doubting.

doubts
675 end in doubts; but if he
5588 you may have some doubts.
10358 in To saucy doubts and fears.

dover
816 cliffs of Dover; you think
1840 cliffs of Dover, Tomorrow,

doves
11595 The moan of doves in

down
3689 a fence down until you
6402 victis. Down with the
6666 people to look down upon.
6778 be brought down by the
7386 Down, down, down into the
7711 meet 'em on your way down.
7883 my coming down let me
7949 the top down. First
8465 head hang down. Never
8653 Just get it down on paper,

downfall
1404 My downfall raises me to

downhearted
5768 Are we downhearted? No! Let

downing street
2014 by Downing Street because it

downs
3863 All in the Downs the fleet

downtrodden
1744 The downtrodden, who are the

dozens
3961 up by dozens, And his

dozes
7327 Here dozes one

dragged
8668 he hadn't dragged her

dragon
5392 a damn big dragon. You kick
10311 between the dragon and his

dragons
11818 Never laugh at live dragons.

drain
11031 by the next town drain.

draining
10821 that of draining money from

drains
11247 the Deity and the Drains.

drake
8147 Drake he's in his hammock

drama
1072 close the drama with the
3943 the drama onto the
4625 Drama is life with the dull
6938 tool. Drama never
12095 talent for drama is not a
12618 of the ear in real drama.

dramatic
5822 as a dramatic work in

drank
6923 well and drank, and the
10658 I work as my father drank.
11314 hungry, and drank without

draughts
12560 susceptible to draughts.

draw
2034 he draws what he
7022 can ye draw but twenty

drawing
5289 Drawing is speaking to the

drawn
6029 that yet may be drawn from.
9370 thou hast drawn together

dread
1105 The dread of beatings!
9991 - I only dread one day at
10622 is why most men dread it.
12774 crowds; I dread the

dreadfully
12248 He is dreadfully married. He's

dreading
1962 Dreading that climax of all

dreadnoughts
6410 up as two Dreadnoughts; and dukes

dream
243 To dream of the person you
1736 and behold it was a dream.
2206 Spayne And dreme of joye,
2987 of a misty dream Our path
3597 I dream of Jeanie with the
3712 You cannot dream yourself
3979 For you dream you are
4246 The dream of reason
4646 ever have a boring dream?
5445 stars, Dream, and so
5503 or a waking dream? Fled is
5642 I have a dream that one day
5738 If you can dream - and not
6226 Lives in a dream. Waits at
7402 is got to dream, boy. It
7741 peace is a dream, and not
7789 Life is a dream; when we
7858 life As love's young dream.
8345 as a bad dream between
8408 age is a dream that is
8807 Is but a dream within a
9333 work and to dream and work
9657 The dream, alone, is of
9902 life is a dream
10100 In a dream you are never
10212 to dream: ay,
10532 This dream of mine, Being
10555 thee, as a dream doth
10673 from the dream of life -
11041 Is a dream a lie if it
11606 like a dream The
12041 I dream my painting, and
12809 the glory and the dream?

dreamed
1728 I dreamed that I dwelt in
4373 than are dreamed of, or can
11195 night I've dreamed of cheese

dreamer
7928 Dreamer of dreams, born out
9887 artist is a dreamer consenting

dreamers
8407 We are the dreamers of dreams
9917 Like all dreamers, I mistook

dreaming
519 with her dreaming spires,
1079 I'm dreaming of a white
2565 Stands dreaming on the
6056 you've been dreaming of Will be
9091 who lose dreaming are lost.
10380 sleep, Dreaming on both.
10701 I slept Dreaming like a
11678 boys are dreaming wicked or

dreams
1234 shall dream dreams, your
1567 of golden dreams had
3655 of dreams is the
3938 by their dreams, Nor feel
5654 Into the land of my dreams.
6615 can lay a hand on our dreams.
6935 is a community of dreams.
7832 beyond the dreams of
9990 all your dreams
10489 stuff As dreams are made
11510 Man dreams of fame while
11516 Than this world dreams of.
11527 a dog, he hunts in dreams.
11680 pulls the legs of his dreams.
11737 of his dreams, and
12188 off of old men's dreams.
12914 spread my dreams under your

dreamt
3937 And dreamt of all
10200 Than are dreamt of in your

dreary
3221 makes life dreary is want of
11186 make you dreary, depend on

dregs
3772 but the dregs of his

dress
2144 and a hundred in dress.
2823 I dress for women - and I
3497 cool white dress after the
6721 put on a dress of guilt
6768 article of dress without
8877 is the dress of
9716 I always dress to match the
9747 gentleman; dresses too
10246 youth did dress
11111 man cannot dress, without
11174 night And dress by yellow
12062 fleshly dress Bright
12396 is the dress of

dressed
8253 was well dressed ever
12290 Let me be dressed fine as I
12463 All dressed up, with nowhere

dresses
7516 neat-handed Phyllis dresses.
12349 a woman dresses up for an
12950 All women's dresses are merely

dressing up
11378 skills - dressing up and

drifted
12408 snow-white .. but I drifted.

drill
350 Drill for oil? You mean

drink
124 we should drink; Good
204 What should we do for drink?
270 a duck a drink if he
1207 eat, and to drink, and to be
1225 us eat and drink; for
1249 Give strong drink unto him
1826 A man may drink and no be
2198 And for to drynken strong
2446 any drop to drink. The very
3491 drove me to drink - and, you
4569 Drink not the third glass -

4986 reason why I never drink it.
5241 Drink to me only with thine
5271 Our drink shall be prepared
6073 bait, don't drink, don't
6098 the heat, To drink there.
6673 them with drink, which
6873 I love drink, so long as it
7266 never to drink by
7973 Drinka Pinta Milka Day.
8010 a man to drink and drive.
8108 I drink to make other
8316 who prefers women to drink
8874 thing; Drink deep, or
9260 Drink nothing without
9344 I drink for the thirst to
9425 "I never drink when I fly."
10849 we could drink all day
11030 Let us drink to the queer
11427 that he has taken to drink.
12305 I drink for it.

drinking
907 Drinking when we are not
3485 too much drinking. That
3544 There is no drinking after
7292 We're drinking my friend, To
10053 not the drinking that is to
11318 true, 'much drinking, little
12608 curse of the drinking classes.

drinks
415 He who drinketh by the inch
1388 is about three drinks behind.
7251 after four drinks; a woman
11663 like who drinks as much as

drive
427 time to drive to the
8010 a man to drink and drive.
11995 way but can't drive the car.

driven
7146 I am driven Into a desperate

driver
915 he was in the driver's seat.

drives
11667 green fuse drives the flower

droopingly
6080 a little droopingly, but with

drop
5104 well to drop, but would
10172 am like a drop of water

dropout
3813 the term dropout' to mean a

dropped
5104 not wish to be dropped by.
7563 setting sun Dropped from the

dropping
11729 dropping from the

drown
1759 a rat may drown a nation.
2752 rains, they drown in every
10461 it was to drown: What
10490 sound, I'll drown my book.

drowned
3816 Bacchus has drowned more men
5200 the chance of being drowned.
9182 a cormorant gets drowned.
11379 do only be drownded now and

drowning
3466 death by drowning, a really
10869 And not waving but drowning.

drowns
729 and drowns things
3156 Whisky drowns some troubles
8557 alone; all drowns in the

drowsy
4290 flight, And drowsy tinklings

drudge
5145 a harmless drudge.
8457 was a genius I was a drudge.

drudgery
10843 love of the drudgery it

drug
8121 Power is a drug on which

drugs
3122 Sex and drugs and rock and
8509 you; And drugs cause

drum
3507 music of a distant drum!
4044 the most effective drum.
8146 'Take my drum to England,
12717 Not a drum was heard, not

drummer
11764 a different drummer. Let him

drums
7886 trumpets, beat the drums!

drunk
1470 he gets drunk; but most
1986 and then drunk.
5100 the art of getting drunk.
5735 If, drunk with sight of
7877 getting drunk, is a sin
8593 Not drunk is he who from
9788 hearts were drunk with a
11043 so think as you drunk I am.
12000 What, when drunk, one sees
12029 from Philip drunk to Philip

drunkard
2258 English drunkard made the
9188 loves the drunkard, but not

drunkards
9347 more old drunkards than old

drunken
11369 We have drunken of things

drunkenness
4998 the sin of drunkenness, which is
6792 feel The drunkenness of things
9762 Drunkenness is temporary suicide:
10072 Drunkenness is nothing but
10522 babbling drunkenness, Or any

dry
124 or being dry, Or lest
1312 and keep your powder dry.
5508 Dry your eyes O dry

dry-dock
8143 it in dry-dock and to

dubiousness
3576 facade every type of dubiousness.

ducats
10396 O my ducats! O my

duchess
6712 every Duchess in London

duck
270 give a duck a drink if
2776 I just forgot to duck.

due
674 have their due, as time,
5360 to every one his due.
10870 when praise is not due.

duenna
2690 is the duenna in the

duke
2627 enough who knows a duke.
6876 treat a duke as an
9907 The Duke returned from the

dukes
3956 in May, And dukes were three
6410 and dukes are just

dull
8 is that he be dull.
3559 is not only dull in
3920 Their dull and deep
5144 Dull. To make
5959 who can be dull in Fleet
8888 oft creep in one dull line.
10980 be too dull to bear,
11069 appears dull there is a
11608 How dull it is to pause,

duller
2781 .. a duller spectacle this

dullness
3578 off the dullness - much as
6187 The devil's name is Dullness.
8827 Gentle Dullness ever loves a
11035 Dullness, occasionally
12657 Dullness is a misdemeanour.

dumb
5065 So dumb he can't fart and
6677 game, and dumb enough to
6748 fruit Dumb As old
8776 or moves it, it is dumb.

9378 but the deep are dumb.
10089 said, I envy dumb people.
11668 And I am dumb to tell the

dunce
2612 How much a dunce that has
8831 A wit with dunces, and a

duncery
7653 tyrannical duncery no free

dunces
11348 that the dunces are all in

dungeon
2518 in the dungeon of self.
3997 In a dungeon cell On a
7480 Himself is his own dungeon.
7549 A dungeon horrible, on all
10432 vapour of a dungeon, Than keep

dungfork
4758 man with a dungfork in his

dunghill
122 crowing on its own dunghill.

dupe
8815 only make a dupe of the

durability
11254 insures vitality and durability.

durable
1537 are too durable, that's

duration
8242 but the duration, of great

dusk
4030 In the dusk with a
8447 each slow dusk a

dusky
11533 shall rear my dusky race.

dust
1070 raised a dust and then
1222 For dust thou art, and
1226 the small dust of the
1419 to ashes, dust to dust;
1582 a richer dust concealed;
3258 rear in a handful of dust.
3508 into the dust descend;
4292 the silent dust, Or
5638 to that dust It so much
6500 its goal; Dust thou art,
6678 The dust of exploded
7072 turn to dust; And into
7841 And dust is for a
8512 Excuse My Dust.
8707 soul the dust of
8843 A heap of dust alone
10028 To the vile dust, from
10672 Dust to the dust! but the
10700 The dust of creeds
11562 scattering dust, And Life,
11570 a little dust of praise.
11614 the unhappy dust thou
11794 of boiling dust up to
12824 Dust as we are, the

dust-heap
1301 The great dust-heap called

dustbin
11889 - into the dustbin of

dutch
2060 of the Dutch Is
9115 but the Dutch made

duties
3018 has its duties as well as
6582 teach new duties: Time
7298 to the duties, yet
8412 the first duties of the
10870 the smaller duties in life, I
11717 to the neglect of his duties.

duty
768 and body to do your DUTY.
2302 to our duty, and so
2416 every man's duty to do all
3912 he had a duty to
4014 as keen A sense of duty?
4711 is not a duty, it is
4745 found that life was duty.
4780 It is the duty of a doctor
6345 to do our duty as we
6362 of official duty and I
6411 forgotten - Duty,

7212 Our duty is to blare like
7453 it is our duty to try to
8129 every man will do his duty.
8131 God, I have done my duty.
8496 right as well as our duty.
9338 will be the duty of some,
9758 A sense of duty is useful
9837 must do our duty as such.
10262 subject's duty is the
10581 that it is his duty.
11118 were in duty both
11201 There is no duty we so much
11603 done my duty as a man
12475 distinction, and of duty.
12565 The one duty we owe to
12891 law, nor duty bade me

dwarf
5271 : and my dwarf shall

dwarfish
2457 epigram? A dwarfish whole, Its

dwarfs
7372 State which dwarfs its men,

dwell
1245 better to dwell in a
12866 not to dwell in

dwelling
2373 left its dwelling place And
12797 Whose dwelling is the

dwelt
12781 She dwelt among the

dwindle
2514 by degrees dwindle into a

dying
131 I am dying with the help of
1473 Smoking is a dying habit.
1570 old, But, dying, has made
1605 indisposeth us for dying.
1655 we fret; Dying, we live.
2583 We are dying of accuracy.
2826 Dying is a wild night and a
3472 death, but dying, which is
3485 of people dying from too
4628 It is always doing or dying.
4780 to prolong the act of dying.
6606 love to those of the dying.
6960 A man's dying is more the
8408 that is dying, Or one
8689 those poor devils are dying.
8756 Dying, Is an art, like
8839 pain, the bliss of dying!
8913 Here am I, dying of a
8988 And she is dying piece-meal
9472 it's about dying, about the
9696 loving and dying - each of
9891 can lose by dying is half so
10028 And, doubly dying, shall go
10164 I am dying, Egypt, dying;
10721 can't stay dying here all
10854 friends for dying: I do not
10872 from dying, with
11243 If this is dying, then I
11513 forgets a dying king.
11664 against the dying of the
12919 new in dying, But nor,

dyke
1759 through a dyke, even a

eagle
127 here. The Eagle has
1492 is not an eagle, it creeps
4840 fly like an eagle with the
6940 and out the Eagle, That's
7464 her as an eagle mewing her
9314 like an eagle that has

ear
579 The ear tends to be lazy,
7483 I was all ear, And took
7504 meant than meets the ear.
7603 close at the ear of Eve.
7899 is to earn to wear
10195 man thine ear, but few
10338 lies in the ear Of him

earful
8043 getting an earful tonight.

earl
3953 be, The Earl, the

early
4796 time to get an early start.
6558 to git up airly Ef you
7097 " Well, it's early yet."
8669 Early to bed, early to
9073 I used to go to bed early.
10471 hate! Too early seen

earn
1495 thee surely will earn it.
4270 be set to earn their
5670 little to earn, and many
9476 you don't earn bonuses

earnest
6305 who are earnest about not
9056 of deadly earnest that can

earning
4300 get money without earning it.

earrings
9395 a pair of earrings for under

ears
1161 that hath ears to hear,
3395 but two ears, that we
5855 hungry stomach has no ears.
8797 since it has no ears.
9155 the ears believe
9717 others is with your ears.
10289 me your ears; I come to
10787 As his ears, keep
11327 tongues, and hedges ears.

earth
115 make terms with the earth!
198 on the earth as other
272 lived on earth, people
463 and I will move the earth.
571 all here on earth to help
584 Earth, receive an honoured
1140 not the earth, neither
1165 salt of the earth: but if
1228 to the earth, and it
1419 the ground; earth to earth,
1428 shall possess the earth.
2571 on earth that allow
3539 last, And earth is but a
3730 Spaceship Earth, and that
4528 thee feel the earth move?
4783 hour when earth's
5684 meet, Till Earth and Sky
5740 is the Earth and
6601 police the earth, a ghost
7469 spot, Which men call earth.
7562 out of the earth a fabric
7611 What if earth Be but the
8650 the whole earth as their
8726 Where on earth do they
9025 stay on earth Which is
9097 made him, earth can find
9409 over the earth, but men
9633 O Earth, lie heavily upon
9638 where this earth Spins like
9781 seen the earth run red at
10200 heaven and earth, Horatio,
10236 the lean earth as he
11501 must have a touch of earth.
12362 scum of the earth - the mere
12414 it is the salt of the earth.
12777 Earth has not anything to
12839 touch of earthly years.

earthquake
1980 eruption prevents an earthquake.
5044 If an earthquake were to engulf
5806 which no earthquake is a
10706 gloom of earthquake and
11586 that world earthquake, Waterloo!

ease
2072 Bring equal ease unto my
6281 seemed at ease and to
6323 greatest of ease, A daring
9238 truth is always at ease.
9615 of ignoble ease, but the
10274 take their ease And sleep
10817 are at ease, our
11010 seas, Ease after war,
11831 and wish to ease his lot by

easier
2270 It will be easier for you.

easiest
10052 they were easiest for his
12045 always the easiest to do
12385 taking the easiest way out.

east
5684 Oh, East is East, and West

east end
3287 look the East End in the

eastern
1745 save in Eastern clime - A
6577 breathed with eastern wind.
7515 against the eastern gate,

eastertide
4787 Wearing white for Eastertide.

easy
1318 It is very easy to say
6074 so easy for
7041 zeal .. all zeal, Mr Easy.
8484 comes easy to me, I
9966 Too easy for children, and
10014 and eye - Easy live and
10583 It is easy - terribly easy
11629 that comes easy, comes

eat
134 Never eat at a place
196 Eat British Lamb: 50,000
223 uncertain - eat dessert
246 To eat is human, to
593 that he eat than that
1190 neither should he eat.
1207 than to eat, and to
1220 me, and I did eat.
1225 Let us eat and drink; for
1825 Some have meat and cannot
2294 it will eat him last.
4960 the verb to eat, in the
6984 Let them eat cake.
7176 one should eat wisely but
7729 One should eat to live,
9379 Eat slowly: only men in
11138 Frogs Eat Butterflies.
12858 that do not eat people are

eaten
5395 waste or eaten within
10341 Or have we eaten on the

eaters
7884 so small eaters, now, as I

eating
1039 over three years in eating.
2064 is like eating an entire
4873 the subject of eating.
9343 The appetite grows by eating.

eats
9620 that eats or needs

eccentric
3429 last bastions of the eccentric.

eccentricity
9898 eccentricity, heresy,

echo
5247 left an echo in the
7037 and waiting for the echo.
8879 seem an echo to the
9859 Hope is an echo, hope ties
9868 Art is a delayed echo.

echoes
11590 Our echoes roll from soul to

eclipse
3955 anon, In a merciful eclipse.
7656 dark, total eclipse Without
10706 of earthquake and eclipse.

ecology
2493 law of ecology is that

econometrician
6866 unfortunate econometrician who, in

economic
4727 and the economic ones are
5545 .. an economic system
5600 forces of economic law on the
5975 shoots of economic spring are
9605 bottom of the economic pyramid.
11436 estimate of economic
11468 of the economic process.
12344 its vital economic interests

economical
493 was being economical with the

economics
146 A study of economics usually
3780 In economics, the majority is
5607 more about economics than my
9508 Economics is the science which

economies
3460 The petty economies of the rich

economist
7044 nothing an economist should

economize
11948 we have. Let us economize it.

economy
4747 Economy is going without
10064 for fear of Political Economy.
11133 Our whole economy is based on

ecstasies
7507 me into ecstasies, And bring

ecstasy
1608 without an ecstasy? Time we
2827 ratio To the ecstasy.
4040 bells of Ecstasy and
7166 is an ecstasy; It is as
8570 this ecstasy, is
12451 a sort of ecstasy. This

ecstatic
2827 For each ecstatic instant We

eden
5525 o'er Eden, That
7544 our woe, With loss of Eden.
7598 The happier Eden, shall
7639 Through Eden took their
10446 This other Eden,

edge
4645 doesn't have clear edges.
10792 sits on the edge of the
10851 to the very edge of their
10998 at the edge of Being.
11152 us to the edge of the

edifice
9817 the edifice of the

edison
2855 devised Edison's

editor
3226 An editor should tell the
4823 An editor - a person

editorial
12065 The editorial job has become,

editors
3259 some editors are failed

educate
2179 work to educate a child,
2638 Educate a man and you educate
8412 is to educate the masses
9829 got to educate him first.

educated
1672 God's - the educated man's!
2169 must be educated, the thumb
3224 really educated without
6715 would have educated their
8385 of stress educated' people
8386 hearing an educated' accent,
9760 most highly educated young men
9873 A child educated only at

educating
12179 Educating a beautiful woman is

education
27 Nothing in education is so
445 is the beginning of education.
744 a part of education; in the
888 of man's education is that he
1259 Education, n: that which
1394 you think education is
1472 What poor education I have
1589 Education makes a people easy
1859 Good education is the essential
2878 Upon the education of the
3045 By education most have been
3227 function of education to help us
3379 are not an education but the
3690 Education is the ability to
3720 notion that education is a
3815 goal of the educational system

4287 capsule of education that
4324 A good education should leave
4930 of all education is the
5032 Education in Britain is a
5290 Education should be gentle and
6329 Most men of education are more
6440 of any to be used in education.
7491 generous education that which
8704 Nothing but education, nothing
8763 kind of education is that a
8871 'Tis education forms the common
8982 Real education must ultimately
9556 movies, and that is education.
9723 is the beginning of education.
10029 hand in their own education.
10801 Education is what survives when
10978 To me education is a leading
10992 Education has for its object
11066 love her is a liberal education.
11665 My education was the liberty I
11881 to which education cannot
11944 Soap and education are not as
11976 with a college education.
12376 between education and
12385 Education ent only books and
12467 a liberal education is
12474 Education with inert ideas is
12526 without education.
12737 Education today, more than ever
12889 Education is not the filling of

educational
4725 kinds of educational
6447 under our educational rules, the

educator
3671 become an educator more

edward
7002 stay, That Edward may be

edwardians
12458 The Edwardians, on the

effect
1260 have a retroactive effect.
4308 with its shattering effect.
8969 that the effect of eating
9988 watch the effect produced

effectiveness
7198 The effectiveness of work increases

effects
4986 and its effects - and that
5784 to. It's the after effects.
12273 the baneful effects of the

effeminate
7047 He that in effeminate invention,

efficiency
10605 the world: efficiency and

efficient
778 next, the efficient parts -
3724 efficient machine
4837 hard to be efficient without
6877 in an efficient state as

efficiently
3013 as doing efficiently that which

effort
132 an intense effort is made,
1019 mental effort would be
2069 Continuous effort - not
3813 up serious effort to meet
5208 without effort is in
8354 than the effort to reduce
12113 was the effort to found
12496 make a new effort necessary.

efforts
6386 direct your efforts more to
9438 be appreciative of my efforts.

egg
628 An egg boiled very soft
1881 is only an egg's way of
2616 the fatal egg by
4588 and hairless as an egg.
5748 eating an egg without
7965 Go to work on an egg.
9293 got a bad egg, Mr Jones.
11968 laid an egg cackles as

eggs
4922 to lay eggs into their
7854 ways to dress eggs?

9247 your rooster will lay eggs.
11933 all thine eggs in one

ego
2251 never the ego; the self

egoism
4305 husband's egoism in order
7306 the Book of Egoism it is

egotism
3378 Take egotism out, and you
4111 often passes for egotism.
4320 it, masking egotism, lust,
4601 is only egotism wrong side

egypt
4842 would still be in Egypt.

eiffel tower
248 The Eiffel Tower is the Empire

eight
7987 We want eight, and we won't
9474 You get eight out of

eighty
159 up is eighty percent of
2144 A man of eighty has outlived
10100 a dream you are never eighty.
11962 the age of eighty and

einstein
8717 genius of Einstein leads to
11044 'Ho! Let Einstein be!'

elasticity
10813 gives elasticity to the

elderly
4716 to all his elderly

elders
4707 of the elders to young

eldest
7581 Night, eldest of things.

elect
12251 Where to elect there is but

elected
2861 1. Get elected. 2. Get
9371 have been elected between
12503 audacity of elected persons.

election
3203 An election is coming.
5359 right of election is the
9009 of the next general election.
10619 substitutes election by the

elections
25 Elections are won by men and
6786 no go the elections, Sit on
10928 You won the elections, but I won

electorate
1322 and the electorate will soon

electric
1003 to mend the Electric Light
11755 you have an electric affinity
12502 I sing the body electric.

electrician
1001 Air - The Electrician is no

electricity
6134 Electricity is of two kinds,
11784 that electricity was

electrification
6214 plus the electrification of the

electronic
6760 The new electronic

elegance
3373 is the main elegance.

elegant
2191 much-loved and elegant friend.
3305 be so elegant as to have

element
10319 sorrow! Thy element's below.
10519 I am not of your element.

elementary
2994 I cried. Elementary,' said he.

elements
7570 of time Become our elements.

elephant
1369 A herd of elephant .. pacing
2956 an elephant, The only
6376 have got an elephant by the

7597 unwieldy elephant To make
11897 with an elephant. No

elephants
3492 are like elephants. They are
9079 When elephants fight it is the

elevates
4634 space that elevates our

eleven
3980 tells you he's only eleven.
6418 At eleven o'clock this
10610 things at eleven at night

elite
2502 has its own elite, its own

elope
4172 about, must elope

elopement
77 an elopement would be

eloquence
5262 Talking and eloquence are not
6408 the finest eloquence is that
7362 say that eloquence is heard,
8544 Continual eloquence is tedious.
10173 Action is eloquence.

eloquent
1297 fails to be eloquent and often
8430 cause any man may be eloquent.

else
9915 someone else. And not

elsewhere
8357 his mind would be elsewhere.
9448 possible to find it elsewhere.
11453 if you are elsewhere, live as

elusive
10977 prime is elusive. You

elvis
3132 I'd be seeing Elvis soon.

elysian
2879 but in the Elysian fields.

elysium
1101 our lost Elysium - rural

emancipation
11215 Every emancipation has in it the

embalmer
5514 O soft embalmer of the still
12094 triumph of the embalmer's art.

embalms
10040 A precedent embalms a

embark
11479 of farewell, When I embark.

embarrassed
6266 royalty .. embarrassed by the

embarrasses
4687 his head out and embarrasses us.

embarrassment
140 The embarrassment of riches
855 the land of embarrassment and
1031 us in our place is embarrassment.

embers
7502 glowing embers through

embittered
4132 harsh and embittered manhood,

embody
3971 I, my Lords, embody the Law.

emboldens
10497 Nothing emboldens sin so much

embossed
11715 and embossed, With His

embrace
7072 I think, do there embrace.
7680 oh as to embrace me she
8901 then pity, then embrace.
11546 I embrace the purpose of God,

embraceable
3896 my sweet embraceable you!

embraced
6262 us; we embraced, and we

embroils
7580 more embroils the fray

emergency
12249 up to the emergency, and cave

emeritus
6131 professor emeritus from the

eminence
7364 His eminence was due to the

emolument
1762 any kind of emolument from it,
3773 of considerable emolument.

emotion
492 not an unknown emotion to us.
1695 He disliked emotion, not
3701 where an emotion has found
3940 thought charged with emotion.
5541 stirred by emotion and take
6165 emotion than a
8110 Love is an emotion
8234 is the epitaph of an emotion.
8506 remembered in emotion.
9429 not being emotional, but
11159 of emotion, but the
11827 is the shorthand of emotion.
12004 a luxurious emotion, it can
12596 of an emotion without
12628 is an emotion for the
12802 origin from emotion

emotional
8760 learning has an emotional base.

emotions
834 To kill the emotions and so
2794 an ocean of emotions entirely
3867 are noble emotions essential
4132 the human emotions! Don't
5790 brothel for emotions.
6967 to control emotions by the
8504 of the emotions from A to
9397 admit our emotions. We think
11450 body and a child's emotions.
12313 basket of the emotions.

emparadised
7598 These two Emparadised in one

emperor
7334 The Emperor is
10761 the Roman Emperor, and am
11137 The only emperor is the
11275 Hail, Emperor, those

empire
10 has lost an Empire and has
248 is the Empire State
1072 course of empire takes its
1693 can be an empire or a
2886 the British Empire to prigs
2928 old Glasgow Empire on a
2996 of the Empire are
3023 All empire is no more than
3806 an unjust empire to save
3887 How's the Empire?
4053 of the Empire, and, I am
4438 of an empire than for
7645 as thy empire must
7811 An empire founded by war has
9622 The Empire is a Commonwealth
9908 lay the empire of the
10147 the ranged empire fall.
12154 Holy Roman Empire was

empires
2306 The empires of the future are
7071 Vaster than empires, and more
7571 here Hatching vain empires.

employed
3747 that might be better employed.

employee
8588 into an employee of Mammon.
8671 every employee tends to

employees
8674 by those employees who have

employer
3569 is not the employer who pays
11033 and harder upon the employer.

employment
1003 man To give employment to the
3790 Employment is nature's
3845 indeed, our employment may be
6356 is the wise employment of

emptied
584 vessel lie Emptied of its

empties
3632 If a man empties his purse

emptiness
8858 smiles his emptiness betray, As

empty
230 indicated by an empty desk?
3801 man with an empty stomach
5460 and line, Empty the
6500 is but an empty dream! For
6519 Fill what's empty. Empty
7927 idle singer of an empty day.
8195 nor in ships empty of men.
12127 through the empty dwellings
12877 All empty souls tend to

emptying
10015 the world, and emptying of it.

enchant
8765 may be said to enchant.

enchanted
9394 not an enchanted place, but

enchanting
7477 such divine enchanting

enchantments
503 the last enchantments of the
958 the last enchantments of the

encores
347 don't respond with encores.

encounter
5324 I go to encounter for the

encountered
808 I even encountered myself.

encourage
12146 to time to encourage the

encumbers
5190 ground, encumbers him with

encyclopedia
12915 charm of an encyclopedia is that it

end
453 The End of every maker is
675 he shall end in doubts;
921 never an end for the
1558 an ulterior end, but an
1657 the world may end tonight?
1858 The end justifies the
2296 is not the end. It is
2372 meets no end, Wastes
2406 for some end or other.
2900 that it can ever end.
3250 In my beginning is my end.
3251 often the end And to
4069 and an end,'
4907 The end cannot justify
6043 a muddle, and an end.
6418 came to an end the
6617 it should end there.
7122 In my end is my
7322 the end of a man's
7366 The sole end for which
7988 with a worker at each end.
8123 means to an end, not the
8320 there's ane end of ane old
9113 but he pays at the end.
9616 In America they end it.
10245 Let the end try the man.
10505 The end crowns all, And
10551 hasten to their end.
11231 it all going to end?
11415 the beginning of the end.
11921 and that's the end of it!
11927 may end, But
12115 grant an end to these
12380 The war that will end war.
12460 the wrong end of time,

endearing
7851 all those endearing young

endeavour
8864 painful an endeavour, Content

endeavours
9057 in great endeavours even to
11737 dreams, and endeavours to live

ended
3289 Lord, is ended, The

ending
1139 and the ending, saith the

2654 A good book has no ending.
9524 alone of ending not

endless
6040 is nowhere, and is endless.
11234 .. the endless time of

endow
8869 Die, and endow a college,
12501 alone, that endows a man to

ends
955 and loose ends.
2777 We may our ends by our
4099 the song that never ends.
5649 the ends for which
9508 between ends and scarce
10230 shapes our ends, Rough-hew

endurance
2104 of being is endurance - to
6483 and patient endurance is
12662 mother, the endurance of an

endure
1136 happy which endure. Ye have
2514 continue to endure you a
3452 not merely endure: he will
4617 is, I now endure but two
5153 life, or better to endure it.
8901 We first endure, then
9276 was hard to endure is sweet
10332 Men must endure Their going
10512 a stuff will not endure.
10691 Nought may endure but
10735 willingness to endure it.

endured
5196 is to be endured, and
9758 not to be endured with

endures
4675 which grows slowly endures.
8211 in love he endures more than

enduring
186 is nothing enduring in life

enemies
715 forgive our enemies; not our
1065 Enemies could become the best
1155 Love your enemies, do good to
1720 mischief, enemies with the
2244 we make our enemies; but God
3760 enough to hold two enemies.
4420 with my enemies. I can
4817 it and your enemies will not
4946 The enemies of Freedom do not
6262 been mortal enemies ever
6509 of our enemies, we should
7227 forgive our enemies; but we do
7759 wish their enemies dead - but
7897 The enemies of the future are
8237 classes: tools and enemies.
8486 perpetual enemies. Our
8647 yesterday's enemies. What is
8698 many friends and few enemies.
9018 the natural enemies of a
10110 More than your enemies.
10941 Enemies' gifts are no gifts
11464 by their enemies. I am
12103 myself from my enemies.
12176 time for making new enemies.
12588 in the choice of his enemies.

enemy
704 terrible enemy, when a
821 than the enemy if you
1130 The last enemy that shall
2475 bitterest enemy in the
2521 more sombre enemy of good
2533 It is the enemy of thought
3424 of an old enemy down on
4651 what your enemy fears most
5535 met the enemy, and he is
7420 is an enemy to the
7428 got a better class of enemy.
8133 ship alongside the enemy.
8135 man your enemy who speaks
8164 towards our enemy as if he
8373 The great enemy of clear
8799 of his enemy, but that
9084 The enemy of my enemy is my
9121 a greater enemy to the
9801 kill him, is his own enemy.
11308 portend, No enemy can match

11952 takes your enemy and your
12001 know the enemy and know
12148 best is the enemy of the
12266 unrelenting enemy leaves us
12364 have on the enemy, but by
12543 hasn't an enemy in the
12894 Have no enemy but time.

energies
3530 mystery are energies of life.

energy
1338 Energy is Eternal Delight.
1881 for the energy which
5308 deal of energy will long
6161 take the energy process
6865 - their energy
9028 himself of energy all over
9796 The energy produced by the

enfants
3835 Les enfants terribles. The

enfold
12906 Rose, Enfold me in my

enforced
7804 Whatever is enforced by command

enfranchised
7653 had once enfranchised herself

engels
5612 of Marx, Engels and Lenin

engendered
10400 ..? It is engendered in the

engine
12326 curious engine, your

engineer
11247 sanitary engineer; and in

engineering
8950 social engineering resembles

engineers
5564 are not engineers of the
11049 are the engineers of human

england
61 We have in England a
165 Speak for England.
231 Coffee in England is just
522 For England, home and beauty.
775 we see that England is a
1348 Walk upon England's
1350 In England's green
1553 England is the mother of
1577 get me to England once
1582 is for ever England. There
1613 I am in England,
1651 to be in England Now that
1851 England is a paradise for
2417 England to me was always the
2464 Rule all England under a
2875 suffer England to be the
2882 England does not love
3003 England's not a bad country
3011 Heart of England well may
3252 History is now and England.
3551 England is the paradise of
3861 and bred in England, I can
4235 In England I would rather be
4527 homes of England, How
4617 my legs, and think of England.
4954 Florence, Elizabethan England.
5047 France and England is - the
5081 that leads him to England.
5189 which in England is
5683 England's on the anvil - hear
5694 know of England who only
5732 fair, Old England to adorn,
6054 grace in England, as (I
6083 make up England today.
6810 history of England is
6920 King born of all England.
7353 food; in England people
7490 Let not England forget her
7835 No place in England where
8026 a bore; he bored for England.
8129 England expects that every
8150 But in England's song for
8152 banks And England's far and
8293 Not only England, but every
8518 be an England While
8748 England has saved herself by
9898 England is the paradise of

11585 This is England's greatest
12013 is nowhere; England one whose
12152 England has forty-two
12546 If England treats her
12745 the stately homes of England.
12804 this hour: England hath need
12843 sea; Nor England! did I

english
104 The English instinctively
511 to her English children
931 The English may not like
1508 The English have the most
1977 The English winter - ending
2026 telling the English some
2308 The English never draw a line
2331 the sort of English up with
3062 of our English nation,
3917 My English text is chaste,
4052 basis of English
4389 The English never smash in a
4391 of the English gentleman,
4885 with the English language,
5666 Breeds hard English men.
5830 In any language but English.
6074 The English people on the
6648
6835 shed one English tear O'er
6939 which the English, not being
6970 that English people
7276 Opera in English is, in the
7430 He speaks English with the
9419 said that English women in
9481 to the English that of
9806 learned English - up to
11018 made our English tongue a
11443 days, A happy English child.
11917 English as she is Spoke.
12203 Only the English make it
12698 learn them a bit of English.
12763 The English have an

englishman
2747 ill-natured thing, an Englishman.
3322 I find the Englishman to be him
3528 The Englishman loves to roll his
3575 that the Englishman can't feel
3966 He is an Englishman! For he
3967 He remains an Englishman!
4019 No Englishman unmoved that
5102 or not; an Englishman is content
5355 rights of an Englishman.
5672 thorough an Englishman as ever
6064 The Englishman respects your
7355 An Englishman, even if he is
7914 An Englishman won't talk
8309 The Englishman has all the
9119 may wet an Englishman to the
10648 can what an Englishman believes
10823 is one Englishman there is a
11114 As an Englishman does not travel
11582 The last great Englishman is low.
11596 genial Englishman.
12010 The Englishman is under no
12296 find an Englishman among the

englishmen
1306 trust all Englishmen except
2591 dogs and Englishmen Go out in
5071 atrophied Englishmen, lacking
5157 When two Englishmen meet, their
5663 be, Honest Englishmen. Do the
6761 One matter Englishmen don't
8630 nature of Englishmen, that
9458 would prefer to be Englishmen.

englishwoman
1505 lover. The Englishwoman simply
10863 This Englishwoman is so refined

enigma
2312 a mystery inside an enigma.

enjoy
472 To enjoy the things we
1902 of life is to enjoy it.
2143 other, and enjoy both
2231 Many people enjoy the
2599 Enjoy the present hour, Be
4734 To really enjoy the better
5039 to enjoy idling

5153 better to enjoy life, or
7618 who can enjoy alone, Or
9027 I don't enjoy them in
9897 save to enjoy the
10839 that, to enjoy it. Only
11848 You never enjoy the world
12453 a desire to enjoy (or

enjoyed
502 To have enjoyed the sun,
4869 I've rather enjoyed them.
5196 and little to be enjoyed.
6854 they may be better enjoyed.
8110 many and enjoyed by the
9483 to be truly enjoyed must be
11271 Women enjoyed (whatsoe'er

enjoyment
4221 Enjoyment is not a goal, it is
5046 with a great deal of enjoyment.
5165 not from enjoyment to
5616 Enjoyment? A
8218 greatest enjoyment from life
11285 it were not for its enjoyments.

enjoys
8209 is that one enjoys several

enlarge
11346 some invent, the rest enlarge.

enmity
9225 be no enmity among

ennui
2476 Ennui has made more
9980 classes, ennui of the

enobles
5648 and enobles the man

enormity
5237 very womb and bed of enormity.

enough
1196 thou hast enough, remember
1702 cared enough, everybody
3832 ought to be enough for
6608 there was enough for
7416 never get enough of is
9348 voice; enough of blood

enrage
12140 solely to enrage those who

enslave
1589 but impossible to enslave.

ensnare
8945 race ensnare, And

entangled
10716 are alone entangled in.

enter
1181 shall not enter into the
8743 storm may enter - the rain

entering
1700 sir, on entering this house

enterprise
3014 criterion of the enterprise.
5563 about free enterprise, or due
5605 to private enterprise on
9535 starship Enterprise . Its
10500 designs, The enterprise is sick.
11774 me is its enterprise and
12882 more enterprise In walking

entertain
3679 you to be entertained in your
4835 only way to entertain some folks
7019 souls, To entertain divine
12204 thee, Could entertain us with no

entertaining
7186 much more entertaining than half

enthusiasm
824 that enthusiasm moves the
2182 enthusiasms, tastes,
2233 Enthusiasm is the greatest asset
3610 errors of enthusiasm to the
5486 height of enthusiasm I have
5970 'Above all no enthusiasm'.
6463 fired with enthusiasm, you'll be

enthusiast
6717 to the enthusiast who keeps

enthusiastic
3986 with enthusiastic tone, All
5659 something to be enthusiastic about.

enthusiasts
6825 how to deal with enthusiasts.

enticing
7663 object more enticing? What

entitled
9609 no man is entitled to, and
11164 and you are entitled to no

entreat
3282 I do entreat heaven daily for

entropy
12954 against the entropy of human

entrusted
4730 populace is entrusted, and who
12088 interests entrusted to the

envies
9761 any peacock envies another

environment
1741 is nothing but stored environment.
3164 The environment is everything
11652 issues like the environment.

environments
12740 human environments; they did

envy
959 dullard's envy of
1198 Envy and wrath shorten the
11559 I envy not in any moods
12923 A show of envy is an

epicure
10891 full, the epicure would say,

epicurean
3114 born stoic and dies epicurean.

epidemics
10598 all, are only induced epidemics.

epigram
2457 What is an epigram? A
6279 Epigram: a wisecrack that has
7156 An epigram is a half-truth so
8231 joke is an epigram on the
11242 A brilliant epigram is a

episode
7292 of a brief episode, Make it

epitaph
1260 Epitaph, n: an inscription on
5723 And the epitaph drear: 'A

epitaphs
10730 a nice derangement of epitaphs!

epitaphy
2780 the taffy than the epitaphy.

epithet
7018 too foul an epithet for thee.

epitome
3026 mankind's epitome. Stiff in

equal
400 free and equal in dignity
476 they may be equal, and
485 form of i equality is to
864 us to be equal upstairs,
2957 comes equally to us
3291 For equal division
3953 All shall equal be, The
4177 Though equal to all
5022 are created equal and
5146 at equal distances,
5357 of freedom we are all equal.
6133 which is equal to
6346 all men are created equal.
7566 be deemed Equal in
8186 opposed an equal reaction:
8368 animals are equal but some
8562 we'll be equal to any
8820 all facts are created equal.
8892 sees with equal eye, as
9033 as fully equal to any
12010 are created equal. The

equality
466 Equality is the result of
2771 settle for equality when sex
5092 in a general state of equality.
9850 Equality of opportunity is an
12673 upon the terms of equality.

equalize
1775 to level never equalize.

equalizer
5982 It is the great equalizer.

equalled
10640 is only equalled by the

equals
710 least of all between equals.
7382 together as equals; claiming
12687 between equals can last.
12917 to be first among equals.

equation
4460 Each equation .. in the book

equator
2317 nation than the Equator.
8283 quarrellin wi' the equator.

equilibrium
9876 a natural equilibrium, of

equity
1497 hear of an equity' in a case

equivocate
3821 I will not equivocate - I will

erased
6280 I have erased this line.

erecting
7076 and there erecting new,

erection
205 gives a judge an erection.

erogenous
12351 can also be an erogenous zone.

eros
8588 converted Eros into an
10163 Unarm, Eros; the long

erotic
3947 the erotic and the

err
3422 men, they needs must err.
8882 To err is human; to

errand
5947 What thy errand here

errands
3954 on little errands for the

erred
1421 We have erred, and strayed
7660 men Have erred, and by

error
764 from error than from
2110 lead to error; many
2370 and made the error double.
2884 act or by one single error.
3652 From error to error one
6430 he is in error, and
6432 positive in error as in
6433 liable to error; and most
7190 and the error is
7333 Error has never approached
10174 mountainous error be too
10561 If this be error, and upon

errors
424 your errors were
1251 weapon: the errors of those
1351 The errors of a wise man
3033 Errors, like straws, upon
3219 Errors look so very ugly in
3634 certain errors of the
4886 our errors, and
4932 harmful than reasoned errors.
5335 His errors are
8349 man whose errors take ten
10757 the common errors of our

erstwhile
7390 all, my erstwhile dear, My

escape
3227 help us to escape, not from
6104 whimper to escape the
6673 for that escape complex
12542 life is to escape the
12911 is the only escape from the

escaped
1229 I am escaped with the skin of
9130 which is escaped now is
10856 to eat and escaped being
10943 I had escaped from a mad

eskimo
2851 about an Eskimo hunter who

espoused
7606 fairest, my espoused, my latest

esprit
51 name - esprit de corps .

espy
4574 And then the heaven espy.

esquires
4243 We are all esquires now, and

essay
4897 The essay is a literary
9627 Non-U, An Essay in

esse
48 In esse I am nothing; in

essence
2714 The essence of life is
6196 than his essence and will
8561 Universe's Essence, With
9927 precedes and rules essence.

essential
1300 The essentials of poetry are
4400 it to be an essential part of
6250 been the essential character

essentiality
11021 eternal and infinite essentiality

estate
2079 were three Estates in
3027 and they had his estate.
6436 out of this estate, and
6807 a fourth estate of the
10374 wish the estate o' the

esteem
7619 Than self esteem, grounded
8628 lessened my esteem of a king,

estimation
1281 him in his estimation, and yours

estranged
6450 you are estranged from it.

eternal
251 The eternal triangle.
1419 to eternal life,
1568 the eternal rocks
4103 Eternal Woman draws us
6604 by doubt is my eternal moon.
8486 We have no eternal allies and
8911 springs eternal in the
10073 Eternal law has arranged
10647 blasted to eternal damnation!
10672 A portion of the Eternal.
10805 eternal and and
11023 and know that we are eternal.
12185 embrace eternal Her blue
12292 blast, And our eternal home.

eternally
2948 we wake eternally, And death
7749 be Thy joy and crown eternally.

eternities
8062 between two eternities of

eternity
34 affects eternity; he can
615 things from eternity are like
618 pinprick of eternity. All
626 from all eternity; and the
1325 hand And eternity in an
1608 speak of eternity without a
1935 sublime The image of eternity.
2035 of an eternity that we
2825 to use again Until Eternity.
5697 here to Eternity, God ha'
6939 some conception of eternity.
7072 of vast eternity. Thy
9368 nothing but eternity hath
9641 the Soul's eternity To one
10152 Eternity was in our lips and
10538 Or sells eternity to get a
11231 Eternity's a terrible thought.
12063 I saw Eternity the other

ethereal
7548 from the ethereal sky With

etherized
3238 a patient etherized upon a

ethical
1516 giants and ethical infants.
11953 Ethical man - a Christian

ethics
6819 a system of ethics,
11045 stop while ethics catches up

ethiopian
1227 Can the Ethiopian change his

etiquette
2665 Etiquette means behaving
6983 no taste, etiquette for people

eton
409 who didn't go to Eton.
8377 of Eton, but the
12357 the playing fields of Eton

etonians
5778 him like Etonians, without a
6867 Attractive Etonians who go

eunuch
3495 between a eunuch and a
4319 the Female Eunuch the world
11224 of the eunuch throughout

eunuchs
964 are like eunuchs in a
3558 Whips. A seraglio of eunuchs.

eureka
462 Eureka! I have got it!

europe
808 people in Europe. I even
2753 not be any European
2761 Yes, it is Europe, from the
3891 at all except another Europe.
4328 all over Europe; we shall
6681 that Europe is the
8748 trust, save Europe by her
9489 over the whole of Europe.
9501 I pine for Europe of the
9837 of Europe and we
9949 Germany is Europe, it is not
10005 large as Europe Silent
11536 years of Europe than a
11892 iron curtain across Europe.
12012 keep up with Western Europe.
12916 Europe is in danger of

european
6903 I am more a European in my head

europeans
7144 are learned Europeans and we
8047 those Europeans upon whom

evanescent
5985 blush, As evanescent too.

evangelism
12874 Decade of Evangelism for

eve
828 delved, and Eve span, Who
4739 When Eve upon the first
7596 of her daughters Eve.
7603 close at the ear of Eve.
11708 sudden - to Eve: Be soon.

even
2861 Don't get mad, get even.

evening
1489 in an evening that the
3238 I, When the evening is spread
3248 The winter evening settles
3918 shade the evening of life.
7635 .. The evening star, Love's
8915 life's cool ev'ning satiate of
9421 the whole evening without

evenings
1647 long dark autumn evenings come.

event
8999 the event, that much
9819 A single event can awaken
10224 too precisely on the event.
10774 Any event, once it has
11578 divine event, To which

events
87 level of events not of
164 train of events has
1261 false, of events, mostly
1685 but three events in his
2353 signs precede certain events.
3443 The events of childhood do
3456 a string of events belonging
6361 controlled events, but
6959 objective events, and

7875 frames events unknown,
9628 momentous events happen in
10425 are many events in the
11828 historical events great men

ever
3959 What, ever? No, never!
9737 that we build for ever.
11474 go, But I go on for ever.

ever-silent
11606 a dream The ever-silent spaces of

everlasting
2934 his first, last, everlasting day
7569 with everlasting groans,
7616 Open, ye everlasting gates,
7841 Beauty is everlasting And dust is
10189 Or that the Everlasting had not

everlastingness
12062 Bright shoots of everlastingness.

every
303 Every woman's man, and

everybody
2659 to make you everybody else -
4257 Everybody has a little bit of
6806 business of everybody is the
10596 happens to everybody sooner or

everyman
252 Everyman, I will go with thee,

everyone
2408 And almost everyone when age,
6265 is what everyone shares.
6743 the way everyone wants to
8683 now that everyone is using
12650 it to everyone, whether

everything
420 only two Everything they say,
961 A place for everything and
1687 Everything has been said, and we
1785 reconciles us to everything.
2008 passes, everything perishes,
3082 Everything that can be invented
3164 in everything that isn't
4897 almost everything about
5562 Everything changes but change
5585 are against everything all the
6465 isn't everything. It is
7705 but everything is always
7757 nothing and buys everything.
7788 A little of everything and
9135 casse. Everything passes;
10118 sans taste, sans everything.
10596 Everything happens to everybody
10611 he knows everything. That
10815 A place for everything, and
10922 a man of everything he's no
10929 Everything's coming up roses.
12134 We can't all do everything.
12150 a bore .. is to tell everything.
12384 'Chips with everything'. Chips

everywhere
6706 Out of the everywhere into here.

evidence
1135 for, the evidence of things
1899 on insufficient evidence.
2997 all the evidence. It
3107 weighs th' 'evidence an' th'
3199 us wordy evidence of the
5402 based on evidence sufficient
8581 for, the evidence of things
9777 is no good evidence either
10940 think, good evidence of life
11742 evidence is very

evil
455 If all evil were
597 to whom evil is done Do
602 When we do evil, We and
1051 in itself is evil.
1167 Resist not evil: but
1192 is the root of all evil.
1420 From all evil and
1426 fear no evil: for thou
1748 nothing for evil to
2017 book is like great evil.
5879 know all the evil he does.
6855 all men are evil and that
7376 it would be an evil still.
7459 of good and evil as two

7553 to find means of evil.
7591 me is lost; Evil, be thou
7984 y pense. Evil be to him
8471 a necessary evil; in its
10273 Men's evil manners live in
10289 him. The evil that men
10637 to profess evil and do
10909 we suffer evil to defend
10924 there were evil people
11150 There is no evil in the

evils
3080 Most of the evils of the
5529 for most evils: but it
9389 Two evils, monstrous either
12178 three great evils, boredom,
12409 between two evils, I always
12585 of two evils, chooses

evolution
2130 call it evolution, And
8409 slowly learned in his evolution.
10987 Evolution .. is - a change

evolutionary
1476 In any evolutionary process, even

ex-patriotism
1119 example (of ex-patriotism) is James

ex-wife
2528 like an ex-wife searching

exacting
9277 is more exacting that God

exactness
6460 with exactness grinds He

exaggerate
3155 Never exaggerate your faults;

exaggerated
7177 he laid an exaggerated stress on
11979 my death are greatly exaggerated.

exaggeration
1290 addicted to exaggeration that they
3935 An exaggeration is a truth that
3945 A work of art is an exaggeration.
10607 is a gross exaggeration of the

exalts
1673 Does which exalts him, but

exam
9474 like an exam. You get

examination
7267 marks his own examination papers.
8269 kind of examination because

examinations
2481 Examinations are formidable even

examine
12747 Examine for a moment an

examiners
5607 economics than my examiners.

example
1119 favourite example (of
9199 'For example' is not proof.
11957 annoyance of a good example.
12554 us a good example, what on

exceed
12290 and flowers, exceed me still.

excel
1518 precedency, and still excel.
2283 so great as daring to excel.

excellence
5478 The excellence of every art is

excellent
2994 Excellent,' I cried.
3971 that's excellent. It has no
6428 never makes excellent things for
9293 you! Parts of it are excellent!

excelsior
6485 the strange device, Excelsior!

exception
7102 case I'll make an exception.

exceptions
2145 consists entirely of exceptions.
4706 the old man knows the exceptions.

excess
296 Nothing in excess.
332 to be practised to excess.
1339 The road of excess leads to
5484 by a fine excess, and not

7164 afraid of excess: excess on
10053 to be blamed, but the excess.
10305 and ridiculous excess.
11863 An excess of law inescapably

excessive
7584 Dark with excessive bright.

exchange
1029 cross, And exchange it some
9015 you cannot exchange food and
10753 By just exchange one for

exchanged
8323 someone exchanged work for
8973 We have exchanged the

exchanges
9691 she exchanges the

excite
8488 than to excite agitation.

excited
2225 get all excited about
2764 his public excited and
6715 have been excited. What

excitement
12461 There is no excitement anywhere

exciting
12254 The most exciting thing is

exclusion
7400 the idea of exclusion and

excuse
4226 If you will excuse me using
6723 said 'excuse me', and
8512 Excuse My Dust.
8667 is no excuse, it's the
10055 of the law excuses no man;
11392 but they make a good excuse.

excuses
4914 Several excuses are always

execrable
7575 what art thou, execrable shape?

execution
4273 as their stringent execution.
9375 some are daily led to execution.
12269 going to the place of execution.

executioner
2941 and yet I am mine own Executioner.

executive
779 to the executive part of
8816 Executive ability is deciding
9357 action an executive must take

exercise
888 in the exercise of his
3040 cure, on exercise depend;
3651 oneself is a good exercise.
5030 possible exercise.
11068 mind what exercise is to the
11898 those who don't exercise it.

exert
3168 that I must exert myself in

exertion
8595 but the exertion is too
8748 by her exertions, and

exhalation
7562 huge Rose like an exhalation.

exhales
1946 her fires, Exhales her

exhaust
4554 they soon exhaust their
11256 genius will never exhaust.

exhausted
2918 a range of exhausted volcanoes.
4058 enemies are not yet exhausted.
4204 I'm exhausted from not talking.

exhibit
10764 strive to exhibit in your

exhibitionism
8329 form of exhibitionism. It is

exhibits
5380 which he exhibits, that

exhilarating
7164 occasion is exhilarating. It
9411 life is so exhilarating as to be

exile
5755 sons to exile To serve

exist
2790 he need not exist in order
5614 or not we exist. If you
8556 thing can exist without
9029 Laski that He doesn't exist.
12007 that didn't exist before,
12086 defeat; they do not exist.

existence
526 condition for our existence.
1337 necessary to human existence.
1974 'Tis woman's whole existence.
1985 the face of Existence; the least
2541 and tempestuous existence.
2607 Existence is a strange bargain.
3673 the problem of human existence.
3828 realize my existence are
4505 a rational existence .. Man
5935 we have existence, and a
7253 about human existence is not
8062 us that our existence is but a
8622 very existence is made
9318 sum of existence is the
9878 fails, existence remains a
9927 Existence precedes and rules

existing
174 already existing in
4908 an organism existing in time,
12615 represents pure existing.

exists
4095 all merely exists for his

exit
8023 a graceful exit at the
10534 Exit, pursued by a bear.
12328 men to take their exits.

expands
8521 Work expands so as to fill

expansion
8519 Expansion means complexity and
11846 expansion coinciding

expansionist
181 of the expansionist

expatiate
8889 and to die) Expatiate free o'er

expect
5298 Don't expect too much: and
12186 Expect nothing. Live

expectation
8385 with some expectation of getting
9597 I have no expectation of making a
11271 .. 'Tis expectation makes a
12163 in the expectation of living.

expected
12429 reasonably be expected to do.

expecting
8809 he is ever expecting that it

expediency
7172 be sacrificed to expediency.

expedient
2912 a principle, but an expedient.

expenditure
8520 Expenditure rises to meet income.

expense
6205 at somebody else's expense.
12263 at the expense of my

expenses
2794 surrounded by expenses.
11227 free but facts are on expenses.

expensive
810 extremely expensive it is to
6134 little more expensive, but is
8728 fruit, when it is expensive.
9572 has got so expensive that it

experience
90 your own experience in
274 comes from experience, and
447 Experience is a good teacher,
737 and are perfected by experience.
744 a part of experience. He that
787 To a great experience one thing
807 Experience, which destroys
881 retire his experience. He must
901 every experience once,
1027 of much experience. Almost
2269 individual experience. Any

The Wordsworth Dictionary of Quotations

2443 most men, experience is like
2477 found by experience that they
2920 Experience is the child of
3294 a poor substitute for experience.
3564 a lot of experience with
3672 we don't have to experience it.
3702 common in experience but
4104 one to experience what is
4431 of the experience than to
4713 logic, it has been experience.
4861 area of richest human experience.
4898 Experience teaches only the
4899 Experience is not what happens
4994 Deep experience is never
5128 triumph of hope over experience.
5324 reality of experience and to
5559 a little experience before he
5588 visual experience today is
5928 to confirm our experience of it.
6070 Experience is the worst teacher;
6429 can go beyond his experience.
6959 lie the experiences of our
7026 has never had much experience.
7508 Till old experience do attain To
7770 seen by experience that
8498 is your own experience, your
8551 nature: instinct and experience.
9092 Experience is the comb that
9842 by the experience of life as
10629 to their experience, but to
10638 the shifty cunning of experience.
11047 The rich experience of history
11505 nurse, Experience, in her
11937 out of an experience only the
12571 Experience is the name every one
12723 inevitable experience of every

experienced
317 of the i experienced giving
2553 it can be experienced - it can
3534 There's an experienced rebel,
4734 first have experienced the things
8110 an emotion experienced by the
9074 that I've experienced my
9210 who have never experienced it.
11154 not an old, experienced hand at

experiences
8045 of his own experiences. No one
12639 appalling experiences are

experiment
9878 a mad and lamentable experiment.

experimentation
3165 amount of experimentation can ever

experimented
2401 I experimented with Marijuana a

expert
1867 An expert is one who knows
9842 trust experts. If you

expiate
6099 to expiate: A

explain
2906 complain and never explain.
3502 Never explain Never
4817 Never explain - your friends
5304 Never explain: never
6469 tobacco to explain it to me.
8834 For thee explain a thing till
12309 and never explain. It's a
12862 I refuse to explain

explained
42 we have explained ourselves
857 things are explained to you;
3408 neither be explained nor
5821 ever yet explained away the
11989 and life stands explained.

explaining
3671 with explaining the news
9815 and forever explaining things to
11074 force in explaining man to

explanation
1379 and with no explanation if he can
9831 saves tons of explanation.

expletive
383 Expletive deleted.
8888 While expletives their feeble

explodes
7211 the end and explodes; and the

exploitation
572 of mutual exploitation, a mental

explore
8902 nature to explore, The fool

explosion
9387 population explosion, and the

exposes
5100 A man who exposes himself

exposing
1269 weather and exposing them to

express
849 content to express itself
5323 will try to express myself in
7802 to better express my own
12892 man but express yourself
12927 and express what is

express-train
11689 Of heat the express-train drew up

expressed
4970 cannot be expressed by any
8887 but ne'er so well expressed.
11454 and not expressed, may take

expressing
4916 nearest to expressing the

expression
939 have an expression of
2578 the finest expression of the
3413 quizzical expression of the
3674 the highest expression of
8877 Expression is the dress of
10652 most perfect expression of scorn.
11239 Of all expression that
11945 natural expression of
12928 is the expression of man's

expurgated
12494 of all is the expurgated book.

extemporanea
8501 A medley of extemporanea; And love

extend
7645 empire must extend, So let

exterior
2609 Less on exterior things

exterminate
11028 will have to exterminate a nation.

extinct
2219 become extinct, the
7168 adultery, are now extinct.

extinction
11079 is on the road to extinction.

extinguish
8350 can quite extinguish, the

extinguished
1776 of Europe is extinguished for ever.

extol
1046 shall we extol thee who

extra
6267 something extra,

extraordinarily
2189 It has been extraordinarily happy and

extraordinary
2971 and extraordinary'. The
3528 the word, extraordinary'. It so
3591 there are extraordinary
5603 This extraordinary figure of our
8616 appear so extraordinary, were it

extravagance
3460 the silly extravagances of the
5220 An extravagance is anything you
8651 not lead to extravagance; our love
12488 a certain extravagance of

extremes
2288 The two extremes appear like
3334 Extremes meet, and there is no
5832 other men's extremes, That know
5838 run to extremes; they are
6700 be whaur Extremes meet -

extremism
4200 you that extremism in the

exuberance
1346 Exuberance is beauty.

eye
544 and his eye on the

579 the eye, on the
1011 and the eye of the
1203 as the apple of his eye.
1217 for life, Eye for eye,
2691 The eye sees only what
4399 keeps his eye fixed on
4574 stay his eye; Or if he
4871 in the eye of the
5295 lack an eye, I look at
6236 neither eye to see,
6696 and by God caught his eye.
7505 me from day's garish eye.
8094 microscopic eye? For this
9249 your own blind eye.
11007 the great eye of heaven
11745 The eye is the jewel of
12354 is an eye in the
12886 in at the eye; That's

eye-deep
8993 .. walked eye-deep in hell

eye-shade
6875 a kind of eye-shade or smoked

eye-wash
10920 you simply gave him eye-wash.

eyeball
9718 We're eyeball to eyeball, and

eyeballs
184 to move his eyeballs again.
8847 and my eyeballs roll, Suck

eyebrows
4064 above 'A' with her eyebrows.

eyeglasses
5291 Words, like eyeglasses, blur

eyeless
7655 find him Eyeless in Gaza at

eyelids
2460 raises her eyelids it's as

eyes
1482 a thousand eyes, And the
2574 takes his eyes off his
3335 The eyes indicate the
3376 daily bread of the eyes
3795 One's eyes are what one
3955 sparkling eyes, Hidden,
4416 Smoke gets in your eyes.
5241 with thine eyes And I will
5455 And her eyes were wild.
5514 Our gloom-pleased eyes.
5831 Oh eyes, no eyes, but
6106 that your eyes might be
6193 evade your eyes, Remember
6659 Night hath a thousand eyes.
7095 "Your eyes shine like the
7464 undazzled eyes at the
8795 the glory of His eyes.
9110 use your eyes and your
9147 friendship closes its eyes.
9155 The eyes believe
9185 with your eyes, don't
9633 upon her eyes; Seal her
9636 Heaven; Her eyes were
9647 cold commemorative eyes.
9788 beauty Our eyes could
10193 them, to men's eyes.
10325 want no eyes; I
10414 with the eyes, but with
10979 a woman's eyes and sees a
11560 Her eyes are homes of
11665 with my eyes hanging
11693 Open your eyes to the air
12049 love men's eyes are always

eyesight
8771 spiritual eyesight improves

eyewitness
431 heard two eyewitness accounts

fabians
4947 civilization of the Fabians.
6215 good man fallen among Fabians.

fables
12141 are but fables that have

fabrication
6919 and not the fabrication of

facade
3576 Chicago - a facade of

face
253 Her face looks as if it
355 Was never a face so pleased
570 My face looks like a
899 The voice is a second face.
1077 Let's face the music
1747 to be young - not her face.
2191 on the face of a
2819 you in the face. Don't
4180 Am I in face to-day?
4846 Her face was her
5240 not always face, Clothes,
5437 Where's the face One would
6255 Accustomed to her face.
6993 this the face that
7820 whose awful face Time's
8375 has the face he
8382 on a human face - for
8539 the whole face of the
8938 Look on her face, and
9121 to the face than
9213 A smiling face is half the
9280 A beautiful face is a mute
9646 Look in my face; my name
9743 paint in the public's face.
10184 you one face, and you
10266 commandments in your face.
10350 False face must hide what
10779 have your face lifted but
10852 on one face after
11007 Her angel's face As the
11029 can't think of your face.
11074 the human face; the
11303 everybody's face but their
11516 see my face again,
11867 recognize me by my face.
12377 clapped on to my face.

face-to-face
11915 going for a face-to-face with

faces
713 and faces are but a
8998 of these faces in the
9031 take their faces from 'em
9626 you forget faces, then you
9643 I know the faces I shall
12815 by their faces see All
12887 with vivid faces From

fact
3868 are in the world of fact.
4929 hypothesis by an ugly fact.
4933 down before fact as a
6853 conceal a fact with
11746 a man fronts a fact.

faction
9791 of a faction should

factor
12475 The factor in human life

factory
9906 factory with

facts
27 in the form of inert facts.
89 is full of facts but it
1125 if the facts had been
1507 Facts in books, statistics
2242 Facts as facts do not
2818 I want is, Facts .. Facts
3650 the full facts of life
5611 is belief in facts.
6165 ask for facts in making
8222 are no facts, only
8814 built up of facts, as a
9628 as the ordinary facts.
9787 - yours, mine and the facts.
10003 free, but facts are
10887 tell me of facts - I never
11227 is free but facts are on
11893 to the facts around
11955 Get your facts first, and

factual
4534 than anything factual can be.

faculties
6431 of their natural faculties.

faculty
2347 when the faculty loses
5590 and parking for the faculty.

fade
3555 die, They simply fade away.
5498 Fade far away, dissolve,

faded
7865 Are faded and gone.
10669 She faded, like a cloud

fades
4290 to me. Now fades the

fading
958 The fading signals and grey
5454 cheeks a fading rose Fast
7489 primrose fading
8150 And she's fading down the

faery
5455 a faery's child
5457 and sing A faery's song.

fail
1041 husbands fail. They
1725 no such word As - fail .
4662 the freedom to fail.
4765 lest he fail in the
5012 can fail and the
5524 were to fail, it would
5587 who dare to fail greatly
5905 a friend must fail.
6859 if he is to fail in one of
10766 if you fail, but you
10918 God, yet fail to
11491 may not fail Through

failed
181 somehow failed to find
2898 who have failed in
7837 what they failed to

failing
6699 To you from failing hands we

fails
3281 thy heart fails thee,
4214 which fails to operate
6719 Nothing fails like success;
9596 it. If it fails, admit it

failure
1477 We learn only from failure.
2594 utterly unspoiled by failure!
5340 failure to attract
7280 His failure is
9008 careers end in failure.
9440 Failure is not our only
9534 and I'll show you a failure.
9586 always pass failure on the way
9849 only one to make it a failure.
10074 Failure changes for the
11374 formula for failure, which is
12519 Thought is born of failure.

failures
19 has made failures of many
2712 suggested to me by my failures.
4434 Half the failures in life
10656 I did were failures. I didn't
12261 nothing but man's failures.

faint
12695 We faint beneath the

fair
569 exceeding fair - he was
1037 remained at 'set fair'.
2752 only in fair weather.
3010 Fair stood the wind for
3031 brave deserves the fair.
5018 Fair shares for all, is
5519 into the fair And open
6014 A faire feeld ful of folk
6254 fair; Who, when
7018 Ah fair Zenocrate, divine
7623 She fair, divinely fair,
10382 made you fair hath made
12700 a lass, a fair one, As
12702 care I how fair she be.
12777 show more fair: Dull

fair play
8391 to do with fair play. It is

fairer
6998 thou art fairer than the

fairest
7626 O fairest of creation, last

fairies
867 was the beginning of fairies.
10058 since the fairies left off

fairy
868 is a little fairy somewhere
5245 Mistress Fairy That doth
7825 and like a fairy, And her
7851 arms, Like fairy gifts

faith
172 of faith, and
183 was of the faith chiefly in
1129 now abideth faith, hope,
1135 Faith is the substance of
1545 sudden explosions of faith.
1633 by faith, For one
1645 A scientific faith's absurd.
2015 through faith, hardly
3326 The faith that stands on
3677 who has faith in himself
3803 of my faith. It is
4689 or even a partial faith.
5402 Faith means intense,
5543 must follow faith, never
6345 Let us have faith that right
6384 still by faith he trod,
6544 a stronger faith embrace A
6642 have faith and
6688 deal of faith for a man
6699 If ye break faith with us
6834 Courage and faith; vain
8581 Faith is the substance of
9605 put their faith once more
10583 a man's faith in
10867 times of faith as best
11331 Faith, that's as well said,
11503 stood, And faith unfaithful
11574 lives more faith in honest
11701 testing his faith On
11801 Faith is the state of being
12108 In this faith I wish to
12522 The simple faith in
12813 .. In the faith that looks

faith-healer
255 There was a faith-healer from Deal

faithful
2986 I have been faithful to thee,
3677 able to be faithful to others.
3931 as a faithful servant.'?
4350 who remains faithful to you but
7493 Ever faithful, ever
9350 done if you had been faithful.

faithless
587 Human on my faithless arm.
10044 only joy, Faithless as the

faked
1705 else did - faked it.

faking
2414 The worst crime is faking it.

falklands
1454 The Falklands thing was a fight

fall
1209 a pit shall fall into it.
1241 spirit before a fall.
1788 they will fall, one by
3131 a hard rain's a gonna fall.
5976 bound to fall off from
6773 imminent fall of the
7610 in this we stand or fall.
8584 to fall in love
9128 Don't fall before you're
9184 Fall seven times, stand up
9373 climb, yet fear I to fall.
10281 Brute? Then fall, Caesar!
10693 a cloud! I fall upon the
10970 by other's fall I deem a
11779 as well fall flat on
12506 is good to fall, battles

fall out
70 should fall out in the
1015 chance that you will fall out.
11587 When we fall out with those

fallacious
8300 lightly, is fallacious, being
10887 was so fallacious as facts,

fallacy
8686 upon a fallacy. The
9730 as the 'Pathetic Fallacy'.

fallen
1197 Many have fallen by the edge
1564 curates has fallen upon the
7552 Fallen cherub, to be weak is
8555 have never fallen or

falling
3154 The falling out of faithful
3186 call the falling domino'
7396 and falling into at

falls
9189 a man who falls on his
10348 itself, And falls on the
11480 like a thunderbolt he falls.

false
748 thou be not false to others.
1173 Beware of false prophets,
1916 Prove false again?
3179 is false. The
3901 as equally false; and by
5917 oneself. False guilt is
10195 not then be false to any
10350 False face must hide what
10424 and most false
11577 out the false, ring in

falsehood
7466 [Truth] and Falsehood grapple;

falseness
9730 in us a falseness in all our

falser
10124 For I am falser than vows

fame
258 test of fame is to have
552 Fame means absolutely
706 to good fame, and
729 Fame is like a river, that
2829 Fame is a bee It has a
2925 Fame is a food that dead
4311 Fame is a powerful
4700 Fame usually comes to
6166 The best fame is a
6716 and Fame with its
7216 and for immortal fame.
7529 Fame is the spur that the
7530 Fame is no plant that
7669 die, her fame survives,
7767 All the fame I look for in
7781 Fame and tranquility can
7861 carelessly smiling at Fame.
8724 rage for fame attends
8830 shall be damned to Fame.
9245 not enjoy fame in two
9492 Fame is the sum of the
9972 Fame is something which
11510 dreams of fame while
11956 Fame is a vapour,

familiar
6045 far too familiar. Get
10704 Familiar acts are beautiful

familiarity
11969 Familiarity breeds contempt - and

families
4578 in the best regulated families.
6294 to run in families.
8281 in the best-regulated families.
11655 women, and there are families.
11821 All happy families resemble

family
389 a wonderful family called
1595 the family of last
2339 does the family start? It
2638 and you educate a family.
4222 The family is the American
5012 world of family life -
5053 peace, the family is sadly
5563 The Family of Man is more
5918 When family relations are no
6122 the family, with its
7220 the family always
7751 head of the family may still
7779 of a family than in
8818 and no family should be
9230 a mule deserves his family.
9945 The family that prays

10826 The family - that dear
11056 of family life, and
11930 left his family, it didn't

famine
11672 fever, And famine grew, and

famous
1016 that time I was too famous.
1200 now praise famous men, and
1949 and found myself famous.
8650 For famous men have the
10171 clip in it A pair so famous.
10588 can become famous without
12174 that has become too famous.
12253 us will be famous for

fan
5807 of becoming his own fan.

fan club
2132 A fan club is a group of

fanatic
2309 A fanatic is one who can't
12900 mother's womb A fanatic heart.

fanaticism
6286 it, so that fanaticism and
9884 Fanaticism consists in

fanatics
5434 Fanatics have their dreams,
9606 Foolish fanatics .. the men

fancies
1669 Fancies that broke through
4317 lust, can many fancies feign.
5520 proud, and full of fancies.

fancy
4789 keep your fancy free.' But
5436 let the fancy roam,
5466 poetry, as fancy is the
6420 of what you fancy does you
10400 where is fancy bred, Or
11523 young man's fancy lightly

fans
5874 a candle and fans a fire.

fantasies
6266 cut in the fantasies of people

fantastic
7475 In a light fantastic round.
7512 the light fantastic toe, And
12518 which the fantastic becomes

fantasy
4320 masochism, fantasy under a
8038 live in a fantasy world, a

far
2422 to know how far one can go
2807 Mexico, so far from God
3598 River, Far, far,
5030 yourself to walk very far.
9096 who are far will come.
11576 so near and yet so far.

farce
7110 the second as farce.
9345 the farce is played
10825 running farce in the

farewell
1806 sever; Ae farewel, and then
7557 Farewell, happy fields Where
7591 So farewell hope, and with
9479 of meeting and of farewell.
10434 Farewell the neighing steed
10554 Farewell! thou art too dear
12627 Piccadilly, Farewell Leicester

farm
116 Life on the farm is a
10959 little snug farm of the

farmer
4558 The Farmer will never be
4796 Even if a farmer intends to
6754 The farmer's way of saving

farmers
4797 Farmers worry only during the
10760 have been farmers for ten

farming
168 and farming the most

farms
1823 wi' the weel-stockit farms.
2632 gazes or for him that farms.

farrow
5320 old sow that eats her farrow.

fart
3273 I had forgot the fart.
5065 he can't fart and chew
11272 Love is the fart Of every

farthest
6578 he goes the farthest who goes

farthing
2644 never pay a farthing for it.

fascinated
12858 people are fascinated by those

fascinating
4554 - the very fascinating ones try

fascination
3998 elbow has a fascination that few
4005 There's a fascination frantic In
12573 have its fascination. When it

fascism
1479 itself into fascism.
4222 is the American fascism.
9624 victims of American Fascism.

fascist
8755 adores a Fascist, The boot

fashion
1056 Fashion, which elevates the
1405 Fashion condemns us to many
2149 does not go out of fashion.
2195 Fashion can be bought Style
2232 is once in fashion, all he
2418 with time. Fashion, on the
2630 Fashion, though Folly's
2986 thee, Cynara! in my fashion.
6983 Fashion exists for women with
10503 out of fashion, like a
10506 nothing else holds fashion.
11278 after the fashion of their
12548 Fashion is that by which the

fashionable
9880 ever to be fashionable is

fashioned
11714 petal!) Fashioned so purely,

fashions
9812 Fashions fade - style is
10598 Fashions, after all, are only

fast
4172 be done too fast; but we,
5049 you run fast. It makes

faster
1712 was far faster than
6335 can write faster, and I can
6954 itself faster and faster

fastidious
6970 I feel as fastidious as though
10960 literature is never fastidious.

fasting
3636 upon hope will die fasting.
7303 Apollo turned fasting friar.

fat
182 every fat man there
1680 Who's your fat friend?
2527 in every fat man a thin
2548 'til the fat lady
3532 A few more fat, old bald
4065 but fat people are
5133 'Who drives fat oxen
6979 if you're fat, is a
8327 Fat, fair and forty were
8351 Fat is a feminist issue.
8371 I'm fat, but I'm thin
10276 me that are fat;

fatal
3643 is more fatal to health
6457 probably fatal to beat it
6702 it is nearly always fatal.
7577 .. Their fatal hands No
7838 is a fatal disease;
10468 forth the fatal loins of
11636 Yes, I am a fatal man,
11985 Travel is fatal to
12566 of it is absolutely fatal.

fate
614 to which fate binds you,
1492 Fate is not an eagle, it

fatigued
8850 good John! fatigued I said,

fattening
12761 immoral, illegal or fattening.

fatter
8594 sheep are fatter; We

fatuous
6107 and fatuous an attempt

fault
1557 is my own fault. Verdi is
1583 it is their fault when
1671 Faultless to a fault.
3216 to find fault with but
5284 at least partly our fault.
5762 they think it's their fault.
5901 long if the fault was only
8322 An artist is his own fault.
8842 glorious fault of angels
9974 fundamental fault of the
10238 sugar be a fault, God help
10275 fates: The fault, dear
10378 Is this her fault or mine?
10492 man has his fault, and
11501 He is all fault who hath no

faultless
1671 Faultless to a fault.
8875 thinks a faultless piece to
11540 Faultily faultless, icily

faults
326 they had no faults at all.
420 have their faults Men have
1874 all thy faults I love
2726 the faults in a
3155 your faults; your
4019 all our faults, we love
4168 are some faults so nearly
4169 All his faults are such that
4648 I may have faults but being
5842 has his faults which he
5865 Of all our faults, the one
5883 we had no faults we should
5893 our little faults to
5991 greater faults than
6050 with the faults they had
8672 correct our faults by
9036 Be to her faults a little
9139 men may have great faults.
9198 the mask of one's own faults.
10166 us Some faults to make us
10385 out of faults, And, for
10411 faults Looks
10853 social faults; they will
12217 events the faults of

faulty
4135 if your face is faulty.

faustus
6994 day That Faustus may repent
6995 come, and Faustus must be

favour
8775 the gods favour dies
12958 as to curry favour with

favourite
160 It's my second favourite organ.
457 My favourite thing is to go
3660 favourite of his

favours
5880 hope for greater favours.
8196 Chance favours only those who
11622 Fortune favours the bold.

fawn
6914 to the afternoon of a fawn.

fear
46 Fear is the foundation of
162 For fear of little
438 lives with fear of
492 Fear is not an unknown
567 Fear has a smell, as Love
703 Men fear death as children
704 masters the fear of death.
718 breedeth fear, but
1096 the direction of our fear.
1138 There is no fear in love;
1410 unite men - fear and
1426 I will fear no evil:
1542 turns into a cry of fear.
1751 the concessions of fear.

1784 and reasoning as fear.
2049 than respect based on fear.
2522 of fear; we fear
2628 hope that never had a fear.
2985 Fear can be headier than
3034 but we fear, To be we
3258 show you fear in a
3450 we call it fear of
4637 continual fear and danger
4653 Fear comes from
5199 from the fear of man;
5259 'Twas only fear first in
5261 The fear of every man that
5314 till the fear of the
5569 out of fear. But let
5842 neither fear nor shame
5885 than the fear of
5987 is not a word of fear.
6025 the people fear, and the
6088 in the world to fear!
6090 by fear. That is
6179 is also the fear of death -
6241 life, fear protects
6604 Fear ringed by doubt is my
6856 himself feared, for
7257 haunting fear that
7686 is left, is left no fear.
7874 the end of what we fear?
7955 me in their fear. What does
8028 And without fear the
8189 And drives away his fear.
8262 they fear you. It
8344 is but his fear of life.
8552 Fear of the policeman is
8577 Courage is fear holding on
9373 climb, yet fear I to fall.
9518 stream of fear trickling
9599 we have to fear is fear
9601 from fear ..
9766 To fear love is to fear
9767 Men fear thought more than
10151 that which we often fear.
10180 Fear no more the heat o'
11008 As if his fear still
11095 Anxiety is fear of one's
11725 died - for fear of dying!
11942 to fear, mastery
12001 need not fear the
12155 Fear succeeds crime - it
12340 live with fear and not be
12530 Unable to fear what is

feared
2667 is to be feared. It is
6146 just as I feared! - Two
6859 to be feared than

fearful
1533 Fearful is the seductive
1958 a lovely and a fearful thing!
10418 not a more fearful wild-fowl

fearfully
1439 for I am fearfully and

fearing
5640 I'm not fearing any man.
10283 many years of fearing death.

fears
693 many fears and
4626 rid of my fears is to make
7795 A man who fears suffering
8170 spite of fears, Pride
10365 do not, Our fears do make us
11491 craven fears of being
12839 no human fears: She

feast
4531 Paris is a movable feast.
5857 someone disturbed the feast.
8114 out, On the Feast of
9169 mind is a perpetual feast.

feat
4398 Only one feat is
10263 What feats he did

feather
5954 ear; not a feather to tickle
10528 I am a feather for each wind

feather-beds
7882 heaven in feather-beds; it is not

fate
1905 we are steered by fate.
2733 their fate: The good
2761 decide the fate of the
2878 country the fate of this
3384 limits us we call Fate.
4265 fears his fate too much,
4699 Fate tried to conceal him
4774 day that Fate allows
5169 jest; Fate never
5638 Till I thy fate shall
6104 which fate carries in
6116 decided by fate, but it
6397 capricious fate, is equal
6475 breathless on thy fate!
6929 revolt against man's fate.
6955 than fate, and she
7346 hung my fate, 'mongst
7414 in life. Fate is what
7615 and what I will is fate.
8092 pick with Fate. Come here
8292 that fate and
8946 of our fate when we
10075 Fate rules the affairs of
10739 against fate; Death
11429 me, but ah! forget my fate.
11507 man and master of his fate.
11598 more: thy fate and mine
12266 The fate of unborn
12922 Their fate is like

fateful
6418 thus, this fateful morning,

fates
4027 See how the Fates their
10275 of their fates: The

father
319 gave her father forty-one!
398 knew my father, My father
1152 unto the Father, but by
1855 struck the father when the
1857 To become a father is not
2345 time the father of the
3650 was 17. My father [Sigmund
4598 thing a father can do for
5179 when his father dies, 'Tis
5332 the limp father of
5396 The father of every good
6517 But the father answered
6594 I meet my Father, my age,
7751 be the father, everyone
7846 My father used to say,
8142 you no longer have a father.
8247 had a good father, one must
9025 Our Father which art in
9145 A father is a banker
9919 is no good father, that's
10252 wish was father, Harry, to
10393 is a wise father that knows
10486 five thy father lies; Of
10658 I work as my father drank.
10831 The father of confederation
11118 either my father or my
11334 that his father was before
11463 unemployed father. He did
11988 my father was so
12299 relation for father and son.
12791 Child is father of the
12848 Father, dear father, come
12876 did you last see your father?

father-like
6670 Father-like, he tends and spares

fatherland
5799 the unity of our fatherland.

fathers
1200 and our fathers that begat
4536 Fathers send their sons to
4851 There are fathers who do not
6346 Our fathers brought forth
6839 of his fathers, And the
6867 on their fathers' advice:
9763 defect of fathers is that
11687 land of my fathers. My

fathom
10486 Full fathom five thy father

fatigue
6464 Fatigue makes cowards of us
8479 undergo the fatigue of
9165 Fatigue is the best pillow.

feature
630 please, every feature works.

february
380 Excepting February alone, And
5823 is not Puritanism but February.

fed
1789 the hand that fed them.
2824 as soon as fed is dead -
10336 He hath not fed of the
11369 and fed on the

feeble
1781 the religion of feeble minds.
3908 of the feeble; and the
6670 Well our feeble frame he
8534 it is feeble if it
10493 to help the feeble up, But to

feed
4564 doth me feed: While He
6230 you still feed me, When
9248 much you feed a wolf, he

feel
255 what I fancy I feel'.
3575 can't feel - it is
4528 did thee feel the earth
4921 think and feel and are is
5926 more to do than feel.
5986 the poor, feel for the
7874 of what we feel. But who
9487 I feel a feeling which I
11023 We feel and know that we

feeling
2468 old as he's feeling. A woman
3622 undisciplined feeling.
3756 but feeling's the
4221 it is a feeling that
4444 thing and a universal feeling.
5284 avoid the feeling that
5305 more true feeling, and
6012 of feeling, and the
8231 on the death of a feeling.
8531 ends in surrender to feeling.
9175 - but feeling is God's
0407 I feel a feeling which I feel
12205 of one's feeling of

feelings
1923 for all feelings: - Man!
4885 to get human feelings right.
6064 never thinks of your feelings.
6533 First feelings are always the
9479 Man's feelings are always
9730 All violent feelings ..
10993 by the feelings, and not
11074 gamut of feelings written on
11824 to others feelings he has
12242 could see some of my feelins.
12802 of powerful feelings: it takes

feels
7093 old as the woman he feels.
8714 but what he feels, what he

fees
986 took their Fees, 'There is
3627 the doctor takes the fees.

feet
318 much work for the feet.
1215 off thy feet, for the
1348 did those feet in ancient
2162 carry the feet, not the
5317 over his feet, humbly
7506 let my due feet never fail
11270 Her feet beneath her
11493 nearer than hands and feet.
12278 with both feet on the

feign
8187 I do not feign

feigning
10120 is feigning, most

felicity
7306 possessed approaches felicity.
8677 Horace's careful felicity.
10231 thee from felicity awhile,
10840 is more felicity on the far
12204 worth, Or shadow of felicity?

fell
1600 Doctor Fell, The
1636 God forgot me, and I fell.

1930 foremost fighting, fell.
6472 the air, It fell to earth,
7563 To noon he fell, from noon

fellow-creature
4327 show to any fellow-creature, let me do

fellow-men
7726 to render our fellow-men better.

fellow-rover
7137 a laughing fellow-rover, And quiet

fellowship
6927 but such a fellowship of good
7925 Fellowship is heaven, and lack
12760 a sense of fellowship with other

felon
310 the great felon loose Who

felt
1695 because he felt lightly,

female
2274 being female put many
3158 shall know a female reign.
5695 The female of the species is
5785 not to the female character,
5816 you it is probably female.
5830 Female empowerment is such
8401 flaming racket of the female.
8938 share some female errors
9974 of the female character
12518 has a faithful female friend.

feminine
3656 into the feminine soul, is
8312 as a really feminine woman.
8326 she's of the feminine gender.
10938 something feminine; what is

feminist
4388 by feminists is making
8351 Fat is a feminist issue.

fence
3689 ever take a fence down until

fences
3699 Good fences make good

ferments
1907 wine, Ferments and frets,

fertility
12446 example in fertility for Nature

fertilize
10775 But fertilize a problem

fervour
9707 retains the fervour of youth
11293 in the full fervour of

fester
3 limbs that fester are not

festivals
1462 of holidays and festivals.

fettered
6538 hair, And fettered to her

fetters
3805 slave, his fetters fall. He

feuds
6835 Forget all feuds, and shed

fever
8118 Love is a fever which
9388 chills and fever she died,

few
824 that so few
1185 called, but few are
2295 owed by so many to so few.
4380 will do few things
8110 and enjoyed by the few.

fib
8852 Destroy his fib, or

fickle
9206 Fortune is fickle and soon
12123 Fickle and changeable always

fickleness
10640 The fickleness of the women I

fiction
1010 developed a fiction that can
1969 Stranger than fiction.
2239 a luxury; fiction is a
2269 through fiction and the
4524 works of fiction produced
4595 history. Fiction gives its
6909 is ultimately fiction.

8455 germs is ridiculous fiction.
9362 but fiction must be
9392 than fiction, but
10520 it as an improbable fiction.
11139 the supreme fiction, madame.
12398 Fiction reveals truth that
12559 That is what fiction means.
12606 thing in fiction the
12756 if she is to write fiction.

fictions
11142 the supreme fictions without

fiddle
1022 He could fiddle all the bugs
5164 learned to fiddle, I should
7843 all this fiddle. Reading
11367 Fiddle, we know, is diddle:

fidelity
4316 injury - fidelity isn't
4534 standard of fidelity to the
5528 but through fidelity to a
9390 idea of fidelity is not
9493 The gnarled fidelity of an old

field
1486 Till the field ring again
1930 into the field, and,
7550 though the field be lost?
7593 that fair field Of Enna,
8518 Beside a field of grain.

fields
11512 of His fields, But in
12808 me from the fields of sleep.

fiend
1360 Like a fiend hid in a
2448 a frightful fiend Doth close
7585 land, the fiend Walked up

fierce
6997 look not so fierce on me.

fifteen
884 is always fifteen years
11193 Fifteen men on the dead man's
12253 be famous for fifteen minutes

fifth
280 the fifth of
5333 And he came fifth and lost
5585 One fifth of the people are

fifties
6593 Fifties , and I am

fifty
2617 sides of fifty has lived
4852 of youth; fifty is the
6590 After fifty the clock can't
11163 knows at fifty that he
11536 Better fifty years of

fig
1008 over a fig leaf yet
6151 We don't care a fig!'
10148 life better than figs.

fight
916 Our cock won't fight.
1350 from mental fight, Nor shall
1454 thing was a fight between
1634 when the fight begins
1826 A man may fight and no be
2311 We shall fight in France,
2338 would fight on alone
2853 bed mad. Stay up and fight.
3042 Fight on, my merry men all,
3190 dog in the fight - it's the
3729 Don't fight forces; use
3774 who will fight and fight
4050 You cannot fight against
4259 fight for its
4369 of us must fight on to the
4856 live are those who fight.
5224 have not yet begun to fight.
5547 is hard to fight an enemy
6607 cost; To fight and not to
6961 no chance to fight for them.
6989 up Never give up the fight.
7614 The better fight, who
7749 Fight the good fight with
7989 when men refuse to fight.
9079 elephants fight it is the
9814 into a fist fight, put your
10255 I dare not fight; but I
10952 this great fight did win.'

11149 easier to fight for
12002 even having to fight them.
12288 out, and chide, and fight.
12891 bade me fight, Nor

fighting
1270 two periods of fighting.
1278 him to his fighting weight.
2659 fight, and never stop fighting.
4658 worth fighting for', they
5406 got to keep fighting - you've
5696 first-class fightin' man; An'
6126 lazy about fighting. They
6932 ways of fighting, there's
7098 you're fighting for this
10095 are WE fighting for?' ..
11031 been caught fighting a liar in
11336 are in imitation of fighting.
12142 they are fighting so

fights
257 He that fights and runs
8227 He who fights with monsters
12613 The fights are the best part

figure
52 what a figure a man

figures
235 He uses figures as if they
10887 as facts, except figures.

filches
10430 But he that filches from me my

filigree
11714 devisal (O filigree petal!)

fill
3329 To fill the hour - that is
5740 If you can fill the
6519 Fill what's
8521 so as to fill the time
11288 I'll fill hup the chinks

filled
3987 can be, Filled to the

filling
8405 is the gold filling in the
10015 and spade; filling the world,

film
2013 The British Film Industry
12354 A film is never really

film-making
6274 Film-making has become a kind of

films
4212 and see bad films when they
4626 is to make films about

filthy
9736 and we are filthy and

final
606 of the world is final.
6035 to be Their final blazon,

finale
11137 Let be be finale of seem.

finality
11106 Finality is death. Perfection

finals
6447 is called Finals, the very

finance
4051 Finance is, as it were, the
10900 without finance is no

financial
155 if only for financial reasons.
12659 the other financial centres

financiers
12659 All these financiers, all the

find
1172 ye shall find; knock,
2116 if you can only find it.
2721 able to find a happy
2980 To find a friend one must
4414 will either find a way, or
5163 we can find
8709 I do not seek. I find.
9438 I shall not find Him, but I
10894 never could find any man
11512 with men I find Him not.
11817 One Ring to find them One

finds
515 that he Who finds himself,

fine
1460 mine has been a fine one.
6913 vital, fine day:
8735 work, runs fine inside but

finery
4174 in all her finery, is the

finest
2302 'This was their finest hour.'
9761 tail is the finest in the

finger
343 Whose finger do you want on
7347 the ring without the finger.
7889 It is God's finger on man's
8410 One finger in the throat and

fingers
1449 under my fingers and I
2169 The fingers must be educated,
3138 and cut their own fingers.
6085 and the fingers of cold
7974 Let your fingers do the
9054 And my fingers wandered

finish
927 and finish together.
2314 and we will finish the job.
3119 Nice guys. Finish last.
11423 thee to finish the work;

finished
3768 married. Then he's finished.
5570 will not be finished in the
7815 of them when they are finished.

finite
6195 it to be finite, like our
7893 of the finite from the

fire
340 water, the fire next time.
509 we will The fire which in
990 shouted Fire!' They
1349 me my chariot of fire.
1819 o' nature's fire, That's a'
1835 awkward squad fire over me.
3633 (and a fire) to put
3691 will end in fire, Some say
4264 Fell in the fire and was
4443 k'n hide de fier, but what
6123 must set yourself on fire.
6879 air is to fire, an
7314 till the fire is dying
7934 C'mon, baby, light my fire.
8330 a muse of fire exist
8604 It is a fire, it is a
8762 wrong to add fire to fire.
9132 Fire tries gold,
9178 house is on fire let us
9317 one of you fire until you
9371 a durable fire, In the
9595 killed by fire. People
10527 makes the fire, Not she
10566 compact of fire, Not gross
10786 The fire was furry as a
12889 but the lighting of a fire.

fired
6463 you aren't fired with

fires
3765 are like fires. They go
4216 redeeming fires have ever

firm
463 Give me a firm spot on
11165 who stands firm is a

firmness
5184 firm, and firmness is

first
760 God's first Creature, which
1148 let him first cast a
1184 that are first shall be
1706 to be first with an
3437 One's first book, kiss,
4185 The first blow is half the
4237 the first kiss after
5049 It makes you run first.
7003 loved not at first sight?
7909 in the first place, or
8536 a work is what to put first.
8912 Be not the first by whom
9001 himself at first sight and
12019 people who got there first.

first-rate
8790 With first-rate sherry flowing

fish
1116 by fish. Only an
1572 Fish say, they have their
2164 I have my own fish to fry.
6599 like fish; a savage
6974 as the fish lives in
8429 expect it, will be a fish.
9083 up with a fish in his
9240 Fish, to taste right, must
10013 It's no fish ye're buying
11094 is like a fish without a

fish-ball
6005 give bread with one fish-ball!'

fish-knives
1100 for the fish-knives, Norman As

fishbone
6600 like a fishbone in the

fisherman
8272 than a fisherman pulled

fishers
5669 Three fishers went sailing

fishes
5940 muteness of fishes.
6539 go free, Fishes, that
6793 like little fishes vanish
10750 lived like fishes; the great

fishing
11418 pleasure of fishing them out.

fit
5186 yourself fit for
5480 to become fit for this
5722 peoples were not fit.
6370 think I am fit for the
6904 I am fit, I am well, I am
7491 that which fits a man to
8642 physically fit can enjoy
10048 world in a fit of absence
10094 and only the Fit survive.

fitter
750 men are fitter to invent

fittest
8481 of the fittest, it seems,
10988 of the fittest implies

five
7933 Five to one, baby, one in

five-cent
26 of good five-cent cigars in

five-pound
6154 up in a five-pound note. The

fix
4041 an angry fix,
5979 ain't broke, don't fix it.

fixed
4458 have they fixed the where
10937 in a flash, fixed forever.

flag
2516 people's flag is deepest
3314 Their flag to April's
12511 country's flag,' she

flame
8570 gemlike flame, to
8604 coal Whose flame creeps in
8839 of heav'nly flame! Quit, oh
9446 that little flame which is
11562 Life, a Fury slinging flame.

flames
7955 itself as flames, but
9639 Went by her like thin flames.

flanders
6554 the Duke in Flanders, In a
6698 In Flanders fields the poppies
11124 terribly in Flanders,' cried my

flash
8039 is the flash which in

flashes
12828 In flashes, and with

flat
2592 Very flat, Norfolk.

flatter
2644 me, and not flatter me at all;
5141 Before you flatter a man so

5908 us, we flatter ourselves
7724 the less we flatter them; it
9482 easier to flatter men than
10555 dream doth flatter, In sleep

flattered
11283 people are flattered into

flatterers
1992 to die; It hath no flatterers.
5851 that all flatterers live at

flatteries
6862 against flatteries except

flattering
11903 his time flattering, kissing

flatters
5188 Nothing flatters a man as much
10604 What really flatters a man is

flattery
2466 of ten to tout for flattery.
2905 likes flattery; and when
4650 of both flattery and
5892 Flattery is false coin that is
6449 in flattery of one's
11162 I suppose flattery hurts no
11341 That flattery's the food
11376 the sincerest form of flattery.
12741 the implied flattery of rapt

flavour
2626 That gives it all its flavour.
4685 A general flavour of mild

flaw
459 about them is the flaw.
5452 It is a flaw In happiness,
11778 We all have flaws, and mine

flayed
11337 saw a woman flayed, and you

flea
5129 between a louse and a flea.
5249 the very flea of his
8304 performing flea.
11330 observe, a flea Hath

fleas
5997 Fleas know not whether they
7888 Great fleas have little
8958 educated fleas do it.
9546 do as the fleas do - skip.
12420 amount o' fleas is good

fled
5433 lovers fled away into
11008 Still as he fled, his eye
11706 I fled Him, down the
12243 my Lions & fled the Seen.

flee
287 follows those who flee it.
2176 passion. Flee it if you
12864 They flee from me, that

fleet
6495 and childhood fleet!

fleet street
5959 who can be dull in Fleet Street.

fleeting
9497 in that fleeting hour How I
10557 of the fleeting year! What

fleetingly
7032 comes fleetingly now and

flesh
450 is the east wind made flesh.
891 The more flesh you show,
1218 bones, and flesh of my
1219 and they shall be one flesh.
3482 delicate white human flesh.
4743 dear, And flesh and blood
6912 The flesh, alas, is
7628 Flesh of flesh, Bone of my
10189 too solid flesh would
10456 my gross flesh sinks
10877 take off my flesh and sit in

flew
1377 something flew between me

flexible
7959 Access, your flexible friend.

flickered
11823 darkness, flickered, grew dim,

flickering
4216 My life began by flickering out.
7808 you are a flickering light, to

flies
259 If it flies, floats or
7010 best, that flies beyond my
9765 him like flies on a
10327 As flies to wanton boys,
10836 shops with large blue flies?
12290 as I will, Flies, worms,

flight
2556 as they take their flight.
2822 Flight is the only true
5319 back from flight. You talk
6493 by sudden flight, But they,
6662 to take a flight into
7038 took their flight, Hear us,

fling
12668 to have a fling For autumn

flinging
9743 guineas for flinging a pot of

flings
3741 He that flings dirt at

flint
1453 Flint must be an extremely

flippant
5520 behold thee flippant, vain,

flirt
10878 How can he flirt? The most

flirtation
1975 innocent flirtation. Not quite
8340 Flirtation - attention without

float
9841 is to float lazily

floating
3597 brown hair, Floating, like a
5332 of his bush floating, floating
7446 be a Cloud Floating in the

floats
3156 and floats a lot

flock
953 standing a flock of sheep
6505 There is no flock, however

flocks
11430 their flocks by night,

flogging
5087 is now less flogging in our
11867 habit of flogging me

flood
1966 at the flood, leads -
4056 and return it as a flood.
7071 before the flood: And you
7215 the second flood we are
10299 at the flood, leads on

flooded
1018 Streets Flooded. Please

floor
4892 becomes a floor, upon
5432 rose along the gusty floor.
6542 saw The floor lay paved
8586 the sanded floor, And

flop
772 a worse flop than the

floppy
11656 a weak, floppy thing in

florida
4330 Florida: God's waiting room.

flourishing
6975 and a flourishing socialist

flow
4556 All things flow, nothing
11850 within did flow With seas

flower
601 I hold The Flower of the
4592 this same flower that
5332 a languid floating flower.
6728 arise flower societies
6928 me is the flower of kings
7489 O fairest flower no sooner
8033 national flower is the
8106 is but a flower Which
10481 sweetest flower of all the
11498 the white flower of a

12285 From every opening flower!
12814 the meanest flower that blows

flowering
3306 The flowering of geometry.

flowerless
11352 in the flowerless fields of

flowers
603 rain, And it won't be flowers.
939 Flowers have an expression of
1940 leaf; The flowers and fruits
4001 The flowers that bloom in the
5500 see what flowers are at my
6120 with the flowers she comes
6506 And the flowers that grow
6626 them all amongst the flowers.
6975 a hundred flowers blossom
7080 with flowers, I fall on
7259 he smells flowers, looks
7384 and strewing flowers.
7592 Flowers of all hue, and
7593 gathering flowers Herself a
7794 other men's flowers, and
8325 Say it with flowers.
8447 pall, Their flowers the
8692 The flowers anew, returning
9541 roots, All flowers keep the
10047 have all the flowers gone?

flowery
5267 come to the flowery plains of
10419 wakes me from my flowery bed?

flowing
1216 A land flowing with milk and

flu
7687 members in bed with flu.

fluency
4495 all the fluency and

flung
6139 He flung himself from the

flushpots
5312 The flushpots of Euston and the

flute
3068 The soft complaining flute.

fly
304 be able to fly over
427 time to fly across the
743 they ever fly by
1932 To fly from, need not be
4573 must lose a fly to catch a
4810 spider to a fly: "Tis the
5151 A fly, Sir, may sting a
5159 Fly fishing may be a very
5319 try to fly by those
5499 for I will fly to thee,
5588 today is to fly over a
6140 hurt a fly. It's not
6323 He'd fly through the air
7685 Fly envious Time, till
8894 reason, man is not a fly.
9239 to cook a fly, he would
9425 never drink when I fly."
9861 wanting to fly in the
9973 The fly ought to be used

fly-bottle
12706 the way out of the fly-bottle.

flying
4134 on earth is flying past, and
5537 flying machines
6378 magic of flying is a
8369 Keep the aspidistra flying.
11785 Man is flying too fast for a
12137 Irretrievable time is flying.
12763 ability for flying into a
12816 in a flying horse,

focus
8025 as the focus of longing

foe
1048 Call no man foe, but never
1361 with my foe: I told it
2059 and manly foe, Bold I
3855 An open foe may prove a
4070 wrong the foe, Good, and
5362 more deadly than any foe.
6544 The first foe in the
7560 overcome but half his foe.
7663 another to let in the foe?

8145 down. The foe that comes
8148 to meet the foe; Where the
8500 a lover, and find a foe.
8861 one worthy man my foe.
9801 has his foe at his
10269 for your foe so hot
11504 who never made a foe.

foemen
10021 feel In foemen worthy of

foes
10468 these two foes A pair of
10808 His chest against his foes:
12104 foes to truth.

fog
1638 the natural fog of the
2812 .. A fog, miss.
2889 subject to fogs and with
9856 The fog comes on little

foggy
403 from the foggy, foggy
3892 A foggy day in London Town
6996 like a foggy mist ..

fold
12515 man! fold to thy

folk
488 music is folk music, I
876 of simple folk to prize
5971 with a folk song is

folks
3598 where the old folks stay.
11172 home and my folks were
12419 in some folks as there

follies
1286 man has his follies - and
2805 explain the follies of
7726 all human follies there's
9687 The follies which a man
10395 The pretty follies that
10655 of inspired follies? The

follow
113 tune and man must follow it.
617 mind and to follow him who
1486 Follow up! Follow up!
1841 pack, and follow at
2847 Follow me, if I advance;
3817 loves his country, follow me.
4933 notion, follow humbly
4957 it does not follow that most
6173 I've got to follow them - I
8068 hearts and minds will follow.
8425 mind seeks to follow through.
8437 approve; I follow the worse.
11499 wrong, follow the King -
11580 After it, follow it, Follow

followed
1421 We have followed too much

followers
554 at least two or three followers.

following
293 Following the sun we left the

folly
1267 funniest folly of the
1342 in his folly he would
1614 piece of folly he hath
2335 so, it is folly not to
2456 fear usually ends in folly.
3264 stoops to folly and Paces
3474 no greater folly than to
4299 bliss 'Tis folly to be
5170 and the folly of the
5909 without folly is not as
6105 be moved to folly by a
6595 Folly comes from something
7494 brood of folly without
7848 nature as folly, and
7864 looks, And folly's all
8603 compound of folly, weakness,
8890 shoot Folly as it
10113 slightest folly That ever
12429 It is a folly to expect men

fond
6186 should grow too fond of it.
7719 like: I am fond of my rags
11319 We are so fond of one

fonder
199 makes the heart grow fonder.
902 heart grow fonder, Isle of

font
5775 second-hand font, would

food
1540 Food comes first, then
2675 age where food has taken
2930 problem is food. When you
3263 and lays out food in tins.
3779 of too much food than of
3801 empty stomach food is god.
6627 What is food to one man is
6937 struggle for room and food.
7353 have good food; in
7718 It's good food and not
9002 and the food a tragedy.
9252 the poor provide food.
9716 the colour of the food.
9892 they have food and drink,
10158 moody food Of us that
10508 be the food of love,
10682 air: Poets' food is love
12712 was a food well in

fool
260 Any fool can make a rule,
448 A fool bolts pleasure,
564 fifty per cent bloody fool.
1257 crime and a fool's excuse
1288 she makes a fool she means
1341 A fool sees not the same
1342 If the fool would persist
1392 A fool can always find a
1879 may make a fool of
1981 genius! damned fool!
2058 has hope for it is a fool.
2481 greatest fool may ask
2608 A fool must now and then
2984 a lie. A fool had better
3029 yet, but was a fool.
3047 that is not fool is rogue.
3454 shouldn't fool with booze
3614 man than a fool who holds
3807 Any fool can criticize,
4118 here, poor fool, with all
4254 than a fool from his
4379 A busy fool is fitter to
4542 The wisest fool in
4815 is a damn fool for at
5159 end and a fool at the
5187 None but a fool worries
5699 the burnt Fool's bandaged
5723 drear: 'A fool lies here
5728 woman to manage a fool.
5752 A fool there was and he
6339 You may fool all the
6631 Remains a fool his whole
7662 of the fool, And no
7708 he's no fool usually
7720 fool is a
8333 marry me, you little fool"
8336 get into a fool or a
8559 to be some fool who will
8849 poet is a fool: But you
8851 smarts so little as a fool.
8853 nor yet a fool to fame, I
8899 thyself, and be a fool!
8902 The fool is happy
9020 And I'm a fool for
9028 Any fool can be fussy and
9466 you're no fool, Walk
9903 man a fool, and of
10104 haste of a fool is the
10550 So true a fool is love
10755 Fool,' said my Muse to
11181 no fool as a
12770 a school To breed a fool.
12932 speed; A fool at forty
12939 himself a fool; Knows it

foolish
229 a need for foolish admirers.
1235 but a foolish son is the
1259 from the foolish their lack
3605 say a foolish thing, it
5131 was more foolish when he
6441 him a very foolish fellow,
6573 The foolish and the dead

7124 wings These foolish things
9431 the most foolish women are
9522 said a foolish thing, Nor
9750 much less foolish than they
11165 and a foolish man who
12512 Forgive our foolish ways!
12901 young and foolish, with her

foolishest
1614 it is the foolishest act a wise

foolishness
4778 a little foolishness with your
4804 the general foolishness of the
11428 of amazing foolishness and

fools
422 is full of fools, and he
429 old men fools and old
686 is the virtue of fools.
2744 Fools out of favour grudge
2962 I am two fools, I know, For
3054 children and from fools.
4155 sway, And fools, who came
4642 they are the money of fools.
4958 kinds of fools: one says,
5231 Fortune, that favours fools.
5631 are made by fools like me,
5645 or perish together as fools.
5925 hath more fools in it than
7233 all the d-d fools said would
7586 Paradise of Fools, to few
8636 these poor fools decoyed
8880 move, For fools admire,
8886 For fools rush in where
9109 is no chance for old fools.
10420 Lord, what fools these
11309 Hated by fools, and fools
11341 the food of fools; Yet now
11411 and fools. The
11932 got all the fools in town on
11983 for the fools. But for
12104 part of fools and
12157 to free fools from the

foot
900 to put your foot tactfully
3501 is 12 inches to a foot.
5688 Foot - foot - foot - foot
10662 rabbit's foot if you

football
1374 is like football - it
3948 Pro football is like nuclear
6725 Oh, he's football crazy, he's
10570 think football is a
10780 to play football they'd

footmen
4490 But of all footmen the lowest

footprints
6503 behind us Footprints on the

footsoles
8757 your footsoles, and your

footsteps
890 in the footsteps of the men
2614 plants his footsteps in the sea
6480 distant footsteps echo

foppery
10313 excellent foppery of the

forbear
6844 Could scarce forbear to cheer.

forbearance
1769 at which forbearance ceases to

forbid
3608 equality, forbids the rich
4093 and God forbid that I

forbidden
7544 Of that forbidden tree,
11401 Things forbidden have a secret
12583 it has forbidden to itself.

force
1752 The use of force alone is
2430 it is of no force in law.
3000 unofficial force - the
3191 appeal to force, there's
4638 Force, and fraud, are in
4777 Force, unaided by
5336 says he. Force, hatred,
6218 use of force by one
6616 and may the force be with

Force
6887 Force is never more
7284 a creative force. The
8185 the motive force impressed;
8354 the use of force to the
9194 You can't force anyone to
10001 - that is a real force.
10646 is a great force - the only
11058 egalitarian force in
11385 powerful force for
11667 The force that through the
11886 in force is the
11890 Where force is necessary,
12267 not eloquence - it is force.
12303 use force'; we
12433 Hence no force however
12482 the use of force is to
12679 others by force that it is

forced
5135 They are forced plants,
10627 you will be forced to like

forces
1410 only two forces that unite
8184 state by forces impressed
9396 he adds to nature's forces.

forcible
6129 always more forcible as an

forebears
1588 in our forebears. It seems

foreboding
9016 filled with foreboding. Like the

forehead
5409 Upon the forehead of the age
5803 on thy forehead, thou wilt
6478 of her forehead, When she
7423 of her forehead; When she

foreign
1117 Britain's Foreign Secretary
1582 corner of a foreign field That
4451 past is a foreign country.
6788 hawk-like foreign faces The
8574 woman is a foreign land, Of
11620 nothing human foreign to me
12272 portion of the foreign world.

foreigners
2724 The more foreigners I saw, the
7704 bloody and foreigners are
11465 forever be foreigners holding
11660 it Vinchy, foreigners always
12698 signed five foreigners over the

forelock
7644 occasion's forelock watchful

foremost
6842 would be foremost To lead

foreplay
1032 all .. No foreplay. No

foresaw
3425 a way for what none foresaw

foresee
8670 enough to foresee something

foreseen
9496 that cannot be foreseen.
11000 I had not foreseen Was the

foresight
2183 in foresight, a

forest
5138 clipped hedge is to a forest.
6149 through the forest goes! The
6382 through the forest with a
6482 This is the forest primeval.
9248 always return to the forest.

forests
1362 In the forests of the
3319 a thousand forests is in one
6511 The forests, with their

forever
2160 the wicked, but not forever.
6951 for they are gone forever.
7747 diamond tiara lasts forever."
10080 Injustice never rules forever.
12192 and segregation forever!

forfeit
10028 shall forfeit fair

forfeiting
8387 has no intention of forfeiting.

forgave
3039 and forgave the

forge
3621 been forged in cases
3712 hammer and forge yourself
4024 a man can't forge his own
9339 and makes it forge ahead.
10713 The arms ye forge, another

forgers
8607 of liars and forgers.

forget
496 And we forget because we
526 power to forget, is a
548 day: if I forget thee, do
943 Never forget what a man says
1655 Best, to forget! Living,
1803 I always forget to include
2125 never forget!' 'You
2193 is the thing you forget with.
2467 whom it will soonest forget.
2572 is to forget it once.
4226 it, fuck it, and forget it.
4520 change and forget to tell
4690 before he can forget it.
5639 hateful art, how to forget.
5733 Lest we forget - lest we
6683 we forget who we
7102 I never forget a face, but
7599 conversing I forget all time.
7926 Forget six counties overhung
8361 don't you forget it,
8938 and you'll forget 'em all.
9144 To want to forget something
9356 but never forget it either.
9442 memory; I forget
9626 First you forget names, then
9632 you should forget and smile
10263 Old men forget: yet all
10725 It is not so easy to forget.
11363 time I shall not forget.
11371 Till life forget and death
11389 forgive nor forget; the naïve
11793 When I forgot my sovereign,
12484 to forget its
12725 book is to forget a book and

forget-me-nots
10790 Forget-me-nots, whose eyes of

forgets
7852 loved never forgets, But as

forgetting
2267 crime of loving is forgetting.
9359 is all; forgetting is another
11182 memory for forgetting, David.
12810 is but a sleep and a forgetting.

forgive
1158 Father, forgive them: for
1281 job to forgive a man,
1655 Good, to forgive; Best, to
2218 Women can't forgive failure.
3471 must learn to forgive himself.
3616 someone, we forgive him
3685 Forgive, O Lord, my little
5868 We often forgive those who
7183 A woman can forgive a man for
7227 we ought to forgive our
7261 my ghost, forgive some
8882 is human; to forgive, divine
9268 If I die, I forgive you: if I
10853 fault and never forgive you.
11389 neither forgive nor
12397 easy to forgive others
12512 of mankind, Forgive our
12523 God of forgiveness, do not
12605 if ever, do they forgive them.

forgiven
3081 What is forgiven is usually
10621 can nor should be forgiven.

forgiveness
1356 Mutual Forgiveness of each vice,
4941 is the forgiveness of nature
7695 seven parts forgiveness of sins.
12023 of endless forgiveness; a tender

forgives
2141 - and God forgives me for it.
10626 everything, forgives itself

forgiving
3705 To be social is to be forgiving.
9359 Forgiving is all; forgetting is

forgot
2776 Honey, I just forgot to duck.
2986 I have forgot much, Cynara!
4565 I am clean forgot, Let me
5450 And she forgot the stars,
7826 sister, And forgot my
8824 ridiculous, and dead forgot?
8884 proposed as things forgot.
10688 accents are soon forgot.

forgotten
444 is any, need to be forgotten.
578 forgotten; none are
4237 men have forgotten the last.
9072 we have forgotten having
9497 afar The forgotten gesture,
9605 more in the forgotten man at the
9884 you have forgotten your aim.
10001 been learnt has been forgotten.
11370 If you have forgotten my kisses

fork
6412 up mercury with a fork.

forlorn
2451 is of sense forlorn: A sadder
7627 in these wild woods forlorn?

form
6207 In form and feature, face
6753 itself is formless
8212 a visible form.
8556 possessing form, and form
11277 Form follows function.
12830 glide; The Form remains,

formalities
1798 in the formalities of the

formation
10992 object the formation of

formed
622 he is not formed by nature

formidable
4391 and equally formidable on both
5006 the most formidable of all the

formula
8177 The formula for complete
9075 fixed the formula: 'Cannot
9703 there is no formula for
11374 you the formula for

fornicated
2043 man: he fornicated and read

fornication
7009 BARABAS: Fornication? But that

forsake
1430 of ago: forsake me not

forsee
118 I clearly forsee the day

forte
10898 is his forte, and

forth
3574 go forth into a
5333 Come forth, Lazarus! And

fortissimo
6889 Fortissimo at last!

fortitude
766 is fortitude, which in
2104 can, with fortitude in any

fortress
10446 This fortress built by

fortunate
10914 he is at best but fortunate.

fortune
650 of a good fortune, must be
711 of a man's fortune is in his
712 shall see Fortune: for
1383 ill-turn of fortune the most
2357 another's fortune so much
3043 great, ere fortune made him
3219 people of fortune may
3447 be a beauty without a fortune.
4295 A youth to fortune and to
4298 method of making a fortune.
5231 Fortune, that favours fools.
5251 Blind Fortune still Bestows
5882 to bear good fortune than bad.

fortune
6141 brought fortune to
6612 but his fortune has
6711 When Fortune empties her
7732 take good fortune where I
9206 Fortune is fickle and soon
9235 If fortune turns against you,
10077 a great fortune is a great
10135 the gift of fortune; but to
10177 Fortune brings in some boats
10313 are sick in fortune - often
11403 rare good fortune that you
11622 Fortune favours the bold.
12130 Fortune assists the bold.
12332 Fortune's a right whore: If
12762 takes your fortune and runs

fortunes
7869 mend your fortunes, nor help
10309 Lest it may mar your fortunes.

forty
440 you are forty, half of
1485 Forty years on, when afar
1747 woman past forty should
3053 young till forty, and then
4721 than to be forty years old.
4852 Forty is the old age of
6593 , and I am forty. Ought I
8327 fair and forty were all
8727 From forty to fifty a man
10625 man over forty is a
12259 when I was forty. I was a

forty-five
6594 At forty-five, What next, what
7899 time he is forty-five

forty-niner
7824 a miner, Forty-niner, And his

forty-three
4030 pass for forty-three In the

forty-two
20 and Everything..is Forty-two.

forward
2277 is going forward. Life is
6842 cried 'Forward!' And
8403 looking forward to the
9272 the lame man, both go forward.
11209 look forward to the
11476 Forward, the Light Brigade!'
11535 Forward, forward let us

forwards
5623 but it must be lived forwards.

foster-child
5488 Thou foster-child of silence

fought
1666 Rats! They fought the dogs
6184 Philip fought men, but
6188 We have fought this fight as
7566 spirit That fought in heaven;
8260 of eventually being fought.
10264 speaks That fought with us
10954 what they fought each other
11490 be met and fought with
11603 I have fought for Queen and
12310 Who fought with us
12621 We have .. fought for our

foul
10193 Foul deeds will rise,
10198 Murder most foul, as in the
10340 So foul and fair a day I

fouled
11505 in her kind Hath fouled me.

found
4950 just before he is found out.
5307 perhaps found it. But
6777 have never found, in a long
8156 is slowly found out.
8188 but now am found, Was
8546 me if you had not found me.
8774 hasn't yet found out what
10717 still has found The
10953 what he had found, That was
12113 effort to found the Roman

foundation
46 Fear is the foundation of most
1050 is the foundation of morals
1782 is the foundation of all
1859 essential foundation of a

3308 on the foundations of the
9851 loses the foundation on which
11219 one foundation Is Jesus

founders
12484 to forget its founders is lost.

founding
1541 compared with founding a bank?

fount
5242 slow, fresh fount, keep time
7017 is the fount whence

fountain
6431 light, and fountain of all
6626 of the fountain of
7083 Here at the fountain's sliding
10672 the burning fountain whence it

fountains
4860 in the fountains of

four
44 The four most miserable
8367 Four legs good, two legs
8503 Four be the things I'd
12025 the age of four with paper

fourscore
12392 day lived fourscore years ..

fox
6288 of a fox at large.
6654 to the fox's sermon.
8643 Crazy like a fox.
9153 When the fox preaches,
11289 I loves the fox less, but
12602 after a fox - the

fox-hunting
4371 them prefer fox-hunting - the

foxed
8627 ever I was foxed it was

foxes
196 50,000 foxes can't be
3750 Old foxes want no tutors.

foxholes
2663 no atheists in the foxholes.

fragile
3292 so fragile, so easy
5509 a day; A fragile dew-drop
5534 most fragile things,
8201 nor can the fragile fingers of

fragmentation
12260 have bitter fragmentation that will

fragments
4035 broken into dependent fragments.
10676 Death tramples it to fragments.

fragrance
11875 sweetest fragrance from the

frail
5252 the most delicate and frail.
11207 men are too frail a thread

frailty
3048 the noblest frailty of the
10103 the noblest frailty of the
10190 Frailty, thy name is woman!

frame
8906 the gen'ral frame, And bade

framed
11765 in was not framed, like that
12216 to have it framed and glazed

france
364 they love France itself but
2092 France was long a despotism
2754 France has lost a battle.
3010 stood the wind for France.
5047 between France and
11113 this matter better in France.
11279 by which France is fed.

frank
6742 frank with them,
6775 Let us be frank about it:
8681 all frank'. I think
11733 I'm frank, brutally frank.

frankly
11104 who says frankly and fully

frankness
10822 secret, wrap it up in frankness.

frauds
6068 men of history are frauds.

freckles
8503 curiosity, freckles, and

fred
313 Here lies Fred, Who was

free
13 is really free is the
102 makes men free is for the
180 They bring it to you, free.
388 such thing as a free lunch.
400 are born free and equal
439 you get free costs too
617 the free agent that
838 a mother is never free.
843 is either free or he is
1012 To be truly free, it takes
1046 of the Free, How shall
1121 but in a free society it
1149 truth shall make you free.
1755 exist in a free country.
2351 order that we may be free.
2949 shall be free, Nor ever
3036 I am as free as nature
3611 and sex for free is that
4072 at least, or set me free.
4666 people are free to do as
4725 should be free to find or
4991 A free man is as jealous
5024 press is free, no one
5064 I am a free man, an
5376 in chains than to be free.
5557 All free men, wherever
5568 If a free society cannot
5597 land of the free, and the
6357 half slave and half free.
6362 everywhere could be free.
6436 nature all free, equal,
6511 so wild and free, That he
6883 should be free than that
6884 Church shall be free.
6885 No free man shall be taken
7116 which the free
7240 is always and wholly free.
7328 Free me, I pray, to go in
7683 naturally were born free.
9264 and let the hawk go free.
9675 was born free, and
9867 herself free who does
9928 I am condemned to be free.
10003 Comment is free, but facts
10921 they're not free either.
10922 power - he's free again.
10932 Ev'rything free in America
11148 of a free society is
11153 man is not a free man.
11297 anyone is free - one
11410 nothing and leaves it free.
12026 This is a free country,
12157 is hard to free fools from

free press
11226 you on the free press. It's the

free-born
11642 as only a free-born Briton can

free-will
1106 This free-will business is a

freed
3664 a man is freed of

freedom
811 Freedom is not something that
883 is freedom. But in
1409 leaves full freedom of
1504 between freedom and
1812 Freedom and Whisky gan
2618 Freedom has a thousand charms
2650 of mankind; freedom, a
3363 inside, the terrible freedom!
3805 to others. Freedom and
3874 O Freedom, what liberties are
4662 be no real freedom without
4910 spiritual freedom in spite
5357 rights of freedom we are all
5622 is the dizziness of freedom.
5625 use of the freedom they have,
5647 toward freedom is not the
5681 stands if freedom fall? Who
5812 Freedom's just another word
5913 name of our freedom and our
6106 To earn you freedom, the seven

freedom (continued)

6219 can be no freedom. When
6334 Freedom of the press is
6351 In giving freedom to the
6354 birth of freedom; and that
6395 of freedom, the
6403 less of the freedom of others
6434 preserve and enlarge freedom.
6647 Freedom is always and
6869 ideal of freedom and
7335 The word 'freedom' means for
7682 can love freedom heartily,
7982 Freedom! Equality!
8041 Freedom is not choosing; that
8243 by freedom of spirit'
8379 is peace. Freedom is
8461 of freedom, equality,
8479 of freedom must, like
8496 fight for freedom. That it
8608 better organised than freedom.
8747 of human freedom: it is the
8947 plan for freedom, and not
9923 Once freedom lights its
9933 birds must find in freedom.
11299 Freedom of the press in
11375 flame of freedom in their
11810 deny that freedom is
11895 our freedom is not
11949 things: freedom of speech,
12650 Freedom is an indivisible
12870 it means freedom to

freedoms

9525 . Natural freedoms are but
9601 human freedoms. The

freehold

6625 to none freehold, but it is

freely

1177 Freely ye have received,
5889 nothing so freely as advice.
7610 Freely we serve, Because we
9015 services freely with a
9774 from living freely and nobly.

freemasonry

960 have a kind of bitter freemasonry.

freemen

12265 are to be freemen or slaves.

frees

10947 One word frees us of all

freeze

5361 praised, then left to freeze.

freezing

2830 As Freezing persons,
10557 year! What freezings have I

french

118
263 The French have a passion
309 no more French, No more
364 that the French didn't
735 The French are wiser than
1306 those who speak French.
1505 A French woman, when
2060 much. The French are with
4241 to speak French, not
4260 by a French Marquis!
7126 and some are fond of French.
9481 to the French the empire
9505 is not clear is not French.
10874 As the French say, there are
11860 If the French noblesse had
11972 to them in French; I never

frenchies

8352 Those Frenchies seek him

frenchman

5102 A Frenchman must be always
8134 with a Frenchman, but
8135 must hate a Frenchman as you
11647 cynical Frenchman has said

frenzy

5606 their frenzy from some
7633 Demoniac frenzy, moping

fresh

6591 variation, fresh as when
7531 Tomorrow to fresh woods, and

fresh air

528 fond of fresh air and

freshmen

6553 The freshmen bring a little

freshness

12498 freshness and

fretful

9638 Spins like a fretful midge.

freud

2928 Freud's theory was that

freudian

6592 had her Freudian papa and

friday

2742 My man Friday.

friend

31 A friend in power is a
35 One friend in a lifetime is
1000 luncheon with a city friend.
1195 A faithful friend is the
1361 with my friend; I told my
1680 Who's your fat friend?
1830 dearest friend, The
2059 me from the candid friend!
2220 a man's friend only in
2372 and homes without a friend
2404 change our friend and not
2485 with your friend when he
2533 and the friend of
2662 A friend is one who knows
3323 A friend is a person with
3324 to have a friend is to be
3337 A friend may well be
3541 O friend unseen, unborn,
3588 my friend, I hope I
3855 a pretended friend is worse.
4049 her as a friend than as a
4622 doorway. Friend' he said,
4755 an old friend for
4798 If a friend is in trouble,
4831 A friend that ain't in need
5119 Of every friendless name
5861 himself a friend, but only
6342 lost every friend on earth,
7436 where a friend-and-relati
7959 Access, your flexible friend.
8164 one day to be our friend.
8450 'Strange friend,' I said,
8652 boy's best friend is his
9004 of my enemy is my friend.
9513 are a girl's best friend.
9617 as you choose a friend.
9912 a portrait I lose a friend.
10290 He was my friend, faithful
10298 A friend should bear his
10963 the last best friend am I.
11308 No enemy can match a friend.
11418 such a good friend that she
11504 He makes no friend who never
12096 Whenever a friend succeeds,

friendless

1727 no man so friendless but what

friendly

8600 world can be friendly pressure.

friends

215 our enemies; not our friends.
473 Without friends no one would
1153 down his life for his friends.
1720 or friends with the
2167 are the friends of their
2231 of their best friends.
2244 We make our friends; we make
2542 a man wins friends for
2772 but choice makes our friends.
3155 your friends will
3198 agreeable friends - they ask
3640 faithful friends: an old
3760 for two friends, but the
4090 by one's friends than to
4420 But my damn friends, my
4465 that their friends say in the
4676 than to be friends with her.
4731 ever meets with friends.
4793 you will make friends for him.
4817 - your friends do not
5110 few of his friends' houses
5295 When my friends lack an eye,
5902 of our best friends, we always
6153 He has many friends, laymen

6228 from my friends, Mm, I get
6248 two close friends, one is
6742 to our friends to believe
7227 ought to forgive our friends.
7428 buy friends but you
7724 we love our friends, the less
7823 it to your friends, to make
8102 Outnumber your friends.
8749 we could be friends, On each
10052 Old friends are best. King
10121 is without three good friends.
10289 Friends, Romans, countrymen,
10371 troops of friends, I must
10441 Whirring me from my friends.
10686 His best friends hear no
10737 are our friends. As for
10853 tell your friends their
10854 forgive my friends for dying:
10857 We need new friends. Some of
11464 by their friends. Judge
11619 Of my friends I am the only
11748 our actual friends, that we
11777 down his friends for his
11806 Friends, I have lost a day.
11918 the best of friends, the same
12019 that friends are
12046 Want of friends argues either
12103 me from my friends - I can
12233 not make friends ashamed to
12543 none of his friends like him.
12673 cannot be friends upon any
12895 glory was I had such friends.
12926 true friends. That

friendship

35 possible. Friendship needs a
634 money, but friendship hardly
710 is little friendship in the
1864 blindness, Friendship from
1979 Friendship is Love without his
2071 kind, to friendship clear, To
2483 Friendship often ends in love;
3022 In friendship false, implacable
3849 A woman's friendship ever ends
3865 Who friendship with a knave hath
4170 Friendship is a disinterested
4701 genial friendship plays The
5080 keep his friendship in
5108 your friendship of his own
5884 like hatred than like friendship.
6742 to friendship that we
8109 infinitely less than friendship.
8252 well form a friendship with a
9147 is blind; friendship closes its
9490 in friendship, sex and
9844 that is indeed true friendship.
9875 Friendship is almost always the
10120 Most friendship is feigning,
10130 Friendship is constant in all

friendships

3202 Friendships begin with liking or
4113 Friendships are precious Hugging
9746 be to dissolve all friendships.
11813 the foundation of friendships.

frighten

1458 why they frighten so easily.
1494 which would frighten two people
2028 street and frighten the
4651 means he uses to frighten you.
12364 but by God, they frighten me .

frightened

10794 It has a frightened look in
11284 killed than frightened to death.

frightening

4116 more frightening
5017 far more frightening than none
9279 only for frightening fish when

frightful

6115 This frightful word [function]
9808 is more frightful than

frigid

8101 a bit Is so frigid upon the

fringe

9606 the lunatic fringe in all

frivolous

9521 that frivolous pretence,
12753 what is frivolous if unpaid

frog-spawn
6083 nothing but frog-spawn - the

frogs
7704 Frogs .. are slightly
11138 Frogs Eat Butterflies.

front
166 bet as to what is out front.
3118 what we see in front of us.
7120 Go in in front of Royalty:
7728 your front to the
9435 Quiet on the Western Front.
12261 the front page
12460 backwards from in front.

frontier
5556 of a new frontier .. But

frontiers
816 the old frontiers are gone.
11746 The frontiers are not east or

frost
10481 an untimely frost Upon the
11715 And His graver of frost.

frosty
9630 mid-winter Frosty wind made

frown
4295 Science frowned not on
10043 without frown or smile,
11317 libel in a frown, And wink

frowzy
10902 pent up in frowzy lodgings,

frozen
3900 Your tiny hand is frozen.
5422 through the frozen grass, And
9950 in general is frozen music.

frugal
2281 Be frugal in the gift of

fruit
2534 the fruit of memory
4853 Sorrow is a fruit; God does
6925 and to bring forth fruit.
7625 to the fruit, she
7754 But the fruit that can fall
8728 I love fruit, when it is
9771 can bear fruit; divorced

fruitfulness
5410 and mellow fruitfulness, Close

fruits
5349 dangerous fruits on the
7857 Dead Sea fruits, that

frustrate
7454 not be frustrate of his

frustration
3469 relieved of fear and frustration.
4890 doomed to frustration at the
9472 and the frustrations that it

fuck
1032 And fuck all in
4226 of find it, fuck it, and
5229 The zipless fuck is
6050 They fuck you up, your mum

fucks
259 floats or fucks...don't

fudge
6572 and two-fifths sheer fudge.

fuel
4791 a wonderful fuel for

fugitive
7192 feel like a fugitive from th'

fulfilled
9990 your dreams fulfilled'. I

fulfilment
3701 to find fulfilment. A
4092 to its fulfilment, where I
8025 and the image of fulfilment.

full
1205 yet the sea is not full.
1815 I wasna fou, but just had
2704 life if, full of care,
10891 Serenely full, the epicure
11175 world is so full of a

fully-equipped
6410 A fully-equipped duke costs as much

fun
120 wits for the fun of it.

149 the most fun I ever had
2093 say, and make fun of it.
2596 Work is more fun than fun.
3463 is the most fun you can
5230 is all the fun you think
5307 But have we had any fun?
5377 time, Ain't we got fun.
5712 taken my fun where I've
6524 Fun is fun but no girl
7816 but the people have fun.
8089 Were more fun to be
8383 amount of fun out of
8956 was great fun, But it
12520 best of my fun I owe it

function
2796 They only function when they
6115 word function| was born
8259 It is the function of art to
9920 that their function in life is
11277 Form follows function.
12830 the Function never

functionary
2397 that of a functionary for his

functions
6866 the major functions of his

fundament
8101 Is so frigid upon the fundament.

funeral
5957 mis-behaved once at a funeral.
6501 are beating Funeral marches to
7088 prince's funeral, Shining
9016 up its own funeral pyre. As I
12717 not a funeral note, As
12951 A solemn funeral is

funerals
7923 I hate funerals, and would not

funny
3493 "It's a funny old world - a
4464 you mean, funny?
6761 the least funny is their
7445 Isn't it funny How a bear
8395 Whatever is funny is
9566 is funny as long as
11151 A funny thing happened to
12743 ragged and funny, But we'll

furnace
7549 one great furnace flamed,
10269 Heat not a furnace for your

furnaces
1471 is your furnaces, Which,

furnish
5522 task, Would furnish all we
9004 Books do furnish a room.

furnished
8664 how poorly furnished you are.

furnishing
11304 wax; thus furnishing mankind

furniture
2990 all the furniture that he is
6066 than the furniture of the
6771 that nice furniture that used
7947 the furniture on the
10875 No furniture so charming as

furrow
9623 must plough my furrow alone.
11594 A shining furrow, as thy
11757 drawn a furrow deep and

furry
10786 fire was furry as a bear.

further
217 are, the further they fall.
5858 did not see further than his
8750 of Hell - but no further.
9391 that's further away from

fury
2513 Nor Hell a fury, like a
2528 There is no fury like an
3030 Beware the fury of a
7529 the blind Fury with
12880 The fury and the

fuse
7211 line is a fuse. The line
9953 when your fuses blew.

fuss
1379 minimum of fuss and with

fustian
8855 he, whose fustian's so

futility
4659 free from a sense of futility.

future
9 The future comes one day at
261 in the future will weigh
621 let the future disturb
1696 putting the future in debt to
1961 The future states of
2306 of the future are the
2681 As for a future life, every
2699 future is, in
3170 of the future. It comes
4066 of the future, of the
4315 opens and lets the future in.
5214 create a future, so the
5595 is in the future because I
5699 be in the future, it was at
6032 a smile with a future in it.
6057 The future is not a gift -
6393 reason its future can never
8214 it is the future that makes
8382 of the future, imagine a
8725 believe the future is only
9383 middle class is its future.
9984 us what the future will be?
10006 my god, The Future of man is
11073 seen the future; and it
11235 seen the future after
11814 Future shock' .. the
12005 together in the future.
12459 The once and future king.
12831 and serve the future hour.

futurity
8794 perpetuity by way of futurity.

fuzzy-wuzzy
2014 status of a fuzzy-wuzzy colony is,
5696 to you, Fuzzy-Wuzzy, at your

gain
1163 if he shall gain the whole
1675 pain ends, gain ends too.
4901 Every gain made by
8920 will) For gain, not
8935 many for the gain of a few.
10222 We go to gain a little
10618 The other is to gain it.
10970 a losing gain; All

gained
8311 we have gained, we have
11585 He that gained a hundred
12164 and once when I gained one.

gaining
8466 may be gaining on you.

gains
698 Light gains make heavy
4590 are our gains. Man's
11157 are no gains without

galaxy
9807 lost in a galaxy tucked

galilee
1941 rolls nightly on deep Galilee.

gallant
558 A very gallant

gallantry
1972 men call gallantry, and gods
10724 to do with gallantry than it
12639 by the gallantry with which

gallery
4012 Grosvenor Gallery,
6807 The gallery in which the

galleys
5296 old Roman galleys;

galling
1827 thou art a galling load,

gallon
342 buys his ink by the gallon.

gallop
1854 and he will ride a gallop.
10864 likes to Gallop about

galloped
1653 and he; I galloped, Dirk

galloping
5404 mad hooves galloping in the

gallows
1777 see nothing but the gallows.
8477 to the gallows, something

gamble
9559 Don't gamble; take all your
11233 Life is a gamble at terrible

gamblers
2476 made more gamblers than

gambling
2727 organize gambling are some

game
250 childish game, it's
914 exciting than any game.
1073 but the game of the
1092 The game isn't over until
3005 to win this game, and to
4847 more than a game. It's an
8145 To love the game beyond the
8151 up! and play the game'.
8659 your little game We are the
9464 how you played the Game.
10632 is a game at which
11592 is his game: The sleek

games
1090 Games people play: the
1105 of all, the dread of games!
6661 It is in games that many
6663 may be the games are silly.
7778 their games should be
10010 it is better than games.

gamesmanship
8977 practice of gamesmanship or the art

gaming
5932 Man is a gaming animal. He

gamut
8504 the whole gamut of the

gangsters
5826 acted like gangsters, and the

gap
2417 endless gap between
3078 is art, art is the gap.
11234 back .. a gap you can't
12456 if gaps are to be

garbo
12000 one sees in Garbo sober.

garden
715 planted a garden; and
1480 Of the garden hard by
4997 a small garden plot to a
5698 is a garden, and such
7089 I have a garden of my own
7693 ourselves Back to the garden.
9095 is like a garden carried in
9126 Is like a garden full of
10823 there is a garden. Where
11364 ghost of a garden fronts the
11543 into the garden, Maud, For
11544 the rosebud garden of girls.
12147 We must cultivate our garden.
12604 woman in a garden. It ends

garden-state
7084 the happy garden-state, While man

gardens
12901 the salley gardens my love

garish
7505 me from day's garish eye.

garland
10165 is the garland of the

garlic
315 thing as a little garlic.
2198 loved he garleek, oynons,

garment
9158 countenance but torn garments.

garrick
4175 Our Garrick's a salad; for in
4176 lies David Garrick, describe

gas
6285 to turn the gas off before
8509 give; Gas smells

gate
4454 at the gate of the
7663 it at one gate to make

8725 through another gate.
11816 new road, or a secret gate.

gates
7073 the iron gates of life.
8750 go to the gates of Hell -

gather
4592 Gather ye rosebuds while ye
4669 wo, we'll gather and go,
11014 Gather therefore the rose,

gathered
586 See us gathered on behalf
1182 three are gathered together

gaudy
10161 one other gaudy night: ..

gave
1230 The Lord gave, and the

gay
2590 He has a gay appeal
8880 not each gay turn thy
9547 not, if I could, be gay.

gaza
7655 Eyeless in Gaza at the

gazelles
7850 the grass, gazelles appear

gazing
9821 consist in gazing at each

geese
9153 look to your geese.

gem
4293 Full many a gem of purest

gems
7471 and various gems inlay The
7863 were the gems she wore,

gender
8326 she's of the feminine gender.

genealogist
266 A genealogist is one who traces

general
9418 war, a general must know
12367 themselves into general use.

generalists
7140 it will be run by generalists.

generally
7758 notions are generally wrong.

generals
7300 her soldiers, her generals too.
8190 has two generals in whom
8915 Our Gen'rals now, retired to
11910 like dead generals, hold the
12025 we're all Generals. Only

generation
90 style of a generation younger
313 the whole generation, Still
950 to the generation that says
2182 Every generation is a secret
2852 history, generation follows
3667 Every generation harvests the
3728 My generation of Canadians grew
5285 from generation to
5589 The beat generation.
6348 dishonour to the last generation.
8031 Every generation revolts against
8559 In every generation there has to
8751 and a new generation grows up
11087 You are all a lost generation.

generations
1211 in their generations and were
1606 Generations pass while some trees
5502 No hungry generations tread thee
6623 while the generations of living
6827 of twenty generations lie

generis
6470 I am sui generis and let

generosity
2543 - has no generosity. No
3867 potential - generosity, service,
5869 Generosity is the vanity of
6746 for generosity and we'd
9920 is to exercise our generosity.
11400 Candour and generosity, unless

generous
4046 leaves no right to be generous.

7129 something generous dies for
7822 they are always generous ones.

genes
2715 the name of genes, and we

genesis
208 rewrites the Book of Genesis.

genius
18 in which a genius would like
170 for talent is genius.
267 The parting genius is with
564 per cent genius, fifty per
846 between the genius which does
894 Genius is childhood
1064 We define genius as the
1333 are roads of genius.
1622 when was genius found
1716 Genius does what it must,
1981 stupendous genius! damned
2855 forget that genius ..
3001 instantly recognizes genius.
3118 immense genius to
3143 Genius is one per cent
3151 Men of genius are the worst
3300 for all men - that is genius.
3387 work of genius we
3408 Genius as such can neither
3512 is the feminine of genius
3811 to be a genius, but a
4187 Gives genius a better
4497 of human genius, we should
4966 mediocrity, genius is
5003 Genius, in truth, means
5206 The true genius is a mind of
5256 Ramp up my genius, be not
5335 A man of genius makes no
6116 Genius is personal, decided
6280 between genius and
6296 Many a genius has been slow
6327 is a genius at least
6331 the name of genius in the
6424 True Genius, like Armida's
6572 of him genius, and
6586 power; genius is that in
6630 man of genius is
7241 Genius, all over the world,
7325 Genius does what it must,
8018 making of genius. I love
8059 Genius is an African who
8063 like a genius, I write
8457 I was a genius I was a
8611 Short of genius, a rich man
8741 invoke the genius of the
9048 The mark of genius is an
9454 taste or genius by rules,
11105 the man of genius rules is
11256 of human genius will never
11348 When a true genius appears in
12498 noblest expressive genius.
12567 I've put my genius into my
12577 to declare except my genius.
12592 everything except genius.
12949 or to his genius, according

geniuses
581 Geniuses are the luckiest of
4085 have nothing but geniuses.
6735 many other geniuses, a greater
12209 greatest geniuses that ever

genteel
1470 is not genteel when he

gentile
5553 is a Gentile problem

gentiles
5735 as the Gentiles use, Or

gentility
1332 marks of gentility When
2343 Gentility is what is left over

gentle
2205 That he is gentil that dooth
2722 all other, Gentle Child of
3206 be they gentle or simple,
5290 should be gentle and stern,
6302 one - the gentle slope,
8872 Of manners gentle, of
10968 not woman, gentle woman dare
11016 The gentle mind by gentle

gentle
11664 Do not go gentle into that
12387 Gentle Jesus, meek and mild,

gentleman
143 (A gentleman) is any man who
211 and a gentleman
268 Gentleman: one who never hurts
558 gallant gentleman....he
785 English gentleman, in his
818 what a gentleman is to a
828 span, Who was then a gentleman?
841 A gentleman does things no
1768 but he cannot make a gentleman.
4391 the English gentleman, the
6281 of the last gentleman in Europe.
6403 A gentleman is mindful no less
6710 a manner befitting a gentleman.
8168 of a gentleman to say
8687 test of a gentleman: his
9747 Not a gentleman; dresses too
10726 Honourable gentleman is
11292 being a gentleman never is
11294 He was a gentleman who was
11967 to call you a gentleman.
12413 Every other inch a gentleman.
12599 A true gentleman is one who is
12602 country gentleman galloping

gentlemanly
523 secondly, gentlemanly conduct;
11188 do a very gentlemanly thing.
11291 one werry gentlemanly ideas, but

gentlemen
4053 that these gentlemen wish to
4207 Gentlemen, include me out.
4243 none of us gentlemen any more.
5194 of conversation among gentlemen.
5731 while the Gentlemen go by!
6733 to behave like gentlemen.
6832 There were gentlemen and there
7239 Gentlemen prefer bonds.
8020 good gentlemen. I want
8517 You gentlemen of England Who
10264 And gentlemen in England, now
11414 Above all, gentlemen, not the
11639 written by gentlemen for
12827 Scholars and gentlemen.

gentleness
11699 such, only a willed gentleness.

genuine
7843 all, a place for the genuine.

geographical
2317 India is a geographical term. It
7336 Italy is a geographical

geography
1054 from Geography. Geography

geometrical
6936 in a geometrical ratio.

geometry
3306 The flowering of geometry.

george
1055 George the Third Ought never
5990 George the First was always

georgia
4233 Georgia, Georgia, no peace I

georgian
6771 of all the Georgian silver
10994 in gentle Georgian Squares.

geraniums
7441 (blue) and geraniums (red), And

german
1305 one ally: the German people.
4079 are under German influence.
9489 is all a German racket,

germans
2585 to the Germans When our
3870 The Germans, if this
4633 the Sudeten Germans, my
5798 Europe, but Germans need it
5799 We Germans now have the
6416 the Germans found the
9481 and to the Germans that of -
11910 grip and Germans, no less

germany
4667 über alles Germany above all.
9949 The soul of Germany is Europe,

germinates
169 springs and germinates no more.

germs
7976 Trap the germs in your
8455 theory of germs is

gesture
1398 a gesture. A

get
1180 Get thee behind me,
4690 A man must get a thing
6989 Get up, stand up Stand up
10627 care to get what you
10839 first, to get what you

gharsley
8094 Parsley is gharsley.

ghost
2953 old lover's ghost, Who died
4639 than the ghost of the
6613 stands the ghost of a great
9800 of the Ghost in the
10678 like a ghost from the

ghosts
8865 round the ghosts of Beauty
10692 like ghosts from an

ghoulies
269 From ghoulies to ghosties and

giant
1487 of lunatic giant -
5997 body of a giant or upon
6063 it was a giant column

giants
8181 on the shoulders of giants.

gibbets
12934 law; And gibbets keep the

gibbon
4551 scribble! Eh! Mr. Gibbon?

gibraltar
3897 crumble, Gibraltar may

giddy
1703 and I turn giddy when I

gift
84 skin is a gift from God.
434 all, the gift of
1401 Guilt: the gift that goes
2038 is a gift to the
3362 The only gift is a portion
4529 essential gift for a good
4729 Zeus, and a gift, though
5274 You have a gift, sir,
5665 every gift, except
6057 is not a gift - it is an
6112 He has the gift of quiet.
6685 a sort of gift or trust
7316 That rarest gift To Beauty,
7332 greatest gift of any
7606 last best gift, my ever
8172 is God's gift, but so
10026 love's the gift which God
11354 Time with a gift of tears,
11878 to make the gift rich by

giftie
1828 Pow'r the giftie gie us To
8030 power the giftie gie us to

gifts
1570 us rarer gifts than gold.
5251 Bestows her gifts on such as
10440 your goodly gifts, And
10941 Enemies' gifts are no gifts
12118 even when they bring gifts.
12784 highest gifts, The

gigantic
6821 The gigantic body, the huge

gild
1963 silly 'To gild refinèd
10305 To gild refinèd gold, to

gilded
5923 She's a bird in gilded cage.
10442 Men are but gilded loam or

gimble
2120 gyre and gimble in the

gin
1384 "Of all the gin joints in
2367 never drink gin. It makes
9422 can get out the gin, eh?

giotto
6488 Giotto's tower, The lily of

girdle
8095 with your girdle when your

girl
212 The average girl would
1104 is the girl of my
1569 find some girl perhaps,
2224 that a girl will wait
2656 a pretty girl who naked is
3458 Claus to a girl of twenty.
4280 If I were a girl, I'd
6478 a little girl Who had a
6522 said a girl with
6524 fun but no girl wants to
7423 a little girl who had a
9809 little girl knows
10976 Give me a girl at an
11880 whether any girl would be
12196 The little girl had the
12452 same as a girl to me - I
12899 can I, that girl standing

girlfriend
2380 All girlfriends are like
8192 your girlfriend and the

girls
120 Girls are so queer, you
2076 Of all the girls that are
2344 looking at girls and
4406 American girls turn into
7701 to the girls, you never
8014 Good girls go to heaven.
8499 If all the girls attending

give
302 Give me a child for the
486 Give them the cold steel,
610 the same, give that I
1177 have received, freely give.
2672 a matter of give and take,
3563 enough to give you
6111 Give me your tired, your
6607 To give and not to
7285 ones who give it and the
7416 we never give enough of
8433 they give or refuse,
8673 I'll give it to you.
9094 Canada or give it back.
12509 I do not give lectures

give in
2325 Never give in, never give in,

given
811 can be given; freedom
1172 it shall be given you; seek,
3475 nothing is given, of him

giver
8223 not the giver be

gives
847 those to whom he gives it.
2843 wit, and gives it to
3176 in what he gives and not in
5889 One gives nothing so freely
9281 He gives the poor man twice

giving
3674 Giving is the highest
5840 less in giving liberally
10464 not in the giving vein

gizzard
11754 is the gizzard of

glacier
3244 as a glacier, will

glad
1436 I was glad when they said
1656 soon made glad, Too
1659 Never glad confident

gladness
10711 me half the gladness That thy
12829 begin in gladness; But

gladsome
7493 us with a gladsome mind

glamorous
3895 my life so glamorous, You can't

glance
5922 a single glance to give

glances
271 The glances over cocktails

glands
4921 ductless glands and our

glass
999 the Sound of Broken Glass
4574 looks on glass, On it may
6787 profit. The glass is falling
10246 indeed the glass Wherein
10676 glass, Stains
11303 a sort of glass, wherein
11648 a looking glass and gives

glass eye
10330 Get thee glass eyes; And, like

glass-bottomed
7709 a sewer in a glass-bottomed boat.
12189 a sewer in a glass-bottomed boat.

glasses
8507 At girls who wear glasses.

gleam
11580 follow it, Follow The Gleam.

glen
162 the rushy glen, We

glide
12830 Still glides the Stream,

glistering
1519 make your glistering gold but

glisters
4296 Nor all, that glisters, gold.

glitterati
12630 for the glitterati or the

glittering
4589 O how that glittering taketh me!
7537 Are seen in glittering ranks with
10830 to offer glittering prizes to

gloamin'
6060 in the gloamin', On the

global
6760 image of a global village.

gloom
323 of glory or gloom to
8986 In the gloom, the gold

glooms
11731 kindred glooms! Congenial

gloomy
338 that gloomy shell He

gloria
234 Sic transit gloria mundi.

glories
10453 You may my glories and my
12061 weaker glories spy Some
12327 Glories, like glow-worms,

glorified
11903 is, is a glorified public

glorious
4013 is, it is a glorious thing To
10457 Made glorious summer by
10809 Glorious the northern lights

glory
202 All glory comes from daring
234 passes the glory of the
323 of glory or gloom
676 for the glory of the
1120 is not the glory of rulers
1211 were the glory of their
1776 and the glory of Europe
1937 The glory and the nothing
2562 there is no glory in the
3006 yields the true glory.
3880 country, I glory in the
4102 is all, the glory nothing.
4758 gives God glory, but a man
4806 seen the glory of the
5465 Glory and loveliness have
6182 calls and glory leads the
7308 but O the glory of the
7958 To the greater glory of God.
8798 but the glory belongs to
8898 hurled; The glory, jest, and
9374 My gown of glory, hope's
9669 the day of glory has
9784 and the chief glory of man.
10495 is the glory of this
10539 Time's glory is to calm

10679 corrupter, glory a bubble,
10734 war as all glory, but,
11268 Waste of Glory, waste of
11430 down, And glory shone
11602 for the glory of the
12056 an air of glory, Whose
12719 him alone with his glory.
12806 away a glory from the
12809 it now, the glory and the
12811 clouds of glory do we come
12826 Not as our glory and our
12828 and with glory not their
12895 where man's glory most

glossy
4195 for a fine glossy surface,

glow
11156 and her glow has warmed

glow-worm
2293 believe that I am a glow-worm.
12327 like glow-worms, afar off

glows
6987 You would even say it glows.

glutton
4363 is just a glutton with
6015 A gloton of wordes.

gluttons
9379 in rags And gluttons old in sin

gnarled
9493 The gnarled fidelity of an

gnashing
1174 weeping and gnashing of teeth.

gnats
5411 the small gnats mourn

gnawing
1759 By gnawing through a dyke,

gnomes
12659 the little gnomes in Zurich

go
3641 thing done, go - if not,
6911 Sir, stop - go away: I
7638 thee to go, Is to
8399 I have a go, lady,
11192 not to go anywhere,
11474 and men may go, But I go

go on
10868 I think you couldn't go on.

go-between
9181 The go-between wears out a

goaded
4075 she has goaded to the

goal
851 The prime goal is to
2574 his eyes off his goal.
3815 ultimate goal of the
4117 have not reached my goal.
6297 his next goal somewhat
6666 a higher goal to attain,
11563 be the final goal of ill.

goals
4224 very modest goals for
5702 muddied oafs at the goals.

goat
997 hairy goat With an
7001 with their goat feet dance

god
106 Even God cannot change
157 is there no God, but try
158 If only God would give me
190 the further from God.
208 April, God rewrites
272 If God lived on earth,
311 all give God a great
337 nature of God is a
408 ask of God when they
454 understands to be God.
842 God has been replaced, as
847 the Lord God thinks of
860 you're .. God? EARL OF
865 God gave us memories that
925 wheresoever God buildeth a
938 dog is the god of frolic.
1078 God bless America, Land
1127 God is no respecter of
1145 was with God, and the

1157 kingdom of God is within
1183 therefore God hath
1186 and unto God the things
1202 Lord our God is one
1277 By God, O King, I will
1429 God is our hope and
1435 Lord he is God: it is he
1441 Those whom God hath
1464 Cabots talk only to God.
1636 No mother, God forgot me,
1729 Thanks to God, I am still
1863 God is usually on the
1870 the case. God has
1878 that though God cannot
1922 God bless the King, I
2088 God Almighty never
2130 And others call it God.
2160 God bears with the
2408 there is a God, Or
2441 'twas that God himself
2670 where does that leave God?
2689 path to God and
2717 deal of God. He
2745 Wherever God erects a
2851 know about God and sin,
2969 terrible. God and devil
3166 God is subtle but he is
3198 over to God's mercy,
3272 God may pardon you, but I
3274 Though God hath raised me
3318 everything God has made.
3592 God is not a cosmic
3603 of God when he
3627 God heals, and the doctor
3801 empty stomach food is god.
3922 a wafer is God than that
4330 Florida: God's waiting
4391 between God and a goat
4397 God does not die on the
4461 know the mind of God.
4564 The God of love my
4783 stay; What God abandoned,
4814 God will not look you
4924 God is
5034 God is the surprise of
5448 makes a god of me.
5522 us, daily, nearer God.
5640 want to do God's will.
5767 God and I both knew what
5772 A man with God is always
5802 Give God time.
5803 That which God writes on
6174 God is love, but get it
6270 If God were to hold out
6373 sir, that God is on our
6384 by the ways of God.
6407 God made me on a morning
6558 you want to take in God.
6598 even God was born
6636 no other. God help me.
6641 that is really your God.
6696 By and by God caught his
6704 we can be alone with God.
6750 be guilty, and God is
6921 God defend me, said
6934 of what God should be.
6952 in order - God does the
7263 God is a comedian whose
7458 creature, God's image;
7594 He for God only, she
7632 O why did God, Creator
7661 the ways of God, And
7735 God it is true, does some
7814 invented a god, they
7953 There's God, angels,
7958 the greater glory of God.
8043 Well, God is certainly
8117 God punishes us mildly by
8208 take himself for a god.
8215 God is dead: but
8334 to the eye of God.
8443 God and the doctor we
8565 himself a god and an
8697 One on God's side is a
8711 God is really only
8767 chooses: God is
8799 he thinks little of God.
8906 Thus God and nature

8908 the noblest work of God.
9029 God can stand being told
9113 God does not pay weekly,
9115 God made the ocean, but
9197 God could not be
9207 God will be present,
9209 is the voice of God.
9323 Our God and soldiers we
9659 and you are a god.
9782 because God put Adam
9847 as 'Call Me God') to the
10051 God keeps the wicked to
10184 God has given you one
10272 served my God with half
10386 God made him, and
10580 man whose God is in the
10599 What God hath joined
10803 God all-bounteous,
10804 beauty, but God, God hath
10847 serve both God and Mammon
10918 than God, yet fail
11021 By God I mean a being
11368 But God, if a God there
11393 you talk to God, you are
11469 that God is only,
11494 Man's word is God in man.
11515 to new, And God fulfils
11565 darkness up to God.
11571 God's finger touched him,
11634 the name of God in the
11805 If God were not a
12039 God created man and,
12058 these looms God ordered
12098 The true God, the mighty
12115 things, God will grant
12153 If God did not exist, it
12165 prayers to God only
12168 God is on the side not of
12232 angler, and now with God.
12287 bite, For God hath made
12523 God of forgiveness, do
12925 to see God in all

god's-acre
6489 The burial-ground God's-Acre!

god-intoxicated
8294 A God-intoxicated man.

god-like
11845 have been God-like in our

goddamm
8983 Lhude sing Goddamm, Raineth

goddess
5243 thy light, Goddess,
8606 Goddess, allow this aged man

godliness
11914 With their godliness they may

godot
923 We're waiting for Godot.

gods
1848 The gods are well pleased
4601 The Gods rank work above
4732 in the lap of the gods.
4763 Not gods, nor men, nor
5259 in the world made gods.
5443 of the early gods!
6284 they first make gods.
6397 to the gods above and
6838 slay; The Gods who live
6839 the temples of his Gods?'
7248 Whom the gods love dies
7623 fair, fit love for gods.
8427 there be gods, and, as
8761 of the gods recognized
8764 by the gods because it
8775 He whom the gods favour
9870 denies only gods fashioned
9923 heart, the gods are
9956 the gods themselves
10092 yet bows to no false gods.
10279 fit for the gods, Not hew
10327 we to the gods; They kill
10333 The gods are just, and of
11184 fame, the gods have
11404 The gods are on the side
11538 hills like Gods together,
12121 The gods thought
12535 So many gods, so many
12792 The gods approve The

goes
1509 God there goes John
11496 to the great deep he goes.

goethe
2669 Goethe said there would be

going
4775 When the going gets rough,
5280 who knows where he is going.
5584 When the going gets tough,
9544 I learn by going where I
9860 where I'm going but I'm on
10332 Their going hence,

gold
1111 their mouths with gold.
6145 sing, This gold, my
6652 is mor than gold or gret
7863 a bright gold ring on
8721 best. But gold shines
8825 truth with gold she
8986 gloom, the gold gathers
9132 Fire tries gold,
10303 back, When gold and silver
12122 cursed craving for gold!

gold-starred
10790 blue, Gold-starred like

golden
1898 that is golden, not
2767 Golden slumbers kiss your
4062 of those golden moments of
4210 that lays the golden egg.
7693 We are golden, And we
10684 anew, The golden years
11489 circle of the golden year.
11923 went into a golden land,

golf
24 to take up golf and too
3254 thousand lost golf balls.'
4754 you work at it, it's golf.
11958 Golf is a good walk

gone
2850 love is gone? If you
5433 they are gone: aye, ages
5540 he is gone. And when
5946 Gone before To that
5964 all are gone, the old
6543 when I am gone, You or I
7526 thou art gone, Now thou
8676 He's gone to join the
9549 dead - but gone before, He
10019 He is gone on the
10529 What's gone and what's
12055 are all gone into the

gongs
2248 Strong gongs groaning as

good
275 is so much good in the
289 But what..is it good for?
414 would do good to
455 much good would be
627 is for the good of that
793 something good and bad of
1007 is only as good as what he
1047 some quite good people who
1056 of the good,
1155 enemies, do good to them
1243 heart doeth good like a
1285 of feeling good all over,
1335 would do good to
1733 is too good for him,
1748 for the good man to do
1895 to have good taste than
2024 as good or as bad
2071 Good to the poor, to
2265 The word good' has many
2459 over, the good is no
2641 for any good you have
2733 fate: The good die early,
2981 is too good for some
3044 prospect of a distant good.
3071 their own good; or
3418 We know the good, we
3738 himself is good when he is
3743 Good is not good, where
3745 Great and good are seldom
3879 for your good, for all
4052 great good for the

4255 see the good in each
4327 once; any good thing
4333 What's the good of a home
4386 The good should be
4517 anything as good as
4585 who feels good about it.
4623 cannot do good, he must
5113 a man a good man , upon
5180 is both good and
5301 man is as good as another
5388 be called good without
6215 A good man fallen among
6468 for all good men to
6478 she was good She was
6518 something good about
6523 while you're looking good.'
6671 Seek to be good, but aim
6729 being a good writer or
6737 never so good or so bad
6775 have never had it so good.
6857 are made good by some
7367 His own good, either
7423 she was good she was
7552 To do aught good never will
7553 And out of good still to
7682 but good men; the
7796 no man so good, who, were
7961 Guinness is good for you.
8001 It's good to talk.
8005 You never had it so good.
8265 needs good farmers,
8572 for the good we do, Not
8655 Every good thing that
9152 Good things are not done
9167 Good is when I steal other
9190 Good men need no
9223 A good man and a good
9281 as much good who gives
9578 down the good things you
9724 do me any good by loving
9748 you're good at
9764 The good life, as I
9827 cook was a good cook, as
9915 And not as good as some
10004 Greek. No good can come
10037 There's a gude time
10105 loves what he is good at.
10206 either good or bad,
10243 they have a good thing, to
10382 fair hath made you good.
10637 profess evil and do good.
10865 A good time was had by
10912 whereas good men eat
10924 dividing good and evil
10971 Good is best when soonest
10984 is to be a good animal.
11488 all men's good Be each
11563 somehow good Will be
11646 could be a good woman if I
11720 universe Of good or ill, of
11744 not simply good; be good
11750 of doing me good, I should
12090 I will be good.
12399 When I'm good, I'm very
12492 I am as good as the
12536 can be good in the
12559 The good ended happily,
12575 but they never become good.
12773 If all the good people
12785 The good die first, And
12849 There's a good time
12920 always the good feel

good will
12651 of good will toward us,

good works
1166 they may see your good works.

good-night
8591 do, till our last good-night.
10478 Good-night, good-night! parting
10683 Good-night? ah! no; the hour is
12896 a gay good-night and

goodbye
950 that says goodbye at the
2719 in every goodbye for every
3077 one says goodbye to what
4281 Goodbye to all that.
6299 we must say Goodbye, my

8956 So goodbye dear, and Amen,
8961 Every time we say goodbye.
12422 Good-bye-ee! - Good-bye-ee! Wipe

goodnatured
10720 one damned goodnatured friend or

goodness
1533 seductive power of goodness.
5866 were quite devoid of goodness.
5873 for his goodness unless he
11820 that beauty is goodness.
11949 is by the goodness of God

goods
473 he had all other goods.
1440 my worldly goods I thee
6148 were all his worldly goods.

goolies
4232 Party by the goolies.

goose
6457 is a gold goose that lays
6654 is a blind goose that

gooseberried
11675 grassgreen gooseberried double-bed

gordian
5461 She was a gordian shape of

gored
1469 tossed and gored several

gorgeousness
6629 the human spirit is gorgeousness.

gorgonised
11542 Gorgonised me from head to foot

gory
12372 I'll make a gory mess of

gospel
7069 boast) The gospel's pearl
7911 The golden Gospel of Silence
10601 of the gospel of getting

gossip
3200 Gossip is a sort of smoke
4602 No gossip ever dies away
4832 Gossip is vice enjoyed
8090 thing about gossip is that it
9250 Gossip needs no carriage.
9825 ill-natured gossip ourselves,
12654 Gossip is when you hear
12692 Gossip is the art of saying

gossips
9261 Whoever gossips to you will

gotten
4422 mess you've gotten me into."

goulash
5619 better to have good goulash?

gourmet
4363 A gourmet is just a glutton

gout
7759 them the gout, give them

govern
989 Go out and govern New South
1589 easy to govern, but
2320 Labour is not fit to govern.
2757 How can you govern a country
6292 To govern is to
7143 that would govern others,
8833 of Kings to govern wrong.
11901 right, to govern himself
12032 but it does not govern.

governed
4744 not so well governed as they
8452 wisdom the world is governed?
10462 land that's governed by a
12430 he who is governed by that

governess
1565 Be a governess! Better be a

governing
1403 The art of governing consists
8016 to the lust of governing.

government
40 of a free Government ought to
43 A government of laws, and not of
45 society is the end of government.
773 is a strong government is that it
780 the first government which made
948 next to anarchy, is government.
1120 object of government in peace

1595 The government is becoming the
1789 looked to government for bread,
1791 forms of Government the people
2094 run every government is the
2291 support the government, the
2301 form of government except all
2337 attack the government of my own
2434 what the government gives, it
2463 pay, the government should
2846 to the government is not a
2870 No Government can be long secure
2873 Government is an
3563 If the Government is big enough
3783 what a government will do if
4055 into a system of Government.
4515 to see the government get out of
4624 toppled the government? Swift
4868 hand of government can never
5023 That government is best which
5024 No government ought to be
5027 for which government ought to
5028 of pure government as sores
5602 thing for Government is not to
5609 work for a Government I despise
5655 Government in the last analysis
6341 existing government, they can
6352 Must a government of necessity
6354 and that government of the
6357 this government cannot
6360 object of government is to do
6367 existing government and form a
6778 no British government should be
6786 no go the Government grants,
6888 have good Government you often
6901 has the government it
6902 a coalition government on my own
6948 regards government as a sort
7950 Government is the only
8268 of our system of government.
8460 A government of the people, by
8471 Government, even in its best
8477 in the system of government.
8488 of a government is to
8620 and government to suffer
8700 under a government of men and
8905 forms of government let fools
9387 The government is concerned
9575 all the government we're
9727 Government and co-operation are
9876 Government is the political
9942 aim of good government to
10061 Government of the busy by the
10577 The art of government is the
10595 A government which robs Peter to
10821 which one government sooner
10919 is to have another government.
10985 form of Government is the
11216 Every government is run by liars
11416 science of government; but that
11765 The government of the world I
11825 Government is an association of
11905 understands government, and it
11909 efficient government you have a
11911 a British government than that
12143 The best government is a
12184 Much of Government's activity is
12267 Government is not reason, it is
12322 people's government, made for
12622 the last government program
12680 ever saw a government. I live

governmental
12674 of governmental power, not

governments
46 foundation of most governments.
1066 Governments last as long as the
3189 these days governments had better
8475 and teach governments humanity.
8698 Governments exist to protect the
12167 Governments need both shepherds

governors
12214 Our supreme governors, the mob.

governs
5023 best which governs the least,
7580 arbiter Chance governs all.
9510 will governs each
11882 who now governs the

gown
8516 heart Like a satin gown?

grace
878 thing to the grace of God.
1509 But for the grace of God
2407 Grace is given of God, but
2722 Give us grace to
2935 hath such grace, As I have
4477 Grace is the absence of
5240 gives the grace, Or the
5246 a grace; Robes
5777 all by Thy grace To
8188 Amazing grace! how sweet
8917 with grace; If not,
10447 Grace me no grace, nor
11071 grow old with a good grace.
12639 are survived with grace.

gracehoper
5316 The Gracehoper was always

graces
10544 all your graces, The age
11012 many Graces sate.

gracious
1437 for he is gracious: and his
10776 Show me a gracious loser and

gradualness
12312 of gradualness cannot

graduate
3728 some day graduate from

graduated
11405 men are graduated from

grail
12003 Product is our Holy Grail.

grain
1325 world in a grain of sand

grammar
2908 posterity talking bad grammar.
4850 bows to success, even grammar.
6020 Grammer, the ground of al.
10761 Emperor, and am above grammar.

grammatical
2328 with a grammatical ending -

grand
6456 Isn't it grand! Isn't it
9913 Ain't it grand to be

grand canyon
7037 down the Grand Canyon and

grandeur
4291 Nor grandeur hear with
4424 and the grandeur underlying
8808 And the grandeur that was

grandfather
12529 through his grandfather or his

grandfathers
8031 friends with its grandfathers.

grandmother
4849 a man, begin with his grandmother.
11651 We have become a grandmother.

grandson
4851 does not adore his grandson.

grant
1423 Grant that this day we fall
1501 knows who's in Grant's tomb.
6916 O grant me, Heaven, a
11922 Great God, grant that twice

granted
2222 liberty for granted, when you
4901 instantly taken for granted.
9745 have long taken for granted.

grape
10538 one sweet grape who will

grapes
4806 where the grapes of wrath
6801 be the grapes of the

grapeshot
2090 A whiff of grapeshot.

grapple
7466 Falsehood grapple; who ever

grapples
11568 And grapples with his

grasp
12228 a better grasp of what is

grasping
96 by grasping at the

grass
373 this grass will
1102 There isn't grass to graze a
4941 Grass is the forgiveness of
9079 it is the grass that
9649 I know the grass beyond the
9857 - I am the grass; I cover
11083 Pigeons on the grass alas.
12132 a snake hidden in the grass.
12507 a leaf of grass is no less
12813 in the grass, of glory

grateful
2156 that anybody can be grateful.
7590 A grateful mind By owing owes
9825 are always grateful to those

gratification
529 not in it for the ego gratification.
2009 is accepting deferred gratification.
4408 the maximum gratification of the
10665 that the gratification of your

gratitude
5880 of mankind gratitude is merely
9143 Gratitude is the heart's

gratuitous
3208 prophecy is the most gratuitous.
3942 I mean: gratuitous. And that

grave
375 O grave, thy
378 in the grave His soul
1131 sting? O grave, where is
2134 And by my grave you'd pray
2323 the cradle to the grave
2940 for we come to seek a grave.
3127 the cradle and the grave.
3698 beyond the grave, But the
4208 he'd turn in his grave.
4291 glory lead but to the grave.
4639 upon the grave thereof.
5046 if I was a grave digger, or
5117 no letters in the grave.
5550 dread The grave as little
5993 on this side of the grave.
6500 And the grave is not its
7072 lust. The grave's a fine
7386 of the grave Gently
7679 Alcestis from the grave.
8569 the secrets of the grave.
8640 go into my grave - for
10171 No grave upon the earth
10703 to the grave Through
10880 is a kind of healthy grave.
11614 upon my grave, To
11855 Even the grave yawns for
12782 is in her grave, and, ho,
12820 Upon his mother's grave?
12907 with O'Leary in the grave.

graves
9023 to me: The graves of little
10810 day dig our graves with our

graveyards
5574 foxholes or graveyards of battle.

gravitation
11886 as not believing in gravitation.

gravity
71 of women, gravity is that of

grazing
11279 Tilling and grazing are the

grease
6599 slides by on grease.

greasy
2868 the top of the greasy pole.

great
14 Great men are
139 you're as great as I am,
543 is not a great man, he
1232 Great men are not always
1352 Great things are done when
1697 Its a great life if you
2450 things both great and small.
3041 soul .. he is always great.
3043 For he was great, ere
3328 To be great is to be
3438 - the great ones who

3745 Great and good are seldom
3831 a nation great is not
4223 Few great men could pass
4710 calling is great when
5991 Great men too often have
6068 If I am a great man, then a
6503 Lives of great men all
6671 not to be great; A woman's
6808 to him great, and
6841 The the great man helped
6982 to be great: since it
7228 You're not that great.
8219 To do great things is
8246 Of what is great, one must
8266 The great silent majority.
8601 every great man there
9139 Only great men may have
10876 Great men hallow a whole
11176 proud and great, And tell
11908 was in the great' class,
12931 think the great unhappy,

greater
4107 himself as greater than he
7726 could be greater Than
11777 Greater love hath no man than

greatest
138 I am the greatest.
4433 The greatest truths are the
7780 The greatest thing in the
9361 to live as the greatest he.
9491 part in the greatest; the more
11452 nothing of its greatest men.
11585 England's greatest son, He

greatness
135 out with my greatness intact.
535 Greatness is a zigzag streak of
2052 ideals and without greatness.
2755 Greatness is a road leading
4816 penalty for greatness, and every
10517 achieve greatness, and some
11491 God our greatness may not

greece
1964 that Greece might
8808 that was Greece And the

greed
1702 enough for everyone's greed.
3669 on greed? The
9048 Genius is a spiritual greed.
12037 against probable greeds.

greediness
12699 how much greediness We seek

greedy
9292 thank goodness, I am greedy.

greek
1957 loving, natural, and Greek.
2190 of a Greek tragedy.
3773 study of Greek
5173 when his wife talks Greek.
5254 small Latin, and less Greek.
6900 is not Greek in its
10004 and half Greek. No good
10277 part, it was Greek to me.
12462 its classic Greek sense -

greeks
111 The Greeks had a word for
1518 Let Greeks be Greeks, and
6183 When Greeks joined Greeks,
12118 I fear the Greeks even when

green
130 There is a green hill far
1348 mountains green? And was
1821 Green grow the rashes, O,
4100 life springs ever green.
6406 How green was my valley.
7082 made To a green thought in
10154 When I was green in
11667 through the green fuse

green-eyed
10431 It is the green-eyed monster

greenery
4012 A greenery-yallery, Grosvenor
5617 There is no greenery. It would

greensleeves
279 Greensleeves was all my joy,

greenwich
1320 Greenwich is the place the

greenwood
10114 Under the greenwood tree Who

grey
2279 little grey cells. It
5829 Nature prematurely grey.
10090 us respect grey hairs,
12735 me over in my grey hairs.

greyhounds
10257 stand like greyhounds in the

grief
669 be the grief, as is the
704 to it; grief flieth to
795 But woman's grief is like a
1213 is much grief: and he
1363 another's grief, And not
1625 hopeless grief is
1940 and the grief Are mine
4160 silent manliness of grief.
5154 While grief is fresh, every
6539 thirsty grief in wine we
6943 with human grief to a
7874 In grief we know the worst
10134 master a grief but he
10516 monument, Smiling at grief.
10529 help Should be past grief.
10670 gone, But grief returns
10699 and vain; Grief for awhile
11354 of tears, Grief with a
11545 After long grief and pain
11719 black with grief eternal
12252 idle is Has most of grief.

griefs
714 and cutteth griefs in halves.
727 are their griefs and fears.
2366 keep his griefs in their
5059 solitary griefs, Desolate
5169 Of all the griefs that
10453 But not my griefs; still am

grievance
6649 doon offte gret greuaunce.
6945 From grievances

grieve
386 parting grieve thee, And
3024 suffer, than a nation grieve.
8465 down and grieve. Find

grieved
12800 And much it grieved my heart

grin
2113 he seems to grin, How
8723 And ev're grin, so merry,

grind
6460 of God grind slowly,

grip
11406 hand With a grip that kills

gristle
6708 yet in the gristle, and it

groan
5498 each other groan; Where

groans
6606 are the groans of love to

grooves
11535 the ringing grooves of change.

grope
3167 How do I work? I grope.

gross
8139 income with my gross habits.
12003 Gross National Product is

groucho
7993 - tendance Groucho. I am a

ground
136 here on the ground while
1500 Ground control to Major Tom.
6020 Grammer, the ground of al.
7062 which drags me to the ground.
8324 the dark and bloody ground.
9992 for the ground. It makes
10222 patch of ground, That hath
11040 was when I hit the ground.
12278 feet on the ground and I'll

group
141 - a group of men who

grouse
1957 they form a group that's
5796 the group-mind takes

grouse
3265 grouse against

grove
7918 And for groves, O! a

grovelled
11642 man he grovelled before

groves
1777 In the groves of their

grow
877 best chance to grow up.
919 We grow neither better nor
1668 Grow old along with me!
4301 man, and grow up with
11590 soul, And grow for ever
12025 of us never grow out of it.

growed
11241 I s'pect I growed. Don't

growing
6265 Growing up is after all only

growl
5124 sit and growl ; let him

grown
3521 Grown up, and that is a
7908 kids - they've all grown up.
11176 When I am grown to man's
12729 exist to be grown out of.

grownups
4125 Unlike grownups, children have
9815 Grownups never understand

grows
3093 from the soil he grows in.
8708 an artist once he grows up.
11088 universe, grows beyond his
11681 Nothing grows in our
12672 either grows or swells,

growth
1 Growth for the sake of
3313 force growth and make
5996 have their growth, their
6110 that it is growth rather
8167 Growth is the only evidence
10811 all genuine growth in the

grubbing
5698 lives At grubbing weeds from

grudge
339 or too fresh the grudge.
8328 will never grudge a
11249 wretch had a grudge against.

grumbling
3265 a piece of rhythmical grumbling.

grundy
6443 God - And more of Mrs Grundy.

grunt
8414 and grunt. Speech

guard
6574 be on his guard, if he
7439 changing guard at

guarded
4197 to be ever guarded is scarce

guardian
11792 As guardian of His majesty's
12629 Be thou my Guardian and my

guardians
7327 good grey guardians of art

guards
2021 The Guards die but do not

guerilla
6974 The guerilla must live amongst

guess
5415 Medical Men guess: if they
9862 through to guess about what

guessing
12360 I called guessing what was

guest
2717 guest in a

guests
198 to be good guests, how to
952 classes: hosts and guests.
10265 Unbidden guests Are often

guide
252 and be thy guide, In thy
2630 child, and guide of fools,
7760 my virtue's guide: In part

guidelines
1450 Guidelines for bureaucrats: (1)

guiding-star
7957 he was the guiding-star of a whole

guilt
769 joyously and without guilt.
1401 Guilt: the gift that goes
4199 art can wash her guilt away?
4671 they don't feel guilt.
5917 True guilt is guilt at the
10926 of war, without its guilt.
11205 circumstance of guilt.
11287 without its guilt, and only

guiltless
1295 only are guiltless

guilty
1316 that ten guilty persons
2498 to be guilty of it.
5370 No guilty man is acquitted
6750 but to be guilty, God is
7138 I can feel guilty about the
8394 be judged guilty until they
9676 is already guilty; true
10268 haunts the guilty mind; The
10313 - we make guilty of our own

guinea
1808 is but the guinea's stamp,
11528 of the guinea helps the

guinea pigs
12632 all of us guinea pigs in the

guinness
7961 Guinness is good for you.

guitar
238 sound, and guitar music is
11140 have a blue guitar, You do

gull
7137 To the gull's way and

gulled
1856 will be gulled, let it be

gullet
7409 This is the gullet of New

gum
12857 is chewing gum for the

gun
998 The Maxim Gun, and they
3187 Every gun that is made,
4867 was founded on the gun.
6231 happiness is a warm gun.
12406 "Is that a gun in your

gunga din
5701 better man than I am, Gunga Din!

gunpowder
280 November, Gunpowder Treason
2085 Gunpowder, Printing,

guns
4077 without guns. If we
4078 butter or guns? ..
5750 when the guns begin to
7933 got the guns but we got
9320 a hundred men with guns.

gunshot
3694 in play far out of gunshot.

gut
11754 full of gut and
12397 takes more gut and

gutless
8389 a sort of gutless Kipling.

guts
2162 The guts carry the feet,
2708 to have the guts to be

gutter
8361 from the gutter and don't
12569 all in the gutter, but some

guys
3119 Nice guys. Finish last.
9710 Guys and dolls.

gypsy
3896 bring out the gypsy in me!

habit
4680 a desperate habit, and one
7164 deadening effect of a habit.
7199 than a bad habit which a
8796 is long-standing habit.
9217 Habit is second nature.
9407 you reap a habit. Sow a
9493 fidelity of an old habit.
9799 of category habits by
9877 Habit is stronger than
12023 look that becomes a habit.

habitation
10422 A local habitation and a

habits
2974 but the habits he has
3046 Ill habits gather by unseen
7872 Small habits, well pursued
8139 income with my gross habits.
8244 without habits, a life
11155 never as effective as habits.
12241 and my other habits are good.

habituation
6954 Habituation is a falling asleep

hack
7744 Do not hack me as you did

hackles
11135 tan with henna hackles, halt!

hades
12127 realms of Hades.

haggis
8417 - head, heart and haggis.

hail
7557 dwells; hail horrors,
10020 Hail to the chief who in
12388 Hail, the heaven-born

hair
3597 light brown hair, Floating,
5455 child Her hair was long,
7921 with hair. The
8945 us with a single hair.
9637 Her hair that lay along
9642 one strangling golden hair.
9937 Hair is another name for

haircut
12715 you get a haircut; you look

hairy
193 a small hairy individual

hale
11291 I should prefer mild hale.

half
1098 cheeriness, Half dead and
2678 The first half of our
2974 the second half of a man's
4185 blow is half the
8299 not that I half knew my
9836 Too clever by half.
11486 Half light, half shade,
12445 more than half of the

half-a-crown
4429 bar is, Or help to half-a-crown.

half-brother
793 thou half-brother of the

half-buried
6487 hound, Half-buried in the

half-create
12798 what they half-create, And what

half-human
5603 bard, this half-human visitor to

half-mental
1094 cent of this game is half-mental.

half-truth
7156 is a half-truth so stated
9193 A half-truth is a whole lie.

half-way
6700 ha'e nae hauf-way hoose, but
9291 The Half-Way House to Rome,

half-wit
6943 smile of a half-wit: an animal

half-witted
11103 . an old half-witted sheep Which

hallow
10876 Great men hallow a whole

halo
12748 a luminous halo, a

halve
4460 book would halve the sales.

ham'n eggs
4228 have your ham'n eggs in

hamlet
874 want him (Hamlet') to be so
4413 said that Hamlet is the
7151 Hamlet is the tragedy of
8331
12871 to produce Hamlet .

hammer
6516 either be anvil or hammer.
9287 it's the 'ammer, 'ammer,
11715 With His hammer of wind,

hammered
5683 being hammered, hammered,
9183 sticks out is hammered down.
10594 getting well hammered yourself.

hamsters
1275 tigress surrounded by hamsters.

hand
65 The hand that makes us
1168 thy left hand know what
1580 With hand made sure,
1811 there's a hand, my trusty
3343 of the hand unless the
3900 Your tiny hand is frozen.
3906 and a hand to
4282 From whose hand it came?
4454 put your hand into the
4868 impersonal hand of
5250 My strict hand Was made to
6156 spoon; And hand in hand,
7639 They hand in hand, with
8233 offers his hand too
9740 which the hand, the head,
10382 The hand that hath made
10748 from hand to hand of
11472 a vanished hand, And the
11672 The hand that signed the
12195 For the hand that rocks
12326 engine, your white hand.
12405 man a free hand and he'll
12655 I think with my right hand.

handbook
5664 constable's handbook - an

handel
10793 they to the tunes of Handel.

handicap
2274 Of my two 'handicaps', being
2674 the first handicap to any

handicraft
9916 sphere of handicraft and placed

handiwork
5322 above his handiwork,

handkerchief
6734 like a damp handkerchief and
7976 the germs in your handkerchief.

handle
356 Some people handle the truth
1804 happiness you can handle.
10351 me, The handle toward my

handles
6135 are no handles to a

handmaid
685 are a good handmaid, but the

hands
711 fortune is in his own hands.
5227 in whatever hands it is
5927 what hands you would
8261 and shaking hands, I want to
9671 Creator's hands;
10399 not a Jew hands, organs,
11457 union of hands and
11493 nearer than hands and feet.
11671 Hands have not tears to

handshakes
875 by secret handshakes than by

handsome
3427 others more handsome by far,
9158 Truth has a handsome
10411 Looks handsome in three

hang
1277 I will neither go nor hang!
3639 indeed all hang together,
5255 peach Hang on thy
5677 come to hang you, lad:
7730 Paris| they hang a man
8985 Hang it all, Robert
10235 Go hang thyself in thine
10519 Go, hang yourselves all!

hanged
4381 Men are not hanged for
5210 he is to be hanged in a
8625 Harrison hanged, drawn,
9941 Men are not hanged for

hanging
1733 Hanging is too good for him,
3449 Hanging and marriage, you
4612 destiny, and hanging likewise.
5312 and the hanging garments
5691 - they're hanging him
7796 not deserve hanging ten times
10510 Many a good hanging prevents a

hangman
5046 or even a hangman, there are

hangs
7068 He hangs in shades the
11205 What hangs people .. is

happen
626 may happen to you was
1838 things happen their own
4066 see what's going to happen.
4581 few things happen at the
5757 that didn't happen has never
6316 It can't happen here.
7233 has not happened, and

happened
4969 things after they've happened.
11151 funny thing happened to me on
11990 whether it had happened or not.
12485 a thing has happened with so

happens
4899 is not what happens to a man.
7823 pleasant happens to you,
10596 Everything happens to

happier
3890 I feel happier now that
4951 are often happier than the
7602 ye seek No happier state, and
8278 day makes that day happier.
11962 infinitely happier if we

happiest
1283 The happiest time in any man's
3213 The happiest women, like the
10680 best and happiest moments of
11411 The fools are the happiest.

happily
1452 He was happily married -
7270 matter how happily a woman

happiness
45 The happiness of society is the
635 often is happiness destroyed
642 recipe for happiness I ever
799 Happiness is a small and
832 All happiness depends on
870 secret of happiness is not in
957 owe their happiness chiefly to
1050 greatest happiness of the
1120 but the happiness of the
1699 the highest happiness?'
1710 Happiness comes more from
1799 ruin of all happiness! There's
1804 Happiness? A good cigar, a
2607 only true happiness comes from
2609 Happiness depends, as Nature
3050 For all the happiness mankind
3282 my people's happiness and their
3329 the hour - that is happiness.
3397 one way to happiness and that
3419 Happiness is brief It will not
3692 Happiness makes up in height
3790 is essential to human happiness.
4127 enjoy his happiness in silence
4225 that happiness is a way
4359 All happiness depends on a
4855 The supreme happiness of life is
4906 about somebody else's happiness.
4913 Who gain a happiness in eyeing
4962 is that: Happiness is the
5022 and the pursuit of happiness.
5083 Happiness consists in the
5088 so much happiness is
5127 to human happiness; it
5156 species of happiness, and,
5188 much as the happiness of his
5389 Happiness is not an ideal of
5528 true happiness. It is
6231 because happiness is a warm
6728 the cult of happiness is
7032 Happiness comes fleetingly now
7033 Happiness is the interval
7081 Withdraws into its happiness.
7182 character; happiness does that
7204 Happiness is the light on the
7383 do without happiness; it is
7808 Happiness, for you we walk on a
8177 complete happiness is to be
8194 Happiness is not wanting to be
8279 a job. Happiness or
8318 Happiness to a dog is what lies
8610 at once his happiness and his
8907 Oh Happiness! our being's end
9404 right to happiness or to be
9424 don't have happiness, you send
9448 to find happiness in
9672 Happiness: a good bank account,
9744 indispensable part of happiness.
9748 at contributes to happiness.
9759 most fatal to true happiness.
9872 of happiness, if one
9878 Happiness is the only sanction
9883 is the beginning of happiness.
9914 greatest happiness you can
9957 will of man is his happiness.
9979 is human happiness in the
9997 Happiness? That's nothing more
10387 is no mean happiness,
10582 to consume happiness without
10613 lifetime of happiness! No man
10664 Happiness is essentially a
11248 Happiness is the perpetual
11388 Happiness is an imaginary
11435 of as much happiness as is good
11492 The happiness of a man in this
12428 Happiness is no laughing
12527 Man's happiness springs mainly

happy
1136 count them happy which
1700 you are as happy, my dear
2044 To be happy, we must not be
2532 to make happy rather
3070 Happy the man, and happy he
3470 so as to be happy, let us at
3846 How happy could I be with
3862 to be very happy, can never
4017 lot is not a happy one.
4027 For A is happy - B is
4151 How happy he who crowns
4479 doing something to be happy.
4558 never be happy again; He
5067 one's wife happy. One is
5092 should be u happy than that
5098 would be as happy in the
5473 me at all happy without
5813 we can't be happy, we must
5870 examine how happy they are,
5904 never as u happy as one
6038 are to be happy in: Where
6981 sure that he is not happy.
7101 who wants a happy marriage
7257 somewhere, may be happy.
7358 you are happy, and you
8809 life is happy, chiefly
8844 Oh happy state! when souls
8902 learn'd is happy nature to
8918 To make men happy, and to
8933 Happy the man, whose wish
9096 Make happy those who are
9764 it, is a happy life. I
9993 and yet I'm happy. I can't
10000 be really happy are those
10092 The happy man is he who
10914 Call no man happy before he
10957 'tis the happy who have
11201 as the duty of being happy.

11334 'Tis happy for him, that
11443 days, A happy English
12014 to make you happy.
12060 Happy those early days,
12246 us all be happy, and live
12707 of the happy is quite

harbinger
7635 evening star, Love's harbinger.

hard
1210 are too hard for thee,
1857 is not hard, To be a
1880 It is hard to come down
3131 .. it's a hard rain's a
4374 is awfully hard to get it
5666 'Tis the hard grey weather
6227 It's been a hard day's
6694 make life hard for all
11593 woman is so hard Upon the

hard-faced
817 a lot of hard-faced men who

harden
1817 But och! it hardens a'
7762 told, We harden like

harder
2633 something harder to shock.
7809 is nothing harder than the
8780 The harder you work, the

hardship
8550 of the hardship of his

hardships
3681 his son the hardships that made

hardware
4827 coming out of a hardware store.

hardy
8132 Kiss me, Hardy.

hare
575 Happy the hare at morning,
6103 and a hare sitting

hark
513 Hark! ah, the Nightingale!

harlot
1985 harlot we have
5721 of the harlot throughout

harlow
541 is silent - as in Harlow'.

harm
2552 said ever did me any harm.
3229 Half of the harm that is
4623 be kept from doing harm.
6017 that moost harm wercheth
6231 do me no harm because
7183 man for the harm he does
7367 to prevent harm to others.
7944 may do you extreme harm.
8256 should do the sick no harm.
9768 supposed to do no harm.
10364 born Shall harm Macbeth.
11434 What harm have I ever done
12948 that more harm is done by

harmful
12474 is above all things harmful.

harmless
2956 The only harmless great
8782 Harmless thunderbolts.

harmonies
4302 who uses harmonies instead of

harmonious
5918 no longer harmonious, we have
6197 and most harmonious and
10711 know, Such harmonious madness

harmony
119 the harmony of the
5933 disposed to harmony. But
12824 grows Like harmony in music;

harp
7856 The harp that once through
7859 his wild harp slung
11554 one clear harp in divers

harpic
1030 As I read the Harpic tin.

harpists
283 Harpists spend half their life

harridan
4805 was the harridan I married.

harry
10257 'God for Harry! England
10260 touch of Harry in the

harshness
8879 enough no harshness gives

harvard
4794 is to send a son to Harvard.
7243 Yale College and my Harvard.
7846 the glass flowers at Harvard'.

harvest
5042 and she laughs with a harvest.
8679 the bite of a harvest apple.
9089 is the season of the harvest.
12822 The harvest of a quiet eye

harvesting
3731 resources we're not harvesting.

harvests
3667 generation harvests the dragon

hashish
9473 I puffed hashish, but I

haste
1248 that maketh haste to be rich
2645 make what haste I can to
4611 The more haste, the less
7608 looks in haste She turns,
10104 The haste of a fool is the
10384 Haste still pays haste, and
11695 marrying in haste, and
12393 always in haste, I am

hasten
1391 Hasten slowly, and without
11273 lente. Hasten slowly.

hat
143 a woman with his hat on.
7971 to get ahead, get a hat.
12306 come out of an empty hat.
12572 the right hat to wear on

hatch
10775 - you'll hatch out

hatched
98 before they are hatched.

hatches
5482 under hatches .. Rain!

hatching
7571 here Hatching vain

hate
472 and to hate the things
718 roughness breedeth hate.
1155 to them which hate you.
1238 his rod hateth his son.
1932 not be to hate, mankind
2478 We hate some persons
2522 Hate is the consequence of
3343 I hate the giving of the
3344 I hate quotations.
3711 and hate what's
3877 I hate all Boets and
4405 eight, To hate all the
4604 If you hate a person, you
5641 Don't hate, it's too big a
6083 God, how I hate them!
6819 were, to hate your
7049 and Envy's raging hate.
7208 Hate is not the opposite
7264 I hate all sports as
7278 Women hate revolutions and
7350 There's no hate lost
7839 town and hate each other
8050 I hate like death the
8135 you must hate a
8271 Those who hate you don't
9427 and without reason we hate.
10079 injured, they also hate.
10151 In time we hate that which
10587 is not to hate them, but
11323 I hate and detest
11338 to make us hate, but not
11397 nature to hate the man
12004 Hate is such a luxurious
12524 love is not hate, it's

hated
3769 I never hated a man enough

8901 As, to be hated, needs but
11309 Hated by fools, and fools

hateful
4999 to the eye, hateful to the
8545 The self is hateful.
12342 A hateful act is the

hates
1886 what a man hates, provided
5405 every poet hates in spite
7913 He who hates vice hates
9507 authority, Hates a
9661 Any man who hates dogs and

hating
1043 he'll end up hating you.
3827 consists in hating all other
8096 a fool, But hating, my boy,
9825 Hating anything in the way

hatless
1097 man lands hatless from the
6036 Hatless, I take off My

hatred
830 Hatred is self-punishment.
1110 burning hatred for the
1976 Now hatred is by far the
2356 Hatred is settled anger.
3426 curable hatred is that
3653 Hatred of Judaism is at
3667 seeds of hatred sown by
4076 mind with perpetual hatred.
4312 Hatred seems to operate on
4656 Passionate hatred can give
5884 more like hatred than like
8391 up with hatred, jealousy,
9349 to feel any hatred for him.
9976 Hatred comes from the heart;
10076 the power to endure hatred.
10602 Hatred is the coward's
11813 of hatred is almost

hatreds
9367 Hatreds are the cinders of
9797 and no real hatreds. Blessed

hats
1099 their hats Come
12366 bad hats in my
12490 Hats divide generally into

haughtily
11316 How haughtily he lifts his

haughtiness
3369 a certain haughtiness. He can

haughty
1241 and an haughty spirit
7472 An old and haughty nation
9680 this that haughty, gallant,

haunt
8865 glide, And haunt the places

haunted
1068 constantly haunted by fears
6006 sea, A haunted town it is
8198 I am haunted by mental decay

haunts
11473 I come from haunts of coot

have
872 If you have it, you
1455 miss, not what you have.
4457 will ever have for
8157 on what we have, since we
9607 what you have, where you
10314 Have more than thou
12666 got to have We plot to

have to
11716 you have to go round.

having
5005 based on having are less
12861 Never satisfied with having.

havoc
10286 Cry, Havoc!' and let slip

hawk
1951 But, like a hawk encumbered
10208 I know a hawk from a

hazard
194 hazard of being a
1817 sin; The hazard of

hazards
7061 The hazards of computing are
7940 underwater hazards through

haze
4537 Purple haze is in my brain

hazy
8400 is so hazy, he really

he
6229 I am he As you are me

head
658 is in my head; to put it
1560 to give them their head.
2114 on your head- Do you
2128 to get one's head cut off.
3276 you shorter by the head.
3283 but for your good head.
3632 into his head, no one
4158 one small head could
4205 have his head examined.
4539 chance My head is bloody,
5706 put his head down close
6044 Inside your head, and
6903 in my head than in my
9537 inside my head. The
11583 O good grey head which all

head-in-air
4668 there, Little Johnny Head-In-Air!

headache
3978 a dismal headache, and

headland
5734 On dune and headland sinks the

headlight
2842 is the headlight of an

headline
8426 they will headline that

headlong
7564 but was headlong sent With

headmaster
2303 Headmasters have powers at their

heads
1507 to use them in men's heads.
1718 all the heads in the
6150 live; Their heads are green,

headstrong
5527 may be headstrong, but it

heal
1154 Physician, heal thyself.
9363 artist is to heal the soul.
12464 they who heal us of

healed
10399 diseases, healed by the

healer
3869 and not as healers with a
9702 powerful healer of them

healing
3 tumour; And healing
585 Let the healing fountain

heals
3627 God heals, and the doctor
5648 It is a sword that heals.

health
23 Health is the thing that
1376 His health, his
1422 And there is no health in us.
2930 you have both it's health.
3643 fatal to health than an
4149 Where health and plenty
4372 yet met a healthy person
6539 steep, When healths and
7773 in the health even of
7975 seriously damage your health.
9122 men when in the worst health.
9997 more than health and a poor

healthy
1525 healthy man, the
1707 It is not healthy when a
8224 One is healthy when one can
10880 it is a kind of healthy grave.
11761 'Tis healthy to be sick
12457 otherwise healthy adult than

heap
7065 But a rude heap together
10723 I was struck all of a heap.
10913 one common heap, whence

hear
102 men prefer not to hear.
607 Hear the other side.
1161 ears to hear, let him
1875 who do not wish to hear it.
2901 come when you will hear me.
3395 that we may hear from
3663 shall also hear of
4465 could they hear all that
4493 You will hear more good
4801 if people ever hear of him.
6002 tho' none hear Beside the
9104 I hear and I forget. I
9653 a first hearing, and I
10720 sure to hear of it from
11763 speak, and another to hear.
11797 I hear a voice you cannot
12629 Guide, And hear me when I

heard
3618 what you heard, not what
3821 inch - and I will be heard!
4026 generally heard, and if it
4492 never have been heard of.
4870 right to be heard does not
5261 man that heard him was,
7345 I never heard Of any true
7613 name Is heard no more in
8954 Have you heard it's in the
9299 The more he heard, the less
12455 never heard of either
12618 the more heard. The eye

hearing
7094 of the best hearing aids a man

hears
4453 If a man hears much that a
7807 and half his that hears it.
8576 too nearly hears The music
9005 One hears about life all
12787 the noisy world Hears least.
12839 She neither hears nor sees;

heart
173 he is man only by the heart.
199 makes the heart grow
505 The same heart beats in
614 do so with all your heart.
687 than in the heart of Man.
854 our last muscle - the heart.
1021 Bury my heart at Wounded
1080 - And my heart beats so
1243 A merry heart doeth good
1250 A man after his own heart.
1279 take their heart in one
1482 And the heart but one;
1581 laughing heart's long
1656 She had A heart - how shall
1684 great no heart .. if I
1718 A good heart is better than
1822 My heart's in the
1993 Though the heart be still
2101 the human heart, is there
2238 eye to the heart that does
2373 before. My heart has left
2568 with all my heart there will
2709 to the collective heart.
2769 where my heart was; And
2811 the human heart that had
2825 up the Heart And
2938 breaks not, it is my heart.
3011 we the Heart of England
3183 solitude of the heart.
3309 private heart is true
3431 But the heart line on my
3525 how much a heart can hold.
3598 where my heart is turning
3820 Heart of oak are our ships,
3906 he had a heart to
3937 Till in my heart the
4101 is gone, My heart is heavy.
4403 Paris Her heart was warm
4750 in your heart, you have
4789 not your heart away; Give
4864 The heart of man is made to
5246 mine eyes, but not my heart.
5279 Fourteen heart attacks and
5325 to your heart - Sleep on
5339 yes and his heart was going
5491 leaves a heart

5729 giving your heart to a dog
5770 tears out the heart of it.
5888 always fooled by the heart.
6062 Follow your heart, and you
6263 of the heart is absurd.
6473 in the heart of a
6504 With a heart for any
6640 of the heart alone make
6641 your heart clings to
6653 As my poor heart doth
6756 My heart is a lonely hunter
6835 A broken heart lies here.
6928 mine heart will not
7118 'Calais' lying in my heart.
7124 still my heart has wings
7662 But the heart of the
7852 No, the heart that has
8516 ease the heart Like a
8542 The heart has its reasons
8828 and a heart of lead.
8955 My heart belongs to Daddy.
9108 smiling, but is the heart?
9156 the mother by the heart.
9316 time! The heart demands
9470 plotting heart in the
9471 A feeling heart is a
9545 tongue. My heart keeps open
9642 round his heart one
9674 when the heart is better
9740 and the heart of man go
9816 with the heart that one
9908 share the heart and hand
9923 in a man's heart, the gods
9952 is like the heart muscle's
10030 or wound a heart that's
10102 language of the heart.
10191 break, my heart, for I
10231 me in thy heart, Absent
10267 than a heart untainted!
10294 then burst his mighty heart.
10350 the false heart doth know.
10400 Or in the heart, or in the
10603 Irishman's heart is nothing
10674 mourn A heart grown
10753 hath my heart and I have
10755 in thy heart and
10924 through the heart of every
11272 Of every heart: It pains
11361 has ached with a heart!
11425 I writ; My heart did do it,
11462 Makes the heart break.
11483 Because my heart is pure.
11673 of the heart Push in
11714 What heart could have
11719 of my heart, In every
11894 the cold of heart or the
11975 his private heart no man
12009 The heart prefers to move
12048 you her heart, you can
12081 wound my heart with a
12514 Indian Summer of the heart!
12778 that mighty heart is lying
12790 My heart leaps up when I
12799 betray The heart that loved
12845 And then my heart with
12881 and bone shop of the heart.
12898 Is hid in the heart of love.
12900 womb A fanatic heart.

heart-break
3938 feel the heart-break in the

heart-easing
5512 tell the most heart-easing things.

hearth
12043 a blazing hearth in one's

hearth-fire
5730 And the hearth-fire and the

hearts
1249 that be of heavy hearts.
1577 with Splendid Hearts may go.
2801 in people's hearts but I
3125 .. True hearts have ears
3973 Hearts just as pure and fair
4387 Two hearts that beat
5870 we set our hearts too much
6176 in the hearts of his
6501 And our hearts, though
6542 lay paved with broken hearts.

6547 Two hearts that beat
7642 draw Hearts after them
7856 o'er; And hearts, that once
8068 their hearts and minds
9645 we to our hearts, for
9788 Our hearts were drunk with a
10802 of their hearts for sins
11457 union of hands and hearts.
11506 but our hearts are great.
11517 good. Kind hearts are more
12122 drive human hearts, cursed
12324 women's hearts So far
12785 they whose hearts are dry as

heat
10877 Heat, ma'am! It was so
12053 stand the heat, get out
12327 neither heat nor light.

heathen
5692 The 'eathen in 'is blindness
5693 The 'eathen in 'is blindness

heaven
53 And all of heaven we have
115 into Heaven ever hope
866 Heaven for climate, hell for
1080 Heaven - I'm in Heaven - And
1181 into the kingdom of heaven.
1187 Heaven and earth shall pass
1325 sand And a heaven in a wild
1603 quincunx of heaven runs low,
1631 death, One heaven, one hell.
1735 from the gates of Heaven.
2000 light Which heaven to gaudy
2513 Heaven has no rage, like
2746 his own by-way to heaven.
2832 we know of heaven, And all
3300 the way to heaven, to be as
3678 concept of heaven is, they
3949 as near to heaven by sea as
4136 hell, you will be in heaven.
4304 Heaven is the place where
4373 things in heaven and earth
4783 day when heaven was
5226 allot and all to Heaven
5238 is the consent of heaven!
5385 the starry heaven above me
5519 fair And open face of heaven.
5848 and heaven will help
5920 god who remembers heaven
6018 For if hevene be on this
6024 out from heaven the beam
6028 Heaven and Earth are not
6181 a kind of heaven to be
6221 there's no heaven, It's easy
6273 raised to heaven Is the
6451 to take you to heaven.
6658 are made in heaven and
6782 cuts to Heaven, only the
6992 be hell that are not heaven.
7507 bring all heaven before
7534 While the heaven-born-child
7555 all-ruling heaven Left him
7556 change for heaven, this
7557 Can make a heaven of hell, a
7589 Warring in heaven against
7611 shadow of heaven, and
7613 Is heard no more in heaven.
7617 Heaven is for thee too high
7634 or short permit to heaven.
7638 under heaven, all
7881 as nigh heaven as my own?
7882 to go to heaven in
8142 is dead! Heaven is empty -
8146 the port o' Heaven, An' drum
8840 Is it, in heav'n, a crime to
9097 If heaven made him, earth
10006 future of man is my heaven.
10025 For love is heaven, and
10194 way to heaven, Whiles,
10218 thoughts never to heaven go.
10641 to be in heaven is to
10707 That from Heaven, or near
10827 But; Heaven will
10969 their place in heaven also.
10980 you, Heaven would be
11190 I seek, the heaven above And
11322 If Heaven had looked upon
11352 flowerless fields of heaven.
11728 O'er heaven and earth, far

11981 cigars in heaven, I shall
12230 be given, Heaven was in
12644 better in heaven, my friend
12789 to be young was very heaven!

heavenly
4129 ye not, ye heavenly powers.
12112 anger in those heavenly minds?

heavens
12280 done though the heavens fall.

heaventree
5338 The heaventree of stars hung

heavier
6295 age, weighs heavier in the

heaviness
1235 son is the heaviness of his

heavy
698 gains make heavy purses.
1249 that be of heavy hearts.
10409 doth make a heavy husband.

hedge
5138 a clipped hedge is to a

hedgehogs
5620 throwing hedgehogs under me.

hedges
11327 tongues, and hedges ears.

heels
7 Time wounds all heels.

heffalump
7451 decided to catch a Heffalump.

height
3692 makes up in height for what
6243 years old is half his height.

heights
1404 raises me to infinite heights.
6493 The heights by great men
12070 great heights only by

heir
11534 I the heir of all the
11848 be the sole heir of the

heir-apparent
10235 in thine own heir-apparent garters!

helen
6993 Sweet Helen, make me
8808 Helen, thy beauty is to me
9681 Like Helen, in the night

helicopters
1378 shot From helicopters, the boy

hell
93 Hell to ships, hell to
285 Hell is truth seen too
794 Hell is more bearable than
866 climate, hell for
1086 Hell, madame, is to love
1359 builds a Hell in
1735 a way to Hell, even from
1847 that's his hell: another
1851 women, and hell for
1931 to quick bosoms is a hell.
2676 places in hell are
2832 And all we need of hell.
2851 I go to hell?' 'No,'
2975 What is hell? I maintain
3225 What is hell? Hell is
3551 and the hell of horses.
4136 to love hell, you will
4304 his carrot: hell is the
4890 A belief in hell and the
6213 Old age is woman's hell.
6221 you try, No hell below us,
6302 road to Hell is the
6451 going to hell. It isn't
6470 Oh hell, say that I am
6597 I myself am hell, nobody's
6992 Hell hath no limits nor is
7034 go through hell to get it.
7209 world can go to hell.
7271 to go to hell without
7539 And hell itself will pass
7557 profoundest hell Receive
7564 crew to build in hell.
7573 that out of hell leads up
7578 out Death! Hell trembled
7604 not all hell broke
7609 the injured lover's hell.

8750 gates of Hell - but no
8993 eye-deep in hell believing
9784 the pit of hell and is not
9925 Hell is other people.
10613 it would be hell on earth.
10639 working definition of hell.
10641 to be in hell is to
10698 Hell is a city much like
10734 but, boys, it is all hell.
10969 said that hell is paved
10980 bear, And Hell would not
11209 to go to hell in such a
11237 the news and raise hell.
11251 connected with it to hell.
11477 Into the mouth of Hell.
11904 public| hell. I just
12128 relent, I shall move Hell.
12352 Hell is not other people,
12626 Hell is indefinite.

hell fire
9364 should be hell fire and sparks

hell-broth
10362 Like a hell-broth boil and

hellhound
12711 you like, a hellhound is always

help
97 The gods help them that
131 with the help of too
240 present help in time of
571 on earth to help others;
1429 present help in
5847 People must help one
5848 t'aidera. Help yourself,
6084 They look on and help.
6228 a little help from my
6369 who has a heart to help.
6669 When other helpers fail,
7818 Worrying helps you some.
8854 To help me through this
11444 Who ran to help me when I
12292 God, our help in ages

helping
5663 at whiles, Helping, when we
12255 without helping himself.

helpless
1360 I leapt: Helpless, naked,
3357 baby - so helpless and

hen
1881 A hen is only an egg's
5615 better take a wet hen.
9266 where the hen crows and

henry viii
2666 Henry VIII had so many wives

heraldry
4291 boast of heraldry, the pomp

herb
11875 from the herb at your

herbs
7516 Of herbs, and other country

herd-instinct
8216 is the herd-instinct in the

herds
9245 not enjoy fame in two herds.

herdsman
12885 And God the herdsman goads them

here
366 Here's tae us; wha's like
372 The buck stops here.
377 We're here because we're
968 We're here because we're
3993 Here's a state of things!
5540 the man is here; tomorrow
6770 j'y reste. Here I am, and
6904 well, I am here - I am
7969 I'm only here for the
11725 Here lies a man who never

hereditary
8341 with an hereditary ill that

heredity
1741 Heredity is nothing but stored
4687 Heredity is an omnibus in

heresies
1545 alive by heresies, which are

heresy
16 is no worse heresy than that
10648 believes be heresy? It is a

heretic
10527 It is a heretic that makes
12954 Heretics are the only bitter

heritage
1571 we have come into our heritage.
5566 our ancient heritage - and

hermit
5462 torment than a hermit's fast.

hermitage
6540 That for an hermitage; If I have

hero
3346 Every hero becomes a bore
3347 A hero is no braver than
3516 Show me a hero and I will
3654 A hero is a man who stands
4108 no man is a hero to his
6045 before The hero arrives,
6894 a hero is a man
7886 conquering hero comes!
8892 of all, A hero perish, or
8963 a villain, Millions a hero.
9562 of being a hero, about the
9563 Being a hero is about the
11236 don't want to be a hero.

heroes
3578 a few heroes stuck
4511 When the heroes go off the
5058 Heroes are created by
6303 favoured heroes attain -
6415 country for heroes to live
7295 Thoughts of heroes were as
7710 the movie heroes are in the
12416 do not make heroes or

heroic
3727 to demand a heroic heart as
4628 In a truly heroic life there
5001 to make heroic decisions
6507 of good, Heroic womanhood.

heroically
7670 Samson, and heroically hath

hertford
6257 In Hertford, Hereford, and

hesitates
9352 wavers, she hesitates. In a

hesitation
11424 yeast, salt and hesitation.

hesperus
5243 keep: Hesperus entreats

heterodoxy
12240 is my doxy; heterodoxy is another

heterogeneity
10987 a definite coherent heterogeneity.

hew
8929 to hew blocks

hi diddle
12275 Hi diddle dee dee (an actor's

hid
8873 laws lay hid in night.
10394 murder cannot be hid long.
11706 of tears I hid from Him,

hidden
2388 can never remain hidden.
3955 eyes, Hidden, ever and
6039 something hidden from us
8456 The hidden persuaders.

hide
1032 trying to hide anything,
7480 But he that hides a dark
7505 Hide me from day's garish
8944 woe; To hide the fault
10179 it is to hide the sparks
10509 a world to hide virtues
11837 me, Let me hide myself in

hideous
7926 of the hideous town;

hierarchy
8671 In a hierarchy every employee

high
2566 true to their high calling.
3500 a permanently high plateau.
7617 thee too high To know

high flyer
8632 and no high flyer, as he

high heels
8401 their high heels, banging

high mass
6851 on her return from High Mass.

high-mindedness
1520 and honourable high-mindedness.

high-tech
4644 thing with high-tech is that

highbrow
4559 A highbrow is the kind of
7159 A highbrow is a person
12191 What is a highbrow? He is a

higher
9037 Stuart or Nassau go higher?
10752 shall shoot higher than who
11554 dead selves to higher things.

highest
9584 The highest and most lofty
10985 is the highest form of

highlands
1822 in the Highlands, my heart

highway
4444 for us a highway between a

hill
2768 beyond the hill lies
8194 or over the next hill.
12854 be on a hill, or on

hills
5635 out on the hills alone. A

hillside
9456 on the hillside .. And

him
11512 I found Him in the

himself
826 about himself and called
1061 is demolished but by himself.
5843 and does not know himself.
6561 party - an' that is himself.
8035 can stand himself. He can
8859 And he himself one vile
9696 of us must do it for himself.

hind
10140 The hind that would be

hindrance
2364 a positive hindrance to those

hindrances
7378 the chief hindrances to human
11751 positive hindrances to the

hindsight
12609 Hindsight is always

hindu
3799 myself a Hindu,
10686 or turns Hindoo, His best

hinges
7579 on their hinges grate
7871 principal hinges on which

hinted
9621 to be hinted that we

hip
2172 feel in my hip pocket.
6898 Hip is the sophistication

hire
1443 and some hire public
7056 are men who hire out their
7890 do. I hire him to

hirelings
9030 twenty-two hirelings kick a

hiroshima
8717 of Einstein leads to Hiroshima.

hiss
7631 universal hiss, the sound

hissing
2432 with the least hissing.

historian
3919 to the historian of the
4581 historian will
8225 The historian looks backward.
10774 by a competent historian.
11097 for a historian is to have
11245 of the historian -

historians
1878 the past, historians can; it is
4438 honoured by historians more for
8987 when the historians left
9058 Give the historians something to

historical
3230 The historical sense involves a
11828 In historical events great men -
12052 a famous historical figure who

histories
740 Histories make men wise; poets,
12141 the ancient histories, as one of

history
15 dignity and worth to history.
83 History is the sum total of
431 you wonder about history.
479 attention than history.
577 Man is a history-making
677 are history defaced,
858 Does history repeat itself,
875 More history's made by secret
1261 History, n: an account mostly
1301 dust-heap called history'.
1510 first rough draft of history.
1761 History is a pact between the
1805 The Thames is liquid history.
1889 The history of art is the
2082 History is the essence of
2136 time in the history of the
2151 History will absolve me.
2158 History doesn't pass the
2340 The whole history of the
2538 History repeats itself, but
2822 achieved in modern history.
2859 History is philosophy learned
2866 changed the history of the
2874 Read no history: nothing but
2927 History needs to be rewritten
3113 lessons of history is that
3213 nations, have no history.
3252 chapel History is now and
3304 All history is but the
3325 properly no history; only
3498 is history seen
3571 History is more or less bunk.
3587 this is why history is so
3621 summary of history to say
3814 History never looks like
3903 History .. is, indeed,
4062 of our history, one of
4344 History repeats itself.
4792 Most history is a record of
4995 deal of history to produce
5330 History, Stephen said, is a
5399 suicide note in history.
5614 it or not, history is on our
5722 traces, And history gives the
5757 The history of things that
6068 men of history are
6348 escape history .. The
6507 the great history of the
6509 the secret history of our
6521 The history of the world is
6728 moments in history, by a
6810 The history of England is
6829 below the dignity of history.
7115 The history of all hitherto
8948 There is no history of
9010 History is littered with the
9256 without history is like
9369 a modern history, shall
9533 eras in history, and to
9822 make more history than they
9959 The world's history is the
9961 The world's history is
10049 History is past politics; and
10066 History is not what you
10118 eventful history, Is second
10249 There is a history in all
10590 What will history say?
10799 I have no history but the
11047 of history teaches
11207 a thread to hang history from.
11437 History gets thicker as it
11438 History is not another name
11439 who study history, he
11440 to shape history than human
11465 British history in their

11811 History is a gallery of
11846 The history of almost every
11889 - into the dustbin of history!
12034 History is the science of
12160 Indeed, history is nothing
12376 Human history becomes more
12565 we owe to history is to
12658 me that history is on

hit
143 wouldn't hit a woman
1091 think and hit at the
9597 of making a hit every time
12962 If he is hit by a

hitler
4597 cancel out Hitler through
6550 war. Even Hitler and
8207 When Hitler attacked the
8659 Mister Hitler? If you
12927 worst, like Hitler, but he

hitting
2558 for loving and not hitting.

hive
2601 this great hive, the city.
11304 to fill our hives with

hoard
11506 Our hoard is little, but

hoarded
7485 must not be hoarded, But must

hobby
286 A hobby is hard work you

hobson
12251 one, 'Tis Hobson's choice,

hodgepodge
11018 or hodgepodge of all

hoe
5042 her with a hoe, and she
6986 Upon his hoe and gazes

hog
7422 the whole hog, you know.

hogs
6731 not be like hogs Hunted and
11138 Eat Frogs. Hogs Eat

hold
2939 God's sake hold your
10973 a woman to hold a man is

holding
3893 Holding hands at midnight
9564 A holding company is the

hole
797 of a better 'ole, go to it.
1543 to the hole when the
6055 maketh a hole in the
7396 there is a hole in the
8337 A hole is nothing at all,
9232 cat there's a hole nearby.

holey
9498 hands in holey pockets;

holiday
7517 to play On a sunshine holiday.
9756 to take a holiday would
10639 A perpetual holiday is a good

holidays
6491 of all holidays are those
10234 playing holidays, To sport

holiness
5467 but the holiness of the
7750 beauty of holiness, Bow down

holland
4741 Holland .. lies so low

hollow
3231 We are the hollow men ..
10450 within the hollow crown That

hollywood
4671 In Hollywood they don't feel
7710 years in Hollywood and I
9424 In Hollywood, if you don't have

holocaust
5553 The Holocaust is a Gentile

holy
100 I'm so holy that when I
1215 standest is holy ground.
6076 And the holy
7538 For if such holy song

8764 which is holy loved by
9436 Man makes holy what he
12154 itself the Holy Roman

homage
1617 and owes no homage unto the

home
91 A House is not a Home.
334 you get home from
503 Ages.. Home of lost
522 England, home and
645 staying at home for real
1070 America, My home sweet
1108 no place to stay home from.
1464 Boston, The home of the
2571 children to come back home.
2612 that has been kept at home!
2837 thou art, that, is Home.
2983 to found a home discovers
3572 Keep the Home-fires
3679 wouldn't have in your home.
3686 Home is the place where,
4190 country ever is, at home.
4323 be outside their own home.
4333 good of a home if you are
4616 Home James, and don't
4627 into the home - where it
4827 his own home is always
4834 it ought t' stay at home.
5323 itself my home, my
5592 you get it home, but it
7834 and returns home to find
7892 Home is not where you live
8169 and I am far from home.
8220 man has no home in Europe
8335 a computer in their home.
8517 Who live at home at ease,
8587 there's no place like home.
8848 there's nobody at home.
8993 came home, home to a
9321 to his wife away from home.
9414 get you home by nine
10109 I was at home, I was in
10835 Sated with home, of wife,
11928 Seek home for rest, For
12617 and envy are in every home.
12811 From God, who is our home.
12848 come home with me

home-fires
3572 Keep the Home-fires burning,

home-keeping
10523 Home-keeping youth have ever

homeland
2774 the more I loved my homeland.
4231 place that's warm is homeland.

homeless
1323 of people homeless on the
6111 these, the homeless,
10961 who are homeless by choice.

homely
1020 face was homely as a
1960 to a very homely household
5071 homely - even, on
8526 makes you homely, make you
10523 youth have ever homely wits.

homer
474 It is Homer who has chiefly
1060 you must not call it Homer.
11328 view In Homer more than

homes
10763 homes of the

homesick
4803 makes them homesick for
12015 you can be homesick for while

homicidal
11229 The great homicidal classics?

homo sapiens
7921 ape self-named Homo sapiens.

homogeneity
10987 incoherent homogeneity, to a

homogenized
3683 against a homogenized society

honest
379 good to be honest and true,
529 are more honest and
2159 he is only honest who is not

2743 makes an honest man a
2804 is that of being honest.
3651 entirely honest with
3753 none but honest men, must
4033 you're an honest man, or
4349 Honest women are
4963 An honest God is the noblest
5663 we will be, Honest
6254 Men are so honest, so
6585 thoroughly honest fellow
7105 if a man is honest - ask him.
7351 Though I be poor, I'm honest.
8626 A good honest and painful
10136 I am as honest as any man
10204 sir; to be honest, as this
10533 naturally honest, I am so
11228 quotable than to be honest.
11600 dine, But honest talk and
11945 the man looked honest enough.
12236 anglers, or very honest men.
12373 To be honest, one must be

honester
9400 The honester the man, the

honestly
4766 If possible honestly, if not,

honesty
1023 Honesty is as rare as a man
2806 easy - honesty most of
4952 that honesty is always
5361 Honesty's praised, then left
7028 honesty is a good thing but
7878 for saving of thine honesty.
8120 than out of the honesty.
9723 capable of honesty is the
9739 Your honesty is not to be
10492 his fault, and honesty is his.
12430 Honesty is the best policy;

honey
1216 flowing with milk and honey.
1579 is there honey still for
6178 and the sun drips honey.
7445 bear likes honey? Buzz!
12179 pouring honey into a
12285 And gather honey all the

honeysuckle
9336 roadside honeysuckle. That's

honour
287 Honour follows those who
1189 not without honour save in
1571 Honour has come back, as a
2246 Of honour and the
2913 a peace I hope with honour.
2970 martyrs and honour those whom
3032 trouble; Honour but an
3317 of his honour, the
3733 and private honour become
3806 to save his honour, his
4236 it, Till honour turned its
4260 loss of honour was a
5273 Honour! tut, a breath,
5715 take mine honour from me if
5764 Fear God. Honour the king.
6347 for the honour of the
6394 A man has honour if he holds
6411 peaks of honour we had
6544 Loved I not honour more.
6678 tribe and honour the
7017 fount whence honour springs.
7098 woman's honour .. which
8138 In honour I gained them, and
8145 prize, To honour, while you
8462 Honour is like a match, you
8865 where their honour died. See
9085 for labour - honour for risk.
9353 Honour, without money, is
9792 with honour, it is no
9972 be won; honour is
10240 Honour pricks me on. Yea,
10371 old age, As honour, love,
10443 Take honour from me, and my
10503 lord, Keeps honour bright: to
10995 air signed with their honour.
11503 His honour rooted in
11528 the hurt that Honour feels.
12716 Your honour is not my

honourable
3473 strictly honourable, as the

4776 Sweet and honourable it is to
6351 the free - honourable alike in
9262 is more honourable than the
10290 And Brutus is an honourable man.

honoured
1211 these were honoured in their
2358 an honoured old age,
11222 so long as it is honoured.

honours
471 possessing honours, but in
3817 you neither honours nor wages;
11946 to deserve honours and not

hoofbeats
10903 you hear hoofbeats, think of

hook
8429 Let your hook be always
12863 Thy baited hooks shall

hookah
5685 from the hookah-mouth.

hoover
4321 onto the board of Hoover.

hope
518 hope, still
546 is despair, hope; Where
649 or when hope is gone.
752 Hope is a good breakfast,
1408 leader is a dealer in hope.
1429 God is our hope and
1985 What is hope? nothing but
2345 his house open to hope.
2458 without hope draws
2581 of hope. That is
2600 Hope! of all ills that men
2628 He has no hope that never
2831 Hope' is the thing with
3636 lives upon hope will die
3839 is the only hope that keeps
3918 failure of hope, will
4572 Hope is the poor man's
4968 said that hope is the
5128 triumph of hope over
5156 Hope is itself a species
5871 Hope, deceitful as it is,
5880 a secret hope for
5988 man would hope no more;
6349 do we hope, fervently
6351 last, best hope of earth.
6353 With high hope for the
6632 the world is done by hope.
6660 is past hope, the heart
6805 The rising hope of those
7074 feeble Hope could
7454 of his hope to write
7549 dwell, hope never
7554 gain from hope; If not,
7656 Without all hope of day!
7686 Where no hope is left, is
8450 years, The hopelessness.
8911 Hope springs eternal in
8951 in the hope of
9859 Hope is an echo, hope ties
10379 But only hope: I have
12227 But not another's hope.
12292 past Our hope for years
12541 And what was dead was Hope.
12623 need not hope in order

hoped
1135 of things hoped for, the

hopeful
6080 but with a hopeful heart.

hopefully
11204 To travel hopefully is a better

hopeless
2372 Hopeless hope hopes on and
5158 is more hopeless than a
7569 Ages of hopeless end.
9460 Only the hopeless are starkly

hopelessness
8450 years, The hopelessness. Whatever

hopes
633 has great hopes from
4456 our fondest hopes is a
6475 all the hopes of future
9485 joys but our hopes cease.

hoppy
3293 Bowery, Hoppy, Croppy,
5316 ajog, hoppy on akkant

horace
8677 Horace's careful felicity.

horatius
6839 spake brave Horatius, The
6845 How well Horatius kept the

horde
1971 polished horde, Formed of

horizon
4399 on the far horizon will find

horizontal
583 none But the horizontal one.
2423 Life is a horizontal fall.
10586 of a horizontal desire.
12433 into an horizontal line which

horn
4277 and his horn in the
8498 come out of your horn.

hornpipes
1816 There's hornpipes and

horny
9358 I get horny for my

horny-handed
9840 Horny-handed sons of toil.

horribilis
3284 out to be an 'annus horribilis'.

horrible
12909 think it horrible that lust

horrid
5459 gloam With horrid warning
6478 she was bad she was horrid.
7510 'Mongst horrid shapes,

horrified
1896 are equally horrified at hearing

horrifying
5766 The more horrifying this world

horror
2125 'The horror of that moment,'
2998 there is no horror.
6891 The horror of the Twentieth
7398 Horror is a feeling that
7540 the scaly horror of his
9351 during the horror of a deep

horrors
10372 full with horrors; Direness,
11731 Congenial horrors, hail!

horse
488 heard no horse sing a
966 A Protestant with a horse.
2485 abuses his horse or his
3734 he'll not come back a horse.
4167 is a good horse in the
4235 be a man, a horse, a dog or
4434 in one's horse as he is
5151 a stately horse and make
5404 - A sick horse nosing
5511 a rocking horse, And
5690 for the horse is drawn
9204 rise and steal a horse.
9208 To spur a willing horse.
9699 about the horse And one of
10466 A horse! a horse! my
10514 indeed, a horse of that
11295 a rider and his horse.
11419 to the horse's
11525 dearer than his horse.
11722 a man a horse he can
12118 trust the horse, Trojans.
12520 I owe it to horse and hound.

horse-sense
7154 Horse-sense is something a horse

horseback
1854 a beggar on horseback, and he

horseguards
9398 be in the Horseguards and still

horsepond
8592 almost always a muddy horsepond.

horses
2732 Horses and jockeys mature
4616 and don't spare the horses.
5189 given to horses, but in
9941 stealing horses, but that

10903 think of horses before
11645 sir, in hosses, dawgs,

horseshit
7953 plants .. and horseshit.

hospitable
7608 turns, on hospitable thoughts

hospital
1616 inn, but an hospital, and a
8256 in a hospital is that it

host
954 all that a host and
12299 Perhaps host and guest is

hostages
721 hath given hostages to
11833 children. Hostages to

hostile
5598 world. A hostile person

hostilities
1490 others by their hostilities.

hostility
4053 in direct hostility one with
8424 irrational hostility that
9066 lurks a hostility

hosts
952 classes: hosts and

hot spot
7694 and a swinging hot spot.

hot-bed
5135 raised in a hot-bed; and they

hot-water
7354 English have hot-water bottles.

hotel
7694 With a pink hotel, A

hotel-keepers
11876 things that hotel-keepers continue

hound
2208 a slepyng hound to wake.
6487 faithful hound,
11289 that I loves the 'ound more.
12520 I owe it to horse and hound.

hounds
4277 With his hounds and his
10279 as a carcass fit for hounds.

hour
4219 minute starts an hour.
4809 in an hour than
4811 only an hour's drive
6303 minutes an hour, whatever
6477 as the Children's Hour.
9129 is but an hour a day
9645 hour When
9712 At such an hour the
9733 of the hour, and the
10016 The hour is come, but not
10116 so, from hour to hour,
10343 and the hour runs
12906 me in my hour of hours.

hour-glass
9644 silence, still as the hour-glass.

hourly
9488 set their hourly rates by

hours
663 Foster, the hours I've put
3115 twenty-four hours and too
3181 for two hours, you think
5059 passions, aching hours.
5919 you, happy hours, stay your
6951 two golden hours, each set
6963 through the course of hours.

house
91 A House is not a Home.
1151 my Father's house are many
1160 If a house be divided
1247 wisdom a house is built
1436 go into the house of the
2431 For a man's house is his
3633 hast a house (and a
3975 in that House MPs
3977 The House of Peers,
4259 That this House will in no
5036 I want a house that has got
6037 A serious house on serious
6117 A house is a machine for
6236 but as the house is pleased

6357 'A house divided against
6710 in the House to teach
7847 'Make my house your inn'.
7881 Is not this house [the Tower
7918 But a house is much more to
8814 facts, as a house is built
9061 my parents' house, in the
9246 buy the house; buy the
9266 Woe to the house where the
9943 is a house built upon
11311 to sell his house, and
11547 Dark house, by which once
12400 man in the house is worth
12854 No house should ever be on

house of lords
11224 The House of Lords, an illusion to

housekeeper
3766 excellent housekeeper. Everytime
12612 to make a housekeeper think

housekeeping
11961 so-called housekeeping where they

houses
1493 In big houses in which
3464 is not the houses. It is
7388 the ugly houses stand:
7930 in your houses that you
10479 A plague o' both your houses!
12778 the very houses seem

housetop
1245 of the housetop, than with

housewife
1108 being a housewife is you
7223 suburban housewife spends her
8813 and love - except the housewife.
9129 a good housewife and a bad
11281 The housewife is the Cinderella

housewives
11927 send, But housewives' affairs
12865 who are housewives, and other

housework
3412 Housework is what woman does

houston
127 Houston, Tranquillity Base

how-de-doo
3992 Here's a how-de-doo!

howl
6692 done and let them howl.

hue
10706 With hue like that when

huff
7099 leave in a huff. If

hugged
3039 She hugged the offender, and

hugging
4113 precious Hugging

hugo
2424 Victor Hugo was a madman

hull
9499 penetrates my wooden hull.

hum
4071 and hideous hum Indicat

human
400 All human beings are born
1584 Every human being has
2346 is simply a human organism
2495 are only human .. But it
2571 Human beings are the only
2711 Only a few human beings
3076 not lose its human face.
3234 Human kind cannot bear very
3299 of predatory human hands.
3607 It is human nature to think
3663 to us as a human being.
3727 mankind is not quite human.
3909 All that is human must
4193 of all that human hearts
4325 The human race has had long
4439 of the human race
4609 recurring human need.
4922 Why should human females
5387 she is a human being, but
5470 fine - but human nature is
5941 The human species,
6239 Human subtlety .. will

6663 then, so are human beings.
6930 The human condition.
6931 made on a human scale; and
6956 A human being who is first
7205 to the human condition.
7496 sense of human sight; And
7734 the less human for being
7919 jungle, it is a human zoo.
8372 thing that human beings
8589 fact of the human condition.
8882 To err is human; to
8911 in the human breast Man
8979 encompass the human race.
9380 I loved the Human Race; I
9682 of human nature,
9775 what human beings
10006 The human race is my
10636 out of the human race.
10923 one remain a human being?
11382 can be human again it
11397 is part of human nature to
11620 nothing human foreign to
11697 .. least human of all
12072 longer be a human quality,
12880 and the mire of human veins.

humanist
5020 A humanist is anyone who

humanities
8282 but the Humanities live for

humanity
85 of individuals and of humanity.
1035 unremitting humanity soon had
6475 and great! Humanity with all
8057 a means of addressing humanity.
8474 The religion of humanity.
8769 Glaucon, of humanity itself,
10166 Did steer humanity; but you,
10818 to their humanity but their
12632 of God. Humanity is just a
12796 still, sad music of humanity.

humanness
3658 cornerstones of our humanness.

humble
139 I am, it's hard to be humble.
5733 An humble and a
6916 Neither too humble nor too
7228 Don't be so humble. You're
8587 it ever so humble, there's

humbles
12498 person that humbles and mocks

humblest
1692 The humblest citizen of all

humbly
6270 I should humbly take His

humbug
2815 said Scrooge. Humbug!'
8492 Yes we have. Humbug.

humdrum
11652 with humdrum issues

humiliation
573 Art is born of humiliation.
1732 valley of Humiliation .. and to
3137 collapse in deepest humiliation.

humiliations
11255 a time of humiliations, the most

humility
1310 Humility is a good quality,
3334 the naughtiness of humility.
3751 perceiving humility
6325 accuracy - whimpering humility.
6942 its own humility, which is
12046 want of humility or of
12852 humility. I chose

humorist
1861 The great humorist forgets
2791 the word humorist - I feel
4585 A humorist is a man who feels

humorous
4577 too humorous to

humour
117 but no sense of humour.
791 or lacking a sense of humour.
1585 Humour is just another
2027 sense of humour from
2688 our needs. Humour has much

2694 at the root of much humour.
3694 Humour is the most engaging
3782 Humour is richly rewarding
3823 Humour is an affirmation of
5626 legitimate humour consists
6125 of humour I know is:
6137 sense of humour is to give
6761 a deep sense of humour.
7893 Humour is the contemplation
8872 With native humour temp'ring
11782 Humour is emotional chaos
12447 Humour can be dissected, as
12448 Humour plays close to the
12487 absence of humour in the

hump
11641 a positive hump, may marry

hunch
2067 A hunch is creativity

hundred
10778 I look a hundred and weigh

hunger
598 alone; Hunger allows no
1164 which do hunger and thirst
1196 remember the time of hunger.
3187 those who hunger and are
4759 Hunger is not debatable.
9137 ought to begin with hunger.
9168 Hunger is the best sauce.
9459 perpetual hunger to be

hungry
9163 you ask the hungry man how
9292 I am not hungry; but thank
10276 a lean and hungry look; He
11153 A hungry man is not a free
12721 life's hungry man, the

huns
7704 better than Huns or Wops,

hunted
6304 by their hunted

hunter
675 road The Hunter's waking
6756 is a lonely hunter that hunts
9236 the prey goes to the hunter.
11592 Man is the hunter; woman is

hunting
162 go a hunting, For fear
1839 my life to hunting and
5203 to call hunting one of
8633 was about hunting, in a
9287 ain't the 'unting as 'urts
11287 'Unting is all that's worth

hunting-field
7942 a decent death on the hunting-field.

hunts
11527 a dog, he hunts in dreams.

hurl
1744 of slang, hurl pithiness

hurled
7065 a rude heap together hurled.

hurly-burly
10339 When the hurly-burly's done,

hurricanes
6257 Hampshire, Hurricanes hardly

hurricanoes
10321 and hurricanoes, spout

hurry
116 you can't hurry the crops
2289 An old man in a hurry.
4657 People in a hurry cannot
6283 'No hurry, no hurry,' said
9152 are not done in a hurry.
11202 He sows hurry and reaps
12393 I am never in a hurry.

hurt
702 doth more hurt in a state
911 power to hurt us, that
1140 Hurt not the earth,
1327 who shall hurt the little
3532 wouldn't hurt the place.
4395 you want to hurt the giver.
4703 enough to hurt itself;
5739 friends can hurt you, If
6377 I know will not hurt me.
6880 someone hurt you that

7330 to your fear of being hurt.
8464 ain't likely to hurt you.
10399 same food, hurt with the
11267 They never hurt a hair of
11397 hate the man you have hurt.
11528 helps the hurt that
11952 to hurt you to the

hurting
8155 stop hurting because

hurts
8069 When you win, nothing hurts.
11625 until it hurts, then

husband
201 surrender value of a husband.
216 having one husband too many.
288 A husband always prefers his
1041 Being a husband is a
2204 over hir housbond as hir
3210 life her husband makes for
3285 the words 'My husband and I'.
3481 animal, a husband and wife.
4688 Husband and wife come to look
4987 A good husband should always
6541 great good husband, little
6980 Between husband and wife a
7101 The husband who wants a happy
8037 left her husband because
8696 yet an eager husband.
9685 A husband is what is left of
9690 trust a husband too far,
10409 doth make a heavy husband.
10866 your dear husband for a
11426 who has an ideal husband.
12256 of her husband, weighed

husbands
835 majority of husbands remind me
3214 reasons for husbands to stay at
6739 way to get husbands to do
8940 cast, When husbands or when
10436 Let husbands know Their wives
11020 Husbands don't really count
11927 respite to husbands the

hush
4610 So hush, little
7444 Hush! Hush! Whisper who
8151 breathless hush in the

hustles
3142 to him who hustles while he

hybrid
12031 is a hybrid of a

hygiene
10841 part of the hygiene of older

hymns
5910 amorous hymns, and
10547 sings hymns at
11144 of the hymns That fall

hyphen
779 - a hyphen which

hypnotize
4939 The sea can hypnotize. Nature

hypnotized
5796 to being hypnotized by slogans
8224 has been hypnotized by any

hypochondria
5 cure for hypochondria is to

hypochondriac
11210 being a hypochondriac these days

hypocrisy
837 are the hypocrisy of a
2873 is an organized hypocrisy.
3311 get rid of cant and hypocrisy.
5877 Hypocrisy is a tribute which
7169 Hypocrisy is the most difficult
7343 they prefer hypocrisy to a
7587 can discern Hypocrisy, the only
8236 oneself is a form of hypocrisy.
10579 they are. Hypocrisy is not the
12550 time. That would be hypocrisy.

hypocrite
5174 No man is a hypocrite in his
9090 Hypocrite - mouth one way,

hypocrites
4472 are the only honest hypocrites.
4478 We are not hypocrites in our
11125 the cant of hypocrites may be the

hypotenuse
4016 the square on the hypotenuse.

hypotheses
8187 Hypotheses non fingo. I do not

hypothesis
4929 a beautiful hypothesis by an ugly
6528 a pet hypothesis every day

hysteria
893 my hysteria with joy
6107 manipulated hysteria as the
8066 the moment of deepest hysteria.
8994 hysterias, trench confessions,

i
138 I am the greatest.
3829 I am I plus my
12090 I will be good.

ice
542 lies to ice a wedding
3327 over thin ice, our
3691 Some say in ice. From what
7808 feet, thin ice that
9021 The ice of her Ladyship's

ice-cream
11137 is the emperor of ice-cream.

icebergs
4342 between passing icebergs.

iced
508 and three parts iced over.
8353 and iced, In the

iceman
8342 The iceman cometh.

icicle
2139 age like an icicle down my

icing
6689 like the icing on cake,

iconoclasm
4698 Rough work, iconoclasm, but the

idea
89 contain a single idea.
112 than an idea, when you
381 that is an idea whose time
390 puts a new idea across he
554 man with an idea has at
658 The idea is in my head; to
1400 merely an idea the mind
1551 the impact of a new idea.
2683 to whom the idea first
3232 Between the idea And the
3695 An idea is a feat of
4126 When an idea is wanting, a
4848 of an idea whose time
4854 invasion by an idea.
5546 say that an idea is
6935 the idea of a
7029 does get an idea he usually
7840 the little idea from clay,
8307 neck of an idea: you
8415 to whom the idea first
9439 suffering than an idea.
9745 a healthy idea, now and
9880 For an idea ever to be
12590 with an idea, and grew
12855 An idea is salvation by

ideal
2916 a boy's ideal of a manly
4106 Love is the ideal thing,
6646 message from an ideal world.
8255 of a worthy ideal.
8565 god and an ideal and who
9498 the realms of the ideal.
11426 An ideal wife is any woman

idealism
5348 or morphine or idealism.

idealist
9860 I am an idealist. I don't

idealistic
12669 is the only idealistic nation in

ideas
467 Ideas, as distinguished
595 You get ideas you have
1057 of genuine ideas, Bright
1890 Our ideas. They are for
2444 possess ideas; the
2729 simple ideas that are

3016 to crown Ideas flow up
3144 am long on ideas, but short
3292 Big ideas are so hard to
3441 A chaos of clear ideas.
3517 of foolish ideas have died
4088 Daring ideas are like
4240 Very simple ideas lie within
7821 Great ideas are not
9449 absorbs and expresses ideas.
10897 What two ideas are more
11111 without his ideas get
11920 no one's ideas. I have
11993 marriage of ideas which,
12098 God, is the God of ideas.
12474 with inert ideas is not
12476 Ideas won't keep: something

identical
6200 things are identical if one can

identity
3675 not to violate one's identity.
6764 sense of identity is our
6769 quest for identity. When
11179 sense of personal identity.

ideology
1 is the ideology of the
5809 pattern or ideology. It means

idiom
9040 For the idiom of words very

idiosyncrasy
5013 Pound - idiosyncrasy on a

idiot
1262 Idiot, n: a member of a
2214 Any idiot can face a crisis
3986 The idiot who praises, with
7384 like an idiot, babbling,
10373 Told by an idiot, full of

idiots
10881 and the fatuity of idiots.

idle
1853 not solitary, be not idle.
3747 He is idle that might be
3911 the most idle and
5090 all be idle if we
5126 If you are idle, be not
6772 also more idle, with more
7927 The idle singer of an
8602 It is no rest to be idle.
9191 hardest work is to go idle.
10002 Never less idle than when
12252 He who most idle is Has
12286 still For idle hands to

idleness
2095 mankind proceed from idleness.
5038 Idleness, like kisses, to be
5306 is a mere excuse for idleness.
5865 excuse most easily is idleness.
8836 and penalties of idleness.
11179 faculty for idleness implies a

idling
5039 to enjoy idling thoroughly

idol
6640 make both God and an idol.
11432 bodies to appease an idol.

idolaters
4693 Men are idolaters, and want

idolatry
10577 the organization of idolatry.

idols
1471 like old idols, lost
3511 Indeed the idols I have
10649 down to idols of wood

idyll
4010 rank as an idyll, If I

if
5739 If you can talk with
10127 Your if' is the only

ifs
9141 enough ifs' we could

ignoramus
1263 Ignoramus, n: a person
6246 people are ignoramuses and

ignorance
27 amount of ignorance it
139ç is expensive - try ignorance.

1654 Ignorance is not innocence but
2655 all ignorance toboggans into
2900 love is our ignorance that it
3112 expanding desert of ignorance.
4116 than ignorance in action.
4250 it is wise to affect ignorance.
4299 Where ignorance is bliss 'Tis
4351 I know, I owe to my ignorance.
4487 is the child of ignorance.
4812 If ignorance is indeed bliss,
5786 a state of ignorance, and yet
6247 ladies; ignorance and
6777 is ever inhibited by Ignorance.
7006 there is no sin but ignorance.
7994 Don't die of ignorance.
8379 slavery. Ignorance is
8667 Ignorance is no excuse, it's
9039 From ignorance our comfort
9219 Ignorance excuses from sin.
10055 Ignorance of the law excuses no
10907 except the fact of my ignorance.
11245 Ignorance is the first
11511 and naked Ignorance Delivers
11830 weapon of ignorance - the
12477 Not ignorance, but ignorance of

ignorant
1063 to be as ignorant today as
1194 Be not ignorant of any thing
1294 people are ignorant: it's that
2350 that I am ignorant of what I
2677 what many ignorant men are
6466 The ignorant man always adores
6715 not only ignorant of these
7720 fool than an ignorant fool.
9560 is ignorant, only on
10376 Most ignorant of what
11988 was so ignorant I could

ignore
8088 nothing to ignore, And
8778 days to ignore what
9332 what to ignore but at the

ignored
3172 I simply ignored axiom.
9824 in life is to be ignored.
9982 side be ignored and not be

ignores
7691 most poetry ignores most

ignoring
37 consists in ignoring facts.
8117 mildly by ignoring our

iliad
11688 wind - an Iliad fought in

Ilium
6993 towers of Ilium? Sweet

ill
1897 being ill is one of
3008 Ill news hath wings, and
4109 discovers that he is ill.
4150 Ill fares the land, to
5679 not to fall ill, and I
10794 if it is ill, It has a
11349 to use us ill, it
12619 what human ill does not

ill-fed
5134 be; it is ill-fed,

ill-housed
9602 of a nation ill-housed, ill-clad,

ill-spent
9670 is a sign of an ill-spent youth.
10990 the sign of an ill-spent youth.

ill-spirit
6597 I hear my ill-spirit sob in

ill-tempered
6152 think him ill-tempered and queer,

illegal
5758 The illegal we do
8270 means that it is not illegal.
12761 immoral, illegal or

illegitimate
561 is| the illegitimate child of

illegitimi
345 carborundum illegitimi (Cod

illiterate
6458 of the illiterate, the

10727 Illiterate him, I say, quite
12498 about an illiterate person

illness
568 mental illness of the
9284 Art is a kind of illness.
10631 that makes illness
10934 Illness is the night-side of

ills
4297 they of ills to come,
9366 a sure one for all ills.

illuminating
11823 light, illuminating for her

illumination
6009 support rather than illumination.

illumine
2443 ship, which illumine only the
7546 me is dark Illumine, what is

illusion
321 child of illusion and the
361 is an illusion caused by
2544 some memory or some illusion.
4074 specious illusions, which
4311 footer the illusion that it is
5794 than the death of an illusion.
7062 An illusion which makes me
8038 a world of illusion. The
8678 the illusion of
8734 prove an illusion for you
11224 Lords, an illusion to which I

illusions
7408 analyzing illusions in order
7692 It's life's illusions I recall;
12423 of his illusions, he grew

illustrated
5506 you till life has illustrated it.

image
4332 a good image of itself.
4466 television, image becomes
7607 Best image of myself and
8992 demanded an image Of its
10926 of kings; Image of war,
11500 with the image of the
11719 thine image dwells,
12156 us in his image, we have
12165 our own image. We treat

imagery
6715 for their imagery. And they

images
4606 take the images outside
5513 words are images of
5817 its loftier images of itself.

imaginary
2269 of the imaginary that we
7844 inspection, imaginary gardens

imagination
109 then the imagination is
653 A lady's imagination is very
1291 their imagination for their
1978 f-gg-g his imagination. I don't
2101 the human imagination, when
2998 there is no imagination there is
3294 Imagination is a poor substitute
4045 the imagination than the
5098 it not for imagination, Sir, a
5292 Imagination is the eye of the
5389 of reason but of imagination.
5420 The imagination of a boy is
5466 sails, and imagination the
5467 truth of imagination - what the
5910 I got my imagination to the
6584 to the imagination as society
6836 His imagination resembled the
7061 limited only by your imagination.
7180 Imagination grows by exercise,
7875 Imagination frames events
8670 we lacked imagination enough to
9068 women to men without imagination.
10421 Are of imagination all
10422 And, as imagination bodies forth
10603 is nothing but his imagination.
10705 and imagination the
10726 and to his imagination for his
12855 idea is salvation by imagination.

imagine
6221 Imagine there's no heaven,
9496 can one imagine

imbecility
6811 moderation in war is imbecility.

imitate
803 never failed to imitate them.
3255 poets imitate; mature
4666 usually imitate each
6318 alternately imitate and mock
8649 We do not imitate, but are a

imitating
3626 between imitating a good man

imitation
3557 his famous imitation of a
5075 from the imitation of those
6424 the art of Imitation, Is
12166 nothing but judicious imitation.
12812 vocation Were endless imitation.

immature
7147 Immature poets imitate: mature
8425 The immature mind hops from

immediately
5758 we do immediately. The
7997 we do immediately - the

immigration
245 not having an immigration bureau.

immodest
9618 Immodest words admit of no

immoral
118 and immoral people
5596 marriage is immoral without
12761 are either immoral, illegal

immorality
1508 code of immorality in the
3476 of all vice and immorality.
6092 predilection, that is immorality.
12472 like, and immorality is what

immortal
7462 He is immortal, not
4941 vanish, but grass is immortal.
5502 for death, immortal bird! No
5992 that gives Immortal youth to
6993 make me immortal with a
8722 do not seek immortal life, but
8920 And grew immortal in his own
10169 I have Immortal longings
10429 lost the immortal part of
10910 the soul is immortal and

immortality
153 to achieve immortality through my
1570 they gave, their immortality.
2835 just Ourselves - And Immortality.
2968 belief in immortality, not only
3435 - milk's leap toward immortality.
4127 believes in immortality enjoy his
4509 Lord for immortality in
5483 heart like a load of immortality.

impartial
2327 to feel impartial about

impassioned
8591 love's impassioned blindness
12801 it is the impassioned expression

impatience
1381 on patience; man on impatience.

impatient
579 tends to be impatient, craves

impediments
721 they are impediments to great
10560 minds Admit impediments. Love is

impending
12754 I have it impending in me:

imperfect
4996 He was imperfect, unfinished,

imperfection
7430 flawless imperfection of a New

imperfections
3391 Dote on his imperfections, though I
3615 your own imperfections, but

imperialism
6216 Imperialism is the monopoly stage

impertinence
9973 symbol of impertinence and
10871 a piece of impertinence in England

implication
626 and the implication of causes

importance
3091 tell me of importance, for God's
4608 of some importance, but is of
4891 to the importance of the
6079 the vast importance of the
6447 nothing of importance can happen
7184 given it a ridiculous importance.
9033 his own importance, will

important
1544 the most important thing in
1873 three most important things a
3134 that was really important.
3229 to feel important. They
4598 The most important thing a
5008 there is is very important .'
7887 to feel important about is
8064 It is only important to the
9203 wildcat is very self important.
9307 want to be important NOW'.
9756 is terribly important, and that
9963 Almost all important questions
10870 one more important than that
12089 The important thing is not what
12952 it is more important to

importunate
7779 is no less importunate for being

imposes
3045 the child imposes on the

imposing
9063 is not imposing it on

imposition
10424 most false imposition; oft got

impossibility
2086 and metaphysical impossibility.
3356 man is an impossibility until he
6545 to thee That fond impossibility.

impossible
170 what is impossible for talent
404 Nothing is impossible for the
1487 giant - impossible socially,
5482 It is impossible to live in a
5537 flying machines are impossible.
7793 poverty of soul, impossible.
7997 - the impossible takes a
8070 time; the impossible is what
8599 is always impossible to live
8629 I see it is impossible for the

imposters
5738 those two imposters just the

impostors
4074 invented by impostors in order

imposture
4474 is affectation and imposture.
7170 them to carry on the imposture.

impotence
3364 peace, but a canting impotence.
5873 indolence or impotence of will.
9775 and our impotence in the
9888 as he is of impotence.
12298 Impotence and sodomy are

impotent
2315 all-powerful to be impotent.
12862 you become impotent. Better

impress
7158 and should impress it on the

impressed
1656 Too easily impressed: she liked

impression
1397 a clear-cut impression of
1983 is preparing for the impression.
2841 left an impression more
3888 to the impression which
4432 novel is an impression, not an

impressionable
10976 girl at an impressionable age, and

impressions
9730 in all our impressions of

imprison
2949 me to you, imprison me, for I

imprisoned
2527 Imprisoned in every fat man a
6885 be taken or imprisoned or

improbability
2714 statistical improbability on a

improper
10845 An improper mind is a

impropriety
7181 Impropriety is the soul of wit.

improve
935 greatly improve his
2477 in cities, improve their
4124 you never improve them. If
11373 ten people improve on
12453 a desire to improve (or save)

improved
11274 He so improved the city that

improvement
1333 Improvement makes straight roads;
4722 social improvement, or read
5085 improvement arises
7359 No great improvements in the lot
10041 children for signs of improvement.

improving
4919 certain of improving and that's

improvisation
8244 continually required improvisation.

impudence
9743 of Cockney impudence before

impulse
6094 out of the impulse of the
12840 One impulse from a vernal
12891 A lonely impulse of delight

impulses
4463 its onward impulses to men ill
7822 with first impulses for they

impunity
7981 one provokes me with impunity.

impure
6075 things are impure, as

impurity
7460 we bring impurity much

in
2282 the one is in, the other

in common
9322 whom one has nothing in common.

in love
10524 more than over shoes in love.

in vain
11598 and all in vain: Let the

inability
4217 with your inability to put on

inaccuracy
1872 lying, but I hate inaccuracy.
9831 A little inaccuracy sometimes

inaction
5575 costs of comfortable inaction.
6240 so does inaction sap the
6736 Disciplined inaction.

inactivity
6738 a wise and masterly inactivity.

inalienable
5022 and inalienable, among

inapprehensible
11711 know thee, Inapprehensible, we clutch

incapable
7398 nature is incapable of
7755 but I am incapable of taking

incapacity
1340 old maid courted by incapacity.
9342 in proportion to his incapacity.

incarnate
10803 Is incarnate, and a

incarnation
4114 the human incarnation of the
8334 thing in incarnation to the eye

incense
5500 what soft incense hangs upon

incensed
7576 Incensed with indignation

incest
901 excepting incest and

incestuous
5069 has got to be almost incestuous.

inch
415 by the inch and
1794 have an inch of dog
3047 Every inch that is not
10328 Every inch a king.
12413 Every other inch a

inches
5234 to their inches.

incisors
786 into incisors and

incites
7784 nourishes them, incites them.

include
4207 Gentlemen, include me out.

incognito
9334 angel travelling incognito.

income
642 A large income is the best
5604 its real income is
8139 my net income with my
8520 rises to meet income.
10859 a good income is of no
11435 leisure and income to enable

income tax
9403 as an income tax refund.

incomes
4035 While the incomes of the
9823 their incomes nowadays,

incommunicable
11163 is for the most part incommunicable.

incompatibility
2190 How awful incompatibility is, and how

incompatible
6308 pen Thought incompatible by men?

incompetence
8671 rise to his level of incompetence.
8674 their level of incompetence.

incompetent
849 Only an incompetent mind is
10619 by the incompetent many for

incomplete
3768 A man is incomplete until he has

incompleteness
85 sense of incompleteness and

incomprehensible
4727 the economic ones are
incomprehensible.

incongruities
6125 of the incongruities of life,

inconsistency
63 eyes of the world as inconsistency.
10833 Inconsistency is the only thing in

inconsistent
9350 you were inconsistent. What
12373 honest, one must be inconsistent.

inconstancy
974 with that inconstancy was born,
11307 world constant, but inconstancy.

inconstant
3862 An inconstant woman, tho' she

inconvenience
632 and the inconvenience is often
9434 through the inconveniences of life.

inconvenient
1289 but the most inconvenient one, too.
10889 it is confoundedly inconvenient.

incorruptible
2091 The seagreen Incorruptible.

increased
2888 Increased means and increased

increases
9310 love for us increases The less

incurable
2598 Life is an incurable disease.

indebted
7212 is always indebted to the
7590 at once Indebted and
10726 is indebted to his

indecent
1978 that he is indecent but

6067 will be Indecent .. 10
91.69 An indecent mind is a

indecision
9078 Indecision is like a stepchild:

indeed
4831 in need is a friend indeed.

indefatigable
10981 That indefatigable and unsavoury

indefensible
8392 the defence of the indefensible.

indefinite
12626 Hell is indefinite.

independence
3450 we call it independence. When men
10078 step toward independence is a

independent
2869 because they are independent.
2893 will all be independent, too, in a
3676 and to become fully independent.
6560 Ain't to be inderpendunt, why, wut
12486 a word is independent of the

india
2317 India is a geographical
6991 them fly to India for gold,

indian
245 American Indians made a
2773 what the Indians called
10718 only good Indian is a dead
12514 The Indian Summer of the

indians
804 off the Indians and,
6427 the huts of Indians: much less
12390 convert the Indians; but oh,

indictment
1754 up an indictment against an

indifference
2106 Indifference may not wreck a man's
6332 fault, then indifference is a
7230 by our indifference to
7809 than the softness of indifference
8036 and its indifference to
9797 is that indifference which is
11187 you with an indifference closely
12524 is not hate, it's indifference.

indifferent
4679 It is simply indifferent.
10587 but to be indifferent to them:
10832 perfectly indifferent whether it

indigestion
448 complains of moral indigestion.
11202 sows hurry and reaps indigestion.

indignation
3339 A good indignation brings out all
3944 greatest indignation would be
8024 mists of righteous indignation.
11312 fierce indignation can no
12381 Moral indignation is jealousy

indignity
996 me the indignity of being

indiscreet
12552 are never indiscreet. Answers

indiscretion
4427 without indiscretion is no
6776 a cliché and an indiscretion.

indispensable
3784 are indispensable when you
4830 that they seem indispensable.
6390 because it is indispensable.
9744 want is an indispensable part of
11751 only not indispensable, but

indistinct
4522 render their purposes indistinct.

individual
2638 educate an individual - educate
3806 a single individual to defy
4762 notions in an individual way.
5358 done to an individual is
5791 of the individual was: a
6467 an individual is
8064 to the individual, and only
8216 herd-instinct in the individual.
9510 governs each separate individual.
10908 both to the individual and to the
11655 There are individual men and

individualism
5814 Individualism is rather like

individuality
9931 not his individuality, but his
12549 pursuit of my own individuality.

individually
141 of men who individually can do

individuals
5602 which individuals are doing
7375 of the individuals composing
8226 Insanity in individuals is rare -

indivisible
6400 Peace is indivisible.

indoctrination
806 is indoctrination, if you're

indolence
4479 Indolence is a delightful but
5873 nothing but indolence or

indoors
2 - clean, indoors and no
6849 given us indoors and

indubitable
9752 change is indubitable, whereas

induce
11133 we induce people to

indulgent
5287 and indulgent to every
11060 makes one very indulgent.

industrial
3898 the able industrial leader who

industrious
7564 With his industrious crew to

industry
2096 Captains of industry.
4245 Quality of life is an industry.
4918 talent. Industry and all
7688 national industry of
9452 talents, industry will
9916 it in that of a major industry.
10091 Love of bustle is not industry.
11436 unless industry is to be
12661 is a labour-intensive industry.

ineffectual
12670 is ineffectual enough at

inefficiency
2717 God of inefficiency, but when

inefficient
10605 the efficient and the inefficient.

inelegance
638 a continual state of inelegance.

inequality
485 form of inequality is to try

inertia
4407 of further inertia and the
8660 The only menace is inertia.

inescapable
8557 of the way inescapable. I am

inevitability
12312 The inevitability of gradualness

inevitable
2174 must seem to be inevitable.
4291 alike th' inevitable hour, The
6570 with the inevitable. The only
10774 to appear inevitable by a
11417 foresee the inevitable and to

inexperienced
317 of the inexperienced giving

infamous
6826 was rich, quiet, and infamous.

infancy
6388 of man are infancy,
9587 in our infancy, and

infant
11564 am I? An infant crying in

infantile
3169 is an infantile sickness.

infantry
7640 That small infantry Warred on

infants
8988 unkillable infants of the
9516 bewildered infants are trying

infatuated
1845 which have infatuated and

infatuation
511 yielded to infatuation at some

infected
8883 All seems infected that
10370 troubles; infected minds To

infection
6595 it's the infection of things

infects
12284 sheep infects the flock,

infelicity
11456 a sense of a constant infelicity.

inferior
9588 you feel inferior without

inferiority
85 feeling of inferiority rules the
2231 enjoy the inferiority of their
5093 of an inferiority, from his

inferiors
476 Inferiors revolt in order that

infernal
7557 hail Internal world, and

infidel
1264 Infidel, n: in New York, one

infidelity
8468 Infidelity does not consist in
12415 people, infidelity feels like

infinite
1347 to man as it is, infinite.
5710 a man of infinite-resource-a
6197 from an infinite number of
7075 Though infinite, can never
7893 point of view of the infinite.
8051 idea of the infinite torments
8540 of these infinite spaces
10157 stale Her infinite variety;
10477 I have, for both are infinite.
11021 absolutely infinite - that is,

infinity
1325 flower Hold infinity in the
12775 shares the nature of infinity.

infirmities
3474 the natural infirmities of those
10209 friend's infirmities, But

infirmity
12826 and a prop To our infirmity.

inflame
10292 It will inflame you, it

inflation
292 Inflation is defined as the
3668 Inflation is one form of
9570 Invest in inflation. It's the

inflections
11145 beauty of inflections Or the

inflict
8454 Why inflict pain on oneself,

inflicts
8168 is one who never inflicts pain.

influence
34 tell where his influence stops.
2108 friends and influence people.
4923 write to influence their
5187 things he cannot influence.
5351 a stronger influence
7520 eyes Rain influence, and judge
8029 had more influence on human
11167 are a good influence in love
12948 to their influence than by

influences
10101 influences and

inform
11 not to inform the reader
6079 It can inform and lead
10223 do inform against

information
3253 we have lost in information?
4446 two words information' and
11077 much common information all day

informed
679 the one informed by the

infuriating
421 A word to the wise is infuriating.

ingenuity
7225 about the ingenuity or the
8578 you with their ingenuity.

inglorious
4792 of mute, inglorious men and

ingrate
6536 malcontents and one ingrate.

ingratitude
10119 so unkind As man's ingratitude.
10294 him stab, Ingratitude, more
10315 Ingratitude, thou marble-hearted
10502 monster of ingratitudes.
10522 I hate ingratitude more in a man

ingredient
11896 essential ingredient of

ingredients
7904 are three ingredients in the
11056 most useful ingredients of family

ingress
6514 Our ingress into the world

inhale
2401 like it, and I didn't inhale.
9473 hashish, but I didn't inhale.
11162 that is, if you don't inhale.

inherit
1164 they shall inherit the earth.
7035 they shall inherit the earth.
10828 meek shall inherit the earth;

inheritance
2185 For an inheritance to be really

inhospitable
9625 notoriously inhospitable to the

inhumanity
1829 Man's inhumanity to man Makes
10587 that's the essence of inhumanity.

iniquity
9919 to have them, what iniquity!

injure
6856 less to injure a man who

injured
7609 the injured lover's
9124 he feels himself injured.
10079 they have injured, they also

injuries
6435 against the injuries and
6858 for slight injuries - for
7831 is adding insult to injuries.

injuring
11766 time without injuring eternity.

injury
2228 An injury is much sooner
6690 greatest injury to the

injustice
1414 taken to maintain injustice.
2680 hates injustice in its own
2775 a lasting power upon injustice.
5358 The injustice done to an
5644 Injustice anywhere is a threat
6690 greatest injustice that has
7265 Injustice is relatively easy to
10080 Injustice never rules forever.

ink
342 buys his ink by the
2368 in the ink that
6653 sea were ink 'Twere not
7950 worthless by applying ink.
9100 The palest ink is better
10336 he hath not drunk ink.
12210 drop of ink in my pen

inn
7847 house your inn'. Inns are
10717 welcome, at an inn.

innings
5334 get me this innings. Warm

innkeeper
9188 The innkeeper loves the

innocence
807 destroys innocence, also
2686 to know we sinn'd is innocence.
5215 state of innocence very
5814 rather like innocence; there
6021 Innocence is next God, and
6042 Never such innocence, Never

7078 here, And Innocence, thy
7460 bring not innocence into the
8246 cynically and with innocence.
9471 a moral security of innocence.
9676 true innocence is ashamed
11298 not speak again of innocence.
11756 recovered innocence we discern

innocent
1248 be rich shall not be innocent.
1295 The truly innocent are those
1316 than one innocent suffer.
1488 The innocent are so few that
2045 The innocent is the person who
3969 As innocent as a new-laid egg.
5837 if an innocent person is
6750 unthinkable if we are innocent.
8394 until they are proved innocent.
12894 The innocent and the beautiful

innocuous
4234 lambent but innocuous.

innovate
1765 To innovate is not to reform.

innovations
688 so are all innovations, which are

innovator
719 time is the greatest innovator.

innuendos
9285 knows That innuendos Will serve
11145 beauty of innuendos, The

inquiries
3913 religious inquiries (aged 17).

inquisition
11601 To these Inquisition dogs and

insane
782 monarch was insane.
4413 obviously he must be insane.

insanity
1266 a temporary insanity often
6280 genius and insanity. I have
6290 Insanity is hereditary - you
8226 Insanity in individuals is

inscription
1260 n: an inscription on a tomb
6498 is the inscription on the

insect
5151 is but an insect, and the

insects
6331 certain insects come by

inseparable
10897 are more inseparable than Beer
12320 and forever, one and inseparable.

inside
351 the lady inside And a
1487 down inside himself, a
2696 lived inside myself,
3363 do; but inside, the
3428 lot of people inside me.
4209 that great inside thing that

insight
4583 to have insight into much
8039 Insight into the truth is the

insignificance
4497 to see the insignificance of human

insignificant
917 that he is insignificant and is
958 to them and insignificant, does yet
4080 we can endure the insignificant.

insincere
7847 Nor was he insincere in saying,

insincerity
8373 language is insincerity. When

insists
8982 to one who INSISTS on

insolence
2891 and that insolence is not

insoluble
2682 things is insoluble by us; and
4727 ones are insoluble and the

insomnia
5311 from an ideal insomnia.

inspiration
3143 per cent inspiration,

9393 at the mercy of inspiration.
9449 a source of inspiration. The only

inspire
2479 you cannot inspire a woman

inspired
679 the other inspired by divine
2324 that I have inspired the

instinct
1891 all healthy instinct for it.
1904 he was, his instinct told him
2944 man and the instinct of the
4271 human instinct is to
8551 nature: instinct and

instincts
1779 our reason, but our instincts.
6102 animal, true to your instincts.

institution
3123 a long term institution I could
3349 An institution is the lengthening
3370 are in the institution wish to
4266 is the institution of the
4847 than a game. It's an institution.
5043 ancient institution, the old
8818 is a great institution, and no
9930 transformed into an institution.
12407 is a great institution, but I am

institutions
4075 her own institutions which, by
9473 of institutions. Even in
12244 greatest instatooshuns of which

instruction
3730 is that no instruction book came

instrument
546 make me an instrument of Your
930 legs an instrument capable of
4074 the blind instruments of their
11046 State is an instrument in the

instruments
2582 of the instruments of war.
5232 Made instruments even of
6320 of their instruments that they
7372 more docile instruments in its
10333 vices Make instruments to plague

insubordination
6726 price of insubordination and

insufferable
956 that has made me insufferable.

insular
2889 An insular country, subject

insulation
6714 a kind of insulation against

insult
2228 forgotten than an insult.
4525 press is to insult a nation;
6093 attempt to insult sex, to do
7831 is adding insult to
10084 to see an insult, than to
11310 too apt to insult them upon
12923 envy is an insult to

insulted
2710 me to get insulted in places
7097 been so insulted in my

insulting
8283

insurance
2323 compulsory insurance for all

intangible
11711 O world intangible, we touch

integration
5800 of European integration is in

integrity
3675 Integrity simply means a

intellect
2238 not go through the intellect.
3177 to make the intellect our god;
5477 one's intellect is to make
5888 The intellect is always fooled
5954 feather to tickle the intellect.
6809 The highest intellects, like the
9977 Intellect is invisible to the
9981 into the place of the intellect.
10936 of the intellect upon art.
10956 The march of intellect.
10993 and not by the intellect.

11024 Will and intellect are one and
12841 meddling intellect Mis-shapes

intellectual
523 thirdly, intellectual ability.
591 The word 'Intellectual' suggests
2048 An intellectual is someone whose
3188 An intellectual is a man who takes
5606 from any intellectual
6665 - the intellectual cripple's
6833 An intellectual is someone whose
7408 of the real intellectual consists
7568 of pain, this intellectual being.
9811 The intellectual should be a
10666 soul may fix its intellectual eye.
11126 passage to the intellectual World.
11884 In intellectual circles
12821 thing, An intellectual

intellectualism
6602 What replaces it? Intellectualism.

intellectuals
108 themselves as intellectuals.
12853 I hate intellectuals. They are

intelligence
173 only by the intelligence, but he is
385 Tact is the intelligence of the
720 have intelligence is a man's
1684 have little intelligence, the great
3783 No intelligence system can predict
4893 for their intelligence and
5543 Intelligence must follow faith,
5586 in battle or great intelligence.
6665 substitute for intelligence.
7159 educated beyond his intelligence.
8032 of intelligence is to take
8548 The more intelligence one has the
9881 Intelligence is quickness in
11428 and amazing intelligence.
12471 Intelligence is quickness to
12526 Intelligence appears to be the

intelligent
818 The intelligent are to the
2462 she is intelligent demands
2725 Many highly intelligent people are
6967 sign of an intelligent person is
8793 Marry an intelligent person.
12343 The intelligent man who is proud
12924 subborn are the most intelligent.

intelligently
9753 use leisure intelligently will be

intemperance
3920 the brisk intemperance of youth.

intense
2046 An intense feeling carries

intensity
9968 of the intensity, never of
12902 full of passionate intensity.

intent
10348 sides of my intent, but only

intention
1308 slightest intention of
4060 of my own intention to keep my
8340 - attention without intention.

intentions
10969 with good intentions. They
11654 had good intentions. He had
12217 by their good intentions.

interaction
6094 male. The interaction of the

interchanging
4701 game of interchanging praise.

intercourse
2731 In her intercourse with
6034 Sexual intercourse began In

interest
1410 unite men - fear and interest.
1597 a reader's interest that the
2347 loses interest in
2561 take it out, you lose interest.
3224 he took no interest. For it
3229 harm does not interest them.
4944 is the interest paid on
6564 But oh, I du in interest.
6823 the natural interest of money.
8426 a vested interest in

10818 their own interest. We
11940 not only interest boys but

interested
5 and get interested in someone
1047 never an interested person who
2278 the more interested he is in
2849 man is more interested in a woman

interesting
1286 the most interesting things he
3492 They are interesting to look
8090 much more interesting than any
8108 to make other people interesting.
8686 the most interesting thoughts,
11259 not nice, but it's interesting.
12191 more interesting than
12759 much more interesting to men

interests
774 it interests the whole
1114 It is the arena of interests.
4992 The interests of childhood and
8486 Our interests are
8533 Our own interests are still an
9895 sharing the interests of others.

interfered
5032 clad and often interfered with."

interference
1838 without interference. They

interior
2168 All our interior world is
4557 by interior blessings.
7247 unless some interior,

interlunar
7657 in her vacant interlunar cave.

international
1270 n: in international affairs, a
8979 demain, L Internationale Sera le

internet
12620 to the Internet, we know

interpretation
8222 are no facts, only interpretations.
10976 Interpretation is the revenge of the

interpreted
7112 have only interpreted the world

interpreter
12434 Man is the interpreter of nature,

interrogate
8409 man can interrogate as well as

interrupt
5379 for itself, don't interrupt.

interrupted
6166 you get interrupted when you
9483 truly enjoyed must be interrupted.

interruptions
7198 if there are no interruptions.

interstices
5146 with interstices between

interval
9897 save to enjoy the interval.

intimacy
825 without intimacy and no
12967 sternness. Intimacy does not

intimate
1104 us, the intimate roof of

intimidate
3587 one can intimidate generals,

intimidated
10602 revenge for being intimidated.

intimidating
11656 should be intimidating. There's

intolerable
8471 worst state, an intolerable one.
12050 possession of it is intolerable.

intolerant
1323 right to be intolerant of people

intoxicate
4905 They intoxicate themselves with
8874 draughts intoxicate the brain,

intoxicated
5100 when he is intoxicated, has not

introduce
11133 introduce something

intrude
7740 may not intrude, To

intrusion
3405 from the intrusion of the
10978 education, I call it intrusion.

intuition
9872 cultivates intuition and
10736 Intuition is a spiritual

invade
3280 dare to invade the

invaded
6204 Remorse, Invaded with a

invalid
666 cannot be invalid
6956 of all an invalid is all
9154 Invalids live longest.
9171 Every invalid is a physician.

invasion
4854 against invasion by an

invent
750 fitter to invent than to
5473 you could invent some means
9185 eyes, don't invent with your
9538 I invent nothing. I
11097 to have no ability to invent.
11346 What some invent, the rest
12153 be necessary to invent him.

invented
2623 necessity invented stools,
3002 that can be invented has been
3724 has ever invented is the
6939 have invented in order
8711 artist. He invented the

invention
1542 Today every invention is
1982 Pure invention is but the
4534 that his invention, out of
5466 a test of invention which I
6239 devise an invention more
7641 but the invention of a
8761 of his own invention instead of
9180 true, it is a happy Invention.
10254 heaven of invention; A kingdom

inventor
8029 the inventor of double

inventory
9385 a reserve inventory of

invertebrates
6083 invertebrates, the

inverted
3510 And that inverted bowl we call

invest
9570 Invest in inflation It's
9620 Never invest your money in

invested
805 it is invested with so
2303 have never yet been invested.

investigation
445 The investigation of the meaning of

investments
308 luxuries rather than investments.

invisible
712 blind, yet she is not invisible.
1694 who has no invisible means of
7587 that walks Invisible, except to
9816 is invisible to the
9977 is invisible to the man
11134 is the priest of the invisible.

invisibly
11784 dripping invisibly all over

invitation
11376 An invitation is the sincerest

invitations
5614 accept our invitations and don't

involuntarily
7383 it is done involuntarily by

involuntary
5565 It was involuntary. They sank my

invulnerable
10673 knife Invulnerable nothings.

ionic
6788 fluted Ionic columns

ira
2379 with the IRA is to kill

ireland
1119 who left Ireland at
4049 to lose Ireland in
4054 mission is to pacify Ireland.
4867 party in Ireland was
5320 Ireland is the old sow that
5999 Ireland never was contented
7300 'Tis Ireland gives England
7838 Ireland is a fatal disease;
10881 name of Ireland is
11034 The real Ireland is walking
12907 Romantic Ireland's dead and

irish
969 that the Irish are
2915 That is the Irish Question.
5214 as the Irish haven't,
7087 And now the Irish are
7842 dissatisfied. I'm Irish.
8316 An Irish queer: a fellow

irishman
10603 An Irishman's heart is nothing

irishmen
965 like true Irishmen - locked

iron
6240 Iron rusts from disuse;
6540 make, Nor iron bars a
6800 iron.
10255 and hold out mine iron.

iron curtain
2332 Adriatic an iron curtain has
11892 There is an iron curtain across

irrational
11143 that the irrational is

irrationality
12316 of the irrationality of the

irregulars
3000 - the Baker Street irregulars.

irrelevancies
955 free of irrelevancies and loose

irrelevant
5953 is the most irrelevant thing in

irreplaceable
3896 me, you irreplaceable you! Just

irresistible
12897 does not explain, is irresistible.

irresponsible
2543 touch its irresponsible

irretrievable
652 a female is irretrievable..one

irreversible
6393 Life is an irreversible process

irritable
10744 some people are very irritable.

irritate
7156 as to irritate the person

irritates
5154 to divert it only irritates.

irritating
8599 and even irritating to live
10744 carry on irritating some

island
1116 This island is made mainly
2311 defend our island, whatever
2809 snug little Island, A right
2942 man is an Island, entire of
7810 age is an island surrounded
8293 Englishman is an island.
11364 an inland island, The ghost
12012 little island huffing
12201 make this island all her

isle
902 fonder, Isle of Beauty,
10446 sceptered isle, This
10927 favoured isle, And

islington
1336 fields from Islington to

israel
1202 Hear, O Israel: The Lord our
4954 states - Israel, Athens,

issues
4455 large-scale issues is no

4521 That the issues may be
8365 All issues are

istanbul
5922 one should gaze on Istanbul.

it
9106 to know it, don't do

italian
1505 rival. The Italian woman
7276 as baseball in Italian.

italians
5056 Italians come to ruin most

italy
1799 here after seeing Italy.
1851 horses: Italy a paradise
5093 not been in Italy, is always
7336 Italy is a geographical
10893 from Italy a greater
11943 made Italy with
12356 "In Italy for thirty years

itch
661 The Seven Year Itch.
6549 once the itch of
9125 As old as the itch.

itches
392 To scratch when it itches.

ivory
7127 a cargo of ivory, And apes
7928 against the ivory gate,

ivy
75 poison ivy is another
9631 pluck an ivy branch for

jabberwock
2120 'Beware the Jabberwock, my son!

jackals
3535 .. Jackals piss at

jackass
9402 Any jackass can kick down a

jade
4167 an arrant jade on a

jail
2961 or the world's thy jail.
5200 being in a jail, with the

jam
2123 rule is, jam tomorrow

jane
10785 Jane, Jane, Tall as a
12348 Me Tarzan, you Jane.

jar
7005 will harshly jar.

jargon
1057 we have jargon; instead
6423 Alone from Jargon born to

jaundiced
8883 yellow to the jaundiced eye.

jaw-jaw
2319 To jaw-jaw is always better

jaws
2113 With gently smiling jaws!
11477 Into the jaws of Death,

jazz
4302 A jazz musician is a

je-ne-sais-quoi
4011 piminy, Je-ne-sais-quoi young

jealous
10433 Are to the jealous
10438 not easily jealous, but being

jealousy
1331 heart, And Jealousy a human
3211 Anger and jealousy can no more
5230 Jealousy is all the fun you
7609 Nor jealousy Was understood,
9808 To jealousy, nothing is more
10431 my lord, of jealousy; It is the
12381 is jealousy with a

jeepers
7293 Jeepers Creepers - where'd

jelly
9235 you, even jelly breaks

jellybeans
9417 by his way of eating jellybeans.

jerusalem
1336 And there Jerusalem's pillars

1348 And was Jerusalem builded
1350 have built Jerusalem, In

jest
475 and a jest which will
5169 a scornful jest; Fate
9372 in earnest, that's no jest.
10229 of infinite jest, of most
10338 A jest's prosperity lies

jesting
6251 empty and meaningless jesting.

jests
10472 He jests at scars, that

jesu
2722 Jesu, good above all

jesuit
5674 a thing, a tool, a Jesuit.

jesus
129 mild, Jesus Christ her
1025 is to blame Jesus for what
1332 Was Jesus gentle or did he
4751 is that Jesus is coming
6220 from Jesus now; I
8658 power of Jesus' Name; Let
10769 Robinson Jesus loves you
11267 When Jesus came to
11412 Jesus wants me for a
11915 a face-to-face with Jesus.
12258 Jesus loves me - this I

jew
2890 Yes, I am a Jew, and when
3178 declare that I am a Jew.
7422 really a Jew . Just
10399 Hath not a Jew eyes? hath

jewel
10112 a precious jewel in his
10470 Like a rich jewel in an
10805 is a jewel which is
11745 eye is the jewel of the
12057 death! the jewel of the
12349 velvet pillow for the jewel.

jewellery
6222 you, just rattle your jewellery.

jewels
11588 odes, and jewels

jewish
1586 Look at Jewish history.
1602 choose A Jewish God, But
4079 of the Jewish question
4983 by the Jewish people
5553 problem not a Jewish one.
7399 think of myself as Jewish.
9662 A Jewish man with parents
10392 upon my Jewish gabardine,
12523 of Jewish children

jews
3432 Of God To choose The Jews.
4141 The Jews have always been
7229 We Jews have a secret
8207 the Jews I was not

jig
8926 upon a jig of heaven.

jigging
7012 From jigging veins of rhyming

jilted
2033 courted and jilted Than never

jingling
11528 But the jingling of the guinea

job
2 the sort of job all
547 The hardest job kids face
1136 of the patience of Job.
2314 we will finish the job.
4275 The job of a citizen is
4355 he creates a job vacancy.
4420 a hell of a job. I have
5333 fifth and lost the job.
5558 seeking a job and can't
7715 It's an odd job, making
7782 is my job and my
10242 as poor as Job, my lord,

jobs
1403 men grow old in their jobs.
3777 - for the jobs - that are

jockeys
2732 Horses and jockeys mature

jog
5972 a man might jog on with.
11119 As we jog on, either

jogging
9992 Jogging is very beneficial.

john brown
378 John Brown's body lies a
8091 this slab John Brown is stowed.

john peel
4277 D'ye ken John Peel with his

john thomas
6080 John Thomas says good-night to

johnny
4668 at little Johnny there,

johnson
4146 with Johnson; for when
8616 Dr Johnson's sayings would

join
1649 two lives join, there is
2118 will you join the dance?
7498 And join with thee calm

joined
1183 God hath joined together,
1441 God hath joined together
10599 God hath joined together

joint
1384 all the gin joints in all
10201 is out of joint; O cursèd
11246 was out of joint, and he

joke
2285 A joke's a very serious
2535 face of a joke upon the
3684 isn't a joke. We only
3988 Life is a joke that's just
8231 A joke is an epigram on
8827 Dullness ever loves a joke.
9056 under cover of a joke.
10892 to get a joke well into

jokes
3685 my little jokes on Thee
4156 At all his jokes, for many
9176 He that jokes confesses.

jollity
7511 youthful jollity, Quips and

jollyrodgered
11678 the night and the jollyrodgered sea.

josephine
8079 Not tonight, Josephine.

joss-sticks
1520 odour of joss-sticks and

jostling
1352 not done by jostling in the

jotting
6143 you. The jotting is

journal
1468 page of my Journal is like a
9861 is the journal of a sea

journalism
507 Journalism is literature in a
4360 essence of journalism is to know
4595 Journalism allows it's readers
7410 are in journalism. You are

journalist
12720 the British journalist. But,
12910 by rote; A journalist makes up

journalists
1302 for the people than journalists.

journey
191 to take a journey, and
855 does this journey seem like
1279 the journey of life,
2768 The journey is never
3235 year For a journey, and such
3980 on that journey you find
6056 Still journey on Till
6969 for a journey I prepare
8343 long day's journey into
9112 part of his journey behind
9416 begin the journey that will

jove
2074 more where Jove bestows.

jove
5259 Tell proud Jove, Between
7468 of Jove's Court My

joy
1156 Joy shall be in heaven
1567 without the aid of joy.
1995 not a joy the world
3066 Joy ruled the day, and
3497 know of no joy,' she
6322 Strength through joy.
6921 for the joy of love is
7651 headlong joy is ever on
10021 the stern joy which
10044 is my only joy, Faithless
10128 to weep at joy than to
10709 an unbodied joy whose race
11624 filled with joy preaches
11829 as pure and complete joy.
12836 Suprised by joy -

joys
714 redoubleth joys, and
727 The joys of parents are
1359 delight, Joys in
1842 All my joys to this are
3044 For present joys are more
6662 greatest joys known to
7494 deluding joys, The brood
7740 can its joys control?
9683 The joys of meeting pay
12518 lasting joys the man

jubilant
7616 ascended jubilant. Open, ye

judas
4312 the jealous Judas or the
12564 is always Judas who writes

judge
205 gives a judge an
339 the living judge - Too
1171 Judge not, that ye be not
3351 Shall we judge a country by
4761 the guilty damns the judge.
6492 We judge ourselves by what
7267 A judge is a law student
7520 and judge the prize
7936 We judge ourselves by our
8654 the final judge. I have
8936 A perfect judge will read
9022 I am no judge of such
9282 The judge is condemned when
9405 Do not judge this movement
9653 One cannot judge
10569 of the human judge.
11464 mistake to judge people by
12605 a time they judge them;

judged
1171 not, that ye be not judged,
4712 of being judged not to
5642 will not be judged by the

judgement
66 give his judgement rashly,
274 Good judgement comes from
917 pronounce a judgement: 'The
1682 nor enough judgement to be
2042 the last judgement. It
2391 are no substitute for judgement.
2759 career, judgement is torn
2997 It biases the judgement.
4445 independent judgement is being
4777 unaided by judgement, collapses
5684 God's great Judgement Seat; But
5887 one complains of his judgement.
6320 personal judgement of hardly
6508 in one's judgement of others.
7007 men of judgement frame
7648 spirit and judgement equal or
7799 of judgement as doth
8044 for your judgement will
8434 Judgement of beauty can err,
9959 is the world's judgement.
10195 reserve thy judgement. Costly
10403 come to judgement! yea, a
12684 to sit in judgement upon any

judgement book
11447 leaves of the Judgement Book unfold.

judgements
2611 differing judgements serve but
3194 beliefs, on judgements of

judgements
3941 Our judgements about things vary
7770 often accompany weak judgements.
7775 To make judgements about great
11511 brawling judgements,
12065 of making judgements on

judges
4607 their own judges obey the
4841 is what the judges say it is.
6237 that which judges the things
7941 [Irritable Judges] suffer
8160 my Accuser, but my judges.
8914 The hungry judges soon the
9285 And were judges of fact,
9335 a hundred judges have

judging
2131 In judging others, folks will
7727 one considers judging others.

judicious
11206 like a little judicious levity.

jug
6656 Jug, jug, jug,

juliet
10472 east, and Juliet is the
10779 the Nurse, not Juliet.

jumblies
6150 were the Jumblies live;

jumbo
10787 Jumbo asleep! Grey leaves

jump
2176 Jump out the window if you
10397 I will not jump with

jumping
11280 the cat is jumping. The

jumps
653 rapid; it jumps from
6409 a chasm in two small jumps.

june
2074 When June is past,
9255 June's too soon, July's

jungle
2038 more than a jungle. This is
2653 for the law of the jungle.
6383 is dead in the jungle.

jupiter
6610 Jupiter is whatever you see,
11774 its hands and pray to Jupiter.

jurisdiction
1416 hath no jurisdiction in this

jury
3696 A jury consists of twelve
3742 be on the jury at a

jurymen
8914 hang that jurymen may dine.

just
301 Just when you thought it
1156 and nine just persons,
1496 on the just And also
2340 not always just, and when
4976 not be a just peace, but
5152 I expected, and less just.
7661 Just are the ways of God,
10740 of the just Smell

justice
304 were any justice in the
604 for justice withheld.
731 of wild justice, which the
1038 price of justice is eternal
1083 fairness or justice or human
1918 For Justice, though she's
2648 Justice was born outside the
2679 thing as justice - in or
2748 sword of justice first lay
2981 Justice is too good for some
3467 Let justice be done, though
4148 seldom has justice enough to
4340 Lord Chief Justice of England
4608 that justice should not
4708 man, not a court of justice.
4843 Liberty and Justice - Huh!-
5360 Justice is the constant and
5644 I justice anywhere is a
5647 than to justice; who
5885 Love of justice in most men
5911 he stand in need of justice.

justice
6261 Justice is such a fine thing
6689 for justice, if one
6826 The Chief Justice was rich,
6886 or delay, right or justice.
7155 In England, justice is open to
7265 I justice is relatively easy
7583 Die he or justice must.
7630 temper so Justice with
8044 you think justice requires,
8203 for justice makes
8206 establish justice in a
8406 line about justice - not only
9974 it has no sense of justice.
10396 ducats! Justice! the law!
11025 confidence, justice.
12280 Let justice be done though

justifiable
7661 of God, And justifiable to men;

justification
12482 The only justification in the use

justified
7368 be no more justified in

justify
4784 can To justify God's ways
7546 And justify the ways

kaiser
3288 put the kibosh on the Kaiser.

keats
1726 and out-glittering Keats.

keener
4973 that grows keener with

keep
370 Keep a thing seven years
1013 she'll have to keep it.
2433 from seeing you keep yours.
2980 eye. To keep him - two.
4356 than to let him keep her.
4467 We should keep the Panama
5549 the light; Keep me, O keep
5736 If you can keep your head
6056 Keep right on to the end
12401 always say, keep a diary
12476 Ideas won't keep: something

keeping
5711 mad all are in God's keeping.
8365 thing as keeping out of

key
1036 for the key. I wonder
5515 Turn the key deftly in
7470 that golden key That opes
7764 while I keep the key?
8556 form is the key to organic
8991 out of key with his

keyhole
12021 size of the keyhole, today's

keys
4263 half that's got my keys.'
9054 idly Over the noisy keys
11557 keeps the keys of all the

khatmandu
4470 north of Khatmandu, There's a

kibosh
3288 put the kibosh on the

kick
1126 for thee to kick against
2291 with a kick and not a
5471 scarcely kick to come to
8261 hands, I want to kick them.
8527 thinks he may kick at him.
8957 I get no kick from
11040 The first kick I took was
12295 They may kick you out,

kicked
74 He had been kicked in the
415 shall be kicketh by the

kicks
7414 is what kicks you in the

kid
1385 looking at you, kid."
12859 you're a kid, you see

kiddie
8096 Any kiddie in school can

kiddies
1100 You kiddies have

kidding
8659 you are kidding, Mister

kids
2633 Trouble is, kids feel they
6051 have any kids yourself.
7908 with our kids - they've

kill
821 you have to kill more women
2081 could only kill you once.
2313 you have to kill a man it
2379 IRA is to kill 600 people
2409 shalt not kill; but
2539 does one kill fear, I
2847 I advance; kill me if I
3216 will kill a man so
3375 a king you must kill him.
6140 get out and kill something.
6175 a sin to kill a
7008 And kill sick
7458 good almost kill a man as
8080 that is to kill me has not
8200 at all but kill animals
8464 may kill you, but
9557 war they kill you in a
9659 Kill a man, and you are an
9801 does not kill him, is
10327 gods; They kill us for
10612 prepared to kill one
10982 trying to kill, but which
11766 you could kill time
12146 well to kill an admiral
12946 likely to kill you is

killed
264 they were only killed.
2326 war you are only killed once.
5763 your being killed, but I
5860 one has killed the beast.
6172 it is people who get killed.
11284 Better be killed than

killing
32 ends by killing the
5680 finished killing Kruger
10795 In reality, killing time Is
10982 but which ends in killing him.

kills
1085 it kills all its
6091 either it kills the novel,
12540 each man kills the thing

kin
696 man is of kin to the
8089 one's own kin and kith
10187 more than kin, and less
10504 makes the whole world kin.

kind
2693 their own kind. The
2705 that's kind - Not for
3462 naturally kind, you
5152 men more kind than I
6614 of learning to be kind.
8258 Too kind, too kind.
9936 always be kind, As you
10187 kin, and less than kind.
10220 be cruel only to be kind.
11407 are cruel, but man is kind.
12535 of being kind Is all the

kindergarten
9516 a kind of kindergarten, where

kindest
9537 head. The kindest words I'll

kindle
509 We cannot kindle when we
2281 you should kindle in return
5347 is to kindle a light in

kindles
1865 small, it kindles the great.

kindlier
1569 wise, but kindlier, And lips

kindling
9257 tree, all making kindling.

kindly
9847 the KCMG (Kindly Call Me
10946 Time is a kindly god.

kindness
1810 a cup o' kindness yet, For
2563 just, where kindness is vain.

kindred
4227 like stone, Kindness in
4327 do, or any kindness that I can
4834 Kindness goes a long way lots
5108 spontaneous kindness. He whose
8591 of you with kindness, And shall
10345 of human kindness To catch
12641 on the kindness of

kindred
2071 poor, to kindred dear, To

king
300 The King over the water.
367 sea hath no king but God
1313 The king never dies.
1315 That the king can do no
1620 The King to Oxford sent a
1768 that a king may make a
2103 is a born king of
2716 The King's life is moving
2779 to be king for a
3280 of a king, and of a
4259 for its King and
4423 seems most kingly is king.
5405 Of being king and
5717 The man who would be king.
6531 I were not king, I should
6705 all were lo king for a king
6834 To my true king I offered
6920 rightwise King born of
7002 still fair England's king.
7015 to be a king, And ride
7442 The King asked The Queen,
7879 hath not offended the king.
8135 ill of your king: and ..
8628 esteem of a king, that he
8629 for the King to have
8743 - but the King of England
8744 than the King himself.
9045 What is a King? - a man
9522 and mighty king Whose
9700 go For your King and your
10054 A king is a thing men have
10219 A king of shreds and
10226 hedge a king, That
10261 I think the king is but a
10272 I served my king, he would
10328 Every inch a king.
10448 an anointed king; The
10452 must the king do now?
10453 still am I king of those.
10715 despised, and dying king.
11499 follow the King - Else,
11500 with the image of the King.
11513 forgets a dying king.
11852 The King, observing with
12459 The once and future king.
12730 A king is always a king -
12735 served the King, he would

king george
6871 King George, passing slowly in a

kingdom
1157 The kingdom of God is within
1164 is the kingdom of heaven.
1170 first the kingdom of God,
1181 into the kingdom of heaven.
2954 land, My kingdom, safeliest
7650 seeking asses found a kingdom.
10077 possesses a kingdom: a great
10466 a horse! my kingdom for a

kings
1778 Kings will be tyrants from
2121 - and kings - And why
2620 wise, Kings would not
2748 When kings the sword of
3020 and ruin kings.
3445 only five Kings left - the
4318 too; For kings have cares
6800 Bind-their kings-in-chains-
8769 become kings in this
8833 Divine of Kings to govern
10076 art of kings is the
10446 throne of kings, this
10450 death of kings: How some
11175 all be as happy as kings.
11931 All kings is mostly

kinquering
11032 Kinquering Congs their titles

kinship
7314 we for any kinship with the

kipling
11102 cease from kipling And the

kippers
11679 like two old kippers in a box.

kiss
912 Kiss till the cow comes
1806 Ae fond kiss, and then we
1826 A man may kiss a bonnie
2657 will never wholly kiss you.
2707 "I'd luv to kiss ya, but I
4237 the first kiss after men
4580 would I kiss my Julia's
4877 this, a kiss is still a
5063 want him to kiss my ass in
5241 Or leave a kiss but in the
5325 My kiss will give peace
6453 And if I kiss he
6712 will be wanting to kiss me!
7020 Yet let me kiss my Lord
7690 A kiss can be a comma, a
7747 say a kiss on the
7763 my deary! kiss me, and be
7929 at last without a kiss?
8132 Kiss me, Hardy,
8573 take his kiss!' ''Tis
9512 A kiss on the hand may be
10512 Then come kiss me, sweet
11372 with her, kiss her and
11444 tell, Or kiss the place
11482 one long kiss my whole
11587 we love And kiss again with
12274 in the magic of a kiss.
12540 it with a kiss, The brave

kissed
419 they are kissed; some call
2178 one wants to be kissed.
2202 mouth he kiste hir naked
4425 We kissed at the barrier,
5339 He kissed me under the
5748 Being kissed by a man who
7826 But I kissed her little
11735 said when she kissed her cow.
11684 Owen who kissed her once
11838 young, I kissed my first

kisses
2946 More than kisses, letters
4753 who throw kisses are
4874 Stolen kisses are always
5719 Christian kisses on an
6655 cards for kisses, Cupid
7251 loses hers after four kisses.
9142 is one who kisses, and the
10164 thousand kisses the poor
11333 bread and cheese, and kisses.
11370 my kisses And I have

kissing
21 wonder who's kissing her now.
6525 Kissing your hand may make
7092 I wasn't kissing her, I was
7320 Kissing don't last: cookery

kitchen
333 Modern kitchen - where the
12053 heat, get out of the kitchen.

kitchener
543 If Kitchener is not a great

kittenish
980 hand, is kittenish and mild,

knave
2744 grudge at knaves in place.
3865 with a knave hath made,
6814 for a knave, and out

knee
2003 you upon my knee, Just tea

kneel
10485 they should kneel for peace.

knees
4936 than to live on your knees.
6344 times to my knees by the

knew
398 George knew my father,
4156 to view; I knew him well,
4157 how much he knew; 'Twas
5767 and I both knew what it

6208 And not a soul knew which.
7647 only, that he nothing knew.
10229 Yorick. I knew him,
11583 head which all men knew!
11734 If people knew what they
11750 If I knew .. that a man

knife
6171 uses knife and fork?
8480 cuchillo. War by the knife.
10687 wound, the knife is lost in

knife edge
7808 walk on a knife edge. To the

knight
559 Earl and a Knight of the
2196 verray, parfit gentil knyght.
8606 now that was your knight.
11006 A gentle knight was pricking

knights
6922 noblest knights of the
6927 for my good knights' loss than

knit
6308 flower, or knit, To mind

knits
10748 Nothing knits man to man,

knives
4630 The night of the long knives.

knock
150 Don't knock it. It's sex
1172 shall find; knock, and it
4248 will knock up against
5101 a right to knock him down
5943 interest a knock at the
8848 will come: Knock as you

knock-down
4872 to receive a knock down blow.

knocked
926 Cromwell knocked about a
4615 Well, we knocked the bastard
6419 Cromwell knocked about a

knocking
520 Tired of knocking at

knotted
10043 Sat and knotted all the

know
17 thing to know is how to
28 They know enough who know
295 Know thyself.
436 and powerful know he is.
489 they don't know, you can't
597 the public know What all
610 give that I know myself,
681 men must know, that in
742 more than to know little.
1129 face: now I know in part;
1158 for they know not what
1294 that they know so much
1647 How well I know what I
2047 I know myself too well to
2051 To know oneself, one
2216 them don't know what to do
2478 we do not know them; and
2524 can get to know a person
2655 into know and
3579 How can I know what I
3781 is to know what you
3850 so once; but now I know it.
4070 therefore I ought to know.
4093 I do not know myself, and
4128 does not know another
4269 at Oxford Know all there
4336 Not to know certain things
4351 little I know, I owe to
4358 You know I know you know I
4360 is to know what you
4404 He must know sumpin',
4447 you need to know about
4474 to know; and
5060 I may not know much, but I
5163 Knowledge is of two kinds;
5493 is all Ye know on earth,
5538 Seek not to know who said
7060 not to know him
7255 one who is known to many
7465 liberty to know, to utter,
7602 state, and know to know no
7690 every woman ought to know.

7739 thing, to know a thing or
7780 world is to know how to be
7790 sais-je? What do I know?
8087 Ask Daddy, He Won't Know.
8154 If you know nothing, be
8262 You know very well that
8338 is to know something
8452 thou not know, my son,
8943 Know then thyself, presume
9088 thing to know the truth
9106 anyone to know it, don't
9160 is good to know is
9224 naturally desire to know.
9550 To know her was to love
9555 Well, all I know is what I
9577 we don't know that gives
9678 poetry for those who know.
9832 don't know better as
10099 I know, and all the world
10660 better to know nothing
10895 you don't know would make
11128 man should know something
11502 I know not if I know what
11772 To know that we know what
11997 you don't know you're
12133 Now I know what Love is.
12582 the shallow know
12862 if you know too much

knowing
829 I think knowing what you
2087 in a man's knowing when to
5062 It's knowing what's

knowingly
6311 Never knowingly undersold.

knowledge
673 For all knowledge and wonder
679 The knowledge of man is as the
753 Knowledge is power.
757 taken all knowledge to be my
759 For also knowledge itself is
1128 Knowledge puffeth up, but
1213 increaseth knowledge increaseth
1263 kinds of knowledge familiar
1554 The knowledge of the ancient
1603 the five ports of knowledge.
2407 of God, but knowledge is bought
2486 all our knowledge not to
2621 Knowledge is proud that he has
2705 Not for the knowledge in thy
3112 Our knowledge is a receding
3253 lost in knowledge? Where is
3503 Knowledge is a process of
3655 road to a knowledge of the
3744 life is not knowledge, but
3787 organized knowledge to
3930 the dawning of your knowledge.
4250 Even knowledge has to be in
4481 is the knowledge of that
4550 but a blind date with knowledge?
4629 harder to shake than knowledge.
4696 province of knowledge to speak
4925 If a little knowledge is
4926 in natural knowledge has
4927 life is not knowledge, but
5163 Knowledge is of two kinds; we
5172 must carry knowledge with him,
5176 not weak - knowledge is more
5448 Knowledge enormous makes a god
5450 She had no knowledge when the
5610 knowledge concerning
6196 and the knowledge of God is
6198 It is the knowledge of
6426 lies in the way of knowledge.
6429 No man's knowledge here can go
6553 a little knowledge in and the
6662 in search of knowledge.
6837 Knowledge advances by steps,
7413 with the knowledge of
7459 that the knowledge of good
7463 men is but knowledge in the
7599 happiest knowledge and her
8350 this is a knowledge which they
8400 His knowledge of life and
8910 All our knowledge is, ourselves
9085 God sells knowledge for labour
9227 of knowledge is the
9332 items of knowledge. Learning
9603 of the knowledge of higher

9749 search for knowledge and
9773 gained from useless knowledge.
9785 want is not knowledge, but
9883 Knowledge of what is possible
9995 more knowledge, things do
10665 seek for knowledge and wisdom
11220 scientific knowledge of the
11375 light of knowledge in their
11532 Knowledge comes, but wisdom
11609 To follow knowledge like a
11772 know, that is true knowledge.
12389 is worth a pound of knowledge.
12435 it for the knowledge of a
12477 is the death of knowledge.

knowledgeable
7720 A knowledgeable fool is a greater

known
368 to have known all your
1244 a child is known by his
1461 world less known by the
2482 would be known, and not
4635 should have known no more
6853 not become known, or, if it
8731 from the known and the
11867 must have known me had he
12905 all things known That is

knows
797 if you knows of a
1820 God knows, I'm no the thing
2662 is one who knows us, but
2944 but the man knows that he
3109 same man knows much of
7373 He who knows only his own
7449 Brain, but he Knows Things.
11163 What a man knows at fifty
11316 what every schoolboy knows.
12915 is that it knows - and I

labels
11828 - are but labels serving to

laboratory
12632 pigs in the laboratory of God.

laboriously
6881 does not laboriously, though

labour
1178 all ye that labour and are
1239 In all labour there is
1321 Labour is the party of law
1558 Labour is not a commodity,
1615 We all labour against our
2320 Labour is not fit to govern.
4590 If a little labour, little
5018 for all, is Labour's call.
7776 ceaseless labour of your
7931 The reward of labour is life.
7948 Vote Labour: Sleep Tory.
8003 Labour isn't working.
8127 in the Labour Party
8695 The Labour Party owes more
8800 is the sweet sauce of labour.
9455 the mental labour employed
11065 labour of doing
11184 loves the labour of his
11204 true success is to labour.
11434 done to the Labour Party?

labourer
8813 No labourer in the world is

labouring
1734 is sweet to the labouring man.

labours
728 sweeten labours, but they
2354 labours are
3168 on the labours of other
5027 of his labours and the
5548 small and necessary labours.
7349 her yellow labours For thee?
10971 Lingered labours come to

labyrinthine
11706 down the labyrinthine ways Of my

lachrymose
2367 bellicose, lachrymose and

lack
126 men than the lack of it.
1425 can I lack nothing.
3595 discover what they lack.
6701 ava', And lacks a proper

7887 Lack of something to feel
11214 what we lack ourselves,

lacking
2107 it is never wholly lacking.
8431 strength is lacking, yet the

lad
3962 I was a lad I served a

ladder
611 ourselves a ladder out of
891 further up the ladder you go.
10500 is the ladder to all
11713 of Jacob's ladder Pitched
12881 Now that my ladder's gone I

laden
1178 are heavy laden, and I

ladies
630 when he has ladies to please,
7520 store of ladies, whose
9399 Ladies were ladies in those
11293 The young ladies entered the
11854 Ladies, just a little more

ladling
9553 See, ladling butter from

lady
351 was an old lady from Riga
355 There is a lady sweet and
428 was a young lady from Kent,
569 him the lady of
3866 little lady comes by.
4448 why the lady is a
5455 I met a lady in the meads
5714 Said our Lady of the
5752 her his lady fair -
6507 A Lady with a Lamp shall
8967 of a great lady may still
9388 Here lies a lady of beauty
9469 catch a bird than a lady.
10216 The lady doth protest too
11653 The lady's not for

laid
4516 getting laid. It's
8499 Prom were laid end to
11211 can get laid, it's just
11429 When I am laid in earth my

lair
10038 the lion from his lair.

laissez-faire
5605 of laissez-faire to dig

laity
10593 against the laity.

lake
6924 came to a lake that was a

lamb
196 Eat British Lamb: 50,000
5001 As Charles Lamb says,
6505 one dead lamb is there!
11110 the wind to the shorn lamb.

lambs
5697 poor little lambs who've

lame
9272 carries the lame man, both
9985 the lame man who

lament
1787 power, to lament the past,

lamp
6111 I lift my lamp beside the
6507 Lady with a Lamp shall
10688 When the lamp is shattered

lamp-posts
6009 man uses lamp-posts - for

lamps
4328 The lamps are going out all
7068 Like golden lamps in a green
10107 Chianti to make into lamps.

lancashire
8386 In a Lancashire cotton-town you

lancelot
11521 greaves Of bold Sir Lancelot.

land
680 there is no land, when they
1046 Land of Hope and Glory,
1078 America, Land that I
1348 upon En land's
3300 water as by land, and

3873 we had the land and they
3949 heaven by sea as by land!
7653 The land had once
7854 loving the land that has
8028 wrong through all the land.
8802 The land too poor for any
9481 of the land, to the
11687 The land of my fathers.
11923 a golden land,
11986 of sighting land again
12766 not of lands, And

landed
127 here. The Eagle has landed.

landlady
6133 The landlady of a
9051 of national landlady and

landlord
5969 marry a landlord's

landscape
1546 the husband the landscape.
3718 The human landscape of the New
4480 Landscape painting is the
5223 The landscape should belong to
6664 yet leave a landscape as it was
7364 of the surrounding landscape.
9720 can mar a landscape, and

landslide
5583 going to pay for a landslide.

language
449 mind what language an opera
977 sense in a language all
1669 through language and
2187 another language is to
2368 Language has not the power to
3978 may use any language you choose
4128 another language, does not
5143 or enlargement of the language.
5240 But the language, and the
5796 weapon is language. He is
5987 his strange language all I know
6101 In such lovely language.
6293 Language is a form of human
6650 off oure language he was the
6803 else in our language should
6835 that dear language which I
7211 In our language rhyme is a
7684 is the language of that
7894 all, our language is
7905 a foreign language: all men
7935 But we do language. That may
8047 the English language and sent
8373 of clear language is
8393 Political language .. is
8683 wonder what language truck
8862 art, No language, but the
9864 Slang is a language that rolls
10572 divided by a common language.
11062 happens not to be his language.
11564 And with no language but a cry.
11803 Language has created the word
11972 understand their own language.
12347 A language is a dialect with
12683 the crude language of deeds.
12703 of my language mean the
12705 by means of language.

languages
242 his tongue in ten languages.
1554 the ancient languages is mainly
9040 and gave languages just as

lap
4295 upon the lap of Earth A
4732 lies in the lap of the
12185 Her green lap immense

lapdogs
8940 or when lapdogs breathe

lapland
5081 and Lapland is

lards
10236 death And lards the lean

large
2124 It's as large as life and

large-hearted
1624 woman and large-hearted man.

larger
292 balloons larger and candy

lark
1667 The lark's on the
7307 The lark ascending.
8961 can hear a lark somewhere
10547 Like to the lark at break

lass
1823 gie me the lass that has
5948 What a lass that were to
6783 lives a lass, More
8326 I love a lass, As a
12700 I loved a lass, a fair

lasses
1821 spent among the lasses, O.

lassie
6058 I love a lassie, a bonnic,
6060 Wae my lassie by my

last
146 buy anything is last year.
1184 shall be last; and the
1837 colour are their last days.
2294 it will eat him last.
2599 Th' approaches of the last.
2950 the world's last night?
3119 Nice guys. Finish last.
4229 be somebody you must last.
4403 The last time I saw Paris
4769 is your last. Some
5551 this day as if thy last.
6889 Fortissimo at last!
8489 that's the last thing I
8912 Nor yet the last to lay the
9395 won't last as long.
10032 Death who comes at last.
11203 are all on our last cruise.
11582 The last great Englishman
12562 I hope it will last.

lasts
416 He who laughs, lasts.
4499 is the love that lasts.
6525 bracelet lasts for ever.

latch
7291 negative Latch on to the

late
1105 of being late! And,
1687 of human thought too late.
5048 when it comes late in life.
6258 you were late. Ah yes!
7866 never too late for
8053 come too late into a
10471 and known too late!
12368 it's too late to live.
12668 never too late to have a

later
10093 slow; It is later than you

lateral
2729 the term 'lateral thinking'

latin
309 No more Latin, no more
1002 Is there no Latin word for
4510 to learn Latin first of
5254 hadst small Latin, and less
5781 and the Devil knows Latin.
9012 who has Latin is a
10004 is half Latin and half
11042 to be able to read Latin.
12359 Don't quote Latin; say what

latrine
3536 the rotten seat of a latrine.

laugh
309 hard to make me laugh.
419 worst are those who laugh.
576 all of them make me laugh.
867 first baby laughed for the
1619 in others, laugh at us
1678 audience laugh, at a
2027 instead of laugh at them.
2154 sillier than a silly laugh.
2506 than to laugh; Jesu,
2635 Never laugh feebly at what
4152 the loud laugh that spoke
5801 makes his companions laugh.
5841 One must laugh before one
5957 makes me laugh. I
6524 wants to laugh all of the
7132 Laugh and be merry,
7263 audience is afraid to laugh.

7715 making decent people laugh.
8224 one can laugh at the
8890 they rise. Laugh where we
9450 at whom we never laugh.
9462 be able to laugh the more
9668 night, a strangled laugh.
10678 I silently laugh at my own
11026 not to laugh at human
11119 on, either laugh with me,
11818 Never laugh at live
12534 Laugh and the world laughs
12648 a woman laugh you can do

laughed
7262 made off is laughed at by
8078 reign, is laughed at in the

laughing
149 I ever had without laughing.
3094 by not laughing at
3601 stops women laughing at them.
3810 get people laughing, they're
6512 her, Minnehaha, Laughing Water.
8630 forbear laughing and
12428 is no laughing matter.

laughs
410 He who laughs, lasts.
4483 animal that laughs and weeps;
9232 the mouse laughs at the cat
9480 than he who laughs too much.
9554 all the good laughs you can.

laughter
67 by the faculty of laughter.
878 Laughter is the closest thing
1005 But laughter and the
1285 Laughter is the sensation of
1451 Laughter is the shortest
1970 Mirth and Laughter Sermons
3290 recipe like Laughter. Laugh it
4133 it through laughter seen by
8595 Laughter is pleasant, but the
8994 laughter out of
9072 will cause laughter even into
9808 more frightful than laughter,
10710 sincerest laughter With some
12018 Laughter .. the most
12022 Laughter would be bereaved if
12239 Laughter can be an
12281 thy girlish laughter; Then, the

laundry-list
9651 Give me a laundry-list and I'll

laurel
4130 and the laurel stands
7000 Apollo's laurel-bough,
9631 youth, And laurel for the

law
310 The law locks up both man
461 Law is a bottomless pit.
731 more ought law to weed it
1142 where no law is, there
1321 party of law and order
1382 can give a law to lovers?
1414 Law and order is one of
2284 the windward of the law.
3468 and I'll show you the law.
3608 The law, in its majestic
3622 limited as law is as the
3971 The Law is the true
4045 study of law. No poet
4230 time will give its law.
4408 The aim of law is the
4563 The Common Law of England
4708 a court of law, young
4713 life of the law has not
5029 be controlled by law.
5559 he starts to practise law.
5735 breeds without the Law.
5743 this is the Law of the
5847 it is nature's law.
6405 Law .. begins when
6423 to rescue Law, From
6434 the end of law is, not to
6438 of the law, and
7192 from th' law of
7219 above the law, he loses
7599 God is thy law, thou
7624 Law to our selves, our
7940 The law seems like a sort
7946 in the law. Nothing

8180 engaged in law suits as
8699 Law is nothing unless
9000 The law must be stable
9017 nothing is law that is
9283 gives the law without
9509 Any law which violates
9608 above the law and no man
9768 The law of causality, I
9947 people not defied the law.
10055 of the law excuses no
10094 This is the law of the
10375 of the law. Setting
10521 the windy side of the law.
11572 dusty purlieus of the law.
11578 God, one law, one
11863 excess of law

lawbreaking
9714 opposed to lawbreaking, he is not

lawful
6885 by the lawful judgement

lawgiver
323 absolute lawgiver and

lawless
8028 fear the lawless roads Ran

laws
43 of laws, and not
1274 that the laws of the
1395 can be made so by laws.
1719 Laws die, books never.
1750 Bad laws are the worst
1790 Laws, like houses, lean on
2686 Had laws not been, we
4192 Laws grind the poor, and
4193 part which laws or kings
4273 obnoxious laws so
4607 obey the laws. Others
6445 broke the laws of God and
6855 arranges laws for it to
7381 to the laws alone,
7796 to the laws, would not
7812 which the laws allow,
7869 or breaking of laws.
8159 war has its laws; there are
8214 that makes laws for our
8284 Laws were made to be
9264 Laws, like the spider's
9305 that not judges of laws.
9727 things the laws of life;
10716 Laws are generally found
10771 to their laws we lie.
11155 Laws are never as
11306 Laws are like cobwebs,

lawsuit
3706 successful lawsuit is the one
12164 I lost a lawsuit, and once

lawyer
1882 A lawyer's dream of heaven -
3696 who has the better lawyer.
4726 knife, as a lawyer's mouth
7890 as I want a lawyer to tell me
9320 A lawyer with his briefcase
12677 to be a lawyer, but now I

lawyers
2810 would be no good lawyers.
3851 I know you lawyers can, with
7056 Lawyers are men who hire out
8820 To some lawyers, all facts
9111 Lawyers and painters can soon
12653 want to be lawyers or

lax
5290 stern, not cold and lax.

lay
1153 that a man lay down his
1903 one can lay it on so
2507 She lays it on with a
5337 that a man lay down his
6723 how when we lay together
10024 The unpremeditated lay.
11777 that he lay down his

lazier
5872 We are lazier in our minds

laziness
5162 doom of laziness and
9440 for laziness: there is

lazy
305 jumped over the lazy dog.

579 tends to be lazy, craves
791 for anyone lazy,
2400 lazy, I
4607 who are too lazy and
4753 kisses are hopelessly lazy.
5303 Men get lazy, and
7685 Call on the lazy
9187 to send a lazy man for
9706 ugly women, only lazy ones.
12069 The lazy are always
12736 The lazy man gets round

lead
1996 we think we lead, we are
2830 the Hour of Lead -
3100 You can lead a man up to
3146 Lead us, Heavenly Father,
5678 I failed to lead you to the
5827 Lead me from death to
6026 To lead the people, walk
6842 foremost To lead such dire
6966 To lead means to direct
8169 Lead, kindly Light, amid

leaden-eyed
5498 sorrow And leaden-eyed despairs.

leader
1408 A leader is a dealer in
2764 A true leader always keeps
3410 is no ethical leader for me.
4603 European leaders actually
6173 them - I am their leader.
6391 test of a leader is that he
8008 one people, one leader.
8646 A leader who rides to war is
12690 of a leader of men,
12927 A leader may symbolize and

leaders
6025 the best leaders, the

leadership
1318 The art of leadership is saying
3797 I suppose leadership at one time
11649 is the negation of leadership.

leading
2922 its light, Leading onward,

leaf
11556 last red leaf is whirled
12772 One only leaf upon the top

leafage
12682 important than his leafage.

league
11475 Half a league, half a

leak
1737 One leak will sink a ship,

lean
1790 houses, lean on one
5284 somehow the lean and
11779 face as lean over too

leaning
3866 I'm leaning on a lamp-post at

leap
380 twenty-nine in a leap year.
491 one giant leap for
1601 you made a leap into the
2016 carnal leap into that
4636 a great leap in the
7397 but we take leap after leap

leaping
4434 one's horse as he is leaping.

leaps
668 in mighty leaps, It leaps
6837 by steps, and not by leaps.

leapt
1360 world I leapt: Helpless,

lear
6152 to know Mr Lear!' Who has

learn
28 who know how to learn.
95 season for old men to learn.
320 To lose Is to learn.
660 a lot to learn about
895 it takes to learn the simple
1477 we don't learn from it.
2197 wolde he lerne and gladly
2700 fly, We learn so little
2920 We cannot learn men from

3157 best way to learn for
3394 First learn the meaning of
3471 A man must learn to forgive
3663 that if we learn more about
4117 it takes to learn to read.
4654 have no time left to learn.
4933 or you shall learn nothing.
5294 To teach is to learn twice.
6073 beerier, do learn to
6504 pursuing, Learn to labour
7463 desire to learn, there of
8720 Learn what you are, and be
8821 We live and learn, but not
9160 know is difficult to learn.
9544 I learn by going where I
9590 somehow we learn who we
9678 those who learn; poetry
10067 don't want to learn - much.
10085 while they teach, men learn.
10594 You don't learn to hold
11080 You have to learn to do
11092 is not to learn, but to
12698 on hand to learn them a bit
12859 more you learn to see
12925 Learn to see God in all

learned
207 have not learned from
368 what you learned this
1398 gesture learned from
2024 If I've learned anything in
2395 I know I learned after I
3357 he has learned the
5087 less is learned there; so
6918 in my life learned anything
7032 who have learned to do
8819 I have learned little from
8902 The learn'd is happy nature
9806 to have learned English -
11154 to have learned that the
11328 As learned commentators view
11988 old man had learned in seven
12368 time we've learned, it's too

learner
12011 of a teacher and a learner.

learning
747 of a state, learning; and then
1884 public and learning the
2630 wisest, and in learning rules.
2919 of liberty, and of learning.
3566 who stops learning is old,
3852 is thy learning? Hath thy
4187 and learning, Good
4481 Learning is the knowledge of
4781 is to keep learning, to enjoy
4911 rampant, and still learning.
5785 That learning belongs not to
6244 that I was learning how to
6426 of learning is not at
6905 order brings good learning.
7904 good life; learning, earning
8596 a little learning was
8760 All learning has an emotional
8874 A little learning is a
9205 By learning you will teach; by
9244 to your own learning, for he
9331 arts and learning down, And
9332 Learning to learn is to know
10484 O! this learning, what a thing
10882 with learning, but stood
10915 old ever learning many
11467 Learning passes for wisdom
11852 loyal body wanted learning.
11914 with their learning they
12930 scraps of learning dote, And

learns
4930 that he learns
5809 is' and learns from 'what

learnt
2526 we have learnt to walk.
4377 I have learnt a good deal
7649 and easiest learnt, What
10088 can be learnt, even
12237 it can never be fully learnt.

leasehold
6625 but it is leasehold for all.

least
710 world, and least of all

leathern
7066 moist Their leathern boats

leave
386 for I must leave thee, Do
1199 Leave off first for
1219 shall a man leave his father
1276 it wiser to leave five
2255 that if you leave things
3021 And all to leave what with
3602 for what we leave behind us
4132 Don't leave them on
6523 old adage, Leave them while
9578 done, and leave out the
10756 Leave me, O Love which
11005 And lend me leave to come
11377 Will not leave me: all

leave-taking
1877 but I don't like the leave-taking.

leaves
5485 as the leaves to a tree
9215 the falling leaves return to
9543 from the leaves, Lewd,
10692 the leaves dead Are
10694 What if my leaves are
12788 Than what it leaves behind.
12883 Though leaves are many, the

leaving
1700 as I am in leaving it and
10344 like the leaving it: he
11172 that I was leaving home and
12199 Leaving the old, both worlds

leavings
11347 to God of the devil's leavings.

lecher
10329 fly Does lecher in my

lechery
10506 Lechery, lechery; still, wars

lecture
11143 from the lecture Pleased

lecturer
12750 duty of a lecturer - to hand

lectures
12509 do not give lectures or a

led
1996 we lead, we are most led.
5706 nose .. Led go! You

lees
10356 the mere lees Is left

left
293 the sun we left the old
402 right - only who is left.
1168 let not thy left hand know
2669 be little left of him if
4425 through She left me, and
7111 less he has left in
8037 Greenfield left her
8127 to become a left winger in
11050 wing, nor left wing nor
11619 the only one I have left.
12324 So far upon the left side.

leg
6376 by the hind leg, and he is

legacy
1906 left him a legacy, the only
10829 known a legacy from a

legal
7378 sexes - the legal

legalized
2892 We have legalized confiscation,

legend
3818 I'm such a legend, then why

legislation
3668 be imposed without legislation.
4052 of English legislation. We look

legislative
779 the legislative part of
3902 when the legislative power is

legislator
1791 people is the true legislator.

legislature
777 that no legislature can

legitimate
12315 by means of legitimate (i.e.

legless
8817 critic is a legless man who

legs
3283 your bad legs, but for
4617 open my legs, and think
8362 with your legs apart.
8367 Four legs good, two legs
9992 for your legs and your

leicester
5343 Farewell, Leicester Square,

leisure
1462 is less leisure now than
5085 arises from leisure.
5160 is never at leisure. He is
6864 than work, leisure time
7499 retired Leisure, That in
7870 with a life of leisure.
9753 able to use leisure
10384 haste, and leisure answers
10650 is to have leisure to bother
11460 is in their leisure time that
11695 at leisure; Not
11842 to fill leisure

lemon
4182 in the squeezing of a lemon.

lemon-trees
4130 where the lemon-trees bloom? In

lend
1252 not well enough to lend to.
3609 Never lend books - nobody
5941 and the men who lend
9194 you or to lend you money.
10289 countrymen, lend me your
10314 knowest, Lend less than
11290 I never lends - my
11925 Few lend (but

length
3417 A line is length without
3692 for what it lacks in length.

lenin
5600 Lenin was right. There is
5612 Engels and Lenin he

lent
521 has been lent To youth

leopard
1227 or the leopard his spots?

less
58 us, had he pleased us less.
442 rights and nothing less.
566 but there's less of you.
1648 the little less, and what
1658 Less is more.
1867 more about less and less.
5700 An' rather less than 'arf
8254 go, the less others let
8931 the less they have
12874 and more in less and less.

lesser
3438 and the lesser ones, who

lesson
4930 the first lesson that ought
6070 before presenting the lesson.
8965 harder lesson! how to
9842 No lesson seems to be so
11004 Love is the lesson which the

lessons
7945 minded the lessons. I just

let in
10008 to be let in many times

lethal
417 at three, and lethal at one.
10108 .. the Average made lethal.

lethargy
7771 a kind of lethargy steals

lethe
5494 go not to Lethe, neither
5935 shores of Lethe millions

letter
701 he wrote a letter he would
724 by speech than by letter.
3937 I read your letter through
6282 have had a letter from her.
6709 write a letter if you can

9988 sight of a letter from him.
10318 zed! thou unnecessary letter!

letters
592 order, Letters for the
2946 kisses, letters mingle
5117 receive no letters in the
6552 to learn their letters.

lettuce
8969 too much lettuce is

level
1775 attempt to level never
3212 The dead level of

levers
11650 pulling the levers there but

levity
10630 it with the utmost levity.
11206 a little judicious levity.

lexicographer
5145 Lexicographer. A writer of

lexicon
1725 In the lexicon of youth,

liar
827 is a seductive liar.
990 'Little Liar!' And
1982 but the talent of a liar.
4968 universal liar who never
9341 A liar should have a good

liars
3009 do prove the greatest liars.
4866 though liars by
9568 made more liars out of the
10749 Liars ought to have good
11216 is run by liars and
12068 truthful, and die liars.

libel
11317 Convey a libel in a frown,

liberal
3697 A Liberal is a man too
3974 a little Liberal, Or else a
8376 Liberal - a power worshipper
11066 her is a liberal education
12467 and a liberal education

liberality
5840 Liberality lies less in giving

liberate
6367 is to liberate the world.
6941 we shall liberate this

liberates
294 macht frei. Work liberates.

liberation
4142 for the liberation of the

liberationists
6526 Women's Liberationists. They keep

liberties
1771 up their liberties but under
3874 what liberties are taken
4991 as he is of his liberties.
11704 been taking liberties, and these

libertine
10194 reckless libertine, Himself

liberty
40 endanger the public liberty.
312 Liberty is always unfinished
717 power and to lose liberty.
979 effective liberty: that what
1083 Liberty is liberty, not
1753 Abstract liberty, like other
1758 effect of liberty on
1766 Liberty too must be limited
1767 corrupt, liberty cannot
1834 Liberty's in every blow! Let
2222 to take liberty for
3117 When liberty destroys order,
3593 Liberty is always dangerous -
3621 of liberty have
3804 name of liberty or
3905 of constitutional liberty.
4072 not with my liberty; Either
4081 deserves liberty and life
4411 spirit of liberty is the
4548 me, give me liberty, or give
4843 us a-tall: Liberty and
4863 have been enemies of liberty.
4964 By physical liberty I mean the

5022 life, and liberty, and the
5355 The liberty of the press is
5567 and the success of liberty.
6217 Liberty is precious - so
6346 in liberty, and
6437 his natural liberty and puts
6511 Shouted of liberty; And he
6538 the air Know no such liberty.
6539 deep, Know no such liberty.
6540 above, Enjoy such liberty.
6562 But libbaty's a kind o'thing
6685 Liberty, as it is conceived
6816 to wait for liberty till they
6879 Liberty is to faction what
7366 with the liberty of action
7370 The liberty of the individual
7371 Liberty consists in doing
7465 Give me the liberty to know,
7512 mountain nymph, sweet Liberty.
7675 of ancient liberty, When
7676 they cry liberty; For who
7812 Liberty is the right to do
9581 O liberty! O liberty! what
9940 for their liberty, they
9946 Of course liberty is not
10622 Liberty means responsibility.
10862 land of liberty, Of thee I
11812 desires in liberty anything
12320 Liberty and Union, now and
12674 history of liberty is a
12691 of political liberty.
12870 If liberty has any meaning it

liberty-hall
4184 This is Liberty-Hall, gentlemen.

libraries
9736 out of circulating libraries!

library
663 the public library and make
664 Like one of his library books.
1028 you build a public library.
2990 room of his library, where he
5195 hopes, than a public library.
9848 A library is thought in cold
11264 time in the library with

licence
6970 the sort of licence that
7676 Licence they mean when they
7682 love not freedom, but licence.
9946 is not licence. Liberty
11735 your own licence to print

licensed
8300 based upon licensed premises.

licentious
3917 and all licentious passages

lick
9133 He who can lick can bite.

lie
86 possible to lie, and even
352 may lie with
493 not a lie. It was
746 of a lie doth ever
1067 come. Lie follows by
1894 whenever we lie to him.
2164 eat the lie and
2386 thriven May lie till
3856 readily can lie with art.
4631 to a big lie than to a
5009 is no worse lie than a
5140 telling a lie to a sick
5263 stone doth lie As much
5300 The lie in the soul is a
6686 writes is a lie, including
6703 Here lie I, Martin
7786 never venture to lie.
8192 You only lie to two
8232 The lie is a condition of
8706 Art is a lie that makes
9075 come, lie follows'.
9192 Truth is the safest lie.
9193 half-truth is a whole lie.
9376 thou must give the lie.
10114 Who loves to lie with me.
11041 a dream a lie if it
11490 That a lie which is all a
11541 can rule and dare not lie.
12264 tell a lie, Pa; you

12765 man sent to lie abroad for
12881 gone I must lie down where

lied
5689 because our fathers lied.
5737 Or being lied about,

lies
410 It produces lies like sand.
474 of telling lies skilfully.
542 white lies to ice a
1328 all the lies you can
1529 only lies are
2399 Here lies wise and valiant
2863 kinds of lies: lies,
4268 The body never lies.
4843 Lies written down For
5026 nothing to fear from lies.
5421 Here lies one whose name
8393 to make lies sound
8993 old men's lies, the
9037 leave, Here lies what once
9093 Who lies for you, will lie
9522 Here lies a great and
10544 say, 'This poet lies.'
10564 though I know she lies.
10590 will tell lies as usual.
10635 the end the lies he tells
11161 telling lies about the
11199 cruellest lies are often
12188 Who tell lies to
12910 tells his lies by rote; A

lieutenant
7883 you, master Lieutenant, see me

life
20 of. Life, the
175 no inner life is the
223 Life is uncertain - eat
276 Life is a sexually
327 husband for life, not for
353 the home life of our own
393 More a Way of Life.
437 - and that is life.
490 What we play is life.
553 Life is seldom as
619 Life is a stranger's
623 any other life than this
800 an unhappy life, thank
851 to prolong life. And if
854 adhering to life now with
857 because. Life says: she
873 with life is that
1036 Life is rather like a tin
1062 A complete life may be one
1150 giveth his life for the
1152 and the life: no man
1153 down his life for his
1198 and wrath shorten the life.
1217 Life for life, Eye for
1418 midst of life we are in
1573 ours; and life burns on
1599 Life is just a bowl of
1631 but one life and one
1685 in his life: to be
1721 Life would be tolerably
1824 Life is all a VARIORUM, We
1827 O Life! thou art a galling
1884 Life is like playing a
1885 If life must not be taken
1887 Life is one long process
1902 business of life is to
1948 art of life is
2056 sin against life, it
2277 essence of life is going
2321 of human life would be
2369 My life hath been one
2423 Life is a horizontal fall.
2500 Real life seems to have no
2526 Life is a maze in which we
2545 Life's too short to stuff
2576 me all my life to
2589 since my life began The
2598 Life is an incurable
2696 an exellent life of
2704 is this life if, full
2765 makes us think about life.
3296 Life is livable because we
3352 Life consists in what a
3409 not fear life if their

3465 Life cannot defeat a
3583 Our life on earth is, and
3634 career of life. All I
3657 Life as we find it is too
3708 about life. It goes
3850 Life is a jest; and all
3932 of Life's longing
3988 Life is a joke that's just
4040 came? Life would ring
4042 Life is ever Since man was
4100 of actual life springs
4227 Life is mostly froth and
4376 but one life to lose
4398 Life only demands from the
4431 of life should be
4531 of your life, it stays
4625 Drama is life with the
4637 and the life of man,
4645 Life doesn't have clear
4712 Life is action and
4714 Life is painting a
4724 worth of life as an end
4786 Life, to be sure, is
4821 Life is just one damned
4822 more out of life than there
4908 moment, life is
4909 of human life is routine
4975 you imagine life as a book,
5004 use of life is to
5019 Life exists in the
5036 rest of my life bringing
5094 is tired of life; for there
5161 The joy of life is
5165 Life is a progress from
5196 Human life is everywhere a
5336 That's not life for men
5404 was how his life happened.
5475 A man's life of any worth
5509 consider! life is but a
5576 to you in life, I find.
5595 the rest of my life there.
5623 Life can only be
5681 each one life to give.
5804 through life; to
5864 Life is what happens to us
5912 business life is.
6039 Life is first boredom,
6087 Life is ours to be spent,
6094 In life .. no new thing
6132 Life, we learn too late,
6159 And that life on the
6169 Life is something to do
6177 terror my life in the
6192 Life is like a sewer.
6232 all my life, though
6241 imperils life, fear
6242 Life well spent is long.
6286 one way of life as when
6309 Life would be tolerable
6380 to creative life, or
6446 children. Life is the
6500 numbers, Life is but an
6625 And life is given to none
6631 a fool his whole life long.
6730 Some forms of life arise.
6753 has to take life as he
6795 Our end is Life. Put out
6959 of our life. But the
7130 My mother's life made me a
7356 copyright on your own life?
7395 true that life is one
7415 Life, as it is called, is
7431 marble leapt to life a god.
7529 slits the thin-spun life.
7634 love thy life, nor hate;
7658 To live a life half dead,
7692 looked at life from both
7772 course of life so weak
7789 Life is a dream; when we
7867 of glorious life Is worth
7902 spend your life in your
7904 in the good life; learning,
7905 Life is a foreign
7920 Life is like a very short
7931 reward of labour is life.
7956 luxuries of life, and we
8061 Life is a great surprise.
8167 the only evidence of life.

8173 fever of life is over,
8218 from life is to
8224 detail of one's life.
8230 Is not life a hundred
8232 lie is a condition of life.
8235 music, life would be a
8244 would be a life without
8344 is but his fear of life.
8345 Life is perhaps most
8481 interest in life, good, bad
8483 a shorter life than
8501 Oh, life is a glorious
8555 virtue is lifeless and it
8560 My sister life's in flood
8613 he dies of his whole life.
8670 better, life would
8809 Man's real life is happy,
8854 this long disease, my life.
9005 hears about life all the
9329 Thou art my life; if thou
9385 lived his life to the
9416 into the sunset of my life.
9451 Art is life rearranged
9523 draught of life go down.
9561 Half our life is spent
9589 Life has got to be lived -
9629 of my life Is come,
9657 What is life, without a
9682 nature, And life without it
9695 The life of a writer is
9703 of life and what
9713 that all life is 6 to 5
9727 the laws of life; anarchy
9728 is no wealth but life.
9764 The good life, as I
9766 is to fear life, and those
9769 is Man's life; on him
9902 waking life is a dream
9922 Human life begins on the
9971 our coming life, we are
9993 My life has no purpose, no
9996 go through life as a man
10017 One hour of life, crowded
10070 a man's life, but no
10073 way in to life, but many
10112 this our life, exempt
10143 web of our life is of a
10148 I love long life better
10241 the time of life is short;
10278 spirit; But life, being
10304 Life is as tedious as a
10320 Man's life is cheap
10344 in his life Became him
10443 me, and my life is done.
10489 our little life Is
10495 is the glory of this life.
10655 What is life but a series
10673 dream of life - 'Tis we,
10676 Life, like a dome of
10714 those who live Call Life.
10757 common errors of our life.
10839 aim at in life: first, to
10846 say that life is
10856 they say my life isn't a
10937 Life is not about
10940 evidence of life. His
10976 and she is mine for life.
10984 success in life is to be a
11158 in your life but the
11233 Life is a gamble at
11285 Life would be very
11325 all the days of your life.
11355 light, And Life, the
11357 reap; His life is a watch
11421 Would that life were like
11455 As our life is very short,
11492 man in this life does not
11498 a blameless life, Before a
11562 dust, And Life, a Fury
11607 No life that breathes with
11677 Oh, isn't life a terrible
11744 out of much life. So aim
11770 Our life is frittered away
11832 of human life, the true
11865 It is now life and not art
11899 old life. I love
11962 Life would be infinitely
11989 and life stands

11994 All of life is more or
12220 'Tisn't that matters!
12360 business of life, is to
12404 men in my life that
12542 one's own life is to
12713 queer thing Life is! So
12739 is not in life but in art
12748 Life is not a series of
12794 good man's life, His
12893 Life is a long preparation
12943 Life is the desert, life
12949 time in his life (it varies

life-blood
11859 is the life-blood of real

life-giving
3802 is exhilarating and life-giving.

life-jacket
856 is the French for life-jacket.

lifeless
8555 virtue is lifeless and it

lifelong
12553 of a lifelong romance.

lifetime
531 Our lifetime may be the last
799 as a whole lifetime, and
2779 than a schmuck for a lifetime."
5570 in our lifetime on this
10613 But a lifetime of happiness!
11159 dedication of a lifetime.
12435 the knowledge of a lifetime.

lift
10693 Oh, lift me as a wave, a
10714 Lift not the painted veil
10876 people, and lift up all who

lifted
10779 your face lifted but there

light
121 put out the light of even
184 The light did him harm, but
760 Creature, which was Light.
1166 Let your light so shine
1482 Yet the light of the
1994 By the light of the
2266 a girl in a light so dim he
2842 that the light at the end
2951 constant light; And his
3713 The dark is light enough.
3748 Light, God's eldest
4094 Mehr Licht! More light!
4454 'Give me a light that I may
4717 the more light you pour
5270 lose this light, 'Tis with
6024 the beam of your light.
6462 The light is better than a
6589 If we see light at the end
7204 is the light on the
7387 - It gives a lovely light.
7502 room Teach light to
7509 I owe no light or leading
7573 of hell leads up to light.
7637 Light out of darkness! full
7677 how my light is spent,
7934 C'mon, baby, light my fire.
7955 gust of light explains
8062 crack of light between
8126 The light has gone out of
8169 kindly Light, amid the
8873 be! and all was light.
8986 gathers the light against
8997 a ball of light in one's
9329 Thou art my light; if hid,
9364 well as sweetness and light.
9526 leaves the light of nature,
9541 All flowers keep the light.
10409 A light wife doth make a
10437 Put out the light, and then
10472 soft! what light through
10566 sink, but light, and will
10785 The morning light creaks
11304 are sweetness and light.
11673 Light breaks where no sun
12055 world of light, And I
12056 Whose light doth
12063 and endless light, All calm,
12307 you can light it again
12783 The light that never was,

light brigade
11476 the Light Brigade!' Was

lighten
4322 learn to lighten up if we

lightened
12795 world, Is lightened.

lightly
2235 they take themselves lightly.

lightness
5828 unbearable lightness of being.

lightning
535 streak of lightning in the
4234 of summer lightning, lambent
4974 to keep the lightning out. But
11947 between lightning and the

lights
2443 the stern lights of a ship,
4546 Turn up the lights; I don't
9420 was an all-the-lights-on man.
9649 sound, the lights around the
11553 but broken lights of thee,

like
179 No wonder we like them
576 whom I like, I can
609 Love and do what you like.
657 like good
1950 the less I like them. If
2408 Or something very like Him.
2848 him, they do not like him.
3462 of people you don't like.
6359 People who like this sort
6405 someone else does not like.
6588 dreadfully like other
7010 That like I best, that
7278 They like men who
9844 To like and dislike the
10627 what you like or you
11335 one as they like; as the
12019 people you like best, they
12543 of his friends like him.

liked
5956 like to be liked, and what
9758 wish to be liked, not to be

likely
9136 certain but it's very likely.

liking
639 trouble of liking them a
870 but in liking what one
897 necessary: a liking for work.
3616 we take a liking to
11695 Not liking the

likings
5936 made up of likings and

lilies
7089 And lilies, that you
7090 have been Lilies without,
9636 had three lilies in her
10556 deeds; Lilies that

lily
1963 gold, or paint the lily.'
5454 I see a lily on thy brow
6488 tower, The lily of
9103 one, and a lily with the
10305 paint the lily, To throw

lily-handed
11596 No little lily-handed baronet he,

limbo
7586 Into a limbo large and

limbs
8104 your lower limbs in pants;

limit
4120 art is to limit and
4815 in not exceeding the limit.
7424 to sharply limit the number
9244 Don't limit a child to your
11606 the quiet limit of the

limitations
3227 emotional limitations of our
8657 We accept our limitations.
10092 knows his limitations, yet bows
11890 know the limitations of force;

limited
7061 are limited only by
7370 be thus far limited; he must

limits
3384 Whatever limits us we call
4463 within ancient limits.
6992 hath no limits nor is
12703 The limits of my language

limp
12749 He is limp and damp and

lincoln
1020 (Abraham Lincoln's) weathered
9855 Abraham Lincoln was

line
2308 draw a line without
6280 is a thin line between
8787 dies sine linea. Not a
8895 and lives along the line.
9793 thin red line tipped

linen
3548 is like linen often
4742 It is not linen you're

liner
5716 The Liner she's a lady, an'

lines
7075 As lines (so loves) oblique

lingering
3999 Something lingering, with

linguistics
9627 Essay in Sociological Linguistics.

lining
862 crowd has a silver lining.

link
2322 Only one link in the
6529 the missing link between

linked
8428 too will be linked with

linnet
11559 rage, The linnet born

lion
2324 had the lion heart. I
2739 to have a lion at the
8327 the old lion is dead,
10038 Rouse the lion from his
10140 with the lion Must die
10418 A lion among ladies, is a
10808 is the lion - like a

lioness
11458 feeds a lioness at home

lions
8576 And, on the other, lions.
12243 up my Lions & fled the

lip
687 in the lip than in

lipless
3268 backward with a lipless grin.

lips
820 for my lips are not
1862 Read my lips: no new
6453 of thy lips And flies
6944 born before my lips.
6993 a kiss! Her lips suck forth
11524 the touching of the lips.
11634 God in the lips and hearts
12945 Yet the lips that touch

lipstick
8095 on too much lipstick, And helps

liquid
11630 no less liquid than their

liquor
4187 Good liquor, I stoutly
4986 I like liquor - its taste
8100 dandy But liquor Is
12635 live in. Liquor is one way
12945 that touch liquor must never

list
3985 a little list - I've got

listen
3690 ability to listen to almost
3826 I'll not listen to reason
3938 things And listen to the
4430 is wonderful to listen to.
4519 say don't listen to writers
4835 folks is to listen to them.
5613 people will listen today,
5851 of those who listen to them.

7991 Stop-look-listen.
9081 Listen or thy tongue will
9530 much more courage to listen.
10711 should listen then - as
11799 duty of love is to listen.
12521 man should listen when his

listened
9551 was listened to with

listener
1557 impatient listener, but in

listening
803 good at listening to their
1526 about him, ain't listening.
3810 they're listening and you
6395 of listening is what
7284 Listening is a magnetic and
8585 when you're listening to someone
10101 After listening to thousands of
10770 without listening ..

listens
7046 Nobody listens, then
9449 A man who listens because he

lit
4328 see them lit again in

literalists
7844 us can be literalists of the

literary
997 an unsuccessful literary man.
2542 so in literary action, a
2559 If a literary man puts
2852 In literary history,
4490 class is literary footmen.
4888 of modern literary forms.
4897 essay is a literary device for
5106 parole of literary men all
7839 A literary movement consists
9023 Of all the literary scenes

literature
273 children's literature appeals
314 Literature is a power to be
507 is literature in a
565 get from literature depend
1459 you, sir: literature is a drug.
2217 wife. Literature is my
2239 Literature is a luxury; fiction
2898 failed in literature and art.
3079 at the great table of literature.
3120 you can turn her into literature.
3368 of rule in literature that a
3947 literature can be
4949 Literature flourishes best when
4995 to produce a little literature.
6000 Literature is the effort of man
6127 primitive literature. They
6312 like their literature clear and
6446 Literature is mostly about
6549 the itch of literature comes over
7200 In literature as in love we are
7944 of much literature is that it
8304 English literature's performing
8389 Socialist literature is W.H.
8981 Literature is news that STAYS
8990 Great literature is simply
9882 Bible is literature, not
10960 lover of literature is never
11075 Remarks are not literature.
11478 louse in the locks of literature.
12036 The rest is literature.
12487 things in all literature.
12610 Literature is the orchestration
12758 Literature is strewn with the
12953 no bronze literature, there can

litigant
1265 Litigant, n: a person about to

litigious
8180 litigious lady that

littered
9010 History is littered with the

little
1468 soup. A little may be
2496 nearly as much as too little.
3126 do crave; I little have, and
3256 are convinced of too little.
3938 we turn to little things And
4162 wants but little here
6420 A little of what you fancy

6808 was little seemed to
7042 it was a very little one.
7373 case knows little of that.
9457 So little done, so much to
10796 may have Is little to say,
11424 are good in little measure
11569 to do, So little done, such
12941 wants but little, nor that

littleness
2098 of his own littleness, than

littlenesses
11498 a thousand peering littlenesses.

live
257 away, May live to fight
473 choose to live, though he
756 I would live to study, and
940 cream and live skim milk.
1324 I was gonna live this long,
1574 strangely, I live on.
1891 To live is like to love -
1933 I live not in myself, but
2482 be known, live in a city.
2484 anything but live for it.
2537 We live, as we dream -
3649 actually live longer; it
3665 dream is to live long and
3941 left us to live - that we
4856 Those who live are those
4936 than to live on your
5167 better to live rich than
5334 yet. Feel live warm
5550 Teach me to live, that I
5551 past, And live this day
5650 for, he isn't fit to live.
6038 where we live. They
6244 how to live, I have
6310 You only live once - but
6994 hour to live, And then
7050 'I shall live to do
7054 I cannot live with you -
7249 We live, not as we wish
7271 may no more live in the
7326 We may live without
7513 thy crew To live with her,
7627 How can I live without
7634 thou liv'st Live well, how
7714 He who lives without
7729 eat to live, and not
8251 a why to live can bear
8275 If a child lives with
8498 you don't live it it
8509 You might as well live.
8599 to live with her,
8664 Live with yourself: get to
8907 we bear to live, or dare
8934 Thus let me live, unseen,
9080 All would live long, but
9098 getting ready to live.
9783 how to live with
10014 eye - Easy live and quiet
10463 say, do never live long.
10535 cannot live together:
10912 Bad men live to eat and
10962 Live as long as you may,
11149 than to live up to
11217 If you live long enough
11325 May you live all the days
11340 desires to live long; but
11453 at Rome, live in the
11499 Live pure, speak true,
11538 Live and lie reclined On
11737 to live the life
11749 have not stood up to live.
11798 us how to live; and (oh!
11963 I can live for two months
12067 we must live as though
12108 I wish to live and to
12163 We never live, but we are
12368 We should live and learn;
12462 - how to live with grace
12926 learn to live for
12965 am here to live out loud.'

lived
502 To have lived light in
1386 left me. I lived a few
2371 well who lived for joys
3070 for I have lived to-day.

3838 should have lived
3847 loved, has never lived.
4677 Well, I've lived my life as
4961 I have lived to thank God
7090 Had it lived long, it would
7767 is to have lived it
7777 he has lived for a long
8996 seen and lived at least
9071 we lived so fully
9589 got to be lived - that's
9781 feel I have lived in vain.
10011 Had we lived, I should have
10031 thou but lived, though
10371 I have lived long enough:
11725 who never lived, Yet still

lives
623 he now lives, nor lives
2678 half of our lives is ruined
4742 But human creatures' lives!
5005 Lives based on having are
5836 of their lives to making
6503 Lives of great men all
7992 Careless talk costs lives.
8383 of their lives, but on
10013 buying - it's men's lives.
10764 in your own lives and
10857 version of their lives.
11168 Everyone lives by selling
11767 of men lead lives of quiet
12538 For he who lives more lives

living
171 in the great art of living.
203 It's living together
339 of the living can the
495 The living need charity more
616 The art of living is more
1605 habit of living
1761 dead, the living, and the
2499 like living together
3240 gone on living, Living
4375 the living dead, the
4610 an' the livin' is easy,
4833 to stop living on account
6041 we shall be living in a
6132 is in the living, in the
6502 act in the living Present!
7397 Living is a form of not
7782 Living is my job and my art.
8805 called Living' Is
9196 make a wonderful living.
9697 peace in your active living.
10741 that, living know No
11897 Living next to the United
12106 Living? The servants will
12169 to the living; to the
12636 I'm not living with you. We
12737 for living and
12804 shouldst be living at this
12919 course, is living any newer.

livingstone
11052 Dr Livingstone, I presume?

llama
997 The Llama is a woolly sort

lloyd george
398 Lloyd George knew my father, My

loafing
11466 cricket as organized loafing.

loan
664 have him on loan from
2001 a brief loan of his own

loathe
2018 I loathe all things held in

loaves
9163 two, he replies four loaves.

lobbyist
11906 the only lobbyist that all

local
4685 But nothing local, as one

location
8459 on location is in

locks
7464 invincible locks. Methinks

lodgings
10902 in frowzy lodgings, where

logic
2720 It is the logic of our
4713 not been logic, it has
6263 The logic of the heart is

logically
553 facts. it logically ought to
3173 to a logically uniform

loitering
5453 and palely loitering? The sedge

london
2472 Oh, London is a fine town, A
2613 was he Of famous London Town.
2812 This is a London particular
2896 London: a nation, not a
2989 alleys in London do not
2996 London, that great cesspool
3892 day in London Town Had
5094 is tired of London, he is
6052 thought of London spread out
6824 arch of London Bridge to
7134 leads to London, One road
7926 dream of London, small and
8742 are the lungs of London
10698 much like London - A
11686 dead lies London's

loneliness
2213 afraid of loneliness, don't
2544 what true loneliness is - not
2580 is to shatter his loneliness.
4652 of the final loneliness.
7699 The arctic loneliness of age.
8344 Man's loneliness is but his fear
10765 The loneliness of the
11626 Loneliness and the feeling of
11803 the word loneliness' to
12723 Loneliness is and always has

lonely
1570 of these so lonely and poor
2441 So lonely 'twas that God
3818 why am I so lonely? Let me
5051 I may be lonely, and
6226 All the lonely people,
6756 heart is a lonely hunter
7898 No man is lonely while
8233 The lonely one offers his
8576 thenceforth lonely, and for
12127 under the lonely night

lonesome
2448 that on a lonesome road Doth
9170 be quarrelling than lonesome.

long
371 is his long staying.
1537 they last too long.
2641 sat too long here for
5121 Mr Long's character is
5343 It's a long way to
5608 In the long run we are all
6180 appear most long and
6242 Life well spent is long.
6321 is his long staying.
7573 Long is the way And hard,
8098 but it's gone on too long.
8130 work, Hardy, to last long.
8343 A long day's journey into
8712 It takes a long time to
9080 would live long, but none
11597 is life but love is long.
12664 a week is a very long time.

long-distance
10765 of the long-distance runner.

longed
11607 ever truly longed for death.

longer
3347 is brave five minutes longer.
3649 live longer; it just
5758 takes a little longer.
8549 [letter] longer than

longest
7163 that lasts longest is the
9154 Invalids live longest.
10962 are the longest half of

longevity
3561 Longevity conquers scandal
4715 Longevity is having a chronic

longing
5031 has cast a longing eye on
9497 Oh longing for places that

longings
10169 I have Immortal longings in me.

look
712 If a man look sharply, and
2673 portrait to look like the
3425 What we look for does not
3433 When I look at a painting
3896 Just one look at you, my
5021 When I look in the glass I
5981 people will look at
6011 Two men look out through
6565 you can look or listen.
7727 One should look long and
9438 shall still look for Him.
10192 I shall not look upon his
10398 Let him look to his bond.
11300 If I look like this, I
11851 Look in my face. My name
12540 a bitter look, Some with

look after
10009 God's sake look after our
11660 is to look after Itself.

looked
1641 never have looked at me, If
5439 all his men Looked at each
5456 She looked at me as she did
7435 The more he looked inside the
7692 I've looked at life from

looker-on
9325 a patient looker-on; Judge not

looking
184 as much as looking at things
557 gives him to keep on looking.
1385 "Here's looking at you, kid."
1497 dark room - looking for a
2819 bad men not looking you in the
3490 I'm looking for loopholes.
5593 you start looking very
7269 that someone may be looking
11100 all night looking for them
11684 she wasn't looking and never
12752 and a woman looking at a girl
12963 Don't go on looking at me like

looking-glass
5327 The cracked looking-glass of a
12757 as looking-glasses

looks
1656 on, and her looks went
2468 A woman as old as she looks.
4874 Stolen looks are nice
7864 woman's looks, And
10390 a fawning publican he looks!
11916 needs good looks. From 35

looms
12058 these looms God

loopholes
3490 I'm looking for loopholes.
11630 through loopholes Less than

loose
4876 I can pry loose is not
5815 Every which way but loose.

lord
81 The good Lord set definite
128 The Lord God made
546 Lord, make me an
548 O Lord! thou knowest how
610 Lord, who art always the
1202 Israel: The Lord our God is
1230 The Lord gave, and the
1425 The Lord is my shepherd:
1434 unto the Lord a new
1709 Lord, dismiss us with Thy
2922 gracious Lord, may we
3273 My Lord, I had forgot the
3442 Fresh from the Lord!
4509 to ask the Lord for
5345 wit thy Lord's meaning
6596 The Lord survives the
6703 o' my soul, Lord God; As I
7020 me kiss my Lord before I
7750 worship the Lord in the
8898 fall; Great lord of all
12766 Lord of himself, though

lordly
8721 supreme of lordly wealth.

lords
4191 I see the lords of human
7667 Lords are lordliest in
7816 Great lords have their
8277 House of Lords as from
10712 For the lords who lay ye

lordship
864 His lordship may compel us to

lordships
206 for their lordships on a hot

lore
5523 And all the lore its

lose
96 you do not lose the
144 when you lose you die a
320 To lose Is to learn.
365 his side shall lose him.
1163 world, and lose his own
2276 disastrous as to lose one!
2433 Many people lose their
2604 that you'll lose your mind
3191 you must never do - lose
4530 You lose it if you talk
4786 much to lose; But young
6157 day you may lose them all';
6160 But to lose our teeth
6271 does not lose his reason
7568 who would lose, Though
7629 flesh; to lose thee were
8384 ending a war is to lose it.
9091 Those who lose dreaming
9700 want to lose you but we
9912 a portrait I lose a friend.
10618 One is to lose your
10657 You can lose a man like
11692 all must lose Their way.
12234 No man can lose what he
12556 To lose one parent, Mr

loser
0531 gracious loser, and I'll
10776 a gracious loser and I'll

loses
515 himself, loses his
623 that no man loses any other
3094 One loses so many laughs by
7251 A man loses his sense of
8248 of them loses his mind

losing
168 ways of losing money -
1459 A losing trade, I assure
5070 face you're losing your ass.
5736 you Are losing theirs and

lost
31 in power is a friend lost.
971 good men lost on both
2262 that it might be lost.
4313 was ever lost by delay.
5107 that I have lost all the
5116 day to be lost, in which
6033 Are you lost daddy I
6342 .. I have lost every
6951 Lost, yesterday, somewhere
7350 no hate lost between
7550 field be lost? All is
7625 of woe That all was lost.
7824 Thou art lost and gone
7901 who have lost their
8041 is already lost. Freedom
8188 I once was lost, but now
8289 balm - Not but gone
8377 wars have been lost there.
9067 In search of lost time.
9076 that we have lost.
9972 which must not be lost.
10019 He is lost to the
10606 She had lost the art of
11087 are all a lost
11381 grief, I've lost him
11548 loved and lost Than never
11585 Nor ever lost an English
11806 Friends, I have lost a day.
12164 once when I lost a lawsuit,
12361 a battle lost can be

8110 Love is an emotion
8118 Love is a fever which
8211 a man is in love he endures
8317 Love lives in sealed
8422 perilous to love than the
8439 an end of love, love will
8501 And love is a thing
8503 without: Love,
8554 experience love, without
8558 Love is not weakness. It
8572 We love, Fool, for the
8591 first love's
8604 thing is love for (well
8645 Love is not the dying moan
8651 Our love of what is
8710 People love the night,
8757 Love set you going like a
8803 Than to love and be
8840 a crime to love too well?
8844 draw, When love is
8958 do it, let's fall in love.
9001 He fell in love with
9024 Love is so simple.
9034 but I love thee in
9035 past making love, When she
9070 of mind in love, since the
9094 Love Canada or give it
9147 les yeux Love is blind;
9172 who did not love it should
9194 anyone to love you or to
9226 Parents love their
9241 The greater love is a
9310 A woman's love for us
9358 by love, but
9371 Love is a durable fire, In
9427 We love without reason,
9432 Work and love - these are
9450 really love anybody at
9495 Love consists in this,
9523 Love .. That cordial drop
9528 Love a woman? You're an
9545 the eyes My love with no
9550 know her was to love her.
9629 Is come, my love is come to
9664 for you to love money -
9667 Love is two minutes and
9742 When love and skill work
9749 longing for love, the
9759 caution in love is perhaps
9766 To fear love is to fear
9809 knows about love. It is
9821 us that love does not
9902 Work and love - these are
9903 Love makes of the wisest
9951 Love is a spendthrift,
10025 Love rules the court, the
10026 True love's the gift which
10042 Love still has something
10050 Love means never having to
10113 That ever love did make
10124 not fall in love with me,
10125 them, but not for love.
10129 low, if you speak love.
10130 office and affairs of love.
10139 I should love a bright
10146 in the love that can
10158 Of us that trade in love.
10203 But never doubt I love.
10297 upon my love; I may do
10312 Love is not love When it
10395 Love is blind, and lovers
10413 of true love never did
10414 Love looks not with the
10432 the thing I love For
10435 But never taint my love.
10439 Few love to hear the sins
10471 My only love sprung from
10475 What love can do that
10477 the sea, My love as deep;
10501 wise, and love, Exceeds
10512 What is love? 'tis not
10515 Let thy love be younger
10518 Love sought is good, but
10547 thy sweet love remembered
10550 a fool is love that in
10560 Love is not
10561 Love alters not with his
10563 I think my love as rare As

10566 Love is a spirit all
10567 Love comforteth like
10607 Love is a gross
10653 would only love one
10704 are beautiful through love.
10722 may be crossed in love!
10742 person who loves you a
10753 My true love hath my heart
10754 They love indeed who quake
10778 - you won't love me when
10790 speak of love still
10947 of life; that word is love.
10950 Love is but discovery:
10974 repent of love. The sin
10997 I must have love enough to
11004 So let us love, dear Love,
11005 leave to come unto my love?
11013 And all for love, and
11019 and eke to love, Is
11066 To love her is a liberal
11167 in love and keep
11214 We love in others what we
11269 will not love, Nothing
11272 Love is the fart Of every
11276 the state of love exists.
11323 I heartily love John,
11338 to make us love one
11355 to smite, Love that
11362 And love is more cruel
11502 what true love is, But if
11510 while woman wakes to love
11523 turns to thoughts of love.
11543 planet of Love is on
11545 of my true love Round me
11592 skins; They love us for it,
11597 is life but love is long.
11598 more, dear love, for at a
11616 Lovers' rows make love
11625 that if I love until it
11627 Christians love one
11633 We love being in love,
11647 to a love
11690 of sight, Love and
11699 There is no love For such,
11747 truth, there is love.
11783 knows what love really is
11799 duty of love is to
11833 through love of their
11837 let us make love deathless.
11872 courage to love should
11883 Love is like any other
12004 be spent on one we love.
12023 Love is an act of endless
12133 Now I know what Love is.
12135 Love conquers all things:
12226 In love alone we hate to
12254 you fall in love with
12274 between love and
12277 I love him not, but show
12356 brotherly love, five
12386 Amazing love! How can it
12389 An ounce of love is worth a
12415 making love to,
12417 suffer is the test of love.
12524 opposite of love is not
12553 To love oneself is the
12668 too late to fall in love.
12694 Love (if such a thing
12770 that love was but a
12842 some have died for love.
12843 then What love I bore to
12861 Love, a child, is ever
12863 Farewell, Love, and all
12886 mouth And love comes in
12898 hid in the heart of love.
12901 gardens my love and I did
12956 lives does Love really

love song
8961 There's no love song finer, But

love-quarrels
7666 Love-quarrels oft in pleasing

love-sick
10155 winds were love-sick with them.

loved
502 To have loved to have
669 I loved thee once, I'll
982 of Balliol loved and led

1386 weeks while you loved me."
1640 We loved, sir - used to
1661 And the loved one all
1710 than being loved; and often
1798 He may have loved before; I
1807 we never lov'd sae
2603 not being loved as a child
2945 till we loved, were we
3182 survival - I merely loved.
3847 has never loved, has never
3848 sighed, he loved, was
3914 I saw and loved.
4348 handle loved, May be
4855 that we are loved.
6106 I loved you, so I drew
6732 because she loved much: one
6743 has ever loved anyone the
6859 feared than loved, if he is
6928 as I have loved thee
7003 Who ever loved that loved
7394 And if I loved you
7801 say why I loved him, I can
7889 of being loved: It is
8440 want to be loved, be
8764 is holy loved by the
8804 sea; But we loved with a
9349 I have loved him too much
9350 I loved you when you were
9380 I wish I loved the Human
9549 whom he loved so long
9899 it can be loved, and it
10288 Not that I loved Caesar
11548 to have loved and lost
12235 him as though you loved him.
12700 I loved a lass, a fair one,
12967 only to be loved, even

loveliest
4787 Loveliest of trees, the cherry

loveliness
3998 miracle of loveliness. People
5417 ever: Its loveliness increases;
10675 of the loveliness Which once

lovely
2221 'You have lovely eyes, you
4769 forward will prove lovely.
4875 has got, A lovely woman in a
6399 Oh what a lovely war
7739 Ah, it's a lovely thing, to
10675 once he made more lovely.

lovemaking
4661 keeping. Lovemaking is

lover
805 face of a lover is
1959 loves her lover, In all
2155 her lusting lover it is best
2528 searching for a new lover.
3332 All mankind love a lover.
3915 sighed as a lover, I obeyed
4009 Peripatetic Lover, he lived
4105 you can still be a lover.
4427 A lover without
5240 Gives the lover weight and
7609 the injured lover's hell.
8500 Scratch a lover, and find a
9685 left of a lover, after the
10459 prove a lover, To
10960 Your true lover of
11781 not a dog lover. To me, a
11880 with her lover's mind if
12225 A lover forsaken A new love
12646 to her lover -

lovers
1573 other lovers, other
2164 two were lovers or no,
2167 and the lovers of their
2661 home .. lovers alone wear
3539 When even lovers find their
6299 And go, as lovers go, for
8772 of men - lovers of wisdom,
8928 And make two lovers happy.
10045 What need lovers wish for
10468 lovers take their
11520 two young lovers lately
11662 Though lovers be lost

loves
1007 as good as what he loves.
1959 woman loves her lover,

2450 well, who loveth well Both
2662 us, but loves us anyway.
3818 around who loves you.
4169 that one loves him still
4504 always loves for other
6631 Who loves not women, wine
6702 that a man loves And when
6964 He who loves the more is
6981 When a man loves his
7075 lines (so loves) oblique
7676 For who loves that, must
7808 one touch you who loves you.
9436 beautiful what he loves.
9797 no real loves and no
10105 Every man loves what he is
10565 Two loves I have of comfort
11409 only may chastise who loves.
11458 He that loves not his wife
11501 For who loves me must
12540 thing he loves, By each

loving
200 the act of loving someone
649 is that of loving longest,
1994 made for loving, And the
2267 crime of loving is
2558 made for loving and not
5598 A loving person lives in a
7854 can help loving the land
8290 had no lovin' Since
9696 is like loving and dying
9724 any good by loving me; I have
10120 most loving mere
11213 a man for loving her,
11448 The loving are the daring.
12605 begin by loving their

low
4741 .. lies so low they're
4812 is a very low grade of

lowbrow
1082 the first militant lowbrow.

lower
7232 is it to lower the price
12554 if the lower orders

lowly
129 Stood a lowly cattle

loyal
6892 in her heart loyal to you.

loyalties
503 names, and impossible loyalties!
4985 by their loyalties and

loyalty
1467 constitute loyalty, a
5063 don't want loyalty. I want
5632 Loyalty is the Tory's secret
9697 sort of loyalty, you
11852 body wanted loyalty; To

lubricates
10039 A dinner lubricates business.

lucifer
6999 come not, Lucifer! I'll burn
7309 Prince Lucifer uprose.

luck
1024 hard luck - well, we
1084 The luck of having talent
1483 average luck to survive
2923 Luck is being ready for
3424 old enemy down on his luck.
3584 much good luck in the
4043 With luck on your side you
4587 their good luck for their
6130 believer in luck. I find
7908 had bad luck with our
9400 the man, the worse luck.
9604 the good luck of the
11064 believes in luck and sends

luckier
8780 you work, the luckier you get.

luckiest
581 are the luckiest of mortals

lucky
3493 - a man's lucky if he gets
9083 Throw a lucky man into the
9247 were born lucky, even your
12136 Lucky is he who has been

luddites
10836 loaf and Luddites rise? Who

luftwaffe
8754 , With your Luftwaffe, your

lumber
2990 away in the lumber room of
8885 of learned lumber in his

luminous
6149 The Dong with a Luminous Nose!'

lumps
11106 There are lumps in it.

lunatic
9606 form the lunatic fringe in
10421 The lunatic, the lover, and

lunatics
6417 lunatic asylum run by lunatics.
9693 The lunatics have taken charge

lunch
327 for life, not for lunch.
388 such thing as a free lunch.
3484 the cork out of my lunch.
8959 unable to lunch today).

luncheon
1000 to spend At luncheon with a

lungs
8742 are the lungs of London.

lurch
6202 me in the lurch, Lor' how

lured
4236 And half I lured it on, and

lust
1344 of God. The lust of the
2141 women with lust. I've
3540 For lust of knowing what
4317 when they lust, can many
5236 do thou lust after that
8016 to the lust of
8675 Delight of lust is gross
8749 But for lust we could be
9525 generous in mere lust.
10562 of shame Is lust in action;
11362 cruel than lust. Time
12699 (so our lust we may
12909 that lust and rage

lusty
12074 clutch, And lusty life away

lute
10688 When the lute is broken,

luxuries
308 are luxuries rather
2387 One of the luxuries of a
7956 Give us the luxuries of life,
11751 Most of the luxuries, and many
12850 to save the luxuries until I

luxurious
3331 are most luxurious. They

luxury
36 a private and costly luxury.
1554 languages is mainly a luxury.
2623 And luxury the
3580 people is a luxury in which
5362 Luxury is more deadly than
6822 They knew luxury; they knew
7047 in fat-fed luxury, And gapes
7817 ends by luxury;
8358 Every luxury was lavished on
8582 Every luxury must be paid
11883 any other luxury. You have

lying
1290 the truth without lying.
1872 do not mind lying, but I
1904 amount of lying go the
3590 the use of lying when
5299 of hard lying in the
6299 an end of lying down
8514 this: One of you is lying.
12370 is legalized lying.

lymphomaniac
2011 Does that mean I'm a lymphomaniac?

lyre
10694 Make me thy lyre, even as

maastricht
4878 debate on the Maastricht treaty.

macaroni
426 his cap And called it macaroni.

macavity
3243 Macavity, Macavity, there's no

macbeth
954 in general Macbeth and Lady

mace
2642 fool's bauble, the mace.

machine
1371 ingenious machine for
3724 efficient machine that man
5536 the machine is fast,
6117 house is a machine for living
7871 the great machine of human
9800 of the Ghost in the Machine.
10576 not a man, you're a machine.
12676 am a broken machine. I am
12818 of the machine; A being

machinery
4041 in the machinery of the
9906 intricate machinery that is

machines
1471 vision is Machines for making
10800 not whether machines think but
12367 that these machines will ever

macho
3767 Macho does not prove mucho.

mad
924 are born mad. Some
1738 count him mad, The more
1844 All poets are mad.
2590 Mad about the boy, It's
2591 Mad dogs and Englishmen
2861 Don't get mad, get even.
3878 Mad, is he? Then I hope
5711 The mad all are in God's
5727 or less mad on one
5833 when I am mad. Then
5924 Mad, bad, and dangerous
6725 football mad And the
7895 cities are mad: but the
8855 poetry, but prose run mad.
9412 This mad dog of the
10208 I am but mad
10292 you, it will make you mad.
10317 me not be mad, not mad,
10715 An old, mad, blind,
10901 nation is mad - and the
11358 bad glad mad brother's
11662 they go mad they shall
11989 we are all mad, the

madding
4294 from the madding crowd's

made
1146 things were made by him;
1435 that hath made us, and
2161 is as God made him and
10458 world, scarce half made up.
11241 think nobody never made me.
11552 Thou madest man, he knows
12800 What man has made of man.

madeira
3533 Have some madeira, M'dear.

madman
2424 Hugo was a madman who
4379 up than a downright madman.
9140 of the madman in every
10850 like a madman in the

madmen
2857 is only the noise of madmen.
3061 which none but madmen know!
5606 economist. Madmen in
8919 worst of madmen is a saint
9446 They were madmen; but they

madness
3372 woman, has a dash of madness.
3670 Madness is part of all of us,
4768 Anger is a short madness.
5914 Madness need not be all
7896 door that leads into madness.
8935 is but the madness of many
10072 nothing but voluntary madness.
10205 this be madness, yet there
10324 O! that way madness lies; let
10495 Like madness is the glory of

10711 harmonious madness From my
11605 death and trance and madness.
12829 end despondency and madness.
12937 to-day; 'tis madness to defer.

magazines
3763 the women's magazines. It may

magdalen
3911 months at Magdalen College:

magic
1609 the secret magic of
1800 have no magic to stir
2175 kiss is magic, the
2385 from magic
5215 a state of magic. The loss
5603 hag-ridden magic and
6210 realism - I want magic."
6378 fundamental magic of flying
7294 That old black magic.
8259 as if by magic, we see a
9746 given by magic the power
10490 this rough magic I here
11390 men mistook magic for
12274 lost in the magic of a kiss.

magical
880 as a purely magical object.
7889 more magical than the

magistrate
3560 and the magistrate there is a

magnet
12926 There is a magnet in your

magnetic
4009 While this magnetic,

magnetized
6952 it is not magnetized. Lay it

magnificent
1463 It is magnificent, but it is not
2046 universe, magnificent or

maid
209 With you fair maid.
244 I heard a maid sing in
1340 ugly, old maid courted by
2666 he saw a maid of honour.
3466 an old maid is like
3836 the simple maid Still
8605 She could not live a maid.
12781 of Dove, A maid whom there

maiden
8803 This maiden she lived with
11518 A simple maiden in her

maidens
2472 And all the maidens pretty.

maids
3989 little maids who, all
10126 they wed: maids are May

mailman
9313 He's the mailman of human

maintenance
5548 the true maintenance class.

majesty
12099 I love the majesty of human
12777 so touching in its majesty.

major
1500 Ground control to Major Tom.

major-general
4015 model of a modern Major-General.

majorities
7318 action Wisdom goes by majorities.

majority
2730 a rule the majority are wrong.
3351 by the majority, or by the
4943 is the tyranny of the majority.
4977 with courage makes a majority.
5342 made by a majority of the
5772 God is always in the majority.
6218 with majority rule.
6861 the great majority of men are
8266 The great silent majority.
8535 The majority is the best way,
8676 to join the majority [the
8697 on God's side is a majority.
9507 Reaching majority, Seizing
10834 in black majority rule in
11105 and self-indulgent majority.
11932 big enough majority in any

12472 is what the majority then and
12943 joins us to the great majority.

make
871 a Scotsman on the make.
935 do not make the man;
3100 you can't make him think.
4414 find a way, or make one.
8685 The man who makes no

make out
10954 for, I could not well make out.

make-believe
4482 Man is a make-believe animal - he

maker
453 of every maker is
8946 become the makers of our

makes
545 mind until he makes it up.
10338 tongue Of him that makes it.

maketh
1248 He that maketh haste to be
12869 Manners maketh man.

making
11354 came to the making of man

maladjusted
5643 of the creatively maladjusted.

malady
1654 It is the malady of our age

malcontents
6536 a hundred malcontents and one

male
874 to be so male that when
6077 the male of the
9770 of the male, except
12521 the true male never yet

malefactors
3749 number of malefactors authorizes

malevolence
6520 is detached malevolence.

malice
1287 with malice than with
5274 men, And malice, to breed
6363 With malice toward none;
9939 Malice is of a low stature,
10438 aught in malice: then,
11345 Yet malice never was his

malicious
3166 subtle but he is not malicious.
4475 out of malicious

malign
5890 had rather malign oneself

malt
4784 Malt does more than Milton

mama
3764 but I believe it is Mama.

mammon
1169 cannot serve God and mammon.
10847 God and Mammon soon

man
302 and I'll give you the man.
303 Every w man's man, and
324 If every man would mend a
344 Man is more mushroom than
481 Man is by nature a
487 The young man who wants
577 Man is a history-making
953 make a man by
1129 I became a man, I put
1134 Every man shall bear his
1159 made for man, and not
1207 A man hath no better
1223 sheddeth man's blood,
1250 A man after his own
1296 When a man comes to me
1297 When a man gets talking
1298 A man is a person who
1417 Man that is born of a
1483 Every man, even the most
1502 Only man, among living
1503 I'm a man more dined
1532 tell me man doesn't
1607 Man is a noble animal,
1631 A man can have but one
1643 Progress, man's
1991 in vain; Man marks the

2200 Ech man for
2216 A man and a woman marry
2219 Man has been endowed with
2742 My man Friday.
2903 Man, my Lord, is a being
3304 shadow of a great man.
3333 Every man is wanted, and
3343 the whole man
3453 happens .. Man performs,
3458 A man of fifty looks as
3659 Man should not strive to
3727 To be a man will continue
3825 A man .. is so in the
3868 heart of man.
4096 Man will err while yet he
4110 A man can stand almost
4121 The right man is the one
4153 A man he was to all the
4162 Man wants but little here
4165 The man recovered of the
4419 To find the Inner man.
4483 Man is the only animal
4605 Every man is more than
4649 there a man with hide
4800 A man should be taller,
4865 philosophy be still a man.
5006 Man, biologically
5175 Every man has, some time
5536 Man is a slow, sloppy and
5709 ever tasted Man?' 'No,'
5713 get to a man in the
5717 The man who would be
5740 - you'll be a Man, my son!
5741 One man in a thousand,
5879 a single man
6051 Man hands on misery to
6054 play the man. We shall
6185 Man, false man, smiling,
6364 Every man over forty is
6365 Every man is said to have
6568 Before Man made us
6701 He's no a man ava', And
6604 Man is a dog's ideal of
7047 'A man, a man!' Teace,
7084 While man there
7093 A man is only as old as
7226 I met a man who wasn't
7275 that is not in the man.
7458 kill a man as kill a
7737 Man, I can assure you, is
7870 Man cannot be safely
8215 the species Man is in,
8301 of plain is your only man.
8312 No man is as
8366 Man is the only creature
8516 Where's the man could ease
8537 author and we find a man.
8580 Angry young man.
8601 every great man there is a
8615 but make a man a woman,
8774 A man is a wolf rather
8835 off, and get out the man.
9059 [That] man is the measure
9328 Man is Heaven's
9817 To be a man is to feel
9915 Every man in the world is
9929 Man is a useless passion.
10016 is come, but not the man.
10026 given To man alone
10105 Every man loves what he
10106 A man isn't a man until
10136 as any man living,
10192 He was a man, take him
10376 Man, proud man, Drest in
10386 let him pass for a man.
10526 were man But
10576 not a man, you're a
10816 Man, an animal that makes
10942 There are many wonderful
11022 Man is a social animal.
11088 Man, unlike any other
11238 That man is an aggressive
11282 forgotten man. He is
11323 called man; although
11368 of men which is man.
11427 of any man
11494 Man's word is God in man.
11507 For man is man and master

11620 I am a man, I count
11632 what a man may do,
11659 Man will ever stand in
11663 A man you don't like who
11785 Man is flying too fast
11950 Man is the Only Animal
12339 Am I not a man and a
12400 'A man in the house is
12418 The only man who can
12442 write about Man, write
12516 A man for all seasons.
12757 figure of a man at twice
12800 think What man has made
12941 Man wants but little, nor
12949 from every man) when a

man-child
2146 keeping the man-child alive.

man-o'-war
5716 'eeds - The Man-o'-War's 'er

managed
7619 just and right Well managed.
7772 which is managed by order,

management
452 Management is now where the
9532 Good management consists of

mandalay
5718 the road to Mandalay, Where the

manfully
2080 decently, but to live manfully.
3654 stands up manfully against

manger
129 baby, In a manger for its
7534 in the rude manger lies;
12059 born in a manger Commands

manhattan
12722 name of the Island of Manhattan.

manhood
2871 a blunder; Manhood a
5526 Years ago, manhood was an
10264 hold their manhoods cheap

manifesto
10996 plain manifesto The black

mankind
491 one giant leap for mankind.
952 Mankind is divisible into two
3332 All mankind love a lover.
3910 by the experience of mankind.
4992 are the interests of mankind.
5113 more of mankind I expect
5578 Mankind must put an end to
7107 Mankind always sets itself
7359 the lot of mankind are
7366 for which mankind are
7368 If all mankind minus one were
8237 divides mankind into two
8475 which corrupt mankind.
8943 study of mankind is man.
10075 affairs of mankind with no
11538 together, careless of mankind.
11751 to the elevation of mankind.
12512 Father of mankind, Forgive

manly
7021 valorous than manly wise.

manna
3055 loathe our manna, and we

manner
6014 Of alle manere of men,
10196 And to the manner born - it

manners
547 good manners without
837 Manners are the hypocrisy of
1199 off first for manners' sake.
2352 the times! Oh, the manners!
3140 Artifical manners vanish the
3310 an egg. Manners are the
3340 Good manners are made up of
3761 of good manners? Being
4023 the manners of a
5017 English manners are far
7353 have good table manners.
7461 to rectify manners, we must
7871 prevailing manners of an age
8890 catch the Manners living as
9021 Ladyship's manners, The ice
10273 Men's evil manners live in

11016 bewrayed, As by his manners.
12297 Manners are especially the
12869 Manners maketh man.

manoeuvre
11890 with a manoeuvre, a blow

manpower
8083 balance of manpower and

mansion
7468 of Jove's Court My mansion is.

mansion-house
7467 refuge, the mansion-house of

mansions
1151 are many mansions .. I go

mantle
7531 his mantle blue:

manure
5391 to clear up all the manure.

manuscript
5180 Your manuscript is both good and

many
1185 For many are called, but
6340 he makes so many of them.
10906 How many things I can do
11712 miss the many-splendoure

many-headed
8923 a wit, The many-headed monster of

map
8746 up that map; it will

marathon
1964 look on Marathon - And
4284 skirmish fought near Marathon.

marble
1728 that I dwelt in marble halls.
7431 the cold marble leapt to
10549 Not marble, nor the gilded
11274 it brick and left it marble.

marble-constant
10168 foot I am marble-constant, now the

marble-hearted
10315 thou marble-hearted fiend,

march
10065 used to march on their
10956 The march of intellect.
11484 in the front of March.

marched
7310 track marched, rank on

marches
8071 An army marches on its

marching
848 soldiers, Marching as to war,
7924 'Tis the people marching on.

marijuana
2401 with Marijuana a time or

marilyn
6893 Marilyn who was every man's

mariner
2445 ancient Mariner! From the
7768 The Ancient Mariner said to

mark
6481 hit the mark, you must
7195 some mark on it
10752 hit the mark; yet as

market
3539 the great markets by the
12279 a world market for maybe

marksmen
9317 you are all marksmen - don't

marquis
6874 A marquis is a sort of

marred
10142 is a man that's marred.

marriage
30 companionship as in marriage.
326 weren't for marriage, men would
354 Marriage is not a finished
589 Any marriage, happy or
636 refuse an offer of marriage.
776 more for a marriage than a
877 Marriage is our last, best
1266 often curable by marriage.
1268 Marriage, n: the state or
1546 In a happy marriage, it is the

1960 love and marriage rarely can
2437 most happy marriage I can
2561 Marriage is like a bank
2672 Marriage is a matter of give
2793 value of marriage is not
2803 us in this marriage, so it was
3370 Is not marriage an open
3449 Hanging and marriage, you know,
3473 her fortune by way of marriage.
3637 there's marriage without
3844 think there is any in marriage?
3928 the long monotony of marriage?
4106 thing, marriage the real
4143 For me, marriage is having
4266 blind and marriage is the
4661 while marriage is
5197 Marriage has many pains, but
5352 does a marriage develop
5525 The primal marriage blessing,
5596 legal marriage, but
6366 Marriage is neither heaven nor
6658 Marriages are made in heaven
7057 Marriage is not a word but a
7101 a happy marriage should
7104 bedfellows, marriage does.
7412 successful marriage and a
7695 Marriage is three parts love
7721 Reading and marriage don't go
7791 It marriage] is like a cage;
8049 about marriage is that it
8118 fever which marriage puts to
8279 Marriage; a job. Happiness or
8558 of marriage can
8592 Marriage may often be a stormy
8818 Marriage is a great
9692 Before marriage, a man will
9771 is only in marriage with the
9849 to make a marriage a success
10057 Marriage is nothing but a
10432 O curse of marriage! That we
10510 prevents a bad marriage.
10560 not to the marriage of true
10623 Marriage is popular because it
10762 not hold a marriage together.
10873 of marriage .. it
11185 Marriage is one long
11196 In marriage, a man becomes
11197 Marriage is like life in this
12011 Every marriage tends to
12170 Marriage is the only adventure
12313 Marriage is the waste-paper
12407 Marriage is a great
12607 years of marriage make her
12612 Marriage is a bribe to make a
12752 So that is marriage, Lily

marriages
203 All marriages are happy. It's
2381 Medieval marriages were
2788 happiest marriages on earth,
5089 Marriages would in general be
5876 are good marriages, but no
6042 of marriages Lasting a
6732 say of most marriages that they

married
327 I married my husband for
550 I married beneath me. All
647 to being married, a girl
1452 was happily married - but his
1563 Reader, I married him.
1847 was never married, and
1952 Married, charming, chaste,
2560 I never married because I
2664 I married in my youth a wife.
2797 Any married man should forget
2904 Commons until he is married.
3768 he has married. Then
3770 because I was always married.
3838 if ever we had been married?
4172 going to be married, think
4194 man who married and
5472 like to be married to a poem
6379 how seldom married people in
6790 they were married - to be
7174 When married people don't get
7252 women than married men; if
7270 may be married, it always
7381 If married life were all that
7743 of Lyme Who married three

8524 of being unhappily married.
8636 delight we married people
9099 Married couples who love each
9658 A married couple are well
10133 live till I were married.
10142 A young man married is a man
10616 Trade Unionism of the married?
10617 to get married as soon as
10731 no taste when you married me.
11127 going to be married to Mrs
11198 you are married, there is
11783 has been married
11879 they are married, and girls
12248 dreadfully married. He's the
12557 In married life three is
12613 part of married life. The

marries
1495 If thee marries for money,
1798 when he marries. He may
4355 When a man marries his
8584 No woman marries for money;
9552 whom one marries, for one
9691 When a girl marries, she
10686 When a man marries, dies or

marry
487 wants to marry happily
723 man should marry? 'A young
790 but some marry them and
836 man should marry until he
1043 Never marry a man who hates
1883 Mrs Carlyle marry one
2213 of loneliness, don't marry.
2216 and a woman marry because
2225 - and then they marry him!
2300 my wife to marry me.
2693 people marry most
2750 You don't marry it
2899 should marry - and no
4547 alone, they'd never marry.
4593 ye may, go marry: For
5074 no man to marry, who is
5638 must Marry my body to
5969 If ever I marry a wife,
6496 that women marry, And why
7059 and women marry those whom
7272 thing, they marry later.
7701 they may marry' is an
8333 you to marry me, you
8752 Will you marry it, marry
8793 Marry an intelligent
9286 about to marry - 'Don't'.
9689 some girls marry, you
11091 the men we wanted to marry.
11581 'Doänt thou marry for munny,
11637 as easy to marry a rich
11641 hump, may marry whom she
12708 When you marry, Sally, grab

marrying
2588 thought of marrying - and then
2668 caught dead marrying a woman
3450 off from marrying men, we
5592 Marrying a man is like buying
6138 mistake of marrying the whole
11695 From marrying in haste, and

mars
7963 A Mars a day, helps you

martini
79 Those dry Martinis did the
3543 Vodka dry Martini - with a
12764 and into a dry Martini.

martyr
9568 you are a crook or a martyr.

martyrdom
834 accept the martyrdom of our
5101 for it. Martyrdom is the
9968 Martyrdom has always been a
10588 Martyrdom .. the only way in

martyred
2516 oft our martyred dead, And

martyrs
1604 and clouts make martyrs.
2970 love their martyrs and honour
11628 of the martyrs is the

marvel
1745 me such marvel, save in
6496 always be A marvel and a

marvellous
1434 he hath done marvellous things.

marvels
4677 done bloody marvels with a bad

marx
265 pretending to be Karl Marx.
561 of Karl Marx and
1025 to blame Marx for what
5612 teaching of Marx, Engels
6461 Said Marx: 'Don't be

marxism
8695 to Methodism than to Marxism.

marxist
7993 Je suis Marxiste - tendance

masculine
5150 been a masculine endowment,
7632 spirits masculine, create at
10938 women is something masculine.

masculinity
9049 of inactive masculinity are places

mask
2544 it wears a mask. The most
9198 is the mask of one's
10690 He had a mask like
12911 therefore a mask - is the

masochism
108 of national masochism prevails,

masochist
1068 is a masochist, a sadist,

masquerade
11242 gone to a masquerade ball.

mass
4541 Paris is well worth a mass.
11767 The mass of men lead lives

massacre
1560 to make a massacre, any day
11944 sudden as a massacre, but they

masses
3970 ye tradesmen, bow, ye masses.
3996 a series Of masses and fugues
4062 back the masses against
6111 huddled masses yearning
9031 about the masses. First

master
1121 or can be master of money,
2523 man who is master of his
2760 become the master, the
4091 You must be master and win,
4242 love is maister wher he
4540 I am the master of my
5754 only the Master shall
6371 not be a master This
7143 be The master of
7534 her great master so to
8116 In his master's steps he
8229 Master-morality
10134 can master a grief
11507 is man and master of his

master-builder
6426 without master-builders, whose

masterpiece
2419 greatest masterpiece in
2956 great masterpiece, an
3337 to be a masterpiece of nature.
9328 Man is Heaven's masterpiece.
9742 together expect a masterpiece.

masterpieces
3606 of his soul among masterpieces.
9970 with the masterpieces of art as

masters
913 Buy old masters. They fetch
1169 serve two masters .. Ye
1322 are not the masters; the
1770 The people are the masters.
6275 servants, but bad masters.
6552 our future masters to learn
9940 their victory but new masters.
10275 time are masters of their

mastery
4111 Mastery often passes for
8205 The mastery of nature is
11492 but in the mastery of his

masturbation
1978 of mental masturbation - he is
11391 Masturbation: the primary sexual

match
5368 and the big match. [usually
8151 and the match to win - A
8462 is like a match, you can

matches
3997 extravagant matches In fitless
4439 a box of matches on a
6941 stick of matches, with our

mate
7084 walked without a mate.

material
3583 to be, material and

materialism
7741 deteriorate into materialism.

materials
3383 incongrous materials, which
6118 The materials of city planning

maternal
194 maternal - it's an

maternity
6385 mother; for Maternity is a

mathematical
2995 Moriarty of mathematical celebrity

mathematician
8766 known a mathematician who was

mathematics
7274 a resort to mathematics, though
12237 so like the mathematics, that it

matrimony
637 argument in favour of matrimony.
653 love to matrimony in a
4198 of love than matrimony in them.
4562 period in matrimony is
10728 safest in matrimony to begin
11873 as that of matrimony.

matter
602 the sum of matter remains
872 much matter what else
1194 in a great matter or a
3006 any great matter, but the
4026 if it is it doesn't matter.
4288 is only matter out of
7443 is the matter with Mary
8972 seem to matter. But the
9303 What is Matter? - Never
9936 Does It matter? - losing

matters
4540 It matters not how strait the
5859 In all matters one must
9777 those about matters as to

matthew
92 Matthew, Mark, Luke and John,

mattress
7401 crack it open on a mattress.

mature
769 mark of a mature man is the
7147 I mature poets imitate:
8425 The i mature mind hops from

maturing
5410 of the maturing sun;
8092 my mind is maturing late, Or

maturity
2009 the sign of maturity is
3494 Maturity is the capacity to
9962 Maturity consists of no longer
11221 high price to pay for maturity.
12205 A mark of maturity seems to be
12340 is the final test of maturity.
12961 sign of maturity is the

maud
11543 the garden, Maud, For the

mausoleum
1267 Mausoleum, n: the final and
9049 Those mausoleums of inactive

mawkishness
5420 thence proceeds mawkishness.

maxim
7664 grounded maxim So rife
11341 'Tis an old maxim in the

maxims
1389 favourite maxims of my

may
6577 May is a pious fraud of
6925 month of May was come,
10545 buds of May, And
11497 world is white with May.
11874 least the seventh of May.

maypole
5281 The organ and the maypole.

maze
2526 Life is a maze in which we
7940 a sort of maze through
8889 A mighty maze! but not

me
4912 - But the One was me.
6229 As you are me And we are
10159 man that will praise me -
12727 now in the Me Decade -

meal
3404 millstone, shuns the meal.
8617 A good meal makes a man
9137 A good meal ought to begin
9213 face is half the meal.

meals
6277 just meals on heels.

mean
6428 things for mean or no
6749 should not mean But be.
9014 most people mean, even if
10387 It is no mean happiness,
11115 ever I do a mean action, it
11900 even if you don't mean it.

meaner
8889 leave all meaner things To

meaning
4025 with hidden meaning - like
4535 The true meaning of life is
4700 to have a meaning that one
5345 thy Lord's meaning in this
7158 its total meaning within
7689 words. The meaning comes
7935 may be the meaning of our
8990 with meaning to the
9734 get at his meaning, not to
12196 sure of her meaning before she
12870 has any meaning it means

meanly
5096 man thinks meanly of himself

meanness
1939 A land of meanness, sophistry,

meannesses
6356 individual meannesses for the

means
38 No one means all he says,
1858 The end justifies the means.
4907 justify the means, for the
5649 The means by which we live
8057 but a means of
8123 are means to an end,
10306 sight of means to do ill
12246 within our means, even if
12601 have to die beyond my means.
12647 Nothing means anything

meant
7504 more is meant than meets
11164 said what I meant and meant

measles
3169 It is the measles of the
5040 is like the measles; we all
5048 like the measles - all the

measure
1162 With what measure ye mete, it
5651 ultimate measure of a man
7935 may be the measure of our
9059 man is the measure of all
9229 Time is the measure of
10384 like, and Measure still for
10702 is the measure of the
11424 in little measure and evil
11611 stateliest measure ever
12256 the exact measure of her

measured
3239 I have measured out my life
3525 has ever measured, even

10747 must be measured from a
11764 however measured or far

measurement
4431 Measurement of life should be

measures
5248 in short measures life may
7076 Trying the measures of the

meat
1825 Some have meat and cannot
8639 dined upon cold meat.
10132 loves the meat in his
12236 The dish of meat is too

mechanism
833 is a giant mechanism operated

meddles
7235 that meddles with art!

meddling
12841 Our meddling intellect

media
11225 The media. It sounds like

medical
452 where the medical profession
5415 In disease Medical Men guess:
12712 in advance of medical thought.

medicinal
668 Medicinal discovery, It moves

medicine
1195 friend is the medicine of life.
1243 doeth good like a medicine.
2217 Medicine is my lawful wife.
3504 practice of medicine is a
6053 sense is in medicine the master
6127 music and primitive medicine.
8411 to take medicine is perhaps
8412 masses not to take medicine.
9952 practice of medicine is like
10379 no other medicine But only
11390 magic for medicine; now, when
11428 history of medicine is a story
11885 In medicine, sins of
12457 all the medicine and

medicos
9388 And of medicos marvelling

medieval
2381 Medieval marriages were

mediocre
3831 its innumerable mediocre ones.
4514 are born mediocre, some men
7412 and a mediocre one

mediocrity
2365 is a festival of mediocrity.
3001 Mediocrity knows nothing higher
4966 republic of mediocrity, genius is

meditate
7528 strictly meditate the

meditation
5168 abstracted meditation, or remote

mediterranean
10107 from the Mediterranean - from

medium
6766 The medium is the message.

medley
8501 of song, A medley of

meek
1164 are the meek: for they
1428 The meek-spirited shall
7035 Pity the meek for they
7884 to be so meek and tame,
10828 that the meek shall

meet
1488 them seldom meet - when
3546 Let's meet, and either do,
3859 We only part to meet again.
5437 One would meet in every
7761 And we meet with champagne
8701 Every man meets his
8956 hoping we meet now and
10339 we three meet again In

meeting
9479 the hour of meeting and of
9683 The joys of meeting pay the

meetings
3784 Meetings are indispensable
11575 Their meetings made December

megalomania
568 States is megalomania, that of

megaphone
6298 is God's megaphone to rouse a

melancholy
477 Melancholy men are of all others
1842 Naught so sweet as Melancholy.
1960 'Tis melancholy, and a fearful
4295 birth, And Melancholy marked him
5496 when the melancholy fit shall
5959 recipe for melancholy, who can
7496 divinest Melancholy, Whose
7510 loathèd Melancholy, Of
7633 moping melancholy And
8141 the black sun of melancholy.
9547 a charm in melancholy, I would
10516 and yellow melancholy, She sat

mellow
7754 Indeed is too mellow for me.
8696 old, but mellow, like good
11481 The mellow lin-lan-lone of

melodies
5489 Heard melodies are sweet, but
5508 To ease my breast of melodies.

melodious
5413 But diving melodious truth.

melody
1833 like the melodie That's
8962 You're a melody From a

melons
7080 on melons, as I

melting-pot
12957 the great Melting-Pot where all

member
3192 a standing member: an
6710 A new Member requires the
7100 will accept me as a member.

members
1132 We are members one of

memoirs
7322 Published memoirs indicate
8666 write one's memoirs is to
9578 did do - well, that's memoirs.

memorable
7086 Upon that memorable scene: But

memorandum
11 A memorandum is written not to
2125 don't make a memorandum of it.'

memorial
8650 whole earth as their memorial.
9641 monument - Memorial from the

memories
865 God gave us memories that we
2137 to recall memories and it is
7770 excellent memories do often
10725 Our memories are independent
10749 ought to have good memories.
11207 The memories of men are too

memory
325 he has a very good memory.
1291 imagination for their memory.
2193 Memory is the thing you
3249 echo in the memory Down the
5111 say, 'His memory is going'.
5205 true art of memory is the art
5252 Memory, of all the powers of
5751 in a man's memory if they
5887 of his memory, but no
7786 good enough memory, he should
7860 me, Fond Memory brings the
8209 of a bad memory is that
8296 am speaking only from memory.
8418 how the memory of a man
8497 mist of a memory you wander
8951 hope of becoming a memory.
8953 back a memory ever
9100 better than the best memory.
9143 is the heart's memory.
9341 should have a good memory.
9442 remarkable memory; I forget
9514 Thanks for the memory.
9595 no force can abolish memory.

9997 health and a poor memory.
10726 to his memory for his
10727 say, quite from your memory.
11182 a grand memory for
12055 Their very memory is fair

men
93 hell to men, hell to
178 We men have got love well
224 his men were
326 marriage, men would
408 What men usually ask of
420 W men have their faults
428 knew what men meant When
641 Men are all so good for
716 Men in great place are
754 studied books than men.
1352 done when men and
1354 What is it men in women
1518 and W men what they
1590 Men build bridges and
1832 o'mice an' men Gang aft
2280 I love men, not because
2484 Men will wrangle for
2610 Men deal with life, as
3136 us that men and
3206 Men's men: be they gentle
3231 We are the hollow men ..
3358 Men are what their
3422 Men are men, they needs
3532 old bald men wouldn't
3732 is obsolete or men are.
4255 Wise men appreciate all
4317 Men, when they lust, can
4643 Men may be linked in
4742 O! men with sisters dear,
5183 Men know that women are
5761 are the President's men.
5836 majority of men devote the
6088 Men! The only animal in
6184 fought men, but
6238 namely men and the
6254 like a man? Men are so
6444 Some men are good for
7230 I want is men who will
7272 Men have a much better
7411 Give us men to match our
7753 consists of men, women,
8084 though he had 200,000 men.
8195 consists in men, and not
8248 a hundred men stand
8621 Men are generally more
8802 is best for raising men.
8893 abodes, Men would be
9224 All men naturally desire
9295 our best men are dead!
9430 men are afraid
9431 the wisest men make fools
9527 For all men would be
9598 We have the men - the
9810 I like men to behave like
9092 to which men, while
10013 buying - it's men's lives.
10025 grove, And men below, and
10029 All men who have turned
10098 I see of men, the more
10259 Men of few words are the
10292 stones, but men; And,
10494 I wonder men dare trust
10663 When men reach their
11091 the men we wanted
11474 For men may come and men
11788 war between men and women.
11839 to know of men, the more
12161 Men argue, nature acts.
12172 not for all men, nor for
12223 All those men have their
12404 not the men in my life
12429 to expect men to do all
12551 Men can be analysed,
12865 sexes: men, women who
12940 All men think all men

menace
8660 The only menace is inertia.

mend
324 man would mend a man,
1003 tried to mend the
7827 worst, they generally mend.

mendacity
12635 Mendacity is a system that we

mendip
6799 to war from mendip's sunless

mental
7288 Mental health problems do

mentality
6288 with the mentality of a fox

mention
5103 recourse to the mention of it.

mentioned
8724 damned than mentioned not at
11862 family that is never mentioned

mentioning
9421 without mentioning a single

mercenary
4783 their mercenary calling

merchandise
747 mechanical arts and merchandise.

merciful
1164 are the merciful: for they

mercury
132 As both the Mercury and Apollo
6412 to pick up mercury with a

mercy
1364 To Mercy Pity Peace and
1365 For Mercy has a human heart
1419 his great mercy to take
1437 and his mercy endureth
1739 Mercy .. laboured much for
2022 the ground Mercy I asked,
3196 to God's mercy, and show
3480 and leaving mercy to heaven.
6670 Widely as his mercy flows.
6703 Hae mercy o' my
7131 everlasting mercy, Christ.
7630 so Justice with mercy.
7876 withhold in mercy what we
8173 Then in His mercy may he
8223 Is not receiving, mercy?
8044 I see, That mercy I to
9801 foe at his mercy, and does
10402 quality of mercy is not
10497 sin so much as mercy.

meridian
1610 and under any meridian.

merit
2087 is endless merit in a man's
3359 The merit claimed for the
8491 What is merit? The opinion
8941 sight, but merit wins the
9478 which merits shine
10424 got without merit, and lost

meritocracy
12947 but a true meritocracy of talent.

mermaid
5487 than the Mermaid Tavern?

merriment
5105 This merriment of parsons is
5158 than a scheme of merriment.

merry
379 good to be merry and wise,
1207 to drink, and to be merry.
1214 Wine maketh merry: but money
1243 A merry heart doeth good
3065 A very merry, dancing,
10058 never was a merry world
10405 I am never merry when I

merry-go-round
6785 no go the merry-go-round, it's no
11716 on the merry-go-round, you have

mess
3228 make of the mess we have
3520 up the mess they had
4422 fine mess you've
7291 Don't mess with
7516 country messes, Which

message
299 pay for a message sent to
656 electric message came: `He
6646 to offer a message from an
6766 The medium is the message.

messages
4206 messages should be
6179 to leave messages saying 'I

messenger
357 Messenger of sympathy and love,

messing
4272 as simply messing about in

met
808 I met a lot of people in
6258 We met at nine. We met at
11470 of all that I have met.
12887 I have met them at close

metal
1900 but more durable metal.

metaphor
3695 of it is a good metaphor.

metaphysic
1910 as high As metaphysic wit can

metaphysics
1951 Explaining metaphysics to the

mete
1162 measure ye mete, it shall

meteor
11594 the silent meteor on, and

method
2999 You know my methods. Apply
10205 yet there is method in't.
10630 My method is to take the

methodism
8695 more to Methodism than to

metre
6445 of God and man and metre.
7641 matter and lame metre.
9336 though its metre was to

mexico
2807 Poor Mexico, so far from God

mice
1832 schemes o mice an' men
11270 Like little mice, stole in

michelangelo
11943 Italy with designs by Michelangelo.

mickey mouse
8962 sonnet, You're Mickey Mouse!

microbe
983 The Microbe is so very small

microbes
330

microscope
983 To see him through a microscope.

microscopic
8894 not man a microscopic eye? For

mid-air
10931 you in mid-air .. Isn't

midday
2591 Go out in the midday sun.

middle
41 the middle way is
1118 stay in the middle of the

middle age
24 centre of middle age. It occurs
331 Middle age is when you have a
958 enchantments of the Middle Age.
2573 Middle age is when your broad
8093 Middle age: when you're sitting
8102 begins And middle age ends, The
9414 Middle age is when you're faced
9705 I am old. Middle age was the

middle ages
1462 than in the Middle Ages, when one
10867 live in the Middle Ages And be

middle class
500 proper or middle class, I name
989 The Middle Class was quite
8390 the sinking middle class .. may
9383 past; the middle class is its
11884 The middle class is the backbone

middle classes
3970 ye lower middle classes! Bow, bow,

middle east
4673 The Middle East is a region where
9412 This mad dog of the Middle East.

middle way
8435 go most safely by the middle way.

middle-aged
4951 Middle-aged people are often
5111 a young or middle-aged man, when
10041 watches her middle-aged children
11775 length, the middle-aged man

middle-class
7894 the term middle-class' connotes
12298 control is flagrantly middle-class.

middlesex
1101 Elysium - rural Middlesex again.
6812 An acre in Middlesex is better

midge
1099 And lightly skims the midge.
9638 Spins like a fretful midge.

midnight
586 room at midnight See us
3852 consumed the midnight oil?
5441 morrow in midnight, There is
5504 moan Upon the midnight hours.
6656 her woes at midnight rise.
8810 Once upon a midnight dreary,
9326 sweat, our midnight oil; We
10250 heard the chimes at midnight.
10511 a-bed after midnight is to be
12308 in to us at midnight very

midst
1182 am I in the midst of them.

midwife
8757 watch. The midwife slapped

might
6345 right makes might, and in
7749 all thy might, Christ is
10501 love, Exceeds man's might.
12303 Britons alone use Might'.
12513 these: 'It might have

might-have-been
9646 my name is Might-have-been; I am also

mightier
6817 imposition of a mightier hand.

mighty
1046 made thee mighty, make thee
3127 proud and mighty have
12489 down the mighty from their

mignonne
9585 See, Mignonne, hath not the

migrations
4196 and all our migrations from the

mile
1794 of dog than miles of
2711 the square mile; they are
9082 walked a mile in his

milestone
12259 that milestone, but an

militancy
2210 more militancy than

militarism
11432 Militarism .. is fetish

military
1303 possible military power,
2393 to entrust to military men.
3552 toys but of no military value.
4879 A military occupation is a
10615 When the military man

milk
1216 with milk and honey.
3965 seem, Skim milk
4343 with the milk of human
7973 Drinka Pinta Milka Day.
8086 is moo, the other, milk.
8115 With milk and honey
10345 full o' the milk of human
10532 But milk my ewes
12006 mother's milk of

millennium
1320 place the millennium
4860

million
4839 to make a million .. the
6317 you make a million? You start

millionaire
3506 And an old-fashioned millionaire.

8584 marrying a millionaire, to fall
10608 I am a Millionaire. That is my

millionaires
3496 All millionaires love a baked
11971 opposed to millionaires, but it

mills
6460 Though the mills of God

millstone
2893 and are a millstone round our
3404 shuns the millstone, shuns the

milton
4784 more than Milton can To
5130 Milton, Madam, was a genius
12804 Milton! thou shouldst be

mime
6977 the air .. Mime is on the

mimic
3353 and a mimic; life is

mind
103 My mind is not a bed to be
123 in the mind Where it
166 see are the mind's best bet
469 has a good mind and sorry
563 but the mind was that
678 erect the mind, by
840 My mind is very, very
949 matter of the made-up mind.
1370 In the mind and nature of
1638 fog of the good man's mind.
1747 make up her mind to be
1934 is the mind diseased.
2015 enters the mind through
2048 whose mind watches
2253 an open mind is
2306 the empires of the mind.
2435 it sinks into, the mind.
2573 your broad mind and narrow
2584 that my mind has not
2604 lose your mind when you
2691 what the mind is
2993 of a noble mind is the
3048 frailty of the mind.
3101 further impaired his mind.
3184 the human mind exists in
3655 activities of the mind.
3680 in your mind that you
3716 of the mind where
4233 keeps Georgia on my mind.
4689 through the mind, no
4896 bad for the mind as it is
4997 having a mind of her own
5112 clear your mind of cant
5369 a sound mind in a sound
5385 fill the mind with ever
5442 seasons in the mind of man.
5477 up one's mind about
5513 an innocent mind, Whose
5540 also is he out of mind.
5881 in the mind and in the
5998 ingenuous mind feels in
6238 the working of man's mind.
6597 My mind's not right. A
6751 of the mind is only
6808 of his mind was such
6833 whose mind watches
7049 My mind disdains the dungy
7464 I see in my mind a noble
7645 extend thy mind o'er all
8092 think my mind is
8248 loses his mind and gets
8331 could not make up his mind.
8357 body, his mind would be
8363 keep your mind
8425 immature mind hops from
8735 classical mind at work,
8753 no way out of the mind?
8773 When the mind is thinking,
8832 padlock on the mind.
9036 your padlock - on her mind.
9048 activity of mind. Genius
9065 what one has in one's mind.
9077 of the mind, happiness
9169 An indecent mind is a
9303 - Never mind. What is
9384 of one's mind; not in
9909 Free your mind and your
10077 A good mind possesses a

10103 frailty of the mind.
10414 with the mind, And
10574 that has a mind and knows
11016 The gentle mind by gentle
11068 is to the mind what
11072 writes her mind but in her
11141 end of the mind, Beyond
11706 Of my own mind; and in
11870 A man's mind will very
11880 her lover's mind if she
12070 The mind reaches great
12282 Conqueror type of mind.
12351 The mind can also be an
12418 change his mind is the man
12532 Mind in its purest play is
12724 sick, it's all in the mind.
12732 the mind shapes
12747 an ordinary mind on an
12788 The wiser mind Mourns less
12797 and in the mind of man; A

minded
11118 to it, had minded what they

minds
1317 many open minds should be
2796 Minds are like parachutes.
3049 is the virtue of weak minds.
4041 the best minds of my
4240 reach only of complex minds.
9732 thoughtful minds are those
10680 the happiest and best minds.
12645 Minds like beds always made
12787 Strongest minds Are often

mine
1384 she walks into mine."
7629 thou art is mine; Our state
10298 makes mine greater
10976 and she is mine for life.

minefield
6979 fat, is a minefield - you have
8648 a wedding night in a minefield.

mineral
4015 animal, and mineral, I am the

miners
6799 The rugged miners poured to

mineworkers
6781 the National Union of Mineworkers.

mingled
10312 When it is mingled with

miniature
8345 day is a life in miniature.

minimum
8360 paper work down to a minimum.

minister
7235 help the Minister that

ministering
10034 the brow, A ministering angel

ministries
781 Times' has made many ministries.

mink
423 needs a mink coat but a
831 of wearing mink is to look

minnehaha
6512 named her, Minnehaha, Laughing

minorities
13 security enjoyed by minorities.
213 like other minorities.
3596 always the minorities that hold
8698 rights of minorities. The

minority
163 people to make a minority.
3351 or by the minority? By the
4937 A minority may be right, and a
9507 How a minority, Reaching
9679 A minority group has 'arrived'

minstrel
3983 A wandering minstrel I - A
7859 The Minstrel Boy to the war is

minute
861 a sucker born every minute.
3181 it's only a minute. But when
4219 Every minute starts an hour.
7099 leave in a minute and a

minuteness
9775 realize our minuteness and our

minutes
6951 diamond minutes. No
10551 So do our minutes hasten to

miracle
812 is an unprecedented miracle.
2439 It was a miracle of rare
7797 monster or miracle in the
11191 existence is a mere miracle.
11922 prays for a miracle. Every

miracles
3892 the age of miracles hadn't
12350 Miracles sometimes occur, but

miraculous
12547 have a miraculous power of

mirage
3112 a receding mirage in an

mirror
4 of a sunlit mirror, I have
422 alone and smash his mirror.
2675 just had a mirror put over
4247 break her mirror early.
5598 you meet is your mirror.
6326 A book is a mirror: if an ass
9904 The mirror is the conscience
9986 toilet without a mirror.
10858 unexpected mirrors, or to
11098 novel is a mirror which
11522 wide; The mirror cracked

mirth
7513 Mirth, admit me of thy crew
7597 make them mirth used all
10512 Present mirth hath
10538 a minute's mirth to wail a
12233 I love such mirth as does

mirthfulness
942 Mirthfulness is in the mind and

mis-spent
5551 Redeem thy mis-spent time

misanthropy
4480 obvious resource of misanthropy.

misbeliever
10392 You call me misbeliever,

miscalculations
11913 is the unfolding of miscalculations.

mischief
1051 is mischief: all
1720 the most mischief, enemies
3906 deed of mischief he had a
4075 tyranny, produce the mischief?
5275 Mischiefs feed Like beasts,
7218 from God to do mischief.
8178 knowest the mischief done!
12286 finds some mischief still For

misdemeanour
12657 Dullness is a misdemeanour.

miser
12614 have the miser who's no

miserable
44 four most miserable years of
1883 two people miserable instead of
2817 is a most miserable thing to
5150 the world miserable has always
10379 The miserable have no other
10650 of being miserable is to have
11455 it is very miserable, and

miseries
2095 of the miseries and vices

misery
1417 live, and is full of misery.
3004 for the misery of being
3907 relation of distant misery.
5103 but pure misery, there
6051 hands on misery to man. It
6082 to be a great kick at misery.
6551 amount of misery which it
9542 All the misery of manilla
10487 Misery acquaints a man with

misfits
9413 of misfits, Looney

misfortune
1258 has had the misfortune to
1682 is a great misfortune neither to
3141 What a misfortune it is to be
5902 In the misfortune of our best

9132 Fire tries gold, misfortune men.
11308 Some great misfortune to
12556 as a misfortune; to lose

misfortunes
728 they make misfortunes more
5103 of his misfortunes there is
5875 to bear the misfortunes of others.
6571 The misfortunes hardest to bear
7188 Few misfortunes can befall a boy
8932 another's misfortunes perfectly
10913 If all our misfortunes were laid

misgovernment
4049 and misgovernment and I

misguided
6007 not, poor misguided souls,

mislead
537 one to mislead the

misleading
493 contains a misleading

misled
3045 have been misled; So they

mispronounce
7905 language: all men mispronounce it

misquotation
8597 Misquotation is, in fact, the

misquote
1944 enough of learning to misquote.

miss
1455 is what you miss, not what
2604 you won't miss it very
3777 we never miss the goods
7396 night. I miss you like

missed
313 would have missed her; Had
3985 would be missed - who

missing
7501 And missing thee, I walk

mission
4054 My mission is to pacify

missionaries
9558 horse racing and missionaries.

missionary
2851 the local missionary priest,
12528 would eat a missionary, Cassock,

misstatement
2070 a certain margin of misstatement.

mist
1664 into a mist with
1939 sophistry, and mist.
9119 A Scotch mist may wet an
11408 seeming defeat by the mist.

mistake
1395 The great mistake is that of
3208 forms of mistake, prophecy
3407 Do not mistake a child for
4021 Man is Nature's sole mistake!
4502 to make a mistake, your
4587 Those who mistake their good
5219 recognize a mistake when you
8235 life would be a mistake.
10814 made a mistake never made
12549 My great mistake, the fault

mistaken
1273 to be mistaken at the top
2646 possible you may be mistaken.

mistakes
347 with making mistakes. Just
2797 forget his mistakes - no use
4349 for the mistakes they
4383 ill effect of their mistakes.
8685 makes no mistakes does not
11439 from the mistakes of the
12397 their mistakes. It takes
12571 one gives to their mistakes.
12851 bury his mistakes, but an

misteach
11991 who would misteach us that to

mistress
685 but the worst mistress.
2188 history not to have a mistress?
3316 Art is a jealous mistress.
4355 marries his mistress, he
4421 and America as my mistress.
5277 So court a mistress, she

5714 house, But mistress in my own.
6544 True; a new mistress now I
8863 A teeming mistress, but a
8866 And mistress of herself,
10681 the crowd a mistress or a
11352 Maiden, and mistress of the
12866 A mistress should be like a

mistresses
913 better price than old mistresses.

mistrust
8484 easy to me, I mistrust it.

mists
1099 And low the mists of evening

misunderstanding
9492 sum of the misunderstanding that

misunderstood
3328 then, to be misunderstood?
5009 a truth misunderstood by those

misused
10989 How often misused words

mix
8348 I mix them with my
11372 her and mix her with

moan
5456 love And made sweet moan.
11705 paid with moan; For we

moanday
5314 All moanday, tearsday,

moat
10446 Or as a moat defensive

mob
12214 governors, the mob.

mobile
8978 being that he is mobile.

mobilized
8047 Churchill) mobilized the

mobs
5028 The mobs of great cities

moccasins
9082 walked a mile in his moccasins

mock
6731 their mock at our
10161 .. Let's mock the

mockeries
8446 orisons. No mockeries now for

mockery
10503 mail In monumental mockery.

mockingbird
6175 It's a sin to kill a mockingbird
12493 Out of the mockingbird's throat,

model
3151 possible models for men
8649 but are a model to others.

moderate
5972 a year a moderate income -

moderation
332 Even moderation ought not to be
608 easier than perfect moderation.
4200 also that moderation in the
5184 Moderation is commonly firm, and
5211 a thing as moderation, even in
5897 Moderation is an ostentatious
6332 If moderation is a fault, then
6811 and that moderation in war is
6873 long as it isn't in moderation.
8311 uniformly lost by moderation.
11400 by due moderation, lead to

modern
516 disease of modern life.
1010 quality of modern
2043 suffice for modern man: he
2344 Modern art is what happens
4413 the first modern man - so
7954 is uniquely modern. It is a
8992 for the modern stage,
12576 being too modern; one is

modernness
3366 Perpetual modernness is the

modest
4174 A modest woman, dressed out
4801 A modest man is usually
9420 Modest? My word no .. He
11936 I was born modest; not all

modesty
540 His modesty amounts to
1701 Enough for modesty - no more.
7787 aside her modesty with her
8573 true.' 'O modesty!' 'Twas
9478 brighter than through modesty.
10791 cultivate modesty .. But I

moloch
7559 First Moloch, horrid king

molten
1471 Have molten bowels;

moment
2567 the present moment what they
4121 one that seizes the moment.
6252 shining moment That was
7393 things that are Of moment.
12218 I am in a moment of pretty

moments
5444 time! O moments big as
9654 has lovely moments but awful

monarch
782 hereditary monarch was
2615 I am monarch of all I survey.
3628 greatest monarch on the
12198 bind; No monarch but would

monarchial
5967 is to enjoy monarchial

monarchical
1467 utility of monarchical power, and

monarchies
7817 by luxury; monarchies by

monarchy
167 A monarchy is a merchantman,
773 reason why monarchy is a
777 to a true monarchy, are
784 monarchy such as
8405 Monarchy is the gold filling
9768 like the monarchy, only
12661 The Monarchy is a

monastery
8730 at the monastery let me

money
39 put your money in your
76 how to get money except by
155 Money is better than
185 body of men money can buy.
266 far as your money will go.
409 really big money, you
532 Money is something you got
634 may bring money, but
733 Money is like muck, not
809 Money, it turned out, was
847 thinks of money, you have
977 Money speaks sense in a
992 Rhyme. But money gives me
1058 Making money is fun, but
1192 The love of money is the
1214 merry: but money answereth
1495 marries for money, thee
1544 poor know that it is money.
1868 demand your money or your
2343 after the money is gone.
2400 have enough money to get by.
2799 make more money in private
2930 have any money, the
3088 It's other people's money.
3129 Money doesn't talk, it
3423 Money is the wise man's
3519 Her voice is full of money.
3611 sex for money and sex
3624 Remember that time is money.
3640 old dog, and ready money.
3678 - all the money to buy
3693 ask of money spent
3898 hard for my money, producing
4144 to make money. There is
4212 pay good money to go out
4285 There's no money in poetry,
4300 how to get money without
4555 between money and sex
4642 they are the money of fools.
4749 lend you money if you can
4766 if not, somehow, make money.
4826 to spend money where it
4985 and ambitions than by money.
4989 there's money in muck."

5049 Running for money doesn't
5091 wrote, except for money.
5217 havin' money made it
6041 for lack of money. The
6124 enough to get money from it.
6224 much for money, For money
6530 don't like money actually,
6754 of saving money: to be
6762 Money is the poor people's
6823 natural interest of money.
7179 Money is like a sixth sense
7343 to make money as the
7428 Money couldn't buy friends
8323 forget that money gives its
8584 marries for money; they are
8638 to see what money will do.
8777 bring money along with
9172 Money swore an oath that
9194 you or to lend you money.
9195 With money in your pocket,
9252 have to eat money, but
9259 me advice, give me money.
9300 pays your money and you
9353 without money, is just a
9434 Money is good for bribing
9564 give your money to while
9572 lots of money to even
9664 you to love money - it's
9711 up against money, for if
9795 got the money, so we've
9852 uses his money as votes
9910 where the money went - it
9979 Money is human happiness in
10483 amiss, so money comes
10745 need the money, he
10908 come from money, but from
11058 Money is the most
11081 Money is always there but
11208 you've got too much money.
11212 Money isn't everything -
11281 to give her money for the
11581
11635 What money is better
11654 He had money as well.
11967 Make money and the whole
12006 Money is the mother's milk
12083 Money has no smell.
12175 question of money, everybody
12743 a barrel of money, Maybe
12753 Money dignifies what is
12756 must have money and a room

mongrels
3499 of energetic mongrels.

monk
1498 he vowed a monk to be; But
7819 solitary monk who shook

monkey
1112 attack the monkey when the
3413 at the monkey at the zoo
3950 best is only a monkey shaved!
11249 a fiendish monkey at an
12529 his descent from a monkey?

monkeys
4270 Monkeys .. very sensibly
12620 a million monkeys banging on

monogamy
216 too many. Monogamy is the

monopoly
2637 power is not a male monopoly.
4613 best of all monopoly profits is
6216 is the monopoly stage of

monotonous
6601 lost in our monotonous sublime.

monotony
3802 Monotony is the law of nature.
3928 in the long monotony of
9484 to a monotony of
11103 articulate monotony, And

monster
7797 a greater monster or miracle
8923 many-headed monster of the
10431 green-eyed monster which doth
10502 great-sized monster of

monsters
4246 of reason produces monsters.
8227 fights with monsters might take

monstrosity
4501 biological monstrosity - an organ

monstrous
2191 A monstrous carbuncle on the
3481 That monstrous animal, a

montezuma
6813 imprisoned Montezuma, and who

monument
2153 Cato has no monument than why
3254 Their only monument the
5013 - idiosyncrasy on a monument.
6426 lasting monuments to the
6600 Their monument sticks like a
9382 York is a monument of a

moo
8086 One end is moo, the

mood
6963 no mood can be

moon
189 over the moon .. We
1457 and a full moon every
1556 promise the moon and mean
1993 And the moon be still
4138 when he landed on the moon.
5043 at the new moon, out of
7501 wandering moon, Riding
7657 as the moon, When she
7746 some full moon descends
8290 on, harvest moon Up in the
10165 Beneath the visiting moon.
10476 not by the moon, the
11520 Or when the moon was
11610 the slow moon climbs:
11775 to the moon, or
11954 is a moon and has a
12638 go to the moon, I went
12769 when the moon shall
12806 rose, The moon doth with
12908 of the moon, The

moon-struck
7633 And moon-struck madness.

moonlecht
6061 braw brecht moonlecht necht, Yer

moonlight
1077 there's moonlight and music
10022 visit it by the pale moonlight.
10404 sweet the moonlight sleeps
10416 Ill met by moonlight, proud

moonshine
9796 atoms is talking moonshine.

moored
3863 fleet was moored, The

moorish
5339 under the Moorish wall and I

moral
2116 got a moral, if you
4122 not have a deep moral basis.
4143 is pure moral turpitude.
5385 me and the moral law within
8056 profoundly moral - more
9069 One becomes moral as soon as
10614 he is moral when he is
11744 not be too moral. You may
12586 thing as a moral or an

moralist
666 gave to the moralist. His
9755 for the moralist, since

morality
36 Morality is a private and
667 No morality can be founded on
1398 Morality's not practical.
5561 is the basis of all morality.
6092 Morality in the novel is the
6818 periodical fits of morality.
7262 standard of morality will
8216 Morality is the herd-instinct
8229 Master morality and
8837 And unawares Morality expires.
9778 kinds of morality side by
10634 Morality is not
10986 Absolute morality is the
11773 What is morality but
12472 What is morality in any given

morals
1114 arena of morals. It is

1540 comes first, then morals.
2477 but weaken their morals.
4023 with the morals of a
7281 even in the field of morals.
9851 by basing morals on myth.
10643 Have you no morals, man?
11186 If your morals make you

more
189 be even more so when
322 loved, now love the more.
1648 the little more, and how
1658 Less is more.
1738 mad, The more he cast
1067 who knows more and more
5729 arrange for more? Brothers
5926 something more to do than
7292 And one more for the
8254 The more you let yourself
8902 that he knows no more.
10200 There are more things in
10349 Who dares do more is none.
11164 man can do more, and you
11759 a good deal more than we
12874 believing more and more

morn
7532 the happy morn Wherein
7563 From morn To noon he fell,

morning
244 Early one morning, just as
1659 glad confident morning again!
3442 Morning has broken Like the
3522 three o'clock in the morning.
6059 up in the mornin', But it's
6407 me on a morning when he
9271 what the morning never
9503 It's morning again in
9552 find next morning that it
10036 with the morning cool
10671 the great morning of the
11698 fact, are better by morning.

moron
369 the happy moron, He
8319 is not a moron; she's

mortal
2978 done the lover mortal hurt.
4166 Her last disorder mortal.
4670 I am mortal, born to love
6624 possess is something mortal.
7063 To make us mortal, and thee
7085 beyond a mortal's share To
7477 Can any mortal mixture of
7530 that grows on mortal soil.
8282 are mortal, but the
8839 quit this mortal frame:
11366 all things mortal With cold
11885 are mortal, sins of
12940 all men mortal, but

mortality
4442 reminder of one's own mortality.
4764 plan Proclaims mortality to man.
4808 .. the mortality of all
5507 Mortality Weighs heavily on me

mortals
53 good that mortals know And
6397 and loftier than mortals.
6957 is only we mortals who ring
10420 what fools these mortals be!

mortified
11169 A mortified appetite is never a

mortify
8923 remains, to mortify a wit, The

moscow
9312 Moscow: those syllables can

moses
4842 If Moses had been a

mosquito
8336 get into a fool or a mosquito.

moth
3836 How, like a moth, the

mother
129 Where a mother laid her
319 gave her mother forty
334 A mother is a person who if
838 A mother who is really a
946 What the mother sings to the

1043 hates his mother, because
1360 My mother groaned! my father
1553 is the mother of
2867 as bad as a mother who talks
3444 pain, dear mother, now; But
4884 The mother of battles.
5396 and its mother is
6385 unmarried mother, as a
7440 Care of his Mother, Though he
7547 The mother of
8299 knew my mother. I knew
8652 best friend is his mother."
9156 takes the mother by the
9179 is the mother of the
9241 love is a mother's; then
9267 An ounce of mother is worth a
9867 will or will not be a mother.
10041 how old a mother is, she
10042 From whence his mother rose.
10541 art thy mother's glass,
11372 great sweet mother, Mother
11444 to make it well? My Mother.
11634 Mother is the name of God in
11784 Her own mother lived the
12185 a beautiful mother Her green
12738 never sailed me mother.
12820 Upon his mother's grave?

mother-child
3676 The mother-child relationship is

mother-in-law
288 his wife's mother-in-law to his
3646 his mother-in-law are
4471 wife and a surprised mother-in-law.
7258 is a mother-in-law whose

mother-wits
7012 of rhyming mother-wits, And such

mothers
3116 Tired mothers find that
3358 what their mothers made them.
9197 and therefore he made mothers.
12558 like their mothers. That is

moths
3518 went like moths among the

motion
454 put in motion by no
5400 Poetry in motion.
8185 of motion is ever
12839 years. No motion has she

motivation
1679 The whole motivation for any

motive
876 the motive, and of
3221 dreary is want of motive.

motives
1560 with enough motives to make a
3868 Motives and purposes are in
7936 by our motives and others

motor
7214 stalled motor has begun

motto
11309 Be that my motto and my

moulded
1490 people are moulded by their
8080 me has not yet been moulded.
11611 ever moulded by the

moulting
8085 they're moulting They're

mountain
162 Up the airy mountain, Down the
5640 up to the mountain. And I've
10096 isn't the mountain ahead that
11408 The mountain remains unmoved

mountains
1078 From the mountains to the
1933 to me, High mountains are a
1964 The mountains look on Marathon
6809 the tops of mountains, are the
7411 match our mountains, Give us
9731 Mountains are the beginning and
9905 toward high mountains - he

mountebanks
6318 prosperous mountebanks who

mourn
1829 countless thousands mourn!
1988 most Must mourn the

5452 skies to mourn: It spoils
8450 no cause to mourn.' 'None,'
10674 can never mourn A heart

mourned
7004 his arm, and for her mourned.

mourners
7923 of mourners he is

mournful
7556 this mournful gloom For

mourns
12788 wiser mind Mourns less for

mouse
7830 not even a mouse; The
9232 When the mouse laughs at

moustache
5748 wax his moustache was - like

mouth
840 open, and so is my mouth.
3175 is keeping your mouth shut.
3795 is, one's mouth what one
7092 whispering in her mouth.
11160 problem with an open mouth.
11477 Into the mouth of Hell.

mouths
4990 they open their mouths.
10322 she made mouths in a
12912 poets keep our mouths shut.

move
463 and I will move the earth.
1491 A high altar on the move.
6610 whichever way you move.
9418 when to move over to

moved
307 We shall not be moved.
1433 that it cannot be moved.

movement
87 Trust only movement. Life
3721 healthy movement within
6899 The movement of the
8794 it is a movement which
9229 is the measure of movement.
9405 judge this movement kindly.
11843 is a movement - not a

movers
8407 We are the movers and

moves
197 If it moves, salute it; if
2614 God moves in a mysterious
6900 nothing moves in this
9856 haunches and then moves on.

movies
4069 Movies should have a
6681 of American movies abroad
8681 All the movies used to be
9556 kill the movies, and that

moving
4686 what direction we are moving.

mozart
846 In Mozart and Salieri we see
1452 Ah Mozart! He was happily
4114 Mozart is the human
6194 that when Mozart was my
8705 swings. Mozart also

mp
2 Being an MP is the sort

mps
3976 lot Of dull MPs in close

mrs robinson
10769 to you, Mrs Robinson Jesus

much
699 that is too much in
3126 have too much, yet still
3256 We know too much and are
9457 little done, so much to do.
10796 to say, and much to hear
11569 worlds, so much to do, So
12047 Much of a muchness.
12403 Too much of a good thing

muchness
3206 they're much of a muchness.
12047 Much of a muchness.

mucho
3767 Macho does not prove mucho.

muck
733 is like muck, not good
4989 there's money in muck."
9610 with the muck-rakes are

mud
6011 sees the mud, and one

muddle
1552 somehow to muddle through.

muddy
8493 is not made muddy by the

mug
3246 Poetry is a mug's game.

muhammed
336 alone and Muhammed is his

mulberry
9102 the mulberry leaf

mule
4057 Sicilian mule was to me,
9230 None but a mule deserves

mules
8105 world of mules there are
9019 The mules of politics:

multifarious
10795 of the multifarious ways By

multiplication
10988 implies multiplication of the

multitude
4744 persuade a multitude, that they
5791 was: a multitude of one
9619 The multitude is always in the
10397 me with the barbarous multitude.

multitudes
12495 I am large, I contain multitudes.

mum
6050 up, your mum and dad.

mumble
1450 (3) When in doubt, mumble.

mumbo-jumbo
6383 Mumbo-Jumbo is dead in the

mummy
5710 He had his Mummy's leave to

mundi
234 gloria mundi. Thus

murder
86 and even to murder, for the
2405 including murder. The best
2508 how love and murder will out.
2783 himself in murder, very soon
3401 stick to murder and leave
4627 back murder into the
4940 Murder is a serious
6294 Murder, like talent, seems
6713 war called murder. It is
8963 .. One murder made a
10198 Murder most foul, as in the
10353 Macbeth does murder sleep.'
10394 to light; murder cannot be
10690 I met Murder on the way - He
12841 things:- We murder to
12934 destroy, is murder by the

murdered
9643 Each one a murdered self, with
10450 killed; All murdered: for

murderers
5393 let the murderers take the
12523 those murderers of Jewish

murmurs
2470 In hollow murmurs died away.
9311 days; Sad murmurs filled the
10930 In the murmurs, in the

muscle
854 our last muscle - the
9770 except his superior muscle.

muscles
3797 time meant muscles; but today
6515 And the muscles of his

muscular
335 Muscular Christianity.
2880 His Christianity was muscular.

muse
3560 Between the muse and the
8330 Can a muse of fire exist

10254 O! for a Muse of fire,
11882 The tenth Muse, who now

museum
9869 may visit a museum but only a
10979 the British Museum Reading

mushroom
344 Man is more mushroom than
2545 too short to stuff a mushroom.
6063 of a supramundane mushroom.
11794 A mushroom of boiling dust up

music
53 Music, the greatest good
238 and guitar music is on the
488 All music is folk music, I
512 Lent it the music of its
931 not like music, but they
932 Music first and last should
1076 since the music began.
1592 Music is only sound
1676 Who hears music, feels his
2449 sank Like music on my
2505 Music produces a kind of
2509 Music alone with sudden
2512 Music has charms to soothe
2559 words about music, one of
2593 how potent cheap music is.
2649 popular music in this
3067 cannot Music raise and
3069 die, And Music shall
3193 There is music in the air.
4067 creates music - the
4634 composed music
4803 hear good music, it makes
4916 the inexpressible is music.
5185 Music .. the only sensual
5425 The music, yearning like a
6338 But finds its food in music.
7419 before the music begins
7456 doth in music lie.
7856 The soul of music shed, Now
8060 clothes. Music is the
8235 Without music, life would
8498 Music is your own
8568 the condition of music.
8576 hears The music of
8637 Music and women I cannot
8705 Good music is everything
8878 but the music there.
8926 quirks of music, broken
9003 dance to the music of time.
9651 and I'll set it to music.
9950 in general is frozen music.
10158 me some music - music,
10404 sounds of music Creep in
10405 when I hear sweet music.
10406 hath no music in
10454 sour sweet music is, When
10508 If music be the food of
10542 Music to hear, why hear'st
11254 Music is given to us
11380 you the music of a poem
11508 make the music mute, And
11764 step to the music which he
11827 Music is the shorthand of
12018 civilized music in the
12796 still, sad music of
12879 swayed to music, O

music makers
8407 We are the music makers, We are

music-hall
3996 The music-hall singer attends a
7189 Music-hall songs provide the

musical
929 A kind of musical Malcolm
7500 folly, Most musical, most
9634 more musical than any

musically
8806 that so musically wells From

musician
6245 below the musician in that of
11980 Wagner, a musician who wrote

musing
11009 the ground, Musing full sadly

mussolini
6550 Hitler and Mussolini were,

mustard
4032 'Pass the mustard', and they

muster
5315 Three quarks for Muster Mark!

mutability
10691 Nought may endure but Mutability.

mute
6773 except that of mute.
9280 face is a mute

my-lorded
11642 him, and my-lorded him as

myrtle
4130 sky, the myrtle is still

myself
659 If I am not myself, who will
860 I find I'm talking to myself.
2549 I like myself the best.
2696 inside myself, and she
3921 alone than when by myself.
7607 image of myself and dearer
7797 in the world than myself.
10791 busy thinking about myself.
11617 closest relation is myself.
11826 always with myself, and it is

mysteries
8036 one of life's major mysteries.
11989 mad, the mysteries disappear

mysterious
9995 but more mysterious.

mystery
509 is still In mystery our soul
783 it .. Its mystery is its
805 It is a mystery,
1515 grasped the mystery of the
2182 which are a mystery both to
6496 and a mystery to the
6510 Comprehend its mystery!'
12581 The true mystery of the
12779 thing, A voice, a mystery.
12795 of the mystery, In which

mystic
4818 Mystic: a person who is

myth
8768 magnificent myth that would
8949 begin with myths, and with
9655 of indestructible myth.
9851 morals on myth. For,
9896 or less myth which it

mythical
4563 about a mythical figure -

mythology
2927 it becomes mythology and then

naiad
8808 .. ...Thy Naiad airs have

nail
6091 you try to nail anything
8723 adds a nail no doubt;
9183 The nail that sticks out

nailed
4876 is not nailed down is

nailing
11701 emptiness, nailing his

nails
6821 hands, the nails bitten and
7946 clean finger nails.
10788 and forty nails Upon the

naked
1117 Secretary naked into the
1957 Half naked, loving,
2656 girl who naked is is
6514 world Was naked and bare;
7921 is a naked ape
10267 And he but naked, though
10272 left me naked to mine
12882 enterprise In walking naked.

nakedness
1344 of God. The nakedness of woman
2937 Full nakedness! All joys are
8732 stratagem to cover nakedness.
12811 in utter nakedness, But

name
328 My name is George
1182 in my name, there am
1446 that his name is worth

1937 and the nothing of a name.
2820 with your own name.
4410 prefer a self-made name.
6613 the ghost of a great name.
6767 The name of a man is a
7613 his former name Is heard
7862 not his name, let it
7867 an age without a name.
8428 Perhaps my name too will
8658 of Jesus' Name; Let
9492 gathers about a new name.
10422 habitation and a name.
10430 me my good name Robs me of
10452 he lose The name of king?
10474 What's in a name? that
10966 a terrible name - A name
11029 your name perfectly,
11265 easier to name 10 artists
11290 'oss, my wife, and my name.
11370 I have forgotten your name.
11851 face. My name is
12174 burden is a name that has

names
9626 you forget names, then you
9918 with their names: that is

napalm
3124 smell of napalm in the

napoleon
2995 .. is the Napoleon of Crime,
4895 man is Napoleon; hence the
10065 Napoleon's armies always used

narcotic
5348 whether the narcotic be alcohol

narrates
3606 is he who narrates the

narrative
1520 The whole narrative is
5015 is a prose narrative of some
9005 very different narrative gifts.

narrow
7357 by narrow minds,
11070 in a very narrow compass

narrow-souled
8931 It is with narrow-souled people as

nasal
6204 tread My nasal organ.

nastiest
4139 and say The nastiest thing in

nasty
3927 Something nasty in the
5071 turn very nasty at short
7737 you, is a nasty creature.

nation
313 Still better for the nation:
1707 when a nation lives
1752 and a nation is not
2324 the nation. It was
2896 London: a nation, not a
3831 makes a nation great is
4631 mass of a nation .. will
4881 up through the nation state.
5567 Let every nation know,
5573 them we neglect the nation.
5714 A Nation spoke to a Nation,
5753 and lazy nation, To puff
6354 that this nation, under
6877 that every nation will at
6935 idea of a nation, but what
7119 the whole nation. It
7464 puissant nation rousing
7472 and haughty nation proud in
7649 makes a nation happy, and
7957 whole brave nation, and when
8073 est une nation de
8525 march of a nation; no man
8823 of the nation. A
9016 watching a nation busily
9045 burden of the nation's care.
9437 A nation is a body of people
9443 Nation shall speak peace
9602 of a nation
9621 we are a nation of
9791 the voice of a nation.
10763 of a nation,
10901 half of the nation is mad -
11028 have to exterminate a nation.

11906 the whole nation and he's
12005 A nation is a body of people
12102 army is a nation within a
12138 book of the nation is the
12679 thing as a nation being so
12684 No nation is fit to sit in

national
221 of grave national stress,
6774 [African] national

nationalism
122 Nationalism is a silly
3169 Nationalism is an infantile

nationality
5319 to me of nationality, language,
9458 man what nationality he would

nations
56 contending nations know What
1226 The nations are as a drop of
2340 that, when nations are
2917 the People formed Two Nations.
3136 men and nations behave
4134 other nations and states
4643 Nations are linked
4954 The nations which have put
5563 one hundred nations. Most of
5722 Nations have passed away and
7490 of teaching nations how to
11807 Of all nations, those submit

native
5084 in his native place.
6264 our ideas about the native.'
7213 over my native land
8933 breathe his native air, In
9050 Yorker is a native of the
10196 though I am native here, And

native land
10027 This is my own, my native land!

natives
10062 were only natives at the
11313 of your natives to be the
12444 natives give it

nativity
6996 at my nativity, Whose
10412 either in nativity, chance or

nato
4501 NATO is now a biological

natural
705 It is as natural to die as to
4178 he was natural, simple,
6286 to be the natural order of
6533 are always the most natural.
8416 The natural man has only two
9033 of his natural rights,
10010 in natural history if

naturally
7683 all men naturally were born

nature
64 production of human nature.
132 with the laws of nature.
470 imitates nature, but also
483 Nature does nothing without
510 Nature, with equal mind,
511 not one of nature's gifts to
622 not formed by nature to bear.
627 universal nature assigns to
737 perfect nature and are
762 Nature cannot be ordered
787 - an experiencing nature.
792 is man's nature; nature is
908 Nature says to a woman: 'Be
947 is human nature so weak as
1288 Nature never makes any
1381 Nature thrives on patience;
1610 for nature is the art
1813 ever, For Nature made her
2105 joy in nature is the
2471 part, Nature in him was
2702 Kind nature first doth cause
2737 Nature has left this
3360 Nature is reckless of the
3395 Nature has given to men one
3802 the law of nature. Look at
3869 helping nature to get a
3926 the hand of Nature and we
3974 comical How Nature always
4021 Man is Nature's sole

4082 art because it is not nature.
4385 people call nature as anyone
4552 Nature, Mr Allnutt, is what
4694 Nature is in earnest when
4695 Nature, when she invented,
4785 Nature, not content with
4896 contrary to nature, contrary
4960 whole of nature is a
4965 In nature there are neither
5273 thing in nature, infinite
5829 Mother Nature
5920 in his nature, infinite
5989 my strife; Nature I loved,
6012 subjectification of nature.
6195 should like Nature to go no
6239 than does Nature, because
6428 Nature never makes excellent
6568 great Nature made us
6579 Nature fits all her children
6730 death, In nature, nothing
6900 forces of Nature, nothing
7016 Nature that framed us of
7311 not Eternities!' Says Nature.
7492 against nature not to go
7625 wound, and Nature from her
7907 the habit from nature.
7996 Death [is] nature's way of
8182 is it that Nature does
8183 course of Nature, which
8205 mastery of nature is vainly
8409 as observe nature, was a
8551 man's nature: instinct
8614 architecture lets nature in.
8873 Nature, and Nature's laws
8876 The naked nature and the
8897 All nature is but art,
8909 looks thro' Nature, up to
9092 comb that Nature gives us
9145 a banker provided by nature.
9212 Nature abhors a vacuum.
9217 Habit is second nature.
9221 Nature gives to each what is
9222 Nature always desires what
9231 Nature, time and patience
9396 to nature and
9890 By nature's kindly
10135 and read comes by nature.
10228 our trick, nature her custom
10300 talk, And nature must obey
10320 Allow not nature more than
10345 do fear thy nature; It is too
10504 touch of nature makes the
10888 is good nature regulated
10991 .. It is a part of nature.
11329 in a state of war by nature.
11461 In nature, there is less
11549 Nature, red in tooth and
11919 Nature is not a temple, but
12161 Men argue, nature acts.
12419 much human nature in some
12437 Yes madam, Nature is
12438 Nature is usually wrong.
12439 that Nature is to be
12642 stuff that nature replaces
12796 To look on nature, not as in
12799 Nature never did betray The
12936 Tired Nature's sweet

natures
3361 Some natures are too good to

naught
1629 it be for naught Except for
6527 for nobody for naught.

naughty
11177 He is a naughty child, I'm

nauseated
12746 We are nauseated by the sight

navel
9177 Below the navel there is

navies
5734 our navies melt away

navigate
9332 know how to navigate in a

navigators
3923 side of the ablest navigators.

navy
1314 The Royal Navy of England

2133 head of the Navy is that I
3962 Ruler of the Queen's Navee!
3964 Rulers of the Queen's Navee!
6832 in the navy of Charles
10837 bless the Navy, bless the

nay
1137 be yea; and your nay, nay.

nbc
12228 information NBC piles on

near
1649 third; One near one is too
9096 who are near, and those
11561 Be near me when my light
11576 He seems so near and yet so

nearly
6534 I was nearly kept

neat
3455 much as a neat, clean,
4586 about baldness - it's neat.
11177 clean and neat, With lots

necessary
1415 do what is necessary at the
2333 in doing what is necessary.
3315 yourself necessary to
5656 but conscription if necessary.
6619 it is not necessary to change,
9337 to be wiser than is necessary.
11805 were not a necessary Being of
12158 a very necessary thing.

necessities
18 necessities call out
7167 for the necessities of
7956 dispense with its necessities.
9858 greatest necessities in America
10323 art of our necessities is
12850 The necessities were going by

necessity
2623 Thus first necessity invented
2643 Cruel necessity.
2741 the door of necessity, not at
2743 Necessity makes an honest man a
3215 Necessity does the work of
3635 Necessity never made a good
4711 a duty, it is only a necessity.
7615 Necessity and chance Approach
8747 Necessity is the plea for every
9283 Necessity gives the law without
9666 is the recognition of necessity.
9980 Necessity is the constant
10445 Teach thy necessity to reason
10991 but a necessity .. It is
11720 I find alone Necessity Supreme.

neck
2338 have her neck wrung like
2503 he sticks his neck out.
7878 office; my neck is very
8337 can break your neck in it.
12225 get, But a neck when once

necklace
6941 with our necklace, we shall

nectar
8494 after all nectar. One

need
252 In thy most need to go by
2104 the first need of being
2651 Women need a reason to
4749 that you don't need it.
4831 ain't in need is a
5798 We all need Europe, but
6230 you still need me, will
8223 giving a need? Is not
9700 Country both need you so.
9724 love than I need, or could
10019 When our need was the
10320 not the need! Our
11300 like this, I need the trip.
11659 ever stand in need of man.

needed
7725 What's needed in this world
9318 of being needed by just
9992 It makes it feel needed.

needle
3760 space in a needle's eye is

needs
1502 says prayers. Or needs to.

6724 one of his needs is
7109 each according to his needs.
7834 of what he needs and
12187 .. Needs grow too fast;

needy
6023 and to be nedy, Since he

negation
4055 This is the negation of God

negative
6681 unfinished negative of which
7291 the negative Latch on
8717 price in negative terms ..
9762 is merely negative, a

neglect
4327 defer or neglect it, for I
5246 Such sweet neglect more
5573 We will neglect our cities to
11717 to the neglect of his

negotiate
5569 us never negotiate out of

negotiating
6412 Negotiating with de Valera .. is

negotiation
12 Negotiation in the classic

negro
2710 the average negro could
5647 The Negro's great stumbling

neigh
192 me to neigh, grind my

neighbour
2244 makes our next-door neighbour.
4868 the helping hand of a neighbour.
9600 policy of the good neighbour.

neighbourhood
5066 into a neighbourhood before it
9246 the house; buy the neighbourhood.

neighbours
3275 have good neighbours, and
3678 little more than the neighbours.
3699 Good fences make good neighbours.
11660 should be good neighbours.
11756 the innocence of our neighbours.

neither
1277 I will neither go nor

nell
8641 Pretty witty Nell.

neptune
7768 said to Neptune during a

nero
7254 by night. Nero fiddled,

nerve
9685 after the nerve has been

nerves
6530 but it quiets my nerves.

nervous
5415 disease, they call it nervous.
6161 take your nervous system

nest
4674 not throw it into the nest.
5429 her soft and chilly nest.
11458 broods a nest of

net
2147 Net - the biggest word in
6794 Within its net of gold,

nets
7642 tangled in amorous nets.
10716 found to be nets of such a
12323 weave but nets to catch

nettle
10237 Out of this nettle, danger,

nettles
12208 to be overrun with nettles.

network
5146 Network. Anything

neuroses
17 is how to use your neuroses.

neurosis
9432 Without them there is neurosis.
11800 Neurosis is the way of
11997 A neurosis is a secret you

neurotic
241 and a neurotic. A

1525 For the neurotic, the
3947 the neurotic, the
7286 Neurotic means he is not as
10773 as a neurotic who

neurotics
9064 to us from neurotics. It is

neuter
11454 may take a neuter gender;

neutral
12688 apart, studiously neutral.

neutrality
2676 maintain their neutrality.
4676 for a word neutrality' - a word
12670 Armed neutrality is ineffectual

never
134 Never eat at a place called
457 to go where I've never been.
1661 Never the time and the
1809 forgot And never brought to
2033 jilted Than never he courted
2325 Never give in, never give
3958 I could never tell why.
3959 What, never? No, never!
6571 are those which never come.
6775 people have never had it so
6880 know would never hurt you.
8005 You never had it so good.
9477 always, by God, never.
9574 used to be and never was.
10050 Love means never having to
11240 Never was born!' persisted
11548 lost Than never to have
12234 can lose what he never had.
12270 I shall never ask, never
12295 but they never let you

nevermore
8811 Quoth the Raven, Nevermore'.

new
379 you are on with the new.
750 fitter for new projects
1212 is nothing new under the
3096 of the new: seven
4958 'This is new, therefore
5490 piping songs for ever new.
5963 New Year's Day is every
6471 something new, to
8530 nothing new. The
8783 brings [us] something new.
11515 place to new, And God
11577 ring in the new, Ring,
12145 shall find something new.
12919 nothing new in dying,

new man
8562 over by New Man' in the

new world
3718 of the New World shows a

new york
1264 n: in New York, one who
2488 New York, New York, a helluva
2800 not in New York you are
5617 here in New York. There is
7409 gullet of New York swallowing
7900 New York, the nation's thyroid
7906 Like so; N'Yawk, N'Yawk.'
9053 word for New York is
9382 skyline of New York is a
9625 New York is notoriously

new yorker
7430 imperfection of a New Yorker.
9050 A natural New Yorker is a native

new-laid
3969 As innocent as a new-laid egg.

newcastle
3884 coals to Newcastle, no more

newest
10253 sins the newest kind of

news
1510 News is the first rough
4016 a lot of news, With many
4751 The good news is that
4945 is good news; not good
6225 I heard the news today, oh
6985 you see is news, what you
7668 For evil news rides post,
8308 All the news that's fit to

8682 tension out of the news.
8981 is news that STAYS
11237 It is a newspaper's duty
11485 News from the humming city
11694 I have no news of her; I
12301 News is what a chap who

newscasters
4594 and it drives newscasters berserk.

newspaper
3436 One newspaper a day ought to be
7031 The art of newspaper
7405 A good newspaper is a nation
8603 and newspaper
11237 It is a newspaper's duty to
12953 only be a newspaper

newspapers
5952 Newspapers always excite
8426 Newspapers have developed what
8700 of men and morning newspapers.
11226 It's the newspapers I can't
12358 impossible? Read the newspapers.

newton
4912 another Newton, a new
8873 said, Let Newton be! and

next
214 happens next is much
2802 with the next thing I
0453 for the call Next please'.

nibbles
6065 than he who nibbles in a low

nice
2152 of saying nice doggie'
3119 Nice guys. Finish last.
3893 starry sky, Nice work if
6059 O! it's nice to get up in
6693 By nice women .. you
7711 Be nice to people on your
9322 thoroughly nice people

nicean
8808 Like those Nicean barks of

nicer
179 really much nicer than men:
2189 be even nicer with a
12667 But it's nicer, much nicer

nicest
4139 thing in the nicest way.
0074 surely the nicest people in
7897 the very nicest people.

nickname
4491 A nickname is the heaviest
8476 are but nicknames, and

nigger
8347 is the nigger of the

niggers
6562 That don't agree with niggers.

night
592 This is the night mail
1330 are born to endless night.
1482 The night has a thousand
1550 All night it fell, and when
2826 is a wild night and a new
3522 a real dark night of the
4630 The night of the long
5270 with us perpetual night.
5313 me, elm! Night night!
6477 When the night is
6485 shades of night were
6513 pass in the night, and speak
6659 Night hath a thousand eyes.
7387 last the night; But ah,
7474 What hath night to do with
7657 deserts the night Hid in her
7680 day brought back my night.
7860 the stilly night, Ere
8169 me on; The night is dark,
8343 day's journey into night.
8960 Night and day, you are the
9351 the horror of a deep night.
9818 Night, when words fade and
10082 Night brings our troubles
10300 The deep of night is crept
10357 seeling night, Scarf up
10408 This night methinks is but
11355 a breath; Night, the
11664 that good night, Old age

11690 you love it not, of night.
11718 City is of Night; perchance
12866 only for a night and away.

nightblue
5338 hung with humid nightblue fruit.

nightingale
513 ah, the Nightingale! The
5413 Where the nightingale doth sing
5452 the singing of the nightingale.
6656 ravished nightingale. Jug, jug,

nightmare
5330 said, is a nightmare from which

nights
6565 makes sech nights, all white

nile
10153 my serpent of old Nile?'

ninety
1094 Ninety per cent of this game
4716 A man over ninety is a great

ninety-nine
3179 and years. Ninety-nine times, the
9458 to be, and ninety-nine out of a

nineveh
5734 Is one with Nineveh, and Tyre!
7127 of Nineveh from

nip
9519 but I'll nip him in the

no
2053 A man who says no.
4251 No' and 'Yes' are words
4600 to say no to
5309 Ulysses | No, it did
8243 will to say No, where it
8619 No pain, no palm; no
11042 to say No'; it will
11658 at saying no than men.

noah
4912 one poor Noah Dare hope

nobility
725 New nobility is but the act of
726 Nobility of birth commonly
1928 all were noble, save Nobility.
6291 oblige. Nobility has its
6965 us still our old nobility!
9891 is man's charter of nobility,

noble
1928 all were noble, save
2473 the spur of noble minds, the
5081 too, has noble wild
5661 clever; Do noble things,
9166 is nothing noble about
10207 a man! How noble in reason!
10246 Wherein the noble youth did
11517 'Tis only noble to be good.

nobleman
3951 Underrated Nobleman, The Duke

noblemen
4018 are all noblemen who have

nobleness
1571 wage; And Nobleness walks in

nobler
10211 'tis nobler in the

nobles
6817 Nobles by the right of an
9037 Nobles and heralds, by your

noblesse
6291 Noblesse oblige. Nobility
11860 the French noblesse had been

noblest
1072 day: Time's noblest offspring
4963 God is the noblest work of

nobly
1652 Nobly, nobly Cape Saint

nobody
299 sent to nobody in
1499 nobody belongs anywhere,
2659 to be nobody but yourself -
3642 Who is that? Nobody.
4532 Nobody knows what's in him
6806 is the business of nobody.
11078 space where nobody is than
11987 he knew nobody had said

nodding
12913 sleep, And nodding by the

noise
931 love the noise it makes.
2522 who fears noises becomes a
2595 The noise, my dear! And the
2631 till they make a noise.
5776 A loud noise at one end and
6923 and the noise was in the
7500 the noise of folly,
7675 a barbarous noise environs
8931 the more noise they make
9315 and all the noise of town Is
11968 Noise proves nothing.

noiseless
4294 kept the noiseless tenor of
5516 A little noiseless noise

noisy
12787 of whom the noisy world

nomadic
12458 on the contrary, were nomadic.

non-being
11800 of avoiding non-being by

non-combatant
7765 hath no fury like a non-combatant.

non-conformists
7222 of the non-conformists is like to

non-creative
6759 of the non-creative. It is

non-fiction
663 use of her non-fiction tickets.
4845 All that non-fiction can do is

non-negotiable
1319 at school is non-negotiable.

non-obvious
11002 organization of the non-obvious.

non-u
9627 U and Non-U, An Essay in

non-violence
772 of non-violence has been
2210 some cases non-violence requires
3803 Non-violence is the first article
5648 Non-violence is a powerful and

nonconformity
8387 history of Nonconformity behind

none
41 middle way is none at all.
2122 answer came there none -
3858 alike, is praising none.
7297 None of your dam
9127 days is none of these
9977 to the man who has none.
12929 a good one and none at all.

nonsense
316 A little nonsense now and then
593 It is nonsense to speak of
957 The nonsense which was
1049 is simple nonsense: natural
1869 home, are nonsense; but some
2819 quantity of nonsense talked
4910 Nonsense is an assertion of
7170 what nonsense this was
9011 A little nonsense now and then
9381 hallmark of nonsense. Nature
9477 your damned nonsense will I put
11131 The nonsense of the old women

nookie
4224 occasional satisfying nookie.

noon
3538 Noon strikes on England,
4807 riser may sleep till noon.
5063 at high noon and tell
7656 blaze of noon,

norfolk
2592 Very flat, Norfolk.

normal
8398 God we're normal, Yes, this

norman
224 While the Norman Baron lay,
664 feel with Norman blood.
11517 faith than Norman blood.

north
599 He was my North, my South,

6085 of the North is dead,
6718 about the North, but live

north-west
11126 There is a North-west passage to

northern
1552 is that the Northern States
6006 by the Northern sea, A

norway
5081 Norway, too, has noble wild

nose
1674 Any nose May ravage with
2453 cause of the human nose.
3746 has a great nose thinks
5706 his little nose .. 'Led
5858 further than his own nose.
8539 Cleopatra's nose been
9189 back and breaks his nose.
9656 A large nose is in fact
9973 lights upon his very nose.
12377 is not a nose at all,

noses
4486 very nice noses, or will

nostalgia
346 Nostalgia ain't what it used to
827 Nostalgia is a seductive liar.

not
723 young man not yet, an
998 Gun, and they have not.
2427 I'm not ok - you're not
2876 is better not, she would
9220 to be than not to be.
12085 We are not amused.
12716 honour is not my honour.

note
3925 had no note, When
5538 but take note of what
6201 the very note, This is

notebooks
12750 of your notebooks and keep

notes
9967 The notes I handle no
10011 These rough notes and our

nothin'
1292 Pity costs nothin' and ain't
5700 'e wore Was nothin' much
5812 word for nothin' left to

nothing
141 can do nothing but as a
296 Nothing in excess.
404 Nothing is impossible for the
407 What costs nothing is worth
484 others have nothing, the
622 Nothing happens to any man
641 so good for nothing, and
663 she was nothing. Nothing
1191 we brought nothing into this
1456 Caesar or nothing.
1937 and the nothing of a name.
2045 person who explains nothing.
2207 than a good womman? Nothyng.
2225 about nothing - and then
2297 I have nothing to offer but
2313 it costs nothing to be
2480 you have nothing to say,
2958 is there nothing, nothing
3113 is that nothing is often a
3594 Nothing in human life, least
3876 does nothing, and can
3977 war, Did nothing in
4212 bad television for nothing?
4253 at eighty, nothing at all.
4272 There is nothing -
4313 Nothing was ever lost by
4380 leaveth nothing to Chance
4393 stand for nothing fall for
4484 There is nothing good to be
4736 Nothing ever tasted any
4813 - do nothing, say
5102 to say nothing, when he
5164 should have done nothing else.
5283 that doing nothing was a sin.
5388 Nothing in the world - indeed
5636 Nothing to do but work,
5935 We are nothing; less than
6046 Nothing, like something,
6199 There is nothing without a

6407 when he had nothing else to
6527 Nobody does nothing for nobody
6622 Nothing can be created out of
7671 Nothing is here for tears,
7705 Nothing is won forever in
7748 true I had nothing on. I had
7757 costs nothing and buys
7788 and nothing
8154 If you know nothing, be
8337 A hole is nothing at all, but
8550 lot, set him to do nothing.
9028 can settle down to do nothing.
9146 Nothing is so burdensome as a
9260 Drink nothing without seeing
9263 it is to do nothing, and then
9298 Nothink for nothink 'ere, and
9496 Nothing in the world can one
9524 Nothing, thou elder brother
9548 Think nothing done while
9842 doctors, nothing is
10165 there is nothing left
10310 Nothing will come of nothing:
10373 and fury, Signifying nothing.
10426 For I am nothing if not
10483 Nothing comes amiss, so money
10611 He knows nothing; and he
10612 Nothing is ever done in this
10626 itself nothing: age,
10660 to know nothing than to
10907 I know nothing except the
11065 labour of doing nothing.
11124 Toby, 'but nothing to this.'
11206 Nothing like a little
11269 not love, Nothing can make
11294 as having nothing a-year,
11452 world knows nothing of its
11618 Nothing has yet been said
11705 Nothing begins, and nothing
11760 there is nothing, not even
11847 but containeth nothing.
12033 void. Nothing in the
12578 Nothing that is worth knowing
12643 them. There's nothing else.
12647 Nothing means anything until
12663 crusade or it is nothing.
12685 Nothing was ever done so
12766 And having nothing, yet hath

nothingness
794 is more bearable than nothingness.
5417 Pass into nothingness; but still

nothings
10673 knife Invulnerable nothings.

notices
3412 that nobody notices unless she

noticing
6684 them without noticing.

notion
3720 and fatuous notion that
3994 seem to suit her notion.
7758 General notions are

nought
9648 to do nought Is in
10691 Nought may endure but

nouns
7845 is all nouns and verbs.

novel
2050 A novel is never anything
4432 A novel is an impression,
5015 The novel is a prose
5472 to be given away by a novel.
6079 of the novel, properly
6091 down in the novel, either it
6095 The novel is the one bright
6755 A novel must be
11076 of the novel is that
11098 A novel is a mirror which

novelist
6092 When the novelist puts his
6163 - the major novelists .. are

novels
2145 My novels point out that the
2174 the mystery novels published
6798 child you lose two novels.
7186 half the novels that are

novelty
7632 last This novelty on earth,

november
2564 Under the November tree

nowadays
6926 was not as love is nowadays.

nowhere
5636 't is gone; Nowhere to fall
5637 Nowhere to go but out,
12463 up, with nowhere to go.

nowness
8972 But the nowness of

noxious
5633 Of all noxious animals, too,

nubbly
5709 Fish. 'Nice but nubbly.'

nuclear
1516 a world of nuclear giants and
8002
8017 The nuclear arms race has no

nude
5636 from going nude. Nothing

nugget
12750 discourse a nugget of pure

nuisance
3295 of one nuisance for
4792 who made no nuisance of
7370 himself a nuisance to other

null
8303 city, is Null an' Void!

number
2360 rather than to their number.
11934 the number of things

numberless
7495 thick and numberless As the gay

numbers
4862 not in the numbers game, so
8853 I lisped in numbers, for the

numbing
6767 a man is a numbing blow from

nun
7497 pensive nun, devout
8356 a nun would envy
12837 quiet as a nun Breathless

nunnery
10214 thee to a nunnery: why

nuptials
5533 day set apart for her nuptials.

nurse
987 a-hold of Nurse For fear
8257 of what a nurse should be
10170 That sucks the nurse asleep?
10779 offered the Nurse, not

nursed
7525 For we were nursed upon the

nurseries
3476 are the nurseries of all

nursery
1773 and not a nursery of future

nurses
722 age, and old men's nurses.

nursing
518 Still nursing the

nursling
10677 And the nursling of the

nutrition
8900 To draw nutrition,

nuts
9149 gives the nuts, but he
11661 - where the nuts come from.

nymph
7511 Haste thee nymph, and bring

o'clock
7425 bed, for it's now ten o'clock?

oak
2102 When the oak is felled
5732 Sun, Than Oak, and Ash,
6569 to make than an oak.

oaks
1606 last not three oaks.
3430 flow, Tall oaks from
5445 woods, Tall oaks
6296 of growth. Oaks that

oar
3872 of grab an oar and row
9116 row with the oars he has.

oases
8067 of isolated oases of

oath
6372 official oath to-day
8799 with an oath
9172 swore an oath that
10647 I utter an oath again may

oaths
1915 Oaths are but words, and
6668 toys, but men with oaths.

oats
5189 Oats: A grain which in

obedience
1517 to tyrants is obedience to God.
6828 reluctant obedience of distant
7750 gold of obedience and

obedient
10771 That here obedient to their

obey
1034 wouldn't obey the rules.
1106 to obey, and make
3052 monarchs must obey.
3149 way parents obey their
5692 'E don't obey no orders
7342 seem to obey the more
9608 when we ask him to obey it.

obeyed
4366 She who must be obeyed.
7219 right to be obeyed, than any
8535 make itself obeyed. Yet it

obeying
762 about, except by obeying her.

obituary
963 except your own obituary.

object
524 My object will be, if
3995 My object all sublime I
5375 You may object that it is
6360 legitimate object of
7306 to the object possessed
9894 Every real object must cease

objectives
12488 extravagance of objectives.
12737 the dual objectives: education

objects
6729 Nobody objects to a woman
12828 as objects

obligation
5917 at the obligation one owes

obligations
6291 Nobility has its obligations.
10824 paying off obligations to people

obliged
5160 is always obliged to go at a

oblivion
7315 if I drink oblivion of a day,
10502 alms for oblivion, A
10681 wise, commend To cold oblivion.
11956 earthly certainty is oblivion.

oblong
6133 that is, an oblong figure,

obnoxious
4837 without being obnoxious.

oboe
349 Oboe - an ill woodwind

obscenities
12921 indulged in obscenities and

obscenity
205 Obscenity is whatever gives a
9779 that 'obscenity' is not a

obscure
7572 palpable obscure find out

obscurity
3917 left in the obscurity of a
5365 rise out of obscurity whose
6716 between Obscurity with
8099 Purity is obscurity.
9342 The obscurity of a writer is

observance
10196 the breach than the observance.

observation
2110 A few observations and much
3461 on the old observation that every
8566 field of observation, chance
9889 opportunities for observation.

observe
1093 You can observe a lot just by
2992 see, but you do not observe.
8409 as well as observe nature,

observed
10656 young man I observed that nine

observer
591 Is a keen observer of life,
7298 acute and balanced observers.

obsolescence
6388 adolescence and obsolescence.
11133 on planned obsolescence .. we

obstacles
2574 Obstacles are things a person
11738 out of the greatest obstacles.

obstinacy
936 and obstinacy is that
1611 Obstinacy in a bad cause, is
9981 Obstinacy is the result of the
11120 - and of obstinacy in a bad

obstruct
5365 whose talents obstruct at home.

obstruction
10381 lie in cold obstruction and to

obvious
5783 of the obvious so as to
5795 the more obvious it seems

occasion
6333 some great occasion will
12572 wear on an occasion like this.

occasionally
3960 it' I may Occasionally say, I

occupation
2605 Absence of occupation is not
8329 quite the occupation of an
10650 The cure for it is occupation.

occupations
2814 us love our occupations, Bless the
6380 normal occupations in general
6477 the day's occupations, That is
11116 are worse occupations in this

occurred
1055 to have occurred. One can

occurrence
11417 and to expedite its occurrence.

occurring
6143 - it is the occurring which is

ocean
1078 To the oceans white
1991 dark blue ocean - roll!
2794 Love is an ocean of
6008 hear like ocean on a
6513 So on the ocean of life we
6997 into the ocean, ne'er be
7820 thou, vast ocean! on whose
7924 on of ocean in the
8179 the great ocean of truth
9115 made the ocean, but the
10172 That in the ocean seeks
10552 the hungry ocean gain
12203 may use the ocean as their
12797 the round ocean and the

octave
11256 in each octave and the

october
3545 the leaf still in October.

octopus
10826 - that dear octopus from whose

odd
359 care of the id by the odd.
1602 But not so odd As those
3432 How odd Of God To choose
5779 exceedingly odd If he

odes
11588 Quoted odes, and jewels

odorous
10137 Comparisons are odorous.

odours
7533 haste with odours sweet.

off
8153 world, I want to get off.

offence
1253 for a future offence.
4997 The real offence, as she
7665 After offence returning,
7736 constitutes offence, and to
8937 What dire offence from

offences
1427 sins and offences of my

offend
6862 they do not offend you by
10542 married, do offend thine ear,
11272 others doth offend, when 'tis

offended
7879 hath not offended the king.
10423 have offended, Think but

offenders
3985 Of society offenders who might
10101 pardon to offenders, I can

offensive
1583 is being offensive. Bad
5105 of parsons is mighty offensive.
8250 he who is offensive to us are
9758 work, but offensive in
12466 Life is an offensive, directed
12490 classes: offensive hats,

offer
636 refuse an offer of
3817 I can offer you neither
4928 instantly with the offer.
9319 make him an offer he can't

office
16 that the office sanctifies
427 time to drive to the office.
1524 important office is that of
3105 th' highest office in th'
4891 in which the office is held,
5580 we got into office, the thing
5974 of being in office but not in
8508 I had an office so tiny
9839 By office boys for office
12672 who takes office in

officer
211 Any Officer who shall behave
7219 inferior officer who acts

offices
7491 all the offices both

official
4244 as that officials are the
4560 This high official, all allow,
10904 The official world, the

officialism
3586 there is officialism every

officious
5119 Officious, innocent, sincere,

offspring
2793 enough for offspring before the
7601 Of human offspring, sole

often
1284 and vote often' is the
7426 'Do you come here often?'

ogle
6289 equal opportunity to ogle.

oil
254 price for oil is
350 Drill for oil? You mean
3619 past is an oil spread by
4175 him we see Oil, vinegar,
4673 where oil is thicker
5265 words; Pour oil into their

oiled
6253 pore, He oiled his way

oily
11724 round, fat, oily man of

ok
2427 I'm not ok - you're not

old
24 and too old to rush up
692 of the Old Testament,
758 may be old in hours,
1299 grow not old, as we

The Wordsworth Dictionary of Quotations

1403 men grow old in their
1745 - 'half as old as Time'!
1837 leaves grow old. How full
2114 'You are old, Father
2146 matter how old you get,
2468 A man is as old as he's
3270 action; The old at the
3380 time to be old, To take
3888 that the Old Country
4172 that are old, and know
4201 they are old, but
4603 ARE old: he just
4722 good out of being old.
4958 'This is old, therefore
5679 warn you not to grow old.
5743 Jungle - as old and as
5899 people know how to be old.
6044 being old is having
6739 they are too old to do it.
7093 is only as old as the
7170 times the old have
7199 Growing old is no more
7361 it on the old plan.
8053 late into a world too old.
8397 it's a very old building.
9007 Growing old is like being
9080 but none would be old.
9125 As old as the itch.
9631 me Grown old before my
9705 I am old. Middle
10597 do for the old, to shock
10915 I grow old ever learning
10975 am putting old heads on
11071 can grow old with a
11203 Old and young, we are all
11259 Growing old - it's not
11340 but no man would be old.
11841 I die before I get old.
11941 than an old bird of
12088 hand of an old, wild, and
12259 but an older friend
12575 Men become old, but they
12913 you are old and grey

old age
72 affronts, Old age is slow in
884 To me, old age is always
2871 a struggle; Old Age a regret.
6213 Old age is woman's hell.
8113 But when old age crept over
8865 frolics, and old age of cards.
8942 of early old age; it
9485 What makes old age so sad is
11255 Old age is a time of
11887 Old age is the most
12598 tragedy of old age is not
12909 upon my old age; They were

old man
1989 Old man! 'tis not so
2289 An old man in a hurry.
3110 that an old man has
4718 called an old man for
5111 in an old man,
6146 was an Old Man with a
9874 an old man, my
10136 that is an old man and no
10367 thought the old man to

old men
95 season for old men to
352 Old men and far
429 men think old men fools and
1097 Old men who never
11310 to old men, in
12948 is done by old men who

old-fashioned
3506 I want an old-fashioned house With
8404 aid of the old-fashioned, grand
9880 afterwards be always old-fashioned.
11133 products old-fashioned, out of
12576 apt to grow old-fashioned quite

olden
8952 In olden days a glimpse of

older
82 is to go on getting older.
2586 As one gets older, one
7803 more, as I grow older.
7938 As I get older .. I become
8420 as you get older. The idea

8569 She is older than the rocks
8686 happier as we grow older.
9944 As I grow older and older,
11033 as you grow older that the
12052 growing older is that it
12859 The older you get, the more

oligarchy
2261 arrogant oligarchy of those

omega
1139 Alpha and Omega, the

omelette
995 admirable omelette and the
9138 as a pretty good omelette.

omens
11298 grievous omens. Great

ominous
8999 much was ominous. With

omit
11171 is but one art, to omit.

omnibus
4687 is an omnibus in which

omnipotence
2790 of God's omnipotence that he

omnipotent
7548 defy the omnipotent to arms.

omnipresent
8182 omnipresent, who in

omniscience
10898 forte, and omniscience his

on guard
10594 by standing on guard, but by

once
129 Once in Royal David's City
6310 only live once - but if
6327 at least once a year; a
8462 you can only use it once.
11924 comes but once a year.
12459 The once and future king.

one
1202 Lord our God is one Lord.
1511 number one is easier
3086 All for one, one for all.
7288 but one out of
7629 we are one, One
8008 Führer. One realm, one
9127 One of these days is none
9390 more than one man in bed
9798 of one gets
10812 to do only one thing at
11578 One God, one law, one

one up
8974 How to be one up - how to

one-and-twenty
4789 When I was one-and-twenty I heard a

one-eyed
3403 blind the one-eyed man is
4470 There's a one-eyed yellow idol

oneness
12925 feel your oneness with every

oneself
3225 Hell is oneself, Hell is
7727 at oneself before one
8042 other than oneself is real.
8236 to talk of oneself is a form

onion
858 that raw onion sandwich
10150 live in an onion that
10890 Let onion atoms lurk within

only
9599 The only thing we have to
9866 It's the only thing.

onset
8663 disease at its onset.

onward
848 Onward, Christian soldiers,
12454 oft in woe, Onward,

oozing
6253 Oozing charm from every

open
456 Open Sesame!
840 very, very open, and so is
1123 If you open that Pandora's
4275 is to keep his mouth open.

4872 yourself open to what is
10410 I with sword will open.

open-breasted
7047 walks all open-breasted, Drawn

opened
5530 which has been opened for us.

opening
2253 object of opening the mind,
8111 Opening night is the night

opening time
11682 is always opening time in the

opens
8691 When a man opens the car

opera
449 language an opera is sung in
2548 The opera ain't over 'til
3809 Opera is when a guy gets
7276 Opera in English is, in the
7877 to the opera, like
9652 wonderful opera would be
12956 than of a grand opera.

operate
10745 really operate unless it

operatic
9062 so romantic, so operatic.'

operations
12478 important operations which we

ophelia
10228 thou, poor Ophelia, And

opinion
590 a whole climate of opinion.
600 into Public Opinion are
1037 His opinion of himself,
1917 Is of his own opinion still.
2181 cannot face public opinion.
2907 Party is organized opinion.
3012 imagination, but by opinion.
4034 what a poor opinion I have of
4194 was ever of opinion, that the
4955 Public opinion: a vulgar,
5555 comfort of opinion without
5655 organized opinion. Where
6583 of public opinion is like
6852 public opinion is all
6985 what you feel is opinion.
7190 erroneous opinion of their
7368 were of one opinion, and only
7376 that the opinion we are
8328 of him by prevalent opinion.
8491 merit? The opinion one man
8535 it is the opinion of the
8603 Public opinion is a compound
8673 I want your opinion I'll give
8881 think the last opinion right.
9558 of opinion is what
9946 to majority opinion.
9988 your true opinion of
10993 Opinion is ultimately
11061 can brave opinion, a woman
11877 a good opinion of a man
12877 souls tend to extreme opinion.

opinions
1873 and his religious opinions.
2245 of men who have no opinions.
2910 Predominant opinions are
3791 great many opinions in this
6064 your opinions, but he
6425 New opinions are always
6573 never change their opinions.
6737 or so bad as their opinions.
6961 Opinions cannot survive if one
7463 many opinions; for
7798 were two opinions alike in
8661 anyone's opinions but your
9750 man's opinions are much
10871 has any opinions at all
11623 are as many opinions as there
12675 made up of opinions and
12758 reason the opinions of others.

opium
2782 subtle, and mighty opium!
5664 - an opium-dose for
7106 .. is the opium of the

opponents
4746 political opponents honored me
8751 its opponents and making

opportunities
4062 of those opportunities which may
9889 matchless opportunities for
10638 My opportunities were still there;
11641 with fair opportunities and

opportunity
755 Opportunity makes a thief.
2223 Equal opportunity is good, but
2384 It is opportunity. Let's
3037 Thou strong seducer, opportunity!
5378 is only opportunity in work
9687 when he had the opportunity.
9850 Equality of opportunity is an
10623 with the maximum of opportunity.

oppose
6860 Let no one oppose this

opposed
9987 it is opposed, in the
11760 crime, more opposed to poetry,

opposing
10211 And by opposing end them?

opposite
1390 The opposite of a correct
5336 the very opposite of that
5435 sheet opposite,
9901 has an opposite one, no
10873 moving in opposite

opposition
780 Majesty's Opposition'; that it
2291 an opposition is
2784 duty of an Opposition [is] very
2870 without a formidable Opposition.
3647 I love an opposition that has

oppression
1660 Oppression makes the wise man
5053 scene of tension and oppression.

oppressor
4983 people against the oppressors.

upprest
8115 Sink heart and voice upprest.

optimism
7141 Optimism is like a spiritual
9872 passions, including optimism.

optimist
2002 The optimist proclaims that we
4820 to live with an optimist.
4836 An optimist is a fellow who
5021 - I remain an optimist
7026 an optimist is a guy that has

oracles
7541 The oracles are dumb, No
11298 green oracles That will

oracular
10730 use of my oracular tongue,

orange
1743 A clockwork orange.
4130 the gold oranges glow; a

orator
7013 play the orators for us.
10537 of men without an orator.

oratory
6804 object of oratory alone is
8212 a sort of oratory of power
8694 Oratory: the art of making

orb
10476 her circled orb, Lest that

orchestra
927 for an orchestra: start
11394 to the orchestra, not

orchid
3093 isn't an orchid, he must

order
33 life, when order breeds
1782 Good order is the
3117 destroys order, the
4069 necessarily in that order.'
4235 in that order. In
6905 Good order brings good
6952 things in order - God does
6969 return, all is in order.
7221 a planned order of

7335 the word order'. Freedom
7369 A party of order or
7772 managed by order, method
8557 Yet the order of the acts
9594 of a new order of
10075 with no recognizable order.
10359 upon the order of your
11113 They order, said I, this
11254 to make order of things,
11515 The old order changeth,
12294 with a wig to keep order.
12468 to preserve order amid

ordered
762 cannot be ordered about,
5764 You are ordered abroad as a

ordering
3872 in just ordering people to

orders
2421 are no longer any orders.

ordinary
2971 into ordinary' and
3347 than an ordinary man, but
4110 a succession of ordinary days.
5679 not to be ordinary, I warn
5997 or upon one of ordinary size.
6782 only the ordinary way of
6876 duke as an ordinary man is
10108 The Ordinary made beautiful;
12747 a moment an ordinary mind on an

organ
160 my second favourite organ.
1112 when the organ grinder is
4501 - an organ without a
7507 the pealing organ blow To
9054 day at the organ, I was

organism
1888 of every organism to live

organization
29 systematic organization of
466 of human organization. We are
772 than the organization of
2247 Large organization is loose
4392 in any organization is to help
6451 This organization (United Nations)
7400 All organization is and must be
8072 to the organization of the
11002 lies in the organisation of the

organized
2907 Party is organized opinion.
5655 analysis is organized opinion.
9573 gets you organized for the
10983 Science is organized knowledge.
12371 are the curse of organized life.

organizing
1116 Only an organizing genius

organs
2186 cry from suffering organs.
4051 the other organs take their
7162 may make other organs weep.

orgasm
8025 The orgasm has replaced the

orgies
4909 routine punctuated by orgies.

orgy
8024 An orgy looks particularly
9475 late. The orgy has moved

orient
6991 the ocean for orient pearl.

original
2697 The most original thing a
3368 capable of original writing,
4307 profoundly original art looks
5180 good and original; but the
5795 The more original a discovery,
8548 one finds original.
12740 not produce original works of
12793 great and original writer, in

original sin
8791 did researches in original sin.

originality
4666 other. Originality is
4959 What is originality? Undetected
7374 are the fruits of originality.
11107 Originality does not consist in
12166 Originality is nothing but

originals
8538 we do not admire the originals.
11811 are few originals and many

originate
3348 as by what he originates.

ornament
1739 poor .. an ornament to her
7641 or true ornament of poem or
8876 hide with ornaments their
9228 is a woman's finest ornament.
12817 sent To be a moment's ornament.

orphan
12374 'I'm a Norfan, both sides,'

orpheus
7503 the soul of Orpheus sing Such

orthodox
4795 preaching, that's not orthodox.
11247 not orthodox. She felt

orthodoxy
12240 Orthodoxy is my doxy;

ostrich
6836 wings of an ostrich. It

other
5309 did lots of other things
6636 I can do no other. God help
6796 on any other human
9441 bourgeois are other people.
11550 was born to other things.

others
571 to help others; what on
4678 is composed of others.
5883 in noticing them in others.
10592 not do unto others as you
11214 We love in others what we

otherwise
12121 The gods thought otherwise.

ought
1422 which we ought to have
4951 that they ought to be..
6131 , 'so he ought to be'.

ounce
9267 An ounce of mother is worth

ours
2773 Indian said simply Ours'.

ourselves
919 old, but more like ourselves.
4115 deceived; we deceive ourselves.
4650 least about ourselves, we are
5346 better be changed in ourselves.
6025 say, 'we did it ourselves!'
6499 But in ourselves, are
8910 knowledge is, ourselves to know.
9448 in ourselves, and it is
11834 in this together - by ourselves.

out
135 want to get out with my
238 music is on the way out.
1892 only just out to those
2282 all their out, Is, that
3765 They go out when
4415 them all out and I
4446 is giving out;
5637 to go but out, Nowhere
6192 you get out of it
8305 to keep it out of as many
8753 no way out of the
10366 Out, damned spot! out, I

out-did
4591 of thine Out-did the meat,

out-manoeuvre
8134 but out-manoeuvre a

out-of-breath
6722 Peaceful out-of-breath death.

out-of-doors
6849 indoors and out-of-doors, we should

outcast
10546 beweep my outcast state, And

outlast
5004 that will outlast it.

outline
2461 on a firmer outline and then
11230 it into outline it is like
11743 to mere outline sketches

outlive
10549 shall outlive this

outlived
2144 eighty has outlived probably

outposts
5547 who has outposts in your

outrageous
11093 Outrageous acts and everyday

outrageously
10851 behave as outrageously as the

outside
182 Outside every fat man there
3363 Outside, among your fellows,
6890 just going outside and may be
8297 just going outside and may be

outstripped
5233 If I have outstripped An old

outweighs
556 that good outweighs evil in

outwept
10669 which had outwept its rain.

outworn
10700 The dust of creeds outworn.

oval
569 Oval face. His eye a dark

over
1092 game isn't over until it's
7395 damn thing over and over.
12405 to put it all over you."

over-canopied
10417 grows Quite over-canopied with

over-prepared
8999 I had over-prepared the event, that

overcare
3643 health than an overcare of it.

overcoat
6570 is to put on your overcoat.
9498 pockets; my overcoat also was

overcome
394 We Shall Overcome.
5350 has never overcome them.
7550 is else not to be overcome?

overcomes
3654 end victoriously overcomes him.
7560 Who overcomes By force, hath

overdeveloped
3788 the more overdeveloped the women.

overdone
1310 but it can be overdone.

overfed
11866 Overpaid, overfed, oversexed,

overflowed
10882 He not only overflowed with

overheateth
4378 but it overheateth the oven.

overloaded
5664 while they are being overloaded.

overlook
5007 of knowing what to overlook.
5057 everything: overlook a great

overmatch
5183 are an overmatch for them,

overpaid
4560 Is grossly overpaid; There
11866 Overpaid, overfed, oversexed,

oversexed
11866 overfed, oversexed, and over

overtaxed
1066 against the overtaxed.

overthrow
3824 so must we overthrow, With
11084 to overthrow my

overthrown
12805 empire overthrown! And we

overtime
290 three overtime hours to
2131 will work overtime for no

owe
7509 I owe no light or leading
10251 once; we owe God a

owed
2295 was so much owed by so many
2669 what he owed to others.
6754 to be owed by someone

owes
2607 Life owes us little;
9064 how much it owes to them

owl
6154 The Owl and the Pussy-Cat
7437 He respects Owl, because
7449 Owl hasn't exactly got
9299 was an old owl lived in

own
142 want to own anything
3492 wouldn't like to own one.
5965 call his own, is that
6334 only to those who own one.
7902 your life in your own way.
8050 but at least it is my own.
10392 of that which is mine own.
11441 other for what they own.
11840 you're on your own.
11920 ideas. I have my own.

ownership
3583 with the desire for ownership.

ox
1327 He who the ox to wrath

oxen
5133 drives fat oxen should
12885 great black oxen tread the

oxford
770 Oxford is on the whole more
956 .. It is Oxford that has
3538 noon on Oxford town,
3644 in the Oxford sense: you
3911 of Oxford I
4269 men at Oxford Know all
4338 it to be a street in Oxford.
4493 London to Oxford than if
5308 long be popular in Oxford.
6278 spires of Oxford As I was
9291 House to Rome, Oxford.
11031 will leave Oxford by the
11064 and sends his son to Oxford.
11852 To Oxford sent a

oxtail
5337 to the university of Oxtail.

oxygen
373 enough oxygen for two

oyster
1019 eating one oyster cracker or
2821 and solitary as an oyster.
4726 open an oyster without a
7401 world is an oyster, but you
10410 mine oyster, Which I
10722 An oyster may be crossed in
11305 man that first ate an oyster.

oysters
9826 Oysters are more beautiful

ozymandias
10697 'My name is Ozymandias, king of

pace
11764 not keep pace with his

pacific
5439 at the Pacific - and all

pacifist
12188 The quietly pacifist peaceful

pacify
8467 down and pacify it with

pack
525 while, So pack up your
1577 I will pack, and take
6299 remains, to pack and fix on
11888 its pack animal.

pack-horse
7926 of the pack-horse on the

pact
1761 is a pact between

paddington
1334 Ever weeping Paddington.
2061 As London is to Paddington.

paddle
5710 leave to paddle, or else
7043 Every man paddle his own

padlock
8832 jingling padlock on the
9036 clap your padlock - on her

pagan
12955 find the pagan - spoiled.

page
1704 They have no page two.
4723 (moving the page back and
4975 the last page should be

paid
1571 earth, And paid his
1689 but he will be well paid.
5746 God, we ha' paid in full!
8582 must be paid for, and
9030 these men paid their
12423 If he paid for each day's

pail
12889 of a pail, but the

pain
255 'Although pain isn't
256 I feel no pain dear mother
513 triumph! hark - what pain!
514 Passion! Eternal Pain!
1141 be any more pain: for the
1675 When pain ends, gain ends
1948 we exist, even in pain.
3050 but in rest from pain.
3444 I have no pain, dear
3657 too much pain, too many
4583 the worst pain a man can
5120 of fiery pain, No cold
5352 consciousness without pain.
5425 like a God in pain.
6298 Pain is God's megaphone to
6831 it gave pain to the
7324 to inflict pain upon
7568 full of pain, this
8168 who never inflicts pain.
8454 Why inflict pain on
8839 Oh the pain, the bliss
9130 now is pain to come.
10059 the intermission of pain.
10231 breath in pain, To tell
10461 what pain it was to
10710 With some pain is
10986 a way that pain shall not
11351 Superflux of pain.
11360 Dolores, Our Lady of Pain.
11602 in their pain, that they
11705 in other's pain, And
11802 us, or the pain against
12695 beneath the aromatic pain.

painful
705 one is as painful as the
4579 the painful publicity
11015 And painful pleasure turns to

pains
4590 are according to his pains.
4906 people's pains, but not
7217 mutual pains, sorrows,
10762 Pains do not hold a
11011 was his pains, so double
11157 are no gains without pains.
11272 heart: It pains a man when

paint
54 those who paint 'em truest
197 pick it up, paint it white.
1380 attempt to paint the colour
2644 skill to paint my picture
2673 I do not paint a portrait
4760 would be no reason to paint.
7949 I paint from the top down.
8713 I paint objects as I think
9445 I paint with my prick.
9743 a pot of paint in the
12041 I dream my painting, and
12042 well as to paint it. There

painted
951 so young as they are painted.

painter
6238 A good painter is to paint
6245 below the painter in the
7157 creative painter than to
8716 is a painter trying to
9447 A painter who has the feel of
9729 sculptor or painter can be an

10706 some great painter dips His
12044 As a painter I shall never
12439 say to the painter that

painters
2344 when painters stop

painting
1269 Painting, n: the art of
2568 will be painting in heaven.
3433 I look at a painting it isn't
6910 things: a painting and a
7689 The painting rises from the
8538 How vain painting is, exciting
8710 understand painting. Why
8714 Painting is a blind man's
8715 Painting is just another way
9061 Chardin's painting, I never
9668 For me, painting is a way to
9911 is a painting with
10772 Painting is silent poetry,

pair
7602 on Blest pair; and O yet

palace
2961 thine own palace, or the
5462 Love in a palace is perhaps
5463 palace of sweet
7470 opes the palace of

palaces
4935 of mock palaces clearly

palatable
3578 pudding to make it palatable.

palates
10436 have their palates both for

pale
4028 I was a pale young curate
10357 bond Which keeps me pale!
11366 Pale, beyond porch and

paleontology
11079 the laws of paleontology is that an

palestine
7127 in sunny Palestine, With a

palette
2170 an artist's palette, which

pall mall
7917 sweet shady side of Pall Mall!
11639 The Pall Mall Gazette is

palladium
5355 is the Palladium of all

palliate
8737 attempt to palliate nor deny.

pallor
8447 The pallor of girls' brows

palm
5282 has won it bear the palm.
11141 The palm at the end of the

paltered
11584 hour, Nor paltered with

pamper
3890 be polite to and to pamper.

pampered
7022 Holla, ye pampered jades of

panama
4467 keep the Panama Canal.

pandemonium
7565 .. Pandemonium, the high capital

pandora
1123 open that Pandora's Box, you

panic
1831 O what a panic's in thy

pansies
10227 there is pansies, that's

panther
8791 in panther skin Mona

pants
1282 wears the pants in a
7095 like the pants of my blue
7391 public with his pants down.
8104 limbs in pants; Yours are
12180 seat of the pants to the
12278 who can't put his pants on.

panzer-man
8754 blue. Panzer-man,

papacy
4639 The papacy is not other than

paper
2749 Voyages in a paper boat.
4676 a scrap of paper, Great
6653 earth were paper white And
6779 we sail in paper boats.
6790 the evening paper, By
7950 like paper, and make
8653 it down on paper, and then
10336 not eat paper, as it
11069 of this paper appears

paper work
8360 to keep the paper work down to a

papers
74 he read in the Sunday papers.
9555 is what I read in the papers.

papist
2399 a mist, A Papist, yet a

par
11974 shall not be taken at par.

parable
7762 sweetly in parable told. We

parachute
2224 with a parachute packed by

paradise
1356 Such are the Gates of Paradise.
1851 is a paradise for women,
2782 the keys of Paradise, oh just,
3551 Is the paradise of women,
5434 weave A paradise for a
5508 taught in Paradise To ease my
5615 the bird of paradise, better
5801 He deserves paradise who makes
5978 Same old glimpse of Paradise.
6661 men discover their paradise.
7085 there: Two paradises 'twere in
7586 called The Paradise of Fools,
7694 They paved paradise And put up
9076 The true paradises are the
9098 is the paradise of
11710 Have blundered into Paradise.

paradox
2315 in strange paradox, decided
5783 what was a paradox but a
11625 found the paradox that if I
12590 and winged it with paradox.

paradoxical
3676 is paradoxical and, in a

paragon
10207 world! the paragon of

paragraphs
12383 revision; paragraphs and whole

parallel
7075 so truly parallel, Though

parallelogram
6133 is a parallelogram - that is,

paralyzed
9783 being paralyzed by

parapets
9501 Europe of the ancient parapets!

paraphrase
8992 Than the classics in paraphrase!

parasites
5269 nature But parasites or

parcels
12332 it in small parcels, That she

pardon
1709 received. Pardon all, their
3272 God may pardon you, but I
4228 Pardon me boy is that the
4508 God will pardon me. It's
10101 pleas for pardon to

parellelism
35 a certain parellelism of life, a

parent
321 and the parent of
2345 Every parent is at some time
8453 death of a parent makes you
12182 As a parent you just hang on
12556 To lose one parent, Mr

parenthesis
11891 secrets in a casual parenthesis.

parenthood
11815 Parenthood remains the greatest

parents
2 class parents want for
207 which parents have not
1332 left his parents in dismay.
2772 makes our parents, but
3149 is the way parents obey their
3434 when your parents die, you
4442 of one's parents is a harsh
5351 unlived lives of the parents.
5918 children and devoted parents.
8088 that's what parents were
8672 our parents'
9226 Parents love their children
10579 seen their parents as they
10999 My parents kept me from
11916 needs good parents. From 18
12605 their parents; after a
12729 and parents exist to
12733 bondage to parents cramps

paring
5322 paring his

paris
451 when they die, go to Paris.
1119 of living in Paris.
4338 a suburb of Paris, until I
4403 time I saw Paris Her heart
4531 lived in Paris as a young
4541 Paris is well worth a mass.
4632 Is Paris burning?
8220 in Europe save in Paris.
9141 could put Paris into a
11912 its history Paris was French
11972 In Paris they simply stared

parish
5524 would be found in my parish.
12391 all the world as my parish.

parking lot
7694 put up a parking lot, With a

parks
8742 The parks are the lungs of

parliament
1449 get here Parliament) was like
2079 Estates in Parliament; but in
8615 A parliament can do any thing
9947 Parliament itself would not
10610 It enables Parliament to do
11529 In the Parliament of man,

parliamentary
4060 as an old parliamentary hand, to
4232 has got the Parliamentary Party by

parlour
4810 into my parlour?' said a

parochial
4996 provincial - he was parochial.
5970 hopelessly parochial when not
7836 Art must be parochial in the

parole
5106 is the parole of

parrot
2560 morning, a parrot that

parsley
8094 Parsley is gharsley.

parson
2258 him the parson ran, the
2627 The parson knows enough who
3002 creed no parson ever knew,
4158 too, the parson owned his
4647 years, If Parson lost his
6422 Turn parson, Colman, that's
10058 and the Parson left

part
3859 We only part to meet
4202 I read part of it all the
4604 him that is part of
5020 to whom the part is greater
5621 I am a part of all I have
6773 to play a part, any part,
7929 this, To part at last
10176 forgot my part, and I am
11470 I am a part of all that I

parted
1485 and asunder Parted are those

1549 I till we parted, how, hard
7628 shall be parted, bliss or

partialities
11939 and our partialities and

partiality
11398 neither anger nor partiality.

participants
9533 as participants in one of

particular
3688 father's. He's more particular.

particulars
414 must do it in minute particulars.
9496 many unique particulars that

parties
1755 Parties must ever exist in a
1986 Like other parties of the

parting
267 The parting genius is with
386 let this parting grieve
3218 In every parting there is an
9975 Every parting gives a
10478 good-night! parting is such
11575 Their every parting was to

partner
1076 you change partners and dance
3865 Is judged a partner in the

partnership
2403 twenty-first century partnership.

parts
7972 the parts other
8896 All are but parts of one
10117 plays many parts, His acts

party
232 huge garden party, faintly
2489 The party's over, it's time
2862 Stick to your party.
2907 Party is organized opinion.
3774 to save the Party we love.
5762 people at a party, they
6672 The party needs a good
6841 was for a party; Then all
8954 What a swell party this is.
9565 that each party is worse
9567 organized party, I'm a
12273 of the spirit of party.
12663 This party is a moral

party-spirit
8935 Party-spirit .. which at best is

pass
1187 earth shall pass away, but
1890 trying to pass them on
3425 not come to pass. God finds
4327 I expect to pass through
5280 let anyone pass who knows
6486 not the Pass!' the old
7120 but never pass in front
7213 I will pass over my
12580 is to pass it on. It

passage
5137 you meet a passage which you
10748 frequent passage from hand
11126 North-west passage to the

passages
5486 some fine passages but that

passed
1141 things are passed away.
5350 who has not passed through
5465 loveliness have passed away.
8591 Has passed away in
12806 there hath passed away a
12887 I have passed with a nod

passes
8507 seldom make passes At girls
8812 don't make passes at female

passing
6871 George, passing slowly in

passing-bells
8446 What passing-bells for these who

passion
498 is the passion for
514 Eternal Passion! Eternal
704 There is no passion in the
1065 the passion for the
1784 No passion so effectually

1959 her first passion woman
2176 object of passion. Flee it
2397 There is no passion like that
2986 of an old passion, Yea, all
3064 into passion, but to be
3067 What passion cannot Music
3581 and the passion, and both
3600 Passion destroys passion; we
4312 of the Passion, would we
4712 action and passion;
5491 human passion far above,
5533 of a passion for a man,
6181 so much passion, swears
6190 about the limit for passion.
6251 What is passion? That
6338 sure no passion in the
6433 points, by passion or
6981 excess of passion, be sure
7672 of mind, all passion spent.
7799 There is no passion so much
8172 so are the passions. Reason
8514 he vows his passion is
9001 and it is a passion to which
9308 science of the tender passion.
9528 insipid passion To choose
9929 Man is a useless passion.
10287 Passion, I see, is catching.
11115 betwixt one passion and
11525 when his passion shall have
11636 hopeless passion is my
12394 Passion and prejudice govern
12956 of a 'grand passion' than of a

passionate
589 any romance, however passionate.
11361 beautiful passionate body That
12902 Are full of passionate intensity.

passionless
1625 hopeless grief is passionless.

passions
2229 but two passions - vanity
3140 the natural passions are
5059 Desolate passions, aching
5350 of his passions has never
5874 little passions and
5903 resist our passions, it is
6275 is with our passions as it is
7312 need be! Passions spin the
8416 two primal passions, to get
9378 Our passions are most like to
9749 Three passions, simple but
11067 their Passions better
11123 but his passions which have
11492 in the mastery of his passions.

passive
8529 competitive is to be passive.

passport
9377 the world without a passport.

past
577 repeat his past nor leave
955 The past is a work of art,
1431 that is past as a watch
1696 debt to the past by putting
1764 the future by the past.
2699 to the idealized past.
4451 The past is a foreign
5214 so the past assumes a
5601 or nothing but the past.
6343 the quiet past are
6393 a repetition of the past.
6909 The past exudes legend:
8403 forward to the past.
8725 is only the past again,
9356 on what's past, but never
9383 a nation's past; the
9625 to the past, disowning
9863 you the past is a
9885 the past are
10469 and I are past our
10685 of the past, Oh, might
10867 the past And
11263 with the past need not
11438 for the past, as many
11537 of the dreadful Past.
11691 The past is the only dead
12321 The past, at least, is
12751 had his past shut in
12918 last day of an era past.

pasteur
8455 Louis Pasteur's theory of

pastime
6720 to a national pastime here.

pastness
3230 only of the pastness of the

pastors
10194 ungracious pastors do, Show

pate
8848 beat your pate, and fancy

paternal
8933 care A few paternal acres

paternity
9919 the bond of paternity, which is

path
2541 To have his path made clear
5811 Truth is a pathless land,
6386 for the path and less
7783 a rough and thorny path.

pathetic
7452 Pathetic,' he said. 'That's

paths
3547 Of all the paths lead to a
11038 and all her paths are Peace.
12535 So many paths that wind

patience
116 a school of patience; you can't
1136 heard of the patience of Job.
1381 thrives on patience; man on
1711 hold out. Patience is genius.
2184 neither respect nor patience.
2230 Patience is a most necessary
3615 Have patience with all things,
4633 Germans, my patience is now at
4981 Patience has its limits. Take
5852 Patience and passage of time
6460 Though with patience He stands
7932 great patience and
8579 Patience makes a woman
9102 time and patience the
9114 handful of patience is worth
9231 time and patience are the
9539 and one must have patience.
9886 It takes patience to
10516 sat like patience on a
12008 in other people's patience.
12662 the patience of a

patient
3030 the fury of a patient man.
5915 traveller with his patient.
8413 sort of a patient has a
10083 that a patient mind
10242 my lord, but not so patient.

patiently
3761 to bear patiently with bad
11262 a week patiently waiting if

patients
7713 time with patients; and if

patrician
3968 crust, A regular patrician.

patriot
3029 Never was patriot yet, but
3931 a devoted patriot, who
4190 Such is the patriot's boast,
8472 sunshine patriot will, in

patriotic
11964 course is patriotic and which

patriotism
122 Patriotism is a lively sense of
2680 True patriotism hates injustice
3827 kind of patriotism which
4902 of patriotism - it
5086 Patriotism is the last refuge of
6121 Patriotism is when you risk your
10636 knock the patriotism out of the
11159 Patriotism is not short,

patrol
7327 of art Patrol the halls

patron
5190 Is not a patron one who

patter
4026 patter Isn't

pattern
9406 Art is .. pattern informed
12473 of a pattern on

patterns
1592 certain patterns, so to
6554 Christ! What are patterns for?

paul
10595 to pay Paul can always

pauper
8274 He's only a pauper, whom

pause
11973 The pause - that impressive

pauses
9967 But the pauses between

paved
2472 streets are paved with gold,

pay
1298 who will pay two
1841 Pay, pack, and follow at
3870 going to pay every
4783 the sum of things for pay.
5712 now I must pay for my
5749 two ye must pay for one by
5753 therefore pay you cash
6261 we cannot pay too dearly,
8006 Crime doesn't pay.
9113 does not pay weekly,
9735 for what pay? Who is
11282 citizen who pays his debts

paying
5221 when they're paying for it.
9575 government we're paying for.
9679 entire group paying for it.
12596 without paying for it.

payroll
10106 he has to meet a payroll.

pc
8978 isn't a PC. It is a

pea-green
6154 a beautiful pea-green boat. They

peace
60 See in what peace a
478 that we may live in peace.
600 there was peace, he was
1095 makers of peace because
1270 Peace, n: in international
1365 divine, And peace, the human
1413 they want peace, nations
1424 Give peace in our time, O
1534 Peace is nothing but
1535 tell me peace has broken
1555 I am for Peace,
2377 on peace that he
2396 make war than to make peace.
2470 Love of peace, and lonely
2913 you back peace - but a
3083 chances for peace, just as
3084 lasting peace so long as
3189 people want peace so much
3364 The peace of the man who
3459 a little peace, even the
3469 not want peace. People
3554 is not a peace treaty, it
3631 a good war, or a bad peace.
3886 of peace upon earth
4047 know the blessings of peace.
4101 My peace is gone, My heart
4426 but Peace is poor
4570 good war makes a good peace.
4582 In peace, sons bury their
4976 be a just peace, but it is
5000 like the peace of God;
5053 vocation of peace, the
5055 and peace go
5325 will give peace now And
5450 not; but in peace Hung over
5566 and bitter peace, proud of
5647 a negative peace which is
5800 of war and peace in the
5827 from war to peace. Let peace
6168 as inner peace. There is
6223 is Give peace a chance.
6260 whatever peace of mind
6262 They made peace between us;
6400 Peace is indivisible.
6601 cone; peace to our

peace of mind
9070 can be no peace of mind in love,

peace-maker
10127 is the only peace-maker, much

peaceable
9761 peacocks are peaceable birds.

peaceful
4994 experience is never peaceful.
5582 who make peaceful revolution
12671 this great peaceful people

peacefully
2716 is moving peacefully towards

peach
5255 and woolly peach Hang on

peacock
4253 a man is a peacock, at thirty
5461 Eyed like a peacock, and all
9761 that any peacock envies
12584 She is a peacock in

peacocks
9738 useless; peacocks and lilies

peal
4647 The wildest peal for years,

peanut
1019 one half of a salted peanut.

pear
12754 like a ripe pear, pendant,

pearl
7004 tears to pearl he turned,
10415 And hang a pearl in every
10438 threw a pearl away

pearls
3033 search for pearls must dive
10486 Those are pearls that were
10804 sent me to sea for pearls.
12432 is not that pearls fetch a

peasant
9251 loud, the peasant forgets to
10760 a stalwart peasant in a

peasantry
11888 made the peasantry its pack

peasants
11860 with their peasants, their

pebble
8179 a smoother pebble or a

peck
10743 trying to peck my eyes

peculiar
4464 Funny peculiar or funny
10927 And Heaven's peculiar care!

pedant
9869 but only a pedant can live

pedestrians
2795 classes of pedestrians in these

pedigree
2833 The pedigree of honey Does not

peel
8310 Peel's smile: like the

peep
12820 that would peep and

peepers
7293 get those peepers? Jeepers

peeping
4740 sun Came peeping in at

peepshow
6785 and a ticket for the peepshow.

peerage
8128 gained a peerage, or
8288 I want a peerage, I shall
12606 study the Peerage, Gerald

peering
7539 mansions to the peering day.

peerless
6445 lies that peerless paper peer

peers
4019 we love our House of Peers.
6326 if an ass peers into it,
6875 Peers: a kind of eye-shade
6885 of his peers or by the

pegasus
5511 horse, And thought it Pegasus.

pelican
7329 bird is the pelican! His beak

pen
1724 great, The pen is
1846 much the pen is worse
4361 Some with a fountain pen.
5131 had not a pen in his
6295 The pen, in our age,
6308 and the pen Thought
6549 the scratching of a pen.
11757 of a pen, could
12054 been rescued by his pen.

penal
7548 chains and penal fire, Who

penalised
9007 penalised for a

penalty
4816 part of the penalty for

pence
1919 not of pounds, but of pence.
6603 care of the pence, and the
11613 want of pence, Which

pencils
9542 sadness of pencils, Neat in

penetrate
9499 green water penetrates my wooden
12038 To penetrate one's being, one

penetrating
3479 requires a penetrating eye to

pennies
9103 only two pennies left in

penny
2619 To turn a penny in the way
3982 are a penny, and ever
6871 worn penny in the
12878 not given a penny for a song

pension
6786 hang your hat on a pension.

penumbras
4039 and what penumbras! Whole

people
304 the world, people would be
489 are some people that if
1435 we are his people, the sheep
1514 Few people would not be the
1584 of separate people living
1684 The people have little
1754 against an whole people.
1770 The people are the masters.
1801 all the people who know
2259 we are the people of
2495 of course, people are only
2595 my dear! And the people!
2699 is full of people whose
2917 and the People formed Two
3095 that when people have no
3205 either give people what they
3237 And other people whom we

3254 godless people: Their
3365 People only see what they
3946 saved by one or two people.
4037 The people people work with
4117 Ordinary people know little
4405 afraid Of people whose eyes
4584 a nice way to start people.
4725 People should be free to
4802 What people say behind your
4883 When people don't want to
5104 there are people whom one
5899 Few people know how to be
5965 is other people's time.
5981 proved that people will look
6044 head, and people in them,
6119 the Little People goes up to
6165 People don't ask for facts
6221 all the people Living for
6339 all the people some of
6354 of the people, by the
6359 People who like this sort of
6367 Any people anywhere, being
6860 on the people builds on
7153 you can give to some people.
7691 Most people ignore most
7949 cattle, and then the people.
7999 Power to the people.
8008 realm, one people, one
8030 to see some people before
8119 People are like birds - from
8460 of the people, by the
8921 The people's voice is odd,
8989 O woe, woe, People are born
9256 A people without history is
9437 a body of people who have
9925 Hell is other people.
10009 sake look after our people.
10175 is the city but the people?
10605 sorts of people: the
10744 some people because
10763 homes of the people.
10770 People talking without
11160 Some people approach every
12322 The people's government,
12352 not other people, hell is
12395 plain truth for plain people.
12595 of the people by the
12922 No people are uninteresting.

peopled
1676 his solitude peopled at once.
7632 wise, that peopled highest
10048 and peopled half the

peradventure
4628 there is no peradventure. It is

perceive
12798 half-create, And what perceive.

perceived
6684 who have perceived them

perceiving
5003 faculty of perceiving in an

percentage
922 It's a reasonable percentage.

perception
1347 doors of perception were
8259 renew our perception. What we
8781 the citadel of sense perception.

perch
10375 it Their perch and not

perdition
7548 bottomless perdition, there to

perennial
10776 I'll show you a perennial loser.

perfect
5054 To be perfect as a woman does
5248 measures life may perfect be.
10526 But constant, he were perfect.
12308 It's perfect when it
12560 of us are perfect. I myself

perfectibility
4073 Perfectibility is one of the most
7377 speak of perfectibility as a

perfecting
2695 task of perfecting himself.

perfection
1797 to think of perfection; but it's

2107 passion for perfection which you
2383 True perfection is achieved only
4052 Ideal perfection is not the true
4181 The very pink of perfection.
4384 Perfection is the child of Time.
6071 upon the perfection of the
6847 in their highest perfection.
7047 soul of all perfection.' 'What,
7165 husbands a perfection that
8055 must function to perfection.
9386 closest to perfection a person
11106 is death. Perfection is
11245 a placid perfection
11540 null, Dead perfection, no more.

perfections
1351 than the perfections of a fool.

perfectly
3613 and try to be that perfectly.

perform
879 correction to perform.
5900 hopes, and perform according
7491 a man to perform justly,
12478 we can perform without

performance
2502 on excellence of performance.
5209 his worst performance; and when
5383 the performance of the job
7149 all words, And no performance.
10247 so many years outlive performance?

performer
1679 for any performer is 'Look

performs
7804 than to him who performs.

perfume
10368 all the perfumes of Arabia
11377 As a perfume doth remain In

pericles
12927 like Pericles, or what

peril
2562 there is no peril in the

perils
8017 only adds to our perils.
11874 through the perils of winter

period
4492 any other period of the

perish
1249 is ready to perish, and wine
2349 Perish the thought!
3467 though the world perish.
3691 it had to perish twice, I
6007 too shall perish
6062 your heart, and you perish.
6803 should perish, would

perished
7390 Now that love is perished?
12054 Caesar had perished from the

perishes
682 really perishes, and that
2008 everything perishes,

perjured
10562 lust Is perjured,

permanence
2148 love permanence more than
5629 a terrible permanence when

permanent
2841 more delightful than permanent.
12775 is permanent, obscure

permission
9608 any man's permission when we

permitted
7732 It is permitted me to take good

pernicious
2606 Pernicious weed! whose scent the
11313 be the most pernicious race of

perpendicular
7700 Perpendicular, precise and
8487 leaning out of the perpendicular.
10586 is] a perpendicular expression

perpetrate
1905 we perpetrate We do but

perpetual
8486 we have no perpetual enemies.
10845 mind is a perpetual feast.

perpetually
6994 be damned perpetually. Stand

perpetuity
8794 which seeks perpetuity by way of

perplexed
10438 wrought, Perplexed in the

perplexing
4658 It is a perplexing and

persecution
1612 Persecution is a bad and indirect

persepolis
7015 in triumph through Persepolis?

perseverance
936 between perseverance and
10503 Perseverance, dear my lord, Keeps
11120 the name of perseverance in a good

persevere
12271 To persevere in one's duty and
12623 succeed in order to persevere.

persians
4284 Persians do not

person
243 of the person you would
590 no more a person now but a
2077 the sort of person you and I
4372 a healthy person who
5921 when one person is
7023 While a person does not give
7030 there is a person born who
12946 The person by far the most

personal
4596 and permanently personal.
4700 be something personal about it.

personalities
7110 events and personalities in world
7221 that the personalities of the two

personality
3177 muscles, but no personality.
7752 develop a personality once and
12501 is native personality, and that
12675 personality, more made

personnel
4223 great men could pass Personnel.

persons
1127 is no respecter of persons.
4486 Persons who undertake to pry

perspiration
1997 course his perspiration was but
3143 ninety-nine per cent perspiration.

perspire
5708 dig till you gently perspire.

persuade
2300 be able to persuade my wife to
5893 faults to persuade people
9717 ways to persuade others is

persuaders
8456 The hidden persuaders.

persuading
5356 By persuading others, we
11105 rules is by persuading an

persuasion
3908 Persuasion is the resource of
6804 is not truth, but persuasion.

perversion
4900 of all the sexual perversions.
6751 The perversion of the mind is
9360 universal perversion .. war

perversity
12009 perversity is the

perverts
2547 art's sake, .. perverts art.

pessimism
4819 Pessimism is only the name that
5021 face means pessimism, but in
9660 My pessimism goes to the point

pessimist
2002 and the pessimist fears this
4820 A pessimist is one who has been
12585 Pessimist - one who, when he

pestilence
1366 but acts not, breeds pestilence.
7576 hair Shakes pestilence and war.
8107 plague and pestilence, good

petals
8998 the crowd; Petals on a wet,

peter
4312 cowardly Peter who loved
6445 peer Lord Peter, Who broke

peter pan
11996 in Peter Pan , and you

petitioner
1274 of a single petitioner

petrified
4083 architecture petrified music'.

petrifies
1817 within, And petrifies the

pets
2560 have three pets at home

petticoat
1984 keep down a single petticoat.
7787 it on again with her petticoat.
11270 beneath her petticoat, Like

pettiness
6099 to expiate: A pettiness.

petulance
2891 learn that petulance is not

phantom
12817 She was a phantom of delight

phenomena
4605 the world's phenomena intersect,
8182 appear from phenomena that there

phenomenon
8622 .. is the phenomenon whereby

philadelphia
3487 I went to Philadelphia, but it

philanthropist
1271 Philanthropist, n: a rich (and

philistine
5373 of the Philistine is his

philistines
500 from the Philistines proper or
4008 Though the Philistines may

philosopher
2355 but some philosopher has said
3153 to be a philosopher; but, I
3420 I hate the philosopher who is not
4865 Be a philosopher but, amid all
6517 is to be a true philosopher.
10138 never yet philosopher That could
10641 The philosopher is Nature's pilot
12704 The philosopher's treatment of a

philosophers
5234 All men are Philosophers, to their
7112 The philosophers have only
8769 till philosophers become
9340 of philosophers into sages

philosophic
12813 that bring the philosophic mind.

philosophical
479 more philosophical and more
5819 die from philosophical calm,
12483 European philosophical tradition

philosophies
1869 All philosophies, if you ride them

philosophize
593 he eat than that he philosophize.

philosophy
695 A little philosophy inclineth
740 natural philosophy, deep;
945 The philosophy of one century is
1953 think 'twas philosophy that this
2050 but a philosophy put into
2859 History is philosophy learned
3134 Philosophy, Wittgenstein
3209 faced with philosophy and
3392 All philosophy lies in two
3393 of philosophy: a
3461 The philosophy behind much
4167 This same philosophy is a good
4373 be dreamed of, in any philosophy.
4948 to enslave a philosophy.
5460 Philosophy will clip an Angel's
5594 to build a philosophy. It
6467 In philosophy an individual is
6519 a simple philosophy. Fill
7800 Philosophy is doubt.

8180 Philosophy is such an
8927 may talk of philosophy; a man who
9780 you know, philosophy is what
9783 thing that philosophy in our age
9799 Philosophy is the replacement of
9900 a system of philosophy to be
9991 a new philosophy - I only
10200 are dreamt of in your philosophy.
10467 sweet milk, philosophy.
11112 Philosophy has a fine saying for
11326 Philosophy! the lumber of the
12705 Philosophy is a battle against

phoebus
7303 A Phoebus Apollo turned

phoenix
1946 like the phoenix midst her

phone
8339 in dozens of phone booths.
11790 did you answer the phone?

phoniness
9964 that phoniness is phony

photograph
458 see if I didn't photograph them.
6910 a great photograph, you find

photographer
8716 Photographers, along with

photographs
10935 reality, photographs have
10937 fixed forever. Photographs are.

photography
4068 Photography is truth. The cinema
11074 Photography records the gamut of

phrases
4007 in novel phrases of your

physical
4109 about his physical or moral
8252 by a little physical antipathy.
8771 as the physical eyesight

physician
1154 Physician, heal thyself.
1689 to live, a physician will be
2581 are the physician's secret
2885 Time is the great physician.
2955 observe the physician with the
3790 is nature's physician, and is
4660 not thy physician,
8412 of the physician is to
9043 died last night of my physician.
9171 Every invalid is a physician
12929 a good physician and a bad

physicians
94 are the physicians of a mind
131 the help of too many physicians.
986 Physicians of the Utmost Fame
9231 are the three great physicians.
9347 drunkards than old physicians.
12330 Physicians are like kings - they

physicists
8350 the physicists have known

physics
1532 the laws of physics. If you
7274 resort to physics and
9794 is either physics or stamp

pianist
9967 than many pianists. But the
12563 shoot the pianist. He is

piano
6096 great black piano
12439 he may sit on the piano.

picardy
12311 in Picardy, But

picasso
4559 sausage and thinks of Picasso.
7429 divides them like Picasso.
12455 can't stand Picasso, those who

piccadilly
4008 walk down Piccadilly with a
5343 Goodbye, Piccadilly, Farewell,

pick
197 move, pick it up; and
329 to' don't pick no cotton.
487 should pick out a good

picked
10204 be one man picked out of ten

picket-guard
4716 he is a picket-guard at the

picking
1271 is picking his

picnic
1530 Bears have their Picnic.

picture
697 which a picture cannot
852 One picture is worth ten
4444 A picture can become for us a
4714 painting a picture, not doing
5258 Not on his picture, but his
7968 Every picture tells a story.
8485 A picture has been said to be

pictures
2111 'without pictures or
4206 Pictures are for
10354 Are but as pictures; 'tis the
11301 It is the pictures got
11811 gallery of pictures in which
12856 Pictures deface walls oftener

piddles
8019 I write as a sow piddles.

pie
136 want no pie in the sky
844 buttons on a custard pie.
8970 put into a pie by Mrs

pie-crust
11332 and pie-crust are made

piecemeal
8950 Piecemeal social engineering

piety
9870 is true piety towards

pig
2273 with a pig. You get
6155 'Dear Pig, are you
11926 selling of pig in a poke.

pig-sty
11684 once by the pig-sty when she

pig-woman
5235 of the pig-woman's booth

pigeons
304 to fly over pigeons for a
11083 Pigeons on the grass alas.

piglet
7435 the more Piglet wasn't

pigs
2121 And whether pigs have

pilate
4309 than water, like Pilate.

pile
9857 Pile the bodies high at

pile-driver
2316 Use a pile-driver. Hit the

pilgrim
1740 avowed Intent To be a pilgrim.

pilgrimage
9374 And thus I'll take my pilgrimage.

pill
11696 take the pill. Roman

pillar
7237 as a pillar, I must be
10145 The triple pillar of the

pillow
4368 the feather pillow, bears the
9165 Fatigue is the best pillow.
10178 Finds the down pillow hard.
12349 velvet pillow for the

pillows
7542 cloudy red, Pillows his chin
9201 faster, we need the pillows.

pills
6170 you bitter pills in sugar
7289 some 'do-give-a-damn' pills.

pilot
10641 is Nature's pilot - and

piloted
7940 he or she must be piloted.

piminy
4011 miminy, piminy,

pimpernel
8352 That demmed, elusive Pimpernel?

pin
9551 have heard a pin drop.

pinch
9140 There's a pinch of the
10144 a lover's pinch, Which

pine
9501 I pine for Europe of the
10710 after. And pine for what

pineapple
10729 is the very pineapple of

pink
4181 The very pink of

pinko-grey
3585 races are really pinko-grey.

pins
5713 as a row of pins - For the

pint
8301 A pint of plain is your

pioneer
8396 the clarity of a pioneer axe.

pioneers
12740 Pioneers did not produce

pious
3019 In pious times, ere

pipe
845 in your pipe, my Lord

piracy
1272 Piracy, n: commerce without

pirate
4013 thing To be a Pirate King.
6313 was his pirate ship but

pirouettes
7327 dancer pirouettes Upon the

piss
3819 a pitcher of warm piss.

pissed
4751 that he's really pissed off.

pissing
5070 the tent pissing out than

pistol
4146 when his pistol misses
5954 pun) is a pistol let off at

pistons
10996 of pistons, without

pit
461 Law is a bottomless pit.
1209 diggeth a pit shall fall
4999 of the pit that is

pitched
11713 ladder Pitched betwixt

pitcher
3819 worth a pitcher of warm

pitiless
4314 can wage a pitiless war, but

pitt
2061 Pitt is to Addington As

pity
1292 Pity costs nothin' and
1365 human heart Pity a human
3028 And pity never
3547 love Pity's the
5321 Pity is the feeling which
6543 I crave Pity from
7035 Pity the meek for they
7955 than all they pity most.
8451 and the pity of War.
10460 knows some touch of pity.
12637 for your pity, but just
12898 A pity beyond all telling,

pivot
6881 to be the pivot of his

place
961 A place for everything and
988 know their place, and not
1031 us in our place is
1715 our own place in the
2651 sex - men just need a place.
3266 And only for one place.
4231 old man any place that's
4962 good. The place to be
5862 to the place one came
8917 Get place and wealth, if

10012 God! this is an awful place.
10815 A place for everything, and
12760 we take our place among

placebos
6688 be cured by his own placebos.

places
1613 All places, all airs make
6232 There are places I'll
11416 the right places is first

plagiarism
4959 Undetected plagiarism.
7712 it's plagiarism; if you

plagiarist
3834 is either plagiarist or
8050 of the plagiarist; the glass

plagiarize
6193 Plagiarize! Let no one else's

plague
1847 is, and that's his plague.
10333 instruments to plague us.
10479 A plague o' both your
12909 not such a plague when I was

plagues
1845 two main plagues, and
2059 But of all plagues, good

plain
1920 is love in plain clothes.
4198 me pretty plain, that they
4554 the really plain people
6256 stays mainly in the plain.
7763 Be plain in dress, and
7916 is that plain' cooking
12395 I design plain truth for

plainer
6159 Tree The plainer than ever

plaintiff
2363 argument, abuse the plaintiff.

plan
1764 can never plan the future
8562 in the wagon of his Plan'.
8889 but not without a plan.
8947 We must plan for freedom,
9935 both by his plan of attack.

planet
5439 When a new planet swims into
6601 Pity the planet, all joy
9807 planet of a
10168 moon No planet is of
12922 of planets. Nothing

planets
7616 The planets in their stations
8891 What other planets circle

planning
6118 of city planning are sky,

plans
1800 no little plans; they have
5864 we are making other plans.
9316 Draw up our plans to live

plant
3336 a weed? A plant whose
7530 Fame is no plant that grows
8739 is a plant of slow
8900 like a plant on his

planted
2711 commonly planted too close.

plateau
3500 a permanently high plateau.

platitude
819 A platitude is simply a truth
7031 to stroke a platitude until it
11242 is a solemn platitude gone to a

platitudes
12610 the orchestration of platitudes.

plato
4008 à la Plato for a
6072 marvellous Plato of
7646 of Acadame, Plato's
11264 with Plato, and more
12483 of footnotes to Plato.

play
490 What we play is life.
510 her sons at play, Sees man
980 a pretty play fellow for
1090 people play: the

2515 to a very dull Play.
3175 is x; y is play; and z is
3245 A play should give you
4370 - the play, the
4754 If you play it, it's
5834 what's a play without a
5971 you have played it
6276 this may be play to you,
7517 forth to play On a
7785 When I play with my cat,
7963 you work, rest and play.
8111 before the play is ready
8151 An hour to play and the
8152 the ranks: Play up! play
8763 should play amongst
9325 not the play before the
9694 is 'Have you come to play?'
9971 for the play to begin.
10210 The play's the thing
10508 of love, play on; Give
11140 You do not play things as
11296 child inside them to play.
12615 A play visibly represents

playboy
11381 the only Playboy of the

played
6655 my Campaspe played At cards
9464 but how you played the Game.
10520 this were played upon a

player
11100 hurt a ball player. It's

players
10117 merely players: They have

playing
283 other half playing out of
5931 only play at playing at them.
7778 are not playing about;
7945 work terribly hard at playing.

playmates
5964 I have had playmates, I have

plays
3836 maid Still plays about the

plaything
5207 retain the playthings of
5966 A child's a plaything for an

pleasant
2354 labours are pleasant.
4176 all that was pleasant in man.
6152 'How pleasant to know Mr
7823 something pleasant happens to
9735 to do the pleasant and clean
11285 be very pleasant if it were
11446 How pleasant it is, at the end
12145 anything pleasant, at least

please
1359 Self to please, To bind
7042 If you please, ma'am, it was
10044 she never fails to please.
11374 is - try to please everybody.

pleased
58 He more had pleased us, had he
3738 is good when he is pleased.
4488 consists in being pleased.
7612 seemed well pleased, all
8154 nothing, be pleased to know
10115 eats, And pleased with what

pleases
8778 in favour of what pleases us.
10979 think it pleases a man when

pleasing
5850 is doubly pleasing to trick
11015 turns to pleasing pain.

pleasurable
2361 something pleasurable in calm

pleasure
448 fool bolts pleasure, then
632 things. The pleasure is not
635 seize the pleasure at once?
673 of pleasure in itself.
746 a lie doth ever add pleasure.
788 The great pleasure in life is
930 of giving pleasure to
973 to be a pleasure, when it
975 is the soul of pleasure.
992 gives me pleasure all the

1258 pursued pleasure that he
1866 To make pleasure pleasant,
1955 Pleasure's a sin, and
2012 only as far as the pleasure."
2505 a kind of pleasure which
2625 There is a pleasure in poetic
2640 only safe pleasure for a
2734 Pleasure is a thief to
3004 and simple pleasure of being
3050 Is not in pleasure, but in
3061 There is a pleasure sure, In
3550 Love's pleasure lasts but a
3864 A miss for pleasure, and a
4543 ball is a pleasure, but
4720 is an enhancement of pleasure.
4771 can give pleasure for long,
4917 one genuinely modern pleasure.
5046 moments of pleasure. Now, if
5208 general read without pleasure.
5371 always the pleasure of a
5436 fancy roam, Pleasure never is
5497 and aching Pleasure nigh,
5839 The pleasure of criticizing
5883 so much pleasure in
5968 greatest pleasure I know, is
6205 ineffable pleasure Of
6379 enough pleasure, surely,
6831 it gave pleasure to the
7081 mind, from pleasure less,
7283 They get pleasure out of the
7377 them no pleasure if it were
7499 gardens takes his pleasure.
7716 all weren't to give pleasure.
7861 Where Pleasure lies,
7882 look at our pleasure to go to
8907 aim! Good, pleasure, ease,
9134 The price spoils the pleasure.
9242 always give pleasure - if not
9324 as much pleasure in the
9384 a demanding pleasure? A
9455 the mental pleasure produced
9773 is much pleasure to be
9907 and did pleasure me in his
10059 Pleasure is nothing else but
10756 but fading pleasure brings.
10950 is made, the pleasure's done.
11640 first; pleasure
11802 of the pleasure with which
12140 is the only pleasure I have
12304 physical pleasure I'd sooner
12589 a perfect pleasure. It is
12867 I say, pleasure, whilst I
12920 rotten. Pleasure's for

pleasure-dome
2438 A stately pleasure-dome decree:
2439 A sunny pleasure-dome with caves

pleasures
593 and 'lower' pleasures. To a
629 the pleasures of life.
715 the purest of human pleasures.
1897 greatest pleasures of life,
2358 than all the pleasures of youth.
2394 the great pleasures in life
2622 owes its pleasures to
2936 some new pleasures prove Of
4906 with their pleasures. There is
5174 is a hypocrite in his pleasures.
5203 of human pleasures should
7073 tear our pleasures with rough
7513 In unreproved pleasures free.
7816 have their pleasures, but the
9871 has its pleasures it
10459 the idle pleasures of these
11278 take their pleasures sadly
11752 whose pleasures are the

pledge
5241 And I will pledge with mine;
9594 I pledge you, I pledge

pledged
804 you have pledged

plenty
1815 fou, but just had plenty.
5334 Plenty to see and hear and
8436 Plenty has made me poor.

pliant
3851 skill made pliant, Will bend

plot
9325 done: Her plot hath many
12105 Ay, now the plot thickens

plots
2500 life seems to have no plots.
3020 Plots, true or false, are

plotting
3062 Still to be plotting some new
9470 is the most plotting heart in

plough
2025 We plough the fields, and
9623 I must plough my furrow
10712 wherefore plough For the
11757 he held a plough instead of

ploughman
4290 lea, The ploughman homeward

ploughshare
9726 of the ploughshare as well as

ploy
8975 us can, by ploy or gambit,

pluck
9150 Old birds are hard to pluck.

plucking
2432 in so plucking the goose

plumber
157 getting a plumber on
7225 of a plumber never got
9012 A plumber who has Latin is a

plums
3570 - much as plums have to be

plunder
6838 man stop to plunder, But slay,
8149 ill-got plunder, and bury

plundered
6715 would have plundered this new

plural
6792 plural. I peel

pluto
7503 tears down Pluto's cheek.

plutocracy
12947 not a plutocracy of wealth,

pm
559 he ended PM, CH and

pneumatic
3269 promise of pneumatic bliss.

pobble
6157 The Pobble who has no toes

pocket
5070 in my pocket. Better
9095 garden carried in the pocket.
12406 gun in your pocket, or are
12665 in your pocket or purse

pockets
9498 in holey pockets; my
10821 from the pockets of the
11081 but the pockets change; it

poe
6572 There comes Poe with his

poem
1060 is a pretty poem, Mr. Pope,
3701 A poem begins with a lump
5472 to a poem and to be
5630 never see A poem lovely as
6748 A Poem should be palpable
7454 himself to be a true poem.
7689 as a poem rises from
8563 the dark tower of a poem.
11380 music of a poem along with
12035 A poem is never finished;
12262 what is a poem but a
12499 the greatest poem.

poems
389 Ein: Gert's poems are bunk,
4278 feel my poems are mine
5631 Poems are made by fools
6476 are living poems, And all
6850 Poem me no poems.

poesy
678 Poesy was ever thought to
5499 wings of Poesy, Though
5510 Myself in poesy; so I may

poet
2086 A poet without love were a

2180 let the Poet be, It is
3233 No honest poet can ever
3247 The poet's mind is .. a
3267 a great poet has lived
3541 I was a poet, I was
4045 of law. No poet ever
5014 A good poet is someone who
5331 Tennyson, gentleman poet.
5405 what every poet hates in
5435 The poet and the dreamer
6245 The poet ranks far below
6846 can be a poet, or can
7212 The poet is always
7896 of the poet is to keep
8445 All a poet can do today is
8849 That every poet is a fool:
9314 than the poet's soul
10421 and the poet, Are of
10422 the poet's pen
10701 On a poet's lips I slept
11134 The poet is the priest of
11142 makes the poet the potent
11330 Thus every poet, in his
11425 made me poet, And this
11526 truth the poet sings,
11743 is the poet's wealth,
12196 making of a poet in her
12354 eye in the head of a poet.
12783 and the Poet's dream.
12878 Did not the poet sing it

poetic
8048 endeavour to make it poetic.
8825 Poetic Justice, with her

poetry
479 So poetry is something more
504 Poetry is at bottom a
584 lie Emptied of its poetry.
595 My poetry doesn't change
1300 of poetry are
1380 Poetry is the impish attempt
1913 that with poetry is won, Is
1980 means rank poetry high in
2420 Poetry is a religion with no
2454 order: - poetry = the best
2525 greatest poetry is given
2962 saying so In whining poetry.
3063 So poetry, which is in
3246 Poetry is a mug's game.
3702 Poetry should be common in
3703 Poetry is a way of taking
4112 is the poetry of life.
4285 no money in poetry, but then
4447 Poetry contains almost all
4805 Poetry was the maiden I
5400 Poetry in motion.
5466 star of poetry, as fancy
5481 Poetry should be great and
5484 Poetry should surprise by a
5485 If poetry comes not as
5581 arrogance, poetry reminds
5994 deal of poetry: on the
6164 rather than of poetry.
6720 Not reading poetry amounts to
6815 advances, poetry almost
6819 From the poetry of Lord
7037 a book of poetry is like
7362 is heard, poetry is
7691 ignore most poetry because
7845 Poetry is all nouns and
8451 of War. The Poetry is in the
8758 For me, poetry is an evasion
8855 It is not poetry, but prose
8991 dead art Of poetry; to
9678 who learn; poetry for those
9861 Poetry is the journal of a
9862 Poetry is the opening and
10680 Poetry is the record of the
10772 is silent poetry, poetry is
11139 Poetry is the supreme
12694 or ecstasy. Poetry's the
12801 Poetry is the breath and
12802 Poetry is the spontaneous
12884 ourselves we make poetry.

poets
474 other poets the art of
740 men wise; poets, witty;
1844 All poets are mad.

2625 pains Which only poets know.
3041 ancient poets, had the
3255 Immature poets imitate;
3257 Poets in our civilization,
3877 I hate all Boets and
4044 to hold the poets back.
4763 put up with poets being
4866 Poets .. though liars by
7302 the brutes, poets are to us.
7844 till the poets among us
8097 Poets aren't very useful,
8826 pensive poets painful
8876 Poets like painters, thus
9893 Popular poets are the
10682 and air: Poets' food is
12197 Poets that lasting marble
12497 have great poets there must
12784 are the Poets that are
12829 We poets in our youth begin
12912 these We poets keep our

point
2316 important point to make,
5727 or less mad on one point.

point of view
8077 an entirely different point of view.

pointless
8404 About as pointless and

points
1374 1-0, you still get 2 points.
10736 but simply points the way.

poise
6578 is in poise, That he

poised
6776 Forever poised between a

poison
3549 The coward's weapon, poison.
4282 There was poison in the cup
5497 Turning to poison while the
6048 sickening poison - Just for
6627 is bitter poison to others.
7008 I go about and poison wells.
8159 it) to poison the wells.
8494 there it is after all poison.
10399 if you poison us, do we

poisoned
11321 like a poisoned rat in a

poisoning
6919 anything is poisoning our lives

poisonous
5494 for its poisonous wine.

poisons
8509 Poisons pain you; Rivers are
12284 flock, And poisons all the

poker
8309 of a poker except its
12184 more like poker than

pole
2868 the top of the greasy pole.

polecat
3557 a semi-house-trained polecat.

police
598 or the police; We must
1107 the police. It's
2850 called the police - it's
8192 and the police. Everyone
8303
8360 among police officers.
10632 which the police can beat

policeman
3706 is the one worn by a policeman.
4017 be done, A policeman's lot is
8257 It would not do for a policeman.
8552 Fear of the policeman is the
9838 than a policeman - whose

policemen
8359 Policemen, like red squirrels,

policy
1124 [foreign] policy is to be
1303 out the policy you wish;
4952 the best policy. It is
9600 of world policy I would
9739 religion or policy. Both
9841 English policy is to float
10637 My only policy is to profess

12272 our true policy to steer
12430 is the best policy; but he

polished
2735 and must be polished, or the
3962 And I polished up the

polite
1690 his own without being polite.
2313 costs nothing to be polite.

politely
3616 treat us politely, we don't

politeness
1998 glance of great politeness.
5774 When suave politeness, tempering
6537 is the politeness of kings.
9982 Politeness is) a tacit
10729 the very pineapple of politeness!
10888 Politeness is good nature

political
481 is by nature a political animal.
785 death of a political economist.
3107 he ducks political meetin's,
4371 that the political struggle
4727 life. The political ones are
5025 in the political world as
5050 to give a political blank
6436 to the political power of
6774 is a political fact.
6879 to political life,
6938 is not a political tool.
6973 the truth, Political power
7280 that of a political aspirant
7369 healthy state of political life.
8263 life. My political life is
8392 our time, political speech and
8393 Political language .. is
8483 shorter life than Political Art.
8495 a major rule of political life.
8590 species of political villainy.
8948 history of political power.
9008 All political careers end in
10064 for fear of Political Economy.
10611 clearly to a political career.
11652 half your political life

politician
1284 is the Politishun's golden
1396 art of a politician is to
2023 An honest politician is one who
2387 of a politician's life is
2660 a politician is an arse upon
2760 master, the politician poses as
2762 Since a politician never
3856 That politician tops his part,
3931 Are you a politician who says to
5616 life of a politician. It means
6413 A politician was a person with
6942 taste, especially a politician.
7029 that when a politician does get
8237 A politician divides mankind
8328 A wise politician will never
8823 is a politician who places
8939 makes the politician wise, And
9013 For a politician to complain
9014 A politician crystallises what
9614 successful politician is he who
10185 A politician .. one that would
10330 a scurvy politician, seem To
11905 A politician is a man who
12241 I'm not a politician and my

politicians
1302 Politicians have a higher claim
3898 notice than politicians or
5618 Politicians are the same all
6978 The politicians of New York ..
8121 which the politicians are
9011 would we politicians be if we
11265 any century than 10 politicians.
12283 successful politicians Clinton
12652 Politicians make good company for

politics
29 Politics, as a practice,
37 Practical politics consists in
41 In politics the middle way is
529 Women in politics are more
644 From politics, it was an easy
791 Politics is not a good
1114 regarded politics as the
1276 In politics I think it wiser

1304 Politics is the art of the
1374 Politics is like football - it
2052 Politics, and the fate of
2326 Politics is more dangerous
2389 of politics with the
2456 In politics, what begins in
2653 Politics. The diplomatic name
2763 Politics are too serious a
2861 Laws of Politics: 1. Get
2872 the mule of politics that
3311 ground of politics, for then
4303 They politics like ours
4618 Politics is the science of how
4620 taken the politics out of
4805 loved, but politics was the
5356 zeal in politics as well as
5976 Politics is like surfing. You
6691 women would have on politics.
6777 of politics, that
6779 cup, but in politics we sail in
6976 Politics is war without
7104 Politics doesn't make strange
7912 Politics is a field where
7952 now in the centre of politics.
8206 sad duty of politics is to
8365 out of politics'. All
8524 enter local politics solely as
8702 Politics is but the common
9009 amateur in politics is the
9415 Politics is supposed to be the
9520 In politics, a straight line
9565 about this Politics thing, you
9569 truth into politics you would
9572 Politics has got so expensive
9579 Ultimately politics in a
10049 is past politics; and
10724 than it has with politics.
11154 hand at politics. But I am
11180 Politics is perhaps the only
11754 Politics is the gizzard of
11813 In politics a community of
11893 truths; in politics you seek
11896 of politics is timing.
12006 the mother's milk of politics.
12040 Politics is the art of
12664 In politics a week is a very
12899 Russian Or on Spanish politics?

pollution
3731 Pollution is nothing but
5829 Air pollution is turning Mother
10981 engine of pollution, the dog.

polly
3837 Our Polly is a sad slut!

polo
8313 Sex - the poor man's polo.

polygamy
3019 Before polygamy was made a
4822 Polygamy: an endeavour to get

pomp
5734 Lo, all our pomp of
7432 In lowly pomp ride on to
8846 all the pomp to flight,

pompous
1607 ashes, and pompous in the

pond
1572 stream and pond; But is

ponder
1450 in charge, ponder. (2) When

pondered
8810 while I pondered, weak and

pondering
8139 find myself pondering on how to

ponderous
8201 Ponderous and uncertain is that

ponies
4647 blind, pit ponies, And
5731 and twenty ponies, Trotting

pony
426 Riding on a pony; Stuck a

pooh
7438 Pooh began to feel a

poor
147 - the best poor man's
637 for being poor - which is
684 but it keeps them poor.

3126 are but poor, though
3580 the poor cannot
3608 well as the poor to sleep
3861 dare to be poor, which is
4161 found'st me poor at first,
4298 Too poor for a bribe, and
4335 I am a poor man, but I
4659 The poor on the borderline
4904 it, 'is the poor man's
4957 saints were poor, it does
5127 not to be poor; whatever
5191 The poor and the busy have
5377 and the poor get
5426 A poor, weak,
5568 who are poor, it cannot
5911 Nobody is poor unless he
5953 A poor relation - is the
5986 save the poor, feel for
6841 helped the poor, And the
7351 Though I be poor, I'm
8436 Plenty has made me poor.
8988 infants of the very poor.
9179 is the mother of the poor.
9196 them, the poor would make
9252 luckily the poor provide
9920 The poor don't know that
9926 war it's the poor who die.
10242 I am as poor as Job, my
10430 And makes me poor indeed.
11177 else his dear papa is poor.
11637 rich woman as a poor woman.

poorer
8124 the poor poorer and thus

poorest
8743 The poorest man may in his
9361 The poorest he that is in

pop
1478 function of pop music is
6940 goes - Pop goes the

pope
1311 should the Pope be any
6633 than of the Pope and all
11048 The Pope! How many
11258 a President, not a Pope.

popish
8738 creed, a Popish liturgy,

poppies
6698 fields the poppies blow
6699 sleep, though poppies grow.

populace
12503 Where the populace rise at

popular
5300 long be popular in Oxford.
7423 had she was very very popular.

popularity
8618 Avoid popularity; it has many
11956 a vapour, popularity an

population
880 by a whole population which
4194 and only talked of population.
4678 the entire population of the
6218 part of the population against
6936 Population, when unchecked,
9387 about the population explosion,

populism
1479 Populism - as we all know -

populous
7622 who long in populous city pent,
10698 London - A populous and smoky

porcelain
7304 A dainty rogue in porcelain.

porcupine
4348 The porcupine, whom one must
5620 a couple of porcupines under

pornography
6093 Pornography is the attempt to
7848 folly, and pornography may be as
9360 stories, the pornography of war.
10939 What pornography is really about,

porpoise
2117 'There's a porpoise close

port
1059 It would be port if it
5099 for boys; port, for men;

11010 after toil, port after
12369 All port tastes the same

portals
5335 and are the portals of

portion
3362 gift is a portion of
10675 He is a portion of the
10913 an equal portion, most
11537 and become Portions and
12794 That best portion of a good

portioned
6041 were fairly portioned, The

portrait
2673 not paint a portrait to look
5775 same, of a portrait, in frame,
9911 A portrait is a painting with
9912 I paint a portrait I lose a

posies
7011 a thousand fragrant posies.

position
4369 Every position must be held to
11685 is only one position for an
11971 to offer me the position.

positive
1273 To be positive: to be mistaken
6432 may be as positive in error
7291 the positive
8717 Every positive value has its

posse
48 nothing; in posse I am

possess
1428 shall possess the earth.
5665 men who possess almost
5870 are, who already possess it.

possessed
1766 in order to be possessed.
2444 mankind are possessed by them.
9389 one apart, Possessed me, and

possesses
2001 A man possesses nothing

possessing
8844 is full, possessing, and

possession
126 The possession of gold has
4316 the act of possession: we are
5264 Than in the glad possession.
6430 put him in possession of truth.
7306 is written: Possession without
9774 with possession, more than
11248 perpetual possession of being
12050 but the possession of it is

possessions
10806 of possessions, and the

possibilities
480 Probable impossibilities are to be
6163 of the possibilities of life.

possibility
4931 to deny the possibility of

possible
35 are hardly possible.
1188 If it be possible, let this
1304 is the art of the possible.
3952 probable, possible shadow of
7705 everything is always possible.
9883 of what is possible is the
12144 best of possible worlds ..
12358 Possible? Is anything

post
1067 come. Lie follows by post.
7668 news rides post, while

postal
6052 sun, Its postal districts

poster
543 is, at least, a great poster.

posterity
73 decided to write for posterity.
1774 forward to posterity, who never
2182 predecessors and to posterity.
2378 upon by posterity as a brave
2908 go down to posterity talking
4279 To evoke posterity Is to weep
6426 of posterity .. 'tis
8418 float to posterity on what he
9019 ancestry, or hope of posterity.

11669 function of posterity is to look
12699 damage to posterity we bring

posthumously
8221 either; some are born posthumously.

postman
2010 The postman always rings

postponed
4836 going to be will be postponed.

postponement
7415 most of us one long postponement.

postscript
701 in the postscript, as if it
11072 her mind but in her postscript.

pot
333 - where the pot calls the
5328 make them in the one pot.

potato
8423 is like a potato - the only

potato-gatherer
5403 Where the potato-gatherers like

potency
3674 highest expression of potency.
7457 contain a potency of life in

potent
2593 how potent cheap

potential
2069 key to unlocking our potential.

potentiality
9888 as full of potentiality as he is

pounce
3812 of itself, waiting to pounce.

pound
9267 is worth a pound of clergy.
12665 now the pound abroad is

pounds
1919 Pounds are the sons, not of
6583 is sixteen pounds to the
6603 and the pounds will take

poverty
155 better than poverty, if only
789 Poverty is an anomaly to rich
810 with poverty knows how
976 Come away; poverty's
1538 Poverty makes you sad as well
1744 colour at poverty and
3446 crime so shameful as poverty.
3534 squadrons Poverty; There's
3567 wrong as a cure for poverty.
4035 Poverty is less a matter of
4046 curses of poverty: it leaves
5037 to say that poverty is no
5127 less. Poverty is a great
5364 of poverty carry with
7793 Poverty of goods is easily
8817 luxury; monarchies by poverty.
8341 I mean poverty - the most
8611 man cannot imagine poverty.
8620 so much poverty and
10633 Modern poverty is not the
10889 Poverty is no disgrace to a
11626 is the most terrible poverty.
11992 honest poverty a little,

powder
1312 and keep your powder dry.

power
14 Power tends to corrupt, and
31 A friend in power is a
32 effect of power and
40 living with power to
187 Power is like a woman you
314 is a power to be
411 who has the power and skill
717 to seek power and to
725 the act of power, but
753 Knowledge is power.
759 knowledge itself is power.
993 accursed power which
1058 use the power it brings.
1533 seductive power of
1760 greater the power, the more
1762 with power, and have
1850 this power and effect
2543 consciousness of power.
2637 Abuse of power is not a

2670 If absolute power corrupts
2674 the power to
2775 a lasting power upon
2805 The power of habit and the
2972 Power is given only to him
3023 no more than power in trust.
3108 The power of the Crown has
4047 when the power to love
4394 Power over a man's
4485 he has you in his power.
4583 much and power over
4660 Power corrupts the few,
4746 economic power by which I
4862 are not in the power game.
4928 some great power would
4939 possesses a power over one's
5227 Power should always be
5229 There is no power game. The
5259 Between his power and thine
5353 no will to power, and where
5581 When power leads man toward
5665 gift of the power to use
5721 Power without
5735 sight of power, we loose
5974 in office but not in power.
6267 a power thrown
6355 We hold the power and bear
6392 is that the power is
6435 by nature a power .. to
6438 This power to act according
6586 in a man's power; genius is
6697 test of power is not
7299 a witty beauty is a power.
7367 for which power can be
7665 strange power, After
7999 Power to the people.
8121 Power is a drug on which
8176 Power tends to connect;
8201 balance of power. The arch
8212 his will to power, assume a
8287 The power of the press is
8376 Liberal - a power worshipper
8381 Power is not a means, it is
8593 Without the power to drink
8745 Unlimited power is apt to
8948 political power. This is
8997 read for power. Man
9655 incredible power but a
9666 Power is the recognition of
9796 a source of power from the
10783 Writing has power, but its
10904 the corridors of power.
10922 in your power - he's
10997 give a city power, or drive
11058 It confers power on whoever
11339 most men's power to be
11385 lies its powerful force
11387 authority and minimal power.
11584 with Eternal God for power.
11604 lead to sovereign power.
11738 a motive power out of the
11898 Power only tires those who
12221 The balance of power.
12338 Power is always right,
12547 miraculous power of turning
12674 power, not the
12731 to have power over men;
12831 hands have power To live,
12832 have the power, And they
12872 Power never takes a back

powerful
2889 and with a powerful middle
3642 Who is powerful? He that
7180 is more powerful in the
7891 Sisterhood is powerful.
10996 the first powerful plain
12101 Lord, I am powerful but alone,

powerless
9769 Brief and Powerless is Man's
11895 is not powerless, passive

powerlessness
9760 of comfort and powerlessness.

powers
2303 have powers at their
3339 brings out all one's powers.
5206 general powers,
5209 his powers by his

5531 the driving powers of life.
8460 whose just powers are
9339 them that powers the
12037 potential powers against
12838 we lay waste our powers.

practical
2149 Practical, simple, cheap and
4942 a most practical plan: You
5606 Practical men, who believe
6378 any of its practical purposes -

practice
3398 Practice yourself, for
9677 a very good practice always to
9778 but do not practice, and the
10653 put it in practice not only

practise
8927 who has none may practise it.
10721 you would practise this

practised
1896 and at seeing it practised.
7169 be practised at spare
9688 is still very much practised.

practises
2249 he not only practises it without

pragmatist
11050 He is a pragmatist. He is not

praise
54 'em truest praise 'em most.
585 the free man how to praise.
941 kind of praise is that
1200 Let us now praise famous
2030 You praise the firm
3361 good to be spoiled by praise.
3573 Praise the Lord and pass the
3638 Praise to the undeserving is
3789 where men praise courage
4640 The praise of ancient
5549 All praise to thee, my God,
5754 shall praise us, and
5807 without the praise of the
5891 To refuse praise reveals a
5998 unmerited praise the
6670 knows .. Praise him!
7052 They praise those works, but
7129 by praise. But
7178 but they only want praise.
7493 mind Praise the Lord.
7643 to be di praised were no
8165 Praise to the Holiest in the
8881 Some praise at morning what
9482 men than to praise them.
10159 I will praise any man that
10559 but lack tongues to praise.
10952 everybody praise the Duke,
11011 so double be his praise.
11570 stir a little dust of praise.
12230 his just praise be given,

praised
5990 God be praised the
9124 another praised, he feels

praising
1903 doing one's praising for
3858 Praising all alike, is
10867 are always praising the past
10870 that of not praising when

pram
2521 than the pram in the

pray
92 and one to pray, And two
408 when they pray is that
860 When I pray to Him I
940 a man to pray cream and
1274 Pray, v: to ask that the
1364 Love, All pray in their
5369 You should pray to have a
6349 do we pray, that this
7038 we humbly pray, And,
8465 And don't pray when it
9583 Pray for the repose of His
10879 going to pray for you at
11516 face again, Pray for my

prayer
50 in on a wing and a pray'r.
228 is the Tory party at prayer.
1087 wish for prayer is a
4758 hands in prayer gives God

5281 Common Prayer, The organ
5752 he made his prayer (Even as
6273 is the most perfect prayer.
6638 words, the better the prayer.
7319 rises from prayer a better
9698 Conservative Party at prayer.
11560 are homes of silent prayer.
11938 relief denied even to prayer.
11974 In prayer we call ourselves

prayers
1089 that has said its prayers.
1502 says prayers. Or needs
4647 with angry prayers For tamed
4961 that all my prayers have not
7444 Robin is saying his prayers.
8117 our prayers and
12165 We offer up prayers to God

praying
8421 No praying, it spoils
11393 you are praying; if God

prays
2450 He prayeth well, who loveth
9945 family that prays together
11922 a man prays for, he

preach
9153 the fox preaches, look to
9615 I wish to preach, not the
9778 which we preach but do not
12427 Preach not because you have

preachers
6469 When I need preachers I buy 'em
10060 Preachers say, Do as I say, not

preaching
5082 A woman's preaching is like a
11624 joy preaches without preaching.

precedence
7490 forget her precedence of

precedency
5129 point of precedency between a

precedent
10040 A precedent embalms a

precious
4113 are precious Hugging
4729 though small, is precious.
6217 Liberty is precious - so
7561 best Deserve the precious bane.
11268 most precious years,
12464 I know of none more precious.

precisian
7148 The devil turned precisian!

predatory
10007 person with predatory instincts

predecessor
1839 Unlike my predecessors I have
3884 to your predecessor: 'You know

predict
4969 can only predict things

predicted
5391 have predicted that by

prediction
6353 future, no prediction is

prefaces
6605 I like prefaces. I read them.

prefer
11145 which to prefer, The

preference
6319 of an enormous preference.

preferment
520 of knocking at Preferment's door.

pregnancy
6274 a kind of hysterical pregnancy.
7274 to avoid pregnancy by a

pregnant
5554 could get pregnant, abortion

prejudice
2846 without prejudice to the
4020 everybody's prejudice I know a
4487 Prejudice is the child of
10886 reason the prejudice out of a
11985 is fatal to prejudice, bigotry

prejudices
2542 by the passion of his prejudices.
5785 and unphilosophical prejudices.

prejudices
5936 a bundle of prejudices - made up
7271 the moral prejudices of the
8045 eliminate prejudices - just
10884 it; it prejudices a man so.

prelaty
7653 yoke of prelaty, under

prelude
6914 faune. Prelude to the

premonition
11836 stirs the premonition felt while

preoccupation
9774 It is preoccupation with

preparation
635 by preparation, foolish
3720 is a preparation for life.
11180 which no preparation is thought
12893 is a long preparation for

prepare
1151 .. I go to prepare a place
8553 live, not to prepare for life.
8640 the good God prepare me!

prepared
145 of being totally prepared.
768 it is: BE PREPARED, which
2481 to the best prepared, for the
3365 what they are prepared to see.
7979 Be Prepared.
8260 much prepared for, has a

preparedness
4078 guns? .. preparedness makes us

prerogative
5721 the prerogative of the
5967 to enjoy monarchial prerogatives.
6438 that which is called prerogative,
10569 is not the prerogative of the

presence
2234 It is the presence of mind
3230 the past, but of its presence.
4984 need your presence more than
9304 better than presence of mind in
12365 that his presence on the
12690 into the presence of a
12797 have felt A presence that

present
306 All present and correct.
2375 The present is the funeral of
2567 do at the present moment
2950 if this present were the
5214 created a present for
5601 but the present, or
6343 the stormy present. As our
6595 - the present, yes, we
6940 No time like the present.
7138 only in the present can I act.
7728 Always present your front to
9207 God will be present, whether

presented
193 One was presented with a small

presents
77 not for the presents, an
4984 more than your presents.
5934 Presents, I often say, endear

preserve
6434 but to preserve and
8355 if I do not preserve the latter

preserved
4657 They are preserved in a state

presidency
844 to make the presidency work these
2553 The presidency does not yield to
3105 Th' prisidincy is th' highest
6370 I am fit for the presidency.
9655 of the presidency lies in

president
47 been chosen president again, I
1860 as the President's spouse.
2390 be right than be President.
2554 ass as a president, and I
4858 by the president it keeps.
5069 way for a president to deal
5599 the President [Woodrow
5761 We are the President's men.
7254 any other President, whether
8269 not their President is a
8270 When the President does it,

11147 may become president, and I
11258 elected a President, not a
11902 being a president is like
11903 All the President is, is a
11906 The president is the
12662 office of president requires

presidential
12461 the American presidential campaign.

presiding
7223 her time presiding over a

press
4525 limit the press is to
5024 where the press is free,
8287 of the press is very
8495 with the Press or the
9013 about the press is like a
9234 It fell dead from the Press.
11299 of the press in Britain
11882 the periodical press.

pressure
3244 pressure of
6583 The pressure of public opinion
8600 strongest pressure in the

prestige
2786 without prestige, or

presume
10297 Do not presume too much upon
11052 Dr Livingstone, I presume?

presumption
11786 be amused by its presumption.

pretend
247 shall not pretend that there
2677 I do not pretend to know what
7660 again, pretend they ne'er

pretender
1922 - the Pretender; But who

pretending
6890 others nod, pretending not to
12550 life, pretending to be

pretexts
1763 Tyrants seldom want pretexts.

prettier
5929 .. but the prettier the kind

pretty
1926 A pretty woman as was ever
3636 is not a pretty thing when
3524 girl can be pretty - but a
8638 But it is pretty to see what
8641 Pretty witty Nell.
9025 Which is sometimes so pretty.
9068 us leave pretty women to
12297 plain. The pretty can get

prevail
3452 he will prevail. He is
6552 you should prevail on our

prevent
5658 many unwise steps I prevent.
6697 but capacity to prevent it.
9786 knowing how to prevent them.

prevented
1125 have been prevented .. The

prevents
2487 but prevents others
7154 has that prevents him

prevision
12383 are subjects of prevision.

prey
4303 The greater prey upon the
7585 alone bent on his prey.
8898 yet a prey to all;
9236 come, the prey goes to
9725 are this man's lawful prey.
10689 thou soon must be his prey.
11330 that on him prey; And these

preys
5006 one that preys

price
254 A fair price for oil is
362 will not raise your price.
1008 have a price tag on the
1038 The price of justice is
1231 The price of wisdom is
2377 have bought it at any price.
3736 me in the price but not in

5218 use at a price you can't
5366 in Rome has its price.
5567 pay any price, bear any
6726 the price of
9134 The price spoils the
9725 consider price only are
10609 Wot prawce Selvytion nah?
11221 is a high price to pay for
11798 high The price for
12223 those men have their price.
12432 a high price because
12570 knows the price of
12660 man's price increase.

prices
10819 contrivance to raise prices.

prick
9445 with my prick. (possibly
10399 is? If you prick us, do we

pricking
10363 By the pricking of my thumbs,
11006 knight was pricking on the

pricks
1126 to kick against the pricks.
5061 has the pricks on the
10240 Honour pricks me on. Yea,

pride
1241 Pride goeth before
1344 The pride of the peacock is
2487 paradox in pride: it makes
2778 Such is our pride, our
3751 Pride, perceiving humility
3752 Pride had rather go out of
3848 Parthenia's pride! He saw,
3984 my family pride is
4191 Pride in their port,
4316 without pride or to be
5124 fellow whom pride, or
5192 Pride is seldom delicate:
6701 a proper pride, Gin less
7338 children to save its pride.
8170 of fears, Pride ruled my
8893 Pride still is aiming at
8897 spite of Pride, in erring
9198 Pride is the mask of one's
9478 noble pride, through
9835 writer's pride in having
9983 Pride is the direct
10428 'Tis pride that pulls the
10434 quality, Pride, pomp, and
12291 contempt on all my pride.
12617 Pride, avarice and envy are

priest
4544 me of this turbulent priest?
11378 actor and a priest both

priests
1670 nature, priests are only
4863 the world, priests have been
6817 and priests by the
9893 the parish priests of the
10965 with women nor with priests.

primal
8416 only two primal passions,

prime
1044 48 - in the prime of my
9631 the perfect prime; But pluck
10541 lovely April of her prime.
10977 One's prime is elusive.
11014 yet is prime, For soon

prime minister
534 the Unknown Prime Minister [Bonar
989 be The next Prime Minister but three:
2303 with which Prime Ministers have
4232 The Prime Minister has got the
7234 girl or a turned-out Prime Minister.
10838 when the Prime Minister tries to
11656 the Prime Minister should be

prime ministers
822 wild flowers, and Prime Ministers.
9833 know that Prime Ministers are wedded

prime mover
454 arrive at a prime mover, put in

primeval
6482 This is the forest primeval.

primitive
76 A people so primitive that they

6127 are only primitive
6678 is the last primitive society in
6898 of the wise primitive in a giant

primrose
5419 Wan as primroses gathered
10194 Himself the primrose path of

primrose hill
1336 To Primrose Hill and Saint

prince
2188 the first Prince of Wales
7219 soon as the prince sets
8078 A prince who gets a
12291 which the prince of glory
12388 heaven-born Prince of Peace!

principality
6812 than a principality in Utopia.

principle
654 though not in principle.
886 is to appeal to a principle.
1315 fundamental principle of the
1323 the basic principle here is to
2567 The Principle of Unripe Time is
2813 one great principle of the
2912 is not a principle, but an
3186 the 'falling domino' principle.
5818 go on the principle that it
6259 a simple principle for the
6392 The first principle of a
6468 men to rise above principle.
6564 believe in princerple, But oh, I
7172 about a principle is that it
7378 The principle which regulates
10040 A precedent embalms a principle.
12109 The first principle of war is:

principles
1074 The same principles which at
2730 when great principles are
2862 Damn your principles! Stick to
5109 Their principles are the
6559 It ain't by princerples nor men My
8268 greatest principles of our
9218 who denies the first principles.
11149 fight for principles than to
11431 by reference to principles.

print
7855 'tis devils must print.
8308 news that's fit to print.
11299 freedom to print such of
11735 own licence to print money.
12746 in the eternity of print.

printed
11830 diffusion of printed material.
12353 bad that's printed about him.

printing
2085 Gunpowder, Printing, and the
5107 for not printing any list
7461 to regulate printing, thereby

printless
7488 I set my printless feet O'er

priorities
1113 language of priorities is the

prism
3498 through the prism of a

prison
1849 What is a ship but a prison?
6540 do not a prison make, Nor
7764 mourn in prison, while I
9375 but a large prison, out of
9516 is not a prison house',
11297 one creates one's own prison.
12732 seeks to adorn its prison.
12771 'Twixt a prison and a

prisoned
9933 delight As prisoned birds must

prisoner
5763 to your being taken prisoner.
8045 is a prisoner of his own
10921 of a prisoner - they're

prisoners
12539 blue Which prisoners call the
12591 is not the prisoners who need

prisons
1343 Prisons are built with stones
1596 Prisons don't rehabilitate,
12591 it is the prisons.

privacy
6122 its narrow privacy and tawdry
6763 is a self-invasion of privacy.

private
36 is a private and costly
360 face: Its private life is a
428 to dine; Private room,
594 Private faces in public
1873 his private parts, his
2799 more money in private life.
3095 for private usefulness
4515 field to private industry.
5297 one of our few private acts.
6563 trusts To very privit uses.
7236 the sphere of private life.
7664 public good Private respects
11385 been a very private, secretive
12656 five most private things in

privation
3778 value of privation for the
9674 Little privations are easily

priviledged
2917 that the Priviledged and the

privilege
649 All the privilege I claim for
993 stands on Privilege (And goes
2223 but special privilege even
3369 It is the privilege of any
3786 People of privilege will always
3954 But the privilege and pleasure
12259 don't have that privilege.'

privileges
5207 claim the privileges of age and
7282 is not rights, but privileges.

prize
4296 is lawful prize; Nor all,
6892 The highest prize in a world
10499 this: Men prize the thing

prizes
10830 glittering prizes to those

probability
4241 the laws of probability, North

probable
480 Probable impossibilities are
3952 doubt - No probable, possible

probe
12425 has only to probe deep

problem
1704 has a real problem. They
2798 are confronted with a problem.
2991 a three-pipe problem, ..
4633 to the problem of the
5526 now it is a problem to be
9814 only one problem at a time.
10775 A problem left to itself
11092 The first problem for all of
11160 every problem with an

problems
4220 in your problems, and they
4364 to have our problems solved for
4727 are two problems in my
5285 Problems reproduce themselves
6882 kinds of problems, except
7107 only such problems as it can

proceed
3398 and thence proceed to

processes
12479 are processes which all

procession
11959 in that procession but
12709 room, a solemn procession of one.

proclaim
7069 that roar, Proclaim the
7867 world proclaim, One

procrastination
2783 to incivility and procrastination.
7025 procrastination is the art of keeping
12938 Procrastination is the thief of time.

procreant
12505 Always the procreant urge of

prodigal
2345 unreturned prodigal, with

produce
5027 and the produce of his

9453 can never produce anything
12871 necessary to produce Hamlet .

produceful
8097 consumeful or very produceful.

producer
3355 and ought to be a producer.
10820 of the producer ought to

producing
8366 that consumes without producing.

product
3569 It is the product that pays
7337 The best ad is a good product.

production
64 the noblest production of human
9942 stimulate production, of bad
9943 to keep production going is a

productions
9546 all the new productions must do as

products
5545 of its products than of

profanity
11938 profanity furnishes

professed
3791 of them are professed by people
7647 of them all professed To know

profession
689 man a debtor to his profession.
9415 oldest profession. I have
9563 profession on earth.
11180 the only profession for which

professional
5383 In a professional once engaged,

professionals
5382 Amateurs hope. Professionals work.

professions
29 its professions, has
10593 All professions are conspiracies
11768 one of the professions which are

professor
596 A professor is one who talks in
5337 regius professor of French

professors
6312 American professors like their

profile
5295 I look at them in profile.

profit
1163 shall it profit a man, if
1239 all labour there is profit.
3942 .. that profit is not
4214 fails to operate at a profit.
6787 blow the profit. The glass
7301 the soul may not profit by.
10222 in it no profit but the
12263 to make any profit from it.

profitability
3014 Profitability is the sovereign

profitable
7028 it is not profitable to its

profits
1399 It profits a man nothing to
7619 nothing profits more Than

profound
1389 of truths, profound truths
5996 turbid look the most profound.

profundity
8238 Profundity of thought belongs to

progeny
7457 was whose progeny they are.

programme
393 So Much a Programme, More a
12630 not making programmes for the

progress
177 retreat; that is progress.
191 no summer progress. A cold
1643 .. Progress, man's
1888 All progress is based upon a
2109 is certain, progress is not.
2503 He makes progress only when
3295 we call progress' is the
3596 the key of progress; it is
4392 way to progress in any
6514 bare; Our progress through
6810 the history of progress.

6975 promoting progress in the
7369 a party of progress or reform,
7964 Technik. Progress through
8098 Progress might have been all
8703 step of progress the world
9698 the path of progress and be no
9752 progress' is
10624 all progress depends on
10991 Progress, therefore, is not an
12468 The art of progress is to
12522 faith in progress is not a
12533 world's best progress springs.
12632 is just a work in progress.

prohibit
4525 nation; to prohibit reading of

prohibition
9576 is like prohibition, it's a

project
4388 The project as understood by

projects
4441 view: it projects the

proletarians
7117 The proletarians have nothing to

proletariat
7113 dictatorship of the proletariat.

prologue
2515 very witty prologue to a very

prolong
4780 a doctor to prolong life and

prolonging
3203 interest in prolonging the lives

promise
1013 about the promise of spring
1556 can promise the moon
3087 boy the promise of a man,
5193 Promise, large promise, is
5613 'Why do you promise us
5618 over. They promise to build a
5619 we should promise people
5900 We promise according to our
9522 king Whose promise none
10091 A promise made is a debt

promised
5640 seen the promised land ..
7233 wise men promised has not

promises
885 the man who promises least;
5556 a set of promises - it is a
5657 The promises of yesterday are
11332 Promises and pie-crust are

promising
2520 they first call promising.

promoted
4392 ahead of you to get promoted.

pronounce
11960 Vinci and pronounce it Vinchy;

proof
5179 'Tis a proof that he
5897 proof of our
9199 'For example' is not proof.
10433 strong As proofs of holy
12741 beings are proof against

prop
12826 and a prop To our

propaganda
172 inevitable and silent propaganda.
4903 triumphs of propaganda have been

propensities
1792 side of their natural propensities.

proper
11324 Proper words in proper

properties
5019 certain exceptional properties.

property
2250 respect property. They
2381 a matter of property, and, as
3018 Property has its duties as
6435 his property - that is,
6861 of either property or honour,
9060 le vol. Property is theft.

prophecy
3208 of mistake, prophecy is the
10695 of a prophecy! O, Wind,

prophesy
6567 Don't never prophesy - onless
10249 a man my prophesy, With a

prophesying
2440 Ancestral voices prophesying war!
6773 He enjoys prophesying the

prophet
1189 A prophet is not without
9984 be called a prophet; for in

prophetic
7508 something like prophetic strain.

prophets
1173 of false prophets, which
2970 reject the prophets and slay
8946 ceased to pose as its prophets.

proportion
5248 In small proportions we just
8522 in inverse proportion to the sum
10629 are wise in proportion, not to
11776 is rich in proportion to the
11941 well the proportion of things.

propose
2784 and propose nothing.

proposes
5544 Man proposes; God disposes.

propositions
6427 General propositions are seldom

prose
2454 Prose = words in their best
2834 me up in prose As when
4705 write in prose you say
5994 Prose on certain occasions
7545 yet in prose or rhyme.
7738 that is not prose is verse;
8048 of a prose style than
8370 Good prose is like a
8758 real job of writing prose.
8855 poetry, but prose run mad.
11101 curse Of a prose which

prospect
3076 The prospect of a lot Of dull

prospects
4035 than of prospects. While

prosper
4436 doth never prosper, what's
5745 keep it may prosper, but the

prosperity
692 Prosperity is the blessing of
693 Prosperity is not without many
694 Prosperity doth best discover
766 virtue of prosperity is
1901 any great prosperity arrived at
4027 say, Of more prosperity than A.
8788 Prosperity tries the fortunate;

prostitutes
5826 small nations like prostitutes.

prostitution
6732 Prostitution. Selling one's body

prostrate
8593 is he, who prostrate lies,

prostration
11432 It is the prostration of men's

protect
11 but to protect the
6875 glass, to protect us from
7885 does not protect you from
7922 me, And I'll protect it now.
9495 solitudes protect and touch
12103 - I can protect myself

protected
8359 squirrels, must be protected.

protecting
1269 the art of protecting flat

protection
2911 Protection is not only dead, but
2912 Protection is not a principle,
7467 surrounded with his protection.
8698 need no protection - they
11951 good protections against

protects
9494 that each protects the

protest
4666 of the nature of a protest.
10216 lady doth protest too much,

protestant
966 PAT: A Protestant with a
2895 A Protestant, if he wants aid or
8207 me and the Protestant church -
11696 Protestant women may take the
12314 The protestant ethic and the

protoplasmal
3984 back to a protoplasmal primordial

proud
3127 Is all the proud and mighty
4298 and too proud to
4494 The truly proud man is
5188 is always proud of himself
5449 were they proud? again we
6715 rather proud of knowing
7472 nation proud in arms.
8843 and all the proud shall be!
8925 Yes, I am proud; I must be
9124 When a proud man hears
9754 are always proud of the
10480 nor proud me no
11176 be very proud and great,
12343 man who is proud of his
12679 being too proud to fight;

prove
3793 I could prove God
5272 let us prove, While we
7260 trying to prove that the
9466 Prove to me that you're no

proved
5980 with having proved you can

proven
4201 return to proven ways - not
11471 can be proven, Nor yet

provence
5431 mute, In Provence called,
12644 Than you found it in Provence?

proverb
5506 A proverb is no proverb to
5844 it is a common proverb.
6860 well worn proverb: 'He who
9789 A proverb is one man's wit

proverbs
8113 wrote the Proverbs And King

provide
4549 the worst and provide for it

providence
2894 thanks to Providence that his
3302 the divine providence has found
9481 Providence has given to the

province
757 knowledge to be my province.
4061 from the province they have

provinces
6828 of distant provinces generally

provincial
3212 level of provincial existence.
4996 worse than provincial - he was

provincialism
4889 in adultery than in provincialism.

provocation
8924 you what provocation I have

provocative
12475 human life provocative of a noble

provokes
7981 No one provokes me with

proximity
8422 trials of incessant proximity.

prudence
646 forced into prudence in her
1340 Prudence is a rich, ugly, old
4778 with your prudence: it's good
11949 and the prudence never to

prussia
1303 the King of Prussia the
1305 Prussia needs only one ally:
7688 national industry of Prussia.

pry
4486 to pry into, or

psalm
1999 the hundredth psalm.

psalms
8113 King David wrote the Psalms.

pseudonym
3603 is the pseudonym of God

pseudopodium
10738 A lonely pseudopodium I wandered

psyche
5495 be Your mournful Psyche.

psychiatrist
4205 goes to a psychiatrist should
5915 The psychiatrist must become a
8424 Psychiatrists today .. see the

psychiatry
359 Psychiatry is the care of the id
8672 Psychiatry enables us to correct

psychoanalysis
2257 Psychoanalysis is confession without

psychology
1090 play: the psychology of human
12457 and psychology in the

psychotherapy
262 word for psychotherapy is 'talk'.

psychotic
7286 I am, and psychotic means he's

pub
2417 and the pub opening

puberty
1953 thinking puberty assisted.

public
537 mislead the public, another
594 faces in public places Are
927 The public doesn't
2530 and have no public, than to
2554 American public wants a
2799 be in public office who
3095 anxious to serve the public?
3476 Public schools are the
4244 of the public; and the
5358 of service to the public.
7175 to let the public behind the
7664 that to the public good
8596 usual, to a public school,
11280 We tell the public which way
12026 privacy in a public place.
12035 say, gives it to the public.
12087 as if I was a public meeting.
12592 The public is wonderfully
12607 like a public building.

public opinion
8699 stands a warm, living public opinion.
9757 respect public opinion in so far

public-school
3574 composed of public-school men or
12295 That's the public-school system all

publican
10390 a fawning publican he looks!

publication
2016 First publication is a pure,
6763 Publication is a self-invasion of

publicity
963 as bad publicity except
1038 of justice is eternal publicity.
4409 The art of publicity is a black
6164 history of publicity rather
6375 is the publicity it gives
11657 oxygen of publicity on which

publish
12363 Publish and be damned.

published
424 counted and published every day,

publisher
2031 Now Barabbas was a publisher.
8719 A publisher is somebody looking

publishers
73 by numerous publishers, he had

publishes
7391 person who publishes a book

pudding
771 or looks like a plum pudding.
7443 lovely rice pudding for dinner
8825 And solid pudding against

puerility
4657 a state of perpetual puerility.

pugnacious
7907 for being pugnacious; he

pull
4532 he tries to pull it out.
7951 never make you pull it up.
11680 sleep he pulls the legs

pulling
11650 I shan't be pulling the levers

pulse
7856 Now feel that pulse no more.
8702 but the common pulse beat.
11116 feeling a woman's pulse.
12818 The very pulse of the

pulse-less
6083 palsied, pulse-less lot that

punches
9814 the other fellow's punches.

punctilio
7297 None of your dam punctilio.

punctuality
6537 Punctuality is the politeness of
12300 Punctuality is the virtue of the
12593 Punctuality is the thief of time.

punctuate
7829 also serve who only punctuate.

punish
1596 they don't punish, they
3021 of rest? Punish a body
3560 last cannot punish the first

punished
2498 is not punished, and that
5037 and is punished as such.

punishment
323 life, his reward, his punishment.
1051 All punishment is mischief: all
2973 terrible punishment so that
3567 Capital punishment is as
3995 To let the punishment fit the
4521 to take the punishment, you're
5266 What a rare punishment Is avarice
5837 The punishment of a criminal is
6856 secured by a dread of punishment.
7877 its own punishment with it
8240 generally, punishment hardens
9401 without punishment, none
9776 effect of punishment is a
9853 not man's punishment. It is
12155 crime - it is its punishment.

punishments
4540 with punishments the
4965 rewards nor punishments - there
8475 sanguinary punishments which

pup
7421 dog has been a pup.

pupil
3757 Today is yesterday's pupil.
4717 is like the pupil of the

pupils
1085 it kills all its pupils.

purchaser
11311 pattern to encourage purchasers.
11383 what its purchaser will pay

pure
5521 are the pure in heart,
6058 She's as pure as the
11483 Because my heart is pure.
12555 is rarely pure, and never

purest
9732 The purest and most

purgatory
3551 women, the purgatory of men,
6366 hell; it is simply purgatory.

purified
6992 shall be purified, All

purifies
7460 that which purifies us is

purifying
6691 what a purifying effect

puritan
6075 To the Puritan all things are
6831 The Puritan hated

puritanism
7257 Puritanism. The haunting fear

purity
2931 and angels' purity, 'Twixt
3499 Purity of race does not
8099 Purity is obscurity.

purple
4537 Purple haze is in my brain
8497 the deep purple falls over
9585 unclose Her purple mantle to

purpose
483 without purpose or
1206 to every purpose under the
2529 a purpose in life.
3590 serves the same purpose?
4144 any other purpose than to
4656 meaning and purpose to an
5347 the sole purpose of human
6362 stated my purpose according
6695 equals risk plus purpose)
9533 a sense of purpose in
10514 My purpose is, indeed, a
10666 as a steady purpose - a point
11531 increasing purpose runs, And
11546 embrace the purpose of God,

purring
7745 eys Is suddenly purring there.

purrs
7031 until it purrs like an

purse
6 Doctor, feel my purse.
3632 empties his purse into his

pursue
3071 good; or knowing it, pursue.
5027 wishes to pursue his

pursued
10534 Exit, pursued by a bear.

pursuit
6162 The common pursuit.
9404 to the pursuit of
11413 with a bias to some pursuit.
12549 obstinate pursuit of my own

push
10792 and a push may send
11200 one brave push and see

pushed
9128 fall before you're pushed.

pushing
660 After pushing them about

pussy
6154 Owl and the Pussy-Cat went

put down
118 will have to be put down.

put off
9297 you can put off till

puzzle
5960 Nothing puzzles me more than
11129 he. Don't puzzle me, said

puzzled
4818 who is puzzled before the

pygmies
833 mechanism operated by pygmies.

pyjamas
6098 and I in pyjamas for the

pyramid
7674 a star-ypointing pyramid?
8082 of these pyramids, forty

pyrenees
6532 The Pyrenees are no more.

pyschopath
241 between a pyschopath and a

pythagoras
1609 way of Pythagoras, and the

quad
5779 no one about in the Quad.'

quails
3055 and we long for quails.

quake
10754 indeed who quake to say

quaker
4622 A gentle Quaker, hearing a

qualification
2133 only great qualification for being

qualified
3929 Who else is better qualified?

qualities
1690 eminent qualities to hold
2299 of human qualities because it
2758 as high qualities, if he can
3084 war the finest human qualities.
4195 but such qualities as would
8309 has all the qualities of a poker
9905 great qualities in others
10605 only two qualities in the
12469 the five qualities of truth,

quality
4245 Quality of life is an
5303 quantity of work for quality.
7722 People of quality know
10402 The quality of mercy is not
10760 chickens, is good quality.
10920 gave them quality; when you
12462 Quality - in its classic

quangle-wangle
6159 gay!' Said the Quangle-Wangle Quee.

quantity
5303 substitute quantity of work

quarks
5315 Three quarks for Muster

quarrel
342 pick a quarrel with a man
3385 When we quarrel, how we wish
3697 his own side in a quarrel.
4953 to make a quarrel. It is
9309 should one quarrel with good
9658 need for a quarrel at the
10654 how they behave in a quarrel.
10659 hath his quarrel just, But

quarrelling
8283
9170 Better be quarrelling than

quarrels
3054 who in quarrels interpose,
4779 fierce quarrels and war to
5901 Quarrels would not last long
9616 Quarrels in France strengthen
12173 the motto of all quarrels.

quarter
26 they cost a quarter. What the

quarterly
11294 nothing a-year, paid quarterly.

quebec
5744 boy of Quebec Who was

queen
353 of our own very dear Queen!
2801 to be a queen in
3279 The queen of Scots is this
4057 I have been to the Queen.
5243 Queen and huntress, chaste
6927 of my fair queen; for
10270 not be a queen For all
10531 She is The queen of curds
10532 awake, I'll queen it no inch
10689 then his queen; Now is
11544 Queen rose of the rosebud

queer
120 are so queer, you never
968 we're queer Because
4037 best are often very queer.
8316 An Irish queer: a fellow
8444 world is queer save thee
11030 drink to the queer old Dean.
12713 What a queer thing Life is!

queerer
4373 is not only queerer than we

quench
10437 light: If I quench thee, thou

quest
798 perfect model for the Quest.
2580 The eternal quest of the

questing
6923 unto the questing of thirty

question
443 The only question left to be
582 the hard question is simple.

1562 impertinent question, and you
2037 asked any clear question.
2404 The urgent question of our
2845 asks a question unless he
2846 A question which can be
3656 The great question that has
4014 The question is, had he not
7338 I question the right of that
10211 that is the question: Whether
10800 The real question is not
11835 you rephrase the question?
11858 political question is: What
12704 of a question is like

question mark
9745 to hang a question mark on things

questioning
5194 Questioning is not the mode of

questions
156 some pretty good questions.
565 upon the questions you pose.
979 and that all questions are open.
2864 They ask so many questions.
3722 simplest questions are the
4845 is answer questions. It's
9890 most questions which it
9963 important questions in
10861 all first questions in 1776:
12385 it's asking questions, all the
12552 Questions are never indiscreet.
12960 questions and turns

queue
7355 an orderly queue of one.

quick
305 The quick brown fox jumped
2795 - the quick, and the

quicker
7713 through quicker than

quickest
7733 is the quickest way.
8384 The quickest way of ending a

quickly
9281 much good who gives quickly.
10347 well It were done quickly.

quiet
1005 From quiet homes and first
1931 Quiet to quick bosoms is a
2212 how to keep quiet when she
4613 profits is a quiet life.
5325 now And quiet to your
6112 He has the gift of quiet.
7078 Fair Quiet, have I found
7344 Anything for a quiet life.
9435 Neues. All Quiet on the
10636 have a quiet world till
10777 keep love affairs quiet
12693 wealth no quiet knows, But
12837 time is quiet as a nun

quietest
6676 Beside the quietest fire in

quietly
7386 the kind; Quietly they go,

quill
5939 said to do, through a quill.

quince
6156 slices of quince, Which

quintessence
10207 is this quintessence of dust?

quit
7670 Samson hath quit himself

quits
297 waste time, so we are quits.
7217 I, we are quits, and there

quixote
5077 Don Quixote, Robinson

quota
3813 would yield its quota.

quotable
11228 to be quotable than to be

quotation
3353 and literature a quotation.
5143 Every quotation contributes

quotations
2304 man to read books of quotations.
3344 I hate quotations.

quote
3618 Don't quote me; that's what
7802 I quote others in order to
10644 I often quote myself. It
12359 Don't quote Latin; say what
12930 grow immortal as they quote.

quoted
11261 very seldom quoted correctly.

rabbit
360 The rabbit has a charming
10662 on the rabbit's foot if

rabbit-like
11845 but rabbit-like in our

rabbits
10789 employed in keeping rabbits.
12306 expecting rabbits to come

rabble
8988 there is a rabble of the

race
1208 The race is not to the
2732 admitted to race tracks at
3321 the human race will be
5115 can run the race with
5574 of his race from
7685 run out thy race, Call on
8995 of the race, but the
9694 another's race, religion
9715 The race is not always to
10006 The human race is my
10709 joy whose race is just
11375 A loftier race Than e'er
11533 shall rear my dusky race.
12650 what their race or colour
12925 of whatever race or creed.

races
5941 distinct races, the men
6623 Some races increase, others
12957 all the races of Europe

racing
168 money - racing being the
9558 makes horse racing and

rack
10817 is on the rack, as long

racket
8401 flaming racket of the
9489 a German racket, designed

radar
4529 writer's radar and all

radiance
4397 the steady radiance, renewed

radiant
7479 By her own radiant light,

radical
460 The most radical
3704 dared be radical when young
12728 Radical Chic .. is only

radicalism
4661 There is a radicalism in all

radio
586 Of the radio-phonograph
6597 A car radio bleats,
7748 on. I had the radio on.
9916 Radio and television ..

radius
7284 in their radius. When we

rag
5752 I!) To a rag and a bone
12772 like a rag blown by

rag and bone
12881 In the foul rag and bone shop of

rag-bag
221 when that rag-bag called the

rage
1326 Puts all Heaven in a rage.
2852 generation in a rage.
8724 What rage for fame attends
11321 here in a rage, like a
11559 of noble rage, The
11664 of day; Rage, rage
11796 Boredom is rage spread

rages
11033 weight of rages will press
11262 but now he rages if he

rags
7719 Rags and tatters, if you

railings
8487 Iron railings leaning out of

raiment
6801 and your raiment all red?

rain
570 left out in the rain.
1496 The rain, it raineth on
3131 it's a hard rain's a gonna
5482 hatches .. Rain! Rain!
6055 The drop of rain maketh a
6256 The rain in Spain stays
8628 able to command the rain.
8983 Goddamm, Raineth drop
9274 will rain on those
10669 which had outwept its rain.
10678 caverns of rain, Like a
10788 falls the Rain - Dark as
11495 Rain, rain, and sun! a
12082 like the rain on the
12202 curse the rain For which

rainbow
4 of a rainbow, In the
340 Noah the rainbow sign, No
4417 Somewhere over the rainbow.
6596 the rainbow of His
10688 The rainbow's glory is
11495 and sun! a rainbow in the
12790 I behold A rainbow in the
12806 The rainbow comes and goes,

raining
6548 It is not raining rain to me,

rains
2752 soon as it rains, they

rainy
2781 show than a rainy Sunday in

raise
678 it doth raise and erect

raised
11240 I was raised by a
12326 Raised by that curious

rake
2026 on the prongs of a rake.
6820 A rake among scholars, and

raking
9610 when to stop raking the muck.

ramble
4361 world I ramble, I see

rampart
12717 to the rampart we

rang
3937 of you Rang like a

rank
1808 The rank is but the
5357 by rank or

ranks
886 split the ranks is to
6844 even the ranks of Tuscany

ransack
6991 for gold, Ransack the ocean

rape
2750 legitimately, you rape it.
9047 rape is said to

raphael
12455 can't stand Raphael and those

raphaels
4179 of their Raphaels,

rapidity
2756 either in scope or in rapidity.

rapping
8810 gently rapping, rapping

rapscallions
11931 All kings is mostly rapscallions.

rapture
3990 Modified rapture!
6986 him dead to rapture and
8328 or a rapture if it is
8880 turn thy rapture move, For

rapturous
6205 The rapturous, wild, and

rare
5367 A rare bird on this earth,

5895 but it is rare to find a
7863 Rich and rare were the
10563 my love as rare As any she
12345 purest, and they are rare.

rarer
5861 nothing rarer than the

rarest
11769 thought was the rarest.

rascality
11035 relieved by rascality.

rash
7625 Her rash hand in evil hour

rat
1492 it creeps like a rat.
9519 I smell a rat; I see him
11321 a poisoned rat in a hole.

rates
9488 hourly rates by

ratiocination
1908 And pay with ratiocination.

rational
630 he can be rational and
2982 work in a rational and

rationalism
12928 just as rationalism is the

rationed
6217 that it must be rationed.

ratomorphic
5792 the rat, a ratomorphic view of

rats
1666 Rats! They fought the dogs
8296 500 million rats in the
8315 sometimes has to eat rats.

rattle
6222 you, just rattle your
8274 Rattle his bones over the
8903 with a rattle, tickled

raven
6572 with his raven like
10346 The raven himself is hoarse

ravish
2949 chaste, except you ravish me.

ravished
6990 'tis thou hast ravished me.

ravishing
972 what a dear ravishing thing is

razor
7756 a polished razor keen,
8929 to hew blocks with a razor.

re-organised
8678 we would be re-organised. I was to

re-read
9969 should be re-read

reach
2855 within its reach, that
3577 beyond his reach. He mixes
5255 that every child may reach.
7010 that flies beyond my reach.
8090 everybody's reach, And it is

react
5035 to act instead of react.

reaction
1064 productive reaction against
8186 an equal reaction: or the

reactionaries
6972 States reactionaries use to

read
533 You should read it, though
738 Read not to contradict and
985 but his books were read.'
1722 you. Read to live,
1862 Read my lips: no new
2043 and the read
3726 would never read or trust
4524 own age, read the works
4635 If I had read as much as
5137 Read over your
5621 a part of all I have read.
6045 Don't read too much now:
6605 I read them.
6912 and I have read all the
7052 works, but read these.
8193 We read to know we are not

8597 A widely read man never
8885 ignorantly read, With
8936 judge will read each word
8997 we should read for power.
9296 I never read books - I
9546 attempts to read all the
9746 power to read each
10413 I could read, Could
11665 I had to read
11861 able to read but unable
11965 does not read good books
12301 wants to read. And it's
12358 Read the
12913 And slowly read and dream
12959 for people who can't read.

reader
1563 Reader, I married him.
3381 the good reader that makes
3399 would be a reader, read; if
5311 That ideal reader suffering
12448 and the reader feels the
12725 reason a reader reads one

readers
850 and his readers a chance
2442 there are readers to be
4502 your readers might like
5077 by its readers, excepting
5797 readers for ten

readiness
768 a state of readiness in mind
9891 as the readiness to die,

reading
739 Reading maketh a full man;
1984 The reading or non-reading a
2921 an art of reading, as well
3171 Reading after a certain
3604 know any reading more easy,
4435 is, there reading makes it
4523 Reading is sometimes an
5297 Reading, like prayer, remains
7721 Reading and marriage don't go
7843 fiddle. Reading it,
8360 Reading isn't an occupation
9324 in the reading, as I had
9722 is worth reading, it is
10719 writing's vile hard reading.
10789 people now reading and
10846 thing, but I prefer reading.
11068 Reading is to the mind what
11121 the soul of reading; take them
12451 Reading is the work of the

reads
7648 Who reads Incessantly, and

ready
2490 and ready for more.
3570 getting ready is the
3820 always are ready; Steady,
7774 spurred and ready to depart.
8111 the play is ready to open.
12407 I am not ready for an
12676 machine. I am ready to go.

real
397 reason and the real reason.
4106 the real thing; a
6500 Life is real! Life is
11144 back To the real: to the

realisation
8042

realism
6210 don't want realism - I want

realist
2150 But I am a realist.

realistic
6682 to make a realistic decision',

reality
361 Reality is an illusion caused
813 cage of reality bequeathed
1069 which masks reality from us,
1525 over reality. For the
2168 world is reality - and that
2242 a spirit of reality, because
3232 And the reality Between
3234 cannot bear very much reality.
3415 to face reality in all its
4308 the hidden reality with its
4505 spiritual reality he

The Wordsworth Dictionary of Quotations

4606 There is no reality except the
4880 Reality is always ahead of
5928 pressure of reality, so much
6919 it is reality - and not
8038 in life is to find reality.
8734 on your reality as you
9362 Reality is prodigal, but
10933 people's reality, and
10935 recording reality,
12398 truth that reality obscures.

realization
8255 progressive realization of a

realize
821 street to realize that there

realm
1416 in this Realm of
3280 the borders of my realm.
8722 exhaust the realm of the
10446 earth, this realm, this

reap
1224 they shall reap the
9407 and you reap a habit.

reaper
6506 There is a Reaper whose name

reappear
7110 history reappear in one

reaps
11202 hurry and reaps

rear
11533 she shall rear my dusky

rearrange
7947 going to rearrange the

rears
662 S-E-X ever rears its ugly

reason
124 are five reasons we should
397 are two reasons for doing
669 What reason I should
1600 Fell, The reason why I
1604 lost their reason in nothing
1891 love - all reason is against
2013 through reason can be
2219 with reason, with the
2430 be against reason, it is of
2651 need a reason to have
2944 between the reason of man and
3184 light of reason and no
3622 Fragile as reason is and
3826 listen to reason .. Reason
3910 preach, but Reason herself
4382 to us than Reason, when it
4458 men Will know the reason why!
4461 of human reason - for then
5722 simple reason in all
5853 The reason of the strongest
6196 ultimate reason of things,
6198 gives us Reason and the
6199 is nothing without a reason.
6251 vanish at reason's
6271 lose his reason over
6431 Reason is natural
6955 Human reason needs only to
7486 pranked in reason's garb.
7624 selves, our reason is our
7652 Reason is also choice.
7880 was neither rhyme nor reason.
8172 Reason is God's gift, but so
8534 advance of reason is to
8542 has its reasons which
8870 conquers reason still.
8897 in erring Reason's spite,
9017 the reason of the
9427 without reason, and
9526 Reason, an ignis fatuus of
9876 a representative of reason.
9877 is stronger than reason.
9984 Reason deserves to be called
10341 takes the reason prisoner?
10445 to reason thus;
10525 a woman's reason: I think
10705 Reason respects the
11123 is not his reason, but his
11266 die than it is to reason why.
11476 not to reason why,
12247 What is the reason of this
12267 is not reason, it is not

12277 but show no reason can
12394 under the name of reason.
12628 Reason is an emotion for the

reasonable
4089 say some reasonable thing.
4563 figure of 'The Reasonable Man'.
7458 man kills a reasonable creature,
10624 The reasonable man adapts

reasoned
10886 It was not reasoned into him,

reasoning
2110 and much reasoning lead to
4396 Man is a reasoning, rather than
5468 consecutive reasoning - and yet
8531 All our reasoning ends in
8766 who was capable of reasoning.
12821 A reasoning, self-sufficing

reasons
4504 for other reasons than he
6293 and has its reasons which are
7339 Reasons are whores.
8044 give your reasons; for your
9786 want better reasons for having
11250 when the reasons for the

reassembles
9818 When man reassembles his

rebel
2053 What is a rebel? A man who
2639 - how to rebel and
6381 Rebel without a cause.

rebelled
2019 Thirteen rebelled and two

rebellion
1517 Rebellion to tyrants is
5025 a little rebellion now and
8395 is a sort of mental rebellion.
10600 secret rebellion against
11093 acts and everyday rebellions.

rebellious
7215 with rebellious treading!

rebirth
9964 need is a rebirth of satire,

reborn
4609 To be reborn is a constantly

rebuild
8143 who must rebuild their ship

rebuilt
7361 to be rebuilt, there is

recall
4770 takes wing beyond recall.
7692 illusions I recall; I really
9276 to endure is sweet to recall.

recalled
2854 spoke can never be recalled.

recaptured
6909 that can be recaptured wholly; as

receipt
4828 like they expected a receipt.

receive
7285 and the ones who receive it.

received
1177 ye have received, freely
8223 receiver received? Is not

receiver
5793 left the receiver off the

receives
3176 is he who receives a great

recent
11437 it approaches recent times.

receptacle
3247 is .. a receptacle for

recession
3777 recessions, or
11907 It's a recession when your

recipe
1045 I feel a recipe is only a
12036 of all the recipes that are

reckless
3360 Nature is reckless of the

reclaimed
1882 - every man reclaimed his

recognition
3393 a recognition of the
7241 shock of recognition runs the
12473 is recognition of the
12637 for your recognition of me in

recognize
5219 you to recognize a mistake
5375 trial if I recognize it as
8534 is to recognize that it is
9999 hardly even recognize the devils
10977 alert to recognize your prime
11867 he did not recognize me by my

recognized
4108 hero can be recognized only by a

recognizing
7332 make, but recognizing when to

recollect
5111 does not recollect where he

recollection
11257 and ten per cent recollection.

recommendation
9190 men need no recommendation and bad

reconcile
4864 is made to reconcile the most
8139 on how to reconcile my net
9892 cannot reconcile

reconciles
8635 feasting reconciles everybody.
12824 that reconciles Discordant

reconciliation
9948 is the secret of reconciliation.

record
2989 dreadful record of sin
3264 And puts a record on the
6521 is the record of a man

recording
10935 of just recording reality,

recover
1882 tried to recover it from
9268 you: if I recover, we shall

recovers
6707 from which he never recovers.

recreations
7461 all recreations and

rectum
8410 one in the rectum makes a

red
2516 is deepest red; It
6802 and red men
8009 Better red than dead.
8402 not even red brick, but
8449 Red lips are not so red
9585 her raiment red, Her
9951 is always 'in the red'.

red-haired
6178 When red-haired girls

red-nosed
6987 the Red-Nosed Reindeer

redeem
4119 can always redeem the man
11146 who will redeem the time

redeemer
10781 or a redeemer of

redemption
7532 Our great redemption from above

rediscover
9538 I invent nothing. I rediscover.

redoubling
9884 consists in redoubling your

reduce
12482 force is to reduce the amount

reed
8543 is only a reed, the

reels
1816 threesome reels, there's

references
9677 to verify your references, sir!

refined
3035 Refined himself to soul, to
5532 people of refined sentiments
10863 is so refined She has no

refining
4177 went on refining, And

reflecting
12757 power of reflecting the figure

reflection
796 all, the reflection of the
5385 seriously reflection
10858 at their reflections in
10979 and sees a reflection of the
11648 man the reflection of his own

reflects
11098 it reflects to your

reflexes
5071 reflexes. They are

reform
275 us ought to reform the rest
1555 retrenchment, and reform'.
1765 To innovate is not to reform.
2078 All reform except a moral
4476 triumph of reform that it
9606 in all reform movements.
12545 thing to reform anyone.
12939 forty, and reforms his plan;

reformation
3062 be plotting some new reformation.
12591 who need reformation, it is the

reformed
12677 now I am a reformed character.

reformer
2272 A reformer is one who sets
12189 A reformer is a guy who rides

reformers
7833 All reformers are bachelors.
10645 Reformers have the idea that

refrain
4389 They merely refrain from

refraining
4903 but by refraining from

refreshes
7972 Refreshes the parts other beers

refreshing
2025 And soft refreshing rain.

refuge
12544 is the last refuge of the

refugees
1707 if its refugees are among
4375 of refugees: the
6788 sorrow of the refugees.

refund
9403 as an income tax refund.

refuse
636 should ever refuse an offer
5302 should refuse a
7266 never to refuse a drink
7989 when men refuse to fight.
9319 him an offer he can't refuse.
9930 writer must refuse .. to
11870 generally refuse to make

refute
8482 Who can refute a sneer?

regard
8305 as great a regard for

regarded
7278 and well regarded at the

regimen
9063 following a regimen is not

regiment
5691 play, The regiment's in
5771 Monstrous Regiment of Women.

region
7556 Is this the region, this the

register
3903 than the register of the

regret
820 greater regret, for my
4376 I only regret that I have
4495 one pang of regret at not
5678 I will regret to my dying
6971 never to regret and never
8317 in sealed bottles of regret.

regrets
8959 Miss Otis regrets (she's

9687 which a man regrets most in
12538 the wild regrets, and the

regular
3537 Be regular and orderly in

regulated
11254 state to a regulated, perfectly

rehabilitate
1596 don't rehabilitate, they

reign
7558 To reign is worth ambition
8078 year of his reign, is

reigned
3274 that I have reigned with your

reigns
7580 By which he reigns; next him

reincarnation
7418 reasons for reincarnation .. The

reinforcement
2054 ended in a reinforcement of the
7554 What reinforcement we may gain from

reins
109 give the reins to reason

reject
996 .. If you reject me on
4982 it is time to reject it.
5646 which rejects revenge,

rejected
1515 atom, and rejected the Sermon
3387 our own rejected thoughts;

rejoice
2327 colours. I rejoice with the
6642 faith and rejoice in Christ.
7637 or rejoice Much more,

rejoicing
7492 in her rejoicing with

related
2493 is related to
8470 so nearly related, that it

relation
11617 My closest relation is myself.
11643 like a relation to do the
11993 perceived to have any relation.
12299 happiest relation for father

relations
2549 my wife's relations I like
4278 them to my relations with other
4342 Their relations sometimes
4342 Their relations sometimes
4455 conduct in private relations.
5675 God's apology for relations.
7378 social relations between
9066 social relations, there

relationship
1548 In any relationship we feel an
3586 every human relationship suffers.
4791 fuel for starting a relationship.
5352 individual relationship smoothly
5478 in close relationship with

relationships
572 all of our relationships begin, and
1090 psychology of human relationships.
8420 Relationships get more difficult as
12095 to articulate human relationships.

relative
1712 day In a relative way And

relativity
3178 theory of relativity is proven
3181 two hours. That's relativity.

relaxation
9709 most natural form of relaxation.

relaxes
1345 Damn braces: Bless relaxes.

release
2719 a kind of release And a kind

relent
12128 gods above relent, I shall

relic
12325 like a holy relic? I have

relics
7674 hallowed relics should be
7862 his relics are laid.

relief
676 and the relief of man's
1363 And not seek for kind relief.
2688 and through laughter, relief.
12807 thought relief, And I

relieved
4154 but relieved their
10221 are relieved, Or not at

religion
61 that regards religion.
232 by a sense of religion.
695 men's minds about to religion.
978 Art and Religion are means to
1368 Religion converts despair,
1604 as their religion, wherein
1612 indirect way to plant religion.
1852 One religion is as true as
1896 Christian religion doubted,
1956 calms As rum and true religion.
2085 and the Protestant Religion.
2420 Poetry is a religion with no
2484 wrangle for religion, write for
2746 In their religion they are so
2881 of the same religion.' ' And
3174 without religion is lame,
3345 which religion is
3423 is the wise man's religion.
3594 of all in religion, is ever
3664 is freed of religion, he has a
4188 I take my religion from the
4371 - the wisest religion.
4839 is to start your own religion.
4948 a popular religion, it is
4956 Religion is a way of walking,
5055 Religion and peace go
5356 well as in religion. By
5810 Religion is the frozen thought
5811 by any religion, by any
6598 the old religion - all
6621 wrong could religion induce.
7006 I count religion but a
7106 Religion .. is the opium of
7236 pass when religion is allowed
7242 a man's religion becomes
7279 fellow's religion, but only
7784 Our religion is made so as to
8305 to bring religion into it.
8469 system of religion that has
8474 The religion of humanity.
8478 and my religion is to do
8620 reproach to religion and
8837 Religion blushing veils her
8971 Religion to me has always been
9177 is neither religion nor truth.
9739 either on religion or policy.
9826 than any religion ..
9896 Each religion, by the help of
10608 That is my religion.
10642 is only one religion, though
10646 Religion is a great force -
10896 England but vice and religion!
10973 is to leave him for religion.
11054 Our religion, laws,
11123 against religion, always
11338 just enough religion to make us
11390 when religion was strong
11469 concerned with religion.
12175 is of the same religion.

religions
1545 Religions are kept alive by
9064 who found religions and create
12152 forty-two religions and only

religious
523 is, first, religious and moral
1493 always the religious element.
1779 a religious animal;
3901 but even religious concord.
8163 in religious enquiries.
12316 of all religious
12727 third great religious wave in

relished
316 and then is relished by the
3106 an' thin is relished by th'
12793 by which he is to be relished.

reluctant
6495 with reluctant feet,

relume
10437 That can thy light relume.

rely
5844 Rely only on yourself; it
6796 Do not rely completely on

remain
924 born mad. Some remain so.
6232 have gone and some remain.
10683 Let us remain together
11377 doth remain In the

remaining
1511 easier than remaining number

remains
5756 cut up what remains Just roll
8843 dust alone remains of thee;
9548 while aught remains to do.

remarkable
4942 This very remarkable man
8554 is anything remarkable about it.

remarks
2929 said our remarks before us.
11075 Remarks are not literature.
11261 Famous remarks are very

remedies
719 apply new remedies must
3657 do without palliative remedies.
10141 Our remedies oft in ourselves
11384 are some remedies worse than

remedy
734 The remedy is worse than the
897 As a remedy against all ills
2055 As a remedy to life in
3457 requires a dangerous remedy.
5832 not how to remedy our own.
9366 a sharp remedy, but a
12954 only bitter remedy against

remember
280 Please to remember the fifth
325 a man can remember what he
526 power to remember, but its
1196 enough, remember the time
1299 morning We will remember them.
1387 you, I'll always remember you."
2434 point to remember is that
2572 best way to remember your
2844 thing to remember: writers
2977 Remember me when I am dead And
3735 may be sweet to remember.
4237 Women still remember the first
4244 nowadays to remember anything
4740 I remember, I remember, The
4877 You must remember this, a kiss
6232 places I'll remember all my
6258 Ah yes! I remember it well.
6285 quite remember whether he
8987 even I can remember A day when
9072 which we remember of our
9104 I see and I remember I do and
9632 Remember me when I am gone
9885 who cannot remember the past
10066 It is what you can remember.
10263 But he'll remember with
11265 good to remember that
11363 I shall remember while the
11371 and death remember, Till thou
11429 thy breast. Remember me, but
11934 that I can remember, as the
11982 have to remember anything.
11990 I could remember anything,
12116 cheering to remember even these
12725 reads one is to remember it.

remembered
578 none are undeservedly remembered.
1438 when we remembered thee, O
5171 will be remembered, and
7837 is to be remembered by what

remembering
2797 two people remembering the same
9936 the terrace remembering And
11526 sorrow is remembering happier

remembrance
5484 and appear almost a remembrance.
6096 flood of remembrance, I weep
9948 Remembrance is the secret of
10227 that's for remembrance; pray,
10548 I summon up remembrance of things

remind
7124 things Remind me of you.

reminiscence
12493 shuttle .. A reminiscence sing.

remorse
79
2616 Remorse, the fatal egg by
7591 Farewell remorse! All good

remote
4153 a year; Remote from towns

render
1186 Render therefore unto Caesar

rendezvous
10046 I have a rendezvous with Death

renew
10684 a snake renew Her winter

renewing
3154 friends, renewing is of
9442 constantly renewing itself for

renounce
3911 cheerfully renounce me for a

rent
259 buy it, rent it.

repair
2066 you can't repair it
3354 keep it in repair the rest

repairing
9620 that eats or needs repairing.

repairs
1317 should be closed for repairs.

repartee
2260 is the unbearable repartee.

repay
980 Tiger well repay the
1144 I will repay, saith the

repeal
4273 secure the repeal of bad or

repeat
2551 be called on to repeat it,
4344 History repeats itself.
5304 never repeat the
9885 are condemned to repeat it.

repeated
819 a truth repeated until

repel
551 and cheek repel me. I am
5340 attitudes which repel them.

repent
7637 I should repent me now of
10051 to give them time to repent.
10437 Should I repent me; but
10699 It doth repent me; words are
10974 to repent of love.
11446 to have to repent; But

repentance
1156 which need no repentance.
1176 but sinners to repentance.
3049 Repentance is the virtue of weak
3059 Repentance is but want of power
3160 Repentance is for little
9087 is the best part of repentance.
10036 the morning cool repentance came.
12875 who feels Repentance on a

repented
1973 and much repented, And

repenting
11695 haste, and repenting at

repertoire
7868 one's repertoire, the

replaced
842 has been replaced, as he has

reply
4517 tempted to reply, 'Who

reporter
3671 Today's reporter is forced to
6807 which the reporters sit has

reports
11979 The reports of my death are

repose
2275 disturb your repose later on.
3338 truth and repose. Take
6497 Has earned a night's repose.

reprehend
10730 Sure, if I reprehend anything

represent
3118 genius to represent, simply

representation
8419 without representation is

representative
1783 Your representative owes you, not
9876 political representative of a
11906 is the representative of the

repression
7379 of forced repression in some

reproach
6829 bear the reproach of having
8620 It is a reproach to religion
9982 made the subject of reproach.

reproduced
2538 is never reproduced. It is

reproof
5998 praise the bitterest reproof.

reptile
8860 face, a reptile all the

republic
52 make in the republic of
167 whilst a republic is a raft
775 a disguised republic we must
7702 in a republic is like a

republican
10763 of a republican nation, is
10985 The Republican form of
11808 by republican government

republics
7817 Republics are brought to their

reputation
225 a tree, and reputation like its
4401 goes by: reputation increases,
6950 know of us; reputation is what
7828 my reputation will take
8078 who gets a reputation for good
9959 I am better than my reputation.
10424 Reputation is an idle and most
10429 lost my reputation. I have
10442 Is spotless reputation; that
11317 And wink a reputation down.

reputations
3204 large home of ruined reputations.

request
7876 be ruined at our own request.

require
1354 in women do require? The
4509 It must require an inordinate
9914 necessarily require happiness.

required
3475 of him can nothing be required.
3612 I am not required to do

requirement
4735 The first requirement for a
8256 very first requirement in a

requirements
5659 the chief requirements of life,

requisite
59 more requisite in

requited
8443 are alike requited, God is

rescued
12054 sword been rescued by his

research
892 Research is the process of
1531 Basic research is when I'm
3656 years of research into the
4550 What is research, but a blind
5306 Research' is a mere excuse
6528 for a research scientist
7712 steal from many, it's research.

resemblance
8538 by its resemblance to things
9415 very close resemblance to the
11063 knowing the resemblance of things
11433 of their resemblance to them.

resemble
1255 that resemble, but do
10399 we will resemble you in
12200 When I resemble her to

resent
2496 don't resent having
11345 could resent, Where

resentment
8158 to get up resentment towards

reservation
6372 no mental reservations, and with
10664 without regret or reservation.

reserved
2406 that I am reserved for some

reservoir
12651 a gigantic reservoir of good

resign
12270 nor ever resign an office.

resignation
7100 accept my resignation. I don't

resigned
7386 And I am not resigned.

resist
1167 Resist not evil: but
4271 strongest is to resist it.
5764 entirely resist both
6074 nothing to resist at all.
10575 I never resist temptation,
12402 unless I can't resist it.
12568 I can resist everything
12583 to it. Resist it, and

resistance
164 of least resistance and has
8240 the power of resistance.
11046 break the resistance of the
12266 of brave resistance, or the

resistible
1539 The resistible rise of Arturo

resisting
5786 on their resisting

resolute
10364 bold, and resolute; laugh to

resolution
1117 carry this resolution you will
7554 not, what resolution from
7627 Certain my resolution is to die;
8217 Christian resolution to find
10168 My resolution's placed, and I
10213 hue of resolution Is

resolutions
1912 Of great and mighty resolutions.

resolve
515 Resolve to be thyself: and
3649 If you resolve to give up
12939 purpose to resolve; In all

resolved
6682 that he has resolved to do

resort
277 is the last resort of the

resorts
6266 Pleasure resorts are like

resources
4058 The resources of civilization
4767 born to consume resources.

respect
247 those who respect and admire
969 lack of respect for
1920 Respect is love in plain
2184 neither respect nor
2250 Thieves respect property.
6862 you fail to get respect.
7279 We must respect the other
8528 and starves your self respect.
8687 his respect for those
9757 as a rule respect public
10090 Let us respect grey hairs,
11441 men are to respect each other
11966 at least respect his
12169 We owe respect to the living;

respectability
842 West, with respectability and
9032 outside respectability and keep
9405 save a shred of its respectability.
10634 Morality is not respectability.

respectable
1622 when was genius found respectable?
1623 most devilish when respectable.
4354 the most respectable woman has

4748 to what is respectable, and the
7835 can go is considered respectable.
8393 and murder respectable, and to
9823 who aren't respectable live

respected
908 to, but be respected, that is
4256 and character are respected.
4348 May be respected, but is
5390 is to be respected as an

respecter
1127 God is no respecter of persons.

respecting
7437 can't help respecting anybody
8041 and respecting things

respects
11975 no man much respects himself.

responsibility
2774 liberty, solidarity, responsibility.
3148 burden of responsibility and to
4400 a man to assume responsibility.
5776 no sense of responsibility at the
6355 power and bear the responsibility.
9813 who assumes responsibility. He says,
10622 means responsibility. That is
11224 subscribe - responsibility without
11736 any sense of personal responsibility.

responsible
6364 forty is responsible for his

rest
380 All the rest have
1021 I shall not rest quiet in
1178 and I will give you rest.
2605 is not rest, A mind
5616 There is no rest, no
8173 and a holy rest, and peace
8184 state of rest, or of
8602 It is no rest to be idle.
8800 Rest is the sweet sauce of
9263 and then rest afterward.
10232 The rest is silence.
10685 it die or rest at last!
11928 home for rest, For home
12080 All the rest is mere fine
12293 needs more rest if one
12613 life. The rest is merely

restaurant
552 a good table at a restaurant.
4140 tablecloth restaurant is still
6166 at a good restaurant, but not

resting
9712 in bed resting up from

restless
10835 tired. The restless soul is

restrain
6434 abolish or restrain, but to

restrained
3296 will be restrained in their

rests
4295 Here rests his head upon

result
9009 knows the result of the
12597 you get the result.

results
3145 Results! Why, man, I have
8684 the results of his own
9961 produce the same results.

resurrection
1419 hope of the Resurrection to eternal
9975 a foretaste of the resurrection.

resuscitate
8991 strove to resuscitate the dead

retainer
988 The Old Retainer night and

retentive
10278 Can be retentive to the

reticulated
5146 Anything reticulated or

retire
1044 my life. Retire? Retire
2492 length of time to retire.
2897 for him to retire from the
7642 Skilled to retire, and in
10663 sixties and retire, they go

retired
2723 role of a retired person is
11114 I retired to my

retirement
4369 must be no retirement. With our
7621 And short retirement urges
8314 Retirement: statutory senility.
11727 content, Retirement, rural

retiring
5149 think of retiring from the

retract
6692 Never retract, never explain,

retreat
177 ninety-nine retreat; that is
3821 I will not retreat a single
8054 me! If I retreat, cut me
8070 a line of retreat: it is a
12866 country retreat near the

retreating
3553 my right is retreating, situation
8104 you seen yourself retreating?

retrograde
5256 be not retrograde; But

return
1222 unto dust shalt thou return.
7526 gone, and never must return!
11213 unless she returns his love.

returned
1712 way And returned on the
7163 love that is never returned.

returning
10921 They keep returning to the

returns
3609 nobody ever returns them; the
5862 One returns to the place one

reveal
3930 No man can reveal to you
11555 half reveal And half

revelation
6431 is natural revelation, whereby

revelations
12604 garden. It ends with Revelations.

revenge
704 of him. Revenge triumphs
731 Revenge is a kind of wild
732 studieth revenge keeps his
1954 Sweet is revenge - especially
2847 I retreat; revenge me if I
4356 no better revenge than to
5371 Revenge is always the
6858 they take revenge for slight
7550 study of revenge, immortal
7955 become revenge by
9262 No revenge is more honourable
10223 my dull revenge! What is
10399 we not revenge? If we
10602 coward's revenge for being
10936 is the revenge of the
12162 he took his revenge by

reverberation
6891 the paucity of its reverberation.

revere
5058 that Paul Revere never

reverence
777 The mystic reverence, the
783 is to be reverenced, and if
4640 from the reverence of the

reverse
2649 made giant strides in reverse.

reversed
4235 the order would be reversed.

reversion
8841 no bright reversion in the

review
6579 write, can surely review.
7216 I pass in review the front
9426 I have your review in front

reviewers
2442 be found reviewers to
2452 Reviewers are usually people

reviewing
10884 book before reviewing it; it

reviews
6324 When the reviews are bad I

revision
12383 subjects of revision;

revivals
1889 art is the history of revivals.

revolt
3445 world is in revolt. Soon
6929 art is a revolt against
6933 Art is a revolt against

revolted
7614 Against revolted multitudes

revolting
8085 They're pretty revolting.

revolts
8031 generation revolts against
11436 recurrent revolts on the

revolution
263 passion for revolution but an
468 radical revolutionary will
1773 Make the Revolution a parent of
3123 sparks the revolution. I could
3297 over a volcano of revolution.
3717 who rejects the Revolution.
5582 peaceful revolution impossible
5619 than only revolution, they
6932 Neither revolution nor war
8381 safeguard a revolution; one makes
9573 One revolution is like one
12079 that the Revolution, like
12316 of all religious revolution.

revolutionary
5613 by fine revolutionary phrases is
6387 fierce and revolutionary in a

revolutionist
3834 either plagiarist or revolutionist.

revolutionists
7278 and revolutionists. They

revolutions
1723 Revolutions are not made with
2054 All modern revolutions have ended
4947 cause of revolutions, and would
9802 like revolutions, should
10099 knows, that revolutions never go
10628 Revolutions have never lightened
10916 All revolutions unleash the most

reward
323 life, his reward, his
3371 The reward of a thing well
3448 are their own rewards.
4719 The reward of a general is
6951 No reward is
7931 The reward of labour is
9853 It is his reward and his
11013 love, and nothing for reward.
12072 its own reward, it would

rewarded
530 truth; and truth rewarded me.

rewrite
3726 do rewrite my central
12565 to history is to rewrite it.

rhetoric
3830 is the rhetoric of the
10758 Death, without rhetoric.
12884 we make rhetoric; of our

rhetorician
1909 For all a rhetorician's rules
2883 sophistical rhetorician,
12890 The rhetorician would deceive his

rheumatism
3414 believe in rheumatism and true

rhine
816 of the Rhine. That is

rhodesia
10834 rule in Rhodesia - not in a

rhubarb
5780 blancmange and rhubarb tart.

rhyme
4705 write in rhyme you say
7641 Rhyme being no necessary
7880 now it is rhyme; before,
7928 murmuring rhyme Beats with
8806 of Runic rhyme, To the
8922 can, All rhyme, and

rhyming
2203 Thy drasty rymyng is nat

rhythm
5051 between two rhythms, the
7125 by means of rhythm and great
11256 of rhythm offer me

rib
9782 his rib. But male

ribs
1474 all his ribs in his
4032 they roar their ribs out!
7483 Under the ribs of death

rice
6226 up the rice in the

rich
110 happy to be rich, I'm
789 anomaly to rich people: it
1248 haste to be rich shall not
1271 n: a rich (and
2157 you aren't rich, you
2243 The rich are the scum of
3126 And I am rich with
3513 the very rich. They are
3608 forbids the rich as well as
3681 are like a rich father who
4153 And passing rich with forty
4192 poor, and rich men rule
5377 surer, The rich get rich
5568 save the few who are rich.
6014 and the riche,
7832 I am rich beyond the
7863 Rich and rare were the
8598 that of the rich for
8611 genius, a rich man cannot
9196 If the rich could hire
9252 The rich would have to eat
9736 ourselves a rich nation,
9926 When the rich wage war
10301 but to be rich; And,
10849 we could be rich and not
10931 Isn't it rich? Are we a
11637 to marry a rich woman as a
11776 A man is rich in
11992 to become rich, so that I
12650 they are rich or poor,

richer
1907 Becomes the richer still, tho
8124 the rich richer and the

riches
140 des richesses The
392 better than riches To scratch
685 Riches are a good handmaid,
708 Riches are for spending.
1411 Riches do not consist in the
3754 Riches enlarge, rather than
6645 gives riches to those
7007 Infinite riches in a
7492 and see her riches, and
7561 admire That riches grow in
11322 looked upon riches to be a

richesse
6652 mor than gold or gret richesse.

richest
11752 That man is richest whose

rid
4544 Will no one rid me of this
10943 indeed am I rid of it all
11101 Which shall rid us from

ridden
6347 and ridden out of
6639 the less have ridden there.

riddle
2271 The riddle of the sands.
2312 It is a riddle wrapped in
5808 can make a riddle out of an
8898 jest, and riddle of the

riddles
2399 .. Riddles lie here,
6206 'I'm bad at riddles; But I

ride
351 from the ride With the
2488 And people ride in a hole
7015 a king, And ride in triumph
7203 you cannot ride two horses
7432 Ride on, ride on in

7433 Ride on, ride on in
11102 the Haggards ride no more.
12182 just hang on for the ride.

rider
11295 between a rider and his

ridiculed
9987 first it is ridiculed, in the

ridiculous
117 of the ridiculous, but no
2487 some men ridiculous, but
4262 the Sublime To the Ridiculous.'
5364 that it makes men ridiculous.
6818 so ridiculous as the
6890 of the ridiculous, the
7160 will only make him ridiculous.
7659 himself, Made arms ridiculous.
8081 the sublime to the ridiculous.
8470 and the ridiculous are often
8824 Alive, ridiculous, and dead
9105 be certain is to be ridiculous.

riding
1367 was spent riding at
12443 life In riding to and

rifle
5756 on your rifle and blow
8446 stuttering rifles' rapid

rift
11508 the little rift within the

right
148 Only if it's done right.
311 going to turn out all right.
402 who is right - only who
839 wrong than weakly right.
1282 has a good right to them.
1667 - All's right with the
1903 exactly in the right places.
2209 is wrong, everyone is right.
2232 all he does is right.
2254 is all right; it is the
2290 fight; Ulster will be right.
2390 rather be right than he
2608 and then be right by chance.
2698 are really right or not
2731 be in the right; but our
3165 prove me right; a single
3179 hundredth time I am right.
3217 To be right in great and
4870 The right to be heard does
4928 do what is right, on
4937 may be right, and a
4964 I mean the right to do
5062 what's right isn't the
5101 man has a right to utter
5724 - of - them - is - right!
6341 right of
6367 have the right to rise up
6700 o' bein' richt That damns
6817 by the right of an
7952 man of the right. My
8144 to say the right thing in
8268 people's right to change
8496 claim our right as women,
8525 man has a right to fix the
8833 The Right Divine of Kings
8897 'Whatever IS, IS RIGHT'.
9338 will be the right of all, so
9404 has the right to
9994 My country, right or wrong;
10909 It is never right to do
11050 He is not right wing, nor
11386 he has a right not only
11392 make a right, but they
11416 putting the right men in the
11901 inalienable right, to govern
11964 what is right and what
12346 greatest right in the
12445 people are right more than
12671 But the right is more
12679 being so right that it

righteous
1176 to call the righteous, but
1376 seen the righteous forsaken,
8024 mists of righteous

righteousness
1170 and his righteousness; and all
12388 Hail, the Sun of Righteousness!

righting
6444 good for righting wrongs,

rights
442 Men their rights and nothing
784 ours, three rights - the
1049 Natural rights is simple
2462 equal rights with men.
3018 duties as well as its rights.
3158 We will our rights in
4496 things to rights have no
4879 is a denial of human rights.
4983 of civil rights struggles
5022 they derive rights inherent
6989 up for your rights Get up,
7282 is not rights, but
9509 inalienable rights of man is
11054 his sexual rights. Our

rimbauds
8505 he was always chasing Rimbauds.

rind
7459 out the rind of one

ring
789 do not ring the bell.
1440 With this Ring I thee wed,
2652 pierced the outer ring.
6155 Your ring?' Said
7347 not get the ring without
8432 a stone, a ring is worn
11577 Ring out the old, ring in
11817 One Ring to rule them all,
12063 a great ring of pure
12222 They now ring the bells,

rings
2010 postman always rings twice.
8776 bell never rings of itself;

rinky-dink
6893 little rinky-dink of a voice

riot
5653 A riot is at bottom the
11463 He did not riot, he got on

ripe
10116 to hour, we ripe and ripe,

ripen
3396 then bear fruit, then ripen.

ripeness
10332 coming hither: Ripeness is all.

rise
1539 resistible rise of Arturo
2386 thrive Must rise at five;
5270 set, may rise again; But
6367 right to rise up and
8593 floor Can rise alone and
10193 deeds will rise, Though
11599 man's: they rise or sink
12124 Rise up from my dead

risen
1037 having once risen, remained

riser
4807 be an early riser may sleep

rising
683 All rising to great places

risk
1691 runs the risk of
4832 without the risk.
5213 at risk from the
5406 got to risk your life
6121 is when you risk your life
6695 equals risk plus
6866 a proxy for risk and a

risks
5575 There are risks and costs
10017 with noble risks, is worth
11147 one of the risks he takes.

ritz
7155 all - like the Ritz Hotel.

rivalry
35 of thought, a rivalry of aim.

river
624 a sort of river of passing
4059 which the river winds.
4404 Ol' man river, dat ol' man
5618 even when there is no river.
8152 The river of death has

river-rounded
4756 rook-racked, river-rounded.

rivers
1205 All the rivers run into the
3046 brooks make rivers, rivers
7762 and like rivers grow cold.

road
1827 a weary road, To
2238 There is a road from the
2755 is a road leading
2826 wild night and a new road.
5742 shut the road through
6056 end of the road, Keep
7134 One road leads to London,
7292 And one more for the road.
7723 Long is the road from
7894 road policy.
8091 the ads, And not the road.
8909 no private road, But looks
11190 And the road below me.
11710 expeditious road To pack
11873 There is no road to wealth

roads
1333 straight roads; but the

roam
2612 sent to roam Excels a
4189 Where'er I roam, whatever
4190 where'er we roam, His
8587 we may roam, Be it
10835 abroad to roam; Sated

roaming
6060 Roamin' in the gloamin', On

roar
2324 upon to give the roar.
3739 your will roar when your
4032 and they roar their ribs

roareth
4071 this that roareth thus? Can

rob
3473 that is, to rob a lady of
4361 men, Some rob you with a
5245 nightly rob the dairy.
6802 he might rob a

robbed
8149 'Ye have robbed,' said he,
8175 once we've robbed a couple
10922 When you've robbed a man of

robbery
1506 the benefit of the robbery.

robbing
1541 What is robbing a bank
2783 little of robbing; and from

robin
1326 A robin red breast in a

robs
10430 good name Robs me of that
10595 which robs Peter to

rock
2152 till you can find a rock.
3122 drugs and rock and roll.
7388 upon solid rock the ugly
11837 Rock of Ages, cleft for
12722 enfabled rock, that ship
12959 Rock journalism is people

rock'n'roll
6220 go first - rock'n'roll or

rocket
3187 every rocket fired
8473 rose like a rocket, he fell
12530 that rocket the mind;

rockies
3897 In time the Rockies may

rockpile
1597 in the hard rockpile labour of

rocks
4561 over but the rocks remain.
9513 These rocks won't lose

rod
1238 spareth his rod hateth his
6440 The rod, which is the

rode
11475 of Death Rode the six
11487 Then she rode forth,
11521 He rode between

rodents
11238 of certain rodents, no other

rogue
3047 that is not fool is rogue.
7304 A dainty rogue in

rogues
9032 keep them rogues and

role
10 has not yet found a role.
2723 The role of a retired

roll
3122 drugs and rock and roll.

rollin'
4404 jus' keeps rollin', He jus'

rolls
12797 And rolls through

roman
2258 Before the Roman came to
2362 I am a Roman citizen.
3901 in the Roman world,
3919 of the Roman empire.
4639 deceased Roman Empire,
9016 Like the Roman, I seem to
10062 The Roman Conquest was,
10149 A Roman thought hath struck
10296 the moon, Than such a Roman.
12154 the Holy Roman Empire was

romance
589 than any romance, however
646 she learned romance as she
1077 love and romance, Let's
2142 historical romance is the
2557 any more. Romance is much
5518 symbols of a high romance.
10900 Romance without finance is no
12553 of a lifelong romance.
12607 years of romance make a

romances
11271 Are like romances read, or

romans
4510 The Romans would never have
6841 sold: The Romans were like
6843 To whom the Romans pray, A

romantic
4005 ruin that's romantic; Do you
6145 of all romantic poets
9468 much more romantic I'd be But
11252 part with romantic' music.

romanticism
12928 Romanticism is the expression of

rome
613 Rome has spoken; the case
1009 decadent Rome, has
1416 Bishop of Rome hath no
5238 voice of Rome. CATO:
5366 in Rome has its
8808 the grandeur that was Rome.
10147 Let Rome in Tiber melt,
10288 but that I loved Rome more.
11453 you are at Rome, live in
12201 Rome, though her eagle

romeo
10473 O Romeo, Romeo! wherefore

roof
12634 a hot tin roof? - I wish

roofs
12510 over the roofs of the

rookery
9052 that cawing rookery of

rooks
11556 away, The rooks are blown

room
2952 one little room an
4323 need a room of their
4334 I left the room with
5991 men can find room for.
6723 time the room smiled,
9613 There is no room in this
10741 How little room Do we take
12319 is always room at the
12756 money and a room of her own

roosevelt
4208 If Roosevelt were alive he'd

roost
7407 birds came home to roost.
10958 always come home to roost.

rooster
9247 even your rooster will lay
9266 and the rooster keeps

root
1192 is the root of all
4998 is the root of all
7083 mossy root, Casting
8475 axe to the root, and teach
9215 leaves return to the root.
10341 the insane root That takes
12883 many, the root is one;

rootage
12682 A man's rootage is more

rooted
11503 His honour rooted in

roots
2140 of these is roots, the
3202 gratitude - roots that can
4558 is destroying his roots.
9541 in their roots, All

rose
1575 An English unofficial rose.
1674 with impunity a rose.
1833 a red, red rose That's
2074 is past, the fading rose;
5430 As though a rose should
6783 surpass, A rose without a
7037 dropping a rose petal down
7157 to paint a rose, because
7592 and without thorn the rose.
7865 the last rose of summer
8515 dies the rose, Buds the
8795 upon the rose And in the
9046 that, says Rose, I'll die:
9237 who wants a rose must
9585 not the rose That this
10160 the blown rose may they
10335 desire a rose Than wish
10474 we call a rose By any
11014 the rose, whilst
11082 Rose is a rose is a rose
12200 Go, lovely rose! Tell her,
12806 is the rose, The moon
12906 inviolate Rose, Enfold me

rosebud
11544 rose of the rosebud garden of

rosebuds
4592 Gather ye rosebuds while ye

rosemary
10227 There's rosemary, that's for

roses
1663 It was roses, roses, all
2907 of wine and roses: Out of a
5063 me it smells like roses.
6178 like roses over the
7011 beds of roses And a
7089 But so with roses overgrown,
7090 without, roses within.
7103 two dozen roses to Room
7853 of the roses will hang
9631 Oh roses for the flush of
10929 coming up roses.
11197 and not a bed of roses.
12311 Roses are flowering in

rosewater
1723 are not made with rosewater.

rot
8662 virtue and rot for having
8900 propagate, and rot.
10116 to hour, we rot and rot:
10381 obstruction and to rot.

rotted
8092 late, Or simply rotted early?

rotten
10197 is rotten in the
10391 apple rotten at the
10775 up or goes rotten. But
12920 good feel rotten.

rottenness
5031 office, a rottenness begins in
9405 of the rottenness of our

rough
4775 going gets rough, remember
7783 demands a rough and thorny
10999 who were rough And who

rough-hew
10230 our ends, Rough-hew them how

roughest
10343 runs through the roughest day.

roughly
2115 Speak roughly to your little

roughness
718 fear, but roughness breedeth

roughnesses
2644 all these roughnesses, pimples,

round
3700 only way round is
11724 A little round, fat, oily
11785 that is round. Soon he

roundheads
10063 and the Roundheads (Right but

rouse
10038 Rouse the lion from his

rousseau
1082 Rousseau was the first

rout
6801 doth your rout send forth

routine
2175 third is routine. After
9333 Man's usual routine is to work

rovers
1104 us are Rovers and

roving
209 A roving! A-roving! Since
1993 no more a roving So late
1994 no more a roving By the
2954 Licence my roving hands, and

row
1905 We do but row, we are
3872 an oar and row with them.
9116 must row with the

rows
11616 Lovers' rows make love

royal
4675 There is no royal road to

royalties
528 fond of fresh air and royalties.

royalty
783 things our royalty is to be
2905 you come to Royalty you should
6875 the full glare of Royalty.
7120 in front of Royalty: but never

rub
9711 try to rub up against
10212 there's the rub; For in

rubbish
2982 deal of rubbish, and yet
8363 a lot of rubbish into it.
10949 was but the rubbish of an

rubies
1231 of wisdom is above rubies.

rubs
282 The hard rubs of the world
7191 that rubs you up the

rude
3792 rude as the
12599 never unintentionally rude.
12633 can stand a rude remark or

rudeness
4663 Rudeness is the weak man's

rudiments
10949 but the rudiments of

rudolph
6987 Rudolph, the Red-Nosed

rug
3629 snug As a bug In as rug.

rugged
1029 to the old rugged cross, And
4261 O'er the rugged mountain's
5097 is a rugged being.

ruin
652 her in endless ruin.
926 a bit of a ruin that

ruin
1991 earth with ruin - his
3883 boy will ruin himself in
5056 come to ruin most
6419 a bit of a ruin that
7582 With ruin upon ruin, rout
7820 can print no ruin-trace.
10970 others' ruins built To
11400 moderation, lead to ruin.
12607 look like a ruin; but

ruined
126 of gold has ruined fewer men
1042 has been ruined by
1792 that are ruined are ruined
2678 lives is ruined by our
7129 man may be ruined or made
7876 should be ruined at our own
12164 I never was ruined but twice

ruins
2993 Of all ruins that of a
10285 art the ruins of the

rule
260 can make a rule, and every
1724 Beneath the rule of men
2123 The rule is, jam tomorrow
2179 word, than to rule a state.
2337 make it a rule never to
2464 our dog Rule all
3159 The first rule of
5604 rule of any
7266 made it a rule never to
7342 to obey the more they rule.
7716 greatest rule of all
8226 and epochs, it is the rule.
8306 It's my rule never to lose
8495 is a major rule of
8849 gen'ral rule That every
8899 how to rule - Then
11250 for the rule change,
11292 infallible rule we know
11488 each man's rule, and
11541 one Who can rule and dare
11723 strain: Rule,
12714 is a good rule in life
12832 good old rule Sufficeth

ruled
9960 world is ruled only by

ruler
4924 not a ruler but the

rulers
1261 about by rulers, mostly
7123 are rulers who always
7218 Rulers have no authority

rules
365 the rules, his side
1242 and he that ruleth his spirit
4706 knows the rules but the
7486 false rules pranked in
8105 of mules there are no rules.
8391 disregard of all the rules.
9834 these sex rules for
9927 precedes and rules essence.
10025 Love rules the court, the
11105 of genius rules is by
12195 hand that rules the world.

ruling
8870 The ruling passion, be it
11046 of the ruling class,

rum
1956 calms As rum and true
11193 a bottle of rum! Drink and
12375 jest what a Rum Go

run
551 of woman I would run from.
1118 road. They get run down.
2463 it over and try to run it.
5594 It doesn't have to run.
6294 to run in
6376 trying to run away, it
6836 him to run, though
8562 have been run over by
8659 on the run? We are
10997 enough to run a factory
11039 baby, we were born to run.
11750 I should run for my

run-way
1097 beyond the run-way Where a

runcible
6153 He weareth a runcible hat.

running
2126 all the running you can do
2934 yesterday, Running it never
7779 in the running of a
8817 man who teaches running.

runs
257 fights and runs away, May

rural
4875 woman in a rural spot!

rush
11721 As we rush, as we rush in

rushed
9561 we have rushed through

russell
7744 me as you did my Lord Russell.

russia
1693 Russia can be an empire or a
2312 action of Russia. It is a
4134 you too, Russia, speeding
8190 Russia has two generals in
12015 Russia is the only country
12917 It is Russia's mission to be

russian
298 Intelligent Russian once
3269 nice: her Russian eye Is
3967 have been a Roosian, A French,
8134 out-manoeuvre a   Russian.
9312 A tumult in the Russian heart.

russians
11780 and the Russians' is that
11809 The Russians and the Americans

rust
69 away the rust of the
10951 aside To rust in peace,
12465 wear out than to rust out.

rustics
4158 the gazing rustics ranged

rut
11991 stick in a rut is

rutherford
11999 Margaret Rutherford is that

ruthful
6028 are not ruthful; To them

rye
1814 thro' the rye, Gin a
8605 When as the rye reach to

sabbath
1159 The sabbath was made for man,

sable-vested
7581 Sable-vested Night, eldest of

sabotage
12075 to a judicious use of sabotage.

sabrina
7487 Sabrina fair, Listen where

sack
10238 If sack and sugar be a

sacrament
2692 minor sacrament .. I am

sacred
8837 veils her sacred fires, And

sacrifice
3386 each sacrifice is made
3796 amount of sacrifice you are
5733 ancient Sacrifice, An humble
6411 pinnacle of Sacrifice, pointing
7173 will always sacrifice herself if
7433 see the approaching sacrifice.
7559 Of human sacrifice, and
11347 only make a sacrifice to God of

sacrificed
8461 patriots sacrificed their

sacrifices
1783 you, if he sacrifices it to your
3340 are made up of petty sacrifices.
4218 to offer sacrifices that are
7119 made such sacrifices during the
7183 him for the sacrifices he makes
9688 times, sacrifices were made
12207 or he who sacrifices an hundred

sad
1640 meet: How sad and bad

2590 something sad about the
2769 Sad winds where your
5794 is more sad than the
9243 every animal is sad.
9480 profoundly sad than he
9632 remember and be sad.
11117 This sad vicissitude of
11358 Villon, our sad bad glad ~
12513 For of all sad words of

saddens
1665 which saddens while it

sadder
1968 of woe, Sadder than

saddest
7280 The saddest life is that of a
9023 scenes Saddest this sight

saddling
10600 law is the saddling of the

sadistic
9776 to our sadistic impulses.

sadness
9542 inexorable sadness of
11479 there be no sadness of

safe
301 it was safe to go back
530 from the safe comfort of
1494 in public - you feel safe.
2792 is like a safe to which
3584 We are none of us safe.
7883 see me safe up, and my
8273 Safe taste is bad taste.
8439 busy, and you will be safe.

safeguard
11220 the surest safeguard against

safeguards
3621 that the safeguards of liberty

safely
8435 go most safely by the

safer
5539 It is much safer to be in a
6859 It is much safer for a

safest
3593 it is the safest thing we

safety
10237 we pluck this flower, safety.
10258 for a pot of ale, and safety.
12120 is to expect no safety.

safety-pin
221 for the big safety-pin at the top

sagacity
9707 who gains sagacity in youth,

sage
8526 you homely, make you sage.
9903 most foolish woman, a sage.

sages
9340 into sages and cranks
12840 Than all the sages can.

said
66 might be said on both
2287 so very little said.
2552 I never said ever did
3015 things are said over
3618 you heard, not what I said.
3966 himself has said it, And
4475 that they have been said.
5538 to know who said this or
7393 After all's said and done,
8530 is not be said that I
10089 what I have said, I envy
11164 I have said what I meant
11331 as well said, as if I
11618 yet been said that's not
11987 - when he said a good

sail
3380 to be old, To take in sail.
7135 the white sail's shaking,
8148 him when ye sail to meet
12452 I liked to sail alone.

sailor
2808 the lass that loves a sailor!
11136 an old sailor, Drunk and
11738 is the best sailor who can

sailors
8143 We are like sailors who must
12202 Vexed sailors curse the rain

sails
167 which sails well, but
3419 God batters at its sails.
7134 To the white dipping sails.
10155 Purple the sails, and so

saint
7679 espousèd saint Brought to
8372 that a saint must
8609 No one, except a saint.
8919 madmen is a saint run mad.
9998 in order to be a saint.

saintly
7496 Whose saintly visage is

saints
4724 against the saints who deny
4957 most of the saints were poor,
8394 Saints should always be
11189 The Saints are the Sinners

sake
10054 their own sakes, for

salad
4175 Garrick's a salad; for in
5060 shit from chicken salad.
10154 My salad days, When I was

salary
3912 he had a salary to
11795 yearly salary, double

salesman
7402 A salesman is got to dream,

salieri
846 Mozart and Salieri we see the

salisbury
3981 crossing Salisbury Plain on a
5050 blank cheque to Lord Salisbury.

sallows
5411 the river sallows, borne

sally
2076 like pretty Sally, She is

salmon-fishers
7066 But now the salmon-fishers moist

salt
1165 Ye are the salt of the
8784 of a grain of salt.
8786 Sal Atticum. Attic salt.
11424 yeast, salt and
12414 having salt rubbed

salt water
11260 is like salt water, good to

salutary
8494 for the salutary in the

salute
197 it moves, salute it; if it
281 are about to die salute you.
1921 awake! Salute the happy
11275 about to die salute you.

salvation
612 There is no salvation outside
5643 Human Salvation lies in the
8610 his happiness and his salvation.
9374 bottle of salvation, My gown
10609 Wot prawce Selvytion nah?
12855 An idea is salvation by

samaritan
11654 the Good Samaritan if he'd

samarkand
3540 the Golden Road to Samarkand.

samarra
6555 with him tonight in Samarra.

same
656 he is much the same'.
2126 keep in the same place. If
2586 exactly the same with
3745 are seldom the same man.
4537 things don't seem the same.
5394 the more they are the same.
5978 Same old slippers, Same
6455 them I'm having the same.
7232 we must all say the same .
9223 are not the same thing.
9456 all look just the same.

9844 dislike the same things,
12369 tastes the same after

samson
7670 Samson hath quit himself

sanctifies
16 the office sanctifies the holder

sanction
3620 in its moral sanctions.
9878 is the only sanction of life;

sanctuary
822 which need sanctuary more than

sand
410 It produces lies like sand.
7388 palace built upon the sand!
9943 is a house built upon sand.
10096 grain of sand in your

sandals
7825 topses, Sandals were for
9181 wears out a thousand sandals.

sandalwood
7127 peacocks, Sandalwood,

sands
2271 The riddle of the sands.
6503 on the sands of time.

sandwiches
1504 freedom and sandwiches they will

sane
10610 that no sane person
11662 shall be sane, Though

sang
11666 Though I sang in my

sanguine
983 But many sanguine people
4052 by those sanguine

sanity
3290 It it's sanity you're after
3372 Sanity is very rare; every
10645 be achieved by brute sanity.

sank
5565 They sank my boat.
7139 Sighted sub, sank same.

sans
3508 to lie, Sans wine, sans

santa claus
3458 as old as Santa Claus to a girl

sarcasm
2891 is not sarcasm, and that

sardines
1036 a tin of sardines - we are

saskatchewan
6136 wheat' and Saskatchewan was born.

sat
2611 You have sat too long
2660 has sat except a
4368 person who has sat on him!

satan
1180 Get thee behind me, Satan.
7565 capital Of Satan and his
7576 indignation Satan stood
7613 Satan, so call him now, his
11966 may not pay Satan reverence,
12286 For Satan finds some

satanic
1348 these dark Satanic mills?

satiety
699 occasion of satiety, maketh

satire
3638 undeserving is severe satire.
5225 it's satire, But when
5397 Satire is what closes
7756 Satire should, like a
7848 vice as satire is to vent
9964 rebirth of satire, of
11303 Satire is a sort of glass,
12944 a satire on today,

satirist
3910 The satirist may laugh, the
4624 What satirist ever toppled the
6675 A satirist is a man who

satisfaction
3311 a certain satisfaction in coming
3469 no genuine satisfaction in life
3844 to give you satisfaction - if you

4832 subtle satisfaction without
6306 than any other satisfaction.
11276 When the satisfaction or the

satisfactory
354 the key to a satisfactory marriage.

satisfied
2305 I am easily satisfied with the
3875 animal that is never satisfied.
4494 man is satisfied with his
5787 to be satisfied with too
8716 never satisfied with what
10157 hungry Where most she satisfied.
10860 since He is satisfied, so am I.
11880 would be satisfied with her
12480 ten are satisfied, he is
12861 Never satisfied with

satisfy
11436 it must satisfy criteria
12769 That poorly satisfy our eyes,

satisfying
2490 be a wholly satisfying link

saturday
2928 Empire on a Saturday night
5397 is what closes Saturday night
8093 at home on Saturday night and

satyr
8727 either a stoic or a satyr.

satyrs
7001 men, like satyrs grazing on

sauce
8800 the sweet sauce of labour.
9168 Hunger is the best sauce.

saucer
7746 The white saucer like some

sauces
12152 and only two sauces.

sauntering
2026 you can go sauntering along for

sausage
4559 looks at a sausage and thinks

savage
2346 A savage is simply a human
3036 woods the noble savage ran.
3646 untutored savage
7040 As savage as a bear with a
10649 The savage bows down to
11533 take some savage woman, she

savaged
4500 Like being savaged by a dead

savagely
12142 they are fighting so savagely.

savages
2890 were brutal savages in an

save
580 To save your world you
707 time is to save time.
1927 And all, save the spirit
2967 Beauty will save the world.
3159 is to save all the
8748 England has saved herself
11459 It takes time to save time.
12103 God save me from my
12453 improve (or save) the world

saved
922 thieves was saved. (Pause)
2241 they only saved the world.
3946 will be saved by one or
6087 be spent, not to be saved.

saves
3582 the idea of death saves him.
9820 What saves a man is to take

saving
5070 you're saving your face

savings
7058 is past savings

saviour
1921 Whereon the Saviour of the
5750 But it's Saviour of 'is

savour
1165 lost his savour, wherewith
5919 Let us savour the swift

saw
2546 I never saw an ugly thing

3914 I saw and loved.
8458 I came, I saw, I
12366 I never saw so many
12680 No man ever saw a

saxon
6489 ancient Saxon phrase,

say
527 you have something to say.
2328 Say what you have to say
2480 nothing to say, say
2551 you don't say anything,
3134 could say something,
3199 nothing to say, abstains
3565 to decide is what to say.
3605 people say a foolish
4533 he has to say, not speak
5202 to find anything to say.
6518 you can't say something
8325 Say it with flowers.
8719 who has something to say.
9515 more to say when I am
10060 Preachers say, Do as I
10326 as we can say, 'This is
10796 little to say, and much
10885 You never say a word of
11403 like and say what you
11451 want of something to say.
12042 to say a thing
12139 of what you say, but I
12359 Latin; say what you
12427 you have to say something,

saying
5580 we'd been saying they were.
9901 every wise saying has an
11107 consist in saying what no
11112 has a fine saying for
12692 the art of saying nothing in

says
38 all he says, and yet
6675 and then says them about
9065 things one says from
10842 not what he says, but what
11104 man who says frankly

scabbard
2376 he threw away the scabbard.

scaffold
6581 on the scaffold, Wrong
8703 been from scaffold to

scalded
3755 The scalded cat fears even

scale
3501 The best scale for an
8825 her lifted scale, Where, in

scales
6793 practising scales, The notes

scallywag
790 Women love scallywags, but some

scalped
6802 and red men scalped each other

scan
8943 not God to scan: The

scandal
3446 There is no scandal like rags,
3477 Love and scandal are the best
3561 conquers scandal every
7736 is public scandal that
8682 public scandal is good
11600 have no scandal while you

scandalous
211 behave in a scandalous manner,

scandals
12921 and scandals In order

scar
1649 is oft a scar, They are

scarce
10458 world, scarce half made
11019 Is granted scarce to God

scare
4799 A good scare is worth more

scarecrow
10375 not make a scarecrow of the

scared
3707 afraid of like scared people.

8754 always been scared of you ,
9486 courage unless you're scared.

scarf
10357 night, Scarf up the

scarfs
8904 Scarfs, garters, gold, amuse

scarlet
985 sins were scarlet, but his
4737 loves a scarlet coat
5257 though clothed in scarlet.
10837 coats of scarlet, God bless

scars
4814 or diplomas, but for scars.
6821 with the scars of

scatter
2025 fields, and scatter The good
10695 Scatter, as from an

scatters
7514 lively din Scatters the rear

scene
4701 is the scene where
10118 Last scene of all, That
10254 behold the swelling scene.

scenery
5470 Scenery is fine - but human
9731 end of all natural scenery.

scenes
7175 behind the scenes. They are

scent
7853 But the scent of the

sceptic
4931 much of a sceptic to deny

scepticism
1074 lead to scepticism, pursued
3114 end with scepticism and
6557 A wise scepticism is the first
8163 scepticism of the
9921 only her scepticism kept her

sceptred
6003 avails the sceptred race! Ah,

scheme
9838 in the scheme of things

schemes
1832 best laid schemes o'mice an'

schizophrenia
568 of Canada is paranoid schizophrenia.
11393 to you, you have schizophrenia.

schlemiel
9189 The poor schlemiel is a man who

schmuck
2779 than a schmuck for a

scholar
6441 before a great scholar.
6820 rake among scholars, and a

school
744 goeth to school, and not
7662 was there school, But the
7792 is but a school of
7945 At school I never minded the
9829 he's been to a good school.
9873 only at school is an

schoolboy
6813 Every schoolboy knows who
8152 voice of a schoolboy rallies
11316 tell what every schoolboy knows.
11454 and every schoolboy knows it.
11635 than that of a schoolboy's tip?

schoolboys
8605 cream, And schoolboys playing in

schoolchildren
597 What all schoolchildren learn

schoolgirl
3987 Pert as a schoolgirl well can

schoolman
8862 he knew no schoolman's subtle

schoolmasters
1506 to some schoolmasters if they
4187 Let schoolmasters puzzle their
12729 Schoolmasters and parents exist to

schoolroom
444 In the schoolroom, more than any

schools
2144 three new schools of
3379 taught in schools are not an
4367 Our state schools were
5087 our great schools than
9574 The schools ain't what they
11326 the lumber of the schools.
11341 in the schools, That

science
132 shown, our science and
1088 Art is I, science is we.
1528 to disturb, science reassures.
1562 essence of science: ask an
2097 The Dismal Science.
2683 In science the credit goes to
2689 my opinion, science offers a
3109 much of science, and about
3138 Science is an edged tool,
3173 Science is the attempt to
3174 Science without religion is
3209 and investigated by science.
3869 as men of science fighting
4618 is the science of how who
4929 tragedy of Science: the
5529 Science may have found a cure
5610 A positive science may be
5821 fact that science, which can
6124 as the science of
8415 In science the credit goes to
8814 Science is built up of facts,
8829 the beams of science fall.
8949 Science must begin with
9022 Of science and logic he
9678 Science is for those who
9780 Science is what you know,
9794 All science is either physics
10898 Science is his forte, and
10983 Science is organized
11045 Science cannot stop while
11390 strong and science weak, men
11530 Science moves, but slowly
11743 and become men of science.
12028 Whenever science makes a
12034 is the science of what
12036 Science means simply the
12434 of nature, science the right
12484 A science which hesitates to
12597 is a science. If you
12826 Science appears but what in

sciences
763 must follow sciences, and not
8564 as applied sciences, only

scientific
1645 averred, A scientific faith's
3542 not very scientific, but it
4015 I know the scientific names of
5649 live. Our scientific power has
8751 A new scientific truth does not
12873 No scientific theory achieves

scientist
9339 between the scientist's laws and
12960 that the scientist who comes

scientists
11697 behavioural scientists .. least

scintillations
4234 Let the scintillations of your wit

scissors
4644 always end up using scissors.

scoff
1619 vices we scoff at in
4155 who came to scoff, remained

score
11787 kept the score Man wants

scorer
9464 One Great Scorer comes to

scorn
3972 virtuous scorn The
7529 mind) To scorn delights,
7631 the sound Of public scorn.
10547 That then I scorn to change
10652 perfect expression of scorn.
12833 Scorn not the Sonnet;

scorned
2513 a fury, like a woman scorned.

scotch
9119 A Scotch mist may wet an
10892 well into a Scotch

scotchman
5081 which a Scotchman ever sees,
5181 made of a Scotchman if he be

scotchmen
5937 to like Scotchmen, and am

scotland
5189 but in Scotland supports

scotsman
871 than a Scotsman on the

scott
9536 us up, Mr Scott. (usually

scoundrel
1335 plea of the scoundrel, hypocrite
5086 the last refuge of a scoundrel.
10625 man over forty is a scoundrel.
11322 given them to such a scoundrel.

scourge
9980 constant scourge of the

scouts
768 The scouts' motto is founded

scow
2860 - an old scow which

scratch
930 all you can do is scratch it.
6519 full. And scratch where it
6910 If you scratch a great
8500 Scratch a lover, and find a

scratching
6549 it but the scratching of a pen.

scream
9582 more thrilling than a scream.

screwing
6448 I gave up screwing around a

scribblative
10955 arts babblative and scribblative.

scribble
4551 Always scribble, scribble,
8922 scrawl, and scribble, to a man.

scripture
5910 texts of scripture, I got my

scrivener
5939 and cropt scrivener - one that

scrooge
2815 'Bah,' said Scrooge.

scrub
1449 and I couldn't scrub it out.
6672 a good scrub with a

scruple
10224 Some craven scruple Of

sculptor
1447 actor is a sculptor who carves
9729 not a great sculptor or painter

sculpture
1522 is inhabited sculpture.

scum
2243 are the scum of the
12362 of the scum of the

scuttled
9543 lives That scuttled under

scythe
7244 last year's scythes flung
12379 Time with a scythe of my own.

sea
204 And all the sea were ink,
367 The sea hath no king but
680 can see nothing but sea.
921 never an end for the sea.
1205 into the sea; yet the
2133 I am very much at sea.
2236 yet And the sea rises
2446 legs Upon the slimy sea.
2543 The sea - the truth must
3964 never go to sea, And you
4669 o'er the sea, We'll
4939 The sea possesses a power
5045 Love the sea? I dote
5047 and England is - the sea.
5096 or not having been at sea.
5326 snotgreen sea. The
5715 if Ye take away the sea!

5745 fed our sea for a
6510 of the sea? Only
7135 down to the sea again, to
7136 down to the sea again, for
7479 in the flat sea sunk ..
8346 The sea hates a coward!
9013 complaining about the sea.
9481 that of the sea, and to
9500 Poem of the Sea, steeped
9861 of a sea animal
10042 of the sea From
11372 of men, the sea. I will go
11480 wrinkled sea beneath
11673 Where no sea runs, the
11836 love the sea. The look
11848 till the sea itself
12452 alone. The sea was the

sea fight
8137 sure in a sea fight beyond all

sea-change
10486 suffer a sea-change Into

sea-down
11364 At the sea-down's edge

sea-shore
8179 on the sea-shore and

seagreen
2091 The seagreen Incorruptible.

seal
1983 The seal is not yet fixed

sealed
820 not yet u sealed. Were

seamen
6832 there were seamen in the

sear
10371 into the sear, the

search
1210 neither search the things
6270 the active search for Truth,
7834 world in search of what he
9067 perdu. In search of lost

searched
9564 to while you're being searched.

seas
3046 rivers, rivers run to seas.
3125 Seas have their source,
3775 troubled seas of
4561 vain: The seas roll over

seaside
6608 to the seaside, is said

season
1206 there is a season, and a
5410 Season of mists and mellow
10335 thing that in season grows.

season-ticket
164 has held a season-ticket on the

seasoned
11154 I am now seasoned enough to

seasons
3443 like seasons of the
5442 Four seasons fill the measure
7311 'I play for Seasons; not
7492 vernal seasons of the
12516 A man for all seasons.

seat
3116 to the seat of the
12180 the seat of the

seatbelts
2706 your seatbelts. It's

seated
5243 to sleep, Seated in thy
5599 wiser when he was seated.

seats
1453 bought two or three seats.

seawards
7134 leads me seawards To the

second
3523 are no second acts in
5576 settle for second, that's
9653 to hear it a second time.

second-rate
933 so many second-rate ones of
4763 up with poets being second-rate.

secrecy
1331 divine, And Secrecy the human
3871 Where secrecy reigns,

secret
727 parents are secret, and so
973 it ceases to be a secret.
1370 of a man a secret is an ugly
2821 Secret, and self-contained,
3644 A secret in the Oxford
5521 God, The secret of the
5632 is the Tory's secret weapon.
6491 apart; The secret
7736 to sin in secret is not to
8218 me! The secret of reaping
8338 The secret of business is to
8561 With secret trembling,
8567 you the secret that has
9146 is so burdensome as a secret.
10822 your secret, wrap it
11295 There is no secret so close
11816 A new road, or a secret gate.
11871 secret of
11997 is a secret you don't
12150 The secret of being a bore
12005 Be secret and exult, Because

secretary
11152 We hear the Secretary of State

secretive
11385 private, secretive activity.

secrets
2631 Secrets with girls, like
3054 For secrets are edged tools,
4256 of secrets. Their
4504 as full of secrets from
6122 and tawdry secrets, is the
7277 so many secrets, we cease
8569 learned the secrets of the
9545 My secrets cry aloud. I have
10370 will discharge their secrets.
11451 of secrets; for there
11891 tells its secrets in a

sect
10681 that great sect, Whose

secure
642 may secure all the
2870 can be long secure without a
10674 stain He is secure, and now
12321 past, at least, is secure.

security
13 amount of security enjoyed by
6587 a sense of security in an old
8736 Our watchword is security.
8947 only for security, if for no
11276 or the security of another

sedge
5453 The sedge has

seduced
7234 from a seduced

seducer
3037 Thou strong seducer,

seductive
12453 were merely seductive, that

see
212 man can see much
458 would see if I
536 had better wait and see.
1070 complain we cannot see.
1166 they may see your good
1813 To see her is to love
1828 gie us To see oursels as
1950 The more I see of men,
2180 him that all men see.
2387 is that you see yourself
2504 can't go to see somebody.
2992 You see, but you do not
3078 what you see that is
3365 People only see what they
3433 that I see but the
3439 you do not see in the
3579 till I see what I
4576 Thee to see, And what
5057 See everything: overlook
5630 shall never see A poem
6610 you see, whichever
8030 gie us to see some
8807 All that we see or seem Is

8939 wise, And see thro' all
9123 as those who won't see.
9643 I do not see them here;
9751 a world one will not see.
10330 politician, seem To see
10395 cannot see The pretty
10858 or to see themselves
11797 not stay; I see a hand you
12411 and see me?"
12859 learn to see what
12876 you last see your

seed
2025 The good seed on the
10713 The seed ye sow, another
11628 is the seed of the

seed-time
6593 Ought I to regret my seed-time?

seeds
10249 in their seeds And weak

seeing
3756 Seeing's believing, but
5122 Worth seeing, yes; but not
9175 Seeing's believing - but
9741 one way of seeing them, and
9881 in seeing things as

seek
890 Do not seek to follow in
1170 Seek ye first the kingdom
1172 given you; seek, and ye
1210 Seek not out the things
3853 alone I seek to please.
8352 We seek him here, we seek
8463 than to seek them out.
8546 would not seek me if you
8709 I do not seek. I find.
9345 am going to seek a great
11190 Wealth I seek not, hope
12864 did me seek With naked

seekers
9225 among seekers after the

seeking
10115 i' the sun, Seeking the food

seem
8179 what I may seem to the

seemed
7612 All seemed well pleased, all

seen
107 if you've seen one city
3072 see and be seen, in heaps
3075 but neither seen nor heard.
5093 not having seen what it is
8158 whom our has never seen.
8181 If I have seen further it
8406 but must be seen to be
8714 about what he has seen.
9862 what is seen during a
11395 has seen and
11694 I have not seen, I have no
12491 when you've seen one
12618 The less seen, the more

sees
2577 woman never sees what we do
5754 Thing as he sees it for the
7806 A wise man sees as much as
8612 what one sees. Above

segregation
12192 Segregation now, segregation

seize
5250 Was made to seize on vice,

seldom
5984 we knew how seldom they did.
10234 when they seldom come, they

select
3348 by what he selects as by
5477 Not a select party.
10681 one should select Out of the

self
720 is a man's self'.
1062 the not self that there
5916 The divided self.
6633 me the great Pope, Self.
8545 The self is hateful.
11095 is fear of one's self.

self-abuse
2789 is the worst form of self-abuse.

self-acceptance
11302 success is successful self-acceptance.

self-command
3373 Self-command is the main elegance.

self-confidence
5198 Self-confidence is the first

self-contained
12508 are so placid and self-contained.

self-defeating
90 is always self-defeating to pretend

self-defence
6988 it was in self-defence I shot the

self-denial
6283 that air of self-denial that

self-discipline
5980 It is self-discipline and
6333 of previous years of self-discipline.

self-enjoyment
12652 do - their self-enjoyment is

self-esteem
1588 to our self-esteem as to find
4655 is a crisis in self-esteem.

self-evident
9987 it is regarded as self-evident.

self-expression
6727 Self-expression is for babies and

self-government
7938 not a substitute for self-government.

self-hate
8424 as chiefly projected self-hate.

self-imposed
4980 the rest is self-imposed by failing

self-indulgence
3800 limits to self-indulgence, none to
7173 her favourite form of self-indulgence.

self-love
8906 And bade self-love and social

self-made
4410 A self-made man may prefer a
11064 A self-made man is one who

self-mastery
8205 substitute for self-mastery.

self-pity
1023 rare as a man without self-pity.

self-possession
8493 lose his self-possession when he is

self-protection
7366 of their number, is self-protection.

self-punishment
830 Hatred is self-punishment.

self-reproach
12574 luxury in self-reproach. When we

self-respect
4600 Self-respect is the root of

self-restraint
3800 none to self-restraint.

self-reverence
11604 Self-reverence, self-knowledge,

self-same
7525 nursed upon the self-same hill.

self-slain
11365 As a god self-slain on his own

self-slaughter
10189 'gainst self-slaughter! O God! O

self-sufficing
12825 much, The self-sufficing power of

selfish
654 have been a selfish being all
6693 mean selfish women who
11196 slack and selfish, and

selfishness
4462 Selfishness is one of the

sell
413 enough to sell the stuff.
5860 Never sell the bear's skin
6886 man will we sell, or deny,
8012 it high, sell it cheap.
10538 a week? Or sells eternity

selling
6732 Selling one's body
11168 lives by selling something.

selves
4665 with their own selves.
9543 my several selves Come
12744 or seven selves, whereas a

seminary
3989 Come from a ladies' seminary.

senate
2860 The U.S. Senate - an old
6678 The Senate is the last

senator
5064 States Senator, and a

send
5068 about to send American
5265 ears, and send them
6576 God'll send the bill to
11251 I could send everyone

senescence
8102 Senescence begins And middle age

senility
8314 Retirement: statutory senility.

senior
9385 time his senior years are

seniors
6553 in and the seniors take none

sensation
1948 of life is sensation, to feel
2822 only true sensation that men
3991 the sensation of a
5469 a life of sensations rather
12274 very same sensation When

sensational
12561 something sensational to read in

sense
117 have a fine sense of the
857 Books make sense of life.
945 the common sense of the
1074 men back to common sense.
1686 good sense and good
2129 care of the sense and the
2785 Common sense is the best
5894 common sense except to
6053 Common sense is in medicine
6423 Common Law to Common Sense!
6725 o' the wee bit sense he had.
7179 a sixth sense without
7251 loses his sense of
7264 sports hates common sense.
7316 To Beauty, Common Sense.
7946 but common sense, and
8350 of crude sense which no
9381 To demand 'sense' is the
9451 until it makes sense.
9521 disease and want of sense.
9618 of decency is want of sense.
10436 wives have sense like them.
10888 regulated by good sense.
11077 lose their common sense.
11157 Let's talk sense to the
12797 thoughts; a sense sublime Of

senseless
3286 about until one is senseless.
4908 completely senseless. But

senses
7771 the finer senses of the
12382 all their senses to

sensibility
9406 pattern informed by sensibility.
9879 to overestimate his sensibility.

sensible
2881 Sensible men are
3374 No sensible person ever made
8779 is enough for a sensible man.

sensitive
4664 and less sensitive than they

sensory
8182 were in his Sensory, sees the

sensual
5185 the only sensual pleasure
5489 Not to the sensual ear, but,

sent
267 is with sighing sent.

sentence
2043 A single sentence will suffice
2518 a life sentence in the

3342 force of a sentence whether a
7057 is not a word but a sentence.
7567 My sentence is for open war:
8779 A sentence is enough for a
8914 soon the sentence sign, And
11757 like that a sentence should
12486 Not a sentence or a word is

sentenced
12640 all of us sentenced to

sentiment
3796 value of a sentiment is the
7125 others the sentiment which he

sentimental
4008 Then a sentimental passion of a
4320 mythology of sentimental postures.
5191 no leisure for sentimental sorrow.

sentimentalist
12596 A sentimentalist is simply one who
12890 The sentimentalist himself;

sentimentality
7191 Sentimentality is only sentiment

sentiments
5155 quiet interchange of sentiments.
8242 of great sentiments that makes
11644 Them's my sentiments!

sentinel
4197 is scarce worth the sentinel.
7019 heaven, As sentinels to warn

separate
1584 hundreds of separate people
4823 it is to separate the wheat
7174 on they can separate, but if

separately
3639 we shall all hang separately.

separateness
3683 of their separateness; I'm

separates
1698 for what separates men rather

separation
1877 bear the separation, but I
9338 for a separation, amicably
10738 Anon came separation, by

separatism
3721 Separatism is a very healthy

sepulchre
2375 the living sepulchre of life.

sequel
114 and the sequel and the
646 the natural sequel of an

sequestered
4294 the cool sequestered vale of

seraphim
7537 And sworded seraphim Are seen

serene
12818 with eye serene The very

serenity
317 is little serenity comparable
3619 apparent serenity of the
8204 give us serenity to accept
8967 Sympathy, and Serenity.

serge
7095 of my blue serge suit."

serious
655 is a very serious business.
2285 A joke's a very serious thing.
2393 War is too serious a matter
2763 are too serious a matter
3601 to look serious; because
4352 to be serious, but you
4468 for serious minds, a
4940 Murder is a serious business.
10570 much more serious than that.
12017 a funny way of being serious.

serious-minded
7778 their most serious-minded activity.

seriousist
2791 with the word seriousist.

seriously
4870 the right to be taken seriously.
6161 of life seriously, if you

sermon
1515 the Sermon on the
8617 whole world than any sermon.

8626 honest and painful sermon.
9346 hearing a sermon or praying
10633 in the Sermon on the

sermons
1970 Laughter Sermons and
10112 brooks, Sermons in stones,

serpent
1220 The serpent beguiled me, and
4513 is at once apple and serpent.
7547 infernal serpent; he it
7620 The serpent subtlest beast of
10153 'Where's my serpent of old
10665 not be a serpent to sting

servant
357 and love, servant of parted
2760 poses as the servant.
4263 said, 'Your servant's cut in
7614 Servant of God, well done,
10181 Every good servant does not
10600 become the servant of a man.
10784 a civil servant. He was
10807 he is the servant of the
11812 is born to be a servant.

servants
718 are thrice servants; servants
864 equality in the servants' hall.
1322 people's servants. Forget
1493 there are servants to do the
6275 are good servants, but bad
12106 The servants will do

serve
55 but once to serve our
1169 No man can serve two
1944 A man must serve his time
5323 I will not serve that in
6607 Lord, to serve Thee as
7558 hell, than serve in heaven.
7610 Freely we serve, Because we
7678 They also serve who only
7829 We also serve who only
10000 and found how to serve.
10847 set out to serve both God
12345 Those who serve a cause are
12831 act, and serve the future

served
10272 Had I but served my God with
12735 Had I but served God as

serves
12177 Whoever serves his country

service
3178 to his service to them.
5658 my greatest service is in the
8472 from the service of their
8687 of no possible service to him.
8823 at the service of the
10951 constant service, thrown
11037 the service of my
11104 is doing a public service.

services
1446 worth more than his services.
2884 Great services are not
12464 Of all services which can

serving
10907 duly and daily serving him.

serving-men
5707 six honest serving-men (They

servitors
7455 and airy servitors trip about

sesame
456 Open Sesame!

sessions
10548 When to the sessions of sweet

setting
4496 are fond of setting things to

settle
3623 war never settles anything.
5576 going to settle for
5712 less will you settle to one.
6780 do was to settle up these

settled
10746 ever gets settled in this

settlements
4988 In small settlements everyone

settlers
6264 When old settlers say 'One has
12444 but the settlers give it

seven
370 a thing seven years and
661 The Seven Year Itch.
2850 be there at seven and get
3617 they are seven and anyone
3973 lowly air Of Seven Dials.
5226 Seven hours to law, to
6190 Seven years is about the
10117 His acts being seven ages.

seventeen
11683 Seventeen and never been sweet

seventies
11191 into his seventies his

seventy
440 you are seventy, nearly
4721 To be seventy years young is

sever
691 and sever it wholly
10683 ill Which severs those it

severe
2071 nothing but herself severe.
4156 A man severe he was, and
5624 little too severe - like

severed
7629 cannot be severed, we are

severity
718 Severity breedeth fear, but

sew
1621 We sew, sew,

sewer
4486 of a common sewer, either
6192 is like a sewer. What you
7709 through a sewer in a
12189 through a sewer in a

sewing
1590 the job of sewing on a

sex
140 Is sex dirty? Only if
150 it It's sex with
151 that sex is a
156 the answer, sex raises
161 Once sex rears its ugly
444 of sex, if there
662 Delia, if S-E-X ever rears
809 like sex, you
859 you darling after sex.
1746 know about sex and how
2490 Sex ought to be a wholly
2557 with sex that sex
2569 Sex is the great amateur
2651 to have sex - men just
2675 place of sex in my
2930 money, it's sex. When you
3122 Sex and drugs and rock
3611 between sex for money
3770 about sex, because I
4347 apart and started sex.
4555 money and sex appeal,
4791 Sex is like petrol. It's
4861 of the same sex or of a
6081 we have sex in the
6108 said about sex, it cannot
6307 Thus each sex regards
6446 having sex and not
6448 that sex is a
6673 Battles and sex are the
6866 risk and a dummy for sex.
7023 give up on sex, sex does
7354 people have sex life; the
7418 Sex is one of the nine
7849 another form of safe sex.
8122 in the sex
8313 Sex - the poor man's
9490 friendship, sex and death.
9834 Sex is something I really
9937 is another name for sex.
10762 than passion or even sex.
10939 isn't sex but death.
11385 sex has been a
12190 is like sex. When
12239 be a substitute for sex.

sexes
2494 within the sexes than

4649 says two sexes aren't
10874 are three sexes - men,
12865 have three sexes: men,

sexless
12628 is an emotion for the sexless.

sexton
4738 told the sexton, and The

sexual
3661 unnatural sexual behaviour
4238 Of all sexual aberrations,
4310 called the sexual life' the
6289 Sexual revolution has
11054 idea of his sexual rights.

sexually
276 Life is a sexually transmitted

shackles
1012 than to be in shackles.
4142 from the shackles and
9675 everywhere he is in shackles.

shades
4151 crowns in shades like

shadow
1426 of the shadow of death,
3232 And the act Falls the Shadow.
3304 lengthened shadow of a great
3349 lengthening shadow of one
5277 Follow a shadow, it still
5353 one is the shadow of the
7611 Be but the shadow of heaven,
8215 which his shadow will be
10373 a walking shadow, a poor
11001 under the shadow of a war,
11012 Under the shadow of her
11421 like the shadow cast by a
11557 The Shadow cloaked from head
12064 Like a vast shadow moved; in

shadows
6180 sun sets, shadows, that
10423 If we shadows have offended,
11520 sick of shadows,' said The
11630 than their shadows, Offer no
12061 spy Some shadows of

shaft
9540 undone; Its shafts remain.
10030 O! many a shaft, at random
11488 Lie like a shaft of light

shake
4003 With a shake of his
12774 power to shake me as they

shaken
3543 peel. Shaken and not
10560 tempests and is never shaken.

shakespeare
1963 But Shakespeare also says, 'tis
3881 part of Shakespeare? Only one
4497 should read Shakespeare. If we
4859 Playing Shakespeare is very
4912 to be Shakespeare, another
5138 is to Shakespeare .. as a
5244 hanging .. Shakespeare wanted
5260 honour to Shakespeare that in
6090 But already Shakespeare is morbid
6101 When I read Shakespeare I am
6715 Shakespeare would have grasped
7674 needs my Shakespeare for his
8334 Shakespeare - the nearest thing
8920 Shakespeare (whom you and ev'ry
12209 existed, Shakespeare.
12620 works of Shakespeare. Now,
12833 this key Shakespeare unlocked

shaking
7754 without shaking, Indeed is

shallow
239 Deep down he is shallow.
2084 speech is shallow as Time.
7648 books and shallow in
10519 are idle shallow things: I
12581 It is only shallow people who
12582 Only the shallow know

shambles
3772 - the human shambles that

shame
2531 but for the shame of it.
3867 Shame and guilt are noble
5199 Shame arises from the fear

6660 the heart is past shame.
7574 O shame to men! Devil with
10228 holds, Let shame say what
10239 it to my shame, I have a
10562 a waste of shame Is lust in
12333 of some deathless shame.

shameful
5886 It is more shameful to

shameless
1780 the most shameless thing in
4075 can be more shameless than for

shanks
469 a good mind and sorry shanks.

shape
813 We take our shape, it is
2330 We shape our buildings;
7575 art thou, execrable shape?
12378 The shape of things to

shaped
2052 are shaped by men

shapes
10422 them to shapes, and gives

share
2135 who can share it,
2189 able to share it
4804 his modest share of the
9908 never share the heart
10742 you don't share it, you
11027 child will share willingly
12026 a right to share your

shared
1702 everybody shared enough,

shares
3982 The shares are a penny, and

sharing
9895 consists in sharing the
10925 does not object to sharing.

shark
5746 To the shark and

sharpened
1960 by time Is sharpened from its

shave
2732 are old enough to shave.
12443 A man who shaves and takes

she
1569 I dare say she will do.
4366 She who must be obeyed.
12702 For, if she be not for

shears
7529 th'abhorrèd shears, And slits
10873 a pair of shears, so joined

sheath
4575 keeps another in the sheath.

sheba
10738 Queen of Sheba, or I King
12700 one, Another Sheba queen.

shed
1223 Whoso sheddeth man's
6021 us and shedde oure
10293 prepare to shed them now.

sheep
99 to the sheep whose skin
1150 his life for the sheep.
1173 to you in sheep's
1421 like lost sheep. We have
1435 people, the sheep of his
2298 A sheep in sheep's
2964 man, while sheep in
4500 savaged by a dead sheep.
4953 for the sheep to pass
7536 else their sheep, Was all
7884 Your sheep, that were wont
8594 mountain sheep are
11103 half-witted sheep Which
12284 One sickly sheep infects
12834 A flock of sheep that

sheep-herding
8982 the rest is mere sheep-herding.

sheet
11668 How at my sheet goes the

shelf life
11864 The shelf life of the modern

shell
338 that gloomy shell He does

shelled
363 We shelled the Turks from 9

shelter
12292 come, Our shelter from the

sheltered
7922 In youth it sheltered me, And

shelterless
2564 tree Shelterless and dim.

shepherd
517 call you, Shepherd, from the
1150 am the good shepherd: the good
1425 Lord is my shepherd: therefore
4318 unto a shepherd as a king,
4564 of love my Shepherd is, And He

shepherds
11430 While shepherds watched their
12167 need both shepherds and
12202 which poor shepherds prayed in

sheriff
6988 I shot the sheriff But I

sherry
8790 first-rate sherry flowing

shewed
5345 Who shewed it thee?

shield
418 often a shield than a
6637 A trusty shield and

shifted
10628 have only shifted it to

shilling
6155 for one shilling Your
9030 paid their shillings to watch

shillings
4335 give ten shillings to find

shine
1166 light so shine before
8290 Oh, shine on, shine on,
10549 you shall shine more
11339 to shine in

shining
7088 funeral, Shining unto no
11594 leaves A shining furrow, as
12057 the just, Shining nowhere

ship
1849 What is a ship but a
4571 A great ship asks deep
5200 Being in a ship is being
5686 to me is a ship's upon the
6475 sail on, O Ship of State!
7135 is a tall ship and a star
8133 places his ship alongside
8143 their ship on the
12722 rock, that ship of life,

ships
93 Hell to ships, hell to men,
906 our bloody ships today,
3820 oak are our ships, Heart of
4339 the little ships of England
6513 Ships that pass in the
6993 a thousand ships, And burnt
11729 Ships, dim-discovered,

shipwreck
677 escaped the shipwreck of time.

shiraz
1371 red wine of Shiraz into

shire
3011 That shire which we the
5660 to see Shires and towns

shirk
11964 You cannot shirk this and

shirt
3981 In your shirt and your

shiver
1040 should shiver on the
8150 breezes shiver, And she's
11519 breezes dusk and shiver.

shock
804 as a great shock around the
2633 have to shock their
3991 sharp shock, From a
4532 little, the shock can kill a

7119 the shock, which the
9396 into shock by the
10597 the old, to shock them and
11755 receive a shock unless you

shocking
8952 something shocking Now,

shocks
8469 in it that shocks the mind
9779 that shocks the

shoe
10096 grain of sand in your shoe.

shoemaker
49 would be a shoemaker rather

shoes
1215 Put off thy shoes from off
2121 things: Of shoes - and
3322 stands firmest in his shoes.
4188 I take my shoes from the
6721 guilt and shoes with
7825 And her shoes were
10052 for his old shoes; they were
10524 than over shoes in love.
11676 in, mind it wipes its shoes.

shoestring
12762 and runs it into a shoestring.

shook
7819 monk who shook the world.
9423 days that shook the world.

shoot
967 they could shoot me in my
2265 man were to shoot his
2539 How do you shoot a spectre
3375 If you shoot at a king you
4429 war is! You shoot a fellow
4622 where I am about to shoot.'
4946 they shout and they shoot.
9006 you could shoot snipe off
10752 Who shoots at the mid-day
11726 the young idea how to shoot.
12511 Shoot, if you must, this
12563 do not shoot the

shooting
8374 sport is war without shooting.
9270 thinking is shooting without

shoots
5975 The green shoots of economic
12062 Bright shoots of

shopkeepers
8073 is a nation of shopkeepers.

shopocracy
8286 hear you abuse the shopocracy.

shopping
798 Shopping is the perfect model
4039 families shopping at night!
7406 main thing today is - shopping.
9910 I don't even like shopping.

shore
5946 unknown and silent shore.
6490 By the shore of Gitche
10552 on the kingdom of the shore.

short
1417 hath but a short time to
4637 nasty, brutish, and short.
5121 is very short . It is
8112 is much too short to live
8230 times too short for us to
8680 up some children is short.
11455 is very short, so it is

short-lived
974 For such a short-lived happiness?

shortage
1116 produce a shortage of coal

shortcoming
371 His shortcoming is his long
6321 His shortcoming is his long

shorten
1198 and wrath shorten the life.
1866 pleasure pleasant, shorten.

shorter
224 crying, Shorter hours and
3276 make you shorter by the
8549 the time to make it shorter.
9311 shrouded; Shorter and

shortest
2788 and one of the shortest lived.
9118 The shortest answer is doing.
9520 line is the shortest distance

shorthand
11827 is the shorthand of

shortness
10241 spend that shortness basely

shot
2265 him a good shot, but not
3314 fired the shot heard
6472 I shot an arrow into the
6988 I shot the sheriff But I
9403 to being shot at and
9411 as to be shot at without

should
1809 Should auld acquaintance be

shoulder-blade
3998 have a left shoulder-blade that is a

shoulders
4783 Their shoulders held the
8181 on the shoulders of giants.
10975 your young shoulders .. all my

shout
4946 argue; they shout and they
12188 for men who shout. Who tell

shouted
5680 When you've shouted 'Rule

shovel
9857 Waterloo. Shovel them under

show
665 someone can show you that
3468 Show me the man and I'll
6430 thing to show a man that
6745 if we are going to show.
12278 Show me a man with both
12706 - To show the fly

show business
1075 no business like show business.
7410 You are in show business.
12190 Show business is like sex. When

shower
1564 an abundant shower of curates
6711 to have a summer shower'.
8398 this is our finest shower!

showery
3293 Blowy, Showery. Flowery;

showing
159 Showing up is eighty percent

shrapnel
12490 defensive hats, and shrapnel.

shreds
10219 A king of shreds and

shrieks
8940 Not louder shrieks to pitying

shrimp
5612 until a shrimp learns to

shrines
4331 sentimental shrines feigning a

shroud
5496 in an April shroud; Then glut

shrug
11344 will give a shrug, and cry,

shrunk
10284 spoils, Shrunk to this

shuffled
6447 pack is shuffled and cut -
10212 we have shuffled off this

shuffling
6907 and not shuffling it off on

shun
10324 lies; let me shun that.

shunting
1839 my life to shunting and

shut
5742 They shut the road through
7101 his mouth shut and his
8850 Shut, shut the door, good
10496 Men shut their doors

shut up
6033 tenderly. Shut up he

shutter
11631 her on a shutter, like a

shutting
5514 midnight, Shutting, with

shuttle
12058 Man is the shuttle, to whose

shy
11451 Shy and unready men are

sick
3080 are always sick. Most of
3367 falls sick but the
5110 to be at when he is sick.
5617 It would make a stone sick.
5967 To be sick is to enjoy
8106 eye. I am sick, I must
9046 you not extremely sick?
10313 when we are sick in fortune
10387 They are as sick that
10500 The enterprise is sick.
10934 in the kingdom of the sick.
11520 'I am half sick of
11561 heart is sick, And all
11725 Who, if not sick, was never
11761 to be sick sometimes.
12073 When we are sick our
12724 think we're sick, It's all

sicker
4915 not much sicker and much

sickle
6506 with his sickle keen, He

sickness
5949 How sickness enlarges the
8942 Sickness is a sort of early

sickroom
3869 come to the sickroom thinking

side
436 is on his side. The rich
607 Hear the other side.
1863 on the side of big
1870 heard one side of the
4382 when it is not of our side.
6373 is on our side, It is
6580 for the good or evil side.
6838 Are on our side to-day.
7373 his own side of the
8697 on God's side is a
11932 town on our side? and ain't
11954 has a dark side which he
12658 history is on their side.
12743 a song, Side by side.

side-fall
5403 Along the side-fall of the

sidearms
4138 carried no sidearms when he

sideways
2728 Think sideways!

sieve
6150 they went to sea in a Sieve.
6151 aloud 'Our Sieve ain't big,

sigh
521 And sigh that one thing
4877 a kiss, A sigh is just a
8907 th'eternal sigh, For which
10131 Sigh no more, ladies sigh
12051 we sigh for an

sighed
11730 Sighed and looked

sighs
10102 of art, Sighs are the

sight
3939 to lose sight of the
5540 is 'out of sight', quickly
5660 pleasant sight to see
6137 be that his sight is not
10306 How oft the sight of means
11486 stood, a sight to make an
11690 universe of sight, Love and
12777 pass by A sight so

sighted
7139 Sighted sub, sank same.

sights
871 impressive sights in the

sign
158 some clear sign! Like

2820 Never sign a walentine
9260 seeing it; sign nothing
9307 wear the sign: 'I want

signal
6513 Only a signal shown and
8136 really do not see the signal!

signals
4342 exchange of signals between
8133 In case signals can neither
11394 suggestive signals to the

signature
3531 The voice is a second signature.

signatures
12616 put their own signatures on them.

significance
917 The significance of man is that he
932 Never mind the inner significance.
3936 The significance of a man is not

signify
12044 shall never signify anything

signposts
6302 milestones, without signposts.

signs
1147 ye see signs and
2353 Certain signs precede
11824 of external signs, hands on
12760 One of the signs of passing

silence
686 Silence is the virtue of
1898 Silence is not always tact,
2084 lies a silence that is
2260 Silence is the unbearable
2769 with me, Silence where hope
3097 about silence: The
3220 that silence is always
4171 Silence is become his mother
4390 more manageable than silence.
4430 That man's silence is
4903 of view, is silence about
4916 After silence, that which
5202 Silence propagates itself.
5260 answered best with silence.
5516 very sigh that silence heaves.
6491 in silence and apart;
6513 darkness again and a silence.
6962 - it is silence which
7201 Men fear silence as they fear
7321 the small change of silence.
7462 who shall silence all the
7914 mind silence. But
8540 The eternal silence of these
9228 Silence is a woman's finest
9634 Silence more musical than any
9644 visible silence, still as
9655 twofold silence was the
10232 The rest is silence.
10578 of silence and could
10652 Silence is the most perfect
10770 do not know Silence like a
10883 flashes of silence, that make
11199 are often told in silence.
11356 rend; But silence is most
11508 widening slowly silence all.
11973 impressive silence, that
12100 Only silence is great; all

silenced
7910 because you have silenced him.

silencing
7368 in silencing that one

silent
541 The 'T' is silent - as in
1986 was first silent, then
2394 pleasures in life are silent.
3886 of silent witnesses
4160 In all the silent manliness
4489 The most silent people are
5422 grass, And silent was the
5778 Absolutely silent and
6748 the thumb Silent as the
6751 in its defence are silent.
7145 speak, Or be for ever silent.
8246 either be silent, or speak
9157 Better silent than stupid.
9632 into the silent land.
9856 and city on silent haunches
11239 work the silent part is

11912 was French - and silent.
12815 see All silent, and all

silently
6479 And as silently steal
6484 Silently one by one, in the

silk
4589 Whenas in silks my Julia
9102 leaf becomes a silk gown.

silk-worm
7349 Does the silk-worm expend her

sillier
2154 is nothing sillier than a

silliest
5728 for it, the silliest woman can
9528 The silliest part of

silly
250 says it's a silly, childish
660 They are silly things and
1307 some damned silly thing in
4778 good to be silly at the
6128 too much, and he gets silly.
9517 are as silly as our

silver
1109 the thirty pieces of silver.
3572 There's a silver lining
7476 forth her silver lining on
8310 like the silver plate on a

similar
3222 and very similar to others.

similies
9044 Similies are like songs of
10233 the most unsavoury similies.
12780 play with similies, Loose

simple
582 the hard question is simple.
3307 which is simple; which has
4032 thus with simple folk - an
4459 seems to be simple and not
8262 It is just as simple as that.
8557 is not as simple as to
9024 Love is so simple.
12555 pure, and never simple.
12832 them, the simple plan, That

simplest
4433 are the simplest, and so

simplicities
2318 intense simplicities emerge.

simplicity
5246 That makes simplicity a grace;
8872 wit, a man; simplicity, a child;

simplify
2977 am dead And simplify me when
11770 detail .. Simplify, simplify.

simply
11758 from him simply and

simultaneously
8380 one's mind simultaneously, and

sin
1030 and full of sin, Cold the
1148 is without sin among you,
1201 sure your sin will find
1423 into no sin, neither
1654 is not innocence but sin.
1737 leak will sink a ship,
1955 a sin, and
2056 there is a sin against
2436 Ere sin could blight or
2692 a sin of some
2989 record of sin than does
3019 polygamy was made a sin.
3059 but want of power to sin.
5283 was a sin. I had to
5344 Sin is behovely, but all
5463 palace of sweet sin.
5749 For the sin ye do by two
6442 ay, as sin, And
7637 me now of sin By me done
7736 and to sin in secret
8350 have known sin; and this
9219 excuses from sin.
9401 none without sin.
9684 greatest sin, except to
9828 beauty is only sin deep.
10301 there is no sin, but to be
10497 emboldens sin so much as

10587 The worst sin towards our
10974 love. The sin of love

since
11996 in Peter Pan ever since.

sincere
3323 I may be sincere. Before
5906 Weak people cannot be sincere.
9460 are starkly sincere and ..
11900 Always be sincere, even if

sincerely
12255 no one can sincerely try to

sincerity
1514 worse for complete sincerity.
7250 of sincerity on
8967 four S's: Sincerity,
9660 the sincerity of the
10805 For sincerity is a jewel which
12566 A little sincerity is a

sinews
12231 the very sinews of virtue.

sinewy
6515 large and sinewy hands; And

sinful
934 but a sinful man who
8206 justice in a sinful world.

sing
1434 O sing unto the Lord a new
3073 and the man I sing ..
4566 corner sing My God and
5457 bend and sing A faery's
9195 and you sing well too.
9635 my dearest, Sing no sad
10862 of liberty, Of thee I sing.
11566 wrong To sing so wildly;
12111 I sing of arms and the
12502 I sing the body electric.
12504 myself, and sing myself.

singe
10269 That it do singe yourself.

singeing
3007 The singeing of the King of

singer
406 The singer not the song.
4064 an aging singer who had to
7927 The idle singer of an empty

singers
7868 For most singers the first
9652 be if there were no singers.

singing
1485 those who are singing to-day.
4795 like the singing better
6002 delight in singing, tho' none
9933 burst out singing; And I was
9934 the singing will never
10708 And singing still dost soar,
12743 along Singin' a song,

single
650 that a single man in
767 wife, But single thraldom,
4194 continued single and only
4387 with but a single thought,
6547 with but a single thought,

singles
1103 strenuous singles we played

sings
3809 of bleeding, he sings.
7389 that in me sings no more.

singularity
2988 Singularity is almost invariably

sink
167 will never sink, but then
7951 Once you sink that first
8390 We of the sinking middle

sinks
2860 very fast, but never sinks.

sinned
2497 The people sinned against

sinner
1156 over one sinner that
6642 Be a sinner and sin
8609 The sinner is at the heart

sinners
1176 but sinners to
9712 an hour the sinners are still

10214 thou be a breeder of sinners?
11189 are the Sinners who keep

sinning
9087 The sinning is the best part
9712 from their sinning of the

sins
1427 not the sins and
2075 business of alloting sins.
4934 sins, in the
6732 of the sins that were
9755 half the sins of mankind
10253 The oldest sins the newest
10378 the tempted, who sins most?
10439 to hear the sins they love
10802 hearts for sins they have
11885 medicine, sins of
12341 All sins are attempts to

sion
1438 we remembered thee, O Sion.

sip
3894 The way you sip your tea,

sipping
12815 Some sipping punch, some

sire
7392 him for a sire, and her

sissy
8792 A rose-red sissy half as

sister
7826 her little sister, And

sisterhood
7891 Sisterhood is powerful.

sisters
3961 so do his sisters, and his
5713 O'Grady Are sisters under
9468 hadn't had sisters How much

sit
1030 Here I sit, alone and
3181 When you sit with a nice
3223 Teach us to sit still.
4535 you do not expect to sit.
4859 get to sit down,
5708 is not to sit still, Or
6518 someone, sit right here
8286 I cannot sit still,
11937 cat that sits down on a
12043 ever comes to sit by it.
12359 to say, and then sit down.
12780 at ease I sit, and play

sits
9302 Sometimes I sits and

sitting
5698 and sitting in the
6010 "Are you sitting comfortably?
7487 thou art sitting Under the

situation
5217 been in no situation where

sitwells
6164 The Sitwells belong to the

six hundred
11475 of Death Rode the six hundred.

sixpence
9298 precious little for sixpence.

sixteen
11853 Sixteen tons, what do you

sixties
6287 they divided up the Sixties.
8027 reach your sixties, you have
10663 reach their sixties and

sixty
3236 done up to sixty or so has
3899 you going sixty miles an

sixty four
6230 feed me, When I'm sixty four?

size
3190 the size of the dog
6891 was the size of each

skating
3327 In skating over thin ice, our

skeleton
928 Like two skeletons copulating
6868 becomes a skeleton in the

skies
6115 under other skies than those

10580 whose God is in the skies.
11556 are blown about the skies.

skill
411 power and skill To stem
2700 Skill comes so slow, and
2804 feats of skill, the most
3871 to hide - skill loves the
7932 and particular skill.
9742 love and skill work

skilled
900 to become a skilled

skills
11378 similar skills - dressing

skin
84 A thick skin is a gift
99 sheep whose skin the wolf
1227 change his skin, or the
1229 with the skin of my
1265 give up his skin for the
5973 In the castle of my skin.
9119 an Englishman to the skin.
12640 our own skins, for

skip
3521 easier to skip it and go

skip-worthy
533 there is much that is skip-worthy.

skirmish
4284 The trivial skirmish fought

skittles
2020 beer and skittles; They are

skull
3268 And saw the skull beneath

skunk
6375 kills a skunk is the

sky
603 The sky is darkening like
2718 past, the sky is
3238 against the sky Like a
3376 The sky is the daily
3510 we call The Sky,
7949 First the sky, then the
9311 The sky breathed autumn.
11410 to her; the sky asks
11740 carries the sky on his
12539 prisoners call the sky.

skye
1481 king, Over the sea to Skye,

skyline
9382 The skyline of New York is a

skyscrapers
905 and rose and green skyscrapers.
4599 remain human in the skyscrapers.

slab
8091 this slab John Brown

slag-heap
3003 slag-heap covered in

slain
3042 I am not slain; I will
6922 is my most noble lord slain.

slamming
991 Little Girls is slamming Doors.
8401 Slamming their doors, stamping

slander
5239 angry at a slander makes it
11952 the one to slander you and

slang
1744 creators of slang, hurl
9864 Slang is a language that

slanted
7213 as a slanted rain

slap
9701 enough to slap, there's

slash
2539 the heart, slash off its

slashing
11638 For a slashing article, sir,

slaughtered
8149 'ye have slaughtered and made

slaughterous
10372 to my slaughterous thoughts,

slave
175 life is the slave of his

1405 to make oneself its slave.
1565 Better be a slave at once!
2057 The slave begins by
2523 passions is Reason's slave.
3805 moment the slave resolves
6248 always the slave of the
6357 half slave and half
6371 not be a slave, so I
7380 No slave is a slave to the
8229 and slave-morality.
8909 Slave to no sect, who takes

slavery
2650 for power. Slavery of the
4038 a state of slavery in which a
6816 and good in slavery, they may
10077 fortune is a great slavery.
11215 of a new slavery, and every

slaves
1268 and two slaves, making,
2618 show, That slaves, howe'er
5642 of former slaves and the
7223 with a hundred slaves.
7655 Gaza at the mill with slaves.
8747 it is the creed of slaves.
11723 never will be slaves.'
12265 are to be freemen or slaves.

slay
6705 a king To slay their
6838 But slay, and slay,

slays
8964 thousands slays, Peace its

sleep
152 girl to sleep with me,
412 his first sleep should be
596 in someone else's sleep.
1618 We term sleep a death, and
1734 Sleep is sweet to the
1929 No sleep till morn,
2374 I sleep with thee, and wake
4478 not hypocrites in our sleep.
4730 not to sleep the whole
4915 all natural graces, sleep.
5243 is laid to sleep, Seated in
5507 on me like unwilling sleep,
6169 to do when you can't sleep.
7137 And quiet sleep and a
7244 may, we all sleep at last on
7474 hath night to do with sleep?
7602 Sleep on Blest pair; and O
7605 His sleep Was airy light
7789 when we sleep we are
7862 let it sleep in the
8826 keep, Sleepless
9201 Sleep faster, we need the
9315 down With sleep, the
9346 I never sleep in comfort
9483 Sleep, riches and health to
9754 men who sleep badly, are
10163 is done, And we must sleep.
10186 some must sleep; thus runs
10212 To sleep: perchance to
10274 ease And sleep an act or
10353 voice cry, Sleep no more!
10380 sleep, Dreaming
10555 flatter, In sleep a king,
10957 called, O Sleep! the
11010 Sleep after toil, port
11357 Between a sleep and a
11605 Sleep - kinsman thou to
11692 borders of sleep, The
12101 Let me sleep the sleep
12293 been to sleep for over a
12808 me from the fields of sleep.
12936 sweet restorer, balmy sleep!

sleeping
587 Lay your sleeping head, my
2208 good a slepyng hound to
8147 art tha sleepin' there
8239 Sleeping is no mean art. For
10354 The sleeping and the dead Are
11679 Sleeping as quiet as death,
12304 fuss about sleeping together.

sleepless
8826 keep, Sleepless
9647 Sleepless with cold
12834 turns, and yet do lie Sleepless!

sleeps
7047 sweetness, Sleeps sound,
7856 fled. So sleeps the pride
9162 An arch never sleeps.
10182 He that sleeps feels not the

sleeves
6679 with its sleeves rolled.
9864 up its sleeves, spits on

sleigh
1079 To hear sleigh bells in

slept
7254 Coolidge] slept more than
8573 thought he thought I slept.'
11571 touched him, and he slept.

slice
12711 Slice him where you like, a

slimy
2446 be! Yes, slimy things did

slings
10211 suffer The slings and arrows

slip
4440 me while I slip into

slipped
4072 I have only slipped away into

slippers
1621 A pair of slippers, sir, To

slippery
12629 Let not my slippery footsteps

slipping
6589 the machine slipping from our

slit
5677 hard to slit, Slit your

slogans
1057 principles, slogans; and,

slop
10882 but stood in the slop.

slop-pail
4758 with a slop-pail, give him

sloppy
11899 Sloppy, raggerly-assed old

sloth
10178 when resty sloth Finds the

slough
1102 and fall on Slough! It isn't
1731 name of the slough was

slovenliness
1534 nothing but slovenliness, only war

slow
1242 He that is slow to anger
6358 I'm a slow walker, but I
6421 Slow and steady wins the
7996 telling you to slow down.
10032 And come he slow, or come
10093 is always slow; It is

slow down
9952 to slow down. The

slowest
5056 family chose the slowest one.
10104 fool is the slowest thing in

slowly
6954 years pass slowly, while
11273 lente. Hasten slowly.
11530 moves, but slowly slowly,

sluggard
12289 of the sluggard; I heard

slum
107 one city slum you've

slumber
5226 to soothing slumber seven, Ten
7860 night, Ere Slumber's chain
12839 A slumber did my spirit seal;

slumbered
10423 have but slumbered here While

slut
3837 is a sad slut! nor heeds

small
502 Is it so small a thing To
5372 reveals how small are men's
7372 that with small men no
7643 were no small praise.
9200 big. You are not so small.
11301 is the pictures got small."

small-endians
11315 Big-endians and small-endians.

smaller
292 larger and candy bars smaller.
4425 moment got Smaller and
4450 out a great many smaller ones.
8508 an inch smaller and it

smallest
9426 in the smallest room in my

smallpox
9121 to the face than smallpox.

smart
6067 its time Smart Dowdy ..
6677 coach who's smart enough to

smart-asses
8812 make passes at female smart-asses.

smarted
6105 our eyes smarted against

smarter
559 themselves smarter. But he
3564 with people smarter than I am.

smarts
8851 No creature smarts so little

smash
4389 never smash in a face.

smashed
3520 - they smashed up things

smell
2137 sense of smell, almost
3124 "I love the smell of napalm
5634 says the smell of fish
6191 Sweet smell of success.
9519 Speaker, I smell a rat; I
9649 sweet keen smell, The
10368 Here's the smell of the
10556 that fester smell far worse
12083 Money has no smell.

smells
10261 the violet smells to him as

smelt
5782 The room smelt of not

smile
351 rode with a smile on a tiger
374 A smile is a curve that can
525 bag, And smile, smile,
2172 gave me a smile I could
2259 Smile at us, pay us, pass
4924 last fading smile of a
6032 other a smile with a
10023 the vain tribute of a smile.
10043 frown or smile, Sat and
12771 'Twixt a prison and a smile.

smiled
5988 You smiled, you spoke, and I

smiles
1357 a Smile of Smiles In which
1627 the breath, Smiles, tears, of
2767 your eyes, Smiles awake you
5419 Their smiles, Wan as
7511 becks, and wreathèd smiles.
8858 Eternal smiles his emptiness

smiling
8261 when I'm smiling and
9108 teeth are smiling, but is
9213 A smiling face is half the

smily
6566 All kin' o' smily round the

smite
1167 shall smite thee on

smith
4699 him by naming him Smith.

smithy
5324 in the smithy of my soul
6515 The village smithy stands;

smoke
845 my Lord Otto, and smoke it.
3200 a sort of smoke that comes
4416 Smoke gets in your eyes.
4443 you guine do wid de smoke?
5427 Its little smoke, in pallid
5687 but a good cigar is a Smoke.
7469 Above the smoke and stir of
7926 with smoke, Forget
11981 If I cannot smoke cigars in

smoked
5235 the brain smoked like the
5782 of not having been smoked in.
11838 woman, and smoked my first

smoking
1473 Smoking is a dying habit.
7975 Smoking can seriously damage

smooth
10413 love never did run smooth.

snaffle
2030 use the snaffle and the

snake
3489 I see a snake - which I
6098 A snake came to my
12132 There's a snake hidden in

snapped
5349 that are easily snapped off.

snapper-up
10530 A snapper-up of unconsidered

snare
11108 is a rabbit in a snare.

snares
8618 it has many snares, and no

snarl
3459 to snarl

snatch
10440 gifts, And snatch them

sneak
5788 works, sneak attack is

sneaky
8199 a little snouty, sneaky mind.

sneer
8482 Who can refute a sneer?

sneering
3984 help it. I was born sneering.

sneeze
6086 like having a good sneeze.

snigger
3495 a eunuch and a snigger.

snob
1698 of a snob is one who
6666 The true snob never rests;

snobbery
12022 be bereaved if snobbery died.

snobbish
6461 'Don't be snobbish, we seek

snobs
101 Snobs talk as if they had
108 of impudent snobs who

snore
10178 Can snore upon the

snorted
2945 Or snorted we in the

snotgreen
5326 The snotgreen sea. The

snow
1447 who carves in snow.
2025 sends the snow in winter,
2435 is like snow; the
4788 the cherry hung with snow.
5310 heard the snow falling
5744 buried in snow to the
8059 African who dreams up snow.
8114 When the snow lay round
8116 Where the snow lay
9781 and the snow shining
10335 Than wish a snow in May's
12846 The snow hath

snow-leopard
6085 one like a snow-leopard waiting to

snow-white
12408 used to be snow-white .. but I
12901 with little snow-white feet. She

snowflakes
5534 Snowflakes are one of nature's

snows
12107 are the snows of

snowy
3293 Snowy, Flowy, Blowy,

snuff
2453 You abuse snuff! Perhaps
4179 and only took snuff.

snuffed
9446 is not to be snuffed out.

snug
965 in the dark Snug of a
2809 Oh! what a snug little
3629 Skugg Lies snug As a bug

soap
1746 and how little about soap.
4967 With soap baptism is a
9301 I used your soap two years
11944 Soap and education are not

soapboxes
6526 up on soapboxes and

soar
1786 can creep as well as soar.
6836 to run, though not to soar.

soaring
10708 soar, and soaring ever

sobbed
4004 He sobbed and he sighed, and

sober
3545 go to bed sober, Falls
4538 a Jesuit, sober as a hymn.
7478 Such sober certainty of
7497 and pure, Sober,
7763 dress, and sober in your
10849 and keep absolutely sober.
12000 one sees in Garbo sober.
12029 drunk to Philip sober.

sobering
850 It is a sobering thought that
6194 It is a sobering thought, that

sobers
8874 largely sobers us again.

social
1880 down the social ladder
3705 To be social is to be
8387 The typical Socialist is ..
11022 Man is a social animal.

socialism
1113 is the religion of Socialism.
2774 Socialism is liberty,
3076 policy that socialism would not
8388 night, Socialism does not
10905 This is not Socialism. It is
11736 Socialism has been preached for
12097 Socialism can only arrive by

socialist
7939 Champagne socialist.
8387 The typical Socialist is .. a
8389 speak, of Socialist literature

societies
6899 progressive societies has
12488 Vigorous societies harbour a
12858 Societies that do not eat

society
45 of society is the end
430 society, and the
482 to live in society, or who
825 Society, dead or alive, can
1009 Our society, like decadent
1971 Society is now one polished
1992 If from Society we learn to
2171 Society is composed of two
3669 kind of society isn't
3867 civilized society, and vital
4038 No society can survive, no
4276 and reliable force in society.
4309 established society, and been
5182 member of a society has a
5548 class. Society is built
5564 In free society art is not a
5676 Society is based on the
6122 of the good society, the
6744 Every society honours its
6906 Society needs to condemn a
6919 our society, it is
7079 Society is all but rude, To
7222 almost any society, I think,
7287 they will do to society.
7361 When society requires to be
7381 laws alone, society would be a
7621 is best society, And short
7871 of human society turns.
8064 whatever to society. It is

9610 of society; but only
9931 the complex society that
9943 A society in which
11055 place in society marks the
11058 force in society. It
11148 of a free society is a
11260 Society, my dear, is like
11411 in society; the
11655 thing as Society. There
11808 action of society upon
12260 of a plural society which
12469 A civilized society is one
12728 is part of Society and its
12786 Society became my glittering
12824 cling together In one society.

socks
4217 put on your socks and ended

socrates
237 and indifferent to Socrates.
8761 Socrates is guilty of

sods
12718 night, The sods with our

sofa
2623 the accomplished sofa last.
8791 On a sofa upholstered in

soft
1240 A soft answer turneth away
6144 flower, Too soft for
8651 mind does not make us soft.

softness
6554 And the softness of my body
7594 formed, For softness she and

soil
7561 hell; that soil may best
11410 The soil, in return for

sojourn
619 stranger's sojourn, a night

sojourner
12450 I am a sojourner in the

solace
10083 find some solace for it.
10797 With solace and gladness

solar
2081 the whole solar and

sold
1445 somehow sold well
2485 is to be sold, and the
11584 Who never sold the truth

soldier
4 Like soldier's ribbon
3390 a single soldier outside
3431 lovers I am a private soldier.
5096 been a soldier, or not
5756 to your Gawd like a soldier.
5764 abroad as a soldier of the
7439 guard. 'A soldier's life is
8472 The summer soldier and the
8550 If a soldier or labourer
10165 war, The soldier's pole is
10377 in the soldier is flat
10589 expect a soldier to think.
10591 The British soldier can stand
11132 say to your soldier, 'Do this'

soldiers
848 Christian soldiers, Marching
3555 Old soldiers never die, They
6041 brought its soldiers home for
7300 England her soldiers, her
9323 Our God and soldiers we alike
9726 Soldiers of the ploughshare as
9932 Soldiers are citizens of

sole
12242 to my Sole, sed I, so

solecism
1608 without a solecism, or think

soliciting
10342 soliciting Cannot be

solicitor
2895 can only go to his solicitor.
4033 on whose solicitor has given

solid
2253 it again on something solid.

solidity
8393 of solidity to pure

solitary
1853 Be not solitary, be not idle.
5126 be not solitary; if you
7085 To wander solitary there: Two
7639 Eden took their solitary way.

solitude
1676 feels his solitude peopled at
1992 live, 'Tis Solitude should
2519 of his solitude or the
3183 From the solitude of the wood,
4286 you of solitude without
6584 Solitude is as needful to the
7079 To this delicious solitude.
7161 own age; in solitude in all
7201 they fear solitude, because
7618 In solitude What happiness?
7621 For solitude sometimes is best
7740 is harmless solitude! What can
8280 There is no solitude in the
8589 Solitude is the profoundest
9159 A great city, a great solitude.
9494 the solitude of the
9858 to discover creative solitude.
11096 in solitude except
11753 so companionable as solitude.
11803 the word 'solitude' to
12039 feel his solitude more
12825 power of Solitude.

solitudes
9495 that two solitudes protect

solomon
2890 in the Temple of Solomon.
5741 a thousand, Solomon says, Will
8113 and King Solomon Led merry,
10738 or I King Solomon, Alone and

solution
2174 that the solution, once
2379 The only solution for dealing
7107 for its solution already
10775 with a solution - you'll

solutions
6260 to cheap solutions instead of

somebody
1527 had class and been somebody."
3957 one is somebodee, Then no
4229 To be somebody you must last.
7030 to happen to somebody else.
9566 is happening to Somebody Else.

someone
3315 yourself necessary to someone.
5983 softly - to someone else.
9552 that it was someone else.
12654 like about someone you don't.

something
1886 provided he hates something.
2465 let us do something today
3150 Something should be done to get
3687 be agnostic - be something.
7447 Time for a little something.
12069 always wanting to do something.
12427 have to say something, but
12654 you hear something you like

sometimes
9302 Sometimes I sits and thinks,

somewhere
2126 want to get somewhere else, you
4417 Somewhere over the rainbow.
10664 of going somewhere,

son
1235 A wise son maketh a glad
3021 two-legged thing, a son.
3279 of a fair son, and I am
3915 lover, I obeyed as a son.
7532 Wherein the son of
9037 Prior, The son of Adam

son-in-law
9188 but not for a son-in-law.

song
406 The singer not the song.
1434 Lord a new song: for he
2703 thinks two notes a song.
3133 man, play a song for me.
3511 my reputation for a song.
4031 It's a song of a merryman,
4099 That is the song that never
4233 old sweet song keeps

4512 On wings of song.
5661 One grand, sweet song.
6473 And the song, from
7132 with a song. Better
7543 our tedious song should
8320 ane end of ane old song.
9151 I eat, his song I sing.
9645 was the song of love.
9934 The song was wordless; the
10809 the song, when
11570 breeze of song To stir a
11702 the carcase of an old song.

songs
5490 ever piping songs for ever
9044 are like songs of love:
9635 Sing no sad songs for me.
10710 sweetest songs are those

sonnet
5955 When my sonnet was rejected,
8962 Shakespeare sonnet, You're
9641 A sonnet is a moment's

sons
4886 Our sons, who so easily
6878 but God's sons are
8324 Sons of the dark and

soon
1276 minutes too soon than to
9255 June's too soon, July's

sooner
631 The sooner every party

soonest
10971 best when soonest wrought,

soothe
2512 charms to soothe a savage

soothes
8189 ear! It soothes his

soothsaying
6328 world on soothsaying but not on

sophistication
6898 Hip is the sophistication of the

sophistry
765 wits to sophistry and

soporific
8969 too much lettuce is soporific'.

sorbonne
11143 day at the Sorbonne. We shall

sordello
8985 can be but the one Sordello'.

sore
2426 who is sore about
7040 as a bear with a sore head.

sorest
10019 When our need was the sorest.

sorriness
4424 to show the sorriness underlying

sorrow
588 here, Nor sorrow take His
1213 knowledge increaseth sorrow.
1221 In sorrow thou shalt bring
1363 not be in sorrow too. Can I
1988 Sorrow is knowledge:
2361 remembrance of a past sorrow.
3286 selfish is sorrow. But it
3550 love's sorrow lasts all
4853 Sorrow is a fruit; God does
4980 of the sorrow in each
5496 glut thy sorrow on a
5498 be full of sorrow And
5729 There is sorrow enough in
6459 hast no sorrow in thy
6483 Sorrow and silence are
6881 fashion the sorrow that is to
6921 and the sorrow thereof,
7162 The sorrow which has no vent
7915 humiliating sorrow, we think
8506 Sorrow is tranquillity
10150 should water this sorrow.
10319 climbing sorrow! Thy
10478 such sweet sorrow That I
10944 The keenest sorrow is to
11298 Sorrow in all lands, and
11420 deeper the sorrow the less
11526 That a sorrow's crown of

11567 O Sorrow, wilt thou live
11829 complete sorrow is as

sorrows
6141 The sorrows and disasters of
9409 and suffer noble sorrows.
10225 When sorrows come, they come
10859 are few sorrows, however
11458 and broods a nest of sorrows.

sorry
1067 Very sorry can't come. Lie
1378 'I felt sorry for him
5149 will be sorry that you
6097 wild thing Sorry for
10050 having to say you're sorry.
10297 that I shall be sorry for.
11831 I am very sorry for him

sort
2331 This is the sort of English

sot
8027 to be a sot or an

sought
890 old; seek what they sought.
10000 will have sought and found

soul
92 two to bear my soul away.
378 grave His soul is
1163 and lose his own soul?
1399 to give his soul for the
1419 himself the soul of our
1632 To try the soul's strength
2089 essence of a human soul.
2187 to possess a second soul.
2368 The soul lies
2457 brevity, and wit its soul.
2735 The soul is placed in the
2828 the Soul contains,
2831 in the soul - And
2856 most surely, on the soul.
3041 soul .. he is
3335 the antiquity of the soul.
4031 mum, Whose soul was sad,
4372 much about his own soul.
5120 freed his soul the
5276 Soul of the Age! The
5292 is the eye of the soul.
5300 lie in the soul is a true
5310 His soul swooned slowly as
5480 of his soul taken off
5513 Is my soul's
5521 Their soul is
6018 ese to any soule, It is
6198 rational soul or Mind .
6500 For the soul is dead
6648 to yiue his soule good
6995 save my soul, half a
6997 O soul, be changed into
7083 aside, My soul into the
7131 which the soul of man is
7301 suffers the soul may not
7457 as that soul was whose
7740 To interrupt the soul.
7775 things, a soul of the
7793 poverty of soul,
7856 halls The soul of music
8707 from the soul the dust
8722 My soul, do not seek
8847 and catch my flying soul!
8896 is, and God the soul.
8926 Make the soul dance upon
9325 My soul, sit thou a
9583 of His soul. He was
9641 from the Soul's eternity
9896 the human soul and
9949 The soul of Germany is
10027 man, with soul so dead,
10262 subject's soul is his
10307 take my soul, and
10456 mount, my soul! thy seat
10647 may my soul be blasted
10666 which the soul may fix
10835 restless soul is driven
10978 the pupil's soul. To Miss
11482 my whole soul through My
11555 conceal the Soul within.
11590 roll from soul to soul,
11791 it has no soul to be
11847 an infant's soul, in which

11853 go I owe my soul to the
12009 is the soul's very
12043 in one's soul, and yet
12059 My soul, there is a
12792 the tumult, of the soul.

souls
2429 for they have no souls.
2946 letters mingle souls.
3271 windows into men's souls.
3932 not their souls, For their
4097 Two souls dwell, alas! in
5726 About their blessed souls.
6547 Two souls with but a single
8844 state! when souls each other
9639 And the souls mounting up
10848 sell their souls, and live
10910 and our souls will
11049 engineers of human souls.
11150 atom; only in men's souls.
12877 All empty souls tend to

sound
238 like their sound, and
4390 they think sound is more
5247 though the sound were
7924 this, the sound and
8148 him up the Sound, Call him
8879 The sound must seem
9055 Like the sound of a great
10901 the other not very sound.
11472 And the sound of a voice
12510 I sound my barbaric yawp
12834 one; the sound of rain,

sounded
11003 hath thrice already sounded.

sounds
2129 and the sounds will take
5943 Not many sounds in life, and
6676 Of all the sounds there are.
8295 is better than it sounds.
9537 sweetest sounds I'll ever
11980 is better than it sounds.

soup
1468 of portable soup. A little
9186 better with soup than

sour
10454 How sour sweet music is,

source
2034 a single source from
11263 tapping old sources of

sourest
10556 things turn sourest by their

south
1448 The South is avenged.
6085 want to go south, where
6718 live as far south as

south african
10571 The South African police would

southerly
10208 the wind is southerly, I know a

sovereign
716 of the sovereign or state,
784 The Sovereign has, under a
1467 for a sovereign which
3275 to be a Sovereign, what to
11793 I forget my sovereign, may God
12194 Ours is a sovereign nation Bows

sovereignty
2204 to have sovereynetee As wel
7338 national sovereignty, to burn

soviet
6214 is Soviet power plus

sow
5320 is the old sow that eats
8019 I write as a sow piddles.
9407 Sow an act, and you reap

sown
1224 They have sown the wind,

sows
11202 He sows hurry and reaps
11357 derision; Sows, and he

space
1532 in space obeys the
1556 of the space age -
3161 All space is slightly

3771 is space structured
3933 there be spaces in your
4419 Outer Space, To find
4811 Space isn't remote at all.
6027 but in the space within to
7400 occupy the same space.
10147 fall. Here is my space.
11078 is more space where
12771 the narrow space 'Twixt a

spade
1630 truth calls spade a spade!
1843 .. I call a spade a spade.
5256 nominate a spade a spade.

spaghetti
7898 eating spaghetti - it

spain
6256 The rain in Spain stays
11601 and the devildoms of Spain.
11602 not left to Spain, To the

spaniards
735 and the Spaniards seem wiser
3005 and to thrash the Spaniards too.

spanish
7126 are fond of Spanish wine, and

spanking
3116 find that spanking takes less

spare
1914 Then spare the rod,
4036 do in his spare time and

spared
11345 vice, but spared the name;

spareth
1238 He that spareth his rod

sparkle
11473 sally And sparkle out among
11588 of all Time Sparkle for ever.

sparkles
5418 is wine, Alive with sparkles.

sparks
1233 as the sparks fly
10179 to hide the sparks of nature!

spartans
10771 tell the Spartans, thou who

spat
12181 The times spat at me. I

speak
165 Speak for England.
1228 Speak to the earth, and it
1302 claim to speak for the
2979 dare not speak its name.
3377 Speak what you think today
3394 you say, and then speak.
4524 in disguise speak freely.
5262 same: to speak, and to
5835 some who speak one moment
5890 than not speak of oneself
6065 upon to speak a
7046 gets up to speak and says
7145 Now speak, Or be for ever
8666 is to speak ill of
9088 thing to speak the truth:
9443 shall speak peace unto
10122 when I think, I must speak.
10129 Speak low, if you speak
10295 I only speak right on;
10310 of nothing: speak again.
10314 showest, Speak less than
10438 Speak of me as I am;
10945 terrible to speak well and
10966 no one can speak, and no
11178 true, And speak when he is
11763 two to speak the truth

speaker
2841 of the speaker have left
4557 A dull speaker, like a plain

speakers
3303 the great speakers were bad

speaking
3746 everybody is speaking of it.
9270 Speaking without thinking is

speaks
415 inch and speaketh by the
6181 He speaks the kindest words,
7807 his that speaks, and half

The Wordsworth Dictionary of Quotations

9238 The man who speaks the truth
12087 He speaks to me as if I was

spear
1349 Bring me my spear: O clouds,
7535 The idle spear and shield

spears
1941 of their spears was like

specialist
3505 The specialist is a man who

speciality
6520 My speciality is detached

specialized
7140 world is specialized the more

species
5006 on its own species.
7921 living species of monkeys

specifications
12256 designs and specifications of her

spectacle
12611 and there's a spectacle.

spectator
4920 an actor as well as a spectator.
12542 become the spectator of one's

spectators
4765 lists and the spectators laugh.

spectre
7114 A spectre is haunting Europe
10813 spirit. Spectres fly

speculator
11240 raised by a speculator, with lots

speech
724 to deal by speech than by
2084 Under all speech that is
3220 Speech may be barren; but it
3285 begin my speech with the
3565 to make a speech, the first
4147 true use of speech is not so
4270 from speech, lest they
4506 make your speech not too
4641 conception caused by speech.
4878 is the last speech, on the
5625 freedom of speech as a
5856 make your speech
5881 as it does in one's speech.
6962 Speech is civilization
7321 Speech is the small change
8050 any other form of speech.
8414 and grunt. Speech was given
8732 looking at speech is to say
9601 freedom of speech and
10018 His ready speech flowed fair
10309 Mend your speech a little,
10606 the power of speech.
10702 He gave man speech, and
10730 my parts of speech! was ever
11062 Speech happens not to be his
11558 could wed itself with Speech.
12149 and speech only to

speeches
1713 giving speeches; it is
2246 the easy speeches That
4869 thought my speeches were too
11018 of all other speeches.

speechless
2399 let it lie Speechless still, and
4752 literally speechless. Where

speed
1481 Speed, bonnie boat, like a
3327 our safety is in our speed.
4611 more haste, the less speed.
4917 Speed provides the one
7678 his bidding speed And post
8065 Unsafe at any speed.

spell
9516 trying to spell God with
9554 here for a spell, get all
11960 They spell it Vinci and

speller
12245 the wuss speller I know of.

spelling
7437 right; but spelling isn't
7448 My spelling is Wobbly. It's
7690 basic spelling that every

spend
5004 life is to spend it for
5595 am going to spend the rest

spender
2342 not free spenders - doesn't
3693 Where the spender thinks it

spending
708 Riches are for spending.
6267 grace, the spending of

spendthrift
9951 Love is a spendthrift, leaves its

spenser
6004 Thee gentle Spenser fondly

spent
3625 can scarce ever be spent.
5107 that I have spent all the
7672 of mind, all passion spent.
7677 my light is spent, E're half
11525 shall have spent its novel

spermatozoa
4912 million Spermatozoa, All of

spheres
6994 ever-moving spheres of heaven,
8576 forfended spheres Is
12064 by the spheres Like a

spherical
6153 perfectly spherical, He

spice
2626 the very spice of life,
10644 It adds spice to my

spicy
7518 Then to the spicy nut-brown

spider
4810 said a spider to a fly:
8095 The spider's touch, how
9131 When spider webs unite, they
9264 like the spider's web,

spiders
309 me; No more spiders in my bath

spies
10225 not single spies, But in

spin
11535 great world spin for ever

spinach
75 ivy is another man's spinach.

spine
6943 but your spine has been

spinster
7701 an English spinster from being

spires
6278 I saw the spires of Oxford

spirit
509 The spirit bloweth
696 God by his spirit, he is a
1956 so much the spirit calms As
2242 create a spirit of
3944 spirit of one's
4098 I am the spirit that always
4411 The spirit of liberty is the
4492 of the Spirit of the
6024 Come, Holy Spirit, and send
6624 of the spirit we possess
7333 never approached my spirit.
7566 fiercest spirit That
10166 A rarer spirit never Did
10278 strength of spirit; But life,
10562 expense of spirit in a waste
10672 the pure spirit shall flow
10707 blithe Spirit! Bird thou
10811 The spirit of self-help is
10948 have a dumb spirit within:
11609 This grey spirit yearning in
12273 of the spirit of party.
12797 and a spirit, that
12925 self, the spirit that

spirits
5409 .. Other spirits there are
5513 two kindred spirits flee.
7878 up thy spirits, man, and
10565 like two spirits do suggest
11524 And our spirits rushed
12527 a cheerful flow of spirits.

spiritual
1997 such other spiritual liquor.

2958 nothing in spiritual things,
5649 outrun our spiritual power. We
7141 is like a spiritual magnet.
7600 Millions of spiritual creatures
8771 The spiritual eyesight improves
10736 is a spiritual faculty

spiritualists
11225 like a convention of spiritualists.

spit
12181 at me. I spit back at
12194 They spit on

spiteful
6086 when I feel spiteful; it's like

spits
9864 sleeves, spits on its

splashing
4860 I'll be splashing around in the

splendid
1607 animal, splendid in ashes,

splendour
12813 the hour Of splendour in the

splendoured
11712 miss the many splendoured thing.

spoil
1914 rod, and spoil the child.

spoiled
1666 And even spoiled the
11958 Golf is a good walk spoiled.
12955 you find the pagan - spoiled.

spoils
6897 for it spoils something
6978 belong the spoils of the

spoke
9299 the less he spoke; The less
11917 English as she is Spoke.

spoken
820 have seldom spoken with
2751 barely be spoken to; they
7684 What I have spoken, is the

spongy
5250 of such spongy souls, As

spontaneity
169 kills spontaneity. The

spoonfed
4364 to be spoonfed, to have

spoonfuls
11249 so much as spoonfuls of boiling

spoons
3239 my life with coffee spoons.
3317 faster we counted our spoons.
10615 up its spoons and packs

sport
2068 that's what sport is all
2622 Detested sport, That owes
4283 love as in sport, the
4779 Sport begets tumultuous
7196 of war and sport.
8374 sport is war
8391 Serious sport has nothing
9694 Sport is one area where no
10234 To sport would be
10327 kill us for their sport.
10926 chase, the sport of kings;
11287 it's the sport of kings,

sports
1591 Sports do not build
7264 I hate all sports as rabidly
12261 The sports page records

sportsman
5824 of God, we call him a sportsman.
6140 A sportsman is a man who, every

spot
4425 my view She was but a spot.
6252 there was a spot - For one
7469 of this dim spot, Which men
10366 Out, damned spot! out, I

spots
1227 or the leopard his spots?
9875 people are friends in spots.
11936 not all over, but in spots.

spouse
1860 President's spouse. I wish

spread
733 not good except it be spread.
11796 Boredom is rage spread thin.

spring
1013 promise of spring is that
1489 hour of spring strikes -
1566 have melted into spring.
1667 at the spring And day's
3262 roots with spring rain.
3926 when the spring comes her
5419 By chilly fingered spring.
5975 of economic spring are
6577 of real Spring Shaped out
8560 us all in the spring rain.
8692 faded has no second spring.
10695 comes, can Spring be far
11353 by blossom the spring begins.
11523 In the spring a young man's
11674 It is spring, moonless
12446 day of spring was once
12779 of the spring! Even yet

springing
679 and some springing from

springlike
3 grass, so springlike, In limbs

springs
5242 O faintly, gentle springs.
12781 Beside the springs of Dove, A

spunk
6083 and their spunk is that

spur
2473 is the spur of noble
7529 Fame is the spur that the
9208 To spur a willing horse.
10223 me, And spur my dull
10348 I have no spur To prick

spurn
1602 God, But spurn the Jews.
3972 Spurn not the nobly born

spurts
12070 great heights only by spurts.

spy
4810 that ever you did spy.'
6114 The spy who came in from

squadrons
7433 The wingèd squadrons of the sky

squandering
3027 In squandering wealth was his
9843 property, and squandering his own.

squares
6052 packed like squares of wheat.

squeak
3870 - until the pips squeak.

squeezed
3870 going to be squeezed as a lemon

squeezing
4182 you in the squeezing of a

squelching
9667 and fifty seconds of squelching.

squire
2814 Bless the squire and his

squirm
8502 a stab nor squirm To tread

squirrels
8359 like red squirrels, must be

st andrews
6006 St Andrews by the Northern sea,

st nicholas
7830 hopes that St Nicholas soon would

st paul's
6824 sketch the ruins of St Paul's.

stab
7245 heart I stab at thee.
10294 saw him stab,

stabbed
3809 a guy gets stabbed in the

stability
5143 to the stability or

stable
5479 is nothing stable in the

staff
9374 quiet, My staff of faith
10490 break my staff, Bury it

stag
6288 The Stag at Bay with the

stage
2597 on the stage, Mrs
3057 for love, but on the stage.
4178 On the stage he was
10117 world's a stage, And all
10254 for a stage, princes
10331 this great stage of fools.
10373 upon the stage And then
10520 upon a stage now, I
12618 unencumbered stage encourages

stagecoach
2726 faults in a stagecoach may
4493 of a stagecoach from

stages
6388 The four stages of man are
9987 three stages before it
10717 his stages may have

stagnation
1796 then keeps life from stagnation.

staid
7496 with black staid wisdom's

stain
603 like a stain; Something
3740 leave a stain behind

stained
8449 red As the stained stones

stains
10676 glass, Stains the white

stair
683 is by a winding stair.
7226 up the stair I met a

stairs
7425 town, Up stairs and down

stake
7951 that first stake, they'll
8703 and from stake to stake.
10867 at the stake as witches

stalk
9120 delight grow on one stalk.

stalking
12864 naked foot, stalking in my

stalks
3812 gropes, it stalks like a

stamp
9794 physics or stamp

stamped
7202 temperament stamped upon the
11500 one of you Stamped with the

stamps
8200 animals and stick in stamps.

stand
1160 that house cannot stand.
2704 no time to stand and stare.
4686 where we stand, as in
4854 A stand can be made against
6269 prepared to stand up for
6636 Amen. Here stand I. I can
6840 who will stand on either
6989 Get up, stand up Stand up
7002 Stand still you watches of
7610 in this we stand or fall.
8035 A man can stand a lot as
9184 seven times, stand up eight.
9970 - stand quietly
10359 Stand not upon the order of
12077 In order to stand well in
12302 I will not stand for being

standard
2516 the scarlet standard high!
9015 identical standard of bathing

standards
1033 of date. Standards are always
9603 raising of standards of modern
11211 of lowering your standards!

standing
4802 is your standing in the

stands
5651 where he stands in moments
11366 leaves, she stands Who

stanza
7211 blown sky-high in a stanza.

star
2251 more distant than any star.
2710 Being a star has made it
2959 a falling star, Get with
6795 By a high star our course
7563 zenith like a falling star.
7635 The evening star, Love's
8141 My only star is dead,
9807 a humdrum star lost in a
10139 particular star And think
11445 little star, How I
11568 with his evil star.
12697 A Star for every State,

star-crossed
10468 A pair of star-crossed lovers

star-led
7533 The star-led wizards haste

star-spangled
5597 'Tis the star-spangled banner; O

stardom
670 Stardom isn't a profession;

stardust
7693 We are stardust, We are

stare
11542 With a stony British stare.

starlit
12880 A starlit or a moonlit dome

stars
904 you can see the stars.
5447 same bright, patient stars.
5474 and the stars through
6011 the mud, and one the stars.
6154 up to the Stars above And
6484 the lovely stars, the
6995 equi. The stars move
6996 You stars that reigned at
6998 beauty of a thousand stars.
7075 And opposition of the stars.
7314 any kinship with the stars.
7346 Beneath the stars, upon yon
7588 all the stars Hide their
7985 struggle to the stars.
8497 And the stars begin to
8795 And in the stars the glory
8954 it's in the stars, Next July
9636 And the stars in her
9804 night with different stars.
10275 not in our stars, But in
11017 touch the stars, Oft
11447 And the stars are old,
11512 of the stars, I marked
11693 eyes of the stars Through
12051 look at the stars without
12059 beyond the stars, Where
12129 that's the way to the stars.
12331 merely the stars'
12507 journey-work of the stars.
12569 us are looking at the stars.

start
927 orchestra: start together
2339 the family start? It
6317 You start with

starter
559 was even a starter. There

startle
5481 does not startle it or

startled
4718 is always startled when he

starvation
4659 of starvation live
9757 to avoid starvation and to

starve
10387 they that starve with

starved
5459 I saw their starved lips in

starving
2824 dead - 'Tis starving makes it
2915 you have a starving

state
598 as the State And no one
1121 The state is or can be
1772 A state without the means
2179 word, than to rule a state.
3022 ruin or to rule the state.
3876 The state, it cannot too
3993 Here's a state of things!
4505 Only in the state does man
5215 I take the state of
6219 While the State exists,
6535 c'est moi. I am the State.
6841 for the state; The the
6907 it off on the state.
7076 a firm state by
7372 A State which dwarfs its
7375 worth of a State, in the
7779 an entire state. And
9052 The State, that cawing
11046 The State is an instrument
11281 affluent state .. She
11704 decades the state has been
12315 The State is a relation of
12697 for every State, and a

stately
7171 and round a stately park and

stately homes
4527 The stately homes of England, How
12745 as the stately homes of

statement
1390 a correct statement is a false
8980 Any general statement is like a
11930 why .. The statement was

states
978 to similar states of mind.
5438 many goodly states and
5995 States, like men, have their

statesman
8 of a statesman is that he
49 than an American Statesman.
1757 be my standard of a statesman.
2753 European statesman who will
3026 fiddler, statesman, and
4177 nice for a statesman, too proud
6413 did agree, he was a statesman.
6574 A genuine statesman should be
8823 A statesman is a politician who
11165 firm is a statesman, and a
11905 A statesman is a
12249 show us a statesman who can
12910 A statesman is an easy man, He

statesmen
2889 class, requires grave statesmen.
12217 faults of statesmen give

station
1101 concrete station With a
2814 know our proper stations.
3857 a private station, A mind
6671 noblest station is
10996 queen, she leaves the station.
12639 A high station in life is

stationary
4340 its horn and each stationary.

statistically
3793 I could prove God statistically.

statisticians
11787 Though statisticians in our time

statistics
1507 in books, statistics in
2391 Statistics are no substitute for
2863 lies, damned lies and statistics.
4767 We are just statistics, born to
6009 He uses statistics as a drunken

statue
236 to die Seldom rates a statue.
4702 of his own statue erected by
8371 there's a statue inside

statues
389 bunk, Epp's statues are junk,
6041 money. The statues will be

stature
7315 I the stature of my
7769 beauty of stature is the
9939 is of a low stature, but it

status
6899 from Status to
11468 Human status ought not to

status quo
11044 be!' restored the status quo.

stay
3419 It will not stay. God
5977 things to stay as they
6233 here to stay, oh I
6770 Here I am, and here I stay.
7638 go, Is to stay here;
8511 I shall stay the way I am
9025 in heaven Stay there And

staying
4824 - a matter of staying power.
6904 I am here - I am staying.
11100 It's staying up all
12634 .. Just staying on it, I

stays
9945 together stays together.

steal
801 and I will steal from
1506 they would steal two hours
2411 shalt not steal; an empty
3255 imitate; mature poets steal.
4356 When a man steals your
5451 she, 'To steal my
7712 If you steal from one
7866 days Is to steal a few
8934 let me die; Steal from the
9167 is when I steal other
9204 rise and steal a horse.
9320 can steal more than

stealing
9941 hanged for stealing horses,

steals
10430 Who steals my purse steals

stealth
5001 good by stealth and being
5968 action by stealth, and to

steam
7976 snorting steam and piston

steamer
3979 about in a steamer from

steed
5457 my pacing steed And

steel
486 them the cold steel, boys!
7481 is clad in complete steel.
9793 red line tipped with steel.

steeped
9500 of the Sea, steeped in stars,

steer
161 it's time to steer clear.
7146 and cannot steer A middle
10641 to be in heaven is to steer.
11738 who can steer within

steering
6589 else were steering; If we see

stein
389 called Stein, There's

stendhal
3940 secret of Stendhal, his great

step
491 one small step for man,
644 was an easy step to
4306 is to take a step back.
6409 take a big step if one is
8081 is only one step from the
8470 One step above the
8704 the first step toward
9820 to take a step. Then
11764 Let him step to the
12872 a back step - only in

step-mother
7673 A stony-hearted step-mother.

stepped in
10360 am in blood Stepped in so far

stepping-stones
11554 may rise on stepping-stones Of their

steps
6837 advances by steps, and not
7470 that by due steps aspire To

sterilized
4468 recognized is a bias sterilized.

stern
6805 of those stern and

sterner
10291 be made of sterner stuff.

stick
910 of it will always stick.
5159 to a stick and a
6726 we going to make it stick!
8364 of a stick inside a
8473 he fell like the stick.
10383 kind of burr; I shall stick.
10920 was like a stick. It had

stifle
7376 to stifle is a false

stigma
4341 Any stigma, as the old

still
2834 they liked me still',
8127 is to stand still for six
9000 yet is must not stand still.
9463 standing still. Like
9644 silence, still as the
11703 merely by standing still."

stillness
1011 of stillness in the
4290 a solemn stillness holds,

stilts
1049 - nonsense upon stilts.

stimulant
3489 a supply of stimulant handy in

stimulated
9943 stimulated in order

stimulation
7379 unnatural stimulation in others.

stimulus
12527 a healthful stimulus, and are

sting
137 butterfly, sting like a
373 Is thy sting-a-ling-a-l
1131 is thy sting? O grave,
8604 it is a sting, It is a

stings
6453 And if I kiss he stingeth me.
8837 dirt that sinks and stings.

stir
4022 You must stir it and stump
10295 speech, To stir men's
12485 with so little stir.

stirred
3543 peel. Shaken and not stirred.

stirrup
1653 to the stirrup, and
2022 Betwixt the stirrup and the
9275 have a foot in the stirrup.

stock
9559 some good stock and hold
10959 see how his stock went on.

stock exchange
6867 onto the Stock Exchange missing

stocking
8952 glimpse of stocking Was looked

stockings
7830 mouse; The stockings were hung

stocks
3500 Stocks have reached what

stoic
8727 either a stoic or a

stole
4467 all we stole it fair

stolen
2510 he that has stolen the
4381 horses may not be stolen.
4874 Stolen kisses are always
5038 to be sweet must be stolen.

stomach
2925 - I have no stomach for such
4051 were, the stomach of the
5855 A hungry stomach has no ears.
8071 army marches on its stomach.
8467 If your stomach disputes you,

10065 on their stomachs shouting:
10078 is a good-humoured stomach.

stone
1148 let him first cast a stone.
4227 stand like stone, Kindness
4491 heaviest stone that the
6488 blossoming in stone.
6920 of this stone and anvil
7759 gout, give them the stone!
8371 inside every block of stone?
8432 out a stone, a ring is
9630 as iron, Water like a stone.
9817 one's own stone
10571 leave no stone unturned
10696 legs of stone Stand in
11712 Turn but a stone, and start

stone age
6211 them back into the Stone Age.

stones
7932 Like stones, words are
8449 the stained stones kissed by
8814 is built of stones; but an
10568 these stones, And curst
10999 words like stones and who

stony
7328 Along that stony path the
12645 up, (more stony than a

stony-hearted
7673 A stony-hearted step-mother.

stood
11486 shade, She stood, a sight

stools
2623 invented stools,

stoops
1644 way; to rise, it stoops.
4199 woman stoops to folly
9310 say - She stoops, she

stop
1708 history yelling Stop!'
2119 to the end: then stop.'
4883 nothing will stop them.
6911 Stop, Sir, stop - go away:
7991 Stop-look-listen.
8153 Stop the world, I want to
8659 who will stop your
9610 when to stop raking the

stopped
6791 (Somebody stopped the moving
7096 or my watch has stopped."
12847 But it stopped short - never

storehouse
676 is] a rich storehouse for the

stories
4677 wicked stories about me.
4972 to believe of my own stories.
10450 tell sad stories of the
11438 name for stories about the

storm
795 a summer storm, Short as
2614 And rides upon the storm.
5025 world as storms in the
5401 Storm and stress.
6779 It was a storm in a tea
7768 a great storm, 'O God,
8510 calm that know the storm.
10441 a ceaseless storm Whirring

stormy
5789 Stormy weather, Since my man
9854 Stormy, husky, brawling,

story
1042 many a good story has been
6741 and the story of the
6845 is the story told, How
7968 Every picture tells a story.
9787 Every story has three sides
10231 in pain, To tell my story.
11130 is all this story about?' 'A
11940 to write a story for boys

story-teller
10781 basically a story-teller, not a

storytellers
2211 acrobats, storytellers, dancers,

stove-lid
11937 on a hot stove-lid. She will

straight
374 that can set things straight.
5386 humanity no straight thing can
6414 to keep him straight.
7928 the crooked straight? Let it
9520 politics, a straight line is

straightfaced
11680 Straightfaced in his cunning sleep

strain
8000 the train take the strain.
12742 Out of the strain of the

strained
10402 is ı.ot strained, It

strains
7483 And took in strains that might
10707 In profuse strains of

strand
1521 the Maypole in the Strand?

strange
1969 'Tis strange - but true; for
2564 think me strange or older,
5203 It is very strange, and very
6471 new, to something strange.
7104 make strange
7393 Strange how few After all's
8623 Strange the difference of
8630 everything that looks strange.
8635 Strange to see how a good
8961 But how strange the change
10487 a man with strange
11514 new men, strange faces,
11632 'Tis strange what a man may
11849 were such strange and

strangeness
751 not some strangeness in the
896 their degree of strangeness to us.

stranger
1048 foe, but never love a stranger.
4790 I, a stranger and afraid In a
8089 of the stranger If one's
9819 within us a stranger totally
12117 No stranger to trouble myself

strangers
2252 things to perfect strangers.
10123 we may be better strangers.
11086 myself and strangers. The
12641 on the kindness of strangers.

stratagem
8732 a constant stratagem to cover

strategy
1027 industrial strategy for the

strauss
8060 style of Strauss. That was

stravinsky
8060 killed by Stravinsky. He

straw
6028 are but as straw dogs.
10056 Take a straw and throw it

strawberries
8605 within, Strawberries swimming

stray
3840 fondly stray. Over the

stream
12681 against the stream knows the
12830 glides the Stream, and shall

streams
8858 As shallow streams run
9378 floods and streams; The

street
459 on the street, and
2028 it in the street and
3483 the sunny side of the street.
12400 is worth two in the street."

streets
1018 Streets Flooded. Please
3464 is not the streets that

strength
949 Strength is a matter of the
1210 that are above thy strength.
1314 and natural strength; the
1430 not when my strength faileth
4398 from the strength you
4663 man's imitation of strength.
5176 mechanics laughs at strength.

5852 do more than strength and fury.
5903 weakness than to our strength.
5944 but the child's strength.
6322 Freude. Strength through
6578 how much strength is in
6745 Our strength is often composed
7073 all our strength, and all
7749 is thy strength and Christ
8242 is not the strength, but the
8431 Though the strength is
8567 goal. My strength lies
9057 Even if strength fail,
11355 Strength without hands to
11419 equal to the horse's strength.
11483 My strength is as the strength
12522 to strength, but one
12681 knows the strength of it.
12813 rather find Strength in what

strengthen
2477 and strengthen their

strenuous
9615 doctrine of the strenuous life.

stress
5401 Storm and stress.
8385 in times of stress 'educated'
11814 shattering stress and

stretched
4692 Man's mind stretched to a new
8836 thee there, Stretched on the
11929 which he stretched, but

strides
2649 made giant strides in

strife
767 thraldom, or a double strife?
2288 for the sake of strife.
4294 ignoble strife, Their
5989 worth my strife; Nature I
6580 In the strife of Truth
8289 ceaseless strife, Beat wild

strike
1393 I write, I strike out three.
5137 fine, strike it out.
7878 thou strike not awry,
8146 the shore, Strike et when
9369 may happily strike out his
10621 If you strike a child take

string
6135 model has a string to each
7794 own but the string to bind

strings
2811 These are strings .. in the
3388 strings of tension
7005 golden strings all women

strip club
7849 The Strip Club is another form

striped
5461 and blue; Striped like a

stripes
5691 an' cut his stripes away, An'

strive
6363 let us strive on to
11017 And he that strives to touch

strives
4096 will err while yet he strives.
4119 man who aspires and strives.

stroke
7577 No second stroke intend.

strong
2340 nations are strong, they are
3698 But the strong are saying
5577 If we are strong, our
5667 Come; and strong within us
5825 against the strong, Is always
5875 We are all strong enough to
6352 be too strong for the
6483 silence are strong, and
8245 destroy me, makes me strong.
8558 It is strong. Only the
10094 only the Strong shall
10465 to keep the strong in awe.
10808 Strong is the lion - like a
11541 One still strong man in a
12807 And I again am strong.

stronger
381 one thing stronger than all

1692 cause, is stronger than all
3904 least the stronger, of the
11404 on the side of the stronger.

strongest
5853 of the strongest is always
7566 .. The strongest and the
12787 Strongest minds Are often those

stronghold
6637 A safe stronghold our God is

struck
1855 Diogenes struck the father
3388 tension waiting to be struck.
5014 to be struck by
6189 Let the tent be struck.
10149 thought hath struck him.
10723 I was struck all of a heap.

structure
7407 The structure of a play is

struggle
85 struggle both of
1788 in a contemptible struggle.
2650 the struggle for power.
3466 after you cease to struggle.
3828 life is the struggle, the
4059 a desperate struggle for food
5571 twilight struggle, year in
6937 perpetual struggle for room
7985 Through struggle to the
9956 themselves struggle in vain.
12950 the eternal struggle between

struggled
810 has ever struggled with
7417 I struggled in the beginning.
12424 People struggled on for years
12489 having struggled so hard to

struggles
6628 the land on another's struggles.

strumpet
10145 Into a strumpet's fool.

stuck
8264 And they stuck it in.

student
382 If the student fails to learn
3541 unknown, Student of our

students
2347 loses interest in students.
4141 always been students, and their
4331 expect our students to become
5590 sex for the students, athletics
9340 Students of the heavens are

studied
314 body of objects to be studied.
754 have rather studied books than
6945 I've studied all the lore of

studies
736 much time in studies is sloth.
7654 air of delightful studies.

studious
3853 Studious of elegance and ease,
11732 Studious let me sit, And hold

study
756 live to study, and not
4894 The proper study of mankind
5267 paths of study, and come
5639 did nothing study but the
6657 you are in some brown study.
7357 often as a study is
8943 The proper study of mankind

stuff
1111 I stuffed their mouths with
2545 short to stuff a
3881 ever such stuff as great
10489 We are such stuff As dreams
10661 are the stuff of which

stumble
3808 you stumble into when
11017 stars, Oft stumbles at a

stumbled
10325 no eyes; I stumbled when I

stumbling block
8072 will be a stumbling block and the

stung
1642 Stung by the splendour of a

stunned
2451 hath been stunned, And is of

stunt
9405 amusing stunt. It is

stupendous
8896 of one stupendous whole,

stupid
7683 can be so stupid to deny
9157 Better silent than stupid.
9467 half as stupid as my
10581 When a stupid man is doing
11389 The stupid neither forgive

stupidest
7360 existence the stupidest party.

stupidity
81 on his stupidity - and
4703 itself; stupidity often
5806 Stupidity is an elemental force
9956 With stupidity the gods

stygian
4999 horrible Stygian smoke of

style
2195 be bought. Style one must
2425 Style is a simple way of
4704 When the style is fully
7202 Style is the hallmark of a
8537 a natural style, we are
8711 has no real style. He just
9812 fade - style is
11324 true definition of a style.
11453 the Roman style: If you
11758 As for the style of writing, if
12396 Style is the dress of
12911 Style, personality -

styled
5277 truly then Styled but the

styles
12159 All styles are good except

stylish
2671 won't be a stylish marriage,

subconscious
3577 into his subconscious, and draws

subdue
1752 It may subdue for a
11067 but Men subdue their
12002 is to subdue the armies

subject
2309 and won't change the subject.
3275 is to be a subject, what to
9889 form on a subject in which
10262 Every subject's duty is the
12425 really good subject, one has

subjects
1778 policy when subjects are rebels
3505 who fears the other subjects.
9560 only on different subjects.
10871 at all upon important subjects.
12652 favourite subjects -

subjugation
806 white - subjugation if you're

sublime
1297 and often reaches the sublime.
1935 and sublime The image
4262 from the Sublime To the
6890 the ridiculous, the sublime.
8081 from the sublime to the
8470 The sublime and the

submission
3207 for submission
7595 with coy submission, modest
9757 voluntary submission to an

submit
11061 a woman must submit to it.

submits
1368 resignation, which submits.
8211 times; he submits to

subordinate
5539 to be in a subordinate position

subscribers
5107 any list of subscribers; one, that

subscription
4702 erected by national subscription.

subsistence
1071 not any subsistence without a
6936 ratio. Subsistence only

substance
4466 more important than substance.
11021 that is, a substance consisting
11368 be, is the substance of men
12696 of some substance and stake

substitute
1057 the age of substitutes: instead
4881 No substitute has been found for
4918 There is no substitute for
7938 is not a substitute for
12239 can also be a substitute for sex.

substituted
6200 one can be substituted for the

substitutes
8036 to substitutes is one of

subtle
2316 try to be subtle or clever.
3166 God is subtle but he is not
3763 may not be subtle, but
4664 are more subtle and less

subtopia
8067 that it will stick - SUBTOPIA.

suburb
1097 At the new suburb stretched

suburbia
9391 I come from suburbia .. and I

subversive
8395 is funny is subversive, every
9767 Thought is subversive and

succeed
1303 cannot succeed through
2333 have got to succeed in doing
2836 who ne'er succeed. To
4412 We shall succeed only so far
4476 that it shall never succeed.
5012 fail and the humblest succeed.
5905 enough to succeed, a friend
7224 How to succeed in business
8022 To succeed pre-eminently in
9444 possible to succeed without
11983 rest of us could not succeed
12162 able to succeed in the
12623 nor succeed in order

succeeds
4621 Nothing succeeds like one's
12096 a friend succeeds, a little

success
19 Success has made failures of
384 Success is not so much what
391 to be a success, but time
672 owes his success to his
1081 thing about success is that
1477 fails like success because we
2310 guarantee success in war,
2836 Success is counted sweetest
3175 If A is a success in life,
3228 Success is relative: It is
3312 which can do without success.
3570 is the secret of success.
4209 From success you get a lot of
4850 bows to success, even
6123 Success is not the result of
6191 Sweet smell of success.
6246 else but success, and to
6620 Success is that old A B C -
7280 and his success is
7902 is only one success - to be
8255 Success is the progressive
8570 ecstasy, is success in life.
9440 is also the success of others.
9586 failure on the way to success.
9703 formula for success except,
9849 marriage a success and only
9996 secret of success is to go
10074 the better, success for the
10856 isn't a success? Have I
10879 very lively hope of success.
10984 to success in life is
11204 the true success is to
11302 greatest success is
11374 formula for success, but I can
11737 meet with a success unexpected
12066 led to extraordinary success.

The Wordsworth Dictionary of Quotations

12496 fruition of success, no matter
12597 Success is a science. If you

successes
9705 to have successes with women

successful
1593 every successful man
2107 that in successful lives it
2173 the title of a successful book.
3176 A successful man is he who
3924 who is successful before he
4131 every successful man you'll
6297 A successful individual
7036 The successful people are the
7943 Being successful in England is a
11734 to do to be successful, most

succession
4675 things in succession. That

successor
4621 like one's own successor.

succumbed
12424 always succumbed to

succumbs
3111 individual succumbs, but he

sucked
2945 then? But sucked on country

sucker
861 There's a sucker born every
3488 give a sucker an even

suckle
10427 To suckle fools and

suckling
2634 art for suckling children

sudden
2877 Departure should be sudden.
7579 On a sudden open fly With
11708 to Dawn: Be sudden - to Eve:

suddenly
5363 No one ever suddenly became
10008 come to me suddenly, It came

suez
5720 east of Suez, where the

suffer
2099 what men suffer, but
3024 Better one suffer, than a
4670 born to love and to suffer.
5204 better to suffer wrong than
5845 Rather suffer than die is
6964 the inferior and must suffer.
7941 judges] suffer from a bad
8801 must also suffer greatly.
9809 capacity to suffer because of
11872 have courage to suffer.
12387 simplicity, Suffer me to come
12417 what we can suffer is the

suffered
7915 that others have suffered too.
9064 they have suffered in order

suffering
851 alleviate suffering, and not
895 way of not suffering in life,
2975 it is the suffering of being
3195 unspeakable suffering may well
3386 Each suffering is
7182 true that suffering ennobles
7330 to avoid suffering the more
7795 who fears suffering is already
8383 life is suffering and only
9439 causes less suffering than an
9749 for the suffering of
12099 the majesty of human suffering.
12542 to escape the suffering of life.
12775 betrayed: Suffering is

sufferings
446 when my sufferings are to
5321 in human sufferings and unites

suffers
6019 Who suffreth moore than
10817 inform us of what he suffers.

sufficiency
11727 An elegant sufficiency, content,

sufficient
482 he is sufficient for
6414 Sufficient conscience to bother

sugar
6170 pills in sugar coating.

suggest
6739 is to suggest that

suicide
425 if it's just a suicide note.
4004 from the suicide's grave
5399 The longest suicide note in
6713 It is not: it is suicide.
6896 invariably suicide, not
7404 A suicide kills two people,
8228 thought of suicide is a great
9762 temporary suicide: the
11198 not even suicide, but to be
11296 commit slow suicide by

suicides
2476 as many suicides as

suit
2266 have chosen a suit by it.

suited
9658 are well suited when both

sum
4714 picture, not doing a sum.
8522 to the sum involved.

summer
206 on a hot summer afternoon.
965 day of high summer like true
1457 Summer ends, and Autumn
1681 it was summer or winter,
2718 the peak of summer's past,
3926 fulness o' summer, when the
4610 Summer time an' the livin'
6013 In a somer seson, whan
7389 know that summer sang in me
9179 Summer is the mother of the
9255 July's too late - for summer.
10545 thee to a summer's day?
11174 In summer, quite the
11559 never knew the summer woods.
12216 to ensure summer in England
12823 bathing of a summer's day.

summer-night
5445 a trancèd summer-night, Those

summits
4882 Summits are odd creatures.

sun
1133 let not the sun go down
1212 nothing new under the sun.
1299 down of the sun and in the
1377 between me and the sun.
1715 our own place in the sun.
2413 front the sun climbs
2447 The Sun's rim dips; the
2570 tired the sun with
2591 Go out in the midday sun.
3299 The sun, moon and stars
4740 where the sun Came
6013 whan softe was the sonne.
6022 is the sonne; Is no
6115 where the sun reigns
7073 make our sun Stand
7515 the great sun begins his
7542 So when the sun in bed,
7657 The sun to me is dark And
8285 which the sun ever sets.
8448 into the sun - Gently
8960 moon and under the sun.
9954 The sun does not set in
10180 heat o' the sun, Nor the
10472 and Juliet is the sun.
10496 against a setting sun.
10751 light a candle to the sun.
10752 the mid-day sun, though he
10995 Born of the sun they
11422 The sun will set without
11447 Till the sun grows cold,
11676 you let the sun in, mind
12211 The best sun we have is
12908 golden apples of the sun.

sun-flower
7852 As the sun-flower turns on

sunbeam
11412 Jesus wants me for a sunbeam.

sunbeams
7495 motes that people the sunbeams.

sunday
69 Sunday clears away the rust
363 it being Sunday, had
3539 that calm Sunday that goes
6793 For this is Sunday morning,
9463 feeling of Sunday is the

sundial
1004 I am a sundial, and I make a

sundown
9571 between Sundown and Sun-up

sung
5680 when you've sung 'God save
6476 ever were sung or said;
8984 Bah! I have sung women in

sunlight
2661 .. lovers alone wear sunlight.
6120 in the sunlight strong,
6794 The sunlight on the garden
11482 My lips, as sunlight drinketh

sunny
3483 feet To the sunny side of

suns
5270 Suns, that set, may rise
8891 planets circle other suns.

sunset
1652 died away: Sunset ran, one
6872 may make a fine sunset.
8150 Now the sunset breezes
9062 a horror of sunsets, they're
9416 me into the sunset of my

sunshine
1650 Fit for the sunshine, so, it
7517 to play On a sunshine holiday.
10567 like sunshine after
11007 And made a sunshine in the
11121 are the sunshine; they are

superfluities
3860 or no, we must have superfluities.
7340 is the purgation of superfluities.

superfluous
8166 is either superfluous or
12158 The superfluous, a very necessary

superflux
11351 Superflux of pain.

superior
328 I am a most superior person.
476 that they may be superior.
5373 for the superior tastes of
7846 to say, Superior people
9166 about being superior to some
9532 do the work of superior people.

superiority
3823 of man's superiority to all
9770 any innate superiority of the
10918 superiority of certain

superman
8241 you the superman. Man is

supernatural
10342 This supernatural soliciting
12072 a human quality, but supernatural.

superstition
741 There is a superstition in
1781 Superstition is the religion of
4112 Superstition is the poetry of
4948 for a superstition to enslave
5611 American superstition is belief

superstitious
6329 are more superstitious than they

supped
10372 I have supped full with

supper
752 but it is a bad supper.
3152 I consider supper as a
9086 after supper walk a

supplied
2785 he is well supplied with it.

supplies
1535 just bought some new supplies.

supply
1293 is, the supply has always
4280 The supply of good
6030 The supply of government

The Wordsworth Dictionary of Quotations

support
2291 to support the
3148 help and support of the
4873 a loss to support a flagging
7237 because I support if from
7238 who will support me when I
8173 May He support us all the day
10493 up, But to support him after.

supportable
1901 is more supportable with

suppose
10849 To suppose, as we all

supposed
188 All you're supposed to do is
11903 they are supposed to do

suppress
8287 great as the power of suppress.

suppressed
210 is all that cannot be suppressed.

suppression
5809 not mean suppression and

supreme
8161 two only supreme and

sure
984 What nobody is sure about!
1433 world so sure: that it
6588 you may be sure of, be

surfeit
10387 sick that surfeit with too

surfing
5976 is like surfing. You are

surgeon
3405 the wise and humane surgeon.
6462 better than a plastic surgeon.

surgery
3504 practice of surgery a

surgical
10892 requires a surgical operation

surname
6814 Out of his surname they have

surpassed
8241 is something to be surpassed.

surprise
1530 of a big surprise If you go
2764 element of surprise up his
2802 get a big surprise with the
5034 God is the surprise of the
5846 wise man by surprise; he is
7889 There is no surprise more
8061 is a great surprise. I do not
11710 strange surprise, Have
12186 Live frugally on surprise.

surprised
905 I am still surprised each time
2762 he is quite surprised to be
5082 but you are surprised to find it
7404 never hurt, Surprised by unjust
8499 I wouldn't be at all surprised.
8601 man there is a surprised woman.

surprises
632 Surprises are foolish things.

surrender
201 the cash surrender value of a
2021 Guards die but do not surrender.
2311 hills; we shall never surrender.
3786 rather than surrender any
4274 immediate surrender can be

surrounding
8355 I plus my surroundings, and if I
12748 envelope surrounding us from

survey
2615 I am monarch of all I survey.

survival
2334 victory, there is no survival.
2636 Survival is triumph enough.
2715 we are their survival machines.
3182 cared about survival - I merely
4890 rumour, and survival a thing
8481 for survival of the
10988 This survival of the fittest

survive
1483 luck to survive this
2281 that may survive Long after

survived
10759 J'ai vécu. I survived.
12639 are survived with

survives
7669 her fame survives, A secular
10801 is what survives when what

surviving
4325 in surviving adversity.

survivors
3948 are no winners, only survivors.
6960 is more the survivors' affair

susceptible
12560 peculiarly susceptible to

suspect
742 makes a man suspect much, more

suspected
6425 are always suspected, and
9271 the morning never suspected.

suspecting
9660 point of suspecting the

suspended
3913 here that I suspended my
5202 has been suspended, the more

suspense
12562 This suspense is terrible. I

suspicion
959 by the suspicion that they
2007 wife must be above suspicion.
5299 characters are above suspicion.
10268 Suspicion always haunts the
12960 than a mere suspicion that the

suspicions
743 Suspicions amongst thoughts are
7708 fool usually has his suspicions.

sustain
3392 two words, sustain and

sustains
6629 What sustains the human spirit

swagger
9032 they would swagger more now,

swagman
8571 a jolly swagman camped by

swallow
11260 swim in but hard to swallow.

swallowed
3723 are being swallowed up by the
11902 to keep riding or be swallowed.

swallowing
3485 act of swallowing, I will

swan
3925 The silver swan, who,
5367 so much as a black swan.

swanee
3598 upon the Swanee River,

swap
6368 not best to swap horses

swat
2380 just a bit harder to swat.

swayed
4014 she be swayed by quite

swear
11977 when very angry, swear.

swears
3129 doesn't talk, it swears,
10564 my love swears that she

sweat
2297 toil, tears and sweat.
2708 it has to sweat. There
8484 I sweat. If anything comes
9326 our midday sweat, our
11703 into a muck sweat merely by

sweats
10236 Falstaff sweats to death And
12538 the bloody sweats, None knew

sweet
1237 is sweet to the
1640 But then, how it was sweet!
1954 Sweet is revenge -
2373 saw so sweet a face As
2671 you'll look sweet upon the
5246 free: Such sweet neglect
5417 Full of sweet dreams,
5517 Here are sweet peas, on
5519 'Tis very sweet to look
5929 know that a sweet child is
6058 She's as sweet as the
6452 a bee Doth suck his sweet.
6628 Sweet is it, when on the
6990 Sweet Analytics, 'tis thou
7858 half so sweet in life As
8188 grace! how sweet the sound
8189 How sweet the name of Jesus
9210 Sweet is war to those who
10444 Things sweet to taste prove
10474 name would smell as sweet.
11589 Sweet and low, sweet and
11683 never been sweet in the
11691 thing that smells sweet.

sweeten
10368 will not sweeten this

sweeteners
3477 are the best sweeteners of tea.

sweeter
9499 Sweeter than the flesh of

sweetest
706 it, the sweetest canticle
1821 O; The sweetest hours that
9537 The sweetest sounds I'll ever
10556 For sweetest things turn

sweetheart
898 A sweetheart is a bottle of
9241 a dog's; then a sweetheart's.

sweetly
10542 They do but sweetly chide

sweetness
498 passion for sweetness and light,
7507 As may with sweetness, through
11304 which are sweetness and light

sweets
2640 is a bag of boiled sweets.

swell
8954 What a swell party this

swells
12672 grows or swells, and when

swept
624 than it is swept by and

swift
1208 not to the swift, nor the
4624 Swift managed to
11709 To all swift things for

swift-flowing
2155 in wind and swift-flowing water.

swifter
7983 fortius. Swifter, higher,

swill
8364 stick inside a swill bucket.

swim
8846 temples, swim before my
9240 right, must swim three
11260 good to swim in but

swimming
4059 Swimming for his life, a man
12114 Odd figures swimming were
12681 man who is swimming against

swimming pool
9466 fool, Walk across my swimming pool.

swindles
4545 all truly great swindles are.

swing
341 Swing low, sweet chariot
10902 room enough to swing a cat.

swings
8705 that swings. Mozart

swish
192 my teeth and swish my tail.

swiss
3455 The Swiss are not a people

switzerland
12356 In Switzerland they had

swoons
5994 sinks and swoons under a

sword
1197 edge of the sword: but not
1350 shall my sword sleep in
1724 is mightier than the sword.
1846 pen is worse than the sword.
2376 drew the sword, he threw
4575 One sword keeps another in
4806 swift sword: His truth
5999 could use the sword and pen.
6295 than the sword of a
6920 out this sword of this
6924 held a fair sword in that
7859 father's sword he has
8264 gave them a sword. And they
9726 as soldiers of the sword.
12540 The brave man with a sword!
12878 he had a sword upstairs.

swords
6556 dreams or swords, You can
7013 Our swords shall play the
10830 hearts and sharp swords.

swore
1855 father when the son swore.
6545 night I swore to thee
11124 'Our armies swore terribly

syllable
10373 To the last syllable of

syllogism
8300 of your syllogism, I said

symbol
1069 aside the symbols of
2094 the exact symbol of its
5327 It is a symbol of Irish art.

symmetry
1362 frame thy fearful symmetry?

sympathetic
7262 with the sympathetic tears of

sympathize
4906 I can sympathize with people's

sympathizer
8590 A Sympathizer would seem to imply

sympathy
3907 Our sympathy is cold to the
6079 lead our sympathy away in
9460 either give or take sympathy.

symptom
3407 a child for his symptom.

symptoms
348 have all your symptoms ready.
2186 Symptoms, then, are in reality
8913 of a hundred good symptoms.

syntax
2657 to the syntax of things
4704 he likes in words or syntax.

system
6116 by means of system. There is
6738 to their system, remained
8072 .. The new system of weights
8469 Any system of religion that
8891 Observe how system into

systematically
12685 done so systematically as nothing

systems
8125 other systems are worse.
11553 Our little systems have their

t-shirt
195 done that, got the T-shirt.

table
2675 put over my kitchen table.

taboos
3296 network of taboos.

taciturn
7700 precise and taciturn.

tact
385 Tact is the intelligence
1898 not always tact, and it is

tail
5392 it in the tail, and two
5690 that the tail must wag
5703 thy tail hangs down
7540 horror of his folded tail.

tailor
3163 leave elegance to the tailor.
4978 and not by his tailor.

taint
10435 But never taint my love.

take
811 people take and people
1412 start to take Vienna -
2434 it must first take away.
2642 Take away that fool's
2672 of give and take, but so
3563 enough to take away
3686 They have to take you in.
3759 bring, a day may take away.
3876 it does not take from
3894 They can't take that away
9820 a man is to take a step.
12251 choice, - take that or
12332 she may take away all

taken
1230 Lord hath taken away;
2222 never had it taken from you.
8596 carefully taken out of
11537 things are taken from us,

taken in
9962 being taken in by

takes
1995 like that it takes away.

taking
2536 means the taking it away

tale
6089 Trust the tale. The
9336 Simple this tale! - but
10011 have had a tale to tell of
10116 And thereby hangs a tale.
10304 twice-told tale, Vexing
10373 it is a tale Told by

talent
104 who has no talent and is
170 is talent; doing
846 and the talent which does
1016 I had no talent for
1084 of having talent is not
1716 must, and talent does what
1802 new talent has no
2215 is the sister of talent.
2589 is just A talent to amuse.
3001 itself, but talent instantly
3151 models for men of talent.
4123 Talent develops in quiet
4918 for talent. Industry
5228 has a talent. What is
6586 Talent is that which is in a
7325 must, and Talent does what
7677 that one talent which is
10844 tomb of a mediocre talent.
10925 Talent is always conscious
12567 only put my talent into my

talented
9022 I'm sure he's a talented man.

talents
2452 tried their talents at one or
5349 Great talents are the most
8832 the talents, or
9452 have great talents, industry
9850 to prove unequal talents.
11966 at least respect his talents.

tales
5171 to tell tales of himself

talk
262 psychotherapy is talk'.
713 and talk but a
738 nor to find talk and
1469 had a good talk. BOSWELL:
2121 said, 'To talk of many
2252 Men always talk about the
2465 world may talk of
2864 Talk as much as possible
2953 I long to talk with some
3025 and who talk too much.
3089 ways of making men talk."
3129 doesn't talk, it
4377 good deal from my own talk.
4530 it if you talk about it.
4652 no longer talk with
5112 You may talk in this

talk
5160 have his talk out as I
5685 And the talk slid north,
5739 If you can talk with
5751 nor good talk
6395 right to talk may be the
6897 it's bad to talk about
7176 well, and talk well but
7992 Careless talk costs lives.
8001 It's good to talk.
8236 Never to talk of oneself
8623 difference of men's talk!
8752 It can talk, talk,
9011 allowed to talk if
9042 They always talk, who never
9088 and to talk about date
9161 easier to talk than to
10300 upon our talk, And
10578 and could talk for hours
12020 Talk as though you have a
12257 wants to hear actors talk?

talkative
2359 is by nature rather talkative.

talked
2287 much they talked, so very
3411 He talked with more claret
4179 When they talked of their
12521 listen when his mate talked.
12587 than being talked about, and

talker
9449 that of the talker who

talkers
4519 fancy talkers about

talking
560 you can stop people talking.
1526 you ain't talking about him,
2212 right, will keep on talking.
4204 exhausted from not talking.
4956 walking, not a way of talking.
5102 be always talking, whether
5289 to the eye; talking is
5983 listen, try talking softly -
6396 to stop talking and find
7405 is a nation talking to itself.
8773 it is talking to itself.
9099 things without talking.
11292 is always talking about

talks
596 is one who talks in someone

taller
4800 should be taller, older,

tambourine
3133 Hey! Mr Tambourine man, play a

tame
4569 can'st not tame when once

tamed
7087 in one year tamed: So much

tangerine
6792 portion A tangerine and spit

tangle
12863 hooks shall tangle me no

tangled
5332 the dark tangled curls of
6538 When I lie tangled in her
7642 after them tangled in amorous

tank
7970 Put a tiger in your tank.

taper
5427 went the taper as she

tapped
2279 Poirot] tapped his

taradiddles
6206 are sent For telling taradiddles.'

target
2652 a moving target; he never

tarred
6347 man who was tarred and

tarry
4593 You may for ever tarry.

tarts
6778 by the action of two tarts.

tarzan
12348 Me Tarzan, you Jane.

task
1415 One's task is not to turn
2650 The main task of a free
2697 his most difficult task.
3354 and a task for life;
3615 day begin the task anew.
3662 a very difficult task.
4400 A task becomes a duty from
5681 is but one task for all -
6415 What is our task? To make
6497 sees some task begun,
7107 that the task itself
7894 the noblest task of the
9494 the highest task for a bond
10180 thy wordly task hast done,
11263 of strength for new tasks.
11726 Delightful task! to rear

tasmanians
7168 that the Tasmanians, who never

taste
1895 have good taste than about
2674 It is good taste, and good
2985 has acquired a taste for it.
3201 of taste in jokes
3512 Taste is the feminine of
5029 Taste cannot be controlled
5305 worse taste, than in a
5784 not the taste of water I
6759 Good taste is the first
6983 with no taste, etiquette
7273 the taste of the
8273 Safe taste is bad taste.
8718 Taste is the enemy of
8976 than the taste, and vice
9042 They never taste who always
9321 is better taste somehow
9454 we teach taste or genius
10444 sweet to taste prove in
10731 You had no taste when you
11399 The arbiter of taste.
12209 undoubtedly wanted taste.

tasted
5709 you ever tasted Man?'
11031 you have tasted two whole

tastes
10592 you. Their tastes may not be
12307 it never tastes quite the

tatters
7719 Rags and tatters, if you

tattoo
1598 attempt to tattoo soap

taught
3716 should be taught so early
4405 got to be taught to be
5707 (They taught me all I
7649 is plainest taught, and
7722 having been taught anything.
7854 that has taught us Six
7864 all they've taught me.
8884 Men must be taught as if you
10653 I was taught when I was
11004 which the Lord us taught.
11798 There taught us how to live;
12578 worth knowing can be taught.
12825 And I was taught to feel,

tavern
386 There is a tavern in the
2983 opened a tavern for his
5088 as by a good tavern or inn.

tax
1749 To tax and to please, no
3390 no income tax, no
4624 one small tax changed in
7045 power to tax involves
9568 The income tax has made

taxation
2432 The art of taxation consists
3668 one form of taxation that can
8419 Taxation without

taxes
248 State Building after taxes.
745 with taxes should
1862 Read my lips: no new taxes.
3630 except death and taxes.
5657 are the taxes of today.
7696 Death and taxes and

taxi
7099 leave in a taxi you can

taxicabs
1801 driving taxicabs and

taxing
6551 less of a taxing machine.

taxpayer
12956 The average taxpayer is no more

tea
1002 word for Tea? Upon my
2003 knee, Just tea for two
5328 I makes tea I makes
6968 warming the teapot. He's
7171 having tea just too
7745 When the tea is brought
9294 I want tea; but if
9422 sooner the tea's out of

teach
585 of his days Teach the free
1228 and it shall teach thee.
1432 So teach us to number our
1909 rules Teach nothing
2197 he lerne and gladly teche.
2364 profess to teach is often a
3157 to teach another is
3223 Teach us to care and not to
4576 Teach me, my God and King,
5294 To teach is to learn twice.
6607 Teach us, good Lord, to
7016 Doth teach us all to
8944 Teach me to feel another's
8965 Teach him how to live, And,
9227 is the ability to teach.
9454 Could we teach taste or
9673 books; they teach us only to
9783 To teach how to live with
10067 wants to teach there are
10085 while they teach, men
10667 Teach him to think for
10711 Teach me half the gladness
11726 thought, To teach the young
12840 wood May teach you more
12857 does not teach, which

teachable
4898 teaches only the teachable.

teacher
34 A teacher affects eternity;
382 learn the teacher fails to
447 is a good teacher, but she
1085 is a great teacher, but
6070 the worst teacher; it gives
10088 even without a teacher.
11387 A teacher should have maximal

teaches
8942 old age; it teaches us a
10020 does. He who cannot, teaches.
11047 of history teaches that up to

teaching
368 secret of teaching is to
887 Teaching is not a lost art,
4076 way of teaching men to
4654 are so busy teaching us that
9205 teach; by teaching you will

teams
8678 up into teams we would

teapot
6968 warming the teapot. He's a

tear
1923 betwixt a smile and tear.
1938 eye the unanswerable tear!
2073 will shine in every tear.
11312 no longer tear his heart.

tears
749 that shed tears when they
1141 away all tears from their
2769 voice was; Tears, tears
4133 world and tears unseen and
5242 my salt tears: Yet,
5450 it with tears unto the
5831 with tears; Oh life,
6120 strong, Her tears are in the
7162 no vent in tears may make
7503 Drew iron tears down
7671 is here for tears, nothing
8561 service In tears of
10150 Indeed the tears live in an

10228 I forbid my tears; but yet
10293 If you have tears, prepare
11539 Her tears fell with the
11591 Tears from the depth of
11615 Hence those tears.
11671 have not tears to flow.
12082 Tears are shed in my heart
12281 Weep thy girlish tears!
12425 enough to come to tears.

teary
6566 lips, An' teary round the

teases
2115 Because he knows it teases.

teat
6948 a full teat for

teatime
3263 home at teatime, clears

technical
12467 between a technical and a

technique
9393 infallible technique and then

technological
531 out in a technological society.
2491 single technological resource
6618 Technological man can't believe in
6769 with technological

technology
2385 advanced technology is
3672 Technology - the knack of so
3787 Technology means the systematic
7964 Progress through Technology.
8950 the province of technology.

tedious
8544 eloquence is tedious.
10304 Life is as tedious as a
10360 were as tedious as go

tediousness
125 his own tediousness has yet to

teenager
3666 The teenager' seems to have
11840 you as a teenager is when

teeth
786 like teeth, are
1229 with the skin of my teeth.
9108 The teeth are smiling, but
9278 bite, don't show your teeth.
10810 our graves with our teeth.
12024 children cut their teeth.
12038 must go armed to the teeth.

teetotaller
8387 a secret teetotaller and often
10584 only a beer teetotaller, not a

telegrams
9075 of those telegrams of which

telephone
89 The telephone book is full of
405 This telephone' has too many
2491 The telephone is the most
7966
8093 and the telephone rings and

television
853 Television is the first truly
900 through the television set.
1704 Television has a real problem.
2211 Television is not the truth.
2587 heavens, television is
3679 Television is an invention that
4212 and see bad television for
4466 the age of television, image
4627 Television has brought back
5981 Television has proved that
6457 Television is a gold goose that
6458 Television is the literature of
10004 Television? The word is half
12857 Television is chewing gum for

tell
489 know, you can't tell 'em.
1353 seek to tell thy love,
3644 you may tell it to only
4360 find out who will tell you.
5313 Tell me, tell me, tell me,
7051 and I can't tell you why;
8578 Never tell people how to
8612 must always tell what one
9099 each other tell each other

9290 doing, and tell her she
9376 Tell zeal it wants
9649 I cannot tell: I know
12200 rose! Tell her, that
12224 I always tell a young man
12603 a woman who tells one her

teller
1646 truth never hurts The teller.

telling
11208 way of telling you you've
12436 with you - I am telling you.

tells
11449 him how he is, tells you.

temper
651 and uncertain temper.
2433 lose their tempers merely
3690 losing your temper or your
3935 that has lost its temper.
4973 A tart temper never mellows
5471 I am in a temper that if I
6531 I should lose my temper.
7630 Yet I shall temper so Justice
8306 to lose me temper till it
8495 lose your temper with the
10317 Keep me in temper; I would
11119 - only keep your temper.

temperament
6643 my whole temperament is
12966 seen through a temperament.

temperance
3410 Temperance is the control of all
5072 for me as temperance would be
7663 this temperance, not

temperature
8459 to the mean temperature of the

tempered
11400 unless tempered by due

tempest
6486 lowers the tempest overhead.'
10560 looks on tempests and is

tempestuous
3146 O'er the world's tempestuous sea;
6511 smiled At their tempestuous glee.

temple
3934 gate of the temple and take
5810 of which they build temples.
6827 That temple of silence and
11919 is not a temple, but a

tempt
7572 Who shall tempt with
7857 that tempt the eye,

temptation
3192 a dangerous temptation to foreign
3241 The last temptation is the
4258 better of temptation is just to
5753 is always a temptation to a rich
6259 to resist an adequate temptation.
6433 interest, under temptation to it.
9530 The temptation is to tune
10575 resist temptation, because I
10623 maximum of temptation with the
11460 Temptation rarely comes in
11951 against temptations, but the
12402 avoid temptation unless I
12568 everything except temptation.
12583 rid of a temptation is to

temptations
331 of two temptations and choose
3967 of all temptations To belong
5764 may find temptations both in
9414 with two temptations and you
10101 pressed by the same temptations.
12536 There are no temptations there.

tempted
5384 I'm tempted to reply,
10378 or the tempted, who sins
12263 could have tempted me to

tempts
4296 all that tempts your

tenacity
8567 lies solely in my tenacity.

tend
7528 care To tend the homely

tender
2000 to that tender light
4132 from the tender years of
5499 with thee! tender is the
7210 tender; not a
12023 a tender look that

tenderness
796 of the tenderness I bear for
8447 flowers the tenderness of patient

tenement
6673 in the tenement dweller's

tennis
3709 playing tennis with the
6797 every tennis player

tennis-balls
12331 the stars' tennis-balls, struck

tennyson
5331 Lawn Tennyson, gentleman poet.

tension
5053 scene of tension and
8682 - takes the tension out of the

tent
5070 inside the tent pissing
6189 Let the tent be struck.
12539 that little tent of blue

tentacles
10826 from whose tentacles we never

tents
6479 fold their tents, like the
7012 to the stately tents of war.

terminated
572 to be terminated when one

terms
4274 No terms except
5113 upon easier terms than I was
11994 one's own terms for what
12673 any other terms than upon

terra firma
5398 I like terra firma - the more

terrible
3472 but dying, which is terrible.
6186 war is so terrible. We
10966 came, A terrible man with a
11677 life a terrible thing,
12562 suspense is terrible. I hope

terrifies
8540 [the heavens] terrifies me.

territory
7402 It comes with the territory.

terror
893 hysteria with joy and terror.
1331 human face; Terror the human
1378 Terror just before death,
2246 all that terror teaches,
2544 the naked terror? To the
4308 The terror of art lies in
5321 sufferer. Terror is the
6788 the ancient terror - Between
6896 The private terror of the
7201 of the terror of life's
10571 the even terror of their
11856 adds a new terror to life
12356 warfare, terror, murder,

terrorist
11657 starve the terrorist and the

terrors
460 of the new terrors of death.
3835 The little terrors.

test
13 certain test by which
962 The test of the ultimate
3761 What is the test of good
4445 The true test of
8101 I test my bath before I
10654 The test of a man or
11431 to test the
11858 the acid test of any
12417 is the test of powers;

testament
1355 Old and New Testaments are the
10451 The purple testament of

tested
11856 I have tested your

testing
6301 virtue at the testing point.

thames
1099 I see the Thames again? The
1805 The Thames is liquid
7926 The clear Thames bordered
11686 the riding Thames. After the
12213 God! the Thames is between

thank
8131 Thank God, I have done my
10480 Thank me no thankings, nor
11443 I thank the goodness and
12318 Thank God, I - I also - am

thanked
1580 Now, God be thanked Who has
1825 Sae let the Lord be thankit.
3491 I never even thanked her.

thankful
2599 hour, Be thankful for the
9575 Be thankful we're not getting
9650 is really thankful, and has
11983 Let us be thankful for the

thankless
10316 it is To have a thankless child!

thanks
1437 O give thanks unto the Lord,
1439 I will give thanks unto thee,
1709 blessing, Thanks for
2156 deserve any thanks from
2894 grateful thanks to
9514 Thanks for the memory.

that
7121 thrown away for that .

thaw
10189 would melt, Thaw, and

theatre
105 goes to the theatre unless he
681 in this theatre of man's
1592 and to what extent theatre?
3833 go to the theatre instead.
4370 in the theatre - the
4970 Theatre is simply what cannot
7403 A theatre where no-one is
9971 in a theatre before the
9986 go to the theatre is like
11998 an evening in the theatre.

theatrical
3353 life is theatrical and

thee
4576 all things Thee to see,
5777 as without Thee We are not

theft
3187 sense, a theft from those
9060 le vol. Property is theft.

theist
666 offer the theist the same

theme
11076 The central theme of the

themselves
97 help them that help themselves.
4141 greatest study is themselves.
12731 over men; but over themselves.

theology
7903 My theology, briefly, Is that

theories
5726 Art, And theories' and

theorize
2997 mistake to theorize before you

theory
2874 that is life without theory.
3178 If my theory of relativity
4100 All theory, dear friend, is
4880 is always ahead of theory.
7279 respect his theory that his
8977 The theory and practice of
11211 in the theory that

therapeutic
5787 of falsely therapeutic and always

therapist
2062 goes to a therapist, is a
4782 a very effective therapist.

therapy
6110 that therapy is
12229 point of therapy is to get

The Wordsworth Dictionary of Quotations

there
154 want to be there when it
220 I? I'm already there.'
2374 And yet thou are not there.
6917 Because it's there.
7226 who wasn't there. He wasn't
11085 you get there, there
12859 a kid, you see what's there.

thereafter
5591 is that thereafter you have

therefore
2786 I think, therefore I am.

thermodynamics
3137 law of thermodynamics I give you

thermometer
4691 of inverted thermometer, the bulb

they
5682 And everyone else is They.

thickens
12105 the plot thickens very much

thief
755 Opportunity makes a thief.
2510 out stop thief, is often
2734 is a thief to
7601 the subtle thief of youth,
10268 mind; The thief doth fear
12593 is the thief of time.
12938 is the thief of time.

thieves
922 One of the thieves was saved.
2250 Thieves respect property.

thin
2527 fat man a thin one is
2529 way to get thin is to
4065 Thin people are beautiful
8371 but I'm thin inside.

thing
315 is no such thing as a
1820 I'm no the thing I should
5674 is become a thing, a tool, a
6359 sort of thing will find
6004 What thing is love for
8644 is such a thing as too
9138 is no such thing as a
11454 This thing .. that can be

things
1106 Guessn the things which are
3145 thousand things that won't
3965 Things are seldom what they
5951 Things in books' clothing.
7374 All good things which exist
7438 Think of Things, you find
8665 Things ain't what they used
8956 was just one of those things.
9918 I confused things with their
11707 All things betray thee, who
12579 beautiful things are the

think
465 easier to act than to think.
1091 You can't think and hit at
2728 Think sideways!
2786 I think, therefore I am.
2798 We only think when we are
3025 of such Who think too little
3100 you can't make him think.
3179 I think and think for
3245 to think about.
3607 nature to think wisely and
4489 those who think most
4785 ability to think, has
4829 what they think wouldn't
4921 What we think and feel and
4942 you don't think you can't,
5112 but don't think
5738 If you can think - and not
5835 moment before they think.
5854 not the one you would think.
5950 Books think for me.
6081 While we think of it, and
6142 begin to think, it is
6268 Think wrongly, if you
6272 but I still think fondly,
6522 with them besides think.
7036 ones who think up things
7661 be who think not God at
8103 I think that I shall never

thinks
8713 as I think them, not
8841 who greatly think, or
9144 something is to think of it.
9772 sooner than think; in fact,
9795 so we've got to think!
10276 look; He thinks too much:
10525 reason: I think him so,
10589 expect a soldier to think.
10667 him to think for
10800 machines think but
10894 who could think for two
11043 I'm not so think as you
11107 what you think yourself.
11172 I could think of, in the
11243 I don't think much of
11403 you may think what you
11970 how much we think of
12089 what they think of me, it
12125 because they think they can.
12196 know what I think till I see
12655 I think with my right hand.
12689 If you think about what you
12892 Think like a wise man but

thinker
2725 are poor thinkers. Many
5536 brilliant thinker; the

thinking
2729 sort of thinking which ..
2921 an art of thinking, and an
3171 into lazy habits of thinking.
3352 a man is thinking of all
3963 thought of thinking for myself
4652 of genuine thinking and the
4709 who are thinking about
4979 stop thinking and go in.
5109 modes of thinking are
5804 ways save us from thinking.
6609 Thinking nothing done while
7240 no deeply thinking mind is
8077 own way of thinking than from
8543 but he is a thinking reed.
8773 the mind is thinking, it is
9020 And I'm a fool for thinking
9385 of unfinished thinking.
9614 is thinking most often
9692 lie awake thinking about
9696 Thinking is like loving and
10206 or bad, but thinking makes it
10224 scruple Of thinking too
11045 do all the thinking for the
12375 I was thinking jest what a Rum

thinks
436 Every man thinks God is on
5178 what he thinks of his
5380 that which he thinks he has.
6647 the one who thinks
7904 be to him who evil thinks.
8875 Whoever thinks a faultless
9302 I sits and thinks, and then

thinner
6160 and keep on growing thinner.
6209 to grow thinner, diminish

third reich
9413 the advent of the Third Reich.

third-rate
933 all these third-rate foreign

thirst
5720 an' a man can raise a thirst.
9344 drink for the thirst to come.
9459 and that thirst to be
11314 the provocation of thirst.

thirteen
11923 I was but thirteen or so I

thirty
380 Thirty days hath September,
508 I am past thirty, and three
2395 I learned after I was thirty.
3101 when he was thirty will get a
7911 in thirty fine

thomas
660 little Thomas. They are

thorn
4042 Licking honey From a thorn.
5732 Oak, and Ash, and Thorn.
6783 A rose without a thorn.

7592 and without thorn the rose.
9237 rose must respect the thorn.

thorns
10693 upon the thorns of life! I

thoroughness
6315 with the thoroughness of a mind

thought
38 and thought is
176 of thought combined
390 ten men who thought of it
809 sex, you thought of nothing
1642 splendour of a sudden thought.
1665 Ah, thought which saddens
2349 Perish the thought!
2588 sometimes thought of
2920 child of Thought, and
3038 he went, for want of thought.
3121 was once thought can never
3680 All thought is a feat of
3701 found its thought and the
3794 a state of thought is unhappy
4251 amount of thought before you
4412 intolerable labour of thought.
4506 If no thought your mind does
4523 device for avoiding thought.
4697 Every real thought on every
4829 be so bad if they thought.
5117 An odd thought stikes me: we
5555 the discomfort of thought.
5625 freedom of thought; instead
5810 the frozen thought of men out
5984 what people thought of us if
6040 comes the thought of high
6273 grateful thought raised to
6975 schools of thought contend is
7359 of their modes of thought.
8238 of thought belongs to
8414 was given to conceal thought.
8485 between a thing and a thought.
8573 kept: He thought me asleep;
8803 no other thought Than to
8846 One thought of thee puts all
0007 oft was thought but ne'er
9020 is worth a thought, And I'm a
9380 I wish I thought What
9750 be if he thought for
9767 Men fear thought more than
9784 Thought looks into the pit of
10001 Thought is the strongest
10149 A Roman thought hath struck
10213 with the pale cast of thought.
10252 Harry, to that thought.
10367 would have thought the old
10702 created thought, Which is
11141 the last thought, rises ..
11377 So the thought of you,
11395 what nobody has thought.
11558 And Thought leapt out to wed
11609 utmost bound of human thought.
11726 the tender thought, To teach
12149 [Men] use thought only to
12481 guide it by taking thought.
12519 Thought is born of failure.
12683 that new thought gets its

thoughts
625 is what our thoughts make it.
5147 man mistake words for thoughts.
5469 rather than of thoughts!
5484 own highest thoughts, and
6427 in the thoughts of
6439 The thoughts that come often
6494 And the thoughts of youth
7049 Of abject thoughts and Envy's
7480 and foul thoughts Benighted
8035 can listen to his own thoughts.
8467 pacify it with cool thoughts.
8565 of great thoughts and great
9517 people's thoughts are as
9746 other's thoughts, I suppose
10218 fly up, my thoughts remain
10921 The thoughts of a prisoner -
10989 generate misleading thoughts.
11531 And the thoughts of men are
11594 furrow, as thy thoughts in me.
12055 And my sad thoughts doth
12336 vexation As man's own thoughts.

647

12449 but his thoughts are still
12814 can give Thoughts that do

thousand
1482 night has a thousand eyes, And
2770 born three thousand years old.
11646 if I had five thousand a year.

thousands
8869 But thousands die, without or
8964 War its thousands slays, Peace

thrall
5458 merci Thee hath in thrall.

thread
626 the thread of your
8895 at each thread, and lives
10337 out the thread of his
11207 too frail a thread to hang

threads
10762 It is threads, hundreds

threat
3087 girl the threat of a
7484 Against the threats Of malice

three
219 half a boy; three boys are
1494 With three or more people
2127 I tell you three times is
2803 There were three of us in
2863 There are three kinds of
3708 In three words I can sum up
3987 Three little maids from
3989 Three little maids who, all
6177 the age of three; and there
6243 man at three years old
7440 he was only three. James

three-fourths
497 Conduct is three-fourths of our

three-pipe
2991 is quite a three-pipe problem,

three-sided
7814 they would make him three-sided.

threshold
12199 upon the threshold of the

thrice
10659 Thrice is he armed that hath

thrilling
9582 and more thrilling than a

thrive
2386 that would thrive Must rise
6422 the way to thrive; Your

throat
997 undulating throat Like an
3703 of taking life by the throat.
5677 if your throat 'tis hard
6600 in the city's throat.
8410 in the throat and one in
12910 you by the throat; So stay

throats
648 My sore throats are always
4173 each other's throats, for pay.

throne
3628 proudest throne is obliged
5747 up to the Throne, He
6581 on the throne, - Yet
8744 behind the throne greater
10155 a burnished throne, Burned on
10446 This royal throne of kings,

through
88 you can get through, but
3700 The only way round is through.
4202 of it all the way through.
4446 is getting through.
5040 we all have to go through it.
11783 you've been through with

throw
920 I would throw it out of
981 do not throw this book
4693 and hug, or throw themselves
8656 You have to throw yourself

thrown
4395 not to be thrown away
7121 All this thrown away for

thrust
4514 mediocrity thrust upon them.
10517 greatness thrust upon them.

thumb
2169 the thumb is born
10363 of my thumbs,

thumbscrew
11602 To the thumbscrew and the

thump
11670 be said to thump the clouds

thunder
5718 up like thunder outer
6008 surge and thunder of the
7579 hinges grate Harsh thunder.
9251 If the thunder is not loud,
9584 reason to dread the thunder.
10809 Glorious the thunder's roar.
11670 clouds are cursed by thunder?

thunderbolt
8782 Harmless thunderbolts.
11480 And like a thunderbolt he falls.

thunderstorm
5014 out in thunderstorms, to be
6957 is never a thunderstorm or blare

thursday
7394 love you Thursday - So much

thus
12247 Why is this thus? What is

thwackum
3480 Thwackum was for doing

thyme
7527 With wild thyme and the

thyroid
7900 the nation's thyroid gland.

thyself
3362 gift is a portion of thyself.
5287 to every one but thyself.
9174 Trust me, but look to thyself.

tiber
6843 Oh, Tiber! father Tiber To
9016 'the River Tiber foaming
12126 and the Tiber foaming

tick
12862 it is that makes you tick.

ticket
1124 to take a ticket at
6785 and a ticket for the

tickled
8903 a rattle, tickled with a

ticky-tacky
9456 made out of ticky-tacky And they

tide
1457 have high tide always and
1836 can tether time or tide.
1966 There is a tide in the
7136 the running tide Is a wild
10299 There is a tide in the
11673 heart Push in their tides.

tidily
8442 are brought to an end tidily.

tidy
7977 Keep Britain Tidy.

tie
7174 It's a tie that only
9131 they can tie up a lion.

tied
11410 the tree tied to her;

tiger
351 smile on a tiger They
980 The Tiger, on the other
1362 Tyger Tyger, burning
6972 is a paper tiger which the
7970 Put a tiger in your tank.
10256 of the tiger; Stiffen
11902 riding a tiger. A man

tigers
2307 and fro on tigers from which
9164 fro upon tigers from which
9203 are no tigers, a wildcat
11136 Catches tigers In red

tigress
1275 She was a tigress surrounded

tile
6639 there are tiles on the
8402 red brick, but white tile.

tiller
7768 holding my tiller straight.'

tilling
11279 Tilling and grazing are the

tilt
1104 With the tilt of her

timbuctoo
12528 plains of Timbuctoo, I would

time
7 Time wounds all heels.
113 Time must needs call the
297 Time wastes our bodies and
391 It takes time to be a
396 is the daughter of time.
618 instant of time is a
624 Time is a sort of river of
707 To choose time is to save
725 is the act of time.
873 women and so little time.
1085 Time is a great teacher,
1206 and a time to every
1424 peace in our time, O Lord.
1521 by Time's
1608 ecstasy? Time we may
1836 can tether time or tide.
2177 There is time for work.
2489 over, it's time to call it
2885 Time is the great
2901 now, the time will come
2926 Time goes, you say? Ah no!
2960 which are the rags of time.
3065 and unthinking time.
3115 too much time on the
3144 short on time. I expect
3266 for one time. And only
3624 that time is money.
3918 of time, and the
3941 to the time left us to
4050 future. Time is on our
4230 Every new time will give
4252 Time and I against any
4267 of his time. He is
4401 Time goes by: reputation
4592 ye may, Old Time is still
4877 apply, As time goes by.
4962 here. The time to be
5253 an age, but for all time!
5793 hook, and time is running
5802 Give God time.
5919 O time, suspend your
5965 only true time which a
6035 Time has transfigured them
6067 before its time Shameless
6100 the new direction of Time.
6258 I was on time. No, you
6339 some of the time; you can
6468 The time has come for all
6501 long, and Time is
6791 Time was away and
6949 No time like the present.
6954 sense of time; which
6957 Time has no divisions to
6958 spaces of time without
6963 Time cools, time
7281 Time is a great legalizer,
7447 Time for a little
7538 fancy long, Time will run
7599 I forget all time.
7681 soon hath time the subtle
7717 it's for such a long time!
7820 awful face Time's iron
7928 of my due time, Why
8055 exactly on time .. From
8221 My time has not yet come
8297 and may be some time.
8403 spend their time mostly
8438 Time the devourer of
8514 By the time you say you're
8522 Time spent on any item of
8526 Let time that makes you
8792 sissy half as old as time.
8806 Keeping time, time, time,
8991 with his time, He strove
9003 dance to the music of time.
9067 In search of lost time.
9073 For a long time I used to
9216 Time gives good advice.

9229 Time is the measure of
9244 was born in another time.
9254 done at any time will be
9316 It's time, my dear, It's
9368 over time, which
9561 do with the time we have
9733 and the books of all time.
10037 There's a gude time coming.
10086 Time discovered truth.
10201 The time is out of joint;
10241 the time of life is
10282 but the time And
10302 Old Time the clock-setter.
10343 come may, Time and the
10425 the womb of time which will
10454 is, When time is broke,
10455 I wasted time, and now
10458 before my time Into this
10502 Time hath, my lord, a
10505 arbitrator, Time, Will one
10539 Time's glory is to calm
10558 of wasted time I see
10596 if there is time enough.
10783 direct it. Time changes
10795 killing time Is only
10865 A good time was had by
10946 Time is a kindly god.
10982 Time: That which man is
11173 never has time to be
11246 The time was out of joint,
11446 That my time has been
11459 It takes time to save
11534 the foremost files of time.
11562 Time, a maniac scattering
11588 of all Time Sparkle
11666 his means, Time held me
11717 What time he can spare
11766 could kill time without
11771 Time is but the stream I
12064 beneath it, Time in hours,
12137 time is flying.
12176 This is no time for making
12379 of Father Time with a
12416 more than half of the time.
12593 is the thief of time.
12637 the enemy, time, in us
12638 - for time is the
12894 Have no enemy but time.
12908 pluck till time and times
12924 Time has a way of
12938 is the thief of time.

time-table
7186 read a time-table or a

timeliness
5840 than in the timeliness of the

timely
12807 A timely utterance gave that

times
18 These are times in which a
387 in illis. Times change,
781 'The Times' has made many
2352 Oh, the times! Oh, the
8472 are the times that try
10972 Times go by turns, and
11403 These times having the rare
12172 all men, nor for all times.
12181 The times spat at me. I
12912 that at times like these

timing
3527 Timing, degree and
11896 of politics is timing.

ting-a-ling
375 is thy ting-a-ling-a-ling O

tinge
3918 will always tinge with a

tinker
6793 expands to tinker with his
10737 don't matter a tinker's cuss.

tinkering
3159 intelligent tinkering is to save

tiny
5371 paltry, feeble, tiny mind.

tip
11194 Tip me the black spot.

tip-toe
5517 peas, on tip-toe for a

tipperary
5343 long way to Tipperary, It's a
12627 long way to Tipperary, but my

tire
9326 oil; We tire the night

tired
643 can ever be tired of Bath!
819 people get tired of hearing
1372 you got tired of
1887 process of getting tired.
4733 Men grow tired of sleep,
5094 a man is tired of London,
6056 Tho' you're tired and weary,
8904 Till tired he sleeps,
9583 His soul. He was so tired.
9704 I am tired before the

tiresome
12159 good except the tiresome kind.

tiring
4859 is very tiring. You
7703 Wooing, so tiring.

titania
10416 by moonlight, proud Titania.

titanic
7947 on the deck of the Titanic.

title
2173 A good title is the title
2748 the crown. Titles are
8476 Titles are but nicknames,
12751 could only read the title.

titled
8598 that of the titled for

titles
10679 Titles are tinsel, power a
11032 Congs their titles take.

tits
10780 have their tits somewhere

titwillow
4003 Willow, titwillow,
4004 'Oh willow, titwillow,

toad
4269 As intelligent Mr. Toad.
5725 The toad beneath the
6048 I let the toad work
6049 arm, old toad; Help me
7603 like a toad, close at
10112 like the toad, ugly and
10432 rather be a toad, And live
12171 Ask a toad what is beauty?

toast
8327 all the toasts of the
8586 a piece of toast

toasted
231 England is just toasted milk.

tobacco
5236 that tawney weed tobacco.
5945 thy sake, Tobacco, I Would
5961 leave off tobacco! Surely
7714 without tobacco is not
11838 any more time on tobacco.

tobacconist
5235 of the tobacconist are

today
79 immense, Today I feel
1626 Light tomorrow with today!
3147 these gave their today.'
3377 you think today in words
3757 Today is yesterday's pupil.
6913 vital, fine day: today.
7050 life's too late; live today.
8445 a poet can do today is warn.
9297 Never do today what you can
9708 not be worth living today.
12918 Today is the last day of an
12944 a satire on today, And shows

toes
6157 who has no toes Had once

together
4449 Just two crazy people together.
5534 do when they stick together.
5789 my man and I ain't together.
6229 are me And we are all together.
6790 be the more together - And
8248 men stand together, each of

9437 done great things together.
9821 in looking together in the
9975 coming together again a
10683 us remain together still,
11599 they rise or sink Together.
11834 all in this together - by
12005 things together in the

togetherness
3933 in your togetherness. And let

toil
5832 must we toil in other
6575 the horny hands of toil!
7244 Aye, toil as we may, we
9840 Horny-handed sons of toil.
10361 double toil and
12454 Bear the toil, maintain

toilet
9986 one's toilet without a

toiling
6493 slept, Were toiling upward in

told
1361 friend; I told my wrath,
1968 phrase, 'I told you so.'
5705 But he never told anybody.
10516 She never told her love,

tolerance
2104 The peak of tolerance is most
4145 Tolerance is a tremendous
6286 and i tolerance reach
12678 was such a thing as tolerance.

tolerant
6508 one more tolerant and
12592 wonderfully tolerant. It

tolerate
9413 going to tolerate these

tolerates
1878 that He tolerates their

tolls
2943 the bell tolls; it tolls

tomb
249 A tomb now suffices him
9855 into the tombs, he
9944 towards the tomb, I find
10844 the gilded tomb of a
11668 the lover's tomb How at my

tombstone
5723 fight is a tombstone white,
6498 on the tombstone where he

tommy
5750 For It's Tommy this, an'

tomorrow
1225 drink; for tomorrow we shall
1626 Light tomorrow with today!
1840 of Dover, Tomorrow, just you
2934 This, no tomorrow hath, nor
3377 balls, and tomorrow speak what
4774 what tomorrow may bring,
5540 is here; tomorrow he is
6272 I suffer, tomorrow I die: but
7050 do that', tomorrow's life's
7698 After all, tomorrow is another
8128 this time to-morrow I shall
9265 Tomorrow is often the busiest
9297 you can put off till tomorrow.
9708 If tomorrow were never to
10373 To-morrow, and to-morrow, and
12308 Tomorrow is the most important
12944 Tomorrow is a satire on today,

tomorrows
3147 'For your tomorrows these gave
9932 dividend from time's tomorrows.
12803 And confident tomorrows.

tone
5489 spirit ditties of no tone.

tongue
242 hold his tongue in ten
1197 as have fallen by the tongue.
2201 wel they tonge, and thenk
3395 to men one tongue, but two
3614 a fool who holds his tongue.
4171 is become his mother tongue.
4973 and a sharp tongue is the
6236 to see, nor tongue to speak
8574 customs, politics and tongue.
9161 than to hold one's tongue.

9185 invent with your tongue.
9273 The tongue ever turns to the
10191 for I must hold my tongue.
10338 in the tongue Of him
11018 our English tongue a
11420 the less tongue it hath.
12933 her eternal tongue, For ever

tongues
7631 innumerable tongues A dismal
10112 Finds tongues in trees,

tonight
8079 Not tonight, Josephine.

tonnage
7409 the tonnage of the

took
2077 you and I took me for.

tool
3138 is an edged tool, with

tools
1909 but to name his tools.
2314 Give us the tools and we
6575 work, And tools to work
11925 fools) Their working tools.

tooth
1217 for eye, tooth for tooth,
9235 jelly breaks your tooth.
9273 turns to the aching tooth.
11549 red in tooth and claw.

tooth-point
5725 where each tooth-point goes; The

toothache
8155 Toothache doesn't stop hurting
10138 endure the toothache patiently.
10182 sleeps feels not the toothache.

toothpaste
4374 Once the toothpaste is out of

top
6447 who comes top of the
8962 You're the top! You're
9474 just about top of the
12319 is always room at the top.
12853 from the top down. I

top-boots
9907 pleasure me in his top-boots.

torch
5505 A bright torch, and a
5566 that the torch has been
6623 relay the torch of life.
6699 throw The torch; be yours
10470 teach the torches to burn

tories
227 Mamma, are Tories born
1467 are both Tories; both
1620 horse, For Tories own no
5071 Tories, in short, are
6805 stern and unbending Tories.

torment
805 the possibility of torment.
2719 a kind of torment in every
5462 grievous torment than a
5833 there's the torment, there's
7242 a positive torment to him;

tormentor
11826 and it is I who am my tormentor.

torments
2348 how many torments lie in the
7570 Our torments also may in
8051 of the infinite torments me.

torn
9158 but torn garments.
10999 and who wore torn clothes.

torontonian
970 A Torontonian is a man who leaves

torrent
4048 down in a torrent of gin and

torrid
2072 The torrid or the

torture
1933 hum Of human cities torture.
5178 put to the torture and is not
7330 begin to torture you in
7419 torture, the
8174 men, as to torture them, into

tortured
1378 the boy Tortured with the

tory
228 is the Tory party at
1110 for the Tory Party ..
5109 A wise Tory and a wise
7948 Vote Labour: Sleep Tory.

tossed
1469 Sir; you tossed and gored

total
83 is the sum total of the
4079 to .. a total solution

totalitarianism
3804 the name of totalitarianism or the

totem
6788 under the totem poles -

touch
356 never touch it at all.
7808 may no one touch you who
10260 A little touch of Harry in
11472 O for the touch of a

touched
6747 Something touched me deep
11571 finger touched him, and

touches
12500 book, Who touches this

touching
11524 at the touching of the

touchstone
5581 as the touchstone of our
9227 The touchstone of knowledge is

tough
1321 today. Tough on crime
5584 going gets tough, the tough
11930 was interesting, but tough.

tougher
12052 tougher to find a

toughest
1081 The toughest thing about

toujours
7027 dame yet toujours gai

tourist
958 to the tourist the last
5633 is a tourist. And of
10933 everyone a tourist in other

tournament
1103 We in the tournament - you

tower
8563 In the dark tower of a poem.

towered
7519 Towered cities please us

towers
503 from her towers the last

towery
4756 Towery city and branchy

town
2624 and man made the town.
4797 season, but town people
6508 least, a town life makes
7055 urbe. Country in the town.
7425 through the town, Up stairs
7440 end of the town, if you
7906 A town that has no ceiling
12441 Art is upon the Town!

towns
1384 in all the towns in all the

toxic
1309 treats me like toxic waste.

toy
7006 a childish toy, And hold

toys
2610 then cast their toys away.
3552 interesting toys but of no
6668 boys with toys, but men
8904 are the toys of age:
11176 Not to meddle with my toys.

toyshop
7920 visit to a toyshop between

traces
266 is one who traces your

track
11721 Come flying on our track.

trade
2619 a penny in the way of trade.
3051 War is the trade of kings.
3063 in London only is a trade.
4560 now There isn't any Trade.
4949 is half a trade and half
5686 of the North-East Trade.
5867 not tired of their trade.
6908 My trade has never been in
10819 of the same trade seldom
11184 of his trade, apart

trade unionism
10616 but the Trade Unionism of the

trade unionist
1122 the British Trade Unionist when you

trades
5046 ugliest of trades have their
10015 live by twa trades ..

tradition
887 for it is a lost tradition.
2101 is tradition! How a
2261 Tradition means giving votes to
2634 Tradition, thou art for

traditions
464 of all our cultural traditions.

trafalgar
4860 of Trafalgar Square

traffic
11713 shine the traffic of Jacob's

tragedies
1961 All tragedies are finished by a
10618 are two tragedies in life.
11229 with the tragedies of

tragedy
64 A perfect tragedy is the
858 time as tragedy, the
1795 Comedy is tragedy - plus
2099 The tragedy of life is not so
3516 I will write you a tragedy.
4439 indeed be a tragedy if the
4499 The tragedy is not that love
5404 way of true tragedy - A sick
5561 triumph and tragedy. A man
5822 True tragedy may be defined
6082 Tragedy ought really to be a
6870 The great tragedy of the
7110 time as tragedy, the
7151 is the tragedy of
7916 The tragedy of English
8331 The tragedy of a man who
8670 would indeed be a tragedy.
11232 That is what tragedy means.
12206 think, a tragedy to those
12470 as yet untouched by tragedy.
12558 is their tragedy. No man
12598 The tragedy of old age is not

tragic
6078 a tragic age, so we
7312 In tragic life, God wot, No
9695 a writer is tragic: the more

tragically
6078 we refuse to take it tragically.

trail
5654 long, long trail awinding

train
164 the train of events
1101 electric train, With a
1246 Train up a child in the way
3899 on a train. Are you
4920 his life in trains and
6589 light of the oncoming train.
8000 Let the train take the
11721 rush in the train, The trees
12355 electric train set any
12443 and takes a train, And then
12561 to read in the train.

trained
6303 We have trained them [men] to
7160 a man has trained himself
8678 We trained hard, but it

training
1064 against one's training.
1278 that severe training has on the
3648 any kind of bad training.
7923 he is training for his

trait
3421 valuable trait Is a
12675 of human traits and red

traitors
10365 Our fears do make us traitors.

tramp
1486 With the tramp of the
4448 why the lady is a tramp.
7215 Tramp squares with
11039 'Cause tramps like us,

trample
11614 grave, To trample round my
12056 light doth trample on my

trance
10673 And in mad trance, strike

tranquilize
10666 so much to tranquilize the mind

tranquillity
3192 of domestic tranquillity but a
3345 of inward tranquillity, which
5162 and drowsy without tranquillity.
8506 Sorrow is tranquillity remembered
11782 chaos remembered in tranquillity.
12002 recollected in tranquillity.

tranquillizers
6260 about tranquillizers is that

transaction
11647 to a love transaction; the one

transcendental
4007 chatter of a transcendental kind.

transferred
3587 to be transferred from an

transformation
625 Universe is transformation; our life
2756 a transformation to which

transformed
12590 the air and transformed it; let it

transforming
3406 steel, of transforming human

transgressing
365 continues transgressing the rules,

transgression
1142 law is, there is no transgression.

transitory
12775 Action is transitory - a step, a

translate
2778 such as cannot write, translate.

translation
11380 'A translation is no
12431 is only a translation of the

translator
9313 despise the translator. He's the

transmit
12525 Not to transmit an experience

transmutation
8183 seems delighted with transmutations.
11461 than death and transmutation.

transport
12836 I turned to share the transport.

transported
11849 first .. transported and

trapeze
6328 man on the flying trapeze.

trappings
10188 but the trappings and the

trash
9943 founded on trash and waste,

travel
744 Travel, in the younger sort,
1017 classes of travel - first
1096 We must travel in the
1280 should go, travel that way
3357 man should travel until he
3382 Though we travel the world
3440 When you travel, remember
4225 is a way of travel - not a
9377 that can travel the world
9475 Wherever I travel, I'm too
11114 does not travel to see
11192 my part, I travel not to go
11204 To travel hopefully is a
11257 Travel is ninety per cent

travel
11985 Travel is fatal to
12743 But we'll travel along

travelled
220 she never travelled, said 'Why
915 way he travelled providing
5438 Much have I travelled in the
10717 Whoe'er has travelled life's
10995 sun they travelled a short
11762 I have travelled a good deal in
12843 I travelled among unknown men,

traveller
770 and the traveller is
4920 The traveller's eye view of men
5407 perfect traveller always
5915 a fellow traveller with his
6487 A traveller, by the faithful
6824 when some traveller from New
10183 bourn no traveller returns.
10696 I met a traveller from an
10703 A traveller from the cradle to
11343 is a young traveller just
12818 breath, A traveller between

travellers
352 men and far travellers may lie
10109 place; but travellers must be

travelling
1799 Travelling is the ruin of all
3734 an ass goes travelling, he'll not

travels
3077 unless one travels to
5747 Throne. He travels the
7834 A man travels the world in

treacherous
5898 are oftener treacherous through

tread
7488 That bends not as I tread.
8886 where angels fear to tread.
12914 your feet; Tread softly

treading
2117 and he's treading on my

treason
280 Gunpowder Treason and Plot
2399 'Twixt treason and
2429 commit treason, nor be
2892 and condoned high treason.
3056 But treason is not owned when
3241 greatest treason: To do the
4436 Treason doth never prosper,
10226 king, That treason can but
10406 Is fit for treasons,

treasure
981 it as your chiefest treasure.
3954 That we treasure beyond
7299 woman is a treasure; a witty
10442 The purest treasure mortal

treasures
1411 of treasures, but in
6016 Whan alle tresors arn tried,

treasury
5605 If the Treasury were to fill

treat
4124 If you treat men the way
6916 left to treat my
12546 If England treats her

treated
6858 be either treated generously

treatment
851 And if your treatment does not
7290 A suitable case for treatment.
12704 treatment of a

treaty
3554 not a peace treaty, it is an

tree
1341 the same tree that a
1988 truth, The Tree of
5416 happy tree Thy
5630 A poem lovely as a tree.
5631 only God can make a tree.
5779 that this tree Continues
6147 Man in a tree, Who was
7918 mind than a tree, And for
7922 spare that tree! Touch not
8103 lovely as a tree. Perhaps,
8871 bent, the tree's
9215 Though a tree grow ever so

9257 a fallen tree, all
11342 like that tree, I shall
11410 keeps the tree tied to
11551 deep where grew the tree.

tree-tops
1079 Where the tree-tops glisten

trees
512 music of its trees at dawn?
1140 the sea, nor the trees.
1606 while some trees stand, and
4535 is to plant trees, under
5673 And all the trees are green:
5732 Of all the trees that grow
9584 most lofty trees have the
10543 When lofty trees I see
11688 between the trees and
11849 The green trees when I saw

trelawny
4458 And shall Trelawny die?

tremble
8847 See my lips tremble, and my

trembling
5168 dinner, or trembling at a
5429 Trembling in her soft and

trenches
10540 dig deep trenches in thy

tresses
8945 Fair tresses man's imperial

trial
3742 the jury at a goose's trial.
5375 it is not a trial at all;
6348 The fiery trial through
7460 us is trial, and trial

trials
8422 terrible trials of

triangle
251 The eternal triangle.

triangles
7814 that if triangles invented a

tribal
5724 tribal lays, And

tribe
1262 powerful tribe whose
10438 Richer than all his tribe.

tribes
1971 two mighty tribes, The Bores

tribunal
1672 a new tribunal now higher

tribute
10023 the vain tribute of a

trick
831 The trick of wearing mink
991 A Trick that everyone
5850 pleasing to trick the
10243 yet the trick of our

tricks
5125 that all tricks are either
10376 fantastic tricks before

tried
1027 has been tried at least
1871 should be tried by a judge
2263 not been tried and found
2301 have been tried from time
6374 the old and tried, against
8912 the new are tried Nor yet
10585 if anyone ever tried it.
12110 Trust one who has tried.
12409 one I've never tried before.

trifle
10344 As 'twere a careless trifle.

trifles
825 an interest in trifles.
10433 Trifles light as air Are to
10530 of unconsidered trifles.

trifling
8418 as the most trifling of his

trigger
343 do you want on the trigger?

trimming
7868 the second half trimming it.

trinkets
5702 to your trinkets; then ye

trip
7512 Come, and trip it as ye go
7709 A trip through a sewer in
8011 Clunk, click, every trip.
11209 look forward to the trip.
11300 like this, I need the trip.

triple
5686 There be triple ways to

triumph
1542 a cry of triumph which soon
1549 the sure triumph of her
2636 Survival is triumph enough.
4461 ultimate triumph of human
5374 the world of one's triumph.
5561 mixture of triumph and
5738 meet with triumph and
6801 ye forth in triumph from the
8212 of man, his triumph over
12094 A triumph of the embalmer's

triumphant
556 gloriously triumphant will

triumphed
9368 hath triumphed over time,

trivia
8072 the people with trivia!!!

trivial
5522 The trivial round, the common
6101 That such trivial people
8937 rise from trivial things.
8972 both more trivial than they

trivialities
1389 contrast to trivialities where

triviality
7844 and triviality and can

trod
8116 steps he trod, Where the

troika
4134 a spirited troika that

trojan
1123 know what Trojan 'orses

trojans
12118 the horse, Trojans. Whatever

trombone
4723 The trombone age (moving the

trophies
8915 their old trophies o'er the
12323 Who seek by trophies and dead

trouble
240 help in time of trouble.
873 The trouble with life is that
1077 may be trouble ahead, But
1429 very present help in trouble.
2693 kind. The trouble lies in
2736 In trouble to be troubled Is
3791 have never been in trouble.
4750 worst kind of heart trouble.
4798 is in trouble, don't
5378 Trouble is only opportunity
5768 there's trouble brewing,
5787 One trouble with a kind of
5960 yet nothing troubles me less,
5982 Trouble is the common
6307 taking trouble for
7024 in time of trouble when it is
8454 ready to save us the trouble?
8655 is accompanied by trouble.
9274 Trouble will rain on those
9577 gives us trouble, it's what
9719 stirring up trouble somewhere.
10362 of powerful trouble, Like a
10630 the utmost trouble to find
10742 Trouble is a part of your
12117 stranger to trouble myself I
12250 women and care and trouble.
12374 of one who had seen trouble.
12534 But has trouble enough of

troubled
7842 I'm troubled. I'm
8631 wretch, is troubled with her
10768 bridge over troubled water I
11836 become inexplicably troubled.

troublemakers
6744 and its dead troublemakers.

troubles
134 woman whose troubles are
525 up your troubles in your
5036 all its troubles; I don't
6233 all my troubles seemed so
8769 end to the troubles of states,
10082 brings our troubles to the
10211 a sea of troubles, And by
12424 years with troubles', but they

troublesome
5532 the most troublesome creatures

trousers
1040 Trousers should shiver on the
4938 one's best trousers to go out

trout
4573 lose a fly to catch a trout.
11742 you find a trout in the

trowel
2507 She lays it on with a trowel.
2905 lay it on with a trowel.

troy
1521 not de troved by
9681 night when Troy was
12904 another Troy for her to

truant
10239 I have a truant been to

truck
5593 hit by a truck - if you

truck drivers
8683 language truck drivers are using,

trudged
3038 He trudged along unknowing

true
124 If all be true that I do
501 let us be true To one
748 Be so true to thyself as
761 like to be true, that he
1635 He said true things, but
1852 is as true as
1916 was proved true before,
2127 you three times is true.
3901 as equally true; by the
4201 but because they are true.
4475 should be true, but that
4684 but be simply true.
5239 at a slander makes it true.
5907 perfectly true is
6561 He's been true to one
7394 Thursday - So much is true.
9180 it is not true, it is a
9900 to be substantially true.
10195 own self be true, And it
11041 don't come true, Or is it
11373 have found his words true.
11500 coins, Some true, some
11502 I know what true love is,
11503 kept him falsely true.
12531 ear, 'You are not true'.
12594 necessarily true because a
12620 we know this is not true.

truly
7852 that has truly loved

trumpet
3069 The trumpet shall be heard on
4179 shifted his trumpet, and only
5571 Now the trumpet summons us
5771 of the Trumpet Against
6895 the small trumpet of your
11003 Spring, His trumpet shrill

trumpets
5423 snarling trumpets 'gan to
6105 The trumpets came out brazenly

trumps
5927 dirt were trumps, what

trust
40 to be to trust no man
87 Trust only movement. Life
1306 You can trust all
1312 Put your trust in God, my
1893 put one's trust in God is
3580 To trust people is a luxury
3758 Trust thyself only, and
5070 ass. Never trust a man
5737 If you can trust yourself
6089 Never trust the artist.
6502 Trust no Future, howe'er
8995 learn to trust their
9174 Trust me, but look to
10494 men dare trust themselves
10562 not to trust; Enjoyed
11222 be taken on trust; truth is
11509 And trust me not at all or
11759 may safely trust a good
12110 Trust one who has tried.
12118 Do not trust the horse,
12603 never trust a woman
12868 to those that trust 'em.
12967 generations - only trust.

trusted
7870 be safely trusted with a

trusty
1811 a hand, my trusty fiere! And

truth
15 Truth is the only merit
86 The truth is often a
102 The truth which makes men
285 Hell is truth seen too
356 handle the truth
396 Truth is the daughter of
493 economical with the truth.
506 This truth - to prove, and
530 my love for truth; and truth
650 It is a truth universally
674 further to discover truth.
764 Truth emerges more readily
824 trusted to speak the truth.
1073 Truth is the cry of all,
1149 know the truth, and the
1152 way, the truth, and the
1293 scarce as truth is, the
1328 A truth that's told with
1390 a profound truth may well
1529 Truth exists; only lies are
1630 stage where truth calls
1646 good is truth, truth
2110 a little reasoning to truth.
2199 Trouthe is the hyeste thyng
2405 and the truth will come
2428 but truth, and too
2611 That truth lies
2652 Truth for him was a moving
2694 The love of truth lies at
3064 to be reasoned into truth.
3163 the truth, leave
3338 between truth and
3590 lying when truth, well
3652 discovers the entire truth.
3715 Beauty and truth may be
3808 Truth is something you
4045 lawyer interprets the truth.
4063 are truth, justice,
4155 Truth from his lips
4495 One truth discovered, one
4518 way of saying the truth.
4549 the whole truth - to know
4698 way to get at the truth.
4806 sword: His truth is
4866 an air of truth to their
4903 Great is truth, but still
5009 lie than a truth
5076 the love of truth by the
5101 he thinks truth, and every
5140 you are to tell the truth.
5178 obliged to speak the truth.
5211 even in telling the truth.
5233 age's truth sometimes,
5307 have sought truth, and
5467 and the truth of
5468 known for truth by
5523 heavenly truth imparts,
5671 Truth, for its own sake,
5811 Truth is a pathless land,
5827 to truth. Lead me
6016 arn tried, Truthe is the
6065 truth, tells it
6072 is the only truth. An
6129 A half truth, like half a
6270 hand all Truth, and in
6328 but not on truth saying.
6430 him in possession of truth.
6431 portion of truth which he
6432 in error as in truth.
6581 Truth forever on the

6582 would keep abreast of Truth.
6644 but truth at any
6804 is not truth, but
6862 you the truth; but when
7296 Caricature is rough truth.
7323 of true wit is truth itself.
7330 The truth that many people
7417 write the truth, so help
7466 Let her Truth] and
7614 cause Of truth, in word
7654 of truth in the
7803 I speak the truth, not so
7909 we put truth in the
8039 into the truth is the
8179 ocean of truth lay all
8192 else you tell the truth to.
8559 speak the truth as he sees
8607 bellow the truth when he
8706 Art is not truth. Art is a
8751 scientific truth does not
8785 veritas. Truth comes out
8897 spite. One truth is clear,
9088 speak the truth: but it is
9158 Truth has a handsome
9175 feeling is God's own truth.
9177 neither religion nor truth.
9192 Truth is the safest lie.
9225 seekers after the truth.
9238 speaks the truth is always
9275 speak the truth you have a
9369 follow truth too near
9377 it is not truth, but
9392 Truth may be stranger than
9540 Truth never is undone; Its
9569 injected truth into
9833 to the truth, but like
9845 is only one truth,
9899 The truth is cruel, but it
9917 disenchantment for truth.
9987 Every truth passes through
10008 The truth did not come to
10086 Time discovered truth.
10174 heaped For truth to
10203 move; Doubt truth to be a
10394 Truth will come to light;
10539 and bring truth to light.
10564 is made of truth, I do
10569 complete truth is not the
10917 the road to truth, and to
11070 speak plain truth, he may
11157 them the truth, that
11161 telling the truth about
11215 and every truth easily
11222 on trust; truth is only
11230 so close to truth, it
11406 to keep truth safe in
11490 is part a truth is a
11526 This is truth the poet
11554 I held it truth, with him
11584 sold the truth to serve
11633 love, that's the truth on't.
11747 is hearty truth, there is
11763 speak the truth - one to
11804 passion for truth is
11904 tell the truth, and they
11929 mainly he told the truth.
11948 Truth is the most valuable
11982 tell the truth you don't
12104 foes to truth.
12169 the dead we owe only truth.
12395 plain truth for plain
12398 reveals truth that
12555 The truth is rarely pure,
12618 the truth operative
12750 of pure truth to wrap up
12883 I may wither into the truth.
truthful
12068 are born truthful, and die
truths
979 fundamental truths without a
1389 sorts of truths, profound
1727 tell him disagreeable truths.
2036 call first truths those we
4433 greatest truths are the
4932 held truths may be
5022 hold these truths to be
5026 fears no truths has
6684 are no new truths, but only

10573 All great truths begin as
11893 absolute truths; in
12172 There are truths that are
truthtelling
358 the honest truthtelling there is
try
3893 you can get it if you try.
7730 first, and try him
9404 right to try but that's
9596 method and try it. If it
10245 Let the end try the man.
10766 doomed if you don't try.
trying
901 a point of trying every
7224 without really trying.
11189 Sinners who keep on trying.
11908 while I was trying to be
tube
4374 out of the tube, it is
tuberculosis
9803 as they are by tuberculosis.
tuesday
7437 can spell TUESDAY, even if
8276 it good - we want it Tuesday.
tug
6183 then was the tug of war!
tumble
9379 bags And tumble victuals
tumbled
4262 time She tumbled off a bus,
tumbling
1880 ladder without tumbling off.
tumour
3 ripens in a tumour; And
32 a sort of tumour that ends
tumult
1010 the full tumult, the
1999 when the tumult dwindled
2440 'mid this tumult Kubla
5733 The tumult and the shouting
5780 The tumult and the shouting
12792 and not the tumult, of the
12891 to this tumult in the
tune
1112 about the tune, there is
1833 sweetly play'd in tune.
2831 sings the tune without
5933 I am incapable of a tune.
tunes
4614 have all the good tunes.
tuning
283 their life tuning and the
tunnel
2842 end of the tunnel is the
6589 end of the tunnel, It's the
turbulence
2384 Turbulence is life force. It is
turd
2203 is nat worth a toord!'
turf
12780 the dappled turf at ease I
turkey
8191 Turkey is a dying man. We
turks
4061 Let the Turks now carry
turn
1167 cheek, turn to him the
6161 you must turn on, tune
12896 and quickly turn away.
turned
73 After being turned down by
2448 having once turned round
turning
6135 face for turning its head
9371 From itself never turning.
11653 The lady's not for turning.
turnip
5179 the man who turnips cries,
7039 blood out of a turnip.
turnpike
3152 supper as a turnpike through

turtle
2503 Behold the turtle. He makes
tutors
3750 Old foxes want no tutors.
6440 that tutors generally
twentieth
6891 of the Twentieth Century
twenty
3625 thinks twenty shillings
10962 the first twenty years are
12776 as long As twenty days are
twenty-twenty
12609 Hindsight is always twenty-twenty.
twice
2124 as life and twice as
2126 at least twice as fast as
5891 to be praised twice over.
7906 name her twice, Like so;
12034 of what never happens twice.
12517 must do twice as well as
twig
5349 slender twigs that are
8871 Just as the twig is bent,
twilight
11479 Twilight and evening bell, And
twin
6208 was born a twin And not a
twinkle
11445 Twinkle, twinkle, little
twins
4261 threw the twins she
6870 is to have been born twins.
twist
3851 with ease, Twist words and
8968 for I have NO MORE TWIST.
two
35 is much; two are many;
151 between two people.
408 is that two and two
2003 too far two and two
2492 Two weeks is about the
4387 Two souls with but a
6791 There were two glasses
6982 has to suffice for two.
7404 kills two people
two-edged
7221 It is a two-edged sword.
type
9074 who wasn't even my type.
11579 of the type she seems,
typewriters
12620 a million typewriters will
typing
2063 not writing, that's typing.
typist
3263 The typist home at teatime,
tyranny
465 of tyranny it is far
1750 are the worst sort of tyranny.
4943 is the tyranny of the
8016 Tyranny is yielding to the
8047 night of tyranny had
8419 representation is tyranny.
8608 Tyranny is always better
9757 to an unnecessary tyranny.
10628 burden of tyranny: they have
12143 benevolent tyranny tempered
tyrant
1257 n: a tyrant's
3922 cruel and capricious tyrant.
4955 anonymous tyrant who
7219 king in the tyrant; he does
8122 of a cruel tyrant. Enjoy!'
tyrants
1763 Tyrants seldom want pretexts.
2737 would be tyrants if they
8747 argument of tyrants; it is the
12958 favour with tyrants, for a
uglier
4382 has an uglier look to us
uglinesses
3350 with its uglinesses the

ugly
161 rears its ugly 'ead it's
1706 with an ugly woman than
2418 produces ugly things
2546 saw an ugly thing in
4029 Elderly ugly daughter.
4307 art looks ugly at first.
8217 the world ugly and bad
9706 are no ugly women,

ulcers
284 He'd give the devil ulcers.

ulster
2014 betrayal of Ulster, the
2290 Ulster will fight; Ulster

umbrage
9288 have taken umbrage. The deuce

umbrella
1496 steals the just's umbrella.

umpire
6007 ball, The umpire, the

un-wholesome
5938 they are un-wholesome companions

unable
482 He who is unable to live in
8959 (she's unable to lunch

unaggressive
6729 well groomed and unaggressive.

unattempted
7545 Things unattempted yet in prose

unattended
3765 They go out when unattended.

unattractive
4002 la, A most unattractive old thing,
4314 but not against the unattractive.
4557 surface so unattractive must be

unavailing
2078 moral one will prove unavailing.

unavoidable
3663 It is unavoidable that if we

unaware
2234 makes me unaware of

unbearable
5828 The unbearable lightness of

unbecoming
2506 more unbecoming a man of

unbelief
1633 then by our unbelief Is a life

unbends
3842 is nothing unbends the mind

unbent
5930 She unbent her mind

unbidden
10265 Unbidden guests Are often

unbodied
2937 As souls unbodied, bodies
10709 Like an unbodied joy whose

unbribed
12720 man will do unbribed, there's

unburnished
11608 To rust unburnished, not to

uncertain
223 Life is uncertain - eat dessert
9105 To be uncertain is to be

uncertainty
2321 perpetual uncertainty, the drama
3494 capacity to endure uncertainty.
4653 comes from uncertainty. When we

unclad
6768 uncertain, unclad and

uncle
10447 grace, nor uncle me no

uncloth'd
2937 bodies uncloth'd must be.

uncomfortable
3814 and it always feels uncomfortable.
7242 of ours an uncomfortable inn to
10614 moral when he is only uncomfortable.

uncommunicating
5940 The uncommunicating muteness of

uncompacted
1550 of its uncompacted lightness,

unconcern
5190 looks with unconcern on a man

unconquerable
5961 which this unconquerable purpose

unconscious
5814 be something unconscious about it.

unconsciousness
9906 Our unconsciousness is like a vast

unconsidered
10530 snapper-up of unconsidered trifles.

uncontrollable
4980 by outside uncontrollable elements,

unconvincing
4000 bald and unconvincing narrative.

uncorseted
3269 emphasis; Uncorseted, her

uncouth
6582 good uncouth; They must
7572 find out His uncouth way.

uncreating
8838 before thy uncreating word: Thy

undecided
2315 only to be undecided, resolved

undemocratic
2014 entirely undemocratic banishment

under
6515 Under a spreading chestnut

under-dogs
12296 among the under-dogs - except

underachieve
5805 United States, you underachieve.

underdeveloped
3788 The more underdeveloped the country,

underfoot
611 the vices themselves underfoot.

undergraduates
957 Undergraduates owe their happiness
4493 with the undergraduates, or heads

underground
8423 belonging to him is underground.

underlings
10275 that we are underlings.

underneath
80 In uplifting, get underneath.

underrate
11201 we so much underrate as the

undersized
3980 He's a bit undersized, and you

undersold
6311 Never knowingly undersold.

understand
389 And no one can understand Ein.
449 is a language I don't understand.
773 of mankind understand it, and
909 to understand things in
977 language all nations understand.
2576 my life to understand that it is
3205 or what they don't understand.
3298 are to understand each
4306 best way to understand a highly
4474 men really understand is
6109 meant to understand - They're
6264 'One has to understand the
6466 adores what he cannot understand.
6906 more and understand a little
7892 but where they understand you.
8046 really understand the
8166 When men understand what each
8574 ne'er quite understand The
8710 wants to understand painting.
9104 remember. I do and I understand.
9834 don't understand too hot.
9874 endeavour to understand him.
11026 them, but to understand them.
11084 I understand you undertake to
11972 idiots understand their own
12136 able to understand the causes

understanding
651 of mean understanding, little
1247 and through understanding it is
2012 "My understanding of Women goes
4641 Understanding is nothing else than
5000 of God; they pass all understanding.
5074 likely to propagate understanding.
5114 to find you an understanding,
6265 only the understanding that one's
11060 be totally understanding makes one
11974 of tacit understanding that the
12637 just your understanding - no, not

understands
174 A man only understands what is
4818 but who understands the
8996 No man understands a deep book
9202 one word and understands two.

understood
2667 It is only to be understood.
7213 want to be understood by my
10277 Those that understood him smiled
12060 Before I understood this place
12967 not to be understood', but only

undertake
6330 Never undertake anything for
12623 in order to undertake; nor

undertaking
5198 requisite to great undertakings.
11084 to overthrow my undertaking.

undertaxed
1066 long as the undertaxed can defend

underwood
11353 in green underwood and cover

undeserving
3638 to the undeserving is severe

undevotional
12091 Dirty, dark, and undevotional.

undisciplined
3622 of unbridled, undisciplined feeling.

undivided
10738 Alone and undivided, we lived

undo
7349 thee does she undo herself?

undone
974 way 'tis we must be undone?
1422 have left undone those
3072 undo, and some to be undone.
8968 .. I am undone and worn
9540 never is undone; Its
10369 What's done cannot be undone.
10374 o' the world were now undone.

undress
1107 you have to undress in front
2823 women - and I undress for men.
12950 unadmitted desire to undress.

undying
8514 Infinite, undying - Lady,

unearned
7363 of the unearned increment

uneasiness
1683 felt in the uneasiness

uneasy
5012 The dark, uneasy world of
5177 makes me uneasy, and I am
10248 Uneasy lies the head that

uneatable
12602 full pursuit of the uneatable.

uneducated
2304 for an uneducated man to
9873 at school is an uneducated child.
12245 was so unedicated. He's the

unemancipated
6592 when the unemancipated woman

unembroidered
7328 of joys Unembroidered by your

unemployed
3390 tax, no unemployed and not a
11463 with our unemployed father.

unemployment
2555 out of work, unemployment results.
5605 be no more unemployment and, with

unendurable
553 seldom as unendurable as, to
8244 The most unendurable thing, to be

unequal
3291 division of unequal earnings.
12324 Unequal nature, to place

unespied
7067 In the ocean's bosom unespied.

unexpected
1409 on an unexpected occasion,
11887 is the most unexpected of all
unexplained
4385 only you're unexplained as yet.
unfair
8250 are we most unfair, but to he
unfaithful
9321 should be unfaithful to his
unfathomable
11692 sleep, The unfathomable deep
unfed
5745 us, still unfed, Though
unfettered
6869 to have an unfettered
unfinished
312 is always unfinished business.
unfit
6440 is the most unfit of any to
7260 party is unfit to rule -
unfold
7284 makes us unfold and
unforgiveness
8789 war An alp of unforgiveness grew.
unforgiving
10733 An unforgiving eye, and a damned
unfortunate
1383 sort of unfortunate man is the
ungained
10499 the thing ungained more than
ungainly
8272 is more ungainly than a
unhabitual
5003 perceiving in an unhabitual way.
unhappily
11232 The bad end unhappily, the good
unhappiness
7033 between periods of unhappiness.
8279 or unhappiness has
9077 For if unhappiness develops the
9762 cessation of unhappiness.
9886 spirits prefer unhappiness.
11986 There is no unhappiness like the
unhappy
62 much more unhappy he might
800 I've had an unhappy life,
1047 who were unhappy, but never
1383 the most unhappy sort of
5092 should be unhappy than that
5329 which make us so unhappy.
5836 their remaining years unhappy.
5904 is never as unhappy as one
9069 as soon as one is unhappy.
9460 only the unhappy can either
9605 These unhappy times call for
9754 Men who are unhappy, like men
11173 never has time to be unhappy.
11614 And vex the unhappy dust thou
11821 but each unhappy family is
12707 from that of the unhappy.
12708 All the unhappy marriages
12931 the great unhappy, but the
unheard
5489 but those unheard Are
5653 the language of the unheard.
unholy
7510 shrieks, and sights unholy.
unhooked
12229 is to get unhooked, not to
unicorn
5229 it is rarer than the unicorn.
uniform
4737 coat Should be more uniform.
5700 The uniform 'e wore Was
unimaginative
12544 last refuge of the unimaginative.
unimportant
7418 The other eight are unimportant.
8177 be very busy with the unimportant.
unintelligible
1986 then unintelligible, then
12795 Of all this unintelligible world, Is

unintentionally
268 anyone's feelings unintentionally.
uninteresting
12922 people are uninteresting. Their
uninterrupted
6103 just uninterrupted grass, and
union
2788 The proper union of gin and
2840 just, our union is
8207 the unions and the
8461 A perfect Union, one and
9875 always the union of a part
11457 The union of hands and
11993 their union, were not
12320 and Union, now and
unique
3222 cases are unique and very
4605 the unique, the very
unitarian
7187 A Unitarian very earnestly
unite
3247 which can unite to form a
6437 to join and unite into a
7117 MEN OF ALL COUNTRIES, UNITE!
9131 spider webs unite, they can
united
2317 no more a united nation
2753 will be united by the
united nations
6451 United Nations) is
united states
399 The United States was born in the
2807 and so close to the United States.
3723 of the United States, but then
3779 die in the United States of too
5558 of the United States
5805 die in the United States, you
8296 rats in the United States; of
11808 in the United States is the
11897 next to the United States is in some
12100 The United States themselves are
12680 of the United States, but I
unites
1698 than for what unites them.
5321 and unites it with
7430 Nothing unites the English
11819 - it unites people.
uniting
2839 all, By uniting we stand,
unity
1475 no cultural unity, no
5799 realize the unity of our
9697 cannot find unity and peace
universal
3203 is coming. Universal peace is
12548 becomes for a moment universal.
universe
455 be absent from the universe.
625 The Universe is
917 part of the universe that asks
2046 it its own universe,
2792 The universe is like a safe to
3162 plays dice with the universe.
4373 is that the universe is not
4459 of the universe on a very
4678 of the universe, with one
4679 The universe is not hostile,
4919 of the universe you can be
5019 in the universe only
5222 back Thy universe and give
5310 through the universe and
5843 knows the universe and does
7903 Is that the universe Was
7953 about the universe. There's
8622 whereby the universe's very
9807 corner of a universe in which
9870 towards the universe and denies
11690 All the universe of sight,
11720 the universe Of good or
12466 mechanism of the Universe.
universities
765 Universities incline wits to
university
181 from university training,
1026 are the one University everyone

1472 gained in the University of Life.
2100 The true university of these
2347 A university is what a college
2566 University printing presses
2919 A University should be a place
3100 up to the university, but you
3185 The university is the last
8402 Jimmy's university.
8596 to the university, where it
11036 the High; We are the University.
unjust
1496 also on the unjust fella: But
9509 essentially unjust and
unkempt
1575 Unkempt about those hedges
unkindest
10294 the most unkindest cut of
unkindness
10435 Unkindness may do much; And his
unknowable
7277 in the unknowable. But
unknown
534 buried the Unknown Prime
2755 leading towards the unknown.
4454 into the unknown.' And he
7978 Toward the Unknown.
8731 and the unknown, what else
8884 And things unknown proposed
unlabelled
4934 to go about unlabelled. The
unlamented
8934 Thus unlamented let me
unlearn
11092 not to learn, but to unlearn.
unlearned
8862
9089 For the unlearned, old age is
unlike
12713 is! So unlike anything
unlove
2661 unlove's the heavenless hell
unlovely
11547 in the long unlovely street.
unluckily
11232 the good unluckily. That is
unlucky
7030 who is so unlucky that he
unmarried
6385 for the unmarried mother, as
10617 to keep unmarried as long as
unmask
10539 kings, To unmask falsehood,
unmourning
11686 by the unmourning water Of
unmoved
9784 proudly, as unmoved as if it
11408 remains unmoved at seeming
unmuzzled
4934 the police do an unmuzzled dog.
unnatural
646 of an unnatural beginning.
3661 The only unnatural sexual
4385 neither unnatural, nor
10370 abroad. Unnatural deeds Do
unnecessary
4437 the unfit, to do the unnecessary.
12860 agree, one of them is unnecessary.
unobtrusive
5481 great and unobtrusive, a thing
unobtrusiveness
9824 respectful unobtrusiveness of one
unoccupied
10002 than when unoccupied, nor less
unofficial
3000 It is the unofficial force - the
unorthodox
1032 anything unorthodox goes on
unpleasant
4080 up with the unpleasant more
4503 The unpleasant and unacceptable
8494 in the unpleasant: if it is
9421 anything unpleasant , at all.

unpleasantness
8077 put up with unpleasantness from a man

unpopular
956 I was not unpopular [at school]
6966 he might be unpopular. What
11148 it is safe to be unpopular.

unprecedented
467 events, are never unprecedented.

unpremeditated
10024 The unpremeditated lay.

unprepared
1409 I mean unprepared courage,
2565 unprepared For the

unprincipled
2065 sold by the unprincipled to the

unprofitable
10189 flat, and unprofitable Seem to me

unpunished
1587 good deed ever goes unpunished.
4106 the ideal never goes unpunished.

unreal
4606 such an unreal life.

unregenerate
4724 side of the unregenerate who affirm

unreprieved
7569 unpitied, unreprieved, Ages of

unsafe
7064 lowness is unsafe as height,
8065 Unsafe at any speed.

unsaid
7412 or four things a day unsaid.
8815 have left unsaid that
12692 practically nothing unsaid.

unsatisfied
12589 leaves one unsatisfied. What

unsavoury
10233 the most unsavoury similies.

unsayable
11884 been absolutely unsayable.

unseen
7501 I walk unseen On the dry
7600 the earth Unseen, both when

unselfishness
6307 means by unselfishness chiefly
9895 Real unselfishness consists in
12926 magnet is unselfishness, thinking

unskilled
8876 thus unskilled to trace

unsought
6439 come often unsought, and, as
10518 but giv'n unsought is better.

unsoundness
6846 a certain unsoundness of mind.

unspeakable
12602 a fox - the unspeakable in full

unspoiled
2594 utterly unspoiled by

unstuck
221 of coming unstuck, thank

unsuccessful
1593 a lot of unsuccessful years.

unsung
10028 unhonoured, and unsung.

unsupportable
8420 again is unsupportable, so I

unsure
10512 is still unsure: In delay

untalented
2065 of the untalented, sold by

unthought
3121 thought can never be unthought.

untie
5293 cut what you can untie.

untimely
12204 came I so untimely forth Into

untouch'd
7005 time lie untouch'd, will

untravelled
4189 My heart untravelled fondly

untried
6374 against the new and untried?

untrodden
5441 show untrodden green,
12781 among the untrodden ways

untrue
591 A man who's untrue to his
5783 as to make it sound untrue?
12183 that is untrue in the
12770 Untrue she was; yet I

untruth
5628 is a crowd there is untruth.

unturned
10571 no stone unturned to see

unutterable
11730 and looked unutterable things.

unwanted
11626 of being unwanted is the

unweave
5460 mine - Unweave a rainbow.

unwholesome
628 very soft is not unwholesome.

unwilling
4437 of the unwilling, picked
7638 to go hence unwilling; thou to

unworthiness
4653 of utter unworthiness can be a

unworthy
799 a small and unworthy goal for
11810 is altogether unworthy of it.

up
3689 know why it was put up.
6940 Up and down the City
7711 on your way up because

up to date
10597 them and keep them up to date.

upbringing
8356 I'd the upbringing a nun would

uplift
856 give gentle uplift and

uplifting
80 In uplifting, get underneath.

upper class
999 many of the Upper Class He liked

upper crust
3968 The other, upper crust, A regular

upright
939 are plain, honest and upright.
11685 and that is, upright.

uproar
5479 the world - uproar's your

upstanding
5677 A clean upstanding chap like

upward
4103 Woman draws us upward.
4811 could go straight upwards.

urban
1578 Being urban, squat,
6768 in the urban compound.

urge
12505 Urge and urge and urge,
12928 of man's urge to rise

urgent
6283 conveys the urgent necessity

urn
4292 Can storied urn or

us
366 Here's tae us; wha's
5535 the enemy, and he is us.

use
370 will find a use for it.
2366 prime; they use themselves
2384 and use it for
3729 fight forces; use them.
5220 no earthly use to your
7179 a complete use of the
8432 ring is worn away by use.
9097 can find some use for him.
11042 be of more use to you
11349 begun to use us ill, it
12235 Use him as though you
12554 earth is the use of them?
12580 never any use to

used
3205 they are used to, or
8665 ain't what they used to be.
9301 I used your soap two years

used up
9996 a man who never gets used up.

useful
660 be a Really Useful Engine.
2157 should always look useful.
3901 as equally useful. And thus
6145 dearest, is an useful thing.
7436 it's always useful to know
7930 know to be useful, or
8097 aren't very useful, Because

usefulness
3095 for private usefulness they

useless
3013 nothing so useless as doing
7677 hide Lodged with me useless.
9738 the most useless; peacocks
9929 Man is a useless passion.
12392 may never live to be useless!
12474 is not only useless; it is

uses
9508 have alternative uses.

usurped
3904 sexes, has usurped the powers

utopia
4052 attained in Utopia, from a
6812 a principality in Utopia.

utopias
4947 the static Utopias and the
12740 not imagine utopias because

utterance
5443 That large utterance of the
6094 the first utterance that was
12807 A timely utterance gave that

uttered
12486 under which it is uttered.

vacancy
4355 he creates a job vacancy.
10156 but for vacancy, Had gone

vacant
6505 But has one vacant chair!
10014 Vacant heart and hand, and

vacuum
4321 behind the vacuum cleaner to
9212 Nature abhors a vacuum.
12642 A vacuum is a hell of a lot

vagabonds
9032 rogues and vagabonds, which is

vagrant
7137 to the vagrant gypsy

vague
2681 conflicting vague
5830 is such vague

vaguery
8400 'For Vaguery in the

vain
4561 is in vain: The seas
6096 now it is vain for the
8538 How vain painting is,
11749 How vain it is to sit down

vainglorious
118 when this vainglorious and

vainly
7077 How vainly men themselves

vales
6389 our lovely vales, Oh, let

valet
4108 hero to his valet. That is

valiant
745 ever become valiant and
10280 deaths; The valiant never
11603 like a valiant man and

validity
962 ultimate validity of what

valley
244 sing in the valley below:
6406 How green was my valley.
11473 To bicker down a valley.
11475 All in the valley of Death

victories
3714 between Our victories and our
7522 hath her victories No less
12002 a hundred victories in a

victorious
6611 The victorious cause pleased the

victory
918 personal victory over
937 so near to victory as when
1131 O grave, where is thy victory?
2334 Victory, victory at all
2341 Victory has a hundred
2398 which result in victory.
2585 When our Victory is
2966 'Dig for Victory' be the
3124 smells like victory."
4824 Victory - a matter of staying
5678 you to the victory you
6350 To give victory to the right,
6674 be no substitute for victory.
8112 moment of victory is much
9924 details of victory, it is
10952 'But 'twas a famous victory.'
11002 of all victory lies in
12037 sustained victory of
12687 without victory .. Only

victuals
2020 to please About their victuals.

vienna
1412 to take Vienna - take
7334 everything, Vienna is

vietnam
11028 To win in Vietnam, we will

view
1639 die, Do I view the world
2617 no other views of the
4441 frame the view:
7441 a wonderful view Of
10022 would'st view fair

viewing
4133 heroes, viewing life in

vigilance
7169 unceasing vigilance and a rare

vigils
8826 painful vigils keep,

vigorous
3331 are least vigorous, or when
6772 people more vigorous than we

vigour
551 My vigour, vitality and

vikings
5667 us Stir the Vikings' blood;

vile
5990 reckoned Vile, but viler
10323 can make vile things

vilely
10244 it not show vilely in me to

vilify
910 Vilify! Vilify! Some of it

villa
7917 must have a villa in summer
9720 A single villa can mar a

village
4149 loveliest village of the
4157 The village all declared how

villain
7312 God wot, No villain need be!
8963 made a villain, Millions
10391 Is like a villain with a
10459 to prove a villain, And hate

villainy
11881 There is no villainy to which
11945 of villainy which we

villon
11358 Villon, our sad bad glad mad

vindicate
8890 we can; But vindicate the ways

vindictive
7182 makes men petty and vindictive.

vine
7527 the gadding vine o'ergrown.

vines
5410 fruit the vines that round

vintage
4806 out the vintage where the

violence
123 Keep violence in the mind
401 Violence is, essentially, a
1594 I say violence is necessary.
2563 Violence is just, where
3278 never be by violence
3830 Today violence is the rhetoric
6055 not by violence, but by
6683 In violence, we forget who we
6769 Violence is the quest for
6811 of war is violence, and that
7331 Violence is essentially
8056 think about violence. For me
11825 men who do violence to the
12315 to be legitimate) violence.

violent
795 storm, Short as it violent is.
3244 the most violent, and
3537 you may be violent and
5582 will make violent revolution

violet
10261 I am: the violet smells to

violets
6548 to me, It's raining violets.

violin
835 trying to play the violin.
1884 playing a violin solo in
8645 a distant violin - it's the

violins
12081 of autumn's violins wound my

virgin
6913 That virgin, vital, fine
7532 maid, and virgin mother
7543 But see the virgin blest,

virgin-choir
5504 Nor virgin-choir to make delicious

virginity
7072 preserved virginity: And your
9046 no; for my virginity, When I
11854 little more virginity, if you

virgins
1927 Where the virgins are soft as
12446 the young virgins into the

virtue
652 Loss of virtue in a female
686 is the virtue of fools.
694 doth best discover virtue.
721 either of virtue or
766 The virtue of prosperity is
1396 to the cause of virtue.
1406 The first virtue in a
1769 ceases to be a virtue.
1876 to keep virtue within
1900 A virtue to be serviceable
2047 to believe in pure virtue.
3049 is the virtue of weak
3324 reward of virtue is virtue;
4145 tremendous virtue, but the
4168 eradicating the virtue.
4197 The virtue which requires to
4200 of justice is no virtue!
5139 maintaining virtue that it is
5662 first upgrowth of all virtue.
5671 been a virtue with the
5877 which vice pays to virtue.
6019 a soverayn vertue, and a
6982 A woman's virtue ought
7017 Virtue is the fount whence
7142 Is in a prince the virtue.
7382 The true virtue of human
7479 Virtue could see to do what
7484 hold firm, Virtue may be
7725 accommodating sort of virtue.
7760 maxim be my virtue's guide:
7783 Virtue shuns ease as a
7805 the best virtue I have has
7944 The virtue of much
8213 makes a necessity of virtue.
8555 Their virtue is
8662 recognize virtue and rot
8864 Virtue she finds too painful
9511 as virtue is the
9721 virtue expressed
10401 mark of virtue on his

10445 There is no virtue like
10616 What is virtue but the Trade
10908 Virtue does not come from
11025 it is a virtue, a state
11283 into virtue than
11359 languors of virtue For the
11431 virtue of
11991 - and a virtue, and that
12071 stirs up war; virtue fights.
12072 If virtue were its own
12219 Virtue knows to a farthing
12268 men have virtue to

virtues
2292 all of the virtues I dislike
3448 like virtues, are their
4557 all the virtues, for we
4601 Gods rank work above virtues.
4638 war the two cardinal virtues.
5127 makes some virtues
5354 have no virtues, their
5882 greater virtues to bear
6301 one of the virtues but the
8040 Only in our virtues are we
9036 Be to her virtues very kind;
10273 their virtues We write
10509 it a world to hide virtues in?
11217 praised for virtues you never
12073 sick our virtues and our
12412 one's virtues and not
12611 about his virtues, and
12614 let your virtues spring up

virtuous
1236 A virtuous woman is a crown to
1395 upon men as virtuous, or
4902 we are profoundly virtuous.
10513 thou art virtuous, there
11347 men grow virtuous in their
12207 is the most virtuous man, he
12646 No woman is virtuous who does

visible
1568 of little visible delight,
5765 the visible; rather,
8535 it is visible, and has
12581 is the visible, not the

vision
1256 faulty vision sees
2713 has no vision, no
4970 convey a vision of the
5503 Was it a vision, or a waking
9805 with his vision, Spring
11146 with a vision of things
12890 Is but a vision of

visionary
12809 is fled the visionary gleam?

visions
1234 young men shall see visions.
10423 While these visions did
10673 in stormy visions, keep With

visit
5947 thy short visit meant, or
7920 very short visit to a
10022 aright, Go visit it by the

visitor
770 ordinary visitor; and the

visits
7846 make long visits, have to
9242 Visits always give pleasure

vital
8417 their three vital parts -
8839 Vital spark of heav'nly

vitality
11179 deficient vitality; and a

vivacity
71 As vivacity is the gift of

vivid
6546 Youth is vivid rather than

vocation
4144 There is no vocation about
10767 but a vocation of
10843 test of a vocation is the
12812 his whole vocation Were

vogue
12016 he'd be working for Vogue .
12212 to totter into vogue.

voice
563 The voice we heard was that
899 The voice is a second face.
1300 dance and the human voice.
2449 No voice; but oh! the
3519 Her voice is full of money.
3531 The voice is a second
5238 The Voice of Cato is
5247 The voice so sweet, the
6513 a distant voice in the
7541 dumb, No voice or hideous
8921 people's voice is odd, It
9209 dei. The voice of the
9348 and a clear voice; enough of
9582 candent voice which was
9791 against the voice of a
11472 sound of a voice that is
11797 I hear a voice you cannot
12337 lost my voice Most
12710 in his voice, and I

voices
11610 Moans round with many voices.

void
8844 No craving void left
12033 a certain void. 'Nothing
12341 are attempts to fill voids.

volatile
9886 bliss; volatile spirits

volcanic
6601 this sweet volcanic cone;

volcano
3536 not on a volcano, but on
9846 We are dancing on a volcano.

volcanoes
2918 a range of exhausted volcanoes.

volume
7706 I am the entire volume.
12961 that the volume knob also

volumes
826 four volumes about
5942 and creators of odd volumes.
6132 such volumes of stuff!

votary
5939 A votary of the desk - a

vote
25 most people vote against
885 Vote for the man who
1284 Vote early and vote
3486 I never vote for
3975 And vote just as
5342 and who vote - a very
5583 a single vote more than
7948 Vote Labour: Sleep Tory.
12910 let the neighbours vote.

voted
3963 I always voted at my

voter
8121 it from the voters, using
9852 each is a voter who uses

voting
6401 If voting changed anything
11223 not the voting that's

vouchsafes
6645 to whom He vouchsafes nothing

vow
11037 I vow to thee, my country

vowels
9502 O blue: vowels, some day

vows
1670 means love, Vows can't
10124 falser than vows made in

voyage
4636 my last voyage, a great
10299 all the voyage of their
11843 a voyage - not a
11986 a cheerful, careless voyage.

voyages
2749 Voyages in a paper boat.
9535 are the voyages of the
12643 Make voyages. Attempt them.

vulgar
1002 let the vulgar stuff
2506 'tis such a vulgar expression
3773 above the vulgar herd, but

7007 from the vulgar trade,
8929 upon the vulgar with fine
9306 wicked, my dear, it's vulgar.
12537 are always vulgar and often
12573 upon as vulgar, it will
12633 remark or a vulgar action.

vulgarity
8973 for the Jacksonian vulgarity.

vulnerable
11833 is vulnerable through

vultures
10743 how many vultures there are

wade
10360 should I wade no more,

wag
5175 an ambition to be a wag.

wage
11795 an hourly wage to an
12660 One man's wage rise is

wages
1143 The wages of sin is death.
3569 who pays wages - he only
8388 than better wages and
10180 ta'en thy wages: Golden

wagner
8295 told that Wagner's music is
9054 Wagner has lovely moments
11980 Richard Wagner, a musician

wail
6056 yet so does wail? O 'tis

waist
544 round your waist and his
2573 and narrow waist begin to
12198 her slender waist confined

wait
536 We had better wait and see.
1387 I'll wait for you.
2224 a girl will wait is just
3085 two words - wait and hope.
5216 Wait a minute, wait a
6707 If you can wait and not be
5935 and must wait upon the
6816 men are to wait for
7644 forelock watchful wait.
7678 who only stand and wait.
7987 eight, and we won't wait.
9970 them and wait till they

waiter
3079 best is a waiter at the
4357 and a dam' good head waiter.
6005 The waiter roars it through

waiting
923 We're waiting for Godot.
1637 are just waiting until the
6202 was I, waiting at the
6534 I was nearly kept waiting.
6958 Waiting we say is long. We
11251 a period of waiting for the

waits
3142 who hustles while he waits.
6226 in a dream. Waits at the

waive
1817 I waive the quantum o' the

wake
2208 a slepyng hound to wake.
2374 thee, and wake with thee,
5503 music: do I wake or sleep?
5638 wilt not wake Till I thy

waked
7680 inclined I waked, she fled,
12289 'You have waked me too

wakes
11510 while woman wakes to love.

waking
1618 yet it is waking that kills
10555 king, but, waking, no such

wales
1399 world .. But for Wales - !
6389 bless the Prince of Wales!'

walk
133 A walk on the wild side.
1193 Can two walk together,
1348 time Walk upon
2117 'Will you walk a little

2629 for a closer walk with God.
4133 powers to walk hand in
5739 virtue, Or walk with Kings
6347 thing, I'd rather walk.'
7008 myself, I walk abroad
7403 allowed to walk out and
7506 fail To walk the
8197 have to walk and live a
8916 men must walk at least
9086 after supper walk a mile.
9466 no fool, Walk across my
11958 is a good walk spoiled.
12457 five-mile walk will do

walked
1730 As I walked through the
5704 He walked by himself, and

walking
4420 keep me walking the floor
5030 Walking is the best possible
5082 a dog's walking on his
7226 As I was walking up the stair
7974 your fingers do the walking.
11034 Ireland is walking in spirit
12056 I see them walking in an air

walks
4892 which one walks as a
6091 gets up and walks away with
7480 Benighted walks under the

wall
2965 is the only wall Between us
6864 climb the wall when they

wallet
6121 when you risk your wallet.
8068 by their wallets, their

wallowing
6971 it's good only for wallowing in.

walls
494 are her wooden walls.
8195 and not in walls nor in
9394 but the walls are
11327 Walls have tongues, and

walrus
6287 them, then, Walrus and

waltzing
8571 come a waltzing, Matilda,

wandered
2584 certainly wandered a good
12844 I wandered lonely as a cloud

wandering
7171 eternity wandering round and
7501 behold the wandering moon,

want
581 what they most want to do.
853 the people want. The most
3600 passion; we want what puts
4747 you do want in case
5165 from want to want,
5274 let you want, while
7034 what they want and are
7436 'I don't want him,' said
7731 unbridled, now Just want.
8276 We don't want it good - we
9601 from want ..
9978 feels the want of what it
11467 among those who want both.
11613 eternal want of pence,
11621 When you want to, they
12050 The want of a thing is

wanted
2818 alone are wanted in life.
3333 man is wanted, and no
3785 tell them what they wanted.
8746 will not be wanted these ten

wanting
2156 Give up wanting to deserve
6724 Man is a wanting animal - as

wanton
7511 cranks, and wanton wiles,

wants
1298 item he wants. A woman
3305 to have few wants, and to
4147 express our wants as to
9684 when a man wants her is a
10121 He that wants money, means,
11451 are few wants more

11787 score Man wants a great
12941 Man wants but little, nor

war

402 War does not determine
410 When war enters a country
464 Human war has been the
478 We make war that we may
555 After each war there is a
600 there was war, he went.
823 War would end if the dead
1095 making of war - at least
1125 has been a war yet which,
1307 another war in Europe,
1463 but it is not war.
1534 only war creates
1536 War is like love. It
2138 In time of war the first
2248 is going to the war.
2276 War settles nothing ..
2310 success in war, but only
2319 better than to war-war.
2326 than war, for in
2335 In war, as in life, it is
2336 War is mainly a catalogue
2342 the cash of war. Whoever
2389 War is nothing but a
2393 War is too serious a
2396 to make war than to
2398 War is a series of
2440 voices prophesying war!
2582 of war increases
2620 But war's a game, which,
2687 vain, For war breeds war
2754 has not lost the war!
3032 War, he sung, is toil and
3051 War is the trade of
3074 are dangerous in war.
3083 must take chances in war.
3084 reserve for war the finest
3102 game is war - crool,
3139 no declaration of war.
3469 court war to escape
3601 Men love war because it
3623 true that war never
3631 was a good war, or a bad
3725 War appeals to young men
3732 Either war is obsolete or
3886 to the desolation of war.
4040 gave a war & Nobody
4044 As soon as war is
4426 War makes rattling good
4429 and curious war is! You
4515 get out of war altogether
4570 a good war makes a
4582 fathers; in war, fathers
4676 which in wartime has so
4733 sooner than of war.
4971 object of war is to
4976 a continuation of war.
5010 So far war has been the
5055 to wage war in the
5566 tempered by war,
5578 an end to war or war
5579 War will exist until that
5685 Horses and Power and War.
6069 inevitable war. If war
6172 In a war of ideas it is
6186 well that war is so
6349 scourge of war may
6399 Oh what a lovely war.
6418 terrible war that has
6550 against war. Even
6554 called a war. Christ!
6560 We've a war, an' a debt,
6601 in small war on the
6674 In war, indeed, there can
6697 to make war but
6713 We hear war called
6799 poured to war from
6811 essence of war is
6922 all this war been
6946 Only in war our fate has
6976 Politics is war without
7014 that first invented war.
7088 portend No war, nor
7196 of war and sport.
7429 like war. Nothing
7522 No less renowned than war.

7523 what can war, but
7535 No war, or battle's sound
7567 is for open war: of wiles
7576 Shakes pestilence and war.
7636 no less than war to waste.
7688 la Prusse. War is the
7741 one; and war is a
7742 veterans of World War III.
7765 War hath no fury like a
7811 founded by war has to
7859 Boy to the war is gone,
7989 been a war yet which
7990 in the Great War, daddy?
8015 Make love, not war.
8083 In war, three-quarters
8260 A war regarded as
8374 sport is war without
8379 War is peace. Freedom is
8384 of ending a war is to lose
8451 subject is War, and the
8480 cuchillo. War by the
8789 unwise war An alp of
8964 War its thousands slays,
9210 Sweet is war to those who
9360 War is, after all, the
9557 in every war they kill
9865 give a war and nobody
9926 rich wage war it's the
10095 devil's madness - War.
10256 blast of war blows in
10286 let slip the dogs of war.
10434 of glorious war!
10451 testament of bleeding war.
10485 To offer war where they
10734 looks on war as all
10926 Image of war, without
10965 We wage no war with women
11001 shadow of a war, What can
11025 absence of war, it is a
11236 War is capitalism with
11268 Glory, waste of God, War!
11287 image of war without
11329 a state of war by nature.
11442 Crimea: The War That Would
11788 The war between men and
11910 prepare for the last war.
11913 War is the unfolding of
12071 stirs up war; virtue
12078 peace, prepare for war.
12109 of war is: For
12193 out of this war - can be
12344 enable it to make war.
12360 business of war, and
12380 The war that will end
12461 short of war, to match
12573 As long as war is
12622 World War II was the last
12671 people into war, into the
12678 people into war and they
12934 name, War's glorious

war office
10591 except the British War Office.

war-drum
11529 Till the war-drum throbbed no

warbled
7503 notes as warbled to the

warfare
3526 is a kind of warfare in mufti.
3948 nuclear warfare. There
8159 legitimate warfare: war has

warm
1947 Be warm but pure: be
5334 Feel live warm beings
5491 For ever warm and still to
8130 This is too warm work,
9178 fire let us warm ourselves.

warmed
11156 glow has warmed the world.

warmer
6022 Is no weder warmer than after

warming
6968 than warming the

warming-pans
7295 were as good as warming-pans.

warmth
5483 is an awful warmth about my
8309 except its occasional warmth.

warn
5679 I warn you not to be
8445 poet can do today is warn.
12273 Let me .. warn you in the
12819 planned, To warn, to

warning
6758 Early Warning System

warns
7269 voice which warns us that

warred
7640 infantry Warred on by

warring
7016 elements, Warring within our
7589 Warring in heaven against

warrior
5579 that the warrior does
10021 joy which warriors feel In

wars
5796 Wars are not fought for
6877 that cause wars but wars
8017 purpose. Wars cannot be
8377 subsequent wars have been
8442 Very few wars are brought
8790 couple Between the wars.
9010 with the wars which
9465 All wars are planned by
9593 sent into any foreign wars.
9907 from the wars today and
10506 still, wars and
12126 I see wars, horrible wars,

wary
9031 feeling wary when I

wash
2237 that wash most are
3242 the sky! wash the wind!
9078 he doesn't wash his hands,

washed
2707 but I just washed my hair."

washes
8707 Art washes away from the

washing
6387 shirts and washing
11681 only washing. And

washing-day
8639 and, being washing-day, dined

washington
3789 Washington is a place where men
4935 Washington is an endless series
12194 cough in Washington They spit
12672 office in Washington either

washup
5317 dumbly, only to washup.

wasps
11306 but let wasps and

waste
243 to be is to waste the person
297 Time wastes our bodies and
1309 treats me like toxic waste.
3123 by, What a waste, what a
6971 appalling waste of energy;
7636 no less than war to waste.
10023 They waste their toil For
10548 wail my dear times' waste.
11268 Waste of Blood, and waste
12838 we lay waste our

waste basket
10782 The waste basket is a writer's

waste-paper
1028 file your waste-paper basket for
12313 is the waste-paper basket of

wasted
3233 he may have wasted his time
4561 Nothing is wasted, nothing
9074 that I've wasted years of
10455 I wasted time, and now doth

wasteful
10305 garnish, Is wasteful and

wasting
9078 does, he is wasting the water.
12701 Shall I, wasting in despair,

watch
1004 done much better by a watch.
1431 past as a watch in the
2587 appear on, you don't watch.
4754 If you watch a game, it's
5731 for a spy, Watch the wall,
6581 keeping watch above his
7096 dead, or my watch has
8757 a fat gold watch. The
10186 some must watch, while
12179 fine Swiss watch:

watchdog
4152 The watchdog's voice that

watcher
5439 I like some watcher of the

watches
5142 are like watches. The
11480 crawls; He watches from his

watching
1093 observe a lot just by watching.
8378 BIG BROTHER IS WATCHING YOU.
9633 eyes weary of watching, Earth.

watchmaker
2713 the role of watchmaker in nature,

watchman
10031 of power, A watchman on the

watchword
8736 Our watchword is security.

water
100 wine, it turns into water.
300 The King over the water.
301 to go back in the water.
2446 Water, water, everywhere,
3300 as ready by water as by
4571 great ship asks deep water.
4669 o'er the water, we'll
4771 by drinkers of water.
5328 I makes water I makes
5471 were under water I would
6240 stagnant water loses it
6997 into little water drops, And
7204 on the water. The
8432 Dripping water hollows out
8721 Water is best. But gold
9240 times - in water, in butter
9279 she falls into the water.
10172 a drop of water That in
10228 Too much of water hast thou,
10273 virtues We write in water.
10355 A little water clears us of
10448 Not all the water in the
10768 troubled water I will lay
11418 into the water for the
12834 sheets of water, and pure

waterfall
6512 From the waterfall he named

watergate
4257 little bit of Watergate in him.

waterloo
8377 battle of Waterloo was won
8701 man meets his Waterloo at last.
11586 world-earthquake, Waterloo!
12357 battle of Waterloo was won on

watermelons
4039 you doing down by the watermelons?

waters
5313 rivering waters of
12114 in the waste of waters.

wave
5745 never a wave of all her

wavers
9352 She wavers, she hesitates.

waves
3923 winds and waves are always
7850 of kindlier waves) With
8560 broken her waves over us
10551 Like as the waves make

waving
10869 And not waving but

waxes
3670 and goes, waxes and wanes.

way
1152 I am the way, the truth,
1536 love. It a ways finds a

3825 so in the way in the
4473 to find my way across the
4682 - but woman has her way.
5067 her own way, and the
5686 be triple ways to take,
5815 Every which way but loose.
6029 The Way is like an empty
6739 The best way to get
8004 All the way, with LBJ.
8058 There is no way to peace.
9329 Thou art my way; I wander,
10325 I have no way, and
10812 shortest way to do many
12706 the fly the way out of the

ways
3089 "We have ways of making
8165 Most sure in all His ways.
10073 to life, but many ways out.
11038 Here ways are ways of
11512 But in His ways with men I

we
307 We shall not be moved.
5682 like us are We, And
11651 We have become a

weak
1251 The weak have one weapon:
2473 end and aim of weak ones.
4383 Weak men are apt to be
4703 A weak mind does not
5136 are too weak to be felt
5176 Man is not weak -
5577 If we are weak, words
5825 The weak against the
5906 Weak people cannot be
6352 or too weak to
7177 Like all weak men he laid
7552 to be weak is
7772 of life so weak and
10094 surely the Weak shall
11690 How weak and little is the

weak-minded
4368 A very weak-minded fellow I am

weaken
1697 life if you don't weaken.

weakening
11000 gradual day Weakening the will

weaker
1918 Is to the weaker side

weakness
4003 'Is it weakness of intellect,
4660 few, while weakness corrupts
5903 to their weakness than to
5944 the man's weakness, but the
6745 of the weakness that we're
10069 cruelty springs from weakness.
12100 is great; all else is weakness.
12173 Weakness on both sides is, as
12309 It's a sign of weakness."
12338 right, weakness always
12522 and thence to weakness.
12944 today, And shows its weakness.

weaknesses
4168 touch his weaknesses with a
7194 the encounter of two weaknesses.

wealth
1523 have great wealth
2727 The solid wealth of
2806 Wealth makes everything easy
3776 greater the wealth, the
3898 about wealth. I have
4150 prey, Where wealth
5264 of my wealth Than in
5605 its capital wealth also,
6965 Let wealth and commerce,
7007 as their wealth
8917 place and wealth, if
9529 with wealth is what
9728 There is no wealth but life.
10582 to consume wealth without
10679 excessive wealth a libel on
10713 reaps; The wealth ye find,
11190 Wealth I seek not, hope nor
11743 the poet's wealth, is so
11873 no road to wealth so easy
12077 standard of wealth.
12693 Thirst of wealth no quiet

wealthy
484 are very wealthy and others
1453 extremely wealthy town; I
2400 wealthy, just
3778 wealthy turn up
6285 wealthy, and yet

weaned
2945 were we not weaned till then?

weapon
86 a terrible weapon of
1251 have one weapon: the
5564 is not a weapon ..
5648 and just weapon. It is a
5796 deadliest weapon is
7229 a secret weapon in our
10838 to select a weapon it is the
11830 powerful weapon of

weaponless
7659 iron, And, weaponless himself,

weapons
621 the same weapons of reason
12530 word of the weapons, their

wear
3894 The way you wear your hat,
4131 who has nothing to wear.
6398 does not wear so well.
7899 to learn to wear it over
12465 better to wear out than
12963 you'll wear your eyes

weariness
5498 known, The weariness, the
8675 brief And weariness treads on
10178 Weariness Can snore upon the

wearing
831 trick of wearing mink is to
3077 a long wearing away of

weary
1621 To put on when you're weary.
5773 world is wearie of me so
8810 weak and weary, Over many
10278 life, being weary of these
10683 world is weary of the
11005 this long weary day have

weasel
3484 Some weasel took the cork
6940 goes - Pop goes the weasel!
6733 The weasel under the

weather
191 deep, the weather sharp, the
638 hot weather we have!
5157 first talk is of the weather.
5666 hard grey weather Breeds
5742 years ago. Weather and rain
6787 you won't hold up the weather.
11136 Catches tigers In red weather.
11927 the weather may send,

weathered
1020 Lincoln's) weathered face was

weave
12323 behind, And weave but nets

weaves
11357 He weaves, and is clothed

web
10033 a tangled web we weave,
10143 The web of our life is of
11522 left the web, she left

wed
1440 Ring I thee wed, with my
2370 trouble I wed again, and
10126 when they wed: maids are
10139 think to wed it, he is
11558 out to wed with

wedded
7601 Hail, wedded love,

wedding
68 bought her wedding clothes.
4612 Wedding is destiny, and

wedding night
8648 is like a wedding night in a

wedding-cake
570 like a wedding-cake left out

wedding-day
5525 earliest wedding-day, The

wedding-ring
2348 the small circle of a wedding-ring!

wedlock
1943 angels, yet wedlock's the

weed
3336 What is a weed? A plant
12208 will not weed their own

weeds
9126 like a garden full of weeds.
10556 smell far worse than weeds.
12187 up like weeds. Through

week
69 the rust of the whole week.
4809 than others can in a week.
12664 politics a week is a very

weekly
9113 not pay weekly, but he

weep
2143 one end and weep for her
4260 Weep not for little Léonie
4279 Is to weep on your
5670 women must weep, And
8142 is empty - Weep, children,
10128 is it to weep at joy
10532 But milk my ewes and weep.
12534 with you; Weep, and you

weeping
1174 shall be weeping and
1334 Ever weeping Paddington.
4129 hours Weeping and
6845 With weeping and with

weigh
738 but to weigh and

weight
2360 to the weight of words
4777 through its own weight.
7076 every weight, Trying
12795 the weary weight Of all

weights
8072 system of weights and

welcome
1826 And aye be welcome back
10717 The warmest welcome, at an

welcomest
10265 Are often welcomest when they

welfare
11832 true source of human welfare.

well
817 done very well out of the
941 speaks well of a man,
1950 too, all would be well.
2249 any hope of doing it well.
3080 are always well and those
3882 I am not well; pray get
3977 And did it very well.
5344 shall be well and all
7053 alive, but being well.
7341 It is well with me only
7443 perfectly well and she
8690 done rather well under very
9295 feeling very well myself.
9530 reasonably well in life,
10934 of the well and in the

well conducted
11631 like a well conducted person,

well managed
7619 on just and right Well managed.

well-aired
1681 the morning well-aired before he

well-bred
1875 thoroughly well-bred and soon

well-connected
3972 virtuous scorn The well-connected.

well-dressed
3345 of being well-dressed gives a

well-looking
4180 one of my well-looking days,

well-organised
4276 the only well-organised and

well-remembered
3081 forgiven is usually well-remembered.

well-spent
2083 as rare as a well-spent one.

well-written
2083 A well-written Life is almost as

wellness
7138 component of mental wellness.
12218 in a moment of pretty wellness.

wenceslas
8114 Good King Wenceslas looked out,

wench
7009 besides, the wench is dead.

wept
1438 down and wept: when we
2570 I wept as I remembered how
7004 And as she wept, her tears

west
4301 Go West, young man, and
5669 away to the west, Away to
5684 East, and West is West,
9098 in the West are always
9760 of the West, results

west end
10825 running farce in the West End.

western
5668 Dee.' The western wind was
9435 Quiet on the Western Front.
12491 seen one Western you've

western union
4206 be delivered by Western Union.

westminster
8128 a peerage, or Westminster Abbey.

westward
1072 Westward the course of empire

wet
4757 bereft Of wet and
9006 He's so wet you could
9274 those who are already wet.

whack
2316 time - a tremendous whack!

whacks
319 forty whacks; When she

whale
7245 whale .. from

whaleship
7243 A whaleship was my Yale College

what
1910 He knew what's what, and
5707 names are What and Why
6234 Ah! What is man?
7990 What did you do in the

wheat
271 amorous Over Shredded Wheat.
4823 the wheat from the
6136 there be wheat' and

wheel
6094 begot the wheel, the
8856 a butterfly upon a wheel?
10334 The wheel is come full

wheels
3556 do not let the wheels show.
11561 And all the wheels of Being

where
2119 Where shall I begin,
2837 Where thou art, that, is
6472 to earth, I knew not where.
9607 you have, where you are.
10047 Where have all the flowers

whereabouts
9288 they have! Whereabouts is that?

wherefore
6234 is man? Wherefore does he
10473 Romeo! wherefore art thou

wherever
180 bed for it; Wherever you may

wherewithal
9041 But had not always wherewithal.

whiff
2090 A whiff of grapeshot.

whig
5109 and a wise Whig, I

whigs
1620 sent, For Whigs admit no
2914 caught the Whigs bathing,

whimper
3261 Not with a bang but a whimper.

whimpering
5694 They are whimpering to and fro

whimsies
9034 have my whimsies, but thou

whip
8249 to woman, take thy whip.

whipping
10209 and who should 'scape whipping?

whirl
5271 my roof whirl around

whirlwind
1224 they shall reap the whirlwind.

whirring
10441 storm Whirring me from my

whiskies
7766 to th' extent of two whiskies.

whisky
1812 Freedom and Whisky gan
2985 than whisky, once man
3156 Whisky drowns some troubles
3485 placed on whisky. Why this
3542 gulp of hot whisky at bedtime

whisper
6944 Perhaps my whisper was
7444 Hush! Hush! Whisper who dares!
7462 that whisper softness
9791 that the whisper of a
11700 The dry whisper of unseen

whispering
503 [Oxford] whispering from her
7092 I was just whispering in her
8448 At home, whispering of fields

whisperings
3518 among the whisperings and the
10370 Foul whisperings are abroad.

whispers
3739 when your power only whispers.
10842 he says, but what he whispers.

whistled
3038 sought, And whistled as he

whistling
10156 sit alone, Whistling to the
11709 to the whistling mane of

white
814 world is white no longer,
1079 of a white Christmas,
2114 become very white; And yet
3585 so-called white races are
4843 down For white folks
5647 is not the White Citizens
5652 to be the white man's
5755 Take up the White Man's
7193 Get black on white.
9317 you see the white of their

white house
1860 over the White House as the
8267 no whitewash at the White House.
11151 me on the way to the White House.

white-collar
8387 man with a white-collar job,

white-haired
11606 world, A white-haired shadow

whitehall
11858 my life in Whitehall, the acid

whitewash
8267 can be no whitewash at the

whithering
6234

who
643 Oh! who can ever be tired
11129 And who are you? said he.

whole
9148 It's the whole, not the
9741 seeing the whole of them.

wholeheartedly
10664 somewhere, wholeheartedly,

wholesome
3664 a normal and wholesome life.

whom
78 Whom are you?' he asked,

whomever
8233 quickly to whomever he

whooped
5690 as he whooped of old:

whore
4362 I am the Protestant whore.
8021 terms, like a chaste whore.
11349 as men do to a whore.
12332 a right whore: If she

whores
7339 Reasons are whores.
8790 second-rate whores, And

whoreson
10318 Thou whoreson zed! thou

why
580 he see you now, ask why?
1677 Why need the other women
5449 Why were they proud?
7051 tell you why; All I can
8251 who has a why to live
11266 than it is to reason why.

wicked
227 Tories born wicked, or do
2160 with the wicked, but not
5873 to be wicked. All
6857 are always wicked at bottom
8298 August is a wicked month
9306 worse than wicked, my dear,
10051 keeps the wicked to give
10238 a fault, God help the wicked!
10363 Something wicked this way
11678 dreaming wicked or of the
11778 and mine is being wicked.
12550 to be wicked and being
12573 regarded as wicked, it will

wickedness
6855 to the wickedness of their
9511 Wickedness is the root of
11440 history than human wickedness.

wicket
5702 at the wicket or the

widow
4353 my dear, will be my widow.
7701 like an Indian widow.
8759 Widow. The word consumes
11057 or Molly Stark's a widow.

widow-maker
5730 go with the old grey Widow-maker?

widowed
6747 about his widowed bride.

widowhood
3839 estate of widowhood, is the

wife
250 his wife can beat
650 must be in want of a wife,
672 his first wife and his
721 that hath wife and
767 or have no wife, But
1219 unto his wife: and they
1452 - but his wife wasn't.
2370 me from my wife, and to
2572 your wife's birthday
2664 my youth a wife. She was
2668 old enough to be my wife.
3110 man has for his old wife.
3481 animal, a husband and wife.
3633 take a wife till
3640 an old wife, and old
4305 A wife encourages her
4350 An ideal wife is one who
4356 steals your wife, there is
4421 as my wife and
4471 is a proud wife and a
4516 your own wife is never
4688 Husband and wife come to
4800 and hoarser than his wife.
5067 keep one's wife happy.
5173 when his wife talks
5233 a young wife and a good
6144 power: A wife in
6201 today, My wife won't let
6819 love your neighbour's wife.
6980 husband and wife a shadow
7380 of the word, as a wife is.
8319 a moron; she's your wife.
8599 with your wife.

wife (continued)
8631 My wife, who, poor wretch,
8668 wife complained
8691 for his wife, it's
10107 All my wife has ever taken
10409 A light wife doth make a
11036 There's my wife; look well
11286 out for a wife, to look
11458 not his wife and
11567 mistress, but a wife.
11879 to suit his wife? And yet
12256 isn't a wife in the

wig
6821 the grey wig with the
12294 man with a wig to keep

wigwam
6490 Stood the wigwam of

wild
133 A walk on the wild side.
5705 the Wet Wild Woods,
6097 never saw a wild thing
10199 are but wild and

wild thyme
10417 whereon the wild thyme blows,

wildcat
9203 tigers, a wildcat is very

wilderness
1730 through the wilderness of this
4757 the woods and the wilderness yet.
7089 guess To be a little wilderness.
11396 They make a wilderness and call

wildness
4757 Of wet and wildness? Let them

wiles
7567 war: of wiles More

will
176 with energy of will.
411 a woman's will? For if
659 am not myself, who will be?
936 a strong will, and the
2118 Will you, won't you, will
3383 obeyed the will of some
3397 the power of our will.
3622 of mere will and the
4024 his own will, whose
4394 to a power over his will.
4682 Man has his will - but
6494 A boy's will is the wind's
6596 the rainbow of His will.
6607 that we do Thy will.
7555 The will And high
7610 as in our will To love or
7777 years but on your will.
8243 will to say No,
8291 is perfectly educated will.
9057 at least will deserve
9510 The general will rules in
9598 all, the will .. We
9957 The will of man is his
9981 of the will forcing
9985 The will is the strong
10292 hearing the will of Caesar,
10550 In your will, Though
11024 Will and intellect are one

willin'
2816 Barkis is willin'.

willingness
3514 is a willingness of the
6863 Where the willingness is great,
8431 yet the willingness is
10735 a mental willingness to endure

willows
11519 Willows whiten, aspens

wills
6197 God wills the things which
10725 of our wills. It is

win
144 time you win, you're
1990 so who would greatly win.
2108 How to win friends and
4081 daily must win them anew.
4265 touch To win or lose it
6254 when you win, will
6932 that's to win. Neither
7077 amaze To win the palm,
7117 a world to win. WORKING

win (continued)
7933 Gonna win, yeah,
8069 When you win, nothing
8271 you don't win unless you
11154 is how to win without

winced
4539 I have not winced nor cried

wind
450 is the east wind made
510 control the wind, The wind
1224 sown the wind, and they
1380 the colour of the wind.
1865 love what wind is to
2808 Was - The wind that
3010 stood the wind for
3130 is blowin' in the wind.
4697 knocks the wind out of
4887 a man with wind and
5411 the light wind lives or
5474 of the wind is my wife
5667 Blow, thou wind of God!
6100 I, but the wind that blows
6120 me in the wind's soft
6570 an east wind is to put
6651 is but wynd; leff
6771 The wind of change is
7924 Like the wind in hollow
9256 is like wind on the
10056 that which way the wind is,
10119 thou winter wind, Thou art
10528 for each wind that
10692 O wild West Wind, thou
10695 O, Wind, If Winter
11110 tempers the wind to the
11589 and low, Wind of the
11709 mane of every wind.
12772 a rag blown by the wind.

winders
12242 thar was winders to my

window
10472 yonder window breaks? It

window-pane
8370 Good prose is like a window pane.

windows
272 would break his windows.
3271 not open windows into men's

winds
3923 The winds and waves are
5694 Winds of the World, give
6628 seas the winds are
10321 Blow, winds, and crack your
12808 The winds come to me from

windward
2284 Just to the windward of the

windy
10521 keep o' the windy side of

wine
100 I touch wine, it turns
124 drink; Good wine, a friend,
562 to put new wine into old
898 a bottle of wine, a wife is
1214 Wine maketh merry: but
1249 perish, and wine unto those
1705 about wine, I did
1907 generous wine, Ferments
1970 Let us have Wine and Women,
2575 drink wine by
2987 the days of wine and roses:
3841 glass, for wine inspires
4591 out-did the frolic wine.
5241 And I'll not look for wine.
5418 Here is wine, Alive with
7667 lordliest in their wine.
8434 with the wine and the
8696 like good wine. Not
8762 all use of wine until
8785 Truth comes out in wine.
9002 - the wine was a
9240 in butter and in wine.
10124 than vows made in wine.
10356 The wine of life is drawn,
11600 talk and wholesome wine.
11850 life, like wine. I nothing
12547 of turning wine into
12886 Wine comes in at the mouth

wing
50 in on a wing and a

2829 - Ah, too, it has a wing.
4002 under my wing, Tra la, A
4770 word takes wing beyond
7074 flapped its tinsel wing.
7651 joy is ever on the wing.
9955 under your tender wing.
11050 not right wing, nor left

wings
1979 is Love without his wings!
2140 is roots, the other, wings.
4512 On wings of song.
5317 whitespread wings like he'd
5446 eagle's wings, Unseen
11700 of unseen wings, Bats not

wink
7261 sinner and wink your eye
10255 but I will wink and hold

winning
145 Winning can be defined as the
1005 the wear of winning, But
4088 they may start a winning game.
6465 Winning isn't everything. It
8977 the art of winning games
9866 Sure, winning isn't

wins
6421 and steady wins the race.
7980 Who dares wins.

winter
70 out in the Middle of Winter.
191 , the very dead of Winter.
1489 at the close of a winter day.
1550 Of the winter dawning.
1977 The English winter - ending
3235 The very dead of winter.
6459 song, No winter in thy
6585 Take a winter as you find
7534 It was the winter wild,
8107 From winter, plague and
8983 Winter is icummen in, Lhude
9089 old age is winter; for the
9389 the furious winter blowing.
10457 Now is the winter of our
10557 How like a winter hath my
10670 Winter is come and gone, But
11174 In winter I get up at night
11874 perils of winter till at

winters
10540 When forty winters shall

wipes
11676 in, mind it wipes its shoes.

wireless
299 The wireless music box has no

wires
656 Across the wires the

wisdom
81 on man's wisdom, but set
171 of wisdom, and one
749 It is the wisdom of the
1213 In much wisdom is much
1231 price of wisdom is above
1247 Through wisdom a house is
1329 Can Wisdom be put in a
1339 to the palace of wisdom.
1432 apply our hearts unto wisdom.
1516 without wisdom, power
2094 with their wisdom and
2207
2621 so much; Wisdom is humble
3085 All human wisdom is summed
3253 is the wisdom we have
3503 up facts; wisdom lies in
3610 the indifference of wisdom.
3781 of economic wisdom is to know
4336 is a great part of wisdom.
4696 of wisdom to listen.
4815 every day; wisdom consists
4819 weak nerves give to wisdom.
5170 Love is the wisdom of the
6069 from failure of human wisdom.
6344 go. My own wisdom, and that
6598 in wisdom, dying in
7189 provide them with wisdom.
7318 In action Wisdom goes by
7645 then By wisdom; as thy
8204 and wisdom to
8452 how little wisdom the world

8552 is the beginning of wisdom.
8899 Eternal Wisdom how to
9611 of wisdom consists
9789 wit and all men's wisdom.
11467 passes for wisdom among
11532 comes, but wisdom lingers.
11741 of wisdom not to do
11937 only the wisdom that is in

wise
702 cunning men pass for wise.
723 one of the wise men that
1232 men are not always wise.
1235 A wise son maketh a glad
1259 to the wise and
1341 tree that a wise man sees.
1342 folly he would become wise.
1538 you sad as well as wise.
1660 makes the wise man mad.
1749 and to be wise, is not
2088 man half as wise as he
2984 It takes a wise man to
3040 The wise, for cure, on
3420 who is not wise for
3527 the three wise men in
3614 more like a wise man than a
3642 Who is wise? He that
4254 A wise man gets more use
4255 Wise men appreciate all
4256 The wise have a solid
4642 Words are wise men's
4789 I heard a wise man say,
5007 of being wise is the art
5119 Obscurely wise, and
5131 or more wise when he
5269 All the wise world is
5909 is not as wise as he
6441 or a wise man,
7233 all the wise men
7617 be lowly wise: Think
7676 first be wise and good.
7806 A wise man sees as much as
8414 Look wise, say nothing,
8634 or be more wise, and not
9039 only wretched are the wise.
9195 you are wise, and you
9202 A wise man hears one word
9299 all like that wise bird!
9337 It is not wise to be wiser
9611 in being wise in time.
10463 So wise so young, they
10498 The beacon of the wise.
10501 To be wise, and love,
10629 Men are wise in
11019 To be wise and eke to
11165 said that a wise man who
11169 is never a wise companion.
11350 No wise man ever wished to
11433 fellows. Wise men are
12892 like a wise man but
12932 Be wise with speed; A fool
12937 Be wise to-day; 'tis

wisecrack
6279 Epigram: a wisecrack that has

wisecracking
8513 between wisecracking and wit.

wisely
3136 behave wisely once they
9327 Be wisely worldly, be not

wiser
594 places Are wiser and nicer
735 French are wiser than they
2451 and a wiser man, He
4118 I stand no wiser than
5599 looked wiser when he
7170 they are wiser than they,
8821 but not the wiser grow.
8930 that he is wiser to-day
11495 man will be wiser by and by;

wisest
316 relished by the wisest men.
7647 first and wisest of them
7660 Wisest men Have erred, and
9431 Even the wisest men make
11373 The wisest man I have ever

wish
1087 The wish for prayer is a
3613 Do not wish to be anything

5084 a lurking wish to appear
5988 this last wish be vain:
7249 not as we wish to, but as
8157 we have not what we wish.
9380 I wish I loved the Human
10252 Thy wish was father,

wishes
2329 with my wishes after

wistful
12539 With such a wistful eye Upon

wit
318 Little wit in the head
418 Wit is far more often a
475 examination is false wit.
1688 more than wit to become
1910 As metaphysic wit can fly.
2192 a great man pass for wit.
2843 it of their wit, and gives
2965 Wit is the only wall
4498 Wit is the salt of
6048 I use my wit as a
7181 is the soul of wit.
7189 the dull with wit, just
7323 of true wit is truth
7653 splendid wit can
8234 Wit is the epitaph of an
8513 and wit. Wit has
8831 A wit with dunces, and a
8848 and fancy wit will come:
8887 True wit is nature to
8908 A wit's a feather, and a
9789 one man's wit and all
10103 And wit's the noblest
10202 is the soul of wit.
10295 neither wit, nor
10687 His fine wit Makes such a
11063 Wit consists in knowing
11425 did do it, And not my wit.
11926 either, let wit bear a
11993 Wit is the sudden
12532 senseless wit Not to

with
1179 that is not with me is
6616 may the force be with you.

withdraw
3400 you should withdraw into

withdrawn
2291 should be withdrawn at the

wither
10157 Age cannot wither her, nor
10899 tree, And wither and
12883 Now I may wither into the

withers
3389 'abolished', it withers away.
5454 fading rose Fast withereth too.

within
1157 kingdom of God is within you.
4569 when once it is within thee.

without
130 far away, Without a city
1146 by him; and without him was
4747 is going without something
7054 with you - or without you.
8035 He can live without hope,
8503 been better without: Love,
9744 To be without some of the
10906 many things I can do without!

withstand
12268 virtue to withstand the

witnessed
12397 for having witnessed your own.

wits
120 out of his wits for the
10523 have ever homely wits.

witticism
1691 away a witticism if he

witty
477 all others the most witty.
684 dull men witty, but it
4352 can't pretend to be witty.
5907 true is perfectly witty.
7299 A witty woman is a
11099 want to be witty, work on

wives
722 Wives are young men's

2666 had so many wives because
4353 only my wives. But you,
4742 mothers and wives! It is not
7743 three wives at a time,
8113 many, many wives; But when
9167 people's wives and
10126 changes when they are wives.
10436 know Their wives have sense

wobbles

7448 but it Wobbles, and the

woe

1363 another's woe, And not
1968 notes of woe, Sadder
7625 signs of woe That all
7628 be parted, bliss or woe.
8944 another's woe; To hide
9266 Woe to the house where
10188 and the suits of woe.
10462 Woe to the land that's
10957 friend of Woe, But 'tis
12084 Woe is me, I think I am
12226 Companions of our woe.

wolf

99 skin the wolf was
1198 The wolf was sick, he
4953 while the wolf remains of
8774 A man is a wolf rather
9248 you feed a wolf, he will
12335 keep the wolf far thence

wolf's-bane

5494 twist Wolf's-bane,

wolves

1173 they are ravening wolves.
2964 are wolves for

woman

57 The woman that deliberates
187 is like a woman you want
229 cleverest woman finds a
640 of ten, a woman had better
651 She was a woman of mean
1218 be called Woman, because
1236 A virtuous woman is a crown
1282 when a woman wears the
1397 beautiful woman hardly
1624 woman and
1804 and a good woman - or a bad
2207 wisedoom? Womman. And what
2212 A woman knows how to keep
2220 A woman can become a man's
2278 husband any woman can have.
2415 If a woman likes another
2455 is for the woman; but the
2462 The woman who thinks she is
2540 thing a woman will
2577 A woman never sees what we
2602 But what is woman? - only
2899 Every woman should marry -
3087 girl the threat of a woman.
3120 done with a woman. You can
3141 be born a woman! .. Why
3148 support of the woman I love.
3207 A woman dictates before
3210 A woman, let her be as good
3264 When lovely woman stoops to
3280 and feeble woman, but I
3447 No woman can be a beauty
3491 It was a woman who drove me
3656 is 'What does a woman want?'
3843 but the woman must have
4131 find a woman who has
4513 Woman is at once apple and
4694 when she makes a woman.
4826 than a woman if you
5054 as a woman does not
5387 a man for a woman is not
5520 Woman! when I behold thee
5533 stages in a woman's life,
5669 on the woman who loved
5687 And a woman is only a woman
5730 What is a woman that you
5834 play without a woman in it?
6144 Woman, a pleasing but a
6254 Why can't a woman be more
6282 know a woman until you
6304 the sort of woman who lives
6377 A woman is the only thing I
6380 Woman's normal occupations

6671 be great; A woman's noblest
6705 That made a woman cry.
6729 to a woman being a
7270 happily a woman may be
7317 expect that Woman will be
7690 that every woman ought to
7787 A woman who goes to bed
8210 Woman was God's second
8249 goest to woman, take thy
8252 A woman may very well form
8253 Has a woman who knew that
8347 Woman is the nigger of the
8441 A woman is always buying
8529 As a woman, to be
8574 A woman is a foreign land,
8579 makes a woman beautiful
8615 a man a woman, and a
8632 A woman sober, and no high
8755 Every woman adores a
8867 Woman's at best a
9074 love for a woman who didn't
9228 is a woman's finest
9279 A beautiful woman who is
9310 A woman's love for us
9352 In a word, she is a woman.
9528 Love a woman? You're an
9684 her is a woman's greatest
9867 No woman can call herself
10034 O Woman! in our hours of
10122 know I am a woman? when I
10168 nothing Of woman in me; now
10190 Frailty, thy name is woman!
10322 yet fair woman but she
10565 spirit a woman, coloured
10617 It is a woman's business to
10968 will not woman, gentle
11054 Woman's degradation is a
11055 that a woman's place in
11072 A woman seldom writes her
11094 A woman without a man is
11426 wife is any woman who has an
11450 I have a woman's body and a
11592 the hunter; woman is his
11593 The woman is so hard Upon
11599 The woman's cause is man's:
11641 A woman with fair
11787 below And Woman even more.
11789 Woman's place is in the
12048 When once a woman has given
12123 changeable always is woman.
12244 The female woman is one of
12250 a bubble; Woman and care,
12302 called a woman in my own
12349 When a woman dresses up for
12603 trust a woman who tells
12730 - and a woman always a
12756 A woman must have money and
12819 A perfect woman, nobly

womanhood

6495 river meet, Womanhood and

womankind

10615 and packs off its womankind.

womanly

10797 So womanly, Her

womb

5237 The very womb and bed of
7130 In the dark womb where I
10425 in the womb of time
12900 my mother's womb A fanatic

women

178 without it. Women don't seem
179 Women are really much nicer
419 Some women blush when they
443 now is, are women persons?
637 Single women have a
641 and hardly any women at all.
776 Women - one half of the
873 beautiful women and so
951 Most women are not so young
1354 it men in women do
1621 works of women are
1677 the other women know so
1868 your life; women require
1943 'Though women are
1950 say so of women too, all
1970 Wine and Women, Mirth and
2012 of Women goes only

2027 humour from women? So that
2204 quod he, Wommen desiren to
2218 Women can't forgive
2229 Women are much more like
2280 because they are not women.
2511 Women are like tricks by
2558 Women are made for loving
2751 are some women who should
2770 Women never have young
2848 Most women set out to try
2864 possible to women. They ask
3209 Plain women he regarded as
3214 function of women, it is a
3402 to 'cuckold' for women.
3842 I must have women. There is
4237 Women still remember the
4321 to get women out from
4322 Women must learn to lighten
4323 Most women still need a
4388 is making women more like
4406 turn into American women.
4547 knew how women pass the
4993 Women never dine alone.
5150 been thrown upon the women.
5472 met with women whom I
5548 Women are the true
5685 things are, Women and Horses
5786 keeping women in a state
5838 Women run to extremes; they
5895 can find women who have
6107 as the Women's
6269 Women are the cowards they
6308 Are simple women only fit
6526 about Women's
6691 effect women would have
6694 Women who set a low value
6733 Women do not find it
6852 Women have one great
7283 Women have simple tastes.
7342 Women are perfectly well
7365 thing women have to do
7379 nature of women is an
7660 and by bad women been
7753 of men, women, and
7871 of the women; this is
8433 or refuse, women are glad
8496 right as women, not only
8637 Music and women I cannot
8984 I have sung women in three
9068 pretty women to men
9430 enough and women are afraid
9431 about women, and even
9468 That all women are
9706 are no ugly women, only lazy
9904 of women; they
10497 that women are so
10499 Women are angels, wooing:
10600 which all women are in
10663 to pieces. Women just go
10780 nice. If women were meant
10802 Women keep a special corner
10965 no war with women nor with
11067 Women dissemble their
11131 of the old women (of both
11271 Women enjoyed (whatsoe'er
11621 nature of women; When you
11658 Women are much better at
11696 Protestant women may take
12410 When women go wrong, men go
12517 Whatever women do they must
12551 analysed, women .. merely
12558 All women become like their
12755 about women in the
12757 Women have served all these
12759 Why are women .. so much
12868 Women and fortune are

women-folk

5726 coo with women-folk About

won

5282 him who has won it bear
7308 the winning were she won!
9464 that you won or lost -
9972 must be won; honour is
10499 Things won are done;
12357 was won on the
12361 as a battle won.
12506 in which they are won.
12621 the sun and have won it.

wonder
21 I wonder who's kissing her
2135 sense of wonder without
5276 the wonder of our
6101 struck with wonder That such
10559 eyes to wonder, but lack

wondered
6206 I wondered hugely what she

wonderful
7185 Something wonderful and strange
7247 without, no wonderful effect is
8332 know it was wonderful, but I
9467 half as wonderful as my
10942 are many wonderful things,
12190 When it's wonderful, it's
12403 a good thing can be wonderful.

wonderfully
1439 am fearfully and wonderfully made.

wondering
3413 from his wondering whether he

wonderment
8101 moved to wonderment That what

wonders
1147 signs and wonders, ye will
2614 way His wonders to
10829 a rich relative work wonders.

wondrous
7329 Oh, a wondrous bird is the
8972 is absolutely wondrous.
12291 survey the wondrous cross On

woo
403 Was to woo a fair
10126 when they woo, December

wood
4693 make it of wood, you must
11675 double-bed of the wood.

woodbine
11543 And the woodbine spices are

woodlands
4788 About the woodlands I will go

woodman
7922 Woodman, spare that tree!

woods
1375 am for the woods against
1530 down in the woods today
5445 of mighty woods, Tall
5705 Wet Wild Woods, waving
5742 through the woods Seventy
7527 The woods, and desert
9805 down the woods and

woodshed
3927 nasty in the woodshed.
11775 to build a woodshed with them.

woodwind
349 - an ill woodwind that

wooing
7703 Wooing, so tiring.
10499 are angels, wooing: Things

woolworth
8197 and live a Woolworth life

wops
7704 Huns or Wops, but

word
111 Greeks had a word for it.
421 A word to the wise is
1145 was the Word, and the
1725 is no such word As - fail
2203 at a word, Thy
3320 with a single word.
3509 wash out a word of it.
4126 wanting, a word can always
4770 sent out a word takes wing
5566 Let the word go forth from
5812 another word for
6651 Woord is but wynd; leff
6686 Every word she writes is a
6962 The word, even the
7038 eternal Word Chaos and
7614 truth, in word mightier
7807 The word is half his that
8838 uncreating word: Thy hand,
9202 hears one word and
9314 the divine word touch his
9355 A single word often

10030 And many a word, at random
10215 to the word, the word
10240 honour? A word. What is
10732 deal at every word.
10947 One word frees us of all
11494 Man's word is God in man.
11947 the right word and the
12540 flattering word. The

wordless
6748 should be wordless As the
7331 essentially wordless, and it
9934 song was wordless; the

words
38 mean, for words are
94 Words are the physicians of
852 is worth ten thousand words.
1187 but my words shall not
1393 every four words I write, I
1915 are but words, and words
2559 two words about
2780 these nice words while I'm
2854 But words once spoke can
3188 takes more words than
3284 In the words of one of my
4158 While words of learned
4249 Words are feminine; deeds
4642 Words are wise men's
4693 you must make it of words.
4760 say it in words there
5147 man mistake words for
5247 sweet, the words so fair,
5265 Give 'em words; Pour oil
5291 Words, like eyeglasses,
5296 Some words are like the old
5329 those big words, Stephen
6015 A gloton of wordes.
6556 dreams or words, You can
6638 fewer the words, the
6878 Words are men's daughters,
7149 been all words, And no
7450 and long words Bother me.
7455 His words .. like so many
7541 roof in words deceiving.
7718 not fine words that keeps
7932 stones, words are
8039 carries one beyond words.
8165 In all his words most
8888 And ten low words oft creep
9040 idiom of words very
9126 A man of words and not of
9409 speak great words and suffer
9537 The kindest words I'll ever
9618 Immodest words admit of no
10102 Words may be false and full
10199 and whirling words, my lord.
10218 My words fly up, my
10259 Men of few words are the
10695 sparks, my words among
10989 misused words generate
11324 Proper words in proper
11356 For words divide and rend;
11555 For words, like Nature,
11973 of words, howsoever
12042 the art of words exists
12383 Words and sentences are
12449 His words leap across
12513 of all sad words of tongue

wordsworth
1726 Out-babying Wordsworth and
1945 Let simple Wordsworth chime his
1981 Wordsworth - stupendous genius!
4492 Mr Wordsworth's genius is a pure
6047 daffodils were for Wordsworth.

wore
1701 She just wore Enough for

work
153 through my work. I want
286 is hard work you
294 frei. Work liberates.
895 truth that work, that
903 Half the work that is done
1000 He has to WORK to keep
1014 amount of work provided
1190 would not work, neither
1391 put your work twenty
1897 obliged to work till one
2040 dignity in work only when

2103 He that can work is a born
2177 is time for work. And time
2237 are those that work least.
2458 Work without hope draws
2555 out of work,
2578 gave man work, not to
2596 Work is more fun than fun.
3145 things that won't work.
3150 to get them at work again.
3167 How do I work? I grope.
3175 y plus z. Work is x; y is
3369 any human work which is
3650 talked about his work.
3658 Love and work are the
3899 Going to work for a large
3934 Work is love made visible.
4037 people work with best
4754 If you work at it,
4825 We work to become, not to
4905 with work so they
4950 his best work just
5039 has plenty of work to do.
5221 like hard work,
5379 When your work speaks for
5395 thing about work in the
5663 Do the work that's
5670 men must work, and women
5863 By the work one knows the
6130 harder I work, the more
6315 She did her work with the
6448 of the work instinct.
6575 whose work Is not
6643 I never work better than
6787 my poppet; Work your hands
7158 A work should contain its
7963 helps you work, rest and
7965 Go to work on an egg.
8130 is too warm work, Hardy, to
8173 and our work is done!
8323 exchanged work for it.
8521 Work expands so as to fill
8669 to rise, work like hell,
8674 Work is accomplished by
8780 harder you work, the
8813 expected to work for room,
8816 else to do the work.
8908 the noblest work of God.
9191 The hardest work is to go
9333 is to work and to
9432 Work and love - these are
9476 I work every day - or at
9539 One must work, nothing but
9612 George, I work harder at
9689 hate to work for a
9709 Work is man's most natural
9735 and dirty work for the
9758 useful in work, but
9853 Work is not man's
9864 its hands and goes to work.
9902 Work and love - these are
10001 we have. Work done by
10207 a piece of work is a man!
10234 as to work; But when
10656 I did ten times more work.
10658 I work as my father drank.
10920 Work was like a stick. It
11088 beyond his work, walks up
11239 every noble work the silent
11423 finish the work; neither
11435 important work, and
11463 bike and looked for work.
11802 about our work is spoiled
11832 Work is the inevitable
12178 Work banishes those three
12252 Work brings its own
12350 one has to work terribly
12608 Work is the curse of the

workaholics
6864 time leaves workaholics at a loss
6865 Workaholics are energized rather
11296 Workaholics commit slow suicide

worker
5613 that the worker can be
7988 with a worker at each

workers
290 day, workers require
10095 we, the Workers, all
10737 organised workers of the

workhouse
8477 to the workhouse and youth

working
76 except by working for it.
599 West, My working week and
850 the inner working of his
4036 and in his working time that
5754 joy of the working, and each,
6227 I've been working like a
7117 to win. WORKING MEN OF ALL
7214 motor has begun working again.
8003 Labour isn't working.

working class
8390 into the working class where we

working man
8388 ordinary working man, the sort

working-day
10111 briers is this working-day world!

workman
5863 work one knows the workman.
11919 and man's the workman in it.

works
1662 Works done least rapidly,
5232 even of the greatest works.
7626 and best Of all God's works.
8752 talk. It works, there is
10697 Look on my works, ye
11073 the future; and it works.
11235 could add: 'and it works'.
12567 put my talent into my works.

workshop
2875 to be the workshop of the
11919 but a workshop, and man's

world
147 man's country in the world.
204 If all the world were
234 the glory of the world.
249 the whole world was not
282 rubs of the world are what
324 all the world would be
376 makes the world go round.
500 save your world you asked
629 half of the world cannot
814 This world is white no
1163 the whole world, and lose
1191 into this world, and it is
1369 at the end of the world.
1375 against the world, But are
1388 The whole world is about
1433 the round world so sure:
1516 The world has achieved
1561 The world can only be
1616 For the world, I count it
1657 but the world may end
1667 All's right with the world!
1856 If the world will be
2145 that the world consists
2286 test; The world wil give
2428 The world is too dangerous
2756 that the world is
2866 the history of the world.
2897 to retire from the world.
3012 The world is not run by
3197 advantage i' this world.
3261 the way the world ends Not
3275 of this world. I know
3493 a funny old world - a man's
3630 In this world nothing can
3946 The world will be saved by
4047 will our world know the
4319 Eunuch the world over.
4419 The world would be a safer
4463 The world owes all its
4552 into this world to rise
4566 Let all the world in ev'ry
4606 allow the world within to
4757 would the world be, once
4790 afraid In a world I never
5066 that the world will not
5673 all the world is young,
5773 As the world is wearie of
5790 regard the world as a sort
5925 can see the world hath more
6103 thought, a world empty of
6417 The world is becoming like
6442 The world's as ugly, ay, as
6717 The world belongs to the

6760 the world in the
6789 eyes, Their world gives way
6792 World is crazier and more
6931 that the world is not
7034 Ours is a world where
7065 it was, the world, But a
7070 Had we but world enough,
7091 the whole world cannot
7140 more the world is
7161 In the world a man lives in
7271 live in the world without
7289 What the world needs is
7401 The world is an oyster, but
7616 his six days' work, a world.
7725 in this world is an
7753 This world consists of men,
7780 in the world is to know
7792 The world is but a school
7937 The world is divided into
8053 late into a world too old.
8153 Stop the world, I want to
8217 to find the world ugly and
8302 The whole worl's in a state
8407 Of the world for ever,
8444 All the world is queer save
8452 wisdom the world is
8478 is the world, and my
8561 World, nature, Universe's
8845 lot! The world
8892 burst, and now a world.
8948 the history of the world.
9277 The world is more exacting
9375 The world itself is but a
9423 days that shook the world.
9463 shall be, world without
9601 to a world founded
9719 of the world are asleep
9751 about a world one will
9960 The world is ruled only by
10006 The world is my country,
10035 half of the warld thinks the
10048 half the world in a fit
10189 all the uses of this world
10270 a queen For all the world.
10410 then the world's mine
10441 This world to me is but a
10491 O brave new world, That has
10509 Is it a world to hide
10636 a quiet world till you
10684 The world's great age
10685 The world is weary of the
10803 Of the very world he made.
10911 or Greece, but of the world,
11175 The world is so full of a
11309 the world has grown
11497 for the world is white
11529 the Federation of the world.
11535 the great world spin for
11606 of the world, A
11648 The world is a looking
11711 O world invisible, we view
11848 enjoy the world aright,
12064 which the world And all
12201 through the world had flown,
12204 Into a world which,
12215 will the world know that
12228 on in the world from one
12250 The world is full of care,
12391 all the world as my
12394 govern the world; only
12453 If the world were merely
12531 cow of the world, and as we
12534 and the world laughs
12535 Is all the sad world needs.
12703 mean the limits of my world.
12773 good, The world would be
12798 the mighty world Of eye and
12838 The world is too much with

worldly
6148 were all his worldly goods.
9327 Be wisely worldly, be not

worlds
11569 So many worlds, so much to
12199 old, both worlds at once

worm
4003 tough worm in your
5159 with a worm at one end
8502 upon a worm. 'Aha, my

9604 bad luck of the early worm.
10516 like a worm i' the
11668 goes the same crooked worm.

worms
2293 We are all worms, but I do
6639 on me in Worms as there
7072 song; then worms shall try
10125 time, and worms have eaten
11974 ourselves worms of the

worn
253 if it had worn out two
8968 I am worn to a ravelling
10951 When we're worn, Hacked

worried
325 what he worried about last

worries
4372 person who worries very much
5187 but a fool worries about
9186 Worries go down better with

worry
4797 Farmers worry only during
5984 We wouldn't worry so much
7027 oh i should worry and fret

worrying
525 the use of worrying? It never
3397 is to cease worrying about
7810 Worrying helps you some. It
11702 Worrying the carcase of an old
12051 without worrying whether

worse
227 born wicked, and grow worse.
648 are always worse than
987 of finding something worse.
2161 a good deal worse.
3645 bad that I don't feel worse.
4838 day - then worse again in
5217 money made it any worse.
5602 or a little worse; but to do
7231 they are certainly no worse.
8125 other systems are worse.
9565 party is worse than the
11041 Or is it something worse?
11337 her person for the worse.
12587 the world worse than being

worship
3901 modes of worship, which
6678 We still worship the elders
7750 O worship the Lord in the
9601 person to worship God in his
11432 is fetish worship. It is

worshipped
8357 if he thee worshipped with his

worst
556 prevent the worst before it
948 The worst thing in this
1513 be good to know the worst.
1650 the best Out of the worst.
2664 hope nobody gets the worst.
3070 do thy worst, for I
4943 suffer, the worst is the
5142 The worst is better
6416 they prepared for the worst.
7827 come to the worst, they
8202 The worst thing, I fear,
9122 when in the worst health.
9136 The worst is not always
10326 The worst is not, So long

worst-bred
11343 the worst-bred person in

worsted
6821 the black worsted stockings,

worth
407 nothing is worth nothing.
812 are not worth very much;
1292 and ain't worth nothin'.
1634 A man's worth something.
2264 a thing is worth doing, it
2656 naked is is worth a million
5122 Worth seeing, yes; but not
6828 it [the territory] is worth.
10029 turned out worth anything
10554 of thy worth gives thee
10604 think him worth
11383 is worth what its
11518 flower Is worth a hundred
12578 that is worth knowing

worthless
7950 and make it worthless by

worthy
706 obtained worthy ends and
4027 Yet B is worthy, I dare
7714 is not worthy to live.
8861 to make one worthy man my
11471 For nothing worthy of proving

wotthehell
7027 but wotthehell wotthehell oh i

would
1673 him, but what man Would do!

wound
2684 Next to the wound, what
4928 clock and wound up every
7625 felt the wound, and
7756 razor keen, Wound with a
8971 been the wound, not the
10687 such a wound, the knife
12414 into their wounds, even if

wounded
4248 show your wounded finger,
5756 When you're wounded and left

wounded knee
1021 Bury my heart at Wounded Knee.

wounds
732 keeps his own wounds green.

wrap
10822 secret, wrap it up in

wrapping
12953 used for wrapping soap

wrath
1133 sun go down upon your wrath.
1198 Envy and wrath shorten the
1240 answer turneth away wrath.
1344 of God. The wrath of the
1361 I told my wrath, my wrath
1420 from thy wrath, and from
10311 the dragon and his wrath.

wreathed
7597 might, and wreathed His lithe

wreck
10684 gleam, Like wrecks of a
10778 you see the wreck that
12479 all but wreck the

wreckage
12758 with the wreckage of men who

wren
1052 Christopher Wren Said, 'I
4840 with the wings of a wren.
10329 The wren goes to't, and

wrestle
2273 never to wrestle with a

wrestled
10110 you have wrestled well, and

wrestling
616 that of wrestling than of

wretch
10028 The wretch, concentred all

wretched
9039 The only wretched are the

wretchedness
832 periods of wretchedness, but with
9879 man's wretchedness if it were

wretches
4071 How shall wretches live like

wring
12222 will soon wring their

wrinkle
3053 the first wrinkle and the

wrinkled
11679 side by wrinkled side,

wrinkles
8106 Which wrinkles will

writ
5421 name was writ in water.
11425 And this I writ; My heart

write
178 enough; They write about it.
425 Write something, even if
962 you can write it down.
2030 which they write - I'm with

2155 is best to write in wind
2530 Better to write for
2697 thing a writer can do is
4157 he could write and cypher
4705 When you write in prose you
4785 with the ability to write.
5079 A man may write at any
5118 know how to write trifles
5132 A man might write such stuff
5476 I sit down to write.
6031 How can you write if you
6086 I like to write when I feel
6179 The urge to write is also
6335 I can write better than
6579 who would write and can't
6653 for me to write As my poor
6709 Law: Never write a letter
7410 The day you write to please
7417 going to write the truth,
7454 his hope to write well
8019 I write as a sow piddles
8060 any longer write in the fat
8656 away when you write.
8834 it, And write about it,
8922 who cannot write, and those
9058 something to write about.
9296 read books - I write them.
10097 to write than
10135 but to write and read
10719 You write with ease, to
10755 in thy heart and write.'
11086 I write for myself and
11749 sit down to write when you
11869 as a man ought to write.
11940 way to write a story
12442 to young writers who want
12683 the men who write; and it is
12959 who can't write

writer
1006 All a writer has to do to
1068 Every writer, without
1843 plain, rude writer .. I call
3348 of a writer's genius
3399 read; if a writer, write.
4529 for a good writer is a
4533 The writer must write what
4885 A writer and nothing else: a
5797 A writer's ambition should
5808 A writer is someone who can
6166 fame is a writer's fame;
6727 A writer's business
8259 see. The writer shakes up
8654 believe the writer .. should
9342 of a writer is
9695 life of a writer is tragic:
9930 A writer must refuse .. to
9931 The writer is committed when
10635 anything a writer tells you
10781 A good writer is basically a
10782 basket is a writer's best
10919 a great writer is to have
11864 hardback writer is
12725 reason a writer writes a
12793 original writer, in

writers
786 Writers, like teeth, are
1009 with writers chief
2844 remember: writers are always
3075 Writers should be read - but
3259 are failed writers - but so
3438 kinds of writers - the
4519 themselves, writers. If I had
4752 are my writers when I
4923 Writers write to influence
5996 Clear writers, like clear
11049 Writers are the engineers of

writes
3509 finger writes; and,
5803 which God writes on thy
12480 man really writes for an

writing
527 said that writing comes more
739 man; and writing an exact
1597 agony of writing comes in.
1705 it came to writing about
2063 That's not writing, that's
2921 and an art of writing.

3465 love with writing - for life
3599 Writing is easy: all you do
3715 of good writing, but if
3726 Writing: I certainly do
3940 in writing at once
5150 faculty of writing has
5153 only end of writing is to
5260 that in his writing,
6143 Writing is no trouble: you
6174 love, but get it in writing.
6444 And some for writing verses.
6938 Writing is not a political
8879 ease in writing comes from
9018 Writing is a solitary
9324 as I had in the writing.
9369 in writing a modern
9472 all writing is about
10767 Writing is not a profession
10783 Writing has power, but its
11122 Writing, when properly
11758 style of writing, if one
12080 the rest is mere fine writing.
12656 business of writing is one of
12754 myself from writing it till I

writings
3368 from the writings of others
3798 academic writings. Action

written
3233 what he has written: he may
4211 the paper it is written on.
5077 anything written by mere
5208 What is written without
5301 until he has written a book.
5757 happen has never been written.
9835 never been written that
11847 may be written. It is
11935 man himself cannot be written.
12586 are well written, or badly

wrong
599 last forever: I was wrong.
665 mind being wrong if someone
839 be strongly wrong than
906 something wrong with our
1315 can do no wrong, is a
1635 called them by wrong names.
2190 I have got it all so wrong?
2209 everyone is wrong, everyone
2254 American who is all wrong.
2402 is nothing wrong with a
2497 kinds of wrong. The
2635 at what you know is wrong.
2787 are always in the wrong.
3165 can prove me wrong.
3780 majority is always wrong.
4018 who have gone wrong!
4496 to setting them wrong.
4619 really wrong with him -
4648 but being wrong ain't one
4937 a majority is always wrong.
4964 the right to think wrong.
5015 has something wrong with it.
6621 So much wrong could
7029 usually gets it all wrong.
7238 me when I am in the wrong.
7448 get in the wrong places.
7758 notions are generally wrong.
8144 unsaid the wrong thing at
8930 been in the wrong, which is
8974 has gone wrong, however
8991 old sense. Wrong from the
9117 The absent are always wrong.
9504 The customer is never wrong.
9619 is always in the wrong.
9911 something wrong with the
9994 right or wrong; if right,
10909 right to do wrong or to
10945 to speak well and be wrong.
11186 depend on it they are wrong.
11386 right but also to be wrong.
11629 comes easy, comes wrong.
11789 place is in the wrong.
11964 and what is wrong, which
12346 is the right to be wrong.
12410 women go wrong, men go
12438 Nature is usually wrong.
12933 most divinely in the wrong.

wrongdoing
4720 A sense of wrongdoing is an

wrongly
6268 Think wrongly, if you please,

wrongs
3028 the people's wrongs his own.
5831 but mass of public wrongs.
11392 Two wrongs don't make a

wrote
6106 hands and wrote my will
9336 tackle, I'm glad I wrote it.
11980 who wrote music

wrought
11516 things are wrought by prayer

xanadu
2438 In Xanadu did Kubla Khan A

xenophobic
8966 are not xenophobic - we are

y-shaped
8362 the grave in a Y-shaped coffin.

yale
7243 was my Yale College
8499 the Yale Prom were

yankee
426 Yankee Doodle came to town

yarn
10143 a mingled yarn, good and

yawn
8836 everlasting yawn confess

yawns
11855 the grave yawns for him.

yawp
12510 my barbaric yawp over the

yea
1137 Let your yea be yea; and

year
23 the best time of the year.
47 have lived another year.
1667 The year's at the spring
3285 time of the year For a
5442 of the year; There are
10553 time of year thou mayst
11489 circle of the golden year.
11577 snow: The year is going,

yearning
3572 hearts are yearning, Though
7904 learning, earning and yearning.
8036 absolute yearning of one
9648 the man of yearning thought

years
601 The years shall run like
3104 at all ivry fifty years.
3115 the last six thousand years.
3330 The years teach much which
3625 and twenty years can scarce
5797 in ten years' time and
7777 of your years but on
8819 from the years that fly;
10283 off twenty years of life
11158 is not the years in your
11514 me, and the years, Among new
12885 The years like great black

yeast
11424 in large: yeast, salt and

yeats
584 Willam Yeats is laid to

yellow
4470 a one-eyed yellow idol to
8883 all looks yellow to the
9637 back Was yellow like ripe

yes
1318 no, not yes. It is
1323 is to say, yes, it is
4251 'No' and 'Yes' are words

yesterday
1431 are but as yesterday: seeing
2934 hath, nor yesterday, Running
5222 universe and give me yesterday.

6233 Yesterday all my troubles
6272 Yesterday I loved, today I
7025 of keeping up with yesterday.
12308 learnt something from yesterday.

yesterdays
10373 And all our yesterdays have
12803 of cheerful yesterdays And

yesteryear
12107 are the snows of yesteryear?

yet
605 continence, but not yet.

yid
9663 PUT THE ID BACK IN YID!

yield
4258 is just to yield to it.
7664 Private respects must yield.
11598 a touch I yield; Ask me no
12583 is to yield to it.

yielded
7595 And by her yielded, by him

yo-ho-ho
11193 man's chest Yo-ho-ho, and a

yoke
7653 impertinent yoke of

yorick
10229 Alas, poor Yorick. I knew

yorkshireman
9204 over a Yorkshireman's grave,

you
375 For you but not
441 'I love you,' we say
2005 tu, Brute? You too,
4358 You know I know you know
7966 It's for you-hoo!
9261 gossips to you will
9711 for if you rub up

young
24 you are too young to take up
82 to make me young again.
758 man that is young in years
1376 I have been young, and now
1636 I was so young, I loved him
1904 Young as he was, his
1953 that one so young should
2421 joy of the young is to
2639 The young always have the
3270 The young feel tired at the
3566 stays young. The
4580 Only the young die good.
5181 if he be caught young.
5673 world is young, lad, And
6528 It keeps him young.
8202 no longer young, is that
8712 a long time to become young.
8775 the gods favour dies young.
9705 When I was young, I used to
9908 If I were young and
10463 So wise so young, they say,
10597 that the young can do for
10841 of the young is a
11039 while we're young, 'Cause
11486 to make an old man young.
11666 Oh as I was young and easy
11838 I was very young, I kissed
11941 to be a young June bug,
12598 old, but that one is young.
12789 But to be young was very
12878 When I was young, I had not

young man
4301 Go West, young man, and grow up
6722 me die a youngman's death
8737 of being a young man .. I
11181 give me the young man who has

young men
72 Young men soon give, and soon
429 Young men think old men fools
750 Young men are fitter to invent
4786 lose; But young men think it
10840 than young men can

young people
7731 civility; Young people
8049 it gets young people to bed at
9533 we enable young people to see

younger
10515 thy love be younger than
11310 to keep the younger at a
11350 man ever wished to be younger.
11990 When I was younger, I could

yourself
3929 Be yourself. Who else is
6740 go to bed with is yourself.
7152 if you have to do it yourself.
8664 Live with yourself: get to
12946 likely to kill you is yourself.

youth
430 This is a youth-oriented
747 In the youth of a state
1427 and offences of my youth.
1460 Youth will be served, every
1570 wine of youth; gave up
1580 caught our youth, and
1670 Youth means love, Vows
2740 age is youth without
2777 Youth, what man's age is
2871 Youth is a blunder; Manhood
3110 have in our youth is
3298 must be laid in youth.
3416 If youth knew; if age was
3944 of one's youth, one's
4095 in his youth that the
4151 these, A youth of labour
5498 Where youth grows
5527 there is youth in the
6386 preparing youth for the
6485 passed A youth, who bore,
6494 thoughts of youth are long,
6546 Youth is vivid rather than
7681 thief of youth, Stol'n on
7915 In extreme youth, in our
8238 belongs to youth, clarity
8477 and youth to the
8686 belief that youth is the
8739 aged bosom: youth is the
9026 grasp of youth, is that
9308 From early youth his
9631 flush of youth, And
9670 sign of an ill-spent youth.
9707 sagacity in youth, has
9971 In early youth, as we
10380 hast nor youth nor age;
10512 and twenty, Youth's a stuff
10535 age and youth cannot
10626 Youth, which is forgiven
10852 laugh at a youth for his
10967 days of my youth I
11775 The youth gets together
12027 Youth has become a class.
12325 I have youth And a
12470 of youth is life as
12796 thoughtless youth; but
12883 days of my youth I swayed

yugoslavia
11465 kingdom will become a Yugoslavia.

zeal
5541 and take it for zeal.
5774 bigot zeal, Corrected
6602 All zeal runs down. What
7041 All zeal .. all zeal, Mr
7365 stir up the zeal of women
9376 Tell zeal it wants
10272 half the zeal I served
11414 not the slightest zeal.

zenocrate
7018 Ah fair Zenocrate, divine

zeus
4729 are from Zeus, and a

zipper
9626 pull your zipper up, then